S0-BIQ-017

THE DELL
CROSSWORD
DICTIONARY

THE DELL CROSSWORD DICTIONARY

COMPILED AND EDITED BY KATHLEEN RAFFERTY

REVISED AND UPDATED BY MARGARET S. DOHERTY

EDITORIAL CONSULTANT, ROSALIND MOORE

A DELL TRADE PAPERBACK

A DELL TRADE PAPERBACK

Published by
Dell Publishing
a division of
The Bantam Doubleday Dell Publishing Group, Inc.
New York, New York 10013

Copyright © 1950, 1960, 1984 by Dell Publishing
Copyright renewed 1978 by Dell Publishing

All rights reserved.
No part of this book may be reproduced or
transmitted in any form or by any means, electronic or
mechanical, including photocopying, recording or by any
information storage and retrieval system, without the written
permission of the Publisher, except where permitted by law.

The trademark Dell® is registered in the U.S. Patent
and Trademark Office.
ISBN: 0-440-56318-6
Printed in the United States of America
August 1984

11

MV

ABOUT THIS BOOK . . .

Looking for an "Assam silkworm"? Can't find a "Brazilian coin"? Don't know a "candlenut tree"? They're easily found —with the aid of this book.

The purpose of this dictionary is to give puzzlers the pleasure of COMPLETING, down to the last two-letter word, every crossword that they begin. It is meant to eliminate the frustration of filling in "all but a few" of those final puzzle squares. Here, in a handy, easy-to-use format, is a complete 432-page reference book, including the exclusive cross-referenced Word-Finder, where puzzle solvers can find all those little-known, but much-used, crossword words.

We believe this book is the most useful book ever published for crossword solvers. It is the outgrowth of many years of exhaustive research and was prepared by Kathleen Rafferty who was, for many years, editor-in-chief of the Dell crossword magazines and books.

ABOUT THIS EDITION

Many of the words and definitions used in crosswords remain the same today as when this dictionary was first compiled. However, new words have come into our language since that time, and today's crosswords utilize these words. Since such words, in the main, are in specialized areas, this edition has been expanded by adding to the Special Section, instead of including additional words and definitions in the general section. This arrangement of the new information will make it easier for you to find the words you need to complete your puzzles!

In this edition, the Special Section now includes such listings as Computer Terminology, Aerospace, and Acronyms and Abbreviations. Though not new to the language, sections on Music and Sports, among others, have also been added. Both the Gazetteer and the First and Last Names sections have been completely revised and updated. You will undoubtedly find the all-new Celebrities' Original Names section entertaining, as well as a handy reference.

These new additions have been compiled from material I have gathered, both as solver and editor, over the past twelve years. The lists are in no way meant to be all-inclusive; they are not intended as exhaustive reference works, but as invaluable puzzle-solving aids.

Margaret S. Doherty

TABLE OF CONTENTS

DEFINITIONS SECTION 5

All the important crossword puzzle words are listed alphabetically by definition.

Look under group headings for these special word listings:

SPECIAL SECTION
READY REFERENCE WORD LISTS

WORD-FINDER 256

Every essential two-, three-, and four-letter word in the English language. Cross-referenced to the Definitions section for utmost aid to
solving. You can complete unfinished puzzle words with this section.

ABBREVIATIONS USED IN THIS BOOK

abbr. .... abbreviation
Abyssin. .... Abyssinia(n)
Afgh. .... Afghanistan
Afr. .... Africa(n)
Am. .... American
Arab. .... Arabia(n)
Arch. .... Architecture
A.-S. .... Anglo-Saxon
Austr. .... Austria(n)
Austral. .... Australia(n)
Babyl. .... Babylonian
Bibl. .... Biblical
biol. .... biology
bot. .... botany; botanical
Braz. .... Brazil(ian)
Cent. Am. ... Central America(n)
Chin. .... Chinese
comb. form .... combining form
Dan. .... Danish
Du. .... Dutch
Du. E. Ind. ... Dutch East Indies
E. .... East
Egyp. .... Egypt(ian)
E. Ind. .... East Indies
Eng. .... England; English
Eur., Europ. .... Europe(an)
fort. .... fortification
Fr. .... France; French
geol. ...... geology; geological
geom. .... geometry
Ger. .... German(y)
Goth. .... Gothic
govt. .... government
Gr. .... Greek
Hebr. .... Hebrew
Her. .... heraldry
Himal. .... Himalayan
Holl. .... Holland
Ind. .... India(n)
Indo-Chin. .... Indo-Chinese
Ir. .... Ireland; Irish
Is. .... Island

Ital. .... Italian; Italy
Jap. .... Japan(ese)
Lat. .... Latin
math. .... mathematics
med. .... medical
Medit. .... Mediterranean
Mex. .... Mexican; Mexico
milit. .... military
Min. .... Minor
mus. .... music; musical
myth. .. mythological; mythology
N., No. .... North
naut. .... nautical
N. Hebr. .... New Hebrides
N. T. .... New Testament
N. Z. .... New Zealand
Nor. .... Norway; Norwegian
O. Eng. .... Old English
P. I. .... Philippine Islands
P. R. .... Puerto Rico
Pacif. .... Pacific
Pers. .... Persian
pert. .... pertaining
pharm. .... pharmacy
philos. .... philosophical
poet. .... poetry
Polyn. .... Polynesia(n)
Port. ..... Portugal; Portuguese
Pruss. .... Prussian
R. C. .... Roman Catholic
Rom. .... Roman
Russ. .... Russian
S. .... South
S. Afr. .... South Africa(n)
Scot. .... Scottish
Sp. .... Spanish
Teut. .... Teutonic
Turk. .... Turkey; Turkish
W. .... West
W. Ind. .... West Indian
WW .... World War
zool. .... zoology

DEFINITIONS
SECTION

CROSSWORD DEFINITIONS
AND ANSWERS

HOW TO USE THIS SECTION:

Here are crossword **DEFINITIONS**, arranged alphabetically.

Look up the **DEFINITION** of a crossword word, and you will find, in bold-face type, the word you want.

There are two kinds of crossword definitions. One is the almost unvarying definition: "Bitter vetch" or "Vetch" is used to define ERS. If you look in this dictionary under "B" for "bitter vetch" or under "V" for "vetch" you will find it there.

The other kind of definition, far more common, is the more varied definition where the puzzle-maker can choose from among many descriptive words when he defines a puzzle word: "India nurse," "Oriental nurse," "Oriental maid," "Oriental nursemaid" are all used in crossword puzzles as definitions for AMAH. For efficiency's sake, crossword words with varying definitions are listed here under the ESSENTIAL definition word. In the case of AMAH, the listing is under "nurse," "maid," and "nursemaid".

So, if you don't find your wanted word under the first word of the definition given, look for it under the other words of the definition.

The length of a word is important to crossword solvers, and so, when a definition fits two or more words the words are arranged according to length. For example: adage .... SAW, MAXIM, PROVERB.

Remember to use also the efficiently-arranged reference word lists in the SPECIAL SECTION, beginning on page 187.

5

A

a
Aaron's brother .... **MOSES**
Aaron's sister .... **MIRIAM**
Aaron's miracle worker ... **ROD**
Aaron's son, oldest .... **NADAB**
abaca .... **LINAGA**
abaca, top-quality ..... **LUPIS**
Abadan's land .... **IRAN**
abalone shell money
　　　　　　　 ULLO, UHLLO
abandon **MAROON, DISCARD**
abandoned .... **DERELICT**
abate .... **EBB, LESSEN**
abatement .... **LETUP**
abbess .... **AMMA**
abbey: Sp. .... **ABADIA**
abbot: Lat. .... **ABBAS**
abbreviations
　　　 PTA, SRO, NATO (1949 pact)
abdominal .... **VENTRAL**
Abel's brother .... **CAIN**
abhor **HATE, DETEST, LOATHE**
Abie's girl .... **ROSE**
Abijah's son .... **ASA**
ability ...... **POWER, TALENT**
abject .... **BASE**

b
abode, blissful .... **EDEN**
abode of dead .. **HADES, SHEOL**
abode of dead: Egypt.
　　　　　　　 AALU, AARU
abound .... **TEEM**
abounding .... **RIFE**
about .. **OF, RE, ANENT, CIRCA**
about: Lat. .... **CIRCITER**
above ..... **O'ER, OVER, UPON**
abrade .... **RUB, CHAFE**
Abraham's birthplace ..... **UR**
Abraham's brother
　　　　　 HARAN, NAHOR
Abraham's father ..... **TERAH**
Abraham's nephew .... **LOT**
Abraham's son
　　　　　 ISAAC, ISHMAEL
Abraham's wife . **SARAH, SARAI**
abrasive .... **EMERY**
abrogate .... **ANNUL**
abrupt flexure .... **GENU**
Absalom's cousin ..... **AMASA**
Absalom's sister ...... **TAMAR**
abscond ...... **ELOPE, LEVANT**
absence, license for .... **EXEAT**
absent ..... **OFF, OUT, AWAY, GONE**
absolute .... **UTTER, PLENARY**
absolve sins .... **SHRIVE**

c
absorbed .... **RAPT**
abstruse .... **ESOTERIC**
abundance, in .... **GALORE**
abundant .... **RIFE, AMPLE**
abuse: India .... **GALI, GALEE**
abuse ... **VIOLATE, MISTREAT**
abusive, be .... **REVILE**
abusive charges .... **MUD**
abut .... **ADJOIN, BORDER**
abyss .... **GULF, HOLE, CHASM**
Abyssinian ..... **KAFA, KAFFA**
Abyssin. fly .... **ZIMB**
Abyssin. grain .... **TEFF**
Abyssin. Hamite . **AFAR, AGAO, BEJA, AFARA**
Abyssin. language ...... **SAHO**
Abyssin. mountain wolf
　　　　　　　 KABERU
Abyssin. ruler's title ... **NEGUS**
Abyssin. ox .. **GALLA, SANGA, SANGU**
Abyssin. Semitic dialect
　　　　 GEEZ, GHESE
Abyssin. tree .... **KOSO**
Abyssin. tribesman ..... **SHOA**
Abyssin. vizier .... **RAS**
accent .... **TONE**
accent, Irish .. **BLAS, BROGUE**

d
access .... **ENTREE**
accommodate .... **LEND**
"— accompli" .... **FAIT**
according to . **ALA, AUX, ALLA**
accost .... **HAIL, GREET**
account entry ...**ITEM, DEBIT, CREDIT**
accumulate .... **AMASS, HOARD, ACCRUE**
accumulation .... **FUND**
accustomed ..... **USED, WONT, ENURED**
acetic acid ester .... **ACETATE**
acetone derivative ... **ACETOL**
acetylene .... **ETHIN, ETHINE**
Achilles' adviser ...... **NESTOR**
Achilles' father .... **PELEUS**
Achilles' mother ...... **THETIS**
Achilles' slayer .... **PARIS**
acid, kind of .. **AMINO, BORIC**
acid radical ... **ACYL, ACETYL**
acidity .... **ACOR**
acknowledge .... **OWN**
acknowledge frankly .. **AVOW**
acorns, dried .... **CAMATA**
acoustics apparatus ... **SIRENE**
acquainted .... **VERSANT**
acquiesce .... **ASSENT**

a acquiesce, fully ..... **ACCEDE**
acquire .... **WIN, GAIN, REAP**
acrobat of India .... **NAT**
Acropolis of Thebes .. **CADMEA**
across: comb. form
TRAN, TRANS
acrostic, Hebrew .... **AGLA**
act ...... **DEED, FEAT, EMOTE**
act: Lat. ...... **ACTU, ACTUS**
action, put into .... **ACTUATE**
action word .... **VERB**
active ... **SPRY, AGILE, BRISK,**
LIVELY, NIMBLE
actor .... **HISTRIO, HISTRION**
actor's group .... **TROUPE**
actor's hint .... **CUE**
actor's valet .... **DRESSER**
actual .... **REAL, TRUE**
actual being .... **ESSE**
actuality .... **FACT**
adage .... **SAW, MAXIM,**
PROVERB
Adam's ale .... **WATER**
Adam's 1st mate: legend
LILITH
Adam's grandson .... **ENOS**
Adam's son . **ABEL, CAIN, SETH**
adapt .... **FIT**
adept .... **ACE**

b add on .... **AFFIX, ANNEX,**
ATTACH
adder, common .... **ASP**
additions .... **ADDENDA**
addition, bill's .... **RIDER**
adequate .... **DUE, FULL,**
AMPLE, EQUAL
adhere .... **CLING, STICK,**
CLEAVE
adherent .... **IST**
adhesive .. **GUM, GLUE, PASTE**
ADJECTIVE ENDING, see SUF-
FIX, ADJECTIVE
adjust ...... **FIX, SET, ADAPT,**
ATTUNE, ORIENT
adjutant .... **AIDE**
adjutant bird .... **ARGALA,**
HURGILA, MARABOU
admonish .... **WARN, EXHORT,**
REPROVE
admonisher .... **MONITOR**
adolescence .... **TEENS,**
YOUTH, NONAGE
adopted son of Mohammed . **ALI**
Adriana's servant ...... **LUCE**
adroit ...... **READY, HABILE,**
SKILLFUL
adulterate .. **DEBASE, DEFILE,**
DENATURE
advance guard .... **VAN**
advantage .... **USE, GAIN,**
PROFIT, BENEFIT

c adventitious lung sound .. **RALE**
adventure ...... **GEST, GESTE**
adviser, woman ...... **EGERIA**
Aeëtes' daughter ..... **MEDEA**
Aegir's wife .... **RAN**
Aeneas' wife .... **CREUSA**
Aeneid author **VERGIL, VIRGIL**
Aesir ... **TIU, TYR, ULL, FREY,**
LOKE, LOKI, ODIN, THOR,
VALE, VALI, DONAR,
FREYA, BRAGI, WODEN,
BALDER
affectionate ... **FOND, WARM,**
LOVING, TENDER
affirm .. **AVER, POSIT, ASSERT**
affirmative .... **AY, AYE,**
YEA, YES
affirmative vote .... **AY, AYE,**
YEA, YES
afflict ...... **TRY, VEX, PAIN,**
DISTRESS
affluence ...... **EASE, RICHES,**
WEALTH
affray .... **BRAWL, FIGHT,**
MELEE
Afghan prince .. **AMIR, AMEER**
Afghan title .... **KHAN**
afresh .... **ANEW**
d afraid: obsolete .... **REDDE**
AFRICAN .... see also SOUTH
AFRICAN and AFRICAN **in**
SPECIAL SECTION
AFRICAN ANTELOPE
see ANTELOPE
Afr. bass .... **IYO**
Afr. bustard .... **KORI**
Afr. cotton garment .... **TOBE**
Afr. disease .... **NENTA**
Afr. worm .... **LOA**
Afr. grass, millet-like .. **FUNDI**
Afr. hornbill .... **TOCK**
Afr. plant .... **ALOE**
Afr. scrub .... **BITO**
Afr. soldier .... **ASKARI**
Afr. squirrel .... **XERUS**
Afr. stockade .... **BOMA**
Afr. tableland .... **KAROO**
Afrikaans ...... **TAAL, BOERS**
aft .... **ABAFT, ASTERN**
after awhile .... **ANON**
aftermath .... **ROWEN**
afterpart of ship's keel
SKAG, SKEG
afterpiece, comic ..... **EXODE**
aftersong .... **EPODE**
again .... **ENCORE**
against .... **CON, ANTI,**
CONTRA, VERSUS
agalloch wood .. **AGAR, ALOE,**
GAROO
Agamemnon's son .... **ORESTES**

a agate stone .... **ACHATE**
age .... **EON, ERA, AERA,
    RIPEN, PERIOD**
aged .... **OLD, ANILE, SENILE**
agave fiber .... **ISTLE**
agency, depression-era .. **N R A**
agency, govt. ... **E C A, F H A**
agency, wage, price .... **E S A**
agency, ration-book .... **O P A**
agency, World-War II .. **O P A**
agent .... **DOER, FACTOR,
    FACIENT**
agents acted through .. **MEDIA**
aggregate . **SUM, MASS, TOTAL**
agitate .... **STIR**
agitation ..... **STIR, DITHER,
    TUMULT**
agitation, be in state of **SEETHE**
agnomen .... **NAME**
agree ..... **GIBE, JIBE, TALLY,
    ASSENT, CONCUR**
agreeable: old Eng. ... **AMENE**
agreeableness of letters **EUTONY**
agreement ...... **MISE, PACT,
    CONCORD, ENTENTE**
agriculture goddess .... **CERES,
    VACUNA, DEMETER**
Agrippina's son .... **NERO**
Ahasuerus' minister .. **HAMAN**
b ahead . **ON, BEFORE, FORWARD**
Ahiam's father .... **SACAR**
aid ... **ABET, ASSIST, SUCCOR,
    FURTHER**
aim ...... **END, GOAL, ASPIRE**
aims, with the same ... **AKIN**
air .. **AER, ARIA, MIEN, TUNE**
air apparatus ...... **AERATOR**
air current, ascending **THERMAL**
air, fill with .... **AERATE**
air, fresh .... **OZONE**
air passage ...... **FLUE, VENT**
air spirit .... **SYLPH**
air, upper .... **ETHER, AETHER**
aircraft, motorless .... **GLIDER**
airplane .... **JET, AERO**
airplane: Fr. .... **AVION**
airport marker .... **PYLON**
airport, Paris .... **ORLY**
airship . **AERO, BLIMP, PLANE**
airy ...... **LIGHT, ETHEREAL**
ait .... **ISLE**
Ajax, tale about ...... **MYTH**
Ajax's father ...... **TELAMON**
akin .... **SIB**
along grass .... **LALANG**
alarm . **SCARE, SIREN, AROUSE**
alas! .. **ACH, HEU, OCH, OIME**
alas: Irish .. **OHONE, OCHONE**
alas: poetic .... **AY**
Alaska glacier .... **MUIR**

c **ALBANIAN** see **COINS, TRIBES,
    GAZETTEER** in SPECIAL
        SECTION
Albanian dialect .. **GEG, CHAM,
    GHEG, TOSK**
albatross, sooty ...... **NELLY**
alchitran .... **TAR, PITCH**
alcohol radical .... **AL**
alcohol, solid . **STERIN, STEROL**
alcoholic drink .... **GIN, RUM,
    RHUM**
Alcott heroine ...... **JO, AMY,
    MEG, BETH**
alcove .... **BOWER, RECESS**
alder tree: Scot .... **ARN**
ale mug .... **TOBY**
ale, sour .... **ALEGAR**
alewife fish .... **POMPANO**
ALEUTIAN see **TRIBES, GAZET-
    TEER** in SPECIAL SECTION
Alexandrian theologian . **ARIUS**
Alexander victory
        ISSUS, ARBELA
alfalfa .... **LUCERN, LUCERNE**
Alfonso's queen .... **ENA**
alga .... **NORI**
alga, one-cell ...... **DIATOM**
algae genus, fan-shaped
        PADINA
algarroba tree ...... **CALDEN**
d Algerian governor .... **DEY**
ALGERIA—see SPECIAL SEC-
    TION
ALGONQUIN .... see Page 192
Ali Baba's word ...... **SESAME**
Ali, caliph descendants **ALIDS**
Alien in Hebrew territory .. **GER**
alienate ... **WEAN, ESTRANGE**
align ... **TRUE, ALINE, RANGE**
alkali ..... **LYE, REH, USAR**
alkaline solution .... **LYE**
alkaloid .. **CAFFEIN, CAFFEINE**
alkaloid, calabar bean
        ESERINE
all: Lat. .... **TOTO**
all religions, believer in
        OMNIST
all right .... **OKAY, OKEH**
allanite .... **CERINE**
allay .... **CALM, ASSUAGE,
    RELIEVE**
alleged force .... **OD**
allegory, religious ... **PARABLE**
Allepo native .... **SYRIAN**
alleviate .... **EASE, ALLAY,
    LESSEN**
alley .... **MIB, MIG**
alliance ..... **UNION, LEAGUE**
alliance, Western ...... **NATO**
alligator .... **LAGARTO**

a alligator pear ..... AVOCADO
alligator, S.A. ...... CAIMAN,
CAYMAN
allot .... METE, GRANT,
ASSIGN, PORTION
allotment .... QUOTA, RATION
allow .... LET
allowance TARE, TRET, RATION
alloy .... MOKUM, OROIDE
alloy, aluminum ...... DURAL
alloy, copper .... BRASS
alloy, copper-tin ..... BRONZE
alloy, gold-silver: Egyp. . ASEM
alloy, lead-tin .. CALIN, TERNE
alloy, non-ferrous ...... TULA
alloy, yellow .... AICH
allspice .... PIMENTO
allure .... TICE, TOLE,
TEMPT, ENTICE
allusion .... HINT
almond emulsion ..... ORGEAT
almost .... ANEAR
alms box or chest ...... ARCA
aloe .... AGAVE
aloe derivative .... ALOIN
aloes product .... ALOIN
alone, on stage .. SOLA, SOLUS
along .... ON, BESIDE
alp .... PEAK
b alpaca .... PACO
alphabet letter, old .... RUNE
Alps, Austro-It.
TIROL, TYROL, TIROLO
Alps, one of .... BLANC
Alps pass .... CENIS
Alps, river rising in .. RHONE
Altar constellation ...... ARA
altar end of church .... APSE
altar screen .... REREDOS
altar shelf . GRADIN, RETABLE
altar side curtain .... RIDDEL
altar top .... MENSA
alternate .... ROTATE
alternative ...... OR, EITHER
alumni .... GRADS
always ... AY, AYE, EER, EVER
amadou .... PUNK
amass ...... HOARD, GATHER
amateur TIRO, TYRO, NOVICE
Amazon cetacean ...... INIA
Amazon tributary .. APA, ICA
ambary .... DA
ambary hemp ...... NALITA
ambassador .. ENVOY, LEGATE
amber fish
RUNNER, MEDREGAL
Amen-Ra's wife .... MUT
amend ALTER, EMEND, REVISE
amendment, document . RIDER
amends, make .... ATONE
ament .... CHAT

c Am. artist ..... WEST, HICKS,
HOMER, MARIN, PEALE, BEN-
TON, COPLEY, INNESS, COR-
BINO, ALBRIGHT
AMERICAN INDIAN ...... see
INDIANS, Page 192
Am. aloe fiber .... PITA, PITO
Am. author . ADE, POE. AMES,
BAUM, HARTE, WYLIE,
YERBY, CORWIN, FERBER,
HERSEY, KANTOR, MORLEY
Am. author, illustrator ... PYLE
Am. capitalist .... ASTOR
Am. caricaturist .. REA, NAST
Am. dramatist . AKINS, BARRY,
ODETS, CROUSE
Am. editor .... BOK
Am. educator .... MANN
Am. explorer . BYRD, FREMONT
Am. general
LEE, OTIS, GREENE
Am. humorist ...... ADE, NYE,
COBB, NASH, ROGERS
Am. jurist .... TANEY
Am. inventor ... IVES, MORSE,
TESLA, EDISON
American: Mex. ..... GRINGO
Am. nature writer BEEBE, SETON
Am. nighthawk .... PISK
AM. PAINTER see AM. ARTIST
d Am. patriot ...... HALE, OTIS,
ALLEN, REVERE
Am. philanthropist ...... RIIS
Am. philosopher ..... EDMAN
Am. pianist
ARRAU, DUCHIN, LEVANT
Am. poet . POE, AUDEN, BENET,
FROST, GUEST, RILEY,
STEIN, MILLAY
Am. poetess ... STEIN, LOWELL
Am. sculptor .... CALDER
AM. SINGER ... see SOPRANO
Am. statesman
CLAY, BARUCH, DULLES
Am. suffragist .... CATT
Am. surgeon .... PARRAN
AM. WRITER see AM. AUTHOR
AMERIND (means any American
Indian) See pages 192, 193
amide, pert. to .... AMIC
a mine: Corn. .... BAL
ammonia compound ... AMIN,
AMIDE, AMINE
ammoniac plant ...... OSHAC
ammunition . SHOT, SHRAPNEL
ammunition, short for: . AMMO,
AMMU
ammunition wagon ... CAISSON
among ...... IN, MID, AMID
amorously, stare .. LEER, OGLE
amount assessed ...... RATAL

Amount

a
amount staked in gambling **MISE**
amuse .... **DIVERT**
ampere................. **WEBER**
amphibian .... **FROG, TOAD,**
ANURAN
amphibian, order **HYLA, ANURA**
amphitheater .... **ARENA**
amphitheater, natural ... **CIRQUE**
amplification factor......... **MU**
amulet ..... **CHARM, PERIAPT**
analyze...... **ASSAY, DISSECT**
analyze grammatically ... **PARSE**
ancestor of Irish .. **IR, ITH, MIL,**
MILED
ancestor of man, Hindu .. **MANU**
ancestral spirit, P. I. ..... **ANITO**
ancestral .... **AVITAL**
ancestral spirits **LARES, MANES**
anchor **FIX, TIE, MOOR, KEDGE**
anchor part............. **FLUKE**
anchor, small, light ..... **KEDGE**
anchor tackle .... **CAT**
ancient Asiatic .... **MEDE**
ancient Briton.......... **CELT**
ancient Chinese......... **SERES**
anchovy sauce........... **ALEC**
ancient city, Asia Minor .. **MYRA,**
NICAEA
ancient country .... **GAUL**
Ancient Egyp. kingdom **SENNAR**
ancient flute .... **TIBIA**
ancient Greece division **AETOLIA**
ancient invader, India .... **SAKA,**
SACAE
b
ancient people of Gaul .... **REMI**
ancient Persian .... **MEDE**
ancient Persian money... **DARIC**
ancient philosophy ...... **YOGA**
ancient race .... **MEDES**
ancient Slav ..... **VEND, WEND,**
VENED
ancient times ...... **ELD, YORE**
ancient tribe of Britons ... **ICENI**
ancient weight .... **MINA**
and .. **TOO, ALSO, PLUS, WITH**
and: Lat.................... **ET**
and not .... **NOR**
and so on: abbr............ **ETC.**
Andes cold higher region . **PUNA**
Andes grass .... **ICHU**
Andes mountain....... **SORATA**
andiron................... **DOG**
"Andronicus,—"......... **TITUS**
anecdotage or anecdotes . **ANA,**
TALES
anent .... **RE, ABOUT, BESIDE**
anent, close— .... **TO**
anesthetic........ **GAS, ETHER**
Angel of Death........ **AZRAEL**
angel, Pers................ **MAH**

c
anger .... **IRE, RAGE, RILE,**
CHOLER
anger, fit of... **PIQUE, TEMPER**
angle, 57 degrees..... **RADIAN**
angle of leaf and axis...... **AXIL**
angle of leafstalk.......... **AXIL**
angle of stem, pert. to... **AXILE**
Anglo-Saxon "G"... **YOK, YOGH**
A.-S. god of peace .... **ING**
A.-S. lord's man **THANE, THEGN**
A.-S. king .... **INE**
A.-S. money (coin) .... **ORA**
A.-S. slave .... **ESNE**
A.-S. warrior... **THANE, THEGN**
Angora goat .... **CHAMAL**
angry .... **HOT, MAD, SORE,**
IRATE
animal, Afr..... **CIVET, GENET,**
POTTO, ZEBRA, GENETTE
animal, ant-eating .... **ECHIDNA**
animal, aquatic.. **SEAL, OTTER,**
WHALE, DUGONG,
WALRUS, MANATEE
animal, arboreal ...... **TARSIER**
animal, Austral....... **ECHIDNA**
animal, badgerlike, Java **TELEDU**
animal body .... **SOMA**
animal, draft .... **OX, OXEN**
d
animal, fabulous...... **DRAGON**
animal, giraffelike .... **OKAPI**
animal, India .... **DHOLE**
animal, Madagascar .... **FOSSA,**
FOUSSA
animals of area .... **FAUNA**
animal-plant life .... **BIOTA**
animal, Peru .... **ALPACA**
animal, sea ..... **SEAL, CORAL,**
WHALE, WALRUS,
DUGONG, MANATEE
animal, S. Afr. .... **ZORIL**
animal, S. Am. . **APARA, COATI**
animal trail . **RUN, SLOT, SPUR,**
SPOOR
animating principle .... **SOUL**
ankle.. **TALUS, TARSI, TARSUS**
ankle, pert. to......... **TARSAL**
Annamese measure .... **TAO**
Annapolis student **PLEB, PLEBE**
annatto seeds: Sp. ... **ACHIOTE**
anneal ... **TEMPER, TOUGHEN**
annex........ **ADD, ELL, WING,**
ATTACH
annihilate........... **DESTROY,**
DISCREATE
ANNIVERSARY .. see WEDDING
announce............. **HERALD**
annoy... **IRK, TRY, VEX, RILE,**
PEEVE, TEASE, BOTHER,
MOLEST, PESTER,
DISTURB

a annual, as winds .... **ETESIAN**
annuity, form of .... **TONTINE**
annul .... **UNDO, VOID,**
CANCEL, REVOKE
annular die .... **DOD**
annulet: Her. .... **VIRE**
anoint ... **OIL, ANELE, ENELE**
another ... **NEW, ADDITIONAL**
ant .... **EMMET, PISMIRE**
antarctic bird ...... **PENGUIN**
antarctic icebreaker .... **ATKA**
antecedent . **PRIOR, ANCESTOR**
antelope, Afr. .... **GNU, KOB,**
BISA, GUIB, KOBA, KUDU,
ORYX, POKU, PUKU, TORA,
ADDAX, ELAND, ORIBI,
RHEBOK
antelope, Afr., large .. **IMPALA**
antelope, Afr., small .. **DUIKER**
antelope, Ind.
SASIN, NILGAI, NILGAU
antelope, Siberian ..... **SAIGA**
antelope, tawny .... **ORIBI**
antenna **HORN, PALP, AERIAL**
FEELER
antenna, with nodose
NODICORN
anthracite, inferior ..... **CULM**
anti-aircraft shells ..... **FLAK**
anti-tank gun .... **PIAT**
b antic ... **DIDO, CAPER, PRANK**
antique red color .. **CHAUDRON**
antiseptic .... **EUPAD, EUSOL,**
IODIN, SALOL, CRESOL,
IODINE
antiseptic, mercury
EGOL, METAPHEN
antitoxin ...... **SERA, SERUM**
antler point .... **SNAG, TINE,**
PRONG
antler, unbranched ...... **DAG**
antlers, stag's .... **ATTIRE**
"Anthony and Cleopatra" character .... **IRAS**
anvil .... **INCUS, TEEST**
anxiety .... **CARE**
any: dialect .... **ONI**
any one .... **AN**
aoudad .... **ARUI**
apathy ... **ENNUI, DOLDRUMS**
ape .... **ORANG**
ape, long-tailed, India ... **KRA**
appelation ..... **NAME, TITLE**
APERTURE . see also OPENING
aperture .... **GAP, HOLE,**
SLOT, VENT, ORIFICE
apex, at the .... **APICAL**
aphasia, motor .... **ALALIA**
aphorism .. **SAW, RULE, SUTRA**
Aphrodite .... **VENUS**

c Aphrodite, got apple from
PARIS
Aphrodite, love of ... **ADONIS**
Aphrodite's mother .... **DIONE**
Aphrodite's son .... **EROS**
apocopate .... **ELIDE**
Apocrypha, book from . **ESDRAS**
Apollo's instrument ..... **BOW,**
LUTE, LYRE
Apollo's mother **LETO, LATONA**
Apollo's sister
DIANA, ARTEMIS
Apollo's son .... **ION**
Apollo's twin .... **ARTEMIS**
Apollo's vale, sacred ... **TEMPE**
apoplexy, plant .... **ESCA**
Apostle (12) .... **JOHN, JUDE**
(THADDEUS), JAMES, JUDAS,
PETER (SIMON PETER), SI-
MON, ANDREW, PHILIP,
THOMAS (DIDYMUS), MAT-
THEW (LEVI), MATTHIAS,
BARTHOLOMEW
Apostle, Capernaum **MATTHEW**
Apostles, teaching of . **DIDACHE**
apparent ..... **OVERT, PLAIN,**
EVIDENT
apparition .. **SPECTER, SPECTRE**
appear .... **LOOK, LOOM, SEEM**
appearance . **AIR, MIEN, GUISE**
d appease ...... **CALM, ALLAY**
PLACATE
appellation ..... **NAME, TITLE**
append .... **ADD, AFFIX,**
ATTACH
appendage, caudal ... ...**TAIL**
appetizer . **CANAPE, APERITIF**
apple ... **POME, TREE, FRUIT,**
PIPPIN
apple acid .... **MALIC**
apple seed .... **PIP**
apple tree .... **SORB**
apple tree genus ...... **MALUS**
apple, winter .... **ESOPUS**
apples, crushed ..... **POMACE**
apple-like fruit .... **POME**
appoint .. **SET, NAME, CHOOSE**
apportion **DEAL, METE, ALLOT**
appraise **RATE, VALUE, ASSESS**
apprise ...... **ADVISE, NOTIFY**
approach ...... **NEAR, ANEAR,**
ACCESS
appropriate, ... **APT, FIT, MEET**
appropriate, not **INAPT, UNFIT**
apricot, Jap. .... **UME**
apricot, Korean . **ANSU, ANZU**
apricots .... **MEBOS**
apropos .... **PAT, FITTING**
apteryx .... **KIWI**
aptitude ..... **FLAIR, ABILITY**

Aptitude

a aptitude, natural
  FLAIR, TALENT
aquamarine .... **BERYL**
AQUATIC . see SEA or MARINE
Arab ....**GAMIN, SEMITE**
Arab cloak, sleeveless .... **ABA**
Arab drink ...... **BOSA, BOZA**
  BOZAH
Arab name .... **ALI**
Arab's state of bliss ..... **KEF**
Arabia, people of ..... **OMANI**
ARABIAN . see ARAB, ARABIA,
  SPECIAL SECTION
Arabian chief . **SAYID, SAYYID**
Arabian chieftain **AMIR, EMIR,**
  AMEER, EMEER
Arabian chieftain's domain
  EMIRATE
Arabian cloth .... **ABA**
Arabian district .... **TEMA**
Arabian garment .... **ABA**
Arabian jasmine .... **BELA**
Arabian judge .... **CADI**
"Arabian Nights" dervish . **AGIB**
Arabian noble .. **AMIR, EMIR,**
  AMEER, EMEER
Arabian nomadic tribesman
  SLEB
Arabian sailboat .. see VESSEL,
  ARAB
Arabian sleeveless garment **ABA**
b Arabian tambourine
  TAAR, DAIRA, DAIRE
Arabic jinni, evil
  AFRIT, AFREET, AFRITE
Arabic letter . **GAF, KAF, MIM,**
  WAW, ALIF, DHAL
Arabic script .... **NESKI**
Arabic surname .... **SAAD**
arachnid . **MITE, TICK, SPIDER**
Arawakan language .... **TAINO**
arbitrator ... **UMPIRE, REFEREE**
arboreal .... **DENDRAL**
arc .... **LINE, CURVE**
arch of heaven .... **COPE**
arch, pointed .... **OGIVE**
archaeology, mound ..... **TERP**
archangel .... **URIEL**
archbishop .... **PRIMATE**
archbishop, Canterbury **BECKET**
archer in Eng. ballad
  CLIM, CLYM
archetype ... **MODEL, PATTERN**
archfiend .... **SATAN**
architect's drawing ..... **EPURE**
architecture, school of
  BAUHAUS
architecture, type
  DORIC, IONIC
ARCTIC ..... see GAZETTEER
Arctic . **NORTH, POLAR, FRIGID**

c arctic air force base .... **THULE**
arctic dog .... **SAMOYED**
arctic gull genus ...... **XEMA**
arctic plain .... **TUNDRA**
Arden .... **FOREST**
ardor ... **ELAN, ZEAL, FERVOR**
area measure .. **RADII, RADIUS**
area, small .... **AREOLA**
areca .... **BETEL**
arena .... **FIELD**
Ares' mother .... **ENYO**
Ares' sister .... **ERIS**
ares, 10 .... **DECARE**
Argonaut ... **JASON, ACASTUS**
Argonauts' leader ...... **JASON**
Argonauts' ship .... **ARGO**
argument .... **AGON,**
  DEBATE, HASSLE
arhat .... **LOHAN**
aria ...... **AIR, SOLO, SONG,**
  TUNE, MELODY
arias .... **SOLI**
aridity, having .... **XERIC**
arikara .... **REE**
arise .... **REBEL, ACCRUE,**
  APPEAR
arista .... **AWN**
Arizona aborigine ...... **HOPI**
ARIZONA INDIAN see page 192
d **ARIZONA** ... see also SPECIAL
  SECTION
Ark, porter of: Bible ..... **BEN**
Ark's landing place .. **ARARAT**
arm .... **LIMB, TENTACLE**
arm, movable with verniers
  ALIDADE
arm of sea . **BAY, FIRTH, FRITH**
armadillo ...... **APAR, APARA**
armadillo, Braz. . **TATU, TATOU**
armadillo, giant . **TATU, TATOU**
armadillo, large 12-banded
  TATOUAY
armadillo, 6-banded .. **PELUDO**
armadillo, small .. **PEBA, PEVA**
armadillo, 3-banded .... **APAR,**
  APARA, MATACO, MATICO
armed band .... **POSSE**
armed galley of old Northmen
  AESC
ARMOR .... see also SPECIAL
  SECTION, page 194
armor bearer .... **ARMIGER**
armor, body .... **CUIRASS**
armor, chain .... **MAIL**
armor, horse .. **BARD, BARDE**
armor, leg .... **JAMB, JAMBE**
armor, leg below knee **GREAVE**
armor, lower body ..... **CULET**

12

a

armor part .... **LORICA**
armor part, throat .... **GORGET**
armor, skirt .... **TACE, TASSE, TASSET**
armor, thigh ... **CUISH, TUILE, CUISSE, TUILLE**
armpit .... **ALA**
army .... **HOST, TROOPS**
army group .... **CADRE**
army provisioner ...... **SUTLER**
aroid, an .... **ARAD, ARUM**
aromatic herb
.... **DILL, MINT, SAGE**
aromatic herb, carrot genus
.... **CARUM**
aromatic herb-plant .... **NARD**
aromatic seed
.... **CUMIN, CUMMIN**
aromatic seed, plant ... **ANISE**
aromatic substance ... **BALSAM**
aromatic weed .... **TANSY**
around .... **CIRCA**
arouse .... **FIRE, STIR, PIQUE**
arpeggio .... **ROULADE**
arquebus support ...... **CROC**
arraign ..... **ACCUSE, INDICT**
arrange ...... **FIX, SET, FILE, DISPOSE**
arrangement: comb. form . **TAX, TAXI, TAXO, TAXEO, TAXIS**

b

arrangement, pert. to. .**TACTIC**
array .. **DECK, ORDER, ATTIRE**
arrest .... **NAB, HALT**
arrest writ .... **CAPIAS**
arris .... **PIEN**
arrow .... **BOLT, DART**
arrow, body of .... **STELE**
arrow, fit string to ..... **NOCK**
arrow, spinning .... **VIRE**
arrow wood .... **WAHOO**
arrowroot .... **PIA, ARARU**
arroyo .... **HONDO**
art: Lat. .... **ARS**
art style .... **DADA, GENRE**
Artemis . **UPIS, DELIA, PHOEBE**
Artemis' twin .... **APOLLO**
Artemis' victim ...... **ORION**
artery, largest .... **AORTA**
artery of neck ...... **CAROTID**
artful .... **SLY, WILY**
arthritis aid **ACTH, CORTISONE**
Arthur's foster brother ... **KAY**
Arthurian lady
.... **ENID, ELAIN, ELAINE**
article .... **AN, THE, ITEM**
article, Fr. ...... **LA, LE, DES, LES, UNE**
article, Ger. .... **DAS, DER**
article, Sp. .. **EL, LA, LAS, LOS**
articulated joint ...... **HINGE**
artifice ... **RUSE, WILE, TRICK**

c

artificial language .... **RO, IDO**
ARTIST .... see also **PAINTER**
and under Country
of each artist
artist, primitive .... **MOSES**
artless .... **NAIVE**
arum family plant **TARO, CALLA**
arum plant ..... **ARAD, AROID**
Aryan .... **MEDE, SLAV**
as .. **QUA, LIKE, SINCE, WHILE**
as far as .... **TO**
as it stands: mus. .... **STA**
as written: mus. .... **STA**
asafetida .... **HING**
asbestos .... **ABISTON**
ascent .... **UPGO, CLIMB**
ascetic, ancient .... **ESSENE**
asceticism, Hindu ...... **YOGA**
ash, fruit, seed ..... **SAMARA**
ash key .... **SAMARA**
ashy pale .... **LIVID**
ASIA .. see also SPECIAL SEC-
TION
Asia Minor district, old **IONIA**
Asia Minor region, pert. to
.... **EOLIC, AEOLIC**
Asia native, S.E. ...... **SHAN**
Asiatic ancient people .. **SERES**

d

Asiatic country .. see page 210
Asiatic cow .... **ZO, ZOH**
Asiatic evergreen ...... **BAGO**
Asiatic fowl .... **SAT**
Asiatic gangster .... **DACOIT**
Asiatic sardine .... **LOUR**
Asiatic shrub .... **TEA, TCHE**
Asiatic tree .... **ACLE, ASAK, ASOK, ASOKA**
"— asinorum" .... **PONS**
askew .... **WRY, AGEE, ALOP, AWRY**
aspect ... **SIDE, FACET, PHASE**
asperse .... **SLANDER**
aspire .... **HOPE**
ass, wild
.... **KULAN, ONAGER, QUAGGA**
assail .... **BESET, ATTACK**
ASSAM ..... see also SPECIAL
SECTION, Page 191
Assam hill tribe .... **AKA**
Assam mongol .... **NAGA**
Assam silkworm .... **ERI, ERIA**
Assam tribe, Naga Hills
.... **AO, NAGA**
assault .... **ONSET, STORM**
assault, prolonged ...... **SIEGE**
assayer .... **TESTER**
assaying cup .... **CUPEL**
assemble .... **MEET, MUSTER, COLLECT**

13

a assembly .... DIET, SYNOD
      SESSION, GATHERING
    assembly, A.-S. GEMOT, GEMOTE
    assembly, China, Hawaii .. HUI
    assembly, Dutch .... RAAD
    assent, solemn .... AMEN
    assert .... AVER, POSIT, STATE
    assert formally .... ALLEGATE
    assess ..... TAX, LEVY, VALUE
    assessment RATE, SCOT, RATAL
    asseverate .... AVER
    assignor of property ... CEDENT
    assimilate .. ABSORB, DIGEST
    assistance AID, HELP, SUPPORT
    assistant .... AIDE
    associate .. ALLY, COLLEAGUE
    association, trade GILD, GUILD
    assuage .... MITIGATE
    ASSYRIAN .. see also SPECIAL
        SECTION, Page 198
    Assyrian king .... PUL
    Assyrian queen, myth.
            SEMIRAMIS
    asterisk .... STAR
    astern ..... AFT, BAFT, ABAFT
    astringent .... ALUM, STYPTIC
    astringent, black ...... KATH
    astringent fruit .... SLOE
    astrologer of India .... JOSHI
b astronomical .... URANIC
    astron. luminous "cloud"
                NEBULA
    Aswan, ancient .... SYENE
    asylum ...... HAVEN, REFUGE
    at all .... ANY
    at any time .... EVER
    at odds .... OUT
    at the home of: Fr. ...... CHEZ
    Atahualpa, king ... ... INCA
    atap palm .... NIPA
    atelier .... STUDIO
    Athamas' wife .... INO
    Athena ... PALLAS, MINERVA
    Athena, appellation, title . ALEA
    Athena, possession of ... EGIS
    Athenian .... ATTIC
    Athenian bronze coin CHALCUS
    Athenian demagogue ... CLEON
    Athens, last king of ... CODRUS
    athlete, famous ...... THORPE
    a-tiptoe .... ATIP
    atmospheric pressure, of BARIC
    at no time: poet. ...... NEER
    atoll's pool .... LAGOON
    atom part .... PROTON
    atomic machine
        BETATRON, RHEOTRON
    atomic physicist .. BOHR, RABI,
            UREY, FERMI, PAULI,
            COMPTON, MEITNER
            MILLIKAN

c atomic submarine .... SKATE,
        SARGO, TRITON, NAUTILUS
    atone for .... REDEEM
    attach .... ADD, FIX, TIE,
                APPEND
    attack .... BESET, ONSET
    attack, mock .... FEINT
    attar .... OTTO
    attempt .... TRY, STAB, ESSAY
    attendant, hunter's
                GILLY, GILLIE
    attention ... EAR, CARE, HEED
    attest ..... VOUCH, CERTIFY
    attic .... LOFT, GARRET
    Attica resident .... METIC
    Attila .... ATLI, ETZEL
    attitudinize .... POSE
    attribute .. IMPUTE, ASCRIBE
    attune .... KEY, ACCORD
    auction .... SALE
    audience ...... EAR, HEARING
    auditory .... OTIC, AURAL
    auger .... BORE, BORER
    augment .... EKE
    augur .... BODE, PORTEND
    augury ...... OMEN, PORTENT
    auk genus .. ALCA, ALLE, URIA
    auk, little ... ROTCH, ROTCHE
    aura, pert. to .... AURIC
d aureola .... HALO
    auric acid salt ...... AURATE
    auricle .... EAR
    auricular ...... OTIC, EARED
    aurochs .. TUR, URUS, AURUS
    aurora .... EOS, DAWN
    auspices .... EGIS, AEGIS
    Australasian harrier-hawk
                KAHU
    Australasian shrub genus
                HOYA
    AUSTRALIA . see also SPECIAL
                SECTION
    Australian boomerang .. KILEY
    Austral. food .... KAI
    Austral. gum tree
                KARI, TUART
    Austral. hut .... MIAM, MIMI
    Austral. marsupial
                TAIT, KOALA
    Austral. scaly-finned fish
                MADO
    Austral. tree, timber .. PENDA
    Austrian folk dance .. DREHER
    Austr. violinist .... MORINI
    author .... PARENT
    author, boys' .. ALGER, HENTY
    author, nature stories .. SETON
    authoritative .... MAGISTRAL
    author unknown: abbr. .. ANON

a authority, name as **CITE, QUOTE**
auto, old .. **JALOPY, JALOPPY**
automaton .... **ROBOT**
automaton: Jew. legend **GOLEM**
automobile "shoe" . **TIRE, TYRE**
ave .... **HAIL**
avena .... **OAT**
avenger: Hebr. .... **GOEL**
average .... **PAR, MEAN,
      NORM, USUAL, MEDIAL**
averse .... **LOTH, LOATH**
Avesta division
   YASNA, GATHAS, YASHTS
avid .... **KEEN, EAGER**
avifauna .... **ORNIS**
avocado, Mex. .... **COYO**
avoid .... **SHUN, ESCHEW**

c avouch .... **AVER, ASSERT**
away .... **OFF, GONE, ABSENT**
aweather, opposed to .... **ALEE**
aweto .... **WERI**
awkward .... **INEPT**
awkward fellow .... **LOUT**
awn .... **ARISTA**
awned .... **ARISTATE**
awry .... **AGEE, AJEE, AGLEY**
axilla .... **ALA**
axilla, pert. to .... **ALAR**
axillary .... **ALAR**
axis deer .... **CHITAL**
Aztec god, sowing ...... **XIPE**
Aztec "Noah" (hero) ... **NATA**
Aztec "Noah's" wife ... **NANA**
Aztec spear .... **ATLATL**

B

babbler: Scot. ...... **HAVEREL**
Babism, founder .... **BAB**
babul tree pods ...... **GARAD**
baby animal: Fr. .... **TOTO**
baby carriage .... **PRAM**
b **BABYLONIAN GODS, DEITY,**
   see also GODS and also SPE-
   CIAL SECTION on page 198
Babylonian abode of dead
        ARALU
Babylonian city .... **IS**
Babylonian chief gods ... **EA,
   ANU, BEL, HEA, ENKI**
Babylonian chief goddess
     ISTAR, ISHTAR
Babylonian chief priest of
  shrine .... **EN**
Babylonian division .... **SUMER**
Babylonian hero ...... **ETANA**
Babylonian lunar cycle
        SAROS
Babylonian neighbor
       ELAMITE
Babylonian numeral .... **SAROS**
Babylonian priestess .. **ENTUM**
Babylonian purgatory .. **ARALU**
Bacchanals' cry .... **EVOE**
bacchante .... **MAENAD**
Bacchus' follower ...... **SATYR**
Bacchus' son .... **COMUS**
back .. **AID, AFT, FRO, ABET,
   HIND, REAR, SPONSOR**
back, call .... **REVOKE**
back door .... **POSTERN**
back, flow ...... **EBB, RECEDE**
back, lying on ...... **SUPINE**
back of neck .... **NAPE**
back, pert. to ...... **DORSAL**

back, take .... **RETRACT**
back, thrust .... **REPEL**
back, toward .... **RETRAL**
back: Zool. **NOTA, NOTUM**
d backbone ...... **CHINE, SPINE**
bacteria-free .... **ASEPTIC**
bacteriologist's wire ..... **OESE**
bacteriostatic subst. . **CITRININ**
badge, Jap. .... **MON**
badger .... **DAS, BAIT**
badgerlike animal
     PAHMI, RATEL
badgers, Old World .... **MELES**
baffle .... **FOIL, POSE, ELUDE**
bag .... **SAC**
bag net .... **FYKE**
bagatelle .... **TRIFLE**
bagpipe, hole in .... **LILL**
bagpipe sound .... **SKIRL**
bailiff, old Eng. .... **REEVE**
baize fabric .... **DOMETT**
baker bird .... **HORNERO**
baking chamber ... **OST, KILN,
     OAST, OVEN**
baking pit .... **IMU**
balance .. **REST, POISE, SCALE**
balance, sentence ... **PARISON**
Balance, The .... **LIBRA**
balancing weight ... **BALLAST**
Balder's killer **LOK, LOKE, LOKI**
Balder's wife .... **NANNA**
baldness .... **ACOMIA**
Balkan .... **SERB**
ball, low .... **LINER**
ball, to hit

    LOB, BUNT, SWAT

a
ball, yarn thread ...... **CLEW**
ballad .... **LAY, DERRY**
ballet jump .... **JETE**
ballet skirt .... **TUTU**
ballet turn .... **FOUETTE**
balloon basket **CAR, NACELLE**
ball-rope missile
　　　　　　　BOLA, BOLAS
balm of Gilead ..... **BALSAM**
balsalike wood .... **BONGO**
balsam .... **FIR, TOLU, RESIN**
Balt .... **ESTH**
BALTIC ... see also SPECIAL
　　SECTION
Baltic Finn .... **VOD**
Baltimore stove .... **LATROBE**
Balto-Slav .... **LETT**
Baluchistan tribe .... **REKI**
Baluchistan tribesman .. **MARI**
"Bambi" author ...... **SALTEN**
bamboo .... **REED**
bamboo shoots, pickled **ACHAR**
Bana's daughter: Hindu **USHA**
banal .... **STALE, TRITE**
banana genus .... **MUSA**
banana, kind of .. **PLANTAIN**
banana, Polyn. .... **FEI**
band .... **BELT, TAPE,**
　　　　　　　STRIP, FILLET
band: Arch. .. **FACIA, FASCIA**
band, muscle, nerve .. **TAENIA**
band, narrow .. **STRIA, STRIAE**
bandage ...... **STUPE, TAENIA**
bandicoot .... **RAT**

b
bandmaster, Am. ..... **SOUSA**
banish ..... **EXILE, RELEGATE**
bank .... **RELY, DEPEND**
bank, of a river ... **RIPARIAN**
bank, river .... **RIPA**
banker, India .. **SARAF, SHROFF**
banner .... **FLAG,**
　　　ENSIGN, BANDEROLE
banter ... **CHAFF, PERSIFLAGE**
BANTU 　 see also TRIBES in
　　SPECIAL SECTION, Page 191
Bantu .... **KAFIR, KAFFIR**
Bantu, Congo ... **RUA, WARUA**
Bantu language .... **ILA**
Bantu nation .... **GOGO**
Bantu-speaking tribe
　　RAVI, RORI, PONDO
Bantu tribesman ..... **DUALA**
baobab, dried .... **LALO**
baobab leaves, powdered **LALO**
baptism font .... **LAVER**
baptismal basin .... **FONT**
bar .... **RAIL, INGOT,**
　　　HINDER, STRIPE
bar legally .... **ESTOP**
bar, supporting .... **FID**
barb, feather .... **HARL, HERL**

c
Barbados native .... **BIM**
barbarian .... **HUN, GOTH**
Barbary ape .... **MAGOT**
barber ..... **SHAVER, TONSOR**
bard, Goth. .... **RUNER**
bare ..... **BALD, MERE, NUDE**
bargain .... **DEAL, PALTER**
bargain: Dutch .... **KOOP**
barge .... **HOY**
bark .... **BAY, YAP, YIP**
bark, bitter .. **NIEPA, NIOTA**
bark, inner .... **CORTEX**
bark, lime tree .. **BAST, BASTE**
bark, medicinal .... **COTO**
bark, paper mulberry .. **TAPA**
bark, pert. to ..... **CORTICAL**
bark remover .... **ROSSER**
bark, rough exterior .... **ROSS**
barking .... **LATRANT**
barn owl genus .... **TYTO**
barometric line ...... **ISOBAR**
barony, Jap. .... **HAN**
barracuda, small **SPET, SENNET**
barrelmaker .... **COOPER**
barrel slat .... **STAVE**
barren land .... **USAR**
Barrie character ...... **ALICE**
barrow, Russ. .... **KURGAN**
base .... **LOW, VILE**
base, architectural
　　　SOCLE, PLINTH

d
base, attached by .... **SESSILE**
baseball position: abbr. .... **LF,**
　　　　　　　RF, SS
Bashan, king of .... **OG**
bashful .... **COY, SHY, TIMID**
basilica, Rome ..... **LATERAN**
basin: Geol. .... **TALA**
basis of argument ... **PREMISE**
basket .... **KISH, CABAS,**
　　　PANIER, PANNIER
basket, coarse .... **SKEP**
basket, Eng. ...... **PED, CAUL**
basket, fish ... **WEEL, CRAIL,**
　　　CREEL, WICKER
basket grass, Mex. ..... **OTATE**
basket, large .... **HAMPER**
basket strip .... **RAND**
basketball player ..... **CAGER**
basketry rod .... **OSIER**
Basra native .... **IRAQI**
bass, Europ. .... **BRASSE**
basswood .... **LINDEN**
bast fiber .... **RAMIE**
bat .... **RACKET**
batfish .... **DIABLO**
bathe .... **LAVE**
bathing-suit .... **MAILLOT**
baths, Roman ..... **THERMAE**
Bathsheba's husband
　　　URIA, URIAH

a baton .... **ROD**
batrachian ...... **FROG, TOAD**
batter .... **RAM**
battering machine ...... **RAM**
battery plate .... **GRID**
battle, Am. Rev. ... **CONCORD**
battle area .... **SECTOR**
battle, Arthur's last .. **CAMLAN**
battle ax ... **TWIBIL, TWIBILL**
battle, Civil War, Tenn. **SHILOH**
battle cry, Irish .. **ABU, ABOO**
battle, Eng.-Fr. **CRECY, CRESSY**
battle formation ...... **HERSE**
battle, Franco-Pruss. .. **SEDAN**
battle, 100 Years War
                CRECY, CRESSY
"Battle Hymn of Republic"
author .... **HOWE**
battle, WWI .. **MARNE, SOMME,**
                YPRES, VERDUN
battlefield .... **ARENA**
bauble .... **BEAD**
bay .... **COVE, BIGHT, INLET**
bay, Orkney, Shetland ... **VOE**
bay tree .... **LAUREL**
bay window .... **ORIEL**
bazaar .... **FAIR**
be foolishly overfond ... **DOAT,**
                DOTE
be silent: music ...... **TACET**
b be still .... **SH, HUSH, QUIET**
beach .... **SHORE, STRAND**
beach cabin .... **CABANA**
beads, prayer .... **ROSARY**
beak .... **NEB, NIB, BILL**
beam, supporting
        TEMPLET, TEMPLATE
bean .... **SOY, URD, LIMA**
bean, E. Ind. .... **URD**
bean, field .... **PINTO**
bean, green .... **HARICOT**
bean, poisonous ... **CALABAR**
bean, S. Am. .... **TONKA**
bean tree .... **CAROB**
bear .. **STAND, YIELD, ENDURE**
Bear constellation ...... **URSA**
bear, nymph changed to
                CALLISTO
bear, Austral. .... **KOALA**
bear witness .. **VOUCH, ATTEST**
beard of grain .. **AWN, ARISTA**
bearded seal .... **MAKLUK**
bearer, Ind. .... **SINDAR**
bearing .... **MIEN, ORLE**
bearing plate .... **GIB**
bear's-ear .... **ARICULA**
beast of burden .... **ASS,**
                BURRO, LLAMA
beat .... **WIN, CANE, DRUB,**
        FLAP, POMMEL, PULSE
beat about: naut. ...... **BUSK**

c beater, mortar .... **RAB**
beauty, goddess of: Hindu
    SRI, SHRI, SHREE, LAKSHMI
beauty, Greek .... **LAIS**
beaver .... **CASTOR**
beaver skin .... **PLEW**
beche-de-mer ...... **TREPANG**
beckon .... **NOD**
bed .... **KIP, PALLET**
bed of dry stream .... **DONGA**
bed of press, handle .. **ROUNCE**
bed: slang .... **DOSS**
Bedouin headband cord .. **AGAL**
bee, honey, genus ...... **APIS**
bee house ..... **APIARY, HIVE**
bee, male .... **DRONE**
bee tree .... **LINDEN**
bees, pert. to .... **APIAN**
bee's pollen brush ..... **SCOPA**
beech tree genus ...... **FAGUS**
beechnuts .... **MAST**
beefwood: Polyn. ...... **TOA,**
                TOOA, BELAH
beehive, straw .... **SKEP**
Beehive State .. see page 209
beer ...... **ALE, BOCK, LAGER**
beer, Afr. millet ..... **POMBE**
beer ingredient .. **HOPS, MALT**
beer mug .... **STEIN**
beer, P. l. rice ..... **PANGASI**
d beet variety .... **CHARD**
Beethoven's birthplace . **BONN**
beetle .... **DOR, ELATER**
beetle, burrowing ...... **BORER**
beetle, click .... **ELATER**
beetle, fruit-loving .... **BORER**
beetle genus, ground .. **AMARA**
beetle, ground .... **CARAB**
beetle, sacred Egyp. .. **SCARAB**
beetle, wood .... **SAWYER**
befall .... **HAP**
before .... **ERE, PRE,**
                ANTERIOR
before: obs. .... **ERER**
before: naut. .... **AFORE**
beget .... **EAN, SIRE**
"Beggar's Opera" dramatist
                GAY
beginner .... **TIRO, TYRO,**
            NOVICE, NEOPHYTE
beginning .... **GERM, ONSET,**
            ORIGIN, INITIAL
beginning .... **NASCENCY**
behave toward .... **TREAT**
behind .... **AFT, AREAR,**
                ASTERN
behold ..... **LO, ECCE, VOILA**
behoove .... **DOW**
beige .... **ECRU**
being .... **ENS, ENTITY**

a being, abstract **ENS, ESSE, ENTIA**
being, essential .... **ENS**
Bela, son of .... **IRI**
beleaguerment .... **SIEGE**
Belem .... **PARA**
belief .... **CREED, FAITH, TENET**
believe .... **TROW, CREDO, CREDIT**
believer in god of reason **DEIST**
bell, alarm .... **TOCSIN**
bell, sacring .... **SQUILLA**
bell tower .... **BELFRY, CAMPANILE**
bell's tongue ...... **CLAPPER**
bellbird, N.Z. .... **MAKO**
bellowing .... **AROAR**
below: nautical .... **ALOW**
belt .... **CEST, SASH**
belt, sword .... **BALDRIC, BAWDRIC, BALDRICK**
ben .... **BENE**
bench ...... **EXEDRA, SETTLE**
bench, judge's .. see JUDGE'S BENCH
bench in a galley ...... **BANK**
bend .... **SNY, FLEX, GENU, STOOP, FLEXURE**
benediction .... **BENISON**
benefactor .... **PATRON**
beneficiary: Law ...... **USES**

b benefit .... **BOON, AVAIL**
Bengal native .... **KOL**
Bengal singer .... **BAUL**
Benjamin's first born .. **BELA**
bent .... **PRONATE**
bequeath .... **WILL**
bequest .... **DOWER**
Berber .... **RIFF**
Bermuda arrowroot **ARARU, ARARAO**
Bermuda grass .. **DOOB, DOUB**
berserk .... **AMOK, AMUCK**
beseech .... **PRAY, OBTEST, ENTREAT**
beside .... **BY**
besides .. **TOO, YET, ALSO, ELSE**
bestow .... **AWARD, CONFER, IMPART**
bets, fail to pay **WELCH, WELSH**
betel leaf ...... **BUYO, PAUN**
betel nut .... **SERI, SIRI, BONGA, SIRIH**
betel palm .. **ARECA, PINANG**
betel pepper ..... **IKMO, ITMO**
Bethuel's son .... **LABAN**
betoken .... **DENOTE**
betroth .... **AFFY**
between: prefix .... **INTER**
Bevan's nickname .... **NYE**

c bevel .... **BEZEL, SLANT**
bevel out .... **REAM**
bevel ship timber ..... **SNAPE**
bevel to join .. **MITER, MITRE**
BEVERAGE ... see also **DRINK**
beverage .... **ADE, ALE, TEA, BEER**
beverage, curdled .... **POSSET**
beverage, hot wine .... **NEGUS**
beverage, Polyn. **KAVA, KAWA**
beverage, S. Am. .... **MATE**
bewitch .... **HEX, SPELL**
beyond: comb. form .. **ULTRA**
Bhutan pine .... **KAIL**
biased person .... **BIGOT**
BIBLICAL .. see also SPECIAL SECTION
Biblical city .... **DAN, BABEL, EKRON**
Biblical character .. **ARA, IRA, ERI, ARAN, ATER, ONAN**
Biblical country . **EDOM, ENON SEBA, SHEBA**
Biblical driver .... **JEHU**
Biblical judge .... **ELI, ELON, GIDEON, SAMSON**
Biblical king **OG, ASA, AGAG, AHAB, ELAH, OMRI, SAUL, HEROD, NADAB**

d Biblical kingdom ...... **ELAM, MOAB, SAMARIA**
Biblical land .... **NOD**
Biblical lion .... **ARI**
BIBLICAL MEASURE ...... see HEBREW MEASURE
BIBLICAL MOUNT see Page 197
Biblical name .... **ED, ER, IRI, ONO, REI, TOI. ABIA, ADER, ANER, ANIM, ASOM, DARA, ENOS, IRAD, IVAH, REBA, ABIAM, AHIRA, AMASA, ASEAS**
Biblical name for part of Arabia **SHEBA**
Biblical ornaments ..... **URIM**
Biblical priest, high ...... **ELI, AARON, ANNAS**
Biblical region .. **ARAM, EDAR**
Biblical ruler .... **IRA**
Biblical sacred objects .. **URIM**
Biblical serpent .. **NEHUSHTAN**
Biblical son .... **HAM**
Biblical spy .... **CALEB**
Biblical tower .... **EDAR**
Biblical town in Samaria **ENON**
BIBLICAL TRIBE .... see Page 197
Biblical weed .... **TARE**
Biblical well; spring . **AIN, ESEK**
Biblical wild ox .... **REEM**

a
Biblical witch's home .. ENDOR
Biblical woman RAHAB, LEAH
Biblical word .. SELAH, MENE
Biblical word of reproach RACA
bicarbonate .... SODA
bice blue .... AZURITE
bicker .... CAVIL
bicycle for two ...... TANDEM
biddy .... HEN
"— bien" .... TRES
big casino .... TEN
bile .... GALL
bill .... DUN, NEB, BEAK
bill of fare ..... MENU, CARTE
bill, part of .... CERE
billiard shot .. CAROM, MASSE
billow .... SEA, WAVE
bind .... TAPE, SWATH
biography ..... LIFE, MEMOIR
biological .. BIOTIC, BIOTICAL
biological reproductive body
                      GAMETE
biotic community ..... BIOME

b
bird .... CLEE, COCK, CROW,
   DOVE, FINK, GLED, HUIA,
   IIWI, JACU, KALA, KIWI,
   KOEL, KORA, KUKU, KYAH,
   LARK, LOON, LORO, LORY,
   LOUN, LOWA, LULU, LUPE,
   MAKO, MAMO, MIRO,
   MOHO, MORO, MYNA,
   NENE, PAPE, PEHO, PISK,
   RAIL, RAYA, ROOK, RUFF,
   RURU, RYPE, SKUA, SMEE,
   SMEW, SORA, STIB, SWAN,
   TEAL, TERN, TOCK, TOCO,
   TODY, UTUM, WAEG,
   WREN, YENI, YUTU,
   DRAKE, ROBIN, SERIN, EL-
   ANET, SHRIKE, SISKIN,
bird, Am. .... TOWHEE
bird, Arctic .. BRANT, FULMAR
bird, Austral. .... EMU, KOEL,
                COOEE, COOEY
bird, black ANI, ROOK, RAVEN
bird, blue .... JAY
bird, C. & S. Am. ...... COIN,
              CONDOR, CONDORES
bird cry .... CAW, COO
bird, diving ...... AUK, LOON,
                    LOUN, SMEW
bird, ducklike .... COOT
bird, extinct .... MOA,
                   DODO, MAMO
bird, Europ. .... GLEDE, TEREK
bird genus ...... CRAX, RHEA
bird, gull-like .... TERN
BIRD, HAWAIIAN .... see
          HAWAIIAN BIRD
bird house .... COTE
bird, hunting .... FALCON

c
bird, India .... SARUS
              SHAMA, ARGALA
bird, laughing .... LOON
bird life .... ORNIS
bird, long-legged
              AGAMI, STILT
bird, marsh .... RAIL,
              SORA, BITTERN
bird, mythical .... ROC
bird, national .... EAGLE
bird nest collector .. OOLOGIST
bird of prey ..... ERN, ERNE,
         HAWK, KITE, EAGLE,
                    CORMORANT
bird, orange .... ORIOLE
bird order ..... PICI, RASORES
bird, oscine .. CHAT, ORIOLE
BIRD, OSTRICHLIKE ...... see
          OSTRICHLIKE BIRD
bird, Persian .... BULBUL
BIRD, SEA ..... see SEA BIRD
bird, shore RAIL, SORA, SNIPE,
      WADER, AVOCET, PLOVER
bird, small .... TIT, PIPIT
bird, small brown ...... WREN
BIRD, S. AM. .... see
              S. AMER. BIRD
bird, swimming .. LOON, GREBE
bird, talking .. MYNA, MYNAH

d
bird, tropical ..... ANI, ANO,
         TROGON, JACAMAR
bird, U. S.
      COLIN, VEERY, TANAGER
BIRD, WADING .... see
         ..WADING BIRD
bird, wading, Afr.
      UMBER, UMBRETTE
bird, water see WADING BIRD
BIRD, WEB-FOOTED .... see
          WEB-FOOTED BIRD
bird, W. Ind. .... TODY
bird, white-plumed .... EGRET
bird, white-tailed .. ERN, ERNE
birds .... AVES
bird's beak .... NEB, NIB
bird's cry .... CAW, WEET
birds of region .... ORNIS
birds' route .... FLYWAY
biretta .... CAP
birth, by .... NEE
birth, of one's .... NATAL
birthmark
      MOLE, NEVUS, NAEVUS
birthplace, Apollo, Diana DELOS
birthplace, Constantine's
                  NIS, NISH
birthplace, Mohammed's MECCA
birthplace, Muses, Orpheus
                    PIERIA

a birthstone .... Jan., **GARNET;**
Feb., **AMETHYST;** March,
**JASPER, AQUAMARINE,
BLOODSTONE;** April, **DIA-
MOND;** May, **AGATE, EM-
ERALD;** June, **PEARL,
MOONSTONE;** July, **ONYX,
RUBY;** Aug., **CARNELIAN,
SARDONYX, PERIDOT;**
Sept., **SAPPHIRE;** Oct.,
OPAL; Nov., **TOPAZ;** Dec.,
TURQUOISE, ZIRCON
birthwort, Europ. .. **CLEMATITE**
bishop .... **PRELATE**
bishop of Róme .... **POPE**
bishopric .... **SEE**
bishop's attendant ... **VERGER**
bishop's hat
  HURA, MITER, MITRE
bishop's office .... **LAWN**
bishop's seat ...... **SEE, APSE**
bishop's title, East ..... **ABBA**
bite .... **CHAM, MORSEL**
bite upon .... **GNAW**
biting .... **ACERB, ACRID**
bitter .... **ACERB, ACRID**
bitter almonds compound
  AMARINE
bitter drug .... **ALOE**
bitter vetch .... **ERS**
b bittern .... **HERON**
bivalve ...... **CLAM, MUSSEL**
bivalve genus .... **PINNA**
bizarre .... **OUTRE**
black ..... **JET, EBON, INKY,
RAVEN, SABLE, TARRY,
NIGRINE**
black and blue .... **LIVID**
black buck .... **SASIN**
black gum tree genus **NYSSA**
black haw .... **SLOE**
black kelpie .... **BARB**
black nightshade .... **DUSCLE**
Black Sea arm ... **AZOF, AZOV**
blackbird
  ANI, MERL, MERLE, RAVEN
blackbird, Europ.
  OSSEL, OUSEL, OUZEL
blackbird: variant ...... **ANO**
blacken .... **INK, SOOT**
black-fin snapper .... **SESI**
blackfish .... **TAUTOG**
Blackmore heroine .... **LORNA**
blacksnake .... **RACER**
blacksmith's block ..... **ANVIL**
blackthorn fruit .... **SLOE**
blackwood, India .... **BITI**
blade .... **OAR**
Blake's symbolic figure .. **ZOA**
Blake's symbolic figures **ZOAS**
blanch .... **ETIOLATE**

c blanket, cloak-like .. **PONCHO**
blanket, coarse wool .. **COTTA**
blanket, horse ...... **MANTA**
blanket, Sp.-Am. ..... **SERAPE**
blast furnace, stone in .. **TYMP**
blaubok, S. Afr. ...... **ETAAC**
blaze star .... **NOVA**
bleach .... **CHLORE**
bleaching vat .... **KEIR, KIER**
bleak .... **RAW**
blesbok .... **NUNNI**
bless .... **SAIN**
bless: Yiddish .... **BENSH**
blessing
  BOON, GRACE, BENEFICE
blight .... **NIP**
blight of drought, India **SOKA**
blind, as hawks .... **SEEL**
blind dolphin .... **SUSU**
blind god, Teut. **HOTH, HODER**
blind impulse to ruin ... **ATE**
blindness .... **CECITY**
blister .. **BLEB, BULLA, BULLAE**
block, small arch
  DENTEL, DENTIL
block, wood .... **NOG**
blockhead .... **ASS, DOLT**
blood factor .... **RH**
blood, lack of red
  ANEMIA, ANAEMIA
d blood of gods .... **ICHOR**
blood, part of .... **SERUM**
blood, pert. to ...... **HEMAL,
HEMIC, HAEMAL, HAEMIC**
blood vessel .... **VEIN**
blood vessel, main .... **AORTA**
blood, watery part of
  SERA, SERUM
blood sucker .... **LEECH**
blood-sucking parasite .. **TICK**
blouse, long .... **TUNIC**
blow..... **COUP, CRIG, ONER,
SWAT, WAFT**
blubber, piece of ..... **LIPPER**
blubber, to strip ..... **FLENSE**
blue .... **CADET, PERSE,
SMALT, COBALT**
blue-dye yielding herb **WOAD**
blue dyestuff .... **WOAD**
"Blue Eagle" .... **NRA**
blue-footed petrel ...... **TITI**
blue grass (genus) ...... **POA**
blue grape anthocyanin
  ENIN, OENIN
blue gray
  CHING, MERLE, SLATE
blue, greenish .... **BICE**
  SAXE, TEAL, EMAIL
blue mineral .... **IOLITE**
blue-pencil .... **EDIT**
blue pointer shark ..... **MAKO**

a blue pine .... LIM
Bluebeard's wife ..... FATIMA
bluebonnet .... LUPINE
bluff .... CRUSTY
bluish-white metal ...... ZINC
blunder .... ERR
blunt .... DULL
blushing .... ROSY
boa, ringed .... ABOMA
boast .... BRAG, VAUNT
boastful air .... PARADO
BOAT . see also SHIP, CANOE,
                GALLEY, VESSEL,
boat .... ARK, TUB, PUNT
boat, assault .... LST
boat, Ceylon, India
                DONI, DHONI
boat, collapsible
        FALTBOAT, FOLDBOAT
boat, dispatch .... AVISO
boat, E. Ind. .... DONI, DHONI
boat, Egypt .... BARIS
boat, Eskimo .. BIDAR, CAYAK,
    KAYAK, UMIAK, OOMIAC,
    OOMIAK, UMIACK
boat, fishing
    TROW, DOGGER, CORACLE
boat, fishing, North Sea COBLE
boat, flat-bottomed
                SCOW, BARGE
b boat, freight .... LIGHTER
boat front ...... BOW, PROW
boat, Ind. landing .. MASOOLA
boat, landing .... LCI, LST
boat, Levantine .... BUM
boat, light .... WHERRY
boat, mail .... PACKET
boat, Malay .... PAHI, PRAH,
        PRAO, PRAU, PROA,
        PRAHU, PRAHO
boat, Manila Harbor .. BILALO
boat, military ..... PONTOON
boat, Nile 2-masted .. SANDAL
boat, P. I. .. BANCA, BANKA
boat, racing .. SCULL, SHELL
boat, river
        BARGE, FERRY, PACKET
boat, river, Chin. ... SAMPAN
boat, small .... DORY
boat, 3-oar .... RANDAN
boat, used on Tigris
                GUFA, KUFA
boat, with decks cut
                RASEE, RAZEE
bob bait for fish .... DIB
bobbin .. PIRN, REEL, SPOOL
bobbins, frame for .... CREEL
bobwhite .... COLIN
Boche .... HUN
bodice, India .... CHOLI
bodily motion, pert. to GESTIC

c body .... SOMA, LICHAM
body, heavenly . STAR, COMET
body of laws .... CODE
body of men .... FORCE
body of persons ...... CORPS
body of retainers .... RETINUE
body of writing .... TEXT
body, part of
        THORAX, THORACES
body, pert. to SOMAL, SOMATIC
body, trunk of .. TORSE, TORSO
body: zool. .... SOMA
Boer general .... BOTHA
bog. FEN, MIRE, QUAG, MARSH
boggy .... FENNY
boil .... STEW, SEETHE
boil down .... DECOCT
boiled rice without salt: P. I.
                CANIN
boiler, disk for hole in .. SPUT
"Bolero" composer .... RAVEL
boll weevil .... PICUDO
Bolshevik leader ...... LENIN
bolt .... SCREEN
bomb, defective .... DUD
bombardment, short, intense
                RAFALE
bombast .... ELA
bombastic TURGID, OROTUND
Bombyx .... ERI
d bond .... NEXUS
bond-stone .... PERPEND
bondman ...... SERF, VASSAL
bonds, chem. with 2 double
                DIENE
bone .... OS
bone, ankle TALUS, ASTRAGAL
bone, arm .... ULNA
bone, arm, pert. to ... ULNAR
bone, breast
    STERNA, STERNAL, STERNUM
bone, ear ..... ANVIL, INCUS
bone: Greek .... OSTE
bone, leg .... FEMUR,
    TIBIA, FIBULA, TIBIAE
bone, pelvic, hip ...... ILIUM
bone, pert. to .... OSTEAL
bone scraper .... XYSTER
bone, skull .... VOMER
bones .... OSSA
bones, dorsal .... ILIA
bones, end of spine .. SACRA
bones, hip .... ILIA
bonnet monkey ŻATI, MUNGA
bonnyclabber .... SKYR
bony .... OSTEAL
book .... MO, TOME, PRIMER
book, case for FOREL, FORREL
book, largest .... FOLIO
book, manuscript
                CODEX, CODICES

a book, map .... **ATLAS**
book, Bible .. see SPECIAL SEC-
TION, Page 196
book of devotions .... **MISSAL**
book of feasts, Catholic **ORDO**
book of hours .. **HORA, HORAE**
book palm, tree .... **TARA**
book, The .... **BIBLE**
books, Bible .... **GOSPEL**
bookbinding style ...... **YAPP**
bookkeeping entry
DEBIT, CREDIT
booklet .... **BROCHURE**
boor **OAF, CLOD, LOUT, CHURL**
boot, Eskimo .... **KAMIK**
booth .... **STALL**
booth, Oriental market
SUQ, SOOK, SOUK
bootlace .... **LACET**
booty ..... **LOOT, PELF, SWAG**
booty, take .... **REAVE**
borax, crude .... **TINCAL**
border ...... **HEM, RIM, EDGE,
RAND, SIDE, MARGE**
border on .... **ABUT**
bore .... **TIRE, EAGRE,
WEARY, CALIBER**
borecole .... **KAIL, KALE**
boredom .... **ENNUI**
boric acid salts ...... **BORATE**
b born .... **NEE**
born, being .... **NASCENT**
born: old Eng. .... **NATE**
Bornean squirrel shrew
PENTAIL
Borneo native .. **DYAK, DAYAK**
boron, pert. to .... **BORIC**
borough .... **BURG**
borrowed stock: Irish law **DAER**
bosh .... **ROT, POOH**
boss .... **STUD**
boss on shield .... **UMBO**
Bostonian .... **HUBBITE**
botanical suffix ...... **ACEAE**
botanist .... **MENDEL**
botch .... **FLUB, MESS**
both ears, involving use of
BINAURAL
bother ... **ADO, FUSS, TODO,
TEASE, MOLEST, PESTER**
bo-tree .... **PIPAL**
bottle, glass water .. **CARAFE**
bottle, oil, vinegar
CRUET, FLASK
bottomless pit .... **ABADDON**
boundary ...... **LINE, MERE,
METE, LIMIT**
boundaries, mark off
DEMARCATE
bounder .... **CAD**
bounding line .... **SIDE**

c bounds .... **AMBIT**
bouquet .... **AROMA**
bovine .... **OX, COW**
bovine, male .... **STEER**
bow of ship .... **PROW**
bow, low Oriental
SALAM, SALAAM
bow-shaped .... **ARCATE**
bower .... **ARBOR**
bowfin .... **AMIA**
bowl: cricket .... **YARK**
bowling term .... **SPARE**
bowstring hemp **IFE, PANGANE**
box .... **BIN, BINN, CASE,
CIST, SPAR, CHEST**
box, ecclesiastic ...... **ARCA**
box canyon: Sp. ...... **CAJON**
box, metal .... **CANISTER**
box opener .... **PANDORA**
box, papyrus rolls, Rom.
CAPSA
box, sacred, ancient Rom. **CIST**
box sleigh .... **PUNG**
boxing glove, Rom. .... **CESTUS**
boxing term .... **KO, TKO**
BOY'S NAME .. see MAN'S
NAME
boy ... **BUB, BUD, LAD, TAD**
boys in blue .... **ELI'S**
B.P.O.E. member .... **ELK**
d brace .... **PAIR, TRUSS**
braced aback: nautical **ABOX**
bracing .... **TONIC**
brag .... **BOAST, VAUNT**
Brahman rule .. **SUTRA, SUTTA**
Brahmany bull .... **ZEBU**
braid ... **PLAT, PLAIT, QUEUE**
braid, kind of .... **LACET**
brain canal-passage .... **ITER**
brain, layer in .... **OBEX**
brain opening .... **LURA, PYLA**
brain part .... **PIA**
brain: P. I. .... **UTAC**
brain ridges .... **GYRI**
brain tissue .... **TELA**
brain ventricle opening **PYLA**
branch .... **ARM, LIMB, RAMI,
RAME, RAMUS, SPRIG**
branch-like **RAMOSE, RAMOUS**
branchia .... **GILL**
branch of learning ...... **ART**
brass, man of .. **TALOS, TALUS**
brassart .... **BRACER**
"Brave Bulls" author .... **LEA**
brawl .... **MELEE, FRACAS**
BRAZIL ..... see also SPECIAL
SECTION
Brazil drink .... **ASSAI**
Brazil red .... **ROSET**
Brazil dance .... **SAMBA**
Brazil heron .... **SOCO**

a
Brazil Negro .... **MINA**
Brazil plant ..... **YAGE, YAJE**
Brazil rubber tree   **ULE, HULE**
Brazil tree ...... **APA, ANDA**
Brazil capital .... **RIO**
breach .... **GAP**
bread, hard-baked ...... **RUSK**
bread crumbs, dish with
                      PANADA
breadfruit: P. I. .... **RIMA**
breadfruit: P. R. ... **CASTANA**
bread-tree seeds .... **DIKA**
break .... **SNAP**
break in .... **STAVE**
breakers .... **SURF**
breakwater ...... **MOLE, PIER**
breastbone, of ...... **STERNAL**
breastplate .... **URIM**
breastwork .... **PARAPET**
breastplate, Gr.
          THORAX, THORACES
breath of life .... **PRANA**
breathed .... **SPIRATE**
breathing, harsh
          RALE, STRIDOR
breech-cloth, Polyn. .. **MALO**
breeches: Scot. .... **TREWS**
breed .... **REAR, RAISE**
Bremen's river ...... **WESER**
breviary .. **PORTAS, PORTASS**
b brewer's ferment .. **LOB, LOBB**
brewer's vat .... **TUN**
brewing .... **MALTING**
brewing, one
          GAAL, GAIL, GYLE
bribe .... **SOP**
brick carrier .... **HOD**
brick, sun-dried ...... **ADOBE**
bricklayer .... **MASON**
bricklayer's helper ..... **CAD**
bridal wreath .... **SPIREA**
bridge .... **SPAN**
bridge, floating .... **PONTOON**
bridge, maneuver .... **FINESSE**
bridge, Mississippi ...... **EADS**
bridge part   **TRESSEL, TRESTLE**
brief .... **SHORT, TERSE**
brigand .... **LATRON**
Brigham Young U. site   **PROVO**
bright .... **APT, NITID**
bright colored fish
          BOCE, OPAH, WRASSE
bright: music .... **ANIME**
brilliance .... **ECLAT, ORIENCY**
brilliant group .... **PLEIAD**
bring forth .... **EAN**
bring on oneself ...... **INCUR**
bring together ...... **COMPILE**
bring up .... **REAR, RAISE**
brisk: music .... **ALLEGRO**
bristle .... **SETA**

c bristles .... **SETAE**
bristle, pert. to .... **SETAL**
bristly .... **SETOSE**
Britain's ancient inhabitant
                      PICT
BRITISH .. also see **ENGLISH**
British conservative ..... **TORY**
British king, legendary .. **LUD,
   BELI, BRAN, BRUT, LUDD,
   NUDD**
Britisher, early .... **PICT**
Brittany; city, ancient ...... **IS**
broach .... **RIMER**
broad band: Her. .... **FESS**
broadbill, E. Ind. ...... **RAYA**
broadbill duck .... **SCAUP**
broken glass to remelt .. **CALX**
broken seed coats ...... **BRAN**
broken spike of grain .. **CHOB**
broken stone, etc. ... **RUBBLE**
Bronte heroine .... **EYRE**
bronze, Rom. money ..... **AES**
brood ...... **SET, NIDE, COVEY**
brook, small ...... **RUN, RILL**
broom of twigs .... **BESOM**
broom-corn millet
          HIRSE, KADIKANE
brother .. **FRA, FRIAR, FRATER**
brought up .... **BRED**
brow of hill; Scot. ...... **SNAB**
d brown ..... **TAN, SEAR, SEPIA,
   UMBER, BISTER, RUSSET,
   SIENNA, SORREL**
brown kiwi .... **ROA**
brown, pale .... **ECRU**
brown, red-yellow ..... **PABLO**
brown, yellowish dull ... **DRAB**
brown-skinned race ... **MALAY**
brown sugar .... **PANELA**
browned .... **RISSOLE**
brownie ..... **NIS, NIX, NISSE**
Browning poem, girl in   **PIPPA**
browse .... **GRAZE**
Brünnhilde's mother .... **ERDA**
brushwood .... **TINET, TINNET**
brusque ...... **BLUNT, TERSE**
Brythonic .... **CORNISH**
Brythonic sea god ...... **LER**
bubble .... **BLEB**
buck, 4th year .... **SORE**
Buddha .... **FO**
Buddha, Jap.   **AMIDA, AMITA**
Buddha's foe .... **MARA**
Buddha's mother ...... **MAYA**
Buddha's tree .... **PIPAL**
Buddhist angel .... **DEVA**
Buddhist language ..... **PALI**
Buddhist church in Jap. .. **TERA**
Buddhist monastery, Jap.   **TERA**
Buddhist Mongol ...... **ELEUT**
Buddhist monk .... **BO, LAMA**

a Buddhist pillar .... **LAT**
Buddhist monument .. **STUPA**
Buddhist novice ...... **GOYIN**
Buddhist priest .... **LAMA**
Buddhist relic .... **STUPA**
Buddhist sacred city .. **LASSA**
Buddhist sacred dialect **PALI**
Buddhist sacred mountain **OMEI**
Buddhist saint **LOHAN, ARHAT**
Buddhist scripture **SUTRA, SUTTA**
Buddhist sect, Jap. ..... **ZEN**
Buddhist shrine **TOPE, STUPA,**
DAGABA, DAGOBA, DAG-
HOBA, DHAGOBA
Buddhist spirit of evil .. **MARA**
buds, pickled .... **CAPERS**
buffalo, India
ARNA, ARNI, ARNEE
buffalo pea .... **VETCH**
buffalo, water, P. I. **CARABAO**
buffet .... **SLAP, SMITE, TOSS**
buffoon .. **FOOL, MIME, ZANY,**
CLOWN, MUMMER, JESTER
bug .... **BEETLE**
bugaboo: S. Afr. **GOGA, GOGO**
bugle call
TATOO, TATTOO, TANTARA
bugle note .... **TIRALEE**
build .... **REAR, ERECT**
builder .... **ERECTOR**
b builder, jetty-dam ...... **EADS**
building site .... **LOT**
building wing .... **ELL, ANNEX**
bulb, edible .... **SEGO**
bulb, Indian food
CAMAS, CAMASS, CAMMAS
bulb-like stem .... **CORM**
BULGARIAN .. see also **SPE-**
CIAL SECTION
Bulgarian czar .... **BORIS**
bulge, as eyes .... **BUG**
bulk .... **MASS**
bull, girl carried off on **EUROPA**
bull, sacred Egyp. .... **APIS**
bullet, size of
CALIBER, CALIBRE
bullet sound ...... **ZIP, PHIT,**
PHUT, PIFF
bullfight .... **CORRIDA**
bullfight cry .... **OLE**
bullfighter on foot .. **TORERO**
bullfighter's queue .... **COLETA**
bullfinch, Eng. .... **ALP**
bully .... **HECTOR**
bulrush .... **TULE**
Bulwer-Lytton heroine .. **IONE**
bumblebee .... **DOR**
bumpkin .... **LOUT**
bunch .... **TUFT, WISP**
bunch grass .... **STIPA**
bundle .... **BALE, PACK**

c bundle, small .... **PACKET**
bundle, twig, stick .... **FAGOT**
bundling machine ...... **BALER**
bungle .... **BOTCH**
bunting .. **ESTAMIN, ETAMINE,**
ORTOLAN, ESTAMENE
bunting bird .... **CIRL**
buoy, Eng. .... **DAN**
buoy, kind of. **CAN, NUN, NUT,**
BELL, SPAR, WHISTLING
buoyancy .... **FLOTAGE**
burbot .... **LING**
burbot genus .... **LOTA, LOTE**
Burchell's zebra ...... **DAUW**
burden ... **LADE, LOAD, ONUS**
burden bearer .... **ATLAS**
burglar .... **YEGG**
burial place, Polyn. ...... **AHU**
BURMA .. see also **SPECIAL**
SECTION
Burma Buddhist (native) **MON**
Burma chief .... **BO, BOH**
Burmese capital, ancient **AVA**
Burmese demon (devil) .. **NAT**
Burmese gibbon .... **LAR**
Burmese governor **WUN, WOON**
Burmese hill-dweller ..... **LAI**
Burmese hills .... **NAGA**
Burmese knife .. **DAH, DHAO**
Burmese language .. **WA, PEGU**
Burmese mongoloid ...... **LAI**
d Burmese native (s) **WA,LAI,WAS**
Burmese premier ...... **UNU**
Burmese 3-string viol ... **TURR**
Burmese wood sprite .... **NAT**
burn incense .... **CENSE**
burn .... **ASH, CHAR, SERE**
Burnett, Frances, heroine **SARA**
burning bush .... **WAHOO**
burning, malicious .... **ARSON**
burnish .... **RUB**
burrowing animal **MOLE, RATEL**
burst asunder .... **SPLIT**
burst forth .... **ERUPT**
bury .... **INTER, INHUME**
bush or bushy clump .... **TOD**
bushel, fourth of ...... **PECK**
Bushmen .... **SAN, SAAN**
bushy .... **DUMOSE**
business .... **TRADE**
business cartel .... **TRUST**
"Bus Stop" author ...... **INGE**
bustard genus .... **OTIS**
bustle .... **ADO, TODO**
bustle about .... **FISK**
busy, to be .... **HUM**
but .... **YET, ONLY, STILL**
butcher's hook .... **GAMBREL**
butter, illipe .... **MAHUA**
butter, India ..... **GHI, GHEE**
butter, liquid ..... **GHI, GHEE**

a
butter tree	**SHEA**
butter tub	**FIRKIN**
butterbur	**OXWORT**
butterfly	**IO, SATYR**
butterfly, large	**IDALIA**
butterfly-lily	**SEGO**
button	**STUD**
button, part of	**SHANK**
buyer	**VENDEE**
buyer: Law	**EMPTOR**

c
buzzard	**BUTEO**
buzzing sound	**WHIR, WHIZ**
by	**AT, PER, PAST, ALONG, BESIDE**
by birth	**NEE**
by hand, bred	**CADE**
by means of	**PER**
bygone	**AGO**
Byron poem	**LARA**
Byzantine capital	**NICAEA**

C

C, mark under	**CEDILLA**
caama	**ASSE**
cab, Near East	**ARABA**
cabal	**PLOT**
cabbage	**COLE, KAIL, KALE, KEAL**
cabbage type	**SAVOY**
cabin, main	**SALOON**
cabinet, open, bric-a-brac	**ETAGERE**
cactus fruit, edible	**COCHAL**
cactus, genus	**CEREUS**
cactus-like	**CACTOID**
caddis fly worm	**CADEW**
Caddoan Indian	**REE**

b
cadet	**LAD**
Cadmus' daughter	**INO**
Caen's river	**ORNE**
Caesar's conspirator-slayer	**CASCA, BRUTUS, CASSIUS**
cafe	**CABARET**
caffein in tea	**THEIN, THEINA, THEINE**
caffein-rich nut	**COLA, KOLA**
cage	**MEW**
Cain's brother	**ABEL**
Cain's land	**NOD**
Cain's son	**ENOCH**
Cain's wife, Byron poem	**ADAH**
cake, rich	**TORTE, TORTEN**
cake, small	**BUN, BUNN**
calabar bean alkaloid	**ESERIN, ESERINE**
calamity	**WOE, DISASTER**
calcium oxide	**LIME**
calf of leg, pert. to	**SURAL**
calf's cry	**BLAT**
caliber	**BORE, DIAMETER**
calico colors, mix	**TEER**
calico horse	**PINTO, PIEBALD**
calico-printing method	**LAPIS**
California army base	**ORD**
Calif. fish	**RENA, REINA**
Calif. fort	**ORD**

Calif. herb	**AMOLE**
Calif. motto	**EUREKA**
Calif. shrub, berry	**SALAL**
Calif. wine valley	**NAPA**
Caliph	**ALI, IMAM**
call	**CRY, DUB, DIAL, NAME, ROUSE, WAKEN, MUSTER**
call for hogs	**SOOK**
call forth	**EVOKE, SUMMON, ELICIT, EVOCATE**
call, to attract attention	**HEY, PST, HIST, PIST**
calling	**METIER, VOCATION**
Calliope's sister	**ERATO**

d
calm	**LAY, COOL, LULL, QUIET, STILL, PLACID, SERENE, SMOOTH, SOOTHE**
calorie	**THERM, THERME**
calumniate	**MALIGN**
calumny	**SLANDER**
Calvinists, Scotch	**BEREANS**
calyx leaf	**SEPAL**
cam	**TAPPET**
cambric	**PERCALE**
cambric grass	**RAMIE**
CAME	see **COME**
camel: Anglo-Ind.	**OONT**
camel hair cloth	**ABA**
camel hair robe	**ABA**
camel-like animal	**LLAMA**
Camelot lady	**ENID**
cameo stone	**ONYX**
camera platform	**DOLLY**
Cameroons tribe	**ABO**
"Camille" author	**DUMAS**
camlet	**PONCHO**
camp, fortified	**TABOR**
camp, pert. to	**CASTRAL**
camphor, kind of	**ALANT**
campus, restrict. to Eng.	**GATED**
Canaanite month	**BUL**
Canada goose	**OUTARDE**
canal bank	**BERM, BERME**
canal betw. N. and Balt. Seas	**KIEL**

a

canary yellow .... **MELINE**
canasta play .... **MELD**
cancel .. **DELE, ANNUL, ERASE**
candid .... **OPEN, FRANK**
candidates list .. **LEET, SLATE**
candle ..... **DIP, TEST, TAPER**
candle holder
       SCONCE, GIRANDOLE
candle wick .. **SNAST, SNASTE**
candlenut tree .... **AMA**
candlenut tree fiber ...... **AEA**
cane ... **RATTAN, MALACCA**
Canio's wife "I Pagliacci"
       NEDDA
canister, tea, alloy for .. **CALIN**
canna plant .... **ACHIRA**
cannabis .... **HEMP**
cannon .... **MORTAR**
cannon, old
       MOYENNE, ROBINET
CANOE .. see also BOAT
canoe, Afr. .. **BONGO, BUNGO**
canoe, Hawaii ...... **WAAPA**
canoe, Malabar ...... **TONEE**
canoe, Malay (South Seas) out-
    rigger ..... **PAHI, PRAH,
    PRAO, PRAU, PROA,
    PRAHO, PRAHU**
canoe, Maori .... **WAKA**

b

canoe, P. I. .. **BANCA, BANKA**
canon .... **LAW, RULE**
canonical hour .. **SEXT** (noon),
    **LAUDS, NONES, PRIME,
    MATINS, TIERCE**
canopy **COPE, SHADE, TESTER**
cant **TIP, TILT, SLANG, CAREEN**
cant-hook .... **PEAVY, PEEVY,
    PEAVEY, PEEVEY**
cantankerous command. . **SCAT**
cantata, pastoral .. **SERENATA**
canticle, Scripture ...... **ODE**
"Cantique de Noel" composer
       ADAM
CANTON .. see the country in
    SPECIAL SECTION
canvas .. **DUCK, TUKE, SAILS**
canvas, piece of .... **TARP**
canvas shelter .... **TENT**
canyon mouth .... **ABRA**
canyon, small ...... **CANADA**
CAP .. see HEADGEAR
capable .... **ABLE**
cape .... **NES, RAS,
    NASE, NAZE, NESS**
cape, early .... **COPE**
cape, fur .... **PALATINE**
Cape Horn native .... **ONA**
cape, Pope's .. **FANON, ORALE**
Cape Verde native ..... **SERER**
Capek creature .... **ROBOT**

c

caper .... **DIDO, LEAP, ANTIC**
CAPITAL .. see SPECIAL SEC-
    TION
caprice **WHIM, FANCY, VAGARY**
captain, fiction .... **AHAB**
captain, Nile ...... **RAIS, REIS**
capture **BAG, NAB, NET, SEIZE**
car .... **SEDAN**
car, last **CABOOSE, CAMBOOSE**
car, old make .... **REO**
caracal .... **LYNX**
Caradoc .... **BALA**
caravan .... **CAFILA**
caravansary
       CHAN, KHAN, SERAI
caravel, Columbus **NINA, PINTA**
carbolic acid .... **PHENOL**
carbon, powdery .... **SOOT**
CARD .. see also GAME, CARD
card .. **ACE, PAM, SIX, TEN,
    TWO, FOUR, JACK, KING,
    NINE, TREY, KNAVE,
    POSTAL**
card game like bridge .. **VINT**
card game, 3-handed ... **SKAT**
card game, old ...... **TAROT**
card game, Sp. ...... **OMBER,
    OMBRE**
card holding .... **TENACE**
card in euchre .... **BOWER**
card, playing
    TAROC, TAROT, TAROCCO

d

card wool ...... **TUM, TEASE**
cards, highest ...... **HONORS**
care for .... **RECK, TEND**
care, heavy .... **CARK**
careen ...... **TIP, LIST, TILT**
caress .... **PET**
cargo .... **LOAD, PORTAGE**
cargo, put on .... **LADE, LOAD**
"Carmen" composer .... **BIZET**
carnation .... **PINK**
carnelian .... **SARD**
carnivore, Afr. .... **RATEL**
carol .... **NOEL, SING**
carol singer .... **WAIT**
carom .... **RICOCHET**
carousal **ORGY, BINGE, SPREE**
carouse .... **REVEL**
carp .... **ID, CAVIL**
carp, Jap. .... **KOI**
carp, red-eyed .... **RUD, RUDD**
carpet, Afgh... **HERAT, HERATI**
carpet, Caucasian **BAKU, KUBA**
carpet, India .... **AGRA**
carpet, Pers. .. **KALI, SENNA**
carriage .. **GIG, MIEN, POISE,
    CALASH, LANDAU, CARIOLE**
carriage: Fr. .... **FIACRE**
carriage, India .... **EKKA**
carriage, Java, Oriental **SADO**

a carried away .... **RAPT**
carrier, of Orient .... **HAMAL**
Carroll heroine .... **ALICE**
carrot-family plant .... **ANISE**
carrot-like herb genus .. **MEUM**
carrot ridges .... **JUGA**
carry ...... **LUG, BEAR, TOTE**
carry across water .... **FERRY**
carry on (a war) ...... **WAGE**
cart, heavy .... **DRAY**
carte .... **MENU**
Carthage, of .... **PUNIC**
Carthage queen .... **DIDO**
cartograph .... **MAP**
cartoonist
     ARNO, CAPP, NAST, KIRBY
carve in itaglio ...... **INCISE**
case, grammatical .... **DATIVE**
case of explosives .... **PETARD**
case, toilet, small
     ETUI, ETWEE
casing, bore-hole ...... **LINER**
cask .. **KEG, TUB, TUN, BUTT,**
     CADE, TIERCE, PUNCHEON
cassava .. **AIPI, JUCA, YUCA**
cassia leaves .... **SENNA**
cast, founded .. **FUSIL, FUSILE**
cast metal mass .. **PIG, INGOT**
cast off **MOLT, SHED, MOULT**
b caste **AHIR, BICE, GOLA, JATI**
caste, agricultural ...... **MEO**
caste, gardener .... **MALI**
caste, low **KOLI, KULI, PARIAH**
caste, Tamil merchant
     CHETTY
caster ...... **CRUET, ROLLER**
casting mold ....**DIE**
castor-oil bean poison **RICIN**
castor-oil plant .... **KIKI**
Castor's killer .... **IDAS**
Castor's mother .... **LEDA**
cat .... **ANGORA**
cat, Afr.
     CIVET, GENET, GENETTE
cat, Am.
     PUMA, COUGAR, OCELET
cat cry .. **MEW, MIAU, MIAW,**
     MIAOU, MIAOW, MIAUL
cat genus .... **FELIS**
cat-headed goddess, Egypt **BAST**
cat, spotted
     PARD, MARGAY, OCELET
cat, tailless .... **MANX**
catalogue ..... **LIST, RECORD**
catamaran ...... **BOAT, RAFT**
catapult .... **ONAGER**
cataract .... **FALLS**
catch .... **NAB, HAUL, HOOK,**
     SNAG, TRAP, DETENT
catchword ..... **CUE, SLOGAN**

c catechu-like resin ...... **KINO**
category .... **GENRE, SPECIES**
cater ...... **PANDER, PURVEY**
caterpillar .... **LARVA**
caterpillar hair .... **SETA**
caterpillar, N. Z. ...... **WERI**
catfish, Egypt ...... **DOCMAC**
catfish, S. Am. ...... **DORAD**
cathedral .... **MINSTER**
cathedral city, Eng. ..... **ELY**
cathedral, famous .. **CHARTRES**
cathedral passage ..... **SLYPE**
cathedral, Russian .... **SOBOR**
Catholic, Greek **UNIAT, UNIATA**
Catholic tribunal ...... **ROTA**
catkin ..... **AMENT, AMENTA**
catnip .... **NEP**
catspaw **DUPE, TOOL, STOOGE**
cattail ...... **TULE, MATREED**
cattail India, narrow .. **REREE**
cattail, N. Z. .... **RAUPO**
cattle, breed of .... **DEVON**
cattle dealer .... **DROVER**
cattle genus .... **BOS**
cattle stealing, crime of
     ABIGEAT
CAUCASIAN .... see
     CAUCASUS NATIVE
Caucasian bharal ...... **TUR**
Caucasian goat .... **TUR, TEHR**
Caucasian ibex ....**ZAC**
d Caucasian language
     ANDI, AVAR
Caucasion Moslem
     LAZ, LAZZI
Caucasian race in China
     LOLO, NOSU
Caucasus native
     SVAN, SVANE, OSSET
caucho tree .... **ULE**
caudal appendage ...... **TAIL**
caulk lightly .... **CHINSE**
cause ...... **CAUSA, REASON**
caustic ... **LYE, LIME, ACRID,**
     ERODENT, MORDANT
caustic poison ...... **PHENOL**
cauterize .... **SEAR**
cautery plant .... **MOXA**
cautious **WARE, WARY, CHARY**
"Cavalleria Rusticana" heroine
     LOLA
cavalryman .... **ULAN, UHLAN**
cavalryman, Turk., Alg.
     SPAHI, SPAHEE
cave: archaic .... **ANTRE**
cave explorer ...... **SPELUNKER**
cave: poet. .... **GROT**
cavern .. **CAVE, GROT, GROTTO**
caviar .... **ROE, IKRA**
caviar fish .... **SHAD, STERLET**
cavil .... **CARP, OBJECT**

a cavity .... **ATRIA, ANTRA, SINUS, ANTRUM**
cavity, ear, nose .... **ANTRUM**
cavity, in a rock .. **VUG, VOOG, YUGG, VUGH, GEODE**
cavy .... **APEREA**
cease! .... **HALT, AVAST**
Cecrops' daughter ...... **HERSE**
cedar, E. Ind. ...... **DEODAR**
Celebes ox .... **ANOA**
celebrated .... **EMINENT**
celery-like plant .... **UDO**
cella .... **NAOS**
cellulose acetate .... **ACETOSE**
cellulose: comb. form .. **CELLO**
Celt .... **ERSE, GAEL**
Celt, legendary **IR, ITH, MILED**
Celtic ... **ERSE, MANX, WELSH**
Celtic church early center **IONA**
Celtic dart .... **COLP**
Celtic god .... **TARANIS**
Celtic goddess
ANA, ANU, DANA, DANU
Celtic mother of gods
ANA, ANU, DANA, DANU
Celtic name meaning black
DHU
Celtic Neptune .... **LER**
b Celtic paradise ...... **AVALON**
Celtic sea god .... **LER**
Celtic sun god .... **LUG, LUGH**
cement..**LUTE, PUTTY, SOLDER**
cement well lining .... **STEEN**
cenobite .... **MONK**
censure.**BLAME, CHIDE, SLATE**
center .... **HUB, CORE, FOCI, FOCUS, HEART**
center, away from .... **DISTAL**
center, toward ...... **ENTAD**
centerpiece .... **EPERGNE**
centesimal unit..**GRAD, GRADE**
centesimi, 100 .... **LIRA**
centipede: Tahiti .... **VERI**
central .... **MID, FOCAL**
Cent. Am. gum tree
TUNO, TUNU
Cent. Am. tree .... **EBO, EBOE**
central line .... **AXIS**
central points .... **FOCI**
century plant .... **AGAVE**
century plant fiber..**PITA, PITO**
cere .... **WAX**
cereal .... **FARINA**
cereal grain .... **OAT, RYE**
cereal grass ...... **OAT, RYE, WHEAT, MILLET**
cereal grass, E. Ind. ... **MAND, RAGI, RAGGI, RAGGEE**

c cereal grass genus ... **SECALE**
cereal plant: obs. ...... **RIE**
cereal spike ...... **COB, EAR**
ceremonial chamber .... **KIVA**
Ceres' mother .... **OPS**
certificate, money ..... **SCRIP**
cerulean blue **COELIN, COELINE**
cervine animal .... **DEER**
cesspool .... **SUMP**
cetacean . **ORC, WHALE, NAR-WAL, NARWHAL, PORPOISE**
cetacean, dolphinlike, genus
INIA
Ceylon ape .... **MAHA**
Ceylon foot soldier ..... **PEON**
Ceylon governor .... **DISAWA**
Ceylon moss .... **AGAR**
Ceylon native
VEDDA, VEDDAH, WEDDAH
Ceylon sandstone ...... **PAAR**
Ceylon trading vessel .. **DONI**
chafe **RUB, FRET, FROT, GALL**
chaff .... **BANTER**
chaffinch ..... **CHINK, SPINK**
chain .... **CATENA**
chain, nautical .... **TYE**
chainlike .... **CATENATE**
chair .... **SEDAN**
chair part ...... **RUNG, SPLAT**
d chaise .... **GIG**
chalcedony .... **ONYX, AGATE**
chalcedony, red .... **SARD**
Chaldean astron. cycle .. **SAROS**
Chaldean city .... **UR**
chalice
AMA, AMULA, CALIX, GRAIL
chalice veil .... **AER**
chalky silicate .... **TALC**
challenge .. **DARE, DEFY, CAGE**
chamber .... **ROOM, CAMERA**
chamber, pert. to ... **CAMERAL**
champagne, Marne ...... **AY**
chance .... **HAP, LOT, LUCK**
chances, excess of ..... **ODDS**
chanced upon .... **MET**
chancel part .... **BEMA**
chancel screen .... **JUBE**
chancel seat .. **SEDILE, SEDILIA**
change .... **FLUX, VARY, ALTER, AMEND**
change appearance .. **OBVERT**
change direction **CANT, KANT, TACK, TURN, VEER**
change: music .... **MUTA**
channel .... **GAT, MEDIA, STRIA, MEDIUM, STRIAL**
Channel Island .... **SARK**
channel marker .... **BUOY**
channels .... **MEDIA**

a chant .... **INTONE**
chanticleer .... **COCK**
chantry .... **CHAPEL**
chaos .... **NU, NUN**
chaos, Babyl. .... **APSU**
chaos, Egypt. ... **NU, NUN**
chaos, Maori myth .... **KORE**
Chaos' son .... **EREBUS**
chap: S. Afr. .... **KEREL**
chapel, private .... **ORATORY**
chapel, sailor's ..... **BETHEL**
chaperon: Sp. **DUENA, DUENNA**
chaplain .... **PADRE**
chaplet .. **ANADEM, WREATH**
chapped .... **KIBY**
character .... **NATURE**
characteristic .... **TRAIT**
charcoal: Pharm. ...... **CARBO**
charge .... **FEE, COST,**
⠀⠀⠀⠀**DEBIT, INDICT**
charge solemnly ..... **ADJURE**
charged particle .... **ION**
charger .... **STEED**
chariot, ancient Briton
⠀⠀**ESSED, ESSEDA, ESSEDE**
chariot race site ...... **CIRCUS**
chariot, religious **RATH, RATHA**
charity .... **ALMS**
Charlemagne, race subdued by
⠀⠀⠀⠀⠀⠀⠀⠀⠀**AVARS**
b Charlemagne's father ... **PEPIN**
Charlotte —, dessert .. **RUSSE**
charm .... **JUJU,**
⠀⠀**SPELL, AMULET, GRIGRI**
Charon, payment for .. **OBOL**
Charon, river of .... **STYX**
chart .... **MAP**
Charybdis, rock opp. .. **SCYLLA**
chasm **GAP, ABYSS, CANYON**
chaste .... **PURE, VESTAL**
chat, friendly .... **COSE, COZE**
Chateaubriand heroine, novel
⠀⠀⠀⠀⠀⠀⠀⠀**ATALA**
chatelaine bag .... **ETUI**
chatter **GAB, GAS, YAP, PRATE**
chatterbox .... **PIET**
cheat .... **RENIG, RENEGE**
cheat .... **BAM,**
CON, FOB, FUB, GIP, GYP,
BILK, MUMP, COZEN, SHARP
cheaters: slang ..... **GLASSES**
check ...... **NIP, TAB, REIN,**
⠀⠀⠀⠀**STEM, BRAKE, STUNT**
checking block .... **SPRAG**
cheek .... **GENA, JOLE, JOWL**
"cheek"..**GALL, BRASS, NERVE**
cheek, pert. to ...... **MALAR**
cheek-bone .... **MALAR**
cheer .... **OLE, RAH,**
⠀⠀**BRAVO, ELATE, ENCORE**
cheer pine .... **CHIR**

c cheer up .... **LIVEN**
cheerless .... **SAD, DRAB**
cheese ..... **EDAM, STILTON**
cheese, Dutch .... **EDAM**
cheese, hard brown .. **MYSOST**
cheese, soft .... **BRIE**
cheesy .... **CASEOUS**
cheetah, Ind. . **YOUSE, YOUZE**
chela .... **CLAW**
Chemical compound ... **IMID,**
⠀⠀**AMIDE, AMINE, IMIDE,**
⠀⠀**IMINE, ESTER**
CHEMICAL ELEMENT .... see
⠀⠀⠀**SPECIAL SECTION**
chemical ending **OL, INE, ENOL**
chemical prefix .... **ACI, OXA,**
⠀⠀⠀⠀**AMIDO, AMINO**
chemical salt .... **SAL, ESTER,**
⠀⠀⠀**NITRE, BORATE**
CHEMICAL SUFFIX .. see **SUF-**
⠀⠀**FIX, CHEMICAL**
chemical unit .... **TITER**
chemist's pot .... **ALUDEL**
cherish ... **FOSTER, TREASURE**
cherry .... **GEAN**
cherry red .... **CERISE**
chess piece .... **MAN**
chess term,—passant ..... **EN**
chessman ..... **KING, PAWN,**
ROOK, QUEEN, BISHOP,
d ⠀**CASTLE, KNIGHT**
chest, acacia wood ...... **ARK**
chest, antique .... **CIST, KIST**
chest, sacred **ARK, ARCA, CIST**
chest sound .... **RALE**
chestnut, Eur. ...... **MARRON**
chestnut, Polyn. .... **RATA**
chevrotain . **NAPU, MEMINNA**
chew .... **BITE, CHAM, GNAW**
chew, leaf to .... **COCA**
chewink .... **TOWHEE**
Chibcha chief's title .... **ZIPA**
chick-pea .... **GRAM**
chicken snake .... **BOBA**
chide **SCOLD, BERATE, REPROVE**
chief ... **ARCH, HEAD, MAIN**
chief, Afr. tribe ...... **KAID**
chief, Am. Ind. ...... **SACHEM**
chief: Chinook .... **TYEE**
chief deity, Panopolis .... **MIN**
chief in Italy .... **DUCE**
chief, India .... **SIRDAR**
Chief Justice 1921-30 ... **TAFT**
Chief Justice 1941-46 .. **STONE**
chief, Moslem ..... **RAIS, REIS**
chief officer, India .. **DEWAN,**
⠀⠀⠀⠀⠀⠀**DIWAN**
chief Norse god ...... **ODIN,**
⠀⠀**WODAN, WODEN, WOTAN**
chief, Pres. .... **MIR**
child .... **TIKE, TYKE**

29

child of streets..**ARAB, GAMIN**
"Child of the Sun" ..... **INCA**
child, pert. to : .... **FILIAL**
child: Scot. .... **BAIRN**
child: Tagalog, P. I. .... **BATA**
Chilean proletariat ..... **ROTO**
Chilean timber tree ..... **PELU**
Chilean volcano ..... **ANTUCO**
chill .... **ICE, AGUE**
chills and fever
             AGUE, MALARIA
chimney: dialect .... **LUM**
chimney pipe .... **FLUE**
chin ...... **MENTA, MENTUM**
China .... **CATHAY**
China blue .... **NIKKO**
China grass .... **BON**
Chinese .. **SERES, SERIC, SINIC**
Chinese aborigine . **YAO, MANS**
Chin. aboriginal population
   division .... **MIAO**
Chin. are .... **MU**
Chin. boat .... **JUNK**
Chin. brick bed .... **K'ANG**
Chin. Causasian tribesman **LOLO**
Chin. characters in Jap. . **MANA**
Chin. club .... **TONG**
CHIN. COIN .. see also **COINS**
              Page 190
Chin., coin, bronze .... **LI**
Chin., coin, early .... **PU**
Chin. Communist .. **MAO, CHOU**
Chin. cult .... **JOSS**
Chin. department .... **FU**
Chin. dialect .... **WU**
Chin. division .... **MIAO**
Chin. dynasty . **HAN, KIN, SUI,**
   WEI, YIN, CH'IN, CHOU,
   HSIA, T'ANG, MING, SUNG,
   TS'IN, YUAN
Chin. factory .... **HONG**
Chin. feudal state .... **WEI**
Chin. flute .... **TCHE**
Chin. god .... **GHOS, JOSS**
Chin. govt. section
           HIEN, HSIEN
Chin. guild .... **HUI**
Chin. idol .... **GHOS, JOSS**
Chin. instrument, stringed . **KIN**
Chin. kingdom, old
        WU, SHU, WEI
CHIN. MEASURE.see also pages
            188, 189
Chin. measure of length . **TSUN**
Chin. mile .... **LI**
Chin. monetary unit .... **YUAN**
CHIN, MONEY see also page 190
Chin. negative principle ... **YIN**
Chin. noodles .... **MEIN**
Chin. official .. **KUAN, KWAN**
Chin. philos. principle.**LI, YANG**

Chin. plant .... **UDO**
Chin. pottery .... **CHUN,**
   KUAN, MING, TING
Chin. ruler .. **YAO, YAU, YAOU**
Chin. secret society ..... **TONG**
Chin. shop: Du. E. Ind. .. **TOKO**
Chin. silk .... **PONGEE**
Chin. wax, wax insect .. **PELA**
Chin. wormwood ...... **MOXA**
Chin. yellow .... **SIL**
chinin .... **COYO**
chink ...... **RIFT, RIMA, RIME**
chink-like .. **RIMAL, RIMATE**
chinky ...... **RIMAL, RIMOSE,**
             RIMOUS
chip .... **NICK**
chip of stone .. **SPALL, GALLET**
chipmunk .... **HACKEE**
chirp **CHEEP, TWEET, TWITTER**
chisel, primitive .... **CELT**
chisel, very broad .... **TOOLER**
chocolate powder ..... **PINOLE**
chocolate source ..... **CACAO**
choice .... **CREAM, ELITE,**
        PRIME, SELECT
choke up .... **DAM, CLOG**
choler .... **IRE, BILE, RAGE**
choose .... **OPT, ELECT**
chop ... **AXE, CUT, HEW, LOP**
chop fine .... **MINCE**
chopped .... **HEWN**
choral music
        MOTET, CANTATA
chord, 3 tones .... **TRINE**
chore .... **JOB, CHARE**
Chosen ...... **COREA, KOREA**
Christ's thorn .. **NABK, NUBK**
Christmas ...... **NOEL, YULE**
Christmas crib ...... **CRECHE**
chromosome .... **IDANT**
chronicle .... **ANNAL, ANNALS**
chrysalis .... **PUPA**
chrysanthemum .. **MUM, KIKU**
chub, Europ. .... **CHEVIN**
chunk .... **GOBBET**
church .... **FANE**
church bench .... **PEW**
church, body of .... **NAVE**
church calendar .... **ORDO**
church contribution .... **TITHE**
church council .... **SYNOD**
church court .... **ROTA**
church dignitary.**POPE, BISHOP,**
      PRELATE, CARDINAL
church dish .... **PATEN**
church, India .... **SAMAJ**
church living .... **BENEFICE**
church maintenance, canon's
           PREBEND
church officer .... **ELDER**

a church official ...... SEXTON, VERGER
church part ..... APSE, BEMA, NAVE, ALTAR
church, Pope's ..... LATERAN
church porch .... PARVIS
church property .... GLEBE
church reader .... LECTOR
church recess .... APSE
church, Scot. .... KIRK, KURK
church vessel .. AMA, PIX, PYX
churchman .... PRELATE
churl. CEORL, VILLAIN, VILLEIN
churl: var. .... CARLE
churn plunger .... DASHER
cibol .... ONION
cicatrix .... SCAR
cigar .... CLARO, SMOKE, CORONA, CHEROOT
cigar, cheap ... STOGY, STOGIE
cigarette, medicinal ... CUBEB
cigarfish .... SCAD
cincture .... BELT
cinnamon, kind of .... CASSIA
cion .... GRAFT
cipher .... ZERO, OUGHT
cipher system .... CODE
Circe's home .... AEAEA
circle .... CIRC, CIRQUE, RONDURE

b circle of light ... HALO, NIMB
circle, part of .... ARC
circle segment .... SECTOR
circuit .... LAP, TOUR, AMBIT, ORBIT
circuit judge, court ...... EYRE
circular motion .... GYRE
circular plate ...... DISC, DISK
circular turn .... LOOP
circular saw .... EDGER
cirque, geol. .... CWM
cistern .... BAC, VAT
citation .... CITAL
cite .... QUOTE, ADDUCE
citron ...... ETROG, CEDRAT, ETHROG
citrus fruit .... LIME, LEMON, ORANGE, SHADOCK, SHADDOCK
CITY .. see also TOWN and GAZETTEER
city, ancient, Asia Min. . MYRA, TYRE, SARDES, SARDIS
city, ancient Thessalian .... LARISSA
city: Gr. .... POLIS
City of a Hundred Towers PAVIA
City of Bridges ...... BRUGES
City of God .... HEAVEN
City of Kings .... LIMA
City of Lights .... PARIS

c City of Luxury ...... SYBARIS
City of Masts .... LONDON
City of Rams .... CANTON
City of Refuge ...... MEDINA
City of Saints .... MONTREAL
City of the Prophet .. MEDINA
City of the Seven Hills .. ROME
City of the Violet Crown .... ATHENS
City of Victory .... CAIRO
city, pert. to .. CIVIC, URBAN
city, Philistines' ...... EKRON
city political division ... WARD
civet, Chinese .... RASSE
civet, Indian .... ZIBET
civet, Java .... DEDES
civet, Madagascar .... FOSSA, FOUSSA
civetlike cat . GENET, GENETTE
civic goddess, Gr. ..... ALEA
Civil War commander ..... LEE, POPE, GRANT, EWELL, MEADE, SCOTT, SYKES, HOOKER, CUSTER, FORREST, JACKSON
civil wrong or injury .... TORT
claim ...... ASSERT, DEMAND
clam genus .... MYA
clam, giant .... CHAMA
clam, razor .... SOLEN
clamor .... DIN, NOISE

d clamp .... VICE, VISE
clan .... GEN, SEPT, TRIBE
clan chieftain successor . TANIST
clan division: Gr. .... OBE
clan, Gr. .... GENOS
clan, head of .... ALDER
clarinet socket .... BIRN
clash .... JAR, COLLIDE
clasp . HASP, ENFOLD, INFOLD
clasp for a cope ..... MORSE
class .... ILK, CASTE, GENUS, GENERA, SPECIES
class leader, Eng. .... DUX
class, lowest Jap. .... HEIMIN
class, scientific .... GENUS, GENERA
classic tongue .... LATIN
classification .... RATING
classification method . SYSTEM
classify .. RANK, RATE, SORT, TYPE, GRADE
claw .... NAIL, TALON, UNGUIS, UNGUES
claw, crustacean's .... CHELA, CHELAE
claw ornament .... GRIFF
claw: zool. .... UNCI, UNCUS
clay ..... BOLE, ARGIL, LOESS
clay, baked .... TILE

clay bed .... **GAULT**
clay, building: Sp.
.... **ADOBE, TAPIA**
clay-covered .... **LUTOSE**
clay, friable .... **BOLE**
clay layer ..... **SLOAM, SLOOM**
clay, melting pot ..... **TASCO**
clay mineral .... **NACRITE**
clay molding plate .... **DOD**
clay pigeon shooting ... **SKEET**
clay pipe .... **TD**
clay plug .... **BOTT**
clay, porcelain ...... **KAOLIN**
clay, potter's .... **ARGIL**
clayey .... **BOLAR**
clayey soil . **BOLE, MALM, MARL**
cleansing agent ..... **BORAX**
clear . **NET, RID, LUCID, LIMPID,
AUDIBLE, TRANSPARENT**
clear, as anchor .... **AWEIGH**
clear of charges ..... **ACQUIT**
clearing of land, Eng. ... **SART**
cleave ... **REND, RIVE, CLING**
cleaving tool .... **FROE**
cleft ..... **REFT, RIFT, RIMA**
Clemenceau's nickname . **TIGRE**
clement .... **MILD**
Cleopatra's attendant ... **IRAS**
Cleopatra's handmaid ... **IRAS**
Cleopatra's needle ... **OBELISK**
Cleopatra's serpent .... **ASP**
clergyman .... **ABBE, CANON,
VICAR, CURATE, PRIEST,
RECTOR**
cleric, Fr. .... **ABBE**
clerical cap .... **BIRETTA**
clerical, not .... **LAIC, LAICAL**
clever .... **APT, HABILE**
click beetle ...... **DOR, DORR,
ELATER**
climb .... **GRIMP, SCALE**
climbing plant .... **IVY, VINE,
LIANA, LIANE**
cling .... **STICK, ADHERE**
clingfish .... **TESTAR**
clinging, for .... **TENENT**
Clio, sister of .... **ERATO**
clip . **CUT, MOW, SNIP, SHEAR**
clique .... **SET**
CLOAK .... see also GARMENT
cloak ... **ABA, WRAP, CAPOT,
CAPOTE, MANTLE**
cloak, Ind. .... **CHOGA**
cloak, Rom. . **SAGUM, ABOLLA,
ABOLLAE**
cloak, woman's ..... **DOLMAN**
clock, ship-form .... **NEF**
clog-like shoe .... **PATTEN**
cloister .... **MONASTERY**
"Cloister-Hearth" author . **READE**

close eyes of .... **SEEL**
close, keep .... **HUG**
close: musical .... **CODA**
close to . **AT, BY, NEAR, ANEAR**
close, to fit ..... **FAY, FADGE**
closed, as wings .... **PLIE**
closing measure, music .. **CODA**
CLOTH .... see also SILK,
COTTON, FABRIC
cloth, bark .... **TAPA**
cloth, figured old ..... **TAPET**
cloth measure .... **ELL**
cloth, old wool ..... **CHEYNEY**
cloth, stout .... **BRIN**
cloth strip, India .... **PATA**
cloth used in mourning ... **CRAPE**
cloth, wrapping ...... **TILLOT**
clothe .... **GIRD, VEST, ENDUE**
clothes moth .... **TINEA**
clothespress, old Dutch ... **KAS**
clothing .. **DUDS, GARB, GEAR,
TOGS, RAIMENT**
cloud .... **SMUR, CIRRI,
NUBIA, CIRRUS**
cloud dragon, Vedic .... **AHI**
cloud, luminous ..... **NIMBUS**
clouds, broken .... **RACK**
clouds, wind-driven . **RACK, SCUD**
cloudberry .... **MOLKA**
cloudy .... **DULL, LOWERY**
clout .... **HIT, SWAT**
cloven-footed .... **FISSIPED**
clover .... **HUBAM,
ALSIKE, MELILOT**
clown .... **APER, GOFF, ZANY**
clown, Shakesperean . **LAVACHE**
cloy .... **PALL, SATE, ACCLOY**
club member, Gr. .... **ERANIST**
club, women's .... **ZONTA**
clubfoot .... **TALIPED, TALIPES**
clumsily, handle . **PAW, BOTCH**
clumsy .... **INEPT, OAFISH**
cluster .... **NEP, TUFT**
cluster, grape .... **RACEME**
cluster pine .... **PINASTER**
coach dog ...... **DALMATIAN**
coach, Eastern .... **ARABA**
coagulate .... **GEL, CLOT**
coal dust ...... **COOM, SMUT**
coal, heat-treated ...... **COKE**
coal, live .... **EMBER**
coal, size of .. **EGG, NUT, PEA**
coal refuse .... **CULM**
coal scuttle .... **HOD**
coalfish .... **CUDDY**
coalition .... **UNION, MERGER**
coarse .... **GROSS**
coarse sugar, E. Ind. ..... **RAAB**
coast bird .... **GULL, TERN**
coast dweller ...... **ORARIAN**
coastal range, India .... **GHAT**

a COAT ..... see also GARMENT
coat .... LAYER
coat, animal .... PELAGE
coat, Arab .... ABA
coat, soldier's .... TUNIC
coat with alloy .... TERNE
cob .... SWAN
cobbler .... SUTOR
cobra ... HAJE, NAGA, MAMBA
cobra genus ..... NAIA, NAJA
cocaine source ... COCA, CUCA
cockatoo, Austral. ..... GALAH
cockatoo, palm .. ARA, ARARA
cockboat .... COG
cockpit .... ARENA
coconut, dried .... COPRA
coconut fiber .... COIR, KOIR,
KYAR, COIRE
coconut, Ind. .... NARGIL
coconut palm, P. I. ..... NIOG
cocoon insect .... PUPA
cocoon, silkworm .... CLEW
cod genus .... GADUS
cod, pert. to .... GADOID
cod, young ... . SCROD
code .... LAW, CIPHER
codfish, Eur. .... POOR
coffee ... RIO, JAVA, MOCHA
coffee-chocolate flavor.MOCHA
coffer-dam, Egypt ...... SADD
b coffin stand .... BIER
cognizant .... AWARE
cognomen ... NAME, EPITHET
cohere .... BIND
coil .... WIND, TWINE
TWIST, WREATHE
COIN ...... see also SPECIAL
SECTION, Page 190
coin .... RIN, YEN, SPECIE
coin, cut edges of .... NIG
coin, edging .... REEDING
coin, gold .... LEV
coin, mill .... NURL
coin money .... MINT
coin, pewter .... TRA
coin, reverse side ...... VERSO
coin, silver .... SCEAT
coin tester, Orient
SARAF, SHROFF
coin, tin .... TRA
coincide .... JIBE, AGREE
colander ....SIEVE
cold .... ALGID, GELID
cold, producing ...... ALGIFIC
cold tableland, Andes ... PUNA
collar .. ETON, FICHU, GORGET
collar, clerical ...... RABAT,
RABATO, REBATO
collar, deep .... BERTHA
collar, wheel-shaped .... RUFF
collect ...... AMASS, GARNER

c collection .... ANA, SET
collection .... SORTITE
collection, motley ..... RAFT
collection of facts .... ANA
collection of sayings .... ANA
COLLEGE DEGREE . see DEGREE
college, Iowa .... COE
college, N.J., East Orange
UPSALA
college official .... DEAN
college quadrangle ..... QUAD
colloquialism .... IDIOM
colonists greeting to Ind. NETOP
colonize .... SETTLE
colonizer .... OECIST
colonnade .... STOA
colony, Eng. ...... CAROLINA
colony, Fr. .... ALGERIA
color .... DYE, HUE, TINT
color .. ASH, BAY, RED, TAN,
BLUE, FAON, FAWN, GRAY,
GREY, HOPI, JADE, LIME,
NAVY, NILE, PINK, PUCE,
ROSE, SAXE, AMBER, BEIGE,
CORAL, CREAM, EBONY,
HENNA, IVORY, MAUVE,
MOCHA, SEPIA, UMBER,
CERISE, CITRON, COBALT,
MAROON, RESEDA, SEVRES,
SIENNA, SORREL, CAR-
MINE, CELESTE, CITRINE,
MAGENTA
d color brown sugar ... CARAIBE
color changer, photo ... TONER
color, neutral .. GREGE, GREIGE
color, purplish-brown ... PUCE
color, slightly .... TINT, TINGE
color, stripe of .... PLAGA
color, terrapin .... FEUILLE
Colorado park .... ESTES
coloring agent .... RUDDLE
coloring matter in fustic.MORIN
colorless .... DRAB
colorless alkaloid ...... ESERIN
colorless oil .... CETANE
columbite, variety of.DIANITE
Columbus' birthplace .. GENOA
Columbus' city sailed from
PALOS
Columbus' ship .. NINA, PINTA
column, Buddhist-Hindu, building
LAT
column, Gr. .... DORIC, IONIC
column, memorial .... LAT
column, twisted . TORSE, TORSO
columns, arranged in TABULAR
coma .... TRANCE
comb horse .... CURRY
comb wool .... CARD, TEASE
combat, field, place of . ARENA
combat, knight's ...... JOUST

Combat

a combat, scene of ..... **ARENA**
combination .. **UNION, CARTEL**
combination, card .... **TENACE**
COMBINING FORMS:
   above .... **SUR**
   air ...... **AER, AERI, AERO**
   all .... **PAN, OMNI**
   ass .... **ONO**
   bad .... **MAL**
   bee .... **API**
   beyond .... **SUR**
   black .... **MELA**
   blood .... **HEMO**
   body ...... **SOMA, SOMATO**
   bone .... **OSTEO**
   both .... **AMBI**
   boundary .... **ORI**
   bread .... **ARTO**
   bristle .... **SETI**
   cetacean .... **CETO**
   Chinese .... **SINO**
   communications .... **TEL**
   contemporary .... **NEO**
   daybreak .... **EO**
   dry .... **XER**
   ear .... **OTO, AURI**
   earth .... **GEO**
   egg .... **OO, OVI**
   eight .... **OCT, OCTO**

b   equal .... **ISO, PARI**
   eye .... **OCULO**
   far .... **TEL, TELE**
   fat ... **SEBI, STEAT, STEATO**
   fearful .... **DINO**
   feast day .... **MAS**
   female .... **GYNE**
   firm .... **STEREO**
   five .... **PENTA**
   follower .... **IST**
   food .... **SITO**
   foot ...... **PED, PEDI, PEDO**
   four-parted .... **TETRA**
   fruit .... **CARPO**
   gas .... **AER, AERO**
   gate .... **PYLE**
   glade .... **NEMO**
   gland .... **ADEN**
   gray .... **POLIO**
   great .... **MEGA**
   gums .... **ULO**
   hair .... **PIL, PILI**
   half .... **DEMI, SEMI**
   heat ..... **THERM, THERMO**
   hundred ..... **CENTI, HECTO**
   idea .... **IDEO**
   ill .... **MAL**
   individual .... **IDIO**
   inner .... **ENTO**
   in zoology .... **EAE**
   late, latest .... **NEO**
   line .... **STICH**

c   many .... **POLY**
   medicine .... **IATRO**
   middle .... **MEDI**
   milk .... **LACT, LACTO**
   monster .... **TERAT**
   mountain .... **ORO**
   mouth ...... **STOM, STOMO**
   moving .... **KINO**
   narrow .... **STENO**
   neck types .... **DERA**
   needle .... **ACU**
   nerve .... **NEURO**
   new .... **NEO**
   nine .... **ENNE, ENNEA**
   nose .... **NASI**
   not .... **UN, NON**
   numerical .... **UNI**
   numerous .... **MULTI**
   oil .... **OLEO**
   one .... **UNI, MONO**
   on this side .... **CIS**
   other .... **HETER**
   outside .... **ECTO**
   peculiar .... **IDIO**
   power .... **DYNA**
   powerful .... **MEGA**
   quality .... **ACY**
   recent .... **NEO, CENE**

d   reversal .... **ALLO**
   ribbon .... **TENE**
   round .... **GYRO**
   sad .... **TRAGI**
   seeds .... **CARPO**
   seizure of illness .... **AGRA**
   self .... **AUT, AUTO**
   shoulder .... **OMO**
   small .... **STENO**
   solid .... **STEREO**
   speak .... **LALO**
   star .... **ASTRO**
   stone .... **LITH**
   strange .... **XENO**
   sun .... **HELIO**
   ten .... **DECA**
   thin .... **SERO**
   third .... **TRIT**
   thread .... **NEMA**
   threefold, thrice .... **TER**
   tooth .... **ODONT**
   touch .... **TAC**
   thought .... **IDEO**
   thousand .... **MILLE**
   up .... **ANO**
   vapor .... **ATMO**
   various .... **VARI, VARIO**
   watery .... **SERO**
   white .... **ALBO**
   whole .... **TOTO**
   wind .... **ANEMO**
   within .... **ENT, ESO,**
      ENDO, ENSO, ENTO

_a_
without	ECT
wood	XYLO
worker	ERGATE
come	ENSUE, ACCRUE, ARRIVE
come back	RECUR
come forth	ISSUE, EMERGE, EMERSE
come forth from	JET, GUSH, SPEW, EMANATE
comedian's foil	STOOGE
comedy	FARCE
"Comedy of Errors" servant	LUCE
comfort	EASE, SOLACE
comfortable	COSH, SNUG
comforter	SCARF
command	BID, FIAT, ORDER, DICTATE
command: archaic	HEST
command to horse	GEE, HAW, HUP
commander, Egypt	SIRDAR
commander, Moslem	AGA, AGHA
commander, fortress	CAID, QAID
commentary: Hebrew	BIUR
commission, milit.	BREVET
commodity	WARE, STAPLE
common	VULGAR, GENERAL
common brant	QUINK

_b_
common: Hawaiian	NOA
common man	PLEB
commonplace	BANAL, TRITE
commotion	ADO, STIR, TO-DO
commune, Dutch, Holland	EDE
COMMUNE	see its country in GAZETTEER
communion cup	AMA
communion dish	PATEN
communion service	MASS
communion table	ALTAR
compact	DENSE, SOLID
companion	PAL, MATE
comparative conjunction	THAN
comparative suffix ending	ER
compass point	NE, SE, SW, ENE, ESE, NNE, NNW, SSE, SSW, WNW, WSW
compass point, mariner's	RHUMB
compassion	PITY, RUTH
compel	MAKE, FORCE, COERCE
compendium	SYLLABUS
compensate	PAY
compensation, N. Z.	UTU
competent	ABLE
complain	FRET, FUSS, GRIPE, REPINE
complainant	RELATOR
complete	TOTAL, UTTER, ENTIRE, PLENARY

_c_
completely	ALL, QUITE
completely occupy	ENGROSS
complication	NODE, NODI
comply	OBEY, YIELD
composer, Am.	NEVIN, SOUSA, FOSTER, COPLAND
composer, Eng.	ARNE, ELGAR, COATES
composer, Fr.	LALO, AUBER BIZET, IBERT, RAVEL
composer, Ger.	ABT, BACH, WEBER
composer, Roum.	ENESCO
COMPOSITION	see also MUSIC
composition	ESSAY, THEME
composition, mus.	OPUS, ETUDE, MOTET, RONDO, SUITE, SONATA, CONCERTO, FANTASIA
composition of selections	CENTO
composition, operatic	SCENA
composition, sacred	MOTET
compositor	TYPO
compound, organic	AMIDE
compound with oxygen	OXIDE
comrade-in-arms	ALLY
concave	DISHED
conceal: law	ELOIN
concealed	INNER, PERDU
concealed obstacle	SNAG
concede	ADMIT, GRANT, YIELD

_d_
conceive	IDEATE
concern	CARE
concerning	RE, INRE, ABOUT, ANENT
conch	SHELL
conciliate	ATONE
conciliatory gift	SOP
concise	BRIEF, SHORT, TERSE
concluding passage music	CODA
concoct	BREW
concrete mixer	PAVER
concur	JIBE, AGREE, ASSENT
condescend	DEIGN, STOOP
condiment	SALT, CURRY, SPICE
condition	IF, STATE, STATUS
condition in agreement	PROVISO
conduct	LEAD, GUIDE
conductor	MAESTRO
conductor's stick	BATON
conduit	MAIN, DRAIN, SEWER
cone	STROBIL, STROBILE
cone of silver	PINA
confection	COMFIT
confection, nut	PRALINE
confederate	ALLY
Confederate soldier	REB
confederation	LEAGUE
conference	PALAVER

a confess .... AVOW, ADMIT
confession of faith .... CREDO
confidence .... FAITH, TRUST
confidences .... SECRETS
confident .... RELIANT
confidential .... ESOTERIC
confine ...... BOX, HEM, PEN, CAGE, CRAMP
confined .... PENT
confront .... MEET
confused, make .... ADDLE
confusion .... BABEL
congealed dew .... RIME
conger .... EEL
congregate .. MEET, GATHER
conical mass of thread ... COP
coniferous tree ..... FIR, YEW, PINE, CEDAR, SPRUCE
conjunction .... OR, AND, BUT, NOR
connect ... JOIN, LINK, UNITE
connecting strip of land
ISTHMUS
connection
NEXUS, CORRELATION
connective .... AND, NOR
connective tissue ..... FASCIA
connubial .... MARITAL
conquer .... MASTER
conqueror, Mex.

b CORTES, CORTEZ
Conrad's "Victory" heroine
LENA
conscript .... DRAFT
consecrate .... BLESS
consecrated .... OBLATE
consequence .... OUTCOME
conservative .... TORY
consider .... DEEM, RATE, TREAT, REGARD
consonant, hard ...... FORTIS
consonant, unaspirated .. LENE
conspire .... PLOT
Constantine VIII's daughter . ZOE
constellation .... ARA, LEO, APUS, ARGO, LYNX, LYRA, PAVO, URSA, VELA, ARIES, CANIS, CETUS, DRACO, LIBRA, MENSA, ORION, VIRGO, AQUILA, GEMINI, PISCES, TAURUS
constellation, Altar ...... ARA
constellation, Aquila ... EAGLE
constellation, Ara ..... ALTAR
constellation, Aries ...... RAM
constellation, Balance .. LIBRA
constellation, Bear ...... URSA
constellation, Bull .... TAURUS
constellation, Crab ... CANCER
constellation, Crane ..... GRUS
constellation, Crow ... CORVUS

c constellation, Dog .... CANIS
constellation, Dragon .. DRACO
constellation, Hunter ... ORION
constellation, Lion .... LEO
constellation near South Pole
APUS
constellation, northern ... LEO
constellation, Peacock ... PAVO
constellation, Ram ..... ARIES
constellation, Southern ... ARA, APUS, ARGO, GRUS, PAVO, VELA, INDUS
constellation's main star .. COR
constitution supporter . CARTIST
constrictor ..... BOA, ABOMA
constructor .... ERECTOR
consume: obs. .... ETE
container .... BOX, CAN, TIN, TUB, VAT, URN, CASE
containing ore .... ORY
contempt, exclamation of . PISH
contempt, look of ..... SNEER
contend .... VIE, COPE, DEAL, COMPETE
contest .... AGON, BOUT
continent: abbr. ...... NA, SA, AFR, EUR
continue .... LAST, ENDURE, RESUME
contort . WARP, GNARL, TWIST

d contradict ..... DENY, REBUT, NEGATE
contrition .... REMORSE
contrive .... MAKE, DEVISE
control .... STEER
controversial .... ERISTIC
controversy .... DEBATE
conundrum .. ENIGMA, RIDDLE
convert to Judaism ...... GER
conveyance of estate .. DEMISE
convoy .... ESCORT
cony .. DAS, DAMAN, GANAM
cook in cream .... SHIR, SHIRR
cooking odor .... NIDOR
cooking pot .... OLLA
cooky .... SNAP
cool .... ICE
coolie woman .... CHANGAR
Cooper novel .... PILOT
copal .... ANIME
copper .... CENT
Copperfield, Mrs. .... DORA
copse .... HOLT, COPPICE
Coptic bishop .... ANBA
copy .... APE, MODEL, ECTYPE
copy, court record ... ESTREAT
coral .... POLYP
cord .... LINE, RAIP, ROPE, WELT
cord, hat of Bedouin .... AGAL
cord, Hawaii .... AEA

a cordage fiber . **DA, COIR, ERUC,**
  FERU, HEMP, IMBE, JUTE,
  RHEA, ABACA, SISAL
cordage tree............... **SIDA**
Cordelia's father .... **LEAR**
"Cordiale, —"........ **ENTENTE**
core ...... **AME, PITH, HEART**
core, casting mold ..... **NOWEL**
core material of earth ..... **NIFE**
core to fashion metal...... **AME**
core, wooden .... **AME**
cork .... **SPILE**
Cork County port......... **COBH**
cork, extract of .... **CERIN**
cork, flat .... **SHIVE**
cork helmet...... **TOPI, TOPEE**
corkwood............... **BALSA**
corm.................... **BULB**
corn crake bird............ **RAIL**
corn crake genus......... **CREX**
corn, hulled............ **HOMINY**
corn, India.... **RAGEE, RAGGEE**
corn lily .... **IXIA**
corn meal .... **MASA**
cornbread .... **PONE**
corner... **NOOK, TREE, ANGLE**
cornerstone ..... **COIN, COYN,**
          COIGN, QUOIN, COIGNE
cornice support .... **ANCON**
b Cornish prefix: town....... **TRE**
Cornish prefix in names.... **LAN,**
          ROS
cornu .... **HORN**
Cornwall mine .... **BAL**
corolla part............. **PETAL**
corona .. **AUREOLA, AUREOLE**
coronach, Scot.......... **DIRGE**
coronation stone .... **SCONE**
corpulent............... **OBESE**
corral: Sp.............. **ATAJO**
correct. **OKEH, TRUE, AMEND,**
          EMEND, REVISE
correct behaviour, Chin. ......**LI**
correlative............ **OR, NOR**
correspond**JIBE, AGREE, TALLY**
corridor .... **HALL**
corrie .... **CWM**
corrode ... **EAT, RUST, ERODE**
corrupt........ **TAINT, VENAL,**
          VITIATE
corrupt with money ..... **BRIBE**
corsair .... **PIRATE**
corset bone.............. **BUSK**
cortege .... **RETINUE**
corundum .... **EMERY**
cos lettuce .... **ROMAINE**
Cos, pert. to .... **COAN**
cosmic cycle.............. **EON**
cosmic order: Vedic .... **RITA**
Cossack............... **TATAR**
Cossack chief........ **ATAMAN**

c Cossack headman.... **HETMAN**
Cossack regiment. **POLK, PULK**
cosset .... **PET**
costa .... **RIB**
coterie .... **SET**
cottage, Ind.............. **BARI**
cotton batting............ **BATT**
cotton, Bengal .... **ADATI**
cotton, Egypt ...... **SAK, PIMA,**
          SAKEL
cotton fabric..... **JEAN, LAWN,**
          LENO, DENIM,
          SURAT, MADRAS
cotton fabric, corded **CANTOON**
cotton machine .... **GIN**
cotton, matted........... **BATT**
cotton tree .... **SIMAL**
cottonwood, Texas ..... **ALAMO**
couch.................... **LAIR**
cougar ...... **PUMA, PANTHER**
council .... **SOVIET**
council, ecclesiastical... **SYNOD**
council, king's .... **WITAN**
"Council of —" .... **TRENT**
counsel .... **REDE**
counselor............ **MENTOR**
count .... **ENUMERATE**
count, Ger. .... **GRAF**
counter .... **BAR**
counter, in cards........ **MILLE**
d countercurrent........... **EDDY**
countermand .... **REVOKE**
counterpart.............. **LIKE**
countersink............. **REAM**
counting frame........ **ABACUS**
COUNTRY see also GAZETTEER,
          SPECIAL SECTION
country, ancient.......... **ELAM**
country, ancient, Asia Min., Gr.
          EOLIS, AEOLIA, AEOLIS
country, ancient, Bib.... **SHEBA**
country, ancient Greek..... **ELIS**
country bumpkin .... **RUBE,**
          YOKEL, RUSTIC
country: law .... **PAIS**
COUNTY see also GAZETTEER,
          SPECIAL SECTION
county: Dan.............. **AMT**
county: Eng............. **SHIRE**
county: Nor. ...... **AMT, FYLKE**
county: Swed............. **LAN**
couple .... **TWO, PAIR**
courage .... **METTLE**
courier.............. **ESTAFET,**
          ESTAFETTE
course .... **WAY, ROAD,**
          TACK, ROUTE
course, complete........ **CYCLE**
course, meal.. **SALAD, ENTREE**
course, part of....... **LAP, LEG**
court.................... **AREA**

37

a
court action .... **SUIT**
court, A.-S. .. **GEMOT, GEMOTE**
court, church .... **ROTA**
court cry .... **OYES, OYEZ**
court hearing .... **OYER**
court, inner .... **PATIO**
court, Jap. ..... **DARI, DAIRO**
court, old English .... **LEET**
court order .... **ARRET**
court panel .... **JURY**
court, pert. to church .. **ROTAL**
court proceeding ...... **TRIAL**
courtly .... **AULIC**
courtship strut, grouse's .. **LAK**
courtway .... **AREA**
courtyard .... **PATIO**
Covenant, — of the .... **ARK**
cover inner surface ..... **LINE**
covering .. **TEGMEN, TEGUMEN**
covey .... **BEVY, BROOD**
cow .... **BOSSY, BOVINE**
cow house .... **BYRE**
cows .... **KINE, BOSSIES**
coward .... **CRAVEN**
cowboy garment ...... **CHAPS**
cowboy, S. Am. ..... **GAUCHO**
cowfish .... **RAY, TORO**
cowl .... **HOOD**
cowlike .... **COUS**
coxcomb .... **FOP**

b
coy .... **ARCH**
coyotillo .... **MARGARITA**
coypu .... **NUTRIA**
cozy .... **HOMY, SNUG**
cozy place .... **DEN, NEST**
crab-eating mongoose .. **URVA**
crab, front of .... **METOPE**
crack . **SNAP, CHINK, CREVICE**
crackling .... **CREPITANT**
crackpot .... **NUT**
craft .... **ART, TRADE**
craftsman .... **ARTISAN**
crafty ...... **SLY, FOXY, WILY**
craggy hill .... **TOR**
cramp .... **KINK**
crane arm .... **GIB, JIB**
crane genus .... **GRUS**
crane, India .... **SARUS**
crane, pert. to ...... **GRUINE**
crane, ship's .... **DAVIT**
cranelike bird ...... **CHUNGA**
cranelike bird, S. Amer.
.... **SERIEMA**
cranial nerve ... **VAGI, VAGUS**
cravat .... **TIE**
crave . **ASK, BEG, LONG, DESIRE**
craw .... **MAW, CROP**
crayon .... **CHALK, PASTEL**
craze .... **FAD, MANIA**
crazy .... **LOCO, LUNY, WILD**

c
cream .... **ELITE**
credit transfer system .. **GIRO**
creed .... **CREDO, NICENE**
creek .... **RIA, KILL**
creek: N.Y. .... **VLEI**
creeper .... **IVY**
creeping .. **REPENT, REPTANT**
Cremona .... **AMATI**
crescent moon's point ... **CUSP**
crescent-shaped ..... **LUNATE**
crescent-shaped figure .. **LUNE**
crescent-shaped mark . **LUNULA**
crest . **TOP, COMB, PEAK, TUFT**
crest, sharp rugged mountain
.... **ARETE**
crested as birds ..... **PILEATE**
Cretan princess .... **ARIADNE**
Cretan spikenard .... **PHU**
CRETE . see SPECIAL SECTION
crevice ... **CREVAS, CREVASSE**
crew .... **MEN, GANG,**
.... **TEAM, EIGHT**
cribbage pin or score ..... **PEG**
cribbage term .... **NOB, NOBS**
cricket .... **GRIG**
cricket, ball in .... **EDGER**
cricket, field parts **ONS, OFFS**
cricket, run in .... **BYE**
cricket term **OVER, TICE, YORK**

d
crime, Eccl. .... **SIMONY**
Crimean river .... **ALMA**
criminal .... **FELON**
crimp .... **CURL, GOFFER**
crimson ..... **RED, CARMINE**
crippled .... **HALT, LAME**
criticize .... **SLATE**
criticize in a small way
.... **CARP, CAVIL**
crocodile, India .... **GAVIAL**
crocodile-head god, Egyp.
.... **SOBK, SEBEK**
crocus .... **IRID**
crocus bulb .... **CORM**
Croesus' land .... **LYDIA**
crony ... **PAL, CHUM, BUDDY**
crony: old Eng. .... **EME**
crooked .... **AGEE, AWRY**
crooner, early .... **VALLEE**
crop .... **MAW, CRAW**
crop, spring, India ..... **RABI**
cross ...... **IRATE, TRAVERSE**
cross, church .... **ROOD**
cross-examine .... **GRILL**
cross of life, Egypt .... **ANKH**
cross oneself .... **SAIN**
cross out .... **DELETE**
cross-stroke .... **SERIF**
cross timber, ship ...... **SPALE**
crossbeam ..... **TRAVE, TREVE**
crossbill genus .... **LOXIA**
crossbow .... **RODD**

a crossing, fence .... STILE
crosspiece . BAR, RUNG, CLEAT
crosspiece, vehicle ... EVENER
crossthreads ..... WEFT, WOOF
crosswise .... THWART
crossword champion, former
                          COOPER
crow .. ROOK, CRAKE, CORVUS
crow: Eng. .... BRAN
crow, Guam .... AGA
crow, kind of .... DAW
crowd, common ... MOB, RUCK
crowd together .. HERD, SERRY
crowded .... SERRIED
crown .... CAP, PATE,
            TIARA, DIADEM
crown colony, Brit.
          ADEN, BAHAMAS
crown of Osiris or Egypt .. ATEF
crown: poetic .... TIAR
crown, Pope's triple TIAR, TIARA
crucial point .... CRUX, PIVOT
crucible .... CRUSET
crucifix .... ROOD
crude . RAW, ROUGH, COARSE
crude metal .... ORE
crude sugar-molasses MELADA
cruel person .... SADIST
cruet .... AMA, CASTER
b cruising .... ASEA
crumbled easily ..... FRIABLE
Crusader's foe ...... SARACEN
Crusader's headquarters . ACRE
crush .... MASH, SUBDUE
crustacean .... CRAB, ISOPOD,
            SHRIMP, LOBSTER
crustacean order, one of
                  DECAPOD
cry .... HO, HOA, SOB, HOWL,
        WAIL, WEEP, LAMENT
cry, Austral. ... COOEE, COOEY
cry for silence, court
                OYES, OYEZ
crystal-clear .... PELLUCID
ctenophores, no tentacle .NUDA
Cuban dance .... CONGA
Cuban rodent ...... PILORI
Cuban secret police ... PORRA
Cuban timber tree ..... CUYA
cubic decimeter .... LITER
cubic measure .. CORD, STERE
cubic meter .... STERE
cubicle .... CELL
cubitus .... ULNA
Cuchulain's wife . EMER, EIMER
cuckoo, black, keel-billed ANI
cuckoo, Oriental .. COEL, KOEL
cuckoopint .... ARUM
cucumber .... CUKE, PEPO
cud .... QUID, RUMEN

c cudgel .... BAT, CLUB, DRUB,
            BASTE, STAVE, STICK
cue .... HINT
cue, music .... PRESA
cuff fastener .... TAB
cuirass .... LORICA
cull .... SORT
culmination ..... ACME, APEX
cultivate land .... HOE, PLOW,
            TILL, HARROW
cultivation method, Bengal
                  JUM, JOOM
cultivation, soil .... TILTH
culture medium .... AGAR
cunning ... ART, CUTE, FOXY,
        WILY, DEDAL, CALLID,
        DAEDAL
cup .... CRUSE
cup, assaying .... CUPEL
cup, ceremonial .... AMA
cup, gem cutting .... DOP
cup stand of metal .... ZARF
cup to hold gem .... DOP
cupbearer .... SAKI
cupbearer of gods ...... HEBE
cupboard .... AMBRY, CLOSET
Cupid .... AMOR, EROS
Cupid's title .... DAN
cupola .... DOME
cur .... MUT, MUTT
d curare ...... URALI, OORALI
curassow .... MITU
curassow genus .... CRAX
curdling powder ...... RENNET
cure-all .... ELIXIR, PANACEA
cure by salting .... CORN
cure with salt grass ..... DUN
curfew .... BELL
curios .... VIRTU
curl COIL, FRIZ, WIND, FRIZZ
curl of hair ...... FEAK, TRESS,
                  RINGLET
curling, mark aimed at ... TEE
currant genus .... RIBES
current .... AC, DC, EDDY,
        RIFE, TIDE, STREAM
curt ...... BRUSK, BRUSQUE
curve .... ARC, BOW, ESS,
        ARCH, BEND, SINUS
curve in a stream . HOEK, HOOK
curve, plane .... ELLIPSE,
                  PARABOLA
curve, sigmoid or double .. ESS
curved handle .... BOOL
curved in .. ADUNC, CONCAVE
curved out .... CONVEX
curved plank, vessel's .... SNY
Cush, son of .... SEBA
cushion ...... PAD, HASSOCK
custard .... FLAN
custard apple .... ANNONA

a custard cake .... **ECLAIR**
custard dish .... **FLAN**
custody .... **CHARGE**
custom .... **LAW, WONT,**
 HABIT, USAGE
custom, India ...... **DASTUR**
custom: Lat. .... **RITUS**
custom: obs. .... **URE**
customer .... **PATRON**
customs .... **MORES**
cut . **HEW, LOP, MOW, DOCK,**
 GASH, HACK, KERF, REAP,
 SLIT, SNEE, SNIP, TRIM,
 SEVER, SHEAR, SLIVE,
 CLEAVE, TREPAN
cut down .... **FELL**
cut edges of coins .... **NIG**
cut of meat .... **LOIN**
cut off ... **DOCK, SNIP, ELIDE**
cut off, as mane ..... **ROACH**
cut out .... **EXCISE**
cut: Shakespeare ...... **SLISH**
cut vertically
 SCARP, ESCARP, ESCARPE
cutter .... **SLED**
cutting .... **SECANT, INCISAL**

c cutting tool .. **AX, ADZ, AXE,**
 HOB, SAW, SAX, SYE, ADZE
cuttlefish ...... **SEPIA, SQUID**
cuttlefish fluid .... **INK**
Cyclades, one of, see GAZET-
 TEER
cycle, astronomical ..... **SAROS**
cyclorama .... **CYKE**
cylinder, moving ...... **PISTON**
cylindrical .... **TERETE**
cyma .... **GOLA**
cyma recta or reversa ... **OGEE**
cymbal, Orient .... **ZEL**
cymbals, India .... **TAL**
Cymbeline's daughter . **IMOGEN**
Cymric deity
 GWYN, LLEU, LLEW
Cymry .... **WELSH**
cypher system .... **CODE**
cyprinoid fish .... **ID, IDE,**
 CARP, CHUB
Cyrus' daughter ..... **ATOSSA**
cyst .... **WEN**
Czar .... **IVAN, FEDOR**
Czech .... **SLAV**
Czech, Eastern .... **ZIPS**

D

b Dadaist .... **ERNST**
dado, pedestal ...... **SOLIDUM**
Daedalus' son .... **ICARUS**
dagger .. **DIRK, SNEE, BODKIN**
dagger, ancient . **SKEAN, SKENE**
dagger, Ir. **DHU, SKENE, SKEAN**
dagger, Malay ... **CRIS, KRIS,**
 CREES, KREES, CREESE,
 KREESE
dagger: obs. .... **SNEE**
dagger, thin ...... **STILETTO**
Dahomey Negro .. **FON, FONG**
daily .... **DIURNAL**
dais .... **ESTRADE**
daisy . **MOON, OXEYE, SHASTA**
Dallas school .... **SMU**
dam .... **WAER, WEIR**
dam, Egypt ...... **SADD, SUDD**
dam site .... **ASWAN**
damage . **MAR, HARM, IMPAIR**
Damascus river .... **ABANA**
damp .... **DANK**
damselfish .... **PINTANO**
dance .... **HOP, JIG, REEL,**
 GALOP, GAVOT, POLKA,
 TANGO, RUMBA, REDOWA,
 RHUMBA, GAVOTTA, GA-
 VOTTE
dance, country . **REEL, ALTHEA**
dance, Gr. .... **HORMOS**
dance, Israeli .... **HORA**

d dance, lively ..... **JIG, REEL,**
 GALOP, POLKA, BOLERO
dance, old Eng. ...... **MORRIS**
dance, Sp. ... **TANGO, BOLERO**
dance, stately, old
 PAVAN, MINUET, PAVANE
dance step ..... **PAS, CHASSE,**
 GLISSADE
dancer .... **KELLY, SHAWN,**
 BOLGER, ZORINA, ASTAIRE
dancing girl, Egypt .... **ALMA,**
 ALME, ALMEH
dancing girl, Jap. ..... **GEISHA**
dandy **FOP, DUDE, JAKE, TOFF**
DANISH ... see also DENMARK
 in SPECIAL SECTION
Danish astronomer .... **BRAHE**
Dan. borough (in Eng.) .. **BORG**
Dan. chieftain .... **JARL, YARL**
Dan. division, territorial . **AMT**
Dan. fjord .... **ISE**
Dan. king ..... **CNUT, KNUT,**
 CANUTE
Dan. measure .... **ALEN**
Dan. money ..... **ORA, ORAS**
Dan. physicist .... **BOHR**
Dan. speech sound ...... **STOD**
dank .... **WET**
Dante's patron .... **SCALA**
Danube city ..... **ULM, LINZ**
Danube, old name of ... **ISTER**

a Danube tributary
INN, OLT, ISAR, PRUT
daring .... BOLD, NERVE
dark .... MIRKY, MURKY
dark horse .... ZAIN
dark rock .... CHERT
dark wood ...... TEAK, EBONY
darkness .... MIRK, MURK
darling: Ir. . ROON, ACUSHLA,
ASTHORE
darnel .... TARE
dart along .... FLIT
"Das Rheingold" role ... ERDA
dash .... ELAN
date, pert. to .... DATAL
date plum .... SAPOTE
date, Roman .... IDES, NONES
"David Copperfield" character
DORA, HEEP, DARTLE
David's captain .... JOAB
David's commander ... AMASA
David's daughter ..... TAMAR
David's father .... JESSE
David's nephew .... AMASA
David's ruler, one of ..... IRA
David's son .... SOLOMON
David's wife .... MICHAL
dawn .... DEW, EOS, AURORA
dawn, pert. to .... EOAN
day, Hebr. .... YOM
b day, Rom. ...... IDES, NONES
day-breeze, It. .... ORA
days: Lat. .... DIES
day's march .... ETAPE
daybreak .... DAWN
dazing larks, device for DARE
deacon's stole ...... ORARION
dead ... FLAT, AMORT, INERT
dead, abode of . HADES, SHEOL
dead, region of: Egypt AMENTI
dead trees .... DRIKI
deadly ...... FATAL, LETHAL
deadly carrot .... DRIAS
deadly sins, 7 ENVY, LUST, AN-
GER, PRIDE, SLOTH, GLUT-
TONY, COVETOUSNESS
dealer .... MONGER
dealer, cloth
DRAPER, MERCER
dean ...... DOYEN, DOYENNE
dearth .... WANT
death .... MORT, DEMISE
death deity: Rom. ...... MORS
death note on hunter's horn
MORT
death notice .... OBIT
death rattle .... RALE
debate—debatable
AGON, MOOT
debauchee ...... RAKE, ROUE
debris, rocky .... SCREE

c decade .... TEN
decamp ..... ELOPE, LEVANT
decay, dental .... CARIES
decay tree ...... CONK, KONK
deceit .... SHAM, WILE,
FRAUD, GUILE
deceive .. BILK, DUPE, FOOL,
GULL, TRICK, ILLUDE
decelerate .... RETARD
deception HOAX, STRATAGEM
decide: Rom. law .... CERN
decimal unit .... TEN
deck, ship's .... POOP
decks, cut away . RASEE, RAZEE
declaim .... RANT, RAVE,
ORATE, RECITE
declaration in whist ... MISERE
declare .... AVER, AVOW,
STATE, AVOUCH
declare, in cards .... MELD
decline .... EBB, SINK,
WANE, REFUSE
declivity ...... SCARP, SLOPE
declivity in menage .. CALADE
decorate ...... DECK, ADORN
decorated letter .... FAC
decorated wall part ..... DADO
decorous ..... STAID, DEMURE
decoy .... LURE, PLANT
decrease .... EBB, WANE,
LESSEN, RECEDE
d decree .... ACT, FIAT,
CANON, EDICT, ORDAIN
decree, Fr. law .... ARRET
decree, Moslem .... IRADE
decree, Rom. law .... DECRETE
decree, Russian .... UKASE
deduce .... INFER
deed .... GEST, GESTE
deeds .... ACTA
deer, Asia ...... AHU, KAKAR,
SAMBAR, SAMBUR,
SAMBHAR, SAMBHUR
deer, barking .... KAKAR
deer, Chile, Andes ..... PUDU
deer, female . DOE, ROE, HIND
deer genus, E. Ind. ..... RUSA
deer, India .... AXIS
deer, Jap. .... SIKA
deer, Kashmir ...... HANGUL
deer, red .... ROE, HART
deer, S. Am. .... GEMUL,
GUEMAL, GUEMUL
deer, spotted .... CHITAL
deer, Tibet .... SHOU
deer track .... SLOT
deerlet .... NAPUS
deerlike .... CERVINE
defamation .... LIBEL
defeat, chess .... MATE
defeat utterly ... BEST, ROUT

Defect

a defect, weaving .... **SCOB**
defendant's plea .... **NOLO**
deference .... **RESPECT**
defraud .... **GYP, BILK,**
             GULL, CHEAT
defy .... **DARE**
degrade ...... **ABASE, LOWER,**
              DEBASE
degrading .... **MENIAL**
degree .... **GRADE, STAGE**
degree .. (dental) DDS, DDSC;
  (engineer) CE, EE; (divinity) DD; (science) BSC;
  (arts) BA, MA, MFA; (law)
  LLB, LLD
degree, extreme .... **NTH**
degree taken, Cambridge
         INCEPTOR
degrees, angle of 57.30. **RADIAN**
deified sky, Rom. ..... **CAELUS**
DEITY . see also GOD, GODDESS
     and SPECIAL SECTION
deity .... **GOD**
deity, Buddhist ... **DEV, DEVA**
deity, Hindu ...... **DEV, DEVA**
deity, Jap. .. **AMIDA, AMITA**
deity, primeval .... **TITAN**
deity, Sumerian .... **ABU**
deity, Syrian .... **EL**
b delay . **WAIT, DETAIN, LINGER**
delay, law .... **MORA, MORAE**
delicacy .... **FINESSE**
delight .... **REVEL**
delusion: Buddhism .... **MOHA**
demand . **NEED, CLAIM, INSIST**
demeanor .... **AIR**
Demeter's daughter **CORA, KORE**
demigod .... **HERO**
demolish .... **RASE, RAZE**
demon ... **IMP, DEVIL, FIEND**
demon, Arab, Moslem, Oriental
     JIN, JINN, GENIE,
    GENII, JINNI, JINNEE
demon, Hindu . **ASURA, DAITYA**
demon, sun-swallowing, Hindu
  myth .... **RAHU**
demon, Zoroastrian
      DEV, DIV, DEVA
demonstrative pronoun
     THAT, THIS, WHOM
den ...... **DIVE, LAIR, HAUNT**
denary .... **TEN**
denial .... **NO, NAY**
DENMARK .. see also DANISH
     and SPECIAL SECTION
denomination .... **SECT**
denote .... **MEAN, SHOW,**
           INDICATE
denoting unfit ships in Lloyd's
  registry .... **AE**

c dense . **CRASS, THICK, STUPID**
density .... **DORD**
dental tool .... **SCALER**
deny .... **NEGATE**
depart .... **BEGONE, DECAMP**
depart fast **VAMOSE, VAMOOSE**
depart: Lat. .... **VADE**
departed ... **GONE, LEFT, WENT**
department, Chin. .. **FU, FOO**
departure .... **EXODUS**
dependent .... **MINION**
depict .... **DRAW, PAINT,**
           DESCRIBE
deplore .... **LAMENT**
deposit, alluvial **DELTA, GEEST**
deposit, clayey .... **MARL**
deposit, geyser .... **SINTER**
deposit, mineral .... **LODE**
deposit, river
    ALLUVIA, ALLUVIUM
deposit, wine cask ... **TARTAR**
depressed .... **SAD**
depression ...... **DENT, FOVEA**
deprivation .... **LOSS**
deprived .... **REFT**
depute .... **SEND**
deputy .... **AGENT, VICAR**
derby .... **BOWLER**
deride .... **GIBE, JIBE**
derrick .... **CRANE, STEEVE**
d dervish, "Arab. Nights" . **AGIB**
dervish, Moslem ...... **SADITE**
descendant .... **SON, CION**
descendant, Fatima's
     SAID, SEID, SAYID
descendants, male line .. **GENS**
descent, deep .... **SCARP**
descriptive term ..... **EPITHET**
desert dweller .... **EREMITE**
desert, Mongolia .... **GOBI**
desert plant .... **AGAVE**
deserter .... **RAT**
deserve .... **EARN, MERIT**
design .... **AIM**
desire .... **YEN, URGE,**
         WANT, WISH
desire eagerly .... **ASPIRE**
desirous .... **FAIN**
desolate .... **LORN, BLEAK**
despoil .... **RUIN**
despot .. **CZAR, TSAR, TZAR,**
    TYRANT, DICTATOR
dessert .... **ICE, PIE, MOUSSE,**
         TRIFLE
destiny . **DOOM, FATE, KARMA**
destroy .... **RASE, RAZE,**
         DECIMATE
destruction .... **RUIN**
detach .... **WEAN**
detachable button ...... **STUD**
detail .... **ITEM**

a detain **CHECK, DELAY, ARREST**
detecting device ...... **SONAR**
detective .... **TEC, DICK**
detent .... **PAWL**
determination .... **WILL**
determine .... **FIX, DECIDE,**
RESOLVE
detest .... **HATE, LOATHE**
dethrone .... **DEPOSE**
detonator .... **CAP**
"— deum" .... **TE**
devaluate .... **DEBASE**
developed compound animal
ZOON
Devi .... **UMA**
deviate ... **ERR, YAW, DIVERGE**
deviation .... **LAPSE**
deviation from course .... **YAW**
devil .. **DEMON, DEUCE, SATAN**
devil: Gypsy .... **BENG**
devil, Moslem
SHAITAN, SHEITAN
devil, Russian folklore .. **CHORT**
devil worship ...... **SATANISM**
devilfish .... **MANTA**
Devon river .... **EXE**
devotee .... **FAN, IST**
devotion, nine-day .. **NOVENA**
devoutness .... **PIETY**
dewberry .... **MAYES**
b dewy .... **RORAL, RORIC**
dexterity .... **ART**
dexterous .... **CLEVER**
diadem .... **TIARA**
diagonal .... **BIAS**
DIALECT . see also LANGUAGE
dialect . **IDIOM, LINGO, PATOIS**
dialect, Chin. .... **CANTON**
dialect, Ethiopic ...... **TIGRE**
dialect, Gr. .... **DORIC, IONIC**
diamond corner .... **BASE**
diamond fragments ..... **BORT**
diamond holder .... **DOP**
diamond, impure industrial **BORT**
diamond, perfect ... **PARAGON**
diamonds, low quality ... **BORT**
Diana .... **ARTEMIS**
Diana's grove .... **NEMUS**
Diana's mother ...... **LATONA**
diaphanous ..... **THIN, SHEER**
diaphragm, pert. to .. **PHRENIC**
diatonic note .... **MI**
diatribe .. **SCREED, HARANGUE**
dibble .... **DAP, DIB**
Dickens character .. **PIP, TIM,**
DORA, GAMP, HEEP,
FAGIN, DORRIT
Dickens' pseudonym ...... **BOZ**
"Die Fledermaus" girl .. **ADELE**
die for making drain pipe . **DOD**
die, gambling .. **TAT, TESSERA**

c "Dies —," "Day of Wrath" **IRAE**
diet .... **BANT, FARE**
differ ...... **VARY, DISAGREE**
difference between solar and
lunar year ...... **EPACT**
different ...... **OTHER, DIVERS**
difficulty .... **RUB, KNOT**
dig ...... **GRUB, PION, DELVE**
digest .... **PANDECT**
digit, foot .... **TOE**
digraph **AE, EA, OA, OE, SH, TH**
dike .... **LEVEE**
dilation .... **ECTASIA**
dilatory ...... **SLOW, TARDY,**
REMISS
dilemma .... **FIX**
dill herb .... **ANET**
dilute .... **THIN, WATER**
dim, become .. **BLEAR, DARKLE**
diminish ... **EBB, BATE, SINK,**
WANE, ABATE, TAPER
diminish front: military **PLOY**
dingle ..... **DALE, DELL, GLEN**
dining room, ancient ... **OECUS**
diocese center .... **SEE**
Dioscuri .... **ANAX**
dip .... **DAP, DIB, DOPP,**
DUNK, LADE
dip out .... **BAIL**
diplomacy .... **TACT**
d diplomat .... **ENVOY, CONSUL,**
ATTACHE
diphthong ..... **AE, IA, OA, UO**
Dipper constellation ..... **URSA**
direct .... **AIM, LEAD**
direct attention .... **REFER**
direct steering of boat .. **CONN**
dirge .... **LINOS, LINUS**
dirigible .... **BLIMP**
dirk .... **SNY, SNEE**
dirty lock .... **FRIB**
disable .... **LAME, MAIM**
disagreeable .... **ILL**
disappear gradually . **EVANESCE**
disavow ...... **DENY, RECANT**
disbeliever .... **ATHEIST**
disburse ...... **SPEND, EXPEND**
discard . **DROP, SCRAP, REJECT**
discernment .... **TACT**
discharge .... **EMIT, FIRE,**
SACK, SHOOT
discharged .... **SHOT**
disciple .... **APOSTLE**
disciple: India .... **CHELA**
disciplinarian ..... **MARTINET**
disclaim .... **DENY**
disclose .... **BARE, REVEAL**
discolored ...... **DOTY, LIVID**
disconcert ..... **FAZE, ABASH**
discourse .. **HOMILY, DESCANT**
discourse, art of ... **RHETORIC**

43

a discover . SEE, SPY, ESPY, FIND
discriminate .... SECERN
discuss ...... TREAT, DEBATE
discussion group ...... FORUM
disease ..... MAL, POX, HIVES
disease, Afr. .... NENTA
disease cause .... VIRUS
disease, diver's .... BENDS
disease, fowl ...... PIP, ROUP,
PEROSIS
disease, fungus .... ERGOT
disease, grape-vine
ESCA, ERINOSE
disease, plant ... SMUT, SCALD
disease, skin .... ECZEMA
disease spreader
VECTOR, CARRIER
disease, tropical .... SPRUE
disembark .... LAND
disembodied spirit: Chin.
KUEI, KWEI
disencumber .... RID
disengage .... FREE
disfigure .... MAR, DEFACE
disgrace .... SCANDAL
disguise .... MASK
disgust, word of .... AW
DISH .... also see VESSEL
dish .... PLATE
dish, Hawaiian .... POI

b dish, highly seasoned
OLIO, OLLA
dish, hominy .... POSOLE
dish, Hungarian .... GOULASH
dish, It. .... RAVIOLI
dish, main .... ENTREE
dish, meat .... STEW, RAGOUT
dish, Mex. .. TAMAL, TAMALE,
TAMALI
dish, stemmed ..... COMPOTE
dishearten .... DAUNT, DETER
dishonor .... SHAME, VIOLATE
dishonorable .... BASE
disinclined .... AVERSE
disinfectant . CRESOL, PHENOL,
CRESSOL, CRESSYL
disk, ice hockey ...... PUCK
disk, like a .. DISCAL, DISCOID
disk, metal .... PATEN
dislocate .... LUXATE
dismal .... DREAR
dismantle .... STRIP
dismay .... APPAL, DAUNT
dismiss .... DEMIT, FIRE
dismounted .... ALIT
disorder .... MESS, DERAY,
CLUTTER
disorderly flight .... ROUT
disparaging .... SNIDE
disparaging remark ...... SLUR
dispatch .... SEND, HASTE

c dispatch boat .... AVISO
dispelled .... GONE
display .... AIR, SHEW, SHOW,
ARRAY, EVINCE
display proudly
VAUNT, OSTENT
displease .... VEX, MIFF,
ANGER, ANNOY
disposed .... PRONE
disposition .... MOOD, TEMPER
dispossess .... OUST, EVICT
disprove .... REFUTE
disputable .... MOOT
dissertation ... THESES, THESIS
dissolute person .. RAKE, ROUE
dissonant .... ATONAL
distance, at-from a . OFF, AFAR
distant ... FAR, YON, REMOTE
distilling vessel .... MATRASS
distinctive air ... AURA, MIEN,
CACHET
distracted .... DISTRAIT
distraint: old Eng. law .. NAAM
distribute .. DEAL, DOLE, METE
DISTRICT .... see also REGION
district .... AREA, ZONE
district, old Eng. court
SOC, SOKE
disturb .... ROIL, MOLEST
disturbance ...... ROW, RIOT

d ditch .... FOSS, RINE,
FOSSE, TRENCH
ditch, castle .... MOAT
ditch, fort. .... RELAIS
ditch millet .... HUREEK
ditto .... SAME
divan .... SOFA
dive .... DEN, HEADER
dive bomber .... STUKA
diverge .... DEVIATE
divers .... SEVERAL
divest .... STRIP, DEPRIVE
divide .... PART, SHARE
divide for study ..... DISSECT
divided .... REFT, SPLIT
divider .... MERIST
dividing wall, membrance, parti-
tion ..... SEPTA, SEPTUM
divination by lots: Lat.
SORS, SORTES
"Divine Comedy" author DANTE
divine favor .... GRACE
divine law: Rom. .... FAS
divine revelation TORA, TORAH
divine utterance ..... ORACLE
divinity .... DEITY
divorce bill, Jewish law
GET, GETT
divorce, Moslem ...... TALAK
"— dixit" .... IPSE
dizziness, pert. to ..... DINIC

a docile .... **TAME**
dockyard barge .... **LUMP**
doctor ...... **INTERN, INTERNE**
Dr. Brown's dog hero .... **RAB**
Dr. Jekyll's other self .. **HYDE**
doctrinaire .... **ISMY**
doctrine .. **ISM, DOGMA, TENET**
documents, box for .. **HANAPER**
dodder .... **AMIL**
dodo genus .... **DIDUS**
doe .... **HIND**
doe, young .... **TAG, TEG**
dog, ... **CANIS, CANINE**
dog ...... **POM, CHOW, PEKE, BASSET, POODLE, SPANIEL**
dog, chops of .... **FLEWS**
dog-faced ape .... **AANI**
dog-fisher .... **OTTER**
DOG, GUN see DOG, HUNTING
dog, Hungarian **PULI, KUVASZ**
dog, hunting (bird) ... **ALAN, ALAND, ALANT, BASSET, BEAGLE, SETTER, COURSER, HARRIER, POINTER**
dog, John Brown's ...... **RAB**
dog, large .... **ALAN**
dog, "Odyssey" ...... **ARGOS**
dog salmon .... **KETA**
dog, small-toy ..... **POM, PUG, PEKE**

b dog snapper, fish ...... **JOCU**
dog, Sputnik's .... **LAIKA**
dog star .... **SEPT, SOPT, SEPTI, SIRIUS**
dog, tropical .... **ALCO**
dog, Welsh .... **CORGI**
dog, wild, Austral. ..... **DINGO**
dog, wild, India ...... **DHOLE**
doge, office of ...... **DOGATE**
dogfish .... **SHARK**
dogma .... **TENET**
dogwood ..... **OSIER, CORNEL**
dole .... **METE**
dolphin fish .... **DORADO**
dolphin genus .... **INIA**
dolphin-like cetacean .. **INIA**
dolt .... **ASS, OAF, CLOD, LOUT, DUNCE**
domain ..... **BOURN, REALM, BOURNE, DEMENE, ESTATE, DEMESNE**
dome .... **CUPOLA**
dome-shaped .... **DOMOID**
Domesday Book money ... **ORA**
domestic .... **MAID, LOCAL**
domestic animal .... **ASS, CAT, COW, DOG, HOG, PIG, RAM, SOW, MULE**
domestic slave .... **ESNE**
domesticated .... **TAME**
dominion .... **REALM, EMPERY**

c domino .... **MASK**
Don Juan's mother ...... **INEZ**
donkey .... **ASS, MOKE, BURRO, NEDDY**
doom .... **CONDEMN, DESTINE**
doom palm, Afr. .... **DUM**
door .... **PORTAL**
door: Lat. .... **JANUA**
door part ...... **JAMB, SASH, SILL, LINTEL**
door section .... **PANEL**
doorkeeper, Masonic .... **TILER**
dorado, color .... **CUIR**
Doric frieze slab ..... **METOPE**
dormant ..... **ASLEEP, LATENT**
dormouse .... **LOIR**
dormouse, garden ...... **LEROT**
dormouse genus .... **GLIS**
dorsal .... **NOTAL**
dote .... **DRIVEL**
dots, paint with ...... **STIPPLE**
dotted with figures ..... **SEME**
double . **DUAL, TWIN, BINATE**
double cocoon ...... **DUPION**
double dagger .... **DIESIS**
double, Egypt .... **KA**
double salt .... **ALUM**
double tooth .... **MOLAR**
doubletree .... **EVENER**

d dovkie ...... **ROTCH, ROTGE, ROTCHE**
Dovyalis .... **ABERIA**
dowel ... **PIN, COAG, COAK**
dower, pert. to .... **DOTAL**
dower property .... **DOS**
down ..... **FUZZ, PILE, EIDER**
down, facing.**PRONE, PRONATE**
down quilt .... **DUVET**
"downunder" native clan .. **ATI**
downward, curve ...... **DEFLEX**
dowry .... **DOS, DOT**
drag ... **LUG, TUG, HAUL, SNIG**
dragnet .... **TRAWL**
dragon, like a ... **DRACONTINE**
dragon of darkness, Bibl. **RAHAB**
drain . **SAP, DEPLETE, VITIATE**
drain .... **SUMP, SEWER**
dram, small .... **NIP**
DRAMA .... see also PLAY
Dravidian **KOTA, MALE, NAIR, TODA, TULU, TAMIL**
draw ...... **TIE, TOW, LIMN, PULL, DEPICT**
draw forth .... **EDUCE**
draw from .... **DERIVE**
draw out . **EDUCE, ATTENUATE**
draw tight: naut. .... **FRAP**
drawing curve .... **SPLINE**
drawing room .... **SALON**
dreadful .... **DIRE**
dream, day .... **REVERIE**

45

a   "Dream Girl" playwright . **RICE**
dregs .... **FAEX, LEES,**
            DROSS, SEDIMENT
drench .... **SOUSE, TOUSE**
drenched .... **WET, DEWED**
DRESS .... see also **GARMENT**
dress .... **GARB, CLOTHE,**
           ACCOUTER
dress, as stone ...... **DAB, NIG**
dress feathers .... **PREEN**
dress leather ...... **DUB, TAN**
dress up .... **TOG, PREEN**
dressed .... **CLAD**
dressing wounds, material for
           LINT, LINTS
dried berry: Sp. .... **PASA**
dried up .... **SERE**
drift .... **TREND**
drill .... **BORE, TRAIN**
drilling rod .... **BAR, BIT**
DRINK .... see also **BEVERAGE**
drink .... **GULP, SWIG,**
          QUAFF, IMBIBE
drink, Christmas **NOG, WASSAIL**
drink, fermented ...... **MEAD**
drink, honey .... **MEAD**
drink, hot .... **TODDY**
drink, hot milk .... **POSSET**
drink of gods .... **NECTAR**
drink of liquor .. **NIP, BRACER**
b   drink, old honey ...... **MORAT**
drink, palm .... **NIPA**
drink, rum-gin .... **BUMBO**
drink slowly .... **SIP, SUP**
drink, small .... **NIP, PEG,**
          DRAM, SLUG
drink to excess .. **TOPE, BOUSE**
drink, whiskey .... **STINGER**
drinking bowl .... **MAZER**
drinking cup, Gr. .... **HOLMOS**
drinking vessel .... **CUP, MUG,**
        TIG, TYG, JORUM,
        STEIN, TANKARD
drive ..... **RIDE, URGE, IMPEL**
drive away ..... **SHOO, DISPEL**
drive back
    ROUT, REPEL, REPULSE
drive in .... **TAMP**
drivel .... **DROOL, SLAVER**
driver, fast reckless ..... **JEHU**
drizzle .. **MIST, SMUR, SMURR**
droll .... **ODD**
dromedary, female .... **DELUL**
dromedary, swift .... **MEHARI**
drone .... **BEE, DOR, HUM**
droop .... **LOP, SAG, WILT**
drooping .... **ALOP**
drop ...... **DRIB, FALL, SINK,**
       GUTTA, GLOBULE
drop a fish line or bait .. **DAP**
drop, one .... **MINIM**

c   drop: Prov. Eng. ...... **SIE, SYE**
dropsy .... **EDEMA**
dross .. **SLAG, SPRUE, SCORIA**
drought-tolerant plant .. **GUAR**
drove .... **HERD, RODE**
drove of horses ...... **ATAJO**
drowse .... **NOD**
drudge ..... **MOIL, TOIL, LABOR**
drug ..... **DOPE, SINA, ALOES,**
       OPIATE, DILANTIN
drug, Hippocrates' .... **MECON**
drugged bliss .... **KEF**
drum-call to arms .... **RAPPEL**
drum roll, reveille .... **DIAN**
drum, small . **TABOR, TABOUR,**
         TABRET
drum, W. Ind. .... **GUMBY**
drumbeat .... **DUB, TATOO,**
        TATTOO
drunkard .... **SOT, SOAK,**
       SOUSE, TOPER
dry .... **SEC, ARID, SERE**
dry, as wine .... **SEC**
dry bed of river .... **WADI**
dry goods dealer .... **DRAPER**
dub .... **NAME, KNIGHT**
duck .... **ANAS, SMEE,**
       TEAL, PEKIN
duck, Arctic .... **EIDER**
d   duck, breed of .... **ROUEN**
duck, diving .... **SMEW**
duck eggs, Chin. ...... **PIDAN**
duck, fresh water .... **TEAL**
duck genus .. **AEX, AIX, ANAS**
duck, like a .... **ANATINE**
duck lure .... **DECOY**
duck, male .... **DRAKE**
duck, Muscovy .... **PATO**
duck, pintail .... **SMEE**
duck, ring-necked ..... **DOGY**
duck, river ..... **TEAL, EIDER,**
        SHOVELER
duck, sea ...... **COOT, SCAUP**
duck, sea, northern ... **SCOTER**
duck-shooting boat ..... **SKAG**
duck to cook: Fr. ... **CANETON**
duct: anat. .... **VAS, VASA**
dude .... **FOP, DANDY**
due, India .... **HAK, HAKH**
duet .... **DUI, DUO**
dugout canoe **BANCA, PIROGUE**
dugout, India . **DONGA, DUNGA**
duke's dominion ...... **DUCHY**
dulcimer .... **CITOLE**
dulcimer, Oriental ..... **SANTIR**
dull . **DRY, DUN, DRAB, LOGY,**
    BLUNT, PROSY, BORING
dull color .. **DUN, MAT, DRAB,**
       MATTE, TERNE
dull in finish .... **MAT, MATTE**

a dull silk fabric .... GROS
   dullard .... BOOR
   Dumas hero
       ATHOS, ARAMIS, PORTHOS
   dummy whist .... MORT
   dung beetle .... DOR
   dunlin bird .... STIB
   dupe .... USE, FOOL
   duration measure .... TIME
   dusk .... EVE
   dusky .... DIM, DARK, SWART
   dusty: Scot. .... MOTTY
   DUTCH see also NETHERLANDS,
                SPECIAL SECTION
   Dutch: bit ....DOIT
       cupboard .... KAS
       donkey .... EZEL
       "mister" .... HEER
       out .... UIT
       woman .... FROW
   Dutch cheese .... EDAM
   Dutch commune .... EDE
   Dutch early geographer .. AA
   Dutch fishing boat .. DOGGER
   Dutch measure, old ..... AAM
   Dutch meter .... EL
   Dutch minor coin .... DOIT
   Dutch news agency, old **ANETA**
   Dutch painter
       LIS, HALS, LELY, STEEN
   Dutch two-masted vessel **KOFF**
   duty .... CHORE, TARIFF
   dwarf .. RUNT, STUNT, TROLL

c dwarf cattle, S. Am.
                   NATA, NIATA
   dwell ...... BIDE, LIVE, ABIDE
   dwelling .... ABODE
   dwindle .... PETER
   Dyak knife .... PARANG
   Dyak, sea .... IBAN
   dye base .... ANILINE
   dye, blue .... WOAD
   dye, blue-red ...... ORSELLE
   dye gum .... KINO
   dye, indigo .... ANIL
   dye, lichen
       ARCHIL, ORCHAL, ORCHIL
   dye plant .... ANIL
   dye, red **AAL, ANATO, AURIN,
       EOSIN, ANATTA, ANATTO,
       AURINE, EOSINE, ANNAT-
       TA, ANNATTO, ANNOTTO,
       ARNATTO**
   dye, red, poisonous
                AURIN, AURINE
   dye stuff .. EOSINE, MADDER
   dye, yellow .... WELD,
               WOLD, WOALD
   dyeing apparatus ...... AGER
   dyeing reagent .... ALTERANT
   dyestuff from lichens .. LITMUS
   dyewood tree .... TUI
   dynamite inventor .... NOBEL
   DYNASTY see CHIN. DYNASTY
   dynasty, first Chin. ...... HSIA
   dynasty, It. .... SAVOY

E

b eager .. AGOG, AVID, ARDENT
   eagle .... ERN, ERNE
   eagle, Bible .... GIER
   eagle, tried to mount to heaven
       on .... ETANA
   eagle, sea .... ERN, ERNE
   eagle's nest
       AERY, EYRY, AERIE, EYRIE
   eaglestone ... ETITE, AETITES
   ear .... LUG, HANDLE
   ear canal .... SCALA
   ear cavity .... UTRICLE
   ear doctor .... AURIST
   ear inflamation .... OTITIS
   ear of wheat: archeol.
                SPICA, SPICAE
   ear, pert. to .... OTIC, AURAL
   ear, prominence **TRAGI, TRAGUS**
   ear shell .. ORMER, ABALONE
   ear stone .. OTOLITE, OTOLITH
   earache ... OTALGY, OTALGIA
   eared seal .... OTARY

d early Britisher .... PICT
   early Christian priest ... ARIUS
   earnest
       ARDENT, INTENT, SINCERE
   earnest money: law .... ARRA,
                ARLES, ARRHA
   earth .... GEO
   earth deposit in rocks .. GUHR
   earth: dial. .... ERD
   earth god, Egypt. **GEB, KEB, SEB**
   earth goddess ..... GE, ERDA,
                GAEA, GAIA
   earth goddess, Khonds' .. TARI
   earth goddess, Rom.
                CERES, TERRA
   earth, kind of .... LOAM
   earth, pert. to .... GEAL
   earth's surface, made on
                      EPIGENE
   earthenware maker ... POTTER
   earthly .... TERRENE
   earthquake .. SEISM, TEMBLOR

a earthquake, pert. to .. **SEISMIC**
earthquake, shock of..**TREMOR**
earthwork, Rom. ...... **AGGER**
East .. **ASIA, LEVANT, ORIENT**
E. African native ... **SOMALI**
E. Afr. spiritual power .. **NGAI**
E. Indian animal .... **TARSIER**
E. Ind. dye tree ...... **DHAK**
E. Ind. fruit **DURIAN, DURION**
E. Ind. grass .... **KASA**
E. Ind. herb .... **PIA, SESAME**
E. Ind. herb root **CHAY, CHOY**
E. Ind. palm .... **NIPA**
E. Ind. plant .. **JUTE, SESAME**
E. Ind. shrubby herb .... **SOLA**
E. Ind. tanning tree .. **AMLA,
AMLI**
E. Ind. term of address **SAHIB**
E. Ind. timber tree..**ACH, SAJ,
SAL, SAIN, SAUL, TEAK**
E. Ind. tree, large ..... **SIRIS**
E. Ind. vine ..... **AMIL, GILO,
ODAL, ODEL, SOMA**
E. Ind. vine, milky ..... **SOMA**
E. Ind. weight .... **TOLA**
E. Ind. wood, strong, heavy **ENG**
E. Ind. woody vine **ODAL, GILO**
East Indies .... **INDONESIA**
east wind .... **EURUS**
east wind's opposite .... **AFER**
Easter ...... **PASCH, PASCHA**
b Eastern .... **ORTIVE**
Eastern Catholic ...... **UNIAT**
Eastern Church doxology **DOXA**
Eastern European ...... **SLAV**
Eastern garment .... **SARI**
Eastern name ..... **ALI, ABOU**
Eastern title ...... **AGA, RAS**
Eastern Turkey tribesman **KURD**
easy .... **SOFT**
easy gait .... **LOPE**
easy job **SNAP,CINCH,SINECURE**
eat away .... **ERODE**
eat voraciously
    RAVEN, RAVIN, RAVINE
eaten away .... **EROSE**
eating away **CAUSTIC, ERODENT**
eccentric person .... **GINK**
eccentric piece, rotating .. **CAM**
ecclesiastic .... **PRELATE**
ECCLESIASTICAL see CHURCH
eclipse .... **DIM**
eclipse demon, Hindu
    KETU, RAHU
ecru .... **BEIGE**
Ecuadorian extinct Indians **CARA**
edentate genus .... **MANIS**
edge .... **HEM, LIP, RIM,
ARRIS, BRINK, MARGE**
edged unevenly .... **EROSE**
edging .... **PICOT**

c edging, make .... **TAT**
edible fungus .... **CEPE**
edible root ...... **OCA, YAM,
TARO, CASAVA, CASSAVA**
edible shoot, Jap. ...... **UDO**
edict .... **LAW, FIAT, DECREE**
Edinburgh: poet ...... **EDINA**
edit .... **REVISE, REDACT**
editorial "I" .... **WE**
Edom district .... **TEMAN**
Edomite .... **OMAR**
Edomite city .... **PAU**
Edomite duke **UZ, ARAN, IRAM**
Edomite king, ruler ..... **BELA**
educated ... **BRED, LETTERED**
educator, Am. .... **MANN**
educe .... **EVOKE, ELICIT**
Edward Bradley's pseudo. **BEDE**
eel, marine .... **CONGER**
eel: old Eng. .... **ELE**
eel-shaped amphibian ... **OLM**
eel, S. Am. .... **CARAPO**
eel, young .... **ELVER**
eelworm .... **NEMA**
Eghbal's land .... **IRAN**
effervescent, to make . **AERATE**
effigy .... **IDOL**
effluvium ... **MIASM, MIASMA**
effort .... **DINT, ASSAY,
NISUS, TRIAL**
d effusive .... **GUSHING**
eft .... **EVET, NEWT**
egg .... **OVUM**
egg dish .. **OMELET, OMELETTE**
egg drink ...... **NOG, NOGG**
egg, insect .... **NIT**
egg-shaped
    OOID, OVAL, OVATE, OVOID
egg-shaped ornaments ... **OVA**
egg white, raw .... **GLAIR**
eggs .... **OVA, ROE**
ego .... **SELF**
Egypt, pert. to ...... **COPTIC**
Egyptian bird .... **IBIS**
Egyp. Christian .... **COPT**
Egyp. city, ancient **SAIS, THEBES**
Egyp. cobra .... **HAJE**
Egyp. crown .... **ATEF**
Egyp. dog-headed ape, deity
    AANI
Egyp. gateway .... **PYLON**
Egyp. god of creation ... **PTAH**
**EGYPTIAN GODS — GODDESSES
—DEITY** see also GODS and
SPECIAL SECTION
Egyp. guard .... **GHAFIR**
Egyp. heaven
    AALU, AARU, IALU, YARU
Egyp. immortal heart **AB, HATI**
Egyp. king .. **MENES, RAMESES**
Egyp. lute .... **NABLA**

Egyp. nationalist party . WAFD
Egyp. precious alloy .... ASEM
Egyp. primeval chaos ..... NU
Egyp. queen of gods .... SATI
Egyp. sacred bird .. BENU, IBIS
Egyp. sacred bull .... APIS
Egyp. season .... AHET
Egyp. tambourine ...... RIKK
Egyp. thorn .... KIKAR
Egyp. writing surfaces PAPYRI
eh?: obs. ....ANAN
eight days after feast .. UTAS
eight, group of
OCTAD, OCTET, OCTAVE
eight, set of .... OGDOAD
eighth day of feast .... UTAS
eighth day, on ...... OCTAN
eighth note .... UNCA
Eire legislature .... DAIL
ejaculation, mystic ...... OM
eject ...... EMIT, OUST, SPEW
elaborate .... ORNATE
Elam, capital of .... SUSA
eland .... IMPOFO
elanet .... KITE
elasmobranch fish RAY, SHARK
Elbe, river to ...... EGER, ISER
Elbe tributary .... EGER, ISER
elbow .... ANCON
elder .... SENIOR
elder son of Zeus ... ARES
elder statesmen, Jap. .. GENRO
eldest: law ...... AINE, EIGNE
electric catfish .... RAAD
electric force .... ELOD
electric force unit ...... VOLT
electric reluctance unit .. REL
electric unit .. ES, AMP, MHO,
OHM, REL, PERM, FARAD,
HENRY, AMPERE
electrified particle ...... ION
electrode .. ANODE, CATHODE
electromagnet .... RELAY
electron tube
TRIODE, KLYSTRON
elegance .... GRACE
elegant .... FINE, POSH
elegist .... POET
elegy .... NENIA
ELEMENT, non-metallic and metallic, gaseous on page 195
elemi .... ANIME
element, radioactive of URANIC
elephant goad .... ANKUS
elephant: India .... HATHI
elephant's cry .... BARR
elephant's ear .... TARO
elevated ground MESA, RIDEAU
elevation of mind .. ANAGOGE
elevator: Brit. .... LIFT

elf .... SPRITE
elf, Egypt. .... OUPHE
elfin .... FEY
Elia .... LAMB
elicit .... EDUCE
elide .... DELE, OMIT
Elija .... ELIAS
eliminate ... DELETE, REMOVE
Elizabeth I, name for ORIANA
elk, Am. .... WAPITI
elk, Europ. .... MOOSE
elk, Europ. genus ... ALCES
elliptical ...... OVAL, OVOID
elm .... ULM, ULME
elm fruit seed ...... SAMARA
elongated .... PROLATE
else .... OTHER
elude .... DODGE, EVADE
elver .... EEL
emaciation .... TABES, MACIES
emanation .... AURA
emanation, star .... BLAS
embankment ... DAM, BUND,
DIKE, DYKE, DIGUE, LEVEE
embellish
GILD, ADORN, DECORATE
embellished .... ORNATE
ember .... ASH, COAL
emblem ... INSIGNE, INSIGNIA
emblem of authority .... MACE
emblem of U.S. .... EAGLE
embrace
HUG, CLASP, ENARM, INARM
embrocation ...... LINIMENT
embroidery frame
TABORET, TABOURET
emend .... EDIT
emerald .... BERYL, SMARAGD
emerge RISE, ISSUE, EMANATE
emetic .... IPECAC
eminent .... NOTED
emit .... REEK, EXUDE
emmer .... SPELT
emmet .... ANT
Emperor of Russia
CZAR, TSAR, TZAR
emphasis .... ACCENT, STRESS
empire .... REALM
employ .... USE, HIRE, PLACE
employed for wine, meas. AAM
employees .... PERSONNEL
employer .... BOSS, USER
employment .... PLACE
emporium ...... MART, STORE
Empress, Byzant. ...... IRENE
Empress, Russian ... CZARINA,
TSARINA, TZARINA
empty .... VOID, INANE,
DEPLETE
emulate .... RIVAL
enamel ware .... LIMOGES

a enchantress .... **CIRCE, MEDEA**
encircle .... **ORB, GIRD, GIRT, RING, EMBAY**
encircled
GIRT, RINGED, SURROUNDED
encircling band .... **ZONE**
enclose .... **MEW**
enclosure .... **MEW, PEN, REE, STY, CORRAL**
enclosure, cattle ..... **ATAJO**
enclosure: Sp. Am. ... **CANCHA**
encomium .... **ELOGE**
encompass .. **GIRD, GIRT, RING**
encompassed by .... **AMID**
encore .... **BIS**
encounter .... **MEET**
encourage .... **ABET**
end **TIP, FINIS, LIMIT, OMEGA**
end: music .... **FINE**
end result .... **PRODUCT**
end, tending to an ..... **TELIC**
endeavor .. **TRY, ESSAY, NISUS**
ENDING ... see also SUFFIX or type of ending
ending, comparative . **IER, IOR**
ENDING, NOUN see SUFFIX, NOUN ENDING
ending, plural .... **EN, ES**
ending, superlative ...... **EST**
endow ...... **DOWER, INVEST**
b endue .... **ENDOW**
endure .... **BEAR, LAST, WEAR**
endure: dial. .... **BIDE**
energy .... **PEP, VIM, ZIP, POWER, VIGOR, VIGOUR**
energy, potential ...... **ERGAL**
energy unit **ERG, RAD, ERGON**
enfeeble **WEAKEN, DEBILITATE**
engage **HIRE, ENTER, CHARTER**
engender .... **BEGET, BREED, PROMOTE, GENERATE**
engine, donkey ...... **YARDER**
engine of war .... **RAM**
engine part .... **STATOR**
engine, rotary ...... **TURBINE**
engineer, Am. .... **EADS**
engineer, military .... **SAPPER**
English actor .... **EVANS**
Eng. actress .... (Nell) **GWYN, TERRY, NEAGLE**
Eng. architect .... **WREN**
Eng. author .... **MORE, WEST, ARLEN, BACON, CAINE, DEFOE, DORAN, ELIOT, HARDY, READE, SHUTE, WAUGH, WELLS, AMBLER, AUSTEN, BARRIE, BELLOC, BRONTE, ORWELL, STERNE**
Eng. car .... **ROVER**
Eng. cathedral city **ELY, YORK**
Eng. city, historic **COVENTRY**

c Eng. college ... **ETON, BALIOL**
ENG. COMPOSER
see COMPOSER, ENG.
Eng. country festival .... **ALE**
Eng. dramatist
SHAW, PEELE, DRYDEN
Eng. emblem .... **ROSE**
Eng. essayist .... **SALA, STEELE**
Eng. explorer ... **ROSS, CABOT**
Eng. historian .... **BEDE**
Eng. king
BRAN, CNUT, KNUT, CANUTE
Eng. monk ..... **BEDE, BAEDA**
Eng. murderer .... **ARAM**
Eng. musician .... **ARNE**
ENG. NOVELIST .... see ENG. AUTHOR
Eng. painter .... **OPIE, ORPEN**
Eng. philosopher ...... **HUME, JOAD, BACON, SPENCER**
Eng. playwright .... **SHAW**
Eng. poet ..... **GRAY, AUDEN, BLAKE, BYRON, CAREW, DONNE, ELIOT**
Eng. queen ..... **ANNE, MARY**
Eng. rebel leader, 1450 .. **CADE**
Eng. royal house **YORK, TUDOR**
Eng. scholar, schoolmaster
ARAM
Eng. school, boys' ...... **ETON**
Eng. sculptor ...... **EPSTEIN**
d Eng. spa .... **BATH, MARGATE**
Eng. spy .... **ANDRE**
Eng. statesman ... **EDEN, PITT**
Eng. theologian ..... **ALCUIN**
Eng. woman politician .. **ASTOR**
ENG. WRITER ..... see ENG. AUTHOR and ENG. ESSAYIST
engraver ... **CHASER, ETCHER, GRAVER**
engraver, famous .. **PYE, DORE**
engraver's tool .... **BURIN**
engrossed .... **RAPT**
enigma .... **RIDDLE**
enlarge
DILATE, EXPAND, INCREASE
enlarge a hole .... **REAM**
enlarging, as chimneys .. **EVASE**
enmity .... **ANIMUS**
Enoch's father .... **CAIN**
enough .... **ENOW**
enrol .... **ENTER, ENLIST**
ensign .... **FLAG**
ensnare .... **NET, WEB**
entangle .... **MAT, MESH**
enter .... **ENROL**
entertain
AMUSE, DIVERT, REGALE
enthusiasm
ELAN, ARDOR, VERVE, SPIRIT
enthusiastic .... **RABID**

a entice .... **BAIT, LURE, TOLE, TEMPT, ALLURE**
enticement .... **TICE**
entire man .... **EGO**
entity .... **ENS, ENTIA**
entomb .... **INURN**
entrance
 ADIT, DOOR, GATE, PORTAL
entrance halls .... **ATRIA**
entreat .... **PRAY, PLEAD**
entreaty .... **PLEA**
entry, separate .... **ITEM**
entwine
 WEAVE, ENLACE, WREATHE
enumerate .... **COUNT**
envelop **WRAP, ENFOLD, INFOLD**
environment .... **MILIEU**
envoy .... **LEGATE**
envy .... **COVET**
enzyme .... **ASE, LOTASE, RENNIN, MALTASE**
eon .... **OLAM**
ephah, 1/10 .... **OMER**
epic poetry .... **EPOS, EPOPEE**
epoch .... **ERA**
epochal .... **ERAL**
epode .... **POEM**
eponymous ancestor .... **EBER**
equal **IS, ARE, TIE, EVEN, PEER**
equality .... **PAR, PARITY**
b equally .... **AS**
equilibrium .... **POISE**
equine .... **HORSE**
equip .... **FIT, RIG**
equitable ... **JUST, IMPARTIAL**
equivalence .... **PAR**
equivocate .... **EVADE**
era .... **EPOCH**
eradicate .... **ERASE, UPROOT**
eral .... **EPOCHAL**
erase .... **DELE, DELETE**
erect .... **REAR, RAISE**
ergo .... **HENCE**
Eris' brother .... **ARES**
ermine, summer .... **STOAT**
Eros .... **CUPID**
errand boy .... **PAGE**
error, publication ...... **TYPO, ERRATA, ERRATE, ERRATUM**
Esau .... **EDOM**
Esau's brother .... **JACOB**
Esau's father-in-law ... **ELON**
Esau's grandson ...... **OMAR**
Esau's home .... **SEIR**
Esau's wife .... **ADAH**
escape .. **LAM, ELUDE, EVADE**
eschew .... **SHUN**
escutcheon band .... **FESS**
Esdra's angel .... **URIEL**
eskers .... **OSAR**
Eskimo .... **ITA**

c Eskimo boat
 KIAK, KYAK, KAYAK
Eskimo boot .... **MUKLUK**
Eskimo coat
 PARKA, NETCHA, TEMIAK
Eskimo curlew .... **FUTE**
Eskimo house
 IGLU, IGLOE, IGLOO, IGLOU
Eskimo settlement ..... **ETAH**
Eskimo summer hut .... **TOPEK**
Eskimos of Asia **YUIT, INNUIT**
esoteric .... **INNER**
espy .... **SEE, SPY**
esquire .... **ARMIGER**
essay ... **TRY, TEST, ATTEMPT**
essay, scholarly
 THESIS, TREATISE
essence: Hindu religion .. **RASA**
essence, rose .... **ATTAR**
essential oils fluid ..... **NEROL**
essential part .... **CORE, PITH**
"— est" (that is) ...... **ID**
establish .... **BASE, FOUND**
established value .... **PAR**
estate, landed, large .. **MANOR**
estate manager .... **STEWARD**
estate, not held by feudal tenure **ALOD, ALLOD, ALODIUM**
esteem .... **HONOR, PRIZE, ADMIRE, HONOUR**
d ester, hydriodic acid ... **IODIDE**
ester, liquid .... **ACETIN**
ester, oleic acid .... **OLEATE**
estimate .... **RATE, APPRAISE**
Estonian .... **ESTH**
estuary .... **RIA**
estuary, Brazil .... **PARA**
estuary, S. Am. .... **PLATA**
Eternal City .... **ROME**
eternity .... **AGE, EON, OLAM**
ether compound .... **ESTER**
ethereal .... **AERY, AERIAL**
ETHIOPIA see also **ABYSSINIA**
Ethiopia .... **CUSH**
Ethiopian title .... **RAS**
Ethiopic .... **GEEZ**
ethos, opposed to .... **PATHOS**
Etruscan god .... **LAR**
Etruscan Juno .... **UNI**
Etruscan Minerva .... **MENFRA**
Etruscan title, peer **LAR, LARS**
eucalyptus secretion
 LAAP, LARP, LERP
eucalyptus tree .... **YATE**
Eucharist case ...... **PIX, PYX**
Eucharist cloth
 FANO, FANON, FANUM
Eucharist spoon .... **LABIS**
Eucharist wafer .... **HOST**
eulogy .... **ELOGE**
euphorbia .... **SPURGE**

Eurasian

a
Eurasian dock plant .. **PARELLE**
eureka red .... **PUCE**
Euripides heroine ..... **MEDEA**
EUROPEAN see also specific
    word, as FISH, ANIMAL,
    etc.
European .... **POLE, SLAV**
Eur. colorful fish .... **BOCE**
EUROP. FISH .. see FISH, EUR.
European, in Moslem East
                FRANGI
Europ. iris .... **ORRIS**
Europ. kite ..... **GLED, GLEDE**
Europ. porgy .... **PARGO**
Eurytus' daughter ...... **IOLE**
evade
  SHUN, DODGE, ELUDE, SHIRK
evaluate .... **RATE, ASSESS**
Evangelist ...... **LUKE, MARK**
Evans, Mary Ann ...... **ELIOT**
Eve's grandson .... **ENOS**
even ..... **EEN, LEVEL, PLANE**
even if .... **THO**
evening party .... **SOIREE**
evening prayer .... **VESPER**
eventual lot .... **FATE**
ever .... **EER**
evergreen .... **FIR, YEW, PINE,**
    CAROB, CEDAR, OLIVE,
    SAVIN, LAUREL, SABINE,

b
    SAVINE, SPRUCE
evergreen, bean ...... **CAROB**
evergreen genus
  OLAX, ABIES, CATHA
evergreen, red-berry
          YEW, WHORT
evergreen, tropical .. **CALABA**
everlasting ... **ETERN, ETERNE**
evict .... **OUST**
evident **CLEAR, PLAIN, PATENT**
evil .... **MAL**
evil god, Egypt. ... **SET, SETH**
evil intent: law .... **DOLUS**
evil spirit, Haiti **BAKA, BOKO**
evil spirit, Hindu ..... **ASURA**
evolve .... **EDUCE**
ewe, old .... **CRONE**
exact **BLEED, DEMAND, EXTORT**
exacerbate .... **IRE**
exact point .... **TEE**
examine ..... **PRY, SPY, SCAN**
excavate .. **DIG, PION, DREDGE**
excavation for extracting ore
           STOPE
excavation, mine .. **PIT, STOPE**
exceed .... **TOP**
exceedingly: music ..... **TRES**
excellence .... **VIRTU**
excellent .... **AONE**
except .... **BUT, SAVE**
excess ...... **LUXUS, NIMIETY**

c
excess, fill to ... **GLUT, SATE**
excess of solar year ... **EPACT**
exchange medium, Chin. **SYCEE**
exchange premium, discount
           AGIO
exchequer .... **FISC, FISK**
excite .... **ELATE, ROUSE**
excited .... **AGOG, MANIC**
excitement, public
      FUROR, FURORE
exclamation .. **AH, EH, HA, HI,**
    MY, OH, OW, UM, ACH,
    AHA, AUH, BAH, BAW, FIE,
    FOH, GRR, HAH, HAW,
    HAY, HEM, HEP, HEU, HEY,
    HIC, HIP, HOI, HOY, HUH,
    OHO, OUF, PAH, PEW, POH,
    PUE, SOH, TCH, TCK, TUT,
    UGH, WEE, WHY, WOW,
    YAH, YOI, YOW, ALAS,
    PHEW, ALACK
exclamation, Fr. .... **HEIN**
exclamation, Ger. ...... **HOCH**
exclamation, Ir. .... **ADAD,**
    AHEY, ARAH, ARRA, ARRO,
    BOOH, EHEU, OCHONE
exclude ... **BAR, OMIT, DEBAR**
exclusive .... **SOLE**
exclusive set .... **ELECT, ELITE**
exclusively .... **ONLY**

d
excoriate .... **ABRADE**
excrete from skin ...... **EGEST**
excuse .. **PLEA, ALIBI, REMIT**
excuse, court **ESSOIN, ESSOINE**
execrated ..... **CURST, SWORE**
exemplar ... **MODEL, PATTERN**
exhaust
  SAP, TIRE, SPEND, DEPLETE
exhausted .... **EFFETE**
exhibits leaping ..... **SALTATE**
exigency .... **NEED**
exist .... **LIVE**
exist .. all forms of verb "BE"
exist, beginning to .. **NASCENT**
existence .... **ENS, ESSE**
existentialist leader ... **SARTRE**
existing **ALIVE, BEING, EXTANT**
exit .. **LEAVE, DEPART, EGRESS**
expand ..... **DILATE, DISTEND**
expanse .... **SEA**
expatriate .... **EXILE**
expectation .... **HOPE**
expedite .... **HURRY, HASTEN**
expedition .. **SAFARI, SUFFARI**
expert ... **ACE, ONER, ADEPT**
expiate .... **ATONE**
explain .... **DEFINE**
explode
  POP, DETONATE, FULMINATE
exploit
    DEED, FEAT, GEST, GESTE

a explosive
CAP, TNT, GAINE, TONITE
explosive sound ... POP, CHUG
expose .... AIR, DISPLAY
expression, elegant . ATTICISM
expression, local .... IDIOM
expressionless ..... WOODEN
expunge DELE, ERASE, DELETE
extend
JUT, LIE, REACH, BEETLE
extend the front ..... DEPLOY
extensive .... AMPLE
extent .... AREA
external .... EXOTERIC
external covering. HIDE, HUSK,
PEEL, PELT, RIND, SKIN
extinct wild ox .... URUS
extirpate .. ROOT, ERADICATE
extort .... BLEED, EXACT
extra .... ODD, SPARE
extra leaf .... INSERT
extra, theatrical .... SUPE
extract DRAW, ELICIT, EVULSE
extraneous .... EXOTIC
extraordinary person, thing
ONER

c extravagance .... ELA
extreme .... ULTRA
extreme unction, give
ANELE, ENELE
exudate, plant
GUM, LAC, RESIN
exude ..... EMIT, OOZE, REEK
exult .... ELATE
eye .... ORB, SEE, OGLE
eye cosmetic ... KOHL, KUHL
eye inflammation STY, IRITIS
eye, inner coat ...... RETINA
eye, layer .... UVEA
eye of bean .... HILA, HILUM
eye of insect .... STEMMA
eye, part of the .... IRIS,
UVEA, CORNEA, RETINA
eye, pert. to .... OPTIC
eye socket .... ORBIT
eye, symbolic .... UTA
eye-worm, Afr. .... LOA
eyelash ...... CILIA, CILIUM
eyes: old Eng. .... NIE
eyestalk .... STIPE
eyewink ...... LOOK, GLANCE
eyot .... ISLE, ISLET

F

b Fabian .... SHAW
fable .... APOLOG, APOLOGUE
fable writer .... ESOP, AESOP
fabled bird .... ROC, RUKH
"Fables in Slang" author ADE
fabric .... REP, ACCA, BAFT,
DRAB, DUCK, IKAT,
LAWN, LENO, MOFF, REPP,
SILK, SUSI, TAPA, TUKE,
CRAPE, CREPE, MOIRE,
NINON, ORLON, RAYON,
CANVAS, COVERT, MAN-
TUA, MOHAIR
farbic, Angora ..... CAMLET,
MOHAIR
fabric, coarse cotton .. SURAT
fabric, coarse wool
TAMIN, TAMINE
fabric, corded REP, REPP, PIQUE
fabric, cotton ... LENO, MULL,
DENIM, MANTA, SCRIM,
CALICO, CRETON, NAN-
KIN, PENANG, NANKEEN,
CRETONNE
fabric, curtain ... NET, SCRIM
fabric, felt-like .... BAIZE
fabric, fig'd DAMASK, PAISLEY
fabric from remnants MUNGO
fabric, Ind. .. SHELA, SHELAH

d fabric, knitted .... TRICOT
fabric, light wool .... ALPACA
fabric, lustrous POPLIN, SATEEN
fabric, mourning ALMA, CRAPE
fabric, net .. TULLE, MALINE
fabric, plaid . MAUD, TARTAN
fabric, printed BATIK, BATTIK
FABRIC, RIBBED
see RIBBED FABRIC
fabric, satin .. PEKIN, ETOILE
fabric, satiny
SATINET, SATINETTE
fabric, sheer .... GAUZE,
BEMBERG, ORGANZA
fabric, short nap .... RAS
fabric, silk .... SURAH,
PONGEE, SAMITE, TOBINE
fabric, silk, gold, medieval ACCA
fabric, silk, thick ...... GROS
fabric, stiff .... WIGAN
fabric stretcher
TENTER, STENTER
fabric, striped .. SUSI, DOREA,
DORIA, DOOREA, MADRAS
fabric, thick .... DRAB
fabric, twilled .... REP
fabric, upholstery .. BROCATEL,
BROCATALL, BROCATELL
BROCATELLE

a fabric, velvet-like .... **PANNE**
fabric, voile-like .... **ETAMINE**
fabric, wool .. **SERGE, TAMIN, TAMIS, MERINO, TAMINE, TAMINY, TAMISE, TAMMIN, ESTAMIN, ETAMINE, STAMMEL, ESTAMINE**
fabric, worsted ...... **ETAMINE**
fabricate .... **MAKE**
fabulist .... **ESOP, AESOP**
fabulous bird .... **ROC, RUKH**
face **MAP, MUG, PHIZ, FACADE**
face with stone ...... **REVET**
facet of gem .. **BEZEL, BEZIL, CULET, COLLET**
facile .... **EASY**
facing glacier .... **STOSS**
fact .... **DATUM**
fact, by the: law ..... **FACTO**
facts .... **DATA**
faction .... **SECT, SIDE, CABAL**
factor .... **GENE**
factory .... **PLANT**
faculty .... **SENSE**
fade ...... **DIE, DIM, WITHER**
"Faerie Queene" iron man **TALUS**
"Faerie Queene" lady .... **UNA**
failure .... **DUD, FLOP**
fainting: med. ...... **SYNCOPE**

b fair . **BAZAR, FERIA, BAZAAR KERMIS, KIRMES**
fair **JUST, CLEAR, IMPARTIAL**
fair-haired .. **BLOND, BLONDE**
fair-lead, naut. .... **WAPP**
fairy .. **ELF, FAY, PERI, SPRITE**
fairy fort .... **LIS, LISS**
fairy king .... **OBERON**
fairy queen .. **MAB, TITANIA**
fairy, Serbo-Croat **VILA, VILY**
fairylike creature .... **PERI**
faith, article of ...... **TENET**
faith, pert. to .... **PISTIC**
faithful .... **LEAL, TRUE, STANCH, STAUNCH**
falcon .... **SACER, SAKER, LANNER, MERLIN, SAKERET**
falcon, Asia **LAGGAR, LUGGAR**
falcon genus .... **FALCO**
falcon-headed god **MENT, MENTU**
falcon, Ind. **SHAHIN, SHAHEEN**
falcon of sea ...... **ERN, ERNE**
falconer's bait .... **LURE**
fall **DROP, PLAP, PLOP, SPILL**
fall back .... **RETREAT**
fallacy ...... **IDOLA, IDOLUM**
fallow-deer, female ...... **TEG**
false excuse .... **SUBTERFUGE**
false friend .. **IAGO, TRAITOR**
false fruit of rose .... **HIP**

c false god .... **IDOL**
Falstaff's follower ...... **NYM**
fame .... **ECLAT, KUDOS, RENOWN, REPUTE**
famed .... **NOTED**
familiar .... **VERSANT**
familiar saying .... **SAW, TAG**
family, Florentine .... **MEDICI**
family, Genoese ...... **DORIA**
family: Scot. .... **ILK**
famous .... **NOTED**
fan .... **ROOTER**
fan palm genus ...... **INODES**
fan's stick .... **BRIN**
fanatical .... **RABID**
fancy ... **IDEA, WHIM, IDEATE**
fanfare .... **TANTARA, TANTARO, TANTARARA**
fanning device **PUNKA, PUNKAH**
fare .... **DIET**
farewell ... **AVE, VALE, ADIEU**
farinaceous .... **MEALY**
farinaceous food **SAGO, SALEP**
farm group .... **GRANGE**
farm, small, Sp. Am. **CHACRA**
farm, Sw. small leased .. **TORP**
farm: Swedish .... **TORP**
farm, tenant .... **CROFT**
farmer .... **KULAK, GRANGER**

d farmyard, S. Afr. .... **WERF**
Faroe Is. wind .... **OE**
Faroe judge .... **FOUD**
Farouk's father .... **FUAD**
fashion .... **FORM, MODE, MOLD, MODEL, STYLE**
fasten ... **BOLT, LOCK, NAIL, SEAL, SNIB, TACK, RIVET**
fasten: naut **BELAY, BATTEN**
fastener .... **NUT, PIN, BRAD, CLIP, HASP, NAIL, SNAP, STUD, CLASP, RIVET, CLEVIS, COTTER**
fastener, wire .... **STAPLE**
fastener, naut. .... **BITT**
fastener, wood **FID, NOG, PEG, PIN**
fastening .... **LATCH**
fastidious .... **NICE**
fasting month .... **RAMADAN**
fasting period .... **LENT**
fat **LARD, LIPA, SUET, OBESE**
fat, animal .. **ADEPS, TALLOW**
fat: comb. form **STEAT, STEATO**
fat, liquid part ...... **ELAIN, OLEIN, ELAINE, OLEINE**
fat, natural .... **ESTER**
fat, of .... **SEBAIC**
fat, solid part **STEARIN, STEARINE**
fatal ...... **FUNEST, LETHAL**

fate .... **LOT, DOOM, KISMET**
Fates, Gr. & Rom. ..... **MOIRA,
MORTA, PARCA, CLOTHO,
DECUMA, MOIRAI, PAR-
CAE, ATROPOS, LACHESIS**
fateful .... **DIRE**
father .... **SIRE, BEGET**
father: Arab. ..... **ABU, ABOU**
father: Hebr. .... **ABBA**
father of modern engraving **PYE**
father's side, kinship on
AGNAT, AGNATE
fathom .... **PROBE, SOUND**
fatigue .. **FAG, TIRE, WEARY**
Fatima's huband .... **ALI**
fatty .... **ADIPOSE**
fatty gland secretion **SEBUM**
fatuous .... **INANE**
faucet ... **TAP, COCK, SPIGOT**
fault find ...... **CARP, CAVIL**
faultfinder .. **MOMUS, CAVILER**
faulty .... **BAD**
faux pas ...... **ERROR, GAFFE**
favor .... **BOON**
favorable vote .. **AY, AYE, YES**
favorite .... **PET, IDOL**
fawn color .... **FAON**
fawning favorite .... **MINION**
fear .... **PHOBIA**
fearful .... **TREPID**
feast .... **REGALE**
feast day: comb. form .... **MAS**
feather **PENNA, PINNA, PLUME**
feather grass .... **STIPA**
feather palms .... **EJOO, IROK**
feather: zool. .... **PLUMA**
feathers, cast .... **MEW**
feathers of o-o .... **HULU**
feathered scarf .... **BOA**
feeble .. **PUNY, WEAK, DEBILE**
feel .... **SENSE**
feel one's way .... **GROPE**
feeler **PALP, PALPI, ANTENNA**
feet, having .... **PEDATE**
feet, pert. to **PEDAL, PEDARY**
feign .... **ACT, SHAM**
feline .... **CAT, PUMA**
felis leo .... **LION**
fellow ..... **GUY, LAD, BOZO,
CHAP, DICK, CHAPPY,
CHAPPIE**
felt .... **GROPED, SENSATE**
female animal, parent
DAM, DOE
female camel .... **NAGA**
female disciple at Joppa
DORCAS
female insect .... **GYNE**
fence of shrubs .... **HEDGE**
fence of stakes .... **PALISADE**
fence step .... **STILE**

fence, sunken, hidden
AHA, HAHA
fence to restrain cattle .. **OXER**
fencer's cry .. **HAI, HAY, SASA**
fencing dummy .... **PEL**
fencing position **CARTE, SIXTE,
QUARTE, QUINTE, TIERCE,
SECONDE, SEPTIME**
fencing sword ...... **EPEE, FOIL**
fencing term .... **TOUCHE**
fencing thrust .... **LUNGE,
PUNTO, REMISE, RIPOST,
RIPOSTE, REPRISE**
fend .... **WARD**
fennel: P. I. .... **ANIS**
"Ferdinand the Bull" author
LEAF
feria, pert. to .... **FERIAL**
ferment .... **YEAST**
ferment: med. .... **ZYME**
fermented milk dessert **LACTO**
fern, climbing, P. I. .... **NITO**
fern, Polyn., edible .... **TARA**
fern root, N. Z. .... **ROI**
fern "seed" .... **SPORE**
fern species .... **WEKI**
fern spore ...... **SORI, SORUS**
Ferrara ducal family .... **ESTE**
ferrum .... **IRON**
ferryboat .... **BAC**
ferryboat, Afr. .... **PONT**
fertilizer ..... **MARL, GUANO**
fervent .... **ARDENT**
fervor ... **ZEAL, ZEST, ARDOR**
fester .... **RANKLE**
festival .... **ALE, FAIR, FETE,
GALA, FERIA, FIESTA, KER-
MIS, KIRMES**
festival, Creek Indian .. **BUSK**
festival, Gr.
AGON, DELIA, HALOA
fetid .... **OLID, RANK**
fetish .... **OBI, JUJU, OBIA,
ZEME, ZEMI, CHARM,
OBEAH, GRIGRI**
fetish, P. I. .... **ANITO**
fetter .... **GYVE, IRON**
feud, opposed to ...... **ALOD,
ALLOD, ALODIUM, ALLODIUM**
feudal benefice .... **FEU**
feudal estate **FEOD, FEUD, FIEF**
feudal land .... **BENEFICE**
feudal service, form of **AVERA**
feudal tax
TAILAGE, TALLAGE, TAILLAGE
feudal tenant .... **VASSAL**
fever, intermittent
AGUE, TERTIAN
feverish .... **FEBRILE**
fez .... **TARBUSH,
TARBOOSH, TARBOUCHE**

a fiber .... **JUTE, PITA, RAFFIA, STAPLE, THREAD**
fiber, bark
TAPA, OLONA, TERAP
fiber, coarse .... **ADAD**
fiber, cordage .... **DA, COIR, FERU, HEMP, IMBE, JUTE, RHEA, ABACA, SISAL**
fiber from palm .... **ERUC**
fiber, hat or basket .... **DATIL**
fiber knot .... **NEP**
fiber plant
ISTLE, IXTLE, IXLE, RAMIE
fiber plant, Brazil .... **CAROA**
fiber plant, E. Ind. **SANA, SUNN**
fiber, textile .... **SABA**
fiber, tropical
IXLE, ISTLE, IXTLE
fiber, woody .... **BAST, BASTE**
fictional submarine character
NEMO
fiddle, medieval .... **GIGA**
fiddler crab genus ...... **UCA**
field **LEA, ACRE, WONG, CROFT**
field deity .:.... **PAN, FAUN**
field, enclosed: law ..... **AGER**
field, stubble .... **ROWEN**
fifth segment crustacean
CARPOS
b fig marigold, Afr. ..... **SAMH**
figs, Smyrna .. **ELEME, ELEMI**
fight
CLEM, FRAY, MELEE, AFFRAY
figurative use of word .. **TROPE**
figure .... **SOLID**
figure, equal angles
ISAGON, ISOGON
figure, 4-sided .... **TETRAGON**
figure, geom. .... **SECTOR**
figure of speech
TROPE, SIMILE, METAPHOR
figure, oval .... **ELLIPSE**
figure, 10-sided .... **DECAGON**
figwort .... **MULLEIN**
Fiji chestnut .... **RATA**
Fiji tree .... **BURI**
filament .... **FIBER, HAIR**
filament, flax ... **HARL, HARLE**
filament, plant
ELATER, THREAD
filch .... **STEAL**
file .... **ROW**
file, coarse .... **RASP**
file, three-square single-cut
CARLET
filled to capacity
SATED, REPLETE
fillet, architectural **ORLE, ORLO**
fillet, narrow heraldic
ORLE, ORLO, LISTEL
fillet, shaft's ..... **ORLE, ORLO**

c fillip .... **SNAP**
film, old green ..... **PATINA**
filthy .... **VILE**
filthy lucre .... **PELF**
finale: music .... **CODA**
finally: Fr. .... **ENFIN**
finback whale .... **GRASO**
finch .. **MORO, LINNET, SISKIN**
finch, Europ.
TARIN, TERIN, SERIN
finch, S. Afr. .... **FINK**
find fault ..... **CARP, CAVIL**
fine, as a line .... **LEGER**
fine, punish by ...... **AMERCE**
fine, record of ...... **ESTREAT**
finesse .... **ART, SKILL**
Fingal's kingdom .... **MORVEN**
finger .... **DIGIT**
finger cymbals ... **CASTANETS**
finger, 5th **PINKIE, MINIMUS**
finger inflammation ... **FELON**
finger nail half-moon
LUNULA, LUNULE
fingerless glove .... **MIT, MITT**
fingerprint pattern .... **WHORL**
finial ornament, slender .. **EPI**
finisher .... **EDGER, ENDER**
finishing tool .... **REAMER**
FINLAND, FINNISH
see also SPECIAL SECTION
d Finland .... **SUOMI**
Finn in Ingria ..... **VOT, VOTE**
Finns .... **SUOMI**
Finnish god .... **JUMALA**
Finnish poetry .... **RUNES**
Finnish steam bath ... **SAUNA**
fire basket .... **CRESSET**
fire bullet .... **TRACER**
fire god .... **VULCAN**
fire god, Hindu .. **AGNI, AKAL, CIVA, DEVA, KAMA, SIVA**
fire in heart: Buddhism .. **RAGA**
fire opal: Fr. ...... **GIRASOL**
fire, sacrificial, Hindu .. **AGNI**
fire worshipper **PARSI, PARSEE**
firearm . **GUN, RIFLE, MAUSER, PISTOL, CARBINE, REVOLVER**
firecracker .... **PETARD**
fired clay .... **TILE**
firedog .... **ANDIRON**
fireplace
GRATE, INGLE, HEARTH
fireplace side shelf .... **HOB**
firewood bundle **BARIN, FAGOT**
firewood, Tex. .... **LENA**
firework .... **GERB**
firm **FAST, STANCH, STAUNCH**
firm: Hawaii .... **HUI**
firmament .... **SKY**
firn .... **NEVE**
firs, true .... **ABIES**

a first **PRIME, INITIAL, ORIGINAL**
first American-born white
    child .... **DARE**
first appearance ...... **DEBUT**
first born: law .... **EIGNE**
first fruits of a benefice
    .... **ANNATES**
first miracle site ...... **CANA**
first mortal, Hindu ..... **YAMA**
first part in duet ..... **PRIMO**
first principles .... **ABCS**
first-rate .... **ACE**
firth: Scot. .... **KYLE**
fish .. **ANGLE, TRAWL, TROLL,**
fish ..... **ID, EEL, IDE, CARP,
DACE, HAKE, HIKU, JOCU,
LIJA, LING, MADO, MASU,
OPAH, ORFE, PEGA, PETO,
PIKE, POGY, ROUD, RUDD,
SCAD, SCUP, SESI, SHAD,
SIER, SKIL, SOLE, SPET,
TOPE, TUNA, ULUA, PAR-
GO, POWAN, POWEN,
ROACH, SKATE, CONGER,
MULLET, SABALO, TOMCOD**
fish, ancient .. **ELOPS, ELLOPS**
fish, Atlant. **TAUTOG, ESCOLAR**
fish, boneless .. **FILET, FILLET**
fish, bony .... **CARP, TELEOST**
fish, butterfly .... **PARU**
b fish by trolling .... **DRAIL**
fish, Calif. surf .... **SPRAT**
fish, carplike
    RUD, DACE, ROUD, RUDD
fish cleaner .... **SCALER**
fish, climbing ...... **ANABAS**
fish, cod-like **CUSK, HAKE, LING**
fish, colorful
    BOCE, OPAH, WRASSE
fish, Congo .... **LULU**
fish, Cuban .... **DIABLO**
fish, cyprinoid
    ID, IDE, ORF, ORFE
fish, edible .... **SPRAT**
fish eggs .... **ROE**
fish, Egypt. .... **SAIDE**
fish, elongated **EEL, GAR, PIKE**
fish, Europ. .. **ID, BOCE, DACE,
BREAM, SPRAT, UMBER,
BARBEL, BRASSE, PLAICE,
SENNET, WRASSE**
fish, flat .. **DAB, RAY, SOLE,
BRILL, FLUKE, FLOUNDER**
fish, Florida .... **TARPON**
fish, food .. **COD, CERO, HAAK,
HAIK, HAKE, LING, SHAD,
TUNA, TUNNY, SARDINE**
fish, food: Ind. .... **HILSA**
fish, fresh water
    IDE, BASS, DACE, ESOX
fish from boat .... **TROLL**

c fish, game .... **BASS,
MARLIN, TARPON, TARPUN**
fish, gobeylike .... **DRAGONET**
fish, Gr. Lakes .. **CISCO, PERCH**
fish, Hawaiian .... **AKU**
fish, herringlike .... **SHAD**
fish, hook for **GIG, GAFF, DRAIL**
fish, lancet .... **SERRA**
fish line ...... **SNELL, TRAWL**
fish line cork .... **BOB**
fish, linglike .... **COD**
fish, long-nosed .... **GAR**
fish, mackerellike
    CERO, TUNNY, TINKER
fish, many .... **SHOAL**
fish, marine **BONITO, TARPON**
fish measure .... **MEASE**
fish, Medit. .... **NONNAT**
fish, nest-building .... **ACARA**
fish net
    SEINE, TRAWL, SPILLER
fish, N. Z. .... **IHI**
fish, No. Pacif. ..... **INCONNU**
fish, parasitic .... **REMORA**
fish, perch-like ...... **DARTER**
fish, Pers. myth .... **MAH**
fish pickle .... **ALEC**
fish, piece of ... **FILET, FILLET**
fish, pikelike .... **GAR**
d fish-pitching prong . **PEW, GAFF**
fish-poison tree .... **BITO**
fish, predatory .... **GAR**
fish, river .... **BLAY**
fish, Russian .... **STERLET**
fish sauce .... **ALEC, GARUM**
fish sign .... **PISCES**
fish, silvery .... **MULLET**
fish, small .. **ID, IDE, DARTER**
fish, snouted .... **SAURY**
fish, S. Am. ...... **ARAPAIMA**
fish, sparoid .... **SAR, SARGO**
fish, spiny ..... **GOBY, PERCH**
fish, sucking .... **REMORA**
fish, trap .... **WEEL, WEIR**
fish, tropical
    SARGO, ROBALO, SALEMA
fish, warm sea
    GUASA, GROUPER
fish, W. Ind.
    BOGA, CERO, TESTAR
fish whisker .... **BARBEL**
fish with moving line .. **TROLL**
fish with net .. **SEINE, TRAWL**
fish, young .... **FRY**
fisherman's hut, Orkney
    SKEO, SKIO
fishhook line-leader ... **SNELL**
fishhook part .... **BARB**
fishing expedition: Scot. **DRAVE**
fishing grounds, Shetlands **HAAF**

fissure............... **RENT, RIFT, RIMA, RIME, CLEFT**
fissures, full of **RIMOSE, RIMOUS**
fist .... **NEAF**
fit .. **APT, RIPE, SUIT, ADAPT**
fit for cultivation .... **ARABLE**
fit for human consumption **POTABLE**
fit of sulks .... **HUFF**
five-dollar bill .... **VEE**
five-franc piece .... **ECU**
five, group of .... **PENTAD**
five in cards .... **PEDRO**
fix or fixed .... **SET**
fixed charge .... **FEE**
fixed income person .. **RENTIER**
fixed payment .... **KIST**
flaccid .... **LIMP**
flag. **JACK, ENSIGN, BANDEROLE**
flag, flower, blue .... **IRIS**
flag, military .... **GUIDON**
flag, pirate .... **ROGER**
flag, small **BANNERET, BANNERETTE**
flagellants .... **ALBI**
flag's corner .... **CANTON**
flank .... **SIDE**
flank: dialect .... **LEER**
flannel .... **LANA**
flap .... **TAB, LOMA**
flap, as sails .... **SLAT**
flare .... **FUSEE, FUZEE**
flaring edge.. .. **LIP, FLANGE**
flashed lightning ... **LEVINED**
flask, drinking ..... **CANTEEN**
flat .... **EVEN, LEVEL, PLANE**
flat-bottomed boat **ARK, DORY, PUNT, SCOW**
flat, music ...... **MOL, MOLLE**
flatfish ..... **DAB, RAY, SOLE, BRILL, FLUKE, FLOUNDER**
flatten out .... **CLAP**
flattened .. **OBLATE, PLANATE**
flatter .... **PALP**
flattery .... **PALAVER**
flavor .... **LACE, TANG, AROMA, SAPOR, SEASON**
flavoring plant .. **HERB, LEEK, MINT, ANISE, BASIL**
flavoring root ...... **LICORICE**
flax fiber .... **TOW**
flax, like .... **TOWY**
flax, prepare .... **RET**
flee .... **LAM, BOLT**
fleece .... **FELL, WOOL**
fleece, poorest .... **ABB**
fleet .... **NAVY**
fleet, esp. Span. **ARMADA, ARMADO, ARMATA**
fleet, merchant ...... **ARGOSY**
fleur-de-lis .... **LIS, LYS, LISS**

fleur-de-lis, obs. ...... **LUCE**
flexible .... **LITHE**
flexible wood: dial. .... **EDDER**
flight ...... **HEGIRA, HEJIRA**
flight of ducks .... **SKEIN**
flight organ .... **WING**
flight, pert. to .... **AERO**
flightless bird **EMU, KIWI, WEKA, PENGUIN**
flip .... **SNAP**
flit .... **FLY, GAD**
float **BUOY, RAFT, SWIM, WAFT**
floating .... **NATANT**
floating vegetation on Nile **SADD, SUDD**
floating wreckage .. **FLOTSAM**
flock of quail .... **BEVY**
flock of swans .... **BANK**
flock, pert. to .... **GREGAL**
flock, small .... **COVEY**
flog **BEAT, LASH, WHIP, SWINGE**
flood .... **SEA, EAGRE, SPATE, FRESHET, TORRENT**
floodgate ..... **CLOW, SLUICE**
flora and fauna .... **BIOTA**
floral leaf .... **BRACT, SEPAL**
Florentine family ..... **MEDICI**
Florida tree .... **MABI**
flounder **DAB, SOLE, FLUKE, PLAICE**
flour sieve .... **BOLTER**
flour, unsorted Ind. **ATA, ATTA**
flourish, music ...... **ROULADE**
flourishing: dialect ..... **FRIM**
flow .... **RUN, FLUX**
flow out .... **EMIT, SPILL**
flow, to stop **STANCH, STAUNCH**
flower cluster **CYME, ANADEM, RACEME**
flower extract **ATAR, OTTO, ATTAR, OTTAR**
flower, fall **ASTER, COSMOS, SALVIA**
flower, field .... **GOWAN**
flower, genus of .... **ROSA**
flower-goddess, Norse **NANNA**
flower-goddess, Rom. .. **FLORA**
flower leaf ... **BRACT, SEPAL**
flower, Oriental ...... **LOTUS**
flower part .... **PETAL, SEPAL, CARPEL, SPADIX**
flower, showy .... **CALLA**
flower spike .... **AMENT**
flowering plant .... **ARUM**
fluctuate .... **WAVER**
fluent .... **GLIB**
fluff, yam .... **LINT**

a fluid, aeriform .... **GAS**
fluid, medical ... **SERA, SERUM**
fluid, serous .... **SERA, SERUM**
fluidity unit .... **RHE**
flume .... **SHUTE, SLUICE**
flushed .... **RED**
flute, ancient Gr. .. **HEMIOPE**
flute, India ... **BIN, MATALAN**
flute, small .... **FIFE**
flutter .. **FLAP, WAVE, HOVER**
fly **GNAT, SOAR, WING, AVIATE**
fly agaric .... **AMANITA**
fly aloft .... **SOAR**
fly, artificial
HARL, HERL, CAHILL, CLARET
fly, kind of .... **BOT**
fly, small ...... **GNAT, MIDGE**
fly, S. Afr. .... **TSETSE**
flycatcher
TODY, ALDER, PEWEE, PHOEBE
flying .... **VOLANT, VOLITANT**
"Flying Dutchman" saver **SENTA**
flying fox .... **KALONG**
flying lemur .... **COLUGO**
flying, of .... **AERO**
flying saucer .... **UFO**
foam .... **SUD, SUDS**
focus .... **CONCENTRATE**
fodder pit .... **SILO**
fodder storage place .... **SILO**
b fodder, to store ...... **ENSILE,
ENSILO, ENSILAGE, ENSILATE**
fog .... **MIST**
fog horn .... **SIRENE**
fog: old Eng. .... **RAG**
foist .... **FOB, PALM**
fold .... **LAP, PLY, PLIE,
RUGA, PLEAT, CREASE**
fold of skin .... **PLICA**
folds, arrange in ...... **DRAPE**
folded .... **PLICATE**
folio .... **PAGE**
folk dance, Slavic ...... **KOLO**
folklore being .... **TROLL**
folkway .... **MOS**
folkways .... **MORES**
follow .... **DOG, TAIL,
ENSUE, TRACE, SHADOW**
follow suit, not **RENIG, RENEGE**
follower .. **IST, ITE, ADHERENT**
foment .... **ABET**
fondle .... **PET, CARESS**
fondness: Ir. .... **GRA**
font .... **LAVER, STOUP**
food .... **FARE, MEAT,
MANNA, ALIMENT, PABULUM**
food bit .... **ORT**
food, farinaceous ...... **SAGO**
food for animals .... **FORAGE**
food forbidden Israelites **TEREFA**

c food, Hawaii .... **POI**
food: Maori, N. Z. ...... **KAI**
food of gods
AMRITA, AMREETA, AMBROSIA
food: Polyn. .... **KAI**
food, provide .... **CATER**
food, soft invalid's ...... **PAP**
foods, choice .... **CATES**
fool..**ASS, DOLT, GABY, RACA,
SIMP, IDIOT, NINNY**
fool's bauble ...... **MAROTTE**
fool's gold .... **PYRITE**
foolish .. **DAFT, ZANY, INANE,
SILLY, HARISH, ASININE**
foot, animal's ..... **PAD, PAW**
foot, Chin. .... **CHEK**
foot, Gr. poet. .... **IONIC**
foot, having .... **PEDATE**
foot part, horse's .. **PASTERN**
foot, poet. ... **IAMB, IAMBIC,
IAMBUS, ANAPEST, ANAPAEST**
foot soldier .... **PEON**
foot soldier, Ir. **KERN, KERNE**
foot, two-syllable
SPONDEE, TROCHEE
foot, verse .... **IAMB,
DACTYL, ANAPEST, ANAPAEST**
football position: abbr. ... **FB,
HB, LE, LT, QB, RE, RT**
d footless .... **APOD, APODAL**
footless animal **APOD, APODE**
footless animal genus .. **APODA**
footlike .... **PEDATE**
footlike part .... **PES**
footpad .... **WHYO**
footstalk, leaf .... **STRIG**
footstool **HASSOCK, OTTOMAN**
for .... **PRO**
for example .... **EG**
for fear that .... **LEST**
for shame .... **FIE**
forage plant .. **GUAR, ALSIKE,
LUCERN, ALFALFA, LUCERNE**
foramen .... **PORE**
foray .... **RAID**
forbidden
TABU, TABOO, BANNED
Forbidden City .... **LASSA**
forbidding .... **STERN**
force ...... **VIS, DINT, DRIVE,
IMPEL, POWER, ENERGY,
VIOLENCE**
force, alleged
OD, BIOD, ELOD, ODYL
force, hypothetical .... **OD**
force, unit of .... **DYNE**
force, with .... **AMAIN**
foreboding .... **OMEN**
forefather .... **SIRE**
forefoot .... **PUD**
forefront .... **VAN**

Forehead

a
forehead, of the .... **METOPIC**
forehead strap .... **TUMP**
foreign in origin ...... **EXOTIC**
foreign trade discount .. **AGIO**
foreigner: Hawaii ..... **HAOLE**
foreigners' quarter, Constanti-
nople .... **PERA**
foremost part
BOW, VAN, FRONT
foremost segment, insect's
ACRON
foreordain .... **DESTINE**
foreshadow .... **BODE**
forest: Brazil .... **MATTA**
forest clearing .... **GLADE**
forest: obsolete .... **WOLD**
forest ox .... **ANOA**
forest partly inundated **GAPO**
forest, pert. to
SILVAN, SYLVAN, NEMORAL
forest, P. I. .... **GUBAT**
forest warden .... **RANGER**
forestall .... **AVERT, PREVENT**
foretell .... **AUGUR, INSEE**
foreteller .... **SEER**
foretoken .... **OMEN**
forever .... **AY, AYE**
forever: Maori .... **AKE**
forever: poet. **ETERN, ETERNE**
forfeit .... **LOSE, LAPSE**

b
forfeits, Jap. .... **KEN**
forgetfulness fruit .... **LOTUS**
forgetfulness water ... **LETHE**
forgive .... **REMIT**
forgiving .... **CLEMENT**
forgo .... **WAIVE**
form a network .... **PLEX**
form: Buddhism .... **RUPA**
form into line **ALIGN, ALINE**
form, pert. to ...... **MODAL**
form, philos. .... **EIDOS**
formal choice .... **VOTE**
formation, military .. **ECHELON**
former .... **ERST**
former ruler **CZAR, TSAR, TZAR**
formerly .... **NEE, ERST, ONCE**
formerly: pref. .... **EX**
formic acid source ...... **ANT**
formicid .... **ANT**
formula .... **LAW**
forsaken .... **LORN**
fort .... **DIX, ORD, REDAN,**
CITADEL, REDOUBT, RAVELIN
fort, N. Z. .... **PA, PAH**
forth .... **OUT**
forth, issuing ..... **EMANANT**
forthwith .... **NOW**
fortification
REDAN, RAVELIN, REDOUBT

c
fortification, ditchside
SCARP, ESCARP, ESCARPE
fortification, felled trees
ABATIS
fortification, slope .... **TALUS**
fortified place ...... **LIS, LISS**
fortify .... **ARM, MAN**
fortunate (India) .... **SRI**
fortune: Gypsy .... **BAHI**
forty days fast ...... **CARENE**
forty: Gr. .... **MU**
forward .... **ON, AHEAD**
fossil, mollusk .... **DOLITE**
fossil resin .... **RETINITE**
fossil worm track ... **NEREITE**
foul smelling
OLID, FETID, REEKY
found .... **BASE**
found, thing .... **TROVE**
foundation .. **BED, BASE, BASIS**
fountain .... **FONS**
four, group of ...... **TETRAD**
four-inch measure ...... **HAND**
fourth calif (caliph) ..... **ALI**
fourth estate .... **PRESS**
fowl .... **HEN, CAPON, POULT**
fowl's gizzard, etc. .... **GIBLET**
fox .... **TOD**
fox, Afr. .... **FENNEC**
fox hunter's coat .... **PINK**

d
fox, S. Afr. .... **ASSE, CAAMA**
"Fra Diavolo" composer **AUBER**
fraction ..... **PART, DECIMAL**
fragment, pottery
SHARD, SHERD, SHEARD
fragments .... **ANA, ORTS**
fragrant .... **OLENT**
frame, supporting
TRESSEL, TRESTLE
framework .... **TRUSS**
France .... **GAUL**
franchise .... **CHARTER**
Franciscan .... **MINORITE**
frank .... **OPEN, HONEST**
Franks, pert. to .... **SALIC**
frankincense ...... **OLIBANUM**
Frankish law .... **SALIC**
Frankish peasant .. **LITI, LITUS**
fraud .... **SHAM**
fraught .... **LADEN**
fray .... **MELEE**
free .... **RID, GRATIS**
free-for-all .... **FRAY, MELEE**
free from discount ..... **NET**
free from knots: obs. .. **ENODE**
freebooter .... **PIRATE**
freedman, Kentish law .. **LAET**
freehold land, Turkey .. **MULK**
freeman ...... **CEORL, THANE**
freight-boat .... **ARK**

a freight car .... **GONDOLA**
   FRENCH WORDS: (accent marks
   omitted throughout)
      according to ..... **ALA, AUX**
      after .... **APRES**
      again .... **ENCORE**
      airplane .... **AVION**
      alas .... **HELAS**
      all .... **TOUT**
      among .... **ENTRE**
      and .... **ET**
      angel .... **ANGE**
      annuity .... **RENTE**
      arm .... **BRAS**
      article .... **LA, LE, DE,**
         (plural) **DES, LAS, LES, UNE**
      at the home of ..... **CHEZ**
      aunt .... **TANTE**
      baby .... **BEBE**
      bacon .... **LARD**
      back .... **DOS**
      ball .... **BAL**
      bang! .... **PAN**
      bath .... **BAIN**
      beach .... **PLAGE**
      beast .... **BETE**
      before .... **AVANT**
      being .... **ETRE**
      bench .... **BANC**

b   between .... **ENTRE**
      beware .... **GARE**
      bitter .... **AMER**
      black .... **NOIR, NOIRE**
      blue .... **BLEU**
      bread crumbs ...... **PANURE**
      bridge .... **PONT**
      business house .... **CIE**
      but .... **MAIS**
      cabbage .... **CHOU**
      cake .... **GATEAU**
      carefully groomed .. **SOIGNE**
      carriage .... **FIACRE**
      charmed .... **RAVI**
      chicken .... **POULE**
      child .... **ENFANT**
      clear .... **NET**
      climax, theatre .... **CLOY**
      cloth .... **DRAP**
      cloud .... **NUAGE**
      coarse cloth .... **BURE**
      connective .... **ET**
      cowardly .... **LACHE**
      cup .... **TASSE**
      dance, formal .... **BAL**
      dare .... **OSER**
      daughter .... **FILLE**
      deal .... **DONNE**
      dear .... **CHER, CHERI**
      deed .... **FAIT**
      defy .... **DEFI**

c department .... see SPECIAL
      SECTION, GAZETTEER
   depot .... **GARE**
   detective force .... **SURETE**
   devil .... **DIABLE**
   dirty .... **SALE**
   donkey .... **ANE**
   down with .... **ABAS**
   dream .... **REVE**
   duck to cook .... **CANETON**
   dugout .... **ABRI**
   duke .... **DUC**
   dungeon .... **CACHOT**
   ear of grain .... **EPI**
   east .... **EST**
   egg .... **OEUF**
   elegance .... **LUXE**
   enamel .... **EMAIL**
   equal .... **PAREIL**
   evening .... **SOIR**
   exaggerated .... **OUTRE**
   exclamation .... **HEIN**
   exist .... **ETRE**
   fabric .... **RAS, DRAP**
   father .... **PERE**
   fear .... **PEUR**
   finally .... **ENFIN**
   fingering .... **DOIGTE**
   fire .... **FEU**

d five .... **CINQ**
   for .... **CAR**
   friend .... **AMI, AMIE**
   froth .... **BAVE**
   full .... **PLEIN**
   game .... **JEU, JEUX**
   gift .... **CADEAU**
   god .... **DIEU**
   golden .... **DORE**
   good .... **BON**
   good-bye **ADIEU, AU REVOIR**
   grain ear .... **EPI**
   gray .... **GRIS**
   gravy .... **JUS**
   grimace .... **MOUE**
   ground .... **TERRE**
   half-mask .... **LOUP**
   hall .... **SALLE**
   handle .... **ANSE**
   head .... **TETE**
   health .... **SANTE**
   here .... **ICI**
   hill .... **PUY**
   his .... **SES**
   house .... **MAISON**
   hunting match .... **TIR**
   husband .... **MARI**
   idea .... **IDEE**

(French words continued on
   pages 62 and 63)

French

a FRENCH:

impetuosity	ELAN
in	DANS
income, annual	RENTE
is	EST
island	ILE
kind	SORTE
king	ROI
lamb	AGNEAU
land	TERRE
laugh	RIRE
laughter	RISEE
law	LOI, DROIT
leather	CUIR
lift	LEVE
lily	LIS
little	PEU
lively	VIF
lodging place	GITE
low	BAS
maid	BONNE
mail	POSTE
mask, half	LOUP
material	DRAP
May	MAI
meat dish	SALMI
milk	LAIT
mine	AMOI
mother	MERE

b

mountain	MONT
museum	MUSEE
nail	CLOU
name	NOM
near	PRES
network	RESEAU
night	NUIT
no	NON
nose	NEZ
nothing	RIEN
number, one	UNE
nursemaid	BONNE
of	DE
one	UNE
our	NOS, NOUS
out	HORS
outbreak	EMEUTE
over	SUR
oyster farm	PARC
petticoat	JUPE, COTTE
picnic spot	BOIS
pinion	AILE
poem	DIT
pork	SALE
pout	MOUE
preposition	DES
pretty	JOLI, JOLIE
pronoun	CES, ILS, MES, TOI, UNE, ELLE
queen	REINE
quickly	VITE

c

rabbit	LAPIN
railway station	GARE
read	LIRE
rear	ARRIERE
reception	ACCUEIL
rent	LOUER
river	RIVIERE
roast	ROTI
royal edict	ARRET
saint: abbr.	STE
salt	SEL
salted	SALE
school	ECOLE, LYCEE
scow	ACON
sea	MER
security	RENTE
senior	AINE
servant	BONNE
she	ELLE
sheath	ETUI
sheep	MOUTON
shelter	ABRI
shine	LUSTRE
shooting match	TIR
sickness	MAL
silk	SOIE
situated	SISE
small	PETIT
smitten	EPRISE

d

soldier	POILU
some	DES
son	FILS
soul	AME
spirit	AME
star	ETOILE
state	ETAT
stocking	BAS
storm	ORAGE
summer	ETE
superior quality	LUXE
superfluous	DETROP
surnamed	DIT
sweetmeat	DRAGEE
that	CE, CET, QUE, QUI, CELA
thee	TE
there!	VOILA
they	ILS
thirty	TRENTE
this	CE
thou	TOI
to be	ETRE
to go	ALLER
to love	AIMER
too much	TROP
under	SOUS
upon	SUR
us	NOUS
verb	ETRE
verse	RONDEL

a **FRENCH:**

very .... **TRES**
vineyard .... **CRU**
wall .... **MUR**
water .... **EAU**
wave .... **ONDE**
weapon .... **ARME**
well .... **BIEN**
wine .... **VIN**
wine, delicacy of .... **SEVE**
wine-plant .... **CEP**
with .... **AVEC**
with the .... **AU**
without .... **SANS**
wing .... **AILE**
wood .... **BOIS**
yesterday .... **HIER**
you .... **TOI**
your .... **VOTRE**

Fr., annuity .... **RENTE**
Fr. art group .... **FAUVES**
Fr. artist .. **DORE, DUFY, GROS, COROT, DEGAS, MANET, MONET, BRAQUE, DERAIN, RENOIR, CHAGALL, CHIR-ICO, MATISSE, UTRILLO**
Fr. artist cult .... **DADA**

b

Fr. author .. **SUE, GIDE, HUGO, LOTI, ZOLA, CAMUS, DUMAS, RENAN, STAEL, VERNE, RACINE, SARTRE, COCTEAU**
Fr. Calvinist .... **CALAS**
Fr. chalk .... **TALC**
Fr. coin, old .... **SOU**
Fr. commercial company .. **CIE**
FR. COMPOSER
          see COMPOSER, FR.
Fr. dramatist .... **RACINE**
Fr. ecclesiastic city ...... **SENS**
Fr. explorer .... **CARTIER**
Fr. fort, battle of Verdun **VAUX**
Fr. general .... **FOCH, HOCHE GAMELIN**
Fr.-Ger. river basin ...... **SAAR**
Fr. guerillas .... **MAQUIS**
Fr. Guiana tribesman .... **BONI**
Fr. historical area ..... **ANJOU**
Fr. honeysuckle .... **SULLA**
Fr. illustrator .... **DORE**
Fr. island .... **ILE**
Fr. lace-making town **CLUNY**
Fr. marshal ..... **NEY, MURAT**
FR. NOVELIST see FR. AUTHOR
FR. PAINTER see FR. ARTIST
Fr. philosopher ...... **COMTE**
Fr. premier, former .... **LAVAL**
Fr. priest .... **ABBE, PERE**
Fr. protectorate ...... **TUNIS**
Fr. psychologist .... **BINET**

c Fr. Revolution month **NIVOSE, FLOREAL, PRAIRAL, VEN-TOSE, BRUMAIRE, FERVI-DOR, FRIMAIRE, MESSIDOR, PLUVIOSE, THERMIDOR**
Fr. revolutionist ..... **MARAT**
Fr. sculptor .... **RODIN**
Fr. security .... **RENTE**
Fr. singer ..... **PIAF, SABLON**
Fr. soprano .... **PONS, CALVE**
Fr. statesman .... **COTY**
FR. WRITER .. see FR. AUTHOR
Frenchman .... **GAUL**
frenzied .... **AMOK**
frequently .... **OFT**
fresh .... **NEW, SPICK**
fresh supply .... **RELAY**
freshet .... **FLOOD, SPATE**
freshwater worm .. **NAID, NAIS**
fretted .... **EROSE**
Frey's wife .... **GERD**
friar .... **FRA, MONK**
friar, mendicant ..... **SERVITE**
friend: law .... **AMY**
friends .... **KITH**
Friendly Islands ...... **TONGA**
friendship .... **AMITY**
frigate bird, Hawaiian ... **IWA**
Frigg's brother-in-law ..... **VE**
d Frigg's husband .... **ODIN**
fright .... **FUNK, PANIC**
frighten **FLEY, ALARM, SCARE**
frill, neck ...... **RUFF, JABOT**
fringe of curls ...... **FRISETTE**
fringe: zool. .... **LOMA**
frisk .... **PLAY, ROMP**
frisky .... **PEART**
FROCK see GARMENT
frog .... **TOAD**
frog genus .... **RANA**
frogs, order of .... **ANURA**
frogs, pert. to .... **RANINE**
frolic ... **LARK, PLAY, ROMP, CAPER, SPORT, SPREE**
from head to foot . **CAP-A-PIE**
from: Lat. .... **DE**
from: prefix .... **AB**
front ... **VAN, FORE, FACADE**
front page weather box .. **EAR**
front, to extend ...... **DEPLOY**
frontier post .... **FORT**
frontiersman **BOONE, CARSON**
frost .... **ICE, HOAR, RIME**
frosty .... **RIMY**
froth .... **FOAM, SPUME**
frothlike .... **SPUMY, YEASTY**
frown .... **LOUR, GLOOM, LOWER, SCOWL, GLOWER**
frugal .... **CHARY**
fruit .... **BERRY, OLIVE**
fruit, Afr. .... **PECEGO**

Fruit

fruit, aggregate ..... ETAERIO
fruit decay .... BLET
fruit dish
　　COMPOTE, COMPOTIER
fruitdots, fern .... SORI, SORUS
fruit, dry .... ACHENE
fruit, fleshy ...... PEAR, PEPO
fruit, hard-shelled NUT, GOURD
fruit, India .... BEL
fruit-jelly .... RHOB
fruit, lemonlike ..... CITRON
fruit of maple ...... SAMARA
fruit pigeon, Polyn. ..... LUPE
fruit, plumlike .... SLOE
fruit, pulpy ..... UVA, DRUPE
fruit shrub, E. Ind. .... CUBEB
fruit, small, 1-seeded
　　AKENE, ACHENE, ACHENIUM
fruit, southern .... PAPAW
fruit squeezer ...... REAMER
fruit, tropical .. DATE, MANGO
fruit, vine .... MELON
fruit, yellow tropical
　　PAPAW, PAPAYA, PAWPAW
fruiting spike .... EAR
frustrate ... SCOTCH, THWART
fry lightly .... SAUTE
Fuegan Indian .... ONA
fuel   LOG, COAL, COKE, PEAT
fuel ship .... OILER, TANKER
fuel, turf .... PEAT, PEET
fugue theme .... DUX
fulcrum, oar .... THOLE
full .... PLENARY
full and clear ..... OROTUND
fullness .... PLENUM
fulmar .... NELLY, MALDUCK
fume .... REEK, SMOKE

fun .... SPORT
function ...... GO, USE, WORK
function, trig. ... SINE, COSINE
fundamental
　　BASIC, ELEMENTAL
funeral bell KNELL, MORTBELL
funeral music .... DIRGE
funeral notice .... OBIT
funeral oration ...... ELOGE
funeral pile .... PYRE
funeral song .... NENIA
fungi, tissue in .... TRAMA
fungus .... AGARIC
fungus, edible
　　MOREL, MORIL, TRUFFLE
fungus, white-spored AMANITA
fur ...... SEAL, VAIR, GENET
　　MARTEN, NUTRIA, MINIVER
fur cape .... PELERINE
fur: Her. PEAN, VAIR, VAIRE
furbelow ...... FRILL, RUFFLE
Furies, Gr. .... ERINYS
ERINNYS, ERINYES, ERINNYES
Furies, one of
ALECTO, MEGAERA, TISIPHONE
Furies, Rom. .... DIRAE
furlongs, eight .... MILE
furnish crew .... MAN
furnish with .... ENDOW
furnishings, mode of .. DECOR
furrows, with RIVOSE, RUTTED
further .... AID, YET
furtive .... SLY, SNEAKY
fury .... IRE
furze ...... WHIN, WHUN,
　　GORSE, GORST, GORSTE
fuse partly .... FRIT
fuss .... ADO, TO-DO

gabi .... TARO
Gad, son of .... ARELI
gadget .... GISMO
Gael .... SCOT
Gaelic .. ERSE, CELTIC, KELTIC
Gaelic poem .... DUAN
Gaelic sea god .... LER
gaff .... SPAR
gain .... GET, WIN, EARN
gait .. LOPE, CANTER, GALLOP
gait, horse's ..... PACE, RACK
Galahad's mother ..... ELAINE
Galatea's beloved ..... ACIS
Galilee town .... CANA
galla ox ...... SANGA, SANGU
gallery, art .... SALON
gallery: hist. .... ALURE

gallery, open .... LOGGIA
gallery protecting troops
　　ECOUTE
galley, armed, old Northmen's
　　AESC
galley, fast
　　DROMON, DROMOND
galley, 1 oar bank UNIREME
galley, 2 oar banks .. BIREME
galley, 3 oar banks TRIREME
gallop, rapid .... TANTIVY
gallop slowly .... LOPE
Galsworthy heroine .... IRENE
Galway Bay, isles in .... ARAN
gamble .... GAME
gambling place ...... CASINO

Gambol

a gambol.......... **DIDO, CAPER**
game ... **LOTO, BINGO, LOTTO**
game, Basque .... **PELOTA**
game, board ... **CHESS, HALMA**
game, card ..... **LU, LOO, NAP,**
PAM, PUT, FARO, CINCH,
MACAO, MONTE, OMBER,
OMBRE, STUSS, TAROT,
WHIST, BASSET, CASINO,
ECARTE, ROUNCE,
CANASTA
game, child's .... **TAG**
game, dice .... **LUDO**
game, follow............ **STALK**
game, gambling... **FARO, PICO,**
STUSS
game, Hawaii .... **HEI**
game, Ind. guessing ... **CANUTE**
game, It. guessing....... **MORA**
game of skill..... **POOL, CHESS**
game piece..... **MAN, DOMINO**
gamecock .... **STAG**
gamekeeper .... **RANGER**
gaming cube..... **DIE, DICE**
Ganges boat........... **PUTELI**
gangplank .... **RAMP**
gangster .. **MUG, THUG, WHYO**
gannet, common .... **SOLAN**
gannet genus .... **SULA**
gap .... **HIATUS, LACUNA**
gap in hedge
b **MUSE, MEUSE, MUSET**
gar fish .... **SNOOK**
garland.......... **LEI, ANADEM**
GARMENT. see **COAT, BLOUSE**
garment.................. **ROBE**
garment, Arab .... **ABA**
garment, bishop's .... **CHIMAR,**
CHIMER, CHIMERE
garment, church .... **COTTA**
GARMENT, CLERICAL OR EC-
CLESIASTIC,.... see GARMENT,
PRIESTLY
garment, fitted........ **REEFER**
garment, India, Hindu..... **SARI,**
SAREE, BANIAN, BANYAN
GARMENT, LITURGICAL.. see
GARMENT, PRIESTLY
garment, loose **CAMIS, CAMUS,**
CYMAR, SIMAR, CAMISE
garment, Malay .... **SARONG**
garment, Moslem .... **IZAR**
garment, N. Afr........... **HAIK**
garment, Old Ir........... **INAR**
garment, outer....... **CAPOTE,**
PALETOT
garment, Polyn......... **PAREU**
garment, priestly .... **ALB, COPE,**
AMICE, EPHOD, STOLE
garment, rain .... **PONCHO**
garment, scarflike ...... **TIPPET**

c garment, Turk........ **DOLMAN**
garment, woman's..... **BODICE,**
MANTUA
garnishment .... **LIEN**
garret................... **ATTIC**
garter snake genus.... **ELAPS**
gas .... **FUEL, NEON**
gas apparatus ...... **AERATOR**
gas, charge with ...... **AERATE**
gas, colorless........... **OXAN**
gas, inert..... **ARGON, XENON**
gas, radioactive .... **RADON,**
NITON
GASEOUS ELEMENT...... see
ELEMENTS, SPECIAL
SECTION, Page 195
gaseous sky "cloud" .. **NEBULA**
GASTROPOD see also MOLLUSK
gastropod .... **WELK, WILK,**
WHELK, LIMPET
gastropod, Haliotis .. **ABALONE**
gate .... **PORTAL**
gate, water .... **SLUICE**
gateway............... **PYLON**
gateway, Buddhist temple
TORAN, TORANA
gateway, Pers............. **DAR**
gateway, Shinto shrine.... **TORII**
gather........ **AMASS, GLEAN,**
GARNER, MUSTER
gather, as grouse .... **LEK**
d gather in bundles ..... **SHEAVE**
gathers, put in .... **SHER, SHIR,**
SHIRR
gaunt .... **SPARE**
Gawain's father .... **LOT**
gazelle .... **ARIEL**
gazelle, Afr....... **ADMI, DAMA,**
MOHR, KORIN, MHORR
gazelle, Asia .... **AHU**
gazelle, black-tailed........ **GOA**
gazelle, Pers............. **CORA**
gazelle, Sudan .... **DAMA**
gazelle, Tibetan .... **GOA**
gear .... **CAM**
gear tooth................. **COG**
gear wheel, smallest.... **PINION**
Geb's consort............. **NUT**
Gelderland city............ **EDE**
gelid .... **ICY, COLD**
GEM........... see also STONE
gem ..... **JADE, ONYX, OPAL,**
RUBY, SARD, AGATE, PEARL,
STONE, GARNET, SPINEL,
EMERALD, PERIDOT
gem-bearing earth, Burma **BYON**
gem, carved .... **CAMEO**
gem facet ...... **BEZEL, BEZIL,**
CULET, COLLET
gem weight............. **CARAT**
Gemini's mortal half ... **CASTOR**

65

a

gender, a .... NEUTER
genealogy .... TREE
GENERAL, CIVIL WAR
 see CIVIL WAR COMMANDER
general, Morocco .... KAID
general Sitting Bull defeated
 CUSTER
generation .... AGE
Genesis matriarch ...... SARAI
genie, Egypt. .... HAPI
genip tree .... LANA
genipap wood .... LANA
gentle . MILD, TAME, TENDER
gentle breeze .... AURA
gentle heat .... TEPOR
genuflect .... KNEEL
GENUS . see PLANT or
 ANIMAL named
genus of plants .... ARUM
geode VUG, VOOG, VUGG, VUGH
geological division . LIAS, LYAS
geol. epoch BALA, ECCA, LIAS,
 MUAV, ERIAN, UINTA,
 PLIOCENE
geol. formation ..... TERRAIN,
 TERRANE, TERRENE
geol. period .... DYAS,
 EOCENE, MIOCENE
geol. stage ...... RISS, ACHEN
geol. vein angle .... HADE

b

geometric ratio .... SINE
geometric solid
 CONE, CUBE, PRISM
geometrical lines ...... LOCI,
 LOCUS, SECANT
geometry rule ...... THEOREM
geometry term .... VERSOR
geophagy .... PICA
George Sand novel ..... LELIA
Geraint's wife .... ENID
geranium lake color . NACARAT
germ .. BUG, VIRUS, MICROBE
germ-free ASEPTIC, ANTISEPTIC
germs, produced by ... SEPTIC
GERMAN . see also TEUTONIC
GERMAN WORDS: (umlauts
 omitted throughout)
"A" .... EIN
above .... UBER
again .... UBER
alas .... ACH
article ...... DAS, DER, EIN
ass .... ESEL
beer .... BIER
blood .... BLUT
conjunction .... UND
count .... GRAF
donkey .... ESEL
dumpling .... KNODEL
eat .... ESSEN

c

eight .... ACHT
evening .... ABEND
everything .... ALLES
exclamation .... HOCH
four .... VIER
gentleman .. HERR, HERREN
hall .... AULA, SAAL
heaven .... HIMMEL
hunter .... JAGER
"I" .... ICH
ice .... EIS
iron .... EISEN
is .... IST
it .... ES
league (s) .... BUND, BUNDE
love .... LIEBE
mister .... HERR
nation .... VOLK
never .... NIE
new .... NEUE
no .... NEIN
noble .... EDEL
old .... ALT
one .... EIN, EINE
out of .... AUS
pronoun .... ICH
people .... VOLK
school hall .... AULA
softly .... LEISE

d

song .... LIED
spirit .... GEIST
state .... STAAT
steel .... STAHL
temperament ...... GEMUT
than .... ALS
the .... DAS, DER
three .... DREI
thunder .... DONNER
title .... VON, PRINZ
town .... STADT
us .... UNS
very .... SEHR
with .... MIT
without .... OHNE
yes .... JA
you .... SIE
your ...... IHR, DEIN, EUER

German .... BOCHE
Ger. admiral .... SPEE
Ger. bacteriologist ...... KOCH
Ger. camp, war ...... STALAG
GER. COMPOSER
 see COMPOSER, GER.
Ger.-Czech region ... SUDETEN
Ger. district, old .... GAU
Ger. dive bomber ...... STUKA
Ger. emperor .... OTTO
Ger. highway ..... AUTOBAHN
Ger. John .... HANS

a Ger. king .... **OTTO**
Ger. landscape painter .. **ROOS**
Ger. name prefix .... **VON**
Ger. philosopher . **KANT, HEGEL**
Ger. physicist .. **OHM, ERMAN**
Ger. president .... **EBERT**
Ger. princely family ..... **WELF**
Ger. theologian .... **ARND**
Ger. title .. **VON, GRAF, PRINZ**
Ger. tribal region
GAU, GAUE, GAUS
Germanic deity .... **DONAR**
Germanic letter .... **RUNE**
gesture dance, Samoa; Fiji **SIVA**
get out! . **SCAT, SHOO, SCRAM**
ghastly .... **LURID**
ghost .... **HANT, SPOOK,**
SPECTER, SPECTRE
ghost, India .... **BHUT**
ghost-town state: abbrev.: **UT**
giant .... **TITAN**
giant, frightful .... **OGRE**
giant, Hindu myth ..... **BANA**
giant, killed by Apollo .. **OTUS**
giant, Norse, Scand. myth **YMER,**
YMIR, JOTUM, MIMIR
giant, Rom. .... **CACA**
giant, 1000-armed, Hindu **BANA**
giants, Bibl. .... **ANAK, EMIM**
gibbon, Malay .... **LAR**
gift, receiver of .... **DONEE**
gig .... **NAPPER**

b gigantic person .... **TITAN**
"Gil —" LeSage novel .. **BLAS**
Gilead's descendant .... **ULAM**
Gilgit language, Kashmir **SHINA**
gills, four .... **PINT**
gilt .... **DORE**
gin .... **TRAP**
gingerbread tree .... **DUM**
ginkgo tree .... **ICHO**
GIPSY .... see **GYPSY**
giraffe-like animal .... **OKAPI**
girasol .... **OPAL**
girder .... **TRUSS**
girdle .... **OBI, CEST, SASH**
girl .... **SIS, CHIT,**
DAME, SKIRT
GIRL'S NAME
see **WOMAN'S NAME**
girth, saddle .... **CINCH**
gist .... **NUB, PITH**
give: law .... **REMISE**
give reluctantly ..... **GRUDGE**
give up .. **CEDE, WAIVE, YIELD**
give up wholly ...... **DEVOTE**
give way .... **YIELD**
glacial hill .... **PAHA**
glacial ice block, pinnacle **SERAC**
glacial ridge ... **AS, OS, ASAR,**
KAME, OSAR, ESCAR,
ESKAR, ESKER

c glacial snow field **FIRN, NEVE**
glacial stage .... **WURM**
glacier chasm
CREVAS, CREVASSE
glacier, facing a .... **STOSS**
gladiolus .... **IRID**
gladly .... **FAIN**
gland .... **PINEAL, THYROID**
gland, edible .... **NOIX**
glass .... **LENS**
glass, blue .... **SMALT**
glass bubble .... **BLEB**
glass defect .... **TEAR**
glass, flatten .... **PLATTEN**
glass furnace mouth .. **BOCCA**
glass ingredient ...... **SILICON**
glass-like material .. .. **PLASS**
glass maker .... **GLAZIER**
glass, molten .... **PARISON**
glass, partly fused **FRIT, FRITT**
glass, transparent ..... **UVIOL**
glass vial .. **AMPULE, AMPOULE**
glassmaker's oven . **LEER, LEHR**
glasswort .... **KALI**
glassy .... **HYALINE**
glazier's tack .... **BRAD**
gleam .... **GLINT**
glide .... **SKIM, SLIP,**
SKATE, SLIDE

d glittering piece ..... **SPANGLE**
globe .... **ORB, SPHERE**
global .... **ROUND, SPHERAL**
gloom .... **MIRK, MURK**
gloomy .... **DARK, DOUR,**
DREAR, DREARY
"Gloomy Dean" .... **INGE**
glossy-surfaced .... **GLACE**
glottal stop: Dan. ...... **STOD**
glove leather ..... **KID, NAPA,**
MOCHA, SUEDE
glove shape, unstitched **TRANK**
glowing .... **CANDENT**
glucoside, root .... **GEIN**
glut ... **SATE, GORGE, SATIATE**
gnarl ..... **NUR, KNUR, NURR**
gnat, small .... **MIDGE**
gnome .... **NIS, GREMLIN**
go .... **WEND**
go astray .... **ABERRATE**
go astray slightly .... **ERR**
go back .... **REVERT**
go forth .... **FARE**
go hence: Lat. .... **VADE**
go on! .... **GARN, SCAT**
go shufflingly .. **MOSY, MOSEY**
goad .... **PROD, SPUR, INCITE**
goal .... **AIM, END**
goat, Alpine mountain .. **IBEX**
goat antelope .... **GORAL**
goat, Asian .... **JAGLA**

a
goat, genus .... **CAPRIA**
goat god .... **PAN**
goat, wild .. **TUR, IBEX, TAHR,**
　　TAIR, TEHR, THAR
goatsucker .... **POTOO**
gob .... **TAR**
Gobi Desert .... **SHAMO**
goblet .... **HANAP**
goblin .... **POOK, PUCA, PUCK**
goblin, Egypt .... **OUPHE**
goblin, Norse **NIS,NISSE,KOBOLD**
goby, small .... **MAPO**
GOD . see also DEITY, and see
　　also SPECIAL SECTION
god, Babyl. **EA, ABU, ANU, BEL**
GOD, CHIEF see CHIEF NORSE
　　GOD, also BABYLONIAN
　　CHIEF GOD
god: Chin. .... **SHEN**
god: Hebrew .... **EL**
god: Jap .... **KAMI**
god: Lat. .... **DEUS**
god of alcoholic drinks, **SIRIS**
god of Arcadia .... **PAN**
GOD OF CHAOS ... see CHAOS
god of darkness—evil, Egyp.
　　SET, SETH
god of dead, Hindu .... **YAMA**
god of dead, Rom. .... **ORCUS**
b
god of discord, Norse
　　LOK, LOKE, LOKI
god of earth, Babyl. .. **DAGAN**
GOD OF EARTH, Egyptian
　　see EARTH GOD
god of evil: Egyp. ... **SET, SETH**
god of evil, to ward off **BES,BESA**
god of fertility, Norse ... **FREY**
god of fields, flocks, forest
　　PAN, FAUN
god of fire ... **AGNI, VULCAN**
god of Hades ..... **DIS, PLUTO**
god of harvests ...... **CRONUS**
god of light, Norse
　　BALDR, BALDER, BALDUR
god of love, Gr. .... **EROS**
god of love, Rom. **AMOR, CUPID**
god of love, Vedic .... **BHAGA**
god of mirth .. **COMUS, KOMOS**
god (goddess) of mischief . **ATE**
god of michief, Norse
　　LOK, LOKE, LOKI
GOD OF MOON see MOON GOD
god of music .... **APOLLO**
god of north wind ... **BOREAS**
god of pleasure ..... **BES, BESA**
god of procreation, Egyp. **MIN**
god of prosperity, Teutonic **FREY**
god of revelry, Gr. ... **COMUS,
　　KOMOS**
god of ridicule .... **MOMUS**
GOD OF SEA .... see SEA GOD
GOD OF SKY .... see SKY GOD

c
God of Southeast Wind: Gr.
　　EURUS
GOD OF STORMS
　　see STORM GOD
GOD OF SUN .... see SUN GOD
god of thunder **THOR, DONAR**
god of Tuesday **TIU, TIW, TYR**
GOD OF UNDERWORLD
　　see UNDERWORLD GOD
god of war, Assyrian
　　ASUR, ASSUR
god of war, Babyl. . **IRA, IRRA**
god of war, Gr. .... **ARES**
god of war, Norse
　　TY, TYR, TYRR
god of war, Rom. .... **MARS**
god of war, Teut. .... **ER**
god of wind, Norse ... **VAYU**
god of wind, storm, Babylonian
　　ZU, ADAD, ADDA, ADDU
god of winds, Gr. ..... **AEOLUS**
god of wisdom, Babyl.
　　NABU, NEBO
god of wisdom, Norse .. **ODIN**
god of youth .... **APOLLO**
god skilled with bow, Norse **ULL**
god, Sumerian .... **ABU**
god, unknown, Hindu ..... **KA**
gods, Chief Teut., Norse **AESIR**
gods: Lat. .... **DI**
d
gods, mother of .... **RHEA**
gods, mother of: Ir. **ANA, ANU**
GODS, QUEEN OF
　　see QUEEN OF GODS
gods, the .... **DEI, DII**
GODDESS see also SPECIAL SECT.
GODDESS, CHIEF see **BABY-
　　LONIAN CHIEF GODDESS**
goddess, cow-headed ..... **ISIS**
goddess: Latin .... **DEA**
GODDESS, MOTHER
　　see MOTHER GODDESS
goddess of agriculture
　　CERES, DEMETER
goddess of art or science . **MUSE**
goddess of astronomy **URANIA**
goddess of beauty: Norse **FREYA**
goddess of betrothal, Norse **VOR**
goddess of chase .**DIAN, DIANA**
goddess of crops, Rom. **ANNONA**
goddess of dawn, Gr. ..... **EOS**
goddess of dawn, Rom.
　　AURORA
goddess of dawn, Vedic .. **USAS**
goddess of dead ... **HEL, HELA**
goddess of deep, Babyl. . **NINA**
goddess of destiny, Norse
　　URD, URTH
goddess of destruction ... **ARA**
goddess of discord .. **ATE, ERIS**
goddess of earth, Teut. . **ERDA**

a goddess of earth ... **GE, ERDA, GAEA, GAIA, TARI**
goddess of earth: Rom. **CERES, TERRA**
goddess of faith, Rom. . **FIDES**
goddess of fate, Rom. **NONA, PARCA**
goddess of fate, Teutonic **NORN**
goddess of fertility **ASTARTE**
goddess of fertility, Anatolian **MA**
goddess of field, Rom. . **FAUNA**
goddess of flowers, Gr. **CHLORIS**
goddess of flowers, Norse **NANNA**
goddess of flowers, Rom. **FLORA**
goddess of grain **CERES, DEMETER**
goddess of harvest ...... **OPS**
goddess of harvest, Attica **CARPO**
goddess of healing ...... **EIR**
goddess of hearth ..... **VESTA**
goddess of heavens, Egyp. . **NUT**
goddess of hope .... **SPES**
goddess of hunt . **DIAN, DIANA**
goddess of infatuation .. **ATE**
goddess of justice . **MA, MAAT**
b goddess of love ...... **VENUS, ASTARTE, APHRODITE**
goddess of love, Babylonian **ISTAR, ISHTAR**
goddess of love, Norse **FREYA, FREYJA**
goddess of magic .... **HECATE**
GODDESS OF MATERNITY
 see MATERNITY GODDESS
goddess of mischief .... **ATE**
GODDESS OF MOON
 see MOON GODDESS
goddess of nature **CYBELE, ARTEMIS**
GODDESS OF NIGHT, NORSE
 see NIGHT, NORSE
goddess of night: Rom.**NOX,NYX**
goddess of peace **IRENE, EIRENE**
goddess of plenty .... **OPS**
goddess of prosperity: Rom. **SALUS**
goddess of retribution .... **ATE**
goddess of retribution, Gr. **ARA**
goddess of revenge .. **NEMESIS**
GODDESS OF SEA
 see SEA GODDESS
goddess of seasons .... **HORAE**
goddess of splendor, Hindu **UMA**
goddess of truth, Egypt **MA, MAAT**
GODDESS OF UNDERWORLD
 see UNDERWORLD GODDESS

c goddess of vegetation .. **CORA, KORE, CERES**
goddess of vengeance .... **ARA**
goddess of victory ...... **NIKE**
goddess of volcanoes, Hawaii **PELE**
goddess of war, Gr. .... **ENYO**
goddess of wisdom **ATHENA, PALLAS**
goddess of woods ...... **DIAN, DIANA, ARTEMIS**
goddess of youth .... **HEBE**
goddess, Queen .. **HERA, JUNO**
goddesses of destiny ... **FATES**
goddesses of fate, Gr. **MOERAE**
goddesses of fate, Norse **NORNS**
Goethe drama .... **FAUST**
Goethe heroine ...... **MIGNON**
golconda .... **MINE**
gold ...... **AU, CYME, GILT**
gold alloy, ancient ..... **ASEM**
Gold Coast Negro .... **GA**
Gold Coast tong. **CHI, TWI, TSHI**
gold-colored metal . **ORMOLU**
gold, cover with .... **GILD**
gold deposit .... **PLACER**
gold district-field, Afr. .. **RAND**
gold: Her. .... **OR**
gold, mosaic .... **ORMOLU**
gold, pert. to .... **AURIC**
golden .... **AUREATE**
d Golden Fleece keeper .. **AEETES**
Golden Fleece seeker .. **JASON**
golden in color .. **DORE, DURRY**
golden oriole .... **PIROL**
golden oriole, Eur. .... **LORIOT**
golden-touch king ..... **MIDAS**
golf attendant .. **CADY, CADDY**
golf club ...... **IRON, CLEEK, MASHIE, PUTTER**
golf club, part .... **TOE**
golf club socket .... **HOSEL**
golf hole .... **CUP**
golf pro .... **SNEAD**
golf score .... **PAR**
golf stroke-shot .. **PUT, BAFF, CHIP, LOFT, PUTT, DRIVE, SCLAFF**
golf term ..... **LIE, PAR, TEE**
golfer .... **TEER**
gomuti .... **ARENGA**
gondolier's song **BARCAROLE, BARCAROLLE**
gone .... **OUT, AWAY**
gone by .... **AGO, PAST, YORE**
gonfalon .... **BANNER**
good-bye: Fr. **ADIEU,AU REVOIR**
good digestion ...... **EUPEPSIA**
good health, in .... **PEART**
"Good King" .... **HAL**
good news **EVANGEL, EVANGILE**

a "Good Queen Bess," name for .... ORIANA
good: Tagalog .... MABUTI
goods .... WARES
goods in sea .... JETSAM
goods sunk at sea
LAGAN, LIGAN
goose barnacle genus .. LEPAS
goose cry ...... HONK, YANG
goose genus .... ANSER
goose, male .... GANDER
goose, sea .... SOLAN
goose, wild .... BRANT
gooseberry .... FABES
gopher tortoise ... MUNGOFA
gorge .... GLUT, CHASM,
FLUME, RAVINE
Gorgons, one of ...... MEDUSA
gorse ... WHIN, WHUN, FURZE
goshawk genus . ASTUR, BUTEO
gospel ... EVANGEL, EVANGILE
gossamer .... WEB
gossip .... EME
gossip: India .... GUP
Gottfried's sister .... ELSA
gourd fruit .... PEPO
gourd rattle .... MARACA
gourmet .... EPICURE
gout of knee ...... GONAGRA
government .... STATE
b government control .... REGIE
STATISM
governor .... REGENT
governor, Mecca
SHERIF, SHEREEF
governor, Persia ..... SATRAP
governor, Turkish .... BEY
GOWN .... see GARMENT
grace .... ADORN
Graces' mother .... AEGLE
Graces, The . AGLAIA, THALIA
graceful .... GAINLY
grackle .... DAW, MINA,
MYNA, MYNAH
grade .... RANK, RATE,
SORT, STEP
gradient .... SLOPE
Graf —, ship .... SPEE
graft .... CION, SCION
grafted: Her. .... ENTE
Grail, Holy, finder of .... BORS
grain .... OAT, RYE, SEED,
WALE, SPELT, MILLET
grain beetle .... CADELLE
grain, chaff of .... BRAN
grain, coarse .... SAMP
grain given Romans . ANNONA
grain, sorghum, Ind., .. DARI,
DORA, DURR, MILO, CHENA,
DARRA, DARSO, DURRA,
DHURRA, DOURAH, HEGARI

c grain, sorghum, U. S. FETERITA
grain, stalks of ...... HAULM
grain to grind .... GRIST
gram molecule .... MOL
grammatically, describe . PARSE
grampus .... ORC
granary, India
GOLA, GUNJ, GUNGE
grandparental .... AVAL
grandson, Adam's, Eve's. . ENOS
grant .... CEDE, MISE, REMISE
grant, India, Hindu .... ENAM
grant of rights
PATENT, CHARTER
granular snow .... FIRN, NEVE
grape .... UVA, MUSCAT,
CATAWBA, CONCORD
grape conserve .... UVATE
grape disease .... ESCA
grape genus .... VITIS
grape jelly .... SAPA
grape juice DIBS, MUST, STUM
grape juice sirup .... SAPA
grape-like .. UVA, UVAL, UVIC
grape-like fruit .... UVA
grape refuse .... MARC
grape, white .... MALAGA
grapefruit .. POMELO, PUMELO
graphite .... KISH
grasp .... SEIZE
d grass .... POA, REED, DARNEL
grass, Andes .... ICHU
grass, blue .... POA
grass, coarse .... REED, SEDGE
grass genus ...... AIRA, COIX,
AVENA, STIPA
grass, kind of .... RIE
grass, marsh .... REED
SEDGE, FESCUE
grass, N. Afr. .... ALFA
grass, pasture .... GRAMA
grass rope: Sp. .... SOGA
grass, rope-making
MUNG, MUNJ
grass, sour .... SORREL
grass stem .... CULM
grass tuft .... HASSOCK
grass, yard, wire .... POA
grasshopper .... GRIG
grassland
SAVANNA, SAVANNAH
grassland, S. Afr. ..... VELDT
grasslands, Western ... RANGE
grate ...... JAR, RASP, GRIDE
gratify . SATE, ARRIDE, PLEASE
grating . GRID, GRILL, GRILLE
gratuitous .... FREE
gratuity .... FEE, TIP
gratuity, customer ..... PILON
grave .... SOBER

a gravestone, Gr. & Rom. **STELA, STELE, STELAE, STELAÍ**
graving tool .... **STYLET**
Gray, botanist .... **ASA**
gray .... **OLD, HOAR, ASHEN, SLATE**
gray kingbird .... **PIPIRI**
gray, mole .... **TAUPE**
gray parrot .... **JAKO**
gray plaid, gray shawl .. **MAUD**
grayish-brown ... **DUN, TAUPE**
graze .... **AGIST, BROWSE**
grease ... **OIL, LARD, AXUNGE**
great barracuda ..... **PICUDA**
Great Barrier Island, N. Z. **OTEA**
"Great Emancipator" .... **ABE**
great: Gypsy .... **BARO**
greater .... **MORE, MAJOR**
Greece, ancient name . **HELLAS**
Greece, modern .... **ELLAS**
greedy .... **AVID**
Greek Letters, Numbers:
Greek A, One .... **ALPHA**
Greek B, Two .... **BETA**
Greek D, Four .... **DELTA**
Greek E, Eight .... **ETA**
Greek I, Ten .... **IOTA**
Greek M, Forty .... **MU**
b Greek N, Fifty .... **NU**
Greek O, 800 .... **OMEGA**
Greek P, Eighty .... **PI**
Greek R, 100 .... **RHO**
Greek T, 300 .... **TAU**
Greek Z, Seven .... **ZETA**
Greek 90 .... **KOPPA**
Greek 900 .... **SAMPI**
Gr. ancient .... **ATTIC**
Gr. assembly .... **AGORA**
Gr. athletic contest ..... **AGON**
Gr. authors .... **ZENO, AESOP, HOMER, PLATO, TIMON, HESIOD, PINDAR, SAPPHO, STRABO, THALES, PLU-TARCH**
Gr. city, ancient **ELIS, SPARTA**
Gr. city, word for ...... **POLIS**
Gr. colony, ancient .... **IONIA**
Gr. column ..... **DORIC, IONIC**
Gr. commonalty ...... **DEMOS**
Gr. community .... **DEME**
Gr. dialect ..... **EOLIC, AEOLIC**
Gr. district, ancient ... **ATTICA**
Gr. drama .... **MIME**
Gr. festival city .... **NEMEA**
Gr. galley **TRIREME, UNIREME**
Gr. garment .... **CHITON**
Gr. ghost .... **KER**
GREEK GODS, GODDESSES . see SPECIAL SECTION and see GODS, GODDESSES
Gr. hero ...... **AJAX, JASON**

c Gr. historian .... **CTESIAS**
Gr. January .... **GAMELION**
Gr. legendary hero ...... **IDAS**
Gr. market place ..... **AGORA**
Gr. meeting place of voters **PNYX**
Gr. musical term .. **MESE, NETE**
Gr. myth flier .... **ICARUS**
Gr. native .... **CRETAN**
Gr. patriarch .... **ARIUS**
Gr. philosopher **PLATO, THALES**
Gr. poet ..... **ARION, HOMER, PINDAR**
Gr. poetess ... **SAPHO, SAPPHO**
Gr. poetry, simple ..... **DORIC**
Gr. priest .... **MYST**
Gr. princess .... **IRENE**
Gr. province .... **NOME**
Gr. resistance group ..... **EDES**
Gr. rose .... **CAMPION**
Gr. sculptor .... **PHIDIAS**
Gr. shield .... **PELTA**
Gr. slave .... **PENEST**
Gr. statesman ..... **ARISTIDES**
Gr. temple .... **NAOS**
Gr. theologian .... **ARIUS**
Gr. township-commune .. **DEME**
Gr. underground .... **ELAS**
Gr. vase .... **PELIKE**
d Gr. weight, old .. **MNA, MINA**
green ..... **NILE, VERD, VERT, OLIVE, RESEDA**
green chalcedony ..... **JASPER**
green cheese .... **SAPSAGO**
green chrysolite ..... **PERIDOT**
green copper arsenate . **ERINITE**
green fly .... **APHID**
green: Her. .... **VERT**
Green Mountain hero ... **ALLEN**
green parrot: P. I. .... **CAGIT**
green stone ... **JADE, PERIDOT**
greenish yellow **OLIVE, RESEDA**
Greenland Eskimo .... **ITA**
Greenland geol. div. .... **KOME**
Greenland settlement, town, base .... **ETAH**
Greenland's colonizer ... **ERIC**
greeting .. **AVE, HAIL, SALUTE**
gridiron .... **GRILL**
grief .... **DOLOR, DOLOUR**
griffon genus .... **GYPS**
grimalkin .... **CAT**
grinding .... **MOLAR**
grindstone, Indian ..... **MANO**
grit .... **SAND**
grivet .... **WAAG**
grivet monkey .... **TOTA**
grommet, naut. ...... **BECKET**
groom, India . **SAIS, SICE, SYCE**
groove .... **RUT, SCARF**

a

groove, pilaster **STRIA, STRIAE**
grooved ..... **LIRATE, STRIATE**
grope .... **FEEL**
gross .... **CRASS**
ground grain .... **MEAL**
ground wheat-husk ..... **BRAN**
groundhog .... **MARMOT**
group .... **BAND, BODY,
CREW, TEAM**
group, animal ..... **NID, NYE,
HERD, NIDE, COVEY,
DROVE, CLUTCH**
grouper .... **MERO**
grouse .... **PTARMIGAN**
grouse, red: Scot. . **MUIRFOWL**
grove, small-tree ..... **COPSE**
grow .... **WAX, RAISE**
grow together ...... **ACCRETE**
growing out .... **ENATE**
growl .... **YAR, GNAR,
YARR, SNARL**
growth, skin .... **WEN**
grub .... **LARVA**
grudge .... **SPITE**
gruel, maize .... **ATOLE**
gruesome .. **GRISLY, MACABRE**
guarantees .... **SURETIES**

b

guard .... **SENTRY**
guard, as door .... **TILE**
guardhouse .... **BRIG**
guardian, alert
ARGUS, CERBERUS
Guatemala fruit .... **ANAY**
guava .... **ARACA**
Gudrun's husband
ATLI, SIGURD
Guenon monkey .... **MONA**
guest house .... **INN**
Guiana tree .... **MORA**
guide .... **LEAD, PILOT, STEER**
guiding .... **POLAR**
guiding rule .... **MOTTO**
Guido's note .... **UT, ELA**
guild, merchants' ..... **HANSE**
guillemot ...... **COOT, MURR,
MURRE**
guilty .... **NOCENT**
guinea fowl's young ..... **KEET**
guinea pig .... **CAVY**
gulch: Sp. .... **ARROYO**
GULF, ... also see **GAZETTEER**
gulf, Ionia sea .... **ARTA**
gulf, Medit. .... **TUNIS**

c

gull ..... **MEW, SKUA, TERN,
WAEG, XEMA**
gull, fork-tailed .... **XEMA**
gull genus ...... **LARI, XEMA**
gulls, of, like .... **LARINE**
gullet .... **MAW, CRAW**
gullible person .. **DUPE, GULL**
"Gulliver's Travels," men
YAHOOS
gully: Afr. .... **DONGA**
gulp .... **SWIG**
gum ...... **RESIN, BALATA**
gum arabic
ACACIA, ACACIN, ACACINE
gum, astringent .... **KINO**
gum resin .... **ELEMI, LOBAN,
MYRRH**
gum resin, aromatic ... **MYRRH**
gum, Somaliland ..... **MATTI**
gums .... **ULA**
gumbo ... **OCRA, OKRA, OKRO**
gumbo limbo tree ... **GOMART**
gun .... **GAT**
gun, British .... **STEN**
gun fire, burst of ..... **SALVO**
gun, Ger. .... **BERTHA**

d

gun, kind of .... **BREN**
gun lock catch .... **SEAR**
gun, P. I. .... **BARIL**
gun, slang ..... **ROD, HEATER
ROSCOE**
gun: S. Afr. ..... **ROER, ROHR**
gunny cloth .... **TAT**
gusto .... **ZEST**
gutta mixture .... **SOH**
gutta, Sumatra .... **SIAK**
guy-rope .. **STAT, STAY, VANG**
gym feat .... **KIP**
gymnast .... **TURNER**
gypsum, kind of . **YESO, GESSO,
YESSO, SELENITE**
gypsy .... **ROM, CALE, CALO,
ROAMER, ROMANY**
gypsy boy .... **ROM**
gypsy gentleman .... **RYE**
gypsy girl .... **CHAI**
gypsy husband .... **ROM**
gypsy lady .... **RANI**
gypsy married woman .. **ROMI**
gypsy: Sp. .... **GITANO**
gypsy tent, camp .... **TAN**
gypsy village .... **GAV**
gypsy word .... **LAY**
gypsy word for paper, book .**LIL**

H

H .... AITCH
habit .... RUT, WONT, USAGE
habitat plant form ..... ECAD
habitation .... ABODE
habituate ..... ENURE, INURE
habituated .... USED
hackney coach, Fr. ..... FIACRE
hackneyed .... STALE, TRITE
Hades ... DIS, ORCUS, PLUTO,
           SHEOL, TARTARUS
Hades: Old Eng. .... ADES
Hades, place before .. EREBUS
Hades river
      STYX, LETHE, ACHERON
hag .... CRONE
haggard .... DRAWN
Haggard, H. Rider, novel .. SHE
hail .... AVE, GREET
hail: naut. .... AVAST
hair, arrange .... COIF
hair, caterpillar .... SETA
hair coat .... MELOTE

hair-do, old .... TETE
hair dressing .... POMADE
hair, false . RAT, WIG, TOUPEE
hair, head of .... CRINE
hair, knot of .. BUN, CHIGNON
hair, lock of .... CURL, TRESS
hair net .... SNOOD
hair, remove .... EPILATE
hair, rigid .... SETA
hair, rough, matted .... SHAG
hair shirt .... CILICE
hair, standing .... ROACH
hair unguent .... POMADE
hairless: Sp. Am. ...... PELON
hairlike process
          CILIA, CILIUM
hairy . PILAR, COMOSE, PILOSE
Haiti bandit .... CACO
Halcyone's husband .... CEYX
half .... MOIETY
half-boot .... PAC
half-breed ... MESTEE, MUSTEE
half-caste .... METIS
half-moon figure .... LUNE
half-way .... MID
halfway house .... INN
halfpenny: Brit. .... MAG
hall: Ger. .... AULA, SAAL
hallow .... BLESS
halo .... NIMB, CORONA,
    NIMBUS, AUREOLA, AUREOLE
halt .... LAME, STOP
halting place, troops' . ETAPE
Hamilton's party .... FEDERAL

Hamite .... SOMAL, BERBER,
                     SOMALI
Hamitic language AGAO, AGAU
hamlet ... BURG, DORP, TOWN
Hamlet's castle .... ELSINORE
hammer .... KEVEL
hammer head part ...... PEEN
hammer, heavy .... MAUL
hammer, large .... SLEDGE
hammer, lead .... MADGE
hammer, tilt .... OLIVER
hamper ..... CRAMP, FETTER,
                   TRAMMEL
Ham's son .... CUSH
hand .... PUD, NEAF, MANUS
hand, pert. to .... CHIRAL
hand, whist .... TENACE
handbill .... LEAF
handcuff .... MANACLE
handle .... EAR, LUG, PAW,
           ANSA, HILT, KNOB,
           HELVE, TREAT
handle, bench plane .... TOTE
handle, having ...... ANSATE
handle roughly ... PAW, MAUL
handle, scythe .... SNATH,
         SNEAD, SNEED, SNATHE

handstone for grinding . MANO
handwriting .... SCRIPT
handwriting on the wall . MENE,
     MENE, TEKEL, UPHARSIN
hang .... DRAPE, DROOP,
           HOVER, IMPEND
hank of twine .... RAN
Hannibal's defeat ...... ZAMA
Hannibal's victory .. CANNAE
happen ...... OCCUR, BEFALL,
           BETIDE, CHANCE
happening .... EVENT
happiness god, Jap.
           EBISU, HOTEI
harangue .... ORATE,
           TIRADE, DIATRIBE
Haran's son .... LOT
harass .... NAG, BESET
harbinger .... HERALD
harbor .... BAY, COVE,
           PORT, HAVEN
hard cash .... SPECIE
harden .... GEL, SET
     ENURE, INURE, INDURATE
hardship .... TRIAL
hardtack .... PANTILE
hardwood .... ASH, OAK
Hardy novel heroine ..... TESS
hare: dialect .... WAT

73

a
hare, genus .... LEPUS
hare, young, 1 year .. LEVERET
harem ... ZENANA, SERAGLIO
harem room .... ODA
harlot of Jericho, Bibl. . RAHAB
harm .BANE, DAMAGE, INJURE
harm: old Eng. .... DERE
harm: poetic .... BALE
harmful .... NOCENT
harmonize .... ATTUNE
harmony .. UNISON, CONCORD
harp, ancient .... TRIGON
Harp constellation ...... LYRA
harp guitar key .... DITAL
harp, kind of .... EOLIC
harp, Nubian .... NANGA
harpy, Gr. myth .... AELLO
harquebus projection .... CROC
harrow .... DRAG
harsh to taste .... ACERB
hartebeeste ..... ASSE, TORA,
    CAAMA, KAAMA
harvest .... REAP
harvest festival, Rom. . OPALIA
harvest goddess .... OPS
harvest, India ... RABI, RABBI
has not: Old Eng. .... NAS
hashish .... BHANG
hasty pudding .... SEPON
HAT .... see HEADGEAR

b
hat: Anglo-Ir. ...... CAUBEEN
hat plant .... SOLA
hat, straw .. MILAN, PANAMA
hatchet, archeol. ...... HACHE
hatchet, stone .... MOGO
hatred .. ODIUM, AVERSION
hatred: Buddhism ...... DOSA
hatter's mallet .... BEATER
haul tight, naut. .. BOUSE, TRICE
haunt, low .. DEN, DIVE, NEST
hautboy .... OBOE
haven .... LEE
having buttery account:
    Oxford .... BATTEL
having holes, as cheese .. EYEY
having true luster when uncut
    NAIF
haw!: P.I. .... MANO
haw, as cattle .... HOI
Hawaiian bird .. IO, O-O, IIWI
Hawaiian bird, extinct . MAMO
Hawaiian bird, red-tailed KOAE
Hawaiian blueberry ... OHELO
Hawaiian chant .... MELE
Hawaiian cloth .. TAPA, KAPA
Hawaiian cudweed ... ENAENA
Hawaiian dance .... HULA
Hawaiian farewell, greeting
    ALOHA
Hawaiian feather cloak . MAMO
Hawaiian fern .... HEII

c
Hawaiian floral emblem LEHUA
Hawaiian food .... POI
Hawaiian food-game fish .ULUA
Hawaiian garland .... LEI
Hawaiian god .... KANE
Hawaiian goddess, fire .. PELE
Hawaiian goose .... NENE
Hawaiian gooseberry .... POHA
Hawaiian governor, 1st . DOLE
Hawaiian grass .... HILO
Hawaiian hawk .... IO
Hawaiian herb .... HOLA
Hawaiian loincloth .... MALO
Hawaiian musical instrument
    PUA
Hawaiian porch .... LANAI
Hawaiian president, 1st .. DOLE
Hawaiian royal chief ... ALII
Hawaiian shrub .... AKIA
Hawaiian staple .... POI
Hawaiian starch .... APII
Hawaiian timber tree ... OHIA
Hawaiian tree
    KOA, AULU, ALANI, ILIAHI
Hawaiian tree, dark .... AALII
Hawaiian tree fern ..... PULU
Hawaiian vine .... IE
Hawaiian volcano goddess.PELE
Hawaiian windstorm .... KONA
hawk .... KITE

d
hawk, falconry .... BATER
hawk, fish .... OSPREY
hawk genus .... BUTEO
hawk-head god, Egypt . HORUS
hawk, India .... SHIKRA
hawk-like bird .... KITE
hawk, Scot. .... ALLAN
hawk, young ..... BRANCHER
hawks .... IOS
hawk's cage .... MEW
hawk's leash .... LUNE
hawthorn .... MAY
hawthorn berry .... HAW
hay, spread to dry .... TED
haystack .... RICK
hazard .... DARE, RISK, PERIL
hazardous .... CHANCY
haze: Old Eng. .... HASE
hazelnut .... FILBERT
hazy, make .. DIM, BEDIM
"he remains": Lat. ... MANET
head ..... NOB, LEAD, PATE,
    POLL, TETE, CAPUT, CHIEF,
    CAPITA, LEADER, NODDLE,
    NOODLE
head covering .... CAP, HAT,
    TAM, HOOD, VEIL, BERET
head covering, fleecy .. NUBIA
head, crown of .... PATE
head, having round ... RETUSE
head, membrane covering CAUL

a head, Moslem .... **RAIS, REIS**
head of Benjamin's clan .. **IRI**
head, shaved .... **TONSURE**
head: slang .... **NOGGIN**
head wrap .... **NUBIA, SHAWL**
headband, Gr. .... **TAENIA**
HEADDRESS
        see also HEADGEAR
headdress, bishop's
        MITER, MITRE
headgear, brimless ..... **TOQUE**
headgear, clerical
        BERETTA, BIRETTA
headgear, dervish .... **TAJ**
headgear, kind of ... **PANAMA**
headgear, military .... **SHAKO**
headgear, Moslem .. **TARBUSH,**
   TARBOOCH, TARBOOSH,
       TARBOUCHE
headgear, poetic .... **TIAR**
headgear, priest's
        BERETTA, BIRETTA
headgear, tropics
     TOPI, TERAI, TOPEE
headgear, Turk. .... **FEZ**
headland .. **RAS, CAPE, NASE,**
        NESS, NOZE
headless: Her. .... **ETETE**
headstrong .... **RASH**
healing goddess .... **EIR**
health, in good .... **FIT**
b health-drinking word
      SALUD, PROSIT
health resort .... **SPA**
heap ...... **PILE, RAFF, RAFT**
hear ye! .... **OYES, OYEZ**
hearing: law .... **OYER**
hearken .. **HEAR, HEED, LIST,**
     ATTEND, LISTEN
heart .... **COR, CORE**
heart auricle . **ATRIA, ATRIUM**
heart contraction .... **SYSTOLE**
heart, immortal, Egyp. .... **AB**
heart trouble .... **ANGINA**
heartleaf .... **MEDIC**
heartless ... **CRUEL, SARDONIC**
heat .... **WARM, CALOR**
heated to whiteness . **CANDENT**
heath .... **MOOR**
heath genus .... **ERICA**
heathen .... **PAGAN**
heathen god .... **IDOL**
heather .... **LING, ERICA**
heating apparatus, vessel. **ETNA**
heave upward .... **SCEND**
heaven .. **SION, ZION, URANO**
heaven, eagle-borne flier to
        ETANA
heaven personified: Babyl.. **ANU**
heavens, pert. to .... **URANIC**
heavenly .... **EDENIC**

c heavenly being .... **ANGEL**
    SERAPH, SERAPHIM
heavenly Jerusalem **SION, ZION**
heavy blow .... **ONER**
HEBREW see also JEWISH
        and BIBLICAL
Hebr. Bible books .... **NEBIIM**
Hebr. Bible pronunciation aid
   GRI, KRI, KERE, KERI,
   QERE, QERI, QUERI
Hebr. drum .... **TOPH**
Hebr. dry measure .. **CAB, KAB**
Hebr. lyre .... **ASOR**
Hebr. measure .... **KOR, EPHA,**
     OMER, EPHAH
Hebr. precept .... **TORA**
HEBREW PROPHETS . see
  SPECIAL SECTION, Page 196
Hebr. proselyte .... **GER**
Hebr. reclaimer .... **GOEL**
Hebr. teacher ...... **RAB, REB**
Hebr. universe .... **OLAM**
Hebrews' ancestor, legend
        EBER
Hector's mother ..... **HECUBA**
hedge plant .... **PRIVET**
hedgerow: Eng. .... **REW**
heed .... **HEAR, MIND,**
     OBEY, RECK
heel .... **CAD, CALX**
d height .... **STATURE**
heir .... **SON, SCION,**
   HERITOR, LEGATEE
held, able to be .... **TENABLE**
Helen: It. .... **ELENA**
Helen of Troy's mother . **LEDA**
Helen's lover .... **PARIS**
helical .... **SPIRAL**
Helios .... **SUN**
hell .... **HADES, SHEOL**
Hellespont swimmer . **LEANDER**
helm position .... **ALEE**
helmet, light .... **SALLET**
helmet, medieval
    ARMET, HEAUME
helmet, Rom. .... **GALEA**
helmet-shaped ..... **GALEATE**
helmet-shaped part ... **GALEA**
helmsman .... **PILOT**
Heloise's husband ... **ABELARD**
help .... **AID, ABET, BACK, TIDE,**
   ASSIST, SUCCOR, SUCCOUR
helper .... **AIDE**
Helvetic .... **SWISS**
hem in .... **BESET**
hemp .... **TOW, RINE, RAMIE**
hemp, Afr. .... **IFE**
hemp, India ..... **KEF, BANG,**
   KEEF, KEIF, KIEF, BHANG,
   DAGGA, RAMIE
hemp, Manila .... **ABACA**

a

hemp narcotic ...... **CHARAS**
hemp shrub, India
PUA, POOA, POOAH
hen .... **LAYER**
hen harrier, Europ. .... **FALLER**
hence .... **SO, OFF, AWAY**
Hengist's brother ..... **HORSA**
Henry IV birthplace ...... **PAU**
"Henry IV" character ... **PETO**
"Henry V" knave ...... **NYM**
"Henry VI" character ... **IDEN**
hep .... **ONTO**
her: obs. .... **HIR**
Hera's son .... **ARES**
herald .... **USHER**
HERALDIC TERMS . see also
SPECIAL SECTION, Page 194
herald's coat .... **TABARD**
heraldic bearing **ORLE, FILLET**
heraldic cross .... **PATEE**
heraldic wreath .... **ORLE**
herb ...... **RUE, LEEK, MINT,**
MOLY, WORT, ANISE, TANSY,
YARROW, OREGANO
herb, aromatic **BASIL, DITTANY**
herb, bitter .... **RUE, ALOE**
herb, carrot family .... **ANISE**
herb eve .... **IVA**
herb, fabulous **MOLY, PANACE**
herb, forage .... **SULLA**

b

herb genus .... **ABFA**
GEUM, RUTA, ALETRIS
herb, medicinal .. **ALOE, SENNA**
herb of grace .... **RUE**
herb, snake-charm ... **MUNGO**
herb with aromatic root .**NONDO**
herb, wooly .... **POLY**
Hercules' captive .... **IOLE**
Hercules, monster slain by
HYDRA
Hercules' mother .. **ALCMENE**
herd .... **DROVE**
herd of horses .... **CAVIYA**
herd of whales .... **GAM, POD**
herdsman, Swiss .... **SENN**
hereditary right .... **UDAL**
hereditary factor .. **GEN, GENE**
heretic, 4th cent.
ARIAN, ARIUS
heretofore .... **ERENOW**
Hermes' mother .... **MAIA**
Hermes' son .... **PAN**
hermit . **EREMITE, ANCHORITE**
hero, legendary .... **PALADIN**
Hero's love .... **LEANDER**
heroic .... **EPIC, EPICAL**
heroic poem **EPIC, EPOS, WORK**
heroic song .... **EDDA**
heron .... **EGRET**
heron brood, flock .... **SEDGE**
heron, kind of ...... **BITTERN**

c

herring .... **ALEC, BRIT, SILL**
herring, grayback ..... **CISCO**
herring keg .... **CADE**
herring small Eur. ...... **SPRAT**
hesitate
DEMUR, FALTER, TEETER
hesitation syllable .... **ER, UM**
Hesperides, one of .... **AEGLE**
Heyward, Du Bose, heroine.**BESS**
Hezekiah's mother ...... **ABI**
hiatus .... **GAP, LACUNA**
hickory tree ...... **SHELLBARK**
hidden ..... **INNER, ARCANE,**
COVERT, LATENT
hide .... **VEIL, CACHE**
hide of beast ..... **FELL, SKIN**
hide, thongs of .... **RIEM**
hide, undressed .... **KIP**
hides, Russian leather ... **JUFTI**
hiding in .... **PERDU**
high in pitch: mus. ...... **ALT**
high on scale .... **ELA**
high priest ...... **ELI, AARON,**
ANNAS
highest note .... **ELA**
highest point .. **APEX, ZENITH**
highway .... **ITER, PIKE**
highway, Alaska-Canada **ALCAN**
highwayman .. **PAD, LADRONE**
hike .... **TRAMP**

d

hill .... **TOR**
hill, broad .... **LOMA, LOMITA**
hill dweller, Ceylon .... **TODA**
hill dweller, India ..... **DOGRA**
hill, flat-topped .... **MESA**
hill fort: Ir. .... **RATH**
hill, isolated .... **BUTTE**
hill, pointed .... **TOR**
hill, Rome
CAELIAN, PALATINE
hill, S. Afr. ...... **KOP, BULT**
hill: Turk. .... **DAGH**
hillock .... **TUMP**
hillside: Scot. .... **BRAE**
hilltop .... **KNAP**
hilt, sword .... **HAFT, HANDLE**
Himalayan animal .... **PANDA**
Himal. broadmouth ..... **RAYA**
Himal. ibex .... **KYL**
Himal. monkshood ...... **ATIS**
Himal. mountain .... **API**
Himal. wild goat . **KRAS, TAHR,**
TAIR, THAR
hind ...... **ROE, BACK, REAR**
hinder by fear .... **DETER**
hindrance .... **BAR, LET**
Hindu age, cycle .... **YUGA**
Hindu ancestor .... **MANU**
Hindu ascetic .... **JOGI,**
YATI, YOGI, FAKIR,
SADHU, FAKEER

a
Hindu bible .... **VEDA**
Hindu charitable gift ... **ENAM**
Hindu cymbal .... **TAL**
Hindu deity .... **DEVA, RAMA,
SIVA, SHIVA**
HINDU DEITY . see also **GOD**
and see SPECIAL SECTION
Hindu divorce law ..... **TALAK**
Hindu female slave ..... **DASI**
Hindu festival .... **HOLI**
Hindu festival, religious . **PUJA**
Hindu gentlemen **BABU, BABOO**
HINDU GODS .... see SPECIAL
SECTION, Page 200, and
also **GOD**
Hindu guitar .... **BINA,
VINA, SITAR**
Hindu holy man .... **SADH**
Hindu laws, giver of ... **MANU**
Hindu legendary hero ... **NALA**
Hindu life energy .... **JIVA**
Hindu, low caste .... **KORI**
Hindu magic .... **MAYA**
Hindu mantra .... **OM**
Hindu mendicant ...... **NAGA**
Hindu monastery ...... **MATH**
Hindu "Olympus" .... **MERU**
Hindu philosophy ...... **YOGA**
Hindu poet .... **TAGORE**
Hindu prince
RAJA, RANA, RAJAH
b
Hindu progenitor, myth **MANU**
Hindu queen .... **RANI, RANEE**
Hindu religious adherent
JAIN, JAINA
Hindu rites .... **ACHARA**
Hindu sacred literature .. **VEDA**
Hindu sacred word .... **OM**
Hindu scripture ...... **AGAMA**
Hindu scriptures, pert. to **VEDIC**
Hindu sect, one of **SEIK, SIKH**
Hindu teacher .... **GURU**
Hindu temple .... **DEUL**
Hindu term of respect **SAHIB**
Hindu title .... **AYA, SRI**
Hindu trader
BANIAN, BANYAN
Hindu unknown god ...... **KA**
Hindu, unorthodox .... **JAINA**
Hindu widow, suicide .. **SUTTEE**
Hindu woman's garment
SARI, SAREE
Hindu word .... **OM**
Hindu writings .... **VEDA**
Hinduism, elixir
AMRITA, AMREETA
Hindustani .... **URDU**
hinge, kind of .... **BUTT**
hint .... **TIP, CLEW, POINTER**
hip .... **COXA, ILIA, ILIAC**
hipbone, of the .... **ILIAC**

c
Hippocrates' birthplace ... **KOS**
Hippodrome .... **ARENA**
hire
LET, RENT, ENGAGE, CHARTER
hired carriage .... **HACK**
hired labor: S. Afr. ..... **TOGT**
history .... **LORE**
hitherto .... **YET**
Hittites ancestor .... **HETH**
hive for bees .... **SKEP**
hives .... **UREDO**
hoard .... **AMASS, STORE**
hoarder .... **MISER**
hoarfrost .... **RIME**
hoarfrost: Eng. .... **RAG**
hoary .... **OLD, GRAY**
hoax .... **RUSE, CANARD**
hobgoblin ..... **PUCK, SPRITE**
hock, horse's ...... **GAMBREL**
hockey ball .... **ORR**
hodgepodge ...... **MESS, OLIO**
hog cholera .... **ROUGET**
hog deer .... **AXIS**
hog, female .... **GILT**
hog plum, W. Ind. **AMRA, JOBO**
hog, wild .... **BOAR, PECCARY**
hog's heart, liver, etc. **HASLET**
Hogan, golfer .... **BEN**
hoist .... **HEAVE**
hold, as in war .... **INTERN**
d
hold back .... **DETER**
hold fast: naut. ...... **BELAY**
holding .... **TENURE**
holding device .. **VISE, TONGS**
hole for molten metal .. **SPRUE**
hole in embankment .... **GIME**
hole in mold .... **GEAT**
hole-in-one .... **ACE**
holidays, Roman ...... **FERIA**
HOLLAND see **NETHERLANDS**
SPECIAL SECTION
hollow .... **DENT, HOWE**
holly .... **HOLM, ILEX**
holly, U. S. .... **ASSI,
YAPON, YUPON, YAUPON**
holm oak .... **ILEX**
"Holy Hill," Gr. ...... **ATHOS**
Holy Land city .... **DAN**
holy orders, give .... **ORDAIN**
holy water font .... **STOUP**
homage .... **HONOR**
home .... **ABODE**
home of gods, Norse .. **ASGARD**
"Home Sweet Home" author
PAYNE
homeopath school-founder
HERING
Homer's epic .... **ODYSSEY**
hominy, Indian coarse .. **SAMP**
honey .... **MEL**
honey-badger .... **RATEL**

a honey buzzard .... **PERN**
honey drink .. **MEAD, MORAT**
honey eater bird
    IAO, MOHO, MANUAO
honeybee .... **DESERET**
honeycomb, like a ... **FAVOSE**
honor .... **EXALT, REVERE**
honorarium .... **TIP**
honorary commission .. **BREVET**
Honshu bay .... **ISE**
Honshu port .... **KOBE**
hooded garment ...... **PARKA**
hoodoo .... **JINX, JYNX**
hoof .... **UNGUES, UNGUIS**
hook, bent into ..... **HAMATE**
hook, double curve .... **ESS**
hook, engine .... **GAB**
hook for pot .... **CLEEK**
hook money .... **LARI, LARIN**
hooks .... **HAMI**
hookah .... **NARGILE**
hooked .... **HAMUS,**
  HAMATE, HAMOSE, FALCATE
Hoover Dam lake ...... **MEAD**
hop-picker's basket ...... **BIN**
hope goddess, Rom. ..... **SPES**
hop plant .... **LUPULUS**
hopscotch stone ...... **PEEVER**
Horae, one of .... **DIKE,**
    EIRENE, EUNOMIA
Horeb .... **SINAI**
b horizontal stripe .... **BAR**
horizontal timber ..... **LINTEL**
horn .... **CORNU**
horn, crescent-moon ..... **CUSP**
horn, Hebr. **SHOFAR, SHOPHAR**
horn quicksilver ..... **CALOMEL**
horn-shaped structure .. **CORNU**
horn sounded for kill .. **MORT**
horn tissue, bit of ..... **SCUR**
horneblende .... **EDENITE**
hornless, Eng. dial. ...... **NOT**
hornless stag .... **POLLARD**
hors d'oeuvre .... **CANAPE**
horse .. **BAY, COB, NAG, ARAB,**
  MARE, MERE, ROAN,
  MOUNT, STEED, EQUINE,
  JENNET
horse, Austral. .... **WALER**
horse, Barbary native ... **BARB**
horse blanket .... **MANTA**
horse breed .... **MORGAN**
horse, brown
    BAY, ROAN, SORREL
horse color **BAY, ROAN, SORREL**
horse dealer, Eng. .... **COPER**
horse, disease of .... **SPAVIN**
horse, draft .... **SHIRE**
horse genus .... **EQUUS**
horse: gypsy .. **GRI, GRY, GRAS**
horse-mackerel .... **SCAD**

c horse-man, myth ... **CENTAUR**
horse, piebald .... **PINTO**
horse, race .... **PACER**
horse-radish, fruit of ... **BEN**
horse, saddle .... **MOUNT**
horse, small .... **GENET,**
  GENNET, JENNET, GENETTE
horse, Sp. Am. ..... **CABALLO**
horse, swift .. **ARAB, COURSER**
horse, talking, Gr. .... **ARION**
horse, war .... **CHARGER**
horse, white-flecked ... **ROAN**
horse, wild Asiatic ... **TARPAN**
horse, young ..... **COLT, FOAL**
horses, goddess of ..... **EPONA**
horse's sideways tread ... **VOLT**
horsehair .... **SETON**
horsemanship, art of **MANEGE**
horseshoe gripper ..... **CALK**
horseshoeing stall
    TRAVE, TREVE
Horus' mother .... **ISIS**
Hosea's wife .... **GOMER**
host .... **ARMY, HORDE**
hostelry .... **INN**
hot air chamber .... **OVEN**
hot iron to sear ..... **CAUTER**
hot spring, eruptive .. **GEYSER**
Hottentot .... **NAMA**
hourly .... **HORAL**
d house **ROOF, VILLA, COTTAGE**
house, like a .... **DOMAL**
house, mud, Afr. ..... **TEMBE**
house urn: Rom. ... **CAPANNA**
housefly genus .... **MUSCA**
housefly genus, lesser **FANNIA**
household **MENAGE, MAINPOST**
household god .... **LAR, LARES**
howl .... **ULULATE**
howling monkey **MONO, ARABA**
hub .. **NAVE, BOSTON, CENTER**
hubbub .. **ADO, STIR, TUMULT**
hue .... **COLOR, TINGE**
huge .... **VAST, ENORM**
Huguenot leader ..... **ADRETS**
hull .... **POD, HUSK**
humble .... **ABASE**
hummingbird
  AVA, TOPAZ, COLIBRI
humorist .... **WIT**
humpback salmon
    HADDO, HOLIA
Humphreys, Mrs. (pseudo.)
    RITA
hundred .... **CENTUM**
hundredweight ...... **CENTAL**
Hungarian dog .... **PULI**
Hungarian hero .... **NAGY**
Hungarian king .... **BELA**
Hungarian people ... **MAGYAR**
Hungarian pianist ... **SANDOR**

Hungarian playwright **MOLNAR**
Hungarian violinist .... **AUER**
Huns, king of
ATLI, ETZEL, ATTILA
hunt, Ind. .... **SHIKAR**
hunter ...... **ORION, NIMROD**
hunter, India .... **SHIKARI**
hunting cry .. **HO, YOI, TOHO,
HALLOO, YOICKS, TALLY-
HO**
hunting hat .... **TERAI**
hunting hound .... **ALAN**
huntress .... **ATALANTA**
huntsman .... **JAGER**
HUNTSMAN'S CRY see HUNT-
ING CRY
hup: army .... **ONE**
hurdy-gurdy ..... **LIRA, ROTA**
hurry .... **HIE, HASTEN**
hurt .... **MAR, ACHE, LESION**

hurt: old Eng. .... **DERE**
hurtful .... **MALEFIC**
husband's brother ...... **LEVIR**
hush .... **SH, HSH**
husk, cereal .... **BRAN**
hut, India .... **BARI**
hut, Mex. .... **JACAL**
hydrate, as lime ..... **SLAKE**
hydraulic pump .... **RAM**
hydrocarbon . **TOLAN, ETHANE,
OCTANE, RETENE, TERPENE**
hydrogen compound ... **IMINE**
hydrogen isotope ... **PROTIUM**
hymn .... **ODE**
hymn of praise ..... **ANTHEM**
hypnotic state ...... **TRANCE**
hypothetical force
OD, BIOD, ELOD, ODYL
hypothetical force of ... **ODIC**
hyson .... **TEA**

I

I .... **EGO**
"I have found it" .... **EUREKA**
"I love": Lat. .... **AMO**
Iago's wife ...... **EMILIA**
Iberians .... **IBERI, IBERES**
ibex .... **KYL, TUR, KAIL**
Ibsen character ... **ASE, NORA**
ice block, glacial ...... **SERAC**
ice mass .... **BERG, FLOE**
ice, slushy ...... **SISH, LOLLY**
iced .... **GLACE**
Iceland epic, literature, tales
EDDA
Icelandic narrative ..... **SAGA**
icy .... **GELID**
"id —" (that is) .... **EST**
idea, Plato .... **EIDOS**
ideal .... **UTOPIAN**
ideal republic, imaginary
OCEANA
ideal state .... **UTOPIA**
identical .... **ONE, SAME**
ideology .... **ISM**
idiocy .... **ANOESIA**
idiot .... **AMENT, CRETIN**
idle .... **OTIANT, OTIOSE**
idle, to be ...... **LAZE, LOAF**
idol: archaic .... **PAGOD**
idol: philos. .... **EIDOLON**
idolatrous .... **PAGAN**
ids, pert. to .... **IDIC**
Idumaea .... **EDOM**
if ever .... **ONCE**
if not .... **ELSE**
ignoble .... **BASE**

ignominy .... **SHAME**
ignorance, Hindu philos. **TAMAS**
ignorant .. **STUPID, UNAWARE**
ignore .... **ELIDE**
Igorot's neighbor tribesman **ATA**
ill .... **EVIL**
ill-will .... **SPITE, RANCOR**
illumination unit .... **LUX**
illusion .... **CHIMERA**
illusory riches .... **MINE**
image .... **IDOL,
IDOLON, IDOLUM, EIDOLON**
image, pert. to .... **ICONIC**
image, religious .. **ICON, IKON**
imagine: arch. .... **WIS**
imbecile .... **AMENT,
ANILE, CRETIN**
imbibe .... **SIP, GULP, DRINK**
imitate ... **APE, MIME, MIMIC**
imitation .... **MIMESIS**
imitation gems .... **PASTE**
immature seed .... **OVULE**
immature: zool. ..... **NEANIC**
immeasurable .... **BOUNDLESS**
immediately ..... **NOW, ANON**
immense .... **VAST**
immerse .. **DIP, DUNK, DOUSE**
immigrant, Greek ..... **METIC**
immunizing substance
SERUM, HAPTEN, HAPTENE
imou pine .... **RIMU**
impair .. **MAR, DAMAGE, SPOIL**
impart .... **GIVE, LEND**
impartial .... **EVEN**
impede ...... **ESTOP, HAMPER**
impel .... **URGE**

a
impertinent ..... **PERT, SAUCY**
IMPLEMENT ... see also TOOL
implement, pounding .. **PESTLE**
implement to skid logs .. **TODE**
implied .... **TACIT**
import .... **SENSE**
important, critically ... **VITAL**
importune .... **URGE**
impose .... **LAY**
impost .... **TAX**
imposture .... **SHAM**
impoverish .... **IMPOOR**
impressionist painter .. **DEGAS**
        MANET, MONET, RENOIR
imprison .... **IMMURE**
improve .... **AMEND**
improvise music .... **VAMP**
impudence .... **LIP,**
        BRASS, CHEEK, NERVE
impure metal product .. **MATTE**
in addition .. **TOO, ALSO, YET**
in agreement .... **UNITED**
in disagreement .... **OUT**
in half, in — .... **TWO**
"in medias —" .... **RES**
in name only ...... **NOMINAL**
in same place .... **IBID**
in so far as .... **QUA**
in the know .... **AWARE**
in the matter of .... **INRE**
in the past .... **OVER**
b
in the very near future.. **ANON**
in unison .... **ONE**
in very truth .... **AMEN**
inability to hear ..... **ASONIA**
inactive .... **INERT**
inadequate .... **SCANT**
inborn .... **NATIVE**
incarnation, Hindu .... **RAMA,**
        AVATAR
incense ingredient
        GUM, SPICE, STACTE
incense receptacle, Rom.**ACERRA**
incense, Somali ...... **MATTI**
incentive .... **GOAD, MOTIVE**
incessantly .... **EVER**
inch, .001 of .... **MIL**
incidentally .... **OBITER**
incinerate .... **CREMATE**
incite ..... **EGG, PROD, URGE,**
        IMPEL, SET ON, SUBORN
inciter .... **EGGER**
inclination .... **BENT**
incline .. **TEND, SLOPE, TREND**
inclined .... **APT, PRONE**
inclined way .... **RAMP**
income, annual, Fr. .... **RENTE**
incompletely .... **SEMI**
inconsiderable ..... **NOMINAL**
increase .... **WAX, RISE**
incrustation .... **SCAB**

c
incursion, predatory .... **RAID**
indeed: Ir. ...... **ARU, AROO**
indentation
    CRENA, CRENAE, CRENELET
index mark .... **FIST**
INDIA, INDIAN ... see also
        SPECIAL SECTION and see
        also HINDU
India farmer .... **MEO**
India minstrel .... **BHAT**
India native chief .... **SIRDAR**
India native servant ... **MATY**
India: poet. .... **IND**
India, swamp belt of .. **TERAI**
INDIAN .. see also page 192
Indian .... **SAC**
INDIAN, ALGONQUIN .... see
        page 192
Indian, Arawak ...... **ARAUA**
Indian, Arikara .... **REE**
Indian, Athapasca ..... **TAKU**
Indian buzzard .... **TESA**
Indian corn .... **MAIZE**
Indian corn: N. Z. ... **KANGA**
Indian elk .... **SAMBAR**
Indian farmer, Fla. .. **CALUSA**
Indian in Chaco .... **TOBA**
Indian mahogany tree .. **TOON**
Indian mulberry **AL, AAL, ACH**
Indian of Jalisco ...... **CORA**
Indian of Keresan ...... **SIA**
Indian of Mex., scattered **CORA**
d
Indian ox .... **ZEBU**
Indian, Panamint .... **KOSO**
INDIAN, PLAINS . see page 193
Indian race .... **JAT**
Indian shell currency
        ULO, UHLLO
INDIAN, SIOUAN see page 193
Indian, S. Peru ..... **CHANCA**
INDIAN TREE.see TREE, INDIA
Indian, warlike ...... **APACHE**
Indian weight ..... **SER, TOLA**
Indian, whaler .... **HOH**
Indian yellow .... **PURI,**
        PIURI, PURREE
indicating succession **ORDINAL**
indict .... **ARRAIGN**
indifferent to pain
        STOIC, STOICAL
indigo plant .... **ANIL**
indistinct, make ...... **BEDIM**
indite .... **PEN, WRITE**
individual .... **ONE, SELF**
Indo-Chin. native **LAO,MRU,TAI**
Indo-Chin. tribe **TAI,LAOS,SHAN**
Indo-Chin. tribes .... **MOI**
Indo-European **ARYA, ARYAN**
Indo-Malayan animal .. **NAPU**
indolent ...... **OTIOSE, SUPINE**
Indonesian ..... **ATA, NESIOT**

a induce .... **LEAD**
Indus tribesman .... **GOR**
ineffectual .... **VAIN**
inelastic .... **LIMP**
inert .... **SUPINE**
infatuation .... **ATE**
infertile moor .... **LANDE**
infinity .... **OLAM**
infirm .... **ANILE, SENILE**
inflamed, be .... **RANKLE**
inflammable liquid .. **ACETONE**
inflammation: med. .. **ANGINA**
inflexible ...... **IRON, RIGID**
inflict .... **DEAL, IMPOSE**
inflorescence **RACEME, SPADIX**
inflorescence, racemose **AMENT**
influence .... **AFFECT**
informer: slang .... **NARK**
infusion .... **TEA**
ingenuous .... **NAIVE**
inhabitant .... **ITE**
inhabitant of a town ..... **CIT**
inheritance .... **ENTAIL**
inheritor .... **LEGATEE**
initiate .. **OPEN, BEGIN, START**
initiate, Gr. .... **EPOPT, EPOPTA**
injure ... **MAR, HARM, MAIM**
injury ..... **LESION, TRAUMA**
inlaid .... **MOSAIC**
inlaid decoration ...... **BUHL**
b inlet .. **ARM, BAY, RIA, FIORD**
inlet: Dutch .... **ZEE**
inlet, Orkneys .... **VOE**
inn .... **KHAN,
HOSTEL, POSADA, HOSPICE**
inn, "Canterbury Tales" **TABARD**
inn, Oriental .... **SERAI**
inn, Turkish .... **IMARET**
inner .... **ENTAL**
inner meaning ... **CORE, HEART**
inner parlor: Scot. ...... **BEN**
innkeeper **PADRONE, BONIFACE**
insect ... **ANT, BEE, BUG, DOR,
FLY, FLEA, GNAT, MITE,
APHID, CADEW, EMESA,
BEETLE, CADDIS, CICADA,
CICALA, MANTIS**
insect, adult .... **IMAGO**
insect body
THORAX, THORACES
insect, immature ...... **PUPA,
LARVA, INSTAR**
insect mature .... **IMAGO**
insect order .... **DIPTERA**
insect, plant sucking .. **APHID**
insect, ruinous **APHID, BORER**
insertion mark .... **CARET**
inset .... **PANEL**
insidious .... **SLY**
insincere talk .... **CANT**
insipid, become .... **PALL**

c insist .... **URGE, PRESS**
inspire .... **IMBUE**
install .... **INSTATE**
instance .... **CASE**
instant .... **MO, TRICE**
instar .. **PUPA, IMAGO, LARVA**
instigate .. **EGG, ABET, INCITE**
instruct ..... **BRIEF, EDUCATE**
INSTRUMENT .. see also MUS-
ICAL INSTRUMENT
instrument, Afr. reed
GORA, GORAH, GOURA
instrument, Chin. ancient **KIN**
instrument, Hebr. ... **TIMBREL**
instrument, India ..... **RUANA**
instrument, Jap. .... **SAMISEN**
instrument, lutelike **BANDORE**
instrument, lyrelike ... **KISSAR**
instrument, math. ..... **SECTOR**
instrument, medieval .. **ROCTA**
instrument, naut.
PELORUS, SEXTANT
instrument, Sp. .... **CASTANET**
instrument, stringed ... **LYRE,
NABLA, REBAB, REBEC,
SAROD, SITAR, VIOLA,
CITHER, CITHARA, CITH-
ERN, CITTERN, GITTERN**
instrument, surveying **TRANSIT**
instrumentality **MEDIA, MEDIUM**
d insulate .... **ISLE**
insult .... **CAG**
insurgent .... **REBEL**
intact .... **WHOLE**
intellect .... **MIND,
NOUS, MAHAT, REASON**
inter .... **BURY, INHUME**
intercharged ..... **PERMUTED**
interdict .... **BAN**
interferometer ...... **ETALON**
interior, ancient temple **CELLA**
interjection for silence .... **TST**
interlace .... **WEAVE**
interlock .... **LINK**
international language **RO, IDO**
inter. money unit .... **BANCOR**
international pact ... **ENTENTE**
interpret .... **REDE**
intersect .... **MEET**
interstice, small
AREOLA, AREOLE
interstices, with .... **AREOLAR**
intervening: law ...... **MESNE**
interweave .. **TWINE, RADDLE**
intimidate **AWE, COW, DAUNT**
intone .... **CHANT**
intoxicant: India ...... **SOMA**
intoxicated .... **SOSH**
intricate .... **DEDAL, DAEDAL,
GORDIAN**

intrigue .... **CABAL**
introduce
    BROACH, INSERT, PRESENT
introducer of jetties for deepen-
   ing .... **EADS**
inundation .... **SPATE**
inveigle ...... **LURE, ENTICE**
inventor, claim of rights **PATENT**
inventor, elevator .... **OTIS**
inventor, sewing machine **HOWE**
inventor, steam engine **WATT**
invest ...... **ENDOW, ENDUE,**
    INDUE, CLOTHE, ORDAIN
invested .... **CLAD**
investigate .... **PROBE**
investigator .... **TRACER**
invite .... **ASK, BID**
involve **ENTAIL, ENTRAMMEL**
Io butterfly .... **KIHO**
iodine source .... **KELP**
ion, negative .... **ANION**
ion, positive .... **CATION**
Ionian city .... **TEOS**
iota .... **JOT, MITE**
Iowa college town ...... **AMES**
ipecac source .... **EVEA**
IRAN .. see also PERSIAN
Iran, former part of .... **ELAM**
Iranian .... **TAT, KURD**
Iranian Turk .... **SART**
irascible .... **TESTY**
irate .... **MAD**
Ireland .... **EIRE, ERIN**
Ireland, old name ..... **IERNE**
Ireland personified .... **IRENA**
iridescent gem .... **OPAL**
iris .... **FLAG**
iris, Florentine, European **ORRIS**
iris, layer of .... **UVEA**
iris, of a layer .... **UVEAL**
iris root .... **ORRIS**
IRISH .. see also IRELAND
Irish .... **ERSE**
Ir. alphabet, early
       OGAM, OGUM
Ir. ancestor **IR, MIL, ITH, MILED**
Ir. assembly .... **DAIL**
Ir. church .... **KIL**
Ir. city, ancient .... **TARA**
Ir. clan, ancient .... **SEPT**
Ir. competitive meet .... **FEIS**
Ir. crowning stone, — Fail **LIA**
Ir. dramatist .... **SYNGE**
Ir. exclamation .... **ARU,**
AROO, ARRA, WHIST, WURRA
Ir. fairies .... **SHEE**
Ir. family .... **CINEL**
Ir. Free State .... **EIRE**
Irish-Gaelic .... **ERSE**
Ir. goddess, battle **BADB, BODB**

IR. GODS' MOTHER see page 200
Ir. kings' home .... **TARA**
Ir. law, tribe .... **CINEL**
Ir. lower house parliament **DAIL**
Ir. nobleman .... **AIRE**
Ir. poet
   AE, COLUM, MOORE, YEATS
Ir. rebel group .... **IRA**
Ir. tribe .... **SIOL**
Ir. writing .... **OGAM, OGHAM**
Irishman .. **AIRE, CELT, MICK**
iron disulfide .... **PYRITE**
iron, pert. to .... **FERRIC**
ironwood ...... **ACLE, COLIMA**
irony .... **SATIRE**
Iroquoian .... **ERIE**
Iroquois demon .... **OTKON**
irrational number ...... **SURD**
irregularity .... **JOG**
irrigation ditch **FLUME, SLUICE**
irritate .... **VEX, GALL, RILE,**
     NETTLE, RANKLE
Isaac's son **EDOM, ESAU, JACOB**
Ishmael .... **PARIAH**
Ishmael, son of ...... **DUMAH**
Ishmael's mother ..... **HAGAR**
isinglass .... **MICA**
Isis, husband of ...... **OSIRIS**
ISLAM .... see MOSLEM
island ... **OE, AIT, CAY, KAY,**
    KEY, EYOT, HOLM, ILOT,
    ISLE, ATOLL, ISLET, ISLOT
ISLAND, AEGEAN .... see
     GAZETTEER
island, Argyll .... **IONA**
island, coral .... **ATOLL**
island, Dodecanese . **COO, KOS,**
    CASO, LERO, SIMI
island, Great Barrier ... **OTEA**
island, Gr. (fine marble) **PAROS**
island, Gr., pert. to ... **CRETAN**
island, inhabiting an . **NESIOTE**
ISLAND, INNER HEBRIDES
   see HEBRIDES GAZETTEER
island, Ionian .... **ZANTE**
island, Micronesia ... **PONAPE**
island near Ireland ..... **ARAN**
island, near Italy ...... **CAPRI**
island off Scotland .... **IONA,**
     ARRAN
island, Riga Gulf ...... **OESEL**
island, river **AIT, EYOT, HOLM**
island, South Seas ...... **ARU,**
  TAITI, TAHITI, OTAHEITE
island, west of Sumatra .. **NIAS**
islands, Gulf of Bothnia **ALAND**
islands, Irish .... **ARAN**
islands, off Timor ...... **LETI**
Isle of Man, pert. to ... **MANX**
islet .... **AIT, CAY, HOLM**
isolate .... **ENISLE**

Israel .... **JACOB**
ISRAEL, KING OF ... see KING
OF ISRAEL
ISRAELITE .. see also HEBREW
and BIBLICAL
ISRAELITE JUDGE ...... see
BIBLICAL JUDGE
ISRAELITE KING .. see KING
OF ISRAEL
Israelite tribe .... **DAN**
Israelites .... **SION, ZION**
issue.**EMIT, EMERGE, EMANATE**
isthmus .... **NECK**
istle fiber .... **PITA, PITO**
it proceeds: music .... **VA**
ITALIAN WORDS: (accent marks
omitted throughout)
arts .... **ARTES**
article .... **LA**
canal (s) **CANALE, CANALI**
chest .... **CASSO**
custom house ..... **DOGANA**
day-breeze .... **ORA**
dear .... **CARA, CARO**
dough .... **PASTA**
drink .... **BEVERE**
enough .... **BASTA**
evening .... **SERA**
enthusiasm .... **ESTRO**
feast .... **FESTINO**
field .... **CAMPO**
food .... **PASTO**
from beginning .... **DACAPO**
gentleman .... **SER**
goodby .... **ADDIO**
gondola cabin ...... **FELZE**
hamlet .... **CASAL, CASALE**
hair .... **PELO**
hand .... **MANO**
harbor .... **PORTO**
harp .... **ARPA**
hatred .... **ODIO**
Helen .... **ELENA**
holiday .... **FESTA, FESTE**
host .... **OSTE**
Italy .... **ITALIA**
judge .... **PODESTA**
lady .... **DONNA, SIGNORA**
lake .... **LAGO**
little .... **POCO**
love .... **AMORE**
lover .... **AMOROSO**
mother .... **MADRE**
mountain peak ...... **CIMA**
nine .... **NOVE**
ninth .... **NONO**

one .... **UNO**
paste .... **PASTA**
peak .... **CIMA**
pronoun .... **MIA**
right .... **DESTRO**
Rome .... **ROMA**
sign .... **SEGNO**
somebody .... **UNO**
street .... **CALLE**
three .... **TRE**
time .... **TEMPO**
tour .... **GIRO**
town ...... **CASAL, CASALE**
you .... **TU**
voice .... **VOCE**
well .... **BENE**
with .... **CON**

Italian actress .... **DUSE**
It., ancient
ITALI, OSCAN, SABINE
It. astronomer ...... **GALILEO**
It. author .... **SILONE**
It. car .... **FIAT**
It. cathedral city .... **MILAN**
It. commune .... **ESTE**
It. composer .... **BOITO,**
GUIDO, VERDI, ROSSINI
It. day breeze .... **ORA**
It. family .... **ESTE,**
CENCI, DORIA, MEDICI
It. family royal name ... **ESTE**
It. gambling game ..... **MORA**
It. gentleman .... **SER**
It. guessing game ..... **MORA**
It. lady ..... **DONA, SIGNORA**
It. millet ...... **BUDA, MOHA**
It. painter .... **RENI,**
LIPPI, VINCI, ANDREA,
CRESPI, GIOTTO
It. poet
DANTE, TASSO, ARIOSTO
It. resort .... **LIDO**
It. rice dish .... **RISOTTO**
It.: Rome .... **ROMA**
It. sculptor .... **LEONI**
It. singer .... **AMATO**
It. title, early .... **SER**
It. university city **BARI, PADUA**
It. violin maker ...... **AMATI**
It. wine .... **ASTI**
Italy .... **ITALIA**
itch .... **PSORA**
itemize .... **LIST**
ivory nut ...... **ANTA, TAGUA**
ivy crowned .... **HEDERATED**
ivy thicket .... **TOD**

J

jack in cribbage .... **NOB**
jack-in-the-pulpit **ARAD, AROID**
jack tree .... **JACA**
jackal, Afr. .... **THOS**
jackal, India .... **KOLA**
jackal, N. Afr. .... **DIEB**
jackdaw .... **DAW**
jackdaw: Scot. .... **KAE**
JACKET .. see also GARMENT
jacket .. **ETON, JUPE, BOLERO**
jacket, armor .... **ACTON**
jacket, Malay .... **BAJU**
Jackson heroine .. **RAMONA**
Jacob's brother .. **EDOM, ESAU**
Jacob's son..**DAN, GAD, ASER,**
                LEVI, ASHER
Jacob's twin brother .... **ESAU**
Jacob's wife .. **LEAH, RACHEL**
jaeger gull ..... **SKUA, ALLAN**
jagged line .... **ZAG, ZIG**
jai alai .... **PELOTA**
Jamashid .... **YIMA**
James II daughter ..... **ANNE**
Janizaries, Chief of ...... **DEY**
JAPANESE: . see also SPECIAL
        SECTION
Jap. aborigine ... **AINO, AINU**
Jap. admiral .... **ITO**
Jap.-Am. .... **ISSEI,**
        KIBEI, NISEI, SANSEI
Jap. army reserve ..... **HOJU**
Jap. army second line ... **KOBI**
Jap. art of self-defense **JUDO**
Jap. badge, family ..... **MON**
Jap. badge, imperial **KIRIMON**
Jap. beer, rice .... **SAKE, SAKI**
Jap. beverage .... **SAKE**
Jap. box, girdle .... **INRO**
Jap. bush clover ...... **HAGI**
Jap. cedar .... **SUGI**
Jap. celery-like vegetable **UDO**
Jap. cherry .... **FUJI**
Jap. clogs .... **GETA**
Jap. deer .... **SIKA**
Jap. drama ..... **NO, KABUKI**
Jap. emperor's title ... **TENNO**
Jap. festival .... **BON**
Jap. fish .... **TAI, FUGU**
Jap. food, seaweed
        KOBU, KOMBU
Jap. gods .... **KAMI**
Jap. happiness god
        EBISU, HOTEI
Jap. harp .... **KOTO**
Jap. herb, stout .... **UDO**

Jap. immigrant .... **ISSEI**
Jap. mile measure .... **RI**
Jap. monastery .... **TERA**
Jap. national park ..... **ASO**
Jap. naval station ..... **KURE**
Jap. news agency ... **DOMEI**
Jap. nobleman .... **KUGE**
Jap. outcast
        ETA, YETA, RONIN
Jap. outer garment
        MINO, HAORI, KIMONO
Jap. parliament .... **DIET**
Jap. perfecture .... **FU**
Jap. persimmon .... **KAKI**
Jap. plant .... **UDO**
Jap. plane .... **ZERO**
Jap. primitive ... **AINO, AINU**
Jap. province, old ... **ISE, KAI**
Jap. receptacle .... **INRO**
Jap. salad plant .... **UDO**
Jap. salmon .... **MASU**
Jap. sash, kimono .... **OBI**
Jap. school of painting **KANO**
Jap. ship name .... **MARU**
Jap. sock .... **TABI**
Jap. statesman .... **ITO**
Jap. straw cape .... **MINO**
Jap. sword .. **CATAN, CATTAN**
Jap. vegetable ... **UDO, GOBO**
Jap. verse .... **UTA**
Jap. village .... **MURA**
Jap. volcano .... **FUJI**
Jap. writing .... **KANA**
Japheth, son of ...... **GOMER**
jar ...... **EWER, OLLA, CRUSE**
jar ring .... **LUTE**
jar, wide-mouthed ...... **OLLA**
jargon **CANT, ARGOT, PATOIS**
Jason's father .... **AESON**
Jason's 2d wife ..... **CREUSA**
Jason's ship .... **ARGO**
Jason's wife .... **MEDEA**
jaunty .... **PERK**
Java plum: P. I. ...... **DUHAT**
Javanese carriage ...... **SADO**
Javanese language **KAVI, KAWI**
Javanese poison tree ... **UPAS**
javelin, Afr. **ASSAGAI, ASSEGAI**
javelin game .. **JERID, JEREED**
javelin, Rom. .... **PILUM**
jeer .... **GIBE, SCOFF**
jeer at ..... **TAUNT, DERIDE**
Jehoshaphat, father of ... **ASA**
Jehovah .... **GOD**
Jehovah: Hebr. .... **JAH,**
        JAVE, JAVEH, YAHWEH

a jejune .. **DRY, ARID, BARREN**
jelly base .... **PECTIN**
jelly fruit .... **GUAVA**
jelly, meat .... **ASPIC**
jeopardize .... **ENDANGER**
Jericho, land opposite .. **MOAB**
jersey, woollen ..... **SINGLET**
Jerusalem, ancient name **SALEM**
Jerusalem: poet. ...... **ARIEL**
jest .... **JAPE**
jester .... **MIME, BUFFOON**
jet, U.S. .... **SABRE, SCORPION**
Jether, son of .... **ARA**
jetty .... **MOLE**
Jew .... **SEMITE**
JEWEL .... see GEM, STONE
jewelry setting .... **PAVE**
jewels, adorn with ..... **BEGEM**
JEWISH .. see also HEBREW
Jewish ascetic ...... **ESSENE**
Jewish benediction ... **SHEMA**
Jewish bride .... **KALLAH**
Jewish ceremony **SEDAR, SEDER**
Jewish feast of tabernacles
SUCCOTH
Jewish festival **PURIM, SEDER**
Jewish law, body of .. **TALMUD**
Jewish marriage contract
KETUBA
Jewish offering ..... **CORBAN**
b Jewish prayer book . **MAHZOR**
Jewish scholar .... **RAB**
Jewish sect, ancient .. **ESSENES**
Jewish teacher ... **REB, RABBI**
Jewish title of honor
RAB, GAON
Jezebel's husband ..... **AHAB**
Joan of Arc's victory **ORLEANS**
Job's-tears .... **COIX**
jog .... **TROT, NUDGE**
John: Gaelic, Scot. **IAN, EOAN**
John: Ir. .... **EOIN, SEAN**
John: Russ. .... **IVAN**
johnny-cake .... **PONE**
Johnson, Dr., hero .. **RASSELAS**
join ..... **LINK, PAIR, SEAM, WELD, YOKE, MERGE, UNITE, ATTACH**
join corners ... **MITER, MITRE**
join wood .... **RABBET**
joining bar .... **YOKE**
joint **HIP, KNEE, NODE, HINGE**
joint part **TENON, MORTISE**
joke with **KID, RIB, JAPE, JOSH**
joker .... **WAG, WIT**
Jordan city, ancient region
PETRA
Joseph's father .... **JACOB**
Joseph's nephew .... **TOLA**

c Joshua tree .... **YUCCA**
Joshua's father .... **NUN**
jostle .... **JOG, ELBOW**
jot .... **IOTA, TITTLE**
journey .... **ITER, RIDE, TOUR, TREK, TRIP, TRAVEL**
journey in circuit .... **EYRE**
joy ...... **DELIGHT, RAPTURE**
joyous .... **GLAD**
Judah, city in ... **ADAR, ENAM**
Judah's son .... **ER, ONAN**
Judaism scriptures
TORA, TORAH
judge .. **DEEM, RATE, ARBITER**
JUDGE, BIB. ... see BIBLICAL JUDGE
judge in Hades ...... **MINOS**
judge of dead, Egypt ... **OSIRIS**
judge's bench .... **BANC**
judge's chamber .... **CAMERA**
judges' rule, Israel **KRITARCHY**
judgment, Fr. law ..... **ARRET**
JUDICIAL see also LEGAL, LAW
judicial assembly ..... **COURT**
jug, large beer ...... **RANTER**
jug shaped like man ... **TOBY**
jug, wide-mouthed .... **EWER**
juice .... **SAP**
juice, thickened .... **RHOB**
jujitsu .... **JUDO**
jujube .... **BER, ELB**
Jules Verne character ... **NEMO**
d Juliet's betrothed ..... **PARIS**
Juliet's father, family **CAPULET**
jumble ...... **PI, PIE, MESS**
jump: music .... **SALTO**
jumping disease, Malay **LATA**
jumping rodent ..... **JERBOA**
juncture, line of .... **SEAM**
June bug .... **DOR**
Jungfrau's site .... **ALPS**
jungle clearing .... **MILPA**
juniper .... **GORSE, SAVIN, SABINE, SAVINE**
juniper, Europ. .... **CADE**
juniper tree, Bibl. **EZEL, RETEM**
Jupiter .... **JOVE**
Jupiter's moon, inner ..... **IO**
Jupiter's wife .... **HERA, JUNO**
jurisdiction .... **VENUE**
jurisdiction, old Eng. **SOC, SOKE**
jurisprudence .... **LAW**
jury list .... **PANEL**
jury, writ summoning **VENIRE**
just .... **MORAL**
justice, goddess of . **MA, MAAT**
jute .... **DESI**
Jutlander .... **DANE**
jutting rock .... **TOR**
juxtaposition, place in **APPOSE**
jynx .... **SPELL**

K

a Kaffir language .... XOSA
Kaffir tribe .... ZULU
Kaffir war club .... KIRI
Kaffir warrior .... IMPI
Kalmuck ..... ELEUT, ELEUTH
Kandh language .... KUI
kangaroo, male ...... BOOMER
kangaroo, young .... JOEY
Katmandu's country ... NEPAL
kava .... AVA
kava bowl .... TANOA
Kaw .... AKHA
Keats poem-1820 .... LAMIA
keel .... CAREEN
keel, at right angle to ABEAM
keel block wedge ... TEMPLET
keel, having no ...... RATITE
keel, kind of .... FIN
keel, part of .... SKEG
keel-shaped part
        CARINA, CARINAE
keen ACUTE, SHARP, ASTUTE
keep account of .... TAB
keepsake .... TOKEN
keeve .... KIVER
b Kentucky coffee tree . CHICOT
Kentucky college ..... BEREA
kerchief .... MADRAS
kernel .... NUT
ketch, Levant .... SAIC
ketone, liquid ...... ACETONE
ketone, oily .... CARONE
kettledrum .. NAKER, ATABAL,
    ATTABAL, TIMPANI, TIM-
    PANO, TYMPANO
key .... ISLE
key fruit .... SAMARA
key notch .... WARD
key part .... BIT
key-shaped ...... URDE, URDY
keyed up .... AGOG
Khedive's estate ...... DAIRA
kid, undressed .... SUEDE
kidney .... NEER
kidney bean .... BON
kidneys, pert. to ..... RENAL
killer whale .... ORCA
kiln ...... OST, OAST, OVEN
kiloliter .... STERE
kind
    ILK, SORT, GENRE, SPECIES
kind: Gr. .... GENOS
kindle: dialect .... TIND
kindly .... BENIGN
kindness .... LENITY
kindred .... SIB

c king .... REX, REY, REGES
king —, cartoon character
                        AROO
King Alfred's city: abbr. .. LON
king, Amalekite .... AGAG
King Arthur's abode
AVALON, AVALLON, CAMELOT
King Arthur's burial place
        AVALON, AVALLON
King Arthur's court   CAMELOT
King Arthur's father .. UTHER
King Arthur's fool .. DAGONET
King Arthur's lance ..... RON
King Arthur's mother IGERNA,
    IGERNE, YGERNE, IGRAINE
King Arthur's queen
        GUINEVER, GUINEVERE
KING, BIBLICAL .... see
            BIBLICAL KING
King Ethelred "The —"
                    UNREADY
king, Gr. .... MINOS
King Gradlon's capital .... IS
king, Hebrew .... HEROD
king, Midianite .... REBA
king, mythical .... MIDAS
king of beasts .... LION
d King of Colchis' daughter
                        MEDEA
king of Crete .... MINOS
king of elves ...... ERLKING
king of gods, Egypt
        AMEN, AMON, AMUN
king of Greece, ancient MINOS
king of Israel ... AHAB, ELAH,
        OMRI, SAUL, NADAB
king of Jews .... HEROD
king of Judah ... ASA, AHAZ,
        AMON, UZZIAH
king of Judea .... HEROD
king of Naples ...... MURAT
king of Persia .... CYRUS
king of Sodom .... BERA
king, pert. to .... REGNAL
king, Phrygian .... MIDAS
king, rich .... CROESUS
king, Spartan AGIS, LEONIDAS
king, Teut. Visigoth .. ALARIC
king's bodyguard ..... THANE
king's yellow ..... ORPIMENT
KINGDOM ..see also COUNTRY
kingdom, ancient ...... MOAB
KINGDOM, BIB. .. see page 197
kingfish .... HAKU, OPAH
kinkajou .... POTTO
kinship, Moslem law ... NASAB
Kipling hero .... KIM

kismet .... FATE
kiss .... BUSS, SMACK
kitchen, ship's ...... GALLEY
kitchen tool
   CORER, RICER, GRATER
kite, bird
   GLED, GLEDE, ELANET
kittiwake gull, Shetlands WAEG
kitty, feed the .... ANTE
kiwi .... ROA
knave .... ROGUE
knave, in cribbage ..... NOBS
knave of clubs .... PAM
knead .... ELT
knead, in massage .... PETRIE
knee: Lat. .... GENU
kneecap ... ROTULA, PATELLA
KNIFE .. see also DAGGER
knife .... CHIV, STAB,
   MACHETE, MACHETTE
knife, Burmese .... DAH, DOW
knife dealer .... CUTLER
knife, Eskimo .... ULU
knife, large ...... SNY, SNEE
knife, loop-cutting
   TREVAT, TRIVAT, TRIVET
knife, P. I. .... BOLO
knife, single-edge .... BOWIE
knife, surgical .... SCALPEL
knight SIR, RITTER, TEMPLAR
knight, heroic ...... PALADIN
knight, make .... DUB
knight, medieval ...... BEVIS
knight's mantel ..... TABARD

knight's wife .... DAME
knitting stitch .... PURL
knob: anat. .... CAPUT
knobbed .... TOROSE
knoblike .... NODAL
knobkerrie .... KIRI
knockout .... KO, KAYO
knot ..... MILE, NODE, NODI,
   SNAG, GNARL, KNURL,
   NODUS
knot, fiber .... NOIL, NOYL
knot in wood .... BURL,
   KNAR, KNOR, KNUR, NURL
knot, insecure ..... GRANNY
knot lace .... TAT, TATT
knot, like a .... NODAL
knot of thread .... BURL
knots, fiber .... NEP
knots, having .... NODED
know .... KEN, WIST
knowledge ...... KEN, LORE
knowledge, pert. to .. GNOSTIC
knowledge, pure ..... NOESIS
known as milo maize, grain
   MILO
knucklebones, sheep ... DOLOS
kobold .... NIS, NISSE
Kol dialect .... HO
kopecks, 100 .... RUBLE
Koran chapter .... SURA
Koran interpreters .... ULEMA
Korea .... CHOSEN
Korean president ..... RHEE
Korean soldier .... ROK
Kronos' wife .... RHEA
kurrajong tree .... CALOOL

L

"La Boheme" heroine ... MIMI
Laban, daughter of .... LEAH
label .... TAG, PASTER
LABOR GROUP ... see UNION
laborer, China . COOLY, COOLIE
laborer, India .... TOTY
Labrador tea .... LEDUM
labyrinth .... MAZE
lac .... RESIN
lace .... BEAT, LASH
lace, barred GRILLE, GRILLEE
lace, Fr. ... CLUNY, ALENCON
lace, gold, silver .... ORRIS
lace, metal tip of
   AGLET, AIGLET
lace, square hole ...... FILET
lacerate .... RIP, TEAR
laceration .... RIP, TEAR
lack .... NEED, WANT
lack of power .... ATONY

Laconian clan group ..... OBE
Laconian subdivision ..... OBE
ladder, scale fort wall with
   SCALADE, SCALADO, ES-
   CALADE, ESCALADO
ladderlike .... SCALAR
lady, India .... BIBI
"Lady of the Lake" outlaw DHU
ladylove, in poetry .... DELIA
lagoon .... LIMAN
lake .... MERE
lake, Afr. salt .. SHAT, SHOTT
lake, Blue Nile source .. TANA
Lake Erie battle officer PERRY
Lake, Great (5) ERIE, HURON,
   ONTARIO, MICHIGAN, SU-
   PERIOR
lake, mountain .... TARN
lake near Galilee sea .. MEROM
lake, resort .... TAHOE

Lake

a lake: Scot. .... **LOCH**
Lake Tahoe trout ...... **POGY**
lake whitefish .... **POLLAN**
lama, head .... **DALAI**
lamb .... **EAN, EWE, YEAN**
lamb, holy .... **AGNUS**
lamb: Lat. .... **AGNI, AGNUS**
lamb, young .... **COSSET**
Lamb's pen name ...... **ELIA**
Lamech, ancestor of ... **CAIN**
Lamech's son
    NOAH, JABAL, JUBAL
lament .... **KEEN, WAIL,**
    WEEP, GRIEVE, PLAINT
lamentation .... **LINOS**
lamp black .... **SOOT**
lamprey .... **EEL**
lance head .... **MORNE**
lance, mythical .... **RON**
lance rest, breastplate **FAUCRE**
lance, short .... **DART**
Lancelot's beloved ... **ELAINE**
lancer, Ger. ... **ULAN, UHLAN**
lancewood .... **CIGUA**
land, absolute property **ALOD,**
    ALLOD, ALODIUM, ALLODIUM
land amid water .. **ISLE, ISLET**
land breeze .... **TERRAL**
land, church's .... **GLEBE**
b land held in fee simple
    ODAL, UDAL
land: law .... **SOLUM**
LAND MEASURE .. see also
    AREA in SPECIAL SECTION
land measure
    AR, ARE, ROD, ACRE, ROOD
land ownership, pert. to **ODAL**
land snail genus ...:. **CERION**
land spring .... **LAVANT**
land, tilled, plowed: Sp.
    ARADA, ARADO
land under tenure: Scot. ... **FEU**
landing place ..... **KEY, PIER,**
    QUAI, QUAY, LEVEE
landing place, India
    GAUT, GHAT
landing ship .... **LST**
landmark .... **COPA**
landmark: Sp. .... **SENAL**
lands .... **ACRES**
language, Aramaic ... **SYRIAC**
language, Assam .... **AO, AKA**
language, dead .... **LATIN**
language, early It. .... **OSCAN**
language, Egypt. ..... **COPTIC**
language, Finnish ..... **UGRIC**
language form, peculiarity
    IDIOM
language, Gilgit ...... **SHINA**
language, Hittite ...... **PALA**
language, Indic .... **HINDI**

c language, Indo-Chin. .... **AO,**
    WA, AKA, ANU, LAI, LAO,
    MRO, MRU, PWO, SAK,
    AHOM, AKHA, AMOY,
    BODO, GARO, KAMI, NAGA,
    RONG, SGAU, SHAN
language, Ir. .. **CELTIC, KELTIC**
language, Kandh .... **KUI**
language, Kashmir .... **SHINA**
language, Mossi .... **MO, MOLE**
language, N. Afr. .... **BERBER**
language of Bible days
    ARAMAIC
language, P. I.
    TAGAL, TAGALOG
language, Scot. **CELTIC, KELTIC**
language, Semitic .... **ARABIC**
language, Siberian
    ENISEI, YENISEI
language, S. Afr. ...... **TAAL**
language, Sudanic ... **MO, MOLE**
language, synthetic .. **RO, IDO**
language, Welsh **CELTIC,KELTIC**
languages, E. Europ. ... **UGRIC**
languish .... **FLAG, PINE**
languor, drug-induced
    KEF, KAIF, KIFF
langur .... **MAHA**
lantern feast .... **BON**
d Laomedon's father ...... **ILUS**
Laomedon's son
    PRIAM, TITHONUS
Laos aborigine ... **KHA, YUN**
lapel .... **REVER**
lapidate .... **STONE**
Lapp's sledge ... **PULK, PULKA**
larboard .... **APORT**
larch **TAMARAC, TAMARACK**
large amount .... **SCAD**
lariat .... **LAZO, ROPE,**
    LASSO, REATA, RIATA
lariat, metal eye of
    HONDA, HONDO, HONDOO
larva .... **GRUB**
larva of fly ...... **BOT, BOTT**
lash .... **TIE, WHIP**
lasso
    ROPE, REATA, RIATA, LARIAT
last .... **FINAL, OMEGA**
last but one .... **PENULT**
"Last Days of Pompeii" char-
    acter .... **IONE**
last Imam .... **MAHDI**
last section .... **FINALE**
Last Supper picture .... **CENA**
Last Supper room .. **CENACLE**
latching: naut. .... **LASKET**
late ... **NEW, TARDY, RECENT**
late, one at school ..... **SERO**
lateen-rigged boat ..... **DOW,**
    DHOW, SETEE, MISTIC

88

a
latent .... **DORMANT**
lateral .... **SIDE**
lath .... **SLAT**
LATIN .... see also ROMAN
LATIN:
abbot .... **ABBAS**
above ...... **SUPER, SUPRA**
about .... **CIRCITER**
across .... **TRANS**
act .... **ACTU, ACTUS**
after .... **POST**
aged .... **AET (abbr.)**
all .... **TOTO**
alone .... **SOLO, SOLUS**
and .... **ET**
and others .... **ETAL (abbr.)**
around .... **CIRCUM**
art .... **ARS**
backward .... **RETRO**
before .... **ANTE**
behold .... **ECCE**
being .... **ESSE**
believe, I .... **CREDO**
beneath .... **INERA**
bird .... **AVIS**
book .... **LIBER**
blessed .... **BEATA**
bronze .... **AES**
but .... **SED**
cattle .... **PECORA**

b
country .... **RUS, RURIS**
cup .... **CALIX**
custom .... **RITUS**
day .... **DIEM**
days .... **DIES**
depart! .... **VADE**
divination by lots .... **SORS, SORTES**
door .... **JANUA**
earth .... **TERRA**
egg .... **OVUM**
eight .... **OCTO**
error .... **LAPSUS**
event .... **REI**
evil .... **MALA, MALUM**
fate .... **NONA**
field .... **AGER**
fields .... **AGRI**
fire .... **IGNIS**
first .... **PRIMUS**
fish .... **PISCES**
force .... **VIS**
from .... **DE**
go! .... **VADE**
god .... **DEUS**
goddess .... **DEA**
gods .... **DI**
gold .... **AURUM**
good ...... **BONUM, BONUS**
grandfather .... **AVUS**
he .... **ILLE**

c
he remains .... **MANET**
he was .... **ERAT**
head .... **CAPUT**
high .... **ALTA**
himself .... **IPSE**
I love .... **AMO**
in so far as .... **QUA**
is .... **EST**
itself .... **IPSO**
ivory .... **EBUR**
journey .... **ITER**
knee .... **GENU**
lamb ...... **AGNI, AGNUS**
land .... **AGER**
learned .... **DOCTUS**
life .... **VITA, ANIMA**
lo .... **ECCE**
man .... **VIR**
mass .... **MISSA**
mine .... **MEUM**
more than .... **SUPER**
mountain .... **MONS**
name .... **NOMEN**
nose, of the .... **NAS**
not .... **NON**
observe .... **NOTA**
offense ..... **MALA, MALUM**

d
once .... **SEMEL**
or .... **AUT**
other .... **ALIA**
over .... **SUPER**
pardon .... **VENIA**
palm .... **VOLA**
part .... **PARS**
partly .... **PARTIM**
peace .... **PAX**
pin .... **ACUS**
pledge .... **VAS**
possessive .... **SUA**
power .... **VIS**
pronoun .... **SUA**
property .... **BONA**
quickly .... **CITO**
rate .... **RATA**
religious law .... **FAS**
right .... **DEXTER**
same .... **IDEM**
scarcely .... **VIX**
see .... **VIDE**
side .... **LATUS**
table .... **MENSA**
tail .... **CAUDA**
that is .... **"ID EST"**
that one .... **ILLE**
the same .... **IDEM**
thing .... **RES**

Latin

LATIN(continued from page 89)

this one .... HIC, HAEC
thus .... SIC
throat .... GULA
to be .... ESSE
to use .... UTOR
tooth .... DENS
toward .... AD
twice .... BIS
under .... SUB
unless .... NISI
vein .... VENA
voice .... VOX
water .... AQUA
we .... NOS
well .... BENE
where .... UBI
within .... INTRA
without .... SINE
wool .... LANA
wrong ...... MALA, MALUM

Latvia, native of .... LETT
laugh .... FLEER
laugh, able to .... RISIBLE
laughing .... RIANT
laughing, pert. to .. GELASTIC
laurel .... BAY, DAPHNE
laurel bark, medicinal .. COTO
lava .... AA, LATITE, SCORIA
lava, rough .... AA
lavender, Eur. .... ASPIC
lavish affection .... DOTE
law
    JURE, RULE, CANON, EDICT
law, abstract .... JUS
law, D. E. Ind. .... ADAT
law excluding women from
    reign .... SALIC
law of Moses .. TORA, TORAH
law, Rom. .... JUS, LEX
lawful .... LEGAL, LICIT
lawgiver, Gr.
    DRACO, MINOS, SOLON
lawgiver, Hebr. .... MOSES
lawmaker .... SOLON
lawyer .... LEGIST
lawyers' patron saint ... IVES
lay .... PUT, DITTY
layer .... PLY,
    LAMINA, STRATA, STRATUM
layer of a plant ..... PROVINE
layer, wood .... VENEER
layman .... LAIC
lazar .... LEPER
lazy .... OTIOSE
lead-colored .... LIVID
lead: music PRESA, PRECENT
lead, ore .... GALENA

lead, pellets of .... SHOT
lead, pencil ...... GRAPHITE
lead sulphide, native GALENA
lead telluride ...... ALTAITE
lead, white .... CERUSE
leaden color, having ... LIVID
leader, fishing .... SNELL
leader of movement .... VAN
leader, Rom. .... DUX
leaf appendage ...... STIPEL
leaf-cutting ant ...... ATTA
leaf division .... LOBE
leaf, fern .... FROND
leaf, flower .... BRACT, SEPAL
leaf-miner beetle ..... HISPA
leaf of book .... FOLIO
leaf vein .... RIB
league, Ger. .... BUND
league, trading ...... HANSE
Leah's father .... LABAN
Leah's son .... LEVI
lean .. CANT, GAUNT, SPARE
lean-to .... SHED
Leander's love .... HERO
"Leaning Tower" city .... PISA
leap LUNGE, VAULT, CURVET
leap: music .... SALTO
leap: Scot. LOUP, LOWP, STEND
leaping .... SALTANT
learned .. ERUDITE, LETTERED
learning .... LORE
learning, man of
    SAGE, PEDANT, SAVANT
Lear's daughter ...... REGAN
Lear's faithful follower KENT
least bit .... RAP
leather bottle .... MATARA
leather flask, Gr. .... OLPE
leather, glove
    KID, NAPA, MOCHA, SUEDE
leather, kind of ... ELK, BOCK
leather, prepare—make into
    TAN, TAW
leather, soft
    NAPA, ALUTA, SUEDE
leather thong, hawk's .. BRAIL
leatherfish .... LIJA
"leatherneck" .... MARINE
leave
    GO, QUIT, EXEAT, DEPART
leave destitute ...... STRAND
leave of absence, school EXEAT
leave-taking .... CONGE
leaves, having: Her. .. POINTE
leaven .... YEAST
leaving .... ORT
leavings .... DREGS, RESIDUE
Lebanese port, old .... TYRE
ledge, fort .... BERM, BERME
ledger entry
    ITEM, DEBIT, CREDIT

lee, opposed to .... **STOSS**
leeangle .. **LEAWILL, LEEWILL**
leer .... **OGLE**
Leeward Island .... **NEVIS**
left: comb. form ...... **LEVO**
left-hand .... **LEVO**
left-hand page ... **VO, VERSO**
left, to turn .... **HAW**
leftover .... **ORT**
leg, covering, ancient **PEDULE**
leg, front of .... **SHIN**
leg joint, animal .... **HOCK**
leg-like part .... **CRUS**
leg of mutton,'lamb .. **GIGOT**
leg, part of .... **SHIN, SHANK**
leg, pert. to calf of ... **SURAL**
legal action suit .. **RES, CASE**
legal claim .... **LIEN**
legal delays .... **MORAE**
legal injury .... **TORT**
legal job .... **CASE**
legal matter .... **RES**
legal offense .. **DELIT, DELICT**
legal order .... **WRIT**
legal paper .... **DEED**
legal profession ... **BAR, LAW**
legal prosecution ...... **SUIT**
legend ... **MYTH, SAGA, TALE**
legion division, Rom. **COHORT**
legislate .... **ENACT**
legislative assembly, Afr. **RAAS**
legislator ... **SOLON, SENATOR**
legislature ... **DIET, SENATE**
legislature: Sp. ...... **CORTES**
legume ..... **PEA, POD, BEAN**
leisure .... **REST, OTIUM**
lemur ...... **MAKI, INDRI,**
   LORIS, AYE-AYE, SEMIAPE
lemur, Afr. .... **GALAGO**
lemur, Asia, Ceylon **LORI, LORIS**
lemur, Ceylonese .... **LORI**
lemur, flying .... **COLUGO**
lemur, ruffed .... **VARI**
lemuroid .... **POTTO**
lengthily, address .. **PERORATE**
Leningrad's river .... **NEVA**
lens, hand .... **READER**
lentil .... **ERVUM**
leopard .... **PARD**
Leporidae, one of the ... **HARE**
leprosy .... **LEPRA**
Lepus genus, one of ..... **HARE**
lerp .... **LAAP**
Lesbos, poet of ...... **ARION**
"Les Etats —" .... **UNIS**
less .... **MINUS**
lessen **BATE, ABATE, MITIGATE**
let **HIRE, RENT, LEASE, PERMIT**
let bait drop .... **DAP**
let it stand! .... **STA, STET**

let up .... **ABATE**
lethal .... **FATAL**
lethargy
   COMA, STUPOR, TORPOR
letter .. **AR (18), EF (6), EM**
   (13), EN (14), EX (24),
   WY (25), BEE (2), CEE
   (3), DEE (4), ESS (19),
   GEE (7), JAY (10), PEE
   (16), TEE (20), VEE (22),
   WYE (25), ZED (26), ZEE
   (26), AITCH (8)
letter, according to .. **LITERAL**
letter, Ang.-Sax. .. **EDH, ETH**
letter, early Gr. .... **SAN**
LETTER, GR. and NUMBER . see
   also GREEK LETTER
letter, Gr. .. **MU, NU, PI, XI,**
   CHI, ETA, PHI, PSI, RHO,
   TAU, BETA, IOTA, ZETA,
   ALPHA, DELTA, GAMMA,
   KAPPA, OMEGA, SIGMA,
   THETA, LAMBDA, EPSILON,
   OMICRON, UPSILON
letter, Hebr. **HE (5), PE (17),**
   AIN (16), MEM (13),
   NUN (14), SIN (21), TAV
   (22), TAW (22), VAU
   (16), WAW (16), ALEF
   (11), AYIN (16), BETH
   (2), CAPH (11), ELEF (1),
   KAPH (11), KOPH (19),
   QOPH (19), RESH (20),
   SADE (18), SHIN (21),
   TETH (9), YODH, (10),
   ALEPH (13), GIMEL (3),
   LAMED (12), DALETH (4),
   LAMEDH (12)
letter of resignation .. **DEMIT**
letters, sloping .... **ITALICS**
lettuce, kind of **COS, ROMAINE**
Levantine ketch .... **SAIC**
levee .... **DIKE, DYKE**
level **EVEN, RASE, RAZE, PLANE**
leveling slip .... **SHIM**
lever .... **PRY, PEVY, PEAVY,**
   PEEVY, PEAVEY, PEEVEY,
   TAPPET
levy .... **TAX, CESS, IMPOST**
Lew Wallace hero .... **HUR**
Lhasa holy man .... **LAMA**
Lhasa's country .... **TIBET**
liability .... **DEBT**
liana .... **CIPO**
liang .... **TAEL**
liar .... **ANANIAS**
Liberian native ..... **VAI, VEI**
Liberian tribes .. **GI, KRA, KRU**
license: slang .... **READER**
lichen .... **MOSS**
lichen genus **USNEA, EVERNIA**

Lichen

a

lichen, kind **PARELLA, PARELLE**
lie in wait .... **LURK**
Liege, town near .... **ANS**
liegeman .... **VASSAL**
lieu .... **STEAD**
life .... **BIOS, BIOTA**
life: Lat. ...... **VITA, ANIMA**
life, of .... **VITAL**
life principle .... **PRANA**
life principle, Hindu .. **ATMAN**
life prolonger .... **ELIXIR**
life, relating to
.... **BIOTIC, BIOTICAL**
life tenant .... **LIVIER**
lifeless **AMORT, AZOIC, INERT**
lifetime .... **AGE**
lifted with effort ...... **HOVE**
ligament .... **BOND**
light .... **LAMP, KLEIG,**
.... **KLIEG, TAPER, ILLUME**
light and fine, as lines .. **LEGER**
light as a line .... **LEGER**
light bulb filler ...... **ARGON**
light, circle of
.... **HALO, NIMB, NIMBUS**
light intensity unit ...... **PYR**
light, kind of .... **ARC**
light ring .... **CORONA**
light, science of ...... **OPTICS**
light, sun's **AUREOLA, AUREOLE**

b

light unit **PYR, LUMEN, HEFNER**
lighter, lamp .... **SPILL**
lighter, make .... **LEAVEN**
lighthouse .... **PHAROS**
lightning: poet. .... **LEVIN**
ligulate .... **LORATE**
like .... **AS, AKIN**
likely .... **APT**
likeness .... **ICON, IMAGE**
likewise not .... **NOR**
lily .... **LIS, LYS, ALOE,**
.... **ARUM, SEGO, CALLA**
lily family plant ..... **CAMAS**
.... **CAMASS, CAMMAS**
lily genus .... **ALOE**
lily genus, plantain .... **HOSTA**
Lily Maid of Astolat
.... **ELAIN, ELAINE**
lily, palm .... **TI**
limb ...... **ARM, LEG, MANUS**
limber .... **LITHE**
lime, to hydrate ..... **SLAKE**
lime tree .... **TEIL, TEYL**
limestone, grainy ..... **OOLITE**
limestone, Irish .... **CALP**
limestone, soft **MALM, CHALK**
limicoline bird **SNIPE, PLOVER**
limit .... **TERM, BOURN,**
.... **STENT, STINT, BOURNE**
limn.......... **DRAW, PAINT**
Lindbergh's book .... **WE**

c

linden .... **LIN, TEIL, TEYL**
line .... **ROW, RANK**
line, cutting .... **SECANT**
line, fine, on type letter **CERIF,**
.... **SERIF, CERIPH**
line, fishing .... **SNELL**
line, in a .... **AROW**
line, intersecting ..... **SECANT**
line inside of .... **CEIL**
line, math. .... **VECTOR**
line, naut. . **EARING, MARLINE**
line not forming angle **AGONE**
line on a letter .... **SERIF**
line, pert. to .... **LINEAR**
line, thin ..... **STRIA, STRIAE**
line, waiting ..... **CUE, QUEUE**
line with stone **STEAN, STEENE**
lines, marked with
.... **RULED, STRIATE, STRIATED**
lines, telescope-lens .. **RETICLE**
linen .... **CREA**
linen, fine ..... **LAWN, TOILE**
linen, household, table **NAPERY**
linen, one caring for royal
.... **NAPERER**
linen tape, braid ...... **INKLE**
linger .... **WAIT, TARRY**
lingo .... **ARGOT**
lingua .... **GLOSSA**
liniment .... **ARNICA**

d

link .... **YOKE, CATENATE**
links connected ..... **CATENAE**
linnet ...... **TWITE, LENARD**
lion .... **LEO, SIMBA**
lion group .... **PRIDE**
lion killed by Hercules **NEMEAN**
lion of God .... **ALI**
lionet .... **CUB**
lips, pert. to .... **LABIAL**
liqueur .... **CREME, NOYAU**
liqueur, sweet .... **GENEPI**
liquid element
.... **BROMIN, BROMINE**
liquid, made ... **FUSIL, FUSILE**
liquid, without ..... **ANEROID**
liquor .. **GIN, RUM, RYE, GROG**
liquor, malt .... **ALE, PORTER**
liquor, oriental ..... **ARRACK**
liquor, P. I. .... **VINO**
liquor, Russian **VODKA, VODKI**
liquor, sugar-cane
.... **TAFIA, TAFFIA**
Lisbon's river .... **TAGUS**
lissome .... **SVELTE**
list .... **ROTA, SLATE,**
ROSTER, CATALOG, CATALOGUE
list of persons
.... **ROTA, PANEL, ROSTER**
list, one of a .... **ITEM**
listen .... **HARK, HEAR**
listless, be .... **MOPE**

a listlessness... **ENNUI, APATHY**
liter, Dutch .... **AAM, KAN**
literary collection........... **ANA**
literary extracts .... **ANALECTA, ANALECTS**
literary master .... **STYLIST**
literary scraps, bits....... **ANA, NOTES**
literate .. **LEARNED, LETTERED**
lithograph .... **CHROMO**
Lithuanian .... **BALT, LETT**
litter, E. Ind. ... **DOOLI, DOOLY, DOOLEE, DOOLEY, DOOLIE**
"Little Boy Blue" poet .... **FIELD**
little casino .... **TWO**
little chief hare........... **PIKA**
little: music............... **POCO**
liturgy.................... **RITE**
live .... **all forms of verb "BE"**
live oak, Calif........... **ENCINA**
lively.... **PERT, BRISK, PEART**
lively, make.............. **PERK**
lively: music ..... **VIVO, DESTO, ANIMATO**
lively person.............. **GRIG**
lively song................ **LILT**
liver..................... **HEPAR**
liver, pert. to......... **HEPATIC**
liverwort genus .... **RICCIA**
b livid..................... **BLAE**
living in currents .... **LOTIC**
Livonian.................. **LIV**
lixivium........... **LYE, LEACH**
lizard........... **GILA, GECKO, GUANA, SKINK, VARAN, IGUANA**
lizard, Am....... **ANOLE, ANOLI**
lizard, beaded............. **GILA**
lizard, changeable **CHAMELEON**
lizard genus ..... **UTA, AGAMA**
lizard, large... **GILA, MONITOR**
lizard, old world .... **SEPS**
lizard, small....... **EFT, GECKO**
lizard, starred .... **AGAMA**
lizard, tropical.......... **AGAMA**
lizardlike............. **SAURIAN**
llamalike animal........ **ALPACA**
load............... **LADE, ONUS**
loadstone............ **MAGNET**
loaf, small: dial. .... **BAP**
loam .... **LOESS**
loam, India............. **REGUR**
loath................. **AVERSE**
loathe.................. **ABHOR**
lobster box .... **CAR**
local .... **TOPICAL**
locale .... **SITE**
locality .... **AREA, LOCUS, VENEW, VENUE**
location ... **SITE, SPOT, PLACE**
lock............. **CURL, TRESS**

c locks, Panama Canal ... **GATUN**
lockjaw... **TETANUS, TRISMUS**
locust...... **ACACIA, CICADA, CICALA**
locust, N. Z. .... **WETA**
lodge, soldier's......... **BILLET**
lofty dwelling .... **AERIE**
log birling contest...... **ROLEO**
log drive, escape work on.. **SNIB**
log, spin floating .... **BIRL**
log splitter............. **WEDGE**
logarithmic unit .... **BEL**
loge.................... **STALL**
logger's implement..... **PEAVY, PEAVEY**
logic, omission of step in proof
  SALTUS
logician .... **DIALECTOR**
Lohengrin's wife .... **ELSA**
Loire, city on .... **BLOIS**
loiter...................... **LAG**
Loki's daughter ..... **HEL, HELA**
Loki's son .... **NARE**
Loki's wife.............. **SIGYN**
London district........... **SOHO**
long...... **YEN, PINE, CRAVE, YEARN, ASPIRE**
long ago .... **ELD, YORE**
long journey .. **TREK, ODYSSEY**
d long line (fishing) with hooks
  TROT
long live! .... **VIVA, VIVE**
long-suffering .... **MEEK**
look.................... **LO, SEE**
look after......... **MIND, TEND**
look askance............. **LEER**
look at ...... **EYE, SCAN, VIEW**
look here! .... **HIST**
look narrowly**PEEK, PEEP, PEER**
look slyly .... **LEER, OGLE**
loom, heddles of .... **CAAM**
loom, lever in .... **LAM**
loon, genus .... **GAVIA**
loon, kind of .... **DIVER**
loop, edging .... **PICOT**
loophole........ **MUSE, MEUSE**
looplike structure, anat.... **ANSA**
loose...................... **LAX**
loose coat**PALETOT, MANTEVIL**
loose robe.............. **SIMAR**
loosen .... **UNDO, UNTIE**
lop.... **SNED, PRUNE, SNATHE**
lopsided.......... **ALOP, ALIST**
loquat tree .... **BIWA**
Lord High Executioner in "Mikado"
  KOKO
Lord: Jacobite Church ..... **MAR**
lord, Oriental............. **KHAN**
lord, Pers. .... **KAAN, KAUN, KAWN, KHAN**
lord, privileged ...... **PALATINE**

a lord, Scot. .... **LAIRD**
lore, Norse .... **RUNE**
lorica .... **CUIRASS**
"Lorna Doone" character **RIDD**
lose .... **AMIT**
"Lost Chord" finale .... **AMEN**
lot .... **FATE**
Lotan's father .... **SEIR**
Lot's birthplace .... **UR**
Lot's father :........ **HARAN**
Lot's son .... **MOAB**
lottery prize .... **TERN**
lotus enzyme .... **LOTASE**
Lotus: poet .... **LOTE**
lotus tree .... **SADR**
loud: music .... **FORTE**
loud-voiced one .... **STENTOR**
loudness, measurement unit
PHON
loudspeaker for high sound
TWEETER
loudspeaker for low sound
WOOFER
Louis XVI's nickname .. **VETO**
Louisiana county ..... **PARISH**
b Louisiana native ..... **CREOLE**
lounge .... **LOAF, LOLL**
love . **JO, GRA, ADORE, AMOUR**
love: Anglo-Irish ...... **GRA**
love apple .... **TOMATO**
love feast .... **AGAPE**
love god
LOVE GOD . see GOD OF LOVE
LOVE GODDESS . see GODDESS
OF LOVE
love, inflame with
ENAMOR, ENAMOUR
love knot .... **AMORET**
love to excess ... **DOAT, DOTE**
lover .... **ROMEO**
"Love's Labour's Lost" constable
DULL
loving
FOND, AMATIVE, AMATORY
low .... **MOO, BASE**
low caste Hindu .. **PASI, TELI**
low caste Indian ...... **DOM,
MAL, GADDI**
Lowell, poetess .... **AMY**
lower **ABASE, DEBASE, NETHER**
lower: arch. .... **VAIL**
lower jaw, bird's ...... **MALA**
lower world gods, Rom. **MANES**
lowest deck .... **ORLOP**
lowest part of base ... **PLINTH**

c lowest point .... **NADIR**
loyal .... **LEAL,
TRUE, STANCH, STAUNCH**
loyalist .... **TORY**
lozenge ..... **PASTIL, ROTULA
TROCHE, PASTILE, PASTILLE**
loyalty fulfilling religious
obligations: Rom. . **PIETAS**
Lubeck, pert. to ...... **LUBS**
lucerne .... **MEDIC, ALFALFA**
luck: Ir. .... **CESS**
luck, pert. to ..... **ALEATORY**
lucky stroke .... **FLUKE**
lugubrious .... **SAD**
lukewarm .... **TEPID**
lumber along .... **LOB, LOBB**
Lumber State .... see page 223
lumberman .... **SAWYER**
lumberman's boot .... **PAC**
lumberman's boots
PACS, OVERS
lumberman's hook ..... **PEVY,
PEAVY, PEEVY, PEAVEY,
PEEVEY**
luminaire .... **LAMP**
luminary .... **STAR**
d lump .... **NUB, WAD,
CLOT, NODE, SWAD**
lunar crater .... **LINNE**
lunar god, Phrygian ..... **MEN**
luncheon .... **TIFFIN**
lurch .... **CAREEN**
lure .... **BAIT, DECOY**
luster .... **GLOSS, SHEEN**
lusterless .. **DIM, MAT, MATTE**
lustrous .... **NITID**
lute, Oriental .... **TAR**
luxuriant .... **LUSH, RANK**
luxuriate .... **BASK**
Luzon native .... **ATA, ITA,
AETA, ATTA, TAGAL,
TAGALA**
Luzon negrito .... **ATA,
AETA, ITA, ATTA**
Luzon pagan .... **ITALON**
Lynette's knight .... **GARETH**
lynx, Afr. .... **SYAGUSH**
lynx, Pers. .... **CARACAL**
lyrebird genus ...... **MENURA**
lyric .... **ODE, MELIC**
lyric Muse .... **ERATO**
Lytton heroine .... **IONE**

M

a macaque Indian **BRUH, RHESUS**
macaw .... **ARA, ARARA**
macaw, Braz.
    ARA, ARARA, MARACAN
mace-bearer .... **BEADLE**
macerate .... **RET, STEEP**
machine, finishing .... **EDGER**
machine, grain cleaner **AWNER**
machine gun .... **BREN, STEN**
machine, hummeling .. **AWNER**
machine, ore-dressing **VANNER**
machine part
    CAM, PAWL, TAPPET
machine, rubber .. **EXTRUDER**
mackerel net .... **SPILLER**
mackerel, young .... **SPIKE**
Madagascar mammal .. **LEMUR**
Madagascar native .... **HOVA**
madam .... **MUM, MAAM**
madder ..... **RUBIA, MUNJEET**
madder, common Eu. **GARANCE**
madder shrub genus ... **EVEA**
madness .... **MANIA**
mafura tree .... **ROKA**
maggot .... **LARVA**
Magi, one of .... **GASPAR**
magic .... **RUNE**
magic: Hindustan **JADU, JADOO**
b magic, pert. to .... **GOETIC**
magic stone .... **AGATE**
magic: W. Ind. .... **OBEAH**
magician .... **MAGE,**
    MAGI, MAGUS, MERLIN
magistrate, Athens **ARCHON**
magistrate, It. .... **DOGE**
magistrate, Rom. ...... **EDILE,**
    AEDILE, CONSUL, PRETOR
magnate ... **MOGUL, TYCOON**
magnifying glass .... **LENS**
Magog, ruler of .... **GOG**
magpie .. **MAG, PIE, MAGG,**
    PIET, PIOT, PYAT, PYET,
    NINUT, PIANET
magpie genus .... **PICA**
mah-jongg piece .... **TILE**
mahatma
    ARAHT, ARHAT, ARAHAT
mahogany pine ...... **TOTARA**
mahogany, Sp. .... **CAOBA**
mahogany streak .... **ROE**
mahogany tree, Ind. ... **TOON**
MAHOMET .. see **MOHAMMED**
MAHOMETAN ... see **MOSLEM**
maid .... **LASS, BONNE**
maid, lady's .... **ABIGAIL**
maid-of-all-work ..... **SLAVEY**
maid, Oriental
    AMA, IYA, AMAH, EYAH
maiden .... **DAMSEL**

c maiden name, signifying ..**NEE**
maiden of myth .... **IO**
mail .... **POST, SEND**
mail, coat of . **BRINIE, BYRNIE**
mail, India **DAK, DAUK, DAWK**
main point ... **NUB, GIST, PITH**
maintain.**AVER, HOLD, ASSERT**
maize .... **CORN**
maize bread .... **PIKI**
maize genus .... **ZEA**
major: music .... **DUR**
major third: Gr. mus. .. **DITONE**
make .... **RENDER**
make as one: obs. ...... **UNE**
make evident .... **EVINCE**
make fast: naut. ...... **BELAY**
make good by action . **REDEEM**
make happy .... **ELATE**
make public: Old Eng. **DELATE**
Makua .... **KUA**
malarial fever .... **AGUE**
malarial poison
    MIASM, MIASMA
Malay apple .... **KAWIKA**
Malay canoe
    PRAH, PRAO, PRAU, PROA
Malay chief or headman.**DATO,**
    DATU, DATTO
d Malay dagger ... **CRIS, KRIS,**
    CREES, KREES, CREESE, KREESE
Malay lanseh tree ..... **DUKU**
Malay law .... **ADAT**
Malay lugger .... **TOUP**
malay negrito ..... **ATA, ITA**
Malay nerve ailment ... **LATA**
MALAY OUTRIGGER see **MALAY**
    CANOE
Malay title of respect .. **TUAN**
Malay ungulate ...... **TAPIR**
Malay verse form ... **PANTUN**
Malay vessel
    PRAH, PRAO, PRAU, PROA
Malay, word meaning dark **AETA**
Malayan ape .... **LAR**
male cat .... **GIB, TOM**
male figure, used as support
    ATLAS, TELAMON
male swan .... **COB**
malefic .... **EVIL**
malic acid, fruit with
    ATTA, APPLE, GRAPE
malign .... **REVILE**
malignant .... **EVIL**
malignant spirit ... **KER, KERES**
malleable ..... **SOFT, DUCTILE**
mallet .... **MALL, GAVEL**
malt drink, pert. to .... **ALY**
malt infusion .... **WORT**
maltreat .... **ABUSE**

MAMMAL .. see also ANIMAL
mammal, sea aquatic .. SEAL,
  OTTER, WHALE, DUGONG,
  MANATEE
mammoth .... GIANT
man-eating monster ... LAMIA
man, handsome ...... ADONIS
man, rich .... CROESUS
man's name .. ELI, GUY, IAN,
  IRA, JOB, LEE, RAY, REX,
  ADAM, ALAN, AMOS,
  BRAM, CARL, DANA, DION,
  EBEN, EMIL, ENOS, ERIC,
  EVAN, EZRA, HANS, HUGH,
  HUGO, IVAN, JOEL, JOHN,
  JOSE, JUAN, JUDE, KARL,
  KNUT, LEON, LUKE, MARC,
  MARK, NEIL, NOEL, OTTO,
  OWEN, PAUL, SEAN, SETH,
  TEIG, BASIL, CALEB,
  CLARE, ENOCH, HIRAM,
  HOMER, SERGE, STEVE,
  TERRY, DEXTER, GASPAR,
  GEORGE, OLIVER, SAMSON,
  STEVEN, WARREN
man's nickname. AL, ABE, ALF,
  BEN, BOB, DON, GUS, JIM,
  JOE, KIT, LEW, LON, LOU,
  MAC, MAT, MAX, MOE,
  NED, PAT, ROB, SAM, SID,
  SIM, TED, TOM, ABIE,
  ALGY, ANDY, BART, BERT,
  BILL, BONY, DAVE, DAVY,
  DICK, DODE, FRED, GENE,
  JACK, JAKE, JOCK, JOEY,
  MART, MIKE, MOSE, NOLL,
  PETE, PHIL, RUBE, TOBY,
  TONY, WALT, ZACH, ZEKE
manageable .... YARE
manager .... GERENT
Manasseh, city of ...... ANER
Manasseh, son of ..... AMON
mandarin's home
  YAMEN, YAMUN
manducate .... EAT
maned .... JUBATE
manger ...... CRIB, CRECHE
mangle .... MAUL
mango. P. I. ...... CARABAO
mania .... CRAZE
manifest .... SHOW,
  OVERT, ATTEST, EVINCE
manifestation .... AURA
manifestation of god of lower
  world .... SERAPIS
maniple FANO, FANON, FANUM
manner
  AIR, WAY, MIEN, MODE
manner of walking ..... GAIT
manners .... MORES
manor .... DEMENE, DEMESNE

mantis crab .... SQUILLA
mantle .... CAPE
manual training, Swed. . SLOID,
  SLOYD
manuao .... IAO
Manxman .... GAEL
many .... MAINT
many-colored
  PIED, PINTO, MOTLEY
many-colored stone ... AGATE
Maori tattooing .... MOKO
Maori village ... KAIK, KAIKA
Maori wages .... UTU
Maori war club MERE, MARREE
Maori war-club wood ... RATA
map .... PLAT
map in a map .... INSET
maple fruit, seed .... SAMARA
maple genus .... ACER
maple tree tap .... SPILE
mar .... DEFACE
marabou .... ARGALA
marble MIB, MIG, TAW, MIGG,
  AGATE, AGGIE, MARMOR,
  MEALIE, SHOOTER
marble, Belgian RANCE, RANSE
marble, choice ALAY, ALLEY
marble, It. .... CARRARA
marble, Rom. .... CIPOLIN
marble, white .... DOLOMITE
marbles, game at ...... TAW
March King .... SOUSA
mare: Gypsy .... GRASNI
margin .... RIM, EDGE, MARGE
marginal reading, Hebrew
  Bible .... KRI
margosa tree .... NIM, NEEM
Marie Wilson, character played
  by .... IRMA
MARINE .. see also SEA
marine annelid .... LURG
marine fish, E. Ind. ... DORAB
marine measure, Jap. ..... RI
marine snail
  WELK, WILK, WHELK
marine snail genus .. NERITA
marine turtle genus.. CARETTA
marine worm ...... SYLLID
marionette maker ...... SARG
mark .... STIGMA, STIGMATA
mark, diacritic TILDE, MACRON
mark of omission ..... CARET
mark, reference
  OBELI, OBELUS, OBELISK
mark, short vowel .... BREVE
marked with spots: bot. NOTATE
marker, Gr. & Rom. ... STELA,
  STELE, STELAE, STELAI

a market .... **MART, SELL, VEND, RIALTO**
market: India .... **PASAR**
market, Oriental **SUQ, SOOK, SOUK**
market place **BAZAR, BAZAAR**
market place, Gr. .... **AGORA**
marksman .... **AIMER**
marmalade tree **MAMEY, SAPOTE**
marmoset .... **MICO**
marmoset, S. Am. .. **TAMARIN**
"Marner, — " Eliot novel **SILAS**
marriage, absence of .. **AGAMY**
marriage notice **BAN, BANNS**
marriage portion, pert. to **DOTAL**
marriage portion: Scot. **DOS, DOTE**
marriage settlement **DOS, DOT, DOWRY, DOWERY**
marriage vows .... **TROTH**
marriageable .... **NUBILE**
marrow .... **PITH**
marry .... **WED, WIVE**
Mars .... **ARES**
Mars' outer satellite .. **DEIMOS**
Mars, pert. to .... **AREAN**
"Marseillaise" author .. **LISLE**

b marsh .... **BOG, FEN, SLUE, LIMAN, SWALE**
marsh elder .... **IVA**
marsh fever .... **HELODES**
marsh gas .... **METHANE**
marsh hen .... **RAIL**
marsh mallow .... **ALTEA**
marsh marigold ...... **CAPER**
marsh plant **REED, SEDGE, FESCUE**
marshal, Waterloo .... **NEY**
marshy . **PALUDAL, PALUDINE**
marsupial, arboreal **COALA, KOALA, POSSUM**
marten .... **SOBOL**
martyr, 1st Christian . **STEPHEN**
marvel .... **MIRACLE**
Mascagni heroine .... **LOLA**
MASCULINE see also MALE, MAN'S
mashy .... **IRON**
masjid ...... **MOSK, MOSQUE**
mask, half .... **DOMINO**
mask topknot, Gr. ..... **ONKOS**
masons' pickax ...... **GURLET**
masquerade cloak ... **DOMINO**
mass ...... **GOB, WAD, BULK**
mass book .... **MISSAL**
mass meeting .... **RALLY**
mass, pert. to .... **MISSATICAL**
mass, rounded .... **BOLUS**
mast .... **SPAR**

c mast: obs. .... **SPIR**
mast, support .... **BIBB**
mast, wood for .... **POON**
master: archaic .... **DAN**
master, India **MIAN, SAHEB, SAHIB**
master, pert. to .... **HERILE**
master, S. Afr. .... **BAAS**
master-stroke .... **COUP**
mastic tree .... **ACOMA**
masticate ...... **CHAW, CHEW**
mat, ornamental ...... **DOILY**
match, friction . **FUSEE, FUZEE**
match, wax .... **VESTA**
matchmaker .... **EROS**
MATERIAL ... see also FABRIC
maternity goddess, Egypt . **APET**
matgrass .... **NARD**
math quantity .**SINE, OPERAND**
math ratio, quantity .. **PI, SINE**
math term, hyperbolic function **COSH, SECH, SINH, TANH**
matter: law .... **RES**
matter-of-fact ...... **LITERAL**
matter: philos. .... **HYLE**
mattress case .... **TICK**
mature ..... **AGE, RIPE, RIPEN**
mature reproductive cell **GAMETE**

d maul .... **MALLET**
Mau Mau territory .... **KENYA**
Mauna — .... **LOA**
mausoleum, at Agra ..... **TAJ**
maw: dialect .... **MAA**
maxilla .... **JAW, MALA**
maxim . **SAW, ADAGE, AXIOM, GNOME, MOTTO, SAYING**
maxwell per ampere turn . **PERM**
May 1, Celtic ...... **BELTANE**
May fly .... **DUN**
MAYAN . see MAYAN INDIAN, page 192
Mayan year .... **HAAB**
Mayan year-end days .. **UAYEB**
mayor, Sp. . **ALCADE, ALCALDE**
meadow .... **LEA, MEAD**
meadow barley .... **RIE**
meadow grass genus ..... **POA**
meadow mouse .... **VOLE**
meadow saxifrage ..... **SESELI**
meadowsweet **SPIREA, SPIRAEA**
meager .... **SCANT, LENTEN, SCANTY**
meal .... **REPAST**
meal, boiled .... **MUSH**
meal, fine .... **FARINA**
meal, grain .. **PINOLA, PINOLE**
meal, Indian, Hindu **ATA, ATTA**
meal, light .... **BEVER**

Meaning

a meaning .... **SENSE, PURPORT**
meantime .... **INTERIM**
MEASURE ... Area, Liquid, Dry
Length, Distance
    see SPECIAL SECTION
measure ...... **EM, EN, GAGE,
METE, PACE, GAUGE**
MEASURE, BIB. .. see **HEBREW
MEASURE**
measure, Chin. length .... **LI**
"Measure for Measure"
character .... **ANGELO**
MEASURE, DRY, BIB. ..... see
HEBREW DRY MEASURE
measure, Jap. distance .... **RI**
measure of distance, Ang.-Ind.
COSS
measure of spirits .... **PEG**
measure, old Arab ...... **SAA**
measure, old length ...... **ELL**
measure, poetry .... **SCAN**
measure, square .... **AR, ARE**
meat, cut of ...... **HAM, RIB,
CHOP, LOIN, FILET,
STEAK, FILLET**
meat on skewer ...... **CABOB,
KABOB, KEBAB**
meat roll, fried ...... **RISSOLE**
Mecca pilgrim garb .... **IHRAM**
b Mecca shrine .... **CAABA,
KAABA, KAABEH**
Mecca, trip to .... **HADJ**
mechanical man ...... **ROBOT**
mechanical part .... **CAM**
mechanics, branch of . **STATICS**
mechanics of motion
DYNAMICS
meddle .... **PRY, TAMPER**
Medea's father .... **AEETES**
median line of valve ... **RAPHE**
medical .... **IATRIC**
medical fluid .... **SERUM**
medicinal capsule .... **CACHET**
medicinal fruit shrub ... **ALEM**
medicinal gum .... **KINO**
medicinal herb .... **ALOE,
IPECAC, BONESET**
medicinal plant .... **ALOE**
medicinal plant, leaves **SENNA**
medicinal tablet ..... **TROCHE**
medicine man ...... **SHAMAN**
medicine man, S. Am.
PEAI, PIAY
medieval lyric .... **ALBA**
medieval society **GILD, GUILD**
medieval tale, poem . **LAI, LAY**
Medina Arab .... **AUS**
MEDITERRANEAN .... see also
GAZETTEER
Mediterranean, East of.**LEVANT**
Medit. grass .... **DISS**

c Medit. herb genus ...... **AMMI**
Medit. island: It. .... **RODI**
Medit. resort .... **NICE**
medlar .... **MESPIL**
medley .... **OLIO**
Medusa's slayer ..... **PERSEUS**
meet .... **SIT**
meeting ..... **TRYST, SESSION**
meeting, political .... **CAUCUS**
megapode .... **MALEO**
melancholy . **SAD, BLUE, DREAR**
melancholy: poet. ...... **DOLOR**
mellow .... **AGE, RIPE**
melodic .... **ARIOSE**
melodious .... **ARIOSO**
melody .... **AIR, ARIA,
TUNE, MELOS**
melon .... **PEPO, CASABA**
melt together ..... **FUSE, FUZE**
melted .... **MOLTEN**
membership .... **SEAT**
membrane .... **WEB, TELA,
VELA, VELUM**
memento .... **RELIC**
memorabilia .... **ANA**
memorandum ... **CHIT, NOTE**
memorial post, Indian .. **TOTEM**
memory, pert. to
MNESIC, MNEMONIC
Memphis chief god .... **PTAH**
d Memphis street, famous.**BEALE**
men .... **SONS**
mendacious person ...... **LIAR**
mender, chief .... **TINKER**
mendicant, Mos.
FAKIR, FAKEER
Menelaus' wife .... **HELEN**
menhaden fish .... **POGY**
menhaden, young ... **SARDINE**
Mennonite .... **AMISH**
Menotti heroine ...... **AMELIA**
men's party .... **STAG**
mental .... **PHRENIC**
mental deficiency ... **AMENTIA**
mental deficient **IDIOT, MORON**
mention .... **CITE**
Mercator .... **MAP, CHART**
mercenary . **VENAL, HIRELING**
merchandise .... **WARES**
merchant .... **TRADER**
merchant: India .... **SETH**
"Merchant of Venice" heiress
PORTIA
merchant ship ...... **ARGOSY**
merchant vessel, Gr. . **HOLCAD**
Mercury, Gr. .... **HERMES**
Mercury's wand ... **CADUCEUS**
mercy, show .... **SPARE**
mere .... **SIMPLE**
merely .... **ONLY**

a merganser duck **SMEW, GARBILL**
merge .... **MELD**
merit .... **EARN**
merriment .... **GLEE**
merry-go-round ... **CAROUSAL,
CAROUSEL, CARROUSAL**
"Merry Widow" composer **LEHAR**
"Merry Wives" character
PISTOL
mesh .... **NET, WEB**
Mesopotamia ..... **IRAK, IRAQ**
Mesopotamian boat **GUFA, KUFA**
Mesopotamian city ..... **URFA**
mesquite bean flour ... **PINOLE**
mess, to make a ...... **BOTCH**
mestizo .... **METIS**
metal .... **TIN, MONEL**

metal alloy .... **BRASS,
MONEL, BRONZE**
metal, bar of .... **INGOT**
metal bar on house door . **RISP**
metal casting .... **PIG, INGOT**
metal, coat with .**PLATE, TERNE**
metal-decorating art .. **NIELLO**
metal disk .... **MEDAL**
metal dross .... **SLAG**
metal filings .... **LEMEL**
metal fissure .... **LODE**
b metal leaf .... **FOIL**
metal mixture .... **ALLOY**
metal refuse .... **SCORIA**
metal spacer: print. ..... **SLUG**
metal suit .... **MAIL**
metal sulfide, impure . **MATTE**
metal, white .... **TIN**
metallic rock .... **ORE**
metalware, lacquered .... **TOLE**
metalwork, god of .. **VULCAN**
metarabic acid ..... **CERASIN**
meteor .... **LEONID**
meteor, exploding
BOLIS, BOLIDE
meter, Dutch .... **EL**
meter, one-millionth .. **MICRON**
meters, 100 sq. ...... **AR, ARE**
metheglin .... **MEAD**
method ...... **PLAN, ORDER**
Methuselah's grandson .. **NOAH**
methyl-phenol
CRESOL, CRESSOL
metric measure ..... **AR, ARE,
GRAM, KILO, LITER, METER,
STERE, DECARE, HECTARE**
metric "quart" .... **LITER**
metrical beat .... **ICTUS**
metrical unit .... **MORA**
metropolitan .... **URBAN**
mew .... **GULL**
mew, cat's .... **MIAU, MIAW,
MIAOU, MIAUL**

c Mexican dollar .... **PESO**
Mex. mush .... **ATOLE**
Mex. painter .... **RIVERA**
Mex. persimmon .... **CHAPOTE**
Mex. plant .... **JALAP**
Mex. president ...... **ALEMAN,
CALLES, MADERO**
Mex. resin tree .... **DRAGO**
Mex. rodent .... **TUCAN**
Mex. slave .... **PEON**
Mex. spiny tree ...... **RETAMA**
Mex. timber tree ...... **ABETO**
Mex. wind instrument . **CLARIN**
mezzanine .... **ENTRESOL**
miasma .... **MALARIA**
mica, kind of .... **BIOTITE**
mica of muscovite ...... **TALC**
microbe .... **GERM**
microspores .... **POLLEN**
middle .... **MESAL,
MESNE, MEDIAN**
middle, in the ...... **ATWEEN**
middle, toward .... **MESAD**
middling .... **SOSO**
Midgard Serpent slayer .. **THOR**
midge .... **GNAT**
midship, off .... **ABEAM**
d "Midsummer Night's Dream"
character .. **PUCK, SNUG**
midwife: India .... **DHAI**
MID-EAST land .. **IRAK, IRAQ**
mien .... **AIR**
might .... **POWER**
mignonette ... **GREEN, RESEDA**
migrate .... **TREK**
migratory worker
OKIE, ARKIE
Mikado's court . **DAIRI, DAIRO**
Milanion's wife ... **ATALANTA**
Milan's "Met" ...... **LA SCALA**
mild ...... **SHY, MEEK, SOFT,
BLAND, GENTLE**
mildness .... **LENITY**
mile: naut. .... **KNOT**
mile, part of, Burma ... **DHA**
Miled, son of .... **IR, ITH, EBER**
milestone .... **STELE**
milfoil .... **YARROW**
military award .... **DSO**
military cap .... **KEPI**
military command ... **AT EASE**
military group . **CADRE, CORPS**
military maneuvers .. **TACTICS**
milk, coagulated ...... **CURD**
milk coagulator ..... **RENNIN**
milk, curdled ...... **CLABBER**
milk, part of **SERUM, LACTOSE**
milk, pert. to .... **LACTIC**
milk: pharm. .... **LAC**
milk protein .... **CASEINE**

Milk

a
milk, watery part of .... **WHEY**
milkfish .... **AWA, SABALO**
Milky Way .... **GALAXY**
mill .... **QUERN**
MILLET
   see also GRAIN SORGHUM
millet, India **JOAR,JUAR,CHENA**
millimeter, 1000th part **MICRON**
millstone support ...... **RYND**
millwheel board .... **LADE**
millwheel bucket .... **AWE**
Milton, masque by .... **COMUS**
Milton rebel angel ..... **ARIEL**
mime .... **APER**
mimic ...... **APE, APER, MIME**
mimicking, practice of . **APISM**
mimosa .... **ACACIA**
minced oath .. **GAD, GED, GEE,**
   LUD, DRAT, EGAD, HECK,
   OONS, SWOW, MAFEY,
   MACKINS
mind .... **CARE, TEND**
mind, opposite of: Hindu
   ATTA, ATMAN
mind: philos. .... **NOUS**
Mindanao native, Indonesian
   ATA, AETA, MORO
mine ceiling .... **ASTEL**
mine entrance .... **ADIT**
mine narrow veins ..... **RESUE**

b
mine passage .... **STULM**
mine roof support .... **NOG**
mine shaft drain pit .... **SUMP**
mine step .... **LOB**
mineral, alkaline ..... **TRONA**
mineral, blue .... **IOLITE**
mineral group ...... **URANITE**
mineral group, pert. to . **SALIC**
mineral, hard **SPINEL, SPINELLE**
mineral, lustrous .... **SPAR**
mineral, raw, native ..... **ORE**
mineral salt .... **ALUM**
mineral, soft .... **TALC**
mineral spring .... **SPA**
mineral tar .... **BREA**
mineral, transparent ... **MICA**
mineral used gun-powder **NITER**
Minerva .... **ATHENA**
minim .... **DROP**
mining refuse .... **ATTLE**
mining road .... **BORD**
mining tool .... **GAD, BEELE**
minister, Moslem **VIZIR, VIZIER**
minister (to) .... **CATER**
mink, Amer. .... **VISON**
minority, legal ...... **NONAGE**
Minos' daughter .... **ARIADNE**
Minotaur's slayer .... **THESEUS**
minstrel .... **RIMER**
minstrel, medieval ... **GOLIARD**
minstrel, Norse . **SCALD, SKALD**

c
mint .... **COIN**
mint, Europ. ... **CLARE, CLARY,**
   CLARRY, HYSSOP, DITTANY
mint genus .... **MENTHA**
mint herb .... **SAGE**
mints, the .... **NEPETA**
minus .... **LESS**
minute .... **WEE, TINY, SMALL**
mira .... **STAR**
miracle, scene of first .. **CANA**
mirage .... **SERAB**
miscellany .... **ANA**
mischief .... **HOB**
mischievous spirit ...... **PUCK**
misconceive .... **ERR**
Mishnah section . **ABOT, ABOTH**
Mishnah section festivals .**MOED**
misinterpret .... **ERR**
mislay .... **LOSE**
misplay .... **ERROR**
misrepresent .... **BELIE**
Miss Dombey's suitor .. **TOOTS**
missile .... **DART, SNARK**
missile, guided ... **JUNO, NIKE,**
   THOR, ATLAS, TITAN,
   BOMARC, JUPITER, PERSH-
   ING, REGULUS, REDSTONE,
   BOLD ORION,MINUTEMAN
mist .... **HAZE, SMUR, MISLE**
mist: Eng. .... **RAG**

d
mistake, stupid .... **BONER**
mistakes .... **ERRATA**
mistakes, make .... **ERR**
mite .... **ACARI, ATOMY,**
   ACARID, ACARUS
mite genus .. **ACARI, ACARUS**
mite, tick, order of
   ACARIDA, ACARINA
mitigate . **EASE, ABATE, ALLAY**
mix .... **STIR, ADDLE. KNEAD**
mixture .... **OLIO**
mixture, mineral ..... **MAGMA**
Moab city, chief .... **UR**
Moab king .... **MESHA**
Moabites, Bibl. .... **EMIM**
moat .... **FOSS, FOSSE**
"Moby Dick" pursuer .. **AHAB**
moccasin .... **PAC**
mock ..... **GIBE, JIBE, FLEER,**
   TAUNT, DERIDE
mock blow .... **FEINT**
mock orange ...... **SYRINGA**
mockingbird genus .... **MIMUS**
model, perfect ..... **PARAGON**
moderate .... **BATE,**
   ABATE, LESSEN
modernist .... **NEO**
modest .... **SHY, DEMURE**
modify .... **VARY, ALTER,**
   EMEND, TEMPER
Mogul emperor ...... **AKBAR**

MOHAMMEDAN .. see MOSLEM
Mohammedanism ...... ISLAM
Mohammed's adopted son . ALI
Mohammed's birthplace .MECCA
Mohammed's daughter .FATIMA
Mohammed's descendant
   SAID, SEID, SAYID
Mohammed's son-in-law .. ALI
Mohammed's supporters .ANSAR
Mohammed's title .... ALI
Mohammed's tomb city MEDINA
Mohammed's uncle .... ABBAS
Mohammed's wife .... AISHA
Mohawk, city on .... UTICA
Mohicans, last of the .. UNCAS
moiety .... HALF
moist .... WET, DAMP, DANK,
  DEWY, UVID, HUMID
moist spot, rock-ledge .... SIPE
moisten ... DAMPEN, IMBRUE
moisture, having medium MESIC
mojarra fish .... PATAO
molasses .. TREACLE, TRIACLE
molasses, rum made from
     TAFIA
mold .... MUST
mold, hole in casting .GIT, GEAT
molded clay .... PUG
molding .. CYMA, GULA, OGEE,
 TORUS, REGLET, REEDING
molding, concave
   CONGE, SCOTIA
molding, convex
 OVOLO, TORUS, ASTRAGAL
molding, curved . CYMA, OGEE
molding, edge of . ARIS, ARRIS
molding, flat .... FILLET
molding, rounded TORI, TORUS
molding, S-shaped ..... OGEE
molding, square ...... LISTEL
moldings, quarter-round .OVOLI
moldy .... MUSTY
mole .... NEVUS, NAEVUS
mole cricket, S. Am. .. CHANGA
mole genus .... TALPA
molecule part .... ION
molelike mammal .... DESMAN
MOLLUSK .see also GASTROPOD
mollusk ...... CLAM, CHITON,
  MUSSEL, ABALONE
mollusk, bivalve ..... SCALLOP
mollusk, chamber-shelled
    NAUTILUS
mollusk, gastropod
  SNAIL, ABALONE
mollusk genus ARCA, MUREX,
  OLIVA, ANOMIA
mollusk, largest ...... CHAMA
mollusk's rasp organ .. RADULA
molt .... MEW, SHED

molten rock ... LAVA, MAGMA
moment ..... MO, JIFF, TRICE
Monaco, pert. to
 MONACAN, MONEGASQUE
monad .... ATOM, UNIT
monastery .... MANDRA
monastery church .. MINSTER
MONEY . see also SPECIAL
   SECTION COINS
money ... CASH, CUSH, GELT
money, Amer. Ind. .. WAMPUM
money, bronze .... AES
money certificate .BOND, SCRIP
money, copper .... AES
money: dialect .... SPENSE
money, early Eng. .... ORA
money drawer .... TILL
money exchange fee .... AGIO
money, fishhook . LARI, LARIN
money, medieval .... ORA
money of account .... ORA
money, piece of .... COIN
money premium .... AGIO
money, put in .... INVEST
money reserve .... FUND
money, shell . SEWAN, SEAWAN
money, trade unit .... UNITAS
moneylender .... USURER
moneylender, Ind. .. MAHAJAN
Mongol ... HU, ELEUT, TATAR,
  ELEUTH, TARTAR
Mongol dynasty .... YUAN
Mongol warrior .... TATAR
Mongolian tent .... YURT
Mongoloid .... TURK, DURBAN
Mongoloid in Indo-China .SHAN
mongrel .... CUR, MUTT
monitor lizard .... URAN
monk .. FRA, FRIAR, CENOBITE
monk, Buddhist ...... ARAHT,
  ARHAT, ARAHAT
monk, Eng. ...... BEDA, BEDE
monk, Gr. Church ... CALOYER
monk, head .... ABBOT
monk settlement.SCETE, SKETE
monk's hood .... COWL
monk's title ..... FRA, ABBOT
monkey .... APE, LAR, SAI,
 SIME, SIMIAN, MARMOSET
monkey, Afr. .... MONA,
  WAAG, GRIVET
monkey, Asia .... LANGUR
monkey, capuchin .... SAI
monkey, Chin. .... DOUC
monkey genus .... CEBUS
monkey, guenon ...... NISNAS
monkey, howling ...... ARABA
monkey, P. I. .... MACHIN
monkey puzzle .... PINON
monkey, red, Afr. ..... PATAS
monkey, small .... LEMUR

a monkey, S. Am. .. **SAKI, TITI,
ACARI, ARABA, SAJOU,
TETEE, PINCHE, SAGUIN,
SAMIRI, SAIMIRI, SAPAJOU**
monkey, spider, genus.**QUATA,
ATELES, COAITA**
monkshood .... **ATIS,
ATEES, ACONITE**
monolith .... **MENHIR**
monopoly ..... **TRUST, CARTEL**
monosaccharide .... **OSE**
Mons, language of ...... **PEGU**
monster .. **GOUL, GOWL, OGRE**
monster, Gr. myth .. **CHIMERA**
monster, half-man-bull
MINOTAUR
monster: med. ...... **TERAS**
monster, 100 eyes ..... **ARGUS**
monster slain by Hercules
HYDRA
month, Egypt. .... **AHET,
APAP, TYBI**
month, first day, Rom.
CALENDS, KALENDS
month, Hindu .... **ASIN, JETH,
KUAR, MAGH**
month, in last .... **ULTIMO**
month, Jewish ancient ..... **AB**
(11th), **BUL** (8th), **ZIF**
(8th), **ABIB** (7th), **ADAR**
(6th), **ELUL** (12th), **IYAR,**
(8th), **NISAN** (7th), **SEBAT**
(5th), **SIVAN** (9th), **TEBET**
(4th), **TIZRI** (1st), **TEBETH**
(4th), **TISHRI** (1st)
month, Moslem .... **RABIA,
RAJAB, SAFAR, SHABAN,
RAMADAN**
month, Nisan .... **ABIB**
monument, stone.**LECH, CAIRN,
DOLMEN, CROMLECH**
moon . **LUNA, DIANA, PHOEBE**
moon, age at beginning of
calendar year ..... **EPACT**
moon angel .... **MAH**
moon flower .... **ACHETE**
moon god, Babyl. .. **SIN, ENZU**
moon goddess ...... **ASTARTE**
moon goddess, Gr. ..... **SELENA,
SELENE, ARTEMIS**
moon goddess, Rom. .. **LUNA,
DIAN, DIANA**
moon nearest earth, point
PERIGEE
moon valley ..... **RILL, RILLE**
moor grass .... **NARD**
moorhen .... **GORHEN**
Moorish .... **MORISCAN**
moose genus .... **ALCES**
mop .... **SWAB, SWOB**

c Moqui, one of .... **HOPI**
morals overseer ...... **CENSOR**
morass .... **QUAG, MARSH**
moray .... **EEL**
Mordecai, enemy of .. **HAMAN**
more .... **PLUS**
more! ...... **BIS, PIU, ENCORE**
more than enough ...... **TOO,
EXTRA, EXCESS**
More's island .... **UTOPIA**
morepork, N. Z. ... **PEHO, RURU**
morindin dye .... **AL**
moringa seed .... **BEN**
morning glory .... **IPOMEA**
morning music ...... **AUBADE**
morning: P. I. .... **UMAGA**
morning prayer ...... **MATINS**
morning song .... **MATIN**
Moro .... **SULU, LANAO**
Moro chief **DATO, DATU, DATTO**
Moro mantle .... **JABUL**
Moroccan Berber .... **RIFF**
Moroccan land, public ... **GISH**
Moroccan native .... **MOOR**
moron .... **AMENT, IDIOT**
morose ... **BLUE, GLUM, GRUM**
morsel .... **ORT**
mortar implement .... **PESTLE**
d mortar ingredient ...... **LIME**
mortar mixer ... ... **RAB**
mortar tray .... **HOD**
mortise insert .... **TENON**
Mosaic law .... **TORA, TORAH**
mosaic piece .... **TESSERA**
Moselle, river to .... **SAAR**
Moses, law given to here
SINA, SINAI
Moses' brother .... **AARON**
Moses' death mountain .. **NEBO**
Moses' father-in-law . **JETHRO**
Moses' spy in Canaan .. **CALEB**
MOSLEM ..... see also **MECCA**
Moslem .... **TURK**
Moslem ablution before prayer
WIDU, WUDU, WUZU
Moslem, Afr. .... **MOOR**
Moslem beggar .**FAKIR, FAKEER**
Moslem bible .... **KORAN**
Moslem call to prayer
ADAN, AZAN
Moslem chief .... **AGA,
IMAM, DATTO**
Moslem chief gold coin.**DINAR**
Moslem converts ..... **ANSAR**
Moslem deity ... **JANN, ALLAH**
Moslem demon .. **JANN, EBLIS**
Moslem Easter .... **EED**
Moslem fast ...... **RAMADAN**
Moslem festival ...... **BAIRAM**

a
Moslem fiat .... **IRADE**
Moslem fourth Caliph .... **ALI**
Moslem grant of property
WAKF, WAQF, WUKF
Moslem guide .... **PIR**
Moslem holy city ..... **MECCA**
Moslem holy man
IMAM, IMAUM
Moslem, hostile to Crusaders
SARACEN
Moslem in Turkestan ... **SALAR**
Moslem judge .. **CADI, CAZI,**
CAZY, KADI, KAZI, KAZY
Moslem leader . **IMAM, IMAUM**
Moslem marriage.**MOTA, MUTA**
Moslem marriage settlement
MAHR
MOSLEM MORO ... see **MORO**
CHIEF
Moslem mystic .... **SUFI**
Moslem name .... **ALI**
Moslem Negroids .... **MABA**
Moslem noble .... **AMIR, EMIR,**
AMEER, EMEER
Moslem, N. W. India ... **SWAT**
Moslem official .... **AGA**
Moslem, orthodox ..... **HANIF**
Moslem, P.I. .... **MORO**
Moslem potentate .... **AGA**
Moslem prayer .... **SALAT**
Moslem prayer place ... **IDGAH**
Moslem priest . **IMAM, IMAUM**
b
Moslem prince ... **AMIR, EMIR,**
AMEER, EMEER
Moslem principle .... **IJMA**
Moslem pulpit ...... **MIMBAR**
Moslem reformer .... **WAHABI**
Moslem religion .... **ISLAM**
Moslem religious college
ULEMA
Moslem ruler .... **HAKIM**
Moslem saber ...... **SCIMITAR**
Moslem saint .... **PIR**
Moslem school ..... **MADRASA**
Moslem spirit ... **JINN, JINNI**
Moslem spiritual guide ... **PIR**
Moslem teacher .. **ALIM, COJA**
Moslem temple.**MOSK, MOSQUE**
Moslem theologians ... **ULEMA**
Moslem title .... **AGA, RAIS,**
REIS, SEID, SIDI, SYED,
SYUD, CALIF, SAYID,
SEYID, CALIPH
Moslem tunic .. **JAMA, JAMAH**
Moslem weight .... **ROTL**
Moslem woman's dress .. **IZAR**
Moslems, Sunnite .... **SART**
Moslemized Bulgarian . **POMAK**
mosque .... **MASJID**
mosque, central .... **JAMI**
mosque, Jerusalem .... **OMAR**
mosque student .... **SOFTA**

c
mosquito, genus, yellow-fever
AEDES
mossbunker fish .... **POGY**
moss of Ceylon .... **AGAR**
moth .... **IO, LUNA,**
EGGER, TINEA
moth, clearwing, genus . **SESIA**
moth, clothes .... **TINEA**
moth, green .... **LUNA**
mother goddess; Baby. . **ERUA**
mother goddesses. Hindu **MATRIS**
mother of Arthur .... **IGRAINE**
mother of gods .... **RHEA**
MOTHER OF IRISH GODS .. see
page 200
mother-of-pearl .... **NACRE**
mother-of-pearl shell.**ABALONE**
mother turned to stone . **NIOBE**
mother's side, related on
ENATE, ENATIC
mother's side, relation on
ENATE, ENATION
motherless calf .. **DOGY, DOGIE**
motion, producing .... **MOTILE**
motionless ..... **INERT, STILL**
motive ...... **CAUSE, REASON**
motmot, S. Am. ...... **HOUTOU**
motor part .... **ROTOR**
mottled .... **PIED, PINTO**
d
mottled, as wood ...... **ROEY**
MOULDING .... see **MOLDING**
mound ...... **TUMP, BARROW**
mound, Polyn. .... **AHU**
Mount of Olives ...... **OLIVET**
mountain, Alps ...... **BLANC**
mountain ash .. **SORB, ROWAN**
mountain, Asia Minor ..... **IDA**
mountain, Bibl. .. **HOR, NEBO,**
SEIR, SINA, HOREB,
SINAI, ARARAT
(see others on page 197)
mountain chain .... **SIERRA**
mountain climbing staff .**PITON**
mountain crest .... **ARETE**
mountain, Crete .... **IDA**
mountain, Edom .... **HOR**
mountain, fabled Hindu . **MERU**
mountain, famous .... **IDA**
mountain, Gr. .... **HELICON**
mountain in Thessaly ... **OSSA**
mountain lion .... **PUMA**
mountain mint .... **BASIL**
mountain, Moab .... **NEBO**
mountain pass .... **COL**
mountain pass, Alps **CENIS**
mountain pass, India
GAUT, GHAT
mountain peak .... **ALP**
mountain pool .... **TARN**
mountain recess .... **CWM**
mountain ridge .... **ARETE**

a mountain ridge, Port. .. **SERRA**
mountain, 2nd highest N.A.
LOGAN
mountain sickness **PUNA, VETA**
mountain spinach ..... **ORACH**
mountain spur .... **ARETE**
mountains, Asia ...... **ALTAI**
mountains, myth ... **KAF, QAF**
mourn .... **WEEP,**
GRIEVE, LAMENT
mournful .... **SAD, DIRE**
mourning band .... **CRAPE**
mouse .... **VOLE**
mouse, field .... **VOLE**
mouse genus .... **MUS**
mousebird ..... **COLY, SHRIKE**
mouth .... **OS, ORA**
mouth, away from .... **ABORAL**
mouth open .... **AGAPE**
mouth, river .... **DELTA**
mouth, tidal river ...... **FRITH**
mouth, toward .... **ORAD**
mouthful .... **SIP, SUP**
mouthlike orifice ...... **STOMA**
mouthpiece ....: **REED, BOCAL**
move .... **STIR, AFFECT**
move a camera .... **PAN**
move back ..... **EBB, RECEDE**
move to and fro
WAG, FLAP, SWAY

b movement: biol. .... **TAXIS**
movement, capable of . **MOTILE**
movement: music ...... **MOTO**
movement,with:music **CONMOTO**
movie: Sp. .... **CINE**
moving part .... **ROTOR**
mow, barn's .... **LOFT**
mow of hay .... **GOAF**
mowed strip .... **SWATH**
Mowgli's bear friend ... **BALU,**
BALOO
Mozambique native ...... **YAO**
muck .... **MIRE**
mud .... **MIRE, MURGEON**
mud deposit .... **SILT**
mud, slimy .... **OOZE**
mud, stick in .... **MIRE**
mud, viscous .... **SLIME**
mud, volcano .... **SALSE**
muddle .... **MESS, ADDLE**
muddy .... **ROIL**
muffin .... **GEM**
mug .... **STEIN, NOGGIN**
mug, small .... **TOBY**
mugger .... **GOA**
mulatto .... **METIS**
mulberry bark cloth .... **TAPA**
mulberry genus ...... **MORUS**
mulberry, India ...... **AL, AAL**
mulct .... **FINE, AMERCE**
mullet, red .... **SUR**

c multiform .... **DIVERSE**
multiplicand: math. . **FACIEND**
multiplier: math. .... **FACIENT**
multitude ...... **HOST, HORDE**
mum .... **ALE**
munch .... **CHAMP**
mundane .... **TERRENE**
Munich's river .... **ISAR**
municipal officer, Sp. . **ALCADE,**
ALCAID, ALCAIDE,
ALCAYDE
muntjac deer . **KAKAR, RATWA**
murder by suffocation . **BURKE**
murder fine, Scot. .... **CRO**
murderer, first .... **CAIN**
murmuring sound
CURR, PURL, PURR
Musci, plant of .... **MOSS**
muscle .... **THEW, SINEW**
muscle coordination, lack of
ATAXIA
muscle, deep, pert. to
SCALENE
muscle, kind of
ERECTOR, LEVATOR
muscle, like .... **MYOID**
muscle, round, rolling .. **TERES**
muscle, stretching .... **TENSOR**
muscles .... **BRAWN**
muscular action, irregular
ATAXIA

d muscular spasm .... **TIC**
Muse, chief .... **CALLIOPE**
muse in reverie .... **REVE**
Muse of astronomy .. **URANIA**
Muse of comedy ..... **THALIA**
Muse of dancing .**TERPSICHORE**
Muse of history .... **CLIO**
Muse of lyric poetry
CLIO, ERATO
Muse of music ..... **EUTERPE**
Muse of poetry .... **ERATO**
Muse of sacred lyric
POLYMNIA
Muse of tragedy . **MELPOMENE**
Muses, 9 .... **PIERIDES**
Muses' region .... **AONIA**
Muses, The .... **NINE**
musette .... **OBOE**
museum head ...... **CURATOR**
mush .... **ATOLE, SEPON**
mushroom .... **MOREL, MORIL**
mushroom cap .... **PILEUS**
music: as written .... **STA**
music character .... **DOT,**
CLEF, REST
music drama .... **OPERA**
music for nine .... **NONET**
music for three .... **TRIO**
music for two .... **DUET**
music from the sign: abbr. . **DS**

music hall .... **ODEA,
ODEON, ODEUM**
music interval ...... **TRITONE**
music: it proceeds .... **VA**
music lines .... **STAFF**
music piece
SERENATA, SERENATE
music, sacred
CHORAL, CHORALE
music symbols, old ... **NEUME**
MUSICAL .... see also MUSIC
musical beat .... **TAKT**
musical composition, India
RAGA
musical direction . **STA, TACET**
musical instrument ..... **ASOR,
DRUM, FIFE, GIGA, HARP,
HORN, LUTE, LYRE, OBOE,
PIPE, REED, TCHE, TUBA,
TURR, VINA, VIOL, CELLO,
RAPPEL, SPINET, CLAVIER,
HELICON, OCARINA**
musical sign .. **DOT, CLEF, REST**
musical study .... **ETUDE**
musical work .... **OPUS**
musician, 11th century . **GUIDO**

musket ball, India ...... **GOLI**
Musketeer .... **ATHOS,
ARAMIS, PORTHOS**
mussel, fresh-water ..... **UNIO**
must .... **STUM**
mustache monkey ... **MOUSTOC**
mustard family plant ... **CRESS**
musteline animal
OTTER, RATEL
mustiness .... **FUST**
mutilate .... **MAIM**
muttonbird .... **OII**
muttonfish .... **SAMA**
"My Name is —" ..... **ARAM**
mysteries .... **ARCANA**
mysterious .... **OCCULT**
mystery .... **RUNE**
mystic word, Hindu ...... **OM**
mystic writing .... **RUNE**
mythical land ...... **LEMURIA**
mythical stream .... **STYX**
mythical submerged island
ATLANTIS
mythical warrior .... **ARES**
MYTHOLOGY .... see SPECIAL
SECTION, Page 198

N

nab .... **GRAB, ARREST**
Nabal's wife: Bibl. ... **ABIGAIL**
NaCl .... **SALT**
nahoor sheep .... **SNA**
nail .... **CLAW, TALON,
UNGUES, UNGUIS**
nail, hooked .... **TENTER**
nail, mining, surveying .. **SPAD**
nail, thin .... **BRAD**
nail with aperture ...... **SPAD**
nails, 100 lbs. .... **KEG**
namaycush .... **TOGUE**
NAME .... see also MAN'S
NAME, WOMAN'S NAME
name .... **DUB, TERM, CLEPE,
NOMEN, TITLE, ENTITLE**
name: Dan. .... **NAAM**
name plate, shop's .... **FACIA**
named ... **Y-CLEPT, Y-CLEPED**
namely .... **VIZ**
Naomi, name claimed by **MARA**
Naomi's daughter-in-law . **RUTH**
naos .... **CELLA**
nap, coarse, long .... **SHAG**
nap-raising device ... **TEASEL,
TEASLE, TEAZEL, TEAZLE**
nap-raising machine ...... **GIG**
nap, to raise .... **TEASE**
napoleon, game like ..... **PAM**

Napoleon's brother-in-law
MURAT
Napoleon's isle .... **ELBA**
Napoleon's marshal general **NEY**
Napoleonic victory .**JENA, LODI**
Narcissus, nymph who loved
ECHO
narcotic .... **DOPE, DRUG,
HEROIN, OPIATE**
narcotic, India . **BANG, BHANG**
narcotic plant .... **DUTRA**
narcotic shrub
KAT, KAAT, KHAT
narcotic shrub, S. Am.
COCA, CUCA
narrate .... **TELL**
narrow ...... **LINEAL, STRAIT**
nasal .... **RHINAL**
Nata's wife: myth ..... **NANA**
nation: Ger. .... **VOLK**
nation, pert. to .... see **STATAL**
NATIVE .... see TRIBES in
SPECIAL SECTION, Page 191
native .... **ITE, RAW, NATAL,
ENDEMIC, INDIGENE**
natural luster, having ... **NAIF**
natural talent . **DOWER, FLAIR**
nature ...... **OUSIA, ESSENCE**
nature goddess ...... **CYBELE**

Nature

nature principal: Hindu... **GUNA**
nature spirit .... **NAT**
nature story writer ..... **SETON**
nautical .... **MARINE**
nautical cry...... **AHOY, OHOY,**
AVAST
Navaho hut............. **HOGAN**
naval hero............. **PERRY**
navy jail................. **BRIG**
near .... **AT, NIGH, ABOUT,**
CLOSE
Near East native .. **ARAB, TURK**
Near East river valley.... **WADI**
near the ear .... **PAROTIC**
near to.............. **BY, ON**
nearest.................. **NEXT**
nearsighted person..... **MYOPE**
nearsightedness ...... **MYOPIA**
neat .... **TIDY, TOSH, TRIG,**
TRIM, SPRUCE
neat cattle.............. **NOWT**
neatly................. **FEATLY**
necessitate .... **ENTAIL**
neck, nape of .... **NUCHA**
necklace ..... **BEADS, RIVIERE**
neckline shape..... **VEE, BOAT,**
CREW
neckpiece ..... **ASCOT, STOLE**
neckpiece, feather......... **BOA**
neckpiece, woman's ..... **FICHU**
NECKTIE .... see TIE
need .... **WANT, REQUIRE**
needle .... **PROD, BODKIN**
needle bug .... **NEPA**
needle case............... **ETUI**
needle-shaped .... **ACUATE,**
ACERATE
needlefish .... **GAR**
needlelike bristle ..... **ACICULA**
negative......... **NE, NO, NAY,**
NON, NOT
negative pole .... **CATHODE**
neglect.................. **OMIT**
neglected school subject: abbr.
LAT.
negligent................. **LAX**
negotiate............... **TREAT**
negrito .... **ATA, ATI, ITA,**
AETA, ATTA
Negro dance............. **JUBA**
Negro: India ...... **HUBSHI**
NEGRO TRIBE .... see SPECIAL
SECTION, AFRICAN TRIBES
Nelson's victory site....... **NILE**
nematocyst.............. **CNIDA**
nemesis.................. **BANE**
Nepal Mongoloid .... **RAIS**
Nepal native .... **KHA**
Nepal people.............. **RAIS**
nephew .... **NEPOTE**

nephew, Fijian .... **VASU**
Neptune.................... **LER**
Neptune's spear...... **TRIDENT**
nerve cell............ **NEURON**
nerve-cell process....... **AXON**
nerve layers, brain ...... **ALVEI**
nervous .... **EDGY**
nervous disease....... **CHOREA**
nest .. **NID, NIDE, NIDI, NIDUS**
nest, eagle's ..... **AERY, AERIE,**
EYRY, EYRIE
nested boxes .... **INRO**
nestling .... **EYAS**
net .... **CLEAR**
net, fishing ..... **SEINE, STENT,**
TRAWL
net of hair-lines .... **RETICLE**
NETHERLANDS... see SPECIAL
SECTION
netlike .... **RETIARY**
nettle family ... **RAMIE, RAMEE**
network .... **WEB, MESH,**
RETE, RETIA
neuroglia .... **GLIA**
neve .... **FIRN**
— Nevis, Gt. Brit. peak .... **BEN**
new........... **NOVEL, RECENT**
New Caledonia bird....... **KAGU**
New England state: abbr. .... **RI**
New Guinea area....... **PAPUA**
New Guinea tribesman.. **KARON**
New Guinea victory...... **GONA**
New Guinea wild hog ..... **BENE**
New Jerusalem foundation
JASPER
new, lover of .... **NEO**
new star .... **NOVA**
new wine .... **MUST**
New York harbor isle ..... **ELLIS**
New Zealand aborigine...... **ATI**
N.Z. bird.......... **HUIA, KAKI,**
PEHO, RURU
N.Z. clan .... **ATI**
N.Z. evergreen .... **TAWA**
N.Z. fruit pigeon.......... **KUKU**
N.Z. laburnum............ **GOAI**
N.Z. mollusk .... **PIPI**
N.Z. native............. **MAORI**
N.Z. native fort....... **PA, PAH**
N.Z. parson bird......... **KOKO**
N.Z. plant............... **KARO**
N.Z. rail bird .... **WEKA**
N.Z. scabbard fish........ **HIKU**
N.Z. shrub .... **KARO**
N.Z. shrub, poisonous..... **TUTU**
N.Z. subtribe............ **HAPU**
N.Z. timber tree ... **GOAI, HINO,**
MIRO, PELU, RATA, RIMU,
HINAU, HINOU, KAURI,
KAURY, TOTARA

a N.Z. tree..... **AKE, KOPI, NAIO, PUKA, TORO, WHAU**
N.Z. tribe.................. **ATI**
N.Z. wages .... **UTU**
N.Z. wood hen .... **WEKA**
news agency, Eng. ... **REUTERS**
news agency, former Dutch **ANETA**
news agency, Jap........ **DOMEI**
news agency, Rus. Soviet. **TASS**
news paragraph.......... **ITEM**
newspaper service ..... **AP, UP, INS, UPI, REUTERS**
newspapers............. **PRESS**
newt...... **EFT, EVET, TRITON**
nibble .... **GNAW, KNAB, KNAP**
niche................. **RECESS**
Nichols' hero .... **ABIE**
Nick Charles' dog .... **ASTA**
Nick Charles' wife....... **NORA**
nickel steel alloy .... **INVAR**
nicotine acid........... **NIACIN**
nictitate .... **WINK**
Niger delta native .... **IJO**
NIGERIA.......... see SPECIAL SECTION
Nigerian Negro....... **ARO, IBO**
Nigerian tribe .... **EDO**
NIGERIAN TRIBE OR PEOPLE see also SPECIAL SECTION page 191

b niggard.................. **MISER**
nigh.................... **NEAR**
night, Norse ...... **NATT, NOTT**
nightingale, Pers....... **BULBUL**
nightjar................ **POTOO**
nightmare demon, Teut. . **MARA**
nightmare, the ...... **INCUBUS**
nightshade, black ...... **MOREL, MORIL**
Nile, as god.............. **HAPI**
Nile island .... **RODA**
Nile native.............. **NILOT**
Nile sailboat .... **CANGIA**
Nile valley depression .... **KORE**
Nile, waste matter on.... **SADD, SUDD**
Nilotic Negro .... **JUR, LUO, LWO, SUK**
nimble .... **SPRY, AGILE**
nimbus........... **HALO, NIMB**
nimrod .... **HUNTER**
nine-angled polygon . **NONAGON**
nine, based on .... **NONARY**
nine, group of......... **ENNEAD**
nine inches .... **SPAN**
nine, music for........ **NONET**
Nineveh's founder....... **NINUS**
ninth day, every........ **NONAN**
ninth: mus. .... **NONA**
niton.................. **RADON**

c nitrogen.......... **AZO, AZOTE**
Noah, pert. to.......... **NOETIC**
Noah's landing......... **ARARAT**
Noah's 1st son .... **SEM, SHEM**
Noah's 2nd son........... **HAM**
Nobel prize, literature '04 **MISTRAL**
Nobel prize, science...... **UREY**
noble, nobleman . **DUKE, EARL, LORD, PEER, BARON, COUNT**
noble: Ger....... **GRAF, RITTER**
NOBLEMAN .... see NOBLE
nobleman, Jap............ **KAMI**
nocturnal mammal **BAT, LEMUR**
nod .... **BOW, BECK**
Nod, west of............. **EDEN**
nodding .... **NUTANT**
noddy tern: Hawaii .... **NOIO**
node .... **KNOB, KNOT, KNUR, NODUS**
"— noire" .... **BETE**
nomad .... **ARAB, SCENITE**
Nome in Greece........... **ELIS**
nomenclature .... **NAME**
nominal value............. **PAR**
nominate .... **NAME**
non-gypsy: Romany....... **GAJO**
non-Jew.............. **GOI, GOY**
non-Moslem of Turkey or
d Ottoman Empire... **RAIA, RAYA**
non-professional .... **LAY, LAIC**
non-union worker......... **SCAB**
nonchalant .... **COOL**
none: dialect............... **NIN**
nonsense. **PISH, POOH, HOOEY**
nonsense creature .... **GOOP**
noodles: Yiddish ...... **FARFEL, FERFEL**
nook, sheltered .... **COVE**
noose.................... **LOOP**
Norn, one of **URD, URTH, WYRD**
Norse "Adam"............ **ASKR**
Norse bard .... **SCALD, SKALD**
Norse chieftain.... **JARL, YARL**
Norse epic.............. **EDDA**
Norse explorer...... **ERIC, LEIF**
NORSE GOD or GODDESSES see also GODS and GODDESSES and see also SPECIAL SECTION Page 200
Norse gods **VANS, AESIR, VANIR**
Norse letter.............. **RUNE**
Norse myth. hero .. **EGIL, EGILL**
Norse myth. king.......... **ATLI**
Norse myth. "Life" force.... **LIF**
Norse myth. woman...... **IDUN**
Norse neighbor .... **FINN**
Norse poetry........... **RUNES**
Norse prose .... **EDDA**
Norse sea goddess........ **RAN**
Norseman ...... **DANE, SWEDE**

a North African .... **BERBER**
N. Afr. outer garment .. **HAIK**
North Carolina college .. **ELON**
North Carolinian .... **TARHEEL**
North Caucasian language
    UDI, AVAR, UDIC, UDISH
North, Mrs. of fiction . **PAMELA**
North Sea fishing boat . **COBLE**
North Sea, river into **ELBE, TEES**
North Star .... **POLARIS**
North Syrian deity .... **EL**
northern .... **BOREAL**
northern Scandinavian ... **LAPP**
northern tribe, China ..... **HU**
northernmost land ..... **THULE**
Northumberland river ... **TYNE**
Norway coin .... **ORE**
Norway territorial division.**AMT**
Norwegian author ... **HAMSUN**
Norwegian composer .... **GRIEG**
Norwegian county **AMT, FYLKE**
Norwegian saint .... **OLAF**
nose .... **CONK, NASI,**
    NASUS, SNOOP
nose, having large ... **NASUTE**
nose, having snub .... **SIMOUS**
nose openings .. **NARES, NARIS**
nose, snub .... **PUG**
nostrils .... **NARES, NARIS**
b nostrils, of .... **NARIC,**
    NARIAL, NARINE
"— Nostrum," Mediterranean
    MARE
not at home .... **OUT**
not ever: poet. .... **NEER**
not genuine .... **TIN**
not in style ...... **OUT, PASSE**
not long ago .... **LATELY**
not moving ... **INERT, STATIC**
not one .... **NARY, NONE**
not so great .... **LESS, FEWER,**
    SMALLER
notch ... **KERF, NICK, NOCK,**
    CRENA, CRENAE
notched .. **SERRATE, SERRATED**
note .... **CHIT, MEMO**
note, double, whole .... **BREVE**
note, Guido's .... **UT, ELA**
note, Guido's low ..... **GAMUT**
note, half .... **MINIM**
note, high, highest .... **ELA**
note, marginal
    POSTIL, APOSTIL
note: music .. **DI, DO, FA, FI,**
    LA, LE, LI, ME, MI, RA, RE,
    RI, SE, SI, SO, TE, TI, SOL
note, old Gr. musical .... **NETE**
note, old musical .... **ELA**
NOTE, SCALE ...... see NOTE:
    MUSIC
notes, furnish with . **ANNOTATE**

c notes in Guido's scale .. **ELAMI**
nothing . **NIL, NIX, NUL, NULL,**
    ZERO, NIHIL
notion .... **BEE, IDEA**
notion, capricious ..... **WHIM**
notional .... **IDEAL**
notorious .... **ARRANT**
Nott's son .... **DAG**
notwithstanding .... **YET**
nought .... **ZERO, NULL**
NOUN ENDING
    see SUFFIX, noun
noun form .... **CASE**
noun suffix of condition .. **ATE**
noun with only 2 cases.**DIPTOTE**
nourish .... **FEED, FOSTER**
nourishment ...... **PABULUM**
Nova Scotia .... **ACADIA**
novel, advocate of ...... **NEO**
novel by A. France ..... **THAIS**
novelty .... **FAD**
novice .... **TIRO, TYRO**
now: dial. .... **NOO**
noxious .... **MIASMIC**
Nubian .... **NUBA**
nucha .... **NAPE**
nuclear element ...... **PROTON**
nudge .... **POKE**
nuisance .... **PEST**
nullify .... **NEGATE**
d nullify, legally .... **VOID**
number, describable by .**SCALAR**
number under 10 ..... **DIGIT**
number, whole ...... **INTEGER**
numbered: Bib. .... **MENE**
numerous .. **MANY, MULTIPLE**
nun, Franciscan .... **CLARE**
nun, head .... **ABBESS**
nun's dress .... **HABIT**
nunbird .... **MONASE**
nuque .... **NAPE**
nurse, Oriental, India .. **AMA,**
    IYA, AMAH, AYAH, EYAH
nurse, Slavic .... **BABA**
nursemaid: Fr. .... **BONNE**
nut ...... **COLA, KOLA, LICHI,**
    ALMOND, CASHEW,
    LICHEE, LITCHI
nut, beverage .... **COLA, KOLA**
nut, hickory .... **PECAN**
nut, pert. to .... **NUCAL**
nut, P. I. .... **PILI**
nut, pine .... **PINON**
nut, stimulating .... **BETEL**
nut tree, Afr. .... **COLA, KOLA**
nuts for food .... **MAST**
nuthatch genus .... **SITTA**
nutlike drupe .... **TRYMA**
nutmeg husk .... **MACE**
nutria .... **COYPU**

a nutriment ... **FOOD, ALIMENT**
nutritive .... **ALIBLE**
nymph .... **MAIA, LARVA**
nymph, fountain ...... **EGERIA**
nymph, laurel .... **DAPHNE**
nymph, Moslem .... **HOURI**

c nymph, mountain ..... **OREAD**
nymph, ocean ...... **OCEANID**
nymph, water . **NAIAD, NEREID**
nymph, wood . **DRYAD, NAPEA,**
NAPAEA, HAMADRYAD
Nyx's daughter .... **ERIS**

O, plural .... **OES**
oaf .... **LOUT**
oak, Calif. .... **ENCINA**
oak, dried fruit of ... **CAMATA**
oak, evergreen .... **HOLM**
oak moss .... **EVERNIA**
oak, Turkey .... **CERRIS**
oakum, seal with .... **CALK**
oar .... **ROW, BLADE, PROPEL**
oar at stern .... **SCULL**
oasis, N. Afr. ... **WADI, WADY**
oat genus .... **AVENA**
oats as rent .... **AVENAGE**
oath, knight's .... **EGAD**
oath, old-fashioned . **ODS, EGAD**
oath, say under ..... **DEPOSE**
obeisance, Oriental
BOW, SALAAM
b obey .... **HEED, MIND**
object ... **AIM, CAVIL, DEMUR**
object of art .... **CURIO**
objection, petty .... **CAVIL**
objective .... **AIM, GOAL**
obligation .... **TIE, DEBT**
DUTY, ONUS
oblique .... **CANT, BEVEL,**
SLANT, SLOPE
obliterate .... **ERASE, EFFACE**
obliteration .... **RASURE**
oblivion ..... **LETHE, LIMBO**
oblivion stream .... **LETHE**
obscure ..... **DIM, FOG, DARK**
BEDIM, CLOUD
obscure, render ...... **DARKLE**
observe .. **SEE, NOTE, BEHOLD,**
REMARK, CELEBRATE
obstinate .... **SET, HARD**
obstruction, petty .... **CAVIL,**
obtain .... **GET**
obvious ..... **OPEN, PATENT**
obvious, not . **SUBTLE, SUBTILE**
occasional .... **ODD**
Occident .... **WEST**
occipital protuberances ... **INIA**
occultism .... **CABALA**
occupant .... **TENANT**
occupation .... **TRADE**
occupy .... **USE, FILL**
occurrence .... **EVENT**

ocean's rise, fall ...... **TIDE**
oceanic .... **PELAGIC**
oceanic tunicate .... **SALP**
ocher, black ..... **WAD, WADD**
octave, designating high .. **ALT**
octave of church feast ... **UTAS**
octopus .... **POULPE**
octoroon **METIS, MESTEE, MUSTEE**
odd-job man .... **JOEY**
Odin. **WODAN, WODEN, WOTAN**
Odin's brother ...... **VE, VILI**
Odin's granddaughter . **NANNA**
Odin's son ... **TY, TYR, THOR,**
TYRR, VALE, VALI
Odin's wife .... **RIND**
odor .... **AROMA, SCENT**
ODYSSEUS ... see also ULYSSES
Odysseus' companion . **ELPENOR**
d Odysseus' friend ..... **MENTOR**
Odyssey beggar .... **IRUS**
Odyssey singer .... **SIREN**
Oedipus' father .... **LAIUS**
Oedipus' mother .... **JOCASTA**
of speed of sound ...... **SONIC**
of the age: abbr. .... **AET**
off .... **AWAY**
offend .... **CAG**
offense .... **CRIME**
offense: law .. **MALA, MALUM**
offer .... **BID, TENDER**
offered up .... **OBLATE**
offhand .... **CASUAL**
office, ecclesiastic .. **MATINS**
office, priest's ...... **MATINS**
office, R. C. curia
DATARY, DATARIA
officer, church ...... **BEADLE**
officer, court: Scot. ... **MACER**
officer, municipal: Scot. **BAILIE**
officer, Rom. .... **LICTOR**
officer, synagogue .... **PARNAS**
officer, university
DEAN, BEADLE, BURSAR
official, Moslem .... **HAJIB**
official, Rom.
EDILE, AEDILE, TRIBUNE
official, subordinate .. **SATRAP**
official, weights ...... **SEALER**
offspring .... **SONS, HEIRS**

a ogygian .... **AGED**
Ohio college town .... **ADA**
oil .... **FAT, LARD, LUBE, ATTAR, OLEUM**
oil beetle .... **MELOE**
oil bottle ..... **CRUCE, CRUET, CRUSE, CRUIZÉ**
oil, cruet .... **AMPULLA**
oil, edible .... **ACEITE**
oil, orange .... **NEROLI**
oil, pert. to .... **OLEIC**
oil, rub with .... **ANOINT**
oil-yielding Chinese tree . **TUNG**
oil-yielding tree ... **EBO, EBOE**
oilfish .... **ESCOLAR**
oilstone .... **HONE**
oily ketone .... **IRONE**
ointment .... **BALM, NARD, SALVE, CERATE, POMADE**
Ojibway secret order **MEDA, MIDE**
O.K. .... **ROGER**
okra .... **GOMBO, GUMBO**
old .... **AGED, ANILE, SENILE**
"Old Curiosity Shop" girl . **NELL**
old English army .... **FYRD**
old Eng. gold piece .... **RYAL**
old Eng. rune .... **WEN, WYN**
old Greek coin .... **OBOL**
old Irish coin .... **RAP**
old Persian money .... **DARIC**
OLD TESTAMENT see BIBLICAL and SPECIAL SECTION
Old Testament objects ... **URIM**
b Old Test. people . **PHUD, PHUT**
old person .... **DOTARD**
old Sp. gold coin ...... **DOBLA**
old times .... **ELD, YORE**
old-womanish .... **ANILE**
oleaginous .... **OILY**
oleander genus ...... **NERIUM**
oleic acid salt ...... **OLEATE**
oleoresin .... **ANIME, ELEMI, BALSAM**
olive fly genus .... **DACUS**
olive genus .... **OLEA**
olive, inferior .... **MORON**
olive, stuffed .... **PIMOLA**
Oliver's nickname ...... **NOLL**
Olympian deity-god-goddess **ARES, HERA, APOLLO, ATHENA, HERMES, ARTEMIS, DEMETER**
Olympus, mountain near . **OSSA**
Olympus queen .... **HERA**
Olympus, region by .... **PIERIA**
omen .... **BODE, PRESAGE**
omission, vowel ...... **ELISION**
omit .... **DELE, PASS, SKIP**
omit in pronunciation .. **ELIDE**

c omitted, having part **ELLIPTIC, ELLIPTICAL**
onager .... **ASS**
once: dial. .... **ANES**
one .... **AIN, UNIT**
one-base hit .... **SINGLE**
one behind other .... **TANDEM**
one-eighth Troy ounce .. **DRAM**
one-eyed giant ..... **CYCLOPS**
one-horse carriage ..... **SHAY**
one hundred sq. meters **AR, ARE**
one hundred thousand rupees **LAKH**
one, music by .... **SOLI, SOLO**
one-spot .... **ACE**
one thousand .... **MIL**
one-year record ...... **ANNAL**
O'Neill heroine .... **ANNA**
onion .... **CEPA**
onion, Welsh .... **CIBOL**
onionlike plant .. **CIVE, LEEK, CHIVE, SHALLOT, ESCHALOT**
only .... **MERE, SAVE, SOLE**
onward .... **AHEAD, FORTH**
onyx, Mex. .... **TECALI**
oorial .... **SHA**
ooze .... **LEAK, SEEP, SEIP, SIPE, SYPE, EXUDE**
open .... **AJAR, OVERT, BROACH, PATENT, UNWRAP**
d open court .... **AREA**
open plain .... **VEGA**
opening .... **GAP, HOLE, RIFT, SLOT, VENT, HIATUS**
opening, long .... **RIMA, SLOT**
opening, mouthlike **STOMA, STOMATA**
opening, slit-like .... **RIMA**
opening, small .... **PORE**
opera ... **AIDA, BORIS, ORFEO**
opera, Beethoven .... **FIDELIO**
opera, Bizet .... **CARMEN**
opera composer, modern **BRITTEN, MENOTTI**
opera, Gounod .... **FAUST**
opera hat .... **GIBUS**
opera heroine ... **AIDA, ELSA, MIMI, SENTA, ISOLDE**
opera house, Milan .... **SCALA**
opera, Massenet **MANON, THAIS**
opera, Puccini .... **TOSCA**
opera scene .... **SCENA**
opera singer .... **MELBA**
opera soprano, star.**ALDA, PONS, BORI, RISE, RAISA, STEBER**
opera star .... **DIVA**
opera, Verdi ... **AIDA, ERNANI**
opera, Wagner .... **RIENZI**
operate .... **RUN, MANAGE**
operetta composer ..... **FRIML**

a opium poppy seed ...... **MAW**
opossum, S. Am. ...... **QUICA**
opponent .. **FOE, ANTI, RIVAL**
opportune .... **TIMELY**
opportunity .... **CHANCE**
oppose .... **IMPUGN**
opposed, one .... **ANTI**
opposed to solo .... **TUTTI**
opposite extremities ... **POLES**
opposite .... **REVERSE**
Ops' daughter .... **CERES**
Ops' husband .... **SATURN**
optical glass .... **LENS**
optical illusion ...... **MIRAGE**
optical instrument lines **RETICLE**
optimistic .... **ROSY, ROSEATE**
oracle, Apollo's .... **DELOS**
oracle, Gr. .. **DELPHI, DELPHOI**
oral .... **PAROL**
orange-red stone .... **SARD**
orange tincture, Her. .. **TENNE**
orangutan, Malay ...... **MIAS**
orarion .... **STOLE**
orator .... **OTIS, RHETOR**
orb of day .... **SUN**
orbit point .... **APSIS, APOGEE**
orchid genus .... **DISA**
orchid leaves for tea
FAAM, FAHAM
orchid tuber .... **SALEP**
b ordain .... **DECREE**
order .... **BID, FIAT,**
ARRAY, EDICT, DECREE
order, one of Catholic. **MARIST**
order, put in .... **TIDY, SETTLE**
orderliness .... **SYSTEM**
ordinance .... **LAW**
ordnance piece ...... **MORTAR**
ore deposit ...... **LODE, MINE**
ore of iron .... **OCHER, OCHRE**
ore receptacle ...... **MORTAR**
organ .... **EAR, EYE**
organ of algae .... **PROCARP**
organ part .... **STOP**
organ pipe .... **REED**
organ pipe, displayed **MONTRE**
organ prelude .... **VERSET**
organ, seed-bearing .... **PISTIL**
organ stop **REED,SEXT,DOLCAN,**
CELESTE, MELODIA
organism, 1-cell
AMEBA, AMOEBA
organism, simple
MONAD, MONAS
organization .... **SETUP**
orgy .... **REVEL**
Orient .... **EAST**
Oriental ...... **ASIAN, TATAR**
Oriental dwelling .... **DAR**

c Oriental lute .... **TAR**
Oriental nursemaid .... **AMA,**
IYA, AMAH, AYAH, EYAH
Oriental plane tree .. **CHINAR**
Oriental porgy .... **TAI**
Oriental potentate ...... **AGA**
Oriental sailing ship ... **DHOW**
Oriental servant ...... **HAMAL**
Oriental ship captain .... **RAS**
Oriental weight .... **ROTL**
orifice. **PORE, STOMA, OSTIOLE**
orifices, sponge ...... **OSCULA**
origin .... **SEED**
original .... **NEW**
original sin .... **ADAM**
originate **ARISE, START, CREATE**
Orinoco tributary .... **ARO**
oriole, golden .... **LORIOT**
ornament .... **FRET**
ornament, curly ..... **SCROLL**
ornament in relief ... **EMBOSS**
ornament, spire .... **EPI**
ornamental border .... **DADO**
ornamental grass ... **EULALIA**
ornamental nailhead .... **STUD**
Orpheus' destination ... **HADES**
Orpheus' instrument ..... **LYRE**
orris .... **IRIS**
orris-root ketone, oil ... **IRONE**
oscillate .... **WAVE**
osier .... **WITHE**
d Osiris' brother .... **SET**
Osiris' wife, sister .... **ISIS**
ostentation .... **POMP**
ostracism ..... **TABU, TABOO**
ostrich, Am. .... **RHEA**
ostrich-like bird
EMU, EMEU, RATITE
Otaheite apple .... **HEVI**
Othello was one .... **MOOR**
Othello's lieutenant, foe **IAGO**
otherwise .... **ELSE**
otic .... **AURAL**
otologist .... **AURIST**
otter brown, color ... **LOUTRE**
otter genus .... **LUTRA**
Ottoman .... **TURK**
Ottoman court .... **PORTE**
Ottoman official ...... **PASHA**
"Our Mutual Friend," ballad-
seller in .... **WEGG**
oust .... **EJECT, EVICT**
out .... **AWAY, FORTH**
out-and-out .... **ARRANT**
out: Dutch .... **UIT**
out of style .... **PASSE**
out of the way .... **ASIDE**
outbreak, unruly .... **RIOT**
outburst, sudden ...... **SPATE**
outcast
LEPER, PARIAH, ISHMAEL

a outcome, final .... **UPSHOT**
outcry .... **CLAMOR**
outer .... **ECTAL**
outer portion of earth ... **SIAL**
outfit .. **KIT, RIG, GEAR, SUIT**
outfit, queer .... **GETUP**
outlet .... **VENT**
outline .... **PERIMETER**
outlook .... **VISTA**
outmoded .... **PASSE**
OUTRIGGER see **MALAY CANOE**
outward .... **ECTAD**
ova .... **EGGS**
oval ... **ELLIPTIC, ELLIPTICAL**
oven .... **KILN, OAST**
oven, annealing .. **LEER, LEHR**
oven, Polyn. native ..... **UMU**
over .... **ATOP, ABOVE,**
   AGAIN, ENDED, ACROSS
over-nice .... **FINICAL**
overnice person .... **PRIG**
over: poet. .... **OER**
over there ..... **YON, YONDER**
overact .... **EMOTE**
overcoat ... **ULSTER, PALETOT**
overdue payment ..... **ARREAR**
overflow .... **DEBORD**
overfond, be ..... **DOAT, DOTE**
overjoy .... **ELATE**
overlay .... **CEIL**
overripe grain .... **BRITE**
overseer, ranch: Sp. Am.
   CAPORAL
overshadow .... **DOMINATE**
overshoe
   GOLOE, GALOSH, GALOSHE
overskirt .. **PANIER, PANNIER**
overspreading mass ..... **PALL**

c overt .... **OPEN, FRANK**
overwhelm .... **DELUGE**
overwhelming amount .... **SEA**
Ovid's "— Amatoria" .... **ARS**
ovule .... **SEED**
ovum .... **EGG**
owala tree .... **BOBO**
owl, barn, Samoa ...... **LULU**
owl, eagle .. **BUBO, KATOGLE**
owl, horned .... **BUBO**
owl, S. Asia .... **UTUM**
owl's cry .... **HOOT**
own up to .... **AVOW**
ownership, of land, old law
   ODAL, UDAL
ox, extinct wild .... **URUS**
ox, forest .... **ANOA**
ox, long-haired .... **YAK**
ox of Caesar's time .... **URUS**
ox, wild .... **ANOA**
ox, wild: India .... **GAUR**
   GOUR, ZEBU, GAYAL
oxalis, S. Amer. .... **OCA**
oxen .... **KINE**
oxhide strap ..... **REIM, RIEM**
oxide .... **CALX**
oxidize .... **RUST**
oxygen compound **OXID, OXIDE**
oxygen, form of ...... **OZONE**
oxygen radical .... **OXYL**
oyster bed material
   CULCH, CUTCH, CULTCH
oyster drill .... **BORER**
oyster farm: Fr. .... **PARC**
oyster, young .... **SPAT**
oysterfish .... **TAUTOG**
Ozarks, town west of in Okla.
   ADA
Oz books author ...... **BAUM**

P

b pace .... **RATE, STEP**
pachisi, kind of .... **LUDO**
pachyderm .... **ELEPHANT**
Pacific aroid food plant **TARO**
Pacific Island cloth ..... **TAPA**
Pacific pine .... **HALA**
Pacific shrub .... **SALAL**
pacify
   CALM, SOOTHE, PLACATE
pack .... **WAD, STOW**
pack animal .... **ASS,**
   BURRO, LLAMA, SUMPTER
pack horse .... **SUMPTER**
pack down .... **RAM, TAMP**
package, India ...... **ROBBIN**
package of spun silk .. **MOCHE**
pad .... **TABLET**

d padded jacket under armor
   ACTON
padnag .... **TROT, AMBLE**
Padua, town near ...... **ESTE**
pagan god .... **IDOL**
page, "Love's Labor Lost" **MOTH**
page number .... **FOLIO**
pageantry .... **POMP**
"Pagliacci" character .. **CANIO**
"Pagliacci" heroine ... **NEDDA**
pagoda, Chinese ..... **TA, TAA**
pagoda ornament ... **EPI, TEE**
paid notice .... **AD**
pail .... **SKEEL**
pain, dull .... **ACHE**
pain reliever **OPIATE, ANODYNE**
paint, face .... **FARD, ROUGE**

pain-killer alkaloid source **COCA**
painted bunting: Creole .. **PAPE**
PAINTER .. see also **ARTIST**
and country of each artist
painter, modernist
KLEE, MIRO, ERNST
painting style .... **GENRE**
painting, wall .... **MURAL**
pair .... **DUO, DIAD,**
DUAD, DYAD, MATE
pair of horses ... **SPAN, TEAM**
pairing .... **MATING**
palanquin .... **JAUN**
palanquin bearer ..... **HAMAL**
palanquin, Jap. .... **KAGO**
palatable, very .... **SAPID**
pale .... **WAN, ASHY,**
ASHEN, PASTY
pale color .... **PASTEL**
pale-colored .... **MEALY**
Palestine in Jewish use **ERETS**
palisade: fort. .... **RIMER**
Pallas .... **ATHENA**
pallid .... **WAN, PALE**
palm .... **TI, COCO, TALA,**
TALIPAT, TALIPOT, TALI-
PUT
palm, Afr. .... **DUM**
palm, Asia .... **ARENG, BETEL**
palm, betel .... **ARECA**
palm, book .... **TARA**
palm, Brazil .... **ASSAI**
palm, climbing ...... **RATTAN**
palm cockatoo .... **ARARA**
palm, dwarf genus .... **SABAL**
palm fiber **DOH, TAL, RAFFIA**
palm fiber, S. Amer. .. **DATIL**
palm genus .... **ARECA**
palm genus, Asia ... **ARENGA**
palm juice, fermented .. **SURA**
palm leaf
OLA, OLE, OLAY, OLLA
palm-leaf mat .... **YAPA**
palm lily .... **TI**
palm, liquor ..... **BENO, BINO**
palm, N. Z. .... **NIKAU**
palm, nipa ..... **ATAP, ATTAP**
palm off .... **FOB, FOIST**
palm, palmyra leaf ..... **OLA,**
OLE, OLLA, OLAY
palm sago, Malay ... **GOMUTI**
palm sap .... **TODDY**
palm starch .... **SAGO**
palm, W. Ind. **GRIGRI, GRUGRU**
palmetto .... **SABAL**
palmyra leaf .... **OLA, OLE,**
OLAY, OLLA
palmyra palm .... **BRAB**
palp .... **FEELER**
palpitation .... **PALMUS**

pamper .... **COSHER, COSSET**
pamphlet .... **TRACT**
panacea .... **ELIXIR**
Panama gum tree **COPA, YAYA**
Panama, old name ... **DARIEN**
Panama tree, large .. **CATIVO**
Panay negrito .... **ATI**
panda .... **WAH, BEAR**
panel .... **PANE**
panel of jurors ...... **VENIRE**
pang .... **THROE**
pangolin .... **MANIS**
panic .... **FEAR, FUNK**
pannier .... **DOSSER**
Panopolis, chief god of .. **MIN,**
KHEM
pant .... **GASP**
pantry .... **AMBRY, LARDER,**
SPENCE, BUTTERY
— Paulo, Brazil .... **SAO**
papal cape ... **FANO, FANON,**
FANUM, ORALE, PHANO,
FANNEL
papal church .... **LATERAN**
papal collar .. **FANO, FANON,**
FANUM, ORALE, PHANO,
FANNEL
papal court ...... **SEE, CURIA**
papal fanon .... **ORALE**
papal letter .... **BULL, BULLA**
papal scarf .... **ORALE**
papal veil .... **FANO, FANON,**
FANUM, ORALE, PHANO,
FANNEL
papal vestment .... **FANO,**
FANON, FANUM, ORALE,
PHANO, FANNEL
paper folded once ..... **FOLIO**
paper, imperfect, poor
CASSE, CASSIE, RETREE
paper, lighting .... **SPILL**
paper measure .. **REAM, QUIRE**
paper mulberry .... **KOZO**
paper mulberry bark .... **TAPA**
paper size
DEMY, POTT, OCTAVO
paper, thin crisp ...... **PELURE**
par, 2 under .... **EAGLE**
Para, Brazil, capital .. **BELEM**
parade .... **MARCH, STRUT**
paradise .... **EDEN**
paradise, Buddhist ...... **JODO**
paradise, like .... **EDENIC**
"Paradise Lost" angel .. **ARIEL**
paragraph .... **ITEM**
parallelogram .... **RHOMB**
paralysis .... **PARESIS**
parapet, solid portion of **MERLON**
parasite .... **LEECH**

a   parasite in blood .... **TRYP**
parasitic insect **MITE, ACARID**
parasitic plant **MOSS, DODDER**
paravane .... **OTTER**
Parcae .... **FATES**
Parcae, one of
  NONA, MORTA, DECUMA
parcel of land .... **LOT, PLAT**
parchment, book
  FOREL, FORREL
pardon .... **REMIT, CONDONE**
pardon, general .... **AMNESTY**
pare .... **PEEL**
Paris art exhibit ...... **SALON**
Paris, first bishop of
  DENIS, DENYS
Paris section .... **PASSY**
Paris subway .... **METRO**
Paris thug .... **APACHE**
Paris' father .... **PRIAM**
Paris' wife .... **OENONE**
parish head .... **RECTOR**
parley .... **PALAVER**
Parliament report .. **HANSARD**
parol .... **ORAL**
paroxysm .... **FIT, SPASM**
parrot
  KEA, LORY, VASA, VAZA
parrot, Brazil ... **ARA, ARARA**
parrot-fish

b   **LORO, LAUIA, SCARID**
parrot, hawk .... **HIA**
parrot, monk .... **LORO**
parrot, N. Z. large **KEA, KAKA**
parrot, P. I., green .... **CAGIT**
parrot, sheep-killing .... **KEA**
parrot's bill, part of .... **CERE**
parrotlike .... **ARINE**
parry .... **FEND, EVADE**
Parsi priest .... **MOBED**
Parsi scripture .... **AVESTA**
parsley camphor ...... **APIOL**
parsley, plant kin to
  ANISE, CELERY
parson bird
  POE, TUE, TUI, KOKO
parsonage .... **MANSE**
part .... **ROLE, SOME, PIECE,
  BREAK, SEVER, SHARE,
  CLEAVE, ELEMENT**
part, Greek play
  EXODE, EXODOS
part of church .... **BEMA
  NAVE, AISLE, ALTAR**
part of horse's foot .. **PASTERN**
part of speech .. **NOUN, VERB**
parted .... **PARTITE**
participle ending .... **ING**
parti-colored .... **PIED, PINTO**

c   parti-colored horse
  ROAN, CALICO
particle ...... **ACE, BIT, ION,
  JOT, ATOM, IOTA, DROP,
  MITE, MOTE, GRAIN,
  SHRED, TITTLE**
particle, electrically charged
  ION
particle in cosmic rays **MESON**
particle of chaff ...... **PALEA**
particle, small
  JOT, ATOM, IOTA, MOTE
particular .... **ITEM**
Partlet .... **HEN, BIDDY**
partnership: Hawaii **HUI, HOEY**
partridge call ... **JUCK, JUKE**
partridge, sand ...... **SEESEE**
partridge, snow ...... **LERWA**
party .... **SECT**
parvenu .... **UPSTART**
pasha .... **DEY**
pass .... **HAND, ELAPSE**
pass a rope through ... **REEVE**
pass between peaks ..... **COL**
pass by .... **BYGO**
pass on .... **RELAY**
pass over ... **OMIT, SKIP, ELIDE**
pass through .... **REEVE**
pass through mountains .. **COL,
  DEFILE**
passable .... **SOSO**

d   passage .... **GUT, ITER,
  CANAL, TRANSIT**
passage, bastion .... **POSTERN**
passage, covered .... **ARCADE**
passage: hist. .... **ALURE**
passage: music **TUTTI, STRETTA**
passage out .... **EXIT, EGRESS**
passageway **ADIT, HALL, AISLE**
Passover .... **PASCH, PASCHA**
Passover meal **SEDAR, SEDER**
passport endorsement **VISA, VISE**
past **AGO, GONE, OVER, AGONE**
paste .... **STRASS**
pasteboard .... **CARD**
pasted-up art work .. **COLLAGE**
pastel .... **TINT**
pastoral .... **IDYLLIC**
pastoral place ...... **ARCADIA**
pastoral poem .... **IDYL, IDYLL**
pastoral staff .. **PEDA, PEDUM**
pastry
  PIE, FLAN, TART, ECLAIR
pasture .... **LEA**
pasture: N. Eng. .... **ING**
pasture, to .... **AGIST**
pasty .... **DOUGHY**
pat .... **DAB, TAP**
pat, very .... **APT**
Patagonian cavy ...... **MARA**
patchwork, literary ..... **CENTO**

a patella .... ROTULA
   paten .... ARCA, ARCAE
   patent from monarch .. BERAT
   path: Anglo-Ir. ..... CASAUN
   path: math. .... LOCUS
   path of planet .... ORBIT
   pathos, false .... BATHOS
   patriarch Jacob ...... ISRAEL
   patriarch's title .... NASI
   patron .... CLIENT
   patron saint of France
                    DENIS, DENYS
   patronage ...... EGIS, AEGIS
   pattern .... NORM, TYPE,
      IDEAL, MODEL, PARAGON
   pattern, large square DAMIER
   Paul, Apostle .... SAUL
   Paul's birthplace ..... TARSUS
   paulownia tree .... KIRI
   pause .... REST
   pause: poet. & music
      SELAH, CESURA, CAESURA
   paver .... TUP
   paver's mallet .... TUP
   pavilion .... TENT
   paving stone .... FLAG, SETT
   paw .... PUD, FOOT
   pawl .... DETENT
b pawn .... HOCK
   Pawnee Indian rite .... HAKO
   Pawnee tribes .... CHAUI
   pay .... ANTE, WAGE, REMIT
   pay dirt .... ORE
   pay, fixed .... STIPEND
   pay for another ...... TREAT
   pay homage: feudal law
                        ATTORN
   pay one's part .... ANTE
   pay out .... SPEND
   payable .... DUE
   paymaster, India ...... BUXY
   payment back .... REBATE
   payment for a bride, S. Afr.
                        LOBOLA
   payment for death, feudal CRO
   payment for homicide ... ERIC
   payment, press for ...... DUN
   payment to owner: Fr. law CENS
   pea .... LEGUME
   peace .... PAX
   peace god, Anglo-Saxon .. ING
   peace of mind .... REST
   peaceful ... IRENE, IRENICAL
   peach, clingstone ...... PAVY
   peacock .... MAO, PAVO
   peacock blue .... PAON
   peacock butterfly .... IO
   peacock fish .... WRASSE
   peacock genus .... PAVO
   peacock: Kipling .... MAO

c peak ...... ALP, TOR, ACME,
          APEX, PITON, ZENITH
   peak: Scot. .... BEN
   peanut .... MANI, GOOBER
   pear, autumn .... BOSC
   pear cider .... PERRY
   pearl blue color ...... METAL
   Pearl Buck heroine ..... OLAN
   pearl, imitation ...... OLIVET
   pearl millet ... BAJRA, BAJRI
   pearlweeds .... SAGINA
   peasant. CARL, CEORL, CHURL
   peasant, India .... RYOT
   peasant, Scot.
              COTTAR, COTTER
   peat .... TURF
   peat spade .... SLADE
   pecan tree .... NOGAL
   peccary, collared ..... JAVALI
   peck ...... DAB, NIP, KNIP
   pedal .... TREADLE
   peddle ... HAWK, SELL, VEND
   peddle: Eng. .... TRANT
   pedestal .... GAINE
   pedestal part .. DADO, PLINTH
   peduncle, plant .... SCAPE
   peel . BARK, PARE, RIND, SKIN
   peep-show .... RAREE
   PEER .... see also NOBLE
   peer .... PEEK, PEEP
d Peer Gynt's mother ...... ASE
   peevish .... PETULANT
   peg .... KNAG
   peg, golf .... TEE
   peg, wooden
        NOG, TRENAIL, TREENAIL
   Pegu ironwood .... ACLE
   Peleg's son .... REU
   pellucid ...... CLEAR, LIMPID
   pelma .... SOLE
   pelota court ...... FRONTON
   pelt ..... FELL, SKIN, STONE
   pelvic bone, pert. to .... ILIAC
   pelvic bones .... ILIA
   pen name, Dickens .... BOZ
   pen name, G. Russell ...... AE
   pen name, Lamb .... ELIA
   pen point .... NEB, NIB
   pen-text .... RONDE
   penman, Yutang .... LIN
   penalty .... FINE
   pendulum weight .... BOB
   Penelope's father .... ICARIUS
   penetrate
        GORE, ENTER, PERMEATE
   penitential season ..... LENT
   penmanship .... HAND
   pennies .... PENCE
   Pennsylvania sect ..... AMISH
   Pentateuch .... TORA, TORAH

115

a **PEOPLE** .. see also TRIBES in
  SPECIAL SECTION
people .... **MEN, FOLK,
      ONES, RACE, DEMOS**
people, ancient Asian ... **SERES**
people: Ger. .... **VOLK**
people: Ir. .... **DAOINE**
people, Nigerian . **BENI, BENIN**
people: Sp. .... **GENTE**
people, spirit of ...... **ETHOS**
people, the .... **DEMOS**
pepper, climbing ...... **BETEL**
pepper, garden .... **PIMIENTO**
pepper plant, Borneo .... **ARA**
pepper shrub
    AVA, CAVA, KAVA, KAWA
pepper vine .... **BETEL**
Pequod's captain ...... **AHAB**
"per —" ..... **DIEM, ANNUM**
perceive .. **SEE, SENSE, DESCRY**
perception . **EAR, TACT, SENSE**
perch .... **SIT, ROOST**
perch genus .... **PERCA**
perchlike fish .... **DARTER**
percolate .. **OOZE, SEEP, LEACH**
peregrine .... **ALIEN**
perenially shifting sands region
                AREG
perfect .... **IDEAL, MODEL**
perforate ...... **BORE, DRILL,
            PUNCH, RIDDLE**
perform .... **RENDER**
performer
b   **DOER, ACTOR, ARTISTE**
perfume
    ATAR, OTTO, AROMA, ATTAR
perfume base .... **MUSK**
perfume with incense .. **CENSE**
perfumed pad .... **SACHET**
Pericles' consort .... **ASPASIA**
periphery ... **RIM, PERIMETER**
period .... **DOT**
period, time
    AGE, EON, ERA, STAGE
periodic as Med. winds **ETESIAN**
permit .. **LET, ALLOW, LICENSE**
permission .... **LEAVE**
pernicious, something .... **PEST**
perplex
  BAFFLE, CONFUSE, BEWILDER
Persephone ..... **CORA, KORE**
Persephone's husband
          HADES, PLUTO
Persia .... **IRAN**
Persian .... **IRANI**
Persian coin, ancient .. **DARIC**
Pers. demigod .... **YIMA**
Pers. elf .... **PERI**
Pers. enameled tile ..... **KASI**
Pers. fairy .... **PERI**
Pers. governor, old ... **SATRAP**
Pers. headdress, ancient **TIARA**

c Pers. lord ..... **KAAN, KHAN**
Pers. mystic .... **SUFI**
Pers. native .... **LUR**
Pers. poet .... **OMAR**
Pers. potentate .... **SHAH**
Pers. priestly caste ..... **MAGI**
Pers. province, ancient .. **ELAM**
Pers. race, tribesman **LUR, KURD**
Pers. rug .. **SENNA, HAMADAN**
Pers. ruler .... **SHAH**
Pers. ruler of dead ..... **YIMA**
Pers. sect .... **BABI**
Pers. sprite .... **PERI**
PERS. TITLE .... see TITLE,
                PERSIAN
Pers. tribe member ..... **LUR**
Pers. weight .... **SER**
persimmon, E. Ind. **GAB, GAUB**
person of mixed blood
        METIS, MESTIZO
person, overnice .... **PRIG**
personage .... **NIBS**
personification of folly ... **ATE**
personification of light: Polyn.
                AO
personnel .... **STAFF**
perspiration .. **SUDOR, SWEAT**
perspire .... **EGEST, SWEAT**
pert girl .... **CHIT, MINX**
pertaining to the chin **MENTAL**
d pertinent .... **APT, PAT**
perturb .... **DERANGE,
  DISTURB, AGITATE, TROUBLE**
PERU INDIAN .. see page 193
peruse ..... **CON, READ, SCAN**
peruser .... **CONNER**
Peruvian fertility goddess **MAMA**
Peruvian plant .... **OCA**
pervade .... **PERMEATE**
pester .... **ANNOY, TEASE**
pestle .... **PILUM**
pestle vessel .... **MORTAR**
pet .... **CADE**
pet lamb ...... **CADE, COSSET**
"Peter Pan" dog ...... **NANA**
"Peter Pan" pirate ...... **SMEE**
petiole .... **STIPE**
Petrarch's love .... **LAURA**
petrol .... **GAS**
peyote .... **MESCAL**
phantoms .... **EIDOLA**
Pharaoh .... **RAMESES**
Pharaoh after Rameses I .. **SETI**
phase .... **FACET, STAGE**
pheasant brood **NID, NYE, NIDE**
pheasant, Himal. . **CHIR, CHEER**
pheasant, India ...... **MONAL**
Phidias statue .... **ATHENA**
philippic .... **TIRADE**
PHILIPPINE ISLANDS
    see also SPECIAL SECTION

a   Philippine Islands attendant
                                ALILA
P.I. bast fiber ...... CASTULI
P.I. cedar .... CALANTAS
P.I. chief DATO, DATU, DATTO
P.I. DWARF see P. I. NEGRITO
P.I. dyewood tree
                    TUI, IPIL, TUWI
P.I. food .... POI, SABA
P.I. fort .... COTA, KOTA
P.I. grass ...... BOHO, BOJO
P.I. lighter .... CASCO
P.I. lizard .... IBID, IBIT
P.I. Moslem .... MORO
P.I. negrito, native, dwarf
                    ATA, ATI, ITA,
                    AETA, ATTA
P.I. palm wine ... BENO, BINO
P.I. peasant .... TAO
P.I. poisonous tree .... LIGAS
P.I. rice ...... PAGA, MACAN
P.I. sash .... TAPIS
P.I. servant .... ALILA
P.I. shrub, rope NABO, ANABO
P.I. skirt .... SAYA
P.I. tree .... DAO, IBA, TUA,
        TUI, BOGO, DITA, IFIL,
        IPIL, YPIL
P.I. warrior .... MORO
Philistine city .... GATH,
                    GAZA, EKRON
b   Philistine deity, principal DAGON
philosopher's stone .... ELIXIR
philosophical element ... RECT
philosophical theory MONISM
philosophy, pert. to Gr. ELEATIC
phloem .... BAST
phoebe .... PEWEE, PEWIT
Phoebus .... SOL, SUN
Phoenician city .... TYRE
Phoenician goddess .. ASTARTE
Phoenician port ...... SIDON
Phoenician princess .. EUROPA
phonetic notation system
                        ROMIC
phonetical sound .... PALATAL
phosphate of lime ... APATITE
photo-developing powder METOL
photography solution ... HYPO
Phrygian god .... ATTIS
Phrygian lunar god ..... MEN
physical ... SOMAL, SOMATIC
physician ..... GALEN, MEDIC
physician's group .... AMA
physician's symbol CADUCEUS
physicist, Am. .... EINSTEIN
physicist, Eng. .... BOYLE
physicist, Fr. .... CURIE
physicist, Nobel prize-winner
        1944 .... RABI
physiological individual .. BION

c   piano, upright ...... CLAVIAL
pick, miner's: Eng.
                MANDREL, MANDRIL
pick out .... CULL, GLEAN
picket .... PALE
pickled bamboo shoots ACHAR
pickled meat .... SOUSE
pickling fluid .... BRINE
pickling herb .... DILL
pickpocket .... DIP
"Picnic" author .... INGE
picture ... DRAW, PORTRAIT
picture border .... MAT
picture, composite .. MONTAGE
picturesque .... SCENIC
pie, meat, small .... PASTY
piebald .... PINTO
piebald pony ... PIED, PINTO
piece of eight .... REALS
piece out .... EKE
piece, thin .... SLAT
pier .... KEY, DOCK,
                MOLE, QUAI, QUAY
pier, architectural ..... ANTA
pier support ... PILE, PILING
pierce ... GORE, STAB, SPEAR
pig. HOG, SOW, SHOAT, SHOTE
pig, wild .... BOAR
pig, young .... ELT, GRICE
pigs .... SUS
d   pigs' feet .... PETTITOES
pigs, litter of .... FARROW
pigs, red .... DUROC
pigeon ... NUN, BARB, DOVE,
                POUTER, ROLLER
pigeon hawk .... MERLIN
pigeon pea. DAL, TUR, GANDUL
piglike animal ... PECCARY
pigment, blue-green ..... BICE
pigment, brown .... SEPIA
pigment, brown, from soot
                BISTER, BISTRE
pigment, deep blue .... SMALT
pigment, red .... LAKE
pigment test crystalline DOPA
pigment, without .... ALBINO
pigmentation, lack of
                    ACHROMA
pigtail .... CUE, QUEUE
pike, full grown . LUCE, LUCET
pike, walleyed .... DORE
pilaster .... ANTA
pilchard .. FUMADO, SARDINE
pilchard-like fish ...... SPRAT
pile ...... NAP, HEAP, SPILE
pile driver .... OLIVER
pile driver ram .... TUP
pile of hay .... RICK, STACK
pilfer .... STEAL
pilgrim .... PALMER

117

Pilgrimage

a
pilgrimage city .... MECCA
pilgrimage to Mecca .... HADJ
pill, large .... BOLUS
pillage .... LOOT, SACK, STEAL
pillage .... RAPINE
pillar, as of ore .... JAMB
pillar, Hindu .... LAT
pillar, resembling ..... STELAR
pillar, tapering ...... OBELISK
pillow .... BOLSTER
pilot .... GUIDE, STEER
pimento or —spice ..... ALL
pin .... BROOCH
pin, firing .... TIGE
pin, gunwale .... THOLE
pin, machine .... COTTER
pin, metal .... RIVET
pin, pivot .... PINTLE
pin, rifle firing .... TIGE
pin, Roman .... ACUS
pin, small, very LILL
pin, splicing .... FID
pin, wooden .. FID, NOG, PEG,
     COAG, COAK, DOWEL
pin wrench .... SPANNER
pinafore .... TIER
pincer claw .... CHELA
pinch .... NIP
pinched with cold ..... URLED
Pindar work .... ODE
b
pine-cone, like a ...... PINEAL
pine, Mex. .... OCOTE, PINON
pine, Scot. .... RIGA
pine, textile screw
                ARA, PANDAN
pineapple NANA, PINA, ANANA
pineapple genus .... PUYA
pinfeather .... PEN
pinion .... WING
pink .... DAMASK
pinnacle .... TOP, APEX
pinnacle, ice .... SERAC
pinniped .... SEAL
pinochle score, term
                DIX, MELD
pint, half .... CUP
pintado fish .... SIER
pintail .... SMEE
pinworm .. ASCARID, ASCARIS
pious Biblical Jew ..... TOBIT
pipe .... TUBE, RISER
pipe, Irish .... DUDEEN
pipe joint, fitting .... TEE
pipe, pastoral .... REED
pipe, tobacco
        BRIAR, BRIER, DUDEEN
pipe, water.HOOKAH, NARGILE
pipe with socket ends
                HUB, HUBB
pipelike .... TUBATE
pique .... PEEVE

c
pirate ...... ROVER, CORSAIR
pirate in War of 1812 LAFITTE
pismire .... ANT, EMMET
pistil part .... CARPEL
pistol .... DAG, DAGG,
        MAUSER, SIDEARM
pistol: slang .... HEATER
pit ..... HOLE, ABYSS, STONE
pit for roots, Maori ..... RUA
pit: medical .... FOSSA
pit, small .. FOVEA, LACUNA
pitch .... KEY, TAR, TONE
pitcher .... JUG, EWER
pitcher's false move .... BALK
pith .... NUB, GIST
pith helmet .... TOPI, TOPEE
pithy .... TERSE
pithy plant .... SOLA
pitiful quality ...... PATHOS
pittance .... DOLE
pitted .... FOVEATE
pity .... RUTH
placard .... POSTER
place ...... SET, LIEU, LOCI,
     SPOT, LOCUS, STEAD, LO-
     CALE
place before .... APPOSE
place, camping .... ETAPE
place case is tried .... VENUE
place in office again .. RESEAT
d
place, in relation .... POSIT
place, market .... FORUM
place of shelter .. GITE, HAVEN
placid .... CALM, SERENE
plagiarize .... STEAL
plague .... PEST, TEASE
plain, arctic .... TUNDRA
plain, Argentine ...... PAMPA
plain, Asia .... CHOL
plain, Palestine .... ONO
plain, Russia .... STEPPE
plain, S. Am. .... LLANO
plain, treeless ...... SAVANNA
plain, treeless Arctic TUNDRA
plain, upland .. WOLD, WEALD
Plains Indian .... see page 193
plainly woven .... UNI
plait .... PLY, BRAID
plan .... PLOT, INTEND
plane, Fr. .... SPAD
plane, Ger. .... STUKA
plane, Jap. .... ZERO
plane part .... FLAP,
        NOSE, TAIL, WING
plane, Russ. fighter ...... MIG
planets (in order of distance from
     sun) MERCURY (1), VE-
     NUS (2), EARTH (3),
     MARS (4), JUPITER (5),
     SATURN (6), URANUS (7),
     NEPTUNE (8), PLUTO (9)

a planets in distance from Earth
    (closest first)

1—VENUS	5—SATURN
2—MARS	6—URANUS
3—MERCURY	7—NEPTUNE
4—JUPITER	8—PLUTO

   planets in size
    (largest first)

1—JUPITER	6—VENUS
2—SATURN	7—PLUTO
3—NEPTUNE	8—MARS
4—URANUS	9—MERCURY
5—EARTH	

planetarium .... ORRERY
planetary aspect CUSP, TRINE
plank's curve on ship ..... SNY
plant .... SOW, SEED
plant, bayonet .... DATIL
plant broom .... SPART
plant, bulb
    CAMAS, CAMASS, CAMMAS
plant cutter bird ...... RARA
plant cutting .. SLIP, PHYTON
plant disease .... RUST, SMUT
plant joined to another GRAFT
plant life .... FLORA
PLANT, LILY ...... see LILY
plant, lily-like
    CAMAS, CAMASS, CAMMAS
plant louse .... APHID
plant, male .... MAS
b plant, medicinal, S. Am.
    ALOE, SENNA, IPECAC
plant modified by environment
    to abnormal development
    ECAD
plant, mustard family
    KALE, CRESS
plant organ .... LEAF
plant pod .... BOLL
plant, poisonous ...... LOCO
plant, sea-bottom ... ENALID
plant stem: bot. ...... CAULIS
plant stem tissue ...... PITH
plant used as soap ... AMOLE
plants of area .... FLORA
plantain lily genus ..... HOSTA
plantation, osier .... HOLT
planter .... SEEDER
plaster .... SMEAR
plaster, artist's painting.GESSO
plaster of Paris .... GESSO
plastic .... LUCITE
plate, battery .... GRID
plate, Eucharist .... PATEN
plate, reptile's .... SCUTE
plate to hurl .... DISCUS
plateau .... MESA
plateau, Andes .... PUNA
platform ...... DAIS, STAGE
platform, ancient ...... BEMA

c platform, mine shaft
    SOLLAR, SOLLER
platinum, of .... OSMIC
platinum wire loop ..... OESE
Plato's "Idea" ... EIDE, EIDOS
play .... DRAMA
play on words .... PUN
play, part of ..... ACT, SCENE
play unskillfully ...... STRUM
player .... ACTOR
playing card, old It. ... TAROT
playwright .... INGE
plea, to end: law .... ABATER
plead .... SUE, ENTREAT
pleading: law .... OYER
please .... SUIT
pleasing .... NICE
pleasure god, Egypt. . BES, BESA
pledge .... VOW,
    GAGE, OATH, PAWN,
    TROTH, ENGAGE
pledge, Rom. law .... VAS
plexus .... RETE, RETIA
pliable .... WAXY
pliant .... LITHE
plinth .... ORLO, SOCLE
plot .... LOT,
    PLAT, CABAL, CONSPIRE
plow, cutter COLTER, COULTER
d plow part .... SHETH, SHEATH
plow, sole of .... SHARE
plowed field .... ERD, ARADA
plug .... BUNG,
    CORK, SPILE, STOPPER
plum .... GAGE, SLOE
plume ..EGRET, PREEN, AIGRET
plummet .... FATHOM
plump child .... FUB
plunder .... ROB, LOOT, PREY,
    SACK, BOOTY, RAVEN,
    RAVIN, REAVE, PILFER,
    RAPINE, RAVAGE, RAVINE
plunder ruthlessly ... MARAUD
plunge .... DIVE, DOUSE
plural ending .... EN, ES
plus .... AND
Pluto .... DIS, HADES, ORCUS
Pluto's mother-in-law DEMETER
pneumonia, kind of .... LOBAR
Po tributary .... ADDA
pochard .... SMEE
pocket billiards .... POOL
pocket gopher, Mex. .... TUZA
pod, cotton .... BOLL
pods for tanning .... PIPI
Poe poem .... RAVEN
poem .... ODE, ELEGY, EPODE
poem division, or part . CANTO
poem, 8 line .... TRIOLET

a
poem, long heroic .. **EPIC, EPOS**
poem, love .... **SONNET**
poem, lyric ...... **ODE, EPODE**
poem, mournful .... **ELEGY**
poem, of a .... **ODIC**
poem, old Fr. .... **DIT**
poem, sacred .... **PSALM**
poet .... **BARD, ODIST**
poet, A.-S. .... **SCOP**
poet, Bengal .... **TAGORE**
poet, blind, epic ..... **HOMER**
poet, lyric .... **ODIST**
poet, Norse ... **SCALD, SKALD**
poet, poor .... **RIMER**
poetry .... **EPOS, POESY**
poetry, early .... **RUNE**
poetry, Finnish .... **RUNES**
poetry, mournful, pert. to
ELEGIAC
poetry, Norse god of
BRAGE, BRAGI
poi, source of .... **TARO**
point **END, TIP, BARB, PUNTO**
point in moon's orbit nearest
earth .... **PERIGEE**
point of curve .... **NODE**
point of land .... **SPIT**
point of moon .... **CUSP**
point of view .... **ANGLE**

b
point on mariner's compass
RUMB
point on tooth's crown ... **CUSP**
point, tennis or golf .... **ACE**
point won .... **GOAL**
pointed ..... **SHARP, ACUATE**
pointed arch .... **OGEE**
pointed end .... **CUSP**
pointed missile **DART, SPEAR**
pointed remark .... **BARB**
pointed staff .... **PIKE**
pointer .... **WAND**
pointless .... **INANE**
poison .... **BANE, TAINT**
poison, arrow ... **INEE, UPAS,**
URALI, URARE, URARI,
CURARE, CURARI
poison, hemlock ...... **CONINE**
poison, India **BISH, BISK, BIKH**
poisonous protein **RICIN, RICINE**
poisonous weed .... **LOCO**
poke ..... **JAB, PROD, NUDGE**
poker stake ...... **POT, ANTE**
pokeweed ..... **POCAN, SCOKE**
Polar explorer .... **BYRD**
pole .... **MAST**
pole, Gaelic games
CABER, CABIR
Pole .... **SLAV**
pole, naut. .... **MAST, SPRIT**
pole to handle fish .... **PEW**
pole to pole, from **AXAL, AXIAL**

c
polecat, Cape **ZORIL, ZORILLA**
police line .... **CORDON**
policeman ...... **COP, PEELER**
policeman, state .... **TROOPER**
policeman, S. Afr. ...... **ZARP**
polish .... **RUB, WAX,**
SHINE, LEVIGATE
POLISH ... see also POLAND
SPECIAL SECTION
Polish assembly ... **SEIM, SEJM**
Polish cake .... **BABA**
Polish general .. **BOR, ANDERS**
Polish title of address
PAN, PANI
polished .... **SHINY, SLEEK,**
URBANE, ELEGANT
polisher .... **EMERY**
polishing material
RABAT, ROUGE
polite .... **CIVIL**
political booty .... **GRAFT**
pollack fish .... **SEY**
pollen brush .. **SCOPA, SCOPAE**
Pollux or Castor .... **ANAX**
Pollux' mother .... **LEDA**
Pollux' twin .... **CASTOR**
polo stick .... **MALLET**
Polynesian .... **MAORI**
Polyn. "Adam" .... **TIKI**
Polyn. chestnut .... **RATA**

d
Polyn. cloth .... **TAPA**
Polyn. dance .... **SIVA**
Polyn. deity, demon
AKUA, ATUA
Polyn. drink .... **AVA**
Polyn. for nature's power **MANA**
Polyn. god .... **ATEO**
Polyn. god of forest .... **TANE**
Polyn. herb .... **PIA**
Polyn. hero .... **MAUI**
Polyn. island group ... **SAMOA**
Polyn. languages
MAORI, MAHORI
Polyn. lily .... **TI**
Polyn. stone heap .... **AHU**
pome .... **APPLE**
"Pomp and Circumstance" Com-
poser .... **ELGAR**
pompous .... **TURGID**
pond .. **MERE, POOL, LOCHAN**
ponder .... **MUSE, PORE**
pontiff .... **POPE**
pony .... **CAVY**
pony, student's .... **CRIB**
pool .... **MERE, TARN,**
LAGOON, PUDDLE
pool: Scot. .... **DIB, CARR,**
LINN, LLYN
poon tree **DILO, DOMBA, KEENA**
poor .... **NEEDY**
poor joe .... **HERON**

poor player .... **DUB**
poorly .... **ILL**
POPE .. see also PAPAL
Pope ... **JOHN, PIUS, ADRIAN**
Pope, English .... **ADRIAN**
Pope John XXIII first name
.... **ANGELO**
Pope John XXIII last name
.... **RONCALLI**
Pope Pius XI .... **RATTI**
Pope Pius XII ...... **PACELLI**
POPE'S CAPE, COLLAR ... see
PAPAL CAPE, COLLAR
Pope's triple crown **TIAR, TIARA**
poplar .... **ALAMO, ASPEN**
poplar, white ... **ABELE, ASPEN**
poppy red .... **GRANATE**
poppy seed .... **MAW**
populace, the .... **DEMOS**
popular girl .... **BELLE**
porcelain
.... **CHINA, SEVRES, LIMOGES**
porcelain, ancient .... **MURRA**
porcelain, Chin. .... **JU, KO**
porcelain, Eng. .... **SPODE**
porch .... **ANTA, STOOP,**
VERANDA, VERANDAH
porch, Gr. .... **STOA**
porch, Hawaiian ...... **LANAI**
porch swing .... **GLIDER**
porcupine anteater .. **ECHIDNA**
porcupine, Canada .... **URSON**
pore .... **PORUS, STOMA,**
OSTIOLE, STOMATA
porgy .... **SCUP**
porgy, Europ. .... **PARGO**
porgy genus .... **PAGRUS**
porgy, Jap. (Oriental) .... **TAI**
porkfish .... **SISI**
porous rock ..... **TUFA, TUFF**
porpoise .... **DOLPHIN**
porridge .... **POB, BROSE**
porridge, corn meal ..... **SAMP**
porridge: Sp. Am. ..... **ATOLE**
Porsena of Clusium ..... **LARS**
PORT .. see also SPECIAL SEC-
TION — GAZETTEER
port .... **HAVEN**
port, banana, Honduras .. **TELA**
port, Black Sea ...... **ODESSA**
Port Moresby land ... **PAPUA**
port of Rome .... **OSTIA**
port opp. Gibraltar .... **CEUTA**
port, South Seas .... **APIA**
port, Suez .... **SAID**
port wine city .... **OPORTO**
portable chair .... **SEDAN**
portal .... **DOOR, GATE**
portend BODE, AUGUR, PRESAGE

portent .... **OMEN, SIGN**
porter, Orient
.... **HAMAL, HAMMAL**
Portia's waiting woman **NERISSA**
portico .... **STOA**
portion.**PART, SOME, SEGMENT**
portion out **DOLE, METE, ALLOT**
portray .... **DRAW,**
LIMN, DEPICT, DELINEATE
Portuguese coin .... **REI**
Port. colony, India ...... **GOA**
Port. folk tune .... **FADO**
Port. lady .... **DONA**
Port. man .... **DOM**
Port. navigator .... **GAMA**
Port. title ..... **DOM, DONNA**
pose .... **SIT**
Poseidon .... **NEPTUNE**
Poseidon's son .... **TRITON**
posited .... **SET**
position ...... **SITUS, STATUS**
position without work **SINECURE**
positive .... **THETIC**
positive pole, terminal **ANODE**
possession, landed .... **ESTATE**
possum .... **COON**
possum, comic-strip ..... **POGO**
post .... **MAIL, SEND**
post-hole digger (slick) ...**LOY**
postpone .... **DEFER**
postulate .... **POSIT**
posture .... **STANCE**
pot .... **OLLA**
pot, chem. .... **ALUDEL**
pot, earthen .... **CRUSE**
pot herb .... **WORT**
pot, India **LOTA, LOTO, LOTAH**
pot liquor .... **BREWIS**
pot metal .... **POTIN**
potassium .... **KALITE**
potassium chloride .. **MURIATE**
potassium nitrate
.... **NITER, GROUGH**
potation, small .... **DRAM**
potato .... **SPUD**
potato, sweet .. **YAM, BATATA**
pother .... **ADO**
potpourri .... **OLIO**
potter's blade .... **PALLET**
pottery fragment .... **SHARD**
pottery, pert. to .... **CERAMIC**
pouch .... **SAC**
pouch-shaped ...... **SACCATE**
poultry .... **HENS, BIRDS**
poultry disease .... **PIP, ROUP**
pounce .... **SWOOP**
pound .... **TUND**
pound down ...... **RAM, TAMP**
pour .... **RAIN, TEEM**
pour off gently ...... **DECANT**

Pour

pour out .... **LIBATE**
poverty .... **NEED, WANT**
powder, astringent .... **BORAL**
powder, mineral ingredient
.... **TALC**
powder of aloes .... **PICRA**
powdered pumice .... **TALC**
power .. **DINT, MANA, FORCE**
practical joke .... **HOAX**
practice .... **HABIT**
practice exercise, musical **ETUDE**
praise **LAUD, EXTOL, EXTOLL**
prance .... **CAPER**
prank .... **DIDO, CAPER**
prate .... **GAB, YAP**
prate: India ..... **BUKH, BUKK**
pray: Yiddish .... **DAVEN**
prayer **AVE, BEAD, BENE, PLEA,**
    CREDO, MATIN, ORISON
prayer form .... **LITANY**
prayer, 9-day ...... **NOVENA**
prayer-rug, Hindu ..... **ASANA**
prayer stick, Am. Ind.
    BAHO, PAHO, PAJO
prayers, deacon's
    ECTENE, EKTENE
prayerbook
    ORDO, PORTAS, PORTASS
praying figure .... **ORANT**
preacher, Gospel .... **EVANGEL**
precepts .... **DICTA**
precipice, Hawaii .... **PALI**
precipitous .... **STEEP**
preclude ...... **AVERT, DEBAR**
preconceive .... **IDEATE**
predicament .... **SCRAPE**
predicate
    BASE, FOUND, AFFIRM
predict
   AUGUR, FORECAST, FORETELL
predisposed .... **PRONE**
preen .... **PLUME, PRINK**
preface .... **PROEM**
prefecture, Jap. .... **KEN**
PREFIX:
  about .... **PERI**
  above .... **HYPER**
  across .... **DIA, TRANS**
  again .... **RE**
  against .... **ANTI**
  ahead .... **PRE**
  an .... **AE**
  apart .... **DIS**
  away .... **DE, DI, APO**
  back .... **ANA**
  backward .... **RETRO**
  bad .... **MAL**
  badly .... **MIS**
  beauty .... **CALLI**
  before ..... **OB, PRE, ANTE**
  blood .... **HAEM, HEMO**

both .... **AMBI**
CHEMICALS .. see page 29
common .... **PRE**
distant .... **TEL, TELE**
double .... **DI**
down .... **DE, CATA**
eight ... **OCT, OCTA, OCTO**
equal .... **ISO**
far .... **TEL, TELE**
faulty .... **MIS**
fire .... **PYR**
former, formerly .... **EX**
four .... **TETRA**
from .... **EC**
half ..... **DEMI, HEMI, SEMI**
ill .... **MIS**
mountain .... **ORO**
negative .... **IR, NON**
new .... **NEO**
not ... **IL, IM, IR, UN, NON**
not fully .... **SEMI**
numerical .... **UNI**
of atmospheric pressure **BARO**
of the stars .... **ASTRO**
on this side .... **CIS**
one .... **UNI**
out of .... **EC, EX**
outer ..... **ECT, EXO, ECTO**
outer skin .... **EPI**
outside .... **ECT, EXO**
over .... **EPI, SUPER,**
    SUPRA, SUPERB
partly .... **SEMI**
people .... **DEMO**
pray .... **ORA**
recent .... **NEO**
same .... **ISO, EQUI, HOMO**
separation .... **DIS**
single .... **MONO**
ten .... **DEC, DECA**
thousand .... **KILO**
three .... **TER, TRI**
thrice .... **TER, TRIS**
threefold .... **TRI**
through .... **DIA, PER**
to .... **AP**
together .... **COM**
town .... **TRE**
turning .... **ROTO**
twice .... **BI**
two .... **DI, DUA**
twofold .... **DI**
under .... **SUB**
upon .... **EPI**
upward .... **ANA, ANO**
with .... **SYN**
within .... **ENDO**
wrong .... **MIS**

a prehistoric implement ... CELT
prehistoric mound ...... TERP
prejudice .... BIAS
prelate, high .... PRIMATE
prelude .... PROEM
premium, exchange ..... AGIO
prepare .... FIT, GIRD,
MAKE, ADAPT, EQUIP
prepare for publication .. EDIT
prepared opium
CHANDU, CHANDOO
preposition ...... AT, IN, ON,
UP, INTO
presage
OMEN, HERALD, PORTEND
prescribed .... THETIC
prescribed quantity ..... DOSE
present .. GIFT, GIVE, DONATE
present, be .... ATTEND
present in brief .... SUM
presently.ANON, ENOW, SOON
preserve .... CAN, JAM, KEEP,
SAVE, PROTECT, MAINTAIN
preserve in brine .. CORN, SALT
Presidential nickname .. ABE,
CAL, IKE, TEDDY
press together .... SERRY
pressure .... DURESS
pressure unit .. BARAD, BARIE
pretend .. FAKE, SHAM, FEIGN
b pretense .... SHAM
pretensions .... AIRS
pretentious .... SIDY
prevail .... WIN
prevail on .... INDUCE
prevalent .... RIFE
prevent ... DETER, PRECLUDE
prevent by law .... ESTOP
prey .... RAVIN
prey upon
RAVEN, RAVIN, RAVINE
Priam's son
PARIS, HECTOR, HEKTOR
price .... RATE
price of transportation .. FARE
prickle .... SETA
prickles .... SETAE
prickly pear
TUNA, NOPAL, CACTUS
prickly plant ... BRIAR, BRIER,
NETTLE
prickly seed coat .. BUR, BURR
pride .... PLUME
PRIEST .. see also CLERGYMAN
priest
FRA, ABBE, CURE, PADRE
priest, Celtic .... DRUID
priest, Gr. .... MYST

c PRIEST, HIGH, see HIGH PRIEST
priest in "Iliad" .... CALCHAS
priest, Mongol .... SHAMAN
priest, Moro SARIP, PANDITA
priestess, Gr. .... AUGE
priestess, Rom. .... VESTAL
priesthood, Rom. ...... SALII
priestly caste ... MAGI, MAGUS
prima donna .... DIVA
PRIMA DONNA ...... see also
OPERA SOPRANO
prime , minister: Brit. ... EDEN,
PEEL
primeval .... OLD,
EARLY, PRIMAL, PRISTINE
prince, Abyssin. .... RAS
prince, Arabian .. EMIR, SAYID,
SAYYID, SHERIF, SHEREEF
prince, India
RAJA, RANA, RAJAH
prince of Argos .... DANAE
Prince of Darkness .... SATAN
prince, Oriental .... KHAN
prince, Persian .. AMIR, AMEER
prince, petty .... SATRAP
prince, Slavic .... KNEZ
Prince Val's father ... AGUAR
princeling .... SATRAP
princely .... ROYAL
princess, Gr. myth ...... IOLE
princess, India .. RANI, RANEE
d principal .... TOP, ARCH
MAIN, CHIEF
principal commodity .. STAPLE
principle, accepted
AXIOM, PRANA, TENET
print .... STAMP
print measure .... EM, EN
printer, 1st colonial .... DAYE
printer's direction ...... STET
printer's mark .... DELE
printer's mistake
TYPO, ERRATUM
printer's mistakes .... ERRATA
printing plate .... STEREO
printing roller .... PLATEN
prison.JUG, GAOL, JAIL, QUOD
prison sentence .... RAP
prison spy .... MOUTON
privation .... LOSS
privilege, commercial .. OCTROI
prize .... PRY, AWARD
pro .... FOR
"— pro nobis" .... ORA
probe, medical .... STYLET
problem .... POSER
proboscis .... SNOUT
proboscis monkey ...... KAHA
proceed ... WEND, ADVANCE
proceedings .... ACTA

procession .... **TRAIN, PARADE, MOTORCADE**
proclaim .... **CRY, VOICE, HERALD, DECLARE**
prod .... **URGE**
produce .... **BEGET, YIELD CREATE, INWORK, GENERATE**
produce as an effect ... **BEGET**
produced, quantity ..... **YIELD**
producing cold ...... **ALGIFIC**
production, artistic .. **FACTURE**
profane .... **VIOLATE**
profane, Hawaiian ...... **NOA**
profession
ART, CAREER, METIER
professional, not **LAIC, LAICAL**
profit ... **GAIN, VAIL, AVAIL**
profit, to yield .... **NET**
profits, taker of: law . **PERNOR**
profitable ...... **FAT, USEFUL**
profound .... **DEEP**
"— profundis" .... **DE**
progenitor ..... **SIRE, PARENT**
progeny .... **ISSUE**
prohibit .... **BAN, BAR, VETO, DEBAR, ESTOP**
prohibition
BAN, VETO, EMBARGO
Prohibition, against ...... **WET**
project ...... **JUT, IDEA, PLAN**
projectile .... **MISSILE**
projecting edge **RIM, FLANGE**
projecting piece
ARM, RIM, TENON, FLANGE
projecting rim .... **FLANGE**
projecting tooth .... **SNAG**
projection . **EAR, BARB, PRONG**
projection, fireplace. **HOB, HOBB**
projection, jagged **SNAG, TOOTH**
projection, studlike .... **KNOP**
promenade .... **MALL**
promise .... **WORD**
promise to pay .... **IOU, NOTE**
"Promised Land" fountain **AIN**
promontory ..... **CAPE, NASE, NAZE, NESS**
promontory, Orkneys .... **NOUP**
promontory, rocky ...... **TOR**
promote .... **FOSTER**
prompt .... **CUE, YARE**
prone .... **APT, FLAT**
prong .... **TINE, TOOTH**
pronghorn .... **CABREE, CABRET, CABRIE, CABRIT**
pronoun .. **IT, ME, US, WE, YE, HER, HIM, ONE, SHE, THAT, THIS, THEE, THEM, THEY, THOU, THESE, THOSE**

pronoun, possessive . **MY, HER, HIS, ITS, OUR, HERS, MINE, OURS, YOUR**
pronounce indistinctly ... **SLUR**
pronounce strongly .... **STRESS**
pronouncement **DICTA, DICTUM**
proof, corrected ...... **REVISE**
proof, printer's .... **GALLEY**
proofreader's mark
DELE, STET, CARET
prop .... **HOLD, STAY, BRACE, BOLSTER, SUSTAIN**
propeller .... **OAR**
proper .... **DUE, FIT**
properly .... **FEATLY**
property, hold on .... **LIEN**
property, India .... **DHAN**
property, item of
ASSET, CHATTEL
property, landed ...... **ESTATE**
property owned absolutely **ALOD, ALLOD, ALODIUM, ALLODIUM**
property, receiver of .. **ALIENEE**
prophesy .... **FORETELL**
prophet .... **SEER, AUGUR, PREDICTOR, FORETELLER**
PROPHETS, BIBLICAL ..... see
SPECIAL SECTION
prophets .... **VATES**
prophetic ... **VATIC, VATICAL**
proportion .... **RATIO**
proportionally assess **PRORATE**
proposition
THESES, THESIS, PREMISE
proposition, logic ..... **LEMMA**
proposition: math. .. **THEOREM**
prosecutor .... **SUER**
prosecutor: abbr. .... **DA**
proselyte to Judaism .... **GER**
"— prosequi," .... **NOLLE**
Proserpina ...... **CORA, KORE**
prospect .... **VISTA**
prosperity .... **WEAL**
prosperity god, Teut. .... **FREY**
Prospero's servant ..... **ARIEL**
prostrate .... **PRONE, REPENT**
protagonist .... **HERO**
protected .... **HOUSED**
protection .... **EGIS, AEGIS**
protection right, Old Eng. **MUND**
protective building .... **REDAN**
protective influence
EGIS, AEGIS
Protestant denomination: abbr.
ME, PE, BAP, PRESB
prototype .... **IDEAL**
protozoan order .... **LOBOSA**
protuberance ..... **JAG, NUB, HUMP, KNOB, KNOT, NODE, WART, KNURL, TORUS**

a protuberant .... **TOROSE**
   prove: law .... **DERAIGN**
   proverb ...... **SAW, ADAGE,**
   AXIOM, MAXIM, SAYING
   provide ...... **ENDOW, ENDUE**
   provided .... **IF**
   provided that .... **SO**
   province, Rom. .... **DACIA**
   provisional clause ... **PROVISO**
   proviso .... **CLAUSE**
   provoke........... **IRE, RILE,**
   ANGER, ANNOY
   prow .... **BOW, STEM**
   prune: prov. Eng. ...... **SNED**
   pruning knife .... **DHAW**
   Prussian spa, town ...... **EMS**
   pry .... **NOSE, LEVER, SNOOP**
   Psalm, 51st .... **MISERERE**
   Psalmist .... **DAVID**
   Psalms, selection of .. **HALLEL**
   Psalms, word in .... **SELAH**
   pseudonym ...... **NOM, ALIAS**
   pseudonym of Louise Del La
   Ramee .... **OUIDA**
   psyche .... **SOUL**
   psychiatrist
   JUNG, ADLER, FREUD
   Ptah, embodiment of ... **APIS**
   ptarmigan .... **RYPE**
b pteropod genus ...... **CLIONE**
   pua hemp ...... **POOA**
   public .... **OPEN, OVERT**
   public: Chin. .... **KUNG**
   public esteem ...... **REPUTE**
   public, make ... **AIR, DELATE**
   public vehicle .... **BUS, TAXI**
   publication, style of . **FORMAT**
   publish .... **ISSUE, PRINT**
   publish illegally ...... **PIRATE**
   Puccini heroine .... **MIMI**
   puck, hockey .... **RUBBER**
   pudding........ **DUFF, SAGO**
   pueblo dweller .... **HOPI**
   Pueblo Indian ... **HOPI, ZUNI,**
   KERES, MOQUI, TANOA
   Pueblo sacred chamber .. **KIVA**
   Pueblo, Tanoan .... **HANO**
   Puerto Rican plant ...... **APIO**
   puff up .... **ELATE**
   puffbird, Brazil .... **DREAMER**
   puffbird genus ..... **MONASA**
   puffer fish .... **TAMBOR**
   Pulitzer poet .... **FROST**
   pull .. **TOW, TUG, DRAG, HALE**
   pull with nautical tackle **BOUSE**
   pulley .... **SHEAVE**
   pulp, fruit .... **POMACE**
   pulpit .... **AMBO, BEMA**
   pulpy mass left in cider **POMACE**
   pulverize .... **MICRONIZE**

c pump handle .... **SWIPE**
   pumpkin .... **PEPO**
   punch .... **JAB**
   "Punch and Judy" dog .. **TOBY**
   punch, engraver's .. **MATTOIR**
   punctuation mark **DASH, COLON**
   pungent .. **TEZ, SPICY, TANGY**
   punish by fine ...... **AMERCE**
   punishment .... **FERULE**
   punishment, of .... **PENAL**
   punitive .... **PENAL**
   Punjab native .... **JAT**
   punk .... **AMADOU**
   pupa .... **INSTAR**
   pupil of eye .... **GLENE**
   puppet .... **DOLL**
   puppet, famous **JUDY, PUNCH**
   puppeteer, famous ...... **SARG**
   pure sirup .... **CLAIRCE**
   pure thought .... **NOESIS**
   purification, ancient Roman
   LUSTRUM
   purloin .... **STEAL**
   purple
   MAUVE, MODENA, TYRIAN
   purple dye source .... **MUREX**
   purple medic
   LUCERN, ALFALFA, LUCERNE
   purple ragwort ...... **JACOBY**
   purple seaweed . **SION, LAVER**
d purport, general ...... **TENOR**
   purpose .... **AIM, END,**
   GOAL, SAKE, INTENT
   purposive .... **TELIC**
   purse net .... **SEINE**
   pursy .... **STOUT**
   push up .... **BOOST**
   put aside .... **DAFF**
   put away .... **STORE**
   put back .... **REPLACE**
   put forth .... **EXERT**
   put in bank .... **DEPOSIT**
   put off .... **DEFER**
   put out ...... **OUST, EJECT**
   put up .... **ANTE**
   puzzle .... **POSER,**
   REBUS, BAFFLE, ACROSTIC
   puzzles .... **CRUCES**
   Pygmalion's statue .. **GALATEA**
   pygmy .... **ATOMY**
   pygmy people, Congo
   AKKA, ACHUAS
   pygmy people, Equatorial Africa
   BATWA, ABONGO, OBONGO
   Pylos, kin of .... **NESTOR**
   Pyramus, lover of .... **THISBE**
   pyromaniac .... **FIREBUG**
   Pythias' friend .... **DAMON**
   python .... **BOA**

Q

a
qua .... AS
"— qua non" .... SINE
quack IMPOSTOR, CHARLATAN
quack medicine .... NOSTRUM
quadrant .... ARC
quadrate .... SQUARE
"quae —" which see .... VIDE
quaff .... DRINK
quail .... COLIN, COWER
quake .... SHAKE,
    SHIVER, TREMOR, TREMBLE
Quaker .... FRIEND
Quaker Poet .... WHITTIER
quaking .... TREPID
qualify .... FIT, ADAPT,
        EQUIP, PREPARE
qualified .... FIT, ABLE
quality .... CALIBER, CALIBRE
quantity, indeterminate . SOME
quantity: math.
            SCALER, VECTOR
b
quarrel .... ROW, FEUD,
            SPAT, TIFF
quarter of a year: Scot. RAITH
quartz .... JASPER
quartz, green .... PRASE
quartz, translucent ... PRASE
quash: law .... CASSARE
quaternion .... TETRAD
quay .... LEVEE
Quebec, district, town ... LEVIS
Quebec's patron saint .. ANNE
Queen .... CLEO
queen: Moslem BEGUM, BEEGUM
queen of gods, Egypt. ... SATI
queen of gods, Rom. ... HERA,
                JUNO
Queen of Italy .... ELENA
Queen of Ithaca ... PENELOPE
Queen of Roumania ... MARIE
Queen of Scots .... MARY
Queen of Spain, last ..... ENA
queen, "Romeo and Juliet"
                MAB

c
queenly .... REGAL, REGINAL
Queensland hemp plant
                SIDA
Queensland tribe .... GOA
quell .... CALM, CRUSH
quench .... SLAKE
quench steel ..... AUSTEMPER
quern .... MILL
query .... ASK
queue .... LINE
question .... ASK, GRILL
question, hard .... POSER
quetzal .... TROGON
quibble .... CAVIL, EVADE
quick .... FAST, AGILE,
            ALIVE, RAPID
quick: music .... TOSTO
quicken ... HASTEN, ENLIVEN
quickly .... CITO, APACE,
            PRESTO, PRONTO
quickly, move
        SCAT, SCUD, SKITE
quicksilver ...... HEAUTARIT
quid .... CUD
d
"quid — quo," equivalent . PRO
quiescent LATENT, DORMANT
quiet .... CALM, LULL,
            STILL, SMOOTH
quiet! .... SH, PST, TST
quilkin .... FROG, TOAD
quill .... PEN, SPINE
quill feathers REMEX, REMIGES
quill for winding silk ..... COP
quilt .... EIDER, COVER
quince, Bengal .... BEL, BHEL
quinine .... KINA
quintessence ... PITH, ELIXIR
quirt, cowboy's ...... ROMAL
quit .... CEASE, LEAVE
quite .... ALL
quivering ... ASPEN, TREMOR
"quod — demonstrandum"
                ERAT
"Quo Vadis" tyrant character
                NERO
quoits, mark of .... MOT
quote .... CITE

126

R

Ra, consort of .... **MUT**
Ra, son of .... **SU, SHU**
rabbi, law-teaching ... **AMORA**
rabbit cage .... **HUTCH**
rabbit, Europ. . **CONY, CONEY**
rabbit, female .... **DOE**
rabbit fur .... **LAPIN**
rabbit home .... **WARREN**
rabbit, small swamp .. **TAPETI**
rabbit, So. Am. .... **TAPETI**
rabble .... **MOB**
rabies .... **LYSSA**
raccoon-like mammal .. **COATI**
RACE .. see also TRIBES in
    SPECIAL SECTION
race, boat .... **REGATTA**
race, kind of .... **RELAY**
race, short .... **SPRINT**
race-track .... **OVAL**
race-track circuit ...... **LAP**
race-track tipster ...... **TOUT**
races, pert. to ...... **ETHNIC**
Rachel's father .... **LABAN**
racing boat .... **GIG**
racket, game .... **PELOTA**
radar screen .... **SCOPE**
radiate .... **EMANATE**
radical .... **RED**
radicle .... **STEMLET**
radio advertiser .... **SPONSOR**
radio bulletin ..... **NEWSCAST**
radio-guided bomb ..... **AZON**
radio wave. ..... **MICROWAVE**
radio wire .... **LITZ**
radio-TV awards ..... **EMMIES**
radioactive counter ... **GEIGER**
radioactive element ... **NITON**
radioactive ray ...... **GAMMA**
radium discoverer ...... **CURIE**
radium emanation .... **NITON**
radius, pert. to ...... **RADIAL**
radon .... **NITON**
raft, kind of ... **CATAMARAN**
raft, Maori .... **MOKI**
rag doll .... **MOPPET**
rage .... **RAMP, RANT,**
           RESE, STORM
ragged person: Sp. ...... **ROTO**
raging monster, Bibl. .. **RAHAB**
ragout, game .... **SALMI**
ragweed genus .... **IVA**
raid .... **FORAY, INROAD**
raid, soldier's .... **COMMANDO**
rail at .... **REVILE**
rail bird **SORA, WEKA, CRAKE**
railing .... **PARAPET**

railroad bridge ...... **TRESSEL,**
              TRESTLE
railroad light .... **FLARE**
railroad signal
    TRIMMER, SEMAPHORE
railroad tie .... **SLEEPER**
railroad timber .... **TIE**
railway station: Fr. ..... **GARE**
rain after sunset ...... **SEREIN**
rain, fine .... **MISLE**
rain forest .... **SELVA**
rain gauge .... **UDOMETER**
rain serpent, Hindu .... **NAGA**
rain spout: Scot. ...... **RONE**
rain tree .... **SAMAN**
rainbow .... **ARC, IRIS**
rainbow goddess .... **IRIS**
rainbow, pert. to ..... **IRIDAL**
raincoat .... **PONCHO**
rainy .... **WET**
raise . **REAR, BREED, ELEVATE**
raised .... **BRED**
raisin: Sp. .... **PASA**
raising device .... **JACK**
Rajah's lady ... **RANI, RANEE**
rake ...... **ROUE, LOTHARIO**
rake with gunfire .. **ENFILADE**
ram . **TUP, BUTT, TAMP, ARIES**
ram, male .... **TUP**
ram-headed god, Egypt
    AMEN, AMON, AMUN
Ramachandra, wife of .. **SITA**
ramble .... **GAD, ROVE**
Ramee, de la, penname . **OUIDA**
rammed earth building material
              PISE
rampart ..... **AGGER, VALLUM**
range .... **AREA, GAMUT,**
        SCOPE, SIERRA
Rangoon's state .... **PEGU**
rank .... **ROW, RATE, DEGREE**
ranks, press in .... **SERRY**
rankle .... **FESTER**
ransom .... **REDEEM**
rapeseed ..... **COLSA, COLZA**
rapid, more: music .. **STRETTA,**
    STRETTE, STRETTI, STRETTO
rapids, river .... **SOO**
rapidly .... **APACE**
rapier .... **BILBO**
rare earth element ... **ERBIUM**
rascal .... **IMP, ROGUE**
rase .... **INCISE**
rasorial .... **GNAWING**
rasp .... **FILE, GRATE**

127

a raspberry, variety . **BLACKCAP**
rasse .... **CIVET**
rat .... **DESERTER**
rat, Ceylon, India . **BANDICOOT**
rat hare .... **PIKA**
rate .... **ESTIMATE**
rate, relative .... **AT**
ratify .... **SEAL**
ratio .... **RATE**
RATIO: MATH see MATH, RATIO
rational .... **SANE**
rational integer .... **NORM**
rational principle ...... **LOGOS**
rationalize .... **THOB**
ratite bird ...... **CASSOWARY**
rattan .... **CANE**
rattlesnake
    RATTLER, CROTALUS
rave .... **RANT**
"Raven" author .... **POE**
"Raven" character .... **LENORE**
ravine
    GAP, DALE, VALE, GORGE
ravine, Afr. .... **WADI, WADY**
ravine, Arabia .. **WADI, WADY**
rawboned .... **LEAN**
rawboned animal ...... **SCRAG**
ray fish .... **SKATE**
rays, like .... **RADIAL**
rayon ... **ACETATE, CELANESE**
b raze .... **DEVASTATE**
razor-billed auk
    ALCA, MURR, MURRE
reach across .... **SPAN**
react .... **RESPOND**
read, inability to ... **ALEXIA**
read metrically .... **SCAN**
read publically ...... **PRELECT**
reader, first .... **PRIMER**
reading desk .... **AMBO**
reading substituted: Bibl.
    KERE, KERI
ready: dialect .... **YARE**
ready-made tie .... **TECK**
real being, pert. to .... **ONTAL**
real thing .... **MCCOY**
reality .... **FACT**
realm .... **DOMAIN**
reamer .... **BROACH**
rear ... **ERECT, RAISE, ARRIERE**
rear, to the
    AFT, ABAFT, ASTERN
rearhorse .... **MANTIS**
rearing of horse ...... **PESADE**
reason .... **NOUS**
reason, deprive of ... **DEMENT**
reasoning .... **LOGIC**
reasoning, deductive .. **APRIORI**
reata
    LAZO, ROPE, LASSO, LARIAT

c rebec of India .... **SAROD**
Rebecca's hairy son ..... **ESAU**
rebound .. **CAROM, RICOCHET**
rebuff .... **SLAP, SNUB**
rebuke
    CHIDE, SCOLD, REPROVE
recalcitrant .... **RENITENT**
recant .... **RETRACT**
recede .... **EBB**
recent
    NEO, NEW, LATE, NEOTERIC
receptacle .... **BIN, BOX,**
                TRAY, VESSEL
reception, a.m. .... **LEVEE**
reception: Fr. .... **ACCUEIL**
reception, India ..... **DURBAR**
recess .... **APSE, ALCOVE**
recess, wall .... **NICHE**
recipient .... **DONEE**
recite metrically .... **SCAN**
reckon .... **ARET, COUNT**
reckoning .... **TALLY**
reclaim .... **REDEEM**
recline .... **LOLL**
recluse .... **ASCETIC, EREMITE,**
    ANCHORET, ANCHORITE
recoil .... **SHY, RESILE**
recommit .... **REMAND**
recompense .. **PAY, FEES, MEED**
reconnaissance **RECCO, RECON**
d reconnoiter .... **SCOUT**
reconstruct .... **REMODEL**
record .. **TAB, NOTE, ENROL,**
    ENTER, ENTRY, REGISTER
record of investigation **REPORT**
record, ship's .... **LOG**
record, year's .... **ANNAL**
records .... **ANNALS**
recorded proceedings ... **ACTA**
recording device .... **TAPE**
records, one who ..... **NOTER**
recourse, have .... **REFER**
recover strength ...... **RALLY**
recovery, legal .... **TROVER**
recruit .... **BOOT**
rectifier, current ...... **DIODE**
rectify ...... **AMEND, EMEND**
recurring pattern ..... **CYCLE**
red .... **CARMINE,**
    MAGENTA, NACARAT
red, Brazil .... **ROSET**
red cedar ... **SAVIN, SAVINE**
red circle: Her. .... **GUZE**
red currant .... **RISSEL**
red deer .... **ELAPHINE**
red dye root ... **CHAY, CHOY**
red garden flower .... **CANNA**
red: Her. .... **GULES**
red horse .... **BAY, ROAN**
red ocher .... **KEEL, KIEL,**
    TIVER, RADDLE, RUDDLE

a red pigment .... ROSET, ASTACIN, ASTACENE
red pine .... RIMU
red planet .... MARS
red powder, India .... ABIR
red, painter's .... ROSET
Red River Rebellion leader ...... RIEL
red: Sp. .... ROJO
red squirrel .... CHICKAREE
red swine .... DUROC
red, Venetian .... SIENA
red-yellow color ...... ALOMA
redact .... EDIT
redbreast .... ROBIN
redcap .... PORTER
reddish yellow .... SUDAN
redeem .... RANSOM
redshank .... CLEE
reduce ...... PARE, DEMOTE
reduce sail .... REEF
reduce taxes .... DERATE
reebok .... PEELE
reedbuck .... NAGOR
reek .... FUG, FUME
reef .... SHOAL
reel, fishing-rod .... PIRN
refer .... PERTAIN
refer to repeatedly ..... HARP
refined grace ...... ELEGANCE
b reflection .... GLARE
refracting device .... LENS
refractor, light .... PRISM
refrain .... FORBEAR
refrain in songs .. FALA, LALA, DERRY, LUDDEN
refrigerant .... FREON
refuge ...... HAVEN, SHELTER
refugee .... EMIGREE
refuse .... DENY
refuse .... ORT, DROSS, SCUM, OFFAL, TRASH
refuse, bit of .... SCRAP
refuse, flax .... POB
refuse: law .... RECUSE
refuse, metal .. DROSS, SCORIA
refuse, wool .... COT
refute .... REBUT, DISPROVE
regale .... FETE
regard ...... ESTEEM, RESPECT
regarding .... RE, ANENT
regenerate .... RENEW
regiment's framework .. CADRE
REGION .... see also DISTRICT
region .... CLIME, SECTOR
region, Afr. .. CONGO, NUBIA
region, Boeotia ...... AONIA
region, Cent. Afr. ...... SUDAN, SOUDAN
region, Fr. .... ALSACE

c region, Gr. .... DORIC
region, Indo-China ..... LAOS
region, pert. to .... AREAL
register .... ENROL, ENROLL, RECORD
reiterate .... REPEAT
regret .... RUE, DEPLORE
reign: India .... RAJ
reign, pert. to .... REGNAL
reigning .... REGNANT
reigning beauty .... BELLE
reimbursed .... PAID
reindeer .... CARIBOU
reindeer, Santa's .... DASHER, DONDER, BLITZEN, PRANCER
reinstate .... REVEST
reject .... SPURN, REPULSE
relate .... TELL, RECITE, NARRATE
related .... AKIN, TOLD, COGNATE, GERMANE
related by blood .... SIB
related on mother's side ENATE
relation .... SIB
relative. SIB, SIS, AUNT, NIECE
relative amount ...... RATION
relative pronoun .... WHO, THAT, WHAT
relative speed .... TEMPO
d relatives .... KIN
relatives, favoring .. NEPOTAL
relax .... EASE
relaxing of state tensions ...... DETENTE
relay of horses ..... REMUDA
release .... LOOSE
release: law .... REMISE
release, phonetic .... DETENTE
relevant .... GERMANE
reliable .... HONEST
relief, — .... BAS
relief .... DOLE
relieve .... EASE, ALLAY
relieve: Scot. .... LISS
religieuse .... NUN
religion .... FAITH
religion, Jap. .... SHINTO
religious art, work of .. PIETA
religious brother ...... FRA, MONK, FRIAR
religious festival ..... EASTER
religious festival, India .. MELA
religious law, Rom. ...... FAS
religious laywoman .. BEGUINE
religious opinion .... DOXY
religious order, one in . OBLATE
religious sayings ...... LOGIA
relinquish .... CEDE, WAIVE, YIELD

a reliquary .... APSE, ARCA,
　　　　　　　　　ARCAE, CHEST
relish .... GUSTO
reluctant ..... LOATH, AVERSE
rely .... TRUST
remain .... BIDE, STAY
remainder .... REST
remaining .... OVER
remark, witty .... MOT, SALLY
remiss .... LAX
remit .... SEND
remnant .... END, SHRED
remora fish . PEGA, LOOTSMAN
remove .. DELE, DOFF, DELETE
remove interior .... GUT
remove: law .... ELOIN,
　　　　　ELOIGN, ELOIGNE
remunerate .... PAY
rend ...... RIP, TEAR, WREST
render fat .... TRY
rendezvous .... TRYST
renegade .... APOSTATE
renounce .... ABNEGATE
renovated hat ..... MOLOKER
renown .... FAME, NOTE,
　　　EMINENCE, PRESTIGE
rent .... LET, HIRE, TEAR,
　　　　　TORN, LEASE
rent, old Eng. law .... TAC
renter .... LESSEE

b repair .... DARN, MEND
repartee .... RIPOST, RIPOSTE
repast .... MEAL
repay .... REQUITE
repay in kind .... RETALIATE
repeat .... ECHO, ITERATE
repeat: music .... BIS
repeat performance .. ENCORE
repeat sign: music .... SEGNO
repeat tiresomely .. DIN, DING
repeated phrase ..... REPRISE
repeatedly hit ...... POMMEL
repetition .... ROTE
replete .... FULL
report, small .... POP
repose .... EASE, REST
representation .... IDOL
representative .... AGENT
reproach ..... BLAME, TAUNT
reproach, old term ..... RACA
reproductive body .. GAMETE
reproductive cell ..... SPORE
reptile, pert. to ..... SAURIAN
repulse .... REPEL
reputation .... NAME, REPUTE
repute .... CHARACTER
request .... PLEA
rescind .... REPEAL
resentment .... IRE
reserve supply .... STORE

c residence ..... HOME, ABODE
residence, ecclesiastical . MANSE
resident of .... ITE
resign .... QUIT, DEMIT
resin ..... GUM, LAC, ANIME,
　　COPAL, ELEMI, JALAP,
　　MYRRH, BALSAM, MASTIC
resin, fossil . AMBER, GLESSITE
resin, fragrant .... ELEMI
resist .... OPPOSE
resist authority .... REBEL
resisting pressure ... RENITENT
resistor, current ... RHEOSTAT
resort .... SPA
resort, Fr. .... PAU,
　　　　NICE, CANNES
resources .... FUND,
　　　　MEANS, ASSETS
respect .... ESTEEM
respond .... REACT
rest .... SIT, EASE, REPOSE
rest, lay at .... REPOSE
restaurant, small ..... BISTRO
resthouse ...... CHAN, KHAN
resting .... ABED
restive .... BALKY
restore .... RENEW
restrain .. CURB, REIN, DETER,
　　　　STINT, TETHER

d restrict .... LIMIT
retaliate .... REPAY
retain .... HOLD, KEEP
retaliation .... TALION
retinue .... SUITE, TRAIN
retort, quick . RIPOST, RIPOSTE
retract .... RECANT
retreat .... RECEDE
retreat, cosy . DEN, NEST, NOOK
retribution .... NEMESIS
retribution, get .... VENGE
retrograde .... RECEDE
return ...... RECUR, RESTORE
return a profit .... PAY
return blow .... TIT
return on investment .. YIELD
returning .... REDIENT
reunion, hold a .... REUNE
reveille, call to .... DIAN
revelry, cry of .... EVOE
revelry, drunken .... ORGY
revenue, church: Scot. ANNAT
reverberate .... ECHO
reverberating .... REBOANT
revere ...... HONOR, HONOUR
reverence .... AWE
reversed in order .. CONVERSE
reversion to type .... ATAVISM

130

a revert to state (land) ...... **ESCHEAT**
revise .... **EDIT, AMEND**
revive wine .... **STUM**
revoke legacy, grant .. **ADEEM**
Revolution hero . **HALE, ALLEN**
revolutions per minute .. **REVS**
revolve . **SPIN, TURN, ROTATE**
revolve: logging .... **BIRL**
revolver.**GAT, GUN, ROD, COLT**
reward .... **MEED**
rhebok .... **PEELE**
Rhine city .... **MAINZ**
Rhine tributary .... **AAR**
rhinoceros beetle ...... **UANG**
rhinoceros, black
       BORELE, NASICORN
rhinoceros: obs.
       ABADA, ABATH
Rhone tributary ...... **SAONE**
rhythm .... **TIME, METER,**
       METRE, CADENCE
rhythmical accent ...... **BEAT**
rhythmical swing .... **LILT**
rib .... **COSTA**
rib. pert. to .... **COSTAL**
rib, woman from .... **EVE**
ribs, with .... **COSTATE**
ribbed fabric ..... **REP, CORD,**
       REPP, PIQUÉ
b ribbon, badge ...... **CORDON**
ribbon: comb. form ..... **TENE**
ribbonfish .... **GUAPENA**
rice .... **PADI, PADDY**
rice dish ...... **PILAU, PILAW**
rice field, Java .... **PADI**
rice grass, P.I. .... **BARIT**
rice in husk .... **PALAY**
rice paste, Jap. .... **AME**
rice polishings .... **DARAC**
rich man .... **MIDAS,**
       NABOB, NAWAB
rich silk cloth .... **CAFFA**
riches .... **PELF**
rid .... **FREE**
riddle .... **ENIGMA**
ridge .... **ARETE,**
       SPINE, MOUNTAIN
ridge, camp's .... **RIDEAU**
ridge, glacial, sandy ...... **OS,**
       OSAR, ESKER, OESAR
ridge on cloth .... **WALE**
ridge on skin .... **WELT**
ridge, stony .... **RAND**
ridges, rounded .... **GYRI**
ridged area, Balkan ..... **BILO**
ridicule .... **GUY, MOCK,**
       RAZZ, DERIDE
ridicule personified, Gr.
       MOMUS

c riding academy ..... **MANEGE**
riding dress .... **HABIT**
rifle .... **KRAG, MINIE,**
       GARAND, CARBINE
rifle ball .... **MINIE**
rifleman, Ger. .... **JAGER**
right conduct, Buddhist ... **TAO**
right conduct: Taoism ..... **TE**
right hand: music .... **DM**
right-hand page .. **RO, RECTO**
right: law .... **DROIT**
right, pert. to .... **DEXTER**
right to speak .... **SAY**
right, turn .... **GEE**
rights, of ...... **JURAL, UDAL**
Rigoletto's daughter ... **GILDA**
rigorous ..... **HARSH, STERN,**
       STRICT, SEVERE, AUSTERE
rim ...... **LIP, EDGE, FLANGE**
rim of wheel .. **FELLY, FELLOE**
"Rime cold giant" .**YMER, YMIR**
ring ..... **PEAL, TOLL, KNELL**
ring, boxing .... **ARENA**
ring for reins . **TERRET, TERRIT**
ring, gun carriage ..... **LUNET**
ring, harness pad
       TERRET, TERRIT
ring, lamp condensing ... **CRIC**
ring, little .... **ANNULET**
ring, naut. .... **GROMMET**
d ring of light .... **HALO, NIMB,**
       NIMBUS, AUREOLA,
       AUREOLE
"Ring of the Nibelung" goddess
       ERDA
"Ring of the Nibelung" smith
       MIME
ring out .... **PEAL**
ring, part of .... **CHATON**
ring, rubber jar .... **LUTE**
ring, seal .... **SIGNET**
ring-shaped .... **CIRCINATE**
ring-shaped piece ..... **QUOIT**
ring, stone of .... **CHATON**
ringlet .... **CURL, TRESS**
ringworm ..... **TINEA, TETTER**
ripening agent .... **AGER**
ripple ...... **LAP, RIFF, WAVE**
rise above .... **TOWER**
rise aloft .... **TOWER**
rise: old Eng. .... **RIS**
risible .... **GELASTIC**
rites, religious .... **SACRA**
ritual .... **RITE**
RIVER . see also GAZETTEER in
       SPECIAL SECTION
river .... **RIO**
river, Balmoral Castle's ... **DEE**
river bank .... **RIPA**
river bank, growing by
       RIPARIAN

River

a
river-bank stair, Ind.
.... **GAUT, GHAT**
river bed, dry, Afr.
.... **WADI, WADY**
river between Europe and Asia
.... **KARA**
river, Bremen's .... **WESER**
river Caesar crossed . **RUBICON**
river, Dutch Meuse ..... **MAAS**
river in Baltic .... **ODER**
river in Essex .... **CAM**
river in Orleans .... **LOIRE**
river in Petrograd ...... **NEVA**
river into Moselle ...... **SAAR**
river into Rhone ...... **SAONE**
river islet .... **AIT**
river, "Kubla Khan" .... **ALPH**
river, Munich's .... **ISAR**
river mouth ..... **LADE, DELTA**
river nymph .... **NAIS**
river to the Humber
.... **OUSE, TRENT**
River of Woe .. **ACHERON**
river, Southwest .... **PECOS**
river: Sp. .... **RIO**
river: Tagalog .... **ILOG**
river to Medit. .... **EBRO**
river valley .... **STRATH**
rivulet .... **RILL**
road .... **VIA, PATH,
                    ITER, AGGER**

b
road: Roman .... **ITER**
road: Gypsy .... **DRUN**
roadhouse .... **INN**
roam .... **GAD, ROVE**
roast .... **CALCINE**
roasted meat strip .... **CABOB**
roasting rod .... **SPIT**
rob .... **REAVE, DESPOIL**
Rob Roy .... **CANOE**
robber .... **THIEF**
ROBE ..... see also **GARMENT**
robe .... **MANTLE**
robe to ankles .... **TALAR**
"Roberta" composer .... **KERN**
robot drama .... **RUR**
rock aggregate .... **AUGE**
rock, basic igneous ..... **SIMA**
rock cavity ..... **VOOG, VUGG,
                    VUGH, GEODE**
rock, dangerous ...... **SCYLLA**
rock, dark .... **BASALT**
rock, fine grained ...... **TRAP**
rock, flintlike .... **CHERT**
rock, granitoid **DUNITE, GNEISS**
rock, hard .... **WHIN**
rock, jutting .... **TOR**
rock, laminated .... **SHALE
                    SLATE, GNEISS**
rock, melted .... **LAVA**
rock, mica-bearing ... **DOMITE**

c
rock, projecting ... **TOR, CRAG**
rock, rugged .... **CRAG**
rock snake .... **PYTHON**
rock whiting genus ..... **ODAX**
rock-wren .... **TURCO**
ROCKET .. see under **MISSILE,
                    GUIDED**
rocket's goal .... **MOON**
rockfish .. **RASHER, TAMBOR**
rockfish, Calif. .. **RENA, REINA**
rockweed .... **FUCI, FUCUS**
Rocky Mt. peak .... **ESTES**
Rocky Mt. range
.... **TETON, UINTA**
rocky peak, eminence,
    pinnacle .... **TOR**
rod ... **POLE, WAND, BATON,
            PERCH, STAFF**
rod, barbecue .... **SPIT**
rod, basketry .... **OSIER**
rod, billiard .... **CUE**
rod, chastening .... **FERULE**
rodent .... **RAT, HARE**
rodent genus .... **MUS**
rodent, rabbit-like ...... **PIKA**
rodent, S. Am. .. **CAVY, DEGU,
            PACA, COYPU, AGOUTI**
rodent, W. Ind. .... **HUTIA**
Rhoderick Dhu .... **SCOT**
rogue .... **PICARO**
roguish .... **SLY, ARCH**

d
roister .... **REVEL**
Roland's destroyer ...... **GAN,
                    GANO, GANELON**
roll and heave .... **TOSS**
roll of bread: dialect. .... **BAP**
roll of cloth .... **BOLT**
roll of paper .... **SCROLL**
roll up .... **FURL**
romaine .... **COS**
ROMAN GODS
        see SPECIAL SECTION
Rom. assembly ...... **COMITIA**
Rom. authors .... **CATO, LIVY,
    OVID, LUCAN, NEPOS,
    PLINY, CICERO, HOR-
    ACE, SENECA, SILIUS,
    VERGIL, SALLUST**
Rom. barracks
.... **CANABA, CANNABA**
Rom. box .... **CAPSA**
Rom. boxing glove ... **CESTUS**
Rom. bronze .... **AES**
Rom. brooch .... **FIBULA**
Rom. building .... **INSULA**
Rom. cap .... **PILEUS**
Rom. cavalry body
.... **TURM, TURMA**
Rom. circus post ...... **META**
Rom. clan ..... **GENS, GENTES**
Rom. cloak ... **TOGA, ABOLLA**

132

a Rom. coin, ancient
SEMIS, DINDER
Rom. coins .... AS, AES,
ASSES, SOLIDUS
Rom. Curia court ...... ROTA
Rom. date ...... IDES, NONES
Rom. dictator .... SULLA
Rom. dish .... LANX
Rom. emperor .... NERO,
OTHO, TITUS
Rom. farce .... EXODE
Rom. galley
TRIREME, UNIREME
Rom. gaming cube ..... TALUS
Rom. garment .. TOGA, STOLA,
TUNIC, PLANETA
Rom. goal post in racing . META
Rom. highway ..... VIA, ITER
Rom. historian ... LIVY, NEPOS
Rom. judge .... EDILE, AEDILE
Rom. law control ..... MANUS
Rom. legendary king ... NUMA
Rom. liquid measure .... URNA
Rom. list ...... ALBE, ALBUM
Rom. magistrate or official
EDILE, AEDILE, ARCHON,
CONSUL, PRETOR, TRIBUNE
Rom. market ... FORA, FORUM
Rom. meal .... CENA
b Rom. money, copper ..... AES
Rom. numerals 1-I, 5-V,
10-X, 50-L, 100-C,
500-D, 1000-M
ROMAN OFFICIAL
see ROMAN MAGISTRATE
Rom. patriot .... CATO
Rom. philosopher
CATO, SENECA
Rom. platter .... LANX
Rom. pledge .... VAS
Rom. poet ..... OVID, LUCAN,
HORACE, VERGIL, VIRGIL
Rom. pound .... AS
Rom. province .... DACIA
Rom. public games ...... LUDI
Rom. public lands ...... AGER
Rom. religious festivals . VOTA
Rom. road .... VIA, ITER
Rom. robe .... TOGA
Rom. room, principal
ATRIA, ATRIUM
Rom. scroll .... STEMMA
Rom. statesman .... CATO
Rom. sword .... FALX
Rom. vessel .... PATERA
Rom. war garb .... SAGUM
Rom. weight .... AS

c Rom. well-curb ...... PUTEAL
Rom. writer .... MACER
romance, tale of . GEST, GESTE
ROMANIA .... see RUMANIA
Rome, a founder of ... REMUS
Rome's cathedral church
LATERAN
Rome's conqueror ..... ALARIC
Rome's river .... TIBER
Romulus' twin .... REMUS
rood .... CROSS
roof .... MANSARD
roof edge .... EAVE
roof of mouth .... PALATE
roof of mouth, pert. to
PALATAL
roof ornament .... EPI
roof, rounded . DOME, CUPOLA
roof, rounded like a ... DOMAL
roof, truncated .... HIP
roofing piece ...... RAG, TILE
roofing slate .... TILE
roofing timber .... PURLIN
rook's cry .... CAWK
room, Eng. college supply
BUTTERY
room, snug .... DEN
room, rooms .... SPACE, SUITE
room, architecture ..... OECUS
room for household goods,
linen, etc. . EWRY, EWERY
d room, main, Rom.
ATRIA, ATRIUM
room, mineshaft . PLAT, PLATT
room, Rom. .... ALA
roomy .... WIDE
roost .... PERCH
rooster .... COCK
root .... RADIX, RADICES
root, drug-yielding ..... JALAP
root, edible ..... OCA, TARO,
CASSAVA
root, tree used for sewing
WATAP
root, word .... ETYM
rootlet .... RADICEL, RADICLE
rootstock, edible ...... TARO
rootstock, fern (Maori) ... ROI
rootstock, fragrant .... ORRIS
rope ...... JEFF, LAZO, LASSO,
LONGE, REATA, RIATA,
LARIAT, MARLINE
rope, cringle
LEEFANG, LEEFANGE
rope fiber .. DA, COIR, FERU,
HEMP, IMBE, JUTE, RHEA,
ABACA, SISAL
rope for animals ..... TETHER
rope guide: naut. ...... WAPP
rope loop .... BIGHT

a rope, naut. ... **FOX, TYE, STAY, VANG, HAWSER, RATLIN, LANIARD, LANYARD, RATLINE, SNOTTER**
rope to tie boat ..... **PAINTER**
rope, weave .... **REEVE**
rope, yardarm ..... **SNOTTER**
ropes, unite .... **SPLICE**
rosary bead .... **AVE**
rose: Byron .... **GUL**
rose fruit .... **HIP**
rose genus .... **ROSA, ACAENA**
rose-like plant .... **AVENS**
rose of Sharon
　　　ALTHEA, ALTHAEA
rose oil derivative ..... **ATAR, OTTO, ATTAR, OTTAR**
rose ornament ...... **ROSETTE**
rose, Pers. .... **GUL**
rosewood .... **MOLOMPI**
rosolic acid ... **AURIN, AURINE**
rostellum .... **ROSTEL**
roster .... **LIST, ROTA**
rotate .... **ROLL, GYRATE**
rotating muscle ..... **EVERTOR**
rotating part .... **CAM, ROTOR**
rotation producer .... **TORQUE**
rotten .... **PUTRID**
rouge ...... **RADDLE, RUDDLE**
b rough .... **RUDE, UNEVEN**
rough, as country ...... **HILLY**
rough copy .... **DRAFT**
rough in voice .... **GRUFF**
rough rock .... **KNAR**
roughness, sea .... **LIPPER**
roulette bet ...... **BAS, NOIR, MILIEU**
round, a ...... **ROTA, ROTULA**
round hand .... **RONDE**
round room .... **ROTUNDA**
Round Table Knight .... **KAY, BORS, BORT, BALAN, BALIN, BOHORT, GARETH, GAWAIN, GALAHAD, PELLEAS**
round-up .... **RODEO**
rounded projection ...... **LOBE**
rounder .... **RAKE, ROUE**
roundworm .... **NEMA, ASCARID, ASCARIS**
rouse . **WAKE, AWAKE, WAKEN**
Rousseau novel, hero ... **EMILE**
route .... **WAY, PATH**
route, plane's fixed ..... **LANE**
routine, fixed .... **ROTE**
row .... **LINE, SPAT, TIER**
rowan tree .... **ASH, SORB**
rowdy: slang .... **B'HOY**
rower .... **OAR**
rower's bench .... **ZYGA, ZYGON, THWART**

c royal authority ...... **SCEPTRE**
royal court, relating to . **AULIC**
royal edict: Fr. .... **ARRET**
royal family, Fr. ..... **VALOIS**
royal rights, having . **PALATINE**
royal rod .. **SCEPTER, SCEPTRE**
royal treasury ...... **FISC, FISK**
royalty, Hawaii .... **ALII**
rub harshly .... **GRATE**
rub off .... **ABRADE**
rub out .... **ERASE**
rub roughly .... **SCRAPE**
rub to polish .... **BUFF, SHINE**
rub to soreness .... **CHAFE**
rubber .... **PARA, LATEX, CAUCHO, ELASTIC**
rubber, black .... **EBONITE**
rubber source ...... **KOKSAGYZ**
rubber, S. Am. . **PARA, CEARA**
rubber tree ...... **ULE, HULE, SERINGA**
rubber, wild .... **CEARA**
rubbery substance
　　　GUTTA, NOREPOL
rubbish .... **ROT, JUNK, CULCH, RUBBLE**
rubble masonry ..... **MOELLON**
rubella .... **MEASLES**
ruby .... **RED**
ruby red quartz ..... **RUBASSE**
d ruby spinel ... **BALAS, BALASS**
rudder bushing .... **PINTLE**
rudder fish .... **CHOPA**
ruddle .... **KEEL, KIEL**
rudiment .... **GERM**
rudiments .... **ABC**
rue .... **REGRET**
rue herb genus .... **RUTA**
ruff, female ..... **REE, REEVE**
ruffed lemur .... **VARI**
ruffer .... **NAPPER**
ruffle .... **CRIMP**
ruffle, neck ... **JABOT, RUCHE**
RUG ...... see also **CARPET**
rug, long narrow
　　　KANARA, RUNNER
ruin .... **DOOM**
rule .... **LAW, DOMINEER**
"Rule Britannia" composer
　　　　　ARNE
rules, dueling .... **DUELLO**
ruler .... **REGENT**
ruler, Afghanistan ...... **EMIR, AMEER, CALIF, EMEER, CALIPH, SULTAN**
ruler, Arabian .. **EMIR, AMEER, CALIF, EMEER, CALIPH, SULTAN**
RULER, BIBLICAL .... see SPECIAL SECTION

RULER IN EAST ... see RULER,
ARABIAN
ruler, India............. **NAWAB**
ruler, Morocco .... **SHERIF,
SHEREEF**
ruler, Moslem... **EMIR, AMEER,
CALIF, EMEER, CALIPH,
SULTAN**
ruler of gods............. **ZEUS**
ruler, Oriental........... **CALIF**
ruler, Tunis .... **DEY**
RUMANIA .... see also
SPECIAL SECTION
Rumanian composer... **ENESCO**
Rumanian folk song ..... **DOINA**
Rumanian king's title .... **DOMN**
rumen.................... **CUD**
ruminant .... **DEER, GOAT,
CAMEL, LLAMA,
ANTELOPE**
ruminant genus .... **CAPRA**
ruminant, horned........ **DEER,
GOAT**
ruminate ...... **MULL, PONDER**
Rumor personified....... **FAMA**
rumor, to..... **BRUIT, NORATE,
REPORT**
rumple .... **MUSS**
run at top speed .... **SPRINT**
run before wind.......... **SCUD**
run of the mill .... **PAR**
run out................. **PETER**
runner .... **SCARF, STOLO,
STOLON**
runner, distance........ **MILER**
runner, plant.. **STOLO, STOLON**
rupees, 100,000.......... **LAC**
rural ..... **RUSTIC, PASTORAL**
rural deity ...... **PAN, FAUNUS**
rural poem........... **GEORGIC**
rush .... **HASTE, SPEED**
rush, marsh .... **SPART**
Russell's viper .... **DABOIA,
DABOYA**
RUSSIA....... see also SOVIET
and SPECIAL SECTION
Russia, most northern town
KOLA
Russian .... **RED, RUSS, SLAV,
KULAK, TATAR**
Russ. basso .... **KIPNIS**
Russ. author............ **BUNIN**

Russ. beer....... **KVAS, QUAS,
KVASS**
Russ. community........... **MIR**
Russ. convention......... **RADA**
Russ. cooperative society **ARTEL**
Russ. council .... **DUMA**
Russ. dress......... **SARAFAN**
Russ. edict ... **UKASE, DECREE**
Russ. emperor .... **CZAR,
TSAR, TZAR**
Russ. fiddle............. **GUDOK**
Russ. folk dance .... **KOLO**
Russ. girl's name......... **OLGA**
Russ. hemp............... **RINE**
Russ. labor union........ **ARTEL**
Russ. lagoon............ **LIMAN**
Russ. Lapland capital ..... **KOLA**
Russ. leather............. **YUFT**
Russ. liquid measure ..... **STOF,
STOFF, STOOF**
Russ. log hut .... **ISBA**
Russ. marsh .... **LIMAN**
Russ. mile .... **VERST**
Russ. mountain range .... **ALAI,
URAL**
Russian mts., pert. to... **ALTAIC**
Russ. name, given.. **AKIM, IGOR**
Russ. news agency....... **TASS**
Russ. official.......... **BERIYA**
Russ. opera........... **BORIS**
Russ. peninsula .... **KOLA**
Russ. sea, inland .... **ARAL,
AZOF, AZOV**
Russ. secret police .... **KGB,
NKVD, OGPU**
Russ. tavern .... **CABACK**
Russ. tax, old .... **OBROK**
Russ. tea urn .... **SAMOVAR**
Russ. trade guild .... **ARTEL**
Russ. vehicle ... **ARBA, ARABA**
Russ. village .... **MIR**
Russ. whip.............. **PLET**
Russ. writer.... **GORKI, GORKY**
Russ. "yes"................ **DA**
rust.............. **EAT, ERODE**
Rustam's father........... **ZAL**
rustic .... **BOOR, RUBE, CARL,
CARLE, YOKEL, BUCOLIC,
PEASANT**
Ruth's husband .... **BOAZ**
Ruth's son............... **OBED**
rye, disease of......... **ERGOT**

135

S

sable .... **SOBOL, MARTEN**
sac .... **BURSA**
saccharine source .... **TAR**
sack fiber .... **JUTE**
sack, to .... **LOOT**
saclike cavity .... **BURSA**
sacred asp, symbol ... **URAEUS**
sacred bull, Egypt . **APIS, HAPI**
sacred chalice .... **GRAIL**
sacred city, India ... **BENARES**
sacred enclosure, Gr. .... **SEKOS**
sacred fig .... **PIPAL**
sacred Hindu word .... **OM**
sacred image .... **ICON, IKON**
sacred lily .... **LOTUS**
sacred object: Oceania .. **ZOGO**
sacred picture .... **ICON, IKON**
sacred place .... **SHRINE**
sacred place, Gr.
     ABATON, HIERON
sacred tree, Hindu .. **BO, PIPAL**
sacrifice, place of ..... **ALTAR**
sacrificial drink, Zoroaster's
     SOMA
sacrificial offerings .... **HIERA**
sad: comb. form ...... **TRAGI**
sad cry .... **ALAS, ALACK**
sad: music .... **MESTO**
saddle horses, fresh . **REMUDA**
saddle knob .... **POMMEL**
saddle, rear of .... **CANTLE**
safe .... **SECURE**
safe place ...... **PORT, HAVEN**
safe: thief's slang ...... **PETE**
safety lamp .... **DAVY**
safflower .... **KUSUM**
saga .... **EDDA**
sage .... **WISE**
sagacious .... **WISE,**
     ASTUTE, SAPIENT
sage genus .... **SALVIA**
sail fastener .... **CLEW**
sail-line .... **EARING**
sail nearer wind .... **LUFF**
sail, square .... **LUG**
sail, square, edge of ... **LEECH**
sail, triangular .... **JIB**
sail yard: Scot. .... **RAE**
sail's corner .... **CLEW**
"Sails" of constellation Argo
     VELA
sailboat .... **YAWL, KETCH**
sailing race .... **REGATTA**
SAILING VESSEL .... see
     VESSEL, SAILING
sailmaker's awl ..... **STABBER**

sailor . **GOB, TAR, SALT, SEADOG**
sailor, India .... **LASCAR**
St. Anthony's cross ...... **TAU**
saint, British .... **ALBAN**
saint, Buddhist
     ARAHT, ARHAT, ARAHAT
St. Catherine's home ... **SIENA**
saint, female: abbr. ...... **STE**
saint, 14th century ..... **ROCH**
St. Francis' birthplace .. **ASSISI**
St. John's-bread ..... **CAROB**
"St. Louis Blues" composer
     HANDY
saint, Moslem .... **PIR**
St. Paul, deserter from . **DEMAS**
St. Vitus dance ...... **CHOREA**
sainte: abbr. .... **STE**
saint's relic box ...... **CHASSE**
salad green ...... **UDO, CRESS,**
     KERSE, CRESSE, ENDIVE
salamander .. **EFT, EVET, NEWT**
salient angle .... **CANT**
Salientia, the .... **ANURA**
sally .... **START, SORTIE**
"Sally in Our Alley" composer
     CAREY
salmon, female .... **HEN**
salmon, male .... **COCK**
salmon net .... **MAUD**
salmon, silver .... **COHO**
salmon, third year ..... **MORT**
salmon, 2 yr. .. **SMOLT, SPROD**
salmon, young .. **PARR, GRILSE**
salt ...... **SAL, HALITE, SALINE**
salt factory .... **SALTERN**
salt lake, Turkestan ..... **SHOR**
salt of tartaric acid .. **TARTAR**
salt pond or spring ... **SALINA**
salt, resembling ...... **HALOID**
salt, rock .... **HALITE**
salt, solution .. **BRINE, SALINE**
salt tax .... **GABELLE**
salt tree, Tamarisk ..... **ATLE**
salted .... **ALAT**
saltpeter ...... **NITER, NITRE**
saltwort .... **KALI**
saltworks ,.......... **SALINA**
salty water .... **BRINE**
salutation .... **AVE**
salutation: Ir. .... **ACHARA**
Salvation Army leader . **BOOTH**
salver .... **TRAY**
salvia .... **CHIA**
Sambal language .... **TINO**
sambar deer .... **MAHA, RUSA**
same .... **ILK, DITTO**

same place: abbr. .... IBID
samlet .... PARR
Samoan maiden ...... TAUPO
Samoan mollusk .... ASI
Samoan political council. FONO
Samuel, king killed by .. AGAG
Samuel, teacher of .... ELI
Samuel's son .... ABIA
samurai, straying ..... RONIN
sanction .... AMEN, FIAT
sanctuary ...... BEMA, FANE,
               NAOS, CELLA
sand .... GRIT
sand bar .... REEF, SHOAL
sand expanses .... AREG
sand hill .... DENE, DUNE
sand island .... BAR
sand, sea bottom .... PAAR
sand snake genus .... ERYX
sandal, Egypt .... TATBEB
sandal, Mex.
   HUARACHE, HUARACHO
sandalwood tree .... MAIRE
sandarac powder .... POUNCE
sandarac tree .... ARAR
sandbox tree genus ..... HURA
sandpiper .... REE, RUFF, STIB,
             REEVE, STINT
sandpiper, Europ. ...... TEREK
sandpiper, red .... KNOT
sandpiper, small ...... KNOT,
          PUME, STINT
sandstone .... GRIT
sandstorm .... HABOOB
sandwich .... HERO
Sandwich Island discoverer
             COOK
sandy .... ARENOSE
Sankhya philos. term ... GUNA
Sanskrit dialect .... PALI
Sanskrit precept
        SUTRA, SUTTA
Sanskrit school .... TOL
Sao —, Brazil .... PAULO
Sao Salvador .... BAHIA
sap spout .... SPILE
sapodilla ... SAPOTA, SAPOTE
sapota tree .... ACANA
Saracen ..... MOOR, MOSLEM
Sarah's slave .... HAGAR
sarcasm .... IRONY
Sardinia gold coin ... CARLINE
sargeant fish .... SNOOK
Sargon's capital ...... ACCAD
Sarmatia cave-dwellers . TAURI
sartor .... TAILOR
sash, C. Amer. .... TOBE
sash, Jap. kimono .... OBI
sassafras tree .... AGUE
Satan .... DEVIL
Satan: Arab .... EBLIS

satellite .... MOON, PLANET
satellite .... LUNIK, SPUTNIK,
    PIONEER, EXPLORER,
    VANGUARD, ATLAS-
    SCORE, DISCOVERER
satellite, navigation . TRANSIT
satellite, television .... TIROS
satellite's path .... ORBIT
satiate .. CLOY, GLUT, SATE
satirical .... DRY
satisfaction Maori ...... UTU
satisfy ... SATE, SUIT, PLEASE
saturate . SOAK, IMBUE, STEEP
Saturn, satellite of ..... DIONE
Saturn's rings projection. ANSA
Saturn's wife .... OPS
Saturnalia .... ORGY
satyr .... FAUN
sauce .... GRAVY
sauce, Chinese, Oriental .. SOY
sauce, fish .... ALEC
sauce, peppery ..... TABASCO
sauce, tomato .... CATSUP,
   CATCHUP, KETCHUP
saucy .... PERT
Saul's army leader .... ABNER
Saul's chief herdsman .. DOEG
Saul's father .... KISH
Saul's grandfather . NER, ABIEL
Saul's successor .... DAVID
Saul's uncle .... NER
Sault Ste. Marie .... SOO
saurel fish .... SCAD
sausage, spiced ..... SALAME,
          SALAMI
savage .... FERAL
Savage Island language . NIUE
save .... HOARD, STINT,
    REDEEM, CONSERVE
saviour .... REDEEMER
savory .... SAPID, TASTY
saw .... ADAGE, AXIOM,
    MAXIM, SAYING
saw-leaved centaury
      BEHN, BEHEN
saw, notched like .... SERRATE
saw notching .... REDAN
saw, surgical TREPAN, TREPHINE
sawbill duck .... SMEW
sawlike organ, or part .. SERRA
sawlike parts . SERRAS, SERRAE
sawtooth ridge .... SIERRA
saxhorn .... TUBA
Saxon god .... ER, EAR
Saxon king ...... INE, ALFRED
Saxony natives .... SORBS
say .... UTTER
say again .... ITERATE
saying ... MOT, SAW, ADAGE,
    AXIOM, MAXIM
sayings .... LOGIA

a scabbard fish .... **HIKU**
scabbard, put into .. **SHEATHE**
scaffolding .... **STAGING**
scale .... **GAMUT**
scale, syllable of .. **DO, FA, LA,
MI, RE, SO, TI, SOL**
scale under blossom
PALEA, PALET
scales, having large . **SCUTATE**
scallop ..... **CRENA, CRENAE**
scallops, cut in small .... **PINK**
scalloped .... **CRENATE**
scalp disease .... **FAVI, FAVUS**
scamp ...... **ROGUE, RASCAL**
SCANDINAVIAN
see also NORSE
SCANDINAVIAN . see also
SWEDEN, NORWAY, in
SPECIAL SECTION
Scandinavian ... **DANE, SWEDE**
Scand., ancient .... **NORSE**
Scand. countryman ..... **GEAT**
Scand. explorer .... **ERIC**
Scand. fertility god .... **NJORD**
Scand. legend .... **SAGA**
Scand. measure .... **ALEN**
Scand. nation .... **GEATAS**
Scandinavians in Russia
ROS, RUS

b scanty .... **SPARSE**
scar, resembling a .... **ULOID**
scarce .... **RARE**
scarcely: Lat. .... **VIX**
scare away .... **SHOO**
scarf .... **BOA, TIE,
ASCOT, ORALE**
scarf, long .... **STOLE**
scarf, Sp. Am. .... **TAPALO**
scarlet flower .... **SALVIA**
Scarlett O'Hara's home .. **TARA**
scatter ... **SOW, TED, STREW**
scatter: dial. .... **SCOAD**
scatter on .... **LITTER**
scattered: Her. .... **SEME**
scenario .... **SCRIPT**
scene ...... **VIEW, TABLEAU**
scene of action.**ARENA, SPHERE**
scenic view .... **SCAPE**
scent .... **ODOR, AROMA**
scented .... **OLENT**
schedule .... **LIST**
scheme .... **PLAN, PLOT**
schism .... **RENT**
scholar .... **PEDANT**
scholars, Moslem .... **ULEMA**
scholarship .... **BURSE**
school, boy's .... **PREP**
school, Fr. ...... **ECOLE, LYCEE**
school grounds ...... **CAMPUS**

c **SCHOONER** ... see also **BOAT,
SHIP, VESSEL**
schooner, 3-masted ..... **TERN**
sciences .... **ARTS**
scientific farmer . **AGRONOMIST**
scientific study: abbr. . **ANAT.**
scientist, Am. . **UREY, HOOTON,
PARRAN, COMPTON,
WAKSMAN, MILLIKAN**
scientist, Austr. .... **MEITNER**
scientist, Czech .... **CORI**
scientist, Dan. .... **BOHR**
scientist, Eng. .... **HOGBEN,
FLEMING, HALDANE**
scientist, Ger. .. **BAADE, HABER**
scientist, Ital. .... **FERMI**
scissors .... **SHEARS**
scoff .... **GIBE, JEER, JIBE,
RAIL, SNEER**
scold .... **JAW, NAG, RATE**
scold: dialect .... **FRAB**
scone: Scot. ..... **FARL, FARLE**
scoop .... **DIP**
scoot: Scot. ..... **SKYT, SKITE**
scope .. **AREA, AMBIT, RANGE**
scorch .... **CHAR, SEAR,
SERE, SINGE**
score .... **TALLY**
scoria .... **SLAG, DROSS**

d scorpion fish .... **LAPON**
Scotch cake .... **SCONE**
scoter .... **COOT**
Scotland .... **SCOTIA**
Scott character .... **ELLEN**
Scott heroine .... **ELLEN**
Scott, poem by .... **MARMION**
SCOTTISH
see Pages of SCOTTISH WORDS
Scot. alderman .... **BAILIE**
Scot. author .... **BARRIE**
Scot. chemist .... **URE, DEWAR**
Scot. chief landholder
THANE, THEGN
Scot. cultural congress ... **MOD**
Scot. explorer .... **RAE**
Scot. highlander ...... **GAEL**
Scot. king .... **BRUCE**
Scot. lord ..... **THANE, THEGN**
Scot. pillory .... **JOUG**
Scot. playwright ...... **BARRIE**
Scot. poet .... **BURNS**
Scot. pottage .... **BROSE**
Scot. proprietor .... **LAIRD**
Scot. scholar .... **NICOLL**
Scot. singer .... **LAUDER**
SCOTTISH WORDS:
accept .... **TAE**
advise .... **REDE**
afraid .... **RAD, RADE**
age .... **EILD**

a
against .... **GIN**
alder tree ..... **ARN, ELLER**
an .... **AE**
animal, lean .... **RIBE**
any .... **ONY**
article .... **TA**
ashes .... **ASE**
ask .... **AX**
at all .... **AVA**
away .... **AWA**
awry .... **AJEE**
babbler .... **HAVEREL**
ball .... **BA**
bank .... **BRAE**
barter .... **TROKE**
beg .... **SORN**
bind .... **OOP**
biscuit .... **BAKE**
blockhead .... **CUIF, NOWT**
bloodhound .... **LYAM**
bone .... **BANE**
bound .... **STEND**
breeches .... **TREWS**
broth .... **BREE, BROO**
brow of hill .... **SNAB**
built .... **BAG**
burden .... **BIRN**
bushel .... **FOU**
calves ...... **CAUR, CAURE**

b
came .... **CAM**
catch .... **KEP**
chalk .... **CAUK**
check .... **WERE**
chest .... **KIST**
child .... **BAIRN**
church ...... **KIRK, KURK**
comb .... **KAME**
contend .... **KEMP**
court, bring to .... **SIST**
cut .... **KNAP, SNEG**
dairymaid .... **DEY**
damage .... **TEEN**
damaged .... **LESED**
dare .... **DAUR**
devil .... **DEIL**
did not know ...... **KENNA**
die .... **DEE**
dig .... **HOWK**
dining room .... **SPENCE**
do .... **DAE, DIV**
do not know .... **KENNA**
dread .... **DREE**
drip .... **SIE, SYE**
dusty .... **MOTTY**
earth .... **EARD**
elder .... **ELLER**
else .... **ENSE**
empty .... **TOOM**
endeavor .... **ETTLE**
endure .... **DREE**

c
extra .... **ORRA**
eye .... **EE**
eyes .... **EEN, EES**
family .... **ILK**
fidget .... **FIKE**
firth .... **KYLE**
fishing expedition ... **DRAVE**
fit of sulks .... **GEE**
flax refuse ..... **PAB, POB**
fog ..... **DAG, HAR, HAAR**
foretell .... **SPAE**
give .... **GIE**
glimpse .... **STIME**
grandchild .... **OY, OYE**
grant as property . **DISPONE**
great-grandchild .... **IEROE**
grief .... **TEEN**
have .... **HAE**
hawk .... **ALLAN**
heavy .... **THARF**
hill . **BEN, DOD, BRAE, DODD**
hillside .... **BRAE**
howl .... **YOWT**
hurt .... **LESED**
injure .... **TEEN**
injured .... **LESED**
intent .... **ETTLE**
keg .... **KNAG**

d
kinsman .... **SIB**
kiss .... **PREE**
knead .... **ELT**
knock .... **KNOIT**
lake .... **LOCH**
leap .. **LOUP, LOWP, STEND**
learning .... **LEAR**
list of candidates ..... **LEET**
loaf .... **SORN**
lop .... **SNATHE**
lout .... **CUIF**
love .... **LOE**
loyal .... **LEAL**
marriage portion ..... **DOTE**
millrace .... **LADE**
mire .... **GLAUR**
mist .... **URE**
mountain .... **BEN**
mouth, river .... **BEAL**
mouth .... **BEAL**
mud .... **GLAIR**
must .... **MAUN**
name .... **IAN**
near, nearest .... **NAR**
no .... **NAE**
none .... **NANE**
not matched .... **ORRA**
now .... **NOO**
nowhere .... **NAEGATE**
oak .... **AIK**

(Scottish words continued 140)

Scottish

a
oatmeal dish . . . . **BROSE**
odd . . . . **ORRA**
old age . . . . **EILD**
once . . . . **ANES**
one . . . . . . **AIN, ANE, YIN**
otherwise . . . . **ELS**
out . . . . **OOT**
own . . . . **AIN, ANE, AWN**
pantry . . . . **SPENCE**
parlor . . . . **BEN**
payment . . . . **MENSE**
paw ground . . . . **PAUT**
peat cutter . . . . **PINER**
pig . . . . **GRICE**
pike . . . . **GED, GEDD**
pillory . . . . **TRONE**
pipe . . . . **CUTTY**
pluck wool . . . . **ROO**
pool . . . . **DIB, CARR,**
LINN, LLYN
present . . . . **GIE**
pretty . . . . **GEY**
prop . . . . **RANCE**
propriety . . . . **MENSE**
prune . . . . **SNED**
puddle . . . . **DUB**
pull . . . . **PU**
quagmire . . . . **HAG**
quarter of a year . . . . . . **RAITH**
relieve . . . . **LISS**

b
revenue, church . . . . . . **ANNAT**
ridge of a hill . . . . **SHIN**
river . . . . **DOON**
rowboat . . . . **COBLE**
sailyard . . . . **RAE**
same . . . . **ILK**
scone . . . . **FARL, FARLE**
scoot . . . . **SKYT, SKITE**
scratch . . . . **RIT**
seep . . . . **SIPE**
seize . . . . **VANG**
self . . . . **SEL**
serve . . . . **KAE**
severe blow . . . . **DEVEL**
sheepfold . . . . **REE**
sheep tick . . . . **KED**
sheep walk . . . . **SLAIT**
shelter . . . . **BIELD, SHEAL**
sift . . . . **SIE**
since . . . . **SIN, SYNE**
slope . . . . **BRAE**
slouch . . . . **LOUCH**
sly . . . . **SLEE**
small . . . . **SMA**
snow . . . . **SNA**
so . . . . **SAE**
son of . . . . **MAC**
song . . . . **STROUD**
sore . . . . **SAIR**
sorrow . . . . **TEEN**
sow . . . . **SOO**

c
steward . . . . **MORMAOR**
stipend . . . . **ANNAT**
stone **STANE, STEAN, STEEN**
stretch . . . . **STENT**
stupid one . . . . **CUIF**
suffer . . . . **DREE**
summit . . . . **DOD, DODD**
sweetheart . . . . **JO**
than . . . . **NA**
to . . . . **TAE**
toe . . . . **TAE**
tone . . . . **TEAN**
trench . . . . **GAW**
truant, play . . . . **TRONE**
try . . . . **ETTLE**
tune . . . . **PORT**
turnip . . . . **NEEP**
uncanny . . . . **UNCO**
uncle . . . . **EME**
urge . . . . **ERT**
very . . . . **VERA**
vex . . . . **FASH**
village . . . . **REW**
void, to render . . . . **CASS**
waterfall . . . . . **LIN, LYN, LINN**
wealthy . . . . **BIEN**
weep . . . . **ORP**
week . . . . **OUK**

d
weighing machine . . . . . **TRON,**
TRONE
well . . . . **AWEEL**
wet . . . . **WAT**
whirlpool . . . . . **WEEL, WIEL**
whiskey drink . . . . **ATHOL,**
ATHOLE
widow's third . . . . **TERCE**
workhouse . . . . **AVER**
year, ¼ of . . . . **RAITH**
yell . . . . **GOWL**
scoundrel . . . . . **ROGUE, VARLET**
scout unit . **DEN, PACK, TROOP**
scow . . . . **BARGE, LIGHTER**
scow: Fr. . . . . **ACON**
scrap, table . . . . **ORT**
scraps of literature . . . . **ANA**
scrape . . . **RAKE, RASP, GRAZE**
scrape bottom . . . . **DREDGE**
scratch . . . . **MAR, RAKE**
scrawny animal . . . . **SCRAG**
screamer bird . . . . **CHAJA**
screed . . . . **TIRADE**
screen . . . . **SIFT, SHADE**
screen, altar . . . . **REREDOS**
screen, wind . . . . **PARAVENT**
script, modern Syriac . . . . **SERTA**
script, upright . . . . **RONDE**
scripture, early . . . . **ITALA**
scripture passage . . . . **TEXT**
scriptures, occult interpretation
CABALA
scrutinize . . . . **EYE, SCAN**

a scuffle .... **MELEE**
sculptor of "Thinker" . **RODIN**
scum, metal .... **DROSS**
scup .... **BREAM, PORGY**
scuppernong ..... **MUSCADINE**
scuttle .... **HOD**
scuttle, coal .... **HOD**
scythe .... **SY, SYE**
scythe handle . **SNATH, SNEAD,
SNEED, SNATHE**
sea anemone .. **POLYP, OPELET**
sea bird ... **ERN, ERNE, GULL,
SKUA, SCAUP, TERN, FUL-
MAR, GANNET, PETREL,
SCOTER**
sea bird, north .... **PUFFIN**
sea cow . **DUGONG, MANATEE**
sea cucumber ...... **TREPANG**
sea demon, Teut. ..... **WATE**
sea duck ...... **COOT, EIDER,
SCAUP, SCOTER**
sea eagle .... **ERN, ERNE**
sea-ear .... **ABALONE**
sea: Fr. .... **MER**
sea girdles .... **CUVY**
sea god .... **LER, TRITON,
NEPTUNE**
sea god, Gr. . **NEREUS, TRITON,
POSEIDON**
sea god, Rom. ...... **NEPTUNE**
sea god, Teut. .. **HLER, AEGIR**
sea goddess, Norse ...... **RAN**

b sea green .... **CELADON**
sea gull, Eur. .... **MEW**
sea, kept bow on . **ATRY, ATRIP**
sea lettuce ..... **ALGA, LAVER**
sea lettuce genus **ULVA, ULUA**
sea marker .... **DAN**
sea pheasant .... **SMEE**
sea robber .... **PIRATE**
sea mile, Austral. ...... **NAUT**
sea nymph .... **NEREID**
sea shell .... **TRITON**
(see also SHELL)
sea skeleton .... **CORAL**
sea slug genus . **DOTO, ELYSIA**
sea snail . **WELK, WILK, WHELK**
sea snake, Asia ...... **KERRIL**
sea soldier .... **MARINE**
sea worm . **SAO, LURG, NEREIS**
seal .... **SIGIL**
seal, eared .... **OTARY**
seal, fur .... **URSAL**
seal, letter .... **CACHET**
seal, official .... **SIGNET**
seal, papal .... **BULLA**
seal, young .... **PUP**
seals, group of .... **POD**
seamark .... **BEACON**
seamen: Brit. .... **RATINGS**
seamlike ridge .... **RAPHE**

c seams of boat, fill ..... **CALK**
SEAPORT .... see **PORT**
search .... **GROPE**
search for .... **HUNT, SEEK**
search for food ...... **FORAGE**
season ...... **AGE, FALL, SALT,
TIDE, SPRING**
season, church . **LENT, ADVENT**
season, Fr. .... **ETE**
seasons, goddesses of .. **HORAE**
seasonal phenomenon .. **EPACT**
seasoning .... **SAGE, SALT**
seasoning herb .... **SAGE,
BASIL, THYME**
seat, chancel .... **SEDILE**
seat, long .... **PEW, SETTEE**
seat of oracle of Zeus. **DODONA**
seat, Rom. .... **SELLA**
seaweed ... **ORE, AGAR, ALGA,
KELP, ALGAE, LAVER,
VAREC**
seaweed ashes .... **KELP**
seaweed, brown .... **KELP**
seaweed, edible .... **AGAR**
seaweed, edible Hawaiian .**LIMU**
seaweed, purple .... **LAVER**
seaweed, purple, Jap. ... **NORI**
seaweed, red .... **DULSE**
Seb, consort of .... **NUT**

d secluded .... **REMOTE**
second . **ABET, TRICE, MOMENT**
second brightest star ... **BETA**
second-growth crop ... **ROWEN**
Second Punic War's end,
site of .... **ZAMA**
second team .... **SCRUB**
secondary .... **BYE, LESS**
secret ...... **RUNE, ARCANE,
COVERT, MYSTERY,
ESOTERIC**
secret agent .... **SPY**
secret society, Afr. . **EGBO, PORO**
secret society in Sierra Leone
PORO
secrets .... **ARCANA**
secrets, one learning ... **EPOPT**
secretion, sweet
LAAP, LERP, LAARP
sect .... **CULT**
sect, Nepal . **ACHAR, ACHARA**
section of journey .... **LEG**
secular ... **LAY, LAIC, LAICAL**
secure .. **FIX, GET, PIN, FAST,
NAIL, SAFE, FASTEN**
secure firmly . **MOOR, ANCHOR**
secure with rope .... **BELAY**
security .... **BOND**
Sec'y of State, 1933-44 .. **HULL**
sedate .... **STAID**
sedative .... **NEMBUTAL**

a sediment .... **LEES, SILT, DREGS, SILTAGE**
see .... **ESPY, LOOK**
see: Lat. .... **VIDE**
seed .... **PIP, PIT, GRAIN, SPORE, PYRENE**
seed coat or covering .. **ARIL, HULL, HUSK, TESTA, TEGMEN, TESTAE, TEGUMEN, TEGIMINA**
seed, edible ...... **PEA, BEAN, LENTIL, PINOLE**
seed, edible, Asia .... **SESAME**
seed, immature .... **OVULE**
seed, lens-shaped ..... **LENTIL**
seed, nutlike .... **PINON**
seed, opium poppy ..... **MAW**
seed plant .... **ENDOGEN**
seeds, remove .... **GIN**
seedless plant .... **FERN**
seek to attain .... **ASPIRE**
seem .... **LOOK**
seesaw .... **TEETER**
segment, last .... **TELSON**
segment of body ..... **SOMITE**
segment of circle .... **ARC**
segment, pert. to ...... **TORIC**
seine .... **NET**
seize .... **NAB, GRAB, GRASP, USURP, ARREST, COLLAR**
b seize: archaic .... **REAVE**
selections, literary **ANA, ANALECTA**
self .... **EGO**
self-assurance .... **APLOMB**
self-defense, art of ..... **JUDO**
self-denying .... **ASCETIC**
self-education doctrine **BIOSOPHY**
self-locking nut ..... **PALNUT**
self-reproach .... **REMORSE**
sell .... **VEND**
seller .... **COSTER, VENDER, VENDOR**
semblance .... **GUISE**
semester .... **TERM**
semi-precious stone **ONYX, SARD**
semicircular room ...... **APSE**
semidiameter .... **RADIUS**
semidiameters .... **RADII**
Seminole chief ..... **OSCEOLA**
Semitic deity .... **BAAL**
sen, tenth of .... **RIN**
senate house .... **CURIA**
senate houses .... **CURIAE**
Senator, former ...... **BORAH**
send back ... **REMIT, REMAND**
send money .... **REMIT**

c send out .... **EMIT, ISSUE**
sending forth .... **EMISSIVE**
Senegambia gazelle .... **KORIN**
senility .... **DOTAGE**
senior .... **ELDER**
senior: Fr. .... **AINE**
senna, source of ...... **CASSIA**
sennet .... **SPET**
sense .... **FEEL**
senseless .... **INANE**
sensitive .... **SORE**
sentence, analyze ...... **PARSE**
sentence part .... **CLAUSE**
"Sentimental Journey" author **STERNE**
sentinel, mounted ... **VEDETTE**
separate . **SIFT, APART, SECERN**
separated .... **APART**
separation .... **SCHISM**
sequence, 3-card ..... **TIERCE**
sequester .... **ISOLATE**
Sequoia national park ... **MUIR**
seraglio .... **HAREM, SERAI**
serene .... **SERENO**
serf .... **ESNE**
serf, Rom. .... **COLONA**
serf, Spartan, ancient .. **HELOT**
sergeant fish .... **COBIA**
series .... **SET, GAMUT**
series, in a .... **SERIATIM**
d series of tones .... **SCALE**
serious ..... **GRAVE, EARNEST**
sermon .... **HOMILY**
serow .... **JAGLA**
SERPENT ..... see also SNAKE
serpent, Egypt. myth .... **APEPI**
serpent goddess, Egypt. . **BUTO**
serpent, Gr. .... **SEPS**
serpent, large .. **BOA, PYTHON**
serpent monster ...... **ELLOPS**
serpent, myth. ...... **BASILISK**
serpent worship ...... **OPHISM**
serpentine .... **OPHITE**
servant......... **BOY, MAN, MAID, MENIAL**
servant, India .... **HAMAL, FERASH, HAMMAL**
servant, man's .... **VALET**
servant, P. I. .... **BATA**
servants, for .... **MENIAL**
serve soup .... **LADLE**
server .... **TRAY**
service, religious .... **MASS**
service tree .... **SORB**
servile .... **MENIAL**
serving boy .... **PAGE**
sesame .... **TIL, TEEL**
sesame oil ...... **BENI, BENNE**
sesame seed .... **GINGILI**
session, hold .... **SIT, MEET**

a
set aside .... **DEFER**
set in type .... **PRINT**
set limits to .... **STINT**
set price .... **RATE**
set system .... **ROTE**
set thickly .... **STUD**
setback .... **REVERSE**
Seth's brother .... **CAIN**
Seth's mother .... **EVE**
Seth's son .... **ENOS**
setting .... **SCENE, MILIEU**
setting sun, Egyp. god of.**TEM,**
TUM, ATMU, ATUM
settled .... **ALIT**
settler .... **BOOMER**
seven .... **SEPT**
Seven Dwarfs ... **DOC, DOPEY,**
HAPPY, GRUMPY, SLEEPY,
SNEEZY, BASHFUL
seven, group of .... **HEPTAD,**
PLEIAD, SEPTET, SEPTETTE
"Seventh Heaven" heroine
DIANE
seventh order, of ...... **SEPTIC**
seventh, pert. to ...... **SEPTAN**
sever .... **CUT, LOP, REND**
severe .... **STERN**
severely criticize ...... **PAN,**
SLATE, ROAST

b
sew hawk's eyelids ...... **SEEL**
"Seward's —," Alaska . **FOLLY**
sexes, common to both.**EPICENE**
shabby .... **WORN**
shabby woman .... **DOWD**
shackle .... **BOND, GYVE,**
IRON, FETTER
shad .... **ALLIS, ALOSA,**
ALOSE, ALLICE
shaddock .. **POMELO, PUMELO**
shade .... **HUE, SCREEN**
shade of difference .. **NUANCE**
shade of meaning ... **NUANCE**
shaded walk .... **MALL**
shadow .... **TAIL**
shadow, eclipse ...... **UMBRA**
shaft .... **POLE, SPINDLE**
shaft column, feather .. **SCAPE**
shaft horse .... **THILLER**
shaft of column .... **FUST**
shaft, wooden .... **ARROW**
shafter .... **HORSE**
shake ..... **JAR, JOLT, NIDGE**
Shakespeare's elf ...... **PUCK**
Shakespeare's river .... **AVON**
Shakespeare's theatre .. **GLOBE**
Shakespeare's wife .... **ANNE**
Shakesperian clown .. **BOTTOM**
Shakesperian forest ... **ARDEN**
Shakesperian king ...... **LEAR**

c
Shakesperian shrew ..... **KATE**
Shakesperian villain ..... **IAGO**
shallow receptacle ...... **TRAY**
sham .... **FAKE**
Shamash, wife of .... **AI, AYA**
"Shane," star of ...... **LADD**
Shang dynasty .... **YIN**
shank .... **CRUS, SHIN**
shanks .... **CRURA**
shanty .... **HUT**
shape .... **FORM, MOLD**
shaped like a club .. **CLAVATE**
shaped like a needle
ACUATE, ACERATE
shaping tool ... **LATHE, SWAGE**
share .... **LOT, RATION**
share .... **PARTAKE**
shark .... **TOPE**
shark, Eur. small .... **TOPE**
shark, long-nosed ..... **MAKO**
shark, nurse .... **GATA**
shark parasite fish ... **REMORA**
sharp .... **ACERB,**
ACUTE, ACUATE
sharp .... **CHEAT**
sharp ridge .... **ARETE**
sharpen ... **EDGE, HONE, WHET**
sharpshooter .. **JAGER, SNIPER**
shavetail: abbr. .... **LT**
shawl ... . **MAUD, PAISLEY**

d
shea tree .... **KARITE**
sheaf of grain: Her. .... **GERB**
shear .... **CLIP**
sheath, petiole .... **OCREA**
Sheba: Lat. .... **SABA**
shed, as feathers **MOLT, MOULT**
shed for sheep .... **COTE**
sheen .... **GLOSS**
sheep .... **EWE, RAM, MERINO**
sheep, Afr. domestic ... **ZENU**
sheep, Afr. wild
ARUI, UDAD, AOUDAD
sheep, Asia wild .... **ARGALI**
sheep, Asia, wild, mountain
SHA, SNA, RASSE, URIAL,
BHARAL, NAHOOR, OORIAL
sheep cry .... **BAA, MAA**
sheep disease .. **COE, GID, ROT**
sheep dog .... **COLLIE**
sheep, Eng. black-faced **LONK**
sheep, female .... **EWE**
sheep genus .... **OVIS**
sheep in 2nd year
TEG, TEGG, BIDENT
sheep, India, wild .. **SHA, SNA,**
URIAL, NAHOOR, OORIAL
sheep, large-horned
AOUDAD, ARGALI
sheep, Leicester ...... **DISHLEY**
sheep, male .... **RAM, TUP**

a

sheep, N. Afr. wild
　　　ARUI, UDAD, AOUDAD
sheep, of .... **OVINE**
sheep owner, Bibl. .... **NABAL**
sheep pasture, old Eng. .. **HEAF**
sheep, pert. to .... **OVINE**
sheep, Tibet .... **SHA, SNA,**
　　URIAL, BHARAL, NAHOOR,
　　OORIAL
sheep tick .... **KED, KADE**
sheep, unshorn .. **HOGG, HEDER**
sheep walk: Scot. .... **SLAIT**
sheep, wild .. **SHA, SNA, ARUI,**
　　UDAD, RASSE, BHARAL,
　　NAHOOR, AOUDAD, AR-
　　GALI, OORIAL
sheep, young ...... **TAG, TEG**
sheepfold ...... **REE, COTE**
sheeplike .... **OVINE**
sheepskin leather ..... **BOCK,**
　　　ROAN, SKIVER
sheerly .... **SOLELY**
shekel, ¼, Hebrew ...... **REBA**
shelf .... **LEDGE**
shelf above altar ... **RETABLE**
shell .... **BOMB**
shell .. **TEST, LORICA, TUNICA**
shell beads .... **PEAG**
shell, large .... **CONCH**
shell, marine .... **TRITON**
shell money .... **ULLO,**

b

　　　COWRY, UHLLO, COWRIE
shellfish, edible
　　CRAB, ABALONE, SCALLOP
shelter .... **LEE, COTE,**
　　　SHED, HAVEN, SCREEN
shelter, hillside .... **ABRI**
shelter: Scot. .. **BIELD, SHEAL**
shelter, to .... **ALEE**
sheltered .... **ALEE**
Shem descendant ..... **SEMITE**
Shem's brother .... **HAM**
Shem's son
　　LUD, ARAM, ELAM, ASSHUR
Sheol .... **HADES**
shepherd prophet ...... **AMOS**
shepherd's crook **PEDA, PEDUM**
shepherd's pipe .... **OAT, REED**
shepherd's song .. **MADRIGAL**
shepherdess, "Winter's Tale"
　　　MOPSA
sheriff substitute ..... **ELISOR**
sheriff's men .... **POSSE**
Sherwood .... **FOREST**
Shetland court president **FOUD**
Shetland hill pasture ... **HOGA**
shield .... **ECU, EGIS, AEGIS,**
　　PAVIS, DEFEND, PROTECT
shield, Athena's .... **AEGIS**
shield, Austral. .... **MULGA**
shield-bearing or border. **ORLE**

c

shield, medieval .... **ECU**
shield, Rom.
　　SCUTA, SCUTUM, CLIPEUS
shield-shaped **PELTATE, SCUTATE**
shield, small .... **ECU**
shield strap .... **ENARME**
shield's corner: Her. **CANTON**
shift .... **VEER**
shift position. **GIBE, GYBE, JIBE**
shin .... **CNEMIS**
shine **GLOW, GLISTEN, ERADIATE**
shingle, wedge-shaped .. **SHIM**
shingles .... **ZONA**
shining .... **NITID**
Shinto deity .... **KAMI**
Shinto temple .... **SHA**
Shinto temple gate .... **TORII**
ship ..... **KEEL, SEND, LINER,**
　　TANKER, TENDER, VESSEL,
　　CARAVEL
ship, back part .... **STERN**
ship boat .... **GIG, DORY**
ship body or frame .... **HULL**
ship bow, curve of ...... **LOOF**
ship canvas .... **SAIL**
ship clock .... **NEF**

d

ship drainage hole .. **SCUPPER**
ship employee ...... **STEWARD**
ship, 1st Northwest Passage
　　　GJOA
ship, forward part **BOW, PROW**
ship, fur-hunting ..... **SEALER**
ship, ironclad ...... **MONITOR**
ship: Jap. ...... **MARO, MARU**
ship keel, rear part ..... **SKEG**
ship, large .... **TONNER**
ship, lowest part ...... **BILGE**
ship, Medit. ... **SETEE, SETTEE**
ship, middle part ...... **WAIST**
ship mooring place
　　　DOCK, BERTH
ship, oar-propelled ... **GALLEY**
ship, part of
　　RIB, DECK, HULL, KEEL
ship plank .... **STRAKE**
ship platform .... **DECK**
ship pole .... **MAST, SPAR**
ship shaped clock .... **NEF**
ship side, opp. middle **ABEAM**
ship timber, bevel ..... **SNAPE**
ship timber curve .... **SNY**
ship timber, extra ..... **RIDER**
ship wheel .... **HELM**
ship, wrecked .... **HULK**
ship, 1-masted .... **SLOOP**
ship, 2-masted ... **BRIG, SNOW**
ship's kitchen .... **GALLEY**
shipboard covering .... **CAPOT**

a shipbuilding curve ..... **SNY**
shipbuilding piece
    SPALE, THWART
shipworm .... **BORER, TEREDO**
shipwreck, causing
    NAUFRAGEOUS
shirk .... **GOLDBRICK**
SHIRT .... see also GARMENT
shirt .... **KAMIS, CAMISE**
shirt, Oriental .... **CAMISE**
shoal .... **REEF**
shoal water deposit .... **CULM**
shock .... **STUN,**
    APPAL, APPALL, TRAUMA
shock absorber ..... **SNUBBER**
shod, as monks ..... **CALCED**
shoe .... **GAITER, SANDAL**
shoe form .... **LAST**
shoe front .... **VAMP**
shoe gripper .... **CLEAT**
shoe, heavy. **BROGAN, BROGUE**
shoe latchet .... **TAB**
shoe, mule .... **PLANCH**
shoe part
  LAST, RAND, WELT, INSOLE

b shoe strip ...... **RAND, WELT**
shoe, wooden ... **GETA, SABOT**
shoe, wooden-soled ..... **CLOG**
shoes .... **SHOON**
shoes, Mercury's winged
    TALARIA
shoelace .... **LACET**
shoemakers' saint ... **CRISPIN**
shoemaker's tool .... **AWL**
shoot .... **BAG, POT**
shoot at from ambush **SNIPE**
shoot at, marble to ...... **MIG**
shoot, cotton .... **RATOON**
shoot, plant .... **BINE, CION,**
    GEMMA, SPRIT,
    STOLO, STOLON
shoot, small .... **SPRIG**
shoot, sugar cane ... **RATOON**
shooter, hidden .... **SNIPER**
shooter marble .... **TAW,**
    AGATE, AGGIE
shooting match .... **TIR**
shooting match: Fr. ...... **TIR**
shooting star .... **LEONID**
shop .... **STORE**
shop, Rom. wine ... **TABERNA**
shops, Rom. wine .. **TABERNAE**
shop's name plate ..... **FACIA**
shore .... **COAST, STRAND**
SHORE BIRD . see BIRD, SHORE
short .... **CURT,**
    BRIEF, TERSE, STUBBY

c short-breathed .... **PURSY**
short comedy sketch .... **SKIT**
short-spoken ... **CURT, TERSE**
short tail .... **SCUT**
shorten .... **CUT, DELE, ELIDE**
shortly
    ANON, SOON, PRESENTLY
Shoshonean .... **UTE**
shoulder blade ..... **SCAPULA**
shoulder, of the
    ALAR, SCAPULAR
shoulder ornament
    EPAULET, EPAULETTE
shoulder, road .... **BERM**
shoulder wrap .... **SHAWL**
shout.**CRY, CALL, ROAR, YELL**
shove .... **PUSH**
shovel .... **SPADE**
show as false .... **BELIE**
show off .... **FLAUNT**
show place, Rom. .... **CIRCUS**
show, street .... **RAREE**
"Showboat" author .... **FERBER**
showy .... **LOUD**
shrew .... **ERD, TARTAR**
shrewd.**SAGE, CANNY, ASTUTE**
shrike genus .... **LANIUS**
d shrill .... **PIPY**
shrill, to .... **STRIDULATE**
shrimplike crustacean **PRAWN**
shrine .... **ALTAR**
shrink .... **CONTRACT**
shroud-stopper: naut. .... **WAPP**
SHRUB .... see also TREE
shrub and tree .... **ALDER**
shrub, Asia .... **CHE**
shrub, berry-bearing ... **ELDER**
shrub, berry, Pacific ... **SALAL**
shrub, Chin. .... **TEA**
shrub, Congo medical .. **BOCCA**
shrub, desert
    RETEM, OCOTILLO
shrub, Eng. .... **HEATH**
shrub, evergreen .. **BOX, YEW,**
  TITI, ERICA, HEATH, SAL-
  AL, OLEANDER
shrub, flowering **ITEA, AZALEA,**
  PRIVET, SPIREA, SPIRAEA,
  SYRINGA
shrub genus **BIXA, INGA, ITEA,**
  ROSA, ALDER, IXORA,
  AZALEA
shrub, Hawaiian ..... **OLONA**
shrub, low spiny .... **GORSE**
shrub, Medit. .... **CAPER**
shrub, poisonous
    SUMAC, SUMACH
shrub, prickly .... **CAPER**

Shrub

a shrub, Rhus genus
          SUMAC, SUMACH
   shrub, strong-scented .. **BATIS**
   shrub with grapelike fruit
          SALAL
   shrub, yellow flowers **OLEASTER**
   shun .... **AVOID, DODGE**
   shut up .... **IMMURE**
   shy .... **JIB, BALK**
   SIAM .. see also SPECIAL SEC-
      TION
   Siamese .... **THAI**
   Siam. coin .... **ATT**
   Siam. garment ...... **PANUNG**
   Siam. group ...... **KUI, LAO**
   Siam. monetary unit .... **BAHT**
   Siamese twin ... **ENG, CHANG**
   SIBERIAN .. see also RUSSIAN
   Siberian .... **TATAR**
   Siberian wild cat ..... **MANUL**
   Siberian squirrel ..... **MINIVER**
   sibilant sound .... **HISS**
   Sicilian resort .... **ENNA**
   sickle, curved like ... **FALCATE**
   sickle: variant .... **SIVE**
   side, jewel's .... **FACET**
   side arm .... **GUN,**
      SWORD, PISTOL, REVOLVER

b side: Lat. .... **LATUS**
   side of head ... **LORA, LORUM**
   side, pert. to
          COSTAL, LATERAL
   side-post, door's ...... **JAMB**
   sidetrack .... **SHUNT**
   side street, Chin. ... **HUTUNG**
   side timber: naut. ..... **BIBB**
   side, toward the .... **LATERAD**
   sidereal .... **ASTRAL**
   sidewalk .... **PAVEMENT**
   sidewalk edge ... **CURB, KERB**
   sidewinder .... **CROTALUS**
   sidle .... **EDGE**
   Siegfried's murderer ... **HAGEN**
   siesta .... **NAP**
   sieve .... **SIFT, PUREE, BOLTER**
   sieve for clay .... **LAUN**
   Sif, son of .... **ULL, ULLR**
   sift .... **SCREEN**
   sift: dialect .... **REE**
   sift: old Eng. .... **LUE**
   sift: Scot. .... **SIE**
   sifter .... **SIEVE**
   sigh .... **SOUF, SOUGH**
   sight, come into .... **LOOM**
   sight, dimness of ..... **CALIGO**
   sight on gun .... **BEAD**
   sight, pert. to .... **OCULAR**
   sign ... **MARK, OMEN, TOKEN**

c sign, music .... **PRESA, SEGNO**
   sign: old Eng. .... **SEIN**
   sign, pert. to .... **SEMIC**
   sign up ..... **ENROL, ENROLL**
   signal for attention ...... **PST**
   signal for parley ... **CHAMADE**
   signal to act .... **CUE**
   signal to begin .... **CUE**
   signature, affix
          SIGN, ENDORSE
   signet .... **SIGIL**
   signify ..... **MEAN, DENOTE**
   "Silas Marner" author .. **ELIOT**
   silence .... **GAG, HUSH**
   silence: music .... **TACET**
   silent ... **MUM, MUTE, TACIT**
   silica .... **SAND, SILEX**
   silica, rich in .... **ACIOLIC**
   silicate .... **MICA**
   silk-cotton tree **CEIBA, KAPOK**
   silk-cotton tree fiber
          KAPOK, KUMBI
   silk fabric ..... **GROS, MOFF,**
      PEKIN, SATIN, TULLE
   silk filament .... **BRIN**
   silk, fine .... **CRIN, TULLE**
   silk, heavy .... **GROS**
   silk in cocoon .... **BAVE**
   silk, India ... **ROMAL, RUMAL**
   silk, old heavy ..... **CAMACA**

d silk, raw .... **GREGE**
   silk substitute .... **NYLON,**
      RAYON, ORLON, DACRON
   silk thread .... **FLOSS**
   silk, twilled .... **ALMA**
   silk, unravel .... **SLEAVE**
   silken .... **SERIC**
   silkworm, Assam ... **ERI, ERIA**
   silkworm, China ...... **TASAR**
   silkworm disease .... **UJI**
   silly .... **INANE**
   silver: Her. .... **ARGENT**
   silver lactate .... **ACTOL**
   silver ore .... **PACO**
   silver, uncoined, in ingots **SYCEE**
   silverfish .. **TARPON, TARPUN**
   silverize .... **PLATE**
   silvery .... **ARGENT**
   silvery-white metal .. **COBALT**
   simian .... **APE**
   similar .... **LIKE, SUCH**
   Simon .... **PETER**
   simper .... **SMIRK**
   simple .... **EASY, MERE**
   simple sugar .... **OSE**
   simpleton .... **ASS, DAW, OAF,**
      BOOB, COOT, FOOL, GABY,
      GAWK, GOWK, SIMP,
      GOOSE
   simulate
      APE, SHAM, FEIGN, PRETEND

a
sin .... ERR, EVIL
sin, grief for ..... ATTRITION
Sinai .... HOREB
Sinbad's bird .... ROC
since .... AGO
since: Scot. .... SIN, SYNE
Sinclair Lewis character CASS
sine — non .... QUA
sine qua — .... NON
sinew .... TENDON
sinewy .... WIRY
sing .... LILT, CAROL
sing, as a round ...... TROLL
sing softly .... CROON
sing, Swiss style
          JODEL, YODEL, YODLE
singer, synagogue ... CANTOR
singing bird .... OSCINE
singing girl, Egyptian .. ALMA,
     ALME, ALMAH, ALMAI,
     ALMEH
singing, suitable for .... MELIC
single .... ONE, BILL, MONO,
                ONLY, UNAL
single out .... CHOOSE
single: prefix .... MONO
single thing ...... ONE, UNIT
singleton .... ACE
sink, as putt .... HOLE
sink: geol. .... DOLINA
b
sinuous .. WAVY, SERPENTINE
sinus cavities .... ANTRA
Sioux, Siouan .... OTO, OTOE
sir: India .... MIAN
sir: Malay .... TUAN
siren, Rhine .... LORELEI
Sisera's killer .... JAEL
sister .... NUN, SIB
"Sistine Madonna" painter
                    RAPHAEL
sitatunga, Afr. ...... NAKONG
sitting
       POSING, SEANCE, SESSION
sitting on .... ASTRIDE
situation, difficult .... STRAIT
siva snake .... COBRA
Siva, wife of DEVI, KALI, SATI
six, group of
    SENARY, SESTET, SEXTET
six-line verse SESTET, SESTINA
six on a die .. CISE, SICE, SISE
six, series of .... HEXAD
six: Sp. .... SEIS
sixpence: slang .... SICE
sixteen annas .... RUPEE
sixth: music .... SEXT
sixth sense: abbr. ...... ESP
size of shot ...... BB, FF, TT
sizing .... SEALER
skate .... RAY
skate genus .... RAIA

c
skating area .... RINK
skegger .... PARR
skein of yarn .... RAP, HANK
skeletal .... BONY
skeleton, sea animal
          CORAL, SPONGE
skeptic .... AGNOSTIC
sketch ...... DRAW, OUTLINE
ski, heel spring .... AMSTUTZ
ski race .... SLALOM
ski run ..... SCHUSS, SLALOM
ski wax .... KLISTER
skier, mark of ..... SITZMARK
skiing position .... VORLAGE
skiing, zigzag .... SLALOM
skilled person .... ADEPT
skillful
   ABLE, DEFT, ADEPT, HABILE
skillfully .... ABLY
skim over .... SKIP
skin .... FLAY, DERMA
skin, deeper layer ..... CUTIS
skin, design on
          TATOO, TATTOO
skin disease ... ACNE, MANGE,
               PSORA, TETTER
skin disease, horse's .. CALORIS
skin disease, Peru ...... UTA
skin infection .... LEPRA
skin layer .... DERM, CUTIS,
d
   DERMA, CORIUM, ENDERON
skin of a beast .... FELL
skin, pert. to .. DERIC, DERMIC
skinflint .... MISER
skink, Egypt. .... ADDA
skip .... OMIT
skip a stone .... DAP
skip happily .... CAPER
skipjack .... ELATER
skirmish .... MELEE
skirt, ballet .... TUTU
skirt section .... PANEL
skittle .... PIN
skulk .... LURK
skull, pert. to .. INIAL, INION
skull protuberance .... INION
skullcap, Arab. ...... CHECHIA
skunk .. CHINCHA, CHINCHE
sky .... FIRMAMENT
sky god, Assyrian ...... ANAT
sky: Chin. .... TIEN
sky god, Babyl. .... ABU, ANU
sky god, Norse .... TIU,
          TIW, TYR, ZIO, ZIU
sky, highest part .... ZENITH
sky: Polyn. .... LANGI
sky serpent, Vedic ...... AHI
slab, engraved .... TABLET
slab, flooring, decorative DALLE
slag .... DROSS, SCORIA

a
slam .... BANG
slam in cards .... VOLE
slander ...... LIBEL, ASPERSE
slang .... ARGOT
slant .... BEVEL, SLOPE
slanted edge .... BEVEL
slanted: naut. .... ARAKE
slanting .... SKEW, ASKEW
slanting type .... ITALIC
slantingly, drive .... TOE
slap .... CUFF, SPANK
slash .... JAG, SLISH
slater's tool, same as slate-
    trimming tool
slate-trimming tool
            SAX, ZAT, ZAX
Slav .... SERB
Slav, ancient
        VEND, WEND, VENED
Slav, E. Ger. .... WEND
Slav in Saxony .... SORB
slave .... ESNE, SERF, THRALL
slave, fugitive ..... MAROON
slave, Spartan .... HELOT
sled, Swiss .... LUGE
sled to haul logs ...... TODE
sleep .... NAP, NOD, DOZE
sleep, deep .... SOPOR
sleep lightly .... DOZE

b
sleeping .... DORMANT
sleeping place BED, COT, BERTH
sleeping sickness fly .. TSETSE
sleeve, large .... DOLMAN
sleigh .... PUNG
sleight-of-hand .... MAGIC
slender .... LANK, LEAN,
            SLIM, THIN, REEDY
slender woman .... SYLPH
slice, bacon .... RASHER
slice of meat .... COLP
slice, thick .... SLAB
slick .... LOY
slide .... SKID, SLUE
sliding door, Jap. ... FUSUMA
sliding piece .... CAM
sliding valve .... PISTON
slight .... MERE, SLIM, FAINT
slight intentionally SLUR, SNUB
slimy .... OOZY
sling around .... SLUE
slip.ERR, BONER, GLIDE, LAPSE
slip by .... ELAPSE
slip out of course ...... SLUE
slip, plant .... CION, CUTTING
slipknot .... NOOSE
slipper .... MULE, MOYLE
slipper, P. I. .... CHINELA
slope ...... RAMP, GRADIENT
slope: fort. .... GLACIS

c
slope of vein or lode ... HADE
slope: Scot. .... BRAE
slope of land ...... VERSANT
slope, steep ... SCARP, ESCARP
sloping edge
        BASIL, BEZEL, BEZIL
sloth, three-toed .... AI
sloth, two-toed .... UNAU
slouch: Scot. .... LOUCH
slow .... POKY
slow loris .... KOKAM
slow: music .. TARDO, LARGO
    LENTO, ADAGIO, ANDANTE
slower: music .... RIT
sluggish .... DOPEY
sluice .... CLOW
slump .... RECESSION
slur over .... ELIDE
slushy mass .... POSH
sly look .... LEER, OGLE
sly: old Eng. ..... SLEE, SLOAN
sly: Scot: .... SLEE
smack ...... BUSS, KISS, SLAP
small .... WEE, TINY,
        PETIT, PETTY, PETITE
small amount .. DRAM, MINIM
small arachnid .... MITE
small bottle .... VIAL
small bunch .... WISP

d
small case .... ETUI
small cluster .... SPRIG
small coin .... MITE
small creature MITE, MINIMUS
small dog .... POM, PUG,
        PUP, PEKE, FEIST
small goby, Atlantic ... MAPO
small: law .... PETIT
small marine animal .... SALP
small monkey .... LEMUR
small pearl .... PEARLET
small poem .... ODELET
small: Scot. .... SMA
small stream RUN, RILL, RILLET
small: suffix .... ING
small weight ... GRAM, MITE
smallest .... LEAST
smallest integer .... ONE
smallpox .... VARIOLA
smaragd .... EMERALD
smart .... STING
smart CHIC, ASTUTE, CLEVER
smartly dressed ... CHIC, TRIG
smear on .... DAUB
smell, disagreeable
        OLID, REEK, FETOR
smelting mixture ..... MATTE
smelting waste .. SLAG, DROSS
smirch .... SULLY
smith, aided Siegfried .. MIME

a smock .... CAMISE
smoke .... FUME, REEK
smoke-colored .... FUMOUS
smoke, wisp of .... FLOC
smoked beef ...... PASTRAMI
smokeless powder ..... FILITE
smoking .... AREEK
smoking pipe ... BRIAR, BRIER
smoking pipe, Oriental
      HOOKAH, NARGILE
smoky .... FUMID
smooth
      EVEN, IRON, LEVEL, PREEN
smooth-breathing ...... LENE
smooth, make ..... LEVIGATE
smooth: phonetics ...... LENE
smooth-spoken .... GLIB
smoothing tool .... PLANE
snail, large. WHELK, ABALONE
snail, marine .... TRITON
snake ..... ASP, BOA, ADDER,
      VIPER, PYTHON, REPTILE
snake, Amer. .. ADDER, RACER
snake-bite antidote
      GUACO, CEDRON
snake, black .... RACER
snake charmer's clarinet BEEN
snake-haired woman GORGON,
      MEDUSA, STHENO, EURYALE
b snake, India .... COBRA,
      KRAIT, DABOIA, DABOYA
snake-like .... SINUOUS
snake, S. Amer. .... ABOMA
snake, tree .... LORA
snake, venomous, Ind.. BONGAR
snakes, pert. to ..... OPHIOID
snakebird .... DARTER
snakeroot, white ...... STEVIA
snap up bargains ...... SNUP
snapper .... SESI, PARGO
snapper fish: Maori .. TAMURE
snapper: N. Z. ...... TAMURE
snare .. GIN, NET, WEB, TRAP
snarl .... GNAR, GNARR
snatch .... GRAB, SEIZE
sneer. GIBE, JIBE, FLEER, SCOFF
sniff .... NOSE
snipe, Europ. .... BLEATER
snipe's cry .... SCAPE
snoring .... STERTOR
snow field, Alpine. FIRN, NEVE
snow goose genus ...... CHEN
snow, ground down .... LOLLY
snow house
      IGLU, IGLOE, IGLOO, IGLOU
snow leopard .... OUNCE
snow lily .... VIOLET
snow, living in .... NIVAL
snow mouse .... VOLE

c snow panther .... OUNCE
snow runner .... SKI, SKEE
snow: Scot. .... SNA
SNOW WHITE
      see SEVEN DWARFS
snuff .... RAPPEE
snuffbox bean
      CACOON, MACKAYBEAN
snug .... COSY, COZY
snuggery .... NEST
so .... THUS, TRUE, VERY
so be it! .... AMEN
so much: music ...... TANTO
so: Scot. .... SAE
soak .... RET, SOG, SOP, WET
soak flax .... RET
soap, fine .... CASTILE
soap-frame bar .... SESS
soap: pharm. .... SAPO
soap plant .... AMOLE
soap substitute ...... AMOLE
soap vine .... GOGO
soapstone .... TALC
soapy mineral .... TALC
sober .... GRAVE, STAID
social affair .... TEA
social division .... CASTE
social unit or group .... SEPT
society, entrance into .. DEBUT
d society swell .... NOB
sock, Jap. .... TABI
sock, Rom. .... UDO
sod .... TURF
sodium alum .... MENDOZITE
sodium carbonate .... TRONA
sodium chloride .... SALT
sodium chloride: pharm. .. SAL
sodium compound ..... SODA
sodium nitrate .. NITER, NITRE
sofa .... DIVAN
soft
      LOW, EASY, WAXY, TENDER
soft area on bill .... CERE
soft drink
      ADE, POP, COLA, SODA
soft feathers ... DOWN, EIDER
soft ice from floes ..... LOLLY
soft job ..... SNAP, SINECURE
soft mass .... WAD
soft palate .... VELUM
soft palate lobe ...... UVULA
soft palate, pert. to
      VELAR, UVULAR
soft palates .... VELA
soft-spoken .... MEALY
soften in temper ..... RELENT
softly: music .... SOAVE
soil: comb. form .... AGRO
soil, organic part .... HUMUS

a
soil, rich .... **LOAM**
soil, sticky .. **GOMBO, GUMBO**
soil, type of .... **PEDOCAL**
solar disc ...... **ATEN, ATON**
solar over lunar year,
excess of .... **EPACT**
soldier: Am. Rev. .. **BUCKSKIN**
soldier, Austral., N. Z. **ANZAC**
soldier, Brit. .... **ATKINS**
soldier, former .... **LANCER**
soldier, Gr. .... **HOPLITE**
soldier, Indo-Brit. ..... **SEPOY**
soldier, native India ... **SEPOY**
soldier's shelter ..... **FOXHOLE**
sole .... **PELMA**
sole of foot .... **VOLA**
sole of plow .... **SLADE**
solemn declaration. **VOW, OATH**
solicit .... **BEG, URGE,**
COURT, CANVASS
solicitor's chamber ...... **INN**
solicitude .... **CARE**
solid .... **CONE, CUBE, PRISM**
solid, become **GEL, SET, HARDEN**
solid: comb. form .... **STEREO**
solidify ... **GEL, SET, HARDEN**
solitary .... **LONE, ONLY, SOLE**
solo .... **ARIA**
Solomon's aid giver ... **HIRAM**

b
Solomon's temple rebuilder
HIRAM
solution .... **KEY**
solution, strength of
TITER, TITRE
solvent .... **ACETONE**
solvent, treat with .. **SOLUTIZE**
some .... **ANY**
somite .... **MEROSOME**
son: Fr. .... **FILS**
son-in-law .... **GENER**
son: Ir. .... **MAC**
son of .... **MAC**
son of Agrippina .... **NERO**
son of Joktan .... **OPHIR**
son of Reuben .... **PALLU**
son of: Scot. .... **MAC**
song .... **LAY, ODE, DITE,**
DITTY, MELOS, TROLL
song, Christmas
NOEL, CAROL, WASSAIL
song for solo voices ..... **GLEE**
song: Ger. .... **LIED**
song, Hawaiian .... **MELE**
song, Jap. .... **UTA**
song, morning: poet. .. **MATIN**
song, of a .... **MELIC**
song of praise, joy
PEAN, PAEAN, ANTHEM
"Song of the South" Uncle
REMUS

c
song, operatic .... **ARIA**
song, religious
HYMN, CHANT, ANTHEM
song, sacred
HYMN, CHANT, ANTHEM
song, sad .... **DIRGE**
song: Scot. .... **STROUD**
song, simple .... **DITTY**
song, Sp. .... **CANCION**
song thrush ... **MAVIE, MAVIS**
sonship .... **FILIETY**
soon .... **ANON**
sooner .... **ERE, ERER**
soot .... **COOM, SMUT**
soot: old Eng. .... **SOTE**
soothe .... **EASE, LULL**
soothing **ANODYNE, LENITIVE**
soothsayer .... **SEER**
Sophocles, play by ... **OEDIPUS**
soprano, prima donna .. **ALDA,**
BORI, PONS, RISE,
RAISA, CALLAS, STEBER
sora bird .... **RAIL**
sorceress .... **CIRCE**
sorceress, Hindu .... **USHA**
sorceress, myth. .... **LAMIA**
sorceress, "Odyssey," Greek
CIRCE

d
sorcery, W. Ind.
OBE, OBI, OBEAH
sore, make .... **RANKLE**
sore: Scot. .... **SAIR**
sorghum variety .... **MILO**
sorrow ..... **DOLOR, REMORSE**
sorrow, feel
RUE, LAMENT, REPENT
sorrowful . **SAD, BLUE, DOLENT**
sort .... **KIND,**
CLASS, GROUP, SPECIES
sortie .... **SALLY**
sortilege .... **LOT**
sorting machine ..... **GRADER**
soul .... **ANIMA**
soul, Egyp. .... **BA, KA**
soul, Hindu ... **ATMA, ATMAN**
sound .. **TONE, NOISE, VALID**
sound, kind of ...... **PALATAL**
sound loudly .. **BLARE, LARUM**
sound, monotonous
HUM, DRONE
sound perception .... **EAR**
sound, pert. to ...... **SONANT**
sound reasoning .... **LOGIC**
sound, resemblance of
ASSONANT
sound, solid .... **KLOP**
sound the ocean
PLUMB, FATHOM

a sound waves, of ...... **AUDIO**
sound, without ..... **ASONANT**
sounding .... **SONANT**
soundless .... **ASONANT**
soup, heavy .. **PUREE, POTAGE**
soup spoon .... **LADLE**
soup, thick .... **BISK,**
    HOOSH, PUREE, BISQUE
soup vessel .... **TUREEN**
soupfin shark .... **TOPE**
sour .... **ACID, ACERB,**
    ACIDIC, ACETOSE
sour curdled milk: Nor. .. **SKYR**
sour-leaved plant ..... **SORREL**
sour milk drink.**LEBAN, LEBEN**
source, mineral .... **ORE**
source, obsidian's ...... **LAVA**
soursop .... **ANNONA**
south: Sp. .... **SUR**
South African .... **BOER**
SOUTH AFRICA ..... see also
    SPECIAL SECTION
S. Afr. assembly .... **RAAD**
S. Afr. dialect .... **TAAL**
S. Afr. Dutch .... **BOER, TAAL**
S. Afr. garter snake .... **ELAPS**
S. Afr. grass country .... **VELD**
S. Afr. greenhorn ..... **IKONA**
S. Afr. gully .... **DONGA**
S. Afr. "out" .... **UIT**
b S. Afr. town .... **STAD**
S. Afr. village .... **KRAAL**
SOUTH AMERICA .... see also
    SPECIAL SECTION
South American animal . **TAPIR**
S. Amer. bird ... **GUAN, JACU,**
    SYLPH, TURCO, SERIEMA
S. Amer. game bird **TINAMOU**
S. Amer. Indian group .... **GES**
S. Amer. lizard .... **TEJU**
S. Amer. tree **VERA, CEBIL, FOTUI**
S. Amer. ungulate .... **TAPIR**
"South Pacific" hero .... **EMILE**
Southern Cross constellation
    CRUX
Southern France .... **MIDI**
Southern river .... **PEEDEE**
Southern state: abbr. .... **ALA**
Southwest river .... **RED**
sovereign (coin) .... **SKIV**
sovereignty .... **EMPERY**
SOVIET .... see also RUSSIAN
Soviet news agency ..... **TASS**
Soviet newspaper .... **PRAVDA**
sow .... **PIG, GILT**
sow .... **SEED, PLANT**
sow: Prov. Eng. .... **YELT**
sow: Scot. .... **SOO**
sower .... **SEEDER**
sown: her. .... **SEME**
soybean .... **SOJA, SOYA**

c spa, Bohemian .... **BILIN**
spa, Eng. .... **BATH**
spa, Ger. .... **EMS, BADEN**
space between bird's eye
    and bill ..... **LORA, LORE,**
    LORUM
space between triglyphs
    METOPE
space, small **AREOLA, AREOLE**
spaces on bird's face
    LORAE, LORES
spade .... **LOY, SHOVEL**
spade, narrow .... **LOY, SPUD**
spade-shaped .... **PALACEOUS**
spade, turf .... **SLANE**
Spain, ancient .... **IBERIA**
SPANISH see also SPAIN, SPE-
    CIAL SECTION
SP. ARTIST
    see SP. PAINTER
Sp. belle .... **MAJA**
Sp. cellist .... **CASALS**
Sp. coin, old .... **PISTOLE**
Sp. dance ..... **JOTA, BOLERO**
Sp. epic .... **CID**
Sp. explorer
    CORTEZ, BALBOA, CORTES
d Sp. fabric .... **CREA**
Sp. fortress commander .. **CAID**
Sp. game of ball .... **PELOTA**
Sp. general, duke.**ALBA, ALVA**
Sp. hero .... **CID**
Sp. kettle .... **OLLA**
Sp. lady ..... **DONA, SENORA**
Sp. length unit .... **VARA**
Sp. man .... **DON, SENOR**
Sp. nun .... **AVILA**
Sp. painter
    GOYA, MIRO, SERT, PICASSO
Sp. poet .... **ENCINA**
Sp. pot .... **OLLA**
Sp. title.**DON, SENOR, SENORA**

SPANISH WORDS:
    (tilde omitted throughout)
abbey .... **ABADIA**
afternoon .... **TARDE**
annatto seeds ... **ACHIOTE**
another .... **OTRO**
article .... **EL, LA, LAS,**
    LOS, UNO
ass .... **ASNO**
aunt .... **TIA**
bay .... **BAHIA**
bean .... **HABA**
before .... **ANTES**
being .... **ENTE**
black .... **NEGRA**
blue .... **AZUL**
box canyon .... **CAJON**

a

boy .... NINO
bravo! .... OLE
bull .... TORO
but .... PERO
canal .... CANO
chaperon . DUENA, DUENNA
chest .... CAJETA
chief .... JEFE, ADALID
child .... NINO
church .... IGLESIA
city .... CIUDAD
clay building.ADOBE, TAPIA
cloak .... CAPA
clothes .... ROPA
corral .... ATAJO
cut .... TAJO
day .... DIA
dining hall .... SALA
dove .... PALOMA
drawing room .... SALA
estuary .... RIA
evening .... TARDE
evil .... MALO
first .... PRIMUS
for .... POR
friend .... AMIGO
funds .... CAJA
girl .... NINA
God .... DIOS
gold .... ORO

b

good-bye .... ADIOS
grass fiber rope ...... SOGA
grille .... REJA
gulch .... ARROYO
gypsy .... GITANO
hall .... SALA
hamlet .... ALDA
harbor entrance ..... BOCA
health .... SANO
hello .... HOLLA
hill . ALTO, CERRO, MORRO
hillside .... FALDA
hotel .... POSADA
house .... CASA
Indian .... INDIO
inlet .... RIA, ESTERO
jail keeper .... CAID
judge .... JUEZ
king .... REY
lady .... DAMA
lake .... LAGO
landmark .... SENAL
latter .... ESTE
lawsuit .... ACTO
letter .... CARTA
lime .... LIMA
love .... AMOR
man .... HOMBRE
manservent .... MOZO
mayor .. ALCADE, ALCALDE

c

mouth .... BOCA
movie house .... CINE
meadow ....,..... VEGA
my .... MIO
of .... DE
open space .... COSO
other .... OTRA
parish priest .... CURA
peak .... PICO
people .... GENTE
pine .... PINO
pole .... PALO
pole, wooden .... PALO
porridge .... ATOLE
post office .... CORREO
pot .... OLLA
priest .... CURA, PADRE
queen .... REINA
ragged person .... ROTO
raisin .... PASA
red .... ROJO
river .... RIO
road .... CAMINO
room .... SALA
rum .... RON
saint, feminine .... SANTA
she .... ELLA
silver .... PLATA
six .... SEIS
snake .... CULEBRA

d

song .... CANCION
south .... SUR
street ..... CALLE, CALLI
sweet potato ..... CAMOTE
tall .... ALTA
this .... ESTA, ESTE
three .... TRES
to be .... SER, ESTE
tomorrow .... MANANA
trench .... TAJO
uncle .... TIO
very .... MUY
water .... AGUA
wax .... CERA
wit .... SAL
with .... DE
work .... OBRA
yes .... SI
you .... TE

spar ...... BOX, BOOM, GAFF,
           MAST, YARD, SPRIT
spar for colors .... GAFF
spar, heavy .... BARITE
spar, loading .... STEEVE
spar, small .... SPRIT
spare .... LEAN, EXTRA,
           GAUNT, LENTEN
sparkle .... GLITTER
sparkling, as wine . MOUSSEUX
sparrow, hedge .... DONEY

Sparta queen .... **LEDA**
Spartan army division .. **MORA**
Spartan magistrate ... **EPHOR**
spasm .... **FIT, TIC, JERK**
spawning place .... **REDD**
speak
    UTTER, ORATE, DECLAIM
speak: comb. form ..... **LALO**
speak, inability to ... **ALALIA**
speak theatrically ..... **EMOTE**
speaker ... **ORATOR, LOCUTOR**
speaking tube, pilot's. **GOSPORT**
spear .... **DART, LANCE**
spear, Afr. **ASSAGAI, ASSEGAI**
spear, fish .... **GIG, GAFF**
spear-like weapon **PIKE, LANCE**
spear-shaped .... **HASTATE**
spear, 3-prong ..... **TRIDENT**
spear thrower, Austral.
    WOMERA
special: Moslem law
    KHAS, KHASS
species .... **KIND, SORT**
specific date .... **DAY**
specified time .... **DATE**
specimen .... **SAMPLE**
speck .... **DOT, MOTE, FLECK**
speckle .... **DOT, STIPPLE**
spectacle .... **PAGEANT**
specter .... **BOGY, BOGEY,**
    GHOST, SHADE
speech ... **LECTURE, ORATION**
speech, art of ..... **RHETORIC**
speech defect
    LISP, ALOGIA, STAMMER
speech goddess, Hindu
    VAC, DEVI, VACH
speech, local .... **PATOIS**
speech, long .... **SPIEL**
speech, loss of ...... **APHASIA**
speech peculiarity ...... **IDIOM**
speech, violent ...... **TIRADE**
speechless ...... **DUMB, MUTE**
speed ..... **HIE, RUN, PACE,**
    RACE, HASTE, HASTEN,
    RAPIDITY
speed, at full .... **AMAIN**
spelt .... **ADOR, EMMER**
Spenser heroine .... **UNA**
Spenser's name for Ireland
    IRENA
sphere .... **ORB**
sphere of action ..... **ARENA**
spice .... **MACE**
spice ball .... **FAGOT, FAGGOT**
spicknel .... **MEU, MEW**
spicy .... **RACY**
spider crab genus **MAIA, MAJA**
spider fluid: Pharm. **ARANEIN**

spider monkey
    QUATA, ATELES, COAITA
spider nest .... **NIDUS**
spigot .... **TAP**
spike .... **EAR, GAD, BROB**
spikenard .... **NARD**
spin
    BIRL, REEL, TWIRL, ROTATE
spinal column ... **AXIS, AXON**
spinal cord .... **MYELON**
spinal membrane ...... **DURA**
spindle .... **COP, AXLE**
spindle, yarn .... **HASP**
spine .... **AXIS, AXON**
spine bones .... **SACRA**
spine, slender .... **SETA**
spineless cactus ...... **CHAUTE**
spiniform .... **SPINATE**
spinning jenny .... **MULE**
spiny shrub genus ...... **ULEX**
spiral formation ..... **VOLUTE**
spire ornament .... **EPI**
spirit .... **ELAN, SOUL, METAL**
spirit: Egyp. myth ..... **BA, KA**
spirit: Ger. .... **GEIST**
spirit, Ir. . **BANSHEE, BANSHIE**
spirit lamp .... **ETNA**
spirit, Moslem ..... **JIN, JINN,**
    GENIE, GENII, JINNI, JINNEE
spirit of air .... **ARIEL**
spirit of evil .. **DEMON, DEVIL**
spirit of man: Egypt ..... **AKH**
spirit raiser .. **ELATER, ELATOR**
spirits and water ...... **GROG**
spirits of the dead .... **MANES**
spirited .... **EAGER, CONMOTO**
spirited horse .... **STEED**
spiritual body: Egypt. ... **SAHU**
spiritual struggle ..... **PENIEL**
spiritualist meeting ... **SEANCE**
splash .... **LAP**
spleen .... **MILT**
splendid .... **GRAND**
splendor .... **ECLAT**
splendor, goddess of: Hindu
    UMA
split .... **RIT, RENT, RIVE,**
    CLEFT, RIVEN, CLEAVE
split pulse .... **DAL**
spoil .... **ROT, BOTCH**
spoil, as eggs .... **ADDLE**
spoils of war .... **LOOT**
spoken .... **ORAL**
spoken word .... **AGRAPH**
spokes, having .... **RADIAL**
sponge, calcareous ... **LEUCON**
sponge gourd ... **LOOF, LOOFA**
sponge on ..... **MUMP, LEACH**
sponge spicule, bow-shaped
    OXEA, TOXA, PINULUS
sponge, young .... **ASCON**

a
spongewood .... **SOLA**
sponsor .... **PATRON**
sponsorship ...... **EGIS, AEGIS**
spool .... **REEL**
spore .... **SEED**
spore cluster .... **SORUS**
spore fruit of rust fungi
    AECIA, TELIA, AECIUM,
              TELIUM
spore sac, fungus **ASCI, ASCUS**
sport .... **RUX, GAME,**
    GOLF, PLAY, POLO
sports arena **STADIA, STADIUM**
sports center ... **RINK, ARENA**
sports hall .... **GYM**
spot in mineral ..... **MACLE**
spot on card .... **PIP**
spotted .... **PIED, PINTO,**
    DAPPLED, MACULOSE
spotted cavy .... **PACA**
spotted deer **KAKAR, CHITAL**
spotted moth ...... **FORESTER**
spotted sting-ray ..... **OBISPO**
spotted, to make
    DAPPLE, STIPPLE
spouse .... **MATE, WIFE**
spray .... **ATOMIZE**
spray, sea .... **LIPPER**
b
spread .... **TED**
spread by peening .... **RIVET**
spread by report
    BRUIT, NORATE
spread out .... **FAN**
spread rumor .... **GOSSIP**
spread the word .... **TELL**
spread to dry, as hay .... **TED**
sprightly .... **PERT, PEART**
spring .... **SPA**
spring back .... **RESILE**
spring: Bible .... **AIN**
spring-like .... **VERNAL**
spring: old Eng. .... **KELD**
spring, mineral .... **SPA**
spring rice, India ...... **BORO**
spring, small .... **SEEP**
springs, warm ...... **THERMAE**
springboard .... **BATULE**
sprinkle **DEG, WATER, SPARGE**
sprinkling: her. .... **SEME**
sprint .... **RUN, RACE**
sprite .. **ELF, FAY, PIXY, PIXIE**
sprite, tricksy .... **ARIEL**
sprout ... **CION, GROW, SCION**
spruce ... **TRIG, TRIM, NATTY**
spruce, Jap. .... **YEDDO**
spruce, white ...... **EPINETTE**
spume .... **FOAM**
spun wool .... **YARN**
spur .... **GAD, GOAD, CALCAR**
spur of mountain ..... **ARETE**

c
spur part .... **ROWEL**
spur wheel .... **ROWEL**
spurs, having .... **CALCARATE**
spurt .... **JET, GUSH**
spy, garment-trade slang **KEEK**
spy, British, Revolution **ANDRE**
squama .... **ALULA**
squander .... **SPEND**
square dance .... **REEL**
square-meshed net ..... **LACIS**
squash .... **PEPO,**
    CRUSH, GOURD, FLATTEN
squash bug .... **ANASA**
squaw .... **MAHALA**
squawfish .... **CHUB**
squid genus .... **LOLIGO**
squirrel fur, Siberian
    CALABAR, CALABER
squirrel, ground Europ. .. **SISEL**
squirrel-like animal **DORMOUSE**
squirrel skin .... **VAIR**
squirrel's nest ... **DRAY, DREY**
ST. .... see **SAINT**
stab .... **GORE**
stabilize .... **STEADY**
stable .... **FIRM, SOLID**
stable compartment ... **STALL**
stable-keeper, royal .. **AVENER**
stables, royal .... **MEWS**
stableman .... **OSTLER**
d
stack of hay .... **RICK**
staff .... **ROD, MACE**
staff-bearer .... **MACER**
staff, bishop's ...... **CROSIER**
staff of office .... **MACE**
staff, royal **SCEPTER, SCEPTRE**
stag ..... **DEER, HART, MALE**
stage direction
    MANET, SENET, EXEUNT
stage equipment ...... **PROPS**
stage extra ..... **SUPE, SUPER**
stage horn signal .... **SENNET**
stage setting .... **SCENE**
stage whisper .... **ASIDE**
stagger .... **REEL**
stagger: Prov. Eng. ...... **STOT**
stagnation .... **STASIS**
stagnation, blood ..... **STASIS**
stain, **DYE, SOIL, SPOT, TASH**
stair part ...... **RISER, TREAD**
stair post .... **NEWEL**
staircase spindle ...... **SPEEL**
stake .... **ANTE, WAGER**
stake, like a .... **PALAR**
stake, pointed ..... **PALISADE**
stake, poker .... **ANTE**
stakes .... **POT**
stakes, —, Epsom Downs Race
            OAKS
stale .... **TRITE**
stalk .... **STEM**

a
stalk, flower . **SCAPE, PEDICEL**
stalk, frond . . . . **STIPE**
stalk, plant . . . . **CAULIS**
stalk, short . . . . **STIPE**
stalk, sugarcane. . . . . . . **RATOON**
stall in mud. . . . . **STOG**
stammer . . . . **HAW, HEM**
stammering sound . . . . **ER**
stamp. . . . . **MARK, SIGIL**
stamp battery block . . . . **VOL**
stamp of approval. . . . . **OK**
stamp-sheet part . . . . **PANE**
stamping device . . . . **DIE**
stamping machine. . . . . . **DATER**
stanch . . . . **STEM**
stand . . . . **RISE**
stand . **BEAR, ABIDE, ENDURE**
stand, cuplike. . . . . **ZARF**
stand in awe of . . . . **FEAR**
stand, small . . . . **TABORET,**
TABOURET
stand, 3-legged . . . . **TRIPOD,**
TRIVET
standard . **PAR, FLAG, ENSIGN**
standard **NORM, TYPE, NORMA**
standard of chemical strength
TITER
standard, Turk . . . . **ALEM**
standing. . . . . **STATUS**
stannum. . . . . **TIN**
stanza, last. . . . . **ENVOY**

b
stanza, Nor. . . . . **STEV**
stanza, part of . . . . **STAVE**
star. . . . . **ASTRO**
star, blue . . . . **VEGA**
star, brightest. . . . . **COR**
star cluster, distant. . . **NEBULA,**
NEBULAE
star, day . . . . **SUN**
star, evening. **VENUS, HESPER,**
VESPER, HESPERUS
star facet. . . . . **PANE**
star, fixed . . . . **SUN, ALYA**
star: Fr. . . . . **ETOILE**
star in Aquarius. . . . . **SKAT**
star in Aquilla. . . . . **ALTAIR**
star in Argo. . . . . **NAOS**
star in Big Dipper . . . . **PHAD**
star in Bootes. . . . . **IZAR**
star in Cetus. . . . . **MIRA**
star in Cygenus . **SADR, DENEB**
star in Draco. . . . . . . **ADIB, JUZA**
star in Eridanus . . . . **AZHA, BEID**
star in Leo. . . **DUHR, REGULUS**
star in Lyra . . . . . . **VEGA, WEGA**
star in Orion. . . . . **RIGEL**
star in Pegasus . . **ENIF, MATAR**
star in Pleiades . . . . **MAIA**
star in Perseus. . . . . **ATIK**
star in Scorpio . . . . **ANTARES**

c
star in Serpens . . . . **ALYA**
star in Taurus. . . **NATH, PLEIAD**
star in Virgo . . . . **SPICA**
star near Mizar. . . . . **ALCOR**
star, new . . . . **NOVA**
star-shaped. . . . . **STELLATE**
star-shaped spicule. . . . . **ACTER,**
ACTINE
star, temporary . . . . **NOVA**
stars, dotted with . . . . **SEME**
stars, pert. to . . . . **ASTRAL**
starch. . . . . **AMYL, ARUM,**
SAGO, FARINA, CASSAVA
starchy rootstock . . . . **TARO**
starfish. . . . . **ASTEROID**
starnose. . . . . **MOLE**
— Starr, comic strip character
BRENDA
starred lizard **AGAMA, HARDIM**
start . . . **BEGIN, SALLY, ROUSE**
starvation . . . . **INEDIA**
starwort. . . . . **ASTER**
state. . . . . **AVER**
STATE. . . . . see also GAZETTEER
STATE FLOWERS. see SPECIAL
SECTION
state, New England: abbr. . . . . . **RI**
state of affairs. . . . . **PASS**
state, pert. to . . . . **CIVIL**

d
state of: suffix . . . . **ERY**
state of being: suffix . . . . . . **URE**
state precisely . . . . **SPECIFY**
stately home. . . **DOME, ESTATE**
statements, confused
RIGMAROLE
statesman, Brit. . . . . **PITT**
station . **POST, DEPOT, PLACE**
stationary . . . . . **FIXED, STATIC**
stationary motor part. . **STATOR**
statistician. . . . . **STATIST**
statute . . . . **ACT, LAW**
stave, barrel . . . . **LAG**
stay. . . . . **WAIT, TARRY**
stay rope. . . . . **GUY**
stays. . . . . **CORSET**
stead . . . . **LIEU, PLACE**
steal . . . . **COP, ROB, GLOM,**
SNITCH
steal cattle . . . . **RUSTLE**
steal: Eng. . . . . **GLOM**
steal, Eng. dialect . . . . **NIM**
steel beam . . . . **GIRDER**
steel: Ger. . . . . **STAHL**
steel splint, armor skirt . . **TACE,**
TASSE, TASSET
steep . . . . **RET, SOP**
steep . . . . **SHEER**
steep in lime. . . . . **BOWK**
steer wildly . . . . **YAW**
steer, young: Prov. Eng. . . . **STOT**

Steering

a steering, direct ship's **COND, CONN**
steersman .... **COX**
stellar ...... **ASTRAL, STARRY**
stem **CION, CORM, SCAPE, STALK**
stem, fungus .... **STIPE**
stem, hollow .... **CANE**
stem, jointed .... **CULM**
stem of hop .... **BINE**
stem, rudimentary .. **CAULICLE**
stem, ship's .... **PROW**
stench .... **ODOR, FETOR**
stentorian .... **LOUD**
step .... **GRADE, PHASE**
step ... **PACE, STAIR, TREAD**
step, dance ..... **PAS, CHASSE**
step up to mark .... **TOE**
step, upright part of .. **RISER**
steps, outdoor .... **PERRON**
steps over fence ...... **STILE**
steppes, storm on ..... **BURAN**
stern **GRIM, HARSH, AUSTERE**
steward: Scot. ..... **MORMAOR**
stick .. **BAR, BAT, ROD, CANE, WAND, BATON, MUNDLE**
stick .... **GLUE, PASTE, ADHERE, CLEAVE**
stick, conductor's ..... **BATON**
stick together ...... **COHERE**
stick used in hurling .. **CAMAN**
b sticks, bundle of ...... **FAGOT**
stickler for formality .. **TAPIST**
sticky substance ... **GOO, GUM**
stiffly nice .... **PRIM**
stigma .... **BRAND**
stigmatic point of mango **NAK**
still .... **BUT, YET**
stimulant, coffee **CAFFEIN, CAFFEINE**
stimulant, tea **THEIN, THEINE**
stimulate .. **FAN, WHET, ELATE**
sting .... **BITE, SMART**
stinging ant .... **KELEP**
stinging herb .... **NETTLE**
stingy .... **MEAN**
stint .... **TASK**
stipend, church ..... **PREBEND**
stipend: Scot. .... **ANNAT**
stipulation .... **CLAUSE**
stir .. **ADO, MIX, TODO, ROUSE**
stir up .... **RILE, ROIL**
stitch .... **PUNTO**
stitchbird .... **IHI**
stitched fold .... **TUCK**
stithy .... **ANVIL**
stock .... **BREED**
stock .... **STORE**
stock exchange, membership in **SEAT**
stock exchange, Paris **BOURSE**

c stock market crash .... **PANIC**
stockade: Russ. .... **ETAPE**
stocking run .... **LADDER**
stockings .... **HOSE**
stocky .... **STUB**
stolen goods .... **SWAG**
stomach .... **MAW, CRAW**
stomach division, ruminant's **OMASUM**
stomach, first .... **RUMEN**
stomach, ruminant's ... **TRIPE**
stone .. **AGATE, LAPIS, SLATE**
Stone Age tool .... **CELT, EOLITH, NEOLITH**
stone, aquamarine .... **BERYL**
stone, breastplate .... **JASPER**
stone chest .... **CIST**
stone chip .... **SPALL**
stone: comb. form ..... **LITH**
stone-cutter's chisel .... **DROVE**
stone fruit .... **DRUPE**
stone, green . **BERYL, OLIVINE**
stone hammer .... **MASH**
stone, hard .... **ADAMANT**
stone heap ..... **CARN, KARN, CAIRN, CARNE, CAIRNE**
stone, hollow .... **GEODE**
stone implement ...... **CELT, EOLITH, NEOLITH**
stone, like a .... **LITHOID**
stone, monument .... **MENHIR**
d stone paving block ..... **SETT**
stone pillar .... **STELE**
stone, red ...... **SARD, SPINEL**
stone roller fish ...... **TOTER**
stone, rough .... **RUBBLE**
stone: Scot. .... **STEAN, STEEN**
stone set .... **PAVER**
stone, squared ...... **ASHLAR**
stone to death .... **LAPIDATE**
stone, woman turned to **NIOBE**
stone worker .... **MASON**
stone, yellow **TOPAZ, CITRINE**
stonecrop **ORPIN, SEDUM, ORPINE**
stonecutter **MASON, LAPICIDE**
stonecutter's chisel ... **DROVE**
stoneware: Fr. .... **GRES**
stool pigeon .... **NARK**
stop ..... **DAM, BALK, HALT, STEM, WHOA, DESIST**
stop, as engine .. **CONK, STALL**
stop by accident ...... **STALL**
stop: naut. ... **AVAST, BELAY**
stop short .... **BALK**
stoppage .... **JAM**
stopper .... **BUNG, PLUG**
storage battery plate ... **GRID**
storage place **BIN, BARN, SILO**
store, army .... **CANTEEN**
store fodder .... **ENSILE**

a storehouse .... **ETAPE**
storehouse, army ..... **DEPOT**
storehouse, India .... **GOLA**
storehouse, public ..... **ETAPE**
stork .... **MARABOU**
storm **FUME, FURY, RAGE, RAVE**
storm, away from ...... **ALEE**
storm, dust .... **SIMOON**
storm: Fr. .... **ORAGE**
storm god, Babyl. **ZU, ADAD,**
ADDA, ADDU
story, Norse .... **SAGA**
story, short .... **CONTE**
stoss, opposite of .... **LEE**
stout .... **BURLY**
stout, kind of .... **PORTER**
stove .... **ETNA, RANGE**
"Stowe" character
EVA, TOM, TOPSY
straight .... **DIRECT**
straight-edge .... **RULER**
strain .... **EXERT**
strained .... **TENSE**
strainer .... **SIEVE**
strainer, wool cloth ... **TAMIS**
Straits Settlement region
PENANG
strange .... **ODD**
strap on falcon's leg .... **JESS**
strap-shaped .... **LORATE**
b strass .... **PASTE**
stratagem .... **RUSE, WILE**
stratagem, sudden ...... **COUP**
stratum .... **LAYER**
straw hat ...... **BAKU, MILAN**
stray .... **ERR**
stray .... **WAIF**
stray animal .... **CAVY**
streak .... **ROE, LINE, VEIN,**
STRIA, STRAKE, STRIAE
streaky .... **LINY, ROWY**
stream
FLOW, RILL, BOURN, RIVER
streamlet ...... **RILL, RUNNEL**
street Arab .... **GAMIN**
street: It., Sp. .. **CALLE, CALLI**
street, narrow .... **LANE**
street roisterer .... **MUN**
street urchin .... **ARAB**
street, Venice water .. **RIO, RII**
strength .... **POWER**
strengthening .... **ROBORANT**
stress .... **ICTUS**
stressed beat, syllable ... **ARSIS**
stretch: Scot. .... **STENT**
stretched out ...... **PROLATE**
stretcher .... **LITTER**
stretching frame .... **TENTER,**
STENTER
strewn with flowers: Her. **SEME**

c strife .... **WAR**
strife, civil .... **STASIS**
strike .. **BAT, HIT, RAP, CONK,**
SLOG, SLUG, SOCK, SWAT,
WHAM, SMITE
strikebreaker ..... **FINK, SCAB**
striking effect .... **ECLAT**
string of mules .... **ATAJO**
stringy .... **ROPY**
strip .. **BARE, DIVEST, STRAKE**
strip of land ... **DOAB, DUAB**
strip of wood .... **LATH**
strip off skin .... **FLAY**
strip, oxhide, S. Afr. ... **RIEM**
strip, wood, metal ... **SPLINE**
stripe .... **BAR, BAND, WALE,**
WEAL, STREAK
stripe of color: zool. .. **PLAGA**
stripling .... **BOY, LAD**
strive .... **AIM, VIE**
strobile .... **CONE**
stroke .... **FIT, ICTUS**
stroke, brilliant .... **COUP**
stroll .... **AMBLE**
strong-arm man ...... **GOON**
strong, as cigars .... **MADURO**
strong desire .... **HUNGER**
strong man .... **SAMSON**
strong man, Gr. .... **ATLAS**
strong point .... **FORTE**
d strong-scented ... **OLID, RANK**
strongbox .... **SAFE**
stronghold .. **FORT, SION, ZION**
struck with horror ... **AGHAST**
structure, tall .... **TOWER**
struggle .... **COPE**
struggle helplessly. **FLOUNDER**
struggled .... **HOVE**
stud .... **BOSS**
student in charge ... **MONITOR**
studio, art .... **ATELIER**
study ... **CON, PORE, READ**
study group .... **SEMINAR**
stuff .... **PAD, RAM, CRAM**
stuffing .... **KAPOK**
stum .... **MUST**
stumble: prov. Eng. ..... **STOT**
stump of branch .... **SKEG**
stunted trees .... **SCRUB**
stupefied .... **MAZED**
stupefy .... **DAZE, MAZE,**
STUN, BESOT
stupid .... **CRASS, DENSE**
stupid person ...... **ASS, OAF**
CLOD, COOT, DOLT, LOON,
LOUT, LOWN, MOKE
stupor .... **COMA, SOPOR**
sturgeon, small ..... **STERLET**
style .... **MODE, NAME**
style of art .... **DADA, GENRE**

a
stylet, surgical ...... **TROCAR**
stymie .... **IMPEDE**
Styx ferryman ...... **CHARON**
subbase .... **PLINTH**
subdued shade .... **PASTEL**
subject ...... **TOPIC, VASSAL**
subject in grammar .... **NOUN**
subjoin .... **ADD**
sublime .... **NOBLE**
submarine **PIGBOAT, SNORKEL**
submit .... **BOW, YIELD**
subordinate
          MINOR, DEPENDENT
subside
   EBB, SINK, ABATE, RELAPSE
substance, lustrous .... **METAL**
substances, class of .... **LIPIN**
substantiate .... **VERIFY**
substantive word .... **NOUN**
substitute
      VICE, PROXY, ERSATZ
substitute for: suffix .... **ETTE**
subtle emanation ...... **AURA**
subtle variation ..... **NUANCE**
subtract .... **DEDUCT**
subway, Eng. .... **TUBE**
subway entrance ...... **KIOSK**
subway, Fr. .... **METRO**
success .... **HIT, WOW**

b
succession .... **LINE**
successively .... **AROW**
succinct .... **TERSE**
succor .... **AID**
succulent plant .. **ALOE, HERB**
such .... **SO**
sucking fish ... **PEGA, REMORA**
Sudan lake .... **CHAD**
Sudan native .... **FUL**
Sudan Negroid .... **SERE**
Sudan people .... **HAUSA**
sudden attack: Med. .. **ICTUS**
suet .... **TALLOW**
suffer .... **LET, BIDE**
suffer from hunger
          CLEM, STARVE
suffer: Scot. .... **DREE**
sufficient: poet. .... **ENOW**

SUFFIXES:
   act of .... **TION**
   action .... **ANCE**
   adjective .... **ENT, IAL, INE,
        ISH, IST, ITE, OUS**
   agent .... **URE**
   alcohol .... **OL**
   carbohydrate .... **OSE**
   chemical or chemistry . **ANE,
     ENE, IDE, INE, OLE, ONE,
     ENOL, ITOL, OLIC**

c
   common ending **ENT, INE,
                ING, ION**
   common suffix ..... **ES, ESE,
        ESS, INE, IVE, ETTE,
        YNONE**
   condition .... **ATE, ILE, ISE,
        ANCE, SION, STER**
   comparative ...... **IER, IOR**
   compound .... **ICAL, ILITY**
   diminutive .... **ET, IE, ULA,
                ULE, ETTE**
   feminine ... **INA, INE, ELLA**
   feminine noun .... **ESS**
   follower .... **IST, ISTE**
   forming nouns from verbs. **ER**
   full of .... **OSE**
   inflammation .... **ITIS**
   inhabitant of .... **ITE**
   into .... **EN**
   like .... **OID**
   little .... **ET**
   made of .... **EN**
   make .... **ISE**
   medical .... **IA, OMA**
   mineral .... **ITE, LITE**
   native of .... **ITE**
   noun .. **IA, OR, ATE, ENT,
     ERY, ESS, IER, ISE, IST,
     ITE, ANCY, ENCE, ENSE,
     STER**

d
   noun ending .... **STER**
   noun forming diminutive. **CLE**
   number .... **TEEN**
   or ordinal number .... **ETH**
   oil .... **OL, OLE**
   one who .... **IST, STER**
   one who does .... **IST**
   order of animals .... **INI**
   ordinal .... **ETH**
   origin, denoting ...... **OTE**
   participle .... **ING**
   person .... **ER**
   plural .... (old EN), **ES**
   quality .... **ANCE, ILITY**
   rocks, of .... **ITE, LITE**
   science of .... **ICS**
   skin .... **DERM**
   small .... **ING**
   state of .... **ERY, ANCE**
   state of being .... **URE**
   substitute for .... **ETTE**
   superlative .... **EST**
   sympathizer .... **ITE**
   town .... **TON**
   tumor .... **OMA**
   verb .... **ISE, ESCE**
   with mineral names ... **LITE**
   zoological .... **ATA**
Sufi disciple .... **MURID**
sugar .... **OSE, SUCROSE**
sugar cane disease ..... **ILIAU**

sugar cane residue .. **BAGASSE**
sugar, crude .... **GUR**
sugar, fruit .... **KETOSE**
sugar, raw ...... **CASSONADE**
sugar, simple .... **OSE**
sugar source .... **CANE**
suggestion .... **CUE, HINT**
suit of mail .... **ARMOR**
suitable.**APT, FIT, PAT, PROPER**
suitcase ... **BAG, GRIP, VALISE**
suitor .... **SWAIN**
sullen .. **DOUR, GLUM, MOROSE**
sullen, act .... **MOPE**
sullen, be ...... **POUT, SULK**
sully .... **SOIL, DIRTY**
sultan, Turkish .... **SELIM**
sultan's order .... **IRADE**
sultan's residence ...... **SERAI**
sultanate .... **OMAN**
sultry .... **HUMID**
Sulu Moslem .... **MORO**
"sum," infinitive following **ESSE**
sum paid as punishment .. **FINE**
sumac genus .... **RHUS**
sumac, P. I. .... **ANAM, ANAN**
Sumatra squirrel shrew .. **TANA**
Sumatra wildcat ...... **BALU**
Sumatran silk .... **IKAT**
"summa — laude" ...... **CUM**
summary
　DIGEST, PRECIS, EPITOME
summer: Fr. .... **ETE**
summer-house
　　ARBOR, PERGOLA
summer, pert. to ..... **ESTIVAL**
summit
　APEX, KNAP, PEAK, SPIRE
summits .... **APICES**
summon .... **CALL, CITE,**
　　PAGE, CLEPE, EVOKE
sun .... **SOL, HELIOS**
sun apartments ...... **SOLARIA**
sun bittern .... **CAURALE**
sun: comb. form .... **HELIO**
sun disk .... **ATEN, ATON**
sun-dried brick
　DOBE, DOBY, ADOBE, DOBIE
sun god, Babyl. .. **UTU, UTUG,**
　　BABBAR, SHAMASH
sun god, Egypt. ..... **RA, TEM,**
　　TUM, AMON, AMEN,
　　AMUN, ATMU, ATUM
sun god, Gr., Rom. ...... **SOL,**
　　APOLLO, HELIOS
sun god, Inca .... **INTI**
sun, halo around .... **CORONA**
sun, pert. to .... **SOLAR**
sun porches .... **SOLARIA**
sun tree, Jap. .... **HINOKI**

sunbaked building
　DOBE, DOBY, ADOBE, DOBIE
Sunday of Lent, 4th .. **LAETARE**
sunder
　PART, REND, SPLIT, DIVIDE
sundial, style of ..... **GNOMON**
sunfish .... **BREAM**
sunfish genus .... **MOLA**
sunken fence .... **AHA, HAHA**
sunset, occurring at **ACRONICAL**
sunspot center
　　UMBRA, UMBRAE
supercilious person ..... **SNOB**
superfluous: Fr. ...... **DE TROP**
superintendent, office
　　　MANAGER
superior, most .... **BEST, TOPS**
superior quality: Fr. .... **LUXE**
superiority, belief in .. **RACISM**
superlative, absolute .. **ELATIVE**
superlative ending ...... **EST**
supernatural .... **OCCULT**
supernatural being, Melanesia
　　　ADARO
supernatural power, E. Afr. **NGAI**
supernatural power, Polyn.
　　　MANA
superscribe .... **DIRECT**
superstition, object of
　　FETICH, FETISH
supper .... **TEA**
supplication, make ..... **PRAY**
supply .... **STOCK, ENDUE**
supply, fresh .... **RELAY**
supply of horses .... **REMUDA**
support ...... **LEG, RIB, ABET,**
　　BACK, PROP, BRACE
support, one-legged .. **UNIPOD**
suppose ... **ASSUME, IMAGINE**
suppose: archaic .... **TROW**
suppress ...... **ELIDE, QUASH**
Supreme Being, Hebrew . **IHVH,**
　JHVH, JHWH, YHVH, YHWH
surety agreement ...... **BOND**
surf, roar of .... **ROTE**
surface, attractive ... **VENEER**
surface of gem .... **FACET**
surface of a tool ...... **FACE**
surfeit .... **CLOY, GLUT, SATE**
surfeited .... **BLASE**
surge ...... **TIDE, BILLOW**
surgeon's instrument :. **TREPAN,**
　TROCAR, ABLATOR, LE-
　VATOR, SCALPEL
surgical thread .... **SETON**
Surinam toad .... **PIPA**
surly .... **GRUFF, SULLEN**
surmise .. **INFER, GUESS, OPINE**
surnamed: Fr. .... **DIT**

a surpass ...... **CAP, TOP, BEST**
surplice, chorister's .... **COTTA**
surplus .... **EXTRA, EXCESS**
surrender
      CEDE, YIELD, DEDITION
surrender: law .... **REMISE**
surround **GIRD, BESET, INARM**
surrounding area ...... **ZONE**
surtout .... **COAT**
survey .... **MAP, POLL**
surveyor's assistant .. **RODMAN**
surveyor's instrument
      ROD, ALIDADE
surveyor's rod, sight on **TARGET**
Susa inhabitant ..... **ELAMITE**
suspend .... **HANG**
suspenders .... **BRACES**
suture .... **SEAM**
svelte .... **SLIM, TRIM**
swab .... **MOP**
swain .... **LOVER**
swallow **BOLT, GULP, MARTIN**
swallow, sea .... **TERN**
swamp ..... **BOG, FEN, MARSH,**
   MORASS, SLEW, SLOO, SLUE
swamp gas .. **MIASM, MIASMA**
swamp, S. Afr. ... **VLEI, VLEY**
swampy belt, India ..... **TERAI**
swan, female .... **PEN**
swan genus .... **OLOR**

b swan, male .... **COB**
swan, whistling .... **OLOR**
swap .... **TRADE**
sward .... **SOD, TURF**
swarm .... **NEST, HORDE**
swarthy .... **DUN, DARK**
swastika .... **FYLFOT**
sway .... **ROCK, ROLL**
swear .... **AVER, CURSE**
sweat ...... **SUDOR, PERSPIRE**
SWEDISH ... see also SPECIAL
   SECTION—SWEDEN
Swedish:
   beer .... **OL**
   tea .... **TE**
   toe .... **TA**
   you .... **ER**
Swedish coin .... **ORE**
Swedish county, district .. **LAN**
Swedish explorer ...... **HEDIN**
Swedish order of merit .. **VASA**
Swedish royal guard **DRABANT**
Swedish sculptor ..... **MILLES**
sweep, scythe's ...... **SWATH**
sweet flag .. **SEDGE, CALAMUS**
sweet gale .... **GAGL**
sweet liquid .... **NECTAR**
sweet potato
   YAM, BATATA, OCARINA
sweet potato: Sp. .... **CAMOTE**

c sweet red wine .... **ALICANTE**
sweet-smelling
   OLENT, REDOLENT
sweet spire .... **ITEA**
sweetfish .... **AYU**
sweetheart: Ir. .... **GRA**
sweetheart: Scot. .... **JO**
sweetmeat: Fr. .... **DRAGEE**
sweetsop .... **ATA,**
   ATES, ATTA, ANNONA
swell .... **DILATE**
swell of water .... **WAVE**
swelling **LUMP, NODE, EDEMA**
swelling on plants .... **GALL**
swerve .... **SHY, SKEW**
swift .... **FAST, FLEET**
swift, common .... **CRAN**
swift horse .. **ARAB, PACOLET**
swiftly, run ...... **DART, SCUD**
swimming .... **NATANT**
swimming bell .. **NECTOPHORE**
swindle **GIP, GYP, DUPE, SWIZ**
swindler .... **COZENER**
swine .. **HOG, PIG, SOW, BOAR**
swine, feeding of ... **PANNAGE**
swine fever .... **ROUGET**
swine genus .... **SUS**
swing music .... **JIVE**
swing musician ...... **HEPCAT**

d swinish .... **PORCINE**
swipe .... **GLOM**
swirl .... **EDDY, GURGE**
SWISS .. see also SPECIAL SEC-
   TION—SWITZERLAND
Swiss capital .. **BERN, BERNE**
Swiss card game .... **JASS**
Swiss critic .... **AMIEL**
Swiss patriot .... **TELL**
Swiss state .... **CANTON**
switch .... **TOGGLE**
swollen .... **TURGID**
swoon .... **FAINT**
swoon: old Eng. .... **SWEB**
sword ... **PATA, EPEE, BLADE,**
   SABER, SABRE, RAPIER
sword, Arthur's
   EXCALIBAR, EXCALIBUR
sword, curved .. **SABER, SABRE**
sword, fencing .... **EPEE**
sword, matador's ... **ESTOQUE**
sword, medieval ...... **ESTOC**
sword, Norse myth. ... **GRAM**
sword, put away ... **SHEATHE**
sword, St. George's
   ASCALON, ASKELON
sword-shaped ...... **ENSATE**
sword, Siegfried's ..... **GRAM**
sword, slender .... **RAPIER**
swordsman's dummy stake **PEL**
syllable, last .... **ULTIMA**

160

a syllable, scale .... DO, FA, LA,
　　　　　MI, RE, SO, TI, SOL
syllable, short .. MORA, MORAE
sylvan deity PAN, FAUN, SATYR
SYMBOL, CHEMICAL .... see
　　SPECIAL SECTION
symbol .... TOKEN
symbol of authority ... MACE
symbol of Crusaders ... CROSS
symbol of protection ... EGIS
sympathizer: suffix ...... ITE
synagogue .... SHUL, TEMPLE
syncopated music .... RAG
syncope ...... FAINT, SWOON
synod, Russian .... SOBOR
syntax, give the .... PARSE

c synthetic fabric or fiber NYLON,
　　ORLON, RAYON, DACRON
synthetic rubber
　　　　BUNA, ELASTOMER
Syria, ancient .... ARAM
Syrian, ancient port ... SIDON
Syrian bear .... DUBB
Syrian bishop's title .... ABBA
Syrian city, old ...... ALEPPO
system .... ISM
system of rule ...... REGIME
system of rules .... CODE
system of weights ..... TROY
system of worship ...... CULT
systematic regulation ... CODE

T

T-shaped .... TAU
tab .... FLAP, LABEL
tabard .... CAPE
table mountain, Abyssin. AMBA
tableland .... MESA
tablet .... PAD, SLATE
taboo, opposite of ...... NOA
b tabor, Moorish
　　　ATABAL, ATTABAL
Tacoma's Sound ...... PUGET
tack: naut. .... BUSK
tact .... FINESSE
tackle, anchor .... CAT
tael, part of LI
tag .... LABEL
tag, metal .... AGLET, AIGLET
Tagalog for river .... ILOG
Tahitian national god ... ORO
Tai race branch .... LAO
tail, of ... CAUDAL, CAUDATE
tail of coin .... VERSO
tail, rabbit's .... SCUT
tail: zool. .... CAUDA
tailor .... SARTOR
Taino fetish ..... ZEME, ZEMI
Taj Mahal site .... AGRA
take away by force ... REAVE
take away: law .... ADEEM
take back .... RECANT
take effect again ..... REVEST
take off .... DOFF
take one's ease .... REST
take on cargo ... LADE, LOAD
take out DELE, ELIDE, EXPUNGE
take part .... SIDE
take up again ...... RESUME
take up weapons .... ARM
tale .... SAGA, YARN, STORY
tale, medieval Fr. .... LAI

tale, Norse .... SAGA
"Tale of Two Cities" girl LUCIE
"Tales of a Wayside —" .. INN
talent .... FLAIR
talented .... SMART
talisman .... CHARM
talisman, Afr. .... GRIGRI
talk .... GAB, GAS, CHAT,
　　　　PRATE, PALAVER
d talk: slang .... YAK
talk freely .... DESCANT
talk pompously
　　　ORATE, HARANGUE
talk, rambling ... RIGMAROLE
talk wildly ..... RANT, RAVE
Tallinn .... REVAL
tallow tree .... CERA
tally .... SCORE
Talmud commentary .. GEMARA
talon .... CLAW, NAIL
tamarack .... LARCH
tamarisk .... ATLE
tame, as hawks .... MAN
tan .... BUFF, BEIGE
tan skins .... TAW
tanager ..... YENI, REDBIRD
tanager, S. Am. HABIA, LINDO
tanbark .... ROSS
tangle ...... SNARL, SLEAVE
tangled mass ..... MAT, SHAG
tanning gum .... KINO
tanning, plant for ..... ALDER
tanning shrub SUMAC, SUMACH
tanning tree, India AMLA, AMLI
tantalize .... TEASE
Tantalus' daughter .... NIOBE
tantra .... AGAMA
tantrum .... RAGE
tap PAT, COCK, SPIGOT, FAUCET

161

Tapering

a
tapering dagger .... **ANLACE**
tapering piece .... **SHIM**
tapestry .... **ARRAS, TAPIS, DOSSER**
tapestry center .... **ARRAS**
tapeworm .... **TAENIA**
tapeworm larva .... **MEASLE**
tapioca-like food .... **SALEP**
tapioca source .... **CASAVA, CASSAVA**
tapir, S. Amer. .... **DANTA**
Tapuyan .... **GE**
tarboosh .... **FEZ**
target .... **BUTT**
Tariff Act writer .... **SMOOT**
Tarkington character ...... **SAM**
tarnish .... **SPOT, SULLY**
taro .... **GABE, GABI, DASHEEN**
taro paste .... **POI**
taro root ... **EDO, EDDO, KALO**
tarpaulin .... **PAULIN**
tarpon .... **SABALO**
tarradiddle .... **FIB, LIE**
tarry .... **BIDE, WAIT, STAY, LINGER**
tarsus .... **ANKLE**
tarsus, insect .... **MANUS**
tart .... **ACID**
tartar, crude ... **ARGAL, ARGOL**
Tartini's B-flat .... **ZA**

b
task .... **DUTY, CHORE, STENT, STINT**
task, punishing .... **PENSUM**
taste .... **SIP, SUP, SAPOR, SNACK, PALATE**
tasteful .... **ELEGANT**
tasty .... **SAPID**
Tatar .... **HU**
Tatar dynasty, China .... **WEI**
Tatar tribe, W. Siberia .... **SHOR**
tattle .... **BLAB**
tattler, idle .... **GOSSIP**
Tattler publisher .... **STEELE**
tau cross .... **ANKH**
taunt ...... **JEER, MOCK, TWIT**
taut .... **TENSE**
taut, pull .... **STRETCH**
tavern .... **INN**
tax .... **CESS, GELD, LEVY, SCOT, SESS, STENT, ASSESS, EXCISE, IMPOST**
tax, church .... **TITHE**
tea .... **CHA, CHAA**
tea, black .... **PECO, BOHEA, PEKOE**
tea bowl .... **CHAWAN**
tea box .... **CADDY, CALIN, CANISTER**
tea, China ... **BOHEA, CONGOU**
tea, Chin. green .... **HYSON**

c
tea genus .... **THEA**
tea-growing region ..... **ASSAM**
tea, kind of . **OOPAK, OOLONG, OOPACK**
tea, Labrador .... **LEDUM**
tea, marsh .... **LEDUM**
tea, medicinal. **PTISAN, TISANE**
tea, Oriental .... **CHA**
tea, Paraguay ... **MATE, YERBA**
tea, rolled ... **CHA, TCHA, TSIA**
tea tree .... **TI**
teacake .... **SCON, SCONE**
teacher .... **DOCENT, MENTOR**
teacher, Hebrew .... **RABBI**
teacher, Islam religious ... **ALIM, MOLLA, MULLA**
teacher, Jewish ...... **RAB, REB**
teacher, Moslem .... **ALIM, MOLLA, MULLA**
teacher, Xenophon's **ISOCRATES**
teacher's association: abbr. **NEA**
team of horses .... **SPAN**
team, 3-horse .... **RANDEM**
teamster's command **GEE, HAW**
tear .... **RIP, REND, RENT**
tear apart ..... **REND, TATTER, DIVULSE**
tease .... **TWIT, BOTHER**
technical name: biol ...... **ONYM**
technique .... **ART**
tedious writer .... **PROSER**

d
teem .... **RAIN, POUR**
teeth, false .... **DENTURES**
teeth, incrustation ..... **TARTAR**
Telamon's son .... **AJAX**
telegraph inventor ...... **MORSE**
telegraph key .... **TAPPER**
telegraph signal .... **DOT, DASH**
telegraph, underwater ... **CABLE**
telegraphic speed unit .... **BAUD**
telephone exchange .. **CENTRAL**
telephone inventor .... **BELL**
telephone wire .... **LINE**
telescope part .... **LENS**
television .... **VIDEO**
television broadcast . **TELECAST**
television cable ...... **COAXIAL**
television recording **KINESCOPE**
television tube .. **MONOSCOPE, ICONSCOPE**
tell .... **IMPART, RELATE, NARRATE**
tell in detail .... **RECOUNT**
Tell, site of legend .... **URI**
telling blow .... **COUP, ONER**
temper .... **ANNEAL**
temper, fit of .... **PET**
temperament: Ger. ...... **GEMUT**
"Tempest" sprite .... **ARIEL**
"Tempest" slave ..... **CALIBAN**
temple .. **FANE, RATH, RATHA**
temple, Asian .... **PAGODA**

162

a temple chamber, Gr. ... **NAOS**
temple, inner part ..... **CELLA**
temple: Siam. .... **VAT, WAT**
temple tower, India .. **SHIKARA**
tempo: music .... **TAKT**
temporary decline ..... **SLUMP**
temporary fashion .... **FAD**
temporary relief ... **REPRIEVE**
tempt .... **LURE, TOLE**
temptation .... **ALLURE**
ten .... **DECAD**
ten ares .... **DECARE**
Ten Commandments
      DECALOG, DECALOGUE
"Ten Days that Shook the
   World" author ..... **REED**
ten million ergs .... **JOULE**
tenant .... **LESSEE**
tenant, early Ir. .... **SAER**
tend .... **SERVE**
tender .... **SOFT, OFFER**
tending toward .... **FOR**
tendril: bot. .... **CAPREOL**
tennis score .... **LOVE, DEUCE**
tennis shoe .... **SNEAKER**
tennis stroke **ACE, LOB, LOBB**
tennis term .... **LET**

b Tennyson character .... **ENID,
                            ARDEN**
Tennyson heroine
      ELAIN, ELAINE
Tennyson sailor ...... **ENOCH**
tenon .... **COG**
tenonlike piece .. **COAG, COAK**
tenor, famous ..... **MELCHIOR**
tense .... **TAUT**
tent dweller
      KEDAR, SCENITE
tent dwelling Arabs ... **KEDAR**
tent flap .... **FLY**
tentmaker, the .... **OMAR**
tents .... **CAMP**
tentacle .... **FEELER**
tenth part .... **DECI, TITHE**
tepid .... **WARM**
Tereus' son .... **ITYS**
term .... **NAME**
term .... **SESSION**
term: algebra .... **NOME**
TERM, GEOMETRY ...... see
      GEOMETRY, GEOMETRIC
term in office .... **TENURE**
term, math. .... **SINE, COSINE**
term of address .... **SIR, SIRE,
                       MADAM**
termagant .... **SHREW**
terminable .... **ENDABLE**
termite, P. I. .... **ANAI, ANAY**
tern .... **SKIRK**

c tern, black .... **DARR**
tern genus .... **STERNA**
tern, Hawaii .... **NOIO**
terpene alcohol ...... **NEROL**
terpene compound . **TEREBENE**
terrapin .... **EMYD,
                  POTTER, SLIDER**
terrapin, red-bellied
            POTTER, SLIDER
terrestrial .... **GEAL**
terrible .... **DIRE**
terrier, kind of .. **SKYE, CAIRN**
terrier, Scottish breed of . **SKYE**
terrified .... **AFRAID**
territorial division .... **AMT**
territory .... **LAND, SOIL**
territory, additional
            LEBENSRAUM
territory, enclosed .. **ENCLAVE**
terror .... **PANIC**
terrorist .... **GOON**
tessellated .... **MOSAIC**
tessera .... **TILE**
test .... **ASSAY, TEMPT,
            TRIAL, EXAMINE**
test ground .... **BOSE**
testament .... **WILL**
testifier .... **DEPONENT**
testify ...... **DEPONE, DEPOSE**

d tetrachord, upper tone of.**NETE**
Teutonic, ancient ...... **GOTH**
Teutonic barbarian ..... **GOTH**
Teutonic deity .... **ER**
Teut. Fate ...... **NORN, URTH**
**TEUTONIC GODS, GODDESSES,
   DEITY** see NORSE SPECIAL
   SECTION
Teut. legendary hero ... **OFFA**
Teut. letter of alphabet . **RUNE**
Teut. people .... **GEPIDAE**
Teut. sea goddess ...... **RAN**
Teut. sky god .. **TY, TIU, TIW,
      TYR, ZIO, ZIU, TYRR**
Texas shrine .... **ALAMO**
textile screw pine
            ARA, PANDAN
texture .... **WALE,
            WOOF, GRAIN**
Thailand .... **SIAM**
Thames estuary .... **NORE**
than: Ger. .... **ALS**
than: Scot. .... **NA**
thankless person .... **INGRATE**
that is: abbr. .... **E.G., I.E.**
that not .... **LEST**
that one: Lat. .... **ILLE**

163

That

a
that which follows .... **SEQUEL**
thatch, grass to .... **NETI**
thatching palm .... **NIPA**
the: Ger. .... **DAS, DER**
"The Ballad of Reading —"
                                      GAOL
"The Jairite" .... **IRA**
"The Lion of God" .... **ALI**
"The Red" .... **ERIC**
the same: Lat. .... **IDEM**
the squint .... **SKEN**
theatre .... **ODEA, ODEON,**
                  ODEUM, STAGE
theatre box seat .... **LOGE**
theatre district ...... **RIALTO**
theatre floor .... **PIT**
theatre, Grecian ...... **ODEA,**
                 ODEON, ODEUM
theatre group .... **ANTA**
theatre, part of Greek . **SKENE,**
     SCENA, SCENAE, SKENAI
theatre sign .... **SRO**
"Theban Bard" ...... **PINDAR**
Thebes deity ... **AMEN, AMON,**
   AMUN, MENT, AMENT, MENTU
Thebes, king of
         CREON, OEDIPUS
theme .... **MOTIF**
theme: music .... **TEMA**
then .... **ANON**

b
then: music .... **POI**
theoretical .... **PLATONIC**
there: Fr. .... **VOILA**
therefore .... **ERGO**
theseli veil ...... **TEMPE**
Theseus' father ..... **AEGEUS**
thesis, opp. of .... **ARSIS**
thespian .... **ACTOR**
Thessaly, king of .... **AEOLUS**
Thessaly mountain ...... **OSSA**
Thessaly valley .... **TEMPE**
they: Fr. .... **ILS**
thick-lipped .... **LABROSE**
thicket .. **BOSK, SHAW, COPSE,**
      COPPICE, SPINNEY
thicket: dialect .... **RONE**
thicket, game .... **COVERT**
thickness .... **PLY**
thief, gypsy .... **CHOR**
thief: Yiddish ...... **GANEF,**
          GANOF, GONOF
thigh bone .... **FEMUR**
thigh, of the ...... **FEMORAL**
thin ...... **LANK, LEAN, RARE,**
   SHEER, DILUTE, PAPERY,
     SPARSE, TENUOUS
thin cake .... **WAFER**
thin: comb. form .... **SERO**
thin disk .... **WAFER**
thin layer .... **FILM**

c
"Thin Man" dog ...... **ASTA**
"Thin Man" wife .... **NORA**
thin-toned .... **REEDY**
thin out .... **ATTENUATE**
thing: law (Latin) .... **RES**
things added ..... **ADDENDA**
things done .... **ACTA**
things to be done
     AGENDA, AGENDUM
think ... **DEEM, TROW, OPINE**
think: archaic .... **WIS**
think (over) .... **MULL, MUSE**
third: comb. form .... **TRIT**
third day, every .... **TERTIAN**
third king of Judah ...... **ASA**
third: music .... **TIERCE**
Third Reich special police: abbr.
                            SS
thirst-tortured king: Gr. myth
            TANTALUS
thirsty .... **DRY, ADRY**
thirty: Fr. .... **TRENTE**
thirty, series of .... **TRENTAL**
this: Fr. .... **CE**
this: Sp. .... **ESTA, ESTE**
this one: Lat. ..... **HIC, HAEC**
thither .... **THERE**
Thomas Hardy heroine ... **TESS**
thong .... **STRAP**
thong, braided .... **ROMAL**
thong-shaped .... **LORATE**

d
thong, S. Afr. .... **RIEM**
Thor's stepson ..... **ULL, ULLR**
Thor's wife .... **SIF**
thorax, crustacean's . **PEREION**
thorn ... **BRIAR, BRIER, SPINE**
thorn apple .... **METEL**
thorn, bearing a ..... **SPINATE**
thornback ray .. **DORN, ROKER**
Thorne Smith character. **TOPPER**
thorny plant ... **BRIAR, BRIER**
thorny shrub ... **NABK, NUBK**
thoroughfare .... **WAY, ROAD,**
        AVENUE, STREET
thoroughgoing ...... **ARRANT**
those .... **YON, YOND**
those in power or office ... **INS**
thou: Fr. .... **TU**
thought .... **IDEA**
thought: comb. form .... **IDEO**
thoughts, form .... **IDEATE**
thousand .... **MIL**
thousand: comb. form . **MILLE**
Thrace, ancient people of **EDONI**
thrall .... **ESNE, SLAVE**
thrash .... **LAM, BEAT**
thread: comb. form .... **NEMA**
thread, cotton .... **LISLE**
thread, guiding ball of .. **CLEW**
thread-like .... **NEMALINE**
thread-like process ..... **HAIR**

a
thread-like structure . . . . . **FILUM**
thread, of a . . . . **FILAR**
threads, cross . . . . **RETICLE**
threads crossed by woof. **WARP**
threads crossing warp . . . **WEFT, WOOF**
threads, lengthwise . . . . . . **WARP**
threaded fastener . . . . **NUT**
threaten . . . . **IMPEND, MENACE**
three . . . . **TER, TRIO, TRIAD**
three: Ger. . . . . **DREI**
three: Ital. . . . . **TRE**
three-legged stand . . . . **TRIPOD, TRIVET**
three-masted ship . . . . . . **XEBEC, FRIGATE**
3 parts, divided into: Her. **TIERCE**
3.1416 . . . . **PI**
three: Sp. . . . . **TRES**
three-spot . . . . **TREY**
threefold . . . . . **TRINE, TREBLE, TERNARY, TERNATE**
threefold: comb. form . . . . . **TER**
threshold . . . . **SILL**
threshold, psychology . . . **LIMEN**
thrice: music . . . . **TER**
thrifty . . . . **FRUGAL, SAVING**
thrive . . . . . **BATTEN, PROSPER**
b
throat . . . . **GORGE, GULLET**
throat: Lat. . . . . **GULA**
throat, pert. to . . . . **GULAR**
throb . . . . **BEAT, PULSE, PULSATE**
throe . . . . **PANG**
throng . . . . **MOB, HORDE, SWARM**
through . . . . **PER**
through: prefix . . . . **DIA**
throw . . . . **CAST, PITCH**
throw aside . . . . **FLING**
throw back . . . . **REPEL**
thrush . . . . **VEERY, MISSEL**
thrush, Hawaiian . . . . **OMAO**
thrush, India . . . . **SHAMA**
thrush, missel . . . **MAVIE, MAVIS**
thrust . . . . **LUNGE**
thrust back . . . . **REPEL**
thrust down . . . . **DETRUDE**
thunderfish . . . . **RAAD**
thurible . . . . **CENSER**
Thuringian city . . . . **JENA**
Thursday, source of name **THOR**
thus . . . . **SO, SIC**
thus far . . . . **YET**
thwart . . . . **FOIL**
Tiber tributary . . . . **NERA**
Tibetan chief . . . . **POMBO**
Tibetan ox . . . . **YAK**
Tibetan priest . . . . **LAMA**
Tibetan tribe . . . . **CHAMPA**

c
tibia . . . . **CNEMIS**
Tichborne Claimant . . . . . **ORTON**
tick . . . . **ACARID**
tick genus . . . . **ARGAS**
tick, S. Amer. . . . . **CARAPATO**
tickets, sell illegally . . . . . . **SCALP**
tickle . . . . **TITILLATE**
Ticonderoga's commander **GATES**
tidal flood . . . . . . **BORE, EAGRE**
tidal wave, flow or bore. **EAGRE**
tidbit . . . . **CATE**
tide, lowest high . . . . **NEAP**
tidings . . . . **NEWS, WORD**
tidings, glad . . . . **GOSPEL, EVANGEL, EVANGILE**
tidy . . . . **NEAT, REDO, TRIM**
tie . . . . **BIND, BOND, LASH, TRUSS, CRAVAT**
tie, kind of . . . . **ASCOT**
tie-breaking game . . . . . **RUBBER**
tie off . . . . **LIGATE**
tie, railroad . . . . **SLEEPER**
tier . . . . **ROW**
tiger cat, S. Amer. . . . . **CHATI**
tiger, Persian . . . . . . **SHER, SHIR**
tight . . . . . **SNUG, TAUT, TENSE**
tight place . . . . **FIX, JAM, MESS**
tighten: naut. . . . . **FRAP**
tightly stretched . . . . **TENSE**
til . . . . **SESAME**
d
tile, hexagonal . . . . **FAVI**
tile, roofing . . . . **PANTILE**
tilelike . . . . **TEGULAR**
till the earth . . . . . **FARM, PLOW**
tilled land . . . . . **ARADA, ARADO**
tiller . . . . **HELM**
tilt . . . . **TIP, CANT, LIST**
tilt . . . . **JOUST**
tilting: naut. . . . . **ALIST**
timber bend . . . . **SNY**
timber, flooring . . . . . . **BATTEN**
timber, nautical . . . . **KEVEL**
timber, pine: Asia . . . . . . **MATSU**
timber rot . . . . **DOAT, DOTE**
timber truck . . . . **WYNN**
timber wolf . . . . **LOBO**
timbrel . . . . . . **TABOR, TABOUR**
time . . . . . **ERA, TEMPI, TEMPO**
time before . . . . **EVE**
time being . . . . **NONCE**
time gone by . . . . **PAST**
time out . . . . **RECESS**
time, space of . . . . **WHILE**
time value, equalling in **DIMORIC**
times, old . . . . **ELD, YORE**
timid . . . . **SHY, PAVID**
timorous . . . . **TREPID**
timothy . . . . **HAY**
Timothy's grandmother: Bib. **LOIS**

a
tin .... **CAN, STANNUM**
tin, containing .... **STANNOUS**
tin foil .... **TAIN**
tin plate .... **TAIN**
tin roofing .... **TERNE**
tinamou .... **YUTU**
tincture: Her. ..... **OR, GULES,
VERT, AZURE, SABLE,
ARGENT, PURPURE**
tinder .... **PUNK, AMADOU**
tine .... **PRONG**
tine of antler .... **SNAG**
tinge .... **TAINT**
tinge deeply .... **IMBUE**
tingle of feeling ...... **THRILL**
tinkle .... **TING**
tiny bird, W. Ind. ...... **TODY**
tip .... **END, FEE, APEX, KNAP**
tip .... **CANT, LEAN,
TILT, CAREEN**
tipping .... **ALIST, ATILT**
tiptoe, on .... **ATIP**
tire .... **FAG, JADE**
tire casing .... **SHOE**
tire, face of .... **TREAD**
tire support .... **RIM**
tissue .... **TELA**
tissue, of a .... **TELAR**
tissue, pert. to .... **TELAR**
TITAN . see SPECIAL SECTION,
b
GREEK MYTH page 200
Titania's husband .... **OBERON**
titanic iron-ore sand . **ISERENE**
titlark .... **PIPIT**
title ..... **EARL, NAME, TERM**
title, baronet's .... **SIR**
title, Benedictine .... **DOM**
title, church .... **PRIMATE**
title, East .... **COJA, HOJA**
title, Ethiopian .... **RAS**
title Hindu gives Moslem
MIAN
title, India .... **AYA, NAWAB,
SAHEB, SAHIB**
title, Jewish . **RAB, REB, RABBI**
title, knight's .... **SIR**
title, king's .... **SIRE**
title, lady's .. **DAME, MADAM**
title, Moslem ...... **AGA, ALI,
MOLLA, MULLA,
SHERIF, SHEREFF**
title of address .. **MME., MRS.,
SIR, MAAM, MADAM**
title of honor, Moslem . **SAYID,
SAIYID, SAYYID**
title of kings of Edessa . **ABGAR**
title of respect ..... **SIR, SIRE,
MADAME**
title of respect, Afr. ..... **SIDI**

c
title of respect, India .... **SRI,
SHRI, SAHIB, SHREE,
HUZOOR**
title of respect, Malay .. **TUAN**
title, Oriental .... **BABA**
title, Persian **MIR, AZAM, KHAN**
title, Spanish **DOM, DON, SENOR**
title to property or land . **DEED**
title, Turkish .. **PACHA, PASHA**
titleholder .... **TITLIST**
titmice, genus of ...... **PARUS**
titmouse .... **MAG, PARUS**
tittle .... **JOT, IOTA, WHIT**
Titus Andronicus' daughter
LAVINIA
Tiwaz .... **ER, TIU**
to .... **FOR, UNTO**
to: prefix .... **AP**
to: Scot. .... **TAE**
to be: Fr. .... **ETRE**
to be: Lat. .... **ESSE**
"to be," part of ...... **AM, IS,
ARE, WAS**
to go: Fr. .... **ALLER**
to love: Fr. .... **AIMER**
to the point that ...... **UNTIL**
to use: Lat. .... **UTOR**
toad genus .... **BUFO**
toad, huge .... **AGUA**
toad, order of .... **ANURA**
d
toad, tree genus .... **HYLA**
toadfish .... **SAPO**
toast, bit of .... **SIPPET**
toasting word .... **SALUD,
SKOAL, PROSIT**
tobacco ash . **DOTTEL, DOTTLE**
tobacco, chewing .... **QUID**
tobacco, coarse
SHAG, CAPORAL
tobacco, Cuban .... **CAPA**
tobacco, low grade ...... **SHAG**
tobacco, Peru .... **SANA**
tobacco, roll .... **CIGAR**
toddy palm juice .... **SURA**
toe .... **DIGIT**
toe, fifth .... **MINIMUS**
toe: Scot. .... **TAE**
togs .... **DUDS**
toilet case .... **ETUI**
Tokyo Bay city .... **CHIBI**
Tokyo, old name ... **EDO, YEDO**
tolerable .... **SOSO**
toll .... **FEE, KNELL**
Tolstoi heroine .... **ANNA**
tomb, Moslem **TABUT, TABOOT**
tomboy .... **HOIDEN, HOYDEN**
tomcat .... **GIB**
tone down .... **SOFTEN**
tone, lack of .... **ATONY**
tone, of .... **TONAL**
tone quality .... **TIMBRE**

a tone: Scot. .... TEAN
tones, series of ...... OCTAVE
tongue, gypsy .... CHIB
tongue of Agni .... KALI
tongue, pert. to ..... GLOSSAL
tongue, using the ..... APICAL
tongue, wagon .... NEAP
tonic .... ROBORANT
tonic, dried India
    CHIRATA, CHIRETTA
tonic herb ...... ALOE, TANSY
Tonkin native .... THO
too early .... PREMATURE
too much: Fr. .... TROP
tool, boring .... AWL, BIT,
    AUGER, GIMLET
tool, cutting .. AX, ADZ, AXE,
    HOB, SAW, SAX, SYE, ADZE
tool, engraver's
    BURIN, MATTOIR
tool, enlarging ...... REAMER
tool, grass-cutting ..... SITHE,
    SCYTHE, SICKLE
tool, machine .... LATHE
tool, molding .... DIE
tool, pointed .... BROACH
tool, post hole digging .... LOY
tool shaper .... SWAGER
tool, splitting .... FROE, FROW
b tool, stone, prehistoric
    CELT, EQLITH
tool, threading ...... CHASER
tool's biting edge .... BIT
tooth ..... COG, TINE, MOLAR,
    CANINE, CUSPID, FANG
tooth-billed pigeon ... DODLET
tooth, canine .... CUSPID
tooth: comb. form .... ODONT
tooth, gear .... COG
tooth: Lat. .... DENS
tooth-like ornament .. DENTIL
tooth, long FANG, TUSH, TUSK
tooth pulp .... NERVE
toothed formation ..... SERRA
toothed margin, having
    DENTATE
toothed wheel .... GEAR
toothless .... EDENTATE
toothless mammals . EDENTATA
top .... APEX, CAP, LID
top-notch .... AONE
top ornament ..... EPI, FINIAL
topaz humming bird ..... AVA
topee material .... SOLA
toper .... SOT, SOUSE
topic .... THEME
topmast crossbar support .. FID
topsail .... RAFFE
torment .... BAIT, ANNOY,
    DEVIL, HARRY, TEASE
torn: archaic .... REFT

c torn place .... RENT
torrid region or zone .. TROPIC
tortoise .... GALAPAGO
tortoise, fresh water .... EMYD
tortoise, marsh genus ... EMYS
tortoise, order of ... CHELONIA
torturer .... RACKER
"Tosca" villain ...... SCARPIA
toss ...... CAST, FLIP, HURL,
    FLING, PITCH
tosspot ... . SOT
total ...... ADD, SUM, UTTER
total abstinence .. NEPHALISM
totalitarian ruler ... DICTATOR
totem pole .... XAT
toucan .... TOCO
toucan, S. Am. .... ARACARI
touch .... ABUT
touch lightly .... PAT
touch, organ of .... PALP
touch, pert. to HAPTIC, TACTIC,
    TACTILE, TACTUAL
touch sense, pert. to .. HAPTIC
touchwood .... PUNK
tough .... WIRY, HARDY,
    ROWDY, CHEWY
tour: It. .... GIRO
tourmaline, colorless
    ACHROITE
d tow .... PULL, DRAW
towai .... KAMAHI
toward: Lat. .... AD
toward stern ..... AFT, ABAFF,
    ABAFT, ASTERN
towel .... WIPER
towel fabric .... HUCK, TERRY
tower, Bibl. .... BABEL
tower, India .... MINAR
tower, little .... TURRET
tower, mosque, slender
    MINARET
towering .... STEEP
towhead .... BLOND, BLONDE
town, Arcadia ancient ... ALEA
town: Cornish prefix ..... TRE
town: Dutch .... STAD
town: Ger. .... STADT
town, India pilgrimage . SORON
town: It. .... CASAL, CASALE
town: Jap. .... MACHI
town: suffix .... TON
township, ancient Attica . DEME
townsman .... CIT
toxic protein .... ABRIN
toy with .... TRIFLE
trace .... TINGE, VESTIGE
track .... TRACE
track, animal ... RUN, SLOT,
    SPUR, SPOOR
track circuit .... LAP

a track of ship .... **WAKE**
track, deer's .... **SLOT**
track, otter's .... **SPUR, SPOOR**
track, put off .... **DERAIL**
track, put on another
     SHUNT, SWITCH
tracker, India .... **PUGGI**
tract .... **LOT, AREA**
tract of farm land ...... **FIELD**
trade .... **SWAP, SWOP**
     BARTER, TRAFFIC
trade .... **METIER**
trade agreement ..... **CARTEL**
trader ..... **DEALER, MONGER**
trader selling to soldiers
     SUTLER
trading exchange .... **PIT**
trading vessel of Ceylon
     DONI, DHONI
traditional story .... **SAGA**
traduce .... **SLUR, DEFAME**
traffic .... **TRADE**
trail .... **SLOT, SPOOR, TRACK**
train of attendants
     SUITE, RETINUE
train, overhead .... **EL**
train, slow, many-stops . **LOCAL**
tramp .... **BO, HOBO**
trample .... **TREAD**
tranquil or tranquilize
b   **SERENE, SOOTHE**
transaction ...... **DEAL, SALE**
transfer .... **CEDE**
transfer, property
     DEED, GRANT
transfer, sovereignty .. **DEMISE**
transferer, property .. **ALIENOR**
transform .... **CONVERT**
transgress .... **ERR, SIN**
transit coach .... **BUS**
"— transit gloria mundi" . **SIC**
translator of Freud, Amer.
     BRILL
transmit .... **SEND**
transom .... **TRAVE**
transpire .... **OCCUR, HAPPEN,**
     DEVELOP
transverse pin .... **TOGGLE**
trap .... **SNARE, ENSNARE**
trap door .... **DROP**
trap, mouse: dial. .... **TIPE**
trap, rabbit: dial. ...... **TIPE**
trappings .... **REGALIA**
travel .... **TREK**
traveler .... **PASSENGER**
tray .... **SALVER, SERVER**
tread softly ...... **PAD, SNEAK**
treasure .... **ROON, TROVE**
treasurer, college ..... **BURSAR**
treasury agents .... **TMEN**
treat .... **USE**

c treat with acid ..... **ACIDIZE**
treat with malice .... **SPITE**
treatment .... **USE**
tree   (3 letters) **ASH, ELM,**
    FIR, LIN, OAK, YEW;
    (4 letters) **AKEE, AMLA,**
    AMLI, ANAM, ANDA,
    ARAR, ASAK, AULU, AUSU,
    AUZU, BARU, BIJA, BITO,
    BIWA, BOBO, BOGO, DALI,
    DILO, DOON, DOUM, DUKU,
    EBOE, EJOO, GOAI, GUAO,
    HINO, IFIL, IPIL, KINO,
    KIRI, KOPI, KOZO, LIME,
    LINN, MAKO, MYXA,
    NAIO, NEEM, NIOG, NIPA,
    ODUM, OHIA, PALM, PELU,
    PINE, PUKA, RATA, RIMU,
    ROKA, SAUL, SHEA, SUPA,
    TALA, TARA, TAWA, TEAK,
    TEIL, TEYL, TOON, TORO,
    TUNG, TUNO, TUWI, UPAS,
    WHAU, YATE, YAYA, YPIL;
    (5 letters) **ASPEN;** (6 let-
    ters) **LINDEN**
tree, African .... **AKEE, BAKU,**
    COLA, KOLA, ROKA,
    SHEA, AEGLE, ARTAR
d tree, Afr. & Asia .... **SIRIS**
tree, Afr. gum .... **BUMBO**
tree, Afr. tallow .... **ROKA**
TREE, AMER. TROPICAL...see
    TREE, TROPICAL AMER.
tree, Argentine timber ... **TALA**
TREE, ASIATIC .. see ASIATIC
    TREE
tree, arrow poison ...... **UPAS**
TREE, AUSTRAL. .... see
    AUSTRAL. TREE
tree, Bengal quince ...... **BEL**
tree, black gum ...... **TUPELO**
tree, body of .... **TRUNK**
tree, boxwood yielding . **SERON**
tree, buckwheat .... **TITI**
tree, butter .... **SHEA**
tree, caucho-yielding ..... **ULE**
tree, chicle .... **SAPOTA**
tree, Chin. ... **GINKO, GINKGO**
tree clump, prairie .... **MOTTE**
tree cobra .... **MAMBA**
tree, coniferous (cone) .. **FIR,**
    YEW, PINE, LARCH
TREE. E. IND. ... see E. IND.
    TREE and TREE, IND.
TREE, EVERGREEN .... see
    EVERGREEN
tree, flowering ..... **CATALPA**
tree genus .... **MABA**
tree genus, Afr. .... **OCHNA**

a tree genus, elms
ULMUS, CELTIS
tree genus, small ... CATALPA
tree, gum .... ICICA
tree, hardwood ASH, OAK, IPIL
tree, India .... DAR, MEE, SAJ,
SAL, AMLA, AMLI, DHAK,
MYXA, NEEM, SHOQ, MA-
HUA, BANYAN
tree knot .... BURL
tree, locust .... ACACIA
tree, maidenhair ..... GINKGO
tree, Malay .... TERAP
tree, Medit. .... CAROB
tree, mimosaceous ...... SIRIS
tree moss .... USNEA
tree, N. Am.
TAMARAC, TAMARACK
TREE, N. Z.
see NEW ZEALAND TREE
tree, oak .... ENCINA
tree of olive family ..... ASH
tree, Pacific .... KOU
tree, palm .. GRIGRI, GRUGRU
tree, palm, Asiatic .... ARENG
TREE, P.I. ..... see P. I. TREE
tree, pod .... CAROB
tree, resinous .... FIR, PINE,
BALSAM
tree, showy Asia .... ASAK
b tree-snake .... LORA
tree, sun, Jap. .... HINOKI
tree, swamp .... ALDER
tree, tamarisk salt ...... ATLE
tree, tea .... TI
tree, thorny .... ACACIA
tree tiger .... LEOPARD
tree toad genus .... HYLA
tree, tropical .... EBOE, PALM,
BALSA, MANGO, COLIMA,
SAPOTA, LEBBEK
tree, tropical Amer. CEBA, DALI,
GUAO, CEIBA, COLIMA,
GUAMA, CEDRON
tree trunk .... BOLE
tree, W. Ind. .... GENIP,
SAPOTE, LIBIDIBI
trees of a region .... SILVA
treeless plain .... PAMPAS,
TUNDRA, STEPPES
tremble ...... QUAKE, DIDDER
trembling ..... ASPEN, TREPID
trench .... SAP
trench extension .... SAP
trench, rear wall of .. PARADOS
trend .... TENOR
trespass .. INFRINGE, INTRUDE

c trespass for game .... POACH
trespass to recover goods
TROVER
triad .... TRIO
trial .... TEST
triangle .... TRIGON, SCALENE
triangle, side of .... LEG
triangular insert .... GORE
tribal symbol .... TOTEM
TRIBE
see also SPECIAL SECTION
tribe ...... CLAN, FOLK, RACE
TRIBE, BIBLICAL .... see
SPECIAL SECTION
tribe: Bib. tent-dwellers.KEDAR
tribe division, Rom.
CURIA, CURIAE
TRIBE, ISRAELITE .... see
ISRAELITE TRIBE
TRIBESMAN .. see TRIBES in
SPECIAL SECTION
tribulation .... TRIAL
tribunal .... BAR, FORUM
tribute .... SCAT, SCATT
tribute: Gaelic .... CAIN
trick FLAM, GAWD, JEST, RUSE,
WILE, DODGE, FICELLE,
STRATAGEM
tricks, game for no .... NULLO
tricks, win all .... CAPOT
d Trieste measure .. ORNA, ORNE
trifle ...... TOY, DOIT, FICO,
STRAW, NIGGLE, PALTER
trifling ...... SMALL, SLIGHT
trig .... NEAT, TRIM
trigonometry function
SINE, COSINE
trigonometry line ..... SECANT
trill, bird's .... TIRALEE
trim .... NEAT, TRIG,
ADORN, DECORATE
trimmed .... SNOD
trimming, dress . GIMP, RUCHE
trimmings, overlapping . FLOTS
Trinidad tree .... CYP
trinket .... GAUD
triple .... TRI, TREBLE
triplet .... TRIN
tripletail, P. R. .... SAMA
tripod, 6-footed .... CAT
Tripoli: measure . see page 188
"Tristram Shandy" author
STERNE
Tristram's beloved .... ISOLT,
YSEUT, ISAUDE, ISAULT,
ISEULT, ISOLDE, ISOLTA,
ISOUDE, ISULTE
trite .. BANAL, CORNY, STALE
triton ...... EFT, EVET, NEWT

a troche ...... **PASTIL, ROTULA,**
PASTILE, PASTILLE
TROJAN .... see also TROY
Trojan hero .. **PARIS, ENEAS,**
AENEAS, AGENOR, DARDAN,
HECTOR, HEKTOR, ACHILLES
trolley .... **TRAM**
troop-carrying group: abbr.
ATS
troop, division, Gr. .... **TAXIS**
troops .... **MEN**
troops, spread .... **DEPLOY**
trophy .... **CUP**
tropic .... **SOLAR**
tropical Am. bird genus
CACICUS
tropical disease . **BUBA, BUBAS**
tropical fever .... **DENGUE**
TROPICAL FRUIT .... see
FRUIT, TROPICAL
tropical plant .... **TARO**
tropical shrub genus **INGA, SIDA**
trot .... **JOG, AMBLE**
trouble ... **ADO, AIL, WORRY,**
EFFORT, MOLEST
troubles .... **ILLS**
troublesome person
PEST, AGITATOR
trough, inclined ...... **CHUTE**
trough, mining .... **SLUICE**
b trout, British .. **SEWEN, SEWIN**
trout, brook .... **CHAR**
trowel, plasterers' ..... **DARBY**
Troy .... **ILION, ILIUM**
Troy, founder of .... **ILUS**
Troy, land of .... **TROAS**
Troy, last king of ...... **PARIS,**
PRIAM, PRIAMOS
Troy, of ancient **ILIAC, ILIAN**
Troy: poetic .... **ILIUM**
truant, play: Scot. .... **TRONE**
truck .... **LORRY, CAMION**
trudge .... **PACE, PLOD, SLOG**
true copy: law .... **ESTREAT**
true olives .... **OLEA**
trumpet ..... **HORN, CLARION**
trumpet call, reveille .... **DIAN**
trumpet, mouth of .... **CODON**
trumpet shell .... **TRITON**
trumpeter perch .... **MADO**
trumpeter, pigeon-like . **AGAMI**
trundle, as ore .... **RULL**
trunk of body .... **TORSO**
trunkfish .... **CHAPIN**
truss up .... **TIE**
trust .... **RELY, TROW,**
RELIANCE
trustee of a wakf.**MUTAWALLI**
trusting .... **RELIANT**
truth: Chin. .... **TAO**

c truth drug ...... **PENTOTHAL**
Truth personified .... **UNA**
try .... **TEST, ESSAY, ATTEMPT**
try to equal ... **VIE, EMULATE**
tsetse fly .... **MAU, KIVU**
tsetse fly genus .... **GLOSSINA**
tub .... **VAT, KNAP, KNOP**
tub, brewer's .... **KEEVE**
tub, broad .... **KEELER**
tub, wooden: dialect ...... **SOE**
tube .... **DUCT**
tube, glass ... **PIPET, PIPETTE**
tube, plane's .... **PITOT**
tuber delicacy .... **TRUFFLE**
tuber, edible **OCA, OKA, YAM,**
TARO, POTATO
tuber, orchid .... **SALEP**
tuber, S. Amer. .... **OCA, OKA**
Tuesday, god who gave name to
TIU, TYR
tuft .... **CREST**
tuft: bot. .... **COMA**
tufted plant .... **MOSS**
tulip tree .... **POPLAR**
TUMERIC ..... see TURMERIC
tumor .... **OMA, WEN**
tumor, skin .... **WEN**
tumult .... **RIOT**
tune .... **AIR, ARIA,**
SONG, MELODY
tune, bagpipe .... **PORT**
d tune: Scot. .... **PORT**
tungstite ..... **OCHER, OCHRE**
tuning fork ...... **DIAPASON**
Tunis, ruler of ...... **BEY, DEY**
tunnel, train, Alps .... **CENIS**
tunny .... **AMIA, TUNA**
turban, Oriental .... **MANDIL**
turbid, make .... **ROIL**
turf .... **SOD**
turf, bit of: golf ...... **DIVOT**
Turkestan town dwellers . **SART**
turkey buzzard .... **AURA**
turkey red .... **MADDER**
turkeys, collection of .. **RAFTER**
Turkic person **TATAR, TARTAR**
Turkic person, 8th century
OGOR
Turkish army corps ..... **ORDU**
Turkish army officer ..... **AGA**
Turkish caliph .... **ALI**
Turkish chamber .. **ODA, ODAH**
Turkish chieftain ...... **AMIR,**
ZAIM, AMEER
Turkish commander . **AGA, ALI**
Turkish copper coin .... **PARA**
Turkish decree .... **IRADE**
Turkish flag .... **ALEM**
Turkish general .... **AGA**
Turkish gold coin .... **LIRA,**
ALTUN, MAHBUB

a Turkish government .... **PORTE**
Turkish govt. summer residence
YALI
Turkish governor .. **VALI, WALI**
Turkish hostelry ..... **IMARET**
Turkish judge .... **CADI, KADI**
Turkish leader .... **AGA**
Turkish liquor .... **MASTIC**
Turkish magistrate. **CADI, KADI**
Turkish military district . **ORDO**
Turkish money of account
ASPER
Turkish officer .. **AGA, AGHA**
Turkish oxcart . **ARBA, ARABA**
Turkish palace .... **SERAI**
Turkish pavilion .... **KIOSK**
Turkish president, former
INONU
Turkish regiment .... **ALAI**
Turkish standard . **ALEM, TOUG**
Turkish sultan .... **SELIM**
Turkish title .... **AGA, AGHA,**
BABA, EMIR, EMEER,
PASHA, BASHAW
Turkish tribesman ..... **TATAR**
Turkish tribesman, Persia
GHUZ
Turkoman tribesman **SEID, SHIK**
turmeric .... **REA, ANGO**
b turmoil .... **WELTER**
turn ..... **BEND, GYRE, VEER,**
ROTATE, SWERVE
turn aside.**SKEW, VEER, SHUNT**
turn back to .... **REVERT**
turn direction .... **VERT**
turn inside out .... **EVERT**
turn over: mus. .... **VERTE**
turning point ... **CRISES, CRISIS**
turning: prefix .... **ROTO**
turnover .... **PIE**
turnip ... **BAGA, NEEP, SWEDE**
turnip: Scot. .... **NEEP**
turpentine derivative
ROSIN, PINENE
turpentine distillate .... **ROSIN**
turpentine resin
ALK, GALLIPOT, GALIPOT
turtle, Amazon .... **ARRAU**
turtle, edible
TERAPIN, TERRAPIN
turtle, edible part of . **CALIPEE**
turtle enclosure ...... **CRAWL**
turtle genus .... **EMYS**
turtle, hawkbill .... **CARET**
turtle, order of .... **CHELONIA**
Tuscany art city ...... **SIENA**
tusk, elephant .... **IVORY**
tutelary god ..... **LAR, LARES**
tutor .... **TUTE**

c TV advertiser ...... **SPONSOR**
"Twelfth Night" clown .. **FESTE**
"Twelfth Night" heroine
VIOLA
twelve and one-half cents . **BIT**
twenty-fourth part
CARAT, KARAT
twenty quires .... **REAM**
twice .... **BIS**
twice: prefix .... **BI**
twig, willow .. **WITHE, WITHY**
twilight .... **EVE, DUSK,**
GLOAM, EVENTIDE
twilled coth .... **REP**
twilled wool fabric ..... **SERGE**
twin .... **GEMEL**
twin crystal .... **MACLE**
twin gods, Teut. .... **ALCIS**
twine .... **COIL, WIND, TWIST**
twining stem .... **BINE**
twist ..... **PLY, COIL, FEAK,**
KINK, SKEW, GNARL,
WREATHE, CONTORT
twist inwards .... **INTORT**
twist out of shape ..... **WARP**
twisted .... **AWRY, SKEW,**
TORTILE
twisted roll of fibers .... **SLUB**
twisted spirally .... **TORSE**
twitch .... **TIC**
d twitching .... **TIC**
two .... **DUO, DUAD, PAIR**
two ears, affecting the **DIOTIC**
two elements, having . **BINARY**
two feet, verse of ..... **DIPODY**
two-footed ... **BIPED, BIPEDAL**
two-horse chariot .... **BIGA**
two-hulled boat . **CATAMARAN**
two-masted ship . **YAWL, ZULU**
two-month period .. **BIMESTER**
two, music for .... **DUET**
two notes, group of .... **DUOLE**
two-pronged, as sponges
DICELLATE
two-pronged weapon .. **BIDENT**
two-spot .... **DEUCE**
two tenacles, having.**DICEROUS**
two-toed sloth .... **UNAU**
two-wheeled vehicle **GIG, CART**
two-year-old sheep
TEG, TEGG, BIDENT
"Two Years Before the Mast"
author .... **DANA**
twofold .. **DUAL, TWIN, BINAL**
twofold: prefix .... **DI**
tycoon .... **NABOB**
tymp arch of furnace ... **FAULD**
Tyndareus, wife of ..... **LEDA**
type collection .... **FONT**

Type

U

a unfadable .... **FAST**
unfair move .... **FOUL**
unfair shove in marbles . **FULK**
unfasten ..... **UNTIE, LOOSEN**
unfavorable .... **BAD, ILL**
unfeeling ... **HARSH, CALLOUS**
unfermented grape juice
       STUM
unfit to eat, make . **DENATURE**
unfledged bird .... **EYAS**
unfold .... **EVOLVE**
unguent, Roman wrestlers'
       CEROMA
ungula .. **CLAW, HOOF, NAIL**
ungulate, S. Am. ...... **TAPIR**
unhappy .... **SAD, BLUE,**
    MOROSE, RUEFUL
unicorn fish ...... **LIJA, UNIE**
uniform .... **EVEN**
uniform in hue .. **FLAT, FLOT**
uninteresting .... **DULL**
union .... **MERGER**
union, labor ... **AFL, CIO, ILA,**
     ITA, ILGWU
union, political .... **BLOC**
union, Russ. workers' ... **ARTEL**
unique person .... **ONER**
unique thing: slang ..... **ONER**
unit .... **ACE, ONE**
b unit of capacity ...... **FARAD**
unit of conductance ..... **MHO**
unit of electrical intensity:
 abbr. .... **AMP**
unit of electrical resistance or
 reluctance .... **REL**
unit of electricity . **OHM, WATT,**
    FARAD, WEBER
unit of electromotive force
       VOLT
unit of energy .... **ERG,**
    RAD, ERGON
unit of fluidity .... **RHE**
unit of force .... **DYNE**
unit of heat .... **CALORIE**
unit of illumination ..... **PHOT**
unit of jet propulsion .... **JATO**
unit of light .... **PYR, LUMEN,**
     HEFNER
unit of power .... **DYNE**
unit of power, electric ... **OHM,**
   WATT, FARAD, WEBER
unit of pressure **BARAD, BARIE**
unit of reluctance .... **REL**
unit of resistance .... **OHM**
unit of weight .... **WEY**
unit of work ..... **ERG, ERGON**
unit, pert. to ...... **MONADIC**
unit, power ratio .... **BEL**

c unite .... **WED, ALLY, JOIN,**
  KNIT, WELD, YOKE,
  MERGE, INTEGRATE
unite edges .... **RABBET**
UNITED STATES
   see **AMERICAN**
unity .... **ONE**
univalent element .... **MONAD**
universal .. **WORLD, GENERAL**
universal language ... **RO, IDO**
universe .... **WORLD, COSMOS**
universe: Hindu .... **LOKA**
universe, pert. to ..... **COSMIC**
university degree-holder
    LICENTIATE
University in Conn. ..... **YALE**
unkeeled .... **RATITE**
unkind .... **ILL**
unknown Hindu god ...... **KA**
unless .... **BUT, SAVE**
unless: Lat. .... **NISI**
unlock .... **OPE, OPEN**
unmarried .... **CELIBATE**
unmatched .... **ODD**
unmixed .... **PURE, SHEER**
unmusical clang ...... **TONK**
unnecessary .... **NEEDLESS**
unplowed strip .... **HADE**
unpredictable .... **ERRATIC**
d unprincipled person .... **CAD,**
  SCAMP, BOUNDER,
   REPROBATE
unprofitable, as rents .... **SECK**
unrefined .... **EARTHY**
unrelenting . **IRON, ADAMANT**
unruffled ..... **CALM, SERENE**
unruly outbreak .... **RIOT**
unruly person .... **RANTIPOLE**
unsophisticated .... **NAIVE**
unsorted flour .... **ATA, ATTA**
unspoken .... **TACIT**
unstable ... **ASTATIC, ERRATIC**
unsuitable ..... **INAPT, INEPT**
untamed .... **WILD, FERAL**
untidy person .... **SLOB**
untidiness .... **MESS, MUSS**
until .... **TILL**
untrained .... **RAW**
unusual .... **RARE, EXOTIC**
unusual person or thing . **ONER**
unwavering .... **SURE, STEADY**
unwholesome .... **ILL**
unwieldly thing .... **HULK**
unwilling .... **LOTH, LOATH,**
    AVERSE
unwilling, be: archaic ... **NILL**
unyielding .. **FIRM, ADAMANT**
unyielding: naut. .... **FAST**

a up: comb. form .... ANO
Upanishad .... ISHA
upland plain .... WOLD
upbraid ...... CHIDE, SCOLD,
REPROACH
upon ...... EPI, ATOP, ONTO
upon: law .... SUR
Upper Nile Negro ...... MADI
Upper Nile tribesman ... MADI
Upper Silurian .... ONTARIAN
uppermost part .... TOP
upright ...... ERECT, HONEST
upright column .... STELE
upright piece .... JAMB, STUD
uprising .... REVOLT
uproar .... DIN
upward, heave: naut. ... SCEND
uraeus .... ASP
Uranus' satellite .... ARIEL
urban office-holder ... MAYOR
urchin ..... IMP, TAD, GAMIN
Urfa, modern .... EDESSA
urge .... EGG, PLY, YEN,
IMPEL, PRESS
urge: Scot. .... ERT

c urial .... SHA
urticaria .... HIVES
urus .... TUR
us: Ger. .... UNS
usage .... WONT
use a divining rod ..... DOWSE
use, be of .... AVAIL
use exertions .... STRIVE
use one's efforts .... EXERT
used up ...... ATE, DEPLETED
useful ..... UTILE, PRACTICAL
useless .... IDLE, FUTILE,
OTIOSE, INUTILE
usual .... NORMAL
Utah State flower .... SEGO
utmost .... LAST, FINAL,
GREATEST
utmost hyperbole .... ELA
utter .... SAY, SHEER,
SPEAK, STARK
utter, as greeting .... BID
utter loudly ..... VOCIFERATE
uttered ... ORAL, SAID, SPOKE
utterly .... STARK
Uz, brother of .... ARAN

V

b V-shaped piece ...... WEDGE
vacant .... IDLE, EMPTY
vacuum .... VOID
vacuum, opposite of .. PLENUM
vacuum tube .... DIODE
vagabond . VAG, HOBO, TRAMP
vague .... HAZY, LOOSE
vainglory .... PRIDE
valance, short .... PELMET
vale ..... DALE, DELL, VALLEY
Vali, mother of .... RIND
valiant ... BRAVE, STALWART
Valkyrie .... DIS, NORN
valley ..... DALE, DELL, VAIL,
VALE, GLADE
valley, deep .... COULEE
valley, Jordan .... GHOR
value .... RATE, PRIZE,
WORTH, APPRAISE
value, thing of little ... TRIFLE
valve .... COCK
vampire .... LAMIA
van .... FORE
vandal .... HUN
vanish .... EVANESCE
vanity .... PRIDE
vanity case .... ETUI
vantage, place of ...... COIGN
vapid .... INANE, STALE

d vapor .... STEAM
vapor: comb. form ..... ATMO
vapor: dialect.......... ROKE
vapor in air ...... HAZE, MIST
Varangians .... ROS
variable .... PROTEAN
variable, most ...... PROTEAN
variable star ... MIRA, NOVA
variation, small
SHADE, NUANCE
variegated .... SHOT
variegated in color
PIED, CALICO
variety .... KIND
variety of bean
SOY, LIMA, PINTO
various: comb. form
VARI, VARIO
varnish ingredient
LAC, COPAL, RESIN
varnish, kind of
SHELLAC, SHELLACK
varnish material .... ELEMI
vase .... URN
vat ...... BAC, TUB, CISTERN
vat, beer ... GAAL, GAIL, GYLE
vat, brewer's ... KIVE, KEEVE
vat, large .... KEIR, KIER
vault .... SAFE

a vault, church .... CRYPT
vaulted alcove .... APSE
vaunt .... BRAG, BOAST
vector, that which turns a
                        VERSOR
Vedic dialect .... PALI
VEDIC GODS
            see SPECIAL SECTION
veer ..... SHY, TURN, SHIFT
veer off .... SHEER
vegetable ... PEA, BEAN, BEET,
    KALE, OCRA, OKRA, OKRO,
    CHARD, ENDIVE, TOMATO,
    WOBBIE, CELTUCE
vegetable fuel .... PEAT
vegetables, pod .... PEASE
vehicle .... CAR, CART,
            CYCLE, HANSOM
vehicle, Am. Ind.
        TRAVOIS, TRAVOISE
vehicle 4-wheeled .... LANDAU
vehicle, light, India ... TONGA
vehicle, Near East ..... ARABA
vehicle, Russ. .... TROIKA
vehicle, war .... TANK
veil, chalice .... AER
vein: Lat. .... VENA
b vein of body .... CAVA
vein, ore .... LODE, SCRIN
vein, ore: prov. Eng. .... ROKE
vein, ore beside .... RIDER
vein, throat .... JUGULAR
vellum .... PARCHMENT
velocity per second ..... VELO
velum .... PALATE
velvet .... PANNE
velvet grass .... HOLCUS
vend .... SELL
vendetta .... FEUD
venerable .... OLD, HOARY
"Venerable" monk ...... BEDE
venerate ..... ESTEEM, REVERE
veneration .... AWE
Venetian nobleman ..... DOGE
Venetian painter ..... TITIAN
Venetian red .... SIENA
Venetian resort .... LIDO
Venetian rose .... SIENA
Venetian traveler ...... POLO
Venezuela copper center AROA
Venezuela Ind. language PUME
vengeance goddess ...... ARA
Venice marble bridge ..RIALTO
Venice canals .... RII
Venice district .... RIALTO
ventral .... HEMAD, HAEMAD
venture .... DARE

c Venus, island of ..... MELOS
Venus' son .... CUPID
Venus, youth loved by ADONIS
veranda, Dutch, S. Afr. STOEP
veranda, Hawaii ...... LANAI
veranda, India .... PYAL
verb form .... IS, AM, ARE,
                    WAS, TENSE
verbal .... ORAL
verbal ending .. ED, ER, ES, ING
verbal noun .... GERUND
verbal rhythm .... METRE
verbally .... ALOUD
Verdi heroine .... AIDA
verily .... YEA, AMEN
verity .... TRUTH
versatile .... MOBILE
verse .... LINE, STICH
verse, Fr. .... RONDEL
verse, Ir. .... RANN
verse, pert. to kind of IAMBIC
version, Bible .... ITALA
vertebral bones SACRA, SACRUM
verticle line, in a ..... APEAK
verticle timber: naut. ... BITT
vertigo .... DINUS
very .... SO
very abundant ... LUXURIANT
very: Fr. .... TRES
very: Scot. .... VERA
d very: Span. .... MUY
Ve's brother .... ODIN
vesicle, skin .... BLISTER
VESSEL .. see also BOAT, SHIP,
    GALLEY
vessel .... ARK
vessel, anat. ...... VAS, VASA
vessel, Arab .... DOW, DHOW
vessel, chemical .... ETNA
vessel, coasting, E. Ind.
                    PATAMAR
vessel, cooking .... PAN, POT
vessel, drinking ...... GOURD
vessel for liquors .. DECANTER
vessel, glass .... BOCAL
vessel, Gr. CADUS, AMPHORA
vessel, heating .... ETNA
vessel, large .... TANK
vessel, liquor .... FLAGON
vessel, Medit. .. SETEE, MISTIC
vessel, Rom. .... PATERA
vessel, sacred ..... PIX, PYX
vessel, sailing .... SAIC,
                    SETEE, XEBEC
vessel, shallow .... BASIN
vessel, supply .... COALER
vessel, 3-masted
            XEBEC, FRIGATE
vessel, 2-masted YAWL, ZULU

175

Vessel

a vessel with two handles, Gr.
DIOTA
vessel's curved planking .. SNY
vestal .... CHASTE
vestige .. IOTA, RELIC, TRACE
vestment .. ALB, COPE, AMICE,
EPHOD, STOLE
vestment, white .. ALB, AMICE
vesuvianite, brown ... EGERAN
vetch .... TARE
vetch, bitter .... ERS
vetch, India .... AKRA
vetiver, grass .... BENA
vex GALL, RILE, ROIL, HARRY
vex persistently ...... NETTLE
vex: Scot. .... FASH
vexed .... RILY
via .... PER
viands .... DIET
viands, dainty .... CATES
Viaud's pseudonym ..... LOTI
vibrate .... THRILL
vibration: music .... TREMOLO
vice .... SIN
viceroy .... VALI
Vichy Premier .... LAVAL
vicious man .... YAHOO
victim .... PREY
victorfish .... AKU
victor's crown .... LAUREL
victory, Eng. .. CRECY, CRESSY
victory trophy .... SCALP

b victuals .... FOOD
"— victus," woe to the con-
quered .... VAE
"—vide," "which see" .. QUAE
vie with .... EMULATE
Viennese park .... PRATER
view .... SCENE, VISTA
vigilant .... WARY, ALERT
vigor .... PEP, VIM,
VIS, ZIP, FORCE
Viking ... ERIC, OLAF, ROLLO
Viking explorer .... ERIC
vilify .... REVILE
village .. DORP, VILL, HAMLET
village, Afr. .... KRAAL
village, Java .... DESSA
village, Russ. .... MIR
village, Scot. .... REW
village, S. Afr. native ... STAD
villain .... KNAVE
villein .... CEORL
vindicate .... AVENGE
vindication .... REVENGE
vine .... IVY, BINE
vine: comb. form .... VITI
vine, N. Z. .... AKA
vine, P. I. .... IYO

c vine, woody .. ABUTA, LIANA
"vin du —," wine of the
country .... CRU
vinegar of ale .... ALEGAR
vinegar, pert. to ...... ACETIC
vinegar worm .... EEL, NEMA
vinous .... WINY
viol, ancient type ...... REBEC
viol, bass .... GAMBA
viol, Shetlands .... GUE
viola .... ALTO
violent .... HOT
violet-odored ketone .. IRONE
violin, bass .... CELLO
violin, early .. REBAB, REBEC
violin, famous .... STRAD
violin, It. .. AMATI, CREMONA
violin, small .... KIT
violin, tenor .... ALTO, VIOLA
violinist ...... ELMAN, YSAYE
viper .... ASP, ADDER
viper genus .... ECHIS
viper, horned ...... CERASTES
Virgil's hero .. ENEAS, AENEAS
Virgin Mary pictured mourning
PIETA
virus-fighting substance
ANTIVIRAL
visage .... FACE
viscous
d LIMY, ROPY, SIZY, SLIMY
viscous substance .. TAR, SLIME
Vishnu, incarnation, 7th RAMA
Vishnu, soul of universe VASU
Vishnu's bow .... SARAN
Vishnu's serpent ...... NAGA
visible juncture .... SEAM
Visigoth king ALARIC, ALARIK
vision, defective ..... ANOPIA
vision, pert. to .... OPTIC
visionary .... AIRY, IDEAL,
DREAMY, UNREAL, IDEALIST
visit ...... SEE, CALL, HAUNT
visit at sea .... GAM
visit between whalers ... GAM
vison .... MINK
vital energy .... HORME
vital fluid .... SAP
vital principle .... SOUL
vitalize .... ANIMATE
vitamin ... CITRIN, ADERMIN,
ANEURIN, TORULIN
vitamin B NIACIN, THIAMINE
vitamin B2 .... FLAVIN
vitamin H .... BIOTIN
vitiate .... SPOIL, TAINT,
POLLUTE, INVALIDATE
vitriol-infused earth .... SORY
vituperate .... SCOLD

a vivacious ..... **AIRY, BRIGHT**
vivacity .... **ELAN, LIFE**
vocal flourish ...... **ROULADE**
vocation .... **CAREER**
"— voce" .... **SOTTO**
voice .... **SAY**
voice
    ALTO, BASS, VOCE, TENOR
voice: It. .... **VOCE**
voice: Lat. .... **VOX**
voice, loss of ...... **APHONIA**
voiced .... **SONANT**
voiced, not .... **ASONANT**
voiceless .... **SPIRATE**
voiceless consonant ..... **SURD**
void .... **NUL, NULL,**
   ABYSS, SPACE, INVALID
void, to make.**ANNUL, CANCEL**
void, to render: Scot. ... **CASS**
voided escutcheon ...... **ORLE**
volcanic cinder ...... **SCORIA**
volcanic islands, Atlantic
    FAROE
volcanic rock
   TUFA, TUFF, LATITE
volcanic scoria-matter
    LAVA, SLAG
volcano .. **ETNA, AETNA, PELEE**
volcano crater .... **MAAR**
volcano hole .... **CRATER**

c volcano, Martinique Is. .. **PELEE**
volcano mouth ...... **CRATER**
volcano, P. I. .... **APO**
volcano pit .... **CRATER**
volcano, Sicily **ETNA, AETNA**
volcano, W. Indies .... **PELEE**
volition .... **WILL**
volt-ampere .... **WATT**
Voltaire .... **AROUET**
Voltaire play: Fr. ..... **ZAIRE**
voluble .... **GLIB**
volume .... **MO, TOME**
vomiting .... **EMESIS**
voodoo charm .... **MOJO**
voodoo snake deity .... **ZOMBI**
vote .... **BALLOT**
vote into office .... **ELECT**
vote, right to .... **FRANCHISE**
vote, take a .... **POLL**
votes ...... **AYES, NOES, YEAS**
vouch for .... **SPONSOR**
voucher .... **CHIT, NOTE**
"vous —": Fr., you are .. **ETES**
vowel, line over ..... **MACRON**
vowel suppression .... **ELISION**
voyaging .... **ASEA**
vulcanite .... **EBONITE**
Vulcan's wife .... **MAIA**
vulgar .... **COARSE**
vulture **AURA, URUBU, CONDOR**

b "W", old English .... **WEN**
wade across .... **FORD**
wading bird **IBIS, RAIL, CRANE,**
  EGRET, HERON, STILT,
  AVOCET, AVOSET, JAC-
  ANA, FLAMINGO
wag .... **WIT**
wages .... **PAY**
Wagner heroine . **ELSA, SENTA,**
    ISOLDE
Wagnerian role .... **ERDA**
wagon .. **CART, DRAY, WAIN**
wagon pin .... **CLEVIS**
wagon, Russ. .... **TELEGA**
wagon shaft .... **THILL**
wagon tongue .... **NEAP, POLE**
wagtail .... **LARK**
wahoo, fish .... **PETO**
wail .... **KEEN, LAMENT**
waist ...... **CAMISA, TAILLE**
waistcoat **VEST, GILET, JERKIN**
wait .... **BIDE**
waken ...... **ROUSE, AROUSE**

d wale .... **WELT**
Wales emblem .... **LEEK**
walk ..... **PACE, STEP, TREAD**
walk affectedly ...... **MINCE**
walk heavily .... **PLOD, SLOG**
walk, inability to .... **ABASIA**
walk lamely .... **LIMP**
walk stiffly .... **STALK**
walk, tree-lined .... **ALAMEDA**
walking stick ... **CANE, STILT**
wall, arena .... **SPINA**
wall around fortified place
    RAMPART
wall, divided by .... **SEPTATE**
wall: Fr. .... **MUR**
wall material .... **COB**
wall, of a .... **MURAL**
wall paneling .... **WAINSCOT**
wall piece **TEMPLET, TEMPLATE**
wall section .... **DADO, PANEL**
wall, squeeze against .. **MURE**
walls .... **SEPTA**
wallaba tree, Brazil ..... **APA**
walled city, Nigeria ..... **KANO**

a wallflower .... **KEIRI**
wallop .... **LAM**
wallow .... **WELTER**
walrus .... **MORSE**
wampum **PEAG,SEWAN,SEAWAN**
wan .... **ASHY, PALE, ASHEN**
wand .... **BATON**
wander .. **ERR, HAAK, ROAM,**
ROVE, RAMBLE, DIGRESS
wander idly .... **GAD**
wanderer .... **VAG, NOMAD**
"Wandering Jew" author .. **SUE**
wane .... **EBB**
want .... **LACK, NEED, DESIRE**
wapiti .... **ELK**
war-club, medieval ..... **MACE**
war correspondent
PYLE, BALDWIN
war cry, ancient Gr. ... **ALALA**
war god .... **ARES, MARS**
war god, Babyl. ... **IRA, IRRA**
war god, Norse **TY, TYR, TYRR**
war god, Teut. .... **ER**
war goddess, Gr. ...... **ENYO**
war horse .... **CHARGER**
war, religious ...... **CRUSADE**
war, Russ.-Eng. ...... **CRIMEA**
war vessel .... **CRUISER**
warble .. **SING, TRILL, YODEL**
b ward off ..... **FEND, AVERT,**
PARRY, REPEL, STAVE
ward politician ...... **HEELER**
warden, fire .... **RANGER**
warehouse .... **DEPOT**
warehouse room .... **LOFT**
warm .... **CALID, TEPID**
warning of danger: biol.
SEMATIC
warning signal .... **SIREN**
warning system, attack
DEW, BMEWS
warp yarn .... **ABB**
warrant, from monarch **BERAT**
warrior, Samoa .... **TOA**
warship, sailing ..... **FRIGATE**
wary .... **CAGY**
was not: dialect .... **NAS**
wash .... **LAVE**
wash leather .... **LOSH**
wash out .... **ELUTE**
washings: chem. ..... **ELUATE**
Washington Irving character **RIP**
wasp .... **HORNET**
wasps, the .... **VESPA**
waste .... **LOSS**
waste allowance ...... **TRET**
waste away **GNAW, ATROPHY**
waste fiber .... **NOIL**
waste land .... **MOOR**
waste matter .... **DROSS**
waste silk ..... **KNUB, FRISON**

c waste time .... **IDLE**
wastes, growing in .. **RUDERAL**
watch .... **SEE, GLOM**
watch chain .... **FOB**
watchdog, Hel's .... **GARM**
watchful .... **ALERT**
watchful guardian ... **ARGUS**
watchful, name meaning **IRA**
watchman, alert ...... **ARGUS**
watchman, night ..... **SERENO**
watchtower .... **MIRADOR**
water ... **SPRINKLE, IRRIGATE**
water arum .... **CALLA**
water chestnut, Chin. ... **LING**
water cock .... **KORA**
water, covered by .... **AWASH**
water: Fr. ..... **EAU, EAUX**
water: Lat. .... **AQUA**
water lily .... **LOTUS**
water passage **SLUICE, STRAIT**
water pipe
HOOKA, HOOKAH, NARGILE
water raising device
TABUT, TABOOT
water reservoir, natural
CENOTE
water scorpion genus ... **NEPA**
water, seek .... **DOUSE**
water, sound of ...... **PLASH**
water: Sp. .... **AGUA**
d water spirit
ARIEL, SPRITE, UNDINE
water sprite ..... **NIX, NIXIE**
water sprite: Gaelic .. **KELPIE**
water surface .... **RYME**
water vessel, India
LOTA, LOTO, LOTAH
water wheel
NORIA, DANAIDE, TURBINE
water wheel, Persian .. **NORIA**
water's surface: naut. ... **RYME**
watercourse ... **LADE, BROOK,**
CANAL, RIVER, STREAM
watered apearance .... **MOIRE**
watered silk .... **MOIRE**
waterfall, Scot. **LIN, LYN, LINN**
watering place .. **SPA, BADEN**
waterproof canvas ..... **TARP**
waterskin .... **MATARA**
watertight, make **CALK, CAULK**
waterway .. **BAYOU, CANAL**
waterway, narrow ..... **STRAIT**
watery .... **SEROUS**
watery: comb. form .... **SERO**
wattle tree .... **BOREE**
wattled honeyeater
IAO, MANUAO
wave .... **FLY, SEA**
wave-crest comb. ...... **COOM**
wave: Fr. .... **ONDE**
wave, huge .... **SEA**

a waver ...... **FALTER, TEETER**
wavy: Her.
    UNDE, UNDY, NEBULE
wax .... **CERE**
wax ointment .... **CERATE**
wax, pert. to .... **CERAL**
wax: Sp. .... **CERA**
wax, yellow or white **CERESIN**
waxy chemical .... **CERIN**
waxy substance .... **CERIN**
way ...... **VIA, MODE, ROUTE**
way of walking .... **GAIT**
way out .... **EGRESS**
wayside — .... **INN**
wayside stop, India .. **PARAO**
we: Lat. .... **NOS**
weak .... **PUNY, FRAIL,**
    DEBILE, EFFETE, FEEBLE
weak cider .... **PERKIN**
weaken .... **SAP, LABEFY,**
    VITIATE, ENERVATE, EN-
    FEEBLE
weakfish, S. Am. .... **ACOUPA**
weakness .... **ATONY**
weal .... **WALE**
wealth, man of .... **NABOB**
wealthy: Scot. .... **BIEN**

b weapon .... **LANCE,**
    SPEAR, SWORD, MUSKET
weapon, ancient .... **CELT**
weapon, dagger-like .. **BALAS**
weapon: Fr. .... **ARME**
weapon, gaucho's **BOLA, BOLAS**
weapon, Maori .... **PATU**
weapon, medieval ..... **ONCIN**
weapon, N. Z. .... **PATU**
weapon, P. I. .... **BOLO**
weapon, S. Am. .. **BOLA, BOLAS**
wear away **EAT, ERODE, ABRADE**
wear away slowly ... **CORRODE**
wear by friction .... **RUB**
wear off .... **ABRADE**
wearing down .... **ATTRITION**
weary .... **BORE, TIRE**
weasel **VARE, ERMINE, FERRET**
weasel: Eng.
    STOT, STOAT, STOTE
weather indicator **BAROMETER**
weathercock .... **VANE**
weaverbird ..... **BAYA, MAYA**
weaverbird, S. Afr. .... **TAHA**
weaver's bobbin on shuttle **PIRN**
weaver's reed .... **SLEY**
weaving frame .... **LOOM**
weaving term .... **LISSE**
weaving tool .... **EVENER**

c web .... **TELA**
web-footed bird . **DUCK, LOON,**
    GOOSE
web-like membrane ..... **TELA**
web-spinning
    RETIARY, TELARIAN
wed .... **MARRY**
wedding anniversaries 1st,
    PAPER; 2nd, COTTON;
    3rd, CANDY OR LEATHER;
    4th, SILK, FRUIT, FLOW-
    ERS, or LEATHER; 5th,
    WOODEN; 6th, IRON OR
    CANDY; 7th, WOOL, COP-
    PER, OR FLORAL; 8th,
    WOOL, BRONZE, OR POT-
    TERY; 9th, WILLOW OR
    POTTERY; 10th, TIN; 11th,
    STEEL; 12th, SILK OR LIN-
    EN; 13th, LACE; 14th,
    IVORY; 15th, CRYSTAL;
    20th, CHINA; 25th, SIL-
    VER; 30th, PEARL; 35th,
    CORAL; 40th, RUBY OR
    EMERALD; 45th, RUBY OR
    SAPPHIRE; 50th, GOLDEN;

d   55th, EMERALD; 75th,
    DIAMOND
wedge, entering . **COIN, COIGN,**
    QUOIN, COIGNE
wedge-like piece ..... **QUOIN**
wedge-shaped ...... **CUNEATE**
wedge-shaped piece **GIB, SHIM**
wedge, steel .... **FROE**
Wednesday, source of name
    WODEN
weed .... **TARE, DARNEL**
weed, coarse .... **DOCK**
week ..... **SENNET, SENNIGHT**
week day .... **FERIA**
weep
    CRY, SOB, BOHO, LAMENT
weep, Scot. .... **ORP**
weeping statue .... **NIOBE**
weeping woman, Gr. myth **NIOBE**
weft .... **WOOF**
WEIGHT .. see also SPECIAL
    SECTION
weight .... **TON, HEFT**
weight allowance **TARE, TRET**
weight, ancient
    MINA, TALENT
weight, ancient: var. ... **MNA**
weight, Asiatic .... **TAEL**
weight, balance .... **RIDER**

Weight

a weight, Danish............. **ORT**
weight, India........ **SER, TOLA**
weight machine: Scot.... **TRON, TRONE**
weight, metric unit of.... **GRAM**
weight of England...... **STONE**
weight of silk before degumming **PARI**
weight, pert. to .... **BARIC**
weight system........... **TROY**
weir...................... **DAM**
weird .... **EERY, EERIE**
welcome .... **GREET**
well, Bib.................. **AIN**
well-bred people....... **GENTRY**
"well done"..... **EUGE, BRAVO**
well done: Eng............ **EUGE**
well: Fr................. **BIEN**
well: It. & Lat.......... **BENE**
well: Scot.............. **AWEEL**
Welsh dog.............. **CORGI**
Welsh god of sea ...... **DYLAN**
Welshman................ **CELT**
welt..................... **WALE**
wen..................... **TALPA**
Wend of Saxony .... **SORB**
wergeld .... **CRO**
W. Australia capital..... **PERTH**
W. Afr. timber tree ... **ODUM**
b W. Afr. tribe .. **IBO, BUBE, BUBI**
W. Ind. bayberry .. **AUSU, AUZU**
W. Ind. fish ...... **BOGA, CERO, TESTAR**
W. Ind. idol .... **ZEME, ZEMI**
W. Ind. isle .... **CUBA, HAITI**
W. Ind. key .... **CAY**
W. Ind. scrapper .... **CAJI**
W. Ind. shrub plant .... **ANIL**
West Point mascot....... **MULE**
West Pointer.... **PLEB, CADET, PLEBE**
West Saxon king ...... **INE**
Western division of Osset **DIGOR**
Western European.. **CELT, KELT**
Western Indian............ **UTE**
Western shrub .... **SAGE**
"Western Star" author... **BENET**
Western state............ **UTAH**
Westphalian city .... **HERNE**
wet: Scot. .... **WAT**
wet .... **ASOP, MOIST**
whale .... **CET, ORC, ORK, CETE, BELUGA, GRAMPUS**
whale carcass .... **KRANG, KRENG**
whale hunter............. **AHAB**
whale oil cask............ **RIER**
whale-shark............. **MHOR**
whale tail part .... **FLUKE**
whale, white .... **BELUGA**

c whale, white Caspian .... **HUSE, HUSO**
whales, order of......... **CETE**
whales, herd of ..... **GAM, POD**
whales, pert. to .... **CETIC**
whales, school of ... **GAM, POD**
whalebone............ **BALEEN**
wharf **KEY, PIER, QUAI, QUAY**
what is it? obs........... **ANAN**
whatnot .... **ETAGERE**
wheal ...... **WALE, WEAL**
wheat disease .... **BUNT**
wheat, German. **EMMER, SPELT**
wheat, India **SUJI, SUJEE**
wheat, kind of . **EMMER, SPELT**
wheat middlings..... **SEMOLINA**
wheedle .... **COG, COAX**
wheedling .... **BUTTERY**
wheel .... **ROTA**
wheel band .... **STRAKE**
wheel center. **HOB, HUB, NAVE**
wheel, furniture ...... **CASTER**
wheel, grooved........ **SHEAVE**
wheel horse .... **POLER**
wheel part.......... **HUB, RIM, FELLY, SPOKE**
wheel projection .... **CAM**
wheel shaft.............. **AXLE**
wheel-shaped .... **ROTATE**
d wheel spindle ... **AXLE, ARBOR**
wheel tread.............. **TIRE**
wheels, pert. to .... **ROTAL**
where: Lat. .... **UBI**
whetstone, fine .. **BUHR, HONE**
whey of milk..... **SERA, SERUM**
which see: abbr. .... **QV**
whiff.................... **PUFF**
while.............. **AS, WHEN**
whimper........ **MEWL, PULE**
whin .... **GORSE**
whine .... **PULE**
whinny .... **NEIGH**
whip . **CAT, BEAT, FLOG, LASH**
whip, cowboy........ **CHICOTE**
whip mark....... **WALE, WEAL**
whip, Russ............ **KNOUT**
whipsocket .... **SNEAD**
whirl .... **REEL, SPIN**
whirlpool .... **EDDY, GURGE, VORTEX**
whirlpool: Scot. ... **WEEL, WIEL**
whirlwind in Atlantic......... **OE**
whirring sound .... **BIRR**
whiskers ..... **BEARD, GOATEE**
whiskey: Ir. .... **POTEEN**
whiskey drink: Scot. ..... **ATHOL, ATHOLE**
whist win................ **SLAM**
whistle .... **PIPE, SIREN**
whit................. **BIT, JOT, ATOM, DOIT, IOTA**

a white acid, pert. to .. **TROPIC**
white alkaline .... **SODA**
white ant, P. I. .. **ANAI, ANAY**
white, bitter compound **LININ**
white: comb. form ..... **ALBO**
"White Elephant" land .. **SIAM**
white ermine **LASSET, MINIVER**
white-flecked .... **ROAN**
White Friar ..... **CARMELITE**
white: Ir. .... **BAWN**
white man: P. I. ... **CACHILA**
white matter, brain .... **ALBA**
white oak .... **ROBLE**
white poplar .... **ABELE**
white spruce ...... **EPINETTE**
white with age .... **HOAR**
whitefish .... **CISCO**
whiten .... **ETIOLATE**
whitish .... **HOARY**
whitlow grass .... **DRABA**
Whittier heroine .... **MAUD**
whiz ..... **PIRR, WHIR, ZIZZ**
whoa .... **HOLLA**
whole amount .... **GROSS**
whole: comb. form ...... **TOTO**
wholesome .... **SALUTARY**
wholly .... **ALL**
wicked .... **EVIL**
wicker basket .... **CESTA,**
KIPSY, PANNIER

b wicker basket, Guiana **PEGALL**
wickerwork .... **RATAN**
wickerwork hut .... **JACAL**
wicket, croquet .... **HOOP**
wide-mouthed vessel
EWER, OLLA
widgeon .... **SMEE**
widgeon genus ...... **MARECA**
widow .... **RELICT**
widow in cards .... **SKAT**
widow monkey .... **TITI**
widow's bit or coin ..... **MITE**
widow's third: Scot. .... **TERCE**
wield .... **PLY, USE**
wife, Moroccan ruler's **SHERIFA**
wife ... **FEME, FRAU, FEMME**
wife's property .... **DOS**
wig .... **PERUKE**
wigwam .. **TIPI, TEPEE, TEEPEE**
wild .... **FERAL, SAVAGE**
wild animals, collection of
ZOO, MENAGERIE
wild animal's trail
SLOT, SPUR, SPOOR
wild apple .... **CRAB, DOUCIN**
wild ass, Afr. ...... **QUAGGA**
wild ass, Asia ...... **ONAGER**
wild boar genus .... **SUS**
wild buffalo, India
ARNA, ARNI, ARNEE

c wild buffalo, Malay ... **GAUR,**
SLADANG, SALADANG,
SELADANG
wild cat, Siberia, Tibet, steppes
MANUL
wild cattle, India **GAUR, GOUR**
wild cry .... **EVOE**
wild dog .... **DHOLE**
wild dog genus .... **THOS**
wild dog, Japan ..... **TANATE**
"Wild Duck" author ... **IBSEN**
wild garlic .... **MOLY**
wild ginger .... **ASARUM**
wild hog .... **BOAR**
wild honeybee, E. Ind. **DINGAR**
wild horse of Tartary **TARPAN**
wild lime .... **COLIMA**
wild olive tree ..... **OLEASTER**
wild ox .... **ANOA**
wild ox, Malay. .... **BANTENG**
wild plum .... **SLOE**
wild plum, Calif. ...... **ISLAY**
wild sheep, Asia
RASSE, ARGALI
wild sheep, horned . **MOUFLON**
wild sheep, India ... **SHA, SNA,**
URIAL, NAHOOR, OORIAL
wild sheep, N. Afr.
ARUI, UDAD, AOUDAD
wild sheep, Tibet .... **SHA**

d **SNA, BHARAL, NAHOOR**
wild turnip .... **NAVEW**
wild vanilla .... **LIATRIS**
wildcat .... **BALU, LYNX**
wildcat, Afr. & India .. **CHAUS**
wildcat, S. Am. .... **EYRA**
wildcat, Sumatra ...... **BALU**
wildebeest .... **GNU**
wile .... **ART**
will addition .... **CODICIL**
will, one inheriting from
DEVISEE
will, one making .... **DEVISOR**
will power, loss of .... **ABULIA**
William: Ir. .... **LIAM**
William I, half brother of **ODO**
William the Conqueror's
daughter .... **ADELA**
willingly .... **LIEF**
willow .... **ITEA, OSIER**
willow, Europ. .... **SALLOW**
willow genus, Virginia ... **ITEA**
Wilson's thrush ...... **VEERY**
wilt .... **FADE, DROOP**
wily .... **FOXY**
wimple .... **GORGET**
win .... **GAIN**
winch .... **WHIN**
wind .... **GALE**
wind, Adriatic .... **BORA**

a wind, Andes ... **PUNA, PUNO**
wind, Austral. ...... **BUSTER**
wind, away from .... **ALEE**
wind, cold Malta .... **GREGALE**
wind, cold Medit. .... **MISTRAL**
wind, cold Swiss Alps **BISE, BIZE**
wind: comb. form .... **ANEMO**
wind-deposited loam ... **LOESS**
wind, dry, from Sahara .. **LESTE**
wind, east .... **EURUS**
wind god, Babyl.
   ADAD, ADDA, ADDU
wind god, Hindu ...... **VAYU**
wind god, pert. to
   EOLIAN, AEOLIAN
wind, hot, dry ...... **KAMSIN,**
 SIMOOM, SIMOON, SIROCCO
wind, hot, Medit. .... **SOLANO**
wind indicator .. **SOCK, VANE**
wind instrument
  HORN, OBOE, PIPE, BUGLE
wind, Levant .... **ETESIAN**
wind, Madeira .... **LESTE**
wind, Medit. .... **ETESIAN**
wind, Medit., poet. ..... **SIROC**
wind, Mesop. .... **SHAMAL**
wind, north .... **BOREAS**
wind off Faroe Islands .... **OE**
wind, Peru Andes **PUNA, PUNO**
wind, sand-laden
 SAMIEL, SIMOOM, SIMOON
b wind, Sahara .... **LESTE**
wind, South .. **NOTUS, AUSTER**
wind, southeast .... **EURUS**
wind, southwest .... **AFER**
wind, Trieste, cold ..... **BORA**
wind, warm dry **FOHN, FOEHN**
wind, west .... **AFER**
winds, south, Peru ..... **SURES**
windborne .... **AEOLIAN**
windflower .... **ANEMONE**
windlass .... **CAPSTAN**
windmill sail .... **AWE**
window lead .... **CAME**
window ledge .... **SILL**
window part .... **SASH**
window, semipolygonal .. **ORIEL**
window setter .... **GLAZIER**
windrow .... **SWATH**
windstorm
 OE, BURAN, TORNADO
windstorm, Asia **BURA, BURAN**
wine ...... **VIN, HOCK, PORT,**
 SACK, VINO, MEDOC, TO-
 KAY, CLARET, MALAGA,
 MUSCAT, SHERRY, MO-
 SELLE
wine, Am. .... **CATAWBA**
wine, ancient .... **MASSIC**
wine cask ...... **TUN, BUTT**
wine city, It. .... **ASTI**

c wine cup .... **AMA**
wine, delicacy of: Fr. ... **SEVE**
wine disorder .... **CASSE**
wine district, Calif. ..... **NAPA**
wine drink .... **NEGUS**
wine, dry .... **SEC, BRUT**
wine, golden .... **BUAL**
wine, heavy .... **TOKAY**
wine, honey and ...... **MULSE**
wine, Madeira .... **BUAL**
wine measure, Trieste
   ORNA, ORNE
wine merchant .... **VINTNER**
wine, new .... **MUST**
wine pitcher, Gr. .... **OLPE**
wine, red **PORT, TINTA, CLARET**
wine, sweet .... **MUSCAT**
wine, sweet: Fr. ..... **MASDEU**
wine, to make .... **VINT**
wine vessel ...... **AMA, OLPE,**
  AMULA, CHALICE
wine, white .... **HOCK,**
  SHERRY, SAUTERNE
wineberry, N. Z. ...... **MAKO**
wing .... **ALA, PENNA,**
  PINNA, PINION
wing, bastard .... **ALULA**
wing, beetle .... **TEGMAN,**
 TEGMINA, TEGUMEN
wing: Fr. .... **AILE**
d wing-footed animal .. **ALIPED**
winglike .... **ALAR**
wing-like part ..... **ALA, ALAE**
wing movement .... **FLAP**
wing tip, pert. to ... **ALULAR**
wings .... **ALAE**
wings, divested of
 DEALATA, DEALATED
wings, having .. **ALAR, ALATE**
wings: her. ...... **VOL, AILE**
winged figure, Gr.
 IDOLON, IDOLUM, EIDOLON
winged fruit, indehiscent
   SAMARA
winged god ..... **EROS, CUPID**
winged seed .... **SAMARA**
winged victory .... **NIKE**
wingless .... **APTERAL**
wingless invertebrates **APTERA**
wink rapidly .... **BAT**
winning at bridge ...... **SLAM**
winnow .... **FAN**
winter, pert. to .... **BRUMAL,**
 HIEMAL, HYEMAL, HIBERNAL
winter squash ...... **CUSHAW**
wipe out .... **ERASE**
wire measure .... **MIL**
wire service .... **AP, UP,**
 INS, UPI, REUTERS

a wires, cross .... **RETICLE**
Wisconsin college .... **RIPON**
wisdom ...... **LORE, GNOSIS**
wisdom god of: Babyl.
NABU, NEBO
wisdom goddess of: Gr.
ATHENA, PALLAS
wisdom, goddess of: Rom.
MINERVA
wise .... **SAGE, SENSIBLE**
wise adviser .... **MENTOR**
wise man
SAGE, SOLON, NESTOR
Wise Men .... **MAGI, GASPAR,**
MELCHIOR, BALTHASAR
wise men, A-S .... **WITAN**
wisecrack .. **GAG, JOKE, QUIP**
wish for ..... **YEARN, DESIRE**
wish undone .... **RUE**
wisp of hair .... **TATE**
wit .... **WAG, HUMOR**
wit: Sp. .... **SAL**
witless chatter .... **GAB**
witch ... **HAG, HECAT, LAMIA,**
HECATE, HECCAT, HEKATE
witch city .... **SALEM**
witch doctor .... **GOOFER**
witch in "Faerie Queene"
DUESSA
witchcraft .... **OBEAH**
with: Fr. .... **AVEC**
b with: Ger. .... **MIT**
with joy .... **FAIN**
with: prefix .... **SYN**
withdraw .. **RECEDE, REMOVE,**
RETIRE, SECEDE, RETRACT
wither .... **FADE**
withered .... **SERE**
within ... **INTO, INTERIOR**
within: comb. form
ESO, ENDO, ENSO, ENTO
within: prefix .... **ENDO**
without: comb. form ..... **ECT**
without energy .... **ATONY**
without: Fr. .... **SANS**
without: Ger. .... **OHNE**
without: Lat. .... **SINE**
without: poetic .... **SANS**
without teeth, claws, lion
MORNE
without veins ...... **AVENOUS**
witness .... **SEE**
witness, law . **TESTE, DEPONENT**
witness, to bear ...... **ATTEST**
witty remark ..... **MOT, QUIP**
witty reply .... **REPARTEE**
wobble .... **TEETER**
Woden .... **ODIN**
woe .... **MISERY**
woe is me .... **ALAS**

c wolf, gray .... **LOBO**
wolf, Odin's ...... **GERE, GERI**
wolf, timber .... **LOBO**
wolfhound .... **ALAN**
wolfish .... **LUPINE**
wolframite .... **CAL**
wolverine genus .... **GULO**
woman diplomat, first U.S.
OWEN
woman: Gr. .... **GYNE**
woman, ill-tempered
SHREW, VIRAGO
woman personified, Ir.
EMER, EIMER
woman's name (3 letters) **ADA,**
AMY, ANN, EVA, EVE, FAY,
IDA, INA, MAE, MAY, NAN,
RAE, UNA, ZOE, (4 let-
ters) **AFRA, ALIX, ALMA,**
ALYS, ANNA, ANNE, AVIS,
BONA, CARA, CLOE, CORA,
DORA, EDNA, ELLA, ELSA,
EMMA, ENID, ERMA, ETTA,
INEZ, JANE, JEAN, JOAN,
JUNE, LEAH, LIDA, LILA,
LOIS, LORA, LUCY, MARY,
MAUD, MYRA, NONA,
NORA, OLGA, RITA, ROSA,
ROSE, RUTH, SARA, VERA,
VIDA, (5 letters) ALICE,
ANITA, CLARE, DELIA,
d **DIANA, ELAIN, ELSIE,**
ERICA, FAITH, FLORA,
GRACE, IRENE, SARAH,
SELMA, (6 letters) AL-
THEA, BERTHA, DAPHNE,
EDWINA, ELAINE, EMILIA,
PHOEBE, (7 letters) ABI-
GAIL, CELESTE, LAVINIA
woman's nickname **CAT, DEB,**
HAT, KIT, LOU, MAB, MAG,
MEG, SAL, SUE, ABBY,
ADDY, BESS, BETH, CARO,
DORA, GAIL, JILL, JOSY,
JUDY, JULE, KATE, KATY,
LINA, LISA, LULU, MART,
MIMI, MINA, MOLL, NELL,
NINA, ROXY, SUSY, TAVE,
TAVY, TESS, TINA, XINA,
SALLY, SALLIE
Wonderland girl ...... **ALICE**
wont .... **HABIT**
wood .... **ALOE**
wood apple, Ind. .... **BEL**
wood, black .... **EBONY**
wood, flexible .... **EDDER**
wood, fragrant . **ALOES, CEDAR**
wood: comb. form .... **XYLO**
wood: Fr. .... **BOIS**
wood gum .... **XYLAN**

a

wood, light .... **BALSA**
wood, long piece .... **POLE**
wood: obsolete .... **WOLD**
wood, piece of .... **SLAT,**
             SPRAG, BILLET
wood pussy .... **SKUNK**
wood robin, N. Z. ...... **MIRO**
wood sorrel .... **OCA, OKA**
wood, timber: P. I. ... **CAHUY**
woodchuck .... **MARMOT**
woodchuck: dialect **MOONACK**
wooden .... **TREEN**
wooden brick .... **DOOK**
wooden collar, convict's **CANG**
wooden pail .... **SOE**
wooden peg .... **SKEG**
wooden shoe **SABOT, PATTEN**
woodland deity **FAUN, SATYR**
woodland god .... **PAN**
woodpecker genus **JYNX, YUNX**
woodpecker, green **HICKWALL**
woodpecker group ...... **PICI**
woodpecker, red-bellied . **CHAB**
woodpecker, small ... **PICULE**
woodpeckers, of ...... **PICINE**
woodwind
    OBOE, BASSOON, CLARINET
woodworking tool ..... **SAPPER**
woodworm .... **TERMITE**
woody fiber .... **BAST**

b

woody hill .... **HOLT**
woody plant .... **TREE**
woof .... **WEFT**
wool ...... **ANGORA, MERINO**
wool cluster .... **NEP**
wool, coarse .... **GARE**
wool fat . **LANOLIN, LANOLINE**
wool: Lat. .... **LANA**
wool measure .... **HEER**
wool package .... **FADGE**
wool, reclaimed ...... **MUNGO**
woolen cloth .... **ETAMINE**
woolen cloth, coarse, twilled
               KERSEY
woolen fabric .... **FRISCA**
woolen thread .... **YARN**
woolly ...... **LANATE, LANOSE**
woolly pyrol .... **URD**
word by word .... **LITERAL**
word expressing action .. **VERB**
word meanings, pert. to
             SEMANTIC
word of affirmation .... **AMEN**
word of choice .... **OR**
word of God .... **LOGOS**
word of honor, promise
        PAROL, PAROLE
word of mouth, by
        PAROL, PAROLE
word of ratification .... **AMEN**
word, scrambled ... **ANAGRAM**

c

work
    MOIL, TOIL, CHARE, LABOR
WORK ..see also COMPOSITION
work aimlessly .... **POTTER**
work at steadily .... **PLY**
work hard
    PEG, MOIL, TOIL, SLAVE
work, in terms of heat **ERGON**
work, musical
    OPUS, OPERA, ORATORIO
work persistently .... **PEG**
work, piece of .... **JOB, STINT**
work: Sp. .... **OBRA**
work unit .... **ERG, ERGON**
workbasket .... **CABA, CABAS**
worker .... **HAND,**
     OPERANT, OPERATOR
worker ant .... **ERGATE**
worker: comb. form .. **ERGATE**
worker's group, worldwide .. **ILO**
worker's union, Soviet .. **ARTEL**
workhorse: Scot .... **AVER**
working boat, Chesapeake Bay
              FLATTIE
workman, mine .... **CAGER**
workman, S. Afr. ...... **VOLK**
workshop .... **ATELIER**
world: Hindu myth ...... **LOKA**
world, holder of .... **ATLAS**
World War I battle site

d

           MONS, MARNE
World War I group . **AEF, AMEX**
World War II area ...... **ETO**
worm .. **ESS, TINEA, ANNELID**
worm, African .... **LOA**
worm, bait .... **LURG**
worm, eye-infesting ...... **LOA**
worm, S-shaped .... **ESS**
worm track, fossil .. **NEREITE**
worn, as rope .... **MAGGED**
worn by friction .... **ATTRITE**
worn out .... **EFFETE**
worn-out horse
      NAG, HACK, PLUG
worry .... **RUX, CARE, CARK,**
            FRET, STEW
worship .... **ADORE**
worship, form of ..... **RITUAL**
worship, house of .... **BETHEL**
worship, object of ...... **IDOL**
worship of saints ...... **DULIA**
worship, place of
      ALTAR, TEMPLE
worthless **BAD, RACA, TRASHY**
worthless bit from table .. **ORT**
worthless rock ...... **GANGUE**
wound: Her. .... **VULN**
wound mark .... **SCAR**
wrangle .... **HAGGLE**
wrap .... **SWATHE, SWADDLE**

a
wrapping	PLIOFILM
wrath	IRE
wrathful	IRATE
wreath	CHAPLET
wreath: Her.	TORSE
wreathe	COIL, WIND
wrest	REND
wrestle	TUSSLE
wrestling throw	HIPE, HYPE
wriggling	EELY
wrinkle	RUCK, RUGA, SEAM, RUGAE, RIMPLE
wrinkled	RUGATE, RUGOSE
wrist	CARPUS
wrists	CARPI
wrist bone	CARPAL
wrist guard	BRACER
writ of execution	ELEGIT
writ, sheriff's	VENIRE
writ to arrest	CAPIAS

c
write	PEN, SCRIVE
write comments	POSTIL
write music	NOTATE
writer	DITER, SCRIBE
writer, Ger.	MANN
writing instrument	PEN
writing on the wall	MENE, TEKEL
writing paper size	CAP
writing table	ESCRITOIRE
writing well, art of	RHETORIC
wrong	OUT, EVIL, AMISS
wrong: Lat.	MALA, MALUM
wrong, legal	TORT
wrong: prefix	MIS
wrongdoing	EVIL
wrongdoing, serious	CRIME
wryneck	LOXIA
Wyoming peak, highest	GANNETT

b
Y, in Middle Eng.	YOK, YOGH
Y's	WIES
yacht	SAIL
yacht pennant	BURGEE
Yale	ELI
yam, Hawaii	HOI
yam, white	UBE, UBI, UVE, UVI
Yang, opposite of	YIN
Yangtze tributary	HAN
Yap Island stone money	FEI
yarn	GARN, TALE, CREWEL
yarn count	TYPP
yarn for warp	ABB
yarn measure	LEA, HEER
yarn projection	KNAP, KNOP
yarn, quantity of	SKEIN
Yarura language	PUME
yataghan	BALAS
yaupon holly	CASSENA
yawn	GAPE
yawn: obs.	GANE
yearly	ETESIAN
yearly church payment	ANNAT
yearn	ACHE, LONG
year's crops	ANNONA
yeast	BEES
yeast, brewer's	BARM
yeast, Jap.	KOJI
yeast, wild	ANAMITE
yell: Scot.	GOWL
yellow	AMBER, OCHER, OCHRE, MELINE, CITRINE
yellow-brown	TOPAZ
yellow bugle	IVA

d
yellow dye plant	AMIL
yellow fish	ORF, ORFE
yellow ide	ORF, ORFE
yellow iris	SEDGE
yellow ocher	SIL
yellow pigment	SIL
yellow wood	AVODIRE
yellowhammer, Eur.	AMMER
yellowish	SALLOW
yelp	KIYI, YOUP
Yemenite	ARAB
Yemen's capital	SANA
yes: Sp.	SI
yesterday: Fr.	HIER
yesterday, pert. to	HESTERNAL
yet	E'EN, STILL
yew, pert. to	TAXINE
yield	CEDE, ACCEDE, CONCEDE
Yogi	SWAMI
yoke bar, S. Afr.	SKEY
yokel	OAF, HICK, RUBE
yolk of egg	VITELLUS
yolky	EGGY
yon	THERE
yorker: cricket	TICE
Yorkshire city	LEEDS
Yorkshire river	URE, OUSE
you: It.	TU
you: Sp.	TE
young animal	CUB, PUP, COLT, WHELP
young female hog	GILT
young girl of Burma	MIMA
young hog	SHOAT, SHOTE
young kangaroo	JOEY

Young

a young man, handsome **ADONIS**
young ox: Eng. .... **STOT**
young plant .... **SET**
young rowdy ...... **HOODLUM**
youngest son .... **CADET**
youngster
    KID, TAD, TOT, SHAVER
youth .... **LAD**
youth .... **GOSSOON**
youth shelter .... **HOSTEL**

c youthful: zool. ...... **NEANIC**
Yucatan Indian .... **MAYA**
yucca-like plant .... **SOTOL**
Yugoslav .... **SERB, CROAT**
Yugoslav leader .... **TITO**
Yum-Yum's friend
    KOKO, NANKIPOO
Yutang .... **LIN**

Z

b zeal .... **ELAN, ARDOR**
zealot .... **BIGOT**
zealous .... **AVID**
Zebedee, son of **JOHN, JAMES**
zebra, young .... **COLT**
zebrawood .... **ARAROBA**
zebu-yak hybrid **ZO, ZOH, ZOBO**
zenith .... **TOP, ACME, PEAK**
zenith, opposite of .... **NADIR**
Zeno's follower .... **STOIC**
zeppelin .... **BLIMP**
Zeppelin .... **GRAF**
zero .... **CIPHER**
zest .... **TANG**
zetetic .... **SEEKER**
Zeus, epithet of ..... **AMMON**
Zeus, maiden loved by
    IO, LEDA, EUROPA
Zeus, mother of .... **RHEA**
Zeus, old Doric name for **ZAN**
Zeus' daughter
    ATE, HEBE, IRENE
Zeus' sister .... **HERA**

d Zeus' son ..... **ARES, ARCAS,**
    MINOS, APOLLO
Zeus' wife ..... **HERA, METIS**
Zilpah's son ..... **GAD, ASHER**
zinc in slabs .... **SPELTER**
zinc ingot .... **SPELTER**
Zionist group .... **ITO**
zipper .... **TALON**
zodiac sign ...... **LEO, ARIES,**
    LIBRA, VIRGO, CANCER,
    PISCES, TAURUS, SCORPIO
Zola novel .... **NANA**
zone .... **AREA**
zone: Lat. .... **ZONA**
zoophyte, marine ...... **CORAL**
Zophah, son of ...... **BEERA**
Zoroastrian .. **PARSI, PARSEE**
Zoroastrian bible .... **AVESTA**
zounds .... **OONS**
Zulu headman ..... **INDUNA**
Zulu language .... **BANTU**

SPECIAL SECTION

READY REFERENCE WORD LISTS

In one compact section, here are lists of the most useful and widely used word categories. Some of these words, having certain customary definitions, are also listed in the DEFINITIONS section of this book, but these word lists will be of greatest help when you are confronted with GENERALIZED definitions such as "Roman goddess," "South American Indian," "Heraldic term," "African tribe," "U.S. author," or "Ice hockey great."

In most cases, the words in each separate listing are placed according to the number of letters in the words. This is a tremendous advantage to puzzle solvers, who are more concerned with the length of a word than with its alphabetical placement. However, in some lists of people's names (U.S. Authors, Award-Winning Ice Hockey Players, and the like) you may be looking for either the first name or the last name, but it was impossible to list both ways, so they are listed alphabetically by the last name.

This section is intended as a handy reference for crossword puzzle solvers, and contains words and names often found in crosswords. Therefore, some of the lists are complete (such as Chemical Elements), but many are not (Some Names from the Baseball Hall of Fame, for example).

The listings for this Special Section are shown on the Table of Contents.

MEASURES

AREA MEASURES

AR, ARE, ACRE, DECARE (10 ARES), CENTIAR, CENTIARE
Annam .... MAU, QUO, SAO
Bengal .... BEGA
Czechoslovakia ... LAN, MIRA
Dutch E. Ind. .... BOUW
England, Old .... HYDE
Japan .... BU, SE, TAN
Norway .... MAL, MAAL
Paraguay .... LINO
Poland .... MORG
Rome, Ancient ...... CLIMA, CLIMATA
Serbia .... RIF, RALO
Shetlands, Orkney .... URE
Siam .... RAI, NGAN
Sweden .... MORGEN

DRY MEASURES

PECK, PINT, STERE
Algeria .... TARRI
Austria .... MUTH
Borneo .... GANTANG
Brazil .... MOIO
Burma .... TENG
Calcutta .... KUNK, RAIK
Channel Is. .... CABOT
China .... HO, HU
Dutch .... KOP, ZAK
Egypt .... KADA, KILAH
Hebrew .... CAB, KAB, KOR, EPHA, OMER, SEAH, EPHAH
Italy .... SALM, SALMA
Japan .... SHO
Morocco .... SAHH
Netherlands .... KOP, ZAK
Portugal .... MEIO, PIPA
Russia .... LOF
Tangier .... MUDD
Tunis ..... SAA, SAAH, UEBA

LENGTH, DISTANCE MEASURES

ELL, ROD, FOOT, HAND, INCH, MILE, YARD, METER, METRE, PERCH, MICRON, FURLONG
Annam .... LY, GON, NGU
Brazil .... PE
Calcutta .... DHAN, JAOB
China .... HU, LI, PU, TU, CH'IH, TCHI, TSUN
Czechoslovakia .. SAH, LATRO
Denmark FOD, MIL, MUL, ALEN
Domin. Repub. .... ONA
Dutch .... DUIM, VOET
D. E. Indies .... DEPA
Egypt .. PIC, PIK, KHET, THEB
Eritrea .... CUBI
Estonia .... LIIN, SULD
France .... AUNE
Greece .. PIC, PIK, BEMA, PIKI POUS, ACAENA
Hebrew .... EZBA
Iceland .... FET, ALIN, LINA
India .. GAZ, GEZ, GUZ, JOW, KOS, JAOB, KOSS
Italy .... CANNA
Japan .. BU, JO, RI (marine), CHO, DJO, KEN, RIN, HIRO

Java .... PAAL
Libya .... DRA, PIK, DRAH
Malabar .... ADY
Malacca .... ASTA
Netherlands .... DUIM, VOET
Norway .... FOT, ALEN
Persia ...... GAZ, GEZ, GUZ, ZAR, ZER
Poland .... MILA, PRET
Prussia .... RUTE
Rangoon . LAN, DAIN, TAUN
Rome, ancient .... ACTUS, .. GRADUS, STADIA, STADIUM
Russia .... FUT, VERST
Siam .... WA, KUP, NIU, SEN, SOK, WAH, NIOU, SAWK
Spain .... BARA, CODO, DEDO, VARA
Sweden ...... FOT, REF, FAMN
Switzerland .... TOISE
Tripoli .... DRA, DRAA
Turkey .... PIC, PIK, KHAT, ZIRA

(liquid measures on page 189)

WEIGHTS

KIP, TON, GRAM, KILO, CARAT,
    GRAIN, OUNCE, CENTRAL
Abyssinia .... KASM, NATR,
    OKET, ALADA, NETER
Annam .... BINH
Arabia .... KELA
Austria .... UNZE
Bavaria .... GRAN
Brazil .... ONCA
Bulgaria .... OKA, OKE
Burma ...... VIS, KYAT, VISS
Calcutta .. PANK, PAWA, RAIK
China .... LI, FEN, HAO, KIN
    SSU, TAN, YIN, TAEL
Columbia .... SACO
Denmark ES, ORT, VOG, ESER,
    PUND
Dutch .... ONS, LOOD
Dutch E. Ind ...... TJI, HOEN,
    TALI, WANG
Egypt ... KAT, KET, OKA, OKE,
    HEML, KHAR, OHIA, OKIEH
England .... STONE
Estonia ...... NAEL, PUUD
Ethiopia .... See Abyssinia
France .... GROS
Germany .... LOT, LOTE,
    LOTH, STEIN
Greece .... MNA, MINA,
    OBOLE, OBOLUS
Guinea .... AKEY, PISO,
    UZAN, SERON

Hebrew .... BEKA, REBA
India .... SER, BHAR, PALA,
    RATI, TOLA, VISS, RATTI
Italian .... SALM, SALMA
Japan ...... KIN, SHI, MORIN
Malay .... CHEE
Malta .... SALM, SALMA
Mexico ...... LIBRA, ONZA
Mongolia .... LAN
Morocco .... ARTEL
Moslem .... ROTL
Netherlands ...... ONS, LOOD
Norway .... PUND
ORIENT ...... MANN, ROTL,
    TAEL, ARTAL
Palestine ...... ROTLA, ZUZA
Persia .... SER
Poland .... LUT
Portugal GRAO, ONCA, LIBRA
Rangoon .... RUAY
Rome, Ancient ...... AS, BES,
    LIBRA, SOLIDUS
Russia .... LAN, PUD,
    DOLA, POOD, POUD
Siam .... PAI, KLAM,
    KLOM, TICAL
Shetland Island .. URE (ounce)
Spain .... ONZA
Sweden ASS, ORT, STEN, UNTZ
Turkey ..... OCK, OKA, OKE,
    KILE, OCHA, KERAT

LIQUID MEASURES

TUN, DRAM, GILL, PINT,
MINIM
Abyssinia ...... CUBA, KUBA
Annam .... TAO
Arabia .... SAA
Austria .... FASS
Brazil .... PIPA
Burma .... BYEE, SEIT
China ...... KO, QUEI, SHIH
Cyprus .... CASS
Dutch .. (old) AAM, AUM, KAN
Egypt .... HIN
England .... PIN, CRAN
Ethiopia .... see ABYSSINIA
Germany .... AAM, EIMER
Hebrew .... HIN

Hungary .... AKO
Japan .... KOKU, SHO
Malaya .... PAU
Netherlands . AAM, AUM, KAN
Portugal .... BOTA, PIPA
Rangoon .... BYEE, SEIT
Rome, Ancient .... URNA
Russia ... STOF, STOFF, STOOF
Somaliland .... CABA
Spain .... COPA
Sweden .:.. AM, AMAR, KAPP
Switzerland ..... IMMI, SAUM
Tangier .... KULA
Trieste .... ORNA, ORNE
Yugoslavia .... AKOV

COINS, MONEY

Abyssinia ..... BESA, GIRSH, TALARI
Afghanistan .... AMANIA
Albania .... LEK
Anglo-Saxon .... ORA, SCEAT
Annam .... QUAN
Austria .... DUCAT
Biblical .. BEKA, MITE (small), SHEKEL, TALENT
Brazil .... REI
Bulgaria ... LEV, LEW, DINAR
Chile .... COLON
China .. LI, CASH, TAEL, TIAO, YUAN, PU (early)
Colombia .... REAL
Costa Rica .... COLON
Czechslovakia ..... DUCAT, KRONE (plural, KRONEN)
Denmark ... ORA, ORE, ORAS, KRONE (plural, KRONER)
Dutch OORD, DALER, GULDEN, STIVER
D. E. Indies ..... BONK, DUIT
Egypt .... GIRSH
England ... ORA, RIAL (gold), RYAL, RYEL, GROAT, PENCE, FLORIN, GUINEA
Equador .... SUCRE
Ethiopia ..... see ABYSSINIA
Europe .... (old) GROS, DUCAT
France .. ECU (old), SOL, SOU, AGNEL (old), FRANC, LIARD (old), LOUIS, OBOLE, BESANT or BEZANT (old).
Genoa .... JANE (old)
Germany ..... MARK, KRONE (former), TALER, THALER
Ger. E. Africa .... PESA
Greece .. OBOL or OBOLI (old), STATER (old)
Hungary ...... GARA, PENGO
Iceland .... AURAR, EYRIR, KRONA
India. LAC, PIE, ANNA, DAWM, FELS, HOON, LAKH, PICE (small bronze), TARA, MOHUR (old), RUPEE
Iran .... see PERSIA
Iraq .... DINAR
Ireland .... RAP (old)

Italy .... LIRA, LIRE, SOLDO, TESTER, TESTON, TESTONE, TESTOON
Japan .... BU, RIN, SEN, YEN, OBAN
Latvia .... LAT, LATU
Lithuania .. LIT, LITAI, LITAS
Macao .... AVO
Malaya TRA (tin, pewter), TRAH
Mexico ...... PESO, CENTAVO
Montenegro .... PARA
Morocco ...... OKIA, RIAL
Nepal .... MOHAR
Netherlands .... DAALDER
Norway .... ORE, KRONE (KRONER)
Oman .... GAJ, GAZ, GOZ, GHAZI
Persia. PUL, KRAN, POUL, RIAL DARIC, DINAR, MOHUR (old), TOMAN, STATER
Peru .... SOL, DINERO
Poland .... DUCAT
Portugal ..... JOE, REI, PECA, DOBRA (former)
Rome, ancient . SEMIS, DINDER
Roman ...... AS, AES, ASSES, SOLIDUS
Rumania .... LEU, LEY, BANI
Russia . COPEC, KOPEK, RUBLE
Siam .... AT, ATT, BAHT, TICAL or TIKAL
Sicily .... TARI
Somaliland .... BESA
South Africa ...... DAALDER
Spain ..... COB, DURO, PESO, REAL, DOBLA (old), PESETA, PISTOLE (old)
Sweden ORE, KRONA (KRONOR), KRONE (KRONER)
Switzerland .... BATZ
Thailand .... see SIAM
Timor .... AVO
Turkey .... LIRA (gold), PARA, ALTUN (gold), ASPER, MAHBUB (gold), PIASTER
United States .. CENT, DIME, EAGLE
Venice .... BETSO (old silver)
Yugoslavia .... DINAR

TRIBES (Including Peoples, Natives)

EUROPE:

Albania............ **GEG, CHAM, GHEG, TOSK**
Balto-Slav................. **LETT**
Celtic on Danube........... **BOII**
Finnish near Volga......... **VEPS, VEPSA**
Finnish, Ingria....... **VOT, VOTE, VOTH, WOTE**
Lithuania.................. **BALT**
Syryenian................. **KOMI**
Teuton, ancient............ **UBII**

MIDDLE EAST:

Arab................. **AUS, IBAD**
Bedouin........... **ABSI, HARB**
Turkey.................... **KURD**
East Turkey............... **KURD**
Persia............ see under **ASIA**

ASIA:

Afghanistan................ **SAFI**
Assam......... **AO, AKA; AHOM, GARO, NAGA**
Borneo.... **DYAK, IBAN; DAYAK**
Burma........... **WA, LAI, KAW, MON, WAS; AKHA, CHIN, KADU, KUKI, TSIN; KAREN**
Caucasus .... **IMER, KURI, LASI, LAZE, LAZI, SVAN; OSSET, SVANE**
Celebes, Malayan.......... **BUGI**
China, Miao................. **HEH**
China, Nord....... **USUN, UZUN; USSUN**
China, Tatar............... **TOBA**
India.............. **AWAN, BHIL, BHEEL, TURI**
Kolarian (India)............ **BHAR**
Japan, aborigine..... **AINO, AINU**
Madagascar.............. **HOVA**
Manchu................... **DAUR**
Mongol................... **CHUD**
Nepal............. **AOUL, KHAS**
Persia.............. **LUR, KURD, FARSI, IRANIAN**
Tibet................. **CHAMPA**

AFRICA:

Abyssinian .... **SHOA**
Bantu....... **KUA; BANE, BAYA, BIHE, BULE, FANG, FUNG, GOGO, GOLO, GOMA, GUHA, HAKU, HEHE, JAGA, LUBA, MAKA, NAMA, SOGA, SUKU,** **VIRA, YAKA, ZULU (largest); KAFIR; KAFFIR**
Bedouin.................... **ABSI**
Berber . **DAZA, RIFF, TEDA, TIBU**
Bushman..... **SAN, SAAN, QUNG**
Congo.............. **FIOT, SUSU**
Central Africa....... **ABO; BULO, DOMA, KALI, KURI, LURI, YAKO; LUREM**
Dahomey........... **FON, FONG**
East Africa...... **JUR, LUR, YAO; AKKA, ALUR, ASHA, BARI, BONI, GOLO, MADI, NUER, VITI**
Ethiopian.................. **SHOA**
Gold Coast........ **AKAN, AKIM, AKRA**
Hamitic ..... **AFAR, BEJA, BENI, BOGO, GALA, HIMA**
Kaffir .... **XOSA, ZULU**
Kenya...................... **BONI**
Lake Albert.......... **ALUR, LURI**
Liberia............ **GI; KRA, KRU, VAI, VEI; KROO, TOMA**
Libya......... **FUL, FULA, MZAB**
Mozambique .... **YAO**
Nigeria...... **ARO, EDO, IBO, IJO; BENI, BINI, EBOE, EKOI, IDJO, IDYO, IDZO, NUPE; BENIN**
Nilotic................ **SUK, BARI**
Pygmy............ **AKKA, DOKO**
Slave Coast............... **EGBA**
Sudan..... **FUL, FUR, VEI; FULA, GOLO, MABA, MEGE, NUBA, SUSU, TAMA**
West Africa...... **GA; AJA, EWE, IBO, KRU, KWA; AGNI, AKIM, APPA, BAGA, BINI, EFIK, EGBA, EKOI, GENG, GOLA, HABE, IKWE, JEBU, JOAT, JOLA, KETU, NALU, ONDO, REMO, SAPE, TCHI, TSHI, VACA, WARI**

ALASKA:

Aleutians.................. **ATKA**

GREENLAND .... **ITA**

AUSTRALIA .... **KOKO**
NEW GUINEA............ **KARON**

SOUTH AMERICA:

Fr. Guiana................. **BONI**

191

INDIANS, INDIAN TRIBES

Alaska .... ALEUT, SITKA

Algonquin or Algonkian Indians ... FOX, SAC, WEA; CREE, SAUK; MIAMI; LENAPE, OTTAWA, PIEGAN; SHAWNEE

Amazon .... (lower) MURA, (upper) ANDOA

Apache .... LIPAN

Araucanian .... AUCA

Arawak ..... ARAUA, CAMPA, INERI

Arikara .... REE

Arizona .. HANO, HOPI, MOKI, PIMA, TEWA, YUMA; MOQUI; APACHE

Athapascan Indians ..... DENE, HUPA, TAKU; LIPAN, TINNE; APACHE, NAVAHO

Aymara .... COLLA

Bolivia ...... ITE, URO, URU; ITEN, LECA, MOJO, MOXO, URAN; CHOLO

Brazil ...... GE; YAO; CAME, DIAU, MAKU, MURA, PURI, PURU, TUPI; ACROA, ANDOA, ARAUA, CARIB, GUANA, SIUSI; ZAPARO

Caddoan Indians .. REE; ADAI; IONI, CADDO, BIDAI; PAWNEE

California ...... HUPA, KOSO, MONO, NOZI, POMO, SERI, TATU, YANA; MAIDU, YANAN; SALINA

Canada .... AHT, CREE, DENE, TAKU; NISKA, TINNE; SARCEE

Carib .... YAO, TRIO

Carolina .... CATAWBA

Chaco .... TOBA

Chile .... AUCA

Colorado .... UTE

Colombia .... BORO, DUIT, MUSO, MUZO, TAMA, TAPA; CHOCO; COLIMA

Costa Rica ...... BOTO VOTO

Cowichan Indians .. NANAIMO

Dakotas .. REE, SIOUX, TETON; MANDAN, SANTEE; ARIKARA

Delaware .... LENAPE

Ecuador: ..... CARA (extinct); ANDOA, ARDAN

Eskimo .... ATKA; ALEUT

Florida: .... CALUSA

Fuegan .... ONA

Great Lakes .... ERIE; HURON

Guatemala ...... MAM; CHOL, ITZA, IXIL, IXLI, MAYA, ULVA, VOTO; KICHE, PIPIL

Honduras .... PAYA

Iowa .... FOX, SAC; SAUK

Indiana .... WEA; MIAMI

Iroquoian Indians,

Iroquois: .... ERIE, HURON, CAYUGA, MOHAWK, ONEIDA, SENECA

Jalisco: .... CORA

Keresan Indians: . SIA; ACOMA

Kusan .... COOS

Lesser Antilles .... INERI

Mayan Indians: ... MAM, CHOL

Mexico ... MAM, CHOL, CORA, MAYA, MIXE, PIMA, PIME, SERI, TECA, TECO, WABI; AZTEC, OTOMI, SERIA; TOLTEC

Miami .... WEA

Mississippi ..... TIOU, BILOXI

Montana ...... CROW, HOHE

Muskohegan Indians: . CREEK, YAMASI, CHOCTAW, SEMINOLE

Nebraska .... KIOWA

Nevada .... PAIUTE

New Mexico . SIA, PIRO, TANO, TAOS, TEWA, ZUNI; ACOMA, KERES, PECOS

New York .... SENECA

Nicaragua . MIXE, RAMA, ULVA

Oklahoma .. KAW, OTO; LOUP, OTOE; CADDO, CREEK, KANSA, KIOWA, OSAGE, PONCA; PAWNEE

Oregon .... COOS, KUSAN, MODOC, CHINOOK

Panamint .... KOSO
Panama .... CUNA, CUEVA
Pawnee Indians .... LOUP
Payaguas .... AGAZ
Peru: .... ANDE, ANTI, BORO,
    CANA, INCA, INKA, LAMA,
    PEBA, PIBA, PIRO, YNCA;
    CAMPA, CHIMU, CHOLO,
    COLAN, YUNCA; CHANCA;
    QUICHU
Peru South .... CANA, COLLA,
    CHANCA
Piman Indians .. CORA, JOVA,
    MAYO, PIMA, XOVA, YAKI,
    YAQUI
Plains Indians ... CREE, CROW;
    KIOWA, OSAGE; PONCA,
    TETON, PAWNEE
Pueblo Indians .. HOPI, MOKI,
    TANO, TAOS, ZUNI;
    KERES, MOQUI
Rio Grande .... TANO
Sacramento Valley ..... YANA
Salishan Indians ..... ATNAH,
    LUMMI
Shoshonean Indians .... UTE;
    HOPI,   KOSO,   MOKI,
    MONO; MOQUI,   PIUTE;
    UINTA, PAIUTE
Siouan Indians ... KAW, OTO;
    CROW,   IOWA,   OTOE;

KANSA, OMAHA, OSAGE,
    PONCA; BILOXI, DAKOTA,
    MANDAN; CATAWBA
Sonora .... JOVA, PIMI, SERI
South America (widely
    distributed) .... GES, ONA,
    YAO; LULE, MOXO, PANO,
    PIRO   TOBA;   CARIB,
    INERI; ARAWAK
South Carolina ..... CATAWBA
Tacanan Indians ..... CAVINA
Tanoan .... TEWA
Tapuyan Indians .... GE, GES,
    GHES, ACROA
Texas .... LIPAN
Tierra del Fuego: .... ONA
Tlingit: .... AUK, SITKA
Tupian .... ANTA
Utah: .... UTE
Washington .... HOH, LUMMI,
    MAKAH
Yucatan .... MAYA
Yukian .... TATU
Yukon .... TAKU
Yuncan .... CHIMU

ARMOR

Head .... COIF, HELM; ARMET, VISOR; BEAVER, CAMAIL;
BASINET, HAUBERK
Neck .... GORGET
Shoulder .... AILETTE, PAULDRON, EPAULIERE, PASSEGARDE
Body .... TACE; CULET, TASSE; CORIUM, GORGET, LORICA,
TASSET; CUIRASS, HAUBERK, SURCOAT; BRAGUETTE
Arm .... BRASSARD, PALLETTE, VAMBRACE;
CUBITIERE, REREBRACE
Hand .... GAUNTLET
Thigh .... CUISH, TASSE, TUILE; CUISSE,
TASSET, TUILLE
Leg, foot .... JAMB, JAMBE; GREAVE; CHAUSSE,
PEDIEUX; SOLLERET
Complete suit .... BARD, MAIL; BARDE

HERALDRY—HERALDIC TERMS

Heraldic bearings: BEND, ENTE,
FESS, ORLE, FESSE, GIRON,
GYRON, LAVER, PHEON;
SALTIRE
Heraldic tinctures:
gold, OR; fur, PEAN, VAIR,
VAIRE; green, VERT; blue,
AZURE; red, GULES; black,
SABLE; orange, TENNE; silver, ARGENT; blood-red,
MURREY; purple, PURPURE
attitude of animal
SEJANT, GARDANT,
PASSANT, RAMPANT
ball .... ROUNDEL
band ..... FESS, ORLE, FESSE
barnacle .... BREY
bend .... COTISE
bird .... MARTLET
circle .... BEZANT, ANNULET
colter .... LAVER
creature .. LION, PARD; BISSE,
WYVER; CANNET, WY-
VERN; GRIFFON, MARTLET
cross .. CRUX, NOWY, PATY;
FLORY, FORMY, PATEE,
PATTE; CLECHE; SALTIRE
curved in middle ...... NOWY
curves, made of ..... NEBULE
division ...... PALE, PALY
dog, short-eared ...... ALANT
drops, seme of .... GUTTE
duck ..... CANNET, CANETTE
fillet .... ORLE
fish trap .... WEEL
flower strewn .... SEME

flying in air .... FLOTANT
fountain .... SYKE
grafted .... ENTE
headless .... ETETE
horizontal band ......see bend
leaves, having ...... POINTE
lines .... UNDE, UNDY,
URDY, NEBULY
lozenge ..... FUSIL, MASCLE
manacle .... TIRRET
pointed .... URDE
powdered .... SEME
scattered .... SEME
sheaf of grain .. GERB, GERBE
shield .... PAVIS
shield division .... ENTE
shield's corner ...... CANTON
silver .... ARGENT
sitting .... ASSIS
snake .... BISSE
sown .... SEME
spangled .... SEME
star-strewn .... SEME
strewn .... SEME
three parts, divided into
TIERCE
triangle ..... GIRON, GYRON
two-winged .... VOL
voided escutcheon ...... ORLE
walking .... PASSANT
wavy .... ONDE, UNDE, UNDY,
UNDEE, NEBULE
winged .... VOL, AILE
wound .... VULN
wreath .... ORLE, TORSE

CHEMICAL ELEMENTS AND SYMBOLS

All elements are natural, metallic elements unless otherwise indicated. The chemical symbol of each element is indicated by the letter or letters in dark type that follow it. (Syn.) indicates synthetically produced.

3 letters
TIN **Sn**

4 letters
GOLD **Au**
IRON **Fe**
LEAD **Pb**
NEON **Ne** (gaseous)
ZINC **Zn**

5 letters
ARGON **Ar** (gaseous)
BORON **B** (nonmetallic)
RADON **Rn** (gaseous)
XENON **Xe** (gaseous)

6 letters
BARIUM **Ba**
CARBON **C**
  (nonmetallic)
CERIUM **Ce**
CESIUM **Cs**
COBALT **Co**
COPPER **Cu**
CURIUM **Cm** (syn.)
ERBIUM **Er**
HELIUM **He** (gaseous)
INDIUM **In**
IODINE **I**
  (nonmetallic)
NICKEL **Ni**
OSMIUM **Os**
OXYGEN **O** (gaseous)
RADIUM **Ra**
SILVER **Ag**
SODIUM **Na**
SULFUR **S**
  (nonmetallic)

7 letters
ARSENIC **As**
  (semimetallic)
BISMUTH **Bi**
BROMINE **Br**
  (nonmetallic)

CADMIUM **Cd**
CALCIUM **Ca**
FERMIUM **Fm** (syn.)
GALLIUM **Ga**
HAFNIUM **Hf**
HOLMIUM **Ho**
IRIDIUM **Ir**
KRYPTON **Kr** (gaseous)
LITHIUM **Li**
MERCURY **Hg**
NIOBIUM **Nb**
RHENIUM **Re**
RHODIUM **Rh**
SILICON **Si**
  (nonmetallic)
TERBIUM **Tb**
THORIUM **Th**
THULIUM **Tm**
URANIUM **U**
YTTRIUM **Y**

8 letters
ACTINIUM **Ac**
ALUMINUM **Al**
ANTIMONY **Sb**
ASTATINE **At**
  (semimetallic)
CHLORINE **Cl** (gaseous)
CHROMIUM **Cr**
EUROPIUM **Eu**
FLUORINE **F** (gaseous)
FRANCIUM **Fr**
HYDROGEN **H** (gaseous)
LUTETIUM **Lu**
NITROGEN **N** (gaseous)
NOBELIUM **No** (syn.)
PLATINUM **Pt**
POLONIUM **Po**
RUBIDIUM **Rb**
SAMARIUM **Sm**
SCANDIUM **Sc**
SELENIUM **Se**
  (nonmetallic)
TANTALUM **Ta**
THALLIUM **Ti**

TITANIUM **Ti**
TUNGSTEN **W**
VANADIUM **V**

9 letters
AMERICIUM **Am** (syn.)
BERKELIUM **Bk** (syn.)
BERYLLIUM **Be**
GERMANIUM **Ge**
LANTHANUM **La**
MAGNESIUM **Mg**
MANGANESE **Mn**
NEODYMIUM **Nd**
NEPTUNIUM **Np** (syn.)
PALLADIUM **Pd**
PLUTONIUM **Pu**
POTASSIUM **K**
RUTHENIUM **Ru**
STRONTIUM **Sr**
TELLURIUM **Te**
  (nonmetallic)
YTTERBIUM **Yb**
ZIRCONIUM **Zr**

10 letters
DYSPROSIUM **Dy**
GADOLINIUM **Gd**
LAWRENCIUM **Lr** (syn.)
MOLYBDENUM **Mo**
PHOSPHORUS **P**
  (nonmetallic)
PROMETHIUM **Pm**
TECHNETIUM **Tc**

11 letters
CALIFORNIUM **Cf**
  (syn.)
EINSTEINIUM **Es**
  (syn.)
MENDELEVIUM **Md**
  (syn.)

12 letters
PRASEODYMIUM **Pr**
PROTACTINIUM **Pa**

BIBLICAL REFERENCES

BOOKS OF THE BIBLE

Names and order of books of the:

OLD TESTAMENT

1 GENESIS	11 KINGS 1	21 ECCLESIASTES	30 AMOS
2 EXODUS	12 KINGS 2	22 SONG OF	31 OBADIAH
3 LEVITICUS	13 CHRONICLES 1	SOLOMON	32 JONAH
4 NUMBERS	14 CHRONICLES 2	23 ISAIAH	33 MICAH
5 DEUTERONOMY	15 EZRA	24 JEREMIAH	34 NAHUM
6 JOSHUA	16 NEHEMIAH	25 LAMENTATIONS	35 HABAKKUK
7 JUDGES	17 ESTHER	26 EZEKIEL	36 ZEPHANIAH
8 RUTH	18 JOB	27 DANIEL	37 HAGGAI
9 SAMUEL 1	19 PSALMS	28 HOSEA	38 ZECHARIAH
10 SAMUEL 2	20 PROVERBS	29 JOEL	39 MALACHI

Names and order of books of the:

NEW TESTAMENT

1 MATTHEW	9 GALATIANS	15 TIMOTHY 1	23 JOHN 1
2 MARK	10 EPHESIANS	16 TIMOTHY 2	24 JOHN 2
3 LUKE	11 PHILIPPIANS	17 TITUS	25 JOHN 3
4 JOHN	12 COLOSSIANS	18 PHILEMON	26 JUDE
5 THE ACTS	13 THESSALON-	19 HEBREWS	27 REVELATION
6 ROMANS	IANS 1	20 JAMES	
7 CORINTHIANS 1	14 THESSALON-	21 PETER 1	
8 CORINTHIANS 2	IANS 2	22 PETER 2	

BIBLICAL PROPHETS

AMOS (minor), ESAY, EZRA, JOEL (minor), HOSEA (minor), JONAH (minor), MICAH (minor), MOSES, DANIEL (major), NAHUM (minor), ELISHA, HAGGAI (minor), ISAIAH (major), EZEKIEL (major), JEREMIAH (major)

BIBLICAL PATRIARCHS

REU; ADAM, EBER, ENOS, NOAH, SETH, SHEM; ISAAC, JACOB, JARED, NAHOR, PELEG, SERUG, TERAH; LAMECH

BIBLICAL RULERS

OG; ASA (Judah), GOG, IRA; AGAG, AHAB, AHAZ, AMON, ELAH, JEHU, OMRI, SAUL; CYRUS, DAVID, DEBIR, HEROD, HIRAM, JORAM, NADAB, PEKAH, PIRAM, REZIN, SIHON, ZIMRI; ABIJAH, BAASHA. CAESAR, DARIUS, HEZION, HOSHEA, JAPHIA, JOSHUA, JOSIAH, JOTHAM, UZZIAH

BIBLICAL PEOPLES—TRIBES

DAN, GOG; ANAK, ARAD, CUSH, EMIM, MOAB, PHUD, PHUT (o.t.); ARKITE, HAMITE, HIVITE, KENITE, SEMITE, SHELAH, SINITE; EDOMITE, HITTITE, LEHABIM, MOABITE, REPHAIM

BIBLICAL PLACES

City . DAN, GATH, GAZA, ZOAR; BABEL, EKRON, SODOM; HEBRON

Country .... EDOM, ENON, SEBA; SHEBA

Hill, Jerusalem's .... ZION

Kingdom .... ELAM, MOAB; SAMARIA

Land .... NOD

Land of plenty .... GOSHEN

Mt. HOR, EBAL, NAIN, NEBO, PEOR; HOREB, SEIR, SINA, SINAI, TABOR; ARARAT, GILEAD, HERMON

Place .... ENON, AENON; JORDAN, SHILOH

Pool .... SILOAM

Region .. ARAM, EDAR; BASHAN

Town ...... CANA (1st miracle), NAIN (miracle site); BETHEL

River .... ARNON, JORDAN

BIBLICAL MEN

OG, UZ; ARA, DAN, ELI, GOG, HAM, IRA, LOT, NUN, URI; ABEL, AMOS, BOAZ, CAIN, CUSH, DOEG, EBAL, ENON, ENOS, ESAU, HETH, IRAD, JADA, JEHU, JOAB, KISH, LEVI, MASH, MOAB, OBAL, OBED, OMAR, OREB, OZEM, SETH, SODI, ULAM, UNNI, URIA; AARON (high priest), ABIAH, ABIEL, AHIRA, AMASA, ANNAS, CALEB, CHUZA, ENOCH, HAMAN, HARAN, HIRAM, HOHAM, IBZAN, ISAAC, JACOB, JAMES, JARED, MASSA, MOREH, NABAL, NAHBI, NAHOR, OPHIR, REZON, SACAR, TERAH, URIAH, ZAHAM; SAMSON; ANANIAS, ISHMAEL

BIBLICAL WOMEN

EVE; ADAH, JAEL, LEAH, MARY, RUTH; DINAH, EGLAH, HAGAR, JULIA, JUNIA, LYDIA, MERAB, NAOMI, PHEBE, RAHAB, SARAH, SARAI, SHUAH, TAMAR; ABITAL, BILHAH, DORCAS, ESTHER, HANNAH, HOGLAH, MAACAH, MAHLAH, MICHAL, MILCAH, MIRIAM, PERSIS, RACHEL, RIZPAH, SALOME, VASHTI, ZILLAH, ZILPAH; ABIGAIL, HAMUTAL

BIBLICAL NAMES

ED, ER; IRI, NER, ONO, REI, TOI; ABIA, ADER, ANER, ANIM, ASOM, DARA, ELON, ENOS, IRAD, IVAH, REBA; ABIAM, AHIRA, AMASA, ASEAS

GODS (DEITIES), GODDESSES
AND MYTHOLOGY

ASSYRIAN GODS
ANAT (sky), ASUR or ASSUR (war)

BABYLONIAN GODS
Chief gods: EA, ABU or ANU, BEL
EA (chief), ZU (wind), ABU or ANU (chief, sky, sun), BEL (chief), HEA
(see EA), IRA (war), SIN (moon), UTU (sun), ADAD or ADDA or ADDU
(wind, storm), APSU (chaos), ENKI (see EA), ENZU (see SIN), IRRA
(war), NABU or NEBO (wisdom), UTUG (sun), DAGAN (earth), ETANA
(eagle rider), SIRIS (alcoholic drinks), BABBAR (sun), SHAMASH (sun)

BABYLONIAN GODDESSES
AI or AYA (consort of Shamash), ERUA (mother), NINA (watery deep),
NANAI (daughter of Anu), ISTAR or ISHTAR (chief, love)

BRYTHONIC GODDESS
DON (ancestress of gods)

CELTIC GODS—GODDESS
ANA, ANU, DANA, DANU (mother, queen), LER (sea), LUG, LUGH
(light, sun), DAGDA (chief)

CYMRIC GODS
GWYN, LLEU, LLEW (solar)

EGYPTIAN GODS
RA (sun), SU (solar deity), BES (evil, pleasure), GEB (earth), KEB
(earth), MIN (procreation), SEB (earth), SET (evil), SHU (see SU), TEM or
TUM (sun), AANI (dog-headed ape, sacred to Thoth), AMEN (king),
AMON (sun and king), AMUN (king), ATMU or ATUM (sun), BESA (see
BES), HAPI (the Nile as a god), KHEM (see MIN), MENT (falcon-headed),
PTAH (Memphis god), SETH (evil), SOBK (crocodile-headed), AMMON
(see AMEN), HORUS (hawk-headed), MENTU (see MENT), SEBEK (see
SOBK), THOTH (wisdom, magic), OSIRIS (underworld), SERAPIS (see
OSIRIS)

EGYPTIAN GODDESSES
MA (same as MAAT), MUT (Amen's wife), NUT (heavens), ANTA,
APET (maternity), BAST (cat- or lion-headed), BUTO (serpent), ISIS
(cow-headed, Horus' mother), MAAT (truth, justice), SATI (queen),
ATHOR (see HATHOR), HATHOR (love, mirth, cow-headed)

EGYPTIAN MYTH

BA (soul of man), KA (body of man), NU (chaos), AKH (spirit of man), NUN (see NU), APIS (sacred bull), ATEN (solar disk), DUAT (see AMENTI), HAPI (Nile or Amenti's jinnee), AMENTI (underworld region)

GREEK GODS

DIS (underworld), PAN (field, flocks, forest), ZAN (old name for Zeus), ARES (war, Eris' brother), EROS (love), ZEUS (chief of Olympian gods), COMUS (mirth and revelry), EURUS (southeast wind), HADES (underworld), KOMOS (see COMUS), MOMUS (ridicule), PLUTO (underworld), AEOLUS (wind), APOLLO (sun, youth), AUSTER (south wind), BOREAS (north wind), CRONUS (a Titan, Rhea's spouse; harvest), HELIOS (sun), HERMES (herald), KRONOS (see CRONUS), NEREUS (sea), PLUTUS (wealth), TRITON (sea), BACCHUS (wine), POSEIDON (sea)

GREEK GODDESSES

GE (earth, mother of Titans), ARA (destruction, retribution, vengeance), ATE (discord, mischief, infatuation), EIR (healing), EOS (dawn), ALEA (ATHENA), CORA (see KORE), DICE or DIKE (one of Horae), ENYO (Ares' mother, war), ERIS (discord, sister of Ares), GAEA or GAIA (see GE), HEBE (youth), HERA (queen), HORA (one of Horae), KORE (vegetation), LEDA (Tyndareus' wife), NIKE (victory), RHEA (mother of gods, wife of Kronos), UPIS, ARTEMIS, HORAE (three goddesses of seasons), IRENE (peace), METIS (Zeus' first wife), MOIRA (fate or Fates), ATHENA (wisdom), CLOTHO (a Fate, thread spinner), CYBELE (nature), EIRENE (see IRENE), HECATE (moon, magic), MOERAE (see MOIRA), PALLAS (wisdom), SELENA and SELENE (moon), ARTEMIS (moon, woods, nature), ATROPOS (one of the Fates, thread cutter), DEMETER (grain, agriculture), CHLORIS (flowers), NEMESIS (revenge), LACHESIS (one of the Fates, thread length), APHRODITE (love)

GREEK MYTH

IO (Zeus' beloved changed to a heifer), INO (Cadmus' daughter), PAN (field, flocks, forest), ANAX (one of Dioscuri), AUGE (Arcadian princess), CEYX (Halcyone's husband turned into kingfisher), CLIO (Muse of History), FAUN (see PAN), IDAS (hero, killed Castor), IOLE (Hercules' captive), LETO (Apollo's mother), MAIA (Hermes' mother), OTUS (giant killed by Apollo), ALTIS (sacred grove, Olympic games), ATLAS (held up heavens), CREON (Oedipus' brother-in-law), DIONE (Aphrodite's mother), ENEAS (Troy's defender), ERATO (Clio's sister), HADES (underworld), HELLE (fell into Hellespont with golden fleece), HYDRA (9-headed monster), MINOS (king), NIOBE (weeping stone), SATYR (part-horse demigod), THEIA (Hyperion's sister, wife), ADONIS (beautiful youth), AENEAS (see ENEAS), AGENOR (Trojan warrior), ALECTO (a Fury), DAPHNE (Apollo's nymph turned into tree), EUROPA (carried off by Zeus in form of white bull), HECTOR (Trojan warrior), NEREID (sea nymph to Poseidon), NESTOR (wise king, fought Troy), THETIS (Achilles' mother), TITHON (see TITHONUS), TRITON (sea demigod,

Poseidon's son), **URANIA** (astronomy), **ARIADNE** (Theseus' love), **ATHAMAS** (Ino's husband), **CENTAUR** (half man, half horse), **CYCLOPS** (1-eyed giant), **ERINYES**, (avenging spirits), **EUTERPE** (Muse of Music), **SILENUS** (woodland deity, horse-goat-human), **ATALANTA** (picked up golden apples—lost the race), **TARTARUS** (infernal regions), **TITHONUS** (immortal king of Troy, Eos' favorite), **TISIPHONE** (one of Erinyes)
The Gorgons: **MEDUSA, STHENO, EURYALE**
The Graces: **AGLAIA, THALIA**
The Titans or Titanesses: primeval deities: **GAEA** or **GE** (mother of Titans). **URANUS** (father of Titans). Titans: **RHEA, COEUS, CREUS, THEIA, CRONUS** or **KRONOS, PHOEBE, THEMIS**

HINDU GODS
KA (unknown), **AGNI** (fire), **AKAL** (immortal), **CIVA** (see SIVA), **DEVA** or **DEWA** (divine being), **KAMA** (love), **RAMA** (incarnation of Vishnu), **SIVA** (supreme), **VAYU** (wind), **YAMA** (judge of dead), **BHAGA** (love), **DYAUS** (heaven, sky), **VISHNU** (supreme), **KRISHNA** (avatar of Vishnu)

HINDU GODDESSES
SRI (beauty, wealth, luck, Vishnu's wife), **UMA** (splendor), **VAC** (speech), **DEVI** (any divinity, Siva's consort), **KALI** (evil), **SHRI** (see SRI), **USAS** (dawn), **VACH** (see VAC), **SHREE** (see SRI), **MATRIS** (mothers), **LAKSHMI** (see SRI)

HINDU MYTH
BANA (1,000-arm giant), **KALI** (tongue of Agni), **KETU** (Rahu's tail), **NAGA** (Vishnu's serpent), **RAHU** (dragon, swallows sun), **USHA** (Bana's daughter)

INCA GOD
INTI (sun)

IRISH—see CELTIC

NORSE GODS
ER (war), **TY** (see TIU), **VE** (Odin's brother, slayed Ymir), **EAR** (see ER), **LOK** (see LOKI), **TIU** (sky, war, Tiwaz), **TIW** (see TIU), **TYR** (sky, war), **ULL** (bow skill), **VAN** (sea), **ZIO** (sky), **ZIU** (see ZIO), **FREY** (fertility), **HLER** (sea), **HOTH** (blind god), **LOKE** or **LOKI** (discord, mischief), **ODIN** chief god, war, wisdom, slayed Ymir), **THOR** (thunder), **TYRR** (war), **ULLR** (see ULL), **VALE** (see VALI), **VALI** (Odin's son), **VANS** (see VANIR), **VILI** (Odin's brother), **AEGIR** (sea), **AESIR** (chief), **ALCIS** (twin gods), **BALDR** (see BALDER), **BRAGE** or **BRAGI** (poetry), **DONAR** (see THOR), **HODER** or **HOTHR** (see HOTH), **VANIR** (early race of gods), **WODAN** or **WODEN** or **WOTAN** (see ODIN), **BALDER** or **BALDUR** (light)
The Aesir or chief gods: **TIU, TYR, ULL, FREY, LOKI, ODIN, THOR, VALI, BRAGI, DONAR, WODEN, BALDER**

NORSE GODDESSES

EIR (healing), HEL (Loki's daughter, underworld, dead), RAN (sea, death, wife of Aegir), SIF (Thor's wife), URD (destiny), VOR (betrothal), ERDA (earth), FREA or FRIA (see FRIGG), GERD (Frey's wife), HELA (see HEL), NORN (fate), RIND (Odin's wife, Vali's mother), SAGA (golden beaker), URTH (see URD), FREYA (love, beauty), FRIGG (Odin's wife), NANNA (flowers), NORNA or NORNS (see NORN), FREYJA (see FREYA)

NORSE MYTH

ASK (see ASKR), DIS (female spirit), ASKR (first man), ATLI (king), EGIL (story hero), GARM (Hel's watchdog, slays Tyr), GERI (Odin's wolf), IDUN (Bragi's wife), MARA (nightmare demon), NATT or NOTT (night), WATE (giant), YMIR or YMER ("rime-cold giant"), EGILL (see EGIL), MIMIR (giant), ASGARD (abode of gods)

PHOENICIAN GODDESS

ASTARTE (fertility, love)

ROMAN GODS

DIS (underworld), SOL (sun), AMOR (love), FAUN (field, herds, half goat), JOVE (chief god), MARS (war), MORS (death), COMUS (mirth, joy), CUPID (love), EURUS (southeast wind), KOMOS (see COMUS), MANES (spirits of dead, gods of underworld), ORCUS (dead), APOLLO (sun, music), AUSTER (south wind), BOREAS (north wind), FAUNUS (rural deity), VULCAN (fire), NEPTUNE (sea)

ROMAN GODDESSES

NOX or NYX (night), OPS (harvest, plenty), DIAN (moon, chase, woods), IRIS (rainbow, Zeus' messenger), JUNO (queen), LUNA (moon), MAIA (Vulcan's consort), NONA (Fate), SPES (hope), CERES (earth, grain, agriculture, vegetation), DIANA (see DIAN), EPONA (horses), FIDES (faith), FAUNA (field), FLORA (flowers), MORTA (a Fate), PARCA (a Fate), SALUS (prosperity), TERRA (earth), VENUS (love), VESTA (hearth), ANNONA (crops), AURORA (dawn), DECUMA (a Fate), PARCAE (the Fates), VACUNA (Sabine huntress)
The Fates or Parcae: NONA, MORTA, DECUMA

TEUTONIC GODS—see NORSE GODS

TEUTONIC GODDESSES—see NORSE GODDESSES

VEDIC GODS—see HINDU GODS

VEDIC GODDESSES—see HINDU GODDESSES

WELSH GOD

DYLAN

FIRST AND LAST NAMES
COMMON TO CROSSWORD PUZZLES

You often find in crossword puzzles definitions like "Writer Aldous ———" or "——— Pavlova." The following list contains the most commonly used names, first names and last names. The part of the name which is usually given in the definition is here in light-face type, arranged alphabetically. The rest of the person's name follows in bold-face type.

Aaron . **BURR, HANK**
Abbot .... **BUD**
Abzug .... **BELLA**
Acheson .... **DEAN**
Adam .... **BEDE**
Adams .... **EDIE, MAUDE**
Addams .... **JANE**
Adoree .... **RENEE**
Agar .... **JOHN**
Alain .... **DELON**
Alan .... **ALDA, KING, LADD, ARKIN, BATES, PATON**
Albert .... **CAMUS**
Albertus ... **MAGNUS**
Albrecht ..... **DURER**
Aldo .... **RAY**
Aldous ..... **HUXLEY**
Alejandro .... **REY**
Alexander .... **POPE, SEROV, CALDER, FLEMING**
Alexandre ... **DUMAS**
Alfred **LUNT, DRAKE**
Alfred B. .... **NOBEL**
Alighieri ..... **DANTE**
Allegra .... **KENT**
Allen .... **MEL, FRED, ETHAN, STEVE, WOODY**
Allison .... **FRAN**
Allyson .... **JUNE**
Alpert .... **HERB**
Ambler .... **ERIC**
Ambrose ... **BIERCE, FLEMING**
Amelia ... **BLOOMER**
Amundsen... **ROALD**
Anais .... **NIN**
Anatole ..... **FRANCE**
Andersen ...... **HANS**
Anderson ...... **LONI**
Andersson ...... **BIBI**
Andre .... **GIDE**
Andrea .... **DORIA**
Andrea del . **SARTO**
Andress .... **URSULA**
Andrew ...... **YOUNG**

Andrews ...... **DANA, JULIE**
Andy .... **HARDY, DEVINE**
Aneurin Bevan.. **NYE**
Angelico .... **FRA**
Angelo ..... **MOSSO, PATRI, GIOTTO**
Anita .... **LOOS**
Anna ... **CASE, HELD, STEN, MOFFO, NEAGLE**
Anouk .... **AIMEE**
Anthony ...... **EDEN, SUSAN, TUDOR**
Anton .... **DOLIN, SUSAN**
Antony .... **MARK**
Anya .... **SETON**
Arden .... **EVE, TONI, ENOCH**
Arlene .... **DAHL**
Arnaz .. **DESI, LUCIE**
Arnold .... **HAP**
Arsene .... **LUPIN**
Artemus ...... **WARD**
Arthur .... **BEA**
Arthur Conan **DOYLE**
Ataturk .... **KEMAL**
Attlee .... **CLEMENT**
Auguste .... **COMTE, RODIN**
Autry .... **GENE**
Ayres .... **LEW**
Baba .... **ALI**
Babe .... **RUTH**
Baer .... **MAX**
Bagnold .... **ENID**
Bailey .... **PEARL**
Bainter .... **FAY**
Baird .... **BIL**
Ballard .... **KAYE**
Balzac ...... **HONORE**
Bambi .... **LINN**
Bara .... **THEDA**
Barbara ...... **EDEN, HALE, RUSH**
Barkley ...... **ALBEN**
Barry ... **GENE, JACK**

Barrymore.... **DREW, JOHN, ETHEL, LIONEL**
Bartok... **EVA, BELA**
Barton .... **CLARA**
Basie .... **COUNT**
Bates .... **ALAN**
Bayes .... **NORA**
Bea, Beatrice . **LILLIE**
Bean .. **ROY, ORSON**
Becky .... **SHARP**
Bede .... **ADAM**
Beerbohm ...... **MAX**
Beery .... **NOAH**
Begley .... **ED**
Beiderbecke ..... **BIX**
Ben **HOGAN, SHAHN**
Bennett ...... **CERF, JOAN, TONY**
Bergen ...... **EDGAR, POLLY**
Bernhardt ... **SARAH**
Berra .... **YOGI**
Bert............ **LAHR**
Best............ **EDNA**
Bette **DAVIS, MIDLER**
Beverly .... **SILLS**
Bevin .... **ERNEST**
Billings ...... **JOSH**
Billy .... **MAY, ROSE, SUNDAY**
Bing .... **CROSBY**
Bjorn .... **BORG**
Blaise ...... **PASCAL**
Blake .... **EUBIE**
Blakeley ..... **RONEE, SUSAN**
Blanc........... **MEL**
Blas.............. **GIL**
Bloch........... **RAY**
Bloomer ... **AMELIA**
Blue........... **BEN**
Blum .... **LEON**
Blyth .... **ANN**
Bobby... **ORR, HULL**
Bogarde ...... **DIRK**
Bohan........ **MARC**
Bohr .... **NIELS**
Boleyn .... **ANNE**

Bolger.......... **RAY**
Bolivar .... **SIMON**
Bonheur....... **ROSA**
Boone. **PAT, DEBBY,**
        DANIEL,
        RICHARD
Bovary .... **EMMA**
Bradley....... **OMAR**
Brendan..... **BEHAN**
Bret.......... **HARTE**
Brice........ **FANNY**
Bridges....... **BEAU,**
   JEFF, LLOYD
Brigham..... **YOUNG**
Brodie........ **STEVE**
Bronte .... **EMILY**
Brooke ..... **SHIELDS**
Brooks ..... **HERB**
Brown........... **LES**
Broz........... **TITO**
Bruce **DERN, CABOT**
Brynner .... **YUL**
Buck .... **FRANK,**
  HENRY, OWENS,
  PEARL, ROGERS
Buddy. **RICH, HOLLY**
Buffalo Bill ... **CODY**
Bull .... **OLE**
Bunche...... **RALPH**
Burbank .... **LUTHER**
Burl .... **IVES**
Burr........ **AARON,**
    RAYMOND
Burrows........ **ABE**
Burstyn .... **ELLEN**
Buttons .... **RED**
Byington .... **SPRING**
Cabeza de..... **VACA**
Caesar .... **SID**
Calloway .... **CAB**
Campbell...... **GLEN**
Canada......... **LEE**
Cannon....... **DYAN**
Cantrell ...... **LANA**
Capek........ **KAREL**
Carl .... **CORI, JUNG,**
  FROST, SAGAN
Carl Marie von
       WEBER
Carnegie ...... **DALE**
Carnera ...... **PRIMO**
Carney .... **ART**
Carpenter ... **KAREN,**
      SCOTT
Carrie Chapman
      CATT
Carrie Jacobs **BOND**
Carrillo .... **LEO**
Carroll **LEO, BAKER,**
     LEWIS
Carson .... **KIT**

Carter... **AMY, CHIP,**
  JACK, JUNE,
    LYNDA
Caruso ..... **ENRICO**
Cass .... **PEGGY**
Casals....... **PABLO**
Castle........ **IRENE,**
    VERNON
Cather .... **WILLA**
Catherine...... **PARR**
Cavalieri........ **LINA**
Celeste....... **HOLM**
Chagall....... **MARC**
Champion ... **GOWER**
Chaney......... **LON**
Channing.... **CAROL**
Chaplin. **LETA, OONA**
Chapman...... **CEIL**
Charisse........ **CYD**
Charles.. **RAY, NICK,**
  NORA, DARWIN
Charlie . **RICH, PRIDE**
Charlotte.. **BRONTE,**
    CORDAY
Chase. **ILKA, CHEVY**
Chekhov..... **ANTON**
Christian ...... **DIOR**
Christie..... **AGATHA**
Cid.............. **EL**
Claire .... **INA**
Clapton......... **ERIC**
Clara **BOW, BARTON**
Clare Booth ... **LUCE**
Clarence ...... **DAY,**
    DARROW
Clark... **ROY, DANE,**
  DICK, KENT,
  MARK, GABLE
Claude ..... **MONET,**
    RAINS
Clay........ **HENRY,**
    CASSIUS
Clemens...... **MARK**
    TWAIN
Clement.... **ATTLEE**
Cleveland... **AMORY,**
    GROVER
Cliburn .... **VAN**
Clifton........ **WEBB**
Cobb........ **TY, LEE**
Cole.. **NAT, PORTER**
Columbo ...... **RUSS**
Como .... **PERRY**
Conde......... **NAST**
Connelly...... **MARC**
Connery...... **SEAN**
Connie .... **MACK,**
    FRANCIS
Conway .. **TIM, TOM,**
    SHIRL
Cooper........ **GARY**

Copland ..... **AARON**
Cordell .... **HULL**
Cornel........ **WILDE**
Costello ...... **LOU**
Cotton .... **MATHER**
Coty .... **RENE**
Count .... **BASIE**
Coward....... **NOEL**
Cox .... **WALLY**
Crane .... **HART**
Cregar ...... **LAIRD**
Crockett...... **DAVY**
Cronyn....... **HUME**
Crosby . **BING, GARY**
Crystal ...... **GAYLE**
Curie... **EVE, MARIE,**
    PIERRE
Curtis .... **TONY**
Dailey .... **DAN**
Dale........ **EVANS**
Daniel....... **BOONE,**
    DEFOE
Daniels........ **BEBE**
Danny......... **KAYE**
Dantes .... **EDMOND**
David.. **SOUL, BOWIE**
Davis.... **MAC, JEFF,**
    BETTE
Dawber......... **PAM**
Day **DORIS, LARAINE**
De l'Enclos ... **NINON**
De Leon..... **PONCE**
De Maupassant. **GUY**
De Valera.... **EAMON**
Dean .. **RUSK, DIZZY,**
  JAMES, MARTIN
Deborah....... **KERR**
Della **REESE, STREET**
Delmar .... **VINA**
Delon .... **ALAIN**
Dennis ... **DAY, KING**
Derek .... **BO, JOHN**
Descartes ..... **RENE**
Devine .... **ANDY**
Dewey .. **TOM, JOHN**
DeLuise .... **DOM**
Diamond Jim **BRADY**
Diana... **DORS, ROSS**
Dickinson..... **EMILY**
Dionne ...... **MARIA,**
  OLIVA, CECILE,
  EMELIE, YVONNE,
    ANNETTE
Disney .... **WALT**
Dolin .... **ANTON**
Don .... **HO, ADAMS,**
    KNOTTS
Donahue **PHIL, TROY**
Donlevy ...... **BRIAN**
Donna........ **REED,**
    SUMMER

Doone....... **LORNA**
Dorfmann ..... **ANIA**
Doris.... **DAY, DUKE**
Dorothy ... **DIX, GISH**
Dors .... **DIANA**
Dostoevsky. **FEODOR**
Doubleday... **ABNER**
Downs .... **HUGH**
Drew......... **ELLEN**
Dreyfus .... **ALFRED**
Dufy .... **RAOUL**
Duke .... **DORIS**
Duke Astin .. **PATTY**
Dunaway ...... **FAYE**
Duncan. **SARA, TODD**
Dunne........ **IRENE**
Durocher .. **LEO, LIP,**
LIPPY
Dvorak ...... **ANTON**
Dwight ...... **MOODY**
Eamon de .. **VALERA**
Earhart..... **AMELIA**
Eartha.......... **KITT**
Eastwood..... **CLINT**
Eddie.......... **FOY**
Edgar . **POE, DEGAS,**
GUEST
Edith .... **PIAF**
Edmond .... **DANTES**
Edmund ..... **BURKE**
Edna **BEST, FERBER,**
MILLAY
Edouard ..... **MANET**
Eduard **LALO, BENES**
Edvard .... **GRIEG**
Edward ...... **ELGAR**
Edward Everett **HALE**
Edwards **GUS, VINCE**
Edwin .... **BOOTH,**
WEEKS
Eisaku......... **SATO**
Ekberg ...... **ANITA**
Ekland........ **BRITT**
Elaine .... **MAY**
Eleanora....... **DUSE**
Elia... **LAMB, KAZAN**
Elias.......... **HOWE**
Elihu ... **ROOT, YALE**
Ellen . **DREW, TERRY**
Ellington....... **DUKE**
Elliott........ **GOULD**
Ellsworth ..... **VINES**
Elmer .. **RICE, CRAIG**
Elmo .... **ROPER**
Emerson ...... **FAYE,**
RALPH WALDO
Emile.......... **ZOLA**
Emily **POST, BRONTE**
En-lai.......... **CHOU**
Enoch **ARDEN, LIGHT**
Enrico........ **FERMI**

Erica .... **JONG**
Erik .... **SATIE**
Erikson......... **LIEF**
Ernest........ **BEVIN,**
BLOCK, SETON
Ernie ... **FORD, PYLE**
Errol ... **LEON, FLYNN**
Estrada......... **ERIK**
Ethan **ALLEN, FROME**
Ethel .... **WATERS**
Ethelbert ..... **NEVIN**
Eugene . **DEBS, FIELD**
Eva .... **GABOR**
Eva Marie .... **SAINT**
Evans .... **DALE**
Everett .... **CHAD**
Evita .... **PERON**
Ewell .... **TOM**
Eydie........ **GORME**
Eyre............ **JANE**
Ezra. **POUND, STONE**
Fanny .... **BRICE**
Farrow .... **MIA**
Ferber......... **EDNA**
Ferde......... **GROFE**
Ferenc .... **MOLNAR**
Fermi ...... **ENRICO**
Fernand .... **LEGER**
Fernando.... **LAMAS**
Ferrer .... **MEL, JOSE**
Field .... **SALLY**
Filippino....... **LIPPI**
Fisher... **BUD, HAM,**
CARRIE, EDDIE
Fitzgerald...... **ELLA,**
BARRY, F. SCOTT
Flynn......... **ERROL**
Foch .... **NINA**
Fonda **JANE, HENRY,**
PETER
Ford.. **EDSEL, ERNIE,**
HENRY
Foscolo .... **UGO**
Fra Filippo..... **LIPPI**
Francesco..... **NITTI**
Franchot ...... **TONE**
Francis..... **BACON,**
DRAKE
Francis Scott... **KEY**
Franck ...... **CESAR**
Francoise.... **SAGAN**
Frank.... **FAY, BUCK,**
CAPRA
Frank Lloyd. **WRIGHT**
Frankie...... **CARLE,**
LAINE
Frans.......... **HALS**
Franz... **KAFKA,**
LEHAR, LISZT
Frederick .... **LOEWE**
Frobe .... **GERT**

Frome....... **ETHAN**
Gabor . **EVA, MAGDA,**
ZSA ZSA
Gagarin .... **YURI**
Gale......... **STORM**
Gam .... **RITA**
Garbo .... **GRETA**
Gardner . **AVA, ERLE**
Garner ..... **JAMES,**
ERROLL
Garson ...... **GREER**
Gavin.......... **MUIR**
Gayle...... **CRYSTAL**
Gazzara .... **BEN**
Gehrig......... **LOU**
Geller .... **URI**
Genghis .... **KHAN**
George.. **ADE, OHM,**
BUSH, RAFT,
SAND, BROWN,
CLARK, DEWEY,
GOBEL, LUCAS,
SCOTT, SEGAL,
CUSTER, PATTON
George Bernard
SHAW
George Frederick
HANDEL
George Herman
RUTH
Georges...... **BIZET,**
SEURAT
Gerald......... **FORD**
Geraldine...... **PAGE**
Gershwin....... **IRA,**
GEORGE
Gert.......... **FROBE**
Gertrude ..... **BERG,**
STEIN
Getz........... **STAN**
Gibson .... **HOOT**
Gil .... **BLAS**
Gillespie...... **DIZZY**
Giuseppe ..... **BELLI,**
VERDI
Gladys ..... **KNIGHT**
Glasgow...... **ELLEN**
Glenn . **FORD, JOHN,**
MILLER
Gluck......... **ALMA**
Golda .... **MEIR**
Goldberg ...... **RUBE**
Goldie........ **HAWN**
Gordon **RUTH, FLASH**
Gorky .... **MAXIM**
Gorme .... **EYDIE**
Gould .... **JAY**
Grace .... **KELLY**
Graham ...... **BILLY,**
GREENE, MARTHA
Grandma .... **MOSES**

Meryl....... **STREEP**
Meyerson...... **BESS**
Mickey ..... **MANTLE**
Midler .... **BETTE**
Miles . **VERA, SARAH,**
 STANDISH
Miller.. **ANN, GLENN,**
 ROGER
Mineo .... **SAL**
Minnelli......... **LIZA**
Minnie........ **PEARL**
Minuit .... **PETER**
Mischa .... **AUER,**
 ELMAN
Mitchell . **GUY, JONI,**
 BILLY
Moffo .... **ANNA**
Mohandas .. **GANDHI**
Mollet .... **GUY**
Mondrian .... **PIET**
Montand....... **YVES**
Montez **LOLA, MARIA**
Montgomery.... **WES**
Monty .... **HALL**
Moorhead ... **AGNES**
Moreno......... **RITA**
Morgana **FATA, NINA**
Morley .... **SAFER**
Mostel........ **ZERO**
Mountbatten.. **EARL,**
 LOUIS
Mowbray ...... **ALAN**
Muhammad...... **ALI**
Munson .... **ONA**
Murray ... **DON, JAN,**
 KEN, MAE, ANNE
Musial......... **STAN**
Myra .... **HESS**
Myrna .... **LOY**
Nagy .... **IMRE**
Nahum .... **TATE**
Nancy....... **HANKS**
Natalie .... **WOOD**
Nathan .... **HALE**
Nazimova...... **ALLA**
Ned .... **SPARKS**
Negri.......... **POLA**
Nelson **EDDY, GENE,**
 MILES, RIDDLE
Nero .... **PETER**
Newton....... **ISAAC**
Newton-John **OLIVIA**
Nicholas...... **AMATI**
Niels .... **BOHR**
Nikola .... **TESLA**
Noel....... **COWARD**
Nora . **KAYE, BAYES**
Norman ...... **LEAR,**
 MAILER
Normand .... **MABEL**
Novarro ..... **RAMON**

Novello........ **IVOR**
O'Casey .... **SEAN**
O'Neal........ **RYAN,**
 TATUM
O'Neill........ **OONA**
O. Henry ... **PORTER**
Ogden.. **NASH, REID**
Oley......... **SPEAKS**
Oliver **REED, HARDY,**
 PERRY
Oliver Wendell
 HOLMES
Olsen........... **OLE**
Omar...... **SHARIF,**
 BRADLEY
Onegin ...... **EUGEN**
Opie........... **READ**
Orson .... **BEAN,**
 WELLES
Orville...... **WRIGHT**
Oscar .... **WILDE,**
 LEVANT
Ott............. **MEL**
Pablo....... **CASALS**
Pacino............ **AL**
Paderewski . **IGNACE**
Page .... **PATTI**
Paine............ **TOM**
Palmer **ARNIE, LILLI,**
 ARNOLD
Pancho...... **SANZA,**
 VILLA
Parker......... **FESS**
Parton....... **DOLLY**
Pasternak .... **BORIS**
Pasteur....... **LOUIS**
Pastor.........**TONY**
Paton .... **ALAN**
Patti .... **PAGE**
Paul... **ANKA, KLEE,**
 MUNI
Pauling ...... **LINUS**
Pavlova ...... **ANNA**
Pearl . **BUCK, WHITE,**
 BAILEY, MINNIE
Pearson .... **LESTER**
Peerce .... **JAN**
Peewee ...... **REESE**
Peggy... **LEE, CASS,**
 WOOD
Peron ... **EVA, JUAN,**
 EVITA
Perry **COMO, MASON**
Pete. **ROSE, SEEGER,**
 FOUNTAIN
Peter.. **ARNO, NERO,**
 ROSE, LORRE
Peter Paul.. **RUBENS**
Petula .... **CLARK**
Phileas .... **FOGG**
Philip.... **HALE, NERI**

Philo .... **VANCE**
Picasso...... **PABLO**
Pickens........ **SLIM**
Picon........ **MOLLY**
Pierre .. **LOTI, CURIE**
Pierre-Auguste
 RENOIR
Pinky............. **LEE**
Pinza........... **EZIO**
Pirandello...... **LUIGI**
Pola.......... **NEGRI**
Polo......... **MARCO**
Ponce de ...... **LEON**
Pons .... **LILY**
Ponselle...... **ROSA**
Porter .... **COLE**
Pound .... **EZRA**
Preminger ..... **OTTO**
Priscilla...... **ALDEN,**
 MULLEN
Prokofiev..... **SERGE**
Proust...... **MARCEL**
Pyle .... **ERNIE**
Radner ...... **GILDA**
Rainer ...... **LUISE**
Rainer Maria.. **RILKE**
Raines........ **ELLA**
Rains....... **CLAUDE**
Ralph....... **NADER,**
 BUNCHE
Rand ... **AYN, SALLY**
Rathbone..... **BASIL**
Ray .. **ALDO, BLOCH,**
 NOBLE
Rayburn .... **SAM**
Raymond ..... **BURR,**
 GENE
Read .... **OPIE**
Rebecca..... **WEST**
Red, the........ **ERIC**
Reed . **ALAN, DONNA**
Reese .... **DELLA,**
 PEEWEE
Rehan.......... **ADA**
Reiner... **ROB, CARL**
Rene .... **COTY**
Rex .... **BELL, REED,**
 STOUT
Reynolds ..... **BURT**
Rhodes....... **CECIL**
Richard.. **DIX, BYRD,**
 LONG, ROWE,
 CONTE, STRAUSS
Ringo........ **STARR**
Rip.. **TORN, TAYLOR**
Rita .... **GAM**
Ritter.... **TEX, JOHN,**
 THELMA
Rivera **CHITA, DIEGO**
Robb .... **INEZ**
Rockne....... **KNUTE**

Roger . . . . **BACON**
Rogers . . **ROY, CARL,**
WILL, KENNY,
GINGER
Romero . . . . . **CESAR**
Ronstadt . . . . . **LINDA**
Root . . **OREN, ELIHU**
Roper . . . . **ELMO**
Rose . . . . **PETE**
Rousseau . . . . . **HENRI**
Rowlands . . . . . . **GENA**
Rubinstein . . **ANTON,**
ARTUR, ARTURO
Ruby . . . . **DEE**
Rudolf . **BING, FRIML,**
DIESEL
Runyon . . . . . **DAMON**
Russell . . . . **SAGE**
Ruth **BABE, GORDON**
Saarinen . . . . **EERO**
Sagan . . . . **CARL**
Saint,—Marie . . . **EVA**
Sally . . **RAND, FIELD**
Salmon P . . . . **CHASE**
Salvador . . . . **DALI**
Sam . . . . **SNEAD,**
HOUSTON
Samuel . . . . . . **MORSE**
Sand . . . . . **GEORGE**
Sandra . . . . **DEE**
Sarah . . . . **MILES**
Saud . . . . **IBN**
Savalas . . . . **TELLY**
Schmeling . . . . . **MAX**
Scholem . . . . **ASCH**
Schulberg . . . . . **BUDD**
Seegar . . . . **ALAN**
Seeger . . . . **PETE**
Seeley . . . . **BLOSSOM**
Segovia . . . . **ANDRES**
Selassie . . . . . . **HAILE**
Serling . . . . **ROD**
Seton . . . . **ANYA**
Sevareid . . . . **ERIC**
Severinsen . . . . . **DOC**
Shahn . . . . **BEN**
Shankar . . . . **RAVI**
Sharif . . . . **OMAR**
Sharp . . . . **BECKY**
Shaw . . . . **ARTIE**
Shawn . . . . **TED**
Shelley . . . . . . **PERCY**
BYSSHE,
WINTERS
Shields . . . . . **BROOKE**
Shire . . . . **TALIA**
Shirley . . . . . . **BOOTH**
Sidney . . . . . . **LANIER**
Sigmund . . . . **FREUD**
Signe . . . . **HASSO**
Silvers . . . . **SID, PHIL**

Sinatra . . . . . . **FRANK,**
NANCY
Sinclair . . . . . . **LEWIS,**
UPTON
Skelton . . . . **RED**
Skinner . . . . **OTIS**
Smith . . . . **AL, ADAM,**
ALEXIS, ALFRED
Snead . . . . **SAM**
Sommer . . . . **ELKE**
Sonja . . . . **HENIE**
Sonny **BONO, TUFTS**
Sophia . . . . . **LOREN**
Sothern . . . . **ANN**
Spacek . . . . **SISSY**
Sparks . . . . **NED**
Speaker . . . . **TRIS**
Speaks . . . . **OLEY**
Spencer . . . . . **TRACY**
Spewack . . . . . **BELLA**
St. John **JILL, ADELA**
St. Vincent Millay
EDNA
Stacy . . . . **KEACH**
Stalin . . . . **JOSIF**
Standish . . . . . . **MILES**
Stanford . . . . . . **WHITE**
Starr . . . **KAY, RINGO**
Steen . . . . **JAN**
Steiger . . . . **ROD**
Stengel . . . . . . **CASEY**
Stephen . . . . . **CRANE**
Stephen V. . . . **BENET**
Sterling . . . . **JAN**
Stern . . . . **ISAAC**
Steve . . . . **ALLEN**
Stevens **CAT, MARK,**
RISE, STELLA
Stevenson . . . . **ADLAI**
Stevie . . . . . **WONDER**
Stewart **ROD, JIMMY**
Stoker . . . . **BRAM**
Stone . . **LUCY, EZRA**
Storm . . **GALE, FIELD**
Stravinsky . . . . . **IGOR**
Streep . . . . . . **MERYL**
Stuart . . . . **JEB**
Styne . . . . **JULE**
Sullivan . . . . **ED**
Sumac . . . . **YMA**
Summer . . . . . **DONNA**
Sunday . . . . . . **BILLY**
Susan . . . . **DEY**
Susan B. . **ANTHONY**
Syngman . . . . . . **RHEE**
Tab . . . . **HUNTER**
Tajo . . . . **ITALO**
Talia . . . . **SHIRE**
Tamiroff . . . . **AKIM**
Tanguay . . . . **EVA**
Tarbell . . . . **IDA**

Tarkington . . . **BOOTH**
Taylor . **LIZ, RIP, ROD**
Teasdale . . . . . . **SARA**
Tebaldi . . . . . **RENATA**
Templar . . . . . . **SIMON**
Templeton . . . . . **ALEC**
Tennessee . . . **ERNIE,**
WILLIAMS
Terry . . . . **ELLEN**
Tex . . . . **RITTER**
Thatcher . . . . **BECKY**
Theda . . . . **BARA**
Thelma . . . . . . **RITTER**
Thelonious . . . **MONK**
Thomas . . . . . . **ARNE,**
GRAY, HOOD,
MANN, NAST,
DYLAN, HARDY,
HICKS, DANNY,
MARLO, MOORE,
WOLFE, HOBBES
Thompson . . . . . **SADA**
Thornton . . . **WILDER**
Tilden . . . . **BILL**
Tillis . . . . **MEL**
Tillstrom . . . . . . **BURR**
Timothy . . **BOTTOMS**
Tito . . . . **BROZ**
Tolstoy . . . . **LEO**
Tom . . . . **MIX, EWELL,**
PAINE
Tomlin . . . . **LILY**
Tony **SARG, CURTIS,**
PASTOR
Toren . . . . **MARTA**
Torme . . . . **MEL**
Torn . . . . **RIP**
Toscanini . . . **ARTURO**
Trotsky . . . . **LEON**
Truex . . . . **ERNIE**
Truman . . . . . **BESS,**
HARRY, CAPOTE
Trygve . . . . **LIE**
Tse-tung . . . . **MAO**
Tuesday . . . . . **WELD**
Tunney . . . . **GENE**
Turner . . . . . **IKE, NAT,**
LANA, TINA
Turpin . . . . **BEN**
Twain . . . . **MARK**
Ty . . . . **COBB**
Ulanova . . . . . **GALINA**
Ullmann . . . . **LIV**
Uriah . . . . **HEEP**
Vallee . . . . **RUDY**
Vance . . . . . . **CYRUS,**
ETHEL, PHILO
Vaughan . . . . . **SARAH**
Velez . . . . **LUPE**
Venerable, the . **BEDE**
Vera . . . . **MILES**

Verdon . . . . **GWEN**
Verdugo . . . . . . **ELENA**
Vereen . . . . **BEN**
Vermeer . . . . **JAN**
Verne . . . . **JULES**
Vernon . . . . . **CASTLE**
Victor **HUGO, BORGE, BUONO**
Vigoda . . . . **ABE**
Vincent . . . . **PRICE**
Virginia . . . . **DARE, MAYO, WOOLF**
Virna . . . . **LISI**
Vivien . . . . **LEIGH**
Vladimir . . . . . . **LENIN**
Voight . . . . **JON**
W.C. **HANDY, FIELDS**
Wallace . . . . **LEW, HENRY, AGARD**
Wallach . . . . **ELI**
Waller . . . . **FATS**
Wally . . . . . . **COX, PIP**
Walter . . **ABEL, REED, BRUNO**
Walton . . . . **IZAAK**
Warburg . . . . **OTTO**
Warhol . . . . **ANDY**
Warren . . . . **EARL**
Washington . . **DINAH, BOOKER T.**
Waters . . . . **ETHEL**
Waugh . . . . **ALEC**
Webb . . . **ALAN, JACK**

Webster . . . . . . **NOAH, DANIEL**
Weill . . . . **KURT**
Weld . . . . . **TUESDAY**
Welles . . . . **ORSON, SUMNER**
Wendell . . . . . **COREY, WILLKIE**
Werner Von . **BRAUN**
Wharton . . . . . . **EDITH**
White . . . . . . **BYRON, PEARL, WILLIAM ALLEN**
Whiteman . . . . . **PAUL**
Whitman . . . . . **WALT**
Whitney . . . . **ELI**
Wilbur . . . . **CROSS, WRIGHT**
Wilde . . . . **OSCAR**
Wilder . . **GENE, BILLY**
Wiley . . . . **POST**
Wilhelm von . . . **OPEL**
Wilkins . . . . **ROY**
Willa . . . . **CATHER**
William **HART, HULL, INGE, PENN, PITT, BOOTH, HANDY, HOLDEN**
William Butler . **YEATS**
William Cullen
                BRYANT
William Randolph
                HEARST

William Rose . . **BENET**
William Sidney
                PORTER
Williams **TED, ROBIN, ROGER**
Wills . . . . **CHILL, HELEN**
Wilson . . . . **FLIP**
Winding . . . . **KAI**
Winslow . . . . . **HOMER**
Winterhalter . . **HUGO**
Wolfgang Amadeus
                MOZART
Wood . . . . **GRANT**
Wray . . . . **FAY**
Wynn . . . . **ED, EARLY**
Wynter . . . . **DANA**
Xavier . . . . **CUGAT**
Yale . . . . **ELIHU**
Yat-sen . . . . **SUN**
Yogi . . . . **BERRA**
Yoko . . . . **ONO**
Young . . . . . . **CY, GIG, ALAN, CHIC**
Youskevitch . . . **IGOR**
Yutang . . . . **LIN**
Zasu . . . . **PITTS**
Zebulon . . . . **PIKE**
Zeppo . . . . **MARX**
Zetterling . . . . **MAI**
Zola . . . . **EMILE**
Zorina . . . . **VERA**
Zubin . . . . **MEHTA**

CELEBRITIES' ORIGINAL NAMES

Abbot, Bud....... **William Abbot**

Adams, Edie..... **Elizabeth Edith Enke**

Adoree, Renee .... **Jeanne de la Fonte**

Aimee, Anouk .. **Francoise Sorya**

Albert, Eddie ..... **Edward Albert Heimberger**

Alda, Robert **Alphonso d'Abruzzo**

Alexander, Jane ... **Jane Quigley**

Allen, Fred ...... **John F. Sullivan**

Allen, Woody .. **Allen Konigsberg**

Allyson, June...... **Ella Geisman**

Anderson, Dame Judith. **Frances Margaret Anderson**

Andrews, Dana .... **Carver Daniel Andrews**

Andrews, Julie........ **Julia Wells**

Angeli, Pier.......... **Anna Maria Pierangeli**

Ann-Margret **Ann-Margret Olsson**

Arden, Eve ..... **Eunice Quedens**

Arlen, Harold ..... **Hyman Arluck**

Arliss, George .. **George Andrews**

Arness, James .. **James Aurness**

Arthur, Jean...... **Gladys Greene**

Astaire, Fred .... **Frederick Austerlitz**

Astor, Mary . **Lucille Langehanke**

Auer, Mischa............ **Mischa Ounskowsky**

Aumont, Jean-Pierre . **Jean-Pierre Salomons**

Avalon, Frankie. **Francis Avallone**

Bacall, Lauren **Betty Joan Perske**

Ballard, Kaye.. **Catherine Balotta**

Bancroft, Anne ...... **Anna Maria Italiano**

Bara, Theda **Theodosia Goodman**

Bardot, Brigitte.... **Camille Javal**

Bari, Lynn....... **Marjorie Fisher**

Barry, Gene .... **Eugene Klass**

Barrymore, John ... **John Blythe**

Barrymore, Lionel . **Lionel Blythe**

Bartholomew, Freddie . **Frederick Llewellyn**

Bayes, Nora...... **Dora Goldberg**

Bennett, Tony.......... **Anthony Benedetto**

Benny, Jack . **Benjamin Kubelsky**

Berg, Gertrude .... **Gertrude Edelstein**

Bergen, Polly...... **Nellie Burgin**

Berkeley, Busby .... **William Berkeley Enos**

Berle, Milton .. **Mendel Berlinger**

Berlin, Irving .... **Israel Baline**

Bishop, Joey ...... **Joseph Gottlieb**

Black, Karen ...... **Karen Ziegler**

Blaine, Vivian **Vivienne Stapleton**

Blair, Janet........ **Martha Janet Lafferty**

Blake, Amanda .... **Beverly Neill**

Blake, Robert... **Michael Gubitosi**

Blue, Ben ... **Benjamin Bernstein**

Bogarde, Dirk ... **Derek Van Den Bogaerde**

Boone, Pat...... **Charles Eugene Boone**

Borgnine, Ernest **Ermes Borgnino**

Bowie, David **David Robert Jones**

Brice, Fanny...... **Fanny Borach**

Bridges, Beau ..... **Lloyd Vernet Bridges III**

Britt, May ..... **Maybritt Wilkens**

Brodie, Steve...... **John Stevens**

Bronson, Charles........ **Charles Buchinsky**

Brooks, Mel ... **Melvin Kaminsky**

Burns, George. **Nathan Birnbaum**

Burstyn, Ellen ... **Edna Gilhooley**

Burton, Richard. **Richard Jenkins**

Buttons, Red ..... **Aaron Chwatt**

Byrnes, Edd (Kookie) .... **Edward Breitenberger**

Caine, Michael.......... **Maurice Micklewhite**

Calhoun, Rory .... **Francis Durgin**

Callas, Maria .... **Maria Kalogeropoulos**

Cannon, Dyan .... **Samille Diane Friesen**

Cantor, Eddie... **Edward Iskowitz**

Capucine.... **Germaine Lefebvre**

Carroll, Diahann .. **Carol Diahann Johnson**

Castle, Irene .... **Irene Foote**

Castle, Vernon ... **Vernon Blythe**

Chandler, Jeff........ **Ira Grossel**

Charisse, Cyd **Tula Ellice Finklea**

Checker, Chubby.. **Ernest Evans**

Cher......... **Cherilyn Sarkisian**

Clark, Dane .... **Bernard Zanville**

Cobb, Lee J.......... **Leo Jacoby**

Colbert, Claudette **Lily Claudette Chauchoin**

Cole, Nat (King) . **Nathaniel Coles**

Connery, Sean **Thomas Connery**

Connors, Michael......... **Kreker Ohanian**

Conrad, Robert... **Conrad Robert Falk**

Cooper, Alice.... **Vincent Furnier**

Cooper, Gary... **Frank J. Cooper**

Cord, Alex..... **Alexander Viespi**

Corday, Mara..... **Marilyn Watts**

Cosell, Howard ... **Howard Cohen**

Costello, Elvis . **Declan McManus**

Costello, Lou ...... **Louis Cristillo**

Crawford, Joan . **Lucille Le Sueur**

Crosby, Bing **Harry Lillis Crosby**
Curtis, Tony.. **Bernard Schwartz**
Damone, Vic .... **Vito Farinola**
Darby, Kim...... **Deborah Zerby**
Darren, James... **James Ercolani**
Davis, Bette...... **Ruth Elizabeth
Davis**
Day, Dennis .... **Eugene McNulty**
Day, Doris. **Doris von Kappelhoff**
Day, Laraine.... **Laraine Johnson**
DaSilva, Howard.......... **Harold
Silverblatt**
De Carlo, Yvonne. **Peggy Yvonne
Middleton**
Dee, Ruby.... **Ruby Ann Wallace**
Dee, Sandra.... **Alexandra Zuck**
Deneuve, Catherine.... **Catherine
Dorleac**
Denver, John........ **Henry John
Deutschendorf Jr.**
Derek, John....... **Derek Harris**
Devine, Andy **Jeremiah Schwartz**
DeWolfe, Billy ..... **William Jones**
Dickinson, Angie **Angeline Brown**
Dietrich, Marlene .... **Maria
von Losch**
Diller, Phyllis ...... **Phyllis Driver**
Donahue, Troy ... **Merle Johnson**
Dors, Diana .... **Diana Fluck**
Douglas, Kirk. **Issur Danielovitch**
Douglas, Melvyn......... **Melvyn
Hesselberg**
Drake, Alfred... **Alfredo Capurro**
Dressler, Marie.... **Leila Koerber**
Drew, Ellen.......... **Terry Ray**
Dylan, Bob .. **Robert Zimmerman**
Ebsen, Buddy ... **Christian Ebsen**
Eden, Barbara . **Barbara Huffman**
Ely, Ron.......... **Ronald Pierce**
Evans, Dale .... **Frances Octavia
Smith**
Everett, Chad **Raymond Cramton**
Ewell, Tom.. **S. Yewell Tompkins**
Fabian . **Fabian Forte Bonaparte**
Fairbanks, Douglas ..... **Douglas
Ullman**
Farrow, Mia .... **Maria Farrow**
Faye, Alice .... **Ann Leppert**
Fernandel ... **Fernand Contandin**
Fetchit, Stepin..... **Lincoln Perry**
Fields, Gracie .. **Grace Stansfield**
Fields, W. C...... **William Claude
Dukinfield**
Finch, Peter.... **William Mitchell**
Fitzgerald, Barry. **William Shields**
Fleming, Rhonda .. **Marilyn Louis**
Fontaine, Joan **Joan de Havilland**
Ford, Glenn .... **Gwyllyn Ford**
Ford, John .... **Sean O'Fearna**
Forsythe, John ..... **John Freund**
Foxx, Redd.. **John Elroy Sanford**

Franciosa, Tony .... **Anthony
Papaleo**
Francis, Arlene ... **Arlene Francis
Kazanjian**
Francis, Connie....... **Constance
Franconero**
Gabor, Zsa Zsa .... **Sari Gabor**
Garbo, Greta .. **Greta Gustafsson**
Gardenia, Vincent ...... **Vincente
Scognamiglio**
Gardner, Ava...... **Lucy Johnson**
Garfield, John ... **Julius Garfinkle**
Garland, Beverly......... **Beverly
Fessenden**
Garland, Judy ... **Frances Gumm**
Garner, James .... **James
Baumgarner**
Gaynor, Janet ..... **Laura Gainer**
Gaynor, Mitzi... **Francesca Mitzi
von Gerber**
Gentry, Bobbie **Roberta Streeter**
Gershwin, George .... **Jacob
Gershowitz**
Gershwin, Ira.. **Israel Gershowitz**
Gilbert, John .... **John Pringle**
Gilford, Jack ..... **Jacob Gellman**
Gish, Dorothy **Dorothy de Guiche**
Gish, Lillian..... **Lillian de Guiche**
Goddard, Paulette .. **Marion Levy**
Goldwyn, Samuel........ **Samuel
Goldfish**
Gordon, Gale .... **Gaylord Aldrich**
Gould, Elliott ... **Elliott Goldstein**
Goulet, Robert........... **Stanley
Applebaum**
Granger, Stewart .... **James
Lablanche Stewart**
Grant, Cary .... **Archibald Leach**
Grant, Kathryn ... **Olive Kathryn
Grandstaff**
Grant, Lee...... **Lyova Rosenthal**
Graves, Peter .... **Peter Aurness**
Grayson, Kathryn......... **Zelma
Kathryn Hedrick**
Grey, Joel............. **Joel Katz**
Hackett, Buddy. **Leonard Hacker**
Harlow, Jean **Harlean Carpentier**
Harris, Barbara .... **Sandra
Markowitz**
Harvey, Laurence...... **Larushka
Mischa Skikne**
Haver, June ..... **June Stovenour**
Hayden, Sterling.. **John Hamilton**
Hayes, Helen .... **Helen Hayes
Brown**
Hayward, Louis... **Seafield Grant**
Hayward, Susan......... **Edythe
Marrener**
Hayworth, Rita .... **Margarita
Carmen Cansino**
Heflin, Van . **Emmett Evan Heflin**

Hepburn, Audrey .... **Audrey Hepburn-Ruston**
Heston, Charlton . **John Charlton Carter**
Holden, William.. **William Beedle**
Holliday, Judy ..... **Judith Tuvim**
Hope, Bob.. **Leslie Townes Hope**
Hopper, Hedda .... **Elda Furry**
Houdini, Harry..... **Ehrich Weiss**
Houseman, John .... **Jacques Haussmann**
Howard, Leslie .... **Leslie Stainer**
Hudson, Rock .. **Roy Scherer, Jr.**
Humperdinck, Engelbert .. **Arnold Dorsey**
Hunter, Jeffrey .... **Henry H. McKinnies**
Hunter, Kim .... **Janet Cole**
Hunter, Ross .... **Martin Fuss**
Hussey, Ruth......... **Ruth Carol O'Rourke**
Hutton, Betty........ **Betty Jane Thornburg**
Hutton, Lauren ..... **Mary Hutton**
Ives, Burl..... **Burle Icle Ivanhoe**
Jagger, Dean...... **Dean Jeffries**
Janssen, David ..... **David Meyer**
John, Elton..... **Reginald Dwight**
Johnson, Van....... **Charles Van Johnson**
Jolson, Al .... **Asa Yoelson**
Jones, Jennifer..... **Phyllis Isley**
Jones, Tom . **Thomas Woodward**
Jourdan, Louis..... **Louis Gendre**
Karloff, Boris...... **William Pratt**
Kaye, Danny .... **David Daniel Kaminsky**
Kazan, Elia .... **Elia Kazanjoglous**
Keel, Howard....... **Harold Leek**
Kerr, Deborah.......... **Deborah Kerr-Trimmer**
King, Alan......... **Irwin Kinberg**
King, Carole........ **Carole Klein**
Knight, Ted .. **Tadeus Wladyslaw Konopka**
Ladd, Cheryl .... **Cheryl Stoppelmoor**
Lahr, Bert...... **Irving Lahrheim**
Laine, Frankie .... **Frank Paul Lo Vecchio**
Lake, Veronica .... **Constance Ockleman**
Lamarr, Hedy.... **Hedwig Kiesler**
Lamour, Dorothy .... **Dorothy Kaumeyer**
Lanchester, Elsa....... **Elizabeth Sullivan**
Lanza, Mario ... **Alfredo Cocozza**
Laurel, Stan..... **Arthur Stanley Jefferson**
Laurie, Piper .... **Rosetta Jacobs**

Lawrence, Gertrude... **Alexandra Dagmar Lawrence-Klasen**
Lawrence, Steve.......... **Sidney Leibowitz**
Lee, Canada.... **Lionel Canegata**
Lee, Gypsy Rose . **Louise Hovick**
Lee, Peggy.... **Norma Egstrom**
Leigh, Janet.. **Jeanette Morrison**
Leigh, Vivien ..... **Vivien Hartley**
Lenya, Lotte.. **Caroline Blamauer**
Lewis, Jerry..... **Joseph Levitch**
Liberace ..... **Wladziu Valentino Liberace**
Lillie, Beatrice........ **Constance Sylvia Munston**
Linden, Hal...... **Harold Lipshitz**
Lisi, Virna .... **Virna Pieralisi**
Lockwood, Gary ...... **John Gary Yusolfsky**
Lombard, Carole...... **Jane Alice Peters**
London, Julie......... **Julie Peck**
Lord, Jack.... **John Joseph Ryan**
Loren, Sophia .. **Sophia Scicoloni**
Lorre, Peter . **Laszlo Loewenstein**
Louise, Tina...... **Tina Blackmer**
Loy, Myrna...... **Myrna Williams**
Lynley, Carol....... **Carolyn Lee**
Lynn, Diana ...... **Dolores Loehr**
Maclaine, Shirley .... **Shirley Maclean Beaty**
Madison, Guy ... **Robert Moseley**
Main, Marjorie.. **Mary Tomlinson**
Malden, Karl. **Malden Sekulovich**
Mansfield, Jayne ..... **Vera Jane Palmer**
March, Frederic .... **Ernest Frederick McIntyre Bickel**
Martin, Dean . **Dino Paul Crocetti**
Martin, Ross . **Martin Rosenblatt**
Martin, Tony .... **Alvin Morris**
May, Elaine........ **Elaine Berlin**
Mayo, Virginia.... **Virginia Jones**
McGee, Fibber.... **James Jordan**
McQueen, Butterfly...... **Thelma McQueen**
Meredith, Burgess....... **George Burgess**
Merman, Ethel **Ethel Zimmerman**
Merrill, Dina..... **Nedenia Hutton Rumbough**
Miles, Vera........ **Vera Ralston**
Milland, Ray.. **Reginald Truscott-Jones**
Miller, Ann ... **Lucille Ann Collier**
Miller, Marilyn........ **Mary Ellen Reynolds**
Monroe, Marilyn.... **Norma Jean Baker**
Montand, Yves.......... **Ivo Levi**

Moore, Garry .. **Thomas Garrison Morfit**
Moreno, Rita ..... **Rosita Dolores Alverio**
Morgan, Dennis . **Stanley Morner**
Morgan, Harry.. **Harry Bratsburg**
Morgan, Helen..... **Helen Riggins**
Mostel, Zero. **Samuel Joel Mostel**
Muni, Paul... **Muni Weisenfreund**
Murray, Mae..... **Marie Adrienne Koenig**
Naldi, Nita.. **Anita Donna Dooley**
Neagle, Anna **Marjorie Robertson**
Nelson, Barry .... **Robert Neilson**
Newmar, Julie.. **Julia Newmeyer**
Nichols, Mike....... **Michael Igor Peschkowsky**
North, Sheree ..... **Dawn Bethel**
Novak, Kim ...... **Marilyn Novak**
Novarro, Ramon.......... **Ramon Samaniegos**
Nuyen, France... **France Nguyen Vannga**
O'Brian, Hugh ..... **Hugh Krampe**
O'Brien, Margaret .... **Angela Maxine O'Brien**
O'Hara, Maureen .... **Maureen Fitzsimmons**
O'Keefe, Dennis......... **Edward Flanagan**
Oakie, Jack..... **Lewis D. Offield**
Oberon, Merle..... **Estelle Merle O'Brien Thompson**
Page, Patti .... **Clara Ann Fowler**
Paige, Janis .. **Donna Mae Jaden**
Palmer, Betsy .. **Patricia Brumek**
Palmer, Lilli .... **Lilli Peiser**
Papas, Irene....... **Irene Lelekou**
Parks, Bert....... **Bert Jacobson**
Pearl, Minnie ..... **Sarah Ophelia Cannon**
Peters, Bernadette .. **Bernadette Lazzaro**
Pickens, Slim. **Louis Bert Lindley**
Pickford, Mary..... **Gladys Smith**
Pinza, Ezio ..... **Fortunato Pinza**
Powell, Jane..... **Suzanne Burce**
Powers, Stefanie .... **Stefania Federkiewicz**
Prentiss, Paula .... **Paula Ragusa**
Preston, Robert .... **Robert Preston Meservey**
Raft, George ...... **George Ranft**
Raines, Ella.......... **Ella Raubes**
Randall, Tony .... **Leonard Rosenberg**
Ray, Aldo .... **Aldo da Re**
Raye, Martha.. **Margaret O'Reed**
Reed, Donna .. **Donna Mullenger**
Reese, Della.......... **Delloreese Patricia Early**

Reynolds, Debbie.. **Mary Frances Reynolds**
Rhue, Madlyn.. **Madeleine Roche**
Ritter, Tex .... **Woodward Ritter**
Rivera, Chita .. **Dolores Conchita Figueroa del Rivero**
Robinson, Edward G. . **Emmanuel Goldenberg**
Rogers, Ginger . **Virginia McMath**
Rogers, Roy....... **Leonard Slye**
Rooney, Mickey .... **Joe Yule, Jr.**
Roth, Lillian ..... **Lillian Rutstein**
Russell, Lillian ...... **Helen Louise Leonard**
Sales, Soupy .... **Milton Hines**
Savalas, Telly . **Aristotle Savalas**
Saxon, John...... **Carmen Orrico**
Scala, Gia..... **Giovanna Scoglio**
Schneider, Romy ..... **Rosemarie Albach-Retty**
Scott, Lizabeth .... **Emma Matzo**
Sharif, Omar ... **Michel Shalhoub**
Shearer, Moira ...... **Moira King**
Sheen, Martin ... **Ramon Estevez**
Shire, Talia....... **Talia Coppola**
Shore, Dinah ...... **Frances Rose Shore**
Signoret, Simone........ **Simone Kaminker**
Sills, Beverly .... **Belle Silverman**
Silverheels, Jay . **Harold J. Smith**
Singleton, Penny ..... **Mariana McNulty**
Skelton, Red ... **Richard Skelton**
Smith, Alexis ..... **Gladys Smith**
Somers, Suzanne....... **Suzanne Mahoney**
Sommer, Elke ...... **Elke Schletz**
Soo, Jack .... **Gogo Suzuki**
Sothern, Ann..... **Harriette Lake**
Sparks, Ned.. **Edward Sparkman**
St. James, Susan... **Susan Miller**
St. John, Jill..... **Jill Oppenheim**
Stack, Robert .... **Robert Modini**
Stanwyck, Barbara **Ruby Stevens**
Stapleton, Jean.. **Jeanne Murray**
Starr, Ringo .... **Richard Starkey**
Sterling, Jan ...... **Jane Sterling Adriance**
Sterling, Robert .... **William John Hart**
Stevens, Connie **Concetta Ingolia**
Stevens, Inger... **Inger Stensland**
Storm, Gale ... **Josephine Cottle**
Streep, Meryl....... **Mary Louise Streep**
Summers, Donna....... **LaDonna Gaines**
Sweet, Blanche.. **Daphne Wayne**
Tati, Jacques.......... **Jacques Tatischeff**

213

Taylor, Robert.......... **Spangler Arlington Brugh**
Terry-Thomas .... **Thomas Terry Hoar-Stevens**
Thomas, Danny .. **Amos Muzyad Jacobs**
Thomas, Marlo .... **Margaret Thomas**
Tiffin, Pamela .... **Pamela Wonso**
Torn, Rip...... **Elmore Rual Torn**
Tucker, Sophie .... **Sophia Kalish**
Turner, Lana .. **Julia Jean Turner**
Twiggy........... **Lesley Hornby**
Twitty, Conway..... **Harold Lloyd Jenkins**
Vague, Vera... **Barbara Jo Allen**
Vallee, Rudy........ **Hubert Prior Vallee**
Valli, Frankie . **Frank Castelluccio**
Van Devere, Trish .... **Patricia Dressel**
Van Doren, Mamie.. **Joan Lucille Olander**
Van, Bobby......... **Robert King**
Velez, Lupe... **Maria Guadeloupe Velez de Villalobos**
Vera-Ellen . **Vera-Ellen Westmeyr Rohe**

Walker, Nancy...... **Ann Swoyer Barto**
Wayne, John .... **Marion Michael Morrison**
Webb, Clifton.. **Webb Hollenbeck**
Welch, Raquel.... **Raquel Tejada**
Weld, Tuesday . **Susan Ker Weld**
Werner, Oskar...... **Oskar Josef Schliessmayer**
West, Adam... **William Anderson**
Wilder, Gene ... **Jerry Silberman**
Windsor, Marie ..... **Emily Marie Bertelson**
Winters, Shelley.. **Shirley Schrift**
Wonder, Stevie. **Stevland Morris**
Wong, Anna May ...... **Wong Liu Tsong**
Wood, Natalie ... **Natasha Gurdin**
Wynn, Ed.. **Isaiah Edwin Leopold**
Wynn, Keenan.... **Francis Xavier Aloysius Wynn**
Wynter, Dana . **Dagmar Spencer-Marcus**
York, Susannah .... **Susannah Yolande Fletcher**
Young, Gig . **Byron Elsworth Barr**
Young, Loretta .... **Gretchen Michaela Young**

SOME FAMOUS PEN NAMES

Boz............ **Charles Dickens**

Bell, Acton......... **Anne Bronte**
Bell, Carter.... **Charlotte Bronte**
Bell, Ellis.......... **Emily Bronte**
Boyd, Nancy ... **Edna St. Vincent Millay**
Elia .... **Charles Lamb**
Loti, Pierre.......... **Louis Viaud**
Saki .... **H. H. Munro**
Sand, George .. **Amandine Dupin Dudevant**
Ward, Artemus **Charles F. Browne**

Eliot, George ... **Mary Ann Evans**
Gorki, Maxim............ **Alexey Maximovich Peshkov**
Nasby, Petroleum ... **David Ross Locke**

Henry, O. **William Sydney Porter**
Ouida .... **Louise de la Ramee**
Twain, Mark.... **Samuel Clemens**

France, Anatole .... **Jacques Thibault**
Orwell, George . **Eric Arthur Blair**

Carroll, Lewis . **Charles Dodgson**
Colette........ **Sidonie Gabrielle Claudine Colette**
LeCarre, John....... **David John Cornwell**

Stendhal............ **Henri Beyle**
Voltaire .. **Francois Marie Arouet**

Westmacott, Mary....... **Agatha Christie**

SOME U.S. AUTHORS

Abbot, George
Ade, George
Albee, Edward
Alcott, Louisa May
Alger, Horatio
Asimov, Isaac
Austen, Jane
Baldwin, James
Barth, John
Baum, L. Frank
Behrman, S.N.
Bellow, Saul
Benchley, Peter
Benchley, Robert
Benet, Stephen
  Vincent
Bierce, Ambrose
Bishop, Jim
Blume, Judy
Bradbury, Ray
Brand, Max
Brown, Dee
Buck, Pearl
Burroughs, Edgar
  Rice
Burrows, Abe
Caldwell, Erskine
Caldwell, Taylor
Capote, Truman
Cather, Willa
Chase, Mary
Chayefsky, Paddy
Cheever, John
Clavell, James
Connelly, Marc
Cooper, James
  Fennimore
Crane, Hart
Crane, Stephen
Crews, Harry
Crichton, Michael
cummings, e.e.
Dickinson, Emily
Didion, Joan
Dos Passos, John
Drury, Allen
Emerson, Ralph
  Waldo
Farrel, James T.
Faulkner, William
Ferber, Edna
Fitzgerald, F. Scott
Frost, Robert
Gardner, Erle Stanley
Grey, Zane
Guest, Edgar A.

Hailey, Arthur
Haley, Alex
Hammett, Dashiell
Harris, Joel Chandler
Hart, Moss
Harte, Bret
Heller, Joseph
Hellman, Lillian
Hemingway, Ernest
Henry, O.
Hersey, John
Holmes, Oliver
  Wendell
Hughes, Langston
Inge, William
Irving, John
Irving, Washington
James, Henry
Kazan, Elia
Kerr, Jean
Kesey, Ken
Kilmer, Joyce
Knowles, John
Lardner, Ring
Lee, Harper
Levin, Ira
Lewis, Sinclair
London, Jack
Longfellow, Henry
  Wadsworth
Loos, Anita
Lowell, Amy
Lowell, James Russell
Lowell, Robert
Ludlum, Robert
MacInnes, Helen
Mailer, Norman
Malamud, Bernard
Masters, Edgar Lee
Matthison, Peter
McCarthy, Mary
McCullers, Carson
Melville, Herman
Mencken, H.L.
Michener, James
Millay, Edna St.
  Vincent
Miller, Arthur
Moore, Clement C.
Moore, Marianne
Nash, Ogden
Oates, Joyce Carol
Odets, Clifford
O'Hara, John
O'Neill, Eugene
Parker, Dorothy

Poe, Edgar Allan
Porter, Katherine Ann
Potok, Chaim
Pound, Ezra
Puzo, Mario
Rice, Elmer
Riley, James
  Whitcomb
Rinehart, Mary
  Roberts
Roth, Philip
Runyon, Damon
Salinger, J.D.
Sandburg, Carl
Saroyan, William
Schary, Dore
Schulberg, Budd
Segal, Erich
Shaw, Irwin
Simon, Neil
Sinclair, Upton
Singer, Isaac
  Bashevis
Slaughter, Frank
Stein, Gertrude
Steinbeck, John
Stone, Irving
Stout, Rex
Stowe, Harriet
  Beecher
Styron, William
Tarkington, Booth
Teasdale, Sara
Thurber, James
Tryon, Thomas
Twain, Mark
Updike, John
Uris, Leon
Vidal, Gore
Vonnegut, Kurt Jr.
Wallace, Irving
Warren, Robert Penn
Welty, Eudora
West, Nathaniel
Wharton, Edith
White, Theodore H.
Whitman, Walt
Whittier, John
  Greenleaf
Wilder, Thornton
Williams, Tennessee
Wolfe, Thomas
Wouk, Herman
Wylie, Elinor
Yerby, Frank

NAMES FROM SHAKESPEARE

Listed by Plays

(Plays are listed alphabetically by the titles that are commonly used. The actual title, if different, follows in parentheses.)

ALL'S WELL THAT ENDS WELL
DIANA, LAFEU; HELENA; BERTRAM, LAVACHE, MARIANA; PAROLLES, VIOLENTA

ANTONY AND CLEOPATRA
EROS, IRAS; MENAS, PHILO; ALEXAS, CAESAR (OCTAVIUS), GALLUS, SCARUS, SEXTUS (POMPEIUS), SILIUS, TAURUS; AGRIPPA, LEPIDUS, MARDIAN, OCTAVIA, THYREUS, VARRIUS; CANIDIUS, CHARMIAN, DERCETAS, DIOMEDES, MAECENAS, SELEUCUS; DEMETRIUS, DOLABELLA, VENTIDIUS; EUPHRONIUS, MENECRATES, PROCULEIUS

AS YOU LIKE IT
ADAM; CELIA, CORIN, PHEBE; AMIENS, AUDREY, DENNIS, JAQUES, LE BEAU, OLIVER; CHARLES, ORLANDO, SILVIUS, WILLIAM; ROSALIND; FREDERICK; TOUCHSTONE

COMEDY OF ERRORS, THE
LUCE; PINCH; AEGEON, ANGELO, DROMIO; ADRIANA, AEMILIA, LUCIANA, SOLINUS; BALTHAZAR; ANTIPHOLUS

CORIOLANUS (The Tragedy of Coriolanus)
CAIUS, TITUS; BRUTUS, JUNIUS, TULLUS; AGRIPPA, LARTIUS, MARCIUS, VALERIA, VELUTUS; AUFIDIUS, COMINIUS, MENENIUS, SICINIUS, VIRGILIA, VOLUMNIA

CYMBELINE
CAIUS (LUCIUS), HELEN; CLOTEN, IMOGEN; IACHIMO, PISANIO; BELARIUS, LEONATUS, PHILARIO; ARVIRAGUS, CORNELIUS, GUIDERIUS, POSTHUMUS

HAMLET (The Tragedy of Hamlet, Prince of Denmark)
OSRIC; HORATIO, LAERTES, OPHELIA; BERNARDO, CLAUDIUS, GERTRUDE, POLONIUS, REYNALDO; CORNELIUS, FRANCISCO, MARCELLUS, VOLTIMAND; FORTINBRAS; ROSENCRANTZ; GUILDENSTERN

JULIUS CAESAR (The Tragedy of Julius Caesar)
CATO, LENA; CASCA, CINNA, VARRO; BRUTUS, CICERO, CLITUS, DECIUS, LUCIUS, MARCUS, PORTIA, STRATO; CASSIUS, FLAVIUS, LEPIDUS, MESSALA, PUBLIUS; CLAUDIUS, LIGARIUS, LUCILIUS, MARULLUS, METELLUS, OCTAVIUS, PINDARUS, POPILIUS, TITINIUS; CALPURNIA, DARDANIUS, TREBONIUS, VOLUMNIUS; ARTEMIDORUS

KING HENRY IV, PART I (The First Part of King Henry IV)
JOHN, PETO; BLUNT, HENRY, PERCY, POINS; MICHAEL, QUICKLY; BARDOLPH, FALSTAFF, GADSHILL; ARCHIBALD, GLENDOWER

KING HENRY IV, PART II (The Second Part of King Henry IV)
DAVY, FANG, JOHN, PETO, WART; BLUNT, GOWER, HENRY, POINS, SNARE; FEEBLE, MORTON, MOULDY, PISTOL, RUMOUR, SCROOP, SHADOW, THOMAS; MOWBRAY, QUICKLY, SHALLOW, SILENCE, TRAVERS; BARDOLPH, BULLCALF, FALSTAFF, HARCOURT, HASTINGS, HUMPHREY; DOLL TEARSHEET

KING HENRY V (The Life of King Henry V)
NYM; GREY, JAMY; ALICE, BATES, COURT, GOWER, LEWIS; ISABEL, PISTOL; SCROOP; CHARLES, MONTJOY, QUICKLY; BARDOLPH, FLUELLEN, GRANDPRE, RAMBURES, WILLIAMS; ERPINGHAM, KATHARINE, MACMORRIS

KING HENRY VI, PART I (The First Part of King Henry VI)
LUCY; BASSET, TALBOT, VERNON; CHARLES, RICHARD; BEAUFORT, FASTOLFE, GARGRAVE, MARGARET, REIGNIER, WOODVILE; GLANSDALE, LA PUCELLE (Joan of Arc), PLANTAGENET

KING HENRY VI, PART II (The Second Part of King Henry VI)
SAY; CADE, DICK, HUME, IDEN, VAUX; BEVIS, GOFFE, PETER, SMITH; EDMUND, EDWARD, HORNER, SCALES, THOMAS; ELEANOR, HOLLAND, MICHAEL, RICHARD, SIMPCOX, STANLEY; BEAUFORT, CLIFFORD, HUMPHREY, JOURDAIN, MARGARET, MORTIMER, STAFFORD; ALEXANDER, SOUTHWELL; BOLINGBROKE, PLANTAGENET

KING HENRY VI, PART III (The Third Part of King Henry VI)
BONA, GREY; HENRY, LEWIS; EDMUND, EDWARD, GEORGE, RIVERS; RICHARD, STANLEY, CLIFFORD, HASTINGS, MARGARET, MORTIMER, STAFFORD; SOMERVILLE; MONTGOMERY; PLANTAGENET

KING HENRY VIII (The Famous History of the Life of King Henry VIII)
VAUX; BUTTS, DENNY, SANDS; LOVELL, WOLSEY; BRANDON, CRANMER; CAMPEIUS, CAPUCIUS, CROMWELL, GARDINER, GRIFFITH, PATIENCE; GUILDFORD, KATHARINE; ANNE BULLEN; ABERGAVENNY

KING JOHN (The Life and Death of King John)
BIGOT, HENRY, JAMES, LEWIS, MELUN, PETER; ARTHUR, BLANCHE, ELINOR, GURNEY, HUBERT, PHILIP, ROBERT; DE BURGH, LYMOGES; PANDULPH; CONSTANCE, CHATILLON

KING LEAR (The Tragedy of King Lear)
CURAN, EDGAR, REGAN; EDMUND, OSWALD; GONERIL; CORDELIA

KING RICHARD II (The Tragedy of King Richard II)
ROSS; BAGOT, BUSHY, GREEN, HENRY, PERCY; EDMUND, PIERCE, SCROOP, THOMAS; AUMERLE, HOTSPUR, MOWBRAY; FITZWATER; WILLOUGHBY; BOLINGBROKE, JOHN OF GAUNT

KING RICHARD III (The Tragedy of King Richard III)
ANNE, GREY; HENRY, LOVEL; BLOUNT, EDWARD, GEORGE, MORTON, RIVERS, TYRREL; BRANDON, CATESBY, HERBERT, RICHARD, STANLEY, TRESSEL, URSWICK, VAUGHAN; BERKELEY, HASTINGS, MARGARET, RATCLIFF; BOURCHIER, ELIZABETH, ROTHERHAM; BRAKENBURY

MACBETH (The Tragedy of Macbeth)
ROSS; ANGUS; BANQUO, DUNCAN, HECATE, LENNOX, SEYTON, SIWARD; FLEANCE, MACDUFF, MALCOLM; MENTEITH; CAITHNESS, DONALBAIN

MEASURE FOR MEASURE
ELBOW, FROTH, LUCIO, PETER; ANGELO, JULIET, POMPEY, THOMAS; CLAUDIO, ESCALUS, MARIANA, VARRIUS; ABHORSON, ISABELLA, OVERDONE; FRANCISCA, VINCENTIO; BARNARDINE

MERCHANT OF VENICE, THE
GOBBO, TUBAL; PORTIA; ANTONIO, JESSICA, LORENZO, NERISSA, SALANIO, SALERIO, SHYLOCK; BASSANIO, GRATIANO, LEONARDO, SALARINO, STEPHANO; BALTHASAR

MERRY WIVES OF WINDSOR, THE
NYM; ANNE, FORD, PAGE; CAIUS, EVANS, ROBIN, RUGBY; FENTON, PISTOL, SIMPLE; QUICKLY, SHALLOW, SLENDER, WILLIAM; BARDOLPH, FALSTAFF

MIDSUMMER-NIGHT'S DREAM, A
MOTH, PUCK, SNUG; EGEUS, FLUTE, SNOUT; BOTTOM, COBWEB, HELENA, HERMIA, OBERON, QUINCE; THESEUS, TITANIA; LYSANDER; DEMETRIUS, HIPPOLYTA; STARVELING; PHILOSTRATE; PEASEBLOSSOM

MUCH ADO ABOUT NOTHING
HERO; URSULA, VERGES; ANTONIO, CLAUDIO, CONRADE, DON JOHN, FRANCIS, LEONATO; BEATRICE, BENEDICK, BORACHIO, DOGBERRY, DON PEDRO, MARGARET; BALTHASAR

OTHELLO (The Tragedy of Othello, The Moor of Venice)
IAGO; BIANCA, CASSIO, EMILIA; MONTANO; GRATIANO, LODOVICO, RODERIGO; BRABANTIO, DESDEMONA

PERICLES (Pericles, Prince of Tyre)
BOULT, CLEON, DIANA, GOWER; MARINA, THAISA; CERIMON, DIONYZA, ESCANES, LEONINE; PHILEMON, THALIARD; ANTIOCHUS, HELICANUS, LYCHORIDA, SIMONIDES; LYSIMACHUS

ROMEO AND JULIET (The Tragedy of Romeo and Juliet)
PARIS, PETER; TYBALT; ABRAHAM, CAPULET, ESCALUS, GREGORY, SAMPSON; BENVOLIO, LAURENCE, MERCUTIO, MONTAGUE; BALTHASAR

TAMING OF THE SHREW, THE
SLY; BIANCA, CURTIS, GREMIO, GRUMIO, TRANIO; BAPTISTA, LU-
CENTIO; BIONDELLO, HORTENSIO, KATHARINA, PETRUCHIO, VIN-
CENTIO; CHRISTOPHER

TEMPEST, THE
IRIS, JUNO; ARIEL, CERES; ADRIAN, ALONSO; ANTONIO, CALIBAN;
GONZALO, MIRANDA; PROSPERO, STEPHANO, TRINCULO; FERDI-
NAND, FRANCISCO, SEBASTIAN

TIMON OF ATHENS (The Life of Timon of Athens)
CUPID, TITUS; CAPHIS, LUCIUS; FLAVIUS, PHRYNIA; LUCILIUS,
LUCULLUS, PHILOTUS, TIMANDRA; APEMANTUS, FLAMINIUS, SER-
VILIUS, VENTIDIUS; ALCIBIADES, HORTENSIUS, SEMPRONIUS

TITUS ANDRONICUS (The Tragedy of Titus Andronicus)
AARON; CHIRON, LUCIUS, MARCUS, MUTIUS, TAMORA; ALARBUS,
LAVINIA, MARTIUS, PUBLIUS, QUINTUS; AEMILIUS; BASSIANUS,
DEMETRIUS; SATURNINUS

TROILUS AND CRESSIDA
AJAX; HELEN, PARIS, PRIAM; AENEAS, HECTOR, NESTOR; AN-
TENOR, CALCHAS, HELENUS, ULYSSES; ACHILLES, CRESSIDA, DI-
OMEDES, MENELAUS, PANDARUS; AGAMEMNON, ALEXANDER,
CASSANDRA, DEIPHOBUS, PATROCLUS, THERSITES; ANDROM-
ACHE, MARGARELON

TWELFTH NIGHT (Twelfth Night; or, What You Will)
BELCH, CURIO, FESTE, MARIA, VIOLA; FABIAN, OLIVIA, ORSINO; AN-
TONIO; MALVOLIO; AGUECHEEK, SEBASTIAN, VALENTINE

TWO GENTLEMEN OF VERONA, THE
JULIA, SPEED; LAUNCE, SILVIA, THURIO; ANTONIO, LUCETTA, PRO-
TEUS; EGLAMOUR, PANTHINO; VALENTINE

WINTER'S TALE, THE
DION; MOPSA; DORCAS, EMILIA; CAMILLO, LEONTES, PAULINA,
PERDITA; FLORIZEL, HERMIONE; ANTIGONUS, AUTOLYCUS, CLEO-
MENES, MAMILLIUS, POLIXENES; ARCHIDAMUS

U.S. PRESIDENTS INFORMATION

Note: State indicates state of birth. First Ladies' maiden or original names are given directly under each president's name.

Name	Party	Vice-Pres.	State	Term
1. WASHINGTON, George Martha Dandridge Custis	Fed.	Adams	VA	1789–1797
2. ADAMS, John Abigal Smith	Fed.	Jefferson	MA	1797–1801
3. JEFFERSON, Thomas Martha Wayles Skelton	Dem.-Rep.	Burr, Clinton	VA	1801–1809
4. MADISON, James Dorothea Payne Todd "Dolley"	Dem.-Rep.	Clinton, Gerry	VA	1809–1817
5. MONROE, James Elizabeth Kortright	Dem.-Rep.	Tompkins	VA	1817–1825
6. ADAMS, John Quincy Louise Catherine Johnson	Dem.-Rep.	Calhoun	MA	1825–1829
7. JACKSON, Andrew Rachel Donelson Robards	Dem.	Calhoun, Van Buren	SC	1829–1837
8. VAN BUREN, Martin Hannah Hoes	Dem.	Johnson	NY	1837–1841
9. HARRISON, William Henry Anna Symmes	Whig	Tyler	VA	1841
10. TYLER, John Letitia Christian and Julia Gardiner	Dem.		VA	1841–1845
11. POLK, James Knox Sarah Childress	Dem.	Dallas	NC	1845–1849
12. TAYLOR, Zachary Margaret Smith	Whig	Fillmore	VA	1849–1850
13. FILLMORE, Millard Abigail Powers and Caroline Carmichael McIntosh	Whig		NY	1850–1853
14. PIERCE, Franklin Jane Mears Appleton	Dem.	King	NH	1853–1857
15. BUCHANAN, James	Dem.	Breckenridge	PA	1857–1861
16. LINCOLN, Abraham Mary Todd	Rep.	Hamlin, Johnson	KY	1861–1865
17. JOHNSON, Andrew Eliza McCardle	Dem.		NC	1865–1869
18. GRANT, Ulysses Simpson Julia Dent	Rep.	Colfax, Wilson	OH	1869–1877
19. HAYES, Rutherford Birchard Lucy Ware Webb	Rep.	Wheeler	OH	1877–1881
20. GARFIELD, James Abram Lucretia Rudolph	Rep.	Arthur	OH	1881
21. ARTHUR, Chester Alan Ellen Lewis Herndon	Rep.		VT	1881–1885
22. CLEVELAND, Stephen Grover Frances Folsom	Dem.	Hendricks	NJ	1885–1889
23. HARRISON, Benjamin Caroline Lavinia Scott and Mary Scott Lord Dimmick	Rep.	Morton	OH	1889–1893

Name	Party	Vice-Pres.	State	Term
24. CLEVELAND, Stephen Grover Frances Folsom	Dem.	Stevenson	NJ	1893–1897
25. MC KINLEY, William Ida Saxton	Rep.	Hobart, Roosevelt	OH	1897–1901
26. ROOSEVELT, Theodore Alice Hathaway Lee and Edith Kermit Carow	Rep.	Fairbanks	NY	1901–1909
27. TAFT, William Howard Helen Herron	Rep.	Sherman	OH	1909–1913
28. WILSON, Thomas Woodrow Ellen Louise Axson and Edith Bolling Galt	Dem.	Marshall	VA	1913–1921
29. HARDING, Warren Gamaliel Florence Kling De Wolfe	Rep.	Coolidge	OH	1921–1923
30. COOLIDGE, John Calvin Grace Anna Goodhue	Rep.	Dawes	VT	1923–1929
31. HOOVER, Herbert Clark Lou Henry	Rep.	Curtis	IA	1929–1933
32. ROOSEVELT, Franklin Delano Anna Eleanor Roosevelt	Dem.	Garner, Wallace Truman	NY	1933–1945
33. TRUMAN, Harry S Elizabeth (Bess) Wallace	Dem.	Barkley	MO	1945–1953
34. EISENHOWER, Dwight David Mamie Geneva Doud	Rep.	Nixon	TX	1953–1961
35. KENNEDY, John Fitzgerald Jacqueline Lee Bouvier	Dem.	Johnson	MA	1961–1963
36. JOHNSON, Lyndon Baines Claudia Alta Taylor "Lady Bird"	Dem.	Humphrey	TX	1963–1968
37. NIXON, Richard Milhous Thelma Catherine Patricia Ryan "Pat"	Rep.	Agnew, Ford	CA	1968–1974
38. FORD, Gerald Rudolph Elizabeth Bloomer Warren "Betty"	Rep.	Rockefeller	NE	1974–1977
39. CARTER, James Earl, Jr. Rosalynn Smith	Dem.	Mondale	GA	1977–1981
40. REAGAN, Ronald Wilson Anne Frances Robbins Davis "Nancy"	Rep.	Bush	IL	1981–

U.S. STATES INFORMATION

STATE	ABBREVIATIONS (official P.O. abbr. appears first)	RANK BY AREA	RANK BY POPULATION
ALABAMA	AL, Ala.	29	22
ALASKA	AK, Alas., Alsk.	1	50
ARIZONA	AZ, Ariz.	6	29
ARKANSAS	AR, Ark.	27	33
CALIFORNIA	CA, Calif., Cal.	3	1
COLORADO	CO, Colo.	8	27
*CONNECTICUT	CT, Conn.	48	25
*DELAWARE	DE, Del., Dela.	49	47
†DISTRICT OF COLUMBIA	DC, D.C.		
FLORIDA	FL, Fla.	22	7
*GEORGIA	GA, Ga.	21	12
HAWAII	HI, H., Haw.	47	40
IDAHO	ID, Id., Ida.	13	41
ILLINOIS	IL, Ill.	24	5
INDIANA	IN, Ind.	38	13
IOWA	IA, Ia.	25	28
KANSAS	KS, Kan., Kans.	14	32
KENTUCKY	KY, Ky.	37	24
LOUISIANA	LA, La.	31	18
MAINE	ME, Me.	39	39
*MARYLAND	MD, Md.	42	19
*MASSACHUSETTS	MA, Mass.	45	11
MICHIGAN	MI, Mich.	23	8
MINNESOTA	MN, Minn.	12	21
MISSISSIPPI	MS, Miss.	32	31
MISSOURI	MO, Mo.	19	15
MONTANA	MT, Mont.	4	45
NEBRASKA	NE, Nebr.	15	36
NEVADA	NV, Nev.	7	44
*NEW HAMPSHIRE	NH, N.H.	44	43
*NEW JERSEY	NJ, N.J.	46	9
NEW MEXICO	NM, N.M.	5	38
*NEW YORK	NY, N.Y.	30	2
*NORTH CAROLINA	NC, N.C.	28	10
NORTH DAKOTA	ND, N.D.	17	46
OHIO	OH, O.	35	6
OKLAHOMA	OK, Okla.	18	26
OREGON	OR, Ore.	10	30
*PENNSYLVANIA	PA, Penna., Penn.	33	4
*RHODE ISLAND	RI, R.I.	50	41
*SOUTH CAROLINA	SC, S.C.	40	24
SOUTH DAKOTA	SD, S.D.	16	45
TENNESSEE	TN, Tenn.	34	17
TEXAS	TX, Tex.	2	3
UTAH	UT, Ut.	11	36
VERMONT	VT, Vt.	43	48
*VIRGINIA	VA, Va.	36	14
WASHINGTON	WA, Wash.	20	20
WEST VIRGINIA	WV, W. Va.	41	34
WISCONSIN	WI, Wisc., Wis.	26	16
WYOMING	WY, Wyo.	9	49

†District   *One of the Thirteen Original States

STATE CAPITAL	STATE NICKNAME(S)	STATE FLOWER
Montgomery	Cotton, Heart of Dixie, Yellowhammer	Camellia
Juneau	The Last Frontier	Forget-Me-Not
Phoenix	Grand Canyon	Seguaro Cactus
Little Rock	Land of Opportunity	Apple Blossom
Sacramento	Golden, El Dorado	Golden Poppy
Denver	Centennial, Silver	Columbine
Hartford	Constitution, Nutmeg	Mountain Laurel
Dover	First, Diamond, Blue Hen	Peach Blossom
		American Beauty Rose
Tallahassee	Sunshine, Peninsular	Orange Blossom
Atlanta	Empire State of the South, Peach	Cherokee Rose
Honolulu	Aloha, Paradise of the Pacific	Hibiscus
Boise	Gem	Syringa
Springfield	Prairie, Sucker, The Inland Empire	Violet
Indianapolis	Hoosier	Peony
Des Moines	Hawkeye	Wild Rose
Topeka	Sunflower, Jayhawker	Sunflower
Frankfort	Bluegrass	Goldenrod
Baton Rouge	Pelican, Creole	Magnolia
Augusta	Pine Tree, Lumber	Pine Cone and Tassel
Annapolis	Old Line, Free, Cockade	Black-Eyed Susan
Boston	Bay, Old Colony	Mayflower
Lansing	Wolverine, Great Lake	Apple Blossom
St. Paul	North Star, Gopher	Lady's-Slipper
Jackson	Magnolia, Bayou	Magnolia
Jefferson City	Show Me, Bullion	Hawthorn
Helena	Treasure, Mountain	Bitterroot
Lincoln	Cornhusker, Blackwater	Goldenrod
Carson City	Sagebrush, Silver, Battle Born	Sagebrush
Concord	Granite	Purple Lilac
Trenton	Garden	Violet
Santa Fe	Sunshine, Land of Enchantment	Yucca
Albany	Empire, Excelsior	Rose
Raleigh	Tar Heel, Old North, Turpentine	Dogwood
Bismarck	Sioux, Flickertail	Wild Prairie Rose
Columbus	Buckeye	Scarlet Carnation
Oklahoma City	Sooner	Mistletoe
Salem	Beaver, Sunset, Valentine, Webfoot	Oregon Grape
Harrisburg	Keystone	Mountain Laurel
Providence	Little Rhody, Ocean	Violet
Columbia	Palmetto	Carolina Jessamine
Pierre	Coyote, Sunshine	Pasque Flower
Nashville	Volunteer	Iris
Austin	Lone Star	Bluebonnet
Salt Lake City	Beehive, Mormon	Sego Lily
Montpelier	Green Mountain	Red Clover
Richmond	Old Dominion, Mother of Presidents	Dogwood
Olympia	Evergreen, Chinook	Western Rhododendron
Charleston	Mountain	Big Rhododendron
Madison	Badger	Wood Violet
Cheyenne	Equality	Indian Paintbrush

GAZETTEER

OR

GEOGRAPHICAL DICTIONARY

Cities, States, Countries, Counties, Provinces, Towns, Rivers, Communes, Ports and Harbors, Regions, Lakes, Mountains, Islands, Volcanoes, Settlements, Kingdoms, Districts, Divisions, Peninsulas, Mountain Ranges, etc.

A

ABYSSINIA . . . . see ETHIOPIA

ADRIATIC . . . . . . port and harbor, **FIUME;** peninsula, **ISTRIA;** resort, **LIDO**

AEGEAN. . . . . gulf, **SAROS;** river, **STRUMA;** island, **IOS, KOS, KEOS, CHIOS, DELOS, KASOS, LEROS, MELOS, NAXOS, PAROS, SAMOS, SYROS, TELOS, TENOS, THIRA, AN-DROS, PATMOS, RHODES, SKYROS**

AFGHANISTAN. . . . . city, **HERAT**

AFRICA. . . . . country, **CHAD, MALI, TOGO, BENIN, CONGO, EGYPT, GABON, GHANA, KENYA, LIBYA, NIGER, SUDAN, ZAIRE, ANGOLA, (THE) GAMBIA, GUINEA, MALAWI, RWANDA, UGANDA, ZAMBIA, ALGERIA, BURUNDI, LESOTHO, LIBERIA, NIGERIA, SENEGAL, SOMALIA, TUNISIA;** lake, **CHAD, TANA, NYASA;** mountains, **ATLAS;** river, **NILE, CONGO, NIGER, ORANGE;** canal, **SUEZ**

ALABAMA . . . . city, **SELMA, ANNISTON**

ALASKA. . . . city, **NOME, SITKA;** island, **ADAK, ATKA, ATTU, UNGA;** mountain, **ADA;** inlet, **COOK;** river, **YUKON;** highest peak in N. America, **MCKINLEY;** glacier, **MUIR**

ALBANIA . . . . . . capital, **TIRANA;** river, **DRIN**

ALEUTIANS. . . . . islands, **ADAK, ATKA, ATTU**

ALGERIA . . . city, **ORAN, SETIF, ALGIERS**

ALPS. . . mountain, **ROSA, VISO, BLANC, LEONE, MATTER-HORN**

ANGOLA . . . . city, **LOBITO, LUANDA;** mountain peak, **MOCO**

ANTARCTIC . . . . sea, **ROSS**

ARABIA . . . . . city, **ADEN, SANA;** district, **TEMA (TAIMA);** nation, **OMAN, QATAR, YEMEN, KU-WAIT;** gulf, **ADEN, OMAN;** old kingdom, **NEJD;** cape, **ASIR**

ARCTIC . . . . gulf, **OB;** sea, **KARA**

ARGENTINA . . . . city, **SALTA, CORDOBA, ROSARIO;** province, **CHACO;** volcano, **MAIPO**

ARIZONA. . . . . city, **MESA, YUMA, TEMPE, TUCSON;** county, **GILA, PIMA, YUMA, PINAL, APACHE, MOHAVE, NAVAJO, COCHISE;** lake, **MEAD;** river, **SALT, GILA**

ARKANSAS. . . . . city, **LITTLE ROCK;** county, **LEE, CLAY, DREW, PIKE, BOONE, CROSS, LOGAN, UNION;** river, **RED, WHITE**

ARMENIA. river, **ARAS (ARAKS)**

ARU ISLANDS....... port, **DOBO**

ASIA ... mountains, **ALTAI**; lake, **ARAL**; sea, **ARAL**; river, **OB, ILI, AMUR, LENA, ONON, TIGRIS**; kingdom, **NEPAL**; old kingdom, **SIAM**; country, **IRAN, IRAQ (IRAK), BURMA, CHINA, KOREA, TIBET**; desert, **GOBI**

ASIA MINOR ..... district, **IONIA**; mountains, **IDA**

ASIATIC.............. see ASIA

AUSTRALIA.... peninsula, **EYRE**; river, **SWAN**; city, **PERTH**

AUSTRIA ..... city, **GRAZ, LINZ, VIENNA (WIEN)**; river, **MUR, ENNS, RABA (RAAB)**; spa, **BADEN**

AZORES........ port and harbor, **HORTA**; island, **PICO, FAYAL (FAIAL), FLORES**; volcano, **PICO (ALTO)**

B

BAHAMAS..... capital, **NASSAU**

BAHRAIN.... capital, **MANAMA**

BALEARIC ISLANDS .... port, **PALMA**; island, **MAJORCA**

BALTIC...... capital, **RIGA**; gulf, **RIGA**; river, **ODER**

BANGLADESH . capital, **DACCA**; river, **GANGES**

BAVARIA ... river, **NAB (NAAB), ISAR**

BELGIUM . city, **GENT (GHENT), LIEGE**; commune or town, **ANS, ATH, HUY, SPA, MONS, NIEL, ROUX, NAMUR, MECHLIN (MA-LINES)**; river, **LYS, YSER, MEUSE, SENNE**; port and harbor, **OSTEND**; province, **LIEGE**

BENIN.......... city, **ABOMEY, COTONOU, PORTO-NOVO**; river, **VOLTA**

BOHEMIA.... river, **ELBE, ISER**;

BORNEO .. mountains, **KAPUAS, MULLER**; river, **BARITO, RA-JANG**; state, **SABAH, SARA-WAK**

BRAZIL...... city, **RIO, BELEM**; port and harbor, **PARA, NATAL, SANTOS, PELOTAS**; state, **PARA, BAHIA**; river, **APA, ICA, PARA**

BRITISH WEST INDIES .... island, **NEVIS**

BULGARIA....... capital, **SOFIA**

BURMA .. capital (former), **AVA**, (present), **RANGOON**; district, **PROME**

C

CALIFORNIA . city, **LODI, NAPA, POMONA, ALAMEDA, SALI-NAS**; town, **OJAI**; county, **NAPA, YOLO, MODOC, MADERA**; lake, **TAHOE**; mountain peak, **LASSEN, SHASTA**; valley, **NAPA**

CAMBODIA (KAMPUCHEA)...... capital, **PNOMPENH**; river, **ME-KONG**

CAMEROON .... river, **SANAGA**

CANADA .... mountain, **LOGAN, ROBSON**; peninsula, **GASPE**; province, **ALBERTA (ALTA.), BRITISH COLUMBIA (B.C.), MANITOBA (MAN.), NEW BRUNSWICK (N.B.), NEW-FOUNDLAND (NFLD.), NOVA SCOTIA (N.S.), ONTARIO (ONT.), PRINCE EDWARD IS-LAND (P.E.I.), QUEBEC (QUE.), SASKATCHEWAN (SASK.)**; na-tional park, **JASPER**

CAPE VERDE ..... island, **FOGO, MAIO (MAYO), BRAVA, SAL REI, BOA VISTA**

CARIBBEAN ...... island, **CUBA, ARUBA**

CAROLINES........ island, **YAP, TRUK, PALAU (PELEW), PONAPE**

CASPIAN .... seaport and harbor, **BAKU**

CENTRAL AMERICA .... river, **LEMPA**

CEYLON........ see SRI LANKA

CHAD ... town, **SARH, ABECHE**

CHANNEL ISLANDS ...... island, **SARK**

CHILE .. river, **LOA**; port, harbor, town, **ARICA**

CHINA (see also TAIWAN) ......
city, **AMOY, IPIN, CANTON**; port and harbor, **AMOY**; old kingdom, **SHU**; river, **SI, WU, HAN, HSI, ILI, KAN, PEI, WEI, AMUR, HUAI (HWAI)**; province, **HONAN, HUNAN**; mountains, **OMEI (OMI)**

COLOMBIA river, **MAGDALENA**; city, **CALI**

COLORADO....... city, **LAMAR, OURAY, PUEBLO, DURANGO**; park, **ESTES**; range, **RATON**; mountain, **OSO, EOLUS**; peak, **OSO**; county, **OTERO, OURAY**; resort, **ASPEN**

CONNECTICUT.. town, **DARIEN, ANSONIA, MERIDEN**; city, **NEW HAVEN, HARTFORD, STAMFORD**; river, **THAMES**

CORSICA....... port and harbor, **BASTIA**

CRETE .... port and harbor, **CANDIA**; capital, **CANEA**; mountain, **IDA**

CRIMEA .... port and harbor, **KERCH**; river, **ALMA**

CUBA ...... town, **GUINES**; city, **HAVANA (HABANA)**

CYCLADES ... island, **IOS (NIO), SYRA (SYROS), DELOS, MELOS (MILO), TENOS, THIRA**

CYPRUS....... capital, **NICOSIA**

CZECHOSLOVAKIA .. city, **BRNO (BRUNN)**; river, **GRAN, HRON, IPEL, ISER, ODER, OHRE (EGER), MOLDAU**; capital, **PRAGUE (PRAHA)**

D

DELAWARE ..... capital, **DOVER**; county, **KENT, SUSSEX**

DENMARK...... island off, **ALS, AERO**; islands, **FAROE**

DOMINICAN REPUBLIC ..... city, **MOCA**

DUTCH...... see NETHERLANDS

DUTCH EAST INDIES .... see INDONESIA

E

EAST ASIA .... former kingdom, **KOREA**

EAST EUROPEAN .. river, **DRAU (DRAVA, DRAVE), TISA (TISZA, THEISS)**

EAST INDIES... island, **BORNEO**

ECUADOR ...... capital, **QUITO**; province, **EL ORO**

EGYPT ...... city, **GIZA, CAIRO**; ancient city, **SAIS, THEBES**; province, **GIZA**; river, **NILE**

ENGLAND .... city, **ELY, BATH, YORK, LEEDS, COVENTRY**; port and harbor, **HULL, DOVER, POOLE**; town, **ETON**; river, **ALN (ALNE), CAM, DEE, EXE, NEN (NENE), URE, AVON, OUSE, TEES, TYNE, TRENT**; county, **KENT, YORK, BERKS, BUCKS, DERBY, DEVON, ESSEX, HANTS, WILTS, DORSET, SURREY, SUSSEX**

ESTONIA ..... capital, **TALLINN**; former capital, **REVAL (REVEL)**; town, **PARNU, TARTU**; river, **NARVA, PARNU, KASARI**

ETHIOPIA........ capital, **ADDIS ABABA**; lake, **TANA (TSANA), ABAYA**; province, **TIGRE**; river, **OMO, AWASH**; town, **HARER, GONDER**

EUROPE...... river, **ISAR, OISE, URAL, DANUBE**; lake, **BALATON**; peninsula, **IBERIA**; resort, **LIDO**

F

FAROE ISLANDS island, **STROMO**

FIJI .... capital, **SUVA**; island, **KORO**; island group, **LAU**

FINLAND .... capital, **HELSINKI**; city, **OULU, ESPOO (ESBO), LAHTI, TURKU**; lake, **ENARE (INARI)**; port and harbor, **ABO, PORI**; islands, **ALAND, KARLO**; town, northern, **ENARE (INARI)**; province, **HAME, OULU, LAPPI, VASSA**

FLANDERS .... city, **LISLE**

FLORIDA .... county, **DADE, DUVAL**; resort, **DE LAND**; city, **MIAMI, OCALA, TAMPA, ORLANDO**; cape, **SABLE**

FRANCE....... city, **AIX, AGEN, ALBI, CAEN, LYON (LYONS), METZ, NICE, OPPY, SENS, VAUX, ARLES, ARRAS, BLOIS, DINAN, LILLE, NANCY, NESLE, PARIS, REIMS, SEDAN, TOURS, TULLE, CANNES, NANTES, SEVRES**; commune, **AY, EU, AIX, AUX, DAX, PAU, AUBY, BRON, ISSY, LAON, LOOS, MERU, ORLY, VIMY**; port and harbor, **CAEN, MEZE, SETE, BREST**; resort, **PAU, NICE, CANNES**; department, **VAR, GARD, JURA, NORD, OISE, ORNE, MEUSE, VENDEE**; river, **AIN, LOT, LYS, AIRE, AUDE, CHER, EURE, LOIR, OISE, ORNE, RHIN (RHINE), SAAR, YSER, AISNE, ISERE, LOIRE** (longest), **MARNE, MEUSE, RHONE, SAONE, SARRE, SEINE, SELLE, VESLE, MOSELLE**; Mount, **BLANC**; mountains, **ALPS, JURA**; region, **ANJOU, ALSACE**

G

GABON.... capital, **LIBREVILLE**; city, **PORT-GENTIL**

GAMBIA (THE) . capital, **BANJUL**

GASCONY .... capital, **AUCH**

GEORGIA .... city, **MACON, SPARTA, AUGUSTA**; county, **BIBB, COBB, DE KALB**; river, **FLINT, OCONEE, SAVANNAH**

GERMANY ... capital E. Germany, **E. BERLIN**; capital W. Germany, **BONN**; city, **AUE, EMS, ULM, GERA, JENA, LAHR, EMDEN, ESSEN, MAINZ, NEUSS**; spa, **AIX**; canal, **KIEL**; river, **EMS, ALLE, EDER, EGER, ELBE, ISAR, MAIN, ODER, REMS, RUHR, SAAR, LIPPE, MOSEL (MOSELLE), REGEN, RHINE (RHEIN), WESER**; mountain, **HARZ**; state, **HESSE**; district, **ALSACE**; former region, **SUDETEN**

GHANA.... capital, **ACCRA**; city, **KUMASI**; lake, **VOLTA**; region, **ASHANTI**; river, **VOLTA**

GREAT BARRIER ISLAND.. **OTEA**

GREECE ...... ancient city, **ELIS**; ancient colony, **IONIA**; city, **SPARTA (SPARTI)**; island, **COS (KOS), IOS, NIO, MILO (MELOS), SCIO (CHIOS), CRETE, DELOS, PAROS, SAMOS, IONIAN**; mountain, **OETA, OSSA, HELICON**; river, **ARTA**; peninsula, **MOREA**; region, **DORIS**; ancient district, **ATTICA**

GREENLAND .... base, town, settlement, **ETAH**

GUAM..... city, capital, **AGANA**; port and harbor, **APRA**

GUATEMALA ... volcano, **AGUA**

GUINEA .... capital, **CONAKRY**; island, **TOMBO**; island group, **LOS**; town, **BOKE, LABE**

H

HAWAII. city, **HILO, HONOLULU**; island, **MAUI, OAHU, KAUAI, LANAI**; district, **HANA**; islet, **KURE**; volcanoes, **MAUNA KEA, MAUNA LOA**

HEBRIDES, INNER . island, **IONA, SKYE**

HOLLAND ... see NETHERLANDS

HONDURAS......... port, **TELA**

HONSHU ..... bay, **ISE**; port and harbor, **KOBE**

HUNGARY... city, **EGER, PECS;** river, **RAAB (RABA)**

I

IDAHO .... town, **ARCO**

ILLINOIS... city, **PANA, ALEDO, CAIRO, ELGIN, PEKIN, CANTON, MOLINE, PEORIA, SPARTA**

INDIA ..... capital, **NEW DELHI;** city, **AGRA, DELHI, POONA (PUNE), SIMLA, BOMBAY, KANPUR, MADRAS;** commune, town, **DHAR, ARCOT, SORON, SATARA;** mountains, **GHATS;** region, **GOA, JIND, BERAR, GWALIOR;** river, **SIND, INDUS, GANGES;** state, **ASSAM, BIHAR, MYSORE, PUNJAB**

INDIANA..... city, **GARY, PERU, MARION**

INDOCHINA........ see BURMA, CAMBODIA, LAOS, MALAYSIA, THAILAND, and VIETNAM

INDONESIA island, **AROE (ARU), BALI, JAVA, CELEBES, TERNATE;** island group, **ARU, KAI, OBI, ALOR, LETI;** gulf, **BONE (BONI);** capital, **DJAKARTA**

IOWA ..... city, **AMES** (college); county, **IDA**

IRAN......... capital, **TEHRAN;** city, **AHVAZ, RASHT, ABADAN, KERMAN, TABRIZ, MASHHAD**

IRAQ......... capital, **BAGDAD (BAGHDAD);** port and harbor, **BASRA;** ancient city, **KISH**

IRELAND (see also NORTHERN IRELAND)..... old capital, **TARA;** capital, **DUBLIN;** county, **CORK, MAYO, CLARE;** islands, **ARAN;** lake, **REE, ERNE;** port and harbor, **COBH, TRALEE;** river, **LEE, BANN, ERNE, NORE;** town, **TARA**

ISLE OF WIGHT ... port, **COWES**

ISRAEL......... port and harbor, **ACRE, HAIFA;** plain, **SHARON (SARON);** desert, **NEGEB (NEGEV)**

ISTRIAN PENINSULA ...... town, **PULA**

ITALY.. capital, **ROMA (ROME);** city, **BARI, COMO, PISA, ROMA (ROME), MILAN, PARMA, SIENA, TRENT, NAPLES, VENICE, CASERTA;** commune, town, **BRA, ALBA, ARCO, ASTI, ATRI, DEGO, ESTE, LARI, NOLA, ORIA, SAVA, TODI, ADRIA, ASOLA, ASOLO, PADUA, TURIN, EMPOLI;** resort, **LIDO;** port and harbor, **OSTIA, TRANI;** province, **ROMA, UDINE;** river, **PO, ADDA, ARNO, NERA, RENO, PIAVE, TIBER;** lake, **COMO, ISEO, NEMI;** strait, **OTRANTO;** gulf, **SALERNO;** isle, **CAPRI;** mountain, **VISO**

IVORY COAST ...... city, capital, **ABIDJAN;** Mount, **NIMBA;** town, **MAN, DALOA**

J

JAMAICA... capital, **KINGSTON;** town, **MAY PEN**

JAPAN capital, **TOKYO (TOKIO,** old name, **EDO);** resort city, **HONSHU;** city, **KOBE, KOFU, NARA, CHIBA, OSAKA, OTARU, TOKYO (TOKIO);** harbor, port, or seaport, **OSAKA, OTARU;** island, **SADO, HONDO (HONSHU,** largest); volcano, **ASO, FUJI;** bay, **ISE;** province, old, **ISE, YAMATO;** mountain, **FUJI;** sea, **IYO**

JAVA .. stream, **SOLO;** mountain peak, **SEMERU**

JORDAN.. capital, **AMMAN;** city, **ZARQA;** gulf, **AQABA**

K

KAI ISLANDS ...... sea, **BANDA**

KANSAS .... city, **ARMA, IOLA, SALINA;** county, **OSAGE;** river, **SALINE**

KENTUCKY...... county, **BATH, BELL, ADAIR, BOONE, LARUE, BUTLER**

KENYA....... capital, **NAIROBI;** river, **TANA, EWASO**

228

KIRIBATI ..... capital, **TARAWA**

KLONDIKE........ river, **YUKON**

KOREA, NORTH . city, **WONSAN;** river, **YALU**

KOREA, SOUTH......... capital, **SEOUL (KEIJO);** city, **PUSAN, SUWON, INCHON**

L

LAOS ..... capital, **VIENTIANE;** river, **MEKONG;** town, **PAKSE**

LATVIA...... capital, port, **RIGA;** river, **AA**

LEBANON .... port, **SIDON**

LESOTHO .... capital, **MASERU;** river, **ORANGE;** town, **HOEK**

LIBERIA ... capital, **MONROVIA;** cape, **PALMAS;** river, **MANO, CESTOS;** town, **HARPER**

LIBYA.......... port and harbor, **DERNA;** capital, **TRIPOLI;** gulf, **SIDRA;** town, **TOBRUK**

LITHUANIA .... capital, **VILNIUS**

LITTLE AMERICA..... sea, **ROSS**

LOUISIANA .. parish, **ORLEANS;** river, **RED, PEARL, SABINE**

LUZON........ province, **ABRA;** mountain, **LABO;** river, **ABRA, AGNO**

M

MAINE ...... bay, **CASCO;** town, **BATH,** (university) **ORONO;** city, river, **SACO**

MALAWI.... town, **ZOMBA;** lake, **NYASA;** river, **SHIRE**

MALAY ARCHIPELAGO.... island, **JAVA, LARAT, LUZON, BORNEO, CELEBES**

MALAYSIA.......... city, **IPOH, KANGAR, PENANG, MALACCA;** state, **KEDAH, PERAK, SABAH, JOHORE, PERLIS, SARAWAK**

MALDIVES....... capital, **MALE**

MALI.... capital, **BAMAKO;** city, **KAYES, SEGOU**

MALTA........... island, **GOZO, COMINO**

MARTINIQUE.... volcano, **PELEE**

MARYLAND... city, **BOWIE, BEL AIR;** Mount, **BACKBONE**

MASSACHUSETTS .... city, **SALEM, NEWTON;** cape, **ANN, COD;** mountain, **TOM;** town, **LENOX**

MAURITANIA ...... town, **ATAR**

MEDITERRANEAN ... island, **IOS, GOZO, RODI (RHODES), CAPRI, CRETE, MALTA;** gulf, **TUNIS;** resort, **LIDO, NICE**

MESOPOTAMIA ... river, **TIGRIS**

MEXICO .. city, **LEON, PUEBLA;** lake, **CHAPALA;** state, **COLIMA, SONORA, TABASCO;** town, **TULA, LERDO**

MICHIGAN......... city, **ALMA, CLARE, FLINT, SPARTA;** county, **LUCE, EATON**

MINDANAO .. volcano, **APO;** gulf, **DAVAO;** town, **MATI**

MINNESOTA ..... city, **DULUTH;** Mount, **EAGLE;** river, **ST. CROIX**

MISSISSIPPI ...... city, **BILOXI;** county, **SCOTT;** river, **LEAF, YAZOO**

MISSOURI .... city, **AVA, LAMAR, LIBERTY, OSCEOLA, SEDALIA**

MONGOLIA .... desert, **GOBI**

MONTANA... city, **BUTTE;** peak, **KOCH;** river, **TETON**

MOROCCO .... capital, port, harbor, **RABAT;** city, **MEKNES, TANGIER;** mountains, **ATLAS;** region, **RIF (RIFF);** river, **TENSIFT;** town, **FES (FEZ), IFNI**

MOZAMBIQUE capital, **MAPUTO;**
port and harbor, **BEIRA;** river,
**SAVE (SABI), LIMPOPO,
LUGENDA**

N

NEBRASKA . . . . capital,
LINCOLN; city, **ORD;** river,
LOUP, PLATTE; county, **LOUP,
OTOE**

NEPAL . . . . mountain, **API;** river,
KOSI

NETHERLANDS . . . . city,
UTRECHT; commune or town,
**EDE, EPE, BEEK, ECHT, EDAM,
ELST, OLST, UDEN, GEMERT;**
port and harbor, **EDAM;** river,
EEM, LEK, MAAS (Dutch
Meuse), **RIJN** (Dutch Rhine),
WAAL

NEVADA . . . . city, **ELY, ELKO,
RENO;** county, **NYE, ELKO,
WASHOE;** lake, **TAHOE**

NEW GUINEA . . . . . city, port, and
harbor, **LAE;** island, **PAPUA**

NEW HAMPSHIRE . . city, **KEENE,
NASHUA, LACONIA;** county,
COOS; lake, **OSSIPEE**

NEW HEBRIDES . . . . capital, port,
harbor, **VILA;** island, **EPI (API),
TANA (TANNA), EFATE**

NEW JERSEY . . . city, **NEWARK,
TRENTON;** river, **RARITAN;**
town, **LODI;** cape, **MAY**

NEW MEXICO . . . . . . town, **TAOS;**
river, **GILA;** resort, **TAOS;** county,
LEA, LUNA, TAOS

NEW YORK . . . city, town, **ROME,
TROY, OLEAN, UTICA, ELMIRA,
OSWEGO;** island, **STATEN;**
county, **TIOGA;** village, **ILION,
MALONE**

NEWFOUNDLAND . . . . peninsula,
AVALON

NEW ZEALAND . . . . bay, **HAWKE;**
lake, **TAUPO;** peninsula, **MAHIA;**
island, **OTEA**

NICARAGUA . . . . city, **LEON**

NIGER . . capital, **NIAMEY;** region,
AIR; town, **MARADI, ZINDER**

NIGERIA . . . capital, **LAGOS;** city,
IWO, KANO, BENIN; river,
NIGER, BENUE; town, **ABA,
KUMO**

NORMANDY . . . . . . town, **ST.-LO**

NORTH CAROLINA . . river, **HAW,
TAR, PEE DEE, YADKIN;** cape,
FEAR; county, **ASHE**

NORTH DAKOTA . . city, **FARGO,
MINOT;** river, **KNIFE**

NORTHERN IRELAND . . . . capital,
BELFAST; city, **DERRY** (Lon-
donderry), **NEWRY, ARMAGH;**
county, **DOWN, TYRONE;** river,
BANN, FOYLE, LAGAN

NORTHUMBERLAND . . . . river,
TYNE

NORWAY . . . capital, **OSLO;** river,
KLAR, TANA, LAGEN; city,
HAMAR

O

OHIO . . county, **ROSS;** city, **ADA**
(college town Ohio Northern),
**KENT, LIMA, AKRON, BEREA,
NILES, XENIA, CANTON, FOS-
TORIA;** river, **MAD, MIAMI**

OKINAWA . . . . . . port and harbor,
NAHA (NAFA, NAWA)

OKLAHOMA . . . city, **ADA, ENID,
TULSA, SHAWNEE;** county,
MAJOR, MAYES; river, **RED**

OMAN . . . . capital, **MUSCAT
(MASQAT);** port, **MATRAH**

OREGON . . . . city, **SALEM,
ASTORIA;** peak, **HOOD**

ORKNEYS . . . . island, **HOY**

P

PACIFIC ISLANDS . . island, **YAP,
GUAM, TRUK, WAKE, LEYTE,
TAHITI;** island group, **FIJI, SULU,
PALAU (PELEW), SAMOA**

PAHANG . . . . capital, **KUANTAN**

PAKISTAN....... city **LAHORE,
KARACHI**; province, **SIND, PUN-
JAB**; river, **SWAT, INDUS,
KABUL, KUNDAR;** mountain
pass, **BOLAN, GUMAL, KHYBER**

PANAMA......... city, **ANCON,
COLON**; lake, **GATUN**

PARAGUAY...... city, **ITA**; river,
APA

PENNSYLVANIA...... city, **ERIE,
EASTON, CHESTER, TYRONE**;
port, **ERIE**

PERSIA, Ancient..... city, **SUSA,
NIRIZ**

PERU .... capital, **LIMA**; city,
department, river, **ICA**; cold district, **PUNO**; port and harbor, **ILO,
CALLAO**; town, **LAMAS**

PHILIPPINE ISLANDS (see also
LUZON and MINDANAO).........
capital, (de facto) **MANILA**; city,
**IBA, CEBU, LIPA, NAGA,
ILOILO**; mountain or peak,
APO, IBA, LABO; volcano, **APO**;
port and harbor, **ILOILO, BATAN-
GAS**; province, **DAPA**; island,
**CEBU, BATAN, SAMAR,
PANAY, LEYTE**; island group,
SULU

POLAND... city, **LODZ, LUBAN,
POSEN, SRODA**; commune,
KOLO, KONIN; river, **SAN,
BIALA, VISLA, STRYPA, VIS-
TULA**; province, **KRAKOW (CRA-
KOW)**

PORTUGAL....... cape, **ROCA**;
capital, **LISBON**; city, **OPORTO**;
river, **LIS (LIZ), DOURO, MINHO,
TAGUS**

PUERTO RICO ..... capital, **SAN
JUAN**; city, **PONCE**; town,
LAJAS, LARES; highest point,
CERRO DE PUNTA

Q

QATAR.......... capital, **DOHA**

QUEBEC... city, **HULL, MAGOG,
LAVAL, VERDUN**; county,
LEVIS; lake, **MINTO**; peninsula,
GASPE

R

RHODE ISLAND .. city, **BRISTOL,
NEWPORT, WARWICK**

ROMANIA (RUMANIA) ...... city,
ARAD, CLUJ, IASI; county,
ALBA; river, **OLT**

RUSSIA .... city, **KEM, KIEV,
LIDA, OMSK, OREL**; port and har-
bor, **OREL, ODESSA**; river, **OB,
OM, DON (DUNA), ILI, KEM,
OKA, UFA, LENA, NEVA, ONON,
SEIM, STYR, URAL, TEREK**;
lake, **ONEGA**; sea, **ARAL, AZOF
(AZOV)**; mountains, **ALAI, URAL,
ALTAI**; peninsula, **KOLA, KRYM
(CRIMEA)**; lake in European
Russia, **SEG**; region, **OMSK**

RWANDA....... capital, **KIGALI**

S

SAMOA .... capital, port, and
harbor, **APIA**

SAUDI ARABIA.... city, **MECCA,
MEDINA**

SAVAGE ISLAND ... island, **NIUE**

SCOTLAND..... port and harbor,
OBAN; seaport, **AYR**; former
county, **AYR, BUTE, FIFE**; river,
DEE, TAY (longest), **DOON,
SPEY, TYNE, AFTON**; city, **AYR**;
lake, **AWE, LOCH (LOCHY), LAG-
GAN**; district, **KYLE, ATHOLE
(ATHOLL)**; island off, **ARRAN**

SENEGAL. capital, port, **DAKAR**;
cape, **VERT**

SERBIA...... former capital, **NIS
(NISH)**

SEYCHELLES ..... island, **MAHE**

SIAM............ see THAILAND

SIBERIA (see also RUSSIA)......
river, **OB, YENISEI (ENISEI)**

SICILY volcano, **ETNA (AETNA)**;
commune, town, **RAGUSA**; city,
province, resort, **ENNA**

SIERRA LEONE......... capital,
FREETOWN; city, **BO**

SOCIETY ISLANDS .... island,
TAHITI

SOMALIA........... gulf, **ADEN**

SOUTH AFRICA .. city, **DURBAN**
region, **RAND**; river, **VAAL**

SOUTH AMERICA ... river, **BENI,
PLATA, JAPURA (YAPURA)**;
district, **CHACO**; mountains,
ANDES

SOUTH CAROLINA .... river,
SANTEE; island, **PARRIS**

SOUTH DAKOTA........ capital,
PIERRE; city, **LEMMON**

SOUTH PACIFIC....... isle, **FIJI,
BALI, COOK, SAMOA**

SOUTHWEST ..... river, **PECOS**

SPAIN....... city, **JACA, JAEN,
LEON, AVILA**; province, **JAEN,
LEON, LUGO, AVILA, MALAGA**;
port and harbor, **ADRA, NOYA,
VIGO, MALAGA**; river, **EBRO,
MINHO, TAGUS**; old kingdom,
LEON, CASTILE; commune,
LALIN, LORCA

SRI LANKA .... city, **KANDY**;
province, **UVA**

SUDAN.... capital, **KHARTOUM**;
desert region, **NUBIA**; river, **NILE**;
town, **JUBA**

SUMATRA........ city, **MEDAN**;
stream, **DELI**

SWEDEN .... city, **LUND,
OREBRO**; river, **DAL, UME,
KLAR, LULE, LAGAN**; island off,
ALAND; port and harbor, **LULEA,
MALMO**; strait, **ORESUND**

SWITZERLAND .... city, **BALE
(BASEL, BASLE), BERN
(BERNE), GENF (GENEVA)**;
commune, town, **BEX, BIEL,
CHUR, SION, AARAU, MORAT**;
canton, **URI, ZUG (ZOUG), BERN
(BERNE), VAUD, BASEL
(BASLE)**; river, **AAR (AARE)**;
lake, **ZUG, JOUX, LUCERNE**;
mountain, **TODI, MATTERHORN**;
resort, **DAVOS**; capital, **BERN
(BERNE)**

SYRIA..... capital, **DAMASCUS**;
city, **ALEP (ALEPPO), HAMA,
HOMS**; river, **EUPHRATES**

T

TAHITI ...... capital, **PAPEETE**;
peak, **OROHENA**

TAIWAN (FORMOSA) .... capital,
TAIPEI; city, **TAI-NAN**

TALAUD ISLANDS.... town, **BEO**

TANIMBAR ISLANDS ..... island,
LARAT

TANZANIA......... capital, **DAR
ES SALAAM**; city, **TANGA,
MOSHI**; lake, **NYASA, RUKWA,
VICTORIA, TANGANYIKA**; is-
land, **MAFIA, PEMBA, ZANZI-
BAR**; region, **MARA**; town,
TABORA

TAPUL ISLANDS .... island,
LAPAC, LUGUS, SIASI

TASMANIA .... capital, **HOBART**

TENNESSEE .... city, **MEMPHIS**;
county, **KNOX, MAURY,
SHELBY**

TEXAS .... city, **WACO,
LAREDO, ABILENE**; county,
**CLAY, LAMB, CARSON, LOV-
ING**; river, **LEON**

THAILAND.. capital, **BANGKOK**;
gulf, **SIAM**; river, **PING, KLONG**;
town, **TAK**

TIBET ... city, **LASSA (LHASA)**;
mountain pass, **DANGLA**; river,
INDUS

TOGO.... capital, **LOME**; Mount,
AGOU; town, **PALIME**

TRINIDAD ...... port, **LA BREA**

TUNISIA......... capital, **TUNIS**

TURKEY...... capital, **ANKARA
(ANGORA)**; city, **ADANA, IZMIR**;
lake, **MANYAS**; river, **ARAS
(ARAKS), KURA**; town, city,
ORDU, URFA; island, **TENEDOS**

TUSCANY .... river, **ARNO**

232

U

UGANDA ... capital, **KAMPALA;** lake, **KYOGA, ALBERT, ED-WARD, GEORGE, VICTORIA;** Mount, **ELGON;** river, **NILE;** town, **LIRA, ENTEBBE**

UNITED ARAB EMIRATES ... city, **ABU DHABI**

URUGUAY .... capital, **MONTEVIDEO;** city, **MELO, MINAS, SALTO, RIVERA;** river, **RIO NEGRO**

U.S.S.R. .... see RUSSIA

UTAH .... city, **LEHI, HEBER, LOGAN, OGDEN, PROVO;** county, **CACHE, DAVIS;** mountains, **UINTA;** peak, **KINGS;** river, **GREEN, SEVIER**

V

VENEZUELA . capital, **CARACAS;** town, **CORO, MERIDA;** island off coast, **ARUBA;** river, **META, APURE, ARAUCA, ORINOCO**

VERMONT .... city, **BARRE, RUTLAND;** creek, **OTTER;** county, **ESSEX, ORANGE, OR-LEANS, WINDSOR;** mountains, **GREEN;** river, **WHITE**

VIETNAM .... capital, **HANOI;** city, **HUE, DA NANG, SAIGON** (now **HO CHI MINH CITY**); region, **ANNAM;** river, **RED (HONG), MEKONG**

VIRGINIA .... city, **SALEM, NORTON, BRISTOL, EMPORIA, FAIRFAX, HAMPTON, RAD-FORD, NORFOLK, ROANOKE;** Mount, **ROGERS;** river, **DAN, JAMES, POTOMAC, RAPIDAN, ROANOKE**

VIRGIN ISLANDS .... capital, **CHARLOTTE AMALIE**

W

WALES .... capital, **CARDIFF;** city, **RHONDDA, SWANSEA;** county, **GWENT;** lake, **BALA;** mountains, **BERWYN, SNOW-DON;** river, **DEE, LUG (LUGG), USK, TAFF**

WASHINGTON .... city, **LACEY, TACOMA, SEATTLE, SPO-KANE;** Mount, **RAINIER;** river, **SNAKE, NACHES, YAKIMA, CO-LUMBIA**

WESTERN AUSTRALIA... capital, **PERTH**

WEST INDIES .... isle, island, **CUBA, HAITI, NEVIS**

WEST VIRGINIA .... city, **ELKINS, WHEELING;** river, **OHIO, POTOMAC, BIG SANDY**

WISCONSIN .... city, **ALMA, RIPON, RACINE, KENOSHA, MADISON, GREEN BAY, EAU CLAIRE;** river, **BLACK;** lake, **MENDOTA**

WYOMING .... city, **CASPER, LARAMIE;** highest mountain peak, **GANNETT;** range, **TETON;** river, **GREEN, SNAKE, POWDER, BIGHORN**

Y

YEMEN, NORTH .... capital, **SAN'A (SANAA);** city, **MOCHA;** ancient ruins, **MARIB**

YEMEN, SOUTH.. capital, **ADEN**

YORKSHIRE.... river, **OUSE;** city, **LEEDS**

YUGOSLAVIA .... island, **RAB (ARBE), SOLTA;** city, **NIS (NISH);** port, **KOPER;** river, **LIM, KUPA, SAVA, DRINA, NERETVA (NARENTA);** former district and province, **BANAT**

YUKON .... city, **DAWSON;** district, **KLONDIKE;** peak, **KEELE;** lake, **TAGISH;** river, **PEEL, TANANA;** creek, **HESS**

Z

ZAIRE ...... capital, **KINSHASA;** province, **KIVU, SHABA;** river, **UELE, CONGO, KASAI, LINDI, LULUA, UBANGI**

ZAMBIA ...... capital, **LUSAKA;** waterfall, **VICTORIA;** river, **KAFUE, ZAMBEZI**

AEROSPACE

SATELLITES, CAPSULES, SPACECRAFT

NOTES: Where the country of origin is other than the U.S., that information is given. Many of these names are from a series of launches. For example, there were hundreds of Soyuz launches. The year given is that of the first launch.

3 letters

AMS.....................	1976
ANS .... Dutch,	1974
ATS	1966
BSE .... see YURI	
CAT .... International,	1979
COS .... International,	1975
CTS .... Canadian,	1976
ETS .... see KIKU	
FR-1 .... French,	1965
GRS .... W. German,	1963
IMP	1973
IUE......... International,	1976
LEM.....................	1967
LES......................	1965
OAO.....................	1966
OFO.....................	1970
OGO.....................	1964
OSO.....................	1962
OTS .... International,	1977
SMS.....................	1974
TIP......................	1975
TTS.....................	1967
UME.......... Japanese,	1976

4 letters

ANIK .... see TELESAT	
ANNA	1962
AURA .... French,	1975
AZUR................. see GRS	
BIOS	1966
DASH...................	1963
DIAL French & W. German,	1970
DMSP	1971
ECHO....................	1960
EOLE .... French,	1971
ERTS	1972
ESRO....... International,	1968
ESSA...................	1966
EXOS............ see KYOKKO	
GEOS....... International,	1976
GOES....................	1975
HEAO....................	1977
HEOS....... International,	1968
IQSY .... International,	1978
IRIS .... International,	1968
ISEE........ International,	1977
ISIS............ Canadian,	1965
ITOS....................	1970
KIKU .... Japanese,	1975
LUNA............ Soviet,	1959
MARS .... Soviet,	1962
NATO ...... International,	1970

NOAA	1970
NOSS....................	1976
NOVA	1981
SAGE....................	1979
SERT....................	1964
SRET............ French,	1972
VELA....................	1963
YURI .... Japanese,	1978
ZOND............ Soviet,	1964

5 letters

AEROS ...... W. German,	1972
ARIEL .... British,	1962
ASTEX	1971
AYAME....... Japanese,	1979
CAMEO..................	1979
DENPA .... Japanese,	1972
DODGE..................	1967
DRIMS.......... see TELESAT	
EKRAN .... Soviet,	1976
FAITH	1963
IDCSP	1966
INJUN	1961
LOFTI	1961
MAGIC ..... see INTERCOSMOS	
MIDAS...................	1960
OSCAR	1961
PEOLE........... French,	1970
RELAY	1962
SAMOS..................	1961
SIGMA..................	1962
SIGNE .... French,	1977
SIRIO........... Italian,	1977
SOYUZ .... Soviet,	1967
TAIYO........ Japanese,	1975
TIROS	1960
TRAAC	1961
TRIAD...................	1972
UOSAT	1981
VENUS	1961

6 letters

APOLLO	1965
ARIANE .... International,	1979
AURORA	1962
BOREAS.... International,	1969
CASTOR......... French,	1975
COMSAT	1969
COSMOS .... Soviet,	1962
GEMINI	1964
HELIOS...... W. German,	1974
KYOKKO ..... Japanese,	1978

LAGEOS 1976
MAGION .... Czech, 1978
MAGSAT 1979
NIMBUS 1964
OHSUMI ...... Japanese, 1970
PAGEOS 1966
PALAPA ..... Indonesian, 1976
POLLUX .... French, 1975
POLYOT .... Soviet, 1963
PROTON ... Soviet, 1965
RADOSE 1963
RANGER 1961
ROHINI .... Indian, 1980
SAKURA ...... Japanese, 1977
SALYUT .... Soviet, 1971
SATCOM 1975
SCATHA 1979
SEASAT 1978
SKYLAB 1973
SKYNET .... British, 1969
SOLRAD 1976
SYNCOM 1963
TANSEI .... Japanese, 1971
VIKING 1975
VOSTOK .... Soviet, 1961
WESTAR 1974
WRESAT ..... Australian, 1967

7 letters
ASTERIX .... French, 1965
AUREOLE .... French, 1971
AURORAE .... see ESRO
BHASKAR .... Indian, 1979
COMSTAR 1976
COURIER 1960
DIADEME .... French, 1967
DIAPSON .... French, 1966
ESA-GEOS .. International, 1977
FREEDOM 1961
HAKUCHO .... Japanese, 1979
HAWKEYE 1974
INTASAT .... Spanish, 1974
JIKIKEN ...... Japanese, 1978
LANDSAT .... see ERTS
MARINER 1962
MARISAT 1976
MERCURY 1960
MIRANDA .... British, 1974
MOLNIYA ...... Soviet, 1965
NAVSTAR 1978
ORBITER . see LUNAR ORBITER
PEGASUS 1965

PIONEER 1958
PROGNOZ .... Soviet, 1972
SHINSEI ...... Japanese, 1971
SOLWIND 1979
SPUTNIK .... Soviet, 1957
STAR-RAD 1962
TELESAT ...... Canadian, 1972
TELSTAR 1962
TRANSAT 1977
TRANSIT 1960
VOSKHOD .... Soviet, 1964

8 letters
ALOUETTE .... Canadian, 1962
COLUMBIA 1981
ELEKTRON ...... Soviet, 1964
EXPLORER 1958
GORIZONT .... Soviet, 1978
HIMAWARI ... Japanese, 1977
INTELSAT .. International, 1965
LANI BIRD.. International, 1966
METEOSAT. International, 1977
PROGRESS ...... Soviet, 1978
PROSPERO ...... British, 1971
SAN MARCO ..... Italian, 1964
SURVEYOR 1966
VANGUARD 1958

9 letters
ARYABHATA ..... Indian, 1975
EARLY BIRD International, 1965
FLTSATCOM 1978
STARLETTE ..... French, 1975
SYMPHONIE .... French &
                W. German, 1974
TOURNESOL .... French, 1971
TRANSTAGE 1964

10 letters
CANNONBALL .... see LAGEOS
CHALLENGER 1983
COPERNICUS 1972
DISCOVERER 1959
DODECAPOLE 1965
FRIENDSHIP 1962

11 letters
INTERCOSMOS .. Soviet, 1969
LIBERTY BELL 1961

12 letters
LUNAR ORBITER 1966

ASTRONAUTS

NOTES: The first Russian Cosmonaut was Yuri Gagarin. The others are not listed because you are not apt to find their names in crosswords. This listing includes all U.S. missions up to June 1983.

Aldrin, Edwin (Buzz) .... Gemini-Titan 12, 1966; Apollo-Saturn 11, 1969
Allen, Joseph .... Columbia, November, 1982
Anders, William .... Apollo-Saturn 8, 1968
Armstrong, Neil .... Gemini-Titan 8, 1966; Apollo-Saturn 11, 1969
Bean, Alan........................ Apollo-Saturn 12, 1969; Skylab 3, 1973
Bobko, Karol..................................... Challenger, April, 1983
Borman, Frank .... Gemini-Titan 7, 1965; Apollo-Saturn 8, 1968
Brand, Vance .... Apollo 18, 1975; Columbia, November, 1982
Carpenter, M. Scott................................ Mercury-Atlas 7, 1962
Carr, Gerald..................................... Skylab 4, 1973–1974
Cernan, Eugene .... Apollo-Saturn 10, 1969; Apollo-Saturn 17, 1972
Collins, Michael .... Gemini-Titan 10, 1966; Apollo-Saturn 11, 1969
Conrad, Charles.............. Gemini-Titan 5, 1965; Gemini-Titan 11, 1966;
                                   Apollo-Saturn 12, 1969; Skylab 2, 1973
Cooper, L. Gordon........... Mercury-Atlas 9, 1963; Gemini-Titan 5, 1965
Crippen, Robert .... Columbia, April, 1981; Challenger, June, 1983
Cunningham, R. Walter............................. Apollo-Saturn 7, 1968
Duke, Charles..................................... Apollo-Saturn 16, 1972
Eisele, Donn .... Apollo-Saturn 7, 1968
Engle, Joe .... Columbia, November, 1981
Evans, Ronald..................................... Apollo-Saturn 17, 1972
Fabian, John..................................... Challenger, June, 1983
Fullerton, C. Gordon .... Columbia, March, 1982
Garriott, Owen .... Skylab 3, 1973
Gibson, Edward .... Skylab 4, 1973–1974
Glenn, John..................................... Mercury-Atlas 6, 1962
Gordon, Richard .... Gemini-Titan 11, 1966; Apollo-Saturn 12, 1969
Grissom, Virgil (Gus)...... Mercury-Redstone 4, 1961; Gemini-Titan 3, 1965
Haise, Fred .... Apollo-Saturn 13, 1970
Hartsfield, Henry .... Columbia, June–July, 1982
Hauck, Frederick (Rick) .... Challenger, June, 1983
Irwin, James .... Apollo-Saturn 15, 1971
Kerwin, Joseph.................................... Skylab 2, 1973
Lenoir, William .... Columbia, November, 1982
Lousma, Jack .... Skylab 3, 1973; Columbia, March, 1982
Lovell, James .... Gemini-Titan 7, 1965; Gemini-Titan 12, 1966;
                                Apollo-Saturn 8, 1968; Apollo-Saturn 13, 1970
Mattingly, Thomas...... Apollo-Saturn 16, 1972; Columbia, June–July, 1982
McDivitt, James .... Gemini-Titan 4, 1965; Apollo-Saturn 9, 1969
Mitchell, Edgar .... Apollo-Saturn 14, 1971

Musgrave, Story....................................... Challenger, April, 1983
Overmeyer, Robert .... Columbia, November, 1982
Peterson, Donald .... Challenger, April, 1983
Pogue, William .... Skylab 4, 1973–1974
Ride, Sally .... Challenger, June, 1983
Roosa, Stuart .... Apollo-Saturn 14, 1971
Schirra, Walter .... Mercury-Atlas 8, 1962; Gemini-Titan 6-A, 1965;
Apollo-Saturn 7, 1968
Schmitt, Harrison................................. Apollo-Saturn 17, 1972
Schweickart, Russell............................... Apollo-Saturn 9, 1969
Scott, David .... Gemini-Titan 8, 1966; Apollo-Saturn 9, 1969;
Apollo-Saturn 15, 1971
Shepard, Alan.......... Mercury-Redstone 3, 1961; Apollo-Saturn 14, 1971
Slayton, Donald (Deke)................................... Apollo 18, 1975
Stafford, Thomas............................... Gemini-Titan 6-A, 1965;
Apollo-Saturn 10, 1969; Apollo 18, 1975
Swigart, John .... Apollo-Saturn 13, 1970
Thagard, Norman.................................. Challenger, June, 1983
Truly, Richard.................................. Columbia, November, 1981
Weitz, Paul........................ Skylab 2, 1973; Challenger, April, 1983
White, Edward... Gemini-Titan 4, 1965
Worden, Alfred...................................... Apollo-Saturn 15, 1971
Young, John .... Gemini-Titan 3, 1965; Gemini-Titan 10, 1966;
Apollo-Saturn 10, 1969; Apollo-Saturn 16, 1972;
Columbia, April, 1981

ROCKETS, LAUNCH VEHICLES

4 letters	5 letters	6 letters	8 letters
ABLE	AGENA	APACHE	ABLESTAR
ARGO	ARCAS	BIG JOE	ASTROBEE
HAWK	ARCON	SATURN	BLUE SCOUT
JUNO	ARIES	THORAD	MALEMUTE
NIKE	ATLAS		REDSTONE
TAID	CAJUN	7 letters	TOMAHAWK
THOR	DELTA	AEROBEE	VANGUARD
	JASON	CENTAUR	
	SCOUT	JAVELIN	9 letters
	TITAN	SHOTPUT	LITTLE JOE
		TERRIER	
			10 letters
			BLACKBRANT
			JOURNEYMAN

COMPUTER TERMINOLOGY

Note regarding computer languages: All computers actually work in machine language, which uses binary code. This is the "lowest" level of the languages. People don't think in binary codes, so "higher" level languages (symbolic languages), which are easier to understand, have been devised. The easier a language is to understand, the higher the level; hence the further it is from the computer's actual language.

3 letters
ADA......... High-level language
APL .... High-level language
BCD ..... Binary Coded Decimal
BIT........ Binary digit (1 or 0)
BOX......... Flow-chart symbol
BUG Error, defect, or malfunction
BUS . Conductor for transmitting signals
CAD.... Computer Aided Design
CAIComputer Assisted Instruction
CAL Computer Assisted Learning
CAM........ Computer Assisted Manufacturing
CAT Computer Assisted Training
COM Computer Output Microfilm
CPS .... Characters Per Second
CPU .... Central Processing Unit
CRT .... Cathode Ray Tube
DMA .... Direct Memory Access
DOS .... Disk Operating System
EDP . Electronic Data Processing
HEX ..... (hexadecimal notation) Number system using 16 as a base
HIT... The finding of a matching record
JCL...... Job Control Language
JOBUnit of work for the computer
LOG .... Record events in chronological sequence
LPM.......... Lines Per Minute
MAC... Multi-Access Computing
MPU....... MicroProcessor Unit
PCM..... Pulse Code Modulation
PL-1........ High-level language
RAM... Random-Access Memory
ROM........ Read-Only Memory
RUNBegin execution of a program
ZAP .... Erase; wipe out

4 letters
ANSI .... American National Standards Institute
BAND Group of recording tracks on a magnetic disk or drum
BAUDMeasurement unit of speed of data transmission
BEAD... Small unit of a program
BLIP.. Erratic signal on a screen

BOOT....... Protective housing
BYTE... Group of bits, usually 8 bits in length
CARD .... Circuit board
CHIP ...... Tiny piece of silicon embedded with many electronic circuits
CODE.... Representation of data or instructions in symbolic form
COPY .... Reproduce data from one storage device onto another
DATA.. Information of any type; computer "food"; computer input
DISK . Magnetic storage medium
DOWN......... Not in operation
DRUM . Magnetic storage device
DUMP . Clear memory and store data elsewhere
ECOM .... Electronic Computer-Oriented Mail
EDIT........... Prepare data for subsequent processing
FIFO.......... First In, First Out
FILE.... Organized collection of related data
FLOW ... Sequence of events in the solution of a problem
GATE......... Electronic switch
GIGO .. Garbage In, Garbage Out
HEAD...... Device used to read, record, or erase data on a magnetic storage medium
HOME ... Starting position for a cursor on a screen (top left-hand corner, usually)
KILO .... Prefix denoting one thousand
LIFO.......... Last In, First Out
LISP........ High-level language
LOAD. Transfer information from a storage device into the computer
LOGO...... High-level language, primarily for children
LOOP...... Closed sequence of instructions performed repeatedly

MEGA Prefix denoting one million
MENU .. List of program options
MODE ..... Method of operation
NODE ..... One component in a network
PACK Compress data in order to save space in storage
PASS. Single execution of a loop
PEEK BASIC language command that displays the value of a specific memory location
POKE BASIC language command that puts a one-byte value into a given memory location
PORT...... Computer outlet for plugging in a peripheral
PROM Programmable Read-Only Memory
READ. Retrieve information from memory
SCAN...... Read; examine each part in sequence
SORT Put data in order according to the desired rule
TAPE Magnetic medium for data storage
TASK..... Single unit of work in multiprocessing
TEXT..... Information part of a message
USER.. Computer network client
WORD..... Group of characters representing a unit of data

5 letters
ALGOL ..... High-level language
ARRAY. Orderly arrangement of data in a list
ASCII....... Standard code that assigns values to numbers and letters; code which enables different computers to communicate
BASIC...... High-level language
BATCH.. Group of similar transactions collected for processing as a single unit
BLANK...... Character used to represent a space
BLOCK Group of records treated as a single unit of data
BOARD........ Sheet on which integrated circuits are mounted
BREAK.............. Interrupt
CHART, FLOW... Diagrammatic representation of a data-processing problem
COBOL..... High-level language
CORAL..... High-level language

COUNT.. Total number of times an instruction is performed
CRASH... Hardware or software malfunction causing system breakdown
DEBUG.... Locate and eliminate errors
DRIVE. Device which causes the movement of a recording medium
ENTRY.... Item of data in a list
EPROM... Electrically Programmable Read-Only Memory
FAULT.. Failure of any part of a system
FIELD Part of a record containing a specific unit of information
FORTH ..... High-level language
FRAME Image in a display system
HERTZ .... Unit of frequency
INPUT Data that goes into a computer or its peripherals
LOG-ON . Sign onto a system or network
MERGE Combine two or more sets of records into a single file
MICRO .... Very small
MODEM ... Device which allows computers to communicate over telephone lines
NEXUS Point in a system where interconnections occur
NOISE........ Spurious signals
OCTAL Number system using 8 as a base
PILOT . High-level language used in classrooms
PIXEL Division of a display screen
QUEUE Waiting list of programs to be run
RADIX Base of a number system
RERUN ... Repeat the execution of a program
SLAVE.. Unit which is under the control of a larger unit
SPACE Empty unit of data storage
STACK .... Area of memory reserved for storage of data; LIFO area
STORE .... Memory medium
TABLE.. Set of data arranged as an array
TRACK .... Channel on a magnetic medium
WRITE........ Record data on a storage medium

6 letters
ACCESS.... Retrieve data from a storage device or a peripheral

ANALOG Method of measurement that uses physical variables

ASSIGN Reserve part of a system for a specific purpose

BABBLE Cross-talk from several interfacing channels

BINARY . Notation system using only 1's and 0's to represent data

BUFFER .... Temporary storage space for data

CATENA .... Series of items in a chained list

CURSOR ... Movable spot on the screen showing where the pointer is

DECADE .... Group of ten items

DUPLEX .. Communications line that allows simultaneous 2-way transmission

ENABLE .... Restore to ordinary operating conditions

ENCODE ..... Represent data in digital form

FORMAT Specified arrangement of data; prepare (a diskette) for use

GLITCH .... Unwanted electronic pulse that causes errors

JITTER .... Signal instability

MASTER ..... Unit that controls smaller (slave) units

MATRIX ... Type of printer that forms letters by printing a pattern of dots

MEMORY The part of a computer that stores information

NIBBLE Four bit word; half a byte

ON-LINE . Under the control of a central processor

OUTPUT Information coming out of the computer; the end product of a program

PASCAL .... High-level language

PROMPT ..... Message from an operating system calling for action from the operator

RECORD . Set of information that contains all data about one item

SCREEN Surface of a CRT that is visible to the operator

SCROLL Move the contents of a screen up or down, one line at a time

SEARCH .... Look for a specific piece of data

SECTOR ...... Defined area of a track or band

SERIAL Pertaining to transmission of data one bit at a time

SNOBOL .... High-level language

STRING ..... Set of consecutive characters

SUBSET .. Group of items which belongs to a larger group

SYNTAX . Grammatical rules that specify how an instruction can be written

THREAD . Group of beads which form a complete program

7 letters

ADDRESS .... Particular number associated with each memory location

CIRCUIT .... Closed-loop electric current path

COMMAND ..... Instruction to a computer

COMPILE ... Translate symbolic language into machine language

COUNTER ...... Device used to accumulate totals and maintain a count

DECODER . Device used to alter data from one coded format to another

DIGITAL Describing a method of measurement using precise quantities to represent variables

DISABLE ... Inhibit or remove a hardware or software feature

DISPLAY . Output on the screen

EXECUTE .... Run a program

FLUTTER ...... Recurring speed variation

FORTRAN .. High-level language

GARBAGE .... Meaningless, unwanted data

MEGABIT ...... One million bits

MONITOR . High-resolution CRT

NESTING Writing a program that has loops within loops

NETWORK ..... System of inter-connecting components

OFF-LINE . Not under the control of a central processor

PLOTTER .... Special printer for graphics

PROGRAM ... Set of instructions given a computer so it may perform a task

RAW DATA .. Information which has not been processed

READOUT Display of processed information on a screen

ROUTINE ... Set of instructions; part of a program

SCANNER Device which samples the status of a file
SEGMENT . Division of a routine
STORAGE .. Place where data is held in the computer or its peripherals

8 letters
ALPHABET ...... Character set
ANNOTATE Add explanatory text to program instructions
ASSEMBLY .... Middle-level language
COMPILER . Program that translates symbolic language into machine language
COMPUTER .. Electronic device capable of accepting data, solving problems, and supplying results
CONSTANT. Item of data which does not vary in value
DATA BASE . Set of information available to the computer
DISCRETE ... Pertaining to data organized in distinct parts
DISKETTE .... Floppy disk
FUNCTION ...... The operation specified in an instruction
GRAPHICS. All non-alphanumeric displays generated by a computer
HARD COPY ... Output on paper
HARDWARE . The physical parts of a computer system
MEGABYTE ... One million bytes
OPERATOR ...... Person who is working the computer
PARALLEL.. Type of data transmission where all parts of an 8-bit word are sent simultaneously
REGISTER .. Specific location in memory
RESIDENT .... Any program permanently stored in the computer
RETRIEVE ... Search for, select, and extract data contained in a file
ROBOTICS..... Area of artificial intelligence pertaining to industrial use of robots
SIMULATE.. Represent physical problems by mathematical formulas
SOFTWARE ... All programs that instruct the computer how to operate
TERMINAL ..... Peripheral of a computer system

VARIABLE. Symbol representing a quantity whose value can change

9 letters
ALGORITHM ...... Step-by-step procedure for giving instructions to a computer
ASSEMBLER Code that converts symbolic language into machine language
CHARACTER ..... Single letter, number, symbol, or space
CONNECTOR Flow-chart symbol
DECREMENT Decrease a variable by a specified amount
HANDSHAKE . Acknowledgment between two computers of ability to communicate
INCREMENT Increase a variable by a specified amount
INTERFACE... Linkage between systems, programs, or between a person and a system
INTERRUPT Temporary break in the running of a program
MAIN FRAME .... Very large computer
PARAMETER Quantity which may be given variable values

10 letters
NANOSECOND.... Billionth of a second
PERIPHERAL ...... Any item of hardware that connects to a computer (printer, monitor, drive, etc.)
PHILOXENIC... Friendly to uninformed users; user-friendly
REPERTOIRE Set of instructions a given computer can execute

11 letters
CYBERNETICS The study of the theory of control systems

12 letters
ALPHANUMERIC . Pertaining to characters that represent numbers, letters, and/or symbols
INTELLIGENCE ..... Processing capability

13 letters
CONFIGURATION ..... Specific makeup of the physical units of a computer system

241

MUSIC
MUSICAL TERMS

3 letters
AIR............ Tune or melody
BAR .... Vertical line dividing the staff
CON..................... With
GAI................ Lively, brisk
PIU...................... More

4 letters
ALLA............. In the style of
BEAT..... Division of a measure
CHEF (D'ORCHESTRA)Conductor
CLEF .... Character on the staff
CODA .... Passage ending a movement
ECCO.................... Echo
FINE....................... End
FINO .... As far as; up to
FLAT .... Character on the staff
GLEE ... English composition for 3 or more voices
HOLD........... Sign indicating prolongation of a note
IDYL ..... Romantic or pastoral composition
LENO.............. Faint; quiet
LIED.............. German song
LOCO................. Place
MANO.................... Hand
POCO .... Little
POLO...... Syncopated Spanish dance
REEL............. Lively dance
REST Pause between two tones; character on the staff
SANS.................. Without
SINO .... As far as; up to
TEMA .... Theme
VAMP .... Improvise an accompaniment
VIVO .... Lively; briskly
VOCE..................... Voice

5 letters
A DEUX .... For two hands
ANCOR........ Again; also; yet
BALLO .... Dance
BATON ...... Conductor's wand
BOCCA .... Mouth
CANTO........ Melody or chant
CHANT...... Short sacred song
CHORD..... A harmony of 2 or more tones
CLOSE....... Cadenza ending a section or piece
DESTO .... Sprightly
DIRGE........... Funeral hymn

DOLCE .... Sweet; soft
ELEGY.. Melancholy composition
FLING .... Scottish dance
FOLIA .... Spanish dance
GALOP .... Lively French dance
JALEO.......... Spanish dance
LARGO .... Slow and stately
LENTO .. Slow, but not dragging
MESTO .... Sad; melancholy
METER, METRE... Symmetrical grouping of musical rhythms
MEZZO .... Half
MINIM................ Half-note
MOLTO .... Very; much
PAUSA .... Rest; pause
PAVAN .. Stately Italian-Spanish dance
PEZZO................... Piece
PIANO............. Soft; softly
PIECE ..... Musical composition
PITCH ..... Position of a tone in the musical scale
POLKA .... Bohemian dance
SAMBA......... Brazilian dance
SCALE.... Series of tones which form any major or minor key
SEGNO .... A sign
SENZA .... Without
SHARP .. Character on the staff
SOAVE ...... Suavely; flowingly
TANGO .... Argentine dance
TANTO ..... As much; so much
TARDO .... Slow; lingering
TEMPO .... Rate of speed
VALSE.................. Waltz

6 letters
ADAGIO Slow; a slow movement
ANTHEM ...... Piece of sacred vocal music
A TEMPO..... At the preceding rate of speed
BOLERO........ Spanish dance
CHIARO .... Clear; pure
COMODO............ Leisurely
CON IRA .... Wrathfully
DA CAPO... From the beginning
DECISO.......... With decision
DI GALA.......... Gaily; merrily
EQUALE... Equal; even; smooth
FACILE............. Easy; fluent
FEBILE .... Feeble; weak
FEROCE .... Wildly
FINALE........ Last movement
FLORID.. Embellished with runs, passages, etc.
GIUSTO................ Proper

INFINO .... As far as; up to
INTIMO .... Heartfelt; fervent
JARABE .... Mexican dance
LEGATO ... Slurred; played with
no break between notes
LITANY .... Song of supplication
MINUET .... Early French dance
form
PAVANA Stately Italian-Spanish
dance
REDOWA ..... Bohemian dance
SEMPRE .... Always; throughout
VELOCE .... Rapid
VIVACE .... Lively; animated

7 letters
AGILITA .... Vivacity
AGILITE .... Vivacity
AGITATO .... Agitated
ALLEGRO .... Lively or rapid
ALLONGE .... Prolonged
AMABILE .... Sweet and tender
ANDANDO .... Easy and flowing
ANDANTE ... Moderately slowly
ANIMATO .... Vivaciously
ANIMOSO .... Spirited
BAROCCO .... Eccentric or
whimsical
CADENCE .... Rhythm
CADENZA .... Elaborate ending
passage
CALMATO .... Calmly
CAMPANA .... Bell
CANTATA ..... Vocal work with
instrumental accompaniment
CANTATO .... Singingly
CANZONE .... Folk song or
part-song in madrigal style
CHANSON .... Song
CLAVIER .... Keyboard
COMPASS .... Range of a voice
or instrument
CON BRIO .... Spiritedly
CON MOTO .. With an energetic
movement
DECIBEL ... Unit of loudness or
intensity of sound
DI COLTA ... Suddenly; at once
DI MOLTO ..... Very; extremely
DOLENTE .... Sad
FERMATA .... A hold, pause, or
interruption
FERVOSO ... In an agitated style
GAVOTTE ... Old French dance
GENTILE .... Gracefully; in a
refined style
HANACCA ..... Moravian dance
HAUTBOY .... Oboe
INTRADA .... Short introduction
or prelude
LEGGERO .... Light; airy

MAESTRO ... Master; conductor
MARCATO .... With distinctness
and emphasis
MAZURKA .... Polish dance
PARLATO .... Spoken
PASSAGE .... Portion or section
of a composition
PENSOSO .. Pensive; thoughtful
PIETOSO .... Pitifully; movingly
PLACIDO .... Smooth; placid
REPLICA ... A repeat or reprise
ROBUSTO .... Firmly and boldly
SCHERZO .. Vivacious movement
in a symphony
SENTITO ...... With expression
SERIOSO In a grave, impressive
style

8 letters
A BALLATA .... In singing style
AFFABILE .... Sweetly and
gracefully
BEL CANTO The art of beautiful
song
BERCEUSE .... Lullaby
CALMANDO ..... Growing calm
CANTICLE .... Sacred chant
CAVATINA .... Short aria
CHACONNE .... Spanish dance
CON AMORE .... Lovingly
CON FURIA .... Furiously; wildly
CON GARBO .... Gracefully;
elegantly
CON GIOCO .... Playfully
CON GIOIA .... Joyously
CON TINTO ...... With shading;
expressively
CON UMORE ...... With humor
DAL SEGNO ..... From the sign
DELICATO ... In a delicate style
DIAPASON .... Octave
DISCRETO ...... Comparatively
subdued
DOLCIATO .... Softer; calmer
ELEGANTE .... Gracefully
ENFATICO ...... With emphasis
FANDANGO .... Lively Spanish
dance
FANTASIA .... Free-form
composition
FERVENTE .. Ardently; fervently
HABANERA .... Cuban
contradance
LARGANDO ... Growing broader
LENTANDO ... Growing slower
LIBRETTO .... The words of an
opera, oratorio, etc.
MACHUCHA ... Dance similar to
the bolero
MADRIGAL .. Vocal setting of a
short lyric poem

243

MODULATE..... Pass from one key or mode into another
NOCTURNE.. Dreamily romantic composition
RHAPSODY....... Instrumental fantasia on folk songs
RIGADOON Lively French dance
RIGOROSO .... In strict time
RISOLUTO... In a decided style
SARABAND.... Stately dance of Spanish or Oriental origin
SEMPLICE.... In a natural style
SERENADE...... Love song for the evening
SOGGETTO..... Subject; theme
VIGOROSO .... Vigorously

9 letters
A CAPPELLA......... Without instrumental accompaniment
ACOUSTICS Science of musical tones
AFTER NOTE...... Unaccented note of a pair
ALL' OTTAVA An octave higher
ANTIPHONY Responsive singing
BAGATELLE.. Short, fairly easy piece of music
BARCAROLE ... Venetian boat-song
BELLICOSO... In a warlike style
BERGAMASK.. Clownish dance
CANTABILE .. In a singing style
CAPRICCIO.......... Free-form instrumental piece
CHROMATIC.. Relating to tones foreign to a given key
CON AFFETO...... With feeling
CON CALORE..... Passionately
CON DOLORE.... Expressive of pain or grief
CON FRETTA........ Hurriedly
CON MAESTA ..... Majestically

CON RABBIA ...... With frenzy
CON RIPOSO ...... Calmly; in a tranquil manner
CON VIGORE .... Vigorously
FARANDOLA ..... Circle dance
GLISSANDO .... With a flowing, sliding move
IMPROMPTU ... Composition of extemporaneous form
MALAGUENA..... Spanish folk music
PIZZICATO ... Plucked with the fingers, as strings
POCO A POCO.... Little by little
POLONAISE ...... Polish dance

10 letters
ACCELERATO ... Livelier; faster
ACCIDENTAL... Chromatic sign not in the key-signature
ALLA MARCIA.. In march style
ALLARGANDO. Growing slower
ALLEGRETTO...... Quite lively
BERGERETTE.... Pastoral song
CAMPANELLO....... Small bell
CLAVICHORD..... Precursor of the pianoforte
CON ANIMATO ..... With spirit
CON AUDACIA .. With boldness
CON DELIRIO..... Deliriously
CON FERVORE ...... Ardently; fervently
CON GRAVITA Slowly; seriously
IMPRESARIO ... Manager of an opera or concert company
LARGAMENTE......... Broadly
LENTAMENTE.......... Slowly
NACHTMUSIK .... Serenade
RITARDANDO . Growing slower and slower
SEGUIDILLA.... Spanish dance
SEMIQUAVER 16th-note
TARANTELLA .... Italian dance

SOME NOTED COMPOSERS

3 letters
ABT .... Franz
BAX .... Arnold
CUI .... Cesar

4 letters
ADAM ..... Adolphe
ARNE...... Thomas
BACH....... Johann Sebastian
BACH.......... Karl
BERG........ Alban

BULL .... John
BYRD....... William
CAGE......... John
FOSS .... Lukas
GADE......... Niels
IVES........ Charles
KERN....... Jerome
LALO ...... Edouard
PERI........ Jacopo
RAFF ...... Joachim
RIES...... Ferdinand

TOCH......... Ernst
WOLF......... Hugo

5 letters
AUBER ..... Daniel-Francois-Esprit
BALFE...... Michael
BIZET...... Georges
BLOCH ...... Ernest
BOITO .... Arrigo
BRUCH .... Max

CESTI.. Marc'Antonio
D'INDY ..... Vincent
DUFAY ... Guillaume
DUKAS .... Paul
ELGAR...... Edward
FALLA... Manuel de
FAURE...... Gabriel-
Urbain
FOOTE........ Arthur
FRIML .... Rudolf
GLUCK ... Christoph
GRIEG ...... Edvard
HAYDN .... Franz
Joseph
HOLST...... Gustav
IBERT ..... Jacques
ISAAK ..... Heinrich
LEHAR........ Franz
LISZT.......... Franz
LOEWE .... Carl
LULLY Jean-Baptiste
MOORE.... Douglas
NEVIN.... Ethelbert
PAINE John Knowles
RAVEL..... Maurice
REGER......... Max
SATIE .... Erik
SOUSA ..John Philip
STILL. William Grant
SUPPE.... Franz von
VERDI .... Giuseppe
WEBER .. Carl Maria
von
WEILL .... Kurt
WIDOR Charles-Marie

6 letters
BARBER .... Samuel
BARTOK....... Bela
BERLIN ...... Irving
BOULEZ ..... Pierre
BRAHMS.. Johannes
CADMAN ... Charles
CARTER ..... Elliott
CHAVEZ .... Carlos
CHOPIN ... Frederic
COWELL..... Henry
DELIUS ... Frederick
DUPARC...... Henri
DVORAK.... Antonin
ENESCO ... Georges
FLOTOW... Friedrich
von
FOSTER ... Stephen
FRANCK..... Cesar
GLIERE .... Reinhold
GLINKA..... Mikhail
GOUNOD ... Charles
GRETRY ..... Andre
HALEVY ... Jacques

HANDEL.... George
Frederick
HANSON.... Howard
HARRIS........ Roy
HILLER ... Ferdinand
JOPLIN .... Scott
KODALY .... Zoltan
KRENEK ...... Ernst
KUHLAU... Friedrich
LASSUS . Roland de
LIADOV...... Anatol
MAHLER.... Gustav
MORLEY... Thomas
MOZART.. Wolfgang
Amadeus
PIERNE Henri Gabriel
PISTON...... Walter
PLEYEL....... Ignaz
PORTER ..... Cole,
Quincy
RAMEAU ..... Jean-
Philippe
ROGERS ..... James
SCHUTZ ... Heinrich
STRAUS ..... Oskar
TAYLOR.... Deems
THOMAS.. Ambroise
VECCHI...... Orazio
VITALI..... Giovanni
WAGNER ... Richard
WALTON ... William
WEBERN..... Anton

7 letters
ALBENIZ...... Isaac
ALLEGRI... Gregorio
ARENSKY ... Anton
BABBITT ... Milton
BELLINI... Vincenzo
BERLIOZ.... Hector
BORODIN Alexander
BRITTEN . Benjamin
CACCINI..... Giulio
CAVALLI. Francesco
COPLAND ... Aaron
CORELLI. Arcangelo
CRESTON...... Paul
DEBUSSY... Claude
DELIBES....... Leo
DES PREZ .. Josquin
DOWLAND.... John
GIBBONS .. Orlando
GRIFFES.... Charles
HASSLER..... Hans
HERBERT... Victor
JANACEK..... Leos
LE JEUNE... Claude
MARTINU. Bohuslav
MENOTTI Gian Carlo
MILHAUD.... Darius

NICOLAI....... Otto
OBRECHT.... Jakob
OKEGHEM Johannes
POULENC... Francis
PUCCINI...Giacomo
PURCELL.... Henry
RIEGGER Wallingford
RODGERS... Richard
ROMBERG . Sigmund
ROSSINI Gioacchino
SCHUMAN.. William
SINDING.. Christian
SMETANA . Bedrich
STRAUSS... Johann
STRAUSS... Richard
THOMSON.... Virgil
VIVALDI .... Antonio
WEELKES.. Thomas
YOUMANS.. Vincent

8 letters
ARCADELT .. Jacob
BRUCKNER.. Anton
CHAUSSON.. Ernest
CLEMENTI... Muzio
COUPERIN. Francois
DIABELLI.... Anton
GABRIELI... Andrea,
Giovanni
GERSHWIN . George
GIORDANO Umberto
GOLDMARK.... Karl
GRANADOS. Enrique
HONEGGER.. Arthur
JOMMELLI.. Niccolo
LOEFFLER.. Charles
LORTZING.. Albert
MACHAUT.........
Guillaume de
MASCAGNI.. Pietro
MASSENET... Jules
MESSIAEN... Oliver
PAGANINI... Nicola
PALMGREN... Selim
PICCINNI .... Nicola
PIZZETTI Ildebrando
RESPIGHI.. Ottorino
SCHUBERT ...Franz
SCHUMANN Robert
SCRIABIN Alexander
SESSIONS ... Roger
SIBELIUS ..... Jean
SPONTINI.. Gasparo
SULLIVAN ... Arthur
TELEMANN.. Georg
Philipp
THOMPSON. Randall
VICTORIA... Tomas
Luis de

245

SPORTS

KENTUCKY DERBY WINNERS

YEAR	HORSE	JOCKEY	YEAR	HORSE	JOCKEY
1908	Stone Street	Pickens	1947	Jet Pilot	Guerin
1909	Wintergreen	Powers	1948	Citation	Arcaro
1910	Donau	Herbert	1949	Ponder	Brooks
1911	Meridian	Archibald	1950	Middleground	Boland
1912	Worth	Shilling	1951	Count Turf	McCreary
1913	Donerail	Goose	1952	Hill Gail	Arcaro
1914	Old Rosebud	McCabe	1953	Dark Star	Moreno
1915	Regret	Notter	1954	Determine	York
1916	George Smith	Loftus	1955	Swaps	Shoemaker
1917	Omar Khayyam	Borel	1956	Needles	Erb
1918	Exterminator	Knapp	1957	Iron Liege	Hartack
1919	Sir Barton	Loftus	1958	Tim Tam	Valenzuela
1920	Paul Jones	Rice	1959	Tomy Lee	Shoemaker
1921	Behave Yourself	Thompson	1960	Venetian Way	Hartack
1922	Morvich	Johnson	1961	Carry Back	Sellers
1923	Zev	Sande	1962	Decidedly	Hartack
1924	Black Gold	Mooney	1963	Chateaugay	Baeza
1925	Flying Ebony	Sande	1964	Northern Dancer	Hartack
1926	Bubbling Over	Johnson	1965	Lucky Debonair	Shoemaker
1927	Whiskery	McAtee	1966	Kauai King	Brumfield
1928	Reigh Count	Lang	1967	Proud Clarion	Ussery
1929	Clyde Van Dusen	McAtee	1968	Dancer's Image	Ussery
1930	Gallant Fox	Sande		(or Forward Pass)	
1931	Twenty Grand	Kurtsinger	1969	Majestic Prince	Hartack
1932	Burgoo King	James	1970	Dust Commander	Manganello
1933	Brokers Tip	Meade	1971	Canonero II	Avila
1934	Cavalcade	Garner	1972	Riva Ridge	Turcotte
1935	Omaha	Saunders	1973	Secretariat	Turcotte
1936	Bold Venture	Hanford	1974	Cannonade	Cordero
1937	War Admiral	Kurtsinger	1975	Foolish Pleasure	Vasquez
1938	Lawrin	Arcaro	1976	Bold Forbes	Cordero
1939	Johnstown	Stout	1977	Seattle Slew	Cruguet
1940	Gallahadion	Bierman	1978	Affirmed	Cauthen
1941	Whirlaway	Arcaro	1979	Spectacular Bid	Franklin
1942	Shut Out	Wright	1980	Genuine Risk	Vasquez
1943	Count Fleet	Longden	1981	Pleasant Colony	Velasquez
1944	Pensive	McCreary	1982	Gato del Sol	Delahoussaye
1945	Hoop, Jr.	Arcaro	1983	Sunny's Halo	Delahoussaye
1946	Assault	Mehrtens			

TRIPLE CROWN WINNERS

YEAR	HORSE	JOCKEY	YEAR	HORSE	JOCKEY
1919	Sir Barton	Loftus	1946	Assault	Mehrtens
1930	Gallant Fox	Sande	1948	Citation	Arcaro
1935	Omaha	Saunders	1973	Secretariat	Turcotte
1937	War Admiral	Kurtsinger	1977	Seattle Slew	Cruguet
1941	Whirlaway	Arcaro	1978	Affirmed	Cauthen
1943	Count Fleet	Longden			

SOME NAMES FROM THE BASEBALL
HALL OF FAME

Aaron, Hank
Alexander, Grover
   Cleveland
Anson, Cap
Appling, Luke
Baker, Home Run
Banks, Ernie
Bell, Cool Papa
Bender, Chief
Berra, Yogi
Boudreau, Lou
Brown, Mordecai
Campanella, Roy
Carey, Max
Chance, Frank
Chandler, Happy
Clarke, Fred
Clemente, Roberto
Cobb, Ty
Cochrane, Mickey
Combs, Earl
Conlan, Jocko
Connor, Roger
Cronin, Joe
Cummings, Candy
Cuyler, Kiki
Dean, Dizzy
Delahanty, Ed
Dickey, Bill
DiMaggio, Joe
Duffy, Hugh
Evers, John
Ewing, Buck
Faber, Urban
Feller, Bob
Flick, Elmer H.
Ford, Whitey
Foxx, Jimmy
Frick, Ford
Frisch, Frank
Gehrig, Lou
Giles, Warren
Gomez, Lefty

Goslin, Goose
Greenberg, Hank
Grove, Lefty
Hafey, Chick
Harridge, Will
Harris, Bucky
Hartnett, Gabby
Hooper, Harry
Hornsby, Rogers
Hoyt, Waite
Hubbard, Cal
Hubbell, Carl
Huggins, Miller
Irvin, Monte
Jackson, Travis
Johnson, Byron
Joss, Addie
Kaline, Al
Keefe, Timothy
Keeler, William
Kell, George
Kelley, Joe
Kelly, George
Kelly, King
Kiner, Ralph
Klein, Chuck
Klem, Bill
Koufax, Sandy
Lajoie, Napoleon
Landis, Kenesaw
   Mountain
Lemon, Bob
Lloyd, Pop
Lopez, Al
Mack, Connie
Mantle, Mickey
Manush, Henry
Marichal, Juan
Maranville, Rabbit
Marquard, Rube
Mays, Willie
McGinnity, Joe
McGraw, John

Medwick, Joe
Mize, Johnny
Musial, Stan
Nichols, Kid
Ott, Mel
Paige, Satchel
Plank, Ed
Rice, Sam
Rickey, Branch
Rixey, Eppa
Roberts, Robin
Robinson, Brooks
Robinson, Frank
Robinson, Jackie
Robinson, Wilbert
Roush, Edd
Ruffing, Red
Rusie, Amos
Ruth, Babe
Sisler, George
Snider, Duke
Spahn, Warren
Speaker, Tris
Stengel, Casey
Terry, Bill
Tinker, Joe
Traynor, Pie
Vance, Dazzy
Waddell, Rube
Wagner, Honus
Walsh, Ed
Waner, Lloyd
Waner, Paul
Ward, John
Weiss, George
Welch, Mickey
Wheat, Zach
Williams, Ted
Wilson, Hack
Wynn, Early
Yawkey, Tom
Young, Cy
Youngs, Ross

SOME NAMES FROM THE PRO FOOTBALL HALL OF FAME

Adderley, Herb
Alworth, Lance
Atkins, Doug
Badgro, Morris (Red)
Battles, Cliff
Baugh, Sammy
Bednarik, Chuck
Bell, Bert
Bell, Bobby
Berry, Raymond
Blanda, George
Brown, Jim
Brown, Paul E.
Brown, Roosevelt
Butkus, Dick
Canadeo, Tony
Carr, Joe
Chamberlin, Guy
Christiansen, Jack
Clark, Earl (Dutch)
Connor, George
Conzelman, Jimmy
Davis, Willie
Donovan, Art
Driscoll, John (Paddy)
Dudley, Bill
Edwards, Albert (Turk)
Ewbank, Weeb
Fears, Tom
Flaherty, Ray
Ford, Leonard (Len)
Fortmann, Daniel J.
George, Bill
Gifford, Frank
Gillman, Sid
Graham, Otto
Grange, Harold (Red)
Gregg, Forrest
Groza, Lou

Guyon, Joe
Halas, George
Healey, Ed
Hein, Mel
Henry, Wilbur (Pete)
Herber, Arnie
Hewitt, Bill
Hinkle, Clarke
Hirsch, Elroy (Crazy-
   legs)
Hubbard, Robert (Cal)
Huff, Sam
Hunt, Lamar
Hutson, Don
Jones, David (Deacon)
Jurgensen, Sonny
Kinard, Frank (Bruiser)
Lambeau, Earl (Curly)
Lane, Richard (Night
   Train)
Lary, Yale
Lavelli, Dante
Layne, Bobby
Leemans, Alphonse
   (Tuffy)
Lilly, Bob
Lombardi, Vince
Luckman, Sid
Lyman, William Roy
   (Link)
Marchetti, Gino
Matson, Ollie
McAfee, George
McElhenny, Hugh
McNally, John (Blood)
Michalski, August
   (Mike)
Millner, Wayne
Mitchell, Bobby

Mix, Ron
Moore, Leonard
   (Lenny)
Motley, Marion
Musso, George
Nagurski, Bronko
Neale, Earle (Greasy)
Nevers, Ernie
Nitschke, Ray
Nomellini, Leo
Olsen, Merlin
Otto, Jim
Owen, Steven
Parker, Jim
Perry, Fletcher (Joe)
Pihos, Pete
Ringo, Jim
Robustelli, Andy
Sayers, Gale
Schmidt, Joe
Starr, Bart
Stautner, Ernie
Strong, Ken
Taylor, Jim
Thorpe, Jim
Tittle, Y.A.
Trafton, George
Trippi, Charley
Tunnell, Emlen
Turner, Clyde
   (Bulldog)
Unitas, Johnny
Van Brocklin, Norm
Van Buren, Steve
Warfield, Paul
Waterfield, Bob
Willis, Bill
Wilson, Larry

SOME NAMES FROM THE BASKETBALL
HALL OF FAME

Barlow, Thomas
Baylor, Elgin
Borgmann, Bennie
Bradley, Bill
Brennan, Joseph
Chamberlain, Wilt
Cooper, Charles
  (Tarzan)
Cousy, Robert
Davies, Robert
DeBernardi, Forrest
DeBusschere, Dave
Endacott, Paul
Foster, Harold (Bud)
Friedman, Max
Gale, Lauren (Laddie)
Gola, Thomas

Greer, Hal
Hagan, Clifford
Hanson, Victor
Holman, Nat
Krause, Edward
Kurland, Robert
Lapchick, Joe
Lucas, Jerry Ray
Luisetti, Angelo
McCracken, Branch
McCracken, Jack
Macauley, Edward
Martin, Slater
Mikan, George
Murphy, Charles
Pettit, Robert
Phillip, Andy

Pollard, James
Ramsey, Frank
Reed, Willis
Robertson, Oscar
Russell, John (Honey)
Russell, William
Schayes, Adolph
Schmidt, Ernest
Sedran, Barney
Sharman, William
Thompson, John
Twyman, Jack
Vandivier, Robert
  (Fuzzy)
West, Jerry Alan
Wooden, John

SOME AWARD-WINNING ICE HOCKEY PLAYERS

Beliveau, Jean
Bossy, Mike
Bourque, Ray
Bucyk, John
Clarke, Bobby
Cloutier, Real
Corlyle, Randy
Cournoyer, Yvan
Crozier, Roger
Devecchio, Alex
Dionne, Marcel
Dryden, Dave
Dryden, Ken
Esposito, Phil
Esposito, Tony
Ftorek, Robbie
Gainey, Bob
Giacomin, Ed
Goring, Butch

Goyette, Phil
Grant, Danny
Gretzky, Wayne
Hall, Glenn
Hawerchuk, Dale
Hodge, Charlie
Howe, Gordie
Howell, Harry
Hull, Bobby
Kasper, Steve
Kehoe, Rick
Keon, Dave
Lacroix, Andre
Lafleur, Guy
Laperriere, Jacques
Leach, Reg
Middleton, Rick
Mikita, Stan
Orr, Bobby

Parent, Bernie
Perreault, Gil
Pilote, Pierre
Plett, Willi
Potvin, Denis
Ratelle, Jean
Robinson, Larry
Sanderson, Derek
Savard, Serge
Selby, Brit
Smith, Billy
Stastny, Peter
Tardif, Marc
Trottier, Bryan
Vail, Eric
Vickers, Steve
Walton, Mike
Wharram, Ken
Wilson, Doug

ACRONYMS, INITIALS, ABBREVIATIONS

Acronyms (words or abbreviations formed by using key letters of the phrases they stand for) are seldom defined by those exact words. Hence, this special listing is arranged in sections to help you find the word you are looking for. For example, you may be given the definition "International pact" and you know it is a 4-letter word. Go to the INTERNATIONAL section and look at the 4-letter words (words are grouped by section, then word size, then alphabetically). Your answer will probably be NATO. You might also be given the definition "The 'A' in G.A.R.''; you can then look for GAR in all the sections (it's in the MILITARY section) and find that A stands for ARMY. In each case, the letters from the acronym or initial-word have been capitalized, so you will know what the letters stand for. NOTE: Some of these organizations, acts, etc., no longer exist, but they have been included because they continue to appear in crossword puzzles.

Abbreviations Used in This Section

Admin.. Administration	Corp ...... Corporation	Inst .... Institute
Amer........ American	Dept ...... Department	Internat'l.. International
Assoc ..... Association	Fed .... Federal	Nat'l .... National
Conf ...... Conference	Govt ..... Government	Org ...... Organization
	Inc .... Incorporated	

GOVERNMENTAL, POLITICAL

3 letters
AAA Agricultural Adjustment Act
AAA.... Agricultural Adjustment Admin.
AEC Atomic Energy Commission (now Nuclear Regulatory Commission)
ARA Area Redevelopment Admin.
BIA..... Bureau of Indian Affairs
BLM............ Bureau of Land Management
BLS .. Bureau of Labor Statistics
CAB.... Civil Aeronautics Board
CCA... Circuit Court of Appeals
CCC Civilian Conservation Corps
CIA. Central Intelligence Agency
CRC... Civil Rights Commission
CSA Community Services Admin.
CSA ..... Confederate States of America
CSC .. Civil Service Commission
CWA .... Civil Works Admin.
DEA .. Drug Enforcement Admin.
DOE .... Dept. of Energy
EDA .... Economic Development Admin.
EOP ..... Economic Opportunity Program
EPA ... Environmental Protection Agency
ERA ... Emergency Relief Admin.
ESA .... Employment Standards Admin.

FAA .... Fed. Aviation Admin.
FAC ...... Fed. Advisory Council
FBI . Fed. Bureau of Investigation
FCC ...... Fed. Communications Commission
FDA ..... Food and Drug Admin.
FEC .. Fed. Election Commission
FET .... Fed. Excise Tax
FHA .... Fed. Housing Admin.
FRB .... Fed. Reserve Board
FRS ...... Fed. Reserve System
FTC ..... Fed. Trade Commission
GAO. General Accounting Office
GPO .... Gov't Printing Office
GSA ... General Services Admin.
HRA ... Health Resources Admin.
HUD........ Housing and Urban Development
IRS .... Internal Revenue Service
NBS .. Nat'l Bureau of Standards
NFS .... Nat'l Forest Service
NRA ..... Nat'l Recovery Admin.
NRC........ Nuclear Regulatory Commission
NSA ...... Nat'l Security Agency
NSC ...... Nat'l Security Council
OEO .... Office of Economic Opportunity
OPA ..... Office of Price Admin.
OSS .... Office of Strategic Services
PHA ..... Public Housing Admin.
REA . Rural Electrification Admin.
RFC .... Reconstruction Finance Corp.

SBA ..... Small Business Admin.
SSA ..... Social Security Admin.
SSS... Selective Service System
TVA . Tennessee Valley Authority
WPA...... Works Project Admin.

4 letters
ADAP . Airport Development Aid
Program
ADEA....... Age Discrimination
Employment Act
AFDC...... Aid to Families with
Dependent Children
ALRB......... Agriculture Labor
Relations Board
BATF........ Bureau of Alcohol,
Tobacco, and Firearms
BEOG.......... Basic Education
Opportunity Grant
CETA.......... Comprehensive
Employment and Training Act
CHAP . Child Health Assessment
Program
CWPS .... Council on Wage and
Price Stability
ECOA.. Equal Credit Opportunity
Act
EEOC........ Equal Employment
Opportunity Commission
FCRA.. Fair Credit Reporting Act
FDIC..... Fed. Deposit Insurance
Corp.
FECA.......... Fed. Employees
Compensation Act
FEPA Fair Employment Practices
Act
FERA.... Fed. Emergency Relief
Admin.
FERC... Fed. Energy Regulatory
Commission
FHLA...... Farmers Home Loan
Admin.
FICA........... Fed. Insurance
Contributions Act
FLRB ..... Farm Labor Relations
Board
FNMA ..... Fed. Nat'l Mortgage
Assoc. (Fannie Mae)
FUTA.. Fed. Unemployment Tax
Act
GNMA .... Gov't Nat'l Mortgage
Assoc. (Ginnie Mae)
HHFA....... Housing and Home
Finance Agency
HOAP .... Home Ownership
Assistance Program
LMSA ...... Labor-Management
Services Admin.
MDTA . Manpower Development
and Training Act
MGIC....... Mortgage Guaranty
Insurance Corp. (Maggie Mae)

NASA..... Nat'l Aeronautics and
Space Admin.
NDSL...... Nat'l Direct Student
Loan
NEPA....... Nat'l Environmental
Policy Act
NLRA.. Nat'l Labor Relations Act
NLRB...... Nat'l Labor Relations
Board
NOAA .... Nat'l Oceanic and
Atmospheric Admin.
NTSB...... Nat'l Transportation
Safety Board
OSHA.... Occupation Safety and
Health Admin.
SEOG... Supplemental Education
Opportunity Grant
USBM .... U.S. Bureau of Mines
USCC......... U.S. Circuit Court
USDA.. U.S. Dept. of Agriculture
USDC.. U.S. Dept. of Commerce
USDE...... U.S. Dept. of Energy
USDI .. U.S. Dept. of the Interior
USDJ ...... U.S. Dept. of Justice
USDL....... U.S. Dept. of Labor
USDT............. U.S. Dept. of
Transportation
USIA .. U.S. Information Agency
USIS... U.S. Information Service

5 letters
FSLIC ... Fed. Savings and Loan
Insurance Corp.
MORGA..... Municipal ORG. Act
NCPAC...... Nat'l Conservative
Political Action Committee
NIOSH............ Nat'l Inst. for
Occupational Safety and Health
VISTA . Volunteers In Service To
America

6 letters
ADAMHA . Alcohol, Drug Abuse,
and Mental Health Agency

MILITARY

3 letters
AAB .... Army Air Base
AAM .... Air-to-Air Missile
ABM........ AntiBallistic Missile
ADC..... Air Defense Command
AEF . Amer. Expeditionary Force
AGM....... Air-to-Ground Missile
AMM .... AntiMissile Missile
APO.......... Army Post Office
ARM.......... AntiRadar Missile
BAR .. Browning Automatic Rifle
CEO .... Chief Executive Officer
CIC........ Commander-In-Chief
CNO .. Chief of Naval Operations
DFC . Distinguished Flying Cross

251

DFM. Distinguished Flying Medal
DSC Distinguished Service Cross
DSM Distinguished Service Medal
DSO Distinguished Service Order
ETO .... European Theater of Operations
FPO .... Fleet Post Office
GAR Grand Army of the Republic
LCT .... Landing Craft Tank
LST .... Landing Ship Tank
MAP Military Assistance Program
MIA .... Missing In Action
NCO. Non-Commissioned Officer
OCS ... Officer Candidate School
PFC .... Private First Class
RAF .... Royal Air Force
SAC .... Strategic Air Command
SAM ...... Surface-to-Air Missile
SUM ..... Surface-to-Underwater Missile
UAM .. Underwater-to-Air Missile
USN .... U.S. Navy
VAD .... Vice Admiral
WAC ..... Women's Army Corps
WAF .... Women in the Air Force

4 letters
AANS ...... Advanced Automatic Navigation System
ADCC ..... Air Defense Control Center
ADIZ . Air Defense Identification Zone
AEAF ... Allied Expeditionary Air Force
AWAC ... Airborne Warning And Control
AWOL ... Absent WithOut Leave
ICBM .. InterContinental Ballistic Missile
ICCM .... InterContinental Cruise Missile
IRBM .... Intermediate Range Ballistic Missile
MASH .... Mobile Army Surgical Hospital
MATS .... Military Air Transport Service
RAAF. Royal Australian Air Force
RCAF. Royal Canadian Air Force
ROTC. Reserve Officers Training Corps
SLAM . Supersonic Low Altitude Missile
SLAR ..... Side-Looking Airborne Radar
SLBM ...... Submarine-Launched Ballistic Missile
STOL Short TakeOff and Landing
TCBM TransContinental Ballistic Missile

USAR .... U.S. Army Reserve
USMA ... U.S. Military Academy
USMC .... U.S. Marine Corps
USMM .... U.S. Merchant Marine
USNA .... U.S. Naval Academy
USNR .... U.S. Naval Reserve
WAAC . Women's Auxiliary Army Corps
WAAF ... Women's Auxiliary Air Force

5 letters
AICBM .... AntiInterContinental Ballistic Missile
CONAD CONtinental Air Defense
MIDAS ... MIssile Defense Alarm System
NAVAR ...... NAVigation radAR
NORAD .... NORth Amer. air Defense command
SHAPE . Supreme Headquarters, Allied Powers, Europe
USACE ..... U.S. Army Corps of Engineers
WAVES ... Women Appointed for Volunteer Emergency Service (Naval Reserve)

6 letters
ACLANT .... Allied Command atLANTic
NAVAIR .... NAVal AIR
NAVCAD . NAVal aviation CADet

7 letters
CINCPAC. Commander-IN-Chief, PACific

INTERNATIONAL

3 letters
AID .... Agency for Internat'l Development
CMN .. Common Market Nations
EEC .... European Economic Community
FAO ...... Food and Agricultural Org. (U.N.)
IDA ...... Internat'l Development Assoc.
ILA ... Internat'l Longshoreman's Assoc.
ILO .... Internat'l Labour Org.
ILU .... Internat'l Laborers Union
IOC .... Internat'l Olympics Committee
IRO ...... Internat'l Refugee Org.
ITO .... Internat'l Trade Org.
MFN ...... Most Favored Nation
OAS ...... Org. of Amer. States
PAU .... Pan Amer. Union

UAE...... United Arab Emirates
UAR...... United Arab Republic
WEU..... Western Europe Union
WHO........ World Health Org.

4 letters
CARE.... Cooperative for Amer.
Relief Everywhere
EFTA..... European Free Trade
Assoc.
METO .. Middle East Treaty Org.
NATO North Atlantic Treaty Org.
OPEC........ Org. of Petroleum
Exporting Countries
SALT . Strategic Arms Limitation
Treaty

5 letters
ASEAN ... Assoc. for SouthEast
Asia Nations
ASPAC ...... ASian and PAcific
Council
CENTO .... CENtral Treaty Org.
LAFTA...... Latin America Free
Trade Assoc.
ODECA........ *Organizacion De
Estados CentroAmericanos* (Org.
of Central Amer. States)
SEATO .. SouthEast Asia Treaty
Org.
START .... STrategic Arms
Reduction Talks
SWAPO...... South West Africa
People's Org.
UNRRA... United Nations Relief
and Rehabilitation Admin.
UNRWA .. United Nations Relief
and Works Agency

6 letters
UNESCO........ United Nations
Educational, Scientific and
Cultural Org.
UNICEF........ United Nations
Internat'l Children's Emergency
Fund

7 letters
BENELUX BElgium, NEtherlands,
LUXembourg

8 letters
INTERPOL.. INTERnat'l criminal
POLice org.

ASSOCIATIONS

3 letters
AAA... Amateur Athletic Assoc.
AAO........... Amer. Assoc. of
Orthodontists
AAP . Assoc. of Amer. Publishers

AAU Assoc. of Amer. Universities
ABA.......... Amer. Bar Assoc.
AEA...... Actors' Equity Assoc.
AFM....... Amer. Federation of
Musicians
AFT .... Amer. Federation of
Teachers
AMA ..... Amer. Medical Assoc.
APA... Amer. Psychiatric Assoc.
APA Amer. Psychological Assoc.
NEA..... Nat'l Education Assoc.
SAG....... Screen Actors Guild

4 letters
AAMC . Amer. Assoc. of Medical
Colleges
AAPS... Amer. Assoc. of Plastic
Surgeons
AARP... Amer. Assoc. of Retired
Persons
AAUP .... Amer. Assoc. of
University Professors
AAUW......... Amer. Assoc. of
University Women
ABLA...... Amer. Business Law
Assoc.
AGVA ... Amer. Guild of Variety
Artists
ALPA..... Air Line Pilots Assoc.
ASTA... Amer. Society of Travel
Agents
ATLA...... Amer. Trial Lawyers
Assoc.
SACM ...... Society of Authors
and Composers of Music

5 letters
AFTRA .... Amer. Federation of
Television and Radio Artists
ASCAP .... Amer. Society of
Composers, Authors, and
Publishers
PATCO . Professional Air Traffic
Controllers Org.

SPORTS

3 letters
AAA... Amateur Athletic Assoc.
AAU.... Amateur Athletic Union
ABA... Amer. Basketball Assoc.
ABC....... Amer. Bowling Congress
AFC....... Amer. Football Conf.
AFL ..... Amer. Football League
ASL .... Amer. Soccer League
ERA....... Earned Run Average
MVP...... Most Valuable Player
NBA..... Nat'l Basketball Assoc.
NFC....... Nat'l Football Conf.
NFL ...... Nat'l Football League
NHL....... Nat'l Hockey League

NIT Nat'l Invitational Tournament (basketball)
PBA Professional Bowlers Assoc.
PGA Professional Golfers' Assoc.
RBI.............. Runs Batted In
WBA ...... World Boxing Assoc.

4 letters
LPGA....... Ladies Professional Golfers Assoc.
NCAA .. Nat'l Collegiate Athletic Assoc.
WPGA... Women's Professional Golfers' Assoc.

MISCELLANEOUS

3 letters
AAA.. Amer. Automobile Assoc.
ABS........ Amer. Bible Society
ACA.... Arts Council of America
ACT..... Amer. College Testing
ADA. Americans for Democratic Action
ADF . Automatic Direction Finder
ADL .... Anti-Defamation League
AHA........ Amer. Heart Assoc.
AKA............. Also Known As
AKC........ Amer. Kennel Club
ALP .... Amer. Labor Party
APB.......... All Points Bulletin
ARC.......... Amer. Red Cross
BBB .... Better Business Bureau
BBC . British Broadcasting Corp.
BMR...... Basal Metabolic Rate
BTU .... British Thermal Unit
CAP............. Civil Air Patrol
CDC. Center for Disease Control
CEA....... Council of Economic Advisers
CED... Committee for Economic Development
CID. Criminal Investigation Dept. (Scotland Yard)
CNS... Central Nervous System
COD.......... Cash On Delivery
CPI...... Consumer Price Index
DAR.... Daughters of the Amer. Revolution
DAV... Disabled Amer. Veterans
DBA........ Doing Business As
DNA..... DeoxyriboNucleic Acid
EAB..... Ethics Advisory Board
EBS ..... Emergency Broadcast System
EEG ..... ElectroEncephaloGram
EKG........ ElectroCardioGram
EMS Emergency Medical Service
EOE Equal Opportunity Employer
ERA .. Equal Rights Amendment
ESP ... ExtraSensory Perception
ETA .. Estimated Time of Arrival

ETV ..... Educational TeleVision
FAF .... Financial Aid Form
FCA .... Farm Credit Assoc.
FFA . Future Farmers of America
FOB .... Free On Board
FTA Future Teachers of America
GIM .... Gross Income Multiplier
GNI......... Gross Nat'l Income
GNP........ Gross Nat'l Product
GOP........... Grand Old Party (Republican)
ICU......... Intensive Care Unit
IFO ..... Identified Flying Object
IFR ..... Instrument Flight Rules
IRA....... Individual Retirement Account
JDL.... Jewish Defense League
KGB . *Komitet Gosudarstvennoye Bezopastnosti* (Russian Security Police)
LCD Least Common Denominator
LCD ...... Liquid Crystal Display
LED .... Light Emitting Diode
MDR Minimum Daily Requirement
NAM .... Nat'l Assoc. of Manufacturers
NET Nat'l Educational Television
NHA. Nat'l Homebuilders Assoc.
NOW ..... Nat'l Org. for Women
NRA.......... Nat'l Rifle Assoc.
OOB.......... Off-Off Broadway
PAL ..... Police Athletic League
PBS Public Broadcasting Service
PLO ... Palestine Liberation Org.
POC................ Port Of Call
POE .... Port Of Entry
PSE .... Pacific Stock Exchange
PTA... Parent-Teacher's Assoc.
RCA.... Radio Corp. of America
RDF ..... Radio Direction Finder
REM...... Rapid Eye Movement
RFD .... Rural Free Delivery
RNA.......... RiboNucleic Acid
ROI...... Return On Investment
SAT ... Scholastic Aptitude Test
SEC .... Securities Exchange Commission
SIG...... Special Interest Group
SOP .... Standard Operating Procedure
SRO .... Standing Room Only
SST ...... SuperSonic Transport
TLC .... Tender Loving Care
TWU.. Transport Workers Union
UFO.. Unidentified Flying Object
UFW..... United Farm Workers
UHF ...... Ultra High Frequency
UPI... United Press International
USO........ United Service Org.
UWA ... United Way of America
VAT.......... Value-Added Tax
VCR... Video Cassette Recorder

VFR .... Visual Flight Rules
VFW .. Veterans of Foreign Wars
VHF ...... Very High Frequency
WPI ..... Wholesale Price Index
ZIP ..... Zone Improvement Plan
(post office)
ZPG .... Zero Population Growth

4 letters
AAAL ... Amer. Academy of Arts
and Letters
ACLU ...... Amer. Civil Liberties
Union
ALMA .... Adoptees Liberty
Movement Assoc.
AMEX ... AMer. stock EXchange
ANRC ... Amer. Nat'l Red Cross
ANSI Amer. Nat'l Standards Inst.
ANTA . Amer. Nat'l Theatre and
Academy
ASAP ...... As Soon As Possible
BMOC ..... Big Man On Campus
BPOE .... Benevolent and
Protective Order of Elks
CATV ...... Community Antenna
TeleVision
CCTV .. Closed-Circuit TeleVision
CEEB .... College Entrance
Examination Board
CLEP . College Level Examination
Program
COLA . Cost Of Living Agreement
CORE .... Congress Of Racial
Equality
CWSP ...... College Work-Study
Program
FIFO .... First In, First Out
GASP ... Group Against Smoking
Pollution
HOLC . Home Owners Loan Corp.
IOOF ..... Independent Order of
Odd Fellows
KMPS ... KiloMeters Per Second
LEEP .... Law Enforcement
Education Program
LIFO .... Last In, First Out
LOOM ... Loyal Order Of Moose
MDAR ..... Minimum Daily Adult
Requirement
MPAA . Motion Picture Assoc. of
America
NCOA ... Nat'l Council On Aging
NIFO .... Next In, First Out
NYSE New York Stock Exchange
OCTV ... Open-Circuit TeleVision
PSAT .... Preliminary Scholastic
Aptitude Test
RADA .... Royal Academy of
Dramatic Arts
RCMP . Royal Canadian Mounted
Police

SASE .. Self-Addressed Stamped
Envelope
SBLI .... Savings Bank Life
Insurance
SCAN .. Senior Citizen Anticrime
Network
SNCC .... Student Nonviolent
Coordinating Committee
SPCA .... Society for the
Prevention of Cruelty
to Animals
SPCC .... Society for the
Prevention of Cruelty
to Children
SWAT .... Special Weapons And
Tactics force
TASS . *Telegraphnoye Agentstvo
Sovyetskovo Soyuza* (Soviet
News Agency)
USOC .. U.S. Olympic Committee
USSR .. Union of Soviet Socialist
Republics
WATS .... Wide Area Telephone
Service
WCTU ...... Woman's Christian
Temperance Union

5 letters
AMPAS ..... Academy of Motion
Picture Arts and Sciences
ASPCA ... Amer. Society for the
Prevention of Cruelty to Animals
ATVAS .. Academy of TeleVision
Arts and Sciences
ENDEX .... ENvironmental Data
indEX
ILGWU .... Internat'l Ladies'
Garment Workers' Union
LASER .... Light Amplification by
Stimulated Emission of Radiation
LORAN . LOng-RAnge Navigation
MOPED ... MOtor-assisted PEDal
cycle
NAACP ..... Nat'l Assoc. for the
Advancement of Colored People
RADAR .... RAdio Detection And
Ranging
SCORE .... Service Corps Of
Retired Executives
SCUBA .... Self-Contained
Underwater Breathing Apparatus
SONAR ...... SOund NAvigation
Ranging

6 letters
AFL-CIO ... Amer. Federation of
Labor—Congress of Industrial
Organizations
AMVETS .... AMer. VETeranS
ENCONA .... ENvironmental
Coalition Of North America

THE WORD-FINDER
with cross-references

FOR THE SOLVER

You can complete any unfinished 2-, 3-, or 4-letter word in the crossword you are working by using this WORD-FINDER. Even though you are at first unable to locate it in the Definition section for some reason, if you have just two letters of your wanted word (just one if it's a 2-letter word) you can find it here.

The WORD-FINDER words are listed according to the following Letter-Combination system:

XX - -	(for cases when the first two letters are known)
- XX -	(when the second and third letters are known)
- - XX	(when the last two letters are known)
X - - X	(when the first and last letters are known)

Let us say that you need to complete a word that is four letters long.

STEP ONE: Find the Letter-Combination that is the same as the letters which you have written into the crossword puzzle. Have you, for example, found "ON" as the end of a 4-letter word? Then turn to the "- - ON" Letter-Combination. Of course, since the WORD-FINDER is thorough-going, a number of words, all containing the same letter combination, are listed under this Letter-Combination.

- - ON   Acon, agon, Amon, anon, Avon, axon, azon, bion, boon, cion, coon, Dion, doon, ebon, Enon, Eton, faon, Gaon, hoon, icon, iron, Leon, lion, loon, moon, neon, etc.

STEP TWO: You may know, after looking through the words listed under your Letter-Combination, the word which is the only correct possibility. If not, you now begin to eliminate words in the list by working with the words in the crossword puzzle which CROSS your unfinished word. You do this by experimentally inserting words from the Letter-Combination list. When the experimental insert produces such impossible-looking combinations with the crossing word as "bv," "pv" etc. it can be discarded.

STEP THREE: After eliminating the words which make highly unlikely or "impossible" combinations with the crossing words, you still may not be sure how to complete your unfinished puzzle. Here you make use of the invaluable CROSS-REFERENCE listings following the words in the WORD-FINDER. Each number following a word is the number of the page of the Definitions Section on which the word and one of its definitions will be found. The alphabetical letters a, b, c, d indicate in exactly which section of the definition page you will be able to locate the word with its meaning.

Example: adat (90b,95d)

On page 90 of this Dictionary, in section b of the page, you will find the word ADAT in bold face type. The definition is "law, D. E. Ind". On page 95, section d, you will find another cross-reference to ADAT. The definition reads "Malay law."

STEP FOUR: Now re-examine the definition in your puzzle. Eliminate words in the WORD-FINDER by comparing definitions until you arrive at the "logical candidate" word for which you have been looking. Definitions in this dictionary and those in your puzzle will not always agree in exact wording. In that case, let the general meaning of the definitions be your guide. Everyday words are not always cross-referenced in this WORD-FINDER, nor are some words of exceptional terminology. Only some of the words listed in the Special Section are cross-referenced. If your definition calls for a word likely to be found in the Special Section, it is recommended that you look there first.

TWO-LETTER WORDS

A -   **Aa** (47a), **aa** (90b), **Ab** (48d,75b,102a), **ab** (63d), **AC** (39d), **ad** (90a,112d,167d), **ae** (42b,43c,d,122b,139a), **Ae** (82c,115d), **ah** (52c), **ai** (143c,148c), **al** (8c,80c,102c,104b), **am** (166c,175c), **an** (11b, 13b), **Ao** (13d,88b,c,116c), **AP** (107a,182d), **ap** (122d,166c), **ar** (88b,91c,98a,99b,110c), **as** (51b,67b,92b,126a,133a,b,180d), **at** (25c,32c,106a,123a,128a), **au** (63a,69c), **aw** (44a), **ax** (40c,139a, 167a), **ay** (7c,8b,9b,28d,55a,60a)

- A   **Aa** (47a), **aa** (90b), **BA** (42a), **Ba** (150d,153c), **ba** (139a), **da** (9b,37a, 56a,133d,135d), **DA** (124d), **ea** (43c), **EA** (15b,68a), **fa** (108b,138a, 161a), **Ga** (69c), **ha** (52c), **ia** (43d,158c), **ja** (66d), **ka** (45c), **Ka** (68c, 77b,150d,153c,173c), **la** (13b,61a,83a,108b,138a,151d,161a), **ma, MA** (42a), **Ma** (69a,b,85d), **na** (140c,163d), **NA** (36c), **oa** (43c,d), **pa** (60b,106d), **ra** (108b), **Ra** (159b), **SA** (36c), **ta** (112d,139a,160b), **VA** (83a), **va** (105a), **wa** (188), **Wa** (24c,d,88c), **ya, za** (162a)

B -   **BA** (42a), **ba** (139a,150d,153c), **bb** (147b), **be, bi** (122d,171c), **bo** (23d,24c,136a,168a), **bu** (190), **by** (18b,32c,106a)

- B   **ab** (63d,) **Ab** (48d,75b,102a), **bb** (147b), **FB** (59c), **HB** (59c), **ob** (122b), **QB** (59c)

C -   **ce** (62d,164c), **CE** (42a)

- C   **DC** (39d), **ec** (122c)

D -   **da** (9b,37a,56a,133d,135d), **DA** (124d), **DC** (39d), **DD** (42a), **de** (63d,89b,122b,122c,124a,152c,d), **di** (68c,89b,108b,122b,122c, 122d,171d), **dm** (131c), **do** (108b,138a,161a)

- D   **ad,** (90a,112d,167d), **DD** (42a), **ed** (175c), **Ed** (18d), **id** (26d, 40c,51c,57a,b,d), **od** (8d,59d,79c), **td** (32a)

E -   **ea** (43c), **EA** (15b,68a), **ec** (122c), **ed** (175c), **Ed** (18d), **ee** (139c), **EE** (42a), **ef** (91c), **eg** (59d,163d), **eh** (52c), **el** (13b,42a,47a,99b, 151d,168a), **El** (68a,108a), **em** (91c,98a,123d,172a,c), **en** (15b, 29c,50a,91c,98a,119d,123d,158c,d,172a), **eo** (34a), **er** (35b,76c, 137d,155a,158c,d,160b,175c), **Er** (18d,68c,85c,163d,166c,172c, 178a), **es** (49b,50a,66c,119d,158c,d,175c), **et** (10b,61a,b,89a,158c), **ex** (60b,91c,122c)

- E   **ae** (42b,43c,d,122b,139a), **Ae** (82c,115d), **be, CE** (42a), **Ce** (62d), **ce** (164c), **de** (63d,89b,122b,c,124a,152c,d), **ee** (139c), **EE** (42a), **Ge** (47d,69a), **he** (91c), **ie** (74c,158c,163d), **LE** (59c), **le** (13b,61a, 108b), **me** (108b,124b), **Me.** (124d), **ne** (35b,106b), **oe** (43c,54d, 82d,180d,182a,b), **pe** (91c), **Pe.** (124d), **re** (6b,10b,35d,108b,122b, 129b,138a,161a), **RE** (59c), **se** (35b,108b), **te** (43a,62d,108b,131c, 152d,160b,185d), **Ve** (63c,109c), **we** (48c,124b), **We** (92b), **ye** (124b)

F -   **fa** (108b,138a,161a), **FB** (59c), **ff** (147b), **Fi** (108b), **Fo** (23d), **fu** (42c,84c), **Fu** (30b)

- F   **ef** (91c), **ff** (147b), **if** (35d,125a), **LF** (16d), **of** (6b), **RF** 16d)

G - Ga (69c), Ge (47d,69a), Gi (91d), go (64c,90d)

- G eg (59d,163d), Og (16d,18c)

H - ha (52c), HB (59c), he (91c), hi (52c), ho (39b,79a), Ho (87c), Hu (101c,108a,162b)

- H ah (52c), eh (52c), oh (52c), Rh (20c), sh (17b,43c,79c,126d), th (43c)

I - Ia (43d,158c), id (26d,40c,51c,57a,b,d), ie (74c,158c,163d), if (35d, 125a), iI (122c), im (122c), in (9d,123a), io (74b,74c,103c,115b), lo (25a,85d,95c,186b), ir (°9d,122c), Ir (10a,28a,82b), is (51a,166c, 175c), Is (15b,23c,86c), it (124b)

- I ai (143c,148c), bi (122d,171c), di (68c,89b,108b,122b,c,d,171d), fi (108b), Gi (91d), hi (52c) i (30a,b,37b,98a,108b,161b), mi (43b, 108b,138a,161a), pi (71b,85d,91c,165a,172a), ri (84c,96d,98a, 108b), RI (106c), si (108b,152d,185d), ti (92b,108b,113a,b,120d, 138a,161a,162c,169b), xi (91c)

J - ja (66d), jo (140c,160c), Jo (8c,94b), ju (121a)

K - ka (45c), Ka (68c,77b,150d,153c,173c), ko (22c,87c,121a)

- K OK (155a)

L - Ia (13b,61a,83a,108b,138a,151d,161a), Ie (13b,61a,108b), LE (59c), Lf (16d), Ii (30a,b,37b,98a,108b,161b), Lt (143c), LT (59c), Iu (65a), Io (17d,93d)

- L al (8c,80c,102c,104b), Al (96b), el (13b,42a,47a,99b,151d,168a), El (68a,108a), il (122c), ol (29c,158b,d,160b)

M - ma, Ma (69a,b,85d), MA (42a), me (108b,124b), Me. (124d), mi (43b,108b,138a,161a), mo (21d,81c,101c), Mo (88c,177c), mu (10a, 30a,60c,71a,91c), my (52c,124c)

- M am (166c,175c), em (91c,98a,123d,172a,c), dm (131c), im (122c), om (49a,77a,77b,105c,136a), um (52c,76c)

N - na (140c,163d), NA (36c), ne (35b,106b), no (42b,106b), No (84b), nu (71b,91c), Nu (29a,49a)

- N an (11b,13b), en (15b,29c,50a,91c,98a,119d,123d,158c,d,172a), in (9d,123a), on (8b,9a,60c106a,123a), un (34c,122c)

O - oa (43c,d), ob (122b), od (8d,59d,79c), oe (43c,54d,82d,180d, 182a,b), of (6b), Og (16d,18c), oh (52c), OK (155a), ol (29c, 158b, d,160b), om (49a,77a,b,105c,136a), on (8b,9a,60c,106a,123a), oo (34a,74b), or (9b,36a,37b,69c,158c,166a,184b), os (21d,67b,104a, 131b), ow (52c), ox (10c,22c), oy (139c)

- O Ao (13d,88b,c,116c), bo (23d,24c,136a,168a), do (108b,138a 161a), eo (34a), Fo (23d), go (64c,90d), ho (39b,79a), Ho (87c), io (74b,c,103c,115b), Io (25a,85d,95c,186b), jo (140c,160c), Jo (8c, 94b), ko (22c,87c,121a), Io (17d,93d), mo (21d,81c,101c), Mo (88c, 177c), no (42b,106b), No (84b), oo (34a,74b), Ro (13c,81d,88c,131c, 173c), so (76a,108b,125a,138a,158b,161a,165b,175c), to (10b, 13c), uo (43d), vo (91a), yo, zo (13d,186b)

P - pa (60b,106d), pe (91c), Pe. (124d), pi (71b,85d,91c,165a,172a), pu (30b,140a)

- P ap (122d,166c), AP (107a,182d), up (123a), UP (107a,182d)

Q - QB (59c), q.v. (180d)

R - ra (108b), Ra (159b), re (6b,10b,35d,108b,122b,129b,138a,161a), RE (59c), RF (16d), Rh (20c), ri (84c,96d,98a,108b), RI (106c), Ro (13c,81d,88c,131c,173c), RT (59c)

- R ar (88b,91c,98a,99b,110c), er (35b,76c,137d,155a,158c,d,160b, 175c), Er (18d,68c,85c,163d,166c,172c,178a), ir (99d,122c), Ir (10a, 28a,82b), or (9b,36a,37b,69c158c,166a,184b), Ur (6b,28d,94a, 100d)

S - SA (36c), se (35b,108b), Se, sh (17b,43c,79c,126d), si (108b,152d, 185d), so (76a,108b,125a,138a,158b,161a,165b,175c), SS (16d, 164c), Su (127a), Sw (35b), Sy (141a)

- S as (51b,67b,92b,126a,133a,b,180d), es (49b,50a,66c,119d,158c, d,175c), is (51a,166c,175c), Is (15b,23c,86c), os (21d,67b,104a, 131b), S.S. (16d,164c), us (124b)

T - ta (112d,139a,160b), td (32a), te (43a,62d,108b,131c,152d,160b, 185d), th (43c), ti (92b,108b,113a,b,120d,138a,161a,162c,169b), to (10b,13c), tt (147b), tu (83c,164d,185d), Ty (68c,109c,163d, 178a)

- T at (25c,32c,106a,123a,128a), et (10b,61a,b,89a,158c), It (124b), Lt (143c), LT (59c), RT (59c), tt (147b), ut (72b,108b), Ut (67a)

U - um (52c,76c), un (34c,122c), Uo (43d), up (123a), Ur (6b,28d, 94a,100d), UP (107a,182d), us (124b), ut (72b,108b), Ut (67a), Uz (48c)

- U au (63a,69c), bu (190), fu (42c,84c), Fu (30b), Hu (101c,108a, 162b), ju (121a), lu (65a), mu (10a,30a,60c,71a,91c), nu (71b, 91c), Nu (29a,49a), pu (30b,140a), Su (127a), tu (83c, 164d, 185d), Wu (30b), Zu (68c,157a)

V - va (105a), Va (83a), Ve (63c,109c), vo (91a)

- V q.v. (180d)

W - wa (188), Wa (24c,d,88c), we (48c,124b), We (92b), Wu (30b), wy (91c)

- W aw (44a), ow (52c), sw (35b)

X - xi (91c)

- X ax (40c,139a,167a), ex (60b,91c,122c), ox (10c,22c)

Y - ya, ye (12-1b), yo

- Y ay (7c,8b,9b,28d,55a,60a), by (18b,32c,106a), my (52c,124c), sy (141a), oy (139c), Ty (68c,109c,163d,178a), wy (91c)

Z - za (162a), zo (13d,186b), Zu (68c,157a)

- Z Uz (48c)

THREE-LETTER WORDS

AA - aal (47c,80c,104b), aam (47a,49d,93a), aar (172d), Aar (131a)

A - A aba (12a,25d,32b,33a,65b), Ada (110a,112c,183c), aea (26a,36d), aga (35a,39a,48b,102d,103a,b,111c,166b,170d,171a), aha (52c,55c, 159c), aka (88b,c,176b), Aka (13d), ala (6d,13a,15c,61a,133d,

182c,d), **Ala** (151b), **ama** (26a,28d,31a,35b,39c,95b,108d,111c, 117b,182c), **ana** (10b,33c,60d,93a,98c,122b,d,140d,142b), **Ana** (28a,68d,100c), **apa** (23a,177d), **ara** (33a,114a,116a,118b,163d), **Ara** (9b,18c,36b,c,68d,69b,c,85a,95a,175b), **Asa** (6a,18c,71a,84d, 86d,164c), **ata** (58d,97d,158d,160c,173d), **Ata** (79c,80d,94d, 95d,100a,106b,117a,), **ava** (78d,86a,116a,120d,139a,167b), **Ava** (24c), **awa** (100a,139a), **aya** (77b,166b)

- AA **baa** (143d), **maa** (97d,143d), **saa** (98a), **taa** (112d)

AB - **aba** (12a,25d,32b,33a,65b), **abb** (58b,178b,185b), **ABC** (134d), **Abe** (71a,96a,123a), **Abi** (76c), **Abo** (25d), **Abt** (34c), **abu** (17a), **Abu** (15b,42a,55a,68a,c,147d)

A - B **abb** (58b,178b,185b), **alb** (65b,176a)

- AB **Bab** (15a), **cab** (75c), **dab** (46a,57b,58b,d,114d,115c), **gab** (29b, 78a,116c,122a,161c,183a), **jab** (120b,125c), **kab** (75c), **lab, Mab** (54b,126b,183d), **nab** (13b,26c,27b,142a), **pab** (139c), **rab** (17c,75c, 85b,102d,162c,166b), **Rab** (45a), **tab** (29b,39c,58b,86a,128d,145a)

AC - **ace** (7a,26c,52d,57a,77d,110c,114c,120b,147a,163a,173a), **ach** (8b, 48a,52c,66b,80c), **aci** (29c), **act** (41d,55b,119c,155d), **acu** (34c), **acy** (34c)

A - C **ABC** (134d), **arc** (31b,39d,92a,126a,127c,142a)

- AC **bac** (31b,55c,174d), **fac** (41c), **lac** (53c,99d,130c,135b,174d), **Mac** (96a,140b,150b), **pac** (73b,94c,100d), **sac** (15d,121d), **Sac** (80c), **tac** (34d,130a), **Vac** (153b), **zac** (27c)

AD - **Ada** (110a,112c,183c), **add** (10d,11d,14c,158a,167c), **ade** (18c, 149d), **Ade** (9c,53b), **ado** (22b,24d,35b,64c,78d,121d,156b,170a), **ady** (188), **adz** (40c,167a)

A - D **aid** (14a,15b,64c,75d,158b), **add** (10d,11d,14c,158a,167c), **and** (36a,119d)

- AD **bad** (55a,173a,184d), **cad** (22b,23b,75c,172c,173d), **dad, fad** (38b, 108c,163a), **gad** (58c,100a,b,127d,132b,153c,154b,178a), **Gad** (84a, 186d), **had, lad** (22c,25b,55b,157c,186a), **mad** (10c,82b), **pad** (39d, 59c,76c,157d,161a,168b), **rad** (50b,138d,173b), **sad** (29c,42c,94c, 98c,104d,150d,173a), **tad** (22c,174a,186a), **wad** (94d,97b,109c, 112b,149d)

AE - **aea** (26a,36d), **AEF** (184d), **aer** (8b,28d,34a,b,175a), **aes** (23c, 89a,101c,132d,133a,b), **aet** (89a,109d), **Aex** (46d)

A - E **Abe** (71a,96a,123a), **ace** (7a,26c,52d,57a,77d,110c,114c,120b, 147a,163a,173a), **ade** (18c,149d), **Ade** (9c,53b), **age** (51d,66a,92a, 97c,98c,116b,141c), **ake** (60a,107a), **ale** (17c,18c,50c,55d,92d, 104c), **ame** (37a,62d,131b), **ane** (61c,140a,158b), **ape** (36d,79d, 100a,101d,146d), **are** (51a,88b,98a,99b,110c,166c,175c), **ase** (51a, 139a), **Ase** (79b,115d), **ate** (81a,108c,158c,174c), **Ate** (20c,68b,d, 69a,b,116c,186b), **ave** (54c,71d,73a,122a,134a,136d), **awe** (81d, 100a,130d,175b,182b), **axe** (30c,40c,167a), **aye** (7c,9b,55a,60a)

- AE **dae** (139b), **eae** (34b), **hae** (139c), **kae** (84a,140b), **Mae** (183c), **nae** (139d), **rae** (136b,138d,140b), **Rae** (183c), **sae** (140b,149c), **tae** (138d,140c,166c,d), **vae** (176b)

AF - **AFL** (173a), **Afr.** (36c), **aft** (14a,15b,17d,128b,167d)

A - F **AEF** (184d), **Alf** (96a)

261

- AF gaf (12b), kaf (12b), Kaf (104a), oaf (22a,45b,146d,157d,185d), Qaf (104a)

AG - aga (35a,39a,48b,102d,103a,b,111c,166b,170d,171a), age (51d, 66a,92a,97c,98c,116b,141c), ago (25a,69d,114d,147a)

- AG bag (26c,139a,145b,159a), cag (81d,109d), dag (11b,118c,139c), Dag (108c), fag (55a,166a), gag (146c,183a), hag (140a,183a), jag (124d,148a), lag (93c,155d), mag (73b,95b,166c), Mag (183d), nag (73d,78b,138c,184d), rag (59b,77c,100c,133c,161a), sag (46b), tag (45a,54c,65a,87b,144a), vag (174b,178a), wag (85b,104a,183a), zag (84a)

AH - aha (52c,55c,159c), Ahi (32c,147d), ahu (24c,41d,65d,103d,120d)

A - H ach (8b,48a,52c,66b,80c), akh (153d), ash (24d,33c,49c,73d,134b, 168c,169a), auh (52c)

- AH bah (52c), dah (24c,87a), hah (52c), Jah (84d), Mah (10b,57c, 102b), pah (52c,60b,106d), rah (29b), sah (188), wah (113c), yah (52c)

AI - aid (14a,15b,64c,75d,158b), aik (139d), ail (170a), aim (42d,43d, 67d,109b,125d,157c), ain (18d,91c,110c,124b,140a,154b,180a), air (11c,12c,42b,44c,53a,96b,98c,99d,125b,170c), ait (82d,132a), Aix (46d)

A - I Abi (76c), aci (29c), Ahi (32c,147d), Ali (7b,12a,25c,48b,55a,60c, 92d,101a,103a,164a,166b,170d), ami (61d), ani (19b,d,20b,39b), api (34a,76d), Ari (18d), asi (137a), ati (106d,107a), Ati (45d,106b, 113c,117a)

- AI hai (55c), kai (59c), Kai (14d,84c), lai (98b,161b), Lai (24c,d,88c), mai (62a), rai (188), sai (101d), tai (84b,111c,121b), Tai (80d), Vai (91d)

- AJ gaj (190), raj (129c), saj (48a,169a), taj (75a,97d)

AK - aka (176b), Aka (13d,88b,c), ake (60a,170a), akh (153d), ako (189), aku (57c,176a)

A - K aik (139d), alk (171b), ark (21a,29d,38a,58b,60d,175d), ask (38b, 82a,126c), auk (19b)

- AK dak (95c), hak (46d), lak (38a), nak (156b), oak (73d,168c,169a), sak (37c), Sak (88c), yak (112c,161d,165b), zak (188)

AL - ala (6d,13a,15c,61a,133d,182c,d), Ala. (151b), alb (65b,176a), ale (17c,18c,50c,55d,92d,104c), Alf (96a), Ali (7b,12a,25c,48b,55a,60c, 92d,101a,103a,164a,166b,170d), alk (171b), all (35c,118a,126d, 181a), alp (24b,103d,115c), als (66d,163d), alt (66c,76c,109c), aly (95d)

A - L aal (47c,80c,104b), AFL (173a), ail (170a), all (35c,118a,126d,181a), awl (145b,167a)

- AL aal (47c,80c,104b), bal (9d,37b,61a,61b), cal (183c), Cal (123a), dal (117d,153d), gal, Hal (69d), ial (158b), mal (34a,b,44a,52b,62c, 122b), Mal (94b), pal (35b,38d), sal (29c,48a,136c,149d,152d, 169a,183a), Sal (183d), tal (40c,77a,113b), Zal (135d)

AM - ama (26a,28d,31a,35b,39c,95b,108d,111c,117b,182c), ame (37a, 62d,131b), ami (61d), amo (79a,89c), amp (49b,173b), amt (37d, 40d,108a,163c), amy (63c), Amy (8c,94b,183c)

262

A - M aam (47a,49d,93a), **aim** (42d,43d,67d,109b,125d,157c), **arm** (22d, 60c,81b,92b,124b,161b), **aum** (189)

- AM aam (47a,49d,93a), **bam** (29b), **cam** (48b,65d,95a,98b,134a,139b, 148b,180c), **dam** (30c,49c,55b,156d,180a), **gam** (76b,176d,180c), **ham** (98a,144b), **Ham** (18d,107c), **jam** (123a,156d,165c), **lam** (51b, 58b,93d,164d,178a), **Mam** (192), **pam** (26c,65a,87a,105b), **Ram** (36b), **ram** (17a,45b,50b,79c,112b,121d,143d,157d), **Sam** (96a, 162a), **tam** (74d), **yam** (48c,121d,160b,170c)

AN - ana (10b,33c,60d,93a,98c,122b,d,140d,142b), **Ana** (28a,68d,100c), **and** (36a,119d), **ane** (61c,140a,158b), **ani** (19b,d,20b,39b), **Ann** (183c), **ano** (19d,20b,34d,122d,174a), **Ans** (92a), **ant** (49d,60b,81b, 118c), **Anu** (15b,28a,68a,d,75b,88c,147d), **any** (14b,150b)

A - N ain (18d,91c,110c,124b,140a,154b,180a), **Ann** (183c), **arn** (8c, 139a), **awn** (12c,17b,140a)

- AN ban (81d,97a,124a), **can** (24c,36c,123a,166a), **dan** (24c,97c), **Dan** (18c,39c,77d,83a,84a,141b), **ean** (17d,23b,88a), **fan** (43a,154b), 156b,182d), **Gan** (132d), **Han** (16c,30b,185b), **lan** (85b,96a,139d), **kan** (93a), **lan** (37b,37d,160b), **man** (29c,60c,64c,65a,142d,161d), **Nan** (183c), **pan** (34a,61a,104a,175d), **Pan** (56a,68a,68b,76b,120c, 135b,161a,184a), **ran** (73d), **Ran** (7c,107d,141a,163d), **san** (91c, **San** (24d), **tan** (23d,33c,46a,72d,90d), **van** (7b,59d,60a,63d,90c), **wan** (113a), **Zan** (186b)

A - O Abo (25d), **ado** (22b,24d,35b,64c,78d,121d,156b,170a), **ago** (25a, 69d,114d,147a), **ako** (189), **amo** (79a,89c), **ano** (19d,20b,34d, 122d,174a), **Apo** (122b,177c), **Aro** (107a,111c), **Aso** (84c), **azo** (107c)

- AO dao (117a), **hao** (189), **iao** (78a,96c,178d), **Lao** (80d,88c,146a, 161b), **mao** (115b), **Mao** (30b), **sao** (141b), **Sao** (113c), **tao** (10d, 131c,170b), **Tao** (117a), **Yao** (30a,c,104b)

AP - apa (23a,177d), **ape** (36d,79d,100a,101d,146d), **api** (34a,76d), **apo** (122b), **Apo** (177c), **apt** (11d,23b,32b,58a,80b,92b,114d,116d, 124b,159a)

A - P alp (24b,103d,115c), **amp** (49b,173b), **asp** (7b,32b,149a,174a, 176c)

- AP bap (93b,132d), **Bap** (124d), **cap** (19d,39a,43a,53a,74d,160a,167b, 185c), **dap** (43b,c,46b,91b,147d), **gap** (11b,23a,29b,76c,110d,128a), **hap** (17d,28d), **Jap, lap** (31b,37d,59b,127a,131d,153d,167d), **map** (27a,29b,54a,98d,160a), **nap** (65a,117d,146a,148a), **pap** (59c), **rap** (90d,110a,147c,157c), **sap** (45d,52d,85c,169b,176d,179a), **tap** (55a,114d,153c), **yap** (16c,29b,122a)

AR - ara (33a,114a,116a,118b,163d), **Ara** (8c,9b,36b,c,68d,69b,c, 85a,95a,175b), **arc** (31b,39d,92a,126a,127c,142a), **are** (51a,88b, 98a,99b,110c,166c,175c), **Ari** (18d), **ark** (21a,29d,38a,58b,60d, 175d), **arm** (22d,60c,81b,92b,124b,161b), **arn** (8c,139a), **Aro** (107a, 111c), **ars** (13b,89a), **Ars** (112c), **art** (22d,38b,39c,43b,56c,124a, 162c,181d), **aru** (80c,82b), **Aru** (82d)

A - R aar (172d), **Aar** (131a), **aer** (8b,28d,34a,b,175a), **Afr.** (36c), **air** (11c,12c,42b,44c,53a,96b,98c,99d,125b,170c)

- AR aar (172d), **Aar** (131a), **bar** (37c,39a,46a,52c,76d,78b,91a,124a,

137a,156a,157c,169c), **car** (16a,61d,93b,175a) **dar,** (65c,111b, 169a), **ear** (14c,d,28c,63d,64a,73c,111b,116a,124b,137d,150d, 153c), **far** (44c), **gar** (57b,c,d,106b), **har** (139c), **jar** (31d,70d,143b), **lar** (24c,51d,67a,78d,95d,101d,171b), **mar** (40b,44a,79a,d,81a, 140d), **Mar** (93d), **nar** (139d), **oar** (20b,124c,134b), **par** (15a,51a, 51b,c,69d,107c,135b,155a) **sar** (57d), **tar** (8c,68a,94d,111c,118c, 136a,c,176d), **war** (157c), **yar** (72a), **zar** (188)

AS - **Asa** (6a,18c,71a,84d,86d,164c), **ase** (51a,139a), **Ase** (79b,115d), **ash** (24d,33c,49c,73d,134b,168c,169a), **asi** (137a), **ask** (38b,82a, 126c) **Aso,** (84c), **asp** (7b,32b,149a,174a,176c), **ass** (17b,20c,45b, c,59c,110c,112b,146d,157d)

A - S **aes** (23c,89a,101c,132d,133a,b), **als** (66d,163d), **Ans** (92a), **ars** (13b,89a), **Ars** (112c), **ass** (17b,20c,45b,c,59c,110c,112b,146d, 157d), **aus** (66c), **Aus** (98b)

- AS **bas** (62a,d,129d,134b), **das** (13b,15d,36d,66b,d,164a), **fas** (44d,89d, 129d), **gas** (10b,29b,59a,116d,161c), **has, kas** (32c,47a), **las** (13b, (151d), **mas** (34b,55b,119a) **nas** (74a,89c,178b), **pas** (40d, 156a), **ras** (6c,26b,48b,51d,53d,61c,75a,111c,123c,166b), **vas** (46d, 89d,119c,133b,175d), **was** (166c,175c), **Was** (24d)

AT - **ata** (58d,97d,158d,160c,173d), **Ata** (79c,80d,94d,95d,100a, 106b,117a), **ate** (81a,108c,158c,174c), **Ate** (20c,68b,d,69a,b, 116c,186b), **ati** (106d,107a), **Ati** (45d,106b,113c,117a), **att** (146a)

A - T **Abt** (35c), **act** (41d,55b,119c,155d), **aet** (89a,109d), **aft** (14a,15b, 17d,128b,167d), **ait** (82d,132a), **alt** (66c,76c,109c), **amt** (37d,40d, 108a,163c), **ant** (49d,60b,81b,118c), **apt** (11d,23b,32b,58a,80b,92b, 114d,116d,124b,159a), **art** (22d,38b,39c,43b,56c,124a,162c,181d), **att** (146a), **aut** (34d,89d)

- AT **bat** (39c,107c,156a,157c,182d), **cat** (10a,45b,55b,71d,161b,169d, 180d,183d), **eat** (37b,96b,135d,179b), **fat** (110a,124a), **gat** (28d, 72c,131a), **hat** (74d), **Hat** (183d), **Jat** (80d,125c), **kat** (105d), **lat** (24a,33d,106b,118a), **mat** (46d,50d,94d,117c,161d), **Mat** (96a), **nat** (7a,24c,24d,106a), **oat** (15a,28b,70b,144b), **pat** (11d,116d, 159a,161d,167c), **Pat** (96a), **rat** 16a,42d,73b,132c), **sat** (13d), **tat** (48c,72d,87c), **Tat** (82a), **vat** (31b,36c,163a,170c), **wat** (73d,140d, 163a,180b), **xat** (167c), **zat** (148a)

AU - **auh** (52c), **auk** (19b), **aum** (189), **aus** (66c), **Aus** (98b), **aut** (34d, 89d), **aux** (6d,61a)

A - U **abu** (17a), **Abu** (15b,42a,55a,68a,c,147d), **acu** (34c), **ahu** (24c,41d, 65d,103d,120d), **aku** (57c,176a), **Anu** (15b,28a,68a,d,75b,88c, 147d), **aru** (80c,82b), **Aru** (82d), **ayu** (160c)

- AU **eau** (63a,178c), **gau** (66d,67a), **mau** (170c,188), **pau** (130c), **Pau** (48c,76a), **tau** (71b,91c,136c,161a), **vau** (91c), **Yau** (30c)

AV - **ava** (78d,86a,116a,120d,139a,167b), **Ava** (24c), **ave** (54c,71d,73a, 122a,134a,136d)

- AV **gav** (72d), **lav** (72d), **tav** (91c)

AW - **awa** (100a,139a), **awe** (81d,100a,130d,175b,182b), **awl** (145b,167a), **awn** (12c,17b,140a)

- AW **baw** (52c), **caw** (19b,d), **daw** (39a,70b,84a,146d), **gaw** (140c), **haw** (35a,52c,74d,91a,155a,162c), **jaw** (97d,138c), **law** (26b,33a,40a,

48c,60b,85d,91a,111b,134d,155d),   maw   (38b,d,72c,111a,121a,
142a,156c), paw (32d,59c,73c), raw (20c,39a,105d,173d), saw (7a,
11b,40c,54c,97d,125a,137d,167a), taw (90d,91c,96c,d,145b,161d),
waw (12b,91c), yaw (43a,155d)

AX -   axe (30c,40c,167a)

A - X   Aex (46d), Aix (46d), aux (6d,61a)

- AX   lax (93d,130a), Max (96a), pax (89d,115b), sax (40c,148a,167a),
tax (13a,14a,80a,91d), wax (28b,72a,80b,120c), zax (148a)

AY -   aya (77b,143c,166b), aye (7c,9b,55a,60a), ayu (160c)

A - Y   acy (34c), ady (188), aly (95d), amy (63c), Amy (8c,94b,183c), any
(14b,150b)

- AY   bay (12d,16c,33c,73d,78b,81b,90a,128d),   cay (82d,180b),   day
(153a), fay (32c,54b,154b), Fay (183c), gay, Gay (17d), hay (52c,
55c,165d), jay (19b,91c), kay (82d), Kay (13b,134b), lay
(16a,25c,80a,98b,107d,141d,150b), may (74d), May (183c), nay
(42b,106b),   pay (35b,128c,130a,d,177b),   ray (38a,49a,57b,
58b,147b), Ray (96a), say (131c,174c,177a), way (37d,96b,134b,
164d)

AZ -   azo (107c)

A - Z   adz (40c,167a)

- AZ   gaz (188,190), Laz (27d)

BA -   baa (143d), Bab (15a), bac (31b,55c,174d), bad (55a,173a,184d),
bag (26c,139a,145b,159a), bah (52c), bal (9d,37b,61a,b), bam
(29b), ban (81d,97a,124a), bap (93b,132d), Bap. (124d), bar (37c,
39a,46a,52c,76d,78b,91a,124a,137a,156a,157c,169c), bas (62a,d,
129d,134b), bat (39c,107c,156a,157c,182d), baw (52c), bay (12d,
16c,33c,73d,78b,81b,90a,128d)

B - A   baa (143d) boa (36c,55b,106a,125d,138b,142d,149a)

- BA   aba (12a,25d,32b,33a,65b), iba (117a)

B - B   Bab (15a), bib, bob (57c,115d), Bob (96a), bub (22c)

- BB   abb (58b,178b,185b), ebb (6a,15b,41c,43c,104a,128c,158a,178a)

B - C   bac (31b,55c,174d), BSC (42a)

- BC   ABC (134d)

B - D   bad (55a,173a,184d), bed (60c,148b), bid (35a,82a,109d,111b,
174c), bud (22c)

BE -   bed (60c, 148b), bee (46b,81b,91c,108c), beg (38b,150a), bel (64a,
93c,168d,173b,183d), Bel (15b,68a,126d), ben (78c,81b,102c,115c),
Ben (12d,77c,96a,106c,139d,140a), ber (85c), Bes (68b,119c), bet,
bey (70b,170d)

B - E   bee (46b,81b,91c), bye (38c,141d)

- BE   Abe 71a,96a,123a), obe (31d,87d,150d), ube (185b)

B - G   bag (26c,139a,145b,159a), beg (38b,150a), big, bog (97a,160a),
bug (24b,66b,81b)

B - H   bah (52c), boh (24c)

BI -   bib, bid (35a,82a,109d,111b,174c), big, Bim (16c), bin (22c,59a,
78a,128c,156d), bis (50a,90a,102c,130b,171c), bit (46a,86b,114c,
167a,b,171c,180d), biz

- BI   Abi (76c), obi (55d,67b,84c,137b,150d), ubi (90a,180d,185b)

B - K   Bok (9c)

B - L   bal (9d,37b,61a,61b), bel (64a,93c,168d,173b,183d), Bel (15b,68a, 126d), Bul (25d,102a)

B - M   bam (29b), Bim (16c), bum (21b)

B - N   ban (81d,97a,124a), ben (78c,81b,102c,115c,139d,140a), Ben (12d, 77c,96a,106c), bin (22a,59a,78a,128c,156d), bon (30a,61d,86b,88c), Bon (84b), bun (25b,73b)

BO -   boa (36c,55b,106a,125d,138b,142d,149a), bob (57c,115d), Bob (96a), bog (97a,160a), boh (24c), Bok (9c), bon (30a,61d,86b,88c), Bon (84b), boo, Bor (120c), Bos (27c), bot (59a,88d), bow (11c,21b, 39d,60a,107c,109a,125a,144d,158a), box (36a,128c,145d,152d), boy (142d,157c), Boz (43b,115d)

B - O   boo

- BO   Abo (25d), ebo (28b,110a), Ibo (107a,180a)

B - P   Bap. (124d), bap (93b,132d)

B - R   bar (37c,39a,46a,52c,76d,78b,91a,124a,137a,156a,157c,169c), ber (85c), Bor (120c), bur (123b)

BS -   BSC (42a)

B - S   bas (62a,d,129d,134b), Bes (68b,119c), bis (50a,90a,102c,130b, 171c), Bos (27c), bus (125b,168b)

B - T   bat (39c,107c,156a,157c,182d), bet, bit (46a,86b,114c,167a,b, 171c,180d), bot (59a,88d), but (36a,52b,156b,173c)

- BT   Abt (35c)

BU -   bub (22c), bud (22c), bug (24b,66b,81b), Bul (25d,102a), bum (21b), bun (25b,73b), bur (123b), bus (125b,168b), but (36a,52b, 156b,173c), buy

- BU   abu (17a), Abu (15b,42a,55a,68a,c,147d)

B - W   baw (52c), bow (11c,21b,39d,60a,107c,109a,125a,144d,158a)

B - X   box (36a,c,128c,145d,152d)

BY -   bye (38c,141d)

B - Y   bay (12d,16c,33c,73d,78b,81b,90a,128d), bey (70b,170d), boy (142d,157c), buy

B - Z   biz, Boz (43b,115d)

CA -   cab (75c), cad (22b,23b,75c,172c,173d), cag (81d,109d), cal (183c), Cal (123a), cam (48b,65d,95a,98b,134a,139b,148b,180c), can (24c, 36c,123a,166a), cap (19d,39a,43a,53a,74d,160a,167b,185c), car (16a,61d,93b,175a), cat (10a,45b,55b,71d,161b,169d,180d), Cat (183d), caw (19b,d) cay (82d, 180b)

C - A   cha (162b,c)

- CA   ECA (8a), oca (48c,112c,116d,133d,170c,184a), Uca (56a)

C - B   cab (75c), cob (28c,78b,95d,160b,177d), cub (92d,185d)

C - D   cad (22b,23b,75c,172c,173d), Cid (151c,d), cod (57b,c), cud (126c, 135a)

CE -   cea (91c), cep (63a), ces (62b), cet (62d,180b)

C - E   cee (91c), che (145d), cie (61b,63b), cle (158d), coe (143d),

Coe (33c), **cue** (7a,27b,92c,117d,124b,132c,146c,159a)

- CE   **ace** (7a,26c,52d,57a,77d,110c,114c,120b,147a,163a,173a), **ice** (30a, 36d,42d,63d)

C - G   **cag** (81d,109d), **cig**, **cog** (33a,65d,163b,167b,180c)

CH -   **cha** (162b,c), **che** (145d), **chi** (91c), **Chi** (69c), **cho** (188)

- CH   **ach** (8b,48a,52c,66b,80c), **ich** (66c), **och** (8b), **tch** (52c)

CI -   **Cid** (151c,d), **cie** (61b,63b), **cig**, **CIO** (173a), **cis** (34c,122c), **cit** (81a,167d)

C - I   **chi** (91c), **Chi** (69c)

- CI   **aci** (29c), **ici** (61d), **lci** (9b), **LCI** (21b)

- CK   **ock** (189), **tck** (52c)

CL -   **cle** (158d)

C - L   **cal** (183c), **Cal** (123a), **col** (103d,114c)

C - M   **cam** (48b,65d,95a,98b,134a,139b,148b,180c), **com** (122d), **cum** (159b), **cwm** (31b,37b,103d)

C - N   **can** (24c,36c,123a,166a), **con** (7d,29b,83c,116d,157d)

CO -   **cob** (28c,78b,95d,160b,177d), **cod** (57b,c), **coe** (143d), **Coe** (33c), **cog** (33a,65d,163b,167b,180c), **col** (103d,114c), **com** (122d), **con** (7d,29b,83c,116d,157d), **coo** (19b), **Coo** (82d), **cop** (36a,120c, 126d,153c,155d), **cor** (36c,75b,155b), **cos** (91d,132d), **cot** (129b, 148b), **cow** (22c,45b,81d), **cox** (156a), **coy** (16d), **coz**

C - O   **cho** (188), **CIO** (173a), **coo** (19b), **Coo** (82d), **cro** (104c,115b,180a)

C - P   **cap** (19d,39a,43a,53a,74d,160a,167b,185c), **cep** (63a), **cop** (36a, 120c,126d,153c,155d), **cup** (46b,69d,118b,170a), **cyp** (169d)

CR -   **cro** (104c,115b,180a), **cru** (63a,176c), **cry** (25c,124a,145c,179d)

C - R   **car** (16a,61d,93b,175a), **cor** (36c,75b,155b), **cur** (101d)

C - S   **ces** (62b), **cis** (34c,122c), **cos** (91d,132d)

- CS   **ics** (158d)

C - T   **cat** (10a,45b,55b,71d,161b,169d,180d,183d), **cet** (62d,180b), **cit** (81a,167d), **cot** (148b), **cut** (30c,32b,145c)

- CT   **act** (41d,55b,119c,155d), **ect** (35a,122d,183b), **oct** (34a,122c)

CU -   **cub** (92d,185d), **cud** (126c,135a), **cue** (7a,27b,92c,117d,124b,132c, 146c,159a), **cum** (159b), **cup** (46b,69d,118b,170a), **cur** (101d), **cut** (30c,32b,145c)

C - U   **cru** (63a,176c)

- CU   **acu** (34c), **ecu** (58a,144b,c)

CW -   **cwm** (31b,37b,103d)

C - W   **caw** (19b,d), **cow** (22c,45b,81d)

C - X   **cox** (156a)

CY -   **cyp** (169d)

C - Y   **cay** (82d,180b), **coy** (16d), **cry** (25c,124a,145c,179d)

- CY   **acy** (34c), **icy** (65d)

C - Z   **coz**

DA -   **dab** (46a,57b,58b,d,114d,115c), **dad**, **dae** (139b), **dag** (11b,118c, 139c), **Dag** (108c), **dah** (24c,87a), **dak** (95c), **dal** (117d,153d), **dam**

267

(30c,49c,55b,156d,180a), **dan** (24c,97c), **Dan** (18c,39c,77d,83a, 84a,141b), **dao** (117a), **dap** (43b,c,46b,91b,147d), **dar** (65c,111b, 169a), **das** (13b,15d,36d,66b,d,164a), **daw** (39a,70b,84a,146d), **day** (153a)

D - A **dea** (68d,89b), **dha** (99d), **dia** (122b,d,152a,165b), **dra** (188), **dua** (122d)

- DA **Ada** (110a,112c,183c), **Ida** (103d,183c), **oda** (74a,170d)

D - B **dab** (46a,57b,58b,114d,115c), **deb**, **Deb** (183d), **dib** (21b,43b,c, 120d,140a), **dub** (25c,46a,c,87a,105b,121a,140a)

D - C **dec** (122d), **doc** (143a), **duc** (61c)

DD - **DDS** (42a)

D - D **dad, did, dod** (11a,32a,43b,140c), **dud** (21c,54a)

- DD **add** (10d,11d,14c,158a,167c), **odd** (46b,53a,109b,157a,172d,173c)

DE - **dea** (68d,89b), **deb**, **Deb** (183d), **dec** (122d), **dee** (91c), **Dee** (131d, 139b), **deg** (154b), **dei** (68d), **den** (38b,44d,74b,130d,133c,140d), **der** (13b,66b,d,164a), **des** (13b,61a,62b,d)', **dev** (42a,b), **dew** (41a), **dey** (8d,84a,114c,135a,139b,170d)

D - E **dae** (139b), **dee** (91c), **Dee** (131d,139b), **die** (27b,54a,65a,155a, 167a), **doe** (41d,55b,127a), **due** (7b,115b,124c), **dye** (33c,154d)

- DE **ade** (18c,149d), **Ade** (9c,53b), **Ede** (35b,65d), **ide** (40c,57a,b,d, 158b), **ode** (26b,79c,94d,118a,119d,120a,150b)

D - G **dag** (11b,118c), **Dag** (108c,139c), **deg** (154b), **dig** (52b), **dog** (10b, 45b,59b), **dug**

DH - **dha** (99d), **dhu** (40b), **Dhu** (28a,87d)

D - H **dah** (24c,87a), **doh** (113b)

- DH **edh** (91c)

DI - **dia** (122b,d,152a,165b), **dib** (21b,43b,c,120d,140a), **did, die** (27b, 54a,65a,155a,167a), **dig** (52b), **dii** (68d), **dim** (47a,48b,54a,74d, 94d,109b), **din** (31c,130b,174a), **dip** (26a,79d,117c,138c), **dis** (122b,d), **Dis** (68b,73a,119d,172d,174b), **dit** (62b,d,120a,159d), **div** (42b,139b), **dix** (118b), **Dix** (60b)

D - I **dei** (68d) **dii** (68d), **dui** (46d)

- DI **Udi** (108a)

DJ - **djo** (188)

D - K **dak** (95c)

D - L **dal** (117d,153d)

D - M **dam** (30c,49c,55b,156d,180a), **dim** (47a,48b,54a,74d,94d,109b), **dom** (121c,166b,c), **Dom** (94b), **dum** (45c,67b,113a)

D - N **dan** (24c,97c), **Dan** (18c,39c,77d,83a,84a,141b), **den** (38b,44d,74b, 130d,133c,140d), **din** (130b,174a), **don** (151d,166c), **Don** (96a), **dun** (19a,39d,46d,71a,97d,115b,160b)

DO - **Doc** (143a), **dod** (11a,32a,43b,140c), **doe** (41d,55b,127a), **dog** (10b, 45b,59b), **doh** (113b), **dom** (121c,166b,c), **Dom** (94b), **don** (151d, 166c), **Don** (96a), **dop** (39c,43b), **dor** (17d,24b,32b,46b,47a,81b, 85d), **dos** (45d,61a,97a,181b), **dot** (45d,97a,104d,105a,116b,153a, 162d), **dow** (17d,87a,88d,175d)

268

D - O   **dao** (117a) **djo** (188), **DSO** (99d), **duo** (46d,113a,171d)

- DO   **ado** (22b,24d,35b,64c,121d,156b,170a), **edo** (162a), **Edo** (107a, 166d), **Ido** (13c,81d,88c,173c), **Odo** (181d), **udo** (28a,30c,48c,84b, c,d,136c,149d)

D - P   **dap** (43b,c,46b,91b,147d), **dip** (26a,79d,117c,138c), **dop** (39c,43b)

DR -   **dra** (188), **dry** (46d,85a,137c,164c)

D - R   **dar** (111b,169a), **der** (13b,66b,d,164a), **dor** (17d,24b,32b,46b,47a, 81b,85d), **dur** (95c)

DS -   **DSO** (99d)

D - S   **das** (13b,15d,36d,66b,d,164a), **DDS** (42a), **des** (13b,61a,62b,d), **dis** (122b,d), **Dis** (68b,73a,119d,172d,174b), **dos** (45d,61a,97a,181b)

- DS   **DDS** (42a), **ods** (109a)

D - T   **dit** (62b,d,120a,159d), **dot** (45d,97a,104d,105a,116b,153a,162d)

DU -   **dua** (122d), **dub** (25c,46a,c,87a,105b,121a,140a), **duc** (61c), **dud** (21c,54a), **due** (7b,115b,124c), **dug, dui** (46d), **dum** (45c,67b,113a), **dun** (19a,39d,46d,71a,97d,115b,160b), **duo** (46d,113a,171d), **dur** (95c), **dux** (31d,64a,90c)

D - U   **dhu** (40b), **Dhu** (28a,87d)

D - V   **dev** (42a,b), **div** (42b,139b)

D - W   **daw** (39a,70b,84a), **dew** (41a), **dow** (17d,87a,88d,175d)

D - X   **dix** (118b), **Dix** (60b), **dux** (31d,64a,90c)

DY -   **dye** (33c,154d)

D - Y   **day** (153a), **dey** (8d,84a,114c,135d,139b,170a), **dry** (46d,85a,137c, 164c)

- DY   **ady** (188)

- DZ   **adz** (40c,167a)

EA -   **eae** (34b), **ean** (17d,23b,88a), **ear** (14c,d,28c,63d,64a,73c,111b, 116a,124b,137d,150d,153c), **eat** (37b,96b,135d,179b), **eau** (63a, 178c)

E - A   **ECA** (8a), **ela** (21c,53c,72b,76c,108b,174c), **Ena** (8c,126b), **era** (8a, 51a,116b,165d), **ESA** (8a), **eta** (71a,84c,91c), **Eva** (157a,183c)

- EA   **aea** (26a,36d), **dea** (68d,89b), **Hea** (15b), **kea** (114a,b), **lea** (56a, 97d,114d,185b), **Lea** (22d), **N.E.A.** (162c), **pea** (32d,91b,142a,175a), **rea** (9c,171a), **sea** (19a,52d,58c,112c,178d), **tea** (13d,18c,79c,81a, 145d,149c,159d), **Wea** (192), **yea** (7c,175c), **zea** (95c)

EB -   **ebb** (6a,15b,41c,43c,104a,128c,158a,178a), **ebo** (28b,110a)

E - B   **ebb** (6a,15b,41c,43c,104a,128c,158a,178a), **elb** (85c)

- EB   **deb, Deb** (183d), **Geb** (47d), **Keb** (47d), **neb** (17b,19a,d,115d), **reb** (35d,75c,85b,162c,166b), **Seb** (47d), **web** (50d,70a,98c,99a,106c, 149b)

EC -   **ECA** (8a), **ect** (35a,122d,183b), **ecu** (58a,144b,c)

E - C   **etc** (10b)

- EC   **dec** (122d), **sec** (46c,182c), **tec** (43a)

ED -   **Ede** (35b,65d), **edh** (91c), **edo** (162a), **Edo** (107a,166d)

E - D   **Eed** (102d), **eid** (10b,93c,110b,165d), **end** (8b,67d,120a,125d,130a, 166a), **erd** (47d,119d,145c)

- ED   **bed** (60c,148b), **Eed** (102d), **fed**, **ged** (100a,140a), **ked** (140b,144a), **led**, **Ned** (96a), **ped** (16d,34b), **red** (33c,38d,59a,127b,134c,135b), **Red** (151b), **sed** (89a), **ted** (74d,138b,154b), **Ted** (96b), **wed** (97a, 173c), **zed** (91c)

EE -   **Eed** (102d), **eel** (36a,49c,57a,b,88a,102c,176c), **een** (52a,139c, 185d), **eer** (9b,52a), **ees** (139c)

E - E   **eae** (34b), **Ede** (35b,65d), **eke** (14c,117c), **ele** (48c), **eme** (38d,70a, 140c,172b), **ene** (35b,158b,c), **ere** (17d,150c), **ese** (35b,158c), **ete** (36c,62d,141c,159b), **eve** (47a,131a,143a,165d,171c), **Eve** (183c), **ewe** (88a,143d), **Exe** (43a), **eye** (93d,111b,140d)

- EE   **bee** (46b,81b,91c,108c), **cee** (91c), **dee** (91c), **Dee** (131d,139b), **fee** (29a,58a,70d,166a,d), **gee** (35a,91c,100a,131c,139c,162c), **lee** (74b, 144b), **Lee** (9c,31c,96a), **mee** (169a), **nee** (19d,22b,25c,60b,95c), **pee** (91c), **ree** (12c,50a,80c,134d,137a,140b,144a,146b), **Ree** (25a), **see** (20a,43c,44a,51c,53c,93d,109b,113c,116a,176d,178c,183b), **tee** (39d,52b,69d,91c,112d,115d,118b,172a), **vee** (58a,91c,106a), **wee** (52c,100c,148c), **zee** (81b,91c)

EF -   **eft** (93b,107a,136c,169d)

E - F   **elf** (54b,154b)

- EF   **AEF** (184d), **kef** (12a,46c,75d,88c), **nef** (32b,144c,d), **ref**

EG -   **egg** (32d,80b,81c,112c,174a), **ego** (51a,79a,142b)

E - G   **egg** (32d,80b,81c,112c,174a), **eng** (48a,146a), **erg** (50b,173b, 184c)

- EG   **beg** (38b,150a), **deg** (154b), **Geg** (8c), **keg** (27a,105b), **leg** (37d, 92b,141d,159d,169c), **Meg** (8c,183d), **peg** (38c,46b,54d,98a,118a, 184c), **teg** (45a,54b,171d)

E - H   **edh** (91c), **eth** (91c,158d)

- EH   **Heh** (191), **reh** (8d)

EI -   **ein** (66b,c), **Eir** (69a,75a), **eis** (66c)

E - I   **Eli** (18c,d,76c,96a,137a,185a), **epi** (56c,61c,d,111c,112d,122d, 133c,153c,167b,174a), **eri** (13d,21c,146d), **Eri** (18c)

- EI   **dei** (68d), **fei** (16a,185b), **hei** (65a), **lei** (65b,74c), **rei** (89b,121c), **Rei** (18d), **Vei** (91d), **Wei** (30b,162b)

EK -   **eke** (14c,117c)

E - K   **elk** (22c,90d,178a)

- EK   **lek** (65c)

EL -   **ela** (21c,53c,72b,76c,108b,174c), **elb** (85c), **eld** (10b,93c,110b, 165d), **ele** (48c), **elf** (54b,154b), **Eli** (18c,d,76c,96a,137a,185a), **elk** (22c,90d,178a), **ell** (10d,24b,32c,98a), **elm** (168c), **els** (140a), **elt** (87a,117c,139d), **Ely** (27c,50b)

E - L   **eel** (36a,49c,57a,b,88a,102c,176c), **ell** (10d,24b,32c,98a)

- EL   **bel** (64a,93c,168d,173b,183d), **Bel** (15b,68a,126d), **eel** (36a,49c, 57a,b,88a,102c,176c), **gel** (32d,73d,150a), **Hel** (68d,93c,172d), **mel** (77d), **pel** (55c,160d), **rel** (49b,173b), **sel** (62c,140b), **tel** (34a, b,122c), **zel** (40c)

EM -   **eme** (38d,70a,140c,172b), **Ems** (125a,151c), **emu** (19b,58c,111d)

270

E - M   **elm** (168c)

- EM   **gem** (104b), **hem** (22a,36a,48b,52c,155a), **mem** (91c), **Sem** (107c), **Tem** (143a,159b)

EN -   **Ena** (8c,126b), **end** (8b,67d,120a,125d,130a,166a), **ene** (35b,158b, c), **eng** (48a,146a) **ens** (17d,18a,51a,52d), **ent** (34d,158b,c)

E - N   **ean** (17d,23b,88a), **een** (52a,139c,185d), **ein** (66b,c), **eon** (8a,37b, 51d,116b), **ern** (19c,d,47b,54b,141a)

- EN   **ben** (78c,81b,102c,115c), **Ben** (12d,77c,96a,106c,139d,140a), **den** (38b,44d,74b,130d,133c,140d), **een** (52a,139c,185d), **fen** (21c,97a, 160a), **gen** (31d,76b), **hen** (19a,60c,114c,136c), **ken** (60b,87c,122b, 172d), **men** (38c,116a,117b,170a), **Men** (94d), **pen** (36a,50a,80d, 118b,126d,160a,185c), **sen** (190), **ten** (19a,26c,41c,42b), **wen** (40c, 72a,110a,170c,177b), **yen** (33b,42d,93c,174a), **Zen** (24a)

EO -   **eon** (8a,37b,51d,116b), **Eos** (14d,41a,68d)

E - O   **ebo** (28b,110a), **edo** (162a), **Edo** (107a,166d), **ego** (51a,79a,142b), **eso** (34d,183b), **ETO** (184d), **exo** (122d)

- EO   **geo** (34a,47d), **Leo** (36b,c,92d,186d), **Meo** (27b,80c), **neo** (34a,b, c,100d,106d,108c,122c,d,128c), **Reo** (26c)

EP -   **epi** (56c,61c,d,111c,112d,122d,133c,153c,167b,174a)

E - P   **e.s.p.** (147b)

- EP   **cep** (63a), **hep** (52c), **kep** (139b), **nep** (27c,32d,56a,87c,184b), **pep** (50b,176b), **rep** (53b,d,131a,171c), **yep**, **Zep**

ER -   **era** (8a,51a,116b,165d), **erd** (47d,119d,145c), **ere** (17d,150c), **erg** (50b,173b,184c), **eri** (13d,21c,146d), **Eri** (18c), **ern** (19c,d,47b,54b, 141a), **err** (21a,43a,67d,100c,d,147a,148b,157b,168b,178a), **ers** (20a,176a), **ert** (140c,174a), **ery** (155d,158c,d)

E - R   **ear** (14c,d,28c,63d,64a,73c,111b,116a,124b,137d,150d,153c), **eer** (9b,52a), **Eir** (69a,75a), **err** (21a,43a,67d,100c,d,147a,148b,157b, 168b,178a), **Eur.** (36c)

- ER   **aer** (8b,28d,34a,b,175a), **ber** (85c), **der** (13b,66b,d,164a), **eer** (9b, 52a), **ger** (8d,36d,75c,124d), **her** (124b,c), **ier** (50a,158c), **Ker** (71b, 95d), **Ler** (23d,28a,b,64b,106c,141a), **mer** (62c;141a), **ner** (137c), **o'er** (6b,112a), **per** (25c,122d,165b,176a), **ser** (80d,83b,d,116c, 152d,180a), **ter** (34d,122d,165a), **xer** (34a), **zer** (188)

ES -   **ESA** (8a), **ese** (35b,158c), **eso** (34d,183b), **esp** (147b), **ess** (39d,78a, 91c,158c,184d), **est** (50a,61c,62a,79b,89c,158d,159c)

E - S   **ees** (139c), **eis** (66c), **els** (140a), **Ems** (125a,151c), **ens** (17d,18a, 51a,52d), **Eos** (14d,41a,68d), **ers** (20a,176a), **ess** (39d,78a,91c,158c, 184d)

- ES   **aes** (23c,89a,101c,132d,133a,b), **Bes** (68b,119c), **ces** (62b), **des** (13b,61a,62b,d), **ees** (139c), **Ges** (151b), **les** (13b,61a), **mes** (62b), **nes** (26b), **oes** (109a), **pes** (59d), **res** (80a,89d,91a,97c,164c), **ses** (61d), **yes** (7c,55a)

ET -   **eta** (71a,84c,91c), **etc** (10b), **ete** (36c,62d,141c,159b), **eth** (91c, 158d), **ETO** (184d)

E - T   **eat** (37b,96b,135d,179b), **ect** (35a,122d,183b), **eft** (93b,107a,136c, 169d), **elt** (87a,117c,139d), **ent** (34d,158b,c), **ert** (140c,174a), **est** (50a,62a,79b,89c,158d,159c)

- ET aet (89a,109d), bet, cet (62d,180b), get (44d,64b,109b,141d), jet (20b,35a,154c), ket (189), let (9a,76d,77c,116b,130a,158b,163a), met (28d), net (26c,32a,50d,53b,60d,99a,124a,142a,149b), pet (26d,37c,55a,59b,162d), ret (58b,95a,149c,155d), set (7b,11d,13a, 23c,32b,33c,37c,58a,73d,109b,118c,121c,142c,150a,186a), Set (52b, 68a,b,111d), vet, wet (40d,46a,101a,124a,127c,149c), yet (18b, 24d,64c,77c,80a,108c,156b,165b)

EU - Eur. (136c)

E - U eau (63a,178c), ecu (58a,144b,c), emu (19b,58c,111d)

- EU feu (55d,61c,88b), heu (8b,30c,52c), jeu (61d), leu (190), meu (153b), peu (62a), Reu (115d)

EV - Eva (157a,183c), eve (47a,131a,143a,165d,171c), Eve (183c)

- EV dev (42a,b), lev (33b) rev

EW - ewe (88a,143d)

- EW dew (41a), few, hew (40a), Jew, lew (190), Lew (96a), mew (25b, 27b,50a,55b,72c,74d,101b,141b,153b), new (11a,63c,88d,111c, 128c), pew (30d,52c,57d,120b,141c), rew (75c,140c,176b), sew, yew (36a,52a,b,145d,168c,d)

EX - Exe (43a), exo (122d)

- EX Aex (46d), hex (18c), lex (90b), rex (86c,96a), sex, vex (7c,10d, 44c,82c)

EY - eye (93d,111b,140d)⁻

E - Y Ely (27c,50b), ery (155d,158c,d)

- EY bey (70b,170d), dey (8d,84a,114c,135a,139b,170d), fey (49c), gey (140a), hey (25c,52c), key (14c,82d,88b,117c,118c,150b,180c), ley (190), Ney (63b,97b,105d), rey (86c,152b), sey (120c), wey (173b)

- EZ fez (75a,162a), gez (188), nez (62b), tez (125c), yez

FA - fac (41c), fad (38b,108c,163a), fag (55a,166a), fan (43a,154b, 156b,182d), far (44c), fas (44d,89d,129d), fat (110a,124a), fay (32c,54b,154b), Fay (183c)

F - A Fha (8a), fra (23c,63c,101d,123b,129d)

- FA MFA (42a)

F - B fib (162a), fob (29b,59b,113b,178c), fub (29b,119d)

F - C fac (41c)

F - D fad (38b,108c,163a), fed, fid (16b,54d,118a,167b), fod (188)

FE - fed, fee (29a,58a,70d,166a,d), fei (16a,185b), fen (21c,97a,160a), feu (55d,61c,88b), few, fey (49c), fez (75a,162a)

F - E fee (29a,58a,70d,166a,d), fie (52c,59d), foe (111a)

- FE ife (22c,75d)

- FF off (6b,15c,44c,76a)

F - G fag (55a,166a), fig, fog (109b), fug (129a)

FH - FHA (8a)

F - H foh (52c)

FI - fib (162a), fid (16b,54d,118a,167b), fie (52c,59d), fig, fin (86a), fir (16a,36a,52a,168c,d,169a), fit (7a,11d,51b,75a,114a,123a, 124c,126a,153a,157c,159a), fix (7b,10a,13a,14c,43a,c,141d,165c)

272

F – I	**fei** (16a,185b)
FL –	**flo, flu, fly** (58c,81b,163b,178d)
F – L	**Ful** (158b)
– FL	**AFL** (173a)
F – N	**fan** (43a,154b,156b,182d), **fen** (21c,97a,160a), **fin** (86a), **Fon** (40b), **fun**
FO –	**fob** (29b,59b,113b,178c), **fod** (188), **foe** (111a), **fog** (109b), **foh** (52c), **Fon** (40b), **foo** (42c), **fop** (38a,40d,46d), **for** (123d,163a,166c), **fot** (188), **fou** (139a), **fox** (134a)
F – O	**Flo, foo** (42c), **fro** (15b)
– FO	**Ufo** (59a)
F – P	**fop** (38a,40d,46d)
FR –	**fra** (23c,63c,101d,123b,129d), **fro** (15b), **fry** (57d)
F – R	**far** (44c), **fir** (16a,36a,52a,168c,d,169a), **for** (123d,163a,166c), **fur**
– FR	**Afr.** (36c)
F – S	**fas** (44d,89d,129d)
F – T	**fat** (110a,124a), **fit** (7a,11d,51b,75a,114a,123a,124c,126a, 153a,157c,159a), **fot** (188), **fut** (188)
– FT	**aft** (14a,15b,17d,128b,167d), **eft** (93b,107a,136c,169d), **oft** (63c)
FU –	**fub** (29b,119d), **fug** (129a), **Ful** (158b), **fun, fur, fut** (188)
F – U	**feu** (55d,61c,88b), **flu, fou** (139a)
F – W	**few**
F – X	**fix** (7b,10a,13a,14c,43a,c,141d,165c), **fox** (134a)
F – Y	**fay** (32c,54b,154b), **Fay** (183c), **fey** (49c), **fly** (58c,81b,163b,178d), **fry** (57d)
F – Z	**fez** (75a,162a)
GA –	**gab** (29b,78a,116c,122a,161c,183a), **gad** (58c,100a,127d,132b, 153c,154b,178a), **Gad** (84a,186d), **gaf** (12b), **gag** (146c,183a), **gaj** (190), **gal, gam** (76b,176d,180c), **Gan** (132d), **gap** (11b,23a,29b, 76c,110d,128a), **gar** (57b,c,d,106b), **gas** (10b,29b,59a,116d,161c), **gat** (28d,72c,131a), **gau** (66d,67a), **gav** (72d), **gaw** (140c), **gay, Gay** (17d), **gaz** (188,190)
G – A	**goa** (65d,104b,126c), **Goa** (121c), **gra** (59b,94b,160c)
– GA	**aga** (35a,39a,48b,102d,103a,b,111c,166b,170d,171a)
– GB	**KGB** (135d)
G – B	**gab** (29b,78a,116c,122a,161c,183a), **Geb** (47d), **gib** (17b,38b,95d, 166d,179d), **gob** (97b,136c)
G – D	**gad** (58c,100a,b,127d,132b,153c,154b,178a), **Gad** (84a,186d), **ged** (140a), **Ged** (100a), **gid** (143d), **god** (42a), **God** (84d)
GE –	**Geb** (47d), **Ged** (100a,140a), **gee** (35a,91c,100a,131c,139c,162c), **Geg** (8c), **gel** (32d,73d,150a), **gem** (104b), **gen** (31d,76b), **geo** (34a, 47d), **ger** (8d,36d,75c,124d), **Ges** (151b), **get** (44d,64b,109b,141d), **gey** (140a), **gez** (188)
G – E	**gee** (35a,91c,100a,131c,139c,162c), **gie** (139c,140a), **gue** (176c)
– GE	**age** (51d,66a,92a,97c,98c,116b,141c)
G – F	**gaf** (12b)

G - G   **gag** (146c,183a), **Geg** (8c), **gig** (26d,28d,57c,105b,127a,144c,153a, 171d), **gog** (95b)

- GG   **egg** (32d,80b,81c,112c,174a)

GH -   **ghi** (24d)

- GH   **ugh** (52c)

GI -   **gib** (17b,38b,95d,166d,179d), **gid** (143d), **gie** (139c,140a), **gig** (26d,28d,57c,105b,127a,144c,153a,171d), **gin** (37c,92d,139a,142a, 149b), **gip** (29b,160c), **git** (101a)

G - I   **ghi** (24d), **goi** (107c), **gri** (75c,78b)

G - J   **gaj** (190)

G - L   **gal, gel** (32d,73d,150a), **gul** (134a)

G - M   **gam** (76b,176d,180c), **gem** (104b), **gum** (7b,53c,80b,130c,156b), **gym** (154a)

GN -   **gnu** (11a,181d)

G - N   **gan** (132d), **gen** (31d,76b), **gin** (37c,92d,139a,142a,149b), **gon** (188), **gun** (56d,131a,146a)

GO -   **goa** (65d,104b,126c), **Goa** (121c), **gob** (97b,136c), **god** (42a), **God** (84d), **gog** (95b), **goi** (107c), **gon** (188), **goo** (156b), **Gor** (81a), **got, goy** (107c), **goz** (190)

G - O   **geo** (34a,47d), **goo** (156b)

- GO   **ago** (25a,69d,114d,147a), **ego** (51a,79a,142b)

G - P   **gap** (11b,23a,29b,76c,110d,128a), **gip** (29b,160c), **gup** (70a), **gyp** (29b,42a,160c)

GR -   **gra** (59b,94b,160c), **gri** (75c,78b), **grr** (52c), **gry** (78b)

G - R   **gar** (57b,c,d,106b), **ger** (8d,36d,75c,124d), **Gor** (81a), **grr** (52c), **gur** (159a)

G - S   **gas** (10b,29b,59a,116d,161c), **Ges** (151b), **Gus** (96a)

G - T   **gat** (28d,72c,131a), **get** (44d,64b,109b,141d), **git** (101a), **got, gut** (114d,130a)

GU -   **gue** (176c), **gul** (134a), **gum** (7b,53c,80b,130c,156b), **gun** (56d, 131a,146a), **gup** (70a), **gur** (159a), **Gus** (96a), **gut** (114d,130a), **guy** (55b,131b,155d), **Guy** (96a), **guz** (188)

G - U   **gau** (66d,67a), **gnu** (11a,181d)

- GU   **ngu** (188

G - V   **gav** (72d)

G - W   **gaw** (140c)

GY -   **gym** (154a), **gyp** (29b,42a,160c)

G - Y   **gay, Gay** (17d), **gey** (140a), **goy** (107c), **gry** (78b), **guy** (55b,131b, 155d), **Guy**\ (96a)

G - Z   **gaz** (188,190), **gez** (188), **goz** (190), **guz** (188)

HA -   **had, hae** (139c), **hag** (140a,183a), **hah** (52c), **hai** (55c), **hak** (46d), **Hal** (69d), **ham** (98a,144b), **Ham** (18d,107c), **Han** (16c,30b,185b), **hao** (189) **hap** (17d,28d), **har** (139c), **has, hat** (74d), **Hat** (183d), **haw** (35a,52c,74d,91a,155a,162c), **hay** (52c,55c,165d)

H - A   **Hea** (15b), **hia** (114b), **hoa** (39b)

- HA aha (52c,55c,159c), cha (162b,c), dha (99c), FHA (8a), Kha (88d, 106b), sha (110c,143d,144a,c,174c,181c)

H - B hob (40c,56d,100c,124b,167a,180c), hub (28b,118b,180c)

H - C hic (52c,90a,164c)

H - D had, hid, hod (23b,32d,102d,141a)

HE - Hea (15b), Heh (191), hei (65a), Hel (68d,93c,172d), hem (22a,36a, 48b,52c,155a), hen (19a,60c,114c,136c), hep (52c), her (124b,c), heu (8b,30c,52c), hew (40a), hex (18c), hey (25c,52c)

H - E hae (139c), hie (79a,153b), hoe (39c), hue (33c,143b)

- HE che (145d), rhe (59a), she (124b), She (73a), the (13b)

H - G hag (140a,183a), hog (45b,117c,160c), hug (32c,49d)

H - H hah (52c), Heh (191), Hoh (80d), hsh (79c), huh (52c)

HI - hia (114b), hic (52c,90a,164c), hid, hie (79a,153b), him (124b), hin (189), hip (52c,54b,85b,133c,134a), hir (76a), his (124c), hit (32d,157c,158a)

H - I hai (55c), hei (65a), hoi (52c,74b,185b), hui (14a,30b,56d,114c)

- HI Ahi (32c,147d), chi (91c), Chi (69c), ghi (24d), ihi (57c,156b), phi (91c)

H - K hak (46d)

H - L Hal (69d), Hel (68d,93c,172d)

H - M ham (98a,144b), Ham (18d,107c), hem (22a,36a,48b,52c,155a), him (124b), hum (24d,46b,150d)

- HM ohm (49b,67a,173b)

H - N Han (16c,30b,185b), hen (19a,60c,114c,136c), hin (189), Hun (16c,21d,174b)

HO - hoa (39b), hob (40c,56d,100c,124b,167a,180c), hod (23b,32d,102d, 141a), hoe (39c), hog (45b,117c,160c), Hoh (80d), hoi (52c,74b, 185b), hop (40b), Hor (103d), hot (10c,176c), how, hoy (16c,52c)

H - O hao (189)

- HO cho (188), mho (49b,173b), oho (52c), Rho (71b,91c), sho (188), tho (52a), Tho (167a), who (129c)

H - P hap (17d,28d), hep (52c), hip (52c,54b,85b,133c,134a), hop (40b), hup (35a), hyp

H - R har (139c), her (124b,c), hir (76a), Hor (103d), Hur (91d)

- HR ihr (66d)

HS - hsh (79c)

H - S has, his (124c)

H - T hat (74d), Hat (183d), hit (32d,157c,158a), hot (10c,176c), hut (143c)

HU - hub (28b,118b,180c), hue (33c,143b,) hug (32c,49d), huh (52c), hui (14a,30b,56d,114c), hum (24d,46b,150d), Hun (16c,21d,174b), hup (35a), Hur (91d), hut (143c)

H - U heu (8b,30c,52c)

- HU ahu (24c,41d,65d,103d,120d), dhu (40b), Dhu (28a,87d), phu (38c), Shu (30b,127a)

H - W	haw (35a,52c,74d,91a,155a,162c), hew (40a), how
H - X	hex (18c)
HY -	hyp
H - Y	hay (52c,55c,165d), hey (25c,52c), hoy (16c,52c)
- HY	shy (16d,99d,128c,160c,165d,175a), thy, why (52c)
IA -	ial (158b), Ian (85b,96a,139d), iao (78a,96c,178d)
I - A	iba (117a), Ida (103d,183c), Ila (16b), ILA (173a), ina (158c), Ina (183c), Ira (18c,d,41a,68c,82c,96a,164a,178a,c), Ita (51b,71d, 94d,95d,106b,117a), ITA (173a), iva (76a,97b,127b,185b) iwa (63c), iya (95b,108d,111c)
- IA	dia (122b,d,152a,165b), hia (114b), Lia (82b), mia (83c), pia (13b, 22d,48a,120d), ria (38c,51d,81b,152a,b), Sia (80c), tia (151d), via (132a,133a,b,179a)
IB -	iba (117a), Ibo (107a,180b)
- IB	bib, dib (21b,43b,c,120d,140a), fib (162a), gib (17b,38b,95d,166d, 179d), jib (38b,136b,146a), mib (8d,96c), nib (17b,19d,115d), rib (37c,85b,90c,98a,144d,159d,172a), sib (86b,129c,139d,147b)
IC -	ice (30a,36d,42d,63d), ich (66c), ici (61d), Ici (9b), ics (158d), icy (65d)
- IC	hic (52c,90a,164c), pic (188), sic (90a,165b,168b), tic (104d,153a, 171c,d)
ID -	Ida (103d,183c), ide (40c,57a,b,d,158b), Ido (13c,81d,88c,173c)
I - D	Ind (80c)
- ID	aid (14a,15b,64c,75d,158b), bid (35a,82a,109d,111b,174c), Cid (151c,d), did, fid (16b,54d,118a,167b), gid (143d), hid, kid (67d, 85b,90d,186a), lid (167b), mid (9d,28b,73b), nid (72a,106b,c,116d), old (158c), rid (32a,44a,60d), Sid (96a)
IE -	ier (50a,158c)
I - E	Ice (30a,36d,42d,63d), Ide (40c,57a,b,d,158b), ife (22c,75d), Ike (123a), ile (62a,63b,158c), ine (29c,158b,c), Ine (10c,137d,180b), ire (10c,30c,52b,64c,125a,130b,185a), ise (40d,158c,d), Ise (78a, 84c), ite (59b,81a,105d,130c,158b,c,d,161a), ive (158c)
- IE	cie (61b,63b), die (27b,54a,65a,155a,167a), fie (52c,59d), gie (139c,140a), hie (79a,153b), lie (53a,69d,162a), nie (53c), pie (42d,85d,95b,114d,171b,172a), rie (28c,70d,97d), sie (46c,66d, 139b,140b,146b), tie (10a,14c,38b,45d,51a,88d,109b,127c,138b, 170b), vie (36c,157c,170c)
IF -	ife (22c,75d)
- IF	Lif (107d), rif (188), Sif (164d), vif (62a), Zif (102a)
I - G	ing (114b,d,148d,158c,d,175c), Ing (10c,115b)
- IG	big, cig, dig (52b), fig, gig (26d,28d,57c,105b,127a,144c, 153a,171d), jig (40b,d), mig (8d,96c,145b), Mig (118d), nig (33b, 40a,46a), pig (27a,45b,99a,151b,160c), rig (51b,112a), tig (46b), wig (73b), zig (84a)
IH -	ihl (57c,156b), ihr (66d)
I - H	ich (66c), ish (158b), Ith (10a,28a,82b,99d)

276

125a,130b,185a), **Iri** (18a,d,75a), **irk** (10d)

I - R ier (50a,158c), **ihr** (66d), **ior** (50a,158c)

- IR air (11c,12c,42b,44c,53a,96b,98c,99d,125b,170c), **Eir** (69a,75a), **fir** (16a,36a,52a,168c,d,169a), **hir** (76a), **mir** (29d,135c,d,166c,176b), **pir** (103a,b,136c), **sir** (163b,166b), **tir** (61d,62c,87a,145b), **vir** (89c)

IS - ise (40d,158c,d), **Ise** (78a,84c), **-ish** (158b), **ism** (45a,79b,161c), **iso** (34a,122c,d), **ist** (7b,34b,43a,59b,66c,158c,d)

I - S ics (158d), **ils** (62b,d,164b), **ins** (164d), **INS** (107a,182d), **ios** (74d), **its** (124c)

- IS bis (50a,90a,102c,130b,171c), **cis** (34c,122c), **dis** (122b,d), **Dis** (68b,73a,119d,172d,174b), **eis** (66c), **his** (124c), **lis** (54b, 58b,60c,62a,92b), **Lis** (47a), **mis** (122b,c,d,185c), **nis** (23d,67d, 68a,87c), **Nis** (19d), **ris** (131d), **sis** (67b,129c), **tis**, **vis** (59d,89b,d, 90b,176b), **wis** (79d,164c)

IT - Ita (51b,71d,94d,95d,106b,117a), **ITA** (173a), **ite** (59b,81a,105d, 130c,158b,c,d,161a), **Ite** (130c), **Ith** (10a,28a,82b,99d), **Ito** (84a, c,186d), **its** (124c)

I - T ist (7b,34b,43a,59b,66c,158b,c,d)

- IT ait (82d,132a), **bit** (46a,86b,114c,167a,b,171c,180d), **cit** (81a, 167d), **dit** (62b,d,120a,159d), **fit** (7a,11d,51b,75a,114a,123a,124c, 126a,153a,157c,159a), **git** (101a), **hit** (32d,157c,158a), **kit** (112a, 176c), **Kit** (96a,183d), **lit**, **mit** (56c,66d,183b), **nit** (48d), **pit** (52b, 142a,164a,168a), **rit** (148c,140b,153d), **sit** (98c,116a,121c,130c, 142d), **tit** (19c,130d), **uit** (47a,111d,151a), **wit** (78d,85b,177b)

I - U imu (15d), **I.O.U.** (124b)

- IU piu (102c), **Tiu** (7c,68c,147d,163d,166c,170c), **Ziu** (147d,163d)

IV - iva (76a,97b,127b,185b), **ive** (158c), **ivy** (32b,38c,176b)

- IV div (42b,139b), **Liv** (93b)

IW - iwa (63c)

- IW Tiw (68c,147d,163d)

- IX Aix (46b), **dix** (118b), **Dix** (60b), **fix** (7b,10a,13a,14c,43a,c,141d, 165c), **mix** (156b), **nix** (23d,108c,178d), **pix** (31a,51d,175d), **six** (26c), **vix** (89d,138b)

IY - iya (95b,108d,111c), **iyo** (7d,176b)

I - Y icy (65d), **ivy** (32b,38c,176b)

- IZ biz, **viz** (105b)

JA - jab (120b,125c) **jag** (124d,148a) **Jah** (84d), **jam** (123a,156d,165c), **Jap**, **jar** (31d,70d,143b), **Jat** (80d,125c), **jaw** (97d,138c), **jay** (19b, 91c)

J - B jab (120b,125c), **jib** (38b,136b,146a), **job** (30d,184c), **Job** (96a)

JE - jet (20b,35a,154c), **jeu** (61d), **Jew**

J - E Joe (96a)

J - G jag (124d,148a), **jig** (40b,d), **jog** (82c,85c,170a), **jug** (118c,123d)

J - H Jah (84d)

JI - jib (38b,136b,146a), **jig** (40b,d), **Jim** (96a), **jin** (42b,153c)

- JI tji (189), **uji** (146d)

278

J – M	**jam** (123a,156d,165c), **Jim** (96a), **jum** (39c)
J – N	**jin** (42b,153c)
JO –	**job** (30d,184c), **Job** (96a), **Joe** (96a), **jog** (82c,85c,170a), **jot** (82a, 114c,166c,180d), **jow** (188), **joy**
– JO	**djo** (188), **Ijo** (107a)
J – P	**Jap**
J – R	**jar** (31d,70d,143b), **Jur** (107b)
J – S	**jus** (61d,90b)
J – T	**Jat** (80d,125c), **jet** (20b,35a,154c), **jot** (82a,114c,166c,180d), **jut** (53a,124a)
JU –	**jug** (118c,123d), **jum** (39c), **Jur** (107b), **jus** (61d,90b), **jut** (53a,124a)
J – U	**jeu** (61d)
J – W	**jaw** (97d,138c), **Jew, jow** (188)
J – Y	**jay** (19b,91c), **joy**
KA –	**kab** (75c), **kae** (84a,140b), **kaf** (12b), **Kaf** (104a), **kai** (59c), **Kai** (14d,84c), **kan** (93a), **kas** (32c,47a), **kat** (105d), **kay** (82d), **Kay** (13b,134b)
K – A	**kea** (114a,b), **Kha** (88d,106b), **koa** (74c), **Kra** (11b,91d), **Kua** (95c)
– KA	**aka** (176b), **Aka** (13d,88b,c), **oka** (170c,184a,189)
K – B	**kab** (75c), **Keb** (47d), **KGB** (135d), **kob** (11a)
K – D	**ked** (140b,144a), **kid** (67d,85b,90d,186a)
KE –	**kea** (114a,b), **Keb** (47d), **ked** (140b,144a), **kef** (12a,46c,75d,88c), **keg** (27a,105b), **ken** (60b,87c,122b,172d), **kep** (139b), **Ker** (71b, 95d), **ket** (189) **key** (14c,82d,88b,117c,118c,150b,180c)
K – E	**kae** (84a,140b)
– KE	**ake** (60a,107a), **eke** (14c,117c), **Ike** (123a), **oke** (189)
K – F	**kaf** (12b), **Kaf** (104a), **kef** (12a,46c,75d,88c)
KG –	**KGB** (135d)
K – G	**keg** (27a,105b)
KH –	**Kha** (88d,106b)
– KH	**akh** (153d)
KI –	**kid** (67d,85b,90d,186a), **kil** (82b), **Kim** (86d), **kin** (30b,81c,129d), **Kin** (30b), **kip** (17c,72d,76c,189), **kit** (112a,176c), **Kit** (96a,183d)
K – I	**kai** (59c), **Kai** (14d,84c), **koi** (26d), **kri** (75c,96d), **Kri** (75c), **Kui** (86a,88c,146a)
– KI	**ski** (149c)
K – L	**kil** (82b), **Kol** (18b), **kyl** (76d,79b)
K – M	**Kim** (86d)
K – N	**kan** (93a), **ken** (60b,87c,122b), **kin** (30b,81c), **Kin** (30b)
KO –	**koa** (74c), **kob** (11a), **koi** (26d), **Kol** (18b), **kop** (76d), **kor** (75c), **Kos** (77c,82d), **kou** (169a)
– KO	**ako** (189), **TKO** (22c)
K – P	**kep** (139b), **kip** (17c,72d,76c,189), **kop** (76d), **kup** (188)

KR - Kra (11b,91d), kri (75c,96d), Kru (91d)

K - R Ker (71b,95d), kor (75c)

K - S kas (32c,47a), Kos (77c,82d)

K - T kat (105d), ket (189), kit (112a,176c), Kit (96a,183d)

KU - Kua (95c), Kui (86a,88c,146a), kup (188)

K - U kou (169a), Kru (91d)

- KU aku (57c,176a)

KY - kyl (76d,79b)

K - Y kay (82d), Kay (13b,134b), key (14c,82d,88b,117c,118c,150b, 180c)

- KY sky (56d)

LA - lab, lac (53c,99d,130c,135b,174d), lad (22c,25b,55b,157c,186a), lag (93c,155d), Lai (24c,d,88c), lai (98b,161b), lak (38a), lam (51b, 58b,93d,164d,178a), lan (37b,d,160b), Lao (80d,88c,146a,161b), lap (31b,37d,59b,127a,131d,153d,167d), lar (24c,51d,67a,78d,95d, 101d,171b), las (13b,151d) lat (24a,33d,106b,118a), lav (72d), law (26b,33a,40a,48c,60b,85d,91a,111b,134d,155d), lax (93d,130a), lay (16a,25c,80a,98b,107d,141d,150b), Laz (27d)

L - A lea (56a,97d,114d,185b), Lea (22d), Lia (82b), loa (7d,53c,97d,184d)

- LA ala (6d,13a,15c,61a,133d,182c,d), Ala. (151b), ela (21c,53c,72b, 76c,108b,174c), lla (16b), ILA (173a), ola (113b), ula (72c,158c)

L - B lab, LLB (42a), lob (15d,23b,94c,100b,163a,172d)

- LB alb (65b,176a), elb (85c), LLB (42a)

LC - LCI (21b)

L - C lac (53c,99d,130c,135b,174d)

L - D lad (22c,25b,55b,157c,186a), led, lid (167b), LLD (42a), lud (100a), Lud (23c,144b)

- LD eld (10b,93c,110b,165d), LLD (42a), old (8a,71a,77c,123c,175b)

LE - lea (56a,97d,114d,185b), Lea (22d), led, lee (74b,144b), Lee (9c, 31c,96a), leg (37d,92b,141d,159d,169c), lei (65b,74c), lek (65c), Leo (36b,c,92d,186d), Ler (23d,28a,b,64b,106c,141a), les (13b, 61a), let (9a,76d,77c,116b,130a,158b,163a), leu (190), lev (33b), lew (190), Lew (96a), lex (90b), ley (190)

L - E lee (74b,144b), Lee (9c,31c,96a), lie (53a,69d,162a), loe (139d), lue (146b), lye (8d,27d,93b)

- LE ale (17c,18c,50c,55d,92d,104c), cle (158d), ele (48c), ile (62a,63b, 158c), ole (24b,29b,113b,152a,158b,d), ule (23a,27d,134c,158c, 168d)

L - F Lif (107d), lof (188)

- LF Alf (96a), elf (54b,154b)

L - G lag (93c,155d), leg (37d,92b,141d,159d,169c), log (64a,128d), lug (27a,45d,47b,73c,136b), Lug (28b)

LI - Lia (82b), lid (167b), lie (53a,69d,162a), Lif (107d), lil (72d), lim (21a), lin (92c,140c,168c,178d), Lin (115d,186c), lip (48b,58b,80a, 131c), lis (54b,58b,60c,62a,92b), Lis (47a), lit, Liv (93b)

280

L - I lai (98b,161b), Lai (24c,d,88c), LCI (21b), lei (65b,74c), loi (62a)

- LI Ali (7b,12a,25c,48b,55a,60c,92d,101a,103a,164a,166b,170d), Eli (18c,d,76c,96a,137a,185a)

L - K lak (38a), lek (65c), Lok (15d,68b)

- LK alk (171b), elk (22c,90d,178a), ilk (31d,54c,86b,136d,139c,140b)

LL - LLB (42a), LLD (42a)

L - L lll (72d)

- LL all (35c,118a,126d,181a), ell (10d,24b,32c,98a), ill (43d,121a,173a, c,d), Ull (7c,68c,146b,164d)

L - M lam (51b,58b,93d,164d,178a), lim (21a), lum (30a)

- LM elm (168c), olm (48c), ulm (49c), Ulm (40d)

L - N lan (37b,d,160b), lin (140c,168c,178d), Lin (115d,186c), Lon (86c, 96a), lyn (140c,178d)

LO - loa (7d,53c,97d,184d), lob (15d,23b,94c,100b,163a,172d), loe (139d), lof (188), log (64a,128d), loi (62a), Lok (15d,68b), Lon (86c, 96a), loo (65a), lop (30c,40a,46b,143a), los (13b,151d), lot (24b, 28d,55a,65d,114a,119c,143c,150d,168a), Lot (6b,73d), Lou (96a, 183d), low (16c,149d), loy (121c,148b,151c,167a)

L - O Lao (80d,88c,146a,161b), Leo (36b,c,92d,186d), loo (65a), Luo (107b), Lwo (107b)

- LO Flo (184c), ILO (184c), ulo (34b,80d)

L - P lap (31b,37d,59b,127a,131d,153d,167d), lip (48b,58b,80a,131c), lop (30c,40a,46b,143a)

- LP alp (24b,103d,115c)

L - R lar (24c,51d,67a,78d,95d,101a,171b), Ler (23d,28a,28b,64b,106c, 141a), Lur (116c)

LS - Lst (21a,b,88b)

L - S las (13b,151d), les (13b,61a), lis (54b,58b,60c,62a,92b), Lis (47a), los (13b,151d), lys (58b,92b)

- LS als (66d,163d), els (140a), ils (62b,d,164b)

L - T lat (24a,33d,106b,118a), let (9a,76d,77c,116b,130a,158b,163a), lit, lot (24b,28d,55a,65d,114a,119c,143c,150d,168a), Lot (6b,73d), Lst (21a,b,88b), lut (189)

- LT alt (66c76c,109c), elt (87a,117c,139d), Olt (41a)

LU - lud (100a), Lud (23c,144b), lue (146b), lug (27a,45d,47b,73c,136b), Lug (28b), lum (30a), Luo (107b), Lur (116c), lut (189), lux (79d)

L - U leu (190), Lou (96a,183d)

- LU flu, ulu (87a)

L - V lav (72d), lev (33b), Liv (93b)

LW - Lwo (107b)

L - W law (26b,33a,40a,48c,60b,85d,91a,111b,134d,155d), lew (190), Lew (96a), low (16c,149d)

L - X lax (93d, 130a), lex (90b), lux (79d)

LY - lye (8d,27d,93b), lyn (140c,178d), lys (58b,92b)

L - Y lay (98b,107d,141d,150b), ley (190), loy (121c,148b,151c,167a)

- LY   **aly** (95d), **Ely** (27c,50b), **fly** (58c,81b,163b,178d), **ply** (59b,90b, 118d,164b,171c,174a,181b,184c), **sly** (13b,38b,64c,81b,132c)

L - Z   **Laz** (27d)

MA -   **maa** (97d,143d), **Mab** (54b,126b,183b), **Mac** (96a,140b,150b), **mad** (10c,82b), **Mae** (183c), **mag** (73b,95b,166c), **Mag** (183d), **Mah** (10b, 57c,102b), **mai** (62a), **mal** (34a,b,44a,52b,62c,122b), **Mal** (94b), **Mam** (192), **man** (29c,60c,64c,65a,142d,161d), **mao** (115b), **Mao** (30b), **map** (27a,29b,54a,98d,160a), **mar** (40b,44a,79a,d,81a,140d), **Mar** (93d), **mas** (34b,55b,119a), **mat** (46d,50d,94d,117c,161d), **Mat** (96a), **mau** (170c,188), **maw** (38b,d,72c,111a,121a,142a,156c), **Max** (96a), **may** (74d), **May** (183c)

M - A   **maa** (97d,143d), **MFA** (42a), **mia** (83c), **mna** (71d,179d), **moa** (19b), **Mya** (31c)

- MA   **ama** (26a,28d,31a,35b,39c,95b,108d,111c,117b,182c), **oma** (158c,d, 170c), **sma** (140b,148d), **Uma** (43a,69b,153d)

M - B   **Mab** (54b,126b,183b), **mib** (8d,96c), **mob** (39a,127a,165b)

M - C   **Mac** (96a,140b,150b)

M - D   **mad** (10c,82b), **mid** (9d,28b,73b), **Mod** (138d), **mud** (6c)

ME -   **mee** (169a), **Meg** (8c,183d), **mel** (77d), **mem** (91c), **men** (38c,116a, 117b,170a), **Men** (94d), **Meo** (27b,80c), **mer** (62c,141a), **mes** (62b), **met** (28d), **meu** (153b), **mew** (25b,27b,50a,55b,72c,74d,101b,141b, 153b)

M - E   **Mae** (183c), **mee** (169a), **Mme.** (166b), **Moe** (96a)

- ME   **ame** (37a,62d,131b), **eme** (38d,70a,140c,172b), **Mme.** (166b), **ume** (11d)

MF -   **MFA** (42a)

M - G   **mag** (73b,95b,166c), **Mag** (183d), **Meg** (8c,183d), **mig** (8d,96c, 145b), **Mig** (118d), **mug** (46b,54a,65a)

MH -   **mho** (49b,173b)

M - H   **Mah** (10b,57c,102b)

MI -   **mia** (83c), **mib** (8d,96c), **mid** (9d,28b,73b), **mig** (8d,96c,145b), **Mig** (118d), **mil** (80b,110c,164d,182d), **Mil** (10a,82b), **mim** (12b), **Min** (29d,68b,113c), **mio** (152c), **mir** (29d,135c,d,166c,176b), **mis** (122b,c,d,185c), **mit** (56c,66d,183b), **mix** (156b)

M - I   **mai** (62a), **Moi** (80d)

- MI   **ami** (61d)

M - L   **mal** (34a,b,44a,52b,62c,122b), **Mal** (94b), **mel** (77d), **mil** (80b,110c, 164d,182d), **Mil** (10a,82b), **mol** (58b,70c), **mul** (188)

MM -   **Mme.** (166b)

M - M   **Mam** (192), **mem** (91c), **mim** (12b), **mom, mum** (30d,95a,146c)

MN -   **mna** (71d,179d)

M - N   **man** (29c,60c,64c,65a,142d,161d), **men** (38c,116a,117b,170a), **Men** (94d), **Min** (29d,68b,113c), **mon** (15d,84b) **Mon** (24c), **mun** (157b)

MO -   **moa** (19b), **mob** (39a,127a,165b), **Mod** (138d), **Moe** (96a), **Moi** (80d), **mol** (58b,70c), **mom, mon** (15d,84b), **Mon** (24c), **moo** (94b), **mop** (160a), **mos** (59b), **mot** (126d,130a,137d,183b), **mow** (32b,40a)

M - O   **mao** (115b), **Mao** (30b), **Meo** (27b,80c), **mho** (49b,173b), **mho** (152c), **moo** (94b), **Mro** (88c)

- MO   **amo** (79a,89c), **omo** (34d)

M - P   **map** (27a,29b,54a,98d,160a), **mop** (160a)

- MP   **amp** (49b,173b), **imp** (42b,127d,174a)

MR -   **Mro** (88c), **Mrs.** (166b), **Mru** (80d,88c)

M - R   **mar** (40b,44a,79a,d,81a,140d), **Mar** (93d), **mer** (62c,141a), **mir** (29d, 135c,d,166c,176b), **mur** (63a,177d)

M - S   **mas** (34b,55b,119a), **mes** (62b), **mis** (122b,c,d,185c), **mos** (59b), **Mrs.** (166b), **Mus** (104a,132c)

- MS   **Ems** (125a,151c)

M - T   **mat** (46d,50d,94d,117c,161d), **Mat** (96a), **met** (28d), **mit** (56c,66d, 183b), **mot** (126d,130a,137d,183b), **mut** (39c), **Mut** (9b,127a)

- MT   **amt** (37d,40d,108a,163c)

MU -   **mud** (6c), **mug** (46b,54a,65a), **mul** (188), **mum** (30d,95a,146c), **mun** (157b), **mur** (63a,177d), **Mus** (104a,132c), **mut** (39c), **Mut** (9b,127a), **muy** (152d,175d)

M - U   **mau** (170c,188), **meu** (153b), **Mru** (80d,88c)

- MU   **emu** (19b,58c,111d), **imu** (15d), **SMU** (40b), **umu** (112a)

M - W   **maw** (38b,d,72c,111a,121a,142a,156c), **mew** (25b,27b,50a,55b,72c, 74d,101b,141b,153b), **mow** (32b,40a)

M - X   **Max** (96a), **mix** (156b)

MY -   **Mya** (31c)

M - Y   **may** (74d), **May** (183c), **muy** (152d,175d)

- MY   **amy** (63c), **Amy** (8c,94b,183c)

NA -   **nab** (13b,26c,27b,142a), **nae** (139d), **nag** (73d,78b,138c,184d), **nak** (156b), **Nan** (183c), **nap** (65a,117d,146b,148a), **nar** (139d), **nas** (74a, 89c,178b), **nat** (7a,24c,d,106a), **nay** (42b,106b)

N - A   **NEA** (162c), **noa** (35b,124a,161a), **NRA** (8a,20d)

- NA   **ana** (10b,33c,60d,93a,98c,122b,d,140d,142b), **Ana** (28a,68d,100c), **Ena** (8c,126b), **ina** (158c), **Ina** (183c), **mna** (71d,179d), **Ona** (26b, 64a), **sna** (105b,140b,143d,144a,149c,181c,d), **Una** (54a,153b, 170c,183c)

N - B   **nab** (13b,26c,27b,142a), **neb** (17b,19a,d,115d), **nib** (17b,19d,115d), **nob** (38c,74d,84a,149d) **nub** (67b,94d,95c,118c,124d)

N - D   **Ned** (96a), **nid** (72a,106c,116d), **nod** (17c,46c), **Nod** (18d,25b)

- ND   **and** (36a), **end** (8b,67d,120a,125d,130a,166a), **Ind** (80c), **und** (66b)

NE -   **N.E.A.** (162c), **neb** (17b,19a,d,115d), **Ned** (96a), **nee** (19d,22b,25c, 60b,95c), **nef** (32b,144c,d), **neo** (34a,b,c,100d,106d,108c,122c,d, 128c), **nep** (27c,32d,56a,87c,184b), **ner** (137c), **nes** (26b), **net** (26c, 32a,50d,53b,60d,99a,124a,142a,149b), **new** (11a,63c,88d,111c, 128c, **Ney** (63b,97b,105d), **nez** (62b)

N - E   **nae** (139d), **nee** (19d,22b,25c,60b,95c), **nie** (53c,66c), **NNE** (35b), **nye** (72a,116d), **Nye** (9c,18b)

- NE   **ane** (61c,140a,158b), **ene** (35b,158b,c), **ine** (29c,158b,c), **Ine** (10c, 137d,180b), **NNE** (35b), **one** (79a,b,80b,d,124b,147a,148d,173a,c), une (13b,61a,62b,95c)

N - F nef (32b,144c,d)

NG - ngu (188)

N- G nag (73d,78b,138c,184d), nig (33b,40a,46a), nog (20c,46a,48d,54d, 100b,115d,118a)

- NG eng (48a,146a), ing (114b,d,148d,158c,d,175c), Ing (10c,115b)

N - H nth (42a)

NI - nib (17b,19d,115d), nid (72a,106c,116d), nie (53c,66c), nig (33b, 40a,46a), nil (108c), nim (96d,155d), nin (107d), nip (20c,29b,45d,46a,b,115c,118a), nis (23d,67d,68a,87c), Nis (19d), nit (48d), nix (23d,108c,178d)

- NI ani (19b,d,20b,39b), ini (158d), oni (11b), uni · (34c,118d,122c), Uni (51d)

N - K nak (156b)

- NK ink (20b,40c)

N - L nil (108c), nul (108c,177a)

N - M nim (96d,155d), nom (62b,125a), Nym (54c,76a)

NN - NNE (35b), NNW (35b)

N - N Nan (183c), nin (107d), non (34c,62b,89c,106b,122c,147a), nun (24c,91c,117d,147b), Nun (29a,85c)

- NN Ann (183c), inn (72b,73b,78c,150a,161c,162b,179a), Inn (41a)

NO - noa (35b,124a,161a), nob (38c,74d,84a,149d), nod (17c,46c,148a), Nod (18d,25b), nog (20c,46a,48d,54d,100b,115d,118a), nom (62b, 125a), non (34c,62b,89c,106b,122c,147a), noo (108c,139d), nor (10b,36a,37b,92b), nos (62b,90a,179a), not (78b,106b), now (60b, 79d), Nox (69b)

N - O neo (34a,b,c,100d,106d,108c,122c,d,128c), noo (108c,139d)

- NO ano (19d,20b,34d,122d,174a), Ino (14b,25b), ono (34a), Ono (18d,118d), uno (83c,151d)

N - P nap (65a,117d,146b,148a), nep (27c,32d,56a,87c,184b), nip (20c, 29b,45d,46a,b,115c,118a)

NR - NRA (8a,20d)

N - R nar (139d), ner (137c), nor (10b,36a,37b,92b), nur (67d)

N - S nas (74a,89c,178b), nes (26b), nis (23d,67d,87c), Nis (19d), nos (62b,90a,179a)

- NS Ans (92a), ens (17d,18a,51a,52d), ins (164d), INS (107a,182d), ons (38c), uns (66d,174c)

NT - nth (42a)

N - T nat (7a,24c,d,106a), net (26c,32a,50b,53d,60d,99a,124a,142a, 149b), nit (48d), not (78b,106b), nut (24c,32d,38b,54d,64a,65d, 86b,141c,165a), Nut (69a)

- NT ant (49d,60b,81b,118c), ent (34d,158b,c), TNT (53a)

NU - nub (67b,94d,95c,118c,124d), nul (108c,177a), nun (24c,91c,117d, 147b), Nun (29a,85c,129d), nur (67d), nut (24c,32d,38b,54d,64a, 65d,86b,141c,165a), Nut (69a)

N - U ngu (188)

- **NU**   **Anu** (15b,28a,68a,d,75b,88c,147d), **gnu** (11a,181d), **Unu** (24d)

N - W   **new** (11a,63c,88d,111c,128c), **NNW** (35b), **now** (60b,79d)

- NW   **NNW** (35b), **WNW** (35b)

N - X   **nix** (23d,108c,178d), **Nox** (69b), **Nyx** (69b)

NY -   **nye** (72a,116d), **Nye** (9c,18b), **Nym** (54c,76a), **Nyx** (69b)

N - Y   **nay** (42b,106b), **Ney** (63b,97b,105d)

- NY   **any** (14b,150b), **ony** (139a), **sny** (18a,39d,43d,87a,119a,144d,145a, 165d,176a)

N - Z   **nez** (62b)

OA -   **oaf** (22a,45b,146d,157d,185d), **oak** (73d,168c,169a), **oar** (20b,124c, 134b), **oat** (15a,28b,70b,144b)

O - A   **oca** (48c,112c,116d,133d,170c,184a), **oda** (74a,170d), **oka** (170c, 184a,189), **ola** (113b) **oma** (158c,d,170c), **Ona** (26b,64a), **OPA** (8a), **ora** (10c,40d,41b,45b,83a,c,101c,104a,122d,123d), **ova** (48d), **oxa** (29c)

- OA   **boa** (36c,55b,106a,125d,138b,142d,149a), **goa** (65d,104b,126c), **Goa** (121c), **hoa** (39b), **koa** (74c), **loa** (7d,53c,184d), **Loa** (97d), **moa** (19b), **noa** (35b,124a,161a), **poa** (20d,70d,97d), **roa** (23d,87a), **toa** (17c,178b), **Zoa** (20b)

OB -   **obe** (31d,87d,150d), **obi** (55d,67b,84c,137b,150d)

O - B   **orb** (50a,53c,67d,153b)

- OB   **bob** (57c,115d), **Bob** (96a), **cob** (28c,78b,95d,160b,177d), **fob** (29b, 59b,113b,178c), **gob** (97b,136c), **hob** (40c,56d,100c,124b,167a, 180c), **job** (30d,184c), **Job** (96a), **kob** (11a), **lob** (15d,23b,94c,100b, 163a,172d), **mob** (39a,127a,165b), **nob** (38c,74d,84a,149d), **pob** (121b,129b,139c), **rob** (119d,155d), **Rob** (96a), **sob** (39b,179d)

OC -   **oca** (48c,112c,116d,133d,170c,184a), **och** (8b), **ock** (189), **oct** (34a, 122c)

O - C   **orc** (28c,70c,180b)

- OC   **Doc** (143a), **roc** (19c,53b,54a,147a), **soc** (44c,85d)

OD -   **oda** (74a,170d), **odd** (46b,53a,109b,157a,172d,173c), **ode** (26b,79c, 94d,118a,119d,120a,150b), **Odo** (181d), **ods** (109a)

O - D   **odd** (46b,53a,109b,157a,172d,173c), **oid** (158c), **old** (8a,71a,77c, 123c,175b), **Ord** (25b,60b)

- OD   **cod** (57b,c), **dod** (11a,32a,43b,140c), **fod** (188), **god** (42a), **God** (84d), **hod** (23b,32d,102d,141a), **Mod** (138d), **nod** (17c,46c), **Nod** (18d,25b), **pod** (76b,78d,91b,141b,180c), **rod** (6a,72d,88b,131a, 154d,156a,160a), **sod** (160b,170d), **tod** (24d,60c,83d), **Vod** (16a)

OE -   **o'er** (6b,112a), **oes** (109a)

O - E   **obe** (31d,87d,150d), **ode** (26b,79c,94d,118a,119d,120a,150b), **oke** (189), **ole** (24b,29b,113b,152a,158b,d), **one** (79a,b,80d,124b,147a, 148d,173a,c), **ope** (172b,173c), **ore** (39a,99b,108a,115b,141c,151a, 160b), **ose** (102a,146d,158b,c,d,159a), **owe, ote** (158d), **oye** (139c)

- OE   **coe** (143d), **Coe** (33c), **doe** (41d,55b,127a), **foe** (111a), **hoe** (39c), **Joe** (96a), **loe** (139d), **Moe** (96a), **poe** (114b), **Poe** (9c,d,128a, 172a), **roe** (27d,41d,48d,57b,76d,95b,157b), **soe** (170c,184a), **toe** (43c,69d,148a,156a), **voe** (17a,81b), **woe** (25b), **Zoe** (36b,183c)

285

OF - off (6b,15c,44c,76a), oft (63c)

O - F oaf (22a,45b,146d,157d,185d), off (6b,15c,44c,76a), orf (57b,185c), ouf (52c)

- OF lof (188)

- OG bog (97a,160a), cog (33a,65d,163b,167c,180c), dog (10b,45b,59b), fog (109b), gog (95b), hog (45b,117c,160c), jog (82c,85c,170a), log (64a,128d), nog (20c,46a,48d,54d,100b,115d,118a), sog (149c), tog (46a), vog (189)

OH - ohm (49b,67a,173b), oho (52c)

O - H och (8b)

- OH boh (24c), doh (113b), foh (52c), Hoh (80d), poh (52c), soh (52c, 72d,) zoh (13d,186b)

OI - oid (158c), oii (105c), oil (11a,71a)

O - I obi (55d,67b,84c,137b,150d), oii (105c), oni (11b), ori (34a), ovi (34a)

- OI goi (107c), hoi (52c,74b,185b), koi (26d), loi (62a), Moi (80d), poi (44a,59c,74c,117a,162a,164b), roi (55c,62a,133d), toi (62b,d,63a), Toi (18d), yoi (52c,79a)

OK - oka (170c,184a,189), oke (189)

O - K oak (73d,168c,169a), ock (189), ork (180b), ouk (140c)

- OK Bok (9c), Lok (15d,68b), Rok (87c), sok (188), yok (10c,185a)

OL - ola (113b), old (8a,71a,77c,123c,175b), ole (24b,29b,113b,152a, 158b,d), olm (48c), Olt (41a)

O - L oil (11a,71a), owl

- OL col (103d,114c), Kol (18b), mol (58b,70c), sol (108b), Sol (117b, 159b), tol (137b), vol (155a,182d)

OM - oma (158c,d,170c), omo (34d)

O - M ohm (49b,67a,173b), olm (48c)

- OM com (122d), dom (121c,166b,c), Dom (94b), mom, nom (62b,125a), pom (45a,148d), rom (72d), tom (95d), Tom (96b,157a), yom (41a)

ON - Ona (26b,64a), one (79a,b,80b,d,124b,147a,148d,173a,c), oni (11b), ono (34a), Ono (18d,118d), ons (38c) ony (139a)

O - N own (6d)

- ON bon (30a,61d,86b,88c), Bon (84b), con (7d,29b,83c,116d,157d), don (151d,166c), Don (96a), eon (8a,37b,51d,116b), Fon (40b), gon (188), ion (11c,29a,49b,101b,114c,158c), Lon (86c,96a), mon (15d,84b), Mon (24c), non (34c,62b,89c,106b,122c,147a), ron (152c), Ron (86c,88a), son (42d,75d), ton (158d,167d,179d), von (66d,67a), won (44c,112a,164d)

OO - oop (139a), oot (140a)

O - O Odo (181d), oho (52c), omo (34d), ono (34a), Ono (18d,118d), oro (34c,122c,152a), Oro (161b), oto (34a) Oto (147b)

- OO boo, coo (19b), Coo (82d), foo (42c), goo (156b), loo (65a), moo (94b), noo (108c,139d), roo (140a), soo (127d,140b,151b), Soo (137c), too (18b,102c), woo, zoo (181b)

OP - OPA (8a), ope (172b,173c), Ops (28c,69a,b,74a,137c), opt (30c)

286

O - P oop (139a), orp (140c,179d)

- OP cop (36a,120c,126d,153c,155d), dop (39c,43b), fop (38a,40d,46d), hop (40b), kop (76d), lop (30c,40a,46b,143a), mop (160a), oop (139a), pop (52d,53a,130b,149d), sop (23b,35d,149c,155d), top (38c,52b,118b,123d,160a,174a,186b), wop

OR - ora (10c,40d,41b,45b,83a,c,101c,104a,122c,123d), orb (50a,53c, 67d,153b), orc (28c,70c,180b), Ord (25b,60b), ore (39a,99b,108a, 115b,141c,151a,160b), orf (57b,185c), ori (34a), ork (180b), oro (34c,122c,152a), Oro (161b), orp (140c,179d), orr (77c), ort (59b, 90d,91a,102c,129b,140d,180a,184d), ory (36c)

O - R oar (20b,124c,134b), oer (6b,112a), orr (77c), our (124c)

- OR Bor (120c), cor (36c,75b,155b), dor (17d,24b,32b,46b,47a,81b,85d), for (123d,163a,166c), Gor (81a), Hor (103d), ior (50a,158c), kor (75c), nor (10b,36a,37b,92b), por (152a), tor (38b,76d,85d,115c, 124b,132b,c), Vor (69a)

OS - ose (102a,146d,158b,c,d,159a), ost (15d,86b)

O - S ods (109a), oes (109a), ons (38c), Ops (28c,69a,b,74a,137c), ous (158b)

- OS Bos (27c), cos (91d,132d), dos (45d,61a,97a,181b), Eos (14d,41a, 68d), ios (74d), Kos (77c,82d), los (13b,151d), mos (59b), nos (62b, 90a,179a), ros (37b), Ros (138a,174d), SOS

OT - ote (158d), oto (34a), Oto (147b)

O - T oat (15a,28b,70b,144b), oct (34a,122c), oft (63c), Olt (41a), oot (140a), opt (30c), ort (59b,90d,91a,102c,129b,140d,180a,184d), ost (15d,86b), out (6b,14b,60b,69d,80a,108b,185c)

- OT bot (59a,88d), cot (129b,148b), dot (45d,97a,104d,105a,116b,153a, 162d), fot (188), got, hot (10c,176c), jot (82a,114c,166c,180d), lot (24b,28d,55a,65d,114a,119c,143c,150d,168a), Lot (6b,73d), mot (126d,130a,137d,183b), not (78b,106b), oot (140a), pot (120b, 145b,154d,175d), rot (22b,134c,143d,153d), sot (46c,167b,c), tot (186a), Vot (56d)

OU - ouf (52c), ouk (140c), our (124c), ous (158b), out (6b,14b,60b,69d, 80a,108b,185c)

- OU fou (139a), IOU (124b), kou (169a), Lou (96a,183d), sou (63b), you

OV - ova (48d), ovi (34a)

OW - owe, owl, own (6d)

- OW bow (11c,21b,39d,60a,107c,109a,125a,144d,158a), cow (22c,45b, 81d), dow (17d,87a,88d,175d), how, jow (188), low (16c,149d), mow (32b,40a), now (60b,79d), pow, row (44c,56b,92c,109a,126b, 127d,165c), sow (45b,117c,119a,138b,160c), tow (45d,58b,75d, 125b), vow (119c,150a), wow (52c,158a), yow (52c)

OX - oxa (29c)

- OX box (36a,c,128c,145d,152d), cox (156a), fox (134a), Nox (69b), pox (44a), vox (90a,177a)

OY - oye (139c)

O - Y ony (139a), ory (36c)

- OY boy (142d,157c), coy (16d), goy (107c), hoy (16c,52c), joy, loy (121c,148b,151c,167a), Roy, soy (17b,137c,74d), toy (169d)

- OZ   **Boz** (43b,115d), **coz, goz** (190)

PA -   **pab** (139c), **pac** (73b,94c,100d), **pad** (39d,59c,76c,157d,161a,168b), **pah** (52c,60b,106d), **pal** (35b,38d), **pam** (26c,65a,87a,105b), **pan** (34a,61a,104a,175d), **Pan** (56a,68a,b,76b,120c,135b,161a,184a), **pap** (59c), **par** (15a,51a,b,c,69d,107c,135b,155a), **pas** (40d,156a), **pat** (11d,116d,159a,161d,167c), **Pat** (96a), **Pau** (48c,76a,130c), **paw** (32d,59c,73c), **pax** (89d,115b), **pay** (35b,128c,130a,d,177b)

P - A   **pea** (32d,91b,142a,175a), **pia** (13b,22d,48a,120d), **poa** (20d, 70d,97d), **pta** (6a), **pua** (74c,76a)

- PA   **apa** (23a,177d), **OPA** (8a), **spa** (75b,100b,130c,154b,178d)

P - B   **pab** (139c), **pob** (121b,129b,139c)

P - C   **pac** (73b,94c,100d), **pic** (188)

P - D   **pad** (39d,59c,76c,157d,161a,168b), **ped** (16d,34b), **pod** (76b,78d, 91b,141b,180c), **pud** (59d,73c,115a)

PE -   **pea** (32d,91b,142a,175a), **ped** (16d,34b), **pee** (91c), **peg** (38c,46b, 54d,98a,118a,184c), **pel** (55c,160d), **pen** (36a,50a,80d,118b,126d, 160a,185c), **pep** (50b,176b), **per** (25c,122d,165b,176a), **pes** (59d), **pet** (26d,37c,55a,59b,162d), **peu** (62a), **pew** (30d,52c,57d,120b, 141c)

P - E   **pee** (91c), **pie** (42d,85d,95b,114d,171b,172a), **poe** (114b), **Poe** (9c, d,128a,172a), **pre** (17d,122b,c), **pue** (52c), **Pye** (50d,55a)

- PE   **ape** (36d,79d,100a,101d,146d), **ope** (172b,173c)

P - G   **peg** (38c,46b,54d,98a,118a,184c), **pig** (27a,45b,99a,151b,160c), **pug** (45a,101a,108a,148d)

PH -   **phi** (91c), **phu** (38c)

P - H   **pah** (52c,60b,106d), **poh** (52c)

PI -   **pia** (13b,22d,48a,120d), **pic** (188), **pie** (42d,85d,95b,114d, 171b,172a), **pig** (27a,45b,99a,151b,160c), **pik** (188), **pil** (34b), **pin** (45d,54d,141d,147d), **pip** (11d,44a,121d,142a,154a), **Pip** (43b), **pir** (103a,b,136c), **pit** (52b,142a,164a,168a) **piu** (102c), **pix** (31a,51d, 175d)

P - I   **phi** (91c), **poi** (44a,59c,74c,117a,162a,164b), **psi** (91c)

- PI   **api** (34a,76d), **epi** (56c,61c,d,111c,112d,122d,133c,153c,167b, 174a), **UPI** (107a,182d)

P - K   **pik** (188)

PL -   **ply** (59b,90b,118d,164b,171c,174a,181b,184c)

P - L   **pal** (35b,38d), **pel** (55c,160d), **pil** (34b), **pul** (190), **Pul** (14a)

P - M   **pam** (26b,65a,87a,105b), **pom** (45a,148d)

P - N   **pan** (34a,61a,104a,175d), **Pan** (56a,68a,b,76b,120c,135b,161a, 184a), **pen** (36a,50a,80d,118b,126d,160a,185c), **pin** (45d,54d,141d, 147d), **pun** (119c)

PO -   **poa** (20d,70d,97d), **pob** (121b,129b,139c), **pod** (76b,78d,91b,141b, 180c), **poe** (114b), **Poe** (9c,d,128a,172a), **poh** (52c), **poi** (44a,59c, 74c,117a,162a,164b), **pom** (45a,148d), **pop** (52d,53a,130b,149d), **por** (152a), **pot** (120b,145b,154d,175d), **pow, pox** (44a)

P - O   **pro** (59d,126d), **Pwo** (88c)

- PO apo (122b), Apo (177c)

P - P pap (59c), pep (50b,176b), pip (11d,44a,121d,154a), Pip (43b), pop (52d,53a,130b,149d), pup (141b,148d,185d)

PR - pre (17d,122b,c), pro (59d,126d), pry (52b,91d,98b,123d)

P - R par (15a,51a,b,c,69d,107c,135b,155a), per (25c,122d,165b,176a), pir (103a,b,136c), por (152a), pur, pyr (92a,b,122c,173b)

PS - psi (91c), pst (25c,126d,146c)

P - S pas (40d,156a), pes (59d), pus

- PS Ops (28c,69a,b,74a,137c)

PT - Pta (6a)

P - T pat (11d,116d,159a,161d,167c), Pat (96a), pet (26d,37c,55a,59b, 162d), pit (52b,142a,164a,168a), pot (120b,145b,154d,175d), pst (25c,126d,146c), put (65a,69d,90b)

- PT apt (11d,23b,32b,58a,80b,92b,114d,116d,124b,159a), opt (30c)

PU - pua (74c,76a), pud (59d,73c,115a), pue (52c), pug (45a,101a,108a, 148d), pul (190), Pul (14a), pun (119c), pup (141b,148d,185d), pur, pus, put (65a,69d,90b), puy (61d)

P - U Pau (48c,76a,130c), peu (62a), phu (38c), piu (102c)

PW - Pwo (88c)

P - W paw (32d,59c,73c), pew (30d,52c,57d,120b,141c), pow

P - X pax (89d,115b), pix (31a,51d,175d), pox (44a), pyx (31a,51d,175d)

PY - Pye (50d,55a), pyr (92a,b,122c,173b), pyx (31a,51d,175d)

P - Y pay (35b,128c,130a,d,177b), ply (59b,90b,118d,164b,171c,174a, 181b,184c), pry (52b,91d,98b,123d), puy (61d)

- PY spy (44a,51c,52b,141d)

QA - Qaf (104a)

Q - A qua (13c,80a,89c,147a)

Q - E que (62d)

Q - F Qaf (104a)

Q - I qui (62d)

Q - O quo (188)

QU - qua (13c,80a,89c,147a), que (62d), qui (62d), quo (188)

RA - rab (17c,75c,85b,102d,162c,166b), Rab (45a), rad (50b,138d,173b), rae (136b,138d,140b), Rae (183c), rag (59b,77c,100c,133c,161a), rah (29b), rai (188), raj (129c), ram (17a,45b,50b,79c,112b,121d, 143d,157d), Ram (36b), ran (73d), Ran (7c,107d,141a,163d), rap (90d,110a,147c,157c), ras (6c,26b,48b,51d,53d,61c,75a,111c,123c, 166b), rat (16a,42d,73b,132c), raw (20c,39a,105d,173d), ray (38a, 49a,57b,58b,147b), Ray (96a)

R - A rea (9c,171a), ria (38c,51d,81b,152a,b), roa (23d,87a), rua (118c), Rua (16b)

- RA ara (33a,114a,116a,118b,163d), Ara (9b,18c,36b,c,68d,69b,c,85a, 95a,175b), dra (188), era (8a,51a,116b,165d), fra (23c,63c,101d, 123b,129d), gra (59b,94b,160c), Ira (18c,d,41a,68c,82c,96a,164a, 178a,c), Kra (11b,91d), NRA (8a,20d), ora (10c,40d,41b,45b,83a,c,

289

101c,104a,122d,123d), **tra** (33b)

R - B   **rab** (17c,75c,85b,102d,162c,166b), **Rab** (45a), **reb** (35d,75c,85b, 162c,166b), **rib** (37c,85b,90c,98a,144d,159d,172a), **rob** (119d, 155d), **Rob** (96a), **rub** (6b,24d,28c,43c,120c,179b)

- RB   **orb** (50a,53c,67d,153b)

R - C   **roc** (19c,53b,54a,147a)

- RC   **arc** (31b,39d,92a,126a,127c,142a), **orc** (28c,70c,180b)

R - D   **rad** (50b,138d,173b), **red** (33c,38d,59a,127b,134c,135b), **Red** (151b), **rid** (32a,44a,60d), **rod** (6a,72d,88b,131a,154d,156a,160a), **rud** (26d,57b)

- RD   **erd** (47d,119d,145c), **Ord** (25b,60b), **urd** (17b,184b), **Urd** (68d,107d)

RE -   **rea** (9c,171a), **reb** (35d,75c,85b,162c,166b), **red** (33c,38d,59a,127b, 134c,135b), **Red** (151b), **ree** (12c,50a,80c,134d,137a,140b,144a, 146b), **Ree** (25a), **ref, reh** (8d), **rei** (89b,121c), **Rei** (18d), **rel** (49b, 173b), **Reo** (26c), **rep** (53b,d,131a,171c), **res** (80a,89d,91a,97c), **ret** (58b,95a,149c,155d), **Reu** (115d), **rev, rew** (75c,140c,176b), **rex** (86c,96a), **rey** (86c,152b)

R - E   **rae** (136b,138d,140b), **Rae** (183c), **ree** (12c,50a,80c,134d,137a, 140b,144a,146b), **Ree** (25a), **rhe** (59a,173b), **rie** (28c,70d,97c), **roe** (27d,41d,48d,57b,76d,95b,157b), **rue** (76a,b,129c,150d,183a), **rye** (28b,70b,72d,92d)

- RE   **are** (51a,88b,98a,99b,110c,166c,175c), **ere** (17d,150c), **ire** (10c, 52b,30c,64c,125a,130b,185a), **ore** (39a,99b,108a,115b,141c,151a, 160b), **pre** (17d,122b,c), **tre** (37b,83c,122d,165a,167d), **ure** (40a, 139d,155d,158b,d), **Ure** (138d,185d)

R - F   **ref, rif** (188)

- RF   **orf** (57b,185c)

R - G   **rag** (59b,77c,100c,133c,161a), **rig** (51b,112a), **rug**

- RG   **erg** (50b,173b,184c)

RH -   **rhe** (59a,173b), **rho** (71b,91c)

R - H   **rah** (29b), **reh** (8d)

RI -   **ria** (38c, 51d, 81b, 152a, b), **rib** (37c, 85b, 90c, 98a, 144d, 159d,172a), **rid** (32a,44a,60d), **rie** (28c,70d,97d), **rif** (188), **rig** (51b, 112a), **rii** (157b,175b), **rim** (22a,48b,96d),116b,124b,166a,180c), **rin** (33b,142b), **rio** (33a,131d,132a,152c,157b), **Rio** (23a), **rip** (87b, 130a,162c), **Rip** (178b), **ris** (131d), **rit** (140b,148c,153d)

R - I   **rai** (188), **rei** (89b,121c), **Rei** (18d), **rii** (157b,175b), **roi** (55c,62a, 133d)

- RI   **Ari** (18d), **eri** (13d,21c,146d), **Eri** (18c), **gri** (75c,78b), **Iri** (18a,d, 75a), **kri** (75c,96d), **ori** (34a), **sri** (60c,77b,166c), **Sri** (17c), **tri** (122d,169d), **Uri** (162d)

R - J   **raj** (129c)

R - K   **Rok** (87c)

- RK   **ark** (21a,29d,38a,58b,60d,175d), **irk** (10d), **ork** (180b)

R - L   **rel** (49b,173b)

R - M   **ram** (17a,45b,50b,79c,112b,121d,143d,157d), **Ram** (36b), **rim** (22a,

48b,96d,116b,124b,166a,180c), **rom** (72d), **rum** (8c,92d)

- RM   **arm** (22d,60c,81b,92b,124b,161b)

R - N   **ran** (73d), **Ran** (7c,107d,141a,163d), **rin** (33b),142b), **ron** (152c), **Ron** (86c,88a), **run** (10d,23c,58d,110d,148d,153b,154b,167d)

- RN   **arn** (8c,139a), **ern** (19c,d,47b,54b,141a), **urn** (36c,174d)

RO -   **roa** (23d,87a), **rob** (119d,155d), **Rob** (96a), **roc** (19c,53b,54a,147a), **rod** (6a,72d,88b,131a,154d,156a,160a), **roe** (27d,41d,48d,57b,76d, 95b,157b), **roi** (55c,62a,133d), **Rok** (87c), **rom** (72d), **ron** (152c), **Ron** (86c,88a), **roo** (140a) **ros** (37b), **Ros** (138a,174d), **rot** (22b, 134c,143d,153d), **row** (44 ,56b,92c,109a,126b,127d,165c), **Roy**

R - O   **Reo** (26c), **rho** (71b,91c), **rio** (33a,131d,132a,152c,157b), **Rio** (23a), **roo** (140a)

- RO   **Aro** (107a,111c), **cro** (104c,115b,180a), **fro** (15b), **Mro** (88c), **oro** (34c,122c,152a), **Oro** (161b), **pro** (59d,126d), **S.R.O.** (6a,164a), **Uro** (192)

R - P   **rap** (90d,110a,147c,157c), **rep** (53b,d,131a,171c), **rip** (87b, 130a,162c), **Rip** (178b)

- RP   **orp** (140c,179d)

R - R   **rur** (132b)

- RR   **err** (21a,43a,67d,100c,d,147a,148b,157b,168b,178a), **grr** (52c), **orr** (77c)

R - S   **ras** (6c,26b,48b,51d,53d,61c,75a,111c,123c,166b), **res** (80a,89d, 91a,97c,164c), **ris** (131d), **ros** (37b), **Ros** (138a,174d), **rus** (89b), **Rus** (138a)

- RS   **ars** (13b,89a), **Ars** (112c), **ers** (20a,176a), **Mrs.** (166b)

R - T   **rat** (16a,42d,73b,132c), **ret** (58b,95a,149c,155d), **rit** (140b,148c, 153d), **rot** (22b,134c,143d,153d), **rut** (73a)

- RT   **art** (22d,38b,39c,43b,56c,124a,162c,181d), **ert** (140c,174a), **ort** (59b,90d,91a,102c,129b,140d,180a,184d)

RU -   **rua** (118c), **Rua** (16b), **rub** (6b,24d,28c,43c,120c,179b), **rud** (26d, 57b), **rue** (76a,b,129c,150d,183a), **rug, rum** (8c,92d), **run** (10d,23c, 58d,110d,148d,153b,154b,167d), **rur** (132b), **rus** (89b), **Rus** (138a), **rut** (73a), **rux** (154a,184d)

R - U   **Reu** (115d)

- RU   **aru** (80c,82b), **Aru** (82d), **cru** (63a,176c), **Kru** (91d), **Mru** (80d,88c), **Uru** (192)

R - V   **rev**

R - W   **raw** (20c,39a,105d,173d), **rew** (75c,140c,176b), **row** (44c,56b,92c, 109a,126b,127d,165c)

R - X   **rex** (86c,96a), **rux** (154a,184d)

RY -   **rye** (28b,70b,72d,92d)

R - Y   **ray** (38a,49a,57b,58b,147b), **Ray** (96a), **rey** (86c,152b), **Roy**

- RY   **cry** (25c,124a,145c,179d), **dry** (46d,85a,137c,164c), **ery** (155d,158c, d), **fry** (57d), **gry** (78b), **ory** (36c), **pry** (52b,91d,98b,123d), **try** (7c, 10d,14c,50a,51c,130a), **wry** (13d)

SA -   **saa** (98a), **sac** (15d,121d), **Sac** (80c), **sad** (29c,42c,94c,98c,104a,

150d,173a), **sae** (140b,149c), **sag** (46b), **sah** (188), **sai** (101d), **saj** (48a,169a), **sak** (37c), **Sak** (88c), **sal** (29c,48a,136d,149d,152d, 169a,183a), **Sal** (183d), **Sam** (96a,162a), **san** (91c), **San** (24d), **sao** (141b) , **Sao** (113c), **sap** (45d,52d,85c,169b,176d,179a), **sar** (57d), **sat** (13d), **saw** (7a,11b,40c,54c,97d,125a,137d,167a), **sax** (40c,148a,167a), **say** (131c,174c,177a)

S - A   **saa** (98a), **sea** (19a,52d,58c,112c,178d), **sha** (110c,143d,144a,c, 174c,181c), **sia** (80c), **sma** (140b,148d), **sna** (105b,140b,143d,144a, 149c,181c,d), **spa** (75b,100b,130c,154b,178d), **sta** (13c,91b,104d, 105a), **sua** (89d),

- SA   **Asa** (6a,18c,71a,84d,86d,164c), **ESA** (8a)

S - B   **Seb** (47d), **sib** (86b,129c,139d,147b), **sob** (39b,179d), **sub** (90a, 122d,172c)

S - C   **sac** (15d,121d), **Sac** (80c), **sec** (46c,182c), **sic** (90a,165b,168b), **soc** (44c,85d)

- SC   **BSC** (42a)

S - D   **sad** (29c,42c,94c,98c,104a,150d,173a), **sed** (89a), **Sid** (96a), **sod** (160b,170d), **sud** (59a)

SE -   **sea** (19a,52c,58c,112c,178d), **Seb** (47d), **sec** (46c,182c), **sed** (89a), **see** (20a,43c,44a,51c,53c,93d,109b,113c,116a,176d,178c,183b), **sel** (62c,140b), **Sem** (107c), **sen** (190) **ser** (80d,83b,d,116c, 152d,180a), **ses** (61d), **set** (7b,11d,13a,23c,32b,33c,37c,58a,73d, 109b,118c,121c,142c,150a,186a), **Set** (52b,68a,b,111d), **sew, sex, sey** (120c)

S - E   **sae** (140b,149c), **see** (20a,43c,44a,51c,53c,109b,113c,116a,176d, 178c,183b), **she** (124b), **She** (73a), **sie** (46c,66d,139b,140b,146b), **soe** (170c,184a), **SSE** (35b), **ste** (62c,136c), **sue** (119c), **Sue** (63a, 178a,183d), **sye** (40c,46c,139b,141a,167a)

- SE   **ase** (51a,139a), **Ase** (79b,115d), **ese** (35b,158c), **ise** (40d,158c,d), **Ise** (78a,84c), **ose** (102a,146d,158b,c,d,159a), **SSE** (35b), **use** (7b, 47a,49d,64c,109b,168b,c,181b)

S - F   **Sif** (164d)

S - G   **sag** (46b), **sog** (149c)

SH -   **sha** (110c,143d,144a,c,174c,181c), **she** (124b), **She** (73a), **sho** (188), **Shu** (30b,127a), **shy** (16d,99d,128c,160c,165d,175a)

S - H   **sah** (188), **soh** (52c,72d)

- SH   **ash** (24d,33c,49c,73d,134b,168c,169a), **hsh** (79c), **ish** (158b), **ush**

SI -   **Sia** (80c), **sib** (86b,129c,139d,147b), **sic** (90a,165b,168b), **Sid** (96a), **sie** (46c,66d,139b,140b,146b), **Sif** (164d), **sil** (30c,185c,d), **Sim** (96b), **sin** (91c,140b,147a,168b,176a), **Sin** (102b), **sip** (46b,79d, 104a,162b), **sir** (87a,163b,166b), **sis** (67b,129c), **sit** (98c,116a,121c, 130c,142d), **six** (26c)

S - I   **sai** (101d), **Sia** (80c), **ski** (149c), **sri** (60c,77b,166c), **Sri** (17c), **sui** (30b)

- SI   **asi** (137a), **psi** (91c)

S - J   **saj** (48a,169a)

SK -   **ski** (149c), **sky** (56d)

S - K sak (37c), Sak (88c), sok (188), Suk (107b)

- SK ask (38b,82a,126c)

SL - sly (13b,38b,64c,81b,132c)

S - L sal (29c,48a,136d,149d,152d,169a,183a), Sal (183d), sel (62c, 140b), sil (30c,185c,d), sol (108b), Sol (117b,159b)

SM - sma (140b,148d), SMU (40b)

S - M Sam (96a,162a), Sem (107c), Sim (96b), sum (8a,123a,167c)

- SM ism (45a,79b,161c)

SN - sna (105b,140b,143d,144a,149c,181c), sny (18a,39d,43d,87a,119a, 144d,145a,165d,176a)

S - N san (91c), San (24d), sen (190), sin (91c,140b,147a,168b,176a), Sin (102b), son (42d,75d), sun (75d,111a,117b,155b), syn (122d,183b)

SO - sob (39b,179d), soc (44c,85d), sod (160b,170d), soe (170c,184a), sog (149c), soh (52c,72d), sok (188), sol (108b) Sol (117b,159b), son (42d,75d), soo (127d,140b,151b), Soo (137c), sop (23b,35d, 149c,155d), SOS, sot (46c,167b,c), sou (63b), sow (45b,117c,119a, 138b,160c), soy (17b,137c,174d)

S - O sao (141b), Sao (113c), sho (188), soo (127d,140b,151b), Soo (137c), S.R.O. (6a,164a)

- SO Aso (84c), DSO (99d), eso (34d,183b), iso (34a,122c,d)

SP - spa (75b,100b,130c,154b,178d), spy (44a,51c,52b,141d)

S - P sap (45d,52d,85c,169b,176d,179a), sip (46b,79d,104a,162b), sop (23b,35d,149c,155d), sup (46b,104a,162b)

- SP asp (7b,32b,149a,174a,176c), e.s.p. (147b)

S - Q suq (22a,97a)

SR - sri (60c,77b,166c), Sri (17c), S.R.O. (6a,164a)

S - R sar (57d), ser (80d,83b,d,116c,152d,180a), sir (87a,163b,166b), sur (34a,62b,d,104b,151a,152d,174a)

SS - SSE (35b), ssu (189), SSW (35b)

S - S ses (61d), sis (67b,129c), SOS, sus (117c), Sus (160c,181b)

- SS ass (17b,20c,45b,c,59c,110c,112b,146d,157d), ess (39d,78a,91c, 158c,184d)

ST - sta (13c,91b,104d,105a), ste (62c,136c), sty (50a,53c)

S - T sat (13d), set (7b,11d,13a,23c,32b,33c,37c,58a,73d,109b,118c, 121c,142c,150a,186a), Set (52b,68a,b,111d), sit (98c,116a,121c, 130c,142d), sot (46c,167b,c)

- ST est (50a,61c,62a,79b,89c,158d,159c), ist (7b,34b,43a,59b,66c,158b, c,d), LST (21a,88b), ost (15d,86b), pst (25c,126d,146c), tst (81d, 126d)

SU - sua (89d), sub (90a,122d,172c), sud (59a), sue (119c), Sue (63a, 178a,183d), Sui (30b), Suk (107b), sum (8a,123a,167c), sun (75d, 111a,117b,155b), sup (46b,104a,162b), suq (22a,97a), sur (34a,62b, d,104b,151a,152d,174a), sus (117c), Sus (160c,181b)

S - U Shu (30b,127a), SMU (40b), sou (63b), ssu (189)

- SU ssu (189)

S - W saw (7a,11b,40c,54c,97d,125a,137d,167a), **sew, sow** (45b,117c, 119a,138b,160c), **SSW** (35b)

- SW SSW (35b), **WSW** (35b)

S - X sax (40c,148a,167a), **sex, six** (26c)

SY - sye (40c,46c,139b,141a,167a), **syn** (122d,183b)

S - Y say (131c,174c,177a), **sey** (120c), **shy** (16d,99d,128c,160c,165d, 175a), **sky** (56d), **sly** (13b,38b,64c,81b,132c), **sny** (18a,39d,43d,87a, 119a,144d,145a,165d,176a), **soy** (17b,137c,174d), **spy** (44a,51c, 52b,141d), **sty** (50a,53c)

TA - taa (112d), **tab** (29b,39c,58b,86a,128d,145a), **tac** (34d,130a), **tad** (22c,174a,186a), **tae** (138d,140c,166c,d), **tag** (45a,54c,65a,87b, 144a), **tai** (84b,111c,121b), **Tai** (80d), **taj** (75a,97d), **tal** (40c,77a, 113b), **tam** (74d), **tan** (23d,33c,46a,72d,90d), **tao** (10d,131c, 170b), **Tao** (117a), **tap** (55a,114d,153c), **tar** (8c,68a,94d,111c,118c, 136a,c,176d), **tat** (43b,48c,72d,87c), **Tat** (82a), **tau** (71b,91c,136c, 161a), **tav** (91c), **taw** (90d,91c,96c,d,145b,161d), **tax** (13a,14a,80a, 91d)

T - A taa (112d), **tea** (13d,18c,79c,81a,145d,149c,159d), **tia** (151d), **toa** (17c,178b), **tra** (33b), **tua** (117a)

- TA ata (58d,97d,158d,160c,173d), **Ata** (79c,80d,94d,95d,100a,106b, 117a), **eta** (71a,84c,91c), **Ita** (51b,71d,94d,95d,106b,117a), **ITA** (173a), **Pta** (6a), **sta** (13c,91b,104d,105a), **uta** (53c,84d,93b,147c, 150b)

T - B tab (29b,39c,58b,86a,128d,145a), **tub** (21a,27a,36c,174d)

TC - tch (52c), **tck** (52c)

T - C tac (34d,130a), **tec** (43a), **tic** (104d,153a,171c,d)

- TC etc (10b)

T - D tad (174a,186a), **ted** (74d,138b,154b), **Ted** (96b), **tod** (24d,60c,83d)

TE - tea (13d,18c,79c,81a,145d,149c,159d), **tec** (43a), **ted** (74d,138b, 154b), **Ted** (96b), **tee** (39d,52b,69d,91c,112d,115d,118b,172a), **teg** (45a,54b,143d,144a,171d), **tel** (34a,b,122c), **Tem** (143a,159b), **ten** (19a,26c,41c,42b), **ter** (34d,122d,165a), **tez** (125c)

T - E tae (138d,140c,166c,d), **tee** (39d,52b,69d,91c,112d,115d,118b, 172a), **the** (13b), **tie** (10a,14c,38b,45d,51a,88d,109b,127c,138b, 170b), **toe** (43c,69d,148a,156a), **tre** (37b,83c,122d,165a,167d), **tue** (114b), **tye** (28c,134a)

- TE ate (81a,108c,158c,174c), **Ate** (20c,68b,d,69a,b,116c,186b), **ete** (36c,62d,141c,159b), **ite** (59b,81a,105d,130c,158b,c,d,161a), **ote** (158d), **ste** (62c,136c), **Ute** (145c,180b)

T - G tag (45a,54c,65a,87b,144a), **teg** (45a,54b,143d,144a,171d), **tig** (46b), **tog** (46a), **tug** (45d,125b), **tyg** (46b)

TH - the (13b), **tho** (52a), **Tho** (167a), **thy**

T - H tch (52c)

- TH eth (91c,158d), **Ith** (10a,28a,82b,99d), **nth** (42a)

TI - tia (151d), **tic** (104d,153a,171c,d), **tie** (10a,14c,38b,45d, 51a,88d,109b,127c,138b,170b), **tig** (46b), **til** (142d), **Tim** (43b), **tin** (36c,99a,b,108b,155a,179c), **tio** (152d), **tip** (26b,d,50a,70d,77b,78a,

294

120a,165d), **tir** (61d,62c,145b), **tis, tit** (19c,130d), **Tiu** (7c,68c, 147d,163d,166c,170c), **Tiw** (68c,147d,163d)

T - I   **tai** (84b,111c,121b), **Tai** (80d), **tji** (189), **toi** (62b,d,63a), **Toi** (18d), **tri** (122d,169d), **tui** (47c,114b,117a), **Twi** (69c)

- TI   **ati** (106d,107a), **Ati** (45d,106b,113c,117a)

TJ -   **tji** (189)

T - J   **taj** (75a,97d)

TK -   **TKO** (22c)

T - K   **tck** (52c)

T - L   **tal** (40c,77a,113b), **tel** (34a,b,122c), **til** (142d), **tol** (137b)

T - M   **tam** (74d), **Tem** (143a,159b), **Tim** (43b), **tom** (95d), **Tom** (96b, 157a), **tum** (26d), **Tum** (143a,159b)

TN -   **TNT** (53a)

T - N   **tan** (23d,33c,46a,72d,90d), **ten** (19a,26c,41c,42b), **tin** (36c,99a,b, 108b,155a,179c), **ton** (158d,167d,179d), **tun** (23b,27a,182b)

TO -   **toa** (17c,178b), **tod** (24d,60c,83d), **toe** (43c,69d,148a,156a), **tog** (46a), **toi** (62b,d,63a), **Toi** (18d), **tol** (137b), **tom** (95d), **Tom** (96b, 157a), **ton** (158d,167d,179d), **too** (18b,102c), **top** (38c,52b,118b, 123d,160a,174a,186b), **tor** (38b,76d,85d,115c,124b,132b,c), **tot** (186a), **tow** (45d,58b,75d,125b), **toy** (169d)

T - O   **tao** (10d,131c,170b), **Tao** (117a), **tho** (52a), **Tho** (167a), **tio** (152d), **TKO** (22c), **too** (18b,102c), **two** (26c,37d,80a,93a)

- TO   **ETO** (184d), **Ito** (84a,c,186d), **oto** (34a), **Oto** (147b)

T - P   **tap** (55a,114d,153c), **tip** (26b,d,50a,70d,77b,78a,120a,165d), **top** (38c,52b,118b,123d,160a,174a,186b), **tup** (115a,117d,127d,143d)

TR -   **tra** (33b), **tre** (37b,83c,122d,165a,167d), **tri** (122d,169d), **try** (7c, 10d,14c,50a,51c,130a)

T - R   **tar** (8c,68a,94d,111c,118c,136a,c,176d), **ter** (34d,122d,165a), **tir** (61d,62c,145b), **tor** (38b,76d,85d,115c,124b,132b,c), **tur** (14d,27c, 68a,79b,117d,174c), **tyr** (7c,68c,147d,163d,170c,178a)

TS -   **tst** (81d,126d)

T - S   **tis**

- TS   **its** (124c)

T - T   **tat** (43b,48c,72d,87c), **Tat** (82a), **tit** (19c,130d), **TNT** (53a), **tot** (186a), **tst** (81d,126d), **tut** (52c)

- TT   **att** (146a)

TU -   **tua** (117a), **tub** (21a,27a,36c,174d), **tue** (114b), **tug** (45d,125b), **tui** (47c,114b,117a), **tum** (26d), **Tum** (143a,159b), **tun** (23b,27a, 182b), **tup** (115a,117d,127d,143d), **tur** (14d,27c,68a,79b,117d, 174c), **tut** (52c)

T - U   **tau** (71b,91c,136c,161a), **Tiu** (7c,68c,147d,163d,166c,170c)

- TU   **utu** (35b,137c), **Utu** (96c,107a,159b)

T - V   **tav** (91c)

TW -   **Twi** (69c), **two** (26c,37d,80a,93a)

T - W   **taw** (90d,91c,96c,d,145b,161d), **Tiw** (68c,147d,163d), **tow** (45d, 58b,75d,125b)

T - X   **tax** (13a,14a,80a,91d)

TY -   **tye** (28c,134a), **tyg** (46b), **Tyr** (7c,68c,109c,147d,163d,170c,178a)

T - Y   **thy, toy** (169d), **try** (7c,10d,14c,50a,51c,130a)

- TY   **sty** (50a,53c)

T - Z   **tez** (125c)

U - A   **Uca** (56a), **ula** (72c,158c), **Uma** (43a,69b,153d), **Una** (54a,153b, 170c,183c), **uta** (53c,84d,93b,147c,150b), **uva** (64a,70c)

- UA   **dua** (122d), **Kua** (95c), **pua** (74c,76a), **qua** (13c,80a,89c,147a), **rua** (118c), **Rua** (16b), **sua** (89d), **tua** (117a)

UB -   **ube** (185b), **ubi** (90a,180d,185b)

- UB   **bub** (22c), **cub** (92d,185d), **dub** (25c,46a,c,87a,105b,121a,140a), **fub** (29b,119d), **hub** (28b,118b,180c), **nub** (67b,94d,95c,118c 124d), **rub** (6b,24d,28c,43c,120c,179b), **sub** (90a,122d,172c), **tub** (21a,27a,36c,174d)

UC -   **Uca** (56a)

- UC   **duc** (61c)

UD -   **Udi** (108a), **udo** (28a,30c,48c,84b,c,d,136c,149d)

U - D   **und** (66b), **urd** (17b,184b), **Urd** (68d,107d)

- UD   **bud** (22c), **cud** (126c,135a), **dud** (21c,54a), **lud** (100a), **Lud** (23c, 144b), **mud** (6c), **pud** (59d,73c,115a), **rud** (26d,57b), **sud** (59a)

U - E   **ube** (185b), **ule** (23a,27d,134c,158c,168d), **ume** (11d), **une** (13b, 61a,62b,95c), **ure** (40a,139d,155d,158b,d), **Ure** (138d,185d), **use** (7b,47a,49d,64c,109b,168b,c,181b), **Ute** (145c,180b), **uve** (185b)

- UE   **cue** (7a,27b,92c,117d,124b,132c,146c,159a), **due** (7b,115b,124c), **gue** (176c), **hue** (33c,143b), **lue** (146b), **pue** (52c), **que** (62d), **rue** (76a,b,129c,150d,183a), **sue** (119c), **Sue** (63a,178a,183d), **tue** (114b)

UF -   **ufo** (59a)

- UF   **ouf** (52c)

UG -   **ugh** (52c)

- UG   **bug** (24b,66b,81b), **dug, fug** (129a), **hug** (32c,49d), **jug** (118c, 123d), **lug** (27a,45d,47b,73c,136b), **Lug** (28b), **mug** (46b,54a,65a), **pug** (45a,101a,108a,148d), **rug, tug** (45d,125b), **vug** (28a,66a)

U - H   **ugh** (52c), **ush**

- UH   **auh** (52c), **huh** (52c)

UI -   **uit** (47a,111d,151a)

U - I   **ubi** (90a,180d,185b), **Udi** (108a), **uji** (146d), **uni** (34c,118d,122c), **Uni** (51d), **UPI** (107a,182d), **Uri** (162d), **uvi** (185b)

- UI   **dui** (46d), **hui** (14a,30b,56d,114c), **Kui** (86a,88c,146a), **qui** (62d), **Sui** (30b), **tui** (47c,114b,117a)

UJ -   **uji** (146d)

- UK   **auk** (19b), **ouk** (140c), **Suk** (107b)

UL -   **ula** (72c,158c), **ule** (23a,27d,134c,158c,168d), **Ull** (7c,68c,146b, 164d), **ulm** (49c), **Ulm** (40d), **ulo** (34b,80d), **ulu** (87a)

U - L   **Ull** (7c,68c,146b,164d)

- UL Bul (25d,102a), Ful (158b), gul (134a), mul (188), nul (108c,177a), pul (190), Pul (14a)

UM - Uma (43a,69b,153d), ume (11d), umu (112a)

U - M ulm (49c), Ulm (40d)

- UM aum (189), bum (21b), cum (159b), dum (45c,67b,113a), gum (7b, 53c,80b,130c,156b), hum (24d,46b,150d), Jum (39c), lum (30a), mum (30d,95a,146c), rum (8c,92d), sum (8a,123a,167c), tum (26d), Tum (143a,159b)

UN - Una (54a,153b,170c,183c), und (66b), une (13b,61a,62b,95c), uni (34c,118d,122c), Uni (51d), uno (83c,151d), uns (66d,174c), Unu (24d)

U - N urn (36c,174d)

- UN bun (25b,73b), dun (19a,39d,46d,71a,97d,115b,160b), fun, gun (56d,131a,146a), Hun (16c,21d,174b), mun (157b), nun (24c,91c, 117d,129d,147b), Nun (29a,85c), pun (119c), run (10d,23c,58d, 110d,148d,153b,154b,167d), sun (75d,111a,117b,155b), tun (23b, 27a,182b), wun (24c), Yun (88d)

U - O udo (28a,30c,48c,84b,c,d,136c,149d), ufo (59a), ulo (34b,80d), uno (83c,151d), Uro (192)

- UO duo (46d,113a,171d), Luo (107b), quo (188)

UP - UPI (107a,182d)

- UP cup (46b,69d,118b,170a), gup (70a), hup (35a), kup (188), pup (141b,148d,185d), sup (46b,104a,162b), tup (115a,117d,127d, 143d)

- UQ suq (22a,97a)

UR - urd (17b,184b), Urd (68d,107d), ure (40a,139d,155d,158b,d), Ure (138d,185d), Uri (162d), urn (36c,174d), Uro (192), Uru (192)

- UR bur (123b), cur (101d), dur (95c), Eur. (36c), fur, gur (159a), Hur (91d), Jur (107b), Lur (116c), mur (63a,177d), nur (67d), our (124c), pur, rur (132b), sur (34a,62b,d,104b,151a,152d,174a), tur (14d,27c,68a,79b,117d,174c)

US - use (7b,47a,49d,64c,109b,168b,c,181b), ush

U - S uns (66d,174c)

-US aus (66c), Aus (98b), bus (125b,168b), Gus (96a), jus (61d,90b), Mus (104a,132c), ous (158b), pus, rus (89b,138a), sus (117c), Sus (160c,181b)

UT - uta (53a,84d,93b,147c,150b), Ute (145c,180b), utu (35b, 137c), Utu (96c,107a,159b)

U - T uit (47a,111d,151a)

- UT aut (34d,89d), but (36a,52b,156b,173c), eut (30c,32b,145c), fut (188), gut (114d,130a), hut (143c), jut (53a,124a), lut (189), mut (39c), Mut (9b,127a), nut (24c,32d,38b,54d,64a,65d,86b,141c, 165a), Nut (69a), out (6b,14b,60b,69d,80a,108b,185c), put (65a, 69d,90b), rut (73a), tut (52c)

U - U ulu (87a), umu (112a), Unu (24d), Uru (192), utu (35b,137c), Utu (96c,107a,159b)

UV - uva (64a,70c), uve (185b), uvi (185b)

- UX   aux (6d,61a), dux (31d,64a,90c), lux (79d), rux (154a,184d)
- UY   buy, guy (55b,131b,155d), Guy (96a), muy (152d,175d), puy (61d)
- UZ   guz (188)
VA -   Vac (153b), vae (176b), vag (174b,178a), Vai (91d), van (7b,59d, 60a,63d,90c), vas (46d,89d,119c,133b,175d), vat (31b,36c,163a, 170c), vau (91c)
V - A   via (132a,133a,b,179a)
- VA   ava (78d,86a,116a,120d,139a,167b), Ava (24c), Eva (157a,183c), iva (76a,97b,127b,185b), ova (48d), uva (64a,70c)
V - C   Vac (153b)
V - D   Vod (16a)
VE -   vee (58a,91c,106a), Vei (91d), vet, vex (7c,10d,44c,82c)
V - E   vae (176b), vee (58a,91c,106a), vie (36c,157c,170c), voe (17a,81b)
- VE   ave (54c,71d,73a,122a,134d,136d), eve (47a,131a,143a,165d,171c), Eve (183c), ive (158c), uve (185b)
V - F   vif (62a)
V - G   vag (174b,178a), vog (189), vug (28a,66a)
VI -   via (132a,133a,b,179a), vie (36c,157c,170c), vif (62a), vim (50b, 176b), vin (63a,182b), vir (89c), vis (59d,89b,d,90b,176b), vix, (89d,138b), viz (105b)
V - I   Vai (91d), Vei (91d)
- VI   ovi (34a), uvi (185b)
V - L   vol (155a,182d)
V - M   vim (50b,176b)
V - N   van (7b,59d,60a,63d,90c), vin (63a,182b), von (66d,67a)
VO -   Vod (16a), voe (17a,81b), vog (189), vol (155a,182d), von (66d, 67a), Vor (68d), Vot (56d), vow (119c,150a), vox (90a,177a)
V - R   vir (89c), Vor (68d)
V - S   vas (46d,89d,119c,133b,175d), vis (59d,89b,d,90b,176b)
V - T   vat (31b,36c,163a,170c), vet, Vot (56d)
VU -   vug (28a,66a)
V - U   Vau (91c)
V - W   vow (119c,150a)
V - X   vex (7c,10d,44c,82c), vix (89d,138b), vox (90a,177a)
V - Z   viz (105b)
- VY   ivy (32b,38c,176b)
WA -   wad (94d,97b,109c,112b,149d), wag (85b,104a,183a), wah (113c), wan (113a), war (157c), was (166c,175c), Was (24d), wat (73d, 140d,163a,180b), waw (12b,91c), wax (28b,72a,80b,120c), way (37d,96b,134b,164d)
W - A   Wea (192)
- WA   awa (100a,139a), iwa (63c)
W - B   web (50d,70a,98c,99a,106c,149b)
W - D   wad (94d,97b,109c,112b,149d), wed (97a,173c)

WE - Wea (192), web (50d,70a,98c,99a,106c,149b), wed (97a,173c), wee (52c,100c,148c), Wei (30b,162b), wen (40c,72a,110a,170c,177b), wet (40d,46a,101a,124a,127c,149c), wey (173b)

W - E wee (52c,100c,148c), woe (25b), wye (91c)

- WE awe (81d,100a,130d,175b,182b), ewe (88a,143d), owe

W - G wag (85b,104a,183a), wig (73b)

WH - who (129c), why (52c)

W - H wah (113c)

WI - wig (73b), win (7a,17b,64b,123b), wis (79d,164c), wit (78d,85b, 177b)

W - I Wei (30b,162b)

- WI Twi (69c)

- WL awl (145b,167a), owl

- WM cwm (31b,37b,103d)

WN - WNW (35b)

W - N wan (113a), wen (40c,72a,110a,170c,177b), win (7a,17b,64b,123b), won, wun (24c) wyn (110a)

- WN awn (12c,17b,140a), own (6d)

WO - woe (25b), won, woo, wop, wow (52c,158a)

W - O who (129c), woo

- WO Lwo (107b), Pwo (88c), two (26c,37d,80a,93a)

W - P wop

WR - wry (13d)

W - R war (157c)

WS - WSW (35b)

W - S was (166c,175c), Was (24d), wis (79d,164c)

W - T wat (73d,140d,163a,180b), wet (40d,46a,101a,124a,127c), wit (78d,85b,177b)

WU - wun (24c)

W - W waw (12b,91c), WNW (35b), wow (52c,158a), WSW (35b)

W - X wax (28b,72a,80b,120c)

WY - wye (91c), wyn (110a)

W - Y way (37d,96b,134b,164d), wey (173b), why (52c), wry (13d)

XA - xat (167c)

- XA oxa (29c)

XE - xer (34a)

- XE axe (30c,40c,167a), Exe (43a)

- XO exo (122d)

X - R xer (34a)

X - T xat (167c)

YA - yah (52c), yak (112c,161d,165b), yam (48c,121d,160b,170c), Yao (30a,c,104b), yap (16c,29b,122a), yar (72a), Yau (30c), yaw (43a, 155d)

Y - A   **yea** (7c,175c)

- YA   **aya** (77b,166b), **Aya** (143c), **Iya** (95b,108d,111c), **Mya** (31c)

YE -   **yea** (7c,175c), **yen** (33b,42d,93c,174a), **yep**, **yes** (7c,55a), **yet** (18b, 24d,64c,77c,80a,108c,156b,165b), **yew** (36a,52a,b,145d,168c,d) **yez**

- YE   **aye** (7c,9b,55a,60a), **bye** (38c,141d), **dye** (33c,154d), **eye** (93d, 111b,140d), **lye** (8d,27d,93b), **nye** (72a,116d), **Nye** (9c,18b), **oye** (139c), **Pye** (50d,55a), **rye** (28b,70b,72d), **sye** (40c,46c,139b,141a, 167a), **tye** (28c,134a), **wye** (91c)

- YG   **tyg** (46b)

Y - H   **yah** (52c)

YI -   **yin** (140a), **Yin** (30b,143c,185b), **yip** (16c)

Y - I   **yoi** (52c,79a)

Y - K   **yak** (112c,161d,165b), **yok** (10c,185a)

- YL   **kyl** (76d,79b)

Y - M   **yam** (48c,121d,160d,170c), **yom** (41a)

- YM   **gym** (154a), **Nym** (54c,76a)

Y - N   **yen** (33b,42d,93c,174a), **yin** (140a), **Yin** (30b,143c,185b), **yon** (44c,112a,164d), **Yun** (88d)

- YN   **lyn** (140c,178d), **syn** (122d,183b), **wyn** (110a)

YO -   **yoi** (52c,79a), **yok** (10c,185a), **yom** (41a), **yon** (44c,112a,164d), **you, yow** (52c)

Y - O   **Yao** (30a,c,104b)

- YO   **iyo** (7d,176b)

Y - P   **yap** (16c,29b,122a), **yep**, **yip** (16c)

- YP   **cyp** (169d), **gyp** (29b,42a,160c), **hyp**

Y - R   **yar** (72a)

- YR   **pyr** (92a,b,122c,173b), **Tyr** (7c,68c,109c,147d,163d,170c,178a)

Y - S   **yes** (7c,55a)

- YS   **lys** (58b,92b)

Y - T   **yet** (18b,24d,64c,77c,80a,108c,156b,165b)

YU -   **Yun** (88d)

Y - U   **Yau** (30c), **you**

- YU   **ayu** (160c)

Y - W   **yaw** (43a,155d), **yew** (36a,52a,b,145d,168c,d), **yow** (52c)

- YX   **Nyx** (69b), **pyx** (31a,51d,75d)

Y - Z   **yez**

ZA -   **zac** (27c), **zag** (84a), **zak** (188), **Zal** (135d), **Zan** (186b), **zar** (188), **zat** (148a), **zax** (148a)

Z - A   **zea** (95c), **Zoa** (20b)

Z - C   **zac** (27c)

Z - D   **zed** (91c)

ZE -   **zea** (95c), **zed** (91c), **zee** (81b,91c), **zel** (40c), **Zen** (24a), **Zep, zer** (188)

Z - E   **zee** (81b,91c), **Zoe** (36b,183c)

Z - F	Zif (102a)
Z - G	zag (84a), zig (84a)
Z - H	zoh (13d,186b)
ZI -	Zif (102a), zig (84a), Zio (147d,163d), zip (24b,50b,!76b), Ziu (147d,163d)
Z - K	zak (188)
Z - L	Zal (135d), zel (40c)
Z - N	Zan (186b), Zen (24a)
ZO -	zoa (20b), Zoe (36b,183c), zoh (13d,186b), zoo (181b)
Z - O	Zio (147d,163d), zoo (181b)
- ZO	azo (107c)
Z - P	Zep, zip (24b,50b,176b)
Z - R	zar (188), zer (188)
Z - T	zat (148a)
Z - U	Ziu (147d,163d)
Z - X	zax (148a)

FOUR-LETTER WORDS

AA - -   Aalu (6b,48d), Aani (45a,48d), Aare, Aaru (6b,48d)

- AA -   baal (142b), baas (97c), caam (93d), Faam (111a), gaal (23b,174d), Haab (97d), haaf (57d), haak (57b,178a), haar (139c), kaan (93d, 116c), kaat (105d), laap (51d,91b,141d), maal (188), ma'am (95a, 166b), maar (177a), Maas (132a), Maat (69a,b,85d), Naab, naam (44c), Naam (105b), paal (188), paar (28c,137a), raab (32d), raad (14a,49b,151a,165b), Raad (151a), raas (91b), Saad (12b), saah (188), saal (66c,73b), Saan (24d), Saar (63b,102d,132a), Taal (7d, 88c,151a), taar (12b), Waac, waag (71d,101d)

- - AA   blaa, chaa (162b), draa (188)

A - - A   Abba (20a,55a,161c), Abfa (76b), Abia (18d,137a), abra (26b), Abra, acca (53b,d), acta (41d,123d,128d,164c), adda (147d), Adda (68c,119d,157a,182a), aera (8a), Aeta (94d,100a,106b,117a), Afra (183c), agha (35a,171a), agla (7a), agra (26d,34d), Agra (161b), agua (152d,166c,178c), Aida (110d,175c), Aira (70d), Akha (86a,c), akia (74c), Akka (125d), akra (176a), Akra (191), akua (120d), alba (98b,181a), Alba (151d), Alca (14c,128b), alda (152b), Alda (110d,150c), Alea (14b,31c,167d), alfa (70d), alga (141b,c), alia (89d), alla (6d), alma (40d,53d,146d,147a), Alma 38d, 183c), alta (89c,152d), Alva (151d), Alya (155b,c), amba (161a), amia (22c,170d), amla (48a,161d,168c,169a), amma (6a), amra (77c), anba (36d), anda (23a,168c), anna (190), Anna (110c,166d, 183c), anoa (28a,60a,112c,181c), ansa (73c,93d,137c), anta (83d, 117c,d,121a), Anta (164a), apia (121b), aqua (90a,178c), arba (135d,171a), arca (9a,22c,29d,115a,130a), Arca (101b), area (37d, 38a,44c,53a,93b,110d,127d,138c,168a,186d), aria (8b,98c,150a,c, 170c), arna (24a,181b), Aroa (175b), arpa (83b), arra (47d,52c,82b),

Arta (72b), **Arya** (80d), **asea** (39b,177c), **Asha** (191), **Asia** (48a), **asta** (188), **Asta** (107a,164c), **Atka** (11a), **atma** (150d), **atta** (58d, 90c,97d,160c,173d), **Atta** (94d,95d,100a,106b,117a), **atua** (120d), **Auca** (192), **aula** (66c,73b), **aura** (44c,49c,66a,96b,158a,170d, 177c), **Ausa, Azha** (155b)

AB - -   **abas** (61c), **Abba** (20a,55a,161c), **abbe** (32b,63b,123b), **Abby** (183d), **ABC's** (57a), **abed** (130c), **Abel** (7a,25b), **abet** (8b,15b,50a, 59b,75d,81c,141d,159d), **Abfa** (76b), **Abia** (18d,137a), **Abib** (102 a,b), **Abie** (96b,107a), **abir** (129a), **able** (26b,35b,126a,147c), **ably** (147c), **aboo** (17a), **Abot** (100c), **Abou** (48b,55a), **abox** (22d), **abra** (26b), **Abra, abri** (61c,62c,144b), **Absi** (191), **abut** (22a, 167c)

- AB -   **baba** (108d,120c,166c,171a), **babe, Babi** (116c), **babu** (77a), **baby**, **caba** (184c), **Faba, gabe** (162a), **gabi** (162a), **gaby** (59c,146d), **haba** (151d), **habe** (191), **Maba** (103a,168d), **mabi** (58d), **nabk** (30d, 164d), **nabo** (117a), **Nabu** (68c,183d), **Raba, rabi** (38d,74a), **Rabi** (14b,117b), **saba** (56a,117a), **Saba** (143d), **sabe, tabi** (84c, 149d), **tabu** (59d,111d), **Wabi** (192)

- - AB   **Ahab** (18c,26c,85b,86d,100d,116a,180b), **Arab** (30a,78b,c,106a, 107c,157b,160c,185d), **blab** (162b), **brab** (113b), **chab** (184a), **crab** (39b,144b,181b), **doab** (157c), **drab** (23d,29c,33d,46d,53b,d), **duab** (157c), **frab** (138c), **grab** (105b,142a,149b), **Haab** (97d), **Joab** (41a), **knab** (107a), **Moab** (18d,85a,86d,94a), **Naab, raab** (32d), **scab** (80b, 107d,157c), **slab** (148b), **snab** (23c,139a), **stab** (14c,87a,117c), **swab** (102b)

A - - B   **Abib** (102a,b), **Adib** (155b), **Agib** (12a,42d), **Ahab** (18c,26c,85b, 86d,100d,116a,180b), **Arab** (30a,78b,c,106a,107c,157b,160c,185d)

AC - -   **acca** (53b,d), **Acer** (96c), **ache** (79a,112d,185b), **acht** (66c), **achy**, **acid** (151a,162a), **Acis** (64b), **acle** (13d,82c,115d), **acme** (39c,115c, 186b), **acne** (147c), **acon** (62c,140d), **acor** (6d), **acre** (39b,56a,88b), **Acre, acta** (41d,123d,128d,164c), **acth** (13b), **acto** (152b), **Acts, actu** (7a,89a), **acus** (89d,118a), **acyl** (6d)

- A C -   **Bach** (35c), **back** (75d,76d,159d), **Caca** (67a), **caco** (73b), **dace** (57a,b), **each, face** (159d,176c), **fact** (7a,128b), **hack** (40a,77c, 184d), **jaca** (84a), **jack** (26c,58a,127c), **Jack** (96b), **jacu** (19a,151b), **lace** (58b,179c), **lack** (178a), **lact** (34c), **lacy, mace** (49d,108d,153b, 154d,161a,178a), **mack, nach, paca** (132c,154a), **pace** (64b,98a, 153b,156a,170b,177d), **pack** (24b,140d), **paco** (9b,146d), **pacs** (94c), **pact** (8a), **raca** (19a,59c,130b,184d), **race** (116a,153b,154b, 169c), **rack** (32c,64b), **racy** (153b), **sack** (43d,118a,119d,182b), **saco** (189), **tace** (13a,155d), **tack** (28d,37d,54d), **tact** (43c,d,116a), **Vach** (153b), **Waco, Zach** (96b)

- - AC   **utac** (22d), **Waac**

A - - C   **aesc** (12d,64d), **alec** (10a,57c,d,76c,137c), **amic** (9d), **avec** (63a, 183a)

AD - -   **adad** (52c,56a), **Adad** (68c,157a,182a), **Adah** (25b,51b), **Adam** (26b,96a,111c) **adan** (102d), **Adar** (85c,102a), **adat** (90b,95d), **adda** (147d), **Adda** (68c,119d,157a,182a), **Addu** (68c,157a,182a), **Addy** (183d), **aden** (34b), **Aden, Ader** (18d), **Ades** (73a), **Adib** (155b), **adit** (51a,100a,114d), **admi** (65d), **ador** (153b), **adry** (164c), **adze** (40c,167a)

- AD -   Badb (82b), bade, cade (25c,27a,76c,85d,116d), Cade (50c), cadi (12a,103a,171a), cady (69d), Dada (13b,63a,157d), dado (41c,111c, 115c,177d), Eads (23b,24b,50b,82a), fade (181d,183b), fado (121c), fady, gade, hade (66a,148c,173c), hadj (98b,118a), jade (33c,65d,71d,166a), jadu (95a), jady, kada (188), kade (144a), kadi (103a,171a), Kadu (191), lade (24c,26d,43c,93b,100a,132a,139d, 161b,178d), Ladd (143c), lady, made, Madi (174a), mado (14d,57a, 170b), padi (131b), rada (135c,172a), rade (138d), sadd (33a,40b, 58c,107b), sade (91d), sadh (77a), sado (26d,84d), sadr (94a), Sadr (155c), vade (42c,67d,89b), wadd (109c), wade, wadi (46c,106a, 109a,128a,132a), wady (109a,128a,132a)

- - AD   adad (52c,56a), Adad (68c,157a,182a), arad (13a,c,84a), bead (17a, 122a,146b), brad (54d,67c,105b), Chad (158b), clad (46a,82a), dead, diad (113a), duad (113a,171d), dyad (113a), ecad (73a, 119b), egad (100a,109a), Fuad (54d), glad (85c), goad (80b,154b), grad (28b), head (29d), Ibad (191), Irad (18d), Joad (50c), lead (35d,43d,72b,74d,81a), load (24c,26d,161b), mead (46a,78a,97d, 99b), Mead (78a), orad (104a), Phad (155b), quad (33c,172a), raad (14a,49b,151a,165b), read (116d,157d), road (37d,164d), Saad (12b), scad (31a,57a,78b,88d,137c), shad (27d,57a,b,c), spad (105b), Spad (118d), stad (151b,167d,176b), swad (94d), toad (10a, 17a,63d,126d), udad (143d,144a,181c), woad (20d,47c)

A - - D   abed (130c), acid (151a,162a), adad (52c,56a), Adad (68c,157a, 182a), aged (110a), alod (51c,55d,88a,124c), amid (9d,50a), apod (59d), arad (13a,c,84a), arid (46c,85a), Arnd (67a), Arod (86c), avid (47b,71a,186b)

AE - -   aera (8a), aeri (34a), aero (8b,34a,b,58c,59a), aery (47b,51d,106c), aesc (12d,64d), Aeta (94d,95d,100a,106b,117a)

- AE -   Caen, daer (22b), daez, faex (46a), Gaea (47d,69a), Gael (28a,96c, 138d), haec (90a,164c), haem (122b), Jael (147b), laet (60d), nael (189), saer (163a), tael (91d,179d), waeg (19b,72c,87a), waer (40b)

- - AE   alae (182d), blae (93b), brae (76d,139a,c,140b,148c), Irae (43c), koae (74b), quae (176b), spae (139c)

A - - E   Aare, abbe (32b,63b,123b), Abie (96b,107a), able (26b,35b,126a, 147c), ache (79a,112d,185b), acle (13d,82c,115b), acme (39c,115c, 186b), acne (147c), acre (39b,56a,88b), Acre, adze (40c,167a), agee (13d,15c,38d), ague (30a,55d,95c,137b), aide (7b,14a,75d), aile (62b,63a,182c,d), aine (49b,62c,142c), aire (82c), Aire, ajee (15c,139a), akee (168c), alae (182d), albe (133a) alee (15c,75d,144b,157a,182a), Alle (14c), alme (40d,147a), aloe (7d,20a,76a,b,92b,98b,119b,158b,167a,183d), amie (61d), ance (158b,c,d), Ande (193), ange (61a), Anne (50c,84a,143b,183c), ante (87a,89a,115b,120b,122b,125d,154d), a-one (52b,167b), apse (9b, 20a,31a,128c,130a,142b,175a), arme (63a,179b), Arne (35c,50c, 134d), asse (25a,60d,74a), atle (136d,161d,169b), Aude, auge (123c,132b), aune (188), axle (153c,180c)

AF - -   afar (44c), Afar (6c), afer (48a,182b), affy (18b), Afra (183c)

- AF -   baff (69d), baft (14a,53b), cafe, daff (125d), daft (59c), gaff (57c, d,152d,153a), haft (76d), Kafa (6c), raff (75b), raft (27b,33c,58c, 75b), safe (141d,157d,174d), Safi (191), Taft (29d), Wafd (49a), waft (20d,58c)

- - AF deaf, goaf (104b), Graf (37c,66b,67a,107c,186b), haaf (57d), heaf (144a), leaf (55c,73c,119b), loaf (79b,94b), neaf (58a,73c), Olaf (108a,176b), Piaf (63c), Wraf

A - - F alef (91c), alif (12b), arif (127d), atef (39a,48d), Azof (20b,135d)

AG - - Agag (18c,86c,137a), agal (17c,36d), Agao (6c,73c), agar (7d,28c, 39c,103c,141c), Agau (73c), Agaz (193), aged (110a), agee (13d, 15c,38d), ager (47c,56a,89b,c,131d,133b), agha (35a,171a), Agib (12a,42d), agio (52c,60a,101c,123a), Agis (86d), agla (7a), agni (88a,89c), Agni (56d,68b), agog (47b,52c,86b), agon (12c,36c,41b, 55d,71b), agra (26d,34d), Agra (161b), agri (89b), agro (149d), agua (152d,166c,178c), ague (30a,55d,95c,137b)

- AG - baga (171b), bago (13d), cage (36a), cagy (178b), dagg (118c), dagh (76d), Dago (76d), gage (28d,98a,119c,d), gagl (160b), hagg, hagi (84b), Iago (54b,111d,143c), Jaga (191), jagg, kago (113a), kagu (106c), lago (83b,152b), mage (95b), magg (95b), Magh (102a), magi (123c), Magi (95b,116c,183a), naga (13d,33a,55b,127c), Naga (24c,77a,88c,176d), Nagy (78d), Paga (117a), page (51b,59b, 142d,159b), raga (56d,105a), rage (10c,30c,157a,161d), ragi (28b), saga (79b,91a,138a,157a,161b,c,168a), Saga, sage (13a,90d,100c, 141c,145c,180b,183a), sago (54c,59b,113b,125b,155c), sagy, vagi (38b), wage (27a,115b), yage (23a)

- - AG Agag (18c,86c,137a), brag (21a,175a), coag (45d,118a,163b), crag (132c), drag (74a,125b), flag (16b,50d,82b,88c,115a,155a), knag (115d,139c), krag (131c), peag (144a,178a), quag (21c,102c), shag (73b,105b,161d,166d), skag (7d,46d), slag (46c,99a,138c,148d, 177a), snag (11b,27b,35c,87c,124b,166a), stag (65a,98d), swag (22a,156c), waag (71d,101d)

A - - G Agag (18c,86c,137a), agog (47b,52c,86b), ajog, areg (116a,137a)

AH - - Ahab (18c,26c,85b,86d,100d,116a,180b), Ahaz (86d), ahem, Ahet (49a,102a), ahey (52c), Ahir (27b), Ahom (88c), ahoy (106a), ahum

- AH - bahi (60c), baho (122a), baht (146a), haha (55c,159c), kaha (123d), kahu (14d), maha (28c,88c,136d), mahr (103a), Oahu, paha (67b), pahi (21b,26a), paho (122a), Rahu (42b,48b), saha, sahh (188), Saho (6c), sahu (153d), taha (179b), tahr (68a,76d)

- - AH Adah (25b,51b), Amah (95b,108d,111c), arah (52c), ayah (108d), blah, drah (188), Elah (18c,86d), Etah (51c,71d), eyah (95b,108d, 111c), Ivah (18d), kyah (19a), Leah (19a,84a,87b,183c), Noah (88a, 99b), odah (170d), opah (23b,57a,b,86d), prah (21b,26a,95c,d), Ptah (48d,98c), saah (188), seah (188), shah (116c), Utah (180b), yeah

A - - H acth (13b), Adah (25b,51b), aich (9a), Alph (132a), amah (95b, 108d,111c), ankh (38d,162b), arah (52c), arch (29d,38b,39d,123d, 132c), ayah (108d)

AI - - aich (9a), Aida (110d, 175c), aide (7b,14a,75d), aile (62b,63a,182c, d), aine (49b,62c,142a), Aino (84a,c), aint, Ainu (84a,c), aipi (27a), Aira (70d), aire (82c), Aire, airs (123b), airy (177a,176d)

- AI - bail (43c), bain (61a), bait (15d,51a,94d,167b), caid (35a,151d, 152b), cain (169c), Cain (6a,7a,50d,88a,104c,143a), Dail (49a, 82b, c), dain (188), dais (119b), fail, fain (42d,67c,183b), fair (17a,55d),

304

fait (6d,61b), Gaia (47d,69a), gail (23b,174d), Gail (183d), gain (7a, b,124a,181d), gait (96b,179a), haik (57b,65b,108a), hail (6d,15a, 71d), hair (56b,164d), jail (123d), Jain (77b), kaid (29d,66a), kaif (88c), kaik (96c), kail (18c,22a.25a,79b), Kain, kair, laic (32b,90b, 107d,124a,141d), laid, lain, lair (37c,42b), Lais (17c), lait (62a), Maia (76b,109a,153b,155b,177c), maid (45b.142d), mail (12d,99b, 121c), maim (43d,81a,105c), mair (29d,35d,123d), mais (61b), Naia (33a), naid (63c), naif (74b,105d). naik, nail (31d,54d,141d,161d, 173a), naio (107a,168c), Nair (45d), nais (63c,132a), paid (129c), pail, pain (7c), pair (22d,37d,85b,171d), pais (37d), qaid (35a), raia (107d), Raia (147b), raid (59d,80c), raik (188,189), rail (16b,19b,c, 37a,97b,138c,150c,177b), rain (121d,162d), raip (36d), rais (26c, 29d,75a,103b), Rais (106b), saic (86b,91d,175d), said (174c), Said (42d,101a,121b), sail (144c,185a), sain (20c,38d,48a), sair (140b, 150d), sais (48d,71d), tail (11d,27d,59b,143b), tain (166a), tair (68a,76d), tait (14d), vail (94b,124a,174b), vain (81a), vair (64c, 154c), waif (157b), wail (39b,88a), wain (177b), Wain, wait (26d, 42b,92c,155d,162a), zaim (170d), zain (41a)

- - AI   alai (171a), Alai (135c), anai (163b,181a), chai (72d), goal (106d, 168c), ngai (48a,159c), peai (98b), quai (88b,117c,180c), Thai (146a)

A - - I   Aani (45a,48d), abri (61c,62c,144b), Absi (191), admi (65d), aeri (34a), agni (88a,89c), Agni (56d,68b), agri (89b), aipi (27a), alai (171a), Alai (135c), Albi (58a), alii (74c,134c), ambi (34a,122c), amii (48a,161d,168c,169a), ammi (98c), amoi (62a), anai (163b, 181a), Andi (27d), anti (7d,111a,122b), Anti (193), apii (74c), arni (24a,181b), arui (11b,143d,144a,181c), asci (154a), assi (77d), Asti 83d,'182b), Atli (14c,72b,79a,107d), Atri, auri (34a)

AJ - -   ajar (110c), Ajax (71b,162d), ajee (15c,139a), ajog

- AJ -   baju (84a), caja (152a), caji (180b), gajo (107c), haje (33a,48d), maja (151c), Maja (153b), majo, Naja (33a), pajo (122a), raja (77a, 123c), Raja, tajo (152a,d), yaje (23a)

AK - -   Akal (56d), Akan (191), akee (168c), akey (189), Akha (86a,c), akia (74c), Akim (135d,191), akin (8b,92b,129c), Akka (125d), akov (189), akra (176a), Akra (191), akua (120d)

- AK -   baka (52b), bake (139a), baku (26d,157b,168c), cake, caky, fake (123a,143c), faky, hake (57a,b), hakh (46d), hako (115b), haku (86d), jake (40d), Jake (96b), jako (71a), kaka (114b), kaki (84c, 106d), lake (117d), lakh (110c), laky, make (35b,36d,54a,123a) maki (91b), mako (18a,19a,20d,143c,168c,182c), Maku (192), oaks (154d), oaky, rake (41b,44c,134b,140d), Saka (10a), sake (84b,125d), saki (39c,84b,102a), take, takt (105a,163a), Taku (80c), taky, waka (26a), wake (134b,168a), wakf (103a), waky, Yaka (191), Yaki (193)

- - AK   Anak (67a), asak (13d,168c,169a), beak (19a), coak (45d,118a, 163b), dhak (48a,169a), Dyak (22b), feak (39d,171c), flak (11a), haak (57b,178a), Irak (99a,d), kiak (51c), kyak (51c), leak (110c), peak (9a,38c,159b,186b), siak (72d), soak (46c,137c), teak (41a, 48a,168c), weak (55b)

A - - K   amok (18b,63c), Anak (67a), asak (13d,168c,169a), asok (13d), Atik (155b)

305

AL - -   alae (182d), alai (171a), Alai (135c), alan (45a,79a,183), Alan, alar (15c,145c,182d), alas (52c,136b,183b), alat (136d), alay (96c), alba (98b,181a), Alba (151d), albe (133a), Albi (58a), albo (34d,181a), Alca (14c,128b), alco (45b), alda (152b), Alda (110d, 150c), Alea (14b,31c,167d), alec (10a,57c,d,76c,137c), alee (15c, 75d,144b,157a,182a), alef (91c), alem (98b,155a,170d,171a), alen (40d,138a), alfa (70d), alga (141b,c), Algy (96b), alia (89d), alif (12b), alii (74c,134c), alim (103b,162c), alin (188), alit (44b,143a), Alix (183c), alky, alla (6d), Alle (14c), allo (34c), ally (14a,35c,d, 173c), alma (40d,53d,146d,147a), Alma (38d,183c), alme (40d, 147a), alms (29a), alod (51c,55d,88a,124c), aloe (7d,20a,76a,b,92b, 98b,119b,158b,167a,183d) alop (13d,46b,93d), alow (18a,172c), Alph (132a), Alps (85d), also (10b,18b,80a), alta (89c,152d), alto (152b,176c,177a), alum (14a,45c), Alur (191), Alva (151d), Alya (155b,c), Alys (183c)

- AL -   Aalu (6b,48d), Bala (26c,66a), bald (16c), bale (24b,74a), bali, Bali, balk (118c,146a,156d), ball, balm (110a,172c), Balt (93a), balu (104b,159a,181d), cale (72d), calf, calk (78c,109a,141c,178d), call (145c,159b,176d), calm (8d,11d,112b,118d,126c,d,172b,173d), calo (72d), calp (92b), calx (23c,75c,112c), dale (43c,128a,174b), dali (168c,169b), fala (129b), fall (46b,141c), falx (133b), gala (55d), Gala (191), gale (181d), gali (6c), gall (19a,28c,29b,82c,160c, 176a), galt, hala (112b), hale (125b), Hale (9d,131a), half (101a), hall (37b,114d), halm, halo (14d,31b,92a,107b,131d), Hals (47a), halt (13b,28a,38d,156d), lalu (48d), kala (19a), kale (22a,25a, 119b,175a), kali (26d,67c,136d,167a), Kali (147b), kalo (162a), lala (129b), lalo (16b,34d,153a), Lalo (35c), mala (89b,c,90a,94b, 97d,109d,185c), male (154d), Male (45d), mali (27b), mall (95d,124b,143b), malm (32a,92b), malo (23a,74c,152a), malt (17c), Nala (77a), pala (189), Pala (88b), pale (113a,117c,178a), pall (122b), Pali (23d,24a,137b,175a), pall (32d,81b,112a), palm (59b, 168c,169b), palo (152c), palp (11a,55b,58b,167c), paly (194), rale (7c,23a,29d,41b), ralo (188), sala (152a,b,c), Sala (50c), sale (14c,61c,62b,c,168b), salp (109c,148d), salt (35d,105b,123a,136c, 141c,149d), tala (16d,113a,168c,d), talc (28d,63b,99c,100b,122a, 149c), tale (91a,185b), tali (189), talk, tall (118d), vale (54c,128a, 174b), Vale (7c,109c), vali (171a,176a), Vali (7c,109c), wale (70b, 131b,157c,163d,179a,180a,c,d), wali (171a), walk, wall, Walt (96b), Yale (173c), yali (171a)

- - AL   agal (17c,36d), Akal (56d), Aral (135d), aval (70c), axal (120b), Baal (142b), beal (139d), bual (182c), coal (49c,64a), cral, deal (11d,16c,36c,44c,81a,168b), dhal (12b), dial (25c), dual (45c,171d), eral (51a), etal (89a), foal (78c), gaal (23b,174d), geal (47d,163c), goal (8b,109b,120b,125d), heal, ical (158c), keal (25a), kral, leal (54b,94c,139d), maal (188), meal (72a,130b), Neal, odal (48a,88b, 112c), opal (20a,65d,67b,82b) oral (114a,153d,174c,175c), oval (48d,49c,127a), paal (188), peal (131c,d), pyal (175c), real (7a), rial (190), ryal (110a,190), saal (66c,73b), seal (10c,d,54d,64c,96a, 118b,128a), sial (112a), Taal (7d,88c,151a), teal (19b,20d,46c,d), udal (76b,88b,131c), unal (147a), ural, Ural (135c), uval (70c), veal, vial (148c), weal (124d,157c,180c,d), zeal (12c,55d)

A - - L   Abel (7a,25b), acyl (6d), agal (17c,36d), Akal (56d), amil (45a,48a,

306

185c), **amyl** (155c), **anil** (47c,80d,180b), **Aoul** (191), **Aral** (135d), **aril** (142a), **aval** (70c), **axal** (120b), **axil** (10c), **azul** (151d)

AM - - amah (95b,108d,111c), amar (189), amba (161a), ambi (34a,122c), ambo (125b,128b), amen (14a,80b,94a,137a,149c,175c,184b), Amen (86d,127d,159b,164a), amer (61b), Ames (9c,82a), Amex (184d), amia (22c,170d), amic (9d), amid (9d,50a), amie (61d), amil (45a,48a,185c), amin (9d), amir (7c,12a,103a,b,123c,170d), amit (94a), amla (48a,161d,168c,169a), amli (48a,161d,168c,169a), amma (6a), ammi (98c), ammo (9d), ammu (9d), amoi (62a), amok (18b,63c), Amon (86d,96d,127d,159b,164a), amor (152b), Amor (39c,68b), Amos (96a,144b), Amoy (88c), amra (77c), Amun (86d,127d,159b,164a), amyl (155c)

- AM - came (182b), Came (192), camp (163b), dama (65d,152b), dame (67b,87c,166b), damn, damp (101a), Fama (135a), fame (130a), famn (188), Gama (121c), game (64d,154a), gamp (172a), hami (78a), iamb (59c), jama (103b), jamb (12d,45c,118a,146b,174a), jami (103b), Kama (56d), kame (67b,139b), kami (68a,84b), Kami (88c,107c,144c), lama (23d,24a,91d,165b), Lamb (49c), lame (38d, 43d,73b), lamp (92a,94c), mama, Mama (116d), mamo (19a,d,74b), Nama (78c), name (8a,11b,d,25c,46c,107c,130b,157d,163b,166b), Rama (77a,80b,176d), rame (22d), rami (22d), ramp (65a,80b, 127b,148b), sama (105c,169d), same (44d,79b), samh (56b), samp (70b,77d,121b), Tama (192), tame (45a,b,66a), Tame, tamp (46b, 112b,121d,127d), vamp (80a,145a), Yama (57a,68a), Zama (73d, 141d)

- - AM Adam (26b,96a,111c), anam (159a,168c), Anam, Aram (18d,50c, 105c,144b,161c), Azam (166c), beam, Bram (96a), caam (93d), cham (20a,29d), Cham (8c), clam (20b,101b), cram (157d), dram (46b,110c,121d,148c), edam (29c), Elam (18d,37d,82a,116c,144b), enam (70c,77a), Enam (85c), exam, Faam (111a), flam (169c), foam (63d,154b), gram (29d,99b,148d,160d,180a), Gram, Guam, imam (25c,102d,103a), klam (189), Liam (181d), loam (47d,150a), lyam (139a), ma'am (95a,166b), miam (14d), naam (44c,105b), ogam (82b,c), olam (51a,d,75c,81a), pram (15a), ream (18c,37d, 50d,113d,171c), roam (178a), seam (85b,d,160a,176d,185a), sham (41c,55b,60d,80a,123a,b,146d), Siam (163d,181a), slam (180d, 182d), swam, team (38c,72a,113a), Tiam, tram (170a), Ulam (67b), wham (157c)

A - - M Adam (26b,96a,111c), ahem, Ahom (88c), ahum, Akim (135d,191), alem (98b,155a,170d,171a), alim (103b,162c), alum (14a,45c), anam (159a,168c), Anam, Anim (18d), Aram (18d,50c,105c,144b, 161c), arum (13a,39b,58d,92b,155c), Arum (66a), asem (9a,49a, 69c), Asom (18d), atom (101c,114c,180d), Atum (143a,159b), Azam (166c)

AN - - anai (163b,181a), Anak (67a), anam (159a,168c), anan (49a,159a, 180c), Anas (46c,d), Anat (138c,147d), Anax (43c,120c), anay (72b,163b,181a), anba (36d), ance (158b,c,d), ancy (158c), anda (23a,168c), Ande (193), Andi (27d), Andy (96b), Aner (18d,96b), anes (110c,140a), anet (43c), anew (7c), ange (61a), ango (171a), anil (47c,80d,180b), Anim (18d), anis (55c), ankh (38d,162b), anna (190), Anna (110c,166d,183c), Anne (50c,84a,143b,183c),

anoa (28a,60a,112c,181c), **anon** (7d,14d,79d,80b,123a,145c,150c, 164a), **ansa** (73c,93d,137c), **anse** (61d), **ansu** (11d), **anta** (83d, 117c,d,121a), **Anta** (164a), **ante** (87a,89a,115b,120b,122b,125d, 154d), **anti** (7d,111a,122b), **Anti** (193), **anzu** (11d)

- AN -   **Aani** (45a,48d), **Bana** (67a), **banc** (61a,85c), **band** (72a,157c), **bane** (74a,106b,120b,139a), **bang** (75d,105d,148a), **bani** (190), **bank** (18a,58c), **bans, bant** (43c), **Cana** (57a,64b,100c), **cane** (17b, 128a,156a,159a,177d), **Cane, cang** (184a), **cano** (152a), **cant** (28d, 81b,84d,90c,109b,136c,165d,166a), **Dana** (28a,96a,171d), **Dane** (85d,107d,138a), **dang, dank** (40b,101a), **dans** (62a), **Danu** (28a), **fana, fane** (30d,137a,162d), **fang** (167b), **Fano** (51d,96b,113c,d), **gane** (185b), **gang** (38c), **Gano** (132d), **hand** (60c,114c,115d,184c), **hang** (160a), **hank** (147c), **Hano** (125b), **Hans** (66d,96a), **hant** (67a), **jane** (190), **Jane** (183c), **Jann** (102d), **kana** (84d), **Kane** (74c), **k'ang** (30a), **Kano** (84c,177d), **kant** (28d), **Kant** (67a), **lana** (58a,66a,90a,184b), **land** (44a,163c), **lane** (134b,157b), **lank** (148b,164b), **lanx** (133a,b), **mana** (30a,120d,122a,159c), **mand** (28b), **mane, mani** (115c), **mann** (189), **Mann** (9c,48c,185c), **mano** (71d,73d,74b,83b), **Mans** (30a), **Manu** (10a,76d,77a,b), **Manx** (27b, 28a,82d), **many** (108d), **nana** (118b), **Nana** (15c,105d,116d,186d), **nane** (139d), **Pana, pane** (113c,155a,b), **pang** (165b), **Pani** (120c), **pank** (189), **pant, rana** (77a,123c), **Rana** (63d), **rand** (16d,22a, 131b,145a,b), **Rand** (69c), **rang, rani** (72d,77b,123c,127c), **rank** (31d,55d,70b,92c,94d,157d), **rann** (175c), **rant** (41c,127b,128a, 161d), **sana** (56a,166d), **Sana** (185d), **sand** (71d,146c), **sane** (128a), **sang, sank, sano** (152b), **sans** (63a,183b), **tana** (159a), **Tana** (87d), **Tane** (120d), **tang** (30b,58b,186b), **tanh** (97c), **tank** (175a,d), **Tano** (192), **uang** (131a), **vane** (179b,182a), **vang** (72d,134a,140b), **Vans** (107d), **wand** (120b,132c,156a), **wane** (41c,43c), **wang** (189), **want** (41b,42d,87b,106b,122a), **wany, Yana** (192,193), **yang** (30b,70a), **yank, Yank, zany** (24a,32b,59c)

- - AN   **adan** (102d), **Akan** (191), **alan** (45a,79a,183c), **Alan** (96a), **anan** (49a,159a,180c), **Aran** (18c,48c,64d,82d,174c), **Awan** (191), **azan** (102d), **bean** (91b,142a,175a), **bran** (23c,39a,72a,79c,70b), **Bran** (23c,50c), **chan** (26c,130c), **clan** (169c), **Coan** (37b), **cran** (160c), **cyan, dean** (33c,109d), **dhan** (124c), **dian** (46c,130d,170b), **Dian** (68d,69a,c,102b), **duan** (64b), **elan** (12c,41a,50d,62a,153c,177a, 186b), **Eoan** (41a,85b), **Evan** (96a), **Ewan, flan** (39d,40a,114d), **gean** (29c), **Goan, gran, guan** (151b), **Iban** (47c), **Iran** (6a,48c, 116b), **Ivan** (40c,85b,96a), **jean** (37c), **Jean** (183c), **Joan** (183c), **juan** (113a), **Juan** (96a), **kaan** (93d,116c), **khan** (7c,26c,81b,93d, 116c,123c,130c,166c), **kran** (190), **kuan** (30b,c), **Kuan, kwan** (30b), **lean** (128a,148b,152d,164b,166a), **loan, mean** (15a,42b, 146c,156b), **mian** (97c,147b,166b), **moan, ngan, oban** (190), **Olan** (115c), **Oman** (159a), **Onan** (18c,85c), **Oran, oxan, pean** (65c), **plan** (99b,124a,138b), **quan** (190), **roan** (78b,c,114c,128d,144a, 181a), **Saan** (24d), **Sean** (85b,96a), **Shan** (13c,80d,88c,101d), **scan** (52b,93d,98a,116d,128b,c,140d), **span** (23b,107b,113a,128b,162c), **Svan** (27d), **swan** (19b,33a), **tean** (140c167a), **than** (35b), **tran** (7a), **tuan** (95d,147b;166c), **ulan** (27d,88a), **uran** (101d), **Uran, uzan** (189), **wean** (8d,42d), **yean** (88a), **yuan** (190), **Yuan** (30b,101d)

A - - N   **acon** (62c,140d), **adan** (102d), **aden** (34b), **Aden, agon** (12c,36c, 41b,55d,71b), **Akan** (191), **akin** (8b,92b,129c), **alan** (45a,79a, 183c), **Alan** (96a), **alen** (40d,138a), **alin** (188), **amen** (14a, 80b,94a,137a,149c,175c,184b), **Amen** (86d,127d,159b,164a), **amin** (9d), **Amon** (86d,96b,127d,159b,164a), **Amun** (86d,127d, 159b,164a), **anan** (49a,159a,180c), **anon** (7d,14d,79d,80b,123a, 145c,150c,164a), **Aran** (18c,48c,64d,82d,174c), **Asin** (102a), **aten** (150a,159b), **aton** (150a,159b), **Avon** (143b), **Awan** (191) **axon** (106c,153c), **ayin** (91c), **azan** (102d), **azon** (127b)

AO - -   **aone** (52b,167b), **Aoul** (191)

- AO -   **faon** (33c,55a), **gaol** (123d), **Gaol** (164a), **Gaon** (85b), **Jaob, Laos** (80d,129c), **naos** (28a,71c,137a,163a), **Naos** (155b), **paon** (115b), **Taos** (192), **Yaou** (30c)

- - AO   **Agao** (6c,73c), **dhao** (24c), **grao** (189), **guao** (168c,169b), **Miao** (30a,b), **omao** (165b), **prao** (21b,26a,95c,d), **tiao**

A - - O   **aboo** (17c), **acto** (152b), **aero** (8b,34a,b,58c,59a), **Agao** (6c,73c), **agio** (52c,60a,101c,123a), **agro** (149d), **Aino** (84a,c), **albo** (34d, 181a), **alco** (45b), **allo** (34c), **also** (10b,18b,80a), **alto** (152b,176c, 177a), **ambo** (125b,128b), **ammo** (9d), **ango** (171a), **apio** (125b), **areo** (34c), **Argo** (12c,36b,c), **Arno** (27a), **aroo** (80c,82b), **arro** (52c), **arto** (34a), **asno** (151d), **Ateo** (120d), **atmo** (34d,174d), **auto** (34d)

AP - -   **Apap** (102a), **apar** (12d), **aper** (32d), **Apet** (97c), **apex** (39c,76c, 115c,118b,159b,166a,167b), **apia** (121b), **apii** (74c), **apio** (125b), **Apis** (17c,24b,49a,125a,136a), **apod** (59d), **apse** (9b,20a,31a,128c, 130a,142b,175a), **Apsu** (29a), **Apus** (36b,c)

- AP -   **capa** (152a,166d), **cape** (75a,96c,124b,161a), **caph** (91c), **capp** (27a), **gape** (185b), **gapo** (60a), **gapy, Hapi** (66a,107b,136a), **hapu** (106d), **jape** (85a,b), **kapa** (74b), **kaph** (91d), **kapp, Lapp** (108a), **mapo** (68a,148d), **napa** (25c,67d,90d), **Napa** (182c), **nape** (15b, 108c,d), **napu** (29d,80d), **papa, pape** (19b,113a), **rapt** (6c,27a,50d), **sapa** (70c), **sapo** (149c,166d), **tapa** (16c,32c,53b,56a,74b,104b,112b, 113d,120d), **tape** (16a,19a,128d), **tapu, wapp** (54b,133d,145d), **yapa** (113b), **Yapp** (22a)

- - AP   **Apap** (102a), **atap** (113b), **chap** (55b), **clap** (58b), **drap** (61b,c, 62a), **flap** (17b,59a,104a,118d,161a,182d), **frap** (45d,165c), **heap** (117d), **knap** (76d,107a,139b,159b,166a,170c,185b), **laap** (51d,91b, 141d), **leap** (26c), **neap** (165c,167a,177b), **plap** (54b), **reap** (7a,40a, 74a), **shap, slap** (24a,128c,148c), **snap** (23a,36d,38b,48b,54d,56c, 58c,149d), **soap, swap** (168a), **trap** (27b,67b,132b,149b), **wrap** (32b,51a)

A - - P   **alop** (13d,46b,93d), **Apap** (102a), **asop** (180b), **atap** (113b), **atip** (14b,166a), **atop** (112a,174a)

AQ - -   **aqua** (90a,178c)

- AQ -   **waqf** (103a)

- - AQ   **Iraq** (99a,d)

AR - -   **Arab** (30a,78b,c,106a,107c,157b,160c,185d), **arad** (13a,c,84a), **arah** (52c), **Aral** (135d), **Aram** (18d,50c,105c,144b,161c), **Aran** (18c, 48c,64d,82d,174c), **arar** (137a,168c), **Aras, arba** (135d,171a), **arca**

(9a,22c,29d,115a,130a), **Arca** (101b), **arch** (29d,38b,39d;123d, 132c), **area** (37d,38a,44c,53a,93b,110d,127d,138c,168a,186d), **areg** (116a,137a), **areo** (34c), **Ares** (49b,51b,68c,76a,97a,105c,110b, 178a,186d), **aret** (128c), **Argo** (12c,36b,c), **aria** (8b,98c,150a,c, 170c), **arid** (46c,85a), **arif** (127d), **aril** (142a), **aris** (101b), **arme** (63a,179b), **arms, army** (78c), **arna** (24a,181b), **Arnd** (67a), **Arne** (35c,50c,134d), **arni** (24a,181b), **Arno** (27a), **arn't**, **Aroa** (175b), **Arod** (86c), **aroo** (80c,82b), **arow** (92c,158b), **arpa** (83b), **arra** (47d,52c,82b), **arro** (52c), **Arta** (72b), **arto** (34a), **arts** (138c), **arty, arui** (11b,143d,144a,181c), **arum** (13a,39b,58d,92b,155c), **Arum** (66a), **Arya** (80d)

- AR - **Aare, Aaru** (6b,48d), **bara** (188), **barb** (20b,57d,78b,117d,120a,b, 124b), **bard** (12d,120a), **bare** (43d,157c), **bari** (79c), **Bari** (37c,83d), **bark** (115c), **barm** (185b), **barn** (156d), **baro** (71a,122c), **barr** (49b), **Bart** (96b), **baru** (168c), **cara** (83a), **Cara** (48b,183c), **card** (33d, 114d), **care** (11b,14c,35d,150a,184d), **cark** (26d,184d), **carl** (115c, 135d), **Carl** (96a), **carn** (156c), **caro** (83a,183d), **carp** (27d,38d, 40c,55a,56c,57a), **carr** (120d,140a), **cart** (171d,175a,177b), **Dara** (18d), **Dard**, **dare** (28d,41b,42a,74d,175b), **Dare** (57a), **dari** (38a, 70b), **dark** (47a,67d,109b,160b), **darn** (130b), **darr** (163c), **dart** (13b,88a,100c,120b,153a,160c), **Dart** (100c), **earl** (107c), **earn** (42d,64b,99a), **fard** (112d), **fare** (43c,59b,67d,123b), **farl** (138c, 140b), **farm** (165d), **faro** (65a), **gara** (190), **garb** (32c,46a), **gare** (61b,c,62c,127c,184b), **Garm** (178c), **garn** (67d,185b), **Garo** (88c), **Harb** (191), **hard** (109b), **hare** (91b,132c), **hark** (92d), **harl** (16b,56b, 59a), **harm** (40b,81a), **harp** (105a,129a), **hart** (41d,154d), **jarl** (40d, 107d), **kara** (132a), **Kari** (14d), **Karl** (96a), **karn** (156c), **karo** (106d), **Lara** (25c), **lard** (54d,61a,71a,110a), **lari** (78a,101c), **Lari** (72c), **lark** (19a,63d,177b), **larp** (51d), **Lars** (51d,121b), **mara** (114d), **Mara** (24a,d,105b,107b), **marc** (70c), **Marc** (96a), **mare** (78b,108b), **mari** (16a,61d), **mark, Mark** (52a,96a,146b,155a), **marl** (32a,42c, 55d), **maro** (144d), **Mars** (68c,118d,119a,178a), **mart** (49d,97a), **Mart** (96b,183d), **maru** (84c,144d), **Mary** (50c,126b,183c), **nard** (13a, 97c,102b,110a,153c), **Nare** (93c), **nark** (81a,156d), **nary** (108b), **oary, para** (134c,170d), **Para** (18a,51d), **parc** (62b,112c), **pard** (27b, 91b), **pare** (115c,129a), **pari** (34a,180a), **park, parr** (136d,147c), **pars** (89d), **part** (44d,60d,121c,159c), **paru** (57a), **rara** (119a), **rare** (138b,164b,172b,173d), **Sara** (24d,183c), **sard** (26d,28d,65d,111a, 142b,156d), **Sarg** (96d,125c), **sari** (48b,65b,77b), **Sark** (28d), **Sart** (82b, 103b, 170d), **tara** (22a, 55c, 113a, 168c), **Tara** (82b,c,138b), **tare** (9a,18d,41a,176a,179d), **tari** (47d,69a), **tarn** (87d,103d,120d), **taro** (13c,48c,49b,64b,112b,120a,133d,155c,170a, c), **tarp** (26b,178d), **tart** (114d), **vara** (151d), **vare** (179b), **vari** (34d,91b,134d,174d), **vary** (28d,43c), **ward** (31c,55c,86b), **ware** (27d,35a), **warf, warm** (7c,75b,163b), **warn** (7b), **warp** (36c,165a, 171c), **wart** (124d), **wary** (27d,176b), **yard** (152d), **yare** (96b,124b, 128b), **yark** (22c), **yarl** (40d,107d), **yarn** (154b,161b,184b), **yarr** (72a), **Yaru** (48d), **zarf** (39c,155a), **zarp** (120c)

- - AR **Adar** (85c,102a), **afar** (44c), **Afar** (6c), **agar** (7d,28c,39c,103c,141c), **ajar** (110c), **alar** (15c,145c,182d), **amar** (189), **apar** (12d), **arar** (137a,168c), **asar** (67b), **atar** (58d,116b,134a), **Avar** (27d,108a), **bear** (27a,50b,113c,155a), **Bhar** (191), **boar** (77c,117c,160c,181c),

310

char (24d,138c,170b), **czar** (42d,49d,60b,135c), **dear, Dhar, duar, Edar** (18d), **fear** (113c,155a), **gear** (32c,112a,167b), **gnar** (72a), **guar** (46c,59d), **haar** (139c), **hear** (75b,c,92d), **hoar** (63d,71a, 181a), **inar** (65b), **Isar** (41a,104c,132a), **Iyar** (102b), **izar** (65b, 103b,155b), **joar** (100a), **juar** (100a), **khar** (189), **knar** (87c,134b), **kuar** (102a), **kyar** (33a), **lear** (139d), **Lear** (37a,143b), **liar** (98d), **maar** (177a), **near** (11d,32c,107b), **omar** (103b), **Omar** (48c,51b, 163b), **osar** (51b,67b,131b), **paar** (28c), **pear** (64a), **rear** (15b,23a, b,24a,51b,76d,127c), **roar** (145c) **Saar** (63b,102d,132a), **scar** (31a, 184d), **sear** (23d,27d,72d,138c), **soar** (59a), **spar** (22c,24c,64b, 97b,100b,144d), **star** (14a,21c,94c,100c), **taar** (12b), **tear** (67c, 87b,130a), **thar** (68a,76d), **tiar** (39a,75a,121a), **tsar** (42d,49d, 60b,135c), **tzar** (42d,49d,60b,135c), **usar** (8d,16c), **wear** (50b), **year, Zoar**

A - - R **Abir** (129a), **Acer** (96c), **acor** (6d), **Adar** (85c,102a), **Ader** (18d), **ador** (153b), **afar** (44c), **Afar** (6c), **afer** (48a,182b), **agar** (7d,28c, 39c,103c,141c), **ager** (47c,56a,89b,c,131d,133b), **Ahir** (27b), **ajar** (110c), **alar** (15c,145c,182d), **Alur** (191), **amar** (189), **amer** (61b), **amir** (7c,12a,103a,b,123c,170d), **amor** (152b), **Amor** (39c,68b), **Aner** (18d,96b), **apar** (12d), **aper** (32d), **arar** (137a,168c), **asar** (67b), **Aser** (84a), **Askr** (107d), **asor** (75c,105a), **Asur** (68c), **atar** (58d,116b,134a), **Ater** (18c), **Auer** (79a), **Avar** (27d,108a), **aver** (7c,14a,15c,41c,95c,140d,155c,160b,184c)

AS - - **asak** (13d,168c,169a), **asar** (67b), **asci** (154a), **asea** (39b,177c), **asem** (9a,49a,69c), **Aser** (84a), **Asha** (191), **ashy** (113a,178a), **Asia** (48a), **Asin** (102a), **Askr** (107d), **asno** (151d), **asok** (13d), **Asom** (18d), **asop** (180b), **asor** (75c,105a), **asse** (25a,60d,74a), **assi** (77d), **asta** (188), **Asta** (107a,164c), **Asti** (83d,182b), **Asur** (68c)

- AS - **base** (6a,43b,44b,51c,60c,79b,94b,122b), **bash, bask** (94d), **bass** (57b,c,177a), **bast** (16c,56a,117b,184a), **Bast** (27b), **casa** (152b), **case** (22c,36c,81c,91a,108c), **cash** (101c), **cask, Caso** (82d), **cass** (140c,177a), **Cass** (147a), **cast** (165b,167c), **dash** (125c,162d), **dasi** (77a), **ease** (7c,8d,35a,100d,129d,130b,c,150c), **East** (111b), **easy** (54a,146d,149d,172b), **fash** (140c,176a), **fass** (189), **fast** (56d, 126c,141d,160c,173a,d), **gash** (40a), **gasp** (113c), **hase** (74d), **hash, hasp** (31d,54d,153c), **hast, jass** (160d), **kasa** (48a), **kasi** (116b), **kasm** (189), **lash** (58c,87b,165c,180d), **Lasi** (191), **lass** (95b), **last** (36c,50b,145a,174c), **masa** (37a), **mash** (39b,156c), **mask** (44a,45c), **mass** (8a,24b,35b,142d), **mast** (17c,108d,120b,144d,152d), **masu** (57a,84c), **nase** (26b,75a,124b), **Nash** (9c), **nasi** (34c,108a,115a), **Nast** (9c,27a), **oast** (15d,86b,112a), **pasa** (46a,127c,152c), **pasi** (94b), **pass** (110b,155c), **past** (25c,69d,165d), **rasa** (51c), **rase** (42b, d,91d), **rash** (75a), **rasp** (56b,70d,140d), **sasa** (55c), **sash** (18a,45c, 67b,182b), **sass, tash** (154d), **task** (156b), **Tass** (107a,135d,151b), **vasa** (46d,114a,160b,175d), **Vasa, vase, vast** (78d,79d), **vasu** (106c), **Vasu** (176d), **wash, wasp, wast**

- - AS **abas** (61c), **alas** (52c,136b,183b), **Anas** (46c,d), **Aras, baas** (97c), **bias** (43b,123a), **blas** (6c,49c), **Blas** (67b), **bras** (61a), **Dyas** (66a), **ELAS** (71c), **eyas** (106c,173a), **gras** (78b), **Idas** (27b,71c), **iras** (11b,32a), **khas** (153a), **kras** (76d), **kvas** (135c), **Lias** (66a), **Lyas** (66a), **Maas** (132a), **mias** (111a), **Nias** (82d), **oras** (40d), **quas**

311

(135c), **upas** (84d,120b,168c,d), **Usas** (68d), **utas** (49a,109c), **Xmas,** **yeas** (177c), **Zoas** (20b)

A - - S   **abas** (61c), **ABC's** (57a), **Acis** (64b), **Acts, acus** (89d, 118a), **Ades** (73a), **Agis** (86d), **Aias, Airs** (123b), **alas** (52c,136b,183b), **alms** (29a), **Alps** (85d), **Alys** (183c), **Ames** (9c,82a), **Amos** (96a,144b), **Anas** (46c,d), **Anes** (110c,140a), **anis** (55c), **Apis** (17c,24b,49a, 125a,136a), **Apus** (36b,c), **Aras, Ares** (49b,51b,68c,76a,97a,105c, 110b,178a,186d), **aris** (101b), **arms, arts** (138c), **ates** (160c), **atis** (76d,102a), **Aves** (19d), **Avis** (89a,183c), **avus** (89b), **axis** (28b, 41d,77c,153c), **ayes** (177c)

AT - -   **atap** (113b), **atar** (58d,116b,134a), **atef** (39a,48d), **aten** (150a, 159b), **Ateo** (120d), **Ater** (18c), **ates** (160c), **Atik** (155b), **atip** (14b,166a), **atis** (76d,102a), **Atka** (11a), **atle** (136d,161d,169b), **Atli** (14c,72b,79a,107d), **atma** (150d), **atmo** (34d,174d), **Atmu** (143a,159b), **atom** (101c,114c,180d), **aton** (150a,159b), **atop** (112a, 174a), **Atri, atry** (141b), **atta** (58d,90c,97d,160c,173d), **Atta** (94d, 95d,100a,106b,117a), **Attu, atua** (120d), **Atum** (143a,159b)

- AT -   **bata** (30a,142d), **bate** (43c,91b,100d), **bath, Bath** (50d,151c), **batt** (37c), **batz** (190), **cata** (122c), **cate** (165c), **Cato** (132d,133b), **data** (54a), **date** (64a,153a), **dato** (95c,102c,117a), **datu** (95c,102c, 117a), **eats, fate** (42d,52a,87a,94a), **gata** (143c), **gate** (51a,121b), **Gath** (117a), **hate** (6a,43a), **hath, Hati** (48d), **jati** (27b), **jato** (173b), **Kate** (143c,183d), **kath** (14a), **Katy** (183d), **lata** (85d,95d), **late** (128c), **lath** (157c), **latu** (190), **mate** (18c,35b,41d,113a,154a,162c), **math** (77a), **Matt, maty** (80c), **Nata** (15c,47c), **Nate** (22b), **Nath** (155c), **Nato** (6a,8d), **natr** (189), **Natt** (107b), **oath** (119c,150a), **pata** (32c,160d), **pate** (39a,74d), **path** (132a,134b), **pato** (46d), **patu** (179b), **rata** (29d,56b,89d,96c,106d,120c,168c), **rate** (11d,14a,31d, 36b,51d,52a,70b,85c,112b,123b,127d,128a,138c,143a,174b), **rath** (29a,76d,162d), **rati** (189), **rats, sate** (32d,52c,67d,70d,137c,159d), **sati, Sati** (49a,126b,147b), **tate** (183a), **tatt** (87c), **tatu** (12d), **Tatu, Wate** (141a), **watt, Watt** (82a,173b,177c), **yate** (51d,168c), **yati** (76d), **zati** (21d)

- - AT   **adat** (90b,95d), **alat** (136d), **Anat** (138c,147d), **beat** (58c,87b,131a, 164d,165b,180d), **bhat** (80c), **blat** (25b), **boat** (27b,106a), **brat, chat** (9b,19c,161c), **coat** (160a), **doat** (17a,94b,112a,165d), **drat** (100a), **Duat** (172d), **erat** (89c), **etat** (62d), **feat** (7a,52d), **fiat** (35a, 41d,48c,111b,137a), **Fiat** (83¢), **flat** (41b,124b,173a), **frat, geat** (77d,101a), **Geat** (138a), **ghat** (32d,88b,103d,132a), **gnat** (59a, 81b,99c), **goat** (135a), **heat, ikat** (53b,159a), **kaat** (105d), **khat** (105d), **kyat** (189), **Maat** (69a,b,85d), **meat** (59b), **moat** (44d), **neat** (165c,169d), **peat** (64a,175a), **piat** (11a), **plat** (22d,96c,114a,119c, 133d), **pyat** (95b), **scat** (26b,67a,d,126c,169c), **seat** (98c,156b), **shat** (87d), **skat** (181b), **Skat** (155b), **slat** (58b,89a,117c,184a), **spat** (112c,126b,134b), **stat** (72d), **swat** (15d,20d,32d,157c), **Swat** (103a), **that** (42b,124b,129c), **what** (129c)

A - - T   **abet** (8b,15b,50a,59b,75d,81c,141d,159d), **Abot** (100c), **abut** (22a, 167c), **acht** (66c), **adat** (90b,95d), **adit** (51a,100a,114d), **Ahet** (49a,102a), **aint, alat** (136d), **alit** (44b,143a), **amit** (94a), **Anat** (138c,147d), **anet** (43c), **Apet** (97c), **aret** (128c), **arn't, aunt** (129c)

AU - -   **Auca** (192), **Aude, Auer** (79a), **auge** (123c,132b), **aula** (66c,73b),

312

aulu (74c,168c), aune (188), aunt (129c), aura (44c,49c,66a,96b, 158a,170d,177c), auri (34a), Ausa, ausu (168c,180b), auto (34d), auza (168c,180b)

- AU - baud (162d), baul (18b), Baum (9c,112c), cauk (139b), caul (16d, 74d), caur (139a), daub (148d), dauk (95c), Daur (139b), dauw (24c), eaux (178c), faun (56a,68b,137c,161a,184a), gaub (116c), gaud (169d), gaue (67a), Gaul (10a,60d,63c), gaup, gaur (112c, 181c), gaus (67d), gaut (88b,103d,132a), haul (27b,45d), jaun (113a), kaun (93d), laud (122a), laun (146b), maud (53d,136d, 143c), Maud (181a,183c), Maui (120d), maul (73c), maun (139d), naut (141b), Paul (96a), paun (18b), paut (140a), Sauk (192), saul (48a,168c), Saul (18c,86d,115a), saum (189), taun (188), taut (163b,165c), Vaux (63b), yaup

- - AU Agau (73c), beau, Diau (192), Drau, Esau (82c,84a,128c), frau (181b), miau (27b,99b), prau (21b,26a,95c,d), sgau (88c), unau (148c,171d), whau (107a,168c)

A - - U Aalu (6b,48d), Aaru (6b,48d), Abou (48b,55a), actu (7a,89a), Addu (68c,157a,182a), Agau (73c), Ainu (84a,84c), ammu (9d), ansu (11d), anzu (11d), Apsu (29a), Atmu (143a,159b), Attu, aulu (74c,168c), ausu (168c,180b), auzu (168c,180b)

AV - - aval (70c), Avar (27d,108a), avec (63a,183a), aver (7c,14a,15c,41c, 95c,140d,155c,160b,184c), Aves (19d), avid (47b,71a,186b), avis (89a), Avis (183c), Avon (143b), avow (6d,36a,41c,112c), avus (89b)

- AV - bave (61d,146c), cava (116a,175b), cave (27d), cavy (72b,120d, 132c,157b), Dave (96b), Davy (96b,136b), eave (133c), favi (138a, 165d), gave, have, Java (33a), Jave (84d), kava (18c,116a), Kavi (84d), lava (101c,132b,151a,177a), lave (16d,178b), nave (30d,31a, 78d,114b,180c), navy (33c,58b), pave (85a), pavo (115b), Pavo (36b,c), pavy (115b), rave (41c,157a,161d), ravi, Ravi (16b), save (52b,110c,123a,173c), Tave (183d), Tavy (183d), wave (19a, 59a,111c,131c,160c,172d), wavy (147b,172d), yava

- - AV Muav (66a), Slav (13c,40c,48b,52a,120b,135b)

A - - V akov (189), Azov (20b,135d)

AW - - Awan (191), away (6b,69d,76a,109d,111d), awry (13d,38d,171c)

- AW - bawl, bawn (181a), cawk (133c), dawk (95c), dawm (190), dawn (14d,41b), fawn (33c), gawd (169c), gawk (146d), gawp, hawk (19c, 115c), jawy, kawa (18c,116a), Kawi (84d), kawn (93d), lawn (20a, 37c,53b,92c), pawa (189), pawl (43a,95a), pawn (29c,119c), sawk (188), sawn, tawa (106d,168c), yawl (136b,171d,175d), yawn, yawp

- - AW chaw (97c), claw (29c,105b,161d,173a), craw (38d,72c,156c), dhaw (125a), draw (42c,53a,92b,117c,121c,167d), flaw, gnaw (20a,107a, 178b), miaw (27b,99b), shaw (164b), Shaw (50c,53b), slaw, thaw

A - - W alow (18a,172c), anew (7c), arow (92c,158b), avow (6d,36a,41c, 112c)

AX - - axal (120b), axil (10c), axis (28b,41d,77c,153c), axle (153c,180c), axon (106c,153c)

- AX - saxe (20d,33c), taxi (13a,125b), taxo (13a), waxy (119c,149d)

▪ ▪ AX   **Ajax** (71b,162d), **Anax** (43c,120c), **coax** (180c), **Crax** (19b,39d), **flax, hoax** (41c,122a), **Odax** (132c), **Olax** (52b)

A ▪ ▪ X   **abox** (22d), **Ajax** (71b,162d), **Alix** (183c), **Amex** (184d), **Anax** (43d,120c), **apex** (39c,76c,115c,118b,159b,166a,167b),

AY ▪ ▪   **ayah** (108d), **ayes** (177c), **ayin** (91c)

▪ AY ▪   **baya** (179b), **Baya** (191), **cayo, Daye** (123d), **days, hayz, kayo** (87c), **maya** (179b), **Maya** (23d,186c), **Mayo** (193), **raya** (19b,23c,76d, 107d), **saya** (117a), **Vayu** (68c,182a), **ways, yaya** (113c,168c)

▪ ▪ AY   **alay** (96c), **anay** (72b), **away** (6b,69d,76a,109d,111d), **blay** (57d), **bray, chay** (48a,128d), **Clay** (9d), **dray** (27a,154c,177b), **esay, flay** (147c,157c), **fray** (56b,60d), **gray** (33c,77c), **Gray** (50c), **okay** (8d), **olay** (113b), **piay** (98b), **play** (63d,154a), **pray** (18b,51a,159d), **quay** (88b,117c,180c), **ruay** (189), **shay** (110c), **slay, stay** (72d, 124c,130a,134a,162a), **sway** (104a)

A ▪ ▪ Y   **Abby** (183d), **ably** (147c), **achy, Addy** (183d), **adry,** (164c), **aery** (47b,51d,106c), **affy** (18b), **ahey** (52c), **ahoy** (106a), **airy** (176d, 177a), **akey** (189), **alay** (96c), **Algy** (96b), **alky, ally** (14a,35c,d, 173c), **Amoy** (88c), **anay** (72b,163b,181a), **ancy** (158c), **Andy** (96b), **army, arty, ashy** (113a,178a), **atry** (141b), **away** (6b,69d,76a,109d, 111d), **awry** (13d,38d,171c)

AZ ▪ ▪   **Azam** (166c), **azan** (102d), **Azha** (155b), **Azof** (20b,135d), **azon** (127b), **Azov** (20b,135d), **azul** (151d)

▪ AZ ▪   **caza, cazi** (103a), **cazy** (103a), **Daza** (191), **daze** (157d), **dazy, faze** (43d), **Gaza** (117a), **gaze, gazi, gazy, haze** (100c,174d), **hazy** (174b), **jazz, Kazi** (103a), **kazy** (103a), **laze** (79b), **Laze** (191), **Lazi** (191), **lazo** (88d,128b,133d), **lazy, maze** (87b,157d), **naze** (26b, 124b), **Nazi, raze** (42b,d,91d), **razz** (131b), **vaza** (114a)

▪ ▪ AZ   **Agaz** (193), **Ahaz** (86d), **Boaz** (135d)

A ▪ ▪ Z   **Agaz** (193), **Ahaz** (86d)

BA ▪ ▪   **Baal** (142b), **baas** (97c), **baba** (108d,120c,166c,171a), **babe, Babi** (116c), **babu** (77a), **baby, Bach** (35c), **back** (75d,76d,159d), **Badb** (82b), **bade, baff** (69d), **baft** (14a,53b), **baga** (171b), **bago** (13d), **bahi** (60c), **baho** (122a), **baht** (146a), **bail** (43c), **bain** (61a), **bait** (15d,51a,94d,167b), **baju** (84a), **baka** (52b), **bake** (139a), **baku** (26d,157b,168c), **Bala** (26c,66a), **bald** (16c), **bale** (24b,74a), **balk** (118c,146a,156d), **ball, balm** (110a,172c), **Balt** (93a), **balu** (104b, 159a,181d), **Bana** (67a), **banc** (61a,85c), **band** (72a,157c), **bane** (74a,106b,120b,139a), **bang** (75d,105d,148a), **bani** (190), **bank** (18a,58c), **bans, bant** (43c), **bara** (188), **barb** (20b,57d,78b,117d, 120a,b,124b), **bard** (12d,120a), **bare** (43d,157c), **bari** (37c,79c), **Bari** (83d), **bark** (115c), **barm** (185b), **barn** (156d), **baro** (71a,122c), **barr** (49b), **Bart** (96b), **baru** (168c), **base** (6a,43b,44b,51c,60c,79b,94b, 122b), **bash, bask** (94d), **bass** (57b,c,177a), **bast** (16c,56a,117b, 184a), **Bast** (27b), **bata** (30a,142d), **bate** (43c,91b,100d), **bath, Bath** (50d,151c), **batt** (37c), **batz** (190), **baud** (162d), **baul** (18b), **Baum** (9c,112c), **bave** (61d,146c), **bawl, bawn** (181a), **baya** (179b), **Baya** (191)

▪ BA ▪   **abas** (61c), **Ibad** (191), **Iban** (47c), **oban** (190)

▪ ▪ BA   **Abba** (20a,55a,161c), **alba** (98a,181a), **Alba** (151d), **amba** (161a), anba (36d), arba (135d,171a), baba (108d,120c,166c,171a), boba (29d), buba (170a), caba (184c), ceba (169b), cuba (189), Cuba (180b), Egba (191), Elba (105d), ezba (188), Faba, haba (151d), isba (135c), juba (106b), koba (11a), kuba (26d,189), Luba (191), Maba (103a,168d), Nuba (108c), peba (12d), Peba (193), Raba, reba (144a), Reba (18d,86c), saba (56a,117a), Saba (143d), Seba (18c,39d), Toba (80c), tuba (105a,137d), ueba (188)

B - - A   baba (108d,120c,166c,171a), baga (171b), baka (52b), Bala (26c, 66a), Bana (67a), bara (188), bata (30a,142d), baya (179b), Baya (191), Beda (101d), bega (188), Beja (6c,191), beka (189), bela (12a), Bela (18b,48c), bema (28d,31a,114b,119b,125b,137a), bena, (176a), Bera (86d), Besa (68b,119c), beta (71a,91c,141d), biga (171d), bija (168c), bina (77a), bisa (11a), biwa (93d,168c), Bixa (145d), blaa, boba (29d), boca (152b,c), boga (57d,180b), bola (16a, 179b), boma (7d), bona (89d,183c), Bona, bora (181d,182b), bosa (12a), bota (189), boza (12a), brea (100b), buba (170a), buda (83d), buna (161c), bura (182b)

- **BB -**   Abba (20a,55a,161c), abbe (32b,63b,123b), Abby (183d)

- - **BB**   bibb (97c,146b), Cobb (9c), dubb (161c), hobb (124b), hubb (118b), jibb, lobb (23b,94c,163a)

B - - B   Badb (82b), barb (20b,57d,78b,117d,120a,b,124b), bibb (97c, 146b), blab (162b), bleb (20c,23d,67c), blob, blub, Bodb (82b), bomb (144a), boob (146d), brab (113b), brob (153c), bulb (37a, 172c)

- **BC -**   ABC's (57a)

B - - C   banc (61a,85c), bloc (173a), Bosc (115c)

B - - D   bald (16c), band (72a,157c), bard (12d,120a), baud (162d), bead (17a,122a,146b), Beld (155b), bend (39d,171b), bind (33b,165c), biod (59d,79c), bird, bled, bold (41a), bond (92a,101c,141d,143b, 159d,165c), bord (100b), brad (54d,67c,105b), bred (23c,48c,127c), bund (49c,66c,90c), Byrd (9c,120b)

BE - -   bead (17a,122a,146b), beak (19a), beal (139d), beam, bean (91b, 142a,175a), bear (27a,50b,113c,155a), beat (58c,87b,131a,164d, 165b,180d), beau, beck (107c), Beda (101d), Bede (48c,50c,101d, 175b), beef, been (149a), beer (18c), bees (185b), beet (175a), bega (188), behn (137d), Beid (155b), Beja (6c,191), beka (189), bela (12a), Bela (18b,48c,78d), Beli (23c), bell (24c,39d), Bell (162d), belt (16a,31a), bema (28d,31a,114b,119b,125b,137a), bena (176a), bend (39d,171b), bene (18a,83c,90a,106d,122a,180a), beng (43a), beni (116a,142d), Beni (191), beno (113b,117a), bent (80b), benu (49a), Bera (86d), berg (79b), berm (25d,90d,145c), Bern (160d), Bert (96b), Besa (68b,119c), Bess (76c,183d), best (41d, 159c,160a), beta (71a,91c,141d), bete (61a,107c), beth (91c), Beth (8c,183d), bevy (38a,58c)

- **BE -**   abed (130c), Abel (7a,25b), abet (8b,15b,50a,59b,75d,81c,141d, 159d), Eben (96a), Eber (51a,75c,99d), ibex (67d,68a), obex (22d), obey (35c,75c), Obed (135d), uber (66b)

- - **BE**   abbe (32b,63b,123b), albe (133a), babe, Bube (180b), cube (66b, 150a), dobe (159b,c,172b), Elbe (108a), gabe (162a), gibe (8a,42c, 84d,100d,138c,144c,149b), gybe (144c), Habe (191), Hebe (39c,

315

69c,186b), **imbe** (37a,56a,133d), **jibe** (8a,33b,35d,37b,42c,100d, 138c,144c,149b), **jube** (28d), **kibe, Kobe** (78a), **lobe** (90c,134b), **lube** (110a), **ribe** (139a), **robe** (65b), **rube** (37d,135d,185d), **Rube** (96b), **sabe, tobe** (7d,137b), **tube** (118b,158a)

B - - E   **babe, bade, bake** (139a), **bale** (24b,74a), **bane** (74a,106b,120b, 139a), **bare** (43d,157c), **base** (6a,43b,44b,51c,60c,79b,94b,122b), **bate** (43c,91b,100d), **bave** (61d,146c), **Bede** (48c,50c,101d,175b), **bene** (18a,83c,90a,106d,122a,180a), **bete** (61a,107c), **bice** (20d, 117d), **Bice** (27b), **bide** (47c,50b,130a,158b), **bike, bile** (30c), **bine** (145b,156a,171c,176b), **bise** (182a), **bite** (29d,156b), **bize** (182a), **blae** (93b), **blue** (33c,98c,102c,150d,173a), **boce** (23b,52a,57b), **bode** (14c,60a,110b,121b), **bole** (31d,32a,169b), **bone, bore** (14c, 25b,46a,116a,165c,179b), **bose** (163c), **brae** (76d,139a,c,140b, 148c), **bree** (139a), **Brie** (29c), **Bube** (180b), **bure** (61b), **byee** (189), **byre** (38a)

- BF -   **Abfa** (76b)

B - - F   **baff** (69d), **beef, biff, buff** (134c,161d)

B - - G   **bang** (75d,105d,148a), **beng** (43a), **berg** (79b), **bing, bong, borg** (40d), **brag** (21a,175a), **brig** (72b,106a,144d), **bung** (119d,156d), **burg** (22b,73c)

BH - -   **Bhar** (191), **bhat** (80c), **bhel** (126d), **Bhil** (191), **b'hoy** (134b), **bhut** (67a)

- - BH   **Cobh** (37a)

B - - H   **Bach** (35c), **bash, bath, Bath** (50d,151c), **beth** (91c), **Beth** (8c, 183d), **bikh** (120b), **binh** (189), **bish** (120b), **blah, booh** (52c), **bosh, both, bruh** (95a), **bukh** (122a), **bush**

BI - -   **bias** (43b,123a), **bibb** (97c,146b), **bibi** (87d), **bice** (20d,117d), **Bice** (27b), **bide** (47c,50b,130a,158b,162a,177b), **bien** (63a,140c,179a, 180a), **bier** (33b,66b), **biff, biga** (171d), **bija** (168c), **bike, bikh** (120b), **bile** (30c), **bilk** (29b,41c,42a), **bill** (17b,147a), **Bill** (96b), **bilo** (131b), **bina** (77a), **bind** (33b,165c), **bine** (145b,156a,171c, 176b), **bing, binh** (189), **Bini** (191), **binn** (22c), **bino** (113b,117a), **biod** (59d,79c), **bion** (117b), **bios** (92a), **bird, birl** (93c,131a,153c), **birn** (31d,139a), **birr** (180d), **bisa** (11a), **bise** (182a), **bish** (120b), **bisk** (120b,151a), **bite** (29d,156b), **biti** (20b), **bito** (7d,57d,168c), **bitt** (54d,175c), **biur** (35a), **biwa** (93d,168c), **Bixa** (145d), **bize** (182a), **bizz**

- BI -   **Abia** (18d,137a), **Abib** (102a,b), **Abie** (96b,107a), **abir** (129a), **ibid** (80a,117a,137a), **ibis** (48d,49a,177b), **ibit** (117a), **obia** (55d), **obit** (41b,64c), **Ubii** (191)

- - BI   **Albi** (58a), **ambi** (34a,122c), **Babi** (116c), **bibi** (87d), **Bubi** (180b), **cubi** (188), **gabi** (162a), **gobi, Gobi** (42d), **kobi** (84b), **mabi** (58d), **rabi** (38d,74a), **Rabi** (14b,117b), **sebi** (34b), **tabi** (84c,149d), **Tybi** (102a), **Wabi** (192), **Yobi**

B - - I   **Babi** (116c), **bahi** (60c), **Bali, bani** (190), **bari** (79c), **Bari** (37c, 83d), **Beli** (23c), **beni** (116a,142d), **Beni** (191), **bibi** (87d), **Bini** (191), **biti** (20b), **Boli** (191), **Boni** (63b), **Bori** (110d,150c), **Bubi** (180b), **Bugi** (191), **buri** (56b)

- - BK   **nabk** (30d,164d), **nubk** (30d,164d), **Sobk** (38d)

316

B - - K   **back** (75d,76d,159d), **balk** (118c,146a,156d), **bank** (18a,58c), **bark** (115c), **bask** (94d), **beak** (19a), **beck** (107c), **bilk** (29b,41c,42a), **bisk** (120b,151a), **bock** (17c,90d,144a), **bonk** (190), **book, bosk** (164b), **bowk** (155d), **buck, bukk** (122a), **bulk** (97b), **bunk, busk** (17b,37b,55d,161b)

BL - -   **blaa, blab** (162b), **blae** (93b), **blah, blas** (6c,49c), **Blas** (67b), **blat** (25b), **blay** (57d), **bleb** (20c,23d,67c), **bled, blet** (64a), **bleu** (61b), **blew, blob, bloc** (173a), **blot, blow, blub, blue** (33c,98c,102c,150d, 173a), **blup, blur, blut** (66b)

- BL -   **able** (26b,35b,126a,147c), **ably** (147c)

B - - L   **baal** (142b), **bail** (43c), **ball, baul** (18b), **bawl, beal** (139d), **bell** (24c,39d), **Bell** (162d), **bhel** (126d), **Bhil** (191), **bill** (17b,147a), **Bill** (96b), **birl** (93c,131a,153c), **boil, boll** (119b,d), **bool** (39d), **bowl, bual** (182c), **buhl** (81a), **bull** (113c), **burl** (87c,169a)

B - - M   **balm** (110a,172c), **barm** (185b), **Baum** (9c,112c), **beam, berm** (25d, 90d,145c), **boom** (152d), **Bram** (96a), **brim**

B - - N   **bain** (61a), **barn** (156d), **bawn** (181a), **bean** (91b,142a,175a), **been** (149a), **behn** (137d), **Bern** (160d), **bien** (63a,140c,179a,180a), **binn** (22c), **bion** (117b), **birn** (31d,139a), **Bonn** (17d), **boon** (18b,20c, 55a), **born, bran** (23c,39a,70b,72a,79c), **Bran** (23c,50c), **bren** (72d, 95a), **brin** (32c,54c,146c), **bunn** (25b), **burn**

BO - -   **boar** (77c,117c,160c,181c), **boat** (27b,106a), **Boaz** (135d), **boba** (29d,) **bobo** (112c,168c), **boca** (152b,c), **boce** (23b,52a,57b), **bock** (17c,90d,144a), **Bodb** (82b), **bode** (14c,60a,110b,121b), **Bodo** (88c), **body** (72a), **Boer** (151a), **boga** (57d,180b), **bogo** (117a,168c), **Bogo** (191), **bogy** (153a), **boho** (117a,179d), **Bohr** (14b,40d,138c), **Boil** (191), **boil, bois** (62b,63a,183d), **bojo** (117a), **boko** (52b), **bola** (16a, 179b), **bold** (41a), **bole** (31d,32a,169b), **boll** (119b,d), **bolo** (87a, 179b), **bolt** (13b,54d,58b,132d,160a), **boma** (7d), **bomb** (144a), **bona** (89d), **Bona** (183c), **bond** (92a,101c,141d,143b,159d,165c), **bone, bong, Boni** (63b), **bonk** (190), **Bonn** (17d), **bony** (147c), **Bony** (96b), **boob** (146d), **booh** (52c), **book, bool** (39d), **boom** (152d), **boon** (18b,20c,55a), **boor** (47a,135d,172c), **boot** (128d), **bora** (181d, 182b), **bord** (100b), **bore** (14c,25b,46a,116a,165c,179b), **borg** (40d), **Bori** (110d,150c), **born, boro** (154b), **Boro** (193), **Bors** (70b,134b), **bort** (43b), **Bort** (134b), **bosa** (12a), **Bosc** (115c), **bose** (163c), **bosh, bosk** (164b), **boss** (49d,157d), **bota** (189), **both, Boto** (192), **bott** (32a,88d), **bout** (36c), **bouw** (188), **bowk** (155d), **bowl, boxy, boza** (12a), **bozo** (55b)

- BO -   **aboo** (17a), **Abot** (100c), **Abou** (48b,55a), **abox** (22d), **eboe** (28b, 110a,168c,169b), **Eboe, ebon** (20b), **oboe** (74b,104d,105a,182a, 184a), **obol** (29b,110a)

- - BO   **albo** (34d,181a), **ambo** (125b,128b), **bobo** (112c,168c), **bubo** (112c), **Egbo** (141d), **Gobo** (84d), **hobo** (168a,174b), **jobo** (77c), **lobo** (165d,183c), **nabo** (117a), **Nebo** (68c,102d,103d,183a), **umbo** (22b), **zobo** (186b)

B - - O   **bago** (13d), **baho** (122a), **baro** (71a,122c), **beno** (113b,117a), **bilo** (131b), **bino** (113b,117a), **bito** (7d,52d,168c), **bobo** (112c,168c), **Bodo** (88c), **bogo** (117a,168c), **Bogo** (191), **boho** (117a,179d), **bojo** (117a), **boko** (52b), **bolo** (87a,179b), **boro** (154b), **Boro** (193), **Boto**

(192), **bozo** (55b), **broo** (139a), **bubo** (112c), **Bufo** (166c), **Buto** (142d), **buyo** (18b), **bygo** (114c)

B - - P   **blup, bump**

BR - -   **brab** (113b), **brad** (54d,67c,105b), **brae** (76d,139a,c,140b,148c), **brag** (21a,175a), **Bram** (96a), **bran** (23c,39a,70b,72a,79c), **Bran** (23c,50c), **bras** (61a), **brat, bray, brea** (100b), **bred** (23c,48c,127c), **bree** (139a), **bren** (72d,95a), **Brer** (172b), **Bres, brew** (35d), **brey** (194), **Brie** (29c), **brig** (72b,106a,144d), **brim, brin** (32c,54c,146c), **brit** (76c), **brob** (153c), **broo** (139a), **brow, bruh** (95a), **brut** (182c), **Brut** (23c)

- BR -   **abra** (26b), **Abra, abri** (61c,62c,144b), **Ebro** (132a), **obra** (152d, 184c)

B - - R   **barr** (49b), **bear** (27a,50b,113c,155a), **beer** (18c), **Bhar** (191), **bier** (33b,66b), **birr** (180d), **biur** (35a), **blur, boar** (77c,117c,160c,181c), **Boer** (151a), **Bohr** (14b,40d,138c), **boor** (47a,135d,172c), **Brer** (172b), **buhr** (180d), **burr** (123b)

- BS -   **Absi** (191)

- - BS   **dibs** (70c), **Lubs** (94c), **nibs** (116c), **nobs** (38c,87a)

B - - S   **baas** (97c), **bans, bass** (57b,c,177a), **bees** (185b), **Bess** (76c,183d), **bias** (43b,123a), **bios** (92a), **blas** (6c,49c), **Blas** (67b), **bois** (62b, 63a,183d), **Bors** (70b,134b), **boss** (49d,157d), **bras** (61a), **Bres, buss** (87a,148c)

- - BT   **debt** (91d,109b)

B - - T   **baft** (14a,53b), **baht** (146a), **bait** (15d,51a,94d,167b), **Balt** (93a), **bant** (43c), **Bart** (96b), **bast** (16c,56a,117b,184a), **Bast** (27b), **batt** (37c), **beat** (58c,87b,131a,164d,165b,180d), **beet** (175a), **belt** (16a, 31a), **bent** (80b), **Bert** (96b), **best** (41d,159c,160a), **bhat** (80c), **bhut** (67a), **bitt** (54d,175c), **blat** (25b), **blet** (64a), **blot, blut** (66b), **boat** (27b,106a), **bolt** (13b,54d,58b,132d,160a), **boot** (128d), **bort** (43b), **Bort** (134b), **bott** (32a,88d), **bout** (36c), **brat, brit** (76c), **brut** (182c), **Brut** (23c), **bult** (76d), **bunt** (15d,180c), **bust, butt** (27a,77b,127d,162a,182b)

BU - -   **bual** (182c), **buba** (170a), **Bube** (180b), **Bubi** (180b), **bubo** (112c), **buck, buda** (83d), **buff** (134c,161d), **Bufo** (166c), **Bugi** (191), **buhl** (81a), **buhr** (180d), **bukh** (122a), **bukk** (122a), **bulb** (37a,172c), **bulk** (97b), **bull** (113c), **bult** (76d), **bump, buna** (161c), **bund** (49c,66c,90c), **bung** (119d,156d), **bunk, bunn** (25b), **bunt** (15d, 180c), **buoy** (28d,58c), **bura** (182c), **bure** (61b), **burg** (22b,73c), **buri** (56b), **burl** (87c,169a), **burn, burr** (123b), **bury** (81d), **bush, busk** (17b,37b,55d,161b), **buss** (87a,148c), **bust, busy, Buto** (142d), **butt** (27a,77b,127d,162a,182b), **buxy** (115b), **buyo** (18b) **buzz**

- BU -   **abut** (22a,167c), **ebur** (89c)

- - BU   **babu** (77a), **kobu** (84b), **Nabu** (68c,183a), **tabu** (59d,111d), **Tibu** (191), **zebu** (22d,80d,112c)

B - - U   **babu** (77a), **baju** (84a), **baku** (26d,157b,168c), **balu** (104b,159a, 181d), **baru** (168c), **beau, benu** (49a), **bleu** (61b)

B - - W   **blew, blow, bouw** (188), **brew** (35d), **brow**

BY - -   byee, (189), bygo (114c), Byrd (9c,120b), byre (38a)

- - BY   Abby (183d), baby, doby (159b,c), gaby (59c,146d), goby (57d), kiby (29a), ruby (20a,65d,179c), toby (8c,85c,104b), Toby (96b, 125c)

B - - Y   baby, bevy (38a,58c), b'hoy (134b), blay (57d), body (72a), bogy (153a), bony (147c), Bony (96b), boxy, bray, brey (194), buoy (28d,58c), bury (81d), busy, buxy (115b)

B - - Z   batz (190), bizz, Boaz (135d), buzz

CA - -   caam (93d), caba (184c), Caca (67a), caco (73b), cade (25c,27a,76c, 85d,116d), Cade (50c), cadi (12a,103a,171a), cady (69d), Caen, cafe, cage (36a), cagy (178b), caid (35a,151d,152b), cain (169c), Cain (6a,7a,50d,88a,104c,143a), caja (152a), caji (180b), cake, caky, cale (72d), calf, calk (78c,109a,141c,178d), call (145c,159b, 176d), calm (8d,11d,112b,118d,126c,d,172b,173d), calo (72d), calp (92b), calx (23c,75c,112c), came (182b), Came (192), camp (163b), Cana (57a,64b,100c), cane (17b,128a,156a,159a,177d), Cane, cang (184a), cano (152a), cant (28d,81b,84d,90c,109b,136c,165d,166a), capa (152a,166d), cape (75a,96c,124b,161a), caph (91c), Capp (27a), cara (83a), Cara (48b,183c), card (33d,114d), care (11b, 14c,35d,150a,184d), cark (26d,184d), carl (115c,135d), Carl (96a), carn (156c), caro (83a), Caro (183d), carp (27d,38d,40c,55a,56c, 57a), carr (120d,140a), cart (171d,175a,177b), casa (152b), case (22c,36c,81c,91a,108c), cash (101c), cask, Caso (82d) cass (140c, 177a), Cass (147a), cast (165b,167c), cata (122c), cate (165c), Cato (132d,133b), Catt (9d), cauk (139b), caul (16d,74d), caup, caur (139a), cava (116a,175b), cave (27d), cavy (72b,120d,132c, 157b), cawk (133c), cayo, caza, cazi (103a), cazy (103a)

- CA -   ecad (73a,119b), ical (158c), scab (80b,107d,157c), scad (31a,57a, 78b,88d,137c), scan (52b,93d,98a,116d,128b,c,140d), scar (31a, 184d), scat (26b,67a,d,126c,169c)

- - CA   acca (53b,d), Alca (14c,128b), arca (9a,22c,29d,115a,130a), Area (101b), Auca (192), boca (152b,c), Caca (67a), coca (29d,33a,105d, 113a), cuca (33a,105d), deca (34d,122d), Ecca (66a), esca (11c, 44a,70c), Inca (14b,30a), jaca (84a), juca (27a), mica (82c,100b, 146c), onca (189), orca (86b), paca (132c,154a), peca (190), pica (66b,95b,172c), puca (68a), raca (19a,59c,130b,184d), Teca (192), unca (49a), Ynca (193), yuca (27a)

C - - A   caba (184c), Caca (67a), caja (152a), Cana (57a,64b,100c), capa (152a,166d), cara (83a), Cara (48b,183c), casa (152b), cata (122c), cava (116a,175b), caza, ceba (169b), cela (62d), cena (88d,133a), cepa (110c), cera (152d,161d,179a), chaa (162b), chia (136d), cima (83b,c), Civa (56d), coca (29d,33a,105d,113a), coda (32c,35d,55d, 56c), coja (103b,166b), cola (25b,108d,149d,168c), coma (91c, 157d,170c,172b), copa (88b,113c), cora (65d), Cora (42b,69c,80c, 116b,124d,183c), cota (117a), coxa (77b), crea (92c,151d), cuba (189), Cuba (180b), cuca (33a,105d), Cuna (193), cura (152c), cuya (39b), cyma (101a,b)

C - - B   chab (184a), chib (167a), chob (23c), chub (40c,154c), club (39c), Cobb (9c), comb (38c), crab (39b,144b,181b), crib (96b,120d), curb (130c,146b)

319

- CC -   acca (53b,d), Ecca (66a), ecce (17d,89a,c)

C - - C   chic (148d), circ (31a), cric (131c), croc (13a,74a)

C - - D   caid (35a,151d,152b), card (33d,114d), Chad (158b), chid, Chud (191), clad (46a,82a), clod (22a,45b,157d), coed, cold (65d), cond (156a), cord (39b,131a), curd (99d)

CE - -   ceba (169b), cede (67b,70c,129d,160a,168b,185d), ceil (92c,112a), cela (62d), cell (39b), celt (30c,123a,156c,167b,179b), Celt (10a, 180a,b), cena (88d,133a), cene (34c), cens (115b), cent (36d), cepa (110c), cepe (48c), cera (152d,161d,179a), cere (19a,114b,149d, 179a), cern (41c), cero (57b,c,d,180b), cess (91d,94c,162b), cest (18a,67b), cete (180b,c), ceto (34a), Ceyx (73b)

- CE -   Acer (96c), icer

- - CE   ance (158b,c,d), bice (20d,117d), Bice (27b), boce (23b,52a,57b), dace (57a,b), dice (65a), duce (29d), ecce (17d,89a,c), ence (158c), esce (158d), face (159d,176c), lace (58b,179c), luce (58c,117d), Luce (7b,35a), mace (49d,108d,153b,154d,161a,178a), mice, nice (54d,119c,130c), Nice (98c), once (60b,79b), pace (64b,98a,153b, 156a,170b,177d), pice (190), puce (33c,d,52a), race (116a,153b, 154b), Rice (46a), sice (71d,147b), syce (71d), tace (13a,155d), tice (9a,38c,51a,185d), vice (31d,158a), voce (83c,177a)

C - - E   cade (25c,27a,76c,85d,116d), Cade (50c), cafe, cage (36a), cake, cale (72d), came (182b), Came (192), cane (17b,128a,156a,159a, 177d), Cane, cape (75a,96c,124b,161a), care (11b,14c,35d,150a, 184d), case (22c,36c,81c,91a,108c), cate (165c), cave (27d), cede (67b,70c,129d,160a,168b,185d), cene (34c), cepe (48c), cere (19a, 114b,149d,179a), cete (180b,c), chee (189), cine (104b,152c), cise (147b), cite (15a,98d,126d,159b), cive (110c), clee (19a,129a), Cloe (183c), clue, code (21c,31a,40c,161c), coke (32d,64a), cole (25a), Cole, come, cone (66b,150a,157c), cope (12b,26b,36c,65b, 157d,176a), core (28b,51c,75b,81b), cose (29b), cote (19b,143d, 144a,b), cove (17a,73d,107d), coze (29b), Cree (192), cube (66b, 150a), cuke (39b), cure (123b,d), cute (39c), cyke (40c), cyme (58d, 69c)

C - - F   calf, chef, clef (104d,105a), coif (73a), cuff (148a), cuif (139a,d, 140c)

C - - G   cang (184a), chug (53a), clog (30c,145b), coag (45d,118a,163b), crag (132c), crig (20d)

CH - -   chaa (162b), chab (184a), Chad (158b), chai (72d), cham (20a,29d), Cham (8c) chan (26c,130c), chap (55b), char (24d,138c,170b), chat (9b,19c,161c), chaw (97c), chay (48a,128d), chee (189), chef, chek (59c), Chen (149b), cher (61b), chew (97c), chez (14b,61a), chia (136d), chib (167a), chic (148d), chid, ch'ih (188), chil, chin, Chin (30b), chip (69d), chir (29b,116d), chit (67b,98c,108b,116c, 177c), chiv (87a), chob (23c), chol (118d), Chol (192), chop (98a), chor (164b), chou (61b), Chou (30b), chow (45a), choy (48a,128d), chub (40c,154c), Chud (191), chug (53a), chum (38d), Chun (30c), chut!

- CH -   ache (79a,112d,185b), acht (66c), achy, echo (130b,d), Echo (105d), icho (67b), ichu (10b,70d), ocha (189), tcha (162c), tche (13d,30b, 105a), tchi, Tchi, tchu

320

- - CH aich (9a), arch (29d,38b,39d,123d,132c), bach, Bach (35c), **each,** etch, Foch (63b), hoch (52c,66c), Hoch, inch, itch, Koch (66d), lech (102b), loch (88a,139d), much, nach, ouch, rich, Roch (136c), sech (97c), such (146d), Tech, Vach (153b), Zach (96b)

C - - H caph (91c), Caph, cash (101c), ch'ih (188), Cobh (37a), cosh (35a, 97c), cush (101c), Cush (51d,73c)

CI - - cima (83b,c), cine (104b,152c), cinq (61d), cion (42d,70b,145b, 148b,154b,156a), cipo (91d), circ (31a), cirl (24c), cise (147b), cist (22c,29d,156c), cite (15a,98d,126d,159b), cito (89d,126c), **cits,** city, Civa (56d), cive (110c)

- CI - acid (151a,162a), Acis (64b), Scio

- - CI asci (154a), deci (163b), foci (28b), fuci (132c), loci (66b,118c), Pici (19c,184a), unci (31d)

C - - I cadi (12a,103a,171a), Cadi, caji (180b), cazi (103a), chai (72d), coli, Coni, Cori (138c), cubi (188)

- - CK back (75d,76d,159d), beck (107c), bock (17c,90d,144a), buck, cock (19a,29a,55a,133d,136d,161d,174b), deck (13b,41c, 144d), dick (43a,55b), Dick (96b), dock (40a,117c,144d,179d), duck (26b,53b,179c), hack (40a,77c,184d), heck (100a), hick (185d), hock (91a,115b,182b,c), huck (167d), jack (26c,58a,127c), Jack (96b), jock (96b), Jock, juck (114c), kick, lack (178a), lick lock (54d), luck (28d), mack, mick (82c), mock (131b,162b), muck, neck (83a), nick (30c,108b), nock (13b,108b), pack (24b,140d), peck (24d), pick, puck (44b,68a,77c,100c), Puck (99d,143b), rack (32c,64b), reck (26d,75c), rick (74d,117d), rock (160b), ruck (39a, 185a), sack (43d,118a,119d,182b), seck (173d), sick, sock (157c, 182a), suck, tack (28d,37d,54d), teck (128b), tick (12b,20d,97c), tock (7d,19b), tuck (156b), wick

C - - K calk (78c,109a,141c,178d), cark (26d,184d), cask, cauk (139b), cawk (133c), chek (59c), coak (45d,118a,163b), cock (19a,29a, 55a,133d,136d), conk (41c,108a,156d,157c), cook (137b), cork (119d), cusk (57b)

CL - - clad (46a,82a), clam (20b,101b), clan (169c), clap (58b), claw (29c, 105b,161d,173a), clay, Clay (9d), clee (19a,129a), clef (104d,105a), clem (56b,158b), Cleo (126b), clew (16a,33a,77b,136b,164d), Clim (12b), Clio (104d), clip (54d,143d), clod (22a,45b,157d), Cloe (183c), clog (30c,145b), clop, clot (32d,94d), clou (62b), clow (58c,148c), cloy (61b,137c,159d), club (39c), clue, Clym (12b)

- CL - acle (13d,82c,115d)

C - - L call (145c,159b,176d), carl (115c,135d), Carl (96a), caul (16d,74d), ceil (92c,112a), cell (39b), chil, chol (118d), Chol (192), cirl (24c), coal (49c,64a), coel (39b), coll (39d,171c,185a), cool (25c,107d), cowl (101d), cral, cull (117c), curl (38d,73b,93b,131d)

- CM - acme (39c,115c,186b)

C - - M caam (93d), calm (8d,11d,112b,118d,126c,d,172b), cham (20a,29d), Cham (8c), chum (38d), clam (20b,101b), clem (56b,158b), Clim (12b), Clym (12b), coom (32d,150c,178d), corm (24b,38d,156a), cram (157d), Crom, culm (11a,32d,70,145a,156a)

CN - - Cnut (40d,50c)

- CN -   **acne** (147c)

C - - N   **Caen, cain** (169c), **Cain** (6a,7a,50d,88a,104c,143a), **carn** (156c), **cern** (41c), **chan** (26c,130c), **Chen** (149b), **chin, Chin** (30b), **Chun** (30c), **cion** (42d,70b,145b,148b,154c,156a), **clan** (169c), **Coan** (37b), **coin** (19b,37a,100c,101c,179d), **conn** (43d,156a), **coon** (121c), **corn** (39d,95c,123a), **coyn** (37a), **cran** (160c), **crin** (146c), **cyan**

CO - -   **coag** (45d,118a,163b), **coak** (45d,118a,163b), **coal** (49c,64a), **Coan** (37b), **coat** (160a), **coax** (180c), **Cobb** (9c), **Cobh** (37a), **coca** (29d, 33a,105d,113a), **cock** (19a,29a,55a,133d,136d,161d,174b), **coco,** (113a), **coda** (32c,35d,56c), **code** (21c,31a,40c,161c), **codo** (188), **coed, coel** (39b), **coho** (136d), **coif** (73a), **coil** (39d,171c,185a), **coin** (19b,37a,100c,101c,179d), **coir** (33a,37a,56a,133d), **Coix** (70d,85b), **coja** (103b,166b), **coke** (32d,64a), **coky, cola** (25b,108a,149d,168c), **cold** (65d), **cole** (25a), **Cole, coli, colp** (28a,148b), **colt** (78c,131a, 185d,186b), **Colt, coly** (104a), **coma** (91c,157d,170c,172b), **comb** (38c), **come, Como, cond** (156a), **cone** (66b,150a,157c), **Coni, conk** (41c,108a,156d,157c), **conn** (43d,156a), **cony** (127a), **cook** (137b), **cool** (25c,107d), **coom** (32d,150c,178d), **coon** (121c), **coop, Coos,** (192), **coot** (19b,46d,72b,138d,141a,146d,157d), **copa** (88b,113c), **cope** (12b,26b,36c,65b,157d,176a), **copt** (48d), **copy, cora** (65d), **Cora** (42b,69c,80c,116b,124d,172b,183c), **cord** (39b,139a), **core** (28b,51c,75b,81b), **Cori** (138c), **cork** (119d), **corm** (24b,38d,156a), **corn** (39d,95c,123a), **cose** (29b), **cosh** (35a,97c), **coso** (152c), **coss** (98a), **cost** (29a), **cosy** (149c), **cota** (117a), **cote** (19b,143d,144a,b), **coto** (16c,90b), **Coty** (63c), **coup** (20d,97c,157b,c,162d), **cous** (38a), **cove** (17a,73d,107d), **cowl** (101d), **coxa** (77b) **coyn** (37a), **coyo** (15a,30c), **coze** (29b), **cozy** (149c)

- CO -   **acon** (62c,140d), **acor** (6d), **icon** (79d,92b,136a), **scob** (42a), **scon** (162c), **scop** (120a), **scot** (14a,162b), **Scot** (64b,132c), **scow** (21a, 58b)

- - CO   **alco** (45b), **caco** (73b), **coco** (113a), **Duco, fico** (169d), **loco** (38b, 119b,120b), **mico** (97a), **paco** (9b,146d), **peco** (162b), **pico** (65a, 152c), **poco** (83b,93a), **saco** (189), **soco** (22d), **Teco** (192), **toco** (19b,167c), **unco** (140c), **Waco**

C - - O   **caco** (73b), **calo** (72d), **cano** (152a), **caro** (83a), **Caro** (183d), **Caso** (82d), **Cato** (132d,133b), **cayo, cero** (57b,c,d,180b), **ceto** (34a), **cipo** (91d), **cito** (89d,126c), **Cleo** (126b), **Clio** (104d), **coco,** (113a), **codo** (188), **coho** (136d), **Como, coso** (152d), **coto** (16c,90b), **coyo** (15a,30c)

C - - P   **calp** (92b), **camp** (163b), **Capp** (27a), **carp** (27d,38d,40c,55a,56c, 57a), **caup, chap** (55b), **chip** (69d), **chop** (98a), **clap** (58b), **clip** (54d,143d), **clop, colp** (28a,148b), **coop, coup** (20d,97c,157b,c, 162d), **crop** (38b), **cusp** (38c,78b,119a,120a,b)

C - - Q   **cinq** (61d)

CR - -   **crab** (39b,144b,181b), **crag** (132c), **cral, cram** (157d), **cran** (160c), **craw** (38d,72c,156c), **Crax** (19b,39d), **crea** (92c,151d), **Cree** (192), **crew** (72a,106a), **Crex** (37a), **crib** (96b,120d), **cric** (131c), **crig** (20d), **crin** (146c), **cris** (40b,95d), **croc** (13a,74a), **Crom, crop** (38b), **crow** (19a), **crus** (91a,143c), **crux** (39a,151b)

322

- **- CR -**   acre (39b,56a,88b), Acre, ecru (17d,23d,172b), ocra (72c,175a)
- **C - - R**   carr (120d,140a), caur (139a), char (24d,138c,170b), cher (61b), chir (29b,116d), chor (164b), coir (33a,37a,56a,133d), cuir (45c,62a), curr (104c), Czar (42d,49d,60b,135c)
- **- - CS**   ABC's (57a), pacs (94c)
- **C - - S**   cass (140c,177a), Cass (147a), cens (115b), cess (91d,94c,162b), cits, Coos (192), coss (98a), cous (38a), cris (40b,95d), crus (91a, 143c), cuss
- **- CT -**   acta (41d,123d,128d,164c), acth (13b), acto (152b), Acts, actu (7a, 89a), ecto (34c,122d), octa (122c), octo (34a,89b,122c)
- **- - CT**   duct (170c), fact (7a,128b), lact (34c), pact (8a), Pict (23c,47d), rect (117b), sect (42b,54a,114c), tact (43c,d,116a)
- **C - - T**   cant (28d,81b,84d,90c,109b,136c,165d,166a), cart (171d,175a, 177b), cast (165b,167c), Catt (9d), celt (30c,82c,123a,156c,167b, 179b), Celt (10a,180a,b), cent (36d), cest (18a,67b), chat (9b,19c, 161c), chit (67b,98c,108b,116c,177c), chut!, cist (22c,29d,156c), clot (32d,94d), coat (160a), colt (78c,131a,185d,186b), Colt (131a), coot (19b,46d,72b,138d,141a,146d,157d), Copt (48d), cost (29a), cult (141d,161c), curt (145b,c), cyst
- **CU - -**   cuba (189), Cuba (180b), cube (66b,150a), cubi (188), cuca (33a, 105d), cuff (148a), cuif (139a,d,140c), cuir (45c,62a), cuke (39b), cull (117c), culm (11a,32d,70d,145a,156a), cult (141d,161c), Cuna (193), cura (152c), curb (130c,146b), curd (99d), cure (123b), curl (38d,73b,93b,131d), curr (104c), curt (145b,c), cush (101c), Cush (51d,73c), cusk (57b), cusp (38c,78b,119a,120a,b), cuss, cute (39c), cuvy (141a), cuya (39b)
- **- CU -**   acus (89d,118a), scud (32c,126c,135b,160c), scum (129b), scup (57a,121b), scur (78b), scut (145c,161b)
- **- - CU**   jacu (19a,151b), jocu (45b,57a)
- **C - - U**   chou (61b), Chou (30b), clou (62b)
- **C - - V**   chiv (87a)
- **C - - W**   chaw (97c), chew (97c), chow (45a), claw (29c,105b,161d,173a), clew (16a,33a,77b,136b,164d), clow (58c,148c), craw (38d,72c, 156c), crew (72a,106a), crow (19a)
- **C - - X**   calx (23c,75c,112c), Ceyx (73b), coax (180c), Coix (70d,85b), Crax (19b,39d), Crex (37a), crux (39a,151b)
- **CY - -**   cyan, cyke (40c), cyma (101a,b), cyme (58d,69c), cyst
- **- CY -**   acyl (6d)
- **- - CY**   ancy (158c), lacy, Lucy (183c), racy (153b)
- **C - - Y**   cady (69d), cagy (178b), caky, cavy (72b,120d,132c,157b), cazy (103a), chay (48a,128d), choy (48a,128d), city, clay, Clay (9d), cloy (61b,137c,159d), coky, coly (104a), cony (127a), copy, cosy (149c), Coty (63c), cozy (149c), cuvy (141a)
- **CZ - -**   czar (42d,49d,60b,135c)
- **C - - Z**   chez (14b,61a)
- **DA - -**   dace (57a,b), Dada (13b,63a,157d), dado (41c,111c,115c, 177d), daer (22b), daez, daff (125d), daft (59c), dagg (118c), dagh

(76d), **Dago, Dail** (49a,82b,c), **dain** (188), **dais** (119b), **dale** (43c, 128a,174b), **dali** (168c,169b), **dama** (65d,152b), **dame** (67b,87c, 166b), **damn, damp** (101a), **Dana** (28a,96a,171d), **Dane** (85d,107d, 138a), **dang, dank** (40b,101a), **dans** (62a), **Danu** (28a), **Dara** (18d), **Dard, dare** (28d,41b,42a,74d,175b), **Dare** (57a), **dari** (38a,70b), **dark** (47a,67d,109b,160b), **darn** (130b), **darr** (163c), **dart** (13b,88a, 100c,120b,153a,160c), **dash** (125c,162d), **dasi** (77a), **data** (54a), **date** (64a,153a), **dato** (95c,102c,117a), **datu** (95c,102c,117a), **daub** (148d), **dauk** (95c), **Daur** (139b), **dauw** (24c), **Dave** (96b), **Davy** (96b,136b), **dawk** (95c), **dawm** (190), **dawn** (14d,41b), **Daye** (123d), **days, Daza** (191), **daze** (157d), **dazy**

- **DA** -   adad (52c,56a), **Adad** (68c,157a,182a), **Adah** (25b,51b), **Adam** (26b,96a,111c), **adan** (102d), **Adar** (85c,102a), **adat** (90b,95d), **Edam** (29c), **Edar** (18d), **Idas** (27b,71c), **odah** (170d), **odal** (48a,88b,112c), **Odax** (132c), **udad** (143d,144a,181c), **udal** (76b, 88b,131c)

- - **DA**   adda (147d), **Adda** (68c,119d), **Aida** (110d,175c), **alda** (152b), **Alda** (110d,150c), **anda** (23a,168c), **Beda** (101d), **Buda** (83d), **coda** (32c,35d,56c), **Dada** (13b,63a,157d), **Edda** (76b,79b,107d), **Erda** (23d,41a,47d,68d,69a,131d,177b), **Juda, kada** (188), **Leda** (27b, 75d,120c,153a,171d,186b), **Lida** (183c), **meda** (110a), **nuda** (39b), **peda** (114d,144b), **rada** (135c,172a), **Roda** (107b), **sida** (37a, 126c,170a), **soda** (19a,149d,181a), **Teda** (191), **Toda** (45d,76d), **Veda** (77a,b), **Vida** (183c)

D - - **A**   Dada (13b,63a,157d), **dama** (65d,152b), **Dana** (28a,96a,171d), **Dara** (18d), **data** (54a), **Daza** (191), **deca** (34d,122d), **depa** (188), **dera** (34c), **deva** (23d,42a,56d,77a), **dewa, dika** (23a), **Disa** (111a), **dita** (117a), **diva** (110d,123c), **dola** (189), **dona** (83d,121c,151d), **dopa** (117d), **dora** (70b), **Dora** (36d,41a,43b), **dosa** (74b), **doxa** (48b), **draa** (188), **Duma** (135c), **dura** (153c), **dyna** (34c)

- - **DB**   Badb (82b), **Bodb** (82b), **Medb**

D - - **B**   daub (148d), **dieb** (84a), **doab** (157c), **doob** (18b), **doub** (18b), **drab** (23d,29c,33d,46d,53b,d), **drib** (46b), **drub** (17b,39c), **duab** (157c), **dubb** (161c), **dumb** (153b)

D - - **C**   disc (31b), **douc** (101d)

DD - -   DDSC (42a)

- **DD** -   adda (147a), **Adda** (68c,119d,157a,182a), **Addu** (68c,157a,182a), **Addy** (183d), **Edda** (76b,79b), **eddo** (162a), **eddy** (37d, 39d,160d, 180d), **odds** (28d,172d)

- - **DD**   dodd (139c,140c), **gedd** (140a), **Ladd** (143c), **ludd** (23c), **mudd** (188), **Nudd** (23c), **Redd** (153a), **Ridd** (94a), **rodd** (38d), **rudd** (26d, 57a,b), **sadd** (33a,40b,58c,107b), **sudd** (40b,58c,107b), **wadd** (109c)

D - - **D**   dard, dead, deed (7a,52d,91a,166c,168b), **diad** (113a), **dord** (42c), **dowd** (143b), **duad** (113a,171d), **dyad** (113a)

DE - -   dead, deaf, deal (11d,16c,36c,44c,81a,168b), **dean** (33c,109d), **dear, debt** (91d,109b), **deca** (34d,122d), **deci** (163b), **deck** (13b, 41c,144d), **dedo** (188), **deed** (7a,52d,91a,166c,168b), **deem** (36b, 85c,164c), **deep** (124a), **deer** (28c,135a,154d) **defi** (61b), **deft** (147c), **defy** (28d), **degu** (132c), **deil** (139b), **dein** (66d), **dele** (26a, 49c,51b,53a,110b,123d,124c,130a,145c,161b), **dell** (43c,174b),

deme (71b,c,167d), **demi** (34b,122c), **demo** (122d), **demy** (113d), **dene** (137a), **Dene** (192), **dens** (90a,167b), **dent** (42c,77d), **deny** (36d,43d,129b), **depa** (188), **dera** (34c), **dere** (74a,79c), **derm** (147c,158d), **desi** (85d), **desk, deul** (77b), **deus** (68a,89b), **Deva** (23d,42a,b,56d,77a), **Devi** (147b,153b), **dewa, dewy** (101a)

- DE -   **aden** (34b), **Aden, Ader** (18d), **Ades** (73a), **edel** (66c), **Eden** (6b,50d, 107c,113d,123c), **Eder, EDES** (71c), **idea** (54c,108c,124a,164d), **idee** (61d), **idem** (89d,164a), **Iden** (76a), **ideo** (34b,d), **ides** (41a, b,133a), **odea** (105a,164a), **odel** (48a,112c), **Oder** (132a)

- - DE   **aide** (7b,14a,75d), **Ande** (193), **Aude, bade, Bede** (48c,50c,101d, 175b), **bide** (47c,50b,130a,158b,162a), **bode** (14c,60a,110b,121b), **cade** (25c,27a,76c,85d,116d), **Cade** (50c), **cede** (67b,70c,129d, 160a,168b,185d), **code** (21c,31a,40c,161c), **Dode** (96b), **dude** (40d), **eide** (119c), **fade** (181d,183b), **fide, gade, Gide** (63a), **hade** (66a, 148c,173c), **hide** (53a), **hyde** (188), **Hyde** (45a), **inde, jade** (33c, 65d,71d,166a), **Jude** (11c,96a), **kade** (144a), **lade** (24c,26d,43c,93b, 100a,132a,139d,161b,178d), **lode** (42c,99a,111b,175b), **made, Mede** (10a,b,13c), **mide** (110a), **mode** (54d,96b,157d,179a), **nide** (23c,72a,106c,116d), **node** (35c,85b,87c,94d,120a,124d,160c), **nude** (16c), **onde** (63a,178d), **rede** (37c,81d,138d), **ride** (46b,85c), **rode** (46c), **rude** (134b,172b), **sade** (91d), **side** (13d,22a,b,54a,58a,89a, 161b), **tide** (39d,75d,109c,141c,159d), **Tide, tode** (80a,148a), **unde** (179a), **urde** (86b), **vade** (42c,67d,89c), **vide** (89d,126a,142a), **wade, wide** (133d)

D - - E   **dace** (57a,b), **dale** (43c,128a,174b), **dame** (67b,87c,166b), **Dane** (85d,107d,138a), **dare** (28d,41b,42a,74d,175b), **Dare** (57a), **date** (64a,153a), **Dave** (96b), **Daye** (123d), **daze** (157d), **dele** (26a,49c, 51b,53a,110b,123d,124c,130a,145c,161b), **deme** (71b,c,167d), **dene** (137a), **Dene** (192), **dere** (74a,79c), **dice** (65a), **dike** (49c, 91d), **Dike** (78a), **dime, dine, dire** (45d,55a,104a,163c), **dite** (150b), **dive** (42b,74b,119d), **dobe** (159b,c,172b), **Dode** (96b), **doge** (95b), **dole** (44c,118c,121c,129d), **Dole** (74c), **dome** (39c,133c,155d), **done, dope** (46c,105d), **dore** (61d,67b,69d,117d), **Dore** (50d,63a,b), **dose** (123a), **dote** (17a,90b,94b,97a,112a,139d,165d), **dove** (19a, 117d), **doze** (148a), **dree** (139b,140c,158b,172c), **duce** (29d), **dude** (40d), **duff** (125b), **duke** (107c), **dune** (137a), **dupe** (27c,41c, 72c,160c), **duse** (83c), **dyke** (49c,91d), **dyne** (59d)

D - - F   **daff** (125d), **deaf, doff** (130a,161b), **duff** (125b)

- DG -   **edge** (22a,96d,131c,143c,146b), **edgy** (106c)

D - - G   **dagg** (118c), **dang, ding** (130b), **Doeg** (137c), **dong, drag** (74a, 125b), **dreg, drug** (105d)

DH - -   **dhak** (48a,169a), **dhal** (12b), **dhan** (124c), **dhao** (24c), **Dhar, dhaw** (125a), **dhow** (88d,111c,175d)

- - DH   **sadh** (77a), **Sadh, yodh** (91d)

D - - H   **dagh** (76d), **Dagh, dash** (125c,162d), **dish, doth, drah** (188)

DI - -   **diad** (113a), **dial** (25c), **dian** (46c,130d,170b), **Dian** (68d,69a,c, 102b), **Diau** (192), **dibs** (70c), **dice** (65a), **dick** (43a,55b), **Dick** (96b), **dido** (11b,26c,65a,122a), **Dido** (27a,172c), **dieb** (84a), **diem** (89b,116a), **dier, dies** (41b,89b), **diet** (14a,54c,84c,91b,176a), **Dieu** (61d), **dika** (23a), **dike** (49c,91d), **Dike** (78a), **dill** (13a,117c), **dilo**

325

(120d,168c), **dime, dine, ding** (130b), **dino** (34b), **dint** (48c,59d, 122a), **Dion** (96a,152a), **dipt, dire** (45d,55a,104a,163c), **dirk** (40b), **dirt, Disa** (111a), **disc** (31b), **dish, disk** (31b), **diss** (98b), **dita** (117a), **dite** (150b), **diva** (110d,123c), **dive** (42b,74b,119d), **divi, dixi**

- DI -   **Adib** (155b, **adit** (51a,100a,114d), **edit** (20d,49d,123a,129a,131a), **idic** (79b), **idio** (34b,c), **odic** (79c,120a), **Odin** (7c,29d,63c,68c,175d, 183b), **odio** (83b), **udic** (108a)

- - DI   **Andi** (27d), **cadi** (12a,103a), **kadi** (103a,171a), **Lodi** (105d), **ludi** (133b), **Madi** (174a), **medi** (34c), **Midi** (151b), **nidi** (106c), **nodi** (35c,87c), **padi** (131b), **pedi** (34b), **rodi** (98c), **sidi** (103b), **wadi** (46c,106a,109a,128a,132a)

D - - I   **dali** (168c,169b), **dari** (38a,70b), **dasi** (77a), **deci** (163b), **defi** (61b), **demi** (34b,122c), **desi** (85d), **Devi** (147b,153b), **divi, dixi, doni** (21a,28c,168a), **drei** (66d,165a)

- DJ -   **Idjo** (191)

- - DJ   **hadj** (98b,118a)

D - - K   **dank** (40b,101a), **dark** (47a,67d,109b,160b), **dauk** (95c), **dawk** (95c), **deck** (13b,41c,144d), **desk, dhak** (48a,169a), **dick** (43a,55b), **Dick** (96b), **dirk** (40b), **disk** (31b), **dock** (40a,117c,144d,179d), **dook** (184a), **duck** (26b,53b,179c), **dunk** (43c,79d), **dusk** (171c), **Dyak** (22b)

- DL -   **idle** (174b,c,178c), **idly**

D - - L   **Dail** (49a,82b,c), **deal** (11d,16c,36c,44c,81a,168b), **dell** (139b), **dell** (43c,174b), **deul** (77b), **dhal** (12b), **dial** (25c), **dill** (13a,117c), **doll** (125c), **dowl, dual** (45c,171d), **duel, dull** (21a,32c,173a), **Dull** (94b)

- DM -   **admi** (65d)

D - - M   **dawm** (190), **deem** (36b,85c,164c), **derm** (147c,158d), **diem** (89b, 116a), **doom** (42d,55a,134d), **dorm, doum** (168c), **dram** (46b,110c, 121d,148c), **drum** (105a), **duim** (188)

- DN -   **Edna** (183c)

D - - N   **dain** (188), **darn, damn, dawn** (14d,41b), **dean** (33c,109d), **dein** (66d), **dhan** (124c), **dian** (46c,130d,170b), **Dian** (68d,69a,c,102b), **Dion** (96a,152a), **Domn** (135a), **doon** (140b,168c), **dorn** (164d), **down** (149d), **duan** (64b)

DO - -   **doab** (157c), **doat** (17a,94b,112a,165d), **dobe** (159b,c,172b), **doby** (159b,c), **dock** (40a,117c,144d,179d), **dodd** (139c,140c), **Dode** (96b), **dodo** (19b), **Doeg** (137c), **doer** (8a,116b), **does, doff** (130a,161b), **doge** (95b,175b), **dogy** (46d,103c), **doit** (47a,169d,180d), **Doko** (191), **dola** (189), **dole** (44c,118c,121c,129d), **Dole** (74c), **doll, doll** (125c), **dolt** (20c,59c,157d), **dome** (39c,133c,155d), **Domn** (135a), **domy, dona** (83d,121c,151d), **done, dong, doni** (21a,28c, 168a), **don't, doob** (18b), **dook** (184a), **doom** (42d,55a,134d), **doon** (140b,168c), **door** (51a,121b), **dopa** (117d), **dope** (46c,105d), **dopp** (43c), **dora** (70b), **Dora** (36d,41a,43b,183c,d), **dord** (42c), **dore** (61d,67b,69d,117d), **Dore** (50d,63a,b), **dorm, dorn** (164d), **dorp** (73c,176b), **dorr** (32b), **dory** (21b,58b,144c), **dosa** (74b), **dose** (123a), **doss** (17c), **dost, dote** (17a,90b,94b,97a,112a,139d,165d),

326

doth, Doto (141b), doty (43d), doub (18b), douc (101d), doum (168c), dour (67d,159a), dove (19a,117d), dowd (143b), dowl, down (149d), doxa (48b), doxy (129d), doze (148a), dozy

- DO - ador (153b), Edom (18c,51b,79b,82c,84a), idol (48c,54c,55a,75b, 79d,112d,130b,184d), odor (138b,156a)

- - DO Bodo (88c), codo (188), dado (41c,111c,115c,177d), dedo (188), dido (11b,26c,65a,122a), Dido (27a,172c), dodo (19b), eddo (162a), endo (34d,122d,183b), fado (121c), Jodo (113d), judo (84b,85c, 142b), Lido (83d,175b), ludo (65a,112b), mado (14d,57a,170b), ordo (22a,30d,122a,171a), pedo (34b), redo (165c), sado (26d, 84d), todo (22b,24d,35b,64c,156b), undo (11a,93d), Yedo (166d)

D - - O dado (41c,111c,115c,177d), Dago, dato (95c,102c,117a), dedo (188), demo (122d), dhao (24c), dido (11b,26c,65a,122a), Dido (27a,172c), dilo (120d,168c), dino (34b), dodo (19b), Doko (191), Doto (141b), Duco, duro (190)

D - - P damp (101a), deep (124a), dopp (43c), dorp (73c,176b), drap (61b, c,62a), drip, drop (43d,54b,100b,114c,168b), dump

DR - - draa (188), drab (23d,29c,33d,46d,53b,d), drag (74a,125b), drah (188), dram (46b,110c,121d,148c), drap (61b,c,62a), drat (100a), Drau, draw (42c,53a,92b,117c,121c,167d), dray (27a,154c,177b), dree (139b,140c,158b,172c), dreg, drei (66d,165a), drew, drey (154c), drib (46b), Drin, drip, drop (43d,54b,100b,114c,168b), drub (17b,39c), drug (105d), drum (105a), drun (132b)

- DR - adry (164c)

- - DR sadr (94a), Sadr (155b)

D - - R daer (22b), darr (163c), Daur (139b), dear, deer (28c,135a,154d), Dhar, dier, doer (8a,116b), door (51a,121b), dorr (32b), dour (67d, 159a), duar, Duhr (155b), durr (70b), dyer

- DS - DDSC (42a)

- - DS duds (32c,166d), Eads (23b,24b,50b,82a), odds (28d,172d), suds (59a)

D - - S dais (119b), dans (62a), days, dens (90a,167b), deus (68a,89b), dibs (70c), dies (41b,89b), diss (98b), does, doss (17c), duds (32c,166d), Duns, Dyas (66a)

D - - T daft (59c), dart (13b,88a,100c,120b,153a,160c), debt (91d,109b), deft (147c), dent (42c,77d), diet (14a,54c,84c,91b,176a), dint (48c,59d,122a), dipt, dirt, doat (17a,94b,112a,165d), doit (47a, 169d,180d), dolt (20c,59c,157d), don't, dost, drat (100a), Duat (172d), duct (170c), duet (104d,171d), duit (190), Duit (192), dunt, dust

DU - - duab (157c), duad (113a,171d), dual (45c,171d), duan (64b), duar, Duat (172d), dubb (161c), duce (29d), duck (26b,53b,179c), Duco, duct (170c), dude (40d), duds (32c,166d), duel, duet (104d,171d), duff (125b), Dufy (63a), Duhr (155b), duim (188), duit (190), Duit (192), duke (107c), duku (95d,168c), dull (21a,32c,173a), Dull (94b), Duma (135c), dumb (153b), dump, dune (137a), dunk (43c, 79d), Duns, dunt, dupe (27c,41c,72c,160c), dura (153c), duro (190), durr (70b), duse (83c), dusk (171c), dust, duty (109b,162b)

- DU - idun (107d), odum (168c,180a)

- - DU   **Addu** (68c,157a,182a), **Jadu** (95a), **Kadu** (191), **kudu** (11a), **ordu** (170d), **pudu** (41d), **Urdu** (77b), **widu** (102d), **wudu** (102d)

D - - U   **Danu** (28a), **datu** (95c,102c,117a), **degu** (132c), **Diau** (192), **Dieu** (61d), **Drau**, **duku** (95d,168c)

D - - W   **dauw** (24c), **dhaw** (125a), **dhow** (88d,111c,175d), **draw** (42c,53a, 92b,117c,121c,167d), **drew**

DY - -   **dyad** (113a), **Dyak** (22b), **Dyas** (66a), **dyer**, **dyke** (49c,91d), **dyna** (34c), **dyne** (59d,173b)

- DY -   **idyl** (114d), **Idyo** (191), **odyl** (59d,79c)

- - DY   **Addy** (183d), **Andy** (96b), **body** (72a), **cady** (69d), **eddy** (37d,39d, 160d,180d), **fady**, **jady**, **Judy** (125c,183d), **lady**, **sidy** (123b), **tidy** (106a,111b), **tody** (19b,d,59a,166a), **undy** (179a), **urdy** (86b), **wady** (109a,128a,132a)

D - - Y   **Davy** (96b,136b), **dazy**, **defy** (28d), **demy** (113d), **deny** (36d,43d, 129b), **dewy** (101a), **doby** (159b,c), **dogy** (46d,103c), **domy**, **dory** (21b,58b,144c), **doty** (43d), **doxy** (129d), **dozy**, **dray** (27a,154c, 177b), **drey** (154c), **Dufy** (63a), **duty** (109b,162b)

- DZ -   **adze** (40c,167a), **Idzo** (191)

- - DZ   **Lodz**

D - - Z   **Daez**

EA - -   **each**, **Eads** (23b,24b,50b,82a), **eard** (139b), **earl** (107c,166b), **earn** (42d,64b,99a), **ease** (7c,8d,35a,100d,129c,130b,c,150c), **east**, **East** (111b), **easy** (54a,146d,149d,172b) **eats**, **eaux** (178c), **eave** (133c),

- EA -   **bead** (17a,122a,146b), **beak** (19a), **beal** (139d), **beam**, **bean** (91b, 142a,175a), **bear** (27a,50b,113c,155a), **beat** (58c,87b,131a,164d, 165b,180d), **beau**, **dead**, **deaf**, **deal** (11d,16c,36c,44c,81a,168b), **dean** (33c,109d), **dear**, **feak** (39d,171c), **fear** (113c,155a), **feat** (7a, 52d), **geal** (47d,163c), **gean** (29c), **gear** (32c,112a,167b), **geat** (77d, 101a), **Geat** (138a), **head** (29d), **heaf** (144a), **heal**, **heap** (117d), **hear** (75b,c,92d), **heat**, **jean** (37c), **Jean** (183c), **keal** (25a), **lead** (35d,43d,72b,74d,81a), **leaf** (55c,73c,119b), **Leah** (19a,84a,87b, 183c), **leak** (110c), **leal** (54b,94c,139d), **lean** (128a,148b,152d, 164b,166a), **leap** (26c), **lear** (139d), **Lear** (37a,143b), **mead** (46a, 78a,97d,99b), **Mead** (78a), **meal** (72a,130b), **mean** (15a,42b,146c, 156b), **meat** (59b), **neaf** (58a,73c), **Neal**, **neap** (165c,167a,177b), **near** (11d,32c,107b), **neat** (165c,169d), **peag** (144a,178a), **peai** (98b), **peak** (9a,38c,159b,186b), **peal** (131c,d), **pean** (64c,150b), **pear** (64a), **peat** (64a,175a), **read** (116d,157d), **real** (7a), **ream** (18c,37d,50d,113d,171c), **reap** (7a,40a,74a), **rear** (15b,23a,b,24a, 51b,76d,127c), **seah** (188), **seal** (10c,d,54d,64c,96a,118b,128a), **seam** (85b,d,160a,176d,185a), **Sean** (85b,96a), **sear** (23d,27d,72d, 138c), **seat** (98c,156b), **teak** (41a,48a,168c), **teal** (19b,20d,46c,d), **team** (38c,72a,113a), **tean** (140c,167a), **tear** (67c,87b,130a), **veal**, **weak** (55b), **weal** (124d,157c,180c,d), **wean** (8d,42d), **wear** (50b), **yeah**, **Yean** (88a), **year**, **yeas** (177c), **zeal** (12c,55d)

- - EA   **Alea** (14b,31c,167d), **area** (37d,38a,44c,53a,93b,110d,127d, 138c,168a,186d), **asea** (39b,177c), **brea** (100b), **crea** (92c,151d), **evea** (82a), **Evea** (95a), **flea** (81b), **Frea**, **Gaea** (47d,69a), **idea** (54c, 108c,124a,164d), **Itea** (145d,160c,181d), **odea** (105a,164a), **olea**

(170b), **Olea** (110b), **Otea** (71a,82d), **oxea** (153d), **plea** (51a,52d,
122a,130b), **rhea** (37a,56a,111d,133d), **Rhea** (19b,68d,87c,103c,
186b), **shea** (25a,168c,d), **Thea** (162c), **uvea** (53c,82b)

E - - A   **Ecca** (66a), **Edda** (76b,79b,107d,136b), **Edna** (183c), **Egba**
(191), **Ekka** (26d), **Elba** (105d), **Elia** (88a,115d), **ella** (152c,
158c), **Ella** (183c), **Elsa** (70a,93c,110d,177b,183c), **Emma** (183c),
Enna (146a), **epha** (75c), **Erda** (23d,41a,47d,68d,69a,131d,177b),
eria (13d,146d), **Erma** (183c), **Erua** (103c), **esca** (11c,44a,70c), **esta**
(152d,164c), **etna** (75b,153c,157a,175d,177a,c), **Etta** (183c), **evea**
(82a,95a), **eyra** (181d), **exba** (188), **Ezra** (96a)

EB - -   **Eben** (96a), **Eber** (51a,75c,99d), **Ebro** (132a), **eboe** (28b,110a,168c,
169b), **Eboe**, **ebon** (20b), **ebur** (89c)

- EB -   **ceba** (169b), **debt** (91d,109b), **Hebe** (39c,69c,186b), **Nebo** (68c,
102d,103d,183a), **peba** (12d), **Peba** (193), **Reba** (18d,86c,144a),
Seba (18c,39d), **sebi** (34b), **ueba** (188), **zebu** (22d,80d,112c)

- - EB   **bleb** (20c,23d,67c), **dieb** (84a), **pleb** (10d,35b,180b), **Sleb** (12a),
sweb (160d), **theb** (188)

EC - -   **ecad** (73a,119b), **Ecca** (66a), **ecce** (17d,89a,c), **echo** (130b,d), **Echo**
(105d), **ecru** (17d,23d,172b), **ecto** (34c,122d)

- EC -   **beck** (107c), **deca** (34d,122d), **deci** (163b), **deck** (13b,41c,144d),
heck (100a), **lech** (102b), **neck** (83a), **peca** (190), **peck** (24d), **peco**
(162b), **reck** (26d,75c), **rect** (117b), **sech** (97c), **seck** (173d), **sect**
(42b,54a,114c), **teca**, **Teca** (192), **Tech**, **teck** (128b), **Teco** (192)

- - EC   **alec** (10a,57c,d,76c), **Alec** (137a), **avec** (63a,183a), **haec** (90a,
164c), **spec**

E - - C   **epic** (76b,120a), **eric** (115b), **Eric** (71d,96a,107d,138a,164a,176b),
eruc (37a,56a)

ED - -   **Edam** (29c), **Edar** (18d), **Edda** (76b,79b,107d,136b), **eddo** (162a),
eddy (37d,39d,160d,180d), **edel** (66c), **Eden** (6b,50d,107c,113d,
123c), **Eder**, **Edes** (71c), **edge** (22a,96d,131c,143c,146b), **edgy**
(106c), **edit** (20d,49d,123a,129a,131a), **Edna** (183c), **Edom** (18c,
51b,79b,82c,84a)

- ED -   **Beda** (101d), **Bede** (48c,50c,101d,175b), **cede** (67b,70c,129d,160a,
168b,185d), **dedo** (188), **gedd** (140a), **Leda** (27b,75d,120c,153a,
171d,186b), **meda** (110a), **Medb**, **Mede** (10a,b,13c), **medi** (34c),
peda (114d,144b), **pedi** (34b), **pedo** (34b), **redd** (153a), **rede** (37c,
81d,138d), **redo** (165c), **Teda** (191), **Veda** (77a,b), **Yedo** (166d)

- - ED   **abed** (130c), **aged** (110a), **bled**, **bred** (23c,48c,127c), **coed**, **deed**
(7a,52d,91a,166c,168b), **feed** (108c), **fled**, **Fred** (96b), **gled** (19a,
52a,87a), **heed** (14c,75b,109b), **hued**, **lied** (66d,150b), **meed** (128c,
131a), **Moed** (100c), **need** (42b,52d,87b,122a,178a), **Obed** (135d),
pied (96c,103c,114b,117c,154a,174d), **reed** (16a,70d,97b,105a,
111b,118b,144b), **Reed** (163a), **roed**, **seed** (70b,111c,112c,119a,
151b,154a), **shed** (27a,90c,101b,144b), **sled** (40a), **sned** (93d,125a,
140a), **sped**, **syed** (103b), **tied**, **toed**, **used** (6d,73a), **weed**

E - - D   **eard** (139b), **ecad** (73a,119b), **egad** (100a,109a), **eild** (138d,140a),
elod (49b,59d,79c), **emyd** (163c,167c), **Enid** (13b,25d,66b,163a,
183c)

EE - -   **eely** (185a), **eery** (172b,180a)

- EE - beef, been (149a), beer (18c), bees (185b), beet (175a), deed (7a, 52d,166c,168b), deem (36b,85c,164c), deep (124a), deer (28c, 135a,154d), feed (108c), feel (72a,142c), fees (128c), Geez (6c, 51d), heed (14c,75b,109b), heel (47a,43b), Heep (41a,43b), heer (47a,184b, 185b), jeel, jeep, jeer (138c,162b), keef (75d), keek (154c), keel (128d,134d,144c,d), keen (15a,88a,177b), keep (123a,130d), keet (72b), leek (58b,76a,110c,177d), leer (9d,58a,67c,93d,112a,148c), lees (46a,142a), leet (26a,38a,139d), meed (128c,131a), meek (93d,99d), meer, meet (11d,13d,36a,50a,81d,142d), need (42b, 52d,87b,122a,178a), neem (96d,168c,169a), neep (140c,171b), neer (14b,86b,108b), peek (93d), peel (53a,114a), peen (73c), peep (93d,115c), peer (51a,107c), peet (64a), reed (16a,70d,97b,105a, 111b,118b,144b), Reed (163a), reef (129a,137a,145a), reek (49d, 53c,64a,148d,149a), reel (21b,40b,d,153c,154a,c,d,180d), reem (18d), seed (70b,111c,112c,119a,151b,154a), seek (141c), seel (20c,32c,143b), seem (11c), seen, seep (110c,116a,154b), seer (60a,124c,150c), teel (142d), teem (6b,121d), teen (139b,c,140b, 158d), teer (25b,69d), Tees (108a), veer (28d,144c,171b), weed week, weel (16d,57d,140d,180d), weep (39b,88a,104a), weet (19d)

- - EE agee (13d,15c,38d), ajee (15c,139a), akee (168c), alee (15c,75d, 144b,157a,182a), bree (139a), byee (189), chee (189), clee (19a, 129a), Cree (192), dree (139b,140c,158b,172c), epee (55c,160d), flee, free (44a,70d,131b), ghee (24d), glee (99a,150b), idee (61d), inee (120b), Klee (113a), knee (85b), ogee (40c,101a,b,120b), pree (139d), Rhee (87c), shee (82b), skee (149c), slee (140b,148c), smee (19b,46c,d,118b,119d,141b,181b), Smee (116d), snee (40a, b,43d,87a), Spee (66d,70b), thee (124b), tree (11d,37a,66a,184b), twee, tyee (29d), usee, whee

E - - E ease (7c,8d,35a,100d,129d,130b,c,150c), eave (133c), eboe (28b, 110a,168c,169b), Eboe, ecce (17d,89a,c), edge (22a,96d,131c, 143c,146b), elde (119c), eine (66c), Eire (82b), Elbe (108a), elle (62b,c), else (18b,79b,111d), ence (158c), enne (34c), ense (139b, 158c), ente (70b,151d), epee (55c,160d), Erie (82c,87d), erne (19c, d,47b,54b,141a) Erse (28a,64b,82b), esce (158d), esne (10c,45b, 142c,148a,164d), esse (7a,18a,52d,89a,90a,159a,166c), este (152b, d,164c), Este (55c,83c,112d), etre (61a,c,62d,166c), ette (158a,c,d), euge (180a), evoe (15b,130d,181c), eyre (23c,31b,85c), Eyre

EF - - Efik (191)

- EF - defi (61b), deft (147c), defy (28d), heft (179d), Heft, jefe (152a), jeff (133d), left (42c), reft (32a,42c,44d,167b), teff (6c), weft (39a,165a,184b)

- - EF alef (91c), atef (39a,48d), beef, chef, clef (104d,105a), elef (91c), fief (55d), keef (75d), kief (75d), lief (181d), reef (129a,137a, 145a), tref (172b)

E - - F elef (91c), Enif (155b)

EG - - egad (100a,109a), Egba (191), Egbo (141d), Eger (49a), eggs (112a), eggy (185d), Egil (107d), egis (14b,d,115a,124d,144b,154a,161a), egol (11b)

- EG - bega (188), degu (132c), hegh, mega (34b,c), pega (57a,130a, 158b), Pegu (24c,102a,127d), sego (24b,25a,92b,174c), tegg (143d,

330

171d), **vega** (110d,152c), **Vega** (155b), **Wega** (155b), **Wegg** (111d), **yegg** (24c)

- - EG **areg** (116a,137a), **Areg, Doeg** (137c), **dreg, Gheg** (8c), **skeg** (7d, 86a,144d,157d,184a), **sneg** (139b), **waeg** (19b,72c,87a)

EH - - **eheu** (52c)

- EH - **behn** (137d), **Hehe** (191), **jehu** (46b), **Jehu** (18c), **lehr** (67c,112a), **peho** (19b,102c,106d), **sehr** (66d), **tehr** (27c,68a)

- - EH **okeh** (8d,37b)

E - - H **each, Elah** (18c,86d), **Esth** (16a,51d), **Etah** (51c,71d), **etch, eyah** (95b,108d,111c)

EI - - **eide** (119c), **eild** (138d,140a), **eine** (66c) **Eire** (82b)

- EI - **Beid** (155b), **ceil** (92c,112a), **deil** (139b), **dein** (66d), **feis** (82b), **gein** (67d), **heii** (74b), **hein** (52c,61c), **heir, keif** (75d), **keir** (20c, 174d), **Leif** (107d), **Leir, mein** (30b), **nein** (66c), **meio** (188), **Neil** (96a), **reim** (112c), **rein** (29b,130c), **reis** (26c,29d,75a,103b), **seid** (103b), **Seid** (42d,101a,171a), **Seik** (77b), **Seim** (120c), **sein** (146c), **seip** (110c), **Seir** (51b,94a,103d), **seis** (147b,152c), **seit** (189), **Teig** (96a), **teil** (92b,c,168c), **veil** (74d,76c), **vein** (20d,157b), **weir** (40b,57d), **zein**

- - EI **drei** (66d,165a), **kuei** (44a), **kwei** (44a), **Omei** (24a), **quei** (189), **vlei** (38c,160a)

E - - I **Ekoi** (191), **Enki** (15b), **equi** (122d), **etui** (27a,29b,62c,106b,148d, 166d,174b)

EJ - - **ejoo** (55b,168c)

- EJ - **Beja** (6c,191), **Nejd, reja** (152b), **Sejm** (120c), **teju** (151b)

EK - - **Ekka** (26d), **Ekoi** (191)

- EK - **beka** (189), **feke, Peke** (45a,148d), **Reki** (16a), **weka** (58c,106d, 107a,127b), **weki** (55c), **Zeke** (96b)

- - EK **chek** (59c), **esek** (18d), **hoek** (39d), **keek** (154c), **leek** (58b,76a, 110c,177d), **meek** (93d,99d), **peek** (93d,115c), **reek** (49d,53c, 64a,148d,149a), **seek** (141c), **trek** (85c,93c,99d,168b)

E - - K **Efik** (191), **esek** (18d)

EL - - **Elah** (18c,86d), **Elam** (18d,37d,82a,116c,144b), **elan** (12c,41a,50d, 62a,153c,177a,186b), **ELAS** (71c), **Elba** (105d), **Elbe** (108a), **elef** (91c), **Elia** (88a,115d), **Elis** (22c,37d,71b,107c), **ella** (152c,158c, **Ella** (183c), **elle** (62b,c), **elmy, elod** (49b,59d,79c), **Elon** (18c,51b, 108a), **Elsa** (70a,93c,110d,177b,183c), **else** (18b,79b,111d), **Elul** (102b)

- EL - **bela** (12a), **Bela** (18b,48c,78d), **Beli** (23c), **bell** (24c,39d), **Bell** (162d), **belt** (16a,31a), **cela** (62d), **cell** (39b), **celt** (30c,82c,123a, 156c,167b,179b), **Celt** (10a,180a,b), **dele** (26a,49c,51b,53a,110b, 123d,124c,130a,145c,161b), **dell** (43c,174b), **eely** (185a), **fell** (40a, 58b,76c,115d,147d), **fels** (190), **felt, geld** (162b), **gelt** (101c), **Hela** (93c), **held, helm** (144d,165d), **help** (14a), **kela** (189), **keld** (154b), **kelp** (82a,141c), **Kelt** (180b), **Lely** (47a), **mele** (74b,150b), **melt, Nell** (110a,183d), **pela** (30c), **Pele** (69c,74c), **pelf** (131b), **pelo** (83b), **pelt** (53a), **pelu** (30a,106d,168c), **rely** (16b,170b), **self** (48d,80d), **sell** (97a,115c,175b), **tela** (22d,98c,121b,166a,179c), **tele** (34b,

331

122c), **tell** (94b), **tell** (105d,129c,154b), **Tell** (160d), **vela** (98c, 136b,149d), **Vela** (36b,c), **veld** (151a), **velo** (175b), **weld** (47c,85b, 173c), **Welf** (67a), **welk** (65c,96d,141b), **well, welt** (36d,131b, 145a,b,177b,d), **yell** (145c), **yelp, yelt** (151b)

- - EL **Abel** (7a,25b), **bhel** (126d), **coel** (39b), **duel, edel** (66c), **esel** (66b), **ezel** (47a,85d), **feel** (72a,142c), **fuel** (65c), **Gael** (28a,96c,138d), **goel** (15a,75c), **heel, Jael** (147b), **jeel, Joel** (96a), **keel** (128d,134d, 144c,d), **kiel** (128d,134d), **Kiel** (25d), **koel** (19a,b,39b), **nael** (189), **noel** (26d,150b), **Noel** (30d,96a), **odel** (48a,112c), **Orel, peel** (53a, 114a), **reel** (21b,40b,d,153c,154a,c,d,180d), **Riel** (129a), **ryel** (190), **seel** (20c,32c,143b), **tael** (91d,179d), **teel** (142d), **tuel, weel** (16d, 57d,140d,180d), **wiel** (140d,180d)

E - - L **earl** (107c), **edel** (66c), **Egil** (107d), **egol** (11b), **Elul** (102b), **Emil** (96a), **enol** (29c,158b), **eral** (51a), **esel** (66b), **etal** (89a), **evil** (79c, 95d,147a,181a,185c), **ezel** (47a,85d)

EM - - **Emer** (39b,183c), **emeu** (111d), **Emil** (96a), **Emim** (67a,100d), **emir** (12a,103a,b,123c,134d,135a,171a), **emit** (43d,49a,53c,58d,83a, 142c), **Emma** (183c), **emyd** (163c,167c), **Emys** (167c,171b)

- EM - **bema** (28d,31a,114b,119b,125b,137a), **deme** (71b,c,167d), **demi** (34b,122c), **demo** (122d), **demy** (113d), **feme** (181b), **hemi** (122c), **hemo** (34a,122b), **hemp** (26a,37a,56a,133d), **kemp** (139b), **memo** (108b), **Nema** (34d,48c,134b,164d,176c), **nemo** (34b), **Nemo** (56a, 85c), **Remi** (10b), **Rems, seme** (45c,138b,151b,154b,155c,157b), **semi** (34b,80b,122c,d), **Tema** (12a,164a), **Tema, xema** (72c), **Xema** (12c), **zeme** (55d,161b,180b), **zemi** (55d,161b,180b)

- - EM **ahem, alem** (98b,155a,170d,171a), **asem** (9a,49a,69c), **clem** (56b, 158b), **deem** (36b,85c,164c), **diem** (89b,116a), **haem** (122b), **idem** (89d,164a), **item** (6d,13b,42d,51a,90d,92d,107a,113d,114c), **Khem** (113c), **neem** (96d,168c,169a), **poem** (51a), **reem** (18d), **riem** (76c, 112c,157c,164d), **seem** (11c), **Shem** (107c), **stem** (29b,125a,154d, 155a,156d), **teem** (6b,121d), **them** (124b)

E - - M **edam** (29c), **Edom** (18c,51b,79b,82c,84a), **Elam** (18d,37d,82a,116c, 144b), **Emim** (67a,100d), **enam** (70c,77a), **Enam** (85c), **etym** (133d), **exam**

EN - - **enam** (70c,77a,85c), **ence** (158c), **endo** (34d,122d,183b), **Enid** (13b,25d,66b,163a,183c), **Enif** (155b), **enin** (20d), **Enki** (15b), **Enna** (146a), **enne** (34c), **enol** (29c,158b), **Enon** (18c,d), **Enos** (7a,18d,52a, 70c,96a,143a), **enow** (50d,123a,158b), **ense** (139b,158c), **enso** (34d,183b), **ente** (70b,151d), **ento** (34b,d,183b), **envy** (41b), **Enyo** (12c,69c,178a), **Enzu** (102b)

- EN - **bena** (176a), **bend** (39d,171b), **bene** (18a,83c,90a,106d,122a, 180a), **beng** (43a), **beni** (116a,142d), **Beni** (191), **beno** (113b,117a), **bent** (80b), **benu** (49a), **cena** (88d,133a), **cene** (34c), **cens** (115b), **cent** (36d), **dene** (137a), **Dene** (192), **dens** (90a,167b), **dent** (42c, 77d), **deny** (36d,43d,129b), **fend** (114b,178b), **gena** (29b), **gene** (54a,76b), **Gene** (96b), **gens** (42d,132d), **gent, genu** (6b,18a,87a, 89c), **hens** (121d), **Jena** (105d,165b), **keno, Kent** (90d), **lena** (56d), **Lena** (36b), **lend** (6d,79d), **lene** (36b,149a,172b), **leno** (37c, 53b), **lens** (67c,95b,111a,129b,162d), **lent** (54d), **Lent** (115d,141c), **mend** (130b), **mene** (19a,73d,108d,185c), **Ment** (54b,164a), **menu**

332

(19a,27a), **Menu, nene** (19b,74c), **pend, pene, pent** (36a), **rena**
(25b,132c), **rend** (32a,159c,162c,185a), **Reni** (83d), **Reno, rent**
(58a,91b,138b,153d,162c,167c), **send** (42c,44b,95c,121c,130a,
144c,168b), **senn** (76b), **Sens** (63b), **sent, tend** (26d,80b,93d,100a),
tene (34d,131b), **teng** (188), **tent** (26b,115a), **vena** (90a,175a),
vend (97a,115c,142b), **Vend** (10b,148a), **vent** (8b,11b,110d,112a),
wend (67d,123d), **Wend** (10b,148a), **went** (42c), **xeno** (34d), **yeni**
(19b,161d), **Zend, Zeno** (71b), **zenu** (143d)

- - EN **aden** (34b), **Aden, alen** (40d,138a), **amen** (14a,80b,94a,137a,149c,
175c,184b), **Amen** (86d,127d,164a), **aten** (150a,159b), **been** (149a),
bien (63a,140c,179a,180a), **bren** (72d,95a), **Caen, Chen** (149b),
Eben (96a), **Eden** (6b,50d,107c,113d,123c), **even** (51a,58b,79d,91d,
149a,173a), **glen** (43c), **hien** (30b), **hoen** (189), **Iden** (76a), **Iren**
(127c), **Iten** (192), **keen** (15a,88a,177b), **lien** (65c,91a,124c), **mien**
(11c,17b,26d,44c,96b), **omen** (14c,59d,60a,121c,123a,146b), **open**
(26a,60d,81a,109b,112c,125b,172b,173c), **oven** (15d,78c,86b),
Owen (96a,183c), **oxen** (10c), **peen** (73c), **pien** (13b), **rien** (62b),
seen, Shen (68a), **sken** (164a), **sten** (72c,95a), **teen** (139b,c,140b,
158d), **then, tien** (147d), **T-men** (168b), **when** (180d), **wren** (19b,c),
Wren (50b)

E - - N **earn** (42d,64b,99a), **Eben** (96a), **ebon** (20b), **Eden** (6b,50d,107c,
113d,123c), **elan** (12c,41a,50d,62a,153c,177a,186c), **Elon** (18c,
51b), **enin** (20d), **Enon** (18c,d), **Eoan** (41a,85b), **Eoin** (85b), **Erin**
(82b), **Eton** (33b,50c,84a), **Evan** (96a), **even** (51a,58b,79d,91d,
149a,173a), **Ewan**

EO - - **Eoan** (41a,85b), **Eoin** (85b)

- EO - **feod** (55d), **Leon** (96a), **meou, meow, neon** (65c), **peon** (28c,59c,
99c), **Teos** (82a)

- - EO **areo** (34c), **Ateo** (120d), **Cleo** (126b), **ideo** (34b,d,164d), **oleo** (34c),
skeo (57d)

E - - O **Ebro** (132a), **echo** (130b,d), **Echo** (105d), **ecto** (34c,122d), **eddo**
(162a), **Egbo** (141d), **ejoo** (55b,168c), **endo** (34d,122d,183b), **enso**
(34d,183b), **ento** (34b,d,183b), **Enyo** (12c,69c,178a), **ergo** (164b)

EP - - **epee** (55c,160d), **epha** (75c), **epic** (76b,120a), **epos** (51a,76b,120a)

- EP - **cepa** (110c), **cepe** (48c), **depa** (188), **kepi** (99d), **kept, Nepa** (106b,
178c), **pepo** (39b,64a,70a,98c,125c,154c), **repp** (53b,131a), **seps**
(93b,142d), **sept** (31d,82b,143a,149c), **Sept** (45b), **Veps** (191), **wept**

- - EP **deep** (124a), **Heep** (41a,43b), **jeep, keep** (123a,130d), **neep** (140c,
171b), **peep** (93d,115c), **prep** (138b), **seep** (110c,116a,154b), **skep**
(16d,17c,77c), **step** (70b,112b,177b,d), **weep** (39b,88a,104a)

EQ - - **equi** (122d)

ER - - **eral** (51a), **erat** (89c), **Erda** (23d,41a,47d,68d,69a,131d,177b), **erer**
(17d,150c), **ergo** (164b), **eria** (13d,146d), **eric** (115b), **Eric** (71d,
96a,107d,138a,164a,176b), **Erie** (82c,87d), **Erin** (82b), **Eris** (12c,
68d,109c), **Erma** (183c), **erne** (19c,d,47b,54b,141a), **Eros** (11c,
39c,68b,97c,182d), **Erse** (28a,64b,82b), **erst** (60b), **Erua** (103c),
eruc (37a,56a), **eryx** (137a)

- ER - **aera** (8a), **aeri** (34a), **aero** (8b,34a,b,58c,59a), **aery** (47b,51d,106c),
Bera (86d), **berg** (79b), **berm** (25d,90d,145c), **Bern** (160d), **Bert**

333

(96b), **cera** (152d,161d,179a), **cere** (19a,114b,149d,179a), **ce** ·
(41c), **cero** (57b,c,d, 180b), **dera** (34c), **dere** (74a,79c), **de** ;,
147c,158d), **eery** (172b,180a), **fern** (142a), **feru** (37a,56a,133d),
gerb (56d,143d), **Gerd** (63c), **Gere** (183c), **Geri** (183c), **germ** (17d,
99c,134d), **Hera** (69c,85d,110b,126b,186b,d), **herb** (58b,158b),
herd (39a,46c,72a), **here**, **herl** (16b,59a), **hero** (42b,124d,137b),
Hero (90c), **Herr** (66c), **hers** (124c), **jerk** (153a), **kerb** (146b), **kere**
(75c,128b), **kerf** (40a,108b), **keri** (75c,128b), **kern** (59c,172a),
Kern (132b), **Kerr, Lero** (82d), **lerp** (51d,141d), **mere** (16c,22b,
62a,78b,87d,96c,110c,120d,146d,148b), **merl** (20b), **mero** (72a),
Meru (77a,103d), **Nera** (165b), **Neri, Nero** (8a,126d,133a,172c),
Pera (60a), **pere** (61c,63b), **peri** (54b,116b,c,122b), **perk** (84d,
93a), **perm** (49b,97d), **pern** (78a), **pero** (152a), **pert** (80a,93a,137c,
154b), **Peru, qere** (75c), **qeri** (75c), **sera** (11b,20d,59a,83a,180d),
Serb (15d,148a,186c), **sere** (24d,46a,46c,138c,183b), **Sere** (158b),
serf (21d,148a), **seri** (18b), **Seri** (192), **sero** (34d,88d,164b,178d),
Sert (151d), **tera** (23d,84c), **term** (92b,105b,142b,166b), **tern** (19b,
32d,72c,94a,138c,141a,160a), **terp** (12b,123a), **vera** (140c,151b,
175c), **Vera** (183c), **verb** (7a,114b,184b), **verd** (71d), **veri** (28b),
vert (71d,166a,171b), **very** (149c), **were** (139b), **werf** (54d), **werl**
(15c,27c), **wert, zero** (31a,84c,108c), **Zero** (118d)

- - ER **Acer** (96c) **Ader** (18d), **afer** (48a,182b), **ager** (47c,56a,89b,c,131d,
133b), **amer** (61b), **aner** (18d,96b), **aper** (32d), **Aser** (84a),
Ater (18c), **Auer** (79a), **aver** (7c,14a,15c,41c,95c,140d,155c,160b,
184c), **beer** (18c), **bier** (33b,66b), **Boer** (151a), **Brer** (172b), **cher**
(61b), **daer** (22b), **deer** (28c,135a,154d), **dier, doer** (8a,116b), **dyer,
Eber** (51a,75c,99d), **Eder, Eger** (49a), **Emer** (39b,183c), **erer** (17d,
150c), **eser, euer** (66d), **ever** (9b,14b,80b), **ewer** (84c,85c,118c,
181b), **eyer, gier** (47b), **goer, heer** (47a, 184b, 185b), **hier** (63a,
185d), **Hier** (141a), **hoer, icer, Imer, Iser** (49a), **iter** (22d,76c,85c,
89c,114d,132a,b,133a,b), **jeer** (138c,162b), **kier** (20c,174d), **leer**
(9d,58a,67c,93d,112a,148c), **meer, neer** (14b,86b,108b), **Oder**
(132a), **omer** (51a,75c), **oner** (20d,53a,75c,162d,173a,d), **oser** (61b),
over (6b,38c,80a,114d,130a), **oxer** (55c), **oyer** (38a,75b,119c), **peer**
(51a,93d,107c), **pier** (23a,88b,180c), **rier** (180b), **roer** (72d), **ruer,
saer** (163a), **seer** (60a,124c,150c), **sher** (65d,165c), **sier** (57a,118b),
ster (158c,d), **suer** (124d), **teer** (25b,69d), **tier** (118a,134b), **tyer,
uber** (66b), **user** (49d), **veer** (28d,144c,171b), **vier** (66c), **waer**
(40b), **Ymer** (67a,131c), **Yser**

E - - R **Eber** (51a,75c,99d), **ebur** (89c), **Edar** (18d), **Eder, Eger** (49a), **Emer**
(39b,183c,), **emir** (12a,103a,b,123c,171a), **erer** (17d,150c), **eser,
euer** (66d), **ever** (9b,14b,80b), **ewer** (84d,85c,118c,181b), **eyer**

ES - - **Esau** (82c,84a,128c), **Esay, esca** (11c,44a,70c), **esce** (158d), **esek**
(18d), **esel** (66b), **eser, esne** (10c,45b,142c,148a,164d), **Esop** (53b,
54a), **esox** (57b), **espy** (44a,142a), **esse** (7a,18a,52d,89a,90a,159a,
166c), **esta** (152d,164c), **este** (152b,d,164c), **Este** (55c,83c,d,112d),
Esth (16a,51d), **Esus**

- ES - **aesc** (12d,64d), **Besa** (68b,119c), **Bess** (76c,183d), **best** (41d,159c,
160a), **cess** (91d,94c,162b), **cest** (18a,67b), **desi** (85d), **desk, euer**
(66d), **fess** (23c,51b), **fest, gest** (7c,41d,52d,133c), **hest** (35a), **jess**
(157a), **jest** (169c), **Jesu, less** (100c,108b,141d), **lest** (59d,163d),

334

mesa (49b,76d,119b,161a), **mese** (71c), **mesh** (50d,106c), **mess** (22b,44b,77c,85d,104b,165c,173d), **ness** (26b,75a,124b), **nest** (38b, 74b,130d,149c,160b), **oese** (15d,119c), **pesa** (190), **peso** (99c), **pest** (108c,116b,118d,170a), **rese** (127b), **resh** (91d), **rest** (15d,91b, 104d,105a,115a,b,130a,b,161b), **sesi** (20b,57a,149b), **sess** (149c, 162b), **Tesa** (80c), **Tess** (73d,164c,183d), **test** (26a,51c,144a,169c, 170c), **vest** (32c,177b), **West** (9c,50b,109b), **Yeso** (72d), **zest** (55d, 72d)

- - ES **Ades** (73a), **Ames** (9c,82a), **anes** (110c,140a), **Ares** (49b,51b,68c, 76a,97a,105c,110b,178a,186d), **ates** (160c), **Aves** (19d), **bees** (185b), **Bres**, **dies** (41b,89b), **does**, **EDES** (71c), **fees** (128c), **Ghes** (193), **gres** (156d), **ides** (41a,b,133a), **Ives** (9c,90b), **lees** (46a, 142a), **ones** (116a), **oyes** (38a,39b,75b), **pres** (62b), **spes**, **Spes** (69a,78a), **Tees** (108a), **tres** (19a,52b,63a,152d,165a,175c), **uses** (18a), **wies** (185a)

E - - S **Eads** (23b,24b,50b,82a), **eats**, **EDES** (71c), **eggs** (112a), **egis** (14b, d,115a,124d,144b,154a,161a), **ELAS** (71c), **Elis** (22c,37d,71b, 107c), **Emys** (167c,171b), **Enns**, **Enos** (7a,18d,52a,70c,96a,143a), **epos** (51a,76b,120a), **Eris** (12c,68d,109c), **Eros** (11c,39c,68b,97c, 182d), **Esus**, **etes** (177c), **eyas** (106c,173a)

ET - - **Etah** (51c,71d), **etal** (89a), **etat** (62d), **etch**, **etes** (177c), **etna** (75b, 153c,157a,175d,177a,c), **Eton** (33b,50c,84a), **etre** (61a,c,62d,166c), **Etta** (183c), **ette** (158a,c,d), **etui** (27a,29b,62c,106b,148d,166d, 174b), **etym** (133d)

- ET - **Aeta** (94d,95d,100a,106b,117a), **beta** (71a,91c,141d), **bete** (61a,107c), **beth** (91c), **Beth** (8c,183d), **cete** (180b,c), **ceto** (34a), **fete** (55d,129b), **geta** (84b,145a), **gett** (44d), **Heth** (77c), **jete** (16a), **Jeth** (102a), **keta** (45a), **Keta**, **Ketu** (48b), **lete**, **Leti** (82d), **Leto** (11c), **Lett** (16a,90a,93a), **meta** (132d,133a), **Meta**, **mete** (9a, 11d,22b,44c,45b,98a,121c), **nete** (71c,108b,163d), **neti** (164a), **nett**, **pete** (136b), **Pete** (96b), **peto** (57a,177b), **Peto** (76a), **rete** (106c,119c), **seta** (23b,27c,73a,b,123b,153c), **seth** (98d), **Seth** (7a, 52b,68a,b,96a,98d), **seti** (34a), **Seti** (116d), **sett** (115a,156d), **tete** (61d,73b,74d), **teth** (91d), **veta** (104a), **veto** (94a,124a), **Veto**, **weta** (93c), **yeta** (84c), **zeta** (71b,91c)

- - ET **abet** (8b,15b,50a,59b,75d,81c,141d,159d), **Ahet** (49a,102a), **anet** (43c), **Apet** (97c), **aret** (128c), **beet** (175a), **blet** (64a), **diet** (14a, 54c,84c,91b,176a), **duet** (104d,171d), **evet** (48d,107a,136c,169d), **fret** (28c,35b,111c,184d), **keet** (72b), **khet** (188), **laet** (60d), **leet** (26a,38a), **meet** (11d,13d,36a,50a,81d,142d), **oket** (189), **peet** (64a), **piet** (29b,95b), **plet** (135d), **poet** (49b), **pret** (188), **pyet** (95b), **spet** (16c,57a,142c), **stet** (91b,123d,124c), **suet** (54d), **tret** (9a,178b,179d), **voet** (188), **weet** (19d), **whet** (143c,156b)

E - - T **east**, **East** (111b), **edit** (20d,49d,123a,129a,131a), **emit** (43d,49a, 53c,58d,83a,142c), **erat** (89c), **erst** (60b), **etat** (62d), **evet** (48d, 107a,136c,169d), **exit** (114d), **eyot** (82d)

EU - - **euer** (66d), **euge** (180a)

- EU - **deul** (77b), **deus** (68a,89d), **feud** (55d,126b,175b), **Geum** (76b), **jeux** (61d), **meum** (27a,89c), **Meum**, **neue** (66c), **peur** (61c), **Zeus** (135a)

- - EU   bleu (61b), Dieu (61d), eheu (52c), emeu (111d), lieu (118c,155d)

E - -U   ecru (17d,23d,172b), eheu (52c), emeu (111d), Enzu (102b), Esau (82c,84a,128c)

EV - -   Evan (96a), even (51a,58b,79d,91d,149a,173a), evea (82a,95a), ever (9b,14b,80b), evet (48d,107a,136c,169d), evil (79c,95d,147a, 181a,185c), evoe (15b,130d,181c)

- EV -   bevy (38a,58c), Deva (23d,42a,b,56d,77a), Devi (147b,153b), hevi (111d), Leve (62a), Levi (84a,90c), levo (91a), levy (14a, 162b), Neva (91b,132a), neve (56d,67c,70c,149b), peva (12d), pevy (91d,94c), reve (61c,104d), revs (131a), seve (63a,182c)

- - EV   Kiev, Stev (155b)

EW - -   Ewan, ewer (84d,85c,118c,181b), ewry (133c)

- EW -   dewa, dewy (101a), hewn, mewl (180d), mews (154c), news (165c), newt (48d,136c,169d), sewn, Tewa (193)

- - EW   anew (7c), blew, brew (35d), chew (97c), clew (16a,33a,77b,136b, 164d), crew (72a,106a), drew, flew, grew, knew, Llew (40c), phew (52c), plew (17c), shew (44c), skew (148a,160c,171c), slew (160a), smew (19b,46d,99a,137d), spew (35a,49a), stew (21c,44b,184d), thew (104c), view (93d,138b), whew

E - - W   enow (50d,123a,158b)

EX - -   exam, exit (114d)

- EX -   next (106a), sext (26b,111b,147b), text (21c,140d)

- - EX   Amex (184d), apex (39c,76c,115c,118b,159b,166a,167b), Crex (37a), faex (46a), flex (18a), ibex (67d,68a), ilex (77d), obex (22d), plex (60b), spex, Ulex (153c)

E - - X   eaux (178c), eryx (137a), esox (57b)

EY - -   eyah (95b,108d,111c), eyas (106c,173a), eyer, eyey (74b), eyot (82d), eyra (181d), eyre (23c,31b,85c), Eyre, eyry (47b,106c)

- EY -   Ceyx (73b), teyl (92b,c,168c)

- - EY   ahey (52c), akey (189), brey (194), drey (154c), eyey (74b), fley (63d), Frey (7c,68b,124d), grey (33c), hoey (114c), joey (86a,185d), Joey (96b,109c), obey (35c,75c), prey (119d,176a), roey (103d), skey (185d), sley (179b), Spey, they (124b), trey (26c,165a), Urey (14b,107c,138c), whey (100a)

E - - Y   easy (54a), eddy (37d,39d,160d,180d), edgy (106c), eely (185a), eery (172b,180a), eggy (185d), elmy, envy (41b), esay, espy (44a, 142a), ewry (133c), eyey (74b), eyry (47b,106c)

EZ - -   ezba (188), ezel (47a,85d), Ezra (96a)

- - EZ   chez (14b,61a), daez, Geez (6c,51d), Inez (45c,183c), juez (152b), knez (123c), oyez (38a,39b,75b)

FA - -   Faam (111a), Faba, face (159d,176c), fact (7a,128b), fade (181d, 183b), fado (121c), fady, faex (46a), fail, fain (42d,67c,183b), fair (17a,55d), fait (6d,61b), fake (123a,143c), faky, fala (129b), fall (46b,141c), falx (133b), Fama (135a), fame (130a), famn (188), fana, fane (30d,137a,162d), fang (167b), fano (51d,96b,113c,d), faon (33c,55a), fard (112d) fare (43c,59b,67d,123b), farl (138c, 140b), farm (165d), faro (65a), fash (140c,176a), fass (189), fast (56d,126c,141d,160c,173a,d), fate (42d,52a,87a,94a), faun (56a,

336

68b,137c,161a,184a), **favi** (138a,165d), **fawn** (33c), **faze** (43d)

- FA -   afar (44c), Afar (6c)

- - FA   Abfa (76b), alfa (70d), gufa (21b,99a), Kafa (6c), kufa (21b,99a), Offa (163d), sofa (44d), tufa (121b,177a), Urfa (99a)

F - - A   Faba, fala (129b), Fama (135a), fana, flea (81b), fora (133a), Frea, Fria, fuga

F - - B   flub (22b), frab (138c), frib (43d)

F - - C   fisc (52c,134c), floc (149a)

- - FD   Wafd (49a)

F - -D   fard (112d), feed (108c), fend (114b,178b), feod (55d), feud (55d, 126b,175b), find (44a), fled, fold, fond (7c,94b), food (109a,176b), ford (177b), foud (54d,144b), Fred (96b), Fuad (54d), fund (6d, 101c,130c), fyrd (110a)

FE - -   feak (39d,171c), fear (113c,155a), feat (7a,52d), feed (108c), feel (72a,142c), fees (128c), feis (82b), feke, fell (40a,58b,76c,115d, 147d), fels (190), felt, feme (181b), fend (114b,178b), feod (55d), fern (142a), feru (37a,56a,133d), fess (23c,51b), fest, fete (55d, 129b), feud (55d,126b,175b)

- FE -   afer (48a,182b)

- - FE   cafe, fife (59a,105a), jefe (152a), life (19a,177a), nife (37a), orfe (57a,b,185c), rife (6b,c,39d,123b), safe (141d,157d,174d), wife (154a)

F - - E   face (159d,176c), fade (181d,183b), fake (123a,143c), fame (130a), fane (30d,137a,162d), fare (43c,59b,67d,123b), fate (42d,52a,87a, 94a), faze (43d), feke, feme (181b), fete (55d,129b), fide, fife (59a,105a), fike (139c), file (13a,127d), fine (49b,50a,104b,115d, 159a), fire (13a,43d,44b), five flee, floe (79b), flue (8b,30a), fore (63d,174b), free (44a,70d,131b), froe (32a,167a,179d), fume (129a, 149a,157a), fuse (98c), fute (51c), fuze (98c), fyke (15d)

- FF -   affy (18b), offa, Offa (163d), offs (38c)

- - FF   baff (69d), biff, buff (134c,161d), cuff (148a), daff (125d), doff (130a,161b), duff (125b), gaff (57c,d,152d,153a), goff (32d), guff, huff (58a), jeff (133d), Jeff, jiff (101c), kiff (88c), koff (47a), luff (136b), miff (44c), moff (53b,146c), muff (53b,146c), puff (180d), raff (75b), riff (131d), Riff (18b,102c), ruff (19b,33b,63d, 137a), teff (6c), tiff (126b), toff (40d), tuff (121b,177a)

F - - F   fief (55d)

F - - G   fang (167b), flag (16b,50d,82b,88c,115a,155a), flog (180d), Fong (40b), frog (10a,17a,126d), Fung (191)

F - - H   fash (140c,176a), fish, Foch (63b)

FI - -   fiat (35a,41d,48c,111b,137a), Fiat (83c), fico (169d), fide, fief (55d), fife (59a,105a), fike (139c), file (13a,127d), fili, fill (109b), film (164b), filo, fils (62d,150b), find (44a), fine (49b,50a,104b, 115d,159a), fink (19a,56c,157c), Finn (107d), Fiot (191), fire (13a,43d,44b), firm (154c,173d), firn (67c,70c,106c,149b), fisc (52c,134c), fish, fisk (24d,52c,134c), fist (80c), five

- FI -   Efik (191), ifil (117a,168c)

- - FI   defi (61b), Safi (191), sufi (103a,116c)

F - - I   favi (138a,165d), **fill, foci** (28b), **fucl** (132c), **fuji** (84b), **Fuji** (84d)

F - - J   Funj

F - - K   feak (39d,171c), fink (19a,56c,157c), fisk (24d,52c,134c), flak (11a), folk (116a,169c), fork, fulk (173a), funk (63d,113c)

FL - -   flag (16b,50d,82b,88c,115a,155a), flak (11a), flam (169c), flan (39d,40a,114d), flap (17b,59a,104a,118d,161a,182d), flat (41b, 124b,173a), flaw, flax, flay (147c,157c), flea (81b), fled, flee, flew, flex (18a), fley (63d), flip (167c), flit (41a), flix, floc (149a), floe (79b), flog (180d), flop (54a), flot (173a), flow (157b), flub (22b), flue (8b,30a), flux (28d,58d)

F - - L   fail, fall (46b,141c), farl (138c,140b), feel (72a,142c), fell (40a, 58b,76c,115d,147d), fill (109b), foal (78c), foil (15d,55c,165b), fool (24a,41c,47a,146d), foul (173a), fowl, fuel (65c), full (7b, 130b), furl (132d)

F - - M   Faam (111a), farm (165d), film (164b), firm (154c,173d), flam (169c), foam (63d,154b), form (54d,143c), frim (58d), from

F - - N   fain (42d,67c,183b), famn (188), faon (33c,55a), faun (56a,68b, 137c,161a,184a), fawn (33c), fern (142a), Finn (107d), firn (67c, 70c,106c,149b), flan (39d,40a,114d), fohn (182b)

FO - -   foal (78c), foam (63d,154b), Foch (63b), foci (28b), fogy, fohn (182b), foil (15d,55c,165b), fold, folk (116a,169c), fond (7c,94b), Fong (40b), fono (137a), fons (60c), font (16b,171d,172a), food (109a,176b), fool (24a,41c,47a,146d), foot (115a), fora (133a), ford (177b), fore (63d,174b), fork, form (54d,143c), fort (63d, 157d), foss (44d,100d), foud (54d,144b), foul (173a), four (26c), fowl, foxy (38b,39c,181d)

- - FO   Bufo (166c)

F - - O   fado (121c), fano (51d,96b,113c,d), faro (65a), fico (169d), filo, fono (137a)

F - - P   flap (17b,59a,104a,118d,161a,182d), flip (167c), flop (54a), frap (45d,165c)

FR - -   frab (138c), frap (45d,165c), frat, frau (181b), fray (56b,60d), Frea, Fred (96b), free (44a,70d,131b), fret (28c,35b,111c,184d), Frey (7c,68b,124d), Fria, frib (43d), frim (58d), frit (64c,67c), friz (39d), froe (32a,167a,179d), frog (10a,17a,126d), from, frot (28c), frow (47a,167a)

- FR -   Afra (183c)

F - - R   fair (17a,55d), fear (113c,155a), four (26c)

- - FS   offs (38c)

F - - S   fass (189), fees (128c), feis (82b), fels (190), fess (23c,51b), fils (62d,150b), fons (60c), foss (44d,100d), fuss (22b,35b)

- - FT   baft (14a,53b), daft (59c), deft (147c), gift (123a), haft (76d), heft (179d), Heft, left (42c), lift (49b), loft (14c,69d,104b,178b), raft (27b,33c,58c,75b), reft (32a,42c,44d,167b), rift (30c,32a,58a, 110d), sift (140d,142c,146b), soft (48b,95d,99d,163a), Taft (29d), tuft (24b,32d,38c), waft (20d,58c), weft (39a,165a,184b), yuft (135c)

338

F - - T   **fact** (7a,128b), **fait** (6d,61b), **fast** (56d,126c,141d,160c,173a,d), **feat** (7a,52d), **felt, fest, Fiat** (83c), **fiat** (35a,41d,48c,111b,137a), **Fiot** (191), **fist** (80c), **flat** (41b,124b,173a), **flit** (41a), **flot** (173a), **font** (16b,171d,172a), **foot** (115a), **fort** (63d,157d), **frat, fret** (28c, 35b,111c,184d), **frit** (64c,67c), **frot** (28c), **fust** (105c,143b)

FU - -   **Fuad** (54d), **fuci** (132c), **fuel** (65c), **fuga, fugu** (84b), **fuji** (84b), **Fuji** (84d), **fulk** (173a), **full** (7b,130b), **fume** (129a,149a,157a), **fumy, fund** (6d,101c,130c), **Fung** (191), **funk** (63d,113c), **furl** (132d), **fury** (157a), **fuse** (98c), **fuss** (22b,35b), **fust** (105c,143b), **fute** (51c), **fuze** (98c), **fuzz** (45d)

F - - U   **feru** (37a,56a,133d), **frau** (181b), **fugu** (84b)

F - - W   **flaw, flew, flow** (157b), **frow** (47a,167a)

F - - X   **faex** (46a), **falx** (133b), **flax, flex** (18a), **flix, flux** (28d,58d)

FY - -   **fyke** (15d), **fyrd** (110a)

- - FY   **affy** (18b), **defy** (28d), **Dufy** (63a)

F - - Y   **fady, faky, flay** (147c,157c), **fley** (63d), **fogy, foxy** (38b,39c,181d), **fray** (56b,60d), **Frey** (7c,68b,124d), **fumy, fury** (157a)

F - - Z   **friz** (39d), **fuzz** (45d)

GA - -   **gaal** (23b,174d), **gabe** (162a), **gabi** (162a), **gaby** (59c,146d), **gade Gaea** (47d,69a), **Gael** (28a,96c,138d), **gaff** (57c,d,152d,153a), **gage** (28d,98a,119c,d), **gagl** (160b), **Gaia** (47d,69a), **gail** (23b, 174d), **Gail** (183d), **gain** (7a,b,124a,181d), **gait** (96b,179a), **gajo** (107c), **gala** (55d), **Gala** (191), **gale** (181d), **gali** (6c), **gall** (19a, 28c,29b,82c,160c,176a), **galt, Gama** (121c), **game** (64d,154a), **gamp** (172a), **gane** (185b), **gang** (38c), **Gano** (132d), **gaol** (123d), **Gaol** (164a), **Gaon** (85b), **gape** (185b), **gapo** (60a), **gapy, gara** (190), **garb** (32c,46a), **gare** (61b,c,62c,127c,184b), **Garm** (178c), **garn** (67d,185b), **Garo** (88c), **Gary, gash** (40a), **gasp** (113c), **gata** (143c), **gate** (51a,121b), **Gath** (117a), **gaub** (116c), **gaud** (169d), **gaue** (67a), **Gaul** (10a,60d,63c), **gaup, gaur** (112c,181c), **gaus** (67a), **gaut** (88b,103d,132a), **gave, gawd** (169c), **gawk** (146d), **gawp, Gaza** (117a), **gaze, gazi, gazy**

- GA -   **Agag** (18c,86c,137a), **agal** (17c,36c), **Agao** (6c,73c), **agar** (7d,28c, 39c,103c,141c), **Agau** (73c), **Agaz** (193), **egad** (100a,109a), **ngai** (48a,159c), **ngan, ogam** (82b,c), **Sgau** (88c)

- - GA   **alga** (141b,c), **baga** (171b), **bega** (188), **biga** (171d), **boga** (57d, 180b), **fuga, giga** (56a,105a), **goga** (24a), **hoga** (144b), **inga** (145d, 170a), **Jaga** (191), **juga** (27a), **mega** (34b,c), **muga, naga** (13d, 33a,55b,127c), **Naga** (24c,77a,88c,176d), **Olga** (135c,183c), **paga** (117a), **pega** (57a,130a,158b), **raga** (56d,105a), **riga** (118b), **ruga** (59b,185a), **saga** (79b,91a,138a,157a,161b,c,168a), **Saga, soga** (70d,152b), **Soga** (191), **toga** (132d,133a,b), **vega** (152c), **Vega** (155b), **Wega** (155b), **yoga** (10b,13c,77a), **Yuga** (76d), **zyga** (134b)

G - - A   **Gaea** (47d,69a), **Gaia** (47d,69a), **gala** (55d), **Gala** (191), **Gama** (121c), **gara** (190), **gata** (143c), **Gaza** (117a), **gena** (29b), **geta** (84b, 145a), **giga** (56a, 105a), **gila** (93b), **Gita, Gjoa** (144d), **glia** (106c), **goga** (24a), **gola** (27b,40c,70c,157a), **Goma** (191), **Gona** (106d), **gora** (81c), **Goya** (151d), **gufa** (21b,99a),

Guha (191), gula (90a,101a,165b), guna (106a,137b)

- **GB -** Egba (191), Egbo (141d)

G - - B garb (32c,46a), gaub (116c), gerb (56d,143d), glib (58d,149a,177c), glub, grab (105b,142a,149b), grub (88d), guib (11a)

G - - D gaud (169d), gawd (169c), gedd (140a), geld (162b), Gerd (63c), gild (14a,49c,69c,98b), gird (32c,50a,123a,160a), glad (85c), gled (19a,52a,87a), goad (80b,154b), gold, Gond, good, grad (28b), grid (17a,70d,119b,156d)

GE - - geal (47d,163c), gean (29c), gear (32c,112a,167b), geat (77d,101a), Geat (138a), gedd (140a), Geez (6c,51d), gein (67d), geld (162b), gelt (101c), gena (29b), gene (54a,76b), Gene (96b), gens (42d, 132d), gent, genu (6b,18a,87a,89c), gerb (56d,143d), Gerd (63c), Gere (183c), Geri (183c), germ (17d,99c,134d), gest (7c,41d,52d, 133c), geta (84b,145a), gett (44d), Geum (76b)

- **GE -** aged (110a), agee (13d,15c,38d), ager (47c,56a,89b,c,131d,133c), Eger (49a), ogee (101a,b,120b)

- **- GE** ange (61a), auge (123c,132b), cage (36a), doge (95b,175b), edge (22a,96d,131c,143c,146b), euge (180a), gage (28d,98a,119c,d), huge, Inge (24d,67d,117c,119c), kuge (84c), loge (164a), luge (148a), mage (95b), page (51b,59b,142d,159b), rage (10c,30c,157a, 161d), sage (13a,90d,100c,141c,145c,180b,183a), tige (118a), urge (42d,46b,79d,80a,b,81c,124a,150a), wage (27a,115b), yage (23a)

G - - E gabe (162a), gade, gage (28d,98a,119c,d), gale (181d), game (64d, 154a), gane (185b), gape (185b), gare (61b,c,62c,127c, 184b), gate (51a,121b), gaue (67a), gave, gaze, gene (54a,76b), Gene (96b), ghee (24d), gibe (8a,42c,84d,100d,138c,144c,149b), Gide (63a), gime (77d), gite (62a,118d), give (79d,123a), glee (99a, 150b), glue (7b,156a), gone (6b,15c,42c,44b,114d), gore (115d, 117c,154c,169c), guze (128d), gybe (144c), gyle (23b,174d), gyne (34b,55b,183c), gyre (31b,171b), gyve (55d,143b)

'G - - F gaff (57c,d,152d,153a), goaf (104b), goff (32d), golf (154a), goof, Graf (37c,66b,67a,107c,186b), guff, gulf (6c)

- **GG -** eggs (112a), eggy (185d)

- **- GG** dagg (118c), hagg, hogg (144a), jagg, magg (95b), migg (96c), nogg (48d), tegg (143d,171d), vugg (28a,66a,132b), Wegg (111d), wigg, yegg (24c)

G - - G gang (38c), Gheg (8c), glug, gong, grig (38c,70d,93a), grog (92d, 153d)

GH - - ghat (32d,88b,103d,132a), ghee (24d), Gheg (8c), Ghes (193), ghor (174b), ghos (30b), Ghuz (171a)

- **GH -** agha (35a,171a)

- **- GH** dagh (76d), hegh, high, Hugh (96a), Lugh (28b), Magh (102a), nigh (106a), ough, pugh, sigh, vugh (28a,66a,136b), yogh (10c, 185a)

G - - H gash (40a), Gath (117a), gish (102c), gosh, Goth (16c), gush (35a, 154c)

GI - - gibe (8a,42c,84d,100d,138c,144c,149b), Gide (63a), gier (47b),

340

gift (123a), **giga** (56a,105a), **gila** (93b), **gild** (14a,49c,69c,98b),
gill (22d), **gilo** (48a), **gilt** (69c,77c,151b,185d), **gime** (77d), **gimp**
(169d), **gink** (48b), **gird** (32c,50a,123a,160a), **girl**, **giro** (38c,83c,
167c), **girt** (50a), **gish** (102c), **gist** (95c,118c), **Gita**, **gite** (62a,
118d), **give** (79d,123a)

- GI -   **Agib** (12a,42d), **agio** (52c,60a,101c,123a), **Agis** (86d), **Egil** (107d),
     egis (14b,d,115a,124d,144b,154a,161a)

- - GI   **Bugi** (191), **hagi** (84b), **jogi** (76d), **magi** (123c), **Magi** (95b,116c,
     183a), **ragi** (28b), **sugi** (84b), **vagi** (38b), **yogi** (76d)

G - - I   **gabi** (162a), **gali** (6c), **gazi**, **Geri** (183c), **goai** (106d,168c), **gobi**,
     Gobi (42d), **goli** (105c), **Guti**, **gyri** (22d,131b)

GJ - -   **Gjoa** (144d)

G - - J   **gunj** (70c)

G - - K   **gawk** (146d), **gink** (48b), **gowk** (146d)

GL - -   **glad** (85c), **gled** (19a,52a,87a), **glee** (99a,150b), **glen** (43c), **glia**
     (106c), **glib** (58d,149a,177c), **glim**, **glis** (45c), **glom** (155d,160d,
     178c), **glow** (144c), **glub**, **glue** (7b,156a), **glug**, **glum** (102c,159a),
     glut (52c,70a,137c,159d)

- GL -   **agla** (7a), **iglu** (51c,149b), **ogle** (9d,53c,91a,93d,148c)

- - GL   **gagl** (160b)

G - - L   **gaal** (23b,174d), **Gael** (28a,96c,138d), **gagl** (160b), **gail** (23b,174d),
     Gail (183d), **gall** (19a,28c,29b,82c,160c,176a), **gaol** (123d), **Gaol**
     (164a), **Gaul** (10a,60d,63c), **geal** (47d,163c), **gill** (22d), **girl**, **goal**
     (8b,109b,120b,125d), **goel** (15a,75c), **Goll**, **goul** (102a), **gowl** (102a,
     140d,185b), **gull** (32d,41c,42a,72c,99b,141a)

G - - M   **Garm** (178c), **germ** (99c,134d), **Geum** (76b), **glim**, **glom** (155d,
     160d,178c), **glum** (102c,159a), **gram** (29d,99b,148d,160d,180a),
     Gram, **grim** (156a), **grum** (102c), **Guam**

GN - -   **gnar** (72a), **gnat** (59a,81b,99c), **gnaw** (20a,107a,178b)

- GN -   **agni** (88a,89c), **Agni** (56d,68b)

- - GN   **sign** (121c,146c)

G - - N   **gain** (7a,b,124a,181d), **Gaon** (85b), **garn** (67d,185b), **gean** (29c),
     gein (67d), **glen** (43c), **Goan**, **goon** (157c,163c), **gown**, **gran**, **grin**,
     guan (151b), **Gwyn** (40c,50b)

GO - -   **goad** (80b,154b), **goaf** (104b), **goai** (106d,168c), **goal** (8b,109b,
     120b,125d), **Goan**, **goat** (135a), **gobi**, **Gobi** (42d), **gobo** (84d), **goby**
     (57d), **goel** (15a,75c), **goer**, **goff** (32d), **goga** (24a), **gogo** (16b,24a,
     149c), **Gogo** (191), **gola** (27b,40c,70c,157a), **gold**, **golf** (154a) **goli**
     (105c), **Goll**, **Golo** (191), **Goma** (191), **Gona** (106d), **Gond**, **gone**
     (6b,15c,42c,44c,114d), **gong**, **good**, **goof**, **goon** (157c,163c), **Goop**
     (107d), **goor**, **gora** (81c), **gore** (115d,117c,154c,169c), **gory**, **gosh**,
     Goth (16c,163d), **goul** (102a), **gour** (112c,181c), **gout**, **gowk** (146d),
     gowl (102a,140d,185b), **gown**, **Goya** (151d)

- GO -   **agog** (47b,52c,86c), **agon** (12c,36c,41b,55d),71b), **egol** (11b), **Igor**
     (135d), **Ogor** (170d)

- - GO   **ango** (171a), **Argo** (12c,36b,c), **bago** (13d), **bogo** (117a,
     168c), **Bogo** (191), **bygo** (114c), **Dago**, **ergo** (164b), **gogo** (16b,24a,

341

149c), **Gogo** (191), **Hugo** (63a,96a), **Iago** (54b,111d,143c), **kago** (113a), **lago** (83b,152b), **mogo** (74b), **Pogo** (121c), **sago** (54c, 59b,113b,125b,155c), **sego** (24b,25a,92b,174c), **upgo** (13c), **zogo** (136a)

G - - O **gajo** (107c), **Gajo, Gano** (132d), **gapo** (60a), **Garo** (88c), **gilo** (48a), **giro** (38c,83c,167c), **gobo** (84d), **gogo** (16b,24a,149c), **Gogo** (191), **Golo** (191), **grao** (189), **guao** (168c,169b), **Gulo** (183c), **gyro** (34d)

- GP - **Ogpu** (135d)

G - - P **gamp** (172a), **gasp** (113c), **gaup, gawp, gimp** (169d), **Goop** (107d), **gulp** (46a,79d,160a), **Gump** (43b), **grip** (159a)

GR - - **grab** (105b,142a,149b), **grad** (28b), **Graf** (37c,66b,67a,107c,186b), **gram** (29d,99b,148d,160d,180a), **grao** (189), **gras** (78b), **gray** (33c, 77c), **Gray** (50c), **gres** (156d), **grew, grey** (33c), **grid** (17a,70d, 119b,156d), **grig** (38c,70d,93a), **grim** (156a), **grin, grip** (159a), **gris** (61d), **grit** (137a,b), **grog** (92d,153d), **gros** (47a,53d,146c), **Gros** (63a), **grot** (27d), **grow** (154b), **grub** (43c,88d), **grum** (102c), **Grus** (36b,c,38b)

- GR - **agra** (26d,34d), **Agra** (161b), **agri** (89b), **agro** (149d), **ogre** (67a, 102a)

G - - R **gaur** (112c,181c), **gear** (32c,167b), **Ghor** (174b), **gier** (47b), **gnar** (72a), **goer, goor, gour** (112c,181c) **guar** (46c,59d), **guhr** (47d)

- - GS **eggs** (112a), **togs** (32c)

G - - S **gaus** (67a), **gens** (42d,132d), **Gens, Ghes** (193), **ghos** (30b), **glis** (45c), **Glis, gras** (78b), **gres** (156d), **gris** (61d), **gros** (47a,53d,146c), **Gros** (63a), **Grus** (36b,c,38b), **gyps, Gyps** (71d)

- - GT **togt** (77c), **Vogt**

G - - T **gait** (96b,179a), **galt, gaut** (88b,103d,132a), **geat** (77d,101a), **Geat** (138a), **gelt** (101c), **gent, gest** (7c,41d,52d,133c), **gett** (44d), **ghat** (32d,88b,103d,132a), **gift** (123a), **gilt** (69c,77c,151b), **girt** (50a), **gist** (95c,118c), **glut** (52c,70a,137c,159d), **gnat** (59a,81b,99c), **goat** (135a), **grit** (137a,b), **grot** (27d), **gust**

GU - - **Guam, guan** (151b), **guao** (168c,169b), **guar** (46c,59d), **gufa** (21b, 99a), **guff, gugu, Guha** (191), **guhr** (47d), **guib** (11a), **gula** (90a, 101a,165b), **gulf** (6c), **gull** (32d,41c,42a,72c,99b,141a), **Gulo** (183c), **gulp** (46a,79d,160a), **Gump** (43b), **guna** (106a,137b), **gunj** (70c), **guru** (77b), **gush** (35a,154c), **gust, Guti, guze** (128d)

- GU - **agua** (152d,166c,178c), **ague** (30a,55d,95c), **ogum** (82b)

- - GU **degu** (132c), **fugu** (84b), **gugu, kagu** (106c), **Pegu** (24c,102a,127d)

G - - U **genu** (6b,18a,87a,89c), **gugu, guru** (77b)

GW - - **Gwyn** (40c,50b)

G - - W **glow** (144c), **gnaw** (20a,107a,178b), **grew, grow** (154b)

GY - - **gybe** (144c), **gyle** (23b,174d), **gyne** (34b,55b,183c), **gyps, Gyps** (71d), **gyre** (31b,171b), **gyri** (22d,131b), **gyro** (34d), **gyve** (55d, 143b)

- - GY **algy, Algy** (96b), **bogy** (153a), **cagy** (178b), **dogy** (46d,103c), **edgy** (106c), **eggy** (185d), **fogy, logy** (46d), **Nagy** (78d), **orgy** (26d,130d, 137c), **pogy** (57a,88a,98d,103c), **sagy**

342

G - - Y   gaby (59c,146d), Gaby, gapy, Gary, gazy, goby (57d), gory, gray (33c,77c), Gray (50c), grey (33c)

G - - Z   Geez (6c,51d), Ghuz (171a)

HA - -   Haab (97d), haaf (57d), haak (57b,178a), haar (139c), haba (151d), Habe (191), hack (40a,77c,184d) hade (66a,148c,173c), hadj (98b,118a), haec (90a,164c), haem (122b), haft (76d), hagg, hagi (84b), haha (55c,159c), haik (57b,65b,108a), hail (6d,15a,71d), hair (56b,164d), haje (33a,48d), hake (57a,b), hakh (46d), hako (115b), haku (86d), hala (112b), hale (125b), Hale (9d,131a), half (101a), hall (37b,114d), halm, halo (14d,31b,92a,107b,131d), Hals (47a), halt (13b,28a,38d,156d), hami (78a), hand (60c,114c,115d,184c), hang (160a), hank (147c), Hano (125b), Hans (66d,96a), hant (67a), Hapi (66a,107b,136a), hapu (106d), Harb (191), hard (109b), hare (91b,132c), hark (92d), harl (16b,56b,59a), harm (40b,81a), harp (105a,129a), hart (41d,154d), hase (74d) hash, hasp (31d, 54d,153c), hast, hate (6a,43a), hath, Hati (48d), haul (27b,45d), have, hawk (19c,115c), hayz, haze (100c,174d), hazy (174b)

- HA -   Ahab (18c,26c,85b,86d,100d,116a,180b), Ahaz (86d), Bhar (191), bhat (80c), chaa (162b), chab (184a), Chad (158b), chai (72d), cham (20a,29d), Cham (8c), chan (26c,130c), chap (55b), char (24d,26c, 170b), chat (9b,19c,161c), chaw (97c), chay (48a,128d), dhak (48a, 169a), dhal (12b), dhan (124c), dhao (24c), Dhar, dhaw (125a), ghat (32d,88b,103d,132a), khan (7c,26c,81b,93d,116c,123c,130c, 166c), khar (189), khas (153a), khat (105d), Phad (155b), shad (27d,57a,b,c), shag (73b,105b,161d,166d), shah (116c), sham (41c, 55b,60d,80a,123a,b,146d), Shan (13c,80d,88c,101d), shap, shat (87d), shaw (164b), Shaw (50c,53b), shay (110c), Thai (146a), than (35b), thar (68a,76d), that (42b,124b,129c), thaw, wham (157c), what (129c), whau (107a,168c)

- - HA   agha (35a,171a), Akha (86a,c), Asha (191), Azha (155b), epha (75c), Guha (191), haha (55c,159c), Isha (174a), kaha (123d), maha (28c,88c,136d), moha (42b,83d), ocha (189), paha (67b), poha (74c), saha, taha (179b), tcha (162c), Usha (16a,150c),

H - - A   haba (151d), Haba, haha (55c,159c), hala (112b), Hela (93c), Hera (69c,85d,110b,126b,186b,d), hila (53c), Hima (191), hoga (144b), hoja (166b), hola (74c,152b), hora (22a,40b), Hova (95a), Hoya (14d), Hsia (30b,47c), huia (19a,106d), hula (74b), Hupa (192), hura (20a,137a), Hura, Hyla (10a,166d,169b)

H - - B   Haab (97d), Harb (191), herb (58b,158b), hobb (124b), hubb (118b)

H - - C   haec (90a,164c)

H - - D   hand (60c,114c,115d,184c), hard (109b), head (29d), heed (14c, 75b,109b), held, herd (39a,46c,72a), Hild, hind (15b,41d,45a), hold (95c,124c,130d), hood (38a,74d), hued

HE - -   head (29d), heaf (144a), heal, heap (117d), hear (75b,c,92d), heat, Hebe (39c,69c,186b), heck (100a), heed (14c,75b,109b), heel, Heep (41a,43b), heer (47a,184b,185b), heft (179d), Heft, hegh, Hehe (191), heil (74b), hein (52c,61c), heir, Hela (93c), held, helm (144d,165d), help (14a), hemi (122c), hemo (34a,122b), hemp (26a, 37a,56a,133d), hens (121d), Hera (69c,85d,110b),126b,186b,d), herb (58b,158b), herd (39a,46c,72a), here, herl (16b,59a), hero

343

(42b,124d,137b), **Hero** (90c), **Herr** (66c), **hers** (124c), **hest** (35a), **Heth** (77c), **hevi** (111d), **hewn**

- HE - ahem, Ahet (49a,102a), ahey (52c), bhel (126d), chee (189), chef, chek (59c), Chen (149b), cher (61b), chew (97c), chez (14b,61a), eheu (52c), ghee (24d), Gheg (8c), Ghes (193), Hehe (191), Khem (113c), khet (188), phew (52c), rhea (37a,56a,111d), Rhea (19b,68d, 87c,103c,186b), Rhee (87c), shea (25a,168c,d), shed (27a,90c,101b, 144b), shee (82b), Shem (107c), Shen (68a), sher (65d,165c), shew (44c), Thea (162c), theb (188), thee (124b), them (124b), then, thew (104c), they (124b), whee, when (180d), whet (143c,156b), whew, whey (100a)

- - HE ache (79a,112d,185b), Hehe (191), Hohe (192), tche (13d,30b,105a)

H - - E Habe (191), hade (66a,148c,173c), haje (33a,48d), hake (57a,b), hale (125b), Hale (9d,131a), hare (91b,132c), hase (74d), hate (6a, 43a), have, haze (100c,174d), Hebe (39c,69c,186b), Hehe (191), here, hide (53a), hike, hipe (185a), hire (49d,50b,91b,130a), hive (17c), Hohe (192), hole (6c,11b,110d,118c,147a), home, hone (110a,143c,180d), hope (13d,52d), hose (156c), hove (92a,157d), howe (77d), Howe (17a,82a), huge, hule (23a,134c), Hume (50c), huse (180c), hyde (188), Hyde (45a), hyke, hyle (97c), hype (185a)

H - - F haaf (57d), half (101a), heaf (144a), hoof (173a), huff (58a)

H - - G hagg, hang (160a), hing (13c), hogg (144a), hong (30b), hung

- - HH sahh (188)

H - - H hakh (46d), hash, hath, hegh, Heth (77c), high, hish, hoch, (52c, 66c), Hoch, hoth, Hoth (20c), Hugh (96a), hunh?, hush (17b,146c)

HI - - hick (185d), hide (53a), hien (30b), hier (63a,185d), high, hike, hiku (57a,106d,138a), hila (53c), Hild, hill, hilo (74c), hilt (73c), Hima (191), hind (15b,41d,45a), hing (13c), hino (106d,168c), hint (9a,39c,159a), hipe (185a), hire (49d,50b,91b,130a), hiro, hish, hiss (146a), hist (25c,93d), hive (17c)

- HI - Ahir (27b), Bhil (191), chia (136d), chib (167a), chic (148d), chid, ch'ih (188), chil, chin, Chin (30b), chip (69d), chir (29b,116d), chit (67b,98c,108b,116c,177c), chiv (87a), jhil, ohia (74c,168c), Ohio, Phil (96b), phit (24b), phiz (54a), Rhin, shih (189), Shik (171a), shim (91d,144c,162a,179a), shin (91a,d,140b,143c), ship, shir (36d, 65d,165c), thin (43b,c,148b), this (42b,124b), Whig, whim (26c, 54c,108c), whin (64c,70a,132b,181d), whip (58c,88d), whir (25c, 181a), whit (166c), whiz (25c)

- - HI bahi (60c), Bahi (21b,26a), pahi (21b,26a), tchi, Tchi, tshi, Tshi (69c)

H - - I hagi (84b), hami (78a), Hapi (66a,107b,136a), Hati (48d), heli (74b), hemi (122c), hevi (111d), Holi (77a), hopi (33c), Hopi (12c, 102c,125b), hoti

H - - J hadj (98b,118a)

H - - K haak (57b,178a), hack (40a,77c,184d), haik (57b,65b,108a), hank (147c), hark (92d), hawk (19c,115c), heck (100a), hick (185d), hock (91a,115b,182b,c), hoek (39d), honk (70a), hook (27b,39d), howk (139b), huck (167d), hulk (144d,173d), hunk, husk (53a,78d, 142a)

HL - - Hler (141a)

- - HL buhl (81a), kohl (53c), kuhl (53c)

H - - L hail (6d,15a,71d), hall (37b,114d), harl (16b 56b,59a), haul (27b, 45d), heal, heel, herl (16b,59a), hill, howl (39b), hull (141d,142a, 144c,d), hurl (167c)

H - - M haem (122b), halm, harm (40b,81a), helm (144d,165d), holm (77d, 82d,109a)

- HN - ohne (66d,183b)

- - HN behn (137d), fohn (182b), John (11c,96a,121a,186b)

H - - N hein (52c,61c), hewn, hien (30b), hoen (189), hoon (190), horn (11a, 105a,170b,182a), hymn (150c)

HO - - hoar (63d,71a,181a), hoax (41c,122a), hobb (124b), hobo (168a, 174b), hoch (52c,66c), hock (91a,115b,182b,c), hoek (39d), hoen (189), hoer, hoey (114c), hoga (144b), hogg (144a), Hohe (192), hoja (166b), hoju (84b), hola (74c,152b), hold (95c,124c,130d), hole (6c,11b,110d,118c,147a), Holi (77a), holm (77d,82d,109a), holt (36d,119b,184b), holy, home, homo (122d), homy (38b), hone (110a,143c,180d), hong (30b), honk (70a), hood (38a,74d), hoof (173a), hook (27b,39d), hoon (190), hoop (181b), hoot (112c), hope (13d,52d), hopi (33c), Hopi (12c,102c,125b), hops (17c), hora (22a, 40b), horn (11a,105a,170b,182a), hors (62b), hose (156c), host (13a,51d,104c), Hoth (20c), hoti, hour, Hova (95a), hove (92a, 157d), howe (77d), Howe (17a,82a), howk (139b), howl (39b), Hoya (14d)

- HO - Ahom (88c), ahoy (106a), b'hoy (134b), chob (23c), chol (118d), Chol (192), chop (98a), chor (164b), chou (61b), Chou (30b), chow (45a), choy (48a,128d), dhow (88d,111c,175d), Ghor (174b), ghos (30b), khot, mhor (180b), ohoy (106a), phon (94a), phoo, phos, phot (173b), rhob (64a,85c), Shoa (6c), shod, shoe (166a), shoo (46b,67a,138b), shop, shoq (169a), shor (136d), Shor (162b), shot (9d,43d,90c,174d), shou (41d), show (42b,44c,96b), thob (128a), Thor (7c,68c,99c,100c,109c,165b), Thos (84a,181c), thou (124b), whoa (156d), whom (42b), whoo

- - HO baho (122a), boho (117a,179d), coho (136d), echo (130b,d), Echo (105d), icho (67b), kiho (82a), moho (19a,78a), otho (133a), paho (122a), peho (19b,102c,106d), Saho (6c), soho!, Soho (93c), toho (79a)

H - - O hako (115b), halo (14d,31b,92a,107b,131d), Hano (125b), hemo (34a,122b), hero (42b,124d,137b), Hero (90c), hilo (74c), hino (106d,168c), hiro, hobo (168a,174b), homo (168a,174b), Hugo (63a,96a), huso (180c), hypo (117b)

H - - P harp (105a,129a), hasp (31d,54d,153c), heap (117d), Heep (41a, 43b), help (14a), hemp (26a,37a,56a,133d), hoop (181b), hump (124d)

- HR - Shri (17c,166c)

- - HR Bohr (14b,40d,138c), buhr (180d), Duhr (155b), guhr (47d), lehr (67c,112a), mahr (103a), mohr (65d), rohr (72d), Ruhr, sehr (66d), tahr (68a,76d), tehr (27c,68a)

H - - R haar (139c), hair (56b,164d), hear (75b,c,92d), heer (47a,184b, 185b), heir, Herr (66c), hier (63a,185d), Hier (141a), hoar (63d,

71a,181a), hoer, hour

HS - - Hsia (30b,47c)

H - - S Hals (47a), Hans (66d,96a), hens (121d), hers (124c), hiss (146a), hops (17c), hors (62b), hyps

- - HT acht (66c), baht (146a)

H - - T haft (76d), halt (13b,28a,38d,156d), hant (67a), hart (41d,154d), hast, heat, heft (179d), Heft, hest (35a), hilt (73c), hint (9a,39c, 159a), hist (25c,93d), holt (36d,119b,184b), hoot (112c), host (13a, 51d,104c), hunt (141c), hurt

HU - - hubb (118b), huck (167d), hued, huff (58a), huge, Hugh (96a), Hugo (63a,96a), huia (19a,106d), hula (74b), hule (23a,134c), hulk (144d,173d), hull (141d,142a,144c,d), hulu (55b), Hume (50c), hump (124d), hung, hunh?, hunk, hunt (141c), Hupa (192), hura (20a,137a), Hura, hurl (167c), hurt, huse (180c), hush (17b,146c), husk (53a,78d,142a), huso (180c), huzz

- HU - ahum, bhut (67a), chub (40c,154c), Chud (191), chug (53a), chum, (38d), Chun (30c), chut!, Ghuz (171a), jhum, Phud (110b), phut (24b), Phut (110b), rhum (8c), Rhus (159a), shul (161a), shun (15a, 51b,52a), shut, thud, thug (65a), thus (149c), whun (64c,70a)

- - HU ichu (10b,70d), jehu (46b), Jehu (18c), kahu (14d), Oahu, Rahu (42b,48b), sahu (153d), tchu

H - - U haku (86d), hapu (106d), hiku (57a,106d,138a), hoju (84b), hulu (55b)

- HV - IHVH (159d), JHVH (159d), YHVH (159d)

- HW - JHWH (159d), YHWH (159d)

H - - X hoax (41c,122c)

HY - - hyde (188), Hyde (45a), hyke, Hyla (10a,166d,169b), hyle (97c), hymn (150c), hype (185a), hypo (117b), hyps

- HY - whyo (59d,65a)

- - HY achy, ashy (113a,178a)

H - - Y hazy (174b), hoey (114c), holy, homy (38b)

H - - Z Hayz, huzz

IA - - Iago (54b,111d,143c), Ialu (48d), Iamb (59c)

- IA - bias (43b,123a), diad (113a), dial (25c), dian (46c,130d,170b), Dian (68d,69a,c,102b), Diau (192), fiat (35a,41d,48c,111b,137a), Fiat (83c), kiak (51c), Liam (181d), liar (98d), Lias (66a), miam (14d), mian (97c,147b,166b), Miao (30a,b), mias (111a), Mias, miau (27b,99b), miaw (27b,99b), Nias (82d), Piaf (63c), piat (11a), piay (98b), rial (190), siak (72d), sial (112a), Siam (163d,181a), Tiam, tiao, tiar (39a,75a,121a), vial (148c)

- - IA Abia (18d,137a), akia (74c), amia (22c,170d), apia (121b), aria (8b,98c,150a,c), Asia (48a), chia (136d), Elia (88a,115d), eria (13d, 146d), Fria, Gaia (47d,69a), glia (106c), Hsia (30b,47c), huia (19a, 106d), ilia (21d,77b,115d), inia (9b,109b), Inia (28c,45b), ixia (37a), Maia (76b,109a,153b,155b,177c), Naia (33a), obia (55d), ohia (74c, 168c), okia (190), raia (107d), Raia (147b), Soia, tsia (162c), Uria (14c,16d)

I - - A idea (54c,108c,124a,164d), ijma (103b), ikra (27d), ilia (21d,77b, 115d), Inca (14b,30a), inga (145d), inia (9b,109b), Inia (28c,45b), Inka (193), Iola, Iona (28a,82d), iota (71a,85c,91c,114c,166c,176a, 180d), Iowa (193), Irra (68c,178a), isba (135c), Isha (174a), Itea (145d,160c,181d), Itza (192), ixia (37a)

IB - - Ibad (191), Iban (47c), ibex (67d,68a), ibid (80a,117a,137a), ibis (48d,49a,177b), ibit (117a)

- IB - bibb (97c,146b), bibi (87d), dibs (70c), gibe (8a,42c,84d,100d,138c, 144c,149b), jibb, jibe (8a,33b,35d,37b,42c,100d,138c,144c,149b), kibe, kiby (29a), nibs (116c), ribe (139a), Tibu (191)

- - IB Abib (102a,b), Adib (155b), Agib (12a,42d), chib (167a), crib (96b, 120d), drib (46b), frib (43d), glib (58d,149a,177c), guib (11a), snib (54d,93c), stib (19b,47a,137a)

I - - B iamb (59c)

IC - - ical (158c), icer, icho (67b), ichu (10b,70d), icon (79d,92b,136a)

- IC - aich (9a), bice (20d,117d), Bice (27b), dice (65a), dick (43a,55b), Dick (96b), fico (169d), hick (185d), kick, lick, mica (82c,100b, 146c), mice, mick (82c), mico (97a), nice (54d,119c,130c), Nice (98c), nick (30c,108b), pica (66b,95b,172c), pice (190), Pici (19c, 184a), pick, pico (65a,152c), Pict (23c,47d), rice, Rice (46a), rich, rick (74d,117d,154d), sice (71d,147b), sick, tice (9a,38c,51a,185d), tick (12b,20d,97c), vice (31d,158a), wick

- - IC amic (9d), chic (148d), cric (131c), epic (76b,120a), eric (115b), Eric (71d,96a,107d,138a,164a,176b), idic (79b), laic (32b,90b,107d, 124a,141d), odic (79c,120a), olic (158b), otic (14c,d,47b), saic (86b, 91d,175d), Udic (108a), Uvic (70c)

I - - C idic (79b)

ID - - Idas (27b,71c), idea (54c,108c,124a,164d), idee (61d), idem (89d, 164a), Iden (76a), ideo (34b,d,164d), ides (41a,b,133a), idic (79b), idio (34b,c), Idjo (191), idle (174b,c,178c), idly, idol (48c,54c,55a 75b,79d,112d,130b,184d), Idun (107d), idyl (114d), Idyo (191), Idzo (191)

- ID - Aida (110d,175c), aide (7b,14a,75d), bide (47c,50b,130a,158b, 162a,177b), dido (11b,26c,65a,122a), Dido (27a,172c), eide (119c), fide, Gide (63a) hide (53a), Lida (183c), Lido (83d,175b), mide (110a), Midi (151b), nide (23c,72a,106c,116d), nidi (106c), Ridd (94a), ride (46b,85c), sida (37a,126c,170a), side (13d,22a,b,54a, 58a,89a,161b), sidi (103b,166b), sidy (123b), tide (39d,75d,109c, 141c,159d), tidy (106a,111b), Vida (183c), vide (89d,126a,142a), wide (133d), widu (102d)

- - ID acid (151a,162a), amid (9d,50a), arid (46c,85a), avid (47b,71a, 186b), Beid (155b), caid (35a,151d,152b), chid, Enid (13b,25d,66b, 163a,183c), grid (17a,70d,119b,156d), ibid (80a,117a,137a), imid (29c), irid (38d,67c), kaid (29d,66a), laid, maid (45b,142d), naid (63c), olid (55d,60c,148d,157d), ooid (48d), Ovid (132d,133b), oxid (112c), paid (129c), qaid (35a), quid (39b,166d), raid (59d,80c), said (174c), Said (42d,101a,121b), seid (103b), Seid (42d,101a, 171a), skid (148b), slid, uvid (101a), void (11a,49d,108d), zoid

I - - D Ibad (191), ibid (80a,117a,137a), imid (29c), Irad (18d), irid (38d, 67c)

347

- IE - bien (63a,140c,179a,180a), bier (33b,66b), dieb (84a), diem (89b, 116a), dier, dies (41b,89b), diet (14a,54c,84c,91b,176a), Dieu (61d), fief (55d), gier (47b), hien (30b), hier (63a,185d), kief (75d), kiel (128d,134d), Kiel (25d), kier (20c,174d), Kiev, lied (66d,150b), lief (181d), lien (65c,91a,124c), lieu (118c,155d), mien (11c,17b, 26d,44c,96b), pied (96c,103c,114b,117c,154a,174d), pien (13b), pier (23a,88b,180c), piet (29b,95b), Riel (129a), riem (76c,112c, 157c,164d), rien (62b), rier (180b), sier (57a,118b), tied, tien (147d), tier (118a,134b), vier (66c), view (93d,138b), wiel (140d, 180d), wies (185a)

- - IE Abie (96b,107a), Amie (61d), Brie (29c), Erie (82c,87d), Okie (99d), Opie (50c), plie (32c,59b), soie (62c), unie (173a)

I - - E idee (61d), idle (174b,c,178c), ille (89b,d,163d), imbe (37a,56a, 133d), inde, inee (120b), Inge (24d,67d,117c,119c), inre (35d,80a), lole (52a,76b,123c), lone (24b,88d,94d), ipse (44d,89c), Irae (43c), isle (8b,53c,81d,82d,86b,88a), ixle (56a)

IF - - ifil (117a,168c)

- IF - biff, fife (59a,105a), gift (123a), jiff (101c), kiff (88c), life (19a,177a), lift (49b), miff (44c), nife (37a), piff (24b), rife (6b,c, 39d,123b), riff (131d), Riff (18b,102c), rift (30c,32a,58a,110d), sift (140d,142c,146b), tiff (126b), wife (154a)

- - IF alif (12b), arif (127d), colf (73a), cuif (139a,d,140c), Enif (155b), kaif (88c), keif (75d), Leif (107d), luif, naif (74b,105d), waif (157b)

IG - - iglu (51c,149b), Igor (135d)

- IG - biga (171d), giga (56a,105a), high, migg (96c), nigh (106a), riga (118b), Riga, sigh, sign (121c,146c), tige (118a), wigg

- - IG brig (72b,106a,144d), crig (20d), grig (38c,70d,93a), prig (112a, 116c), snig (45d), swig (46a,72c), Teig (96a), trig (106a,148d,154b, 169d), twig, Whig

I - - G ilog (132a,161b)

IH - - IHVH (159d)

- IH - kiho (82a)

- - IH ch'ih (188), shih (189)

I - - H IHVH (159d), inch, itch, Ivah (18d)

II - - iiwi (19a,74b)

- II - Ilin (188), Riis (9d)

- - II alii (74c,134c), apii (74c), Boii (191), heli (74b), Ubii (191)

I - - I iiwi (19a,74b), immi (189), impi (86a), Inti (159b), Ioni (192)

IJ - - ijma (103b)

- IJ - bija (168c), Ilja (57a,90d,173a)

IK - - ikat (53b,159a), ikmo (18b), ikon (79d,136a), ikra (27d)

- IK - bike, bikh (120b), dika (23a), dike (49c,91d), Dike (78a), fike (139c), hike, hiku (57a,106d,138a), kiki (27b), kiku (30d), like (13c,37d,146d), mike, Mike (96b), Nike (69c,100c,182d), pika (93a,128a,132c), pike (57a,b,76c,120b,153a), piki (95c), piky,

rikk (49a), **sika** (41d,84b), **Sikh** (77b), **tike** (29d), **Tiki** (120c)

- - IK **Atik** (155b), **Efik** (191), **haik** (57b,65b,108a), **kaik** (96c), **naik, raik** (188,189), **Seik** (77b), **Shik** (171a)

I - - K **Irak** (99a,d), **irok** (55b)

IL - - **ilex** (77d), **ilia** (21d,77b,115d), **ille** (89b,d,163d), **ills** (170a), **ilog** (132a,161b), **ilot** (82d), **Ilus** (88d,170b)

- IL - **aile** (62b,63a,182c,d), **bile** (30c), **bilk** (29b,41c,42a), **bill** (17b,147a), **Bill, bilo** (131b), **dill** (13a,117c), **dilo** (120d,168c), **eild** (138d,140a), **file** (13a,127d), **fili, fill** (109b), **film** (164b), **filo, fils** (62d,150b), **gila** (93b), **gild** (14a,49c,69c,98b), **gill** (22d), **gilo** (48a), **gilt** (69c,77c,151b,185d), **hila** (53c), **Hild, hill, hilo** (74c), **hilt** (73c), **Jill** (183d), **jilt, kile** (189), **kill** (38c), **kiln** (15d,112a), **kilo** (99b, 122d), **kilt, Lila** (183c), **lill** (15d,118a), **lilt** (93a,131a,147a), **lily, mila** (188), **mild** (32a,66a), **mile** (64c), **milk, mill** (126c), **milo** (70b, 87c,150d), **Milo, milt** (153d), **nile** (33c,71d), **Nile** (106b), **nill** (173d), **oily** (110b,172c), **pile** (45d,75b,117c), **pili** (34b,108d), **pill, pily, rile** (10c,d,82c,125a,156b,176a), **rill** (23c,102b,132a,148d,157b), **rily** (176a), **silk** (53b,179c), **sill** (45c,76c,165a,182b), **silo** (59a, 156d), **silt** (104b), **tile** (31d,56d,72b,95b,133c,163c), **till** (39c,101c, 173d), **tilt** (26b,d,166a), **vila** (54b), **vile** (16c,56c), **vili** (54b), **Vili** (109c), **vill** (176b), **vily** (54b), **wild** (38b,173d), **wile** (13b,41c,157b, 169c), **wilk** (65c,96d,141b), **will** (18b,43a,163c,177c), **wilt** (46b), **wily** (13b,38b,39c)

- - IL **amil** (45a,48a,185c), **anil** (47c,80d,180b), **aril** (142a), **axil** (10c), **bail** (43c), **Bhil** (191), **boil, ceil** (92c,112a), **chil, coil** (39d,171c, 185a), **Dail** (49a,82b,c), **deil** (139b), **Egil** (107d), **Emil** (96a), **evil** (79c,95d,147a,181a,185c), **fail, foil** (15d,55c,165b), **gail** (23b, 174d), **Gail** (183d), **hail** (6d,15a,71d), **ifil** (117a,168c), **ipil** (117a, 168c,169a), **Ixil** (192), **jail** (123d), **jhil, kail** (8c,22a,25a,79b), **mail** (12d,99b,121c), **moil** (46c,184c), **nail** (31d,54d,141d,161d,173a), **Neil** (96a), **noil** (87c,178b), **pail Phil** (96b), **rail** (16b,19b,c,37a,97b, 138c,150c,177b), **roil** (44c,104b,156b,170d,176a), **sail** (144c,185a), **skil** (57a), **soil** (154d,159a,163c), **tail** (11d,27d,59b,143b), **teil** (92b, c,168c), **toil** (46c,184c), **vail** (94b,124a,174b), **veil** (74d,76c), **wail** (39b,88a), **ypil** (117a,168c)

I - - L **ical** (158c), **idol** (48c,54c,55a,75b,79d,112d,130b,184d), **idyl** (114d), **ifil** (117a,168c), **ipil** (117a,168c,169a), **itol** (158b), **Ixil** (192)

IM - - **imam** (25c,102d,103a), **imbe** (37a,56a,133d), **Imer, imid** (29c), **immi** (189), **impi** (86a)

- IM - **cima** (83b,c), **dime, gime** (77d), **gimp** (169d), **Hima** (191), **lima** (17b,152b,174d), **Lima** (31b), **limb** (12d,22d), **lime** (25b,27d,31b, 33c,102d,168c), **limn** (45d,121c), **limp** (58a,81a,177d), **limu** (141c), **limy** (176d), **mima** (185d), **mime** (24a,71b,85a,100a), **Mime** (131d, 148d), **mimi** (14d), **Mimi** (87b,110d,125b,183d), **nimb** (31b, 73b,92a,107b,131d), **oime** (8b), **pima** (37c), **Pima** (192), **rima** (23a,30c,32a,58a,110d), **rime** (30c,36a,58a,63d,77c), **rimu** (79d,106d,129a,168c), **rimy** (63d), **sima** (132b), **sime** (101d), **Simi** (82d), **simp** (59c,146d), **time** (47a,131a), **Yima** (84a,116b,c), **Zimb** (6c)

349

- - IM Anim (18d), Akim (135d,191), alim (103b,162c), brim, Clim (12b), duim (188), Emim (67a,100d), frim (58d), glim, grim (156a), maim (43d,81a,105c), prim (156b), Seim (120c), shim (91d,144c,162a, 179d), skim (67c), slim (148b,160a), swim (58c), trim (40a,106a, 154b,160a,165c,169d), urim (18d,23a,110a), wﬅim (26c,54c,108c), zaim (170d)

I - - M idem (89d,164a), imam (25c,102d,103a), item (6d,13b,42d,51a, 90d,92d,107a,113d,114c)

IN - - inar (65b), Inca (14b,30a), inch, inde, inee (120b), Inez (45c,183c), inga (145d,170a), Inge (24d,67d,117c,119c), inia (9b,109b), Inia (28c,45b), Inka (193), inky (20b), inly, inre (35d,80a), inro (84b,c, 106c), Inti (159b), into (123a,183b)

- IN - aine (49b,62c), Aine (142c), Aino (84a,c), aint, Ainu (84a,c), bina (77a), bind (33b,165c), bine (145b,156a,171c,176b), bing, binh (189), Bini (191), binn (22c), bino (113b,117a), cine (104b, 152c), cinq (61d), dine, ding (130b), dino (34b), dint (48c,59d, 122a), fine (49b,50a,104b,115d,159a), fink (19a,56c,157c), Finn (107d), gink (48b), hind (15b,41d,45a), hing (13c), hino (106d, 168c), hint (9a,39c,159a), jink, jinn (42b,103b,153c), jinx (78a), kina (126d), kind (150d,153a,174d), kine (38a,112c), king (26c, 29c), kink (38b,171c), kino (27c,34c,47c,72c,98b,161d,168c), lina (188), Lina (183d), line (12b,22b,36d,38a,126c,134b,157b,158b, 162d,175c), ling (24c,57a,b,75b,178c), link (36a,81d,85b), Linn (120d,140a,c,168c,178d), lino, lint (46a,58d), liny (157b), Linz (40d), mina (10b,70b,71d), Mina (23a,183d), mind (75c,81d,93d, 109b), mine (69c,79d,111b,124c), Ming (30b,c), mink (176d), mino (84c), mint (13a,33b,58b,76a), minx (116c), miny, nina (152a), Nina (26c,33d,68d,183d), nine (26c,104d), nino (152a), pina (35d,118b), pine (36a,52a,88c,93c,168c,d,169a), ping, pink (26d,33c,60c,138a), pino (152c), pint (67b), piny, rind (53a, 115c), Rind (109c,174b), rine (44d,75d,135c), ring (50a), rink (147c,154a), sina (46c), Sina (102d,103d), Sind, sine (64c,66b,90a, 97c,126a,163b,169d,183b), sing (26d,178a), sinh (97c), sink (41c, 43c,46b,158a), sino (34a), Tina (183d), tind (86b), tine (11b,124b, 167b), ting (166a), Ting (30c), Tino (136d), tint (33c,d,114d), tiny (100c,148c), vina (77a,105a), vine (32b), vino (92d,182b), vint (26c,182c), viny, wind (33b,39d,171c,185a), wine, wing (10d,58c, 59a,118b,d), wink (107a), winy (176c), Xina (183d), zinc (21a), zing

- - IN akin (8b,92b,129c), alin (188), amin (9d), Asin (102a), ayin (91c), bain (61a), brin (32c,54c,146c), cain (169c), Cain (6a,7a,50d,88a, 104c,143c), chin, Chin (30b), coin (19b,37a,100c,101c,179d), crin (146c), dain (188), dein (66d), Drin, enin (20d), Eoin (85b), Erin (82b), fain (42d,67c,183b), gain (7a,b,124a), gein (67d), grin, hein (52c,61c), Jain (77b), join (36a,173c), Kain, Iain, Iiin (188), loin (98a), main (29d,35d,123d), mein (30b), nein (66c), Odin (7c, 29d,63c,68c,175d,183b), pain (7c), rain (121d,162d), rein (130c), Rhin, ruin (42d), sain (20c,38d,48a), sein (146c), shin (91a,d,140b, 143c), skin (53a,76c,115c,d), spin (131a,180d), tain (166a), thin (43b,c,148b), trin (169d), Tsin (30b), twin (45c,171d), vain (81a), vein (20d,157b), wain (177b), Wain, whin (64c,70a,132b,181d),

350

zain (41a), zein

I - - N   Iban (47c), icon (79d,92b,136a), Iden (76a), Idun (107d), ikon (79d,136a), Iran (6a,48c,116b), Iren (127c), iron (55c,d,69d,81a, 97b,143b,149a,173d,179c), Iten (192), Ivan (40c,85b,96a)

IO - -   Iola, Iole (52a,76b,123c), Iona (28a,82d), Ione (24b,88d,94d), Ioni (192), iota (71a,85c,91c,114c,166c,176a,180d), Iowa (193)

- IO -   biod (79c,59d), bion (117b), bios (92a), cion (42d,70b,145b,148b, 154b,156a), Dion (96a,152a), Fiot (191), lion (55b,86c), niog (33a,168c), niou (188), pion (43c,52b), piot (95b), riot (44c, 111d,170c,173d), siol (82c), sion (125c,158c), Sion (75b,c,83a,157d), tion (158b), Tiou (192), viol (105a), Zion (75b,c,83a,157d)

- - IO   agio (52c,60a,101c,123a), apio (125b), Clio (104d), idio (34b,c), meio (188), moio (188), naio (107a,168c), noio (107c,163c), odio (83b), Ohio, olio (44b,77c,98c,100d,121d), Scio, skio (57d), trio (104d,165a,169c), Unio (105c)

I - ʊ O   Iago (54b,111d,143c), icho (67b), ideo (34b,d,164d), idio (34b,c), Idjo (191), Idyo (191), Idzo (191) ikmo (18b) inro (84b,c,106c), into (123a), ipso (89c), itmo (18b)

IP - -   ipil (117a,168c,169a), ipse (44d,89c), ipso (89c)

- IP -   aipi (27a), cipo (91d), dipt, hipe (185a), kipp, lipa (54d), nipa (14b, 46b,48a,164a,168c), pipa (159d) pipe (105a,180d,182a), pipi (106d, 119d), pipy (145d), ripa (16b,131d), ripe (58a,97c,98c), Sipe (101a, 110c,140b), tipe (168b), tipi (181b), wipe, Xipe (15c), Zipa (29d), zipp, Zips (40c)

- - IP   atip (14b,166a), chip (69d), clip (54d,143d), drip, flip (167c), grip (159a), knip (115c), quip (183a,b), raip (36d), seip (110c), ship, skip (110b,114c,147c), slip (67c,119a), snip (32b,40a), trip (85c), whip (58c,88d)

I - - Q   Iraq (99a,d)

IR - -   Irad (18d), Irae (43c), Irak (99a,d), Iran (6a,48c,116b), Iraq (99a,d), Iras (11b,32a), Iren (127c), irid (38d,67c), iris (53c,58a,111c), Iris (127c), Irma (96d), irok (55b), iron (55c,d,69d,81a,97b,143b,149a, 173d,179c), Irra (68c,178a), irus (109d)

- IR -   Aira (70d), aire (82c), Aire, airs (123b), airy (176d,177a), bird, birl (93c,131a,153c), birn (31d,139a), birr (180d), cirl (24c), circ (31a), dire (45d,55a,104a,163c), dirk (40b), dirt, Eire (82b), fire (13a,43d,44b), firm (154c,173d), firn (67c,70c,106c,149b), gird (32c,50a,123a,160a), girl, giro (38c,83c,167c), girt (50a), hire (49d,50b,91b,130a), hiro, kiri (86a,87c,115a,168c), kirk (31a,139b), lira (28b,79a,170d), lire (62c), Mira (155b,174d), mire (21c,104b), mirk (41a,67d), miro (19a,106d,184a), Miro (113a, 151d), miry, pirn (21b,129a,179b), Piro (192), pirr (181a), rire (62a), sire (17d,55a,59d,124a,163b,166b), siri (18b), tire (15a,22a, 52d,55a,179b,180d), tiro (9b,17d,108c), Vira (191), vire (11a,13b), wire, wiry (147a,167c), zira (188)

- - IR   Abir (129a), Ahir (27b), amir (7c,12a,103a,b,123c,170d), chir (29b,116d), coir (33a,37a,56a,133d), cuir (45c,62a), emir (12a, 103a,b,123c,134d,135a,171a), fair (17a,55d), hair (56b,164d), heir, kair, keir (20c,174d), koir (33a), lair (37c,42b), Leir, loir (45c),

Loir, Muir (8b,142c), **Nair** (45d), **noir** (61b,134b), **pair** (22d,37d, 85b,171d), **sair** (140b,150d), **Seir** (51b,94a,103d), **shir** (36d,65d, 165c), **skir, soir** (61c), **spir** (97c), **stir** (8a,13a,35b,78d,100d), **tair** (68a,76d), **vair** (64c,154c), **weir** (40b,57d), **whir** (25c,181a), **Ymir** (67a,131c)

I - - R **icer, Igor** (135d), **Imer, inar** (65b), **Isar** (41a,104c,132a), **Iser** (49a), **iter** (22d,76c,85c,89c,114d,132a,b,133a,b), **Iyar** (102b), **izar** (65b,103b), **Izar** (155b)

IS - - **Isar** (41a,104c,132a), **isba** (135c), **Iser** (49a), **Isha** (174a), **Isis** (68d, 78c,111d), **isle** (8b,53c,81d,82d,86b,88a), **ismy** (45a)

- IS - **bisa** (11a), **bise** (182a), **bish** (120b), **bisk** (120b,151a), **cise** (147b), **cist** (22c,29d,156c), **Disa** (111a), **disc** (31b), **dish, disk** (31b), **diss** (98b), **fisc** (52c,134c), **fish, fisk** (24d,52c,134c), **fist** (80c), **gish** (102c), **gist** (95c,118c), **hish, hiss** (146a), **hist** (25c,93d), **kish** (16d,70c), **Kish** (137c), **kiss** (148c), **kist** (29d,58a,139b), **Lisa** (183d), **lisp** (153b), **liss** (54b,58b,60c,129d,140a), **list** (26d,27b, 75b,83d,134a,138b,165d), **mise** (8a,10a,70c), **miss, mist** (46b,59b, 59b,174d), **Nish** (19d), **nisi** (90a,173c), **Oise, Pisa** (90c), **pise** (127d), **pish** (36c,107d), **pisk** (9c,19b), **piso** (189), **pist** (25c), **rise** (49d,80b,155a), **Rise** (110d,150c), **risk** (74d), **risp** (99a), **Riss** (66a), **sise** (62c,147b), **sish** (79b), **sisi** (121b), **sist** (139b), **visa** (114d), **vise** (31d,77d,114d), **viss** (189), **wise** (136b), **wish** (42d), **wisp** (148c), **wist** (87c)

- - IS **acis** (64b), **Agis** (86d), **anis** (55c), **Apis** (17c,24b,49a,125a,136a), **aris** (101b), **atis** (76d,102a), **avis** (89a), **Avis** (183c), **axis** (28b, 41d,77c,153c), **bois** (62b,63a,183d), **Bois, cris** (40b,95d), **dais** (119b), **egis** (14b,d,115a,124d,144b,154a,161a), **Elis** (22c,37d, 71b,107c), **Eris** (12c,68d,109c), **feis** (82b), **glis** (45c), **gris** (61d), **ibis** (48d,49a,177b), **iris** (53c,58a,111c), **Iris** (127c), **kris** (40b,95d), **Isis** (68d,78c,111d), **itis** (158c), **Lais** (17c), **Lois** (165d,183c), **mais** (61b), **nais** (63c,132a), **Otis** (9c,d,24d,82a,111a), **Ovis** (143d), **pais** (37d), **rais** (26c,29d,75a,103b), **Rais** (106b), **reis** (26c,29d,75a, 103b), **Riis** (9d), **sais** (48d,71d), **seis** (147b,152c), **this** (42b,124b), **tris** (122d), **unis** (91b), **Upis** (13b)

I - - S **ibis** (48d,49a,177b), **Ibis, Idas** (27b,71c), **ides** (41a,b,133a), **ills** (170a), **Ilus** (88d,170b), **Iras** (11b,32a), **iris** (53c,58a,111c), **Iris** (127c), **Irus** (109d), **Isis** (68d,78c,111d), **Itys** (163b), **Ives** (9c,90b)

IT - - **itch, Itea** (145d,160c,181d), **item** (6d,13b,42d,51a,90d,92d,107a, 113d,114c), **Iten** (192), **iter** (22d,76c,85c,89c,114d,132a,b,133a,b), **itis** (158c), **itmo** (18b), **itol** (158b), **Itys** (163b), **Itza** (192)

- IT - **bite** (29d,156b), **biti** (20b), **bito** (7d,57d,168c), **bitt** (54d,175c), **cite** (15a,98d,126d,159b), **cito** (89d,126c), **cits, city, dita** (117a), **dite** (150b), **Gita, gite** (62a,118d), **jiti, kite** (19c,49a,74c,d), **kith** (63c), **lite** (158c,d), **lith** (34d,156c), **liti** (60d) **litz** (127b), **mite** (12b,81b,82a,114a,c,148c,d,181b), **mitt** (56c), **mitu** (39d), **mity, nito** (55c), **pita** (9c,28b,56a,83a), **pith** (37a,51c,67b,95c,97a, 119b,126d), **pitt** (50d), **Pitt** (155d), **pito** (9c,28b,83a), **pity** (35b), **rita, Rita** (37b,78d,183c), **rite** (93a,131d), **Sita** (127d), **site** (93b), **sito** (34b), **titi** (20d,102a,145d,168d,181b), **Tito** (186c), **vita** (89c, 92a), **vite** (62b), **viti** (176b), **with** (10b)

--IT adit (51a,100a,114d), alit (44b,143a), amit (94a), bait (15d,51a, 94d,167b), brit (76c), chit (67b,98c,108b,116c,177c), doit (47a, 169d,180d), duit (190), **Duit** (192), edit (20d,49d,123a,129a,131a), emit (43d,49a,53c,58d,83a,142c), exit (114d), fait (6d,61b), flit (41a), frit (64c,67c), gait (96b,179a), grit (137a,b), ibit (117a), knit (173c,179b), lait (62a), nuit (62b), obit (41b,64c), omit (49c, 52c,106b,114c,147d), phit (24b), quit (90d,130c), seit (189), skit (145c), slit (40a), spit (120a,132b,c), suit (38a,58a,91a,112a,119c, 137c), tait (14d), trit (34d,164c), twit (162b,c), unit (101c,110c, 147a), wait (26d,42b,92c,155d,162a), whit (166c), writ (91a), **Yuit** (51c)

I--T ibit (117a), ikat (53b,159a), ilot (82d)

-IU- biur (35a), **Niue** (137d), **Pius** (121a)

I--U lalu (48d), ichu (10b,70d), iglu (51c,149b)

IV-- Ivah (18d), **Ivan** (40c,85b,96a), **Ives** (9c,90b)

-IV- **Civa** (56d), cive (110c), diva (110d,123c), dive (42b,74b,119d), divi, five, give (79d,123a), hive (17c), jiva (77a), jive (160c), kiva (28c,125b), kive (174d), kivu (170c), live (47c), **Livy** (132d,133a), rive (32a,153d), siva (67a,120d), **Siva** (56d,77a), sive (146a), viva (93d), vive (93d), vivo (93a), wive (97a)

--IV chiv (87a), skiv (151b)

-IW- **Biwa** (93d,168c), iiwi (19a,74b), kiwi (11d,19a,58c)

IX-- ixia (37a), **Ixil** (192), ixle (56a)

-IX- **Bixa** (145d), dixi, **Mixe** (192), mixy, pixy (154b)

--IX **Alix** (183c), **Coix** (70d,85b), flix, noix (67c)

IY-- iyar (102b)

-IY- kiyi (185d)

I--Y idly, inky (20b), inly, ismy (45a)

IZ-- izar (65b,103b), **Izar** (155b)

-IZ- bize (182a), bizz, sixe, sizy (176d), sizz, tiza (172a), zizz (181a)

--IZ friz (39d), phix (54a), swiz (160c), whiz (25c)

I--Z Inez (45c,183c)

JA-- jaca (84a), jack (26c,58a,127c), **Jack** (96b), jacu (19a,151b), jade (33c,65d,71d,166a), jadu (95a), jady, **Jael** (147b), **Jaga** (191), jagg, jail (123d), **Jain** (77b), jake (40d), **Jake** (96b), jako (71a), jama (103b), jamb (12d,45c,118a,146b,174a), jami (103b), jane (190), **Jane** (183c), jann (102d), jaob, jape (85a,b), jarl (40d,107d), jass (160d), jati (27b), jato (173b), jaun (113a), **Java** (33a), **Jave** (84d), jawy, jazz

-JA- ajar (110c), **Ajax** (71b,162d)

--JA **Beja** (6c,191), bija (168c), caja (152a), coja (103b,166b), hoja (166b), lija (57a,90d,173a), maja (151c), **Maja** (153b), **Naja** (33a), puja (77a), raja (77a,123c), reja (152b), sɔja (151b)

J--A jaca (84a), **Jaca**, **Jaga** (191), jama (103b), **Java** (33a), **Jena** (105d, 165b), jiva (77a), jota (151c), **Jova** (193), juba (106b), juca (27a), **Juda**, juga (27a), jula, jura, **Juza** (155b)

J--B jamb (12d,45c,118a,146b,174a), jaob, jibb, **Joab** (41a)

353

- - JD **Nejd**

J - - D Joad (50c)

JE - - jean (37c), Jean (183c), jeel, jeep, jeer (138c,162b), jefe (152a), jeff (133d), Jeff, jehu (46b), Jehu (18c), Jena (105d,165b), jerk (153a), jess (157a), jest (169c), Jesu, jete (16a), Jeth (102a), jeux (61d)

- JE - ajee (15c,139a)

- - JE haje (33a,48d), yaje (23a)

J - - E jade (33c,65d,71d,166a), jake (40d), Jake (96b), jane (190), Jane (183c), jape (85a,b), Jave (84d), jefe (152a), jete (16a), jibe (8a, 33b,35d,37b,42c,100d,138c,144c,149b), jive (160c), joke (183a), jole (29b), Jose (96a), Jove (85d), jube (28d), Jude (11c,96a), juke (114c), Jule (183d), June (183c), jupe (62b,84a), jure (90b), jute (37a,48a,56a,133d,136a), Jute

J - - F jeff (133d), Jeff, jiff (101c)

J - - G jagg, joug (138d), Jung (125a)

JH - - Jhil, jhum, JHVH (159d), JHWH (159d)

J - - H Jeth (102a), josh (85b), JHVH (159d), JHWH (159d)

JI - - jibb, jibe (8a,33b,35d,37b,42c,100d,138c,144c,149b), jiff (101c), Jill (183d), jilt, jink, jinn (42b,103b,153c), jinx (78a), jiti, jiva (77a), jive (160c)

- - JI caji (180b), Caji, fuji (84b), Fuji (84d), koji (185b), suji (180c)

J - - I jami (103b), jati (27b), Jati, jiti, jogi (76d), joli (62b), joti

J - - K jack (26c,58a,127c), Jack (96b), jerk (153a), jink, jock, Jock (96b), jonk, juck (114c), junk (30a,134c)

J - - L Jael (147b), jail (123d), jarl (40d,107d), jeel, jhil, Jill (183d), Joel (96a), jowl (29b)

- JM - ijma (103b)

- - JM Sejm (120c)

J - - M jhum, joom (39c)

J - - N Jain (77b), jann, Jann (102d), jaun (113a), jean (37c), Jean (183c), jinn (42b,103b,153c), Joan (183c), John (11c,96a,121a,186b), join (36a,173c), juan (113a), Juan (96a)

JO - - Joab (41a), Joad (50c), Joan (183c), joar (100a), jobo (77c), jock, Jock (96b), jocu (45b,57a), Jodo (113d), Joel (96a), joey (86a, 185d), Joey (96b,109c), jogi (76d), John (11c,96a,121a,186b), join (36a,173c), joke (183a), joky, jole (29b), joli (62b), jolt (143b), jonk, joom (39c), Jose (96a), josh (85b), joss (30b), Josy (183d), jota (151c), joti, joug (138d), Jova (193), Jove (85d), jowl 29b), Jozy

- JO - ajog, ejoo (55b,168c), Gjoa (144d)

- - JO bojo (117a), gajo (107c), Idjo (191), majo, mojo (177c), pajo (122a, rojo (129a,152c), tajo (152a,d)

J - - O jako (71a), Jako, jato (173b), jobo (77c), Jodo (113d), judo (84b, 85c,142b), Juno (69c,85d,100c,126b)

J - - P jeep, jump

J - - R   **jeer** (162b), **joar** (100a), **juar** (100a)

J - - S   **jass** (160d), **jess** (157a), **joss** (30b)

J - - T   **jest** (169c), **jilt, jolt** (143b), **just** (51b,54b)

JU - -   **juan** (113a), **Juan** (96a), **juar** (100a), **juba** (106b), **jube** (28d), **juca** (27a), **juck** (114c), **Juda, Jude** (11c,96a), **judo** (84b,85c,142b), **Judy** (125c,183d), **juez** (152b), **juga** (27a), **juju** (29b,55d), **juke** (114c), **jula, Jule** (183d), **jump, June** (183c), **Jung** (125a), **junk** (30a,134c), **Juno** (69c,85d,100c,126b), **jupe** (62b,84a), **jura, Jura, jure** (90b), **jury** (38a), **just** (51b,54b), **jute** (37a,48a,56a,133d, 136a), **Jute, Juza** (155b)

- - JU   **baju** (84a), **hoju** (84b), **juju** (29b,55d), **teju** (151b)

J - - U   **jacu** (19a,151b), **jadu** (95), **jehu** (46b), **Jehu** (18c), **Jesu, jocu** (45b,57a), **juju** (29b,55d)

J - - X   **jeux** (61d), **jinx** (78a), **jynx** (78a), **Jynx** (184a)

JY - -   **jynx** (78a), **Jynx** (184a)

J - - Y   **jady, jawy, joey** (86a,185d), **Joey** (96b,109c), **joky, Josy** (183d), **Jozy, Judy** (125c,183d), **July, jury** (38a)

J - - Z   **jazz, juez** (152b)

KA - -   **kaan** (93d,116c), **kaat** (105d), **kada** (188), **kade** (144a), **kadi** (103a, 171a), **Kadu** (191), **Kafa** (6c), **kago** (113a), **kagu** (106c), **kaha** (123d), **kahu** (14d), **kaid** (29d,66a), **kaif** (88c) **kaik** (96c), **kail** (18c, 22a,25a,79b), **Kain, kair, kaka** (114b), **kaki** (84c,106d), **kala** (19a), **kale** (22a,25a,119b,175a), **kali** (26d,67c,136d,167a), **Kali** (147b), **kalo** (162a), **Kama** (56d), **kame** (67b,139b), **Kami** (68a,84b,88c, 107c,144c), **kana** (84d), **Kane** (74c), **k'ang** (30a), **Kano** (84c,177d), **kant** (28d), **Kant** (67a), **kapa** (74b), **kaph** (91d), **Kapp, Kara** (132a), **Kari** (14d), **Karl** (96a), **karn** (156c), **karo** (106d), **kasa** (48a), **kasi** 116b), **kasm** (189), **Kate** (143c,183d), **kath** (14a), **Katy** (183d), **kaun** (93d), **kava** (18c,116a), **Kavi** (84d), **kawa** (18c,116a), **Kawi** (84d), **kawn** (93d), **kayo** (87c), **kazi** (103a), **kazy** (103a)

- KA -   **Akal** (56d), **Akan** (191), **ikat** (53b,159a), **okay** (8d), **skag** (7d, 46d), **skat** (181b), **Skat** (155b)

- - KA   **Akka** (125d), **Atka** (11a), **baka** (52b), **beka** (189), **dika** (23a), **Ekka** (26d), **Inka** (193), **kaka** (114b), **loka** (173c,184c), **pika** (93a, 128a,132c), **puka** (107a,168c), **roka** (95a,168c,d), **Saka** (10a), **sika** (41d,84b), **soka** (20c), **waka** (26a), **weka** (58c,106d,107a,127b), **Yaka** (191)

K - - A   **kada** (188), **Kafa** (6c), **kaha** (123d), **kaka** (114b), **kala** (19a), **Kama** (56d), **kana** (84d), **kapa** (74b), **kara** (132a), **kasa** (48a), **kava** (18c 116a), **kawa** (18c,116a), **kela** (189), **keta** (45a), **kina** (126d), **kiva** (28c,125b), **koba** (11a), **kola** (25b,84a,108d), **Kola** (135b,c,d), **kona** (74c), **kora** (19a,178c), **kota** (117a), **Kota** (45d), **kuba** (26d,189), **kufa** (21b,99a), **kula** (189), **kusa**

K - - B   **kerb** (146b), **knab** (107a), **knob** (73c,107c,124d), **knub** (178b)

K - - D   **kaid** (29d,66a), **keld** (154b), **kind** (150d,153a,174d), **Kurd** (48b, 82a)

KE - -   **keal** (25a), **keef** (75d), **keek** (154c), **keel** (128d,134d,144c,d), **keen** (15a,88a,177b), **keep** (123a,130d), **keet** (72b), **keif** (75d), **keir**

355

(20c,174d), **kela** (189), **keld** (154b), **kelp** (82a,141c), **Kelt** (180b), **kemp** (139b), **keno**, **Kent** (90d), **kepi** (99d), **kept**, **kerb** (146b), **kere** (75c,128b), **kerf** (40a,108b), **keri** (75c,128b), **kern** (59c,172a), **Kern** (132b), **Kerr, keta** (45a), **Ketu** (48b)

- KE - akee (168c), akey (189), okeh (8d,37b), oket (189), skee (149c), skeg (7d,86a,144d,157d,184a), sken (164a), skeo (57d), skep (16d,17c,77c), skew (148a,160c,171b,c), skey (185d)

- - KE bake (139a), bike, cake, coke (32d,64a), cuke (39b), cyke (40c), dike (49c,91d), Dike (78a), duke (107c), dyke (49c,91d), fake (123a,143c), feke, fike (139c), fyke (15d), hake (57a,b), hike, hyke!, jake (40d), Jake (96b), joke (183a), juke (114c), lake (117d), like (13c,37d,146d), Loke (15d,68b), luke, Luke (52a, 96a), make (35b,36d,54a,123a), mike, Mike (96b), moke (45c, 157d), Nike (69c,100c,182d), Peke (45a,148d), pike (57a,b,76c, 120b,153a), poke (108c), rake (41b,44c,134b,140d), roke (174d, 175b), sake (84b,125d), soke (44c,85d), syke (194), take, tike (29d), tuke (26b,53b), tyke (29d), wake (134b,168a), woke, yoke (85b,92d,173c), Zeke (96b)

K - - E kade (144a), kale (22a,25a,119b,175a), kame (67b,139b), Kane (74c), Kate (143c,183d), kere (75c,128b), kibe kile (189), kine (38a,112c), kite (19c,49a,74c,d), kive (174d), Klee (113a), knee (85b), koae (74b), Kobe (78a), Kome (71d), kore (107b) Kore (29a, 42b,116b,124d), kuge (84c), Kure (84c), kyle (57a,139c)

- - KF wakf (103a), wukf (103a)

K - - F kaif (88c), keef (75d), keif (75d), kerf (40a,108b), kief (75d), kiff (88c), koff (47a)

K - - G k'ang (30a), king (26c,29c), knag (115d,139c), krag (131c), kung (125b)

KH - - khan (7c,26c,81b,93d,116c,123c,130c,166c), khar (189), khas (153a), khat (105d), Khem (113c), khet (188), khot

- KH - Akha (86a,c)

- - KH ankh (38d,162b), bikh (120b), bukh (122a), hakh (46d), lakh (110c), rukh (53b,54a), Sikh (77b)

K - - H kaph (91d), kath (14a), kish (16d,70c), Kish (137c), kith (63c), Koch (66d), koph (91d), Kush, kyah (19a)

KI - - kiak (51c), kibe, kiby (29a), kick, kief (75d), kiel (128d,134d), Kiel (25d), kier (20c,174d), Kiev, kiff (88c), kiho (82a), kiki (27b), kiku (30d), kile (189), kill (38c), kiln (15d,112a), kilo (99b,122d), kilt, kina (126d), kind (150d,153a,174d), kine (38a,112c), king (26c,29c), kink (38b,171c), kino (27c,34c,47c,72c,98b,161d,168c), kipp, kiri (86a,87c,115a,168c), kirk (31a,139b), kish (16d,70c), Kish (137c), kiss (148c), kist (29d,58a,139b), kite (19c,49a,74c,d), kith (63c), kiva (28c,125b), kive (174d), kivu (170c), kiwi (11d, 19a,58c), kiyi (185d)

- KI - akia (74c), Akim (135d,191), akin (8b,92b,129c), okia (190), Okie (99d), skid (148b), skil (57a), skim (67c), skin (53a,76c,115c, d), skio (57d), skip (110b,114c,147c), skir, skit (145c), skiv (151b)

- - KI Enki (15b), kaki (84c,106d), kiki (27b), Kuki (191), Loki (7c,15d, 68b), maki (91b), moki (127b), piki (95c), Reki (16a), saki (39c,

356

84b,102a), **Tiki** (120c), **weki** (55c), **yaki** (193)

K - - I kadi (103a,171a), kaki (84c,106d), kali (26d,67c,136d,167a), **Kali** (147b), **Kami** (68a,84b,88c,107c,144c), **Kari** (14d), kasi (116b), **Kavi** (84d), **Kawi** (84d), **kazi** (103a), **kepi** (99d), **keri** (75c,128b), **kiki** (27b), **kiri** (86a,87c,115a,168c), **kiwi** (11d,19a,58c), **kiyi** (185d), **kobi** (84b), **koji** (185b), **Koli** (27b), **Komi** (191), **kopi** (107a, 168c), **Kopi** (172a), **kori** (7d,77a), **kuei** (44a), **Kuki** (191), **Kuli** (27b), **Kuri** (191), **kwei** (44a)

- KK - Akka (125d), Ekka (26d)

- - KK bukk (122a), rikk (49a)

K - - K kaik (96c), kiak (51c), keek (154c), kick, kink (38b,171c), kirk (31a,139b), konk (41c), kunk (188), kurk (31a,139b), kyak (51c)

KL - - klam (189), Klee (113a), klom (189), klop (150d)

K - - L kail (18c,22a,25a,79b), Karl (96a), keal (25a), keel (128d,134d, 144c,d), kiel (128d,134d), Kiel (25d), kill (38c), koel (19a,b,39b), kohl (53c), kral, kuhl (53c)

- KM - ikmo (18b)

K - - M kasm (189), Khem (113c), klam (189), klom (189)

KN - - Knab (107a), knag (115d,139c), knap (76d,107a,139b,159b,166a, 170c,185b), knar (87c,134b), knee (85b), knew, knez (123c), knip (115c), knit (173c,179b), knob (73c,107c,124d), knop (124b,170c, 185b), knor (87c), knot (43c,99d,107c,124d,137b), knub (178b), knur (67d,87c,107c), knut, Knut (40d,50c,96a)

K - - N kaan (93d,116c), Kain, karn (156c), kaun (93d), kawn (93d), keen (15a,88a,177b), kern (172a), Kern (132b), khan (7c,26c,81b,93d, 116c,123c,130c,166c), kiln (15d,112a), kran (190), kuan (30b), Kuan (30c), kwan (30b)

KO - - koae (74b), koba (11a), Kobe (78a), kobi (84b), kobu (84b), Koch (66d), koel (19a,b,39b), koff (47a), kohl (53c), koir (33a), koji (185b), koko (106d,114b), Koko (93d,186c), koku (189), kola (25b,84a,108d,168c), Kola (135b,c,d), Koli (27b), kolo (59b,135c), Kome (71d), Komi (191), kona (74c), konk (41c), koop (16c), koph (91d), kopi (107a,168c), Kopi (172a), kora (19a,178c), Kora, kore (107b), Kore (29a,42b,116b,124d), kori (7d,77a), koso (6c,80d), Koso (192,193), koss (188), kota (117a), Kota (45d), koto (84b), kozo (113d,168c)

- KO - akov (189), Ekoi (191), ikon (79d,136a)

- - KO boko (52b), Doko (191), hako (115b), jako (71a), koko (106d,114b), Koko (93d,186c), mako (18a,19a,20d,143c,168c,182c), moko (96c), toko (30c)

K - - O kago (113a), kalo (162a), Kano (84c,177d), karo (106d), kayo (87c), keno, kiho (82a), kilo (99b,122d), kino (27c,34c,47c,72c, 98b,161d,168c), koko (106d,114b), Koko (93d,186c), kolo (59b, 135c), koso (6c,80d), Koso (192,193), koto (84b), kozo (113d,168c), Kroo (191)

K - - P Kapp, keep (123a,130d), kelp '82a,141c), kemp (139b), kipp, klop (150d), knap (76d,107a,139b,159b,166a,170c,185b), knip (115c), knop (124b,170c,185b), koop (16c)

357

KR - - krag (131c), kral, kran (190), kras (76d), kris (40b,95d), Kroo (191)

- KR - akra (176a), Akra (191), ikra (27d), okra (72c,175a), okro (72c, 175a)

- - KR Askr (107d)

K - - R kair, keir (20c,174d), Kerr, khar (189), kier (20c,174d), knar (87c,134b), knor (87c), knur (67d,87c,107c), koir (33a), Kuar (102a), kyar (33a)

- - KS oaks (154d)

K - - S khas (153a), kiss (148c), koss (188), kras (76d), kris (40b,95d), kvas (135c)

- - KT takt (105a,163a)

K - - T kaat (105d), kant (28d), Kant (67a), keet (72b), Kelt (180b), Kent (90d), kept, khat (105d), khet (188), khot, kilt, kist (29d,58a, 139b), knit (173c,179b), knot (43c,99d,107c,124d,137b), knut, Knut (40d,50c,96a), kyat (189)

KU - - Kuan (30c), kuan (30b), Kuar (102a), kuba (26d,189), kudu (11a), kuei (44a), kufa (21b,99a), kuge (84c), kuhl (53c), Kuki (191), kuku (19a,106d), kula (189), Kuli (27b), kung (125b), kunk (188), Kurd (48b,82a), Kure (84c), Kuri (191), kurk (31a,139b), kusa, Kush

- KU - akua (120d), skua (19b,72c,84a,141a)

- - KU baku (26d,157b,168c), duku (95d,168c), ḥaku (86d), hiku (57a, 106d,138a), kiku (30d), koku (189), kuku (19a,106d), Maku (192), poku (11a), puku (11a), Suku (191), Taku (80c)

K - - U Kadu (191), kagu (106c), kahu (14d), Ketu (48b), kiku (30d), kivu (170c), kobu (84b), koku (189), kudu (11a), kuku (19a,106d)

KV - - kvas (135c)

- KV - NKVD (135d)

K - - V Kiev

KW - - kwan (30b), kwei (44a)

K - - W knew, know

KY - - kyah (19a), kyak (51c), kyar (33a), kyat (189), kyle (57a,139c)

- KY - Skye (163c), skyr (21d,151a), skyt (138c,140b)

- - KY alky, caky, coky, faky, inky (20b), joky, laky, oaky, piky, poky (148c), taky, waky

K - - Y Katy (183d), kazy (103a), kiby (29a)

K - - Z knez (123c)

LA - - laap (51d,91b,141d), lace (58b,179c), lack (178a), lact (34c), lacy, Ladd (143c), lade (24c,26d,43c,93b,100a,132a,139d,161b,178d), lady, laet (60d), lago (83b,152b), laic (32b,90b,107d,124a,141d), laid, lain, lair (37c,42b), Lais (17c), lait (62a), lake (117d), lakh (110c), laky, lala (129b), lalo (16b,34d,153a), Lalo (35c), lama (23d,24a,91d,165b), lamb, Lamb (49c), lame (38d,43d,73b), lamp (92a,94c), lana (58a,66a,90a,184b), land (44a,163c), lane (134b, 157b), lank (148b,164b), lant, lanx (133a,b), Laos (80d;129c), Lapp (108a), Lara (25c), lard (54d,61a,71a,110a), lari (78a,101c),

Lari (72c), **lark** (19a,63d,177b), **larp** (51d), **Lars** (51d,121b), **lash** (58c,87b,165c,180d), **Lasi** (191), **lass** (95b), **last** (36c,50b,145a, 174c), **lata** (85d,95d), **late** (128c), **lath** (157c), **latu** (190), **laud** (122a), **laun** (146b), **lava** (101c,132b,151a,177a), **lave** (16d,178b), **lawn** (20a,37c,53b,92c), **laze** (79b), **Laze** (191), **Lazi** (191), **lazo** (88d,128b,133d), **lazy**

- LA - **alae** (182d), **alai** (171a), **Alai** (135c), **alan** (45a,79a,183c), **Alan,** **alar** (15c,145c,182d), **alas** (52c,136b,183b), **alat** (136d), **alay** ˙c), **blaa, blab** (162b), **blae** (93b), **blah, blas** (6c,49c), **Blas** (˙ 7b), **blat** (25b), **blay** (57d), **clad** (46a,82a), **clam** (20b,101b), **clan** (169c), **clap** (58b), **claw** (29c,105b,161d,173a), **Clay** (9d), **Elah** (18c,86d), **elan** (12c,41a,50d,62a,153c,177a,186b), **Elam** (18d,37d, 82a,116c,144b), **ELAS** (71c), **flag** (16b,50d,82b,88c,115a,155a), **flak** (11a), **flam** (169c), **flan** (39d,40a,114d), **flap** (17b,59a,104a, 118d,161a,182d), **flat** (41b,124b,173a), **flaw, flax, flay** (147c,157c), **glad** (85c), **klam** (189), **Olaf** (108a,176b), **olam** (51a,d,75c,81a), **Olan** (115c), **Olax** (52b), **olay** (113b), **plan** (99b,124a,138b), **plap** (54b), **plat** (22b,96c,114a,119c,133d), **play** (63d,154a), **slab** (148b), **slag** (46c,99a,138c,148d,177a), **slam** (180d,182d), **slap** (24a,128c, 148c), **slat** (58b,89a,117c,184a), **Slav** (13c,40c,48b,52a,120b,135b), **slaw, slay, Ulam** (67b), **ulan** (27d,88a)

- - LA **agla** (7a), **alla** (6d), **amla** (48a,161d,168c,169a), **aula** (66c,73b), **Bala** (26c,66a), **bela** (12a), **Bela** (18b,48c,78d), **bola** (16a,179b), **cela** (62d), **cola** (25b,108d,149d,168c), **dola** (189), **ella** (152c, 158c), **Ella** (183c), **fala** (129b), **gala** (55d), **Gala** (191), **gila** (93b), **gola** (27b,40c,70c,157a), **gula** (90a,101a,165b), **hala** (112b), **Hela** (93c), **hila** (53c), **hola** (74c,152b), **hula** (74b), **Hyla** (10a,166d, 169b), **lola, jula, kala** (19a), **kela** (189), **kola** (25b,84a,108d,168c), **Kola** (135b,c,d), **kula** (189), **lala** (129b), **Lila** (183c), **Lola** (27d,97b), **mala** (89c,90a,94b,97d,109d,185c), **mela** (34a,129d), **mila** (188), **Mola** (159c), **Nala** (77a), **Nola, olla** (36d,44b,84d,113b,121d, 151d,152c,181b), **pala** (189), **Pala** (88b), **pela** (30c), **Pola,** **pyla** (22d), **sala** (50c,152a,b,c), **Sala** (50c), **sola** (9a,48a,74b,118c, 154a,167b), **Sula** (65a), **tala** (16d,113a,168c,d), **tela** (22d,98c, 121b,166a,179c), **tola** (48a,80d,180a), **Tola** (85b), **tula** (9a), **Tula,** **upla, vela** (98c,136b,149d), **Vela** (36b,c), **vila** (54b), **vola** (89d), **Zola** (63a)

L - - A **lala** (129b), **lama** (23d,24a,91d,165b), **lana** (58a,66a,90a,184b), **Lara** (25c), **lata** (85d,95d), **lava** (101c,132b,151a,177a), **Leda** (27b, 75d,120c,153a,171d,186b), **lena** (56d), **Lena** (36b), **Lida** (183c), **lija** (57a,90d,173a), **Lila** (183c), **lima** (17b,152b,174d), **Lima** (31b), **lina** (188), **Lina** (183d), **lipa** (54d), **lira** (28b,79a,170d), **Lisa** (183d), **loka** (173c,184c), **Lola** (27d,97b), **loma** (58b,63d), **lora** (146b,149b, 151c,169b), **Lora** (183c), **lota** (24c,121d,178d), **Lota, Iowa** (19a), **Luba** (191), **luna** (103c), **Luna** (102b), **lura** (22d,82a), **lyra, Lyra** (36b,74a)

- LB - **alba** (98b,181a), **Alba** (151d), **albe** (133a), **Albi** (58a), **albo** (34d, 181a), **Elba** (105d), **Elbe** (108a)

- - LB **bulb** (37a,172c)

L - - B **lamb, Lamb** (49c), **limb** (12d,22d), **lobb** (23b,94c,163a)

- LC - **Alca** (14c,128b), **alco** (45b)

- - LC   **talc** (28d,63b,99c,100b,122a,149c)

L - - C   **laic** (32b,90b,107d,124a,141d)

- LD -   **Alda** (110d,150c), **alda** (152b)

- - LD   **bald** (16c), **bold** (41a), **cold** (65d), **eild** (138d,140a), **fold, geld** (162b), **gild** (14a,49c,69c,98b), **gold, held, Hild, hold** (95c,124c, 130d), **Keld** (154b), **meld** (26a,41c,99a,118b), **mild** (32a,66a), **mold** (54d,143c), **sold, suld** (188), **told** (129c), **veld** (151a), **weld** (47c, 85b,173c), **wild** (38b,173d), **wold** (47c,60a,118d,174a,184a)

L - - D   **Ladd** (143c), **laid, land** (44a,163c), **lard** (54d,61a,71a,110a), **laud** (122a), **lead** (35d,43d,72b,74d,81a), **lend** (6d,79d), **lied** (66d,150b), **load** (24c,26d,161b), **lood** (189) **lord** (107c), **loud** (156a), **Ludd** (23c)

LE - -   **lead** (35d,43d,72b,74d,81a), **leaf** (55c,73c,119b), **Leah** (19a,84a, 87b,183c), **leak** (110c), **leal** (54b,94c,139d), **lean** (128a,148b,152d, 164b,166a), **leap** (26c), **lear** (139d), **Lear** (37a,143b), **lech** 102b), **Leda** (27b,75d,120c,153a,171d,186b), **leek** (58b,76a,110c,177d), **leer** (9d,58a,67c,93d,112a,148c), **lees** (46a,142a), **leet** (26a, 38a,139d), **left** (42c), **lehr** (67c,112a) **Leif** (107d), **Leir, Lely** (47a), **lena** (56d), **Lena** (36b), **lend** (6d,79d), **lene** (36b,149a, 172b), **leno** (37c,53b), **lens** (67c,95b,111a,129d,162b), **lent** (54d), **Lent** (115d,141c), **Leon** (96a), **Lero** (82d), **lerp** (51d,141d), **less** (100c,108b,141d), **lest** (59d,163d), **lete, Leti** (82d), **Leto** (11c), **Lett** (16a,90a,93a), **leve** (62a), **Levi** (84a,90c), **levo** (91a), **levy** (14a, 162b)

- LE -   **Alea** (14b,31c,167d), **alec** (10a,57c,d,76c,137c), **alee** (15c,75d, 144b,157a,182a), **alef** (91c), **alem** (98b,155a,170d,171a), **alen** (40d, 138a), **bleb** (20c,23d,67c), **bled, blet** (64a), **bleu** (61b), **blew, clee** (19a,129a), **clef** (104d,105a), **clem** (56b,158b), **clew** (16a,33a,77b, 136b,164d), **elef** (91c), **flea** (81b), **fled, flee, flew, flex** (18a), **fley** (63d), **gled** (19a,52a,87a), **glee** (99a,150b), **glen** (43c), **Hler** (141a), **ilex** (77d), **Klee** (113a), **Lleu** (40c), **Llew** (40c), **olea** (170b), **Olea** (110b), **oleo** (34c), **plea** (51a,52d,122a,130b), **pleb** (10d,35b,180b), **plet** (135d), **plew** (17c), **plex** (60b), **Sleb** (12a), **sled** (40a), **slee** (140b,148c), **slew** (160a), **sley** (179b), **Ulex** (153c), **vlei** (38c, 160a), **vley** (160a)

- - LE   **able** (26b,35b,126a,147c), **acle** (13d,82c,115d), **aile** (62b,63a,182c, d), **Alle** (14c), **atle** (136d,161d,169b), **axle** (153c,180c), **bale** (24b, 74a), **bile** (30c), **bole** (31d,32a,169b), **cale** (72d), **cole** (25a), **Cole, dale** (43c,128a,174b), **dele** (26a,49c,51b,53a,110b,123d,124c,130a, 145c,161b), **dole** (44c,118c,121c,129d), **Dole** (74c), **elle** (62b,c), **file** (13a,127d), **gale** (181d), **gyle** (23b,174d), **hale** (125b), **Hale** (9d,131a), **hole** (6c,11b,110d,118c,147a), **hule** (23a,134c), **hyle** (97c), **idle** (174b,c,178c), **ille** (89b,d,163d), **Iole** (52a,76b,123c), **isle** (8b,53c,81d,82d,86b,88a), **ixle** (56a), **jole** (29b), **Jule** (183d), **kale** (22a,25a,119b,175a), **kile** (189), **kyle** (57a,139c), **male** (154d), **Male** (45d), **mele** (74b,150b), **mile** (64c), **mole** (19d,23a,24d,85a, 117c,155c), **Mole** (88c), **mule** (45b,148b,153c,180b), **nile** (33c, 71d), **Nile** (106b), **ogle** (9d,53c,91a,93d,148c), **orle** (17b,56b,76a, 144b,177a), **pale** (113a,117c,178a), **Pele** (69c,74c), **pile** (45d,75b, 117c), **pole** (132c,143b,177b,184a), **Pole** (52a), **pule** (180d), **pyle** (34b), **Pyle** (9c,178a), **rale** (7c,23a,29d,41b), **rile** (10c,d,82c,125a,

360

156b,176a), **role** (114b), **rule** (11b,26b,90b), **sale** (14c,61c,62b,c, 168b), **sole** (52c,57a,b,58b,d,110c,115d,150a), **tale** (91a,185b), **tele** (34b,122c), **tile** (31d,56d,72b,95b,133c,163c), **tole** (9a,51a,99b, 163a), **tule** (24b,27c), **vale** (54c,128a,174b), **Vale** (7c,109c), **vile** (16c,56c), **vole** (97d,104a), **wale** (70b,131b,157c,163d,179a,180a, c,d), **wile** (13b,41c,157b,169c), **Yale** (173c), **Yule** (30d)

L - - E   **lace** (58b,179c), **lade** (24c,26d,43c,93b,100a,132a,139d,161b), 178d), **lake** (117d), **lame** (38d,43d,73b), **lane** (134b,157b), **late** (128c), **lave** (16d,178b), **laze** (79b), **Laze** (191), **lene**(36b,149a, 172b), **lete**, **leve** (62a), **life** (19a,177a), **like** (13c,37d,146d), **lime** (25b,27d,31b,33c,102d,168c), **line** (12b,22b,36d,38a,126c,134b, 157b,158b,162d,175c), **lire** (62c), **lite** (158c,d), **live** (47c), **lobe** (90c,134b), **lode** (42c,99a,111b,175b), **loge** (164a), **Loke** (15d,68b), **Lome**, **lone** (150a), **lope** (48b,64b,d), **lore** (77c,87c,90d,151c,183a), **lose** (60a,100c), **lote** (24c,94a), **love** (163a), **lube** (110a), **luce** (58c,117d), **Luce** (7b,35a), **luge** (148a), **luke**, **Luke** (52a,96a), **lune** (38c,73b,74d), **lupe** (19a,64a), **lure** (41c,51a,54b,163a), **lute** (11c, 28b,84d,105a,131d), **luxe** (61c,62d,159c), **lyre** (11c,81c,105a,111c), **lyse**

- LF -   **alfa** (70d)

- - LF   **calf**, **golf** (154a), **gulf** (6c), **half** (101a), **pelf** (22a,56c,131b), **self** (48d,80d), **Welf** (67a), **wolf**

L - - F   **leaf** (55c,73c,119b), **Leif** (107d), **lief** (181d), **loaf** (49b,94b), **loof** (144c,153d), **luff** (136b), **luif**

- LG -   **alga** (141b,c), **Algy** (96b), **Olga** (135c,183c)

L - - G   **ling** (24c,57a,b,75b,178c), **long** (38b,185b), **lung**, **lurg** (96d,141b, 184d)

L - - H   **lakh** (110c), **lash** (58c,87b,165c,180d), **lath** (157c), **Leah** (19a,84a, 87b,183c), **lech** (102b), **lith** (34d,156c), **loch** (88a,139d), **losh** (178b), **loth** (15a,173d), **Lugh** (28b), **lush** (94d)

LI - -   **Liam** (181d), **liar** (98d), **Lias** (66a), **lick**, **Lida** (183c), **Lido** (83d, 175b), **lied** (66d,150b), **lief** (181d), **lien** (65c,91a,124c), **lieu** (118c, 155d), **life** (19a,177a), **lift** (49b), **liin** (188), **lija** (57a,90d,173a), **like** (13c,37d,146d), **Lila** (183c), **lill** (15d,118a), **lilt** (93a,131a, 147a), **lily**, **lima** (17b,152b,174d), **Lima** (31b), **limb** (12d,22d), **lime** (25b,27d,31b,33c,102d,168c), **limn** (45d,121c), **limp** (58a,81a,177d), **limu** (141c), **limy** (176d), **lina** (188), **Lina** (183d), **line** (12b,22b,36d,38a,126c,134b,157b,158b,162d,175c), **ling** (24c,57a,b,75b,178c), **link** (36a,81d,85b), **linn** (120d,140a,c, 168c,178d), **lino**, **lint** (46a,58d), **liny** (157b), **Linz** (40d), **lion** (55b, 86c), **lipa** (54d), **lira** (28b,79a,170d), **lire** (62c), **Lisa** (183d), **lisp** (153b), **liss** (54b,58b,60c,129d,140a), **list** (26d,27b,75b,83d,134a, 138b,165d), **lite** (158c,d), **lith** (34d,156c), **liti** (60d), **litz** (127b), **live** (47c), **Livy** (132d,133a)

- LI -   **alia** (89d), **alif** (12b), **alii** (74c,134c), **alim** (103b,162c) **alin** (188), **alit** (44b,143a), **Alix** (183c), **Clim** (12b), **Clio** (104d), **clip** (54d, 143d), **Elia** (88a,115d), **Elis** (22c,37d,71b,107c), **flip** (167c), **flit** (41a), **flix**, **glia** (106c), **glib** (58d,149a,177c), **glim** (45c), **ilia** (21d,77b,115d), **ille** (89b,d), **olic** (158b), **olid** (55d,60c,148d,157d), **olio** (44b,77c,98c,100d,121d), **plie** (32c,59b), **slid**, **slim** (148b,

160a), **slip** (67c,119a), **slit** (40a)

- - LI   **amli** (48a,161d,168c,169a), **Atli** (14c,72b,79a,107d), **Bali, Beli** (23c), **coli, dali** (168c,169b), **doli, fili, gali** (6c), **goli** (105c), **Holi** (77a), **joli** (62b), **kali** (26d,67c,136d,167a), **Kali** (147b), **Koli** (27b, **Kuli** (27b), **mali** (27b), **pali** (122b), **Pali** (23d,24a,137b,175a), **pili** (34b,108d), **puli** (45a,78d), **soli** (12c,110c), **tali** (189), **teli** (94b), **vali** (171a,176a), **Vali** (7c,109c), **vili** (54b), **Vili** (109c), **wali** (171a), **yali** (171a)

L - -I   **Lari** (72c), **lari** (78a,101c), **Lasi** (191), **Lazi** (191), **Leti** (82d), **Levi** (84a,90c), **liti** (60d), **loci** (66b,118c), **Lodi** (105d), **Loki** (7c,15d, 68b), **lori** (91b), **Loti** (63a,176a), **ludi** (133b), **Luri** (191)

- LK -   **alky**

- - LK   **balk** (118c,146a,156d), **bilk** (29b,41c,42a), **bulk** (97b), **calk** (78c, 109a,141c,178d), **folk** (116a,169c), **fulk** (173a), **hulk** (144d,173d), **milk, mulk** (60d), **polk** (37c), **pulk** (37c,88d), **silk** (53b,179c), **sulk** (159a), **talk, volk** (66c,105d,116a), **Volk, walk, welk** (65c,96d, 141b), **yolk**

L - - K   **lack** (178a), **lank** (148b,164b), **lark** (19a,63d,177b), **leak** (110c), **leek** (58b,76a,110c,177d), **lick, link** (36a,81d,85b), **lock** (54d), **lonk** (143d), **look** (11c,53c,142a), **luck** (28d), **lurk** (92a, 147d)

LL - -   **llyn** (120d,140a), **Lleu** (40c), **Llew** (40c)

- LL -   **alla** (6d), **Alle** (14c), **allo** (34c), **ally** (14a,35c,d,173c), **ella** (152c, 158c), **Ella** (183c), **elle** (62b,c), **ille** (89b,d,163d), **ills** (170a), **olla** (36d,44b,84d,113b,121d,151d,152c,181b), **ullo** (6a,144a), **Ullr** (146b,164d)

- - LL   **ball, bell** (24c,39d), **Bell** (162d), **bill** (17b,147a), **Bill** (96b), **boll** (119b,d), **bull** (113c), **call** (145c,159b,176d), **cell** (39b), **cull** (117c), **dell** (43c,174b), **dill** (13a,117c), **doll** (125c), **dull** (21a,32c,173a), **Dull** (94b), **fall** (46b,141c), **fell** (40a,58b,76c,115d,147d), **fill** (109b), **full** (7b,130b), **gall** (19a,28c,29b,82c,160c,176a), **gill** (22d), **Goll, gull** (32d,41c,42a,72c,99b,141a), **hall** (37b,114d), **hill, hull** (141d,142a,144c,d), **Jill** (183d), **kill** (38c), **lill** (15d,118a), **loll** (94b,128c), **lull** (126d,150c), **mall** (95d,124b,143b), **mill** (126c), **moll, Moll** (183d), **mull** (53b,135a,164c), **Nell** (110a,183d), **nill** (173d), **Noll** (96b,110b), **null** (108c,177a), **pall** (32d,81b,112a), **pill, poll** (74d,160a,177c), **pull** (45d,167d), **rill** (23c,102b,132a,148d, 157b), **roll** (134a,160b), **rull** (170b), **sell** (97a,115c,175b), **sill** (45c, 76c,165a,182b), **tall** (118d), **tell** (105d,129c,154b), **Tell** (160d), **till** (39c,101c,173d), **toll** (131c), **vill** (176b), **wall, well, will** (18b,43a, 163c,177c), **yell** (145c)

L - - L   **leal** (54b,94c,139d), **lill** (15d,118a), **loll** (94b,128c), **lull** (25c,126d,150c)

- LM -   **alma** (40d,53d,146d,147a), **Alma** (38d,183c), **alme** (40d,147a), **alms** (29a), **elmy, ulme** (49c)

- - LM   **balm** (110a,172c), **calm** (8d,11d,112b,118d,126c,d,172b,173d), **culm** (11a,32d,70d,145a,156a), **film** (164b), **halm, helm** (144d, 165d), **holm** (77d,82d,109a), **malm** (32a,92b), **palm** (59b,168a,169b)

L - - M   **Liam** (181d), **loam** (47d), **loom** (11c,146b,179b), **lyam** (139a)

- LN - ulna (21d,39b)

- - LN kiln (15d,112a), vuln (184d)

L - - N Lain, laun (146b), lawn (20a,37c,53b,92c), lean (128a,148b,152d, 164b,166a), Leon (96a), lien (65c,91a,124c), liin (188), limn (45d, 121c), linn (120d,140a,c,168c,178d), lion (55b,86c), llyn (120d, 140a), loan, loin (40a,98a), loon (19a,b,c,157d,179c), lorn (42d, 60b), loun (19a,b), lown (157d)

LO - - load (24c,26d,161b), loaf (79b,94b), loam (47d,150a), loan, lobb (23b,94c,163a), lobe (90c,134b), lobo (165d,183c), loch (88a,139d), loci (66b,118c), lock (54d), loco (38b,119b,120b), lode (42c,99a, 111b,175b), Lodi (105d), Lodz, loft (14c,69d,104b,178b), loge (164a), logy (46d), loin (40a,98a), loir (45c), Loir, Lois (165d,183c), loka (173c,184c), Loke (7c,15d,68b), Loki (7c,15d,68b), Lola (27d, 97b), loll (94b,128c), Lolo (27d,30a), loma (58b,63d), Lome, lone (150a), long (38b,185b), Lonk (143d), lood (189), loof (144c,153d) look (11c,53c,142a), loom (11c,146b,179b), loon (19a,b,c,157d, 179c), loop (31b,107d), Loos, loot (22a,118a,119d,136a,153d), lope (48b,64b,d), lora (146b,149b,151c,169b), Lora (183c), lord (107c), lore (77c,87c,90d,151c,183a), lori (91b), lorn (42d,60b), loro (19a,114b), lory (19a,114a), lose (60a,100c), losh (178b), loss (42c,123d,178b), lost, lota (24c,121d,178d), lote (24c,94a), loth (15a,173d), Loti (63a,176a), loto (65a,121d,178d), lots, loud (156a), loun (19a,b), loup (61d,62a,90c,139d), Loup (193), lour (13d,63d), lout (15c,22a,24b,45b,109a,157d), love (163a), Iowa (19a), lown (157d), lowp (90c,139d)

- LO - alod (51c,55d,88a,124c), aloe (7d,20a,76a,b,92b,98b,119b,158b, 167a,183d), alop (13d,46b,93d), alow (18a,172c), blob, bloc (173a), blot, blow, clod (22a,45b,157d), Cloe (183c), clog (30c,145b), clop, clot (32d,94d)', clou (62b), clow (58c,148c), cloy (61b,137c, 159d), elod (49b,59d,79c), Elon (18c,51b,108a), floc (149a), floe (79b), flog (180d), flop (54a), flot (173a), flow (157b), glom (155d, 160d,178c), glow (144c), ilog (132a,161b), ilot (82d), klom (189), klop (150d), Olor (160a,b), plod (170b), plop (54b), plot (25a,36b, 118d,138b), plow (39c,165d), ploy (43c), slob (173d), sloe (14a,20b, 64a,119d,181c), slog (157c,170b,177d), sloo (160a), slop, slot (10d, 11b,41d,110d,167d,168a,181b), slow (43c)

- - LO allo (34c), bilo (131b), bolo (87a), calo (72d), dilo (120d,168c), filo, gilo (48a), Golo (191), Gulo (183c), halo (14d,31b,92a), hilo (74c), kalo (162a), kilo (99b,122d), kolo (59b,135c), lalo (16b,34d), Lalo (35c), Lolo (27d,30a), malo (23a,74c,152a), milo (70b,87c), Milo, nolo (42a), orlo (56b,119c), Oslo, palo (152c), pelo (83b), polo (154a), Polo (175b), ralo (188), silo (59a), solo (12c,89a,110c), ullo (6a,144a), velo (175b)

L - - O lago (83b,152b), lalo (16b,34d), Lalo (35c), lazo (88d,128b,133d), leno (37c,53b), Lero (82d), Leto (11c), levo (91a), Lido (83d,175b), lino, lobo (165d,183c), loco (38b,119b,120b), Lolo (27d,30a), loro (19a,114b), loto (65a,121d), ludo (65a,112b)

- LP - Alph (132a), Alps (85d), olpe (90d,182c)

- - LP calp (92b), colp (28a,148b), gulp (46a,79d,160a), help (14a), kelp (82a,141c), palp (11a,55b,58c,167c), pulp, salp (148d), yelp

363

L - - P   laap (51d,91b,141d), lamp (92a,94c), Lapp (108a), larp (51d), leap (26c), lerp (51d,141d), limp (58a,81a,177d), lisp (153b), loop (31b,107d), loup (61d,62a,90c,139d), Loup (193), lowp (90c,139d), lump (45a,160c)

- - LR   Ullr (146b,164d)

L - - R   lair (37c,42b), lear (139d), Lear (37a,143b), leer (9d,58a,67c,93d, 112a,148c), lehr (67c,112a), Leir, liar (98d), loir (45c), Loir, lour (13d,63d)

- LS -   also (10b,18b,80a), Elsa (70a,93c,110d,177b,183c), else (18b,79b, 111d)

- - LS   fels (190), fils (62d,150b), Hals (47a), ills (170a)

L - - S   Lais (17c), Laos (80d,129c), Lars (51d,121b), lass (95b), lees (46a, 142a), lens (95b,111a,129b,162d), less (100c,108b,141d), Lias (66a), liss (54b,58b,60c,129d,140a) Lois (165d,183c), Loos, loss (42c,123d,178b), lots, Lubs (94c), Lyas (66a)

- LT -   alta (89c,152d), alto (152b,176c,177a)

- - LT   Balt (93a), belt (16a,31a), bolt (13b,54d,58b,132d,160a), bult (76d), celt (30c,82c,123a,156c,167b,179b), Celt (10a,180a,b), colt (78c,131a,185d,186b), Colt, cult (141d,161c), dolt (20c,59c,157d), felt, galt, gelt (101c), gilt (69c,77c,151d,185d), halt (13b,28a,38d, 156d), hilt (73c), holt (36d,119b,184b), jilt, jolt (143b), Kelt (180b), kilt, lilt (93a,131a,147a), malt (17c), melt, milt (153d), molt (27a, 143d) pelt (53a), salt (35d,105b,123a,136c,141c,149d), silt (104b, 142a), tilt (26b,d,166a), tolt, volt (49b,78c), Walt (96b), welt (36d,131b,145a,b,177b,d), wilt (46b), yelt (151b)

L - - T   lact (34c), laet (60d), lait (62a), lant, last (36c,50b,145a,174c), leet (26a,38a,139d), left (42c), lent (54d), Lent (115d,141c), lest (59d, 163d), Lett (16a,90a,93a), lift (49b), lilt (93a,131a,147a), lint (46a, 58d), list (26d,27b,75b,83d,134a,138b,165d), loft (14c,69d,104b, 178b), loot (22a,118a,119d,136a,153d), lost, lout (15c,22a,24b,45b, 109a,157d), lust (41b)

LU - -   Luba (191), lube (110a), Lubs (94c), luce (58c,117d), Luce (7b,35a), luck (28d), lucy, Lucy (183c), Ludd (23c), ludi (133b), ludo (65a, 112b), luff (136b), luge (148a), Lugh (28b), luif, luke, Luke (52a, 96a), lull (25c,126d,150c), lulu (19a,57b,112c), Lulu (183d), lump (45a,160c), luna (103c), Luna (102b), lune (38c,73b,74d), lung, luny (38b), lupe (19a,64a), lura (22d,82a), lure (41c,51a,54b,163a), lurg (96d,141b,184d), Luri (191), lurk (92a,147d), lush (94d), lust (41b), lute (11c,28b,84d,105a,131d), luxe (61c,62d,159c)

- LU -   alum (14a,45c), Alur (191), blub, blue (33c,98c,102c,150d,173a), blup, blur, blut (66b), club (39c), clue, Elul (102b), flub (22b), flue (8b,30a), flux (28d,58d), glub, glue (7b,156a), glug, glum (102c, 159a), glut (52c,70a,137c,159d), Ilus (88d,170b), plug (156d,184d), plum, plup, plus (10b,102c) slub (171c), slue (97b,148b,160a), slug (46b,99b,157c), slum, slur (44b,124c,148b,168a), ulua (57a,74c), Ulua (141b)

- - LU   Aalu (6b,48d), aulu (74c,168c), balu (104b,159a,181d), hulu (55b), lalu (48d), iglu (51c,149b), lulu (19a,57b,112c), Lulu (183d), pelu (30a,106d,168c), pulu (74c), Sulu (102c), tolu (16a), Tulu (45d), zulu (171d,175d), Zulu (86a)

L - - U latu (190), lieu (118c,155d), limu (141c), Lieu (40c), lulu (19a,57b, 112c), Lulu (183d)

- LV - Alva (151d), Ulva (141b)

LW - - Lwow

L - - W Liew (40c), Lwow

- - LX calx (23c,75c,112c), falx (133b)

L - - X lanx (133a,b), lynx (26c,181d), Lynx (36b)

LY - - lyam (139a), Lyas (66a), lynx (26c,181d), Lynx (36b), Lyra (36b, 74a), lyre (11c,81c,105a,111c), lyse

- LY - Alya (155b,c), Alys (183c), Clym (12b), Ilyn (120d,140a)

- - LY ably (147c), ally (14a,35c,d,173c), coly (104a), eely (185a), holy, idly, inly, July, Lely (47a), lily, moly (76a,181c), oily (110b, 172c), only (24d,52c,98d,147a,150a), Orly (8b), paly (194), pily, poly (34c,76b), puly, rely (16b,170b), rily (176a), ugly, vily (54b), wily (13b,38b,39c)

L - - Y Lacy, lady, laky, lazy, Lely (47a), levy (14a,162b), lily, limy (176d), liny (157b), livy (132d,133a), logy (46d), lory (19a,114a), lucy, Lucy (183c), luny (38b)

L - - Z Linz (40d), litz (127b), Lodz

MA - - maal (188), ma'am (95a,166b), maar (177a), Maas (132a), Maat (69a,b,85d), Maba (103a,168d), mabi (58d), mace (49d,108d,153b, 154d,161a,178a), mack, made, Madi (174a), mado (14d,57a,170b), mage (95b), magg (95b), Magh (102a), magi (123c), Magi (95b, 116c,183a), maha (28c,88c,136d), mahr (103a), Maia (76b,109a, 153b,155b,177c), maid (45b,142d), mail (12d,99b,121c), maim (43d,81a,105c), main (29d,35d,123d), mais (61b), maja (151c), Maja (153b), majo, make (35b,36d,54a,123a), maki (91b), mako (18a,19a,20d,143c,168c,182c), Maku (192), mala (89b,c,90a,94b, 97d,109d,185c), male (154d), Male (45d), mali (27b), mall (95d, 124b,143b), malm (32a,92b), malo (23a,74c,152a), malt (17c), mama, Mama (116d), mamo (19a,74b), mana (30a,120d,122a, 159c), mand (28b), mane, mani (115c), mann (189), Mann (9c, 48c,185c), mano (71d,73d,74b,83b), Mans (30a), Manu (10a,76d, 77a,b), Manx (27b,28a,82d), many (108d), mapo (68a,148d), mara (114d), Mara (24a,d,105b,107b), marc (70c), Marc (96a) mare (78b), Mare (108b), mari (61d), Mari (16a), mark (146b,155a), Mark (52a, 96a), marl (32a,42c,55d), maro (144d), Mars (68c,118d,119a,129a, 178a), mart (49d,97a), Mart (96b,183d), maru (84c,144d), Mary (50c,126b,183c), masa (37a), mash (39b,156c), mask (44a,45c), mass (8a,24b,35b,142d), mast (17c,108d,120b,144d,152d), masu (57a,84c), mate (18c,35b,41d,113a,154a,162c), math (77a), Matt, maty (80c), maud (53d,71a,136d,143c), Maud (181a,183c), Maui (120d), maul (73c,96b), maun (139d), maya (77a,179b), Maya (23d, 186c), Mayo (193), maze (87b,157d)

- MA - amah (95b,108d,111c), amar (189), imam (25c,102d,103a), Oman (159a), omao (165b), omar (103b), Omar (48c,51b,116c,163b), Xmas

- - MA alma (40d,53d,146d,147a), Alma (38d,183c), amma (6a), atma (150d), bema (28d,31a,114b,119b,125b,137a), boma (7d),

cima (83b,c), **coma** (91c,157d,170c,172b), **cyma** (101a,b), **dama** (65d,152b), **Duma** (135c), **Emma** (138c), **Erma** (183c), **Fama** (135a), **Gama** (121c), **Goma** (191), **Hima** (191), **ijma** (103b), **Irma** (96d), **jama** (103b), **Kama** (56d), **lama** (23d,24a,91d,165b), **lima** (17b,152b,174d), **Lima** (31b), **loma** (58b,63d), **mama, Mama** (116d), **mima** (185d), **Nama** (78c), **Nema** (34d,48c,134b,164d,176c), **Numa** (133a), **pima** (37c), **Pima** (192), **puma** (27b,37c,55b,103d), **Rama** (77a,80b,176d), **rima** (23a,30c,32a,58a,110d), **Roma** (83c,d), **sama** (105c,169d), **sima** (132b), **soma** (10c,21c,34a,48a,81d,136b), **Tama** (192), **tema** (12a,164a), **Toma** (191), **xema** (72c), **Xema** (12c), **Yama** (57a,68a), **Yima** (84a,116b,c), **Yuma, Zama** (73d, 141d)

M - - A   **Maba** (103a,168d), **maha** (28c,88c,136d), **Maia** (76b,109a,153b, 155b,177c), **maja** (151c), **Maja** (153b), **mala** (89b,c,90a,94b,97d, 109d,185c), **mama, Mama** (116d), **mana** (30a,120d,122a,159c), **mara** (114d), **Mara** (24a,d,105b,107b), **masa** (37a), **maya** (77a, 179b), **Maya** (23d,186c), **meda** (110a), **mega** (34b,c), **mela** (34a, 129d), **mesa** (49b,76d,119b,161a), **meta** (132d,133a), **Meta, mica** (82c,100b,146c), **mila** (188), **mima** (185d), **mina** (10b,70b,71d, 179d), **Mina** (23a,183d), **mira** (174d), **Mira** (155b), **moha** (42b, 83d), **Mola** (159c), **mona** (72b,101d), **mora** (42b,65a,72b,83d,99b, 153a,161a), **mota** (103a), **moxa** (27d,30c), **muga, mura** (84d), **Mura** (192), **Musa** (16a), **muta** (28d,103a), **myna** (19a,c,70b), **Myra** (10a, 31b,183c), **myxa** (168c,169a)

- MB -   **amba** (161a), **ambi** (34a,122c), **ambo** (125b,128b), **imbe** (37a,56a, 133d), **umbo** (22b)

- - MB   **bomb** (144a), **comb** (38c), **dumb** (153b), **iamb** (59c), **jamb** (12d, 45c,118a,146b,174a), **lamb, Lamb** (49c), **limb** (12d,22d), **nimb** (31b,73b,92a,107b,131d), **numb, rumb** (120b), **tomb, Zimb** (6c)

M - - B   **medb, Moab** (18d,85a,86d,94a)

M - - C   **marc** (70c), **Marc** (96a)

M - - D   **maid** (45b,142d), **mand** (28b), **maud** (53d,71a,136d,143c), **Maud** (181a,183c), **mead** (46a,78a,97d,99b), **Mead** (78a), **meed** (128c, 131a), **meld** (26a,41c,99a,118b), **mend** (130b), **mild** (32a,66a), **mind** (75c,81d,93d,109b), **Moed** (100c), **mold** (54d,143c), **mood** (44c), **mudd** (188), **mund** (124d)

ME - -   **mead** (46a,78a,97d,99b), **Mead** (78a), **meal** (72a,130b), **mean** (15a, 42b,146c,156b), **meat** (59b), **meda** (110a), **Medb, Mede** (10a,b,13c), **medi** (34c), **meed** (128c,131a), **meek** (93d,99d), **meer, meet** (11d, 13d,36a,50a,81d,142d), **mega** (34b,c), **mein** (30b), **meio** (188), **mela** (34a,129d), **meld** (26a,41c,99a,118b), **mele** (74b,150b), **melt, memo** (108b), **mend** (130b), **mene** (19a,73d,108d,185c), **Ment** (54b,164a), **menu** (19a,27a), **Menu, meou, meow, mere** (16c,22b, 62a,78b,87d,96c,110c,120d,146d,148b), **merl** (20b), **mero** (72a), **Meru** (77a,103d), **mesa** (49b,76d,119b,161a), **mese** (71c), **mesh** (50d,106c), **mess** (22b,44b,77c,85d,104b,165c,173d), **meta** (132d, 133a), **Meta, mete** (9a,11d,22b,44c,45b,98a,121c), **meum** (27a, 89c), **Meum, mewl** (180d), **mews** (154c)

- ME -   **amen** (14a,80b,94a,137a,149c,175c,184b), **Amen** (86d,127d,159b, 164a), **amer** (61b), **Ames** (9c,82a), **Amex** (184d), **Emer** (39b,183c),

emeu (111d), **Imer, Omei** (24a), **omen** (14c,59d,60a,121c,123a, 146b), **omer** (51a,75c), **smee** (19b,46c,d,118b,119d,141b,181b), **Smee** (116d), **smew** (19b,46d,99a,137d), **T-men** (168b), **Ymer** (67a, 131c)

- - ME **acme** (39c,115c,186b), **alme** (40d), **arme** (63a,179b), **came** (182b), **Came** (192), **come, cyme** (58d,69c), **dame** (67b,87c,166b), **deme** (71b,c,167d), **dime, dome** (39c,133c,155d), **fame** (130a) **feme** (181b), **fume** (129a,149a,157a), **game** (64d,154a), **gime** (77d), **home, Hume** (50c), **kame** (67b,139b), **Kome** (71d), **lame** (38d,43d, 73b), **lime** (25b,27d,31b,102d,168c), **Lome, mime** (24a,71b,85a, 100a), **Mime** (131d,148d), **name** (8a,11b,d,25c,46c,107c,130b,157d, 163b,166b), **nome** (71c,163b), **Nome, oime** (8b), **pome** (11d), **Pume** (137b,175b,185b), **rame** (22d), **rime** (30c,36a,58a,63d,77c), **Rome** (31c,51d), **ryme** (178d), **same** (44d,79b), **seme** (45c,138b,151b, 154b,155c,157b), **sime** (101d), **some** (114b,121c,126a), **tame** (45a, 66a), **Tame, time** (47a,131a), **tome** (21d,177c), **ulme** (49c), **zeme** (55d,161b,180b), **zyme** (55c)

M - - E **mace** (49d,108d,153b,154d,161a,178a), **made, mage** (95b), **make** (35b,36d,54a,123a), **male** (154d), **Male** (45d), **mane, mare** (78b), **Mare** (108b), **mate** (18c,35b,41d,113a,154a,162c), **maze** (87b, 157d), **Mede** (10a,b,13c), **mele** (74b,150b), **mene** (19a,73d,108d, 185c), **mere** (16c,22b,62a,78b,87d,96c,110c,120d,146d,148b), **mese** (71c), **mete** (9a,11d,22b,44c,45b,98a,121c), **mice, mide** (110a), **mike, Mike** (96b), **mile** (64c), **mime** (24a,71b,85a,100a), **Mime** (131d,148d), **mine** (69c,79d,111b,124c), **mire** (21c,104b), **mise** (8a, 10a,70c), **mite** (12b,81b,82a,114a,c,148c,d,181b), **Mixe** (192), **mode** (54d,96b,157d,179a), **moke** (45c,157d), **mole** (19d,23a,24d,85a, 117c,155c), **Mole** (88c), **mope** (92d,159a), **more** (71a), **More** (50b), **Mose** (96b), **mote** (114c,153a), **moue** (61d,62b), **move, mule** (45b, 148b,153c,180b), **mure** (177d), **muse** (65b,93d,120d,164c), **Muse** (68d), **mute** (146c,153b)

M - - F **miff** (44c), **moff** (53b,146c), **muff**

M - - G **magg** (95b), **migg** (96c), **Ming** (30b,c), **morg** (188), **mung** (70d)

MH - - **mhor** (180b)

- - MH **samh** (56b)

M - - H **Magh** (102a), **mash** (39b,156c), **math** (77a), **mesh** (50d,106c), **moth, Moth** (112d), **much, mush** (97d), **muth** (188), **myth** (8b,91a)

MI - - **miam** (14d), **mian** (97c,147b,166b), **Miao** (30a,b), **mias** (111a), **miau** (27b,99b), **miaw** (27b,99b), **mica** (82c,100b,146c), **mice, mick** (82c), **mico** (97a), **mide** (110a), **Midi** (151b), **mien** (11c, 17b,26d,44c,96b), **miff** (44c), **migg** (96c), **mike, Mike** (96b), **mila** (188), **mild** (32a,66a), **mile** (64c), **milk, mill** (126c), **milo** (70b,87c, 150d), **Milo, milt** (153d), **mima** (185d), **mime** (24a,71b,85a,100a), **Mime** (131d,148d), **mimi** (14d), **Mimi** (87b,110d,125b,183d), **mina** (10b,70b,71d,179d), **Mina** (23a,183d), **mind** (75c,81d,93d,109b), **mine** (69c,79d,111b,124c), **ming** (30b,c), **mink** (176c), **mino** (84c), **mint** (13a,33b,58b,76a), **minx** (116c), **miny, Mira** (155b,174d), **mire** (21c,104b), **mirk** (41a,67d), **miro** (19a,106d,184a), **Miro** (113a, 151d), **miry, mise** (8a,10a,70c), **miss, mist** (46b,59b,174d), **mite** (12b,81b,82a,114a,c,148c,d,181b), **mitt** (56c), **mitu** (39d), **mity, Mixe** (192), **mixy**

367

- MI - amia (22c,170d), amic (9d), amid (9d,50a), amie (61d), amil (45a, 48a,185c), amin (9d), amir (7c,12a,103a,b,123c,170d), amit (94a), Emil (96a), Emim (67a,100d), emir (12a,103a,b,123c,134d,135a, 171a), emit (43d,49a,53c,58d,83a,142c), imid (29c), omit (49c, 52c,106b,114c,147d)

- - MI admi (65d), ammi (98c), demi (34b,122c), hami (78a), hemi (122c), immi (189), jami (103b), kami (68a,84b), Kami (88c,107c,144c), Komi (191), mimi (14d), Mimi (87b,110d,125b,183d), rami (22d), Remi (10b), romi (72d), semi (34b,80b,122c,d), Simi (82d), zemi (55d,161b,180b)

M - - I Mabi (58d), Madi (174a), magi (123c), Magi (95b,116c,183a), maki (91b), mali (27b), mani (115c), mari (61d), Mari (16a), Maui (120d), medi (34c), Midi (151b), mimi (14d), Mimi (87b,110d,125b,183d), moki (127b), Moki

M - - J munj (70d)

M - - K Mack, mark (146b,155a), Mark (52a,96a), mask (44a,45c), meek (93d,99d), mick (82c), milk (82c), mink (176d), mirk (41a,67d), mock (131b,162b), monk (28b,63c,129d), mosk (97b,103b), muck, mulk (60d), murk (41a,67d), musk (116b)

- ML - amla (48a,161d,168c,169a), amli (48a,161d,168c,169a)

M - - L maal (188), mail (12d,99b,121c), mall (95d,124b,143b), marl (32a, 42c,55d), maul (73c,96b), meal (72a,130b), merl (20b), mewl (180d), mill (126c), moil (46c,184c), moll, Moll (183d), mull (53b, 135a,164c)

- MM - amma (6a), ammi (98c), ammo (9d), ammu (9d), Emma (183c), immi (189)

M - - M ma'am (95a,166b), maim (43d,81a,105c), malm (32a,92b), meum (27a,89c), Meum, miam (14d)

- MN - omni (34a)

- - MN damn, Domn (135a), famn (188), hymn (150c), limn (45d,121c)

M - - N main (29d,35d,123d), mann (189), Mann (9c,48c,185c), maun (139d), mean (15a,42b,146c,156b), mein (30b), mian (97c,147b, 166b), mien (11c,17b,26d,44c,96b), moan, moon (40b,132c,137c), morn, mown

MO - - Moab (18d,85a,86d,94a), moan, moat (44d), mock (131b,162b), mode (54d,96b,157d,179a), Moed (100c), moff (53b,146c), mogo (74b), moha (42b,83d), moho (19a,78a), mohr (65d), moil (46c, 184c), moio (188), mojo (177c), moke (45c,157d), moki (127b), moko (96c), Mola (159c), mold (54d,143c), mole (19d,23a,24d,85a, 117c,155c), Mole (88c), moll, Moll (183d), molt (27a,143d), moly (76a,181c), mona (72b,101d), monk (28b,63c,129d), mono (34c, 78d,122d,147a), Mono (193), mons (89c), Mons (184d), mont (62b), mood (44c), moon (40b,132c,137c), moor (10a,75b,137b,141d, 178b), Moor (102c,d,111d), moot (41b,44c), mope (92d,159a), mora (42b,65a,72b,83d,99b,153a,161a), more (71a), More (50b), morg (188), morn, moro (19a,56c), Moro (100a,103a,117a,159a), Mors (41b), mort (41b,47a,78b,136d), Mose (96b), mosk (97b,103b), moss (91d,104c,114a,170c), most, mosy (67d), mota (103a), mote (114c,153a), moth, Moth (112d), moto (104b), moue (61d,62b), move, mown, moxa (27d,30c), Moxo (192), mozo (152b)

- MO - amol (62a), amok (18b,63c), Amon (86d,96b,127d,159b,164a), amor (152b), Amor (39c,68b), Amos (96a,144b), Amoy (88c)

-- MO ammo (9d), atmo (34d,174d), Como, demo (122d), hemo (34a, 122b), homo (122d), ikmo (18b), itmo (18b), mamo (19a,b,74b), memo (108b), nemo (34b), Nemo (56a,85c), Pomo (192), Sumo

M -- O mado (14d,57a,170b), majo, mako (18a,19a,20d,143c,168c,182c), malo (23a,74c,152a), mamo (19a,74b), mano (71d,73d,74b,83b), mapo (68a,148d), maro (144d), Mayo (193), meio (188), memo (108b), mero (72a), Miao (30a,b), mico (97a), milo (70b,87c, 150d), Milo, mino (84c), miro (19a,106d,184a), Miro (113a,151d), mogo, (74b), moho (19a,78a), moio (188), mojo (177c), moko (96c), mono (34c,78d,122d,147a), Mono (193), moro (19a,56c), Moro (100a,103a,117a,159a), moto (104b), Moxo (192), mozo (152b), Muso (192), Muzo (192), myxo

- MP - impi (86a), umph

-- MP bump, camp (163b), damp (101a), dump, gamp (172a), gimp (169d), Gump (43b), hemp (26a,37a,56a,133d), hump (124d), jump, kemp (139b), lamp (92a,94c), limp (58a,81a,177d), lump (45a, 160c), mump (29b,153d), pomp (111d,112d), pump, ramp (65a, 80b,127b,148b), romp (63d), rump, samp (70b,77d,121b), simp (59c,146d), sump (28c,45d,100b), tamp (46b,112b,121d), tump (60a,76d,103d), tymp (20c), vamp (80a,145a)

M -- P mump (29b,153d)

- MR - amra (77c), Omri (18c,86d)

M -- R maar (177a), mahr (103a), meer, mhor (180b), mohr (65d), moor (10a,75b,137b,141d,178b), Moor (102c,d,111d), Muir (8b, 142c), murr (72b,128b)

- MS - Omsk

-- MS alms (29a), arms, Rems

M -- S Maas (132a), Mais (61b), Mans (30a), Mars (68c,118d,119a,129a, 178a), mass (8a,24b,35b,142d), mess (22b,44b,77c,85d,104b,165c, 173d), mews (154c), mias (111a), miss, mons (89c), Mons (184d), Mors (41b), moss (91d,104c,114a,170c), muss (135b,173d)

M -- T Maat (69a,b,85d), malt (17c), mart (49d,97a), Mart (96b,183d), mast (17c,108d,120b,144d,152d), Matt, meat (59b), meet (11d,13d,36a,50a,81d,142d), melt, Ment (54b,164a), milt (153d), mint (13a,33b,58b,76a), mist (46b,59b,174d), mitt (56c), moat (44d), molt (27a,143d), mont (62b), moot (41b,44c), mort (41b,47a, 78b,136d), most, must (70c,101a,106d,157d,182c), mutt (39c, 101d), myst (71c,123b)

MU -- Muav (66a), much, muck, mudd (188), muff, muga, Muir (8b, 142c), mule (45b,148b,153c,180b), mulk (60d), mull (53b,135a, 164c), mump (29b,153d), mund (124d), mung (70d), munj (70d), mura (84d), Mura (192), mure (177d), murk (41a,67d), murr (72b, 128b), Musa (16a), muse (65b,93d,120d,164c), Muse (68d), mush (97d), musk (116b), Muso (192), muss (135b,173d), must (70c,101a, 106d,157d,182c), muta (28d,103a), mute (146c,153b), muth (188), mutt (39c,101d), Muzo (192)

- MU -   **Amun** (86d,127d,159b,164a), **smug, smur** (32c,46b,100c), **smut** (32d,44a,119a,150c)

- - MU   **ammu** (9d), **Atmu** (143a,159b), **limu** (141c), **rimu** (79d, 106d,129a, 168c)

M - - U   **Maku** (192), **Manu** (10a,76d,77a,b), **maru** (84c,144d), **masu** (57a, 84c), **menu** (19a,27a), **Menu, meou, Meru** (77a,103d), **miau** (99b), **mitu** (39d), **Mitu**

M - - V   **Muav** (66a)

M - - W   **meow, miaw** (27b,99b)

M - - X   **Manx** (27b,28a,82d), **minx** (116c)

MY - -   **myna** (19a,c,70b), **Myra** (10a,31b,183c), **myst** (71c,123b), **myth** (8b,91a), **myxa** (168c,169a), **myxo**

- MY -   **amyl** (155c), **emyd** (163c,167c), **Emys** (167c,171b)

- - MY   **army** (78c), **demy** (113d), **domy, elmy, fumy, homy** (38b), **ismy** (45a), **limy** (176d), **rimy** (63d)

M - - Y   **many** (108d), **Mary** (50c,126b,183c), **maty** (80c), **miny, miry, mity, mixy, moly** (76a,181c), **mosy** (67d)

NA - -   **Naab, naam** (44c,150b), **nabk** (30d,164d), **nabo** (117a), **Nabu** (68c, 183a), **nach, nael** (189), **naga** (13d,33a,55b,127c), **Naga** (24c,77a, 88c,176d), **Nagy** (78d), **Naia** (33a), **naid** (63c), **naif** (74b,105d), **naik, nail** (31d,54d,141d,161d,173a), **naio** (107a,168c), **Nair** (45d), **nais** (63c,132a), **Naja** (33a), **Nala** (77a), **Nama** (78c), **name** (8a, 11b,25c,46c,107c,130b,157d,163b,166b), **nana** (118b), **Nana** (15c, 105d,116d,186d), **nane** (139d), **naos** (28a,71c,137a,163a), **Naos** (155b), **napa** (25c,67d,90d), **Napa** (182c), **nape** (15b,108c,d), **napu** (29d,80d), **nard** (13a,97c,102b,110a,153c), **Nare** (93c), **nark** (81a, 156d), **nary** (108b), **nase** (26b,75a,124b), **Nash** (9c), **nasi** (34c,108a, 115a), **Nast** (9c,27a), **nata** (47c), **Nata** (15c), **Nate** (22b), **Nath** (155c), **Nato** (6a,8d), **natr** (189), **Natt** (107b), **naut** (141b), **nave** (30d,31a,78d,114b,180c), **navy** (33c,58b), **naze** (26b,124b), **Nazi**

- NA -   **anai** (163b,181a), **Anak** (67a), **anam** (159a,168c), **Anam, anan** (49a,159a,180c), **Anas** (46c,d), **Anat** (138c,147d), **Anax** (43c, 120c) **anay** (72b,163b,181a), **enam** (70c,77a), **Enam** (85c), **gnar** (72a), **gnat** (59a,81b,99c), **gnaw** (20a,107a,178b), **inar** (65b), **knab** (107a), **knag** (139c), **knap** (76d,107a,139b,159b,166a,170c,185b), **knar** (87c,134b), **Onan** (18c,85c), **snab** (23c,139a), **snag** (11b, 27b,35c,87c,124b,166a), **snap** (23a,36d,38b,48b,54d,56c,58c,149d), **unal** (147a), **unau** (148c,171d)

- - NA   **anna** (190), **Anna** (110c,166d), **arna** (24a,181b), **Bana** (67a), **bena** (176a), **bina** (77a), **bona** (89d), **Bona** (183c), **buna** (161c), **Cana** (57a,64b,100c), **cena** (88d,133a), **Cuna** (193), **Dana** (28a,96a, 171d), **dona** (83d,121c,151d), **dyna** (34c), **Edna** (183c), **Enna** (146a), **etna** (75b,153c,157a,175d,177a,c), **fana, gena** (29b), **Gona** (106d), **guna** (106a,137b), **Iona** (28a,82d), **Jena** (105d,165b), **kana** (84d), **kina** (126d), **kona** (74c), **lana** (58a,66a,90a,184b), **lena** (56d), **Lena** (36b), **lina** (188), **Lina** (183d), **luna** (103c), **Luna** (102b), **mana** (30a,120d,122a,159c), **mina** (10b,70b,71d,179d), **Mina** (23a, 183d), **mona** (72b,101d), **myna** (19a,c,70b), **nana** (118b), **Nana** (15c,105d,116d,186d), **nina** (152a), **Nina** (26c,33d,68d,183d),

370

nona (89b,107b), **Nona** (69a,114a,183c), **orna** (169d,182c), **Pana, pina** (35d,118b), **puna** (10b,33b,104a,119b,182a), **rana** (77a,123c), **Rana** (63d), **rena** (132c), **sana** (56a,166d), **Sana** (185d), **sina** (46c), **Sina** (102d,103d), **tana** (159a), **Tana** (87d), **Tina** (183d), **tuna** (57a, b,123b,170d), **ulna** (21d,39b), **urna** (133a), **vena** (90a,175a), **vina** (77a,105a), **Xina** (183d), **Yana** (192,193), **zona** (144c,186d)

N - - A   **naga** (13d,33a,55b,127c), **Naga** (24c,77a,88c,176c), **Naia** (33a), **Naja** (33a), **Nala** (77a), **Nama** (78c), **nana** (118b), **Nana** (15c,105d, 116d,186d), **napa** (25c,67d,90d), **Napa** (182c), **nata** (47c), **Nata** (15c), **nema** (34d,48c,134b,164d,176c), **Nepa** (106b,178c), **Nera** (165b), **Neva** (91b,132a), **Nina** (26c,33d,68d,183d), **nipa** (14b, 46b,48a,164a,168c), **Nola, nona** (89b,107b), **Nona** (69a,114a,183c), **Nora** (79b,107a,164c,183c), **nota** (15c,89c), **nova** (20c,106d,155c, 174d), **noxa, Nuba** (108c), **Nuda** (39b), **Numa** (133a)

- NB -   **anba** (36d)

N - - B   **Naab, nimb** (31b,73b,92a,107b,131d), **numb**

- NC -   **ance** (158b,c,d), **ancy** (158c), **ence** (158c), **Inca** (14b,30a), **inch, onca** (189), **once** (60b,79b), **unca** (49a), **unci** (31d), **unco** (140c), **Ynca** (193)

- - NC   **banc** (61a,85c), **zinc** (21a)

- ND -   **anda** (23a,168c), **Ande** (193), **Andi** (27d), **Andy** (96b), **endo** (34d, 122d,183b), **inde, onde** (63a,178d), **unde** (179a), **undo** (11a,93d), **undy** (179a)

- - ND   **Arnd** (67a), **band** (72a,157c), **bend** (39d,171b), **bind** (33b,165c), **bond** (92a,101c,141d,143b,159d,165c), **bund** (49c,66c,90c), **cond** (156a), **fend** (114b,178b), **find** (44a), **fond** (7c,94b), **fund** (6d,101c, 130c), **Gond, hand** (60c,114c,115d,184c), **hind** (15b,41d,45a), **kind** (150d,153a,174d), **land** (44a,163c), **lend** (6d,79d), **mand** (28b), **mend** (130b), **mind** (75c,81d,93d,109b), **mund** (124d), **pend, pond, pund** (189), **rand** (16d,22a,131b,145a,b), **Rand** (69c), **rend** (32a, 159c,162c,185a), **rind** (53a,115c), **Rind** (109c,174b), **rynd** (100a), **sand** (71d,146c), **send** (42c,44b,95c,121c,130a,144c,168b), **Sind, tend** (26d,80b,93a,100a), **tind** (86b), **tund** (121d), **vend** (97a,115c, 142b), **Vend** (10b,148a), **wand** (120b,132c,156a), **wend** (67d,123d), **Wend** (10b,148a), **wind** (33b,39d,171c,185a), **yond** (164d), **Zend**

N - - D   **naid** (63c), **nard** (13a,97c,102b,110a,153c), **need** (42b,52d,87b, 122a,178a), **Nejd, NKVD** (135d), **Nudd** (23c)

NE - -   **neaf** (58a,73c), **Neal, neap** (165c,167a,177b), **near** (11d,32c,107b), **neat** (165c,169d), **Nebo** (68c,102d,103d,183a), **neck** (83a), **need** (42b,52d,87b,122a,178a), **neem** (96d,168c,169a), **neep** (140c, 171b), **neer** (14b,86b,108b), **Neil** (96a), **nein** (66c), **Nejd, Nell** (110a, 183d), **nema** (34d,48c,134b,164d,176c), **nemo** (34b), **Nemo** (56a,85c), **nene** (19b,74c), **neon** (65c), **Nepa** (106b,178c), **Nera** (165b), **Neri, Nero** (8a,126d,133a,150b,172c), **ness** (26b,75a,124b), **nest** (38b,74b,130d,149c,160b), **nete** (71c,108b,163d), **neti** (164a), **nett, neue** (66c), **Neva** (91b,132a), **neve** (56d,67c,70c,149b), **news** (165c), **newt** (48d),136c,169d), **next** (106a)

- NE -   **Aner** (18d,96b), **anes** (110c,140a), **anet** (43c), **anew** (7c), **inee** (120b), **Inez** (45c,183c), **knee** (85b), **knew, knez** (123c), **oner** (20d, 53a,75c,162d,173a,d), **ones** (116a), **sned** (93d,125a,140a), **snee**

(40a,43d,87a), **sneg** (139b)

- - NE acne (147c), aine (49b,62c,142c), Anne (50c,84a,143b,183c), a-one (52b,167b), Arne (35c,50c,134d), aune (188), bane (74a,106b,120b, 139a), bene (18a,83c,90a,106d,122a,180a), bine (145b,156a,171c, 176b), bone, cane (17b,128a,156a,159a,177d), Cane, cene (34c), cine (104b,152c), cone (66b,150a,157c), Dane (85d,107d,138a), dene (137a), Dene (192), dine, done, dune (137a), dyne (59d,173b), eine (66c), enne (34c), erne (19c,d,47b,54b,141a), esne (10c, 45b,142c,148a,164d), fane (30d,137a,162d), fine (49b,50a,104b, 115d,159a), gane (185b), gene (54a), Gene (96b), gone (6b,15c,42c, 44c,114d), gyne (34b,55b,183c), hone (110a,143c,180d), lone (24b,88d,94d), jane (190), Jane (183c), June (183c), kane (74c), kine (38a,112c), lane (134b,157b), lene (36b,149a,172b), line (12b, 22b,36d,38a,126c,134b,157b,158b,162d,175c), lone (150a), lune (38c,73b,74d), mane, mine (69c,79d,111b,124c), mene (19a,73d, 108d,185c), nene (19b,74c), nine (26c,104d), none (108b), ohne (66d,183b), orne (169d,182c), Orne (25b), pane (113c,155a,b), pene, pine (36a,52a,88c,93c,168c,d,169a), pone (37a,85b), rine (44d,75d, 135c), rone (127c,164b), rune (9b,67a,94a,95a,105c,107d,120a, 141d,163d), sane (128a), sine (64c,66b,90a,97c,126a,163b,169d, 183b), syne (140b,147a), Tane (120d), tene (34d,131b), tine (11b, 124b,167b), tone (6c,118c,150d), tune (8b,12c,98c), tyne, Tyne (108a), vane (179b,182a), vine (32b), wane (41c,43c), wine, zone (44c,50a,160a)

N - - E name (8a,11b,d,25c,46c,107c,130b,157d,163b), nane (139d), nape (15b,108c,d), Nare (93c), nase (26b,75a,124b), Nate (22b), nave (30d,31a,78d,114b,180c), naze (26b,124b), nene (19b,74c), nete (71c,108b,163d), neue (66c), neve (56d,67c,70c,149b), nice (54d, 119c,130c), Nice (98c), nide (23c,72a,106c,116d), nife (37a), Nike (69c,100c,182d), nile (33c,71d), Nile (106b), nine (26c,104d), Niue (137d), node (35c,85b,87c,94d,120a,124d,160c), nome (71c,163b), Nome, none (108b), Nore (163d), nose (118d,125a,149b), note (98c,109b,124b,128d,130a,177c), nove (83b), noze (75a), nude (16c,172d), Nupe (191)

N - - F naif (74b,105d), neaf (58a,73c)

NG - - ngai (48a,159c), ngan

- NG - ange (61a), ango (171a), inga (145d,170a), Inge (24d,67d,117c 119c)

- - NG bang (75d,105d,148a), beng (43a), bing, bong, bung (119d,156d), cang (184a), dang, ding (130b), dong, fang (167b), Fong (40b), Fung (191), gang (38c), gong, hang (160a), hing (13c), hong (30b), hung, Jung (125a), k'ang (30a), king (26c,29c), kung (125b), ling (24c,57a,b,75b,178c), long (38b), lung (70d), Ming (30b,c), mung (70d), pang (165b), ping, pong, pung (22c,148b), Qung (191), rang, ring (50a), Rong (88c), rung (28c,39a), sang, sing (26d,178a), song (12c,170c), sung, Sung (30b), tang (30b,58b,186b), teng (188), ting (166a), Ting (30c), tong (30a,c), tung (110a,168c), uang (131a), vang (72d,134a,140b), wang (189), wing (10d,58c,59a, 118b,d), wong (56a), yang (30b,70a), zing

N - - G niog (33a,168c), nogg (48d)

- - NH   binh (189), hunh?, sinh (97c), tanh (97c)

N - - H   Nach, Nash (9c), Nath (155c), nigh (106a), Nish (19d), Noah (88a, 99b)

NI - -   Nias (82d), nibs (116c), nice (54d,119c,130c), Nice (98c), nick (30c,108b), nide (23c,72a,106c,116d), nidi (106c), nife (37a), nigh (106a), Nike (69c,100c,182d), nile (33c,71d), Nile (106b), nill (173d), nimb (31b,73b,92a,107b,131d), nina (152a), Nina (26c, 33d,68d,183d), nine (26c,104d), nino (152a), niog (33a,168c), niou (188), nipa (14b,46b,48a,164a,168c), Nish (19d), nisi (90a, 173c), nito (55c), Niue (137d)

- NI -   anil (47c,80d,180b), Anim (18d), anis (55c), Enid (13b,25d,66b, 163a,183c), Enif (155b), enin (20d), inia (9b,109b), Inia (28c,45b), knip (115c), knit (173c,179b), snib (54d,93c), snig (45d), snip (32b,40a), unie (173a), Unio (105c), unis (91b), unit (101c,110c, 147a)

- - NI   Aani (45a,48d), agni (88a,89c), Agni (56d,68b), arni (24a,181b), bani (190), beni (116a,142d), Beni (191), Bini (191), Boni (63b), Coni, doni (21a,28c,168a), Ioni (192), mani (115c), omni (34a), Pani (120c), rani (72d,77b,123c,127c), Reni (83d), yeni (19b,161d), Zuni (125b)

N - - I   nasi (34c,108a,115a), Nazi, Neri, neti (164a), ngai (48a,159c), nidi (106c), nisi (90a,173c), nodi (35c,87c), nori (8c,141c)

- - NJ   Funj, gunj (70c), munj (70d)

NK - -   NKVD (135d)

- NK -   ankh (38d,162b), Enki (15b), Inka (193), inky (20b)

- - NK   bank (18a,58c), bonk (190), bunk, conk (41c,108a,156d,157c), dank (40b,101a), dunk (43c,79d), fink (19a,56c,157c), funk (63d, 113c), gink (48b), hank (147c), honk (70a), hunk, jink, jonk, junk (30a,134c), kink (38b,171c), konk (41c), kunk (188), lank (148b, 164b), link (36a,81d,85b), lonk (143d), mink (176d), monk (28b, 63c,129d), pank (189), pink (26d,33c,60c,138a), punk (9b,166a, 167c), rank (31d,55d,70b,92c,94d,157d), rink (147c,154a), sank, sink (41c,43c,46b,158a), sunk, tank (175a,d), tonk (173c), wink (107a), yank, Yank

N - - K   nabk (30d,164d), naik, nark (81a,156d), neck (83a), nick (30c, 108b), nock (13b,108b), nook (37a,130d), nubk (30d,164d)

- NL -   inly, only (24d,52c,98d,147a,150a)

N - - L   nael (189), nail (31d,54,141d,161d,173a), Neal, Neil (96a), Nell (110a,183d), nill (173d), noel (26d,150b) Noel (30d,96a), noil (87c, 178b), Noll (96b,110b), noyl (87c), null (108c,177a), nurl (33b,87c)

N - - M   naam (44c,105b), Naam, neem (96d,168c,169a), norm (15a,115a, 128a,155a)

- NN -   Anna (110c,166d,183c), anna (190), Anne (50c,84a,143b,183c), Enna (146a), enne (34c), Enns

- - NN   binn (22c), Bonn (17d), bunn (25b), conn (43d,156a), Finn (107d), Jann (102d), jinn (42b,103b,153c), linn (120d,140a,c,168c,178d), mann (189), Mann (9c,48c,185c), rann (175c), senn (76b), sunn (56a), wynn (165d)

N - - N **nein** (66c), **neon** (65c), **ngan, noon, Norn** (69a,163d,174b), **noun** (114b,158a)

NO - - **Noah** (88a,99b), **nobs** (38c,87a), **nock** (13b,108b), **node** (35c,85b, 87c,94d,120a,124d,160c), **nodi** (35c,87c), **noel** (26d,150b), **Noel** (30d,96a), **noes** (177c), **nogg** (48d), **noil** (87c,178b), **noio** (107c, 163c), **noïr** (61b,134b), **noix** (67c), **Nola, Noll** (96b,110b), **nolo** (42a), **nome** (71c,163b), **Nome, nona** (89b,107b), **Nona** (69a,114a, 183c), **none** (108b), **nono** (83b), **nook** (37a,130d), **noon, Nora** (79b, 107a,164c,183c), **Nore** (163d), **nori** (8c,141c), **norm** (15a,115a, 128a,155a), **Norn** (69a,163d,174b), **nose** (118d,125a,149b), **Nosu** (27d), **nosy, nota** (15c,89c), **note** (98c,109b,124b,128d,130a,177c), **Nott** (107b), **noun** (114b,158a), **noup** (124b), **nous** (81d,100a, 128b), **nova** (20c,106d,155c,174d), **nove** (83b), **nowt** (106a,139a), **nowy** (194), **noxa, noyl** (87c), **noze** (75a)

- NO - **anoa** (28a,60a,112c,181c), **anon** (7d,14d,79d,80b,123a,145c,150c, 164a), **enol** (29c,158b), **Enon** (18c,d), **Enos** (7a,18d,52a,70c,96a, 143a), **enow** (50d,123a,158b), **knob** (73c), **knop** (124b,170c,185b), **knor** (87c), **knot** (43c,99d,107c,124d,137d), **know, snob** (159c), **snod** (169d), **snow**

- - NO **Aino** (84a,c), **Arno** (27a), **asno** (151d), **beno** (113b,117a), **cano** (152a), **dino** (34b), **fano** (51d,96b,113c,d), **fono** (137a), **Gano** (132d), **Hano** (125b), **hino** (106d,168c), **Juno** (69c,85d,100c,126b), **Kano** (84c,177d), **keno** (161d,168c), **kino** (27c,34c,47c,72c,98b), **leno** (37c,53b), **lino, mano** (71d,73d,74b,83b), **mino** (84c), **mono** 34c,78d,122d,147a), **Mono** (193), **nino** (152a), **nono** (83b), **pino** (152c), **puno** (182a), **Reno, sano** (152b), **sino** (34a), **Tano** (192), **Tino** (136d), **tuno** (28b,168c), **vino** (92d,182b), **xeno** (34d), **Zeno** (71b)

N - - O **nabo** (117a), **naio** (107a,168c), **Nato** (6a,8d), **Nebo** (68c,102d,103d, 183a), **nemo** (34b), **Nemo** (56a,85c), **Nero** (8a,126d,133a,150b, 172c), **nino** (152a), **nito** (55c), **noio** (107c,163c), **nolo** (42a), **nono** (83b)

N - - P **neap** (165c,167a,177b), **neep** (140c,171b), **noup** (124b)

- - NQ **cinq** (61d)

- NR - **inre** (35d,80a), **inro** (84b,c,106c)

N - - R **Nair** (45d), **natr** (189), **near** (11d,32c,107b), **neer** (14b,86b,108b), **noir** (61b,134b), **nurr** (67d)

- NS - **ansa** (73c,93d,137c), **anse** (61d), **ansu** (11d), **ense** (139b,158c), **enso** 34d,183b)

- - NS **bans, cens** (115b), **dans** (62a), **dens** (90a,167b), **Duns, Enns, fons** (60c), **gens** (42d,132d), **Hans** (66d,96a), **hens** (121d), **lens** (67c, 95b,111a,129b,162d), **Mans** (30a), **mons** (89c), **Mons** (184d), **oons** (100a,186d), **Pons** (13d,63c,110d,150c), **sans** (63a,183b), **Sens** (63b), **sons** (98d,109d), **Vans** (107d)

N - - S **nais** (63c,132a), **naos** (28a,71c,137a,163a), **Naos** (155b), **ness** (26b, 75a,124b), **news** (165c), **Nias** (82d), **nibs** (116c), **nobs** (38c,87a), **noes** (177c), **nous** (81d,100a,128b)

- NT - **anta** (83d,117c,d,121a), **Anta** (164a), **ante** (87a,89a,115b,120b, 122b,125d,154d), **anti** (7d,111a,122b), **Anti** (193), **ente** (70b,151d),

ento (34b,d,183b), **Inti** (159b), **into** (123a,183b), **onto** (76a,174a), **unto** (166c), **untz** (189)

- - NT **aint, arn't, aunt** (129c), **bant** (43c), **bent** (80b), **bunt** (15d,180c), **cant** (28d,81b,84d,90c,109b,136c,165d,166a), **cent** (36d), **dent** (42c,77d), **dint** (48c,59d,122a), **dont, dunt, font** (16b,171d,172a), **gent, hant** (67a), **hint** (9a,39c,159a), **hunt** (141c), **kant** (28d), **Kant** (67a), **Kent** (90d), **lant, lent** (54d), **Lent** (115d,141c), **lint** (46a,58d), **Ment** (54b,164a), **mint** (13a,33b,58b,76a), **mont** (62b), **oont** (25d), **pant, pent** (36a), **pint** (67b), **pont** (55d,61b), **punt** (21a,58b), **rant** (41c,127b,128a,161d), **rent** (58a,77c,91b,138b, 153d,162c,167c), **runt** (47a,172d), **sent, tent** (26b,115a), **tint** (33c, d,114d), **vent** (8b,11b,110d,112a), **vint** (26c,182c), **want** (41b, (38b,74b,106b,122a), **went** (42c), **wont** (6d,40a,73a,174c)

N - - T **Nast** (9c,27a), **Natt** (107b), **naut** (141b), **neat** (165c,169d), **nest** (38b,74b,130d,149c,160b), **nett, newt** (48d,136c,169d), **next** (106a), **Nott** (107b), **nowt** (106a,139a), **nuit** (62b)

NU - - **Nuba** (108c), **nubk** (30d,164d), **nuda** (39b), **Nudd** (23c), **nude** (16c, 172d), **nuit** (62b), **null** (108c,177a), **Numa** (133a), **numb, Nupe** (191), **nurl** (33b,87c), **nurr** (67d)

- NU - **Cnut** (40d,50c), **knub** (178b), **knur** (67d,87c,107c), **knut, Knut** (40d,50c,96a), **onus** (24c,93b,109b), **snub** (128c,148b), **snug** (35a, 38b,165c), **Snug** (99d), **snup** (149b)

- - NU **Ainu** (84a,c), **benu** (49a), **Danu** (28a), **genu** (6b,18a,87a,89c), **Manu** (10a,76d,77a,b), **menu** (19a,27a), **Menu, tunu** (28b), **zenu** (143d)

N - - U **Nabu** (68c,183a), **napu** (29d,80d), **niou** (188), **Nosu** (27d)
- NV - **envy** (41b)
- - NX **jinx** (78a), **jynx** (78a), **Jynx** (184a), **lanx** (133a,b), **lynx** (26c,181d), **Lynx** (36b), **Manx** (27b,28a,82d), **minx** (116c), **Yunx** (184a)
N - - X **noix** (67c)
- NY - **Enyo** (12c,69c,178a), **onym** (162c), **onyx** (25d,28d,65d,142b), **Pnyx** (71c)

- - NY **bony** (147c), **Bony** (96b), **cony** (127a), **deny** (36d,43d,129b), **liny** (157b), **luny** (38b), **many** (108d), **miny, piny, pony, puny** (55b, 179a), **tiny** (100c,148c), **tony, Tony** (96b), **tuny, viny, wany, winy** (176c), **zany** (24a,32d,59c)

N - - Y **Nagy** (78d), **nary** (108b), **navy** (33c,58b), **nosy, nowy** (194)
- NZ - **anzu** (11d), **Enzu** (102b), **onza** (189), **unze** (189)
- - NZ **Linz** (40d)

OA - - **Oahu, oaks** (154d), **oaky, oary, oast** (15d,86b,112a), **oath** (119c, 150a)

- OA - **boar** (77c,117c,160c,181c), **boat** (27b,106a), **Boaz** (135d), **coag** (45d,118a,163b), **coak** (45d,118a,163b), **coal** (49c,64a), **Coan** (37b), **coat** (160a), **coax** (180c), **doab** (157c). **doat** (17a,94b,112a,165d), **Eoan** (41a,85b), **foal** (78c), **foam** (63d,154b), **goad** (80b,154b), **goaf** (104b), **goai** (106d,168c), **goal** (8b,109b,120b,125d), **Goan, goat** (135a), **hoar** (63d,71a,181a), **hoax** (41c,122a), **Joab** (41a), **Joad** (50c), **Joan** (183c), **joar** (100a), **koae** (74b), **load** (24c,26d,161b), **loaf** (79b,94b), **loam** (47d,150a), **loan, Moab** (18d,85a,86d,94a), moan, moat (44d), Noah (88a,99b), road (37d,164d), roam (178a), roan (78b,c,114c,128d,144a,181a), roar (145c), soak (46c,137c), soap, soar (59a), toad (10a,17a,63d,126d), woad (20d,47c), Zoar, Zoas (20b)

- - OA anoa (28a,60a,112c,181c), Aroa (175b), Gjoa (144d), pooa (76a, 125b), proa (21b,26a,95c,d), Shoa (6c) stoa (33c,121a,c), tooa (17c), whoa (156d)

O - - A obia (55d), obra (152d,184c), ocha (189), ocra (72c,175a), octa (122c), odea (105d,164a), Offa (163d), ohia (74c,168c), okia (190), okra (72c,175a), olea (170b), Olea (110b), Olga (135c,183c), olla (36d,44b,84d,113b,121d,151d,152c,181b), onca (189), onza (189), orca (86b), orna (169d,182c), orra (139c,d,140a), ossa (21d), Ossa (103d,110b,164b), Otea (71a,82d), otra (152c), oxea (153d)

OB - - oban (190), Obed (135d), obex (22d), obey (35c,75c), obia (55d), obit (41b,64c), oboe (74b,104d,105a,182a,184a), obol (29b,110a), obra (152d,184c)

- OB - boba (29d), bobo (112c,168c), Cobb (9c), Cobh (37a), dobe (159b, c,172b), doby (159b,c), gobi, Gobi (42d), gobo (84d), goby (57d), hobb (124b), hobo (168a,174b), jobo (77c), Koba (11a), Kobe (78a), kobi (84b), kobu (84b), lobb (23b,94c,163a), lobe (90c, 134b), lobo (165d,183c), nobs (38c,87a), robe (65b), Sobk (38d), Toba (80c), tobe (7d,137b), toby (8c,85c,104b), Toby (96b,125c), Yobi, zobo (186b)

- - OB blob, boob (146d), brob (153c), chob (23c), doob (18b), jaob, knob (73c,107c,124d), rhob (64a,85c), scob (42a), slob (173d), snob (159c), swob (102b), thob (128a)

OC - - ocha (189), ocra (72c,175a), octa (122c), octo (34a,89b,122c)

- OC - boca (152b,c), boce (23b,52a,57b), bock (17c,90d,144a), coca (29d, 33a,105d,113a), cock (19a,29a,55a,133d,136d,161d,174b), coco, dock (40a,117c,144d,179d), Foch (63b), foci (28b), hoch (52c, 66c), hock (91a,115b,182b,c), jock, Jock (96b), jocu (45b,57a), Koch (66d), loch (88a,139d), loci (66b,118c), lock (54d), loco (38b, 119b,120b), mock (131b,162b), nock (13b,108b), poco (83b,93a), Roch (136c), rock (160b), sock (157c,182a), soco (22d), tock (7d, 19b), toco (19b,167c), voce (83c,177a)

- - OC bloc (173a), croc (13a,74a), floc (149a)

O - - C odic (79c,120a), olic (158b), otic (14c,d,47b)

OD - - odah (170d), odal (48a,88b,112c), Odax (132c), odds (28d,172d), Odea (105a,164a), odel (48a,112c), Oder (132a), odic (79c,120a), Odin (7c,29d,63c,68c,175d,183b), odio (83b), odor (138b,156a), odum (168c,180a), odyl (59d,79c)

- OD - Bodb (82b), bode (14c,60a,110b,121b), Bodo (88c), body (72a), coda (32c,35d,56c), code (21c,31a,40c,161c), codo (188), dodd (139c,140c), Dode (96b), dodo (19b), Jodo (113d), lode (42c,99a,111b,175b), Lodi (105d), Lodz, mode (54d,96b,157d, 179a), node (35c,85b,87c,94d,120a,124d,160c), nodi (35c,87c), Roda (107b), rodd (38d), rode (46c), rodi (98c), soda (19a,149d, 181a), Toda (45d,76d), tode (80a,148a), todo (22b,24d,35b,64c, 156b), tody (19b,d,59a,166a), yodh (91d)

- - OD alod (51c,55d,88a,124c), apod (59d), Arod (86c), biod (59d,79c),

376

clod (22a,45b,157d), **elod** (49b,59d,79c), **feod** (55d), **food** (109a, 176b), **good, hood** (38a,74d), **lood** (189), **mood** (44c), **plod** (170b, 177d), **pood** (189), **prod** (67d,80b,106b,120b), **quod** (123d), **rood** (38d,39a,88b), **shod, snod** (169d), **stod** (40d,67d), **trod, wood**

O - - D   **obed** (135d), **olid** (55d,60c,148d,157d), **ooid** (48d), **oord** (190), **orad** (104a), **Ovid** (132d,133b), **oxid** (112c)

OE - -   **oese** (15d,119c)

- OE -   **Boer** (151a), **coed, coel** (39b), **Doeg** (137c), **doer** (8a,116b), **does, goel** (15a,75c), **goer, hoek** (39d), **hoen** (189), **hoer, hoey** (114c), **Joel** (96a), **joey** (86a,185d), **Joey** (96b,109c), **koel** (19a,b,39b), **Moed** (100c), **noel** (26d,150b), **Noel** (30d,96a), **noes** (177c), **poem** (51a), **poet** (49b), **roed, roer** (72d), **roey** (103d), **toed, voet** (188)

- - OE   **aloe** (7d,20a,76a,b,92b,98b,119b,158b,167a,183d), **Cloe** (183c), **eboe** (28b,110a,168c,169b), **evoe** (15b,130d,181c), **floe** (79b), **froe** (32a,167a,179d), **oboe** (74b,104d,105a,182a,184a), **Otoe** (147b), **shoe** (166a), **sloe** (14a,20b,64a,119d,181c)

O - - E   **oboe** (74b,104d,105a,182a,184a), **oese** (15d,119c), **ogee** (40c,101a, b,120b), **ogle** (9d,53c,91a,93d,148c), **ogre** (67a,102a), **ohne** (66d, 183b), **Oime** (8b), **Oise, Okie** (99d), **olpe** (90d,182c), **once** (60b, 79b), **onde** (63a,178d), **ooze** (53c,104b,116a), **orfe** (57a,b,185c), **orle** (17b,56b,76a,144b,177a), **orne** (169d,182c), **Orne** (25b), **oste** (21d,83b), **Otoe** (147b), **Ouse** (132a,185d), **owse**

OF - -   **Offa** (163d), **offs** (38c)

- OF -   **doff** (130a,161b), **goff** (32d), **koff** (47a), **loft** (14c,69d,104b, 178b), **moff** (53b,146c), **sofa** (44d), **soft** (48b,95d,99d,163a), **toff** (40d)

- - OF   **Azof** (20b,135d), **goof, hoof** (173a), **loof** (144c,153d), **poof, roof** (78d), **stof** (135c), **woof** (39a,163d,165a,179d)

O - -F   **Olaf** (108a,176b)

OG - -   **ogam** (82b,c), **ogee** (40c,101a,b,120b), **ogle** (9d,53c,91a,93d,148c), **Ogor** (170d), **Ogpu** (135d), **ogre** (67a,102a), **ogum** (82b)

- OG -   **boga** (57d,180b), **bogo** (117a,168c), **Bogo** (191), **bogy** (153a), **doge** (95b,175b), **dogy** (46d,103c), **fogy, goga** (24a), **gogo** (16b,24a, 149c), **Gogo** (191), **hoga** (144b), **hogg** (144a), **jogi** (76d), **loge** (164a), **logy** (46d), **mogo** (74b), **nogg** (48d), **Pogo** (121c), **pogy** (57a,88a,98d,103c), **soga** (70d,152b), **Soga** (191), **toga** (132d,133a, b), **togs** (32c), **togt** (77c), **Vogt, yoga** (10b,13c,77a), **yogh** (10c, 185a), **yogi** (76d), **zogo** (136a)

- - OG   **agog** (47b,52c,86b), **ajog, clog** (30c,145b), **flog** (180d), **frog** (10a, 17a,126d), **grog** (92d,153d), **ilog** (132a, 161b), **niog** (33a,168c), **slog** (157c,170b,177d), **stog** (155a), **voog** (28a,66a,132b)

OH - -   **ohia** (74c,168c), **Ohio, ohne** (66d,183b), **ohoy** (106a)

- OH -   **boho** (117a,179d), **Bohr** (14b,40d,138c), **coho** (136d), **fohn** (182b), **Hohe** (192), **John** (11c,96a,121a,186b), **kohl** (53c), **moha** (42b,83d), **moho** (19a,78a), **mohr** (65d), **poha** (74c), **rohr** (72d), **soho!, Soho** (93c), **toho** (79a)

- - OH   **booh** (52c), **pooh** (22b,107d)

O - - H   **oath** (119c,150a), **odah** (170d), **okeh** (8d,37b), **opah** (23b,57a,b, 86d), **ouch!, ough**

Ol - -   oily (110b,172c), oime (8b), Oise

- Ol -   Boil (191), boil, bois (62b,63a,183d), coif (73a), coil (39d,171c, 185a), coin (19b,37a,100c,101c,179d), coir (33a,37a,56a,133d), Coix (70d,85b), doit (47a,169d,180d), Eoin (85b), foil (15d,55c, 165b), join (36a,173c), koir (33a), loin (40a,98a), loir (45c), Loir, Lois (165d,183c), moil (46c,184c), moio (188), noil (87c,178b), noio (107c,163c), noir (61b,134b), noix (67c), ooid (48d), roil (44c, 104b,156b,170d,176a), Soia, soie (62c), soil (154d,159a,163c), soir (61c), toil (46c,184c), void (11a,49d,108d,174b), zoid

- - Ol   amoi (62a), Ekoi (191)

O - - I   Omei (24a), omni (34a), Omri (18c,86d)

- OJ -   bojo (117a), coja (103b,166b), hoja (166b), hoju (84b), koji (185b), mojo (177c), rojo (129a,152c), soja (151b)

OK - -   okay (8d), okeh (8d,37b), oket (189), okia (190), Okie (99d), okra (72c,175a), okro (72c,175a)

- OK -   boko (52b), coke (32d,64a), coky, Doko (191), joke (183a), joky, koko (106d,114b), Koko (93d,186c), koku (189), loka (173c,184c), Loke (15d,68b), Loki (7c,15d,68b), moke (45c,157d), moki (127b), Moki, moko (96c), poke (108c), poku (11a), poky (148c), roka (95a,168c,d), roke (174d,175b), soka (20c), soke (44c,85d), toko (30c), woke, yoke (85b,92d,173c)

- - OK   amok (18b,63c), asok (13d), book, cook (137b), dook (184a), hook (27b,39d), irok (55b), look (11c,53c,142a), nook (37a,130d), pook (68a), rook (19b,29c,39a), sook (22a,25c,97a), took

O - - K   Omsk

OL - -   Olaf (108a,176b), olam (51a,d,75c,81a), Olan (115c), Olax (52b), olay (113b), Olea (110b,170b), oleo (34c), Olga (135c,183c), olie (158b), olid (55d,60c,148d,157d), olio (44b,77c,98c,100d,121d), olla (36d,44b,84d,113b,121d,151d,152c,181b), Olor (160a,b), olpe (90d,182c)

- OL -   bola (16a), bold (41a), bole (31d,32a,169b), boll (119b,d), bolo (87a,179b), bolt (13b,54d,58b,132d,160a), cola (25b,108d,149d, 168c), cold (65d), cole (25a), Cole, coli, colp (28a,148b), colt (78c, 131a,185d,186b), Colt, coly (104a), dola (189), dole (44c,118c, 121c,129d), Dole (74c), doli, doll (125c), dolt (20c,59c,157d), fold folk (116a,169c), gola (27b,40c,70c,157a), gold, golf (154a), goll (105c), Goll, Golo (191), hola (74c,152b), hold (95c,124c,130d), hole (6c,11b,110d,118c,147a), Holi (77a), holm (77d,82d,109a), holt (36d,119b,184b), holy, lola, lole (52a,76b,123c), jole (29b), joli (62b), jolt (143b), kola (25b,84a,108d,168c), Kola (135b,c,d), Koli (27b), kolo (59b,135c), Lola (27d,97b), loll (94b,128c), Lolo (27d,30a), Mola (159c), mold (54d,143c), mole (19d,23a,24d,85a, 117c,155c), Mole (88c), moll, Moll (183d), molt (27a,143d), moly (76a,181c), Nola, Noll (96b,110b), nolo (42a), Pola, pole (132c,143b,177b,184a), Pole (52a), polk (37c), poll (74d,160a, 177c), polo (154a), Polo (175b), poly (34c,76b), role (114b), roll (134a,160b), sola (9a,48a,74b,118c,154a,167b), sold, sole (52c, 57a,b,58b,d,110c,115d,150a), soli (12c,110c), solo (12c,89a,110c), tola (48a,80d), Tola (85b,180a), told (129c), tole (9a,51a,99b,163a), toll (131c), tolt, tolu (16a), vola (89d,150a), vole (97d,104a,148a,

378

149b), **volk** (66c,105d,116a,184c), **Volk, volt** (49b,78c,173b), **wold** (47c,60a,118d,174a,184a), **wolf, yolk, Zola** (63a)

- - OL **bool** (39d), **chol** (118d), **Chol** (192), **cool** (25c,107d), **egol** (11b), **enol** (29c,158b), **fool** (24a,41c,47a,146d), **gaol** (123d), **Gaol** (164a), **idol** (48c,54c,55a,75b,79d,112d,130b,184d), **itol** (158b), **obol** (29b, 110a), **pool** (65a,119d,120d), **siol** (82c), **tool** (27c), **viol** (105a), **wool** (58b,179c)

O - - L **obol** (29b,110a), **odal** (48a,88b,112c), **odel** (48a,112c), **odyl** (59d, 79c), **opal** (20a,65d,67b,82c), **oral** (114a,153d,174c,175c), **Orel, oval** (48d,49c), **oxyl** (112c)

OM - - **Oman** (159a), **omao** (165b), **omar** (103b), **Omar** (48c,51b,116c, 163b), **Omei** (24a), **omen** (14c,59d,60a,121c,123a,146b), **omer** (51a,75c), **omit** (49c,52c,106b,114c,147d), **omni** (34a), **Omri** (18c, 86d), **Omsk**

- OM - **boma** (7d), **bomb** (144a), **coma** (91c,157d,170c,172b), **comb** (38c), **come, Como, dome** (39c,133c,155d), **Domn** (135a), **domy, Goma** (191), **home, homo** (122d), **homy** (38b), **Kome** (71d), **Komi** (191), **loma** (58b,63d), **Lome, nome** (71c,163b), **Nome, pome** (11d), **Pomo** (192), **pomp** (111d,112d), **Roma** (83c,d), **Rome** (31c,51d), **romi** (72d), **romp** (63d), **soma** (10c,21c,34a,48a,81d,136b), **some** (114b, 121c,126a), **Toma** (191), **tomb, tome** (21d,177c)

- - OM **Ahom** (88c), **asom** (18d), **atom** (101c,114c,180d), **boom** (152d), **coom** (32d,150c,178d), **Crom, doom** (42d,55a,134d), **Edom** (18c, 51b,79b,82c,84a), **from, glom** (155d,160d,178c), **joom** (39c), **klom** (189), **loom** (11c,146b,179b), **room** (28d), **stom** (34c), **toom** (139b), **whom** (42b), **zoom**

O - - M **odum** (168c,180a), **ogam** (82b,c), **ogum** (82b), **olam** (51a,d,75c, 81a), **onym** (162c), **ovum** (48d)

ON - - **Onan** (18c,85c), **onca** (189), **once** (60b,79b), **onde** (63a,178d), **oner** (20d,53a,75c,162d,173a,d), **ones** (116a), **only** (24d,52c,98d, 147a,150a), **onto** (76a,174a), **onus** (24c,93b,109b), **onym** (162c), **onyx** (25d,28d,65d,142b), **onza** (189)

- ON - **a-one** (52b,167b), **bona** (89d), **Bona** (183c), **bond** (92a,101c,141d, 143b,159d,165c), **bone, bong, Boni** (63b), **bonk** (190), **Bonn** (17d), **bony** (147c), **Bony** (96b), **cond** (156a), **cone** (66b,150a,157c), **Coni, conk** (41c,108a,156d,157c), **conn** (43d,156a), **cony** (127a), **dona** (83c,121c,151d), **done, dong, doni** (21a,28c,168a), **don't, fond** (7c,94b), **Fong** (40b), **fono** (137a), **fons** (60c), **font** (16b,171d,172a), **Gona** (106d), **Gond, gone** (6b,15c,42c,44c,114d), **gong, hone** (110a, 143c,180d), **hong** (30b), **honk** (70a), **Iona** (28a,82d), **Ione** (24b, 88d,94d), **Ioni** (192), **jonk, kona** (74c), **konk** (41c), **lone** (150a), **long** (38b,185b), **lonk** (143d), **mona** (72b,101d), **monk** (28b,63c, 129d), **mono** (34c,78d,122d,147a), **Mono** (193), **mons** (89c), **Mons** (184d), **mont** (62b), **nona** (89b,107b), **Nona** (69a,183c), **none** (108b), **nono** (83b), **oons** (100a,186d), **oont** (25d), **pond, pone** (37a,85b), **pong, Pons** (13d,63c,110d,150c), **pont** (55d,61b), **pony, rone** (127c,164b), **Rong** (88c), **song** (12c,170c), **sons** (98d,109d), **tone** (6c,118c), **tong** (30a,c), **tonk** (173c), **tony, Tony** (96b), **wong** (56a), **wont** (6d,40a,73a), **yond** (164d), **zona** (144c,186d), **zone** (44c,50a,160a)

379

--ON acon (62c,140d), agon (12c,36c,41b,55d,71b), Amon (86d,96b,
127d,159b,164a), anon (7d,14d,79d,80b,123a,145c,150c,164a),
aton (150a,159b), Avon (143b), axon (106c,153c), azon (127b),
bion (117b), boon (18b,20c,55a), cion (42d,70b,145b,148b,154b,
156a), coon (121c), Dion (96a,152a), doon (140b,168c), ebon (20b),
Elon (18c,51b,108a), Enon (18c,d), Eton (33b,50c,84a), faon (33c,
55a), Gaon (85b), goon (157c,163c), hoon (190), icon (79d,92b,
136a), ikon (79d,136a), iron (55c,d,69d,81a,97b,143b,149a,173d,
179c), Leon (96a), lion (55b,86c), loon (19a,b,c,157d,179c), moon
(40b,132c,137c), neon (65c), paon (115b), peon (28c,59c,99c),
phon (94a), pion (43c,52b), poon (97c), roon (41a,168b), scon
(162c), sion (125c,158c), Sion (75b,c,83a,157d), soon (123a), tion
(158b), toon (80c,95b,168c), tron (180a), upon (6b), woon (24c),
Zion (75b,c,83a,157d) zoon (43a)

O--N oban (190), Odin (7c,29d,63c,68c,175d,183b), Olan (115c), Oman
(159a), omen (14c,59d,60a,121c,123a,146b), onan (18c), Onan
(85c), open (26a,60d,81a,109b,112c,125b,172b,173c), Oran, oven
(15d,78c,86b), Owen (96a,183c), oxan (65c), oxen (10c)

OO-- ooid (48d), oons (100a,186d), oont (25d), oord (190), ooze (53c,
104b,116a), oozy (148b)

-OO- boob (146d), booh (52c), book, bool (39d), boom (152d), boon
(18b,20c,55a), boor (47a,135d,172c), boot (128d), cook (137b),
cool (25c,107d), coom (32d,150c,178d), coon (121c), coop, Coos
(192), coot (19b,46d,72b,138d,141a,146d,157d), doob (18b), dook
(184a), doom (42d,55a,134d), doon (140b,168c), door (51a,121b),
food (109a,176b), fool (24a,41c,47a,146d), foot (115a), good, goof,
goon (157c,163c), Goop (107d), goor, hood (38a,74d), hoof (173a),
hook (27b,39d), hoon (190), hoop (181b), hoot (112c), joom (39c),
koop (16c), lood (189), loof (144c,153d), look (11c,53c,142a), loom
(11c,146b,179b), loon (19a,b,c,157d,179c), loop (31b,107d),
Loos, loot (22a,118a,119d,153d), mood (44c), moon (40b,132c,
137c), moor (10a,75b,137b,141d,178b), Moor (102c,d,111d), moot
(41b,44c), nook (37a,130d), noon, pooa (76a,125b), pood (189),
poof, pooh (22b,107d), pook (68a), pool (65a,119d,120d), poon
(97c), poop (41c), poor (33a), poot!, rood (38d,39a,88b), roof
(78d), rook (19b,29c,39a), room (28d), roon (41a,168b), root
(53a), Roos (67a), sook (22a,25c,97a), soon (123a,145c), soot (20b,
26c,88a), tooa (17c), took, tool (27c), toom (139b), toon (80c,
95b,168c), toot, voog (28a,66a,132b), wood, woof (39a,163d,
165a,179d), wool (58b,179c), woon (24c), yoop, zoon (43a)

--OO aboo (17a), aroo (80c,82b), broo (139a), ejoo (55b,168c), Kroo
(191), phoo, shoo (46b,67a,138b), sloo (160a), whoo

O--O octo (34a,89b,122c), odio (83b), Ohio, okro (72c,175a), oleo (34c),
olio (44b,77c,98c,100d,121d), omao (165b), onto (76a,174a), ordo
(22a,30d,122a,171a), orlo (56b,119c), Oslo (133a), otho (133a), otro
(151d), otto (58d,116b,134a), Otto (14c,66d,67a,96a)

OP-- opah (23b,57a,b,86d), opal (20a,65d,67b,82b), open (26a,60d,
81a,109b,112c,125b,172b,173c), Opie (50c), opus (35c,105a,184c)

-OP- copa (88b,113c), cope (12b,26b,36c,65b,157d,176a), Copt (48d), copy, dopa (117d), dope (46c,105d), dopp (43c), hope (13d,52d), hopi (33c), Hopi (12c,102c,125b), hops (17c), koph (91d), kopi (107a,168c), Kopi (172a), lope (48b,64b,d), mope (92d,159a), pope (20a,30d,31c,120d), qoph (91d), rope (36d,88d,128b), ropy (157c, 176d), soph, Sopt (45b), tope (24a,46b,57a,143c,151a), toph (75c), topi (37a,75a,118c), tops (159c)

- - OP alop (13d,46b,93d), asop (180b), atop (112a,174a), chop (98a), clop, coop, crop (38b), drop (43d,54b,100b,114c,168b), Esop (53b,54a), flop (54a), Goop (107d), hoop (181b), klop (150d), knop (124b,170c,185b), koop (16c), loop (31b,107d), plop (54b), poop (41c), prop (159d), scop (120a), shop, slop, stop (73b,111b), swop (168a), trop (62d,167a), yoop

- - OQ shoq (169a)

OR - - orad (104a), oral (114a,153d,174c,175c), Oran, oras (40d), orca (86b), ordo (22a,30d,122a,171a), ordu (170d), Orel, orfe (57a,b, 185c), orgy (26d,130d,137c), orle (17b,56b,76a,144b,177a), orlo (56b,119c), Orly (8b), orna (169d,182c), orne (169d,182c), Orne (25b), orra (139c,d,140a), orts (60d), oryx (11a)

- OR - bora (181d,182b), bord (100b), bore (14c,25b,46a,116a,165c, 179b), borg (40d), Bori (110d,150c), born, boro (154b), Boro (193), Bors (70b,134b), bort (43b), Bort (134b), cora (65d), Cora (42b, 69c,80c,116b,124d,172b,183c), cord (39b,131a), core (28b,51c, 75b,81b), cork (119d), Cori (138c), corm (24b,38d,156a), corn (39d,95c,123a), dora (70b), Dora (36d,41a,43b,183c,d), dord (42c), dore (61d,67b,69d,117d), Dore (50d,63a,b), dorm, dorn (164d), dorp (73c,176b), dorr (32b), dory (21b,58b,144c), fora (133a), ford (177b), fore (63d,174b), fork, form (54d,143c), fort (63d,157d), gora (81c), gore (115d,117c,154c,169c), gory, hora (22a,40b), horn (11a,105a,170b,182a), hors (62b), kora (178c), Kora, kore (107b), Kore (29a,42b,116b,124d), kori (7d,77a), lora (146b,149b,151c,169b), Lora (183c), lord (107c), lore (77c,87c, 90d,151c,183a), lori (91b), lorn (42d,60b), loro (19a,114b), lory (19a,114a), mora (42b,65a,72b,83d,99b,153a,161a), more (71a), More (50b), morg (188), morn, moro (19a,56c), Moro (100a,103a, 117a,159a), Mors (41b), mort (41b,47a,78b,136d), Nora (79b, 107a,164c,183c), Nore (163d), nori (8c,141c), norm (15a,115a, 128a,155a), Norn (69a,163d,174b), oord (190), pore (59d,110d, 111c,120d,157d), pork, Poro (141d), port (73d,136b,140c,170c,d, 182b,c), Rori (16b), sora (19b,c,127b), sorb (11d,103d,134b,142d), Sorb (148a,180a), sore (23d,142c), sori (55c,64a), sorn (139a,d), sors (44d,89b), sort (31d,39c,70b,86b,153a), sory (176d), tora (11a,44d,74a,75c,85c,90b,102d,115d), tore, tori (101b), torn (130a), toro (38a,107a,152a,168c), torp (54c), tort (31c,91a,185c), Tory (23c,36b,94c,172a), word (124b,165c), wore, work (64c,76b), worm, worn (143b), wort (76a,95d,121d), yore (10b,69d,93c,110b, 165d), york (38c), York (50b,c)

- - OR acor (6d), ador (153b), amor (152b), Amor (39c,68b), asor (75c, 105a), boor (47a,135d,172c), chor (164b), door (51a,121b), Ghor (174b), goor, Igor (135d), knor (87c), mhor (180b), moor (10a, 75b,137b,141d,178b), Moor (102c,d,111d), odor (138b,156a), Ogor (170b), Olor (160a,b), poor (33a), shor (136d), Shor (162b), Thor

(7c,68c,99c,100c,109c,165b), **utor** (90a,166c)

O - - R   **Oder** (132a), **odor** (138b,156a), **Ogor** (170d), **Olor** (160a,b), **omar** (103b), **Omar** (48c,51b,116c), **omer** (51a,75c), **oner** (20d,53a,75c, 162d,173a,d), **osar** (51b,67b,131b), **oser** (61b), **over** (6b,38c,80a, 114d), **oxer** (55c), **oyer** (38a,75b,119c)

OS - -   **osar** (51b,67b,131b), **oser** (61b), **Oslo, ossa** (21d) **Ossa** (103d,110b, 164b), **oste** (21d,83b)

- OS -   **bosa** (12a), **Bosa, Bosc** (115c), **bose** (163c), **bosh, bosk** (164b), **boss** (49d,157d), **cosh** (35a,97c), **cose** (29b), **coso** (152c), **coss** (98a), **cost** (29a), **cosy** (149c), **dosa** (74b), **dose** (123a), **doss** (17c), **dost, foss** (44d,100d), **gosh, hose** (156c), **host** (13a,51d,104c), **Jose** (96a), **josh** (85b), **joss** (30b), **Josy** (183d), **koso** (6c,80d), **Koso** (192,193), **koss** (188), **lose** (60a,100c), **losh** (178b), **loss** (42c,123d, 178b), **lost, Mose** (96b), **mosk** (97b,103b), **moss** (91d,104c,114a, 170c), **most, mosy** (67d), **nose** (118d,125a,149b), **Nosu** (27d), **nosy, pose** (14c,15d), **posh** (49b,148c), **post** (89a,95c,155d), **Rosa** (58d, 134a,145d,183c), **rose** (33c), **Rose** (6a,50c,183c), **ross** (16c,161d), **Ross** (50c), **rosy** (21a,111a), **sosh** (81d), **soso** (99c,114c,166d), **tosh** (106a), **Tosk** (8c), **toss** (24a,132d, **Xosa** (86a)

- - OS   **Amos** (96a,144b), **bios** (92a), **Coos** (192), **Enos** (7a,18d,52a,70c, 96a,143a), **epos** (51a,76b,120a), **Eros** (11c,39c,68b,97c,182d), **ghos** (30b), **gros** (47a,53d,146c), **Gros** (63a), **Laos** (80d,129c), **Loos, naos** (28a,71c,137a,163a), **Naos** (155b), **phos, Taos** (192), **Teos** (82a), **Thos** (84a,181c)

O - - S   **oaks** (154d), **odds** (28d,172d), **offs** (38c), **ones** (116a), **onus** (24c, 93b,109b), **oons** (100a,186d), **opus** (35c,105a,184c), **oras** (40d), **orts** (60d), **Otis** (9c,d,24d,82a,111a), **Otus** (67a), **ours** (124c), **Ovis** (143d), **oyes** (38a,39b,75b)

OT - -   **Otea** (71a,82d), **Otho** (133a), **otic** (14c,d,47b), **Otis** (9c,d,24d,82a, 111a), **Otoe** (147b), **otra** (152c), **otro** (151d), **otto** (58d,116b,134a), **Otto** (14c,66d,67a,96a), **Otus** (67a)

- OT -   **bota** (189), **both, Boto** (192), **bott** (32a,88d), **cota** (117a), **cote** (19b,143d,144a,b), **coto** (16c,90b), **Coty** (63c), **dote** (17a,90b,94b, 97a,112a,139d,165d), **doth, Doto** (141b), **doty** (43d), **Goth** (16c, 163d), **Hoth** (20c), **hoti, iota** (71a,85c,91c,114c,166c,176a,180d), **jota** (151c), **joti, kota** (117a), **Kota** (45d), **koto** (84b), **Iota** (24c, 121d,178d), **loth** (15a,173d), **lote** (24c,94a), **Loti** (63a,176a), **loto** (65a,121d,178d), **lots, mota** (103a), **mote** (114c,153a), **moth, Moth** (112d), **moto** (104b), **nota** (15c,89c), **note** (98c,109b,124b, 128d,130a,177c), **Nott** (107b), **pott** (113d), **rota** (27c,30d,38a,79a, 92d,133a,134a,b,180c), **rote** (130b,134b,143a,159d), **roti** (62c), **roti** (103b,111c), **roto** (30a,122d,127b,152c,171b), **sote** (150c), **tota** (71d), **tote** (27a,73c), **toto** (8d,15a,34d,89a,181a), **toty** (87b), **vota** (133b), **vote** (60b), **Vote** (56d), **Voth** (191), **Voto** (192), **Wote** (191)

- - OT   **Abot** (100c), **blot, boot** (128d), **clot** (32d,94d), **coot** (19b,46d,72b, 138d,141a,146d,157d), **eyot** (82d), **Fiot** (191), **flot** (173a), **foot** (115a), **frot** (28c), **grot** (27d), **hoot** (112c), **ilot** (82d), **khot, knot** (43c,99d,107c,124d,137b), **loot** (22a,118a,119d,136a,153d), **moot** (41b,44c), **phot** (173b), **piot** (95b), **plot** (25a,36b,118d,138b), **poot!, riot** (44c,111d,170c,173d), **root** (53a), **ryot** (115c), **scot** (14a,

162b), **Scot** (64b,132c), **shot** (9d,43d,90c,174d), **slot** (10d,11b,41d, 110d,167d,168a,181b), **soot** (20b,26c,88a), **spot** (93b,118c,154d, 162a), **stot** (154d,155d,157d,179b,186a), **swot, toot, trot** (85b, 93d,112d)

O - - T   **oast** (15d,86b,112a), **obit** (41b,64c), **oket** (189), **omit** (49c,52c, 106b,114c,147d), **oont** (25d), **oust** (44c,49a,52b,125d)

OU - -   **ouch!, ough!, ours** (124c), **Ouse** (132a,185d), **oust** (44c,49a,52b, 125d)

- OU -   **Aoul** (191), **bout** (36c), **bouw** (188), **coup** (20d,97c,157b,c,162d), **cous** (38a), **doub** (18b), **douc** (101d), **doum** (168c), **dour** (67d, 159a), **foud** (54d,144b), **foul** (173a), **four** (26c), **goul** (102a), **gour** (112c,181c), **gout, hour, joug** (138d), **loud** (156a), **loun** (19a,b), **loup** (61d,62a,90c,139d), **Loup** (193), **lour** (13d,63d), **lout** (15c, 22a,24b,45b,109a,157d), **moue** (61d,62b), **noun** (114b,158a), **noup** (124b), **nous** (81d,100a,128b), **pouf, poul** (190), **pour** (162d), **pous** (188), **pout** (159a), **roud** (57a,b), **roue** (41b,44c,127c,134b), **roup** (44a,121d), **rout** (41d,44b,46b), **souf** (146b), **souk** (22a,97a), **soul** (10d,125a,153c,176d), **soup, sour, sous** (62d,172c), **toug** (171a), **toup** (95d), **tour** (31b,85c), **tout** (61a,127a), **youp** (185d), **your** (124c)

- - OU   **Abou** (48b,55a), **chou** (61b), **Chou** (30b), **clou** (62b), **meou, niou** (188), **shou** (41d), **thou** (124b), **Tiou** (192), **Yaou** (30c)

O - - U   **Oahu, Ogpu** (135d), **ordu** (170d)

OV - -   **oval** (48d,49c,127a), **oven** (15d,78c,86b), **over** (6b,38c,80a,114d, 130a), **Ovid** (132d,133b), **Ovis** (143d), **ovum** (48d)

- OV -   **cove** (17a,73d,107d), **dove** (19a,117d), **Hova** (95a), **hove** (92a, 157d), **Jova** (193), **Jove** (85d), **love** (163a), **move, nova** (20c,106d, 155c,174d), **nove** (83b), **rove** (127d,132b,178a), **wove, Xova** (193)

- - OV   **akov** (189), **Azov** (20b)

OW - -   **Owen** (96a,183c), **owse**

- OW -   **bowk** (155d), **bowl, cowl** (101d), **dowd** (143b), **dowl, down** (149d), **fowl, gowk** (146d), **gowl** (102a,140d,185b), **gown, howe** (77d), **Howe** (17a,82a), **howl** (39b), **howk** (139b), **Iowa** (193), **jowl** (29b), **lowa** (19a), **lown** (157d), **lowp** (90c,139d), **mown, nowt** (106a,139a), **nowy** (194), **powe, rowy** (157b), **town** (73c), **towy** (58b), **yowl, yowt** (139c)

- - OW   **alow** (18a,172c), **arow** (92c,158b), **avow** (6d,36a,41c,112c), **blow, brow, chow** (45a), **clow** (58c,148c), **crow** (19a), **dhow** (88d,111c, 175d), **enow** (50d,123a,158b), **flow** (157b), **frow** (47a,167a), **glow** (144c), **grow** (154b), **know, Lwow, meow, plow** (39c,165d), **prow** (21b,22c,144d,156a), **scow** (21a,58b), **show** (42b,44c,96b), **slow** (43c), **snow, stow** (112b), **swow** (100a), **trow** (18a,21a,159d,164c, 170b)

OX - -   **oxan** (65c), **oxea** (153d), **oxen** (10c), **oxer** (55c), **oxid** (112c), **oxyl** (112c)

- OX -   **boxy, coxa** (77b), **doxa** (48b), **doxy** (129d), **foxy** (38b,39c,181d), **moxa** (27d,30c), **Moxo** (192), **noxa, Roxy** (183d), **toxa** (153d)

- - OX   **abox** (22d), **esox** (57b)

O - - X   **obex** (22d), **Odax** (132c), **Olax** (52b), **onyx** (25d,28d,65d,142b), oryx (11a)

OY - -   oyer (38a,75b,119c), oyes (38a,39b,75b), oyez (38a,39b,75b)

- OY -   coyn (37a), coyo (15a,30c), Goya (151d), Hoya (14d), noyl (87c), soya (151b)

- - OY   ahoy (106a), Amoy (88c), b'hoy (134b), buoy (28d,58c), choy (48a,128d), cloy (61b,137c,159d), ohoy (106a), ploy (43c), troy (161c,180a), Troy

O - - Y   oaky, oary, obey (35c,75c), ohoy (106a), oily (110b,172c), okay (8d), olay (113b), only (24d,52c,98d,147a,150a), oozy (148b), orgy (26d,130d,137c), Orly (8b)

- OZ -   boza (12a), bozo (55b), coze (29b), cozy (149c), doze (148a), dozy, Jozy, kozo (113d,168c), mozo (152b), noze (75a), ooze (53c, 104b,116a), oozy (148b)

O - - Z   oyez (38a,39b,75b)

PA - -   paal (188), paar (28c), paca (132c,154a), pace (64b,98a,153b,156a, 170b,177d), pack (24b,140d), paco (9b,146d), pacs (94c), pact (8a), padi (131b), paga (117a), page (51b,59b,142d,159b), paha (67b), pahi (21b,26a), paho (122a), paid (129c), pail, pain (7c), pair (22d,37d,85b,171d), pais (37d), pajo (122a), pala (189), Pala (88b), pale (113a,117c,178a), pali (122b), Pali (23d,24a,137b,175a), pall (32d,81b,112a), palm (59b,168c,169b), palo (152c), palp (11a,55b, 58b,167c), paly (194), Pana, pane (113c,155a,b), pang (165b), Pani (120c), pank (189), pant, paon (115b), papa, pape (19b,113a), para (134c,170d), Para (18a,51d), parc (62b,112c), pard (27b, 91b), pare (115c,129a), pari (34a,180a), park, parr (136d,137a, 147c), pars (89d), part (44d,60d,121c,159c), paru (57a), pasa (46a,127c,152c), pasi (94b), pass (110b,155c), past (25c,69d,165d), pata (32c,160d), pate (39a,74d), path (132a,134b), pato (46d), patu (179b), paul, Paul (96a), paun (18b), paut (140a), pave (85a), pavo (115b), Pavo (36b,c), pavy (115b), pawa (189), pawl (43a, 95a), pawn (29c,119c)

- PA -   Apap (102a), apar (12d), opah (23b,57a,b,86d), opal (20a,65d,67b, 82b), spad (105b), Spad (118d), spae (139c), span (23b,107b,113a, 128b,162c), spar (22c,24c,64b,97b,100b,144d), spat (112c,126b, 134b), upas (84d,120b,168c,d)

- - PA   arpa (83b), capa (152a,166d), cepa (110c), copa (88b,113c), depa (188), dopa (117d), Hupa (192), kapa (74b), lipa (54d), napa (25c,

67d,90d), Napa (182c), Nepa, 106b,178c), nipa (14b,46b,48a,164a, 168c), papa, pipa (159d), pupa (30d,81b,c), ripa (16b,131d), ropa (152a), rupa (60b), sapa (70c), supa (168c), tapa (16c,32c,53b, 56a,74b,104b,112b,113d,120d), yapa (113b), Zipa (29d)

P - - A   paca (132c,154a), paga (117a), paha (67b), pala (189), Pala (88b), Pana, papa, para (134c,170d), Para (18a,51d), pasa (46a, 127c,152c), pata (32c,160d), pawa (189), peba (12d), Peba (193), peca (190), peda (114d,144b), pega (57a,130a), pela (30c), Pera (60a), pesa (190), peva (12d), pica (66b,95b,172c), pika (93a,128a, 132c), pima (37c), Pima (192), pina (35d,118b), pipa (159d), Pisa (90c), pita (9c,28b,56a,83a), plea (51a,52d,122a,130b), poha (74c), pola, pooa (76a,125b), proa (21b,26a,95c,d), puca (68a),

384

puja (77a), **puka** (107a,168c), **puma** (27b,37c,55b,103d), **puna** (10b,33b,104a,119b,182a), **pupa** (30d,81b,c), **Puya** (118b), **pyla** (22d)

P - - B   **pleb** (10d,35b,180b)

P - - C   **parc** (62b,112c)

P - - D   **paid** (129c), **pard** (27b,91b), **pend, Phad** (155b), **Phud** (110b), **pied** (96c,103c,114b,117c,154a,174d), **plod** (170b,177d), **pond, pood** (189), **prod** (67d,80b,106b,120b), **pund** (189), **puud** (189)

PE - -   **peag** (144a,178a), **peai** (98b), **peak** (9a,38c,159b,186b), **peal** (131c,d), **pean** (64c,150b), **pear** (64a), **peat** (64a,175a), **peba** (12d), **Peba** (193), **peca** (190), **peck** (24d), **peco** (162b), **peda** (114d,144b), **pedi** (34b), **pedo** (34b), **peek** (93d,115c), **peel** (53a,114a), **peen** (73c), **peep** (93d,115c), **peer** (51a,93d,107c), **peet** (64a), **pega** (57a,130a,158b), **Pegu** (24c,102a,127d), **peho** (19b,102c,106d), **Peke** (45a,148d), **pela** (30c), **Pele** (69c,74c), **pelf** (22a,56c,131b), **pelo** (83b), **pelt** (53a), **pelu** (30a,106d,168c), **pend, pene, pent** (36a), **peon** (28c,59c,99c), **pepo** (39b,64a,70a,98c,125c,154c), **Pera** (60a), **pere** (61c,63b), **peri** (54b,116b,c,122b), **perk** (84d,93a), **perm** (49b,97d), **pern** (78a), **pero** (152a), **pert** (80a,93a,137c,154b), **Peru,** **pesa** (190), **peso** (99c), **pest** (108c,116b,118d,170a), **pete** (136b), **Pete** (96b), **peto** (57a,177b), **Peto** (76a), **peur** (61c), **peva** (12d), **pevy** (91d,94c)

- PE -   **aper** (32d), **Apet** (97c), **apex** (39c,76c,115c,118b,159b,166a,167b), **epee** (55c,160d), **open** (26a,60d,81a,109b,112c,125b,172b,173c), **spec, sped, Spee** (66d,70b), **spes, Spes** (69a,78a), **spet** (16c,57a, 142c), **spew** (35a,49a), **spex, Spey**

- - PE   **cape** (75a,96c,124b,161a), **cepe** (48c), **cope** (12b,26b,36c,65b,157d, 176a), **dope** (46c,105d), **dupe** (27c,41c,72c,160c), **gape** (185b), **hipe** (185a), **hope** (13d), **hype** (185a), **jape** (85a,b), **jupe** (62b, 84a), **lope** (48b,64b,d), **lupe** (19a,64a), **mope** (92d), **nape** (15b,108c,d), **Nupe** (191), **olpe** (90d), **pape** (19b,113a), **pipe** (105a,180d,182a), **pope** (20a,30d,31c,120d), **ripe** (58a,97c,98c), **rope** (36d,88d,128b), **rype** (19b,125a), **sipe** (101a,110c,140b), **supe** (53a,154d), **sype** (110c), **tape** (16a,19a,128d), **tipe** (168b), **tope** (24a,46b,57a,143c, 151a), **type** (31d,115a,155a), **wipe, Xipe** (15c)

P - - E   **pace** (64b,98a,153b,156a,170b,177d), **page** (51b,59b,142d,159b), **pale** (113a,117c,178a), **pane** (113c,155a,b), **pape** (19b,113a), **pare** (115c,129a), **pate** (39a,74d), **pave** (85a), **Peke** (45a,148d), **Pele** (69c,74c), **pene, pere** (61c,63b), **pete** (136b), **Pete** (96b), **pice** (190), **pike** (57a,b,76c,120b,153a), **pile** (45d,75b,117c), **pine** (36a, 52a,88c,93c,168c,d,169a), **pipe** (105a,180d,182a), **pise** (127d), **pile** (32c,59b), **poke** (108c), **pole** (132c,143b,177b,184a), **Pole** (52a), **pome** (11d), **pone** (37a,85b), **pope** (20a,30d,31c, 120d), **pore** (59d,110d,111c,120d,157d), **pose** (14c,15d), **powe,** **pree** (139d), **puce** (33c,d,52a), **pule** (180d), **pume** (137b), **Pume** (175b,185b), **pure** (29b,172b,173c), **pyle** (34b), **Pyle** (9c,178a), **pyre** (64c)

P - - F   **pelf** (22a,56c,131b), **Piaf** (63c), **piff** (24b), **poor, pouf, puff** (180d)

- PG -   **upgo** (13c)

P - - G   **pang** (165b), **peag** (144a,178a), **ping, plug** (156d,184d), **pong,**

prig (112a,116c), **pung** (22c,148b)

PH - - **Phad** (155b), **phew** (52c), **Phil** (96b), **phit** (24b), **phiz** (54a), **phon** (94a), **phoo, phos, phot** (173b), **Phud** (110b), **phut** (24b), **Phut** (110b)

- PH - epha (75c)

- - PH **Alph** (132a), **caph** (91c), **kaph** (91d), **koph** (91d), **qoph** (91d), **soph, toph** (75c), **umph**

P - - H path (132a,134b), **pish** (36c,107d), **pith** (37a,51c,67b,95c,97a, 119b,126d), **pooh** (22b,107d), **posh** (49b,148c), **prah** (21b, 26a,95c,d), **Ptah** (48d,98c), **pugh!**, **push** (145c)

PI - - **Piaf** (63c), **piat** (11a), **piay** (98b), **pica** (66b,95b,172c), **pice** (190), **Pici** (19c,184a), **pick, pico** (65a,152c), **Pict** (23c,47d), **pied** (96c, 103c,114b,117c,154a,174d), **pien** (13b), **pier** (23a,88b,180c), **piet** (29b,95b), **piff** (24b), **pika** (93a,128a,132c), **pike** (57a,b,76c,120b, 153a), **piki** (95c), **piky, pile** (45d,75b,117c), **pili** (34b,108d), **pill, pily, pima** (37c), **Pima** (192), **pina** (35d,118b), **pine** (36a,52a,88c, 93c,168c,d,169a), **ping, pink** (26d,33c,60c,138a), **pino** (152c), **pint** (67b), **piny, pion** (43c,52b), **piot** (95b), **pipa** (159d), **pipe** (105a, 180d,182a), **pipi** (106d,119d), **pipy** (145d), **pirn** (21b,129a,179b), **Piro** (192), **pirr** (181a), **Pisa** (90c), **pise** (127d), **pish** (36c,107d), **pisk** (9c, 19b), **piso** (189), **pist** (25c), **pita** (9c,28b,56a,83a), **pith** (37a, 51c,67b,95c,97a,119b,126d), **pito** (9c,28b,83a), **Pitt** (50d,155d), **pity** (35b), **Pius** (121a), **pixy** (154b)

- PI - apia (121b), apii (74c), apio (125b), **Apis** (17c,24b,49a,125a,136a), epic (76b,120a), **ipil** (117a,168c,169a), **Opie** (50c), **spin** (131a, 180d), **spir** (97c), **spit** (120a,132b,c), **Upis** (13b), **ypil** (117a,168c)

- - PI **aipi** (27a), **Hapi** (66a,107b,136a), **Hopi** (12c,102c,125b), **hopi** (33c), **impi** (86a), **kepi** (99d), **kopi** (107a,168c), **Kopi** (172a), **pipi** (106d,119d), **tipi** (181b), **topi** (37a,75a,118c), **Tupi** (192)

P - - I padi (131b), **pahi** (21b,26a), **pali** (122b), **Pali**, (23d,24a,137b,175a), **Pani** (120c), **pari** (34a,180a), **pasi** (94b), **peai** (98b), **pedi** (34b), **peri** (54b,116b,c,122b), **Pici** (19c,184a), **piki** (95c), **pili** (34b, 108d), **pipi** (106d,119d), **puli** (45a,78d), **puri** (80d)

P - - K **pack** (24b,140d), **pank** (189), **park, peak** (9a,38c,159b,186b), **peck** (24d), **peek** (93d,115c), **perk** (84d,93a), **pick, pink** (26d,33c,60c, 138a), **pisk** (9c,19b), **polk** (37c), **pook** (68a), **pork, puck** (44b,68a, 77c,100c), **Puck** (99d,143b), **pulk** (37c,88d), **punk** (9b,166a,167c)

PL - - **plan** (99b,124a,138b), **plap** (54b), **plat** (22d,96c,114a,119c,133d), **play** (63d,154a), **plea** (51a,52d,122a,130b), **pleb** (10d,35b,180b), **plet** (135d), **plew** (17c), **plex** (60b), **plie** (32c,59b), **plod** (170b, 177d), **plop** (54b), **plot** (25a,36b,118d,138b), **plow** (39c,165d), **ploy** (43c), **plug** (156d,184d), **plum, plup, plus** (10b,102c)

- PL - upla

P - - L **paal** (188), **pail, pall** (32d,81b,112a), **paul, Paul** (96a), **pawl** (43a, 95a), **peal** (131c,d), **peel** (53a,114a), **Phil** (96b), **pill, poll** (74d, 160a,177c), **pool** (65a,119d,120d), **poul** (190), **pull** (45d,167d), **purl** (87c,104c), **pyal** (175c)

P - - M **palm** (59b,168c,169b), **perm** (49b,97d), **plum, poem** (51a), **pram** (15a), **prim** (156b)

386

PN - -   **Pnyx** (71c)

P - - N   **pain** (7c), **paon** (115b), **paun** (18b), **pawn** (29c,119c), **pean** (64c, 150b), **peen** (73c), **peon** (28c,59c,99c), **pern** (78a), **phon** (94a), **pien** (13b), **pion** (43c,52b), **pirn** (21b,129a,179b), **plan** (99b,124a, 138b), **poon** (97c)

PO - -   **poco** (83b,93a), **poem** (51a), **poet** (49b), **Pogo** (121c), **pogy** (57a, 88a,98d,103c), **poha** (74c), **poke** (108c), **poku** (11a), **poky** (148c), **pola, pole** (132c,143b,177b,184a), **Pole** (52a), **polk** (37c), **poll** (74d,160a,177c), **polo** (154a), **Polo** (175b), **poly** (34c,76b), **pome** (11d), **Pomo** (192), **pomp** (111d,112d), **pond, pone** (37a,85b), **pong, Pons** (13d,63c,110d,150c), **pont** (55d,61b), **pony, pooa** (76a,125b), **pood** (189), **poof, pooh** (22b,107d), **pook** (68a), **pool** (65a,119d, 120d), **poon** (97c), **poop** (41c), **poor** (33a), **poot!, pope** (20a,30d, 31c,120d), **pore** (59d,110d,111c,120d,157d), **pork, Poro** (141d), **port** (73d,136b,140c,170c,d,182b,c), **pose** (14c,15d), **posh** (49b, 148c), **post** (89a,95c,155d), **pott** (113d), **pouf, poul** (190), **pour** (162d), **pous** (188), **pout** (159a), **powe**

- PO -   **apod** (59d), **epos** (51a,76b,120a), **spot** (93b,118c,154d,162a), **upon** (6b)

- - PO   **cipo** (91d), **gapo** (60a), **hypo** (117b), **mapo** (68a,148d), **pepo** (39b, 64a,70a,98c,125c,154c), **sapo** (149c,166d), **typo** (35c,51b)

P - - O   **paco** (9b,146d), **paho** (122a), **pajo** (122a), **palo** (152c), **pato** (46d), **pavo** (115b), **Pavo** (36b,c), **peco** (162b), **pedo** (34b), **peho** (19b, 102c,106d), **pelo** (83b), **pepo** (39b,64a,70a,98c,125c,154c), **pero** (152a), **peso** (99c), **peto** (57a,177b), **Peto** (76a), **phoo, pico** (65a, 152c), **pino** (152c), **Piro** (192), **piso** (189), **pito** (9c,28b,83a), **poco** (83b,93a), **Pogo** (121c), **polo** (154a), **Polo** (175b), **Pomo** (192), **Poro** (141d), **prao** (21b,26a,95c,d), **puno** (182a), **pyro**

- - PP   **Capp** (27a), **dopp** (43c), **kapp, kipp, Lapp** (108a), **repp** (53b,131a), **typp** (185b), **wapp** (54b,133d,145d), **Yapp** (22a), **zipp**

P - - P   **palp** (11a,55b,58b), **peep** (93d,115c), **plap** (54b), **p'op** (54b), **plup, pomp** (111d,112d), **poop** (41c), **prep** (138b), **prop** (159d), **pulp, pump**

PR - -   **prah** (21b,26a,95c,d), **pram** (15a), **prao** (21b,26a,95c,d), **prau** (21b, 26a,95c,d), **pray** (18b,51a,159d), **pree** (139d), **prep** (138b), **pres** (62b), **pret** (188), **prey** (119d,176a), **prig** (112a,116c), **prim** (156b), **proa** (21b,26a,95c,d), **prod** (67d,80b,106b,120b), **prop** (159d), **prow** (21b,22c,144d,156a), **prut!, Prut** (41a)

- PR -   **spry** (7a,107b)

P - - R   **paar** (28c), **pair** (22d,37d,85b,171d), **parr** (136d,137a,147c), **pear** (64a), **peer** (51a,93d,107c), **peur** (61c), **pier** (23a,88b,180c), **pirr** (181a), **poor** (33a), **pour** (162d), **purr** (104c)

- PS -   **apse** (9b,20a,31a,128c,130a,142b,175a), **Apsu** (29a), **ipse** (44d, 89c), **ipso** (89c)

- - PS   **Alps** (85d), **gyps, Gyps** (71d), **hops** (17c), **hyps, seps** (93b,142d), **tops** (159c), **Veps** (191), **Zips** (40c)

P - - S   **pacs** (94c), **pais** (37d), **pars** (89d), **pass** (110b,155c), **phos, Pius** (121a), **plus** (10b,102c), **Pons** (13d,63c,110d,150c), **pous** (188), **pres** (62b), **puss**

PT - -   **Ptah** (48d,98c)

- - PT   **Copt** (48d), **dipt, kept, rapt** (6c,27a,50d), **sept** (31d,82b,143a,149c), **Sept** (45b), **Sopt** (45b), **wept**

P - - T   **pact** (8a), **pant, part** (44d,60d,121c,159c), **past** (25c,69d,165d), **paut** (140a), **peat** (64a,175a), **peet** (64a), **pelt** (53a), **pent** (36a), **pert** (80a,93a,137c,154b), **pest** (108c,116b,118d,170a), **phit** (24b), **phot** (173b), **phut** (24b), **Phut** (110b), **piat** (11a), **Pict** (23c, 47d), **piet** (29b,95b), **pint** (67b), **piot** (95b), **pist** (25c), **Pitt** (50d, 155d), **plat** (22d,96c,114a,119c,133d), **plet** (135d), **plot** (25a,36b, 118d,138b), **poet** (49b), **pont** (55d,61b), **poot!, port** (73d,136b, 140c,170c,d,182b,c), **post** (89a,95c,155d), **pott** (113d), **pout** (159a), **pret** (188), **prut!, Prut** (41a), **punt** (21a,58b), **putt** (69d), **pyat** (95b), **pyet** (95b)

PU - -   **puca** (68a), **puce** (33c,d,52a), **puck** (44b,68a,77c,100c), **Puck** (99d,143b), **pudu** (41d), **puff** (180d), **pugh!, puja** (77a), **puka** (107a,168c), **puku** (11a), **pule** (180d), **puli** (45a,78a), **pulk** (37c, 88d), **pull** (45d,167d), **pulp, pulu** (74c), **puly, puma** (27b,37c,55b, 103d), **pume** (137b), **Pume** (175b,185b), **pump, puna** (10b,33b, 104a,119b,182a), **pund** (189), **pung** (22c,148b), **punk** (9b,166a, 167c), **puno** (182a), **punt** (21a,58b), **puny** (55b,179a), **pupa** (30d, 81b,c), **pure** (29b,172c,173c), **puri** (80d), **purl** (87c,104c), **purr** (104c), **Puru** (192), **push** (145c), **puss, putt** (69d), **puud** (189), **puxy, Puya** (118b)

- PU -   **Apus** (36b,c), **opus** (35c,105a,184c), **spud** (121d,151c), **spun, spur** (10d,67d,167d,168a,181b), **sput** (21c)

- - PU   **hapu** (106d), **napu** (29d,80d), **Ogpu** (135d), **tapu**

P - - U   **paru** (57a), **patu** (179b), **Pegu** (24c,102a,127d), **pelu** (30a,106d, 168c), **Peru, poku** (11a), **prau** (21b,26a,95c,d), **pudu** (41d), **puku** (11a), **pulu** (74c), **Puru** (192)

P - - W   **phew** (52c), **plew** (17c), **plow** (39c,165d), **prow** (21b,22c,144d, 156a)

P - - X   **plex** (60b), **Pnyx** (71c)

PY - -   **pyal** (175c), **pyat** (95b), **pyet** (95b), **pyla** (22d), **pyle** (34b), **Pyle** (9c,178a), **pyre** (64c), **pyro**

- - PY   **copy, espy** (44a,142a), **gapy, pipy** (145d), **ropy** (157c,176d), **typy**

P - - Y   **paly** (194), **pavy** (115b), **pevy** (91d,94c), **piay** (98b), **piky, pily, piny, pipy** (145d), **pity** (35b), **pixy** (154b), **play** (63d,154a), **ploy** (43c), **pogy** (57a,88a,98d,103c), **poky** (148c), **poly** (34c,76b), **pony, pray** (18b,51a,159d), **prey** (119d,176a), **puly, puny** (55b,179a), **puxy**

P - - Z   **phiz** (54a)

QA - -   **Qaid** (35a)

Q - - D   **Qaid** (35a), **quad** (33c,172a), **quid** (39b,166d), **quod** (123d)

QE - -   **qere** (75c), **qeri** (75c)

Q - - E   **qere** (75c), **quae** (176b)

- - QF   **waqf** (103a)

Q - - G   **quag** (21c,102c), **Qung** (191)

Q - - H   **qoph** (91d)

Q - - I qeri (75c), quai (88b,117c,180c), quei (189)

Q - - N quan (190)

QO - - qoph (91d)

Q - - P quip (183a,b)

Q - - S quas (135c)

Q - - T quit (90d,130c)

QU - - quad (33c,172a), quae (176b), quag (21c,102c), quai (88b,117c, 180c), quan (190), quas (135c), quay (88b,117c,180c), quei (189), quid (39b,166d), quip (183a,b), quit (90d,130c), quiz, Qung (191), quod (123d)

- QU - aqua (90a,178c), equi (122d)

Q - - Y quay (88b,117c,180c).

Q - - Z quiz

RA - - raab (32d), raad (14a,49b,151a,165b), raas (91b), Raba, rabi (38d, 74a), Rabi (14b,117b), raca (19a,59c,130b,184d), race (116a,153b, 154b,169c), rack (32c,64b), racy (153b), rada (135c,172a), rade (138d), raff (75b), raft (27b,33c,58c,75b), raga (56d,105a), rage (10c,30c,157a,161d), ragi (28b), Rahu (42b,48b), Raia (107d,147b), raid (59d,80c), raik (188,189), rail (16b,19b,c,37a,97b,138c,150c, 177b), rain (121d,162d), raip (36d), rais (26c,29d,75a,103b), Rais (106b), raja (77a,123c), rake (41b,44c,134b,140d), rale (7c,23a, 29d,41b), ralo (188), Rama (77a,80b,176d), rame (22d), rami (22d), ramp (65a,80b,127b,148b), rana (77a,123c), Rana (63d), rand (16d,22a,131b,145a,b), Rand (69c), rang, rani (72d,77b,123c,127c), rank (31d,55d,70b,92c,94d,157d), rann (175c), rant (41c,127b, 128a,161d), rapt (6c,27a,50d), rara (119a), rare (138b,164b,172b, 173d), rasa (51c), rase (42b,91d), rash (75a), rasp (56b,70d,140d), rata (29d,56b,89d,96c,106d,120c,168c), rate (11d,14a,31d,36b,51d, 52a,70b,85c,112b,123b,127d,128a,138c,143a,174b), rath (29a, 76d,162d), rati (189), rats, rave,(41c,157a,161d), ravi (61b), Ravi (16b), raya (19b,23c,76d,107d), raze (42b,91d) razz (131b)

- RA - Arab (30a,78b,c,106a,107c,157b,160c,185d), arad (13a,c,84a), arah (52c), Aral (135d), Aram (18d,50c,105c,144b,161c), Aran (18c,48c,64d,82d,174c), arar (137a,168c), Aras, brab (113b), brad (54d,67c,105b), brae (76d,139a,c,140b,148c), brag (21a,175a), Bram (96a), bran (23c,39a,70b,72a,79c), Bran (23c,50c), bras (61a), brat, bray, crab (39b,144b,181b), crag (132c), crai, cram (157d), cran (160c), craw (38d,72c,156c), Crax (19b,39d), draa, drab (23d,29c,33d,46d,53d), drag (74a,125b), drah (188), dram (46b,110c,121d,148c), drap (61b,c,62a), drat (100a), Drau, draw (42c,53a,92b,117c,121c,167d), dray (27a,154c), eral (51a), erat (89c), frab (138c), frap (45d,165c), frat, frau (181b), fray (56b,60d), grab (105b,142a,149b), grad (28b), Graf (37c,66b,67a, 107c,186b), gram (29d,99b,148d,160d,180a), grao (189), gras (78b), gray (33c,77c), Gray (50c), Irad (18d), Irae (43c), Irak (99a,d), Iran (6a,48c,116b), Iraq (99a,d), Iras (11b,32a), krag (131c), kral, kran (190), kras (76d), orad (104a), oral (114a,153d, 174c,175c), Oran, oras (40d), prah (21b,26a,95c,d), pram (15a), prao (21b,26a,95c,d), prau (21b,26a,95c,d), pray (18b,51a,159d), tram (170a), tran (7a), trap (27b,67b,132b,149b), tray (128c,136d,

389

142d,143c), **ural, Ural** (135c), **uran** (101d), **Wraf, wrap** (32b,51a)

- - RA **abra** (26b), **Abra, aera** (8a), **Afra** (183c), **agra** (26d,34d), **Agra** (161b), **Aira** (70d), **akra** (176a), **Akra** (191), **amra** (77c), **arra** (47d, 52c,82b), **aura** (44c,49c,66a,96b,158a,170d,177c), **bara** (188), **Bera** (86d), **bora** (181d,182b), **bura** (182b), **cara** (83a), **Cara** (48b, 183c), **cora** (65d), **Cora** (42b,69c,80c,116b,124d,172b,183c), **cura** (152c), **Dara** (18d), **dera** (34c), **dora** (70b), **Dora** (36d,41a,43b, 183c,d), **dura** (153c), **eyra** (181d), **Ezra** (96a), **fora** (133a), **gara** (190), **gora** (81c), **Hera** (69c,85d,110b,126b,186b,d), **hora** (22a,40b), **hura** (20a,137a), **Hura, ikra** (27d), **Irra** (68c, 178a), **jura, Jura, Kara** (132a), **kora** (19a,178c), **Kora, Lara** (25c), **lira** (28b,79a,170d), **lora** (146b,149b,151c,169b), **Lora** (183c), **lura** (22d,82a), **Lyra** (36b,74a), **mara** (114d), **Mara** (24a,d,105b,107b), **mira** (174d), **Mira** (155b), **mora** (42b,65a,72b,83d,99b,153a,161a), **mura** (84d), **Mura** (192), **Myra** (10a,31b,183c), **Nera** (165b), **Nora** (79b,107a,164c,183c), **ocra** (72c,175a), **okra** (72c,175a), **orra** (139c,d,140a), **otra** (152c), **para** (134c,170d), **Para** (18a,51d), **Pera** (60a), **Sara** (24d,183c), **sera** (11b,20d,59a,83a,180d), **sora** (19b,c, 127b), **sura** (87c,113b,166d), **Syra, tara** (22a,55c,113a,168c), **Tara** (82b,c,138b), **tera** (23d,84c), **tora** (11a,44d,74a,75c,85c,90b,102d, 115d), **vara** (151d), **vera** (140c,151b,175c), **Vera** (183c) **Vira** (191), **zira** (188)

R - - A **Raba, raca** (19a,59c,130b,184d), **rada** (135c,172a), **raga** (56d,105a), **Raia** (107d,147b), **raja** (77a,123c), **Rama** (77a,176d), **rana** (77a,123c), **Rana** (63d), **rara** (119a), **rasa** (51c), **rata** (29d,56b,89d), 96c,106d,120c,168c), **raya** (19b,23c,76d,107d), **reba** (144a), **Reba** (18d,86c), **rede** (37c,81d), **reja** (152b), **rena** (25b,132c), **rhea** (37a, 56a,111d,133d), **Rhea** (19b,68d,87c,103c,186b), **riga** (118b), **Riga, rima** (23a,30c,32a,58a,110d), **ripa** (16b,131d), **rita, Rita** (37b, 78d,183c,), **Roda** (107b), **roka** (95a,168c,d), **Roma** (83c,d), **ropa** (152a), **Rosa** (58d,134a,145d,183c), **rota** (27c,30d,38a,79a,92d, 133a,134a,b,180c), **ruga** (59b,185a), **rupa** (60b), **rusa, Rusa** (41d, 136d), **Ruta** (76b,134d)

- RB - **arba** (135d,171a)

- - RB **barb** (20b,57d,78b,117c,120a,b,124b), **curb** (130c,146b), **garb** (32c,46a), **gerb** (56d,143d), **Harb** (191), **herb** (58b,158b), **kerb** (146b), **Serb** (15d,148a,186c), **sorb** (11d,103d,134b,142d), **Sorb** (148a,180a), **verb** (7a,114b,184b)

R - - B **raab** (32d), **rhob** (64a,85c), **rumb** (120b)

- RC - **arca** (9a,22c,29d,115a,130a), **Arca** (101b), **arch** (29d,38b,39d,123d, 132c), **orca** (86b)

- - RC **circ** (31a), **marc** (70c), **Marc** (96a), **parc** (62b,112c)

- RD - **Erda** (23d,41a,47d,68d,69a,131d,177b), **ordo** (22a,30d,122a,171a), **ordu** (170d), **urde** (86b), **Urdu** (77b), **urdy** (86b)

- - RD **bard** (12d,120a), **bird, bord** (100b), **Byrd** (9c,120b), **card** (33d,114d), **cord** (39b,131a), **curd** (99d), **Dard, dord** (42c), **eard** (139b), **fard** (112d), **ford** (177b), **fyrd** (110a), **Gerd** (63c), **gird** (32c,50a,123a,160a), **hard** (109b), **herd** (39a,46c,72a), **Kurd** (48b, 82a), **lard** (54d,61a,71a,110a), **lord** (107c), **nard** (13a,97c,102b, 110a,153c), **oord** (190), **pard** (27b,91b), **sard** (26d,28b,65d,111a),

390

142b,156d), **Sard, surd** (82c,177a), **verd** (71d), **ward** (31c,55c,86b), **word** (124b,165c), **Wurd, Wyrd** (107d), **yard** (152d)

R - - D   **raad** (14a,49b,151a,165b), **Raad** (151a), **raid** (59d,80c), **rand** (16d, 22a,131b,145a,b), **Rand** (69c), **read** (116d,157d), **redd** (153a), **reed** (16a,70d,97b,105a,111b,118b,144b), **Reed** (163a), **rend** (32a,159c, 162c,185a), **Ridd** (94a), **rind** (53a,115c), **Rind** (109c,174b), **road** (37d,164d), **rodd** (38d), **roed, rood** (38d,39a,88b), **roud** (57a,b), **rudd** (26d,57a,b), **rynd** (100a)

RE - -   **read** (116d,157d), **real** (7a), **ream** (18c,37d,50d,113d,171c), **reap** (7a,40a,74a), **rear** (15b,23a,b,24a,51b,76d,127c), **reba** (144a), **Reba** (18d,86c), **reck** (26d,75c), **rect** (117b), **redd** (153a), **rede** (37c, 81d,138d), **redo** (165c), **reed** (16a,70d,97b,105a,111b,118b,144b), **Reed** (163a), **reef** (129a,137a,145a), **reek** (49d,53c,64a,148d,149a), **reel** (21b,40b,d,153c,154a,c,d,180d), **reem** (18d), **reft** (32a,42c, 44d,167b), **reim** (112c), **rein** (29b,130c), **reis** (26c,29d,75a,103b), **reja** (152b), **Reki** (16a), **rely** (16b,170b), **Remi** (10b), **Rems, rena** (25b,132c), **rend** (32a,159c,162c,185a), **Reni** (83d), **Reno, rent** (58a,77c,91b,138b,153d,162c,167c), **repp** (53b,131a), **rese** (127b), **resh** (91d), **rest** (15d,91b,104d,105a,115a,b,130a,b,161b), **rete** (106c,119c), **reve** (61c,104d), **revs** (131a)

- RE -   **area** (37d,38a,44c,53a,93b,110d,127d,138c,168a,186d), **areg** (116a, 137a), **areo** (34c), **Ares** (49b,51b,68c,76a,97a,105c,110b), **aret** (128c), **brea** (100b), **bred** (23c,48c,127c), **bree** (139a), **bren** (72d, 95a), **Brer** (172b), **Bres, brew** (35d), **brey** (194), **crea** (92c), **Cree** (192), **crew** (72a,106a), **Crex** (37a), **dree** (139b,140c,158b,172c), **drei** (66d,165a), **dreg, drew, drey** (154c), **erer,** (17d,150c), **Frea, Fred** (96b), **free** (44a,70d,131b), **fret** (28c,35b,111c,184d), **Frey** (7c, 68b,124d), **gres** (156d), **grew, grey** (33c), **Iren** (127c), **Orel, pree** (139d), **prep** (138b), **pres** (62b), **pret** (188), **prey** (119d), **tree** (11d, 37a,66a,184b), **tref** (172b), **trek** (85c,93c,99d,168b), **tres** (19a,52b, 63a,152d,165a,175c), **tret** (9a,127b,179d), **trey** (26c,165a), **Urey** (107c,138c), **wren** (19b,c), **Wren** (50b)

- - RE   **Aare, acre** (39b,56a,88b), **Acre, aire** (82c), **Aire, bare** (43d,157c), **bore** (14c,25b,46a,116a,165c,179b), **bure** (61b), **byre** (38a), **care** (11b,14c,35d,150a,184d), **cere** (19a,149d,179a), **core** (28b,51c, 75b,81b), **cure** (123b), **dare** (28d,41b,42a,74d,175b), **Dare** (57a), **dere** (74a,79c), **dire** (45d,55a,104a,163c), **dore** (61d,67b,69d, 117d), **Dore** (50d,63a,b), **Eire** (82b), **etre** (61a,c,62d,166c), **eyre** (23c,31b,85c), **Eyre** (43c,59b,67d,123b), **fare** (43c,59b,67d,123b), **fire** (13a,43d, 44b), **fore** (63d,174b), **gare** (61b,c,62c,127c), **Gere** (183c), **gore** (115d,117c,154c,169c), **gyre** (31b,171b), **hare** (91b,132c), **here,** **hire** (49d,50b,91b,130a), **inre** (35d,80a), **jure** (90b), **kere** (75c, 128b), **kore** (107b), **Kore** (29a,42b,116b,124d), **Kure** (84c), **lire** (62c), **lore** (77c,87c,90d,151c,183a), **lure** (41c,51a,54b,163a), **lyre** (11c,81c,105a,111c), **mare** (78b), **Mare** (108b), **mere** (16c,22b,62a, 78b,87d,96c,110c,120d,146d,148b), **mire** (21c,104b), **more** (71a), **More** (50b), **mure** (177d), **Nare** (93c), **Nore** (163d), **ogre** (67a,102a), **pare** (115c,129a), **pere** (61c,63b), **pore** (59d,110d,111c,120d,157d), **pure** (29b,172b,173c), **pyre** (64c), **qere** (75c), **rare** (138b,164b, 172b,173d), **rire** (62a), **sere** (24d,46a,c,138c,183b), **Sere** (158b), **sire** (17d,55a,59d,124a,163b,166b), **sore** (23d,142c), **sure** (173d), **tare** (9a,18d,41a,176a,179d), **tire** (15a,22a,52d,55a,179b,180d),

391

tore, tyre (15a), Tyre (31b,90d,117b), vare (179b), vire (11a,13b), ware (27d,35a), were (139b), wire, wore, yare (96b,124b,128b), yore (10b,69d,93c,110b,165d)

R - - E race (116a,153b,154b,169c), rade (138d), rage (10c,30c,157a, 161d), rake (41b,44c,134b,140d), rale (7c,23a,29d,41b), rame (22d), rare (138b,164b,172d,173d), rase (42b,d,91d), rate 11d,14a,31d,36b,51d,52a,70b,85c,112b,123b,127d,128a,138c,143a, 174b), rave (41c,157a,161d), raze (42b,d,91d), rede (37c,81d,138d), rese (127b), rete (106c,119c), reve (61c,104d), ribe (139a), Rice (46a), ride (46b,85c), rife (6b,c,39d,123b), rile (10c,d,82c,125a, 156b,176a), rime (30c,36a,58a,63d,77c), rine (44d,75d,135c), ripe (58a,97c,98c), rire (62a), rise (49d,80b,155a), Rise (110d,150c), rite (93a,131d), rive (32a,153d), robe (65b), rode (46c), role (114b), Rome (31c,51d), rone (127c,164b), rope (36d,88d,128b), rose (33c), Rose (6a,50c,183c), rote (130b,134b,143a,159d), roue (41b,44c,127c,134b), rove (127d,132b,178a), rube (37d,135d, 185d), Rube (96b), rude (134b,172b), rule (11b,26b,90b), rune (9b,67a,94a,95a,105c,107d,120a,141d,163d), ruse (13b,77c,157b, 169c), rute (188), ryme (178d), rype (19b,125a)

- RF - orfe (57a,b,185c), Urfa (99a)

- - RF kerf (40a,108b), serf (21d,148a), surf (23a), turf (115c,149d, 160b), warf, werf (54d), zarf (39c,155a)

R - - F raff (75b), reef (129a,137a,145a), riff (131d), Riff (18b,102c), roof (78d), ruff (19b,33b,63d,137a)

- RG - Argo (12c,36b,c), ergo (164b), orgy (26d,130d,137c), urge (42d, 46b,79d,80a,b,81c,124a,150a)

- - RG berg (79b), borg (40d), burg (22b,73c), lurg (96d,141b,184d), morg (188), Sarg (96d,125c)

R - - G rang, ring (50a), Rong (88c), rung (28c,39a)

RH - - rhea (37a,56a,111d,133d), Rhea (19b,68d,87c,103c,186b), Rhee (87c), Rhin, rhob (64a,85c), rhum (8c), Rhus (159a)

R - - H rash (75a), rath (29a,76d,162d), resh (91d), rich, Roch (136c), rukh (53b,54a), rush, ruth (35b,118c), Ruth (105b,183c)

RI - - rial (190), ribe (139a), rice, Rice (46a), rich, rick (74d,117d,154d), Ridd (94a), ride (46b,85c), Riel (129a), riem (76c,112c,157c,164d), rien (62b), rier (180b), rife (6b,c,39d,123b), riff (131d), Riff (18b, 102c), rift (30c,32a,58a,110d), riga (118b), Riga, Riis (9d), rikk (49a), rile (10c,d,82c,125a,156b,176a), rill (23c102b,132a,148d, 157b), rily (176a), rima (23a,30c,32a,58a,110d), rime (30c,36a,58a, 63d,77c), rimu (79d,106d,129a,168c), rimy (63d), rind (53a,115c), Rind (109c,174b), rine (44d,75d,135c), ring (50a), rink (147c, 154a), riot (44c,111d,170c,173d), ripa (16b,131d), ripe (58a,97c, 98c), rire (62a), rise (49d,80b,155a), Rise (110d,150c), risk (74d), risp (99a), Riss (66a), rita, Rita (37b,78d,183c), rite (93a,131d), rive (32a,153d)

- RI - aria (8b,98c,150a,c,170c), arid (46c,85a), arif (127d), aril (142a), aris (101b), Brie (29c), brig (72b,106a,144d), brim, brin (32c,54c,146c), brit (76c), crib (96b,120d), cric (131c), crig (20d), crin (146c), cris (40b,95d), drib (46b), Drin, drip, eria (13d,146d), eric (115b), Eric (71d,96a,107d,138a,164a,176b), Erie (82c,87d),

392

Erin (82b), **Eris** (12c,68d,109c), **Fria, frib** (43d), **frim** (58d), **frit** (64c,67c), **friz** (39d), **grid** (17a,70d,119b,156d), **grig** (38c,70d, 93a), **grim** (156a), **grin, grip** (159a), **gris** (61d), **grit** (137a,b), **irid** (38d,67c), **iris** (53c,58a,111c) **Iris** (127c), **kris** (40b,95d), **prig** (112a, 116c), **prim** (156b), **trig** (106a,148d,154b,169d), **trim** (40a,106a, 154b,160a,165c,169d), **trin** (169d), **trio** (104d,165a,169c), **trip** (85c), **tris** (122d), **trit** (34d,164c), **Uria** (14c,16d), **urim** (18d,23a, 110a), **writ** (91a)

- - R I **abri** (61c,62c,144b), **aeri** (34a), **agri** (89b), **Atri, auri** (34a), **bari** (37c,79c), **Bari** (83d), **Bori** (110d,150c), **buri** (56b), **Cori** (138c), **dari** (38a,70b), **Geri** (183c), **gyri** (22d,131b), **kari** (14d), **keri** (75c,128b), **kiri** (86a,87c,115a,168c), **kori** (7d,77a), **Kuri** (191), **lari** (78a,101c), **Lari** (72c), **lori** (91b), **Luri** (191), **mari** (61d), **Mari** (16a), **Neri, nori** (8c,141c), **Omri** (18c,86d), **pari** (34a, 180a), **peri** (54b,116b,c,122b), **puri** (80d), **qeri** (75c), **Rori** (16b), **sari** (48b,65b,77b), **seri** (18b), **Seri** (192), **Shri** (17c,166c), **siri** (18b), **sori** (55c,64a), **Tari** (47d,69a), **tori** (101b), **Turi** (191), **vari** (34d,91b,134d,174d), **veri** (28b), **weri** (15c,27c)

R - - I **rabi** (38d,74a), **Rabi** (14b,117b), **ragi** (28b), **rami** (22d), **rani** (72d, 77b,123c,127c), **rati** (189), **ravi** (61b), **Ravi** (16b), **Reki** (16a), **Remi** (10b), **Reni** (83d), **rodi** (98c), **romi** (72b), **Rori** (16b), **roti** (62c)

- - R K **bark** (115c), **cark** (26d,184d), **cork** (119d), **dark** (47a,67d,109b, 160b), **dirk** (40b), **fork, hark** (92d) **jerk** (153a), **kirk** (31a,139b), **kurk** (31a,139b), **lark** (19a,63d), **lurk** (92a,147d), **mark** (146b, 155a), **Mark** (52a,96a), **mirk** (41a,67d), **murk** (41a,67d), **nark** (81a, 156d), **park, perk** (84d,93a), **pork, Sark** (28d), **Turk** (101d,102d, 106a,111d), **work** (64c,76b), **yark** (22c), **york** (38c), **York** (50b,c)

R - - K **rack** (32c,64b), **raik** (188,189), **rank** (31d,55d,70b,92c,94d,157d), **reck** (26d,75c), **reek** (49d,53c,64a,148d,149a), **rick** (74d,117d, 154d), **rikk** (49a), **rink** (147c,154a), **risk** (74d), **rock** (160b), **rook** (19b,29c,39a), **ruck** (39a,185a), **rusk** (23a)

- R L - **orle** (17b,56b,76a,144b,177a), **orlo** (56b,119c), **Orly** (8b)

- - R L **birl** (93c,131a,153c), **burl** (87c,169a), **carl** (115c,135d), **Carl** (96a), **cirl** (24c), **curl** (38d,73b,93b,131d), **earl** (107c), **farl** (138c,140b), **furl** (132d), **girl, harl** (16b,56b,59a), **herl** (16b,59a), **hurl** (167c), **jarl** (40d,107d), **Karl** (96a), **marl** (32a,42c,55d), **merl** (20b), **nurl** (33b,87c), **purl** (87c,104c), **yarl** (40d,107d)

R - - L **rail** (16b,19b,c,37a,97b,138c,150c,177b), **real** (7a), **reel** (21b,40b,d, 153c,154a,c,d,180d), **rial** (190), **Riel** (129a), **riil** (23c,102b,132a, 148d,157b), **roil** (44c,104b,156b,170d,176a), **roll** (134a,160b), **rotl** (103b,111c), **rull** (170b), **ryal** (110a,190), **ryel** (190)

- R M - **arme** (63a,179b), **arms, army** (78c), **Erma** (183c), **Irma** (96d)

- - R M **barm** (185b), **berm** (25d,90d,145c), **corm** (24b,38d,156a), **derm** (147c,158d), **dorm, farm** (165d), **firm** (154c,173d), **form** (54d, 143c), **Garm** (178c), **germ** (17d,99c,134d), **harm** (40b,81a), **norm** (15a,115a,128a,155a), **perm** (49b,97d), **term** (92b,105b,142b,166b), **turm** (132d), **warm** (7c,75b,163b), **worm, wurm** (67c)

R - - M **ream** (18c,37d,50d,113d,171c), **reem** (18d), **reim** (112c), **rhum** (8c), **riem** (76c,112c,157c,164d), **roam** (178a), **room** (28d)

- R N - **arna** (24a,181b), **Arnd** (67a), **Arne** (35c,50c,134d), **arni** (24a,181b),

393

Arno (27a), **arn't, erne** (19c,d,47b,54b,141a), **orna** (169d,182c), **orne** (169d,182c), **Orne** (25b), **urna** (133a)

- - RN   **barn** (156d), **Bern,** 160d), **birn** (31d), **born, burn, carn** (156c), **cern** (41c), **corn** (39d,95c,123a), **darn** (130b), **dorn** (164d), **earn** (42d, 64b,99a), **fern** (142a), **firn** (67c,70c,106c,149b), **garn** (67d,185b), **horn** (11a,105a,170b,182a), **karn** (156c), **kern** (59c,172a), **Kern** (132b), **lorn** (42d,60b), **morn, Norn** (69a,163d,174b), **pern** (78a), **pirn** (21b,129a,179b), **sorn** (139a,d), **tarn** (87d,103d,120d), **tern** (19b,32d,72c,94a,138c,141b,160a), **torn** (130a), **turn** (28d,131a, 175a), **warn** (7b), **worn** (143b), **yarn** (154b,161b,184b)

R - - N   **rain** (121d,162d), **rann** (175c), **rein** (29b,130c), **Rhin, rien** (62b), **roan** (78b,c,114c,128d,144a,181a), **roon** (41a,168b), **ruin** (42d)

RO - -   **road** (37d,164d), **roam** (178a), **roan** (78b,c,114c,128d,144a, 181a), **roar** (145c), **robe** (65b), **Roch** (136c), **rock** (160b), **Roda** (107b), **rodd** (38d), **rode** (46c), **rodi** (98c), **roed, roer** (72d), **roey** (103d), **rohr** (72d), **roil** (44c,104b,156b,170d,176a), **rojo** (129a, 152c), **roka** (95a,168c,d), **roke** (174d,175b), **role** (114b), **roll** (134a, 160b), **Roma** (83c), **Rome** (31c,51d), **romi** (72d), **romp** (63d), **rone** (127c, 164b), **Rong** (88c), **rood** (38d,39a,88b), **roof** (78d), **rook** (19b,29c,39a), **room** (28d), **roon** (41a,168b), **Roos** (67a), **root** (53a), **ropa** (152a), **rope** (36d,88d,128b), **ropy** (157c,176d), **Rori** (16b), **Rosa** (58d,134a,145d,183c), **rose** (33c), **Rose** (6a,50c,183c), **ross** (16c,161d), **Ross** (50c), **rosy** (21a,111a), **rota** (27c,30d,38a,79a,92d, 133a,134a,b,180c), **rote** (130b,134b,143a,159d), **roti** (62c), **roti** (103b,111c), **roto** (30a,122d,127b,152c,171b), **roud** (57a,b), **roue** (41b,44c,127c,134b), **roup** (44a,121d), **rout** (41d,44b,46b), **rove** (127d,132b,178a), **rowy** (157b), **Roxy** (183d)

- RO -   **Aroa** (175b), **Arod** (86c), **aroo** (80c,82b), **arow** (92c,158b), **brob** (153c), **broo** (139a), **brow, croc** (13a,74a), **Crom, crop** (38b), **crow** (19a), **drop** (43d,54b,100b,114c,168b), **Eros** (11c,39c,68b,97c,182d), **froe** (32a,167a,179d), **frog** (10a,17a,126b), **from, frot** (28c), **frow** (47a,167a), **grog** (92d,153d), **gros** (47a,53d), **Gros** (63a), **grot** (27d), **grow** (154b), **irok** (55b), **iron** (55c,d,69d,81a,97b,143b, 149a,173d,179c), **Kroo** (191), **proa** (21b,26a,95c,d), **prod** (67d,80b, 106b,120b), **prop** (159d), **prow** (21b,22c,144d,156a), **trod, tron** (140d,180a), **trop** (62d,167a), **trot** (85b,93d,112d), **trow** (18a,21a, 159d,164c,170b), **trey** (161c,180a)

- - RO   **aero** (8b,34a,b,58c,59a), **agro** (149d), **arro** (52c), **baro** (71a,122c), **boro** (154b), **Boro** (193), **caro** (83a), **Caro** (183d), **cero** (57b,c,d, 180b), **duro** (190), **Ebro** (132a), **faro** (65a), **Garo** (88c), **giro** (38c, 167c), **gyro** (34d), **hero** (42b,124d,137b), **Hero** (90c), **hiro, inro** (84b,c,106c), **karo** (106d), **Lero** (82d), **loro** (19a,114b), **maro** (144d), **mero** (72a), **miro** (19a,106d,184a), **Miro** (113a,151d), **moro** (19a,56c), **Moro** (100a,103a,117a,159a), **Nero** (8a,126d,133a,150b, 172c), **okro** (72c,175a), **otro** (151d), **pero** (152a), **Piro** (192), **Poro** (141d), **pyro, sero** (34d,88d,164b,178d), **taro** (13c,48c,49b,64b, 112b,120a,133d,155c,170a,c), **tiro** (9b,17d,108c), **toro** (38a,107a, 152a,168c), **tyro** (9b,17d,108c), **zero** (31a,84c,108c), **Zero** (118d)

R - - O   **ralo** (188), **redo** (165c), **Reno, rojo** (129a), **roto** (30a,122d,127b)

- RP -   **arpa** (83b)

- - RP   **carp** (27d,38d,40c,55a,56c,57a), **dorp** (73c,176b), **harp** (105a,129a),

larp (51d), **lerp** (51d,141d), **tarp** (26b,178d), **terp** (12b,123a), **torp** (54c), **turp**, **warp** (36c,165a,171c), **zarp** (120c)

R - - P **raip** (36d), **ramp** (65a,80b,127b,148b), **rasp** (56b,70d,140d), **reap** (7a,40a,74a), **repp** (53b,131a), **risp** (99a), **romp** (63d), **roup** (44a, 121d), **rump**

- RR - **arra** (47d,52c,82b), **arro** (52c), **Irra** (178a), **orra** (139c,d,140a)

- - RR **barr** (49b), **birr** (180d), **burr** (123b), **carr** (120d,140a), **curr** (104c), **darr** (163c), **dorr** (32b), **durr** (70b), **Herr** (66c), **Kerr**, **murr** (72b,128b), **nurr** (67d), **parr** (136d,137a,147c), **pirr** (181a), **purr** (104c), **turr** (24d,105a), **Tyrr** (68c,109c,163d,178a), **yarr** (72a)

R - - R **rear** (15b,23a,b,24a,51b,76d,127c), **rier** (180b), **roar** (145c), **roer** (72d), **rohr** (72d), **ruer**, **Ruhr**

- RS - **Erse** (28a,64b,82b), **erst** (60b), **Ursa** (17b,36b,43d)

- - RS **airs** (123b), **Bors** (70b,134b), **hers** (124c), **hors** (62b), **Lars** (51d, 121b), **Mars** (68c,118d,119a,129a,178a), **Mors** (41b), **ours** (124c), **pars** (89d), **sors** (44d,89b)

R - - S **raas** (91b), **rais** (26c,29d,75a,103b), **Rais** (106b), **rats**, **reis** (26c, 29d,75a,103b), **Rems**, **revs** (131a), **Rhus** (159a), **Riis** (9d), **Riss** (66a), **Roos** (67a), **ross** (16c,161d), **Ross** (50c), **Russ** (135b)

- RT - **Arta** (72b), **arto** (34a), **arts** (138c), **arty**, **orts** (60d), **Urth** (68d, 107d,163d)

- - RT **Bart** (96b), **Bert** (96b), **bort** (43b), **Bort** (134b), **cart** (171d,175a, 177b), **curt** (145b,c), **dart** (13b,88a,100c,120b,153a,160c), **dirt**, **fort** (63d,157d), **girt** (50a), **hart** (41d,154d), **hurt**, **mart** (49d,97a), **Mart** (96b,183d), **mort** (41b,47a,78b,136d), **part** (44d,60d,121c, 159c), **pert** (80a,93a,137c,154b), **port** (73d,136d,140c,170c,d,182b, c), **Sart** (82b,103b,170d), **Sert** (151d), **sort** (31d,39c,70b,86b,153a), **tart** (114d), **tort** (31c,91a,185c), **vert** (71d,166a,171b), **wart** (124d), **wert**, **wort** (76a,95d,121d), **yurt** (101d)

R - - T **raft** (27b,33c,58c,75b), **rant** (41c,127b,128a,161d), **rapt** (6c,27a, 50d), **rect** (117b), **reft** (32a,42c,44d,167b), **rent** (58a,77c,91b,138b, 153d,162c,167c), **rest** (15d,91b,104d,105a,115a,b,130a,b,161b), **rift** (30c,32a,58a,110d), **riot** (44c,111d,170c,173d), **root** (53a), **rout** (41d,44b,46b), **runt** (47a,172d), **rust** (37b,112c,119a), **ryot** (115c)

RU - - **ruay** (189), **rube** (37d,135d,185d), **Rube** (96b), **ruby** (20a,65d, 179c), **ruck** (39a,185a), **rudd** (26d,57a,b), **rude** (134b,172b), **ruer** **ruff** (19b,33b,63d,137a), **ruga** (59b,185a), **Ruhr**, **ruin** (42d), **rukh** (53b,54a), **rule** (11b,26b,90b), **rull** (170b), **rumb** (120b), **rump**, **rune** (9b,67a,94a,95a,105c,107d,120a,141d,163d), **rung** (28c,39a), **runt** (47a,172d), **rupa** (60b), **ruru** (19b,102c,106d), **rusa**, **Rusa** (41d, 136d), **ruse** (13b,77c,157b,169c), **rush**, **rusk** (23a), **Russ** (135b), **rust** (37b,112c,119a), **Ruta** (76b,134d); **rute** (188), **ruth** (35b,118c), **Ruth** (105b,183c)

- RU - **arui** (11b,143d,144a,181c), **arum** (13a,39b,58d,92b,155c), **Arum** (66a), **bruh** (95a), **brut** (182c), **Brut** (23c), **crus** (91a,143c), **crux** (39a,151b), **drub** (17b,39c) **drug** (105d), **drum** (105a), **drun** (132b), **erua** (103c), **eruc** (37a,56a), **grub** (43c,88d), **grum** (102c), **Grus** (36b,c,38b), **irus** (109d), **prut!**, **Prut** (41a), **true** (7a,8d,37b,54b, 94c,149c), **urus** (14d,53a,112c)

- - RU Aaru (6b,48d), baru (168c), ecru (17d,23d,172b), feru (37a,56a, 133d), guru (77b), maru (84c,144d), Meru (77a,103d), paru (57a), Peru, Puru (192), ruru (19b,102c,106d), Yaru (48d)

R - - U Rahu (42b,48b), rimu (79d,106d,129a,168c), ruru (19b,102c,106d)

- RV - urva (38b)

RY - - ryal (110a,190), ryel (190), ryme (178d), rynd (100a), ryot (115c), rype (19b,125a)

- RY - Arya (80d), eryx (137a), oryx (11a), tryp (114a)

- - RY adry (164c), aery (47b,51d,106c), airy (177a,176d), atry (141b), awry (13d,38d,171c), bury (81d), dory (21b,58b,144c), eery (172b, 180a), ewry (133c), eyry (47b,106c), fury (157a), Gary, gory, jury (38a), lory (19a,114a), Mary (50c,126b,183c), miry, nary (108b), oary, sory (176d), spry (7a,107b), Tory (23c,36b,94c,172a), vary (28d,43c), very (149c), wary (27d,176b), wiry (147a,167c)

R - - Y racy (153b), rely (16b,170b), rily (176a), rimy (63d), roey (103d), ropy (157c,176d), rosy (21a,111a), rowy (157b), Roxy (183d), ruay (189), ruby (20a,65d,179c)

R - - Z razz (131b)

SA - - Saad (12b), saah (188), saal (66c,73b), Saan (24d), Saar (63b,102d, 132a), saba (56a,117a), Saba (143d), sabe, sack (43d,118a,119d, 182b), saco (189), sadd (33a,40b,58c,107b), sade (91d), sadh (77a), sado (26d,84d), sadr (94a), Sadr (155b), saer (163a), safe (141d,157d,174d), Safi (191), saga (79b,91a,138a,157a,161b,c, 168a), Saga, sage (13a,90d,100c,141c,145c,180b,183a), sago (54c, 59b,113b,125b,155c), sagy, saha, sahh (188), Saho (6c), sahu (153d), saic (86b,91d,170d), said (174c), Said (42d,101a,121b), sail (144c,185a), sain (20c,38d,48a), sair (140b,150d), sais (48d, 71d), Saka (10a), sake (84b,125d), saki (39c,84b,102a), sala (152a, b,c), Sala (50c), sale (14c,61c,62b,c,168b), salp (109c,148d), salt (35d,105b,123a,136c,141c,149d), sama (105c,169d), same (44d, 79b), samh (56b), samp (70b,77d,121b), sana (56a,166d), Sana (185d), sand (71d,146c), sane (128a), sang, sank, sano (152b), sans (63a,183b), sapa (70c), sapo (149c,166d), Sara (24d,183c), sard (26d,28d,65d,111a,142b,156d), Sard, Sarg (96d,125c), sari (48b,65b,77b), Sark (28d), Sart (82b,103b,170d), sasa (55c), sash (18a,45c,67b,182b), sass, sate (32d,52c,67d,70d,137c,159d), sati, Sati (49a,126b,147b), Sauk (192), saul (48a,168c), Saul (18c,86d, 115a), saum (189), save (52b,110c,123a,173c), sawk (188), sawn saxe (20d,33c), saya (117a)

- SA - asak (13d,168c,169a), asar (67b), Esau (82c,84a,128c), Esay, Isar (41a,104c,132a), osar (51b,67d,131b), tsar (42d,49d,60b,135c), usar (8d,16c), Usas (68d)

- - SA ansa (73c,93d,137c), Ausa, Besa (68b,119c), bisa (11a), bosa (12a), casa (152b), Disa (111a), dosa (74b), Elsa (70a,93c,110d, 177b,183c), kasa (48a), kusa, Lisa (183d), masa (37a), mesa (49b, 76d,119b,161a), Musa (16a), ossa (21d), Ossa (103d,110b,164b), pasa (46a,127c,152c), pesa (190), Pisa (90c), rasa (51c), Rosa (58d,134a,145d,183c), rusa, Rusa (41d,136d), sasa (55c), Susa (49a), Tesa (80c), Ursa (17b,36b,43d), vasa (46d,114a,160b,175d), Vasa, visa (114d), Xosa (86a)

S - - A   saba (56a,117a), Saba (143d), saga (79b,91a,138a,157a,161b,c, 168a), saha, Saka (10a), sala (152a,b,c), Sala (50c), sama (105c, 169d), sana (56a,166d), Sana (185d), sapa (70c), Sara (24d,183c), sasa (55c), saya (117a), Seba (18c,39d), sera (11b,20d,59a,83a, 180d), seta (23b,27c,73a,b,123b,153c), shea (25a,168c,d), Shoa (6c), sida (37a,126c,170a), sika (41d,84b), sima (132b), sina (46c), Sina (102d,103d), Sita (127d), siva (67a,120d), Siva (56d,77a), skua (19b,72c,84a,141a), soda (19a,149d,181a), sofa (44d), soga (70d,152b), Soga (191), Soia, soja (151b), soka (20c), sola (9a,48a, 74b,118c,154a,167b), soma (10c,21c,34a,48a,81d,136b), sora (19b, c,127b), soya (151b), stoa (33c,121a,c), Sula (65a), supa (168c), sura (87c,113b,166d), Susa (49a), Syra

- SB -   isba (135c)

S - - B   scab (80b,107d,157c), scob (42a), Serb (15d,148a,186c), slab (148b), Sleb (12a), slob (173d), slub (171c), snab (23c,139a), snib (54d,93c), snob (159c), snub (128c,148b), sorb (11d,103d,134b, 142d), Sorb (148a,180a), stab (14c,87a,117c), stib (19b,47a,137a), stub (156c), swab (102b), sweb (160d), swob (102b)

SC - -   scab (80b,107d,157c), scad (31a,57a,78b,88d,137c), scan (52b,93d, 98a,116d,128b,c,140d), scar (31a,184d), scat (26b,67a,d,126c, 169c), Scio, scob (42a), scon (162c), scop (120a), scot (14a,162b), Scot (64b,132c), scow (21a,58b), scud (32c,126c,135b,160c), scum (129b), scup (57a,121b), scur (78b), scut (145c,161b)

- SC -   asci (154a), esca (11c,44a,70c), esce (158d)

- - SC   aesc (12d,64d), Bosc (115c), DDSC (42a), disc (31b), fisc (52c,134c)

S - - C   saic (86b,91d,175d), spec

S - - D   Saad (12b), sadd (33a,40b,58c,107b), said (174c), Said (42d,101a, 121b), sand (71d,146c), sard (26d,28d,65d,111a,142b,156d), Sard, scad (31a,57a,78b,137c), scud (32c,126c,135b,160c), seed (70b, 111c,112c,119a,151b,154a), seid (103b), Seid 42d,101a, 171a), send (42c,44b,95c,121c,130a,144c,168b), shad (27d,57a, b,c), shed (27a,90c,101b,144b), shod, Sind, skid (148b), sled (40a), slid, sned (93d,125a), snod (169d), sold, spad (105b), Spad (118d), sped, spud (121d,151c), stad (151b,167d,176b), stod (40d,67d), stud (22b,25a,42d,54d,111c,143a,174a), sudd (40b,58c,107b), suld (188), surd (82c,177a), swad (94d), syed (103b), syud (103b)

SE - -   seah (188), seal (10c,d,54d,64c,96a,118b,128a), seam (85b,d,160a, 176d,185a), Sean (85b,96a), sear (23d,27d,72c,138c), seat (98c, 156b), Seba (18c,39d), sebi (34b), sech (97c), seck (173d), sect (42b,54a,114c), seed (70b,111c,112c,119a,151b,154a), seek (141c), seel (20c,32c,143b), seem (11c), seen, seep (110c,116a, 154b), seer (60a,124c,150c), sego (24b.25a,92b,174c), sehr (66d), seid (103b), Seid (42d,101a,171a), Seik (77b), Seim (120c), sein (146c), seip (110c), Seir (51b,94a,103d), seis (147b,152c), seit (189), Sejm (120c), self (48d,80d), sell (97a,115c,175b), seme (45c, 138b,151b,154b,155c,157b), semi (34b,80b,122c,d), send (42c, 44b,95c,121c,130a,144c,168b), senn (76b), Sens (63b), sent, seps, (93b,142d), sept (31d,82b,143a,149c), Sept (45b), sera (11b,20d, 59a,83a,180d), Serb (15d,148a,186c), sere (24d,46a,c,138c,183b), Sere (158b), serf (21d,148a), seri (18b), Seri (192), sero (34d,88d,

397

164b,178d), **Sert** (151d), **sesi** (20b,57a,149b), **sess** (149c,162b), **seta** (23b,27c,73a,b,123b,153c), **seth** (98d), **Seth** (7a,52b,68a,b,96a, 98d), **seti** (34a), **Seti** (116d), **sett** (115a,156d), **seve** (63a,182c), **sewn, sext** (26b,111b,147b)

- SE - asea (39b,177c), asem (9a,49a,69c), Aser (84a), esek (18d), esel (66b), eser, Iser (49a), oser (61b), used (6d,73a), usee, user (49d), uses (18a), yser

- - SE anse (61d), apse (9b,20a,31a,128c,130a,142b,175a), asse (25a, 60d,74a), base (6a,43b,44b,51c,60c,79b,94b,122b), bise (182a), bose (163c), case (22c,36c,81c,91a,108c), cise (147b), cose (29b), dose (123a), duse (83c), ease (7c,8d,35a,100d,129d,130b,c,150c), else (18b,79b,111d), ense (139b,158c), Erse (28a,64b,82b), esse (7a,18a,52d,89a,90a,159a,166c), fuse (98c), hase (74d), hose (156c), huse (180c), ipse (44d,89c), Jose (96a), lose (60a,100c), lyse, mese (71c), mise (8a,10a,70c), Mose (96b), muse (65b,93d, 120d,164c), Muse (68d), nase (26b,75a,124b), nose (118d,125a, 149b), oese (15d,119c), Oise, Ouse (132a,185d), owse, pise (127d), pose (14c,15d), rase (42b,d,91d), rese (127b), rise (49d,80b,155a), Rise (110d,150c), rose (33c), Rose (6a,50c,183c), ruse (13b,77c, 157b,169c), sise (62c,147b), vase, vise (31d,77d,114d), wise (136b)

S - - E sabe, sade (91d), safe (141d,157d,174d), sage (13a,90d,100c,141c, 145c,180b,183a), sake (84b,125d), sale (14c,61c,62b,c,168b), same (44d,79b), sane (128a), sate (32d,52c,67d,70d,137c,159d), save (52b,110c,123a,173c), saxe (20d,33c), seme (45c,138b,151b,154b, 155c,157b), sere (24d,46a,c,138c,183b), Sere (158b), seve (63a, 182c), shee (82b), shoe (166a), sice (71d,147b), side (13d,22a,b, 54a,58a,89a,161b), sime (101d), sine (64c,66b,90a,97c,126a,163b, 169d,183b), sipe (101a,110c,140b), sire (17d,55a,59d,124a,163b, 166b), sise (62c,147b), site (93b), sive (146a), size, skee (149c), Skye (163c), slee (140b,148c), sloe (14a,20b,64a,119d,181c), slue (97b,148b,160a), smee (19b,46c,d,118b,119d,141b,181b), Smee (116d), snee (40a,b,43d,87a), soie (62c), soke (44c,85d), sole (52c, 57a,b,58b,d,110c,115d,150a), some (114b,121c,126a), sore (23d, 142c), sote (150c), spae (139c), Spee (66d,70b), supe (53a,154d), sure (173d), syce (71d), syke (194), syne (140b,147a), sype (110c)

S - - F self (48d,80d), serf (21d,148a), souf (146b), stof (135c), surf (23a)

SG - - Sgau (88c)

S - - G sang, Sarg (96d,125c), shag (73b,105b,161d,166d), sing (26d,178a), skag (7d,46d), skeg (7d,86a,144d,157d,184a), slag (46c,99a,138c, 148d,177a), slog (157c,170b,177d), slug (46b,99b,157c), smug, snag (11b,27b,35c,87c,124b,166a), sneg (139b), snig (45d), snug (35a,38b,165c), Snug (99d), song (12c,170c), stag (65a,98d), stog (155a), sung, Sung (30b), swag (22a,156c), swig (46a,72c)

SH - - shad (27d,57a,b,c), shag (73b,105b,161d,166d), shah (116c), sham (41c,55b,60d,80a,123a,b,146d), Shan (13c,80d,88c,101d), shap, shat (87d), shaw (164b), Shaw (50c,53b), shay (110c), shea (25a, 168c,d), shed (27a,90c,101b,144b), shee (82b), Shem (107c), Shen (68a), sher (65d,165c), shet, shew (44c), shih (189), Shik (171a), shim (91d,144c,162a,179d), shin (91a,d,140b,143c), ship, shir (36d, 65d,165c), Shoa (6c), shod, shoe (166a), shoo (46b,67a,138b), shop, shoq (169a), shor (136d), Shor (162b), shot (9d,43d,90c,174d), shou

(41d), **show** (42b,44c,96b), **Shri** (17c,166c), **shul** (161a), **shun** (15a, 51b,52a), **shut**

- SH - **Asha** (191), **ashy** (113a,178a), **Isha** (174a), **Tshi** (69c), **Usha** (16a, 150c)

- - SH **bash, bish** (120b), **bosh, bush, cash** (101c), **cosh** (35a,97c), **cush** (101c), **Cush** (51d,73c), **dash** (125c,162d), **dish, fash** (140c,176a), **fish, gash** (40a), **gish** (102c), **gosh, gush** (35a,154c), **hash, hish, hush** (17b,146c), **josh** (85b), **kish** (16d,70c), **Kish** (137c), **Kush lash** (58c,87b,165c,180d), **losh** (178b), **lush** (94d), **mash** (39b, 156c), **mesh** (50d,106c), **mush** (97d), **Nash** (9c), **Nish** (19d), **pish** (36c,107d), **posh** (49b,148c), **push** (145c), **rash** (75a), **resh** (91d), **rush, sash** (18a,45c,67b,182b), **sish** (79b), **sosh** (81d), **tash** (154d), **tosh** (106a), **tush** (167b), **wash, wish** (42d)

S - - H **saah** (188), **sadh** (77a), **sahh** (188), **samh** (56b), **sash** (18a,45c,67b, 182b), **seah** (188), **sech** (97c), **seth** (98d), **Seth** (7a,52b,68a,b,96a, 98d), **shah** (116c), **shih** (189), **sigh, Sikh** (77b), **sinh** (97c), **sish** (79b), **soph, sosh** (81d), **such** (146d)

SI - - **siak** (72d), **sial** (112a), **Siam** (163d,181a), **sice** (71d,147b), **sick, sida** (37a,126c,170a), **side** (13d,22a,b,54a,58a,89a,161b), **sidi** (103b, 166b), **sidy** (123b), **sier** (57a,118b), **sift** (140d,142c,146b), **sigh, sign** (121c,146c), **sika** (41d,84b), **Sikh** (77b), **silk** (53b,179c), **sill** (45c,76c,165a,182b), **silo** (59a,156d), **silt** (104b,142a), **sima** (132b), **sime** (101d), **Simi** (82d), **simp** (59c,146d), **sina** (46c), **Sina** (102d, 103d), **Sind, sine** (64c,66b,90a,97a,126a,163b,169d,183b), **sing** (26d,178a), **sinh** (97c), **sink** (41c,43c,46b,158a) **sino** (34a), **siol** (82c), **sion** (125c,158c), **Sion** (75b,c,83a,157d), **sipe** (101a,110c, 140b), **sire** (17d,55a,59d,124a,163b,166b), **sirí** (18b), **sise** (62c, 147b), **sish** (79b), **sisi** (121b), **siss, sist** (139b), **Sita** (127d), **site** (93b), **sito** (34b), **siva** (67a,120d), **Siva** (56d,77a), **Sive** (146a), **size, sizy** (176d), **sizz**

- SI - **Asia** (48a), **Asin** (102a), **Hsia** (30b,47c), **Isis** (68d,78c,111d), **tsia** (162c), **Tsin** (30b)

- - SI **Absi** (191), **assi** (77d), **dasi** (77a), **desi** (85d), **kasi** (116b), **Lasi** (191), **nasi** (34c,108a,115a), **nisi** (90a,173c), **pasi** (94b), **sesi** (20b,57a), **sisi** (121b), **susi** (53b,d)

S - - I **Safi** (191), **saki** (39c,84b,102a), **sari** (48b,65b,77b), **sati, Sati** (49a, 126b,147b), **sebi** (34b), **semi** (34b,80b,122c,d), **seri** (18b), **Seri** (192), **sesi** (20b,57a,149b), **seti** (34a), **Seti** (116c), **Shri** (17c,166c), **sidi** (103b,166b), **Simi** (82d), **siri** (18b), **sisi** (121b), **soli** (12c,110c), **sori** (55c,64a), **sufi** (103a,116c), **sugi** (84b), **suji** (180c), **susi** (53b,d)

SK - - **skag** (7d,46d), **skat** (181b), **Skat** (155b), **skee** (149c), **skeg** (7d,86a, 144d,157d,184a), **sken** (164a), **skeo** (57d), **skep** (16d,17c,77c), **skew** (148a,160c,171b,c), **skey** (185d), **skid** (148b), **skil** (57a), **skim** (67c), **skin** (53a,76c,115c,d), **skio** (57d), **skip** (110b,114c,147c), **skir, skit** (145c), **skiv** (151b), **skua** (19b,72c,84a,141a), **Skye** (163c), **skyr** (21d,151a), **skyt** (138c,140b)

- SK - **Askr** (107d)

- - SK **bask** (94d), **bisk** (120b,151a), **bosk** (164b), **busk** (17b,37b,55d, 161b), **cask, cusk** (57b), **desk, disk** (31b), **dusk** (171c), **fisk** (24d,52c,134c), **husk** (53a,78d,142a), **mask** (44a,45c), **mosk** (97b,

399

103b), **musk** (116b), **Omsk, pisk** (9c,19b), **risk** (74d), **rusk** (23a), **task** (156b), **Tosk** (8c), **tusk** (167b)

S - - K **sack** (43d,118a,119d,182b), **sank, Sark** (28d), **Sauk** (192), **sawk** (188), **seck** (173d), **seek** (141c), **Seik** (77b), **Shik** (171a), **siak** (72d), **sick, silk** (53b,179c), **sink** (41c,43c,46b,158a), **soak** (46c,137c), **Sobk** (38d), **sock** (157c,182a), **sook** (22a,25c,97a), **souk** (22a,97a), **suck, sulk** (159a), **sunk**

SL - - **slab** (148b), **slag** (46c,99a,138c,148d,177a), **slam** (180d,182d), **slap** (24a,128c,148c), **slat** (58b,89a,117c,184a), **Slav** (13c,40c,48b,52a, 120b,135b), **slaw, slay, Sleb** (12a), **sled** (40a), **slee** (140b,148c), **slew** (160a), **sley** (179b), **slid, slim** (148b,160a), **slip** (67c,119a), **slit** (40a), **slob** (173d), **sloe** (14a,20b,64a,119d,181c), **slog** (157c,170b, 177d), **sloo** (160a), **slop, slot** (10d,11b,41d,110d,167d,168a,181b), **slow** (43c), **slub** (171c), **slue** (97b,148b,160a), **slug** (46b,99b,157c), **slum, slur** (44b,124c,148b,168a)

- SL - **isle** (8b,53c,81d,82d,86b,88a), **Oslo**

S - - L **saal** (66c,73b), **sail** (144c,185a), **saul** (48a,168c), **Saul** (18c,86d, 115a), **seal** (10c,d,54d,64c,96a,118b,128a), **seel** (20c,32c,143b), **sell** (97a,115c,175b), **shul** (161a), **sial** (112a), **sill** (45c,76c,165a, 182b) **siol** (82c), **skil** (57a), **soil** (154d,159a,163c), **soul** (10d,125a, 153c,176d)

SM - - **smee** (19b,46c,d,118b,119d,141b,181b), **Smee** (116d), **smew** (19b, 46d,99a,137d), **smug, smur** (32c,46b,100c), **smut** (32d,44a,119a, 150c)

- SM - **ismy** (45a)

- - SM **kasm** (189)

S - - M **saum** (189), **scum** (129b), **seam** (85b,d,160a,176d,185a), **seem** (11c), **Seim** (120c), **Sejm** (120c), **sham** (41c,55b,60d,80a,123a,b, 146d), **Shem** (107c), **shim** (91d,144c,162a,179d), **Siam** (163d,181a), **skim** (67c), **slam** (180d,182d), **slim** (148b,160a), **slum, stem** (29b, 125a,154d,155a,156d), **stom** (34c), **stum** (70c,105c,131a,173a), **swam, swim** (58c), **swum**

SN - - **snab** (23c,139a), **snag** (11b,27b,35c,87c,124b,166a), **snap** (23a, 36d,38b,48b,54d,56c,58c,149d), **sned** (93d,125a,140a), **snee** (40a, b,43d,87a), **sneg** (139b), **snib** (54d,93c), **snig** (45d), **snip** (32b, 40a), **snob** (159c), **snod** (169d), **snow, snub** (128c,148b), **snug** (35a,38b,165c), **Snug** (99d), **snup** (149b)

- SN - **asno** (151d), **esne** (10c,45b,142c,148a,164d)

S - - N **Saan** (24d), **sain** (20c,38d,48a), **sawn, scan** (52b,93d,98a,116d, 128b,c,140d), **scon** (162c), **Sean** (85b,96a), **seen, sein** (146c), **senn** (76b), **sewn, Shan** (13c,80d,88c,101d), **Shen** (68a), **shin** (91a,d,140b, 143c), **shun** (15a,51b,52a), **sign** (121c,146c), **sion** (125c,158c), **Sion** (75b,c,83a,157d), **sken** (164a), **skin** (53a,76c,115c,d), **soon** (123a, 145c), **sorn** (139a,d), **span** (23b,107b,113a,128b,162c), **spin** (131a, 180d), **spun, sten** (72c,95a), **stun** (145a,157d), **sunn** (56a), **Svan** (27d), **swan** (19b,33a)

SO - - **soak** (46c,137c), **soap, soar** (59a), **Sobk** (38d), **sock** (157c,182a), **soco** (22d), **soda** (19a,149d,181a), **sofa** (44d), **soft** (48b,95d,99d, 163a), **soga** (70d,152b), **Soga** (191), **soho!, Soho** (93c), **Soia, soie**

400

(62c), **soll** (154d,159a,163c), **solr** (61c), **soja** (151b), **soka** (20c), **soke** (44c,85d), **sola** (9a,48a,74b,118c,154a,167b), **sold**, **sole** (52c,57a,b, 58b,d,110c,115d,150a), **soli** (12c,110c), **solo** (12c,89a,110c), **soma** (10c,21c,34a,48a,81d,136b), **some** (114b,121c,126a), **song** (12c, 170c), **sons** (98d,109d), **sook** (22a,25c,97a), **soon** (123a,145c), **soot** (20b,26c,88a), **soph**, **Sopt** (45b), **sora** (19b,c,127b), **sorb** (11d,103d, 134b,142d), **Sorb** (148a,180a), **sore** (23d,142c), **sori** (55c,64a), **sorn** (139a,d), **sors** (44d,89b), **sort** (31d,39c,70b,86b,153a), **sory** (176d), **sosh** (81d), **soso** (99c,114c,166d), **sote** (150c), **souf** (146b), **souk** (22a,97a), **soul** (10d,125a,153c,176d), **soup, sour, sous** (62d,172c), **soya** (151b)

- SO - **asok** (13d), **asom** (18d), **asop** (180b), **asor** (75c,105a), **Esop** (53b, 54a), **esox** (57b)

- - SO **also** (10b,18b,80a), **Caso** (82d), **coso** (152c), **enso** (34d,183b), **huso** (180c), **ipso** (89c), **koso** (6c,80d), **Koso** (192,193), **Muso** (192), **peso** (99c), **piso** (189), **soso** (99c,114c,166d), **yeso** (72d)

S - - O **saco** (189), **sado** (26d,84d), **sago** (54c,59b,113b,125b,155c), **Saho** (6c), **sano** (152b), **sapo** (149c,166d), **Scio**, **sego** (24b,25a,92b,174c), **sero** (34d,88d,164b,178d), **shoo** (46b,67a,138b), **silo** (59a,156d), **sino** (34a), **sito** (34b), **skeo** (57d), **skio** (57d), **sloo** (160a), **soco** (22d), **soho!**, **Soho** (93c), **solo** (12c,89a,110c), **soso** (99c,114c,166d), **Sumo**

SP - - **spad** (105b), **Spad** (118d), **spae** (139c), **span** (23b,107b,113a,128b, 162c), **spar** (22c,24c,64b,97b,100b,144d), **spat** (112c,126b,134b), ~~**spec, sped, Spee**~~ (66d,70b), **spes**, **Spes** (69a,78a), **spet** (16c,57a, 142c), **spew** (35a,49a), **spex**, **spey**, **spin** (131a,180d), **spir** (97c), **spit** (120a,132b,c), **spot** (93b,118c,154d,162a), **spry** (7a,107b), **spud** (121d,151c), **spun**, **spur** (10d,67d,167d,168a,181b), **sput** (21c)

- SP - **espy** (44a,142a)

- - SP **cusp** (38c,78b,119a,120a,b), **gasp** (113c), **hasp** (31d,54d,153c), **lisp** (153b), **rasp** (56b,70d,140d), **risp** (99a), **wasp, wisp** (24b,148c)

S - - P **salp** (109c,148d), **samp** (70b,77d,121b), **scop** (120a), **scup** (57a, 121b), **seep** (110c,116a,154b), **seip** (110c), **shap, ship, shop, simp** (59c,146d), **skep** (16d,17c,77c), **skip** (110b,114c,147c), **slap** (24a, 128c,148c), **slip** (67c,119a), **slop, snap** (23a,36d,38b,48b,54d,56c, 58c,149d), **snip** (32b,40a), **snup** (149b), **soap, soup, step** (70b,112b, 177b,d), **stop** (73b,111b), **sump** (28c,45d,100b), **swap** (168a), **swop** (168a)

S - - Q **shoq** (169a)

S - - R **Saar** (63b,102d,132a), **sadr** (94a), **Sadr** (155b), **saer** (163a), **sair** (140b,150d), **scar** (31a,184d), **scur** (78b), **sear** (23d,27d,72d,138c), **seer** (60a,124c,150c), **sehr** (66d), **Seir** (51b,94a,103d), **sher** (65d, 165c), **shir** (36d,65d,165c), **shor** (136d), **Shor** (162b), **sier** (57a, 118b), **skir, skyr** (21d,151a), **slur** (44b,124c,148b,168a), **smur** (32c,46b,100c), **soar** (59a), **soir** (61c), **sour, spar** (22c,24c,64b,97b, 100b,144d), **spir** (97c), **spur** (10d,67d,167d,168a,181b), **star** (14a, 21c,94c,100c), **ster** (158c,d), **stir** (8a,13a,35b,78d,100d,104a), **suer** (124d)

- SS - **asse** (25a,60d,74a), **assi** (77d), **esse** (7a,18a,52d,89a,90a,159a, 166c), **ossa** (21d), **Ossa** (103d,110b,164b)

- - SS bass (57b,c,177a), Bess (76c,183d), boss (49d,157d), buss (87a, 148c), cass (140c,177a), Cass (147a), cess (91d,94c,162b), coss (98a), cuss, diss (98b), doss (17c), fass (189), fess (23c,51b), foss (44d,100d), fuss (22b,35b), hiss (146a), jass (160d), jess (157a), joss (30b), kiss (148c), koss (188), lass (95b), less (100c,108b,141d), liss (54b,58b,60c,129d,140a), loss (42c,123d,178b), mass (8a,24b, 35b,142d), mess (22b,44b,77c,85d,104b,165c,173d), miss, moss (91d,104c,114a,170c), muss (135b,173d), ness (26b,75a,124b), pass (110b,155c), puss, Riss (66a), ross (16c,161d), Ross (50c), Russ (135b), sass, sess (149c,162b), siss, Tass (107a,135d,151b), Tess (73d,164c,183d), toss (24a,132d), viss (189)

S - - S sais (48d,71d), sans (63a,183b), sass, seis (147b,152c), sens (63b), seps (93b,142d), sess (149c,162b), siss, sons (98d,109d), sors (44d, 89b), sous (62d,172c), spes, Spes (69a,78a), suds (59a)

ST - - stab (14c,87a,117c), stad (151b,167d,176b), stag (65a,98d), star (14a,21c,94c,100c), stat (72d), stay (72d,124c,130a,134a,162a), stem (29b,125a,154d,155a,156d), sten (72c,95a), step (70b,112b, 177b,d), ster (158c,d), stet (91b,123d,124c), stev (155b), stew (21c,44b,184d), stib (19b,47a,137a), stir (8a,13a,35b,78d,100d, 104a), stoa (33c,121a,c), stod (40d,67d), stof (135c), stog (155a), stom (34c), stop (73b,111b), stot (154d,155d,157d,179b,186a), stow (112b), stub (156c), stud (22b,25a,42d,54d,111c,143a,174a), stum (70c,105c,131a,173a), stun (145a,157d), Styx (29b,73a,105c)

- ST - asta (188), Asta (107a,164c), Asti (83d,182b), esta (152d,164c), este (152b,d,164c), Este (55c,83c,d,112d), Esth (16a,51d), oste (21d,83b)

- - ST bast (16c,56a,117b,184a), Bast (27b), best (41d,159c,160a), bust, cast (165b,167c), cest (18a,67b), dost, dust, east, East (111b), erst (60b), fast (56d,126c,141d,160c,173a,d), fest, fist (80c), fust (105c,143b), gest (7c,41d,52d,133c), gist (95c,118c), gust, hast, hest (35a), hist (25c,93d), host (13a,51d,104c), jest (169c), just (51b,54b), kist (29d,58a,139b), last (36c,50b,145a,174c), lest (59d, 163d), list (26d,27b,75b,83d,134a,138b,165d), lost, lust (41b), mast (17c,108d,120b,144d,152d), mist (46b,59b,174d), most, must (70c,101a,106d,157d,182c), myst (71c,123b), Nast (9c,27a), nest (38b,74b,130d,149c,160b), oast* (15d,86b,112a), oust (44c, 49a,52b,125d), past (25c,69d,165d), pest (108c,116b,118d,170a), pist (25c), post (89a,95c,155d), rest (15d,91b,104d,105a,115a,b, 130a,b,161b), rust (37b,112c,119a), sist (139b), test (26a,51c,144a, 169c,170c), vast (78d,79d), vest (32c,177b), wast, west, West (9c, 50b,109b), wist (87c), zest (55d,72d)

S - - T salt (35d,105b,123a,136c,141c,149d), Sart (82b,103b,170d), scat (26b,67a,d,126c,169c), scot (14a,162b), Scot (64b,132c), scut (145c,161b), seat (98c,156b), sect (42b,54a,114c), seit (189), sent, sept (31d,82b,143a,149c), Sept (45b), Sert (151d), sett (115a,156d), sext (26b,111b,147b), shat (87d), shot (9d,43d,90c, 174d), shut, sift (140d,142c,146b), silt (104b,142a), skat (181b), Skat (155b), skit (145c), skyt (138c,140b), slat (58b,89a,117c, 184a), slit (40a), slot (10d,11b,41d,110d,167d,168a,181b), smut (32d,44a,119a,150c), soft (48b,95d,99d,163a), soot (20b,26c,88a), Sopt (45b), sort (31d,39c,70b,86b,153a), spat (112c,126b,134b),

402

spet (16c,57a,142c), **spit** (120a,132b,c), **spot** (93b,118c,154d,162a), **sput** (21c), **stat** (72d), **stet** (91b,123d,124c), **stot** (154d,155d,157d, 179b,186a), **suet** (54d), **suit** (38a,58a,91a,112a,119c,137c), **swat** (15d,20d,32d,157c), **Swat** (103a), **swot**

SU - -   **such** (146d), **suck**, **sudd** (40b,58c,107b), **suds** (59a), **suer** (124d), **suet** (54d), **sufi** (103a,116c), **sugi** (84b), **suit** (38a,58a,91a,112a, 119c,137c), **suji** (180c), **Suku** (191), **Sula** (65a), **suld** (188), **sulk** (159a), **Sulu** (102c), **Sumo, sump** (28c,45d,100b), **sung, Sung** (30b), **sunk, sunn** (56a), **supa** (168c), **supe** (53a,154d), **sura** (87c,113b, 166d), **surd** (82c,177a), **sure** (173d), **surf** (23a), **Susa** (49a), **susi** (53b,d), **susu** (20c), **Susu** (191), **Susy** (183d)

- SU -   **Asur** (68c), **Esus, tsun** (30b), **Usun** (191)

- - SU   **ansu** (11d), **Apsu** (29a), **ausu** (168c,180b), **Jesu, masu** (57a,84c), **Nosu** (27d), **susu** (20c), **Susu** (191), **vasu** (106c), **Vasu** (176d)

S - - U   **sahu** (153d), **Sgau** (88c), **shou** (41d), **Suku** (191), **Sulu** (102c), **susu** 20c), **Susu** (191)

SV - -   **Svan** (27d)

S - - V   **skiv** (151b), **Slav** (13c,40c,48b,52a,120b,135b), **stev** (155b)

SW - -   **swab** (102b), **swad** (94d), **swag** (22a,156c), **swam, swan** (19b,33a), **swap** (168a), **swat** (15d,20d,32d,157c), **Swat** (103a), **sway** (104a), **sweb** (160d), **swig** (46a,72c), **swim** (58c), **swiz** (160c), **swob** (102b), **swop** (168a), **swot, swow** (100a), **swum**

S - - W   **scow** (21a,58b), **shaw** (164b), **Shaw** (50c,53b), **shew** (44c), **show** (42b,44c,96b), ~~skew~~ (148a,160c,171b,c), **siaw, slew** (160a), **slow** (43c), **smew** (19b,46d,99a,137d), **snow, spew** (35a,49a), **stew** (21c, 44b,184d), **stow** (112b), **swow** (100a)

S - - X   **spex, Styx** (29b,73a,105c)

SY - -   **syce** (71d), **syed** (103b), **syke** (194), **syne** (140b,147a), **sype** (110c), **Syra, syud** (103b)

- - SY   **busy, cosy** (149c), **easy** (54a,146d,149d,172b), **Josy** (183d), **mosy** (67d), **nosy, rosy** (21a,111a), **Susy** (183d)

S - - Y   **sagy, shay** (110c), **sidy** (123b), **sizy** (176d), **skey** (185d), **slay, sley** (179b), **sory** (176d), **Spey, spry** (7a,107b), **stay** (72d,124c,130a, 134a), **Susy** (183d), **sway** (104a)

S - - Z   **sizz, swiz** (160c)

TA - -   **Taal** (7d,88c,151a), **taar** (12b), **tabi** (84c,149d), **tabu** (59d,111d), **tace** (13a,155d), **tack** (28d,37d,54c), **tact** (43c,d,116a), **tael** (91d, 179d), **Taft** (29d), **taha** (179b), **tahr** (68a,76d), **tail** (11d,27d,59b, 143b), **tain** (166a), **tair** (68a,76d), **tait** (14d), **tajo** (152a,d), **take, takt** (105a,163a), **Taku** (80c), **taky, tala** (16d,113a,168c,d), **talc** (28d,63b,99c,100b,122a,149c), **tale** (91a,185b), **tali** (189), **talk, tall** (118d), **Tama** (192), **tame** (45a,b,66a), **Tame, tamp** (46b,112b, 121d,127d), **tana** (159a), **Tana** (87d), **Tane** (120d), **tang** (30b,58b, 186b), **tanh** (97c), **tank** (175a,d), **Tano** (192), **Taos** (192), **tapa** (16c, 32c,53b,56a,74b,104b,112b,113d,120d), **tape** (16a,19a,128d), **tapu, tara** (22a,55c,113a,168c), **Tara** (82b,c,138b), **tare** (9a,18d,41a, 176a,179d), **Tari** (47d,69a), **tarn** (87d,103d,120d), **taro** (13c,48c, 49b,64b,112b,120a,133d,155c,170a,c), **tarp** (26b,178d), **tart** (114d), **tash** (154d), **task** (156b), **Tass** (107a,135d,151b), **tate** (183a), **tatt**

(87c), **tatu** (12d), **Tatu, taun** (188), **taut** (163b,165c), **Tave** (183d), **Tavy** (183d), **tawa** (106d,168c), **taxi** (13a,125b), **taxo** (13a)

- TA -   **atap** (113b), **atar** (58d,116b,134a), **Etah** (71d,51c), **etal** (89a), **etat** (62d), **Ptah** (48d,98c), **stab** (14c,87a,117c), **stad** (151b,167d,176b), **stag** (65a,98d), **star** (14a,21c,94c,100c), **stat** (72d), **stay** (72d,124c, 130a,134a,162a), **utac** (22d), **Utah** (180b), **utas** (49a,109c)

- - TA   **acta** (41d,123d,128d,164c), **Aeta** (94d,95d,100a,106b,117a), **alta** (89c,152d), **anta** (83d,117c,d,121a), **Anta** (164a), **Arta** (72b), **asta** (188), **Asta** (107a,164c), **atta** (58d,90c,97d,160c,173d), **Atta** (94d,95d,100a,106b,117a), **bata** (30a,142d), **beta** (71a, 91c,141d), **bota** (189), **cata** (122c), **cota** (117a), **data** (54a), **dita** (117a), **esta** (152d,164c), **Etta** (183c), **gata** (143c), **geta** (84b,145a), **Gita, iota** (71a,85c,91c,114c,166c,176a,180d), **jota** (151c), **keta** (45a), **kota** (117a), **Kota** (45d), **lata** (85d, 95d), **lota** (24c,121d,178d), **Lota meta** (132d,133a), **Meta, mota** (103a), **muta** (28d,103a), **nata** (47c), **Nata** (15c), **nota** (15c, 89c), **octa** (122c), **pata** (32c,160d), **pita** (9c,28b,56a,83a), **rata** (29d,56b,89d,96c,106d,120c,168c), **rita, Rita** (37b,78d,183c), **rota** (27c,30d,38a,79a,92d,133a,134a,b,180c), **Ruta** (76b,134d), **seta** (23b,27c,73a,b,123b,153c), **Sita** (127d), **tota** (71d), **veta** (104a), **vita** (89c,92a), **vota** (133b), **weta** (93c), **yeta** (84c), **zeta** (71b,91c)

T - - A   **taha** (179b), **tala** (16d,113a,168c,d), **Tama** (192), **tana** (159a), **Tana** (87d), **tapa** (16c,32c,53b,56a,74b,104b,112b,113d,120d), **tara** (22a, 55c,113a,168c), **Tara** (82b,c,138b), **tawa** (106d,168c), **tcha** (162c), **teca, Teca** (192), **Teda** (191), **tela** (22d,98c,121b,166a,179c), **tema** (12a,164a), **Tema, tera** (23d,84c), **tesa** (80c), **Tewa** (193), **Thea** (162c), **Tina** (183d), **tiza** (172a), **Toba** (80c), **Toda** (45d,76d), **toga** (132d,133a,b), **tola** (48a,80d,180a), **Tola** (85b), **Toma** (191), **tooa** (17c), **tora** (11a,44d,74a,75c,85c,90b,102d,115d), **tota** (71d), **toxa** (153d), **tsia** (162c), **tuba** (105a,137d), **tufa** (121b,177a), **tula** (9a), **Tula, tuna** (57a,b,123b), **tuza** (119d)

T - - B   **theb** (188), **thob** (128a), **tomb**

TC - -   **tcha** (162c), **tche** (13d,30b,105a), **tchi, Tchi, tchu**

- TC -   **etch, itch**

T - - C   **talc** (28d,63c,99c,100b,122a,149c)

T - - D   **tend** (26d,80b,93d,100a), **thud, tied, tind** (86b), **toad** (10a,17a, 63d,126d), **toed, told** (129c), **trod, tund** (121d)

TE - -   **teak** (41a,48a,168c), **teal** (19b,20d,46c,d), **team** (38c,72a,113a), **tean** (140c,167a), **tear** (67c,87b,130a), **teca, Teca** (192), **Tech, teck** (128b), **Teco** (192), **Teda** (191), **teel** (142d), **teem** (6b,121d), **teen** (139b,c,140b,158d), **teer** (25b,69d), **Tees** (108a), **teff** (6c), **tegg** (143d,171d), **tehr** (27c,68a), **Teig** (96a), **teil** (92b,c,168c), **teju** (151b), **tela** (22d,98c,121b,166a,179c), **tele** (34b,122c), **teli** (94b), **tell** (105d,129c,154b), **Tell** (160d), **tema** (12a,164a), **Tema, tend** (26d,80b,93d,100a) **tene** (34d,131b), **teng** (188), **tent** (26b), 115a), **Teos** (82a), **tera** (23d,84c), **term** (92b,105b,142b,166b), **tern** (19b,32d,72c,94a,138c,141a,160a), **terp** (12b,123a), **tesa** (80c), **Tess** (73d,164c,183d), **test** (26a,51c,144a,169c,170c), **tete** (61d,73b,74d), **teth** (91d), **Tewa** (193), **text** (21c,140d), **teyl** (92b, c,168c)

404

- TE - atef (39a,48d), aten (150a,159b), Ateo (120d), Ater (18c), ates (160c), Itea (145d,160c,181d), item (6d,13b,42d,51a,90d,92d,107a, 113d,114c), Iten (192), iter (22d,76c,85c,89c,114d,132a,b,133a,b), Otea (71a,82d), stem (29b,125a,154d,155a,156d), sten (72c,95a), step (70b,112b,177b,d), ster (158c,d), stet (91b,123d,124c), stev (155b), stew (21c,44b,184d)

- - TE ante (87a,89a,115b,120b,122b,125d,154d), bate (43c,91b,100d), bete (61a,107c), bite (29d,156b), cate (165c), cete (180b,c), cite (15a,98d,126d,159b), cote (19b,143d,144a,b), cute (39c), date (64a,153a), dite (150b), dote (17a,90b,94b,97a,112a,139d,165d), ente (70b,151d), este (152b,d,164c), Este (55c,83c,d,112d), ette (158a,c,d), fate (42d,52a,87a,94a), fete (55d,129b), fute (51c), gate (51a,121b), gite (62a,118d), hate (6a,43a), jete (16a), jute (37a,48a,56a,133d,136a), Jute, Kate (143c,183d), kite (19c,49a, 74c,d), late (128c), lete, lite (158c,d), lote (24c,94a), lute (11c,28b, 84d,105a,131d), mate (18c,35b,41d,113a,154a,162c), mete (9a, 11d,22b,44c,45b,98a,121c), mite (12b,81b,82a,114a,c,148c,d,181b), mote (114c,153a), mute (146c,153b), Nate (22b), nete (71c,108b, 163d), note (98c,109b,124b,128d,130a,177c), oste (21d,83b), pate (39a,74d), pete (136b), Pete, rate (11d,14a,31d,36b,51d,52a,70b, 85c,112b,123b,127d,128a,138c,143a,174b), rete (106c,119c), rite (93a,131d), rote (130b,134b,143a,159d), rute (188), sate (32d,52c, 67d,70d,137c,159d), site (93b), sote (150c), tate (183a), tete (61d, 73b,74d), tote (27a,73c), tute (171b), vite (62b), vote (60b), Vote (56d), Wate (141a), Wote (191), yate (51d,168c)

T - - E tace (13a,155d), take, tale (91a,185b), tame (45a,b,66a), Tame, Tane (120d), tape (16a,19a,128c), tare (9a,18d,41a,176a,179d), tate (183a), Tave (183d), tche (13d,30b,105a), tele (34b,122c), tene (34d,131b), tete (61d,73b,74d), thee (124b), tice (9a,38c,51a, 185d), tide (39d,75d,109c,141c,159d), tige (118a), tike (29d), tile (31d,56d,72b,95b,133c,163c), time (47a,131a), tine (11b,124b, 167b), tipe (168b), tire (15a,22a,52d,55a,179b,180d), tobe (7d, 137b), tode (80a,148a), tole (9a,51a,99b,163a), tome (21d,177c), tone (6c,118c,150d), tope (24a,46b,57a,143c,151a), tore, tote (27a, 73c), tree (11d,37a,66a,184b), true (7a,8d,37b,54b,94c,149c), tube (118b,158a), tuke (26b,53b), tule (24b,27c), tune (8b,12c, 98c), tute (171b), twee, tyee (29d), tyke (29d), tyne, Tyne (108a), type (31d,115a,155a), tyre (15a), Tyre (31b,90d,117b)

T - - F teff (6c), tiff (126b), toff (40d), tref (172b), tuff (121b,177a), turf (115c,149d,160b)

T - - G tang (30b,58b,186b), tegg (143d,171d), Teig (96a), teng (188), thug (65a), ting (166a), Ting (30c), tong (30a,c,), toug (171a), trig (106a,148d,154b,169d), tung (110a,168c), twig

TH - - Thai (146a), than (35b), thar (68a,76d), that (42b,124b,129c), thaw, Thea (162c), theb (188), thee (124b), them (124b), then, thew (104c), they (124b), thin (43b,c,148b), this (42b,124b), thob (128a), Thor (7c,68c,99c,100c,109c,165b), Thos (84a,181c), thou (124b), thud, thug (65a), thus (149c)

- T H - Otho (133a)

- - TH acth (13b), bath, Bath (50d,151c), beth (91c), Beth (8c,183d), both, doth, Esth (16a,51d), Gath (117a), Goth (16c,163d), hath,

405

Heth (77c), Hoth (20c), Jeth (102a), kath (14a), kith (63c), lath (157c), lith (34d,156c), loth (15a,173d), math (77a), moth, Moth (112d), muth (188), myth (8b,91a), Nath (155c), oath (119c,150a), path (132a,134b), pith (37a,51c,67b,95c,97a,119b,126d), rath (76d,162d), ruth (35b,118c), Ruth (105b,183c), seth (98d), Seth (7a,52b,68a,b,96a,98d), teth (91d), Urth (68d,107d,163d), Voth (191), with (10b)

T - - H tanh (97c), tash (154d), Tech, teth (91d), toph (75c), tosh (106a), tush (167b)

TI - - Tiam, tiao, tiar (39a,75a,121a), Tibu (191), tice (9a,38c,51a,185d), tick (12b,20d,97c), tide (39d,75d,109c,141c,159d), tidy (106a, 111b), tied, tien (147d), tier (118a,134b), tiff (126b), tige (118a), tike (29d), Tiki (120c), tile (31d,56d,72b,95b,133c,163c), till (39c, 101c,173d), tilt (26b,d,166a), time (47a,131a), Tina (183d), tind (86b), tine (11b,124b,167b), ting (166a), Ting (30c), Tino (136d), tint (33c,d,114d), tiny (100c,148c), tion (158b), Tiou (192), tipe (168b), tipi (181b), tire (15a,22a,52d,55a,179b,180d), tiro (9b,17d, 108c), titi (20d,102a,145d,168d,181b), Tito (186c), tiza (172a)

- TI - Atik (155b), atip (14b,166a), atis (76d,102a), itis (158c), otic (14c, d,47b), Otis (9c,d,24d,82a,111a), stib (19b,47a,137a), stir (8a, 13a,35b,78d,100d,104a)

- - TI anti (7d,111a,122b), Anti (193), Asti (83d,182b), biti (20b), Guti, Hati (48d), hoti, Inti (159b), jati (27b), jiti, joti, Leti (82d), liti (60d), Loti (63a,176a), neti (164a), rati (189), roti (62c), sati, Sati (49a,126b,147b), seti (34a), Seti (116d), titi (20d,102a,145d,168d, 181b), viti (176b), yati (76d), zati (21d)

T - - I tabi (84c,149d) tali (189), Tari (47d,69a), taxi (13a,125b), tchi, Tchi, teli (94b), Thai (146a), Tiki (120c), tipi (181b), titi (20d,102a, 145d,168d,181b), topi (37a,75a,118c), tori (101b), tshi, Tshi (69c), Tupi (192), Turi (191), tuwi (117a,168c), Tybi (102a)

- TK - Atka (11a)

T - - K tack (28d,37d,54d), talk, tank (175a,d), task (156b), teak (41a, 48a,168c), teck (128b), tick (12b,20d,97c), tock (7d,19b),tonk (173c), took, Tosk (8c), trek (85c,93c,99d,168b), tuck (156b), Turk (101d,102d,106a,111d), tusk (167b)

- TL - atle (136d,161d,169b), Atli (14c,72b,79a,107d)

- - TL rotl (103b,111c)

T - - L Taal (7d,88c,151a), tael (91d,179d), tail (11d,27d,59b,143b), tall (118d), teal (19b,20d,46c,d), teel (142d), teil (92b,c,168c), tell (105d,129c,154b), Tell (160d), teyl (92b,c,168c), till (39c,101c, 173d), toil (46c,184c), toll (131c), tool (27c), tuel

TM - - T-men (168b)

- TM - atma (150d), atmo (34d,174d), Atmu (143a,159b), itmo (18b)

T - - M team (38c,72a,113a), teem (6b), term (92b,105b,142b,166b), them (124b), tiam, toom (139b), tram (170a), trim (40a,106a,154b, 160a,165c,169d), turm (132d)

- TN - etna (75b,153c,157a,175d,177a,c)

T - - N tain (166a), tarn (87d,103d,120d), taun (188), tean (140c,167a), teen (139b,c,140b,158d), tern (19b,32d,72c,94a,138c,141a,160a),

406

than (35b), then, thin (43b,c,148b), tien (147d), tion (158b), T-men (168b), toon (80c,95b,168c), torn (130a), town (73c), tran (7a), trin (169d), tron (140d,180a), Tsin (30b), tsun (30b), tuan (95d,147b,166c), turn (28d,131a,175a), twin (45c,171d)

TO - -   toad (10a,17a,63d,126d), Toba (80c), tobe (7d,137b), toby (8c, 85c,104b), Toby (96b,125c), tock (7d,19b), toco (19b,167c), Toda (45d,76d), tode (80a,148a), todo (22b,24d,35b,64c,156b), tody (19b,d,59a,166a), toed, toff (40d), toga (132d,133a,b), togs (32c), togt (77c), toho (79a), toil (46c,184c), toko (30c), tola (48a,80d,180a), Tola (85b), told (129c), tole (9a,51a,99b,163a), toll (131c), tolt, tolu (16a), Toma (191), tomb, tome (21d,177c), tone (6c,118c,150d), tong (30a,c), tonk (173c), tony, Tony (96b), tooa (17c), took, tool (27c), toom (139b), toon (80c,95b,168c), toot, tope (24a,46b,57a,143c,151a), toph (75c), topi (37a,75a, 118c), tops (159c), tora (11a,44d,74a,75c,85c,90b,102d,115d), tore, tori (101b), torn (130a), toro (38a,107a,152a,168c), torp (54c), tort (31c,91a,185c), Tory (23c,36b,94c,172a), tosh (106a), Tosk (8c), toss (24a,132d), tota (71d), tote (27a,73c), toto (8d,15a,34d, 89a,181a), toty (87b), toug (171a), toup (95d), tour (31b,85c), tout (61a,127a), town (73c), towy (58b), toxa (153d)

- TO -   atom (101c,114c,180d), aton (150a,159b), atop (112a,174a), Eton (33b,50c,84a), itol (158b), Otoe (147b), stoa (33c,121a,c), stod (40d,67d), stof (135c), stog (155a), stom (34c), stop (73b,111b), stot (154d,155d,157d,179b,186a), stow (112b), utor (90a,166c)

- - TO   acto (152b), alto (152b,176c), auto (34d), bito (7d,57d,168c), Boto (192), Buto (142d), Cato (132d,133b), ceto (34a), cito (89d,126c), coto (16c,90b), dato (95c,102c,117a), Doto (141b), ecto (34c,122d), ento (34b,d), into (123a,183b), jato (173b), koto (84b), Leto (11c), loto (65a,121d,178d), moto (104b), Nato (6a,8d), nito (55c), octo (34a,89b,122c), onto (76a,174a), otto (58d,116b,134a), Otto (14c,66d,67a,96a), pato (46d), peto (57a,177b), Peto (76a), pito (9c,28b,83a), roto (30a,122d,127b,152c,171b), sito (34b), Tito (186c), toto (8d,15a,34d,89a,181a), Tyto (16c), unto (166c), veto (94a,124a), Veto, Voto (192)

T - - O   tajo (152a,d), Tano (192), taro (13c,48c,49b,64b,112b,120a,133d, 155c,170a,c), taxo (13a), Teco (192), tiao, Tino (136d), tiro (9b, 17d,108c), Tito (186c), toco (19b,167c), todo (22b,24d,35b,64c, 156b), toho (79a), toko (30c), toro (38a,107a,152a,168c), toto (8d,15a,34d,89a,181a), trio (104d,165a,169c), tuno (28b,168c), typo (35c,51b,123d), tyro (9b,17d,108c), Tyto (16c)

T - - P   tamp (46b,112b,121d,127d), tarp (26b,178d), terp (12b,123a), torp (54c), toup (95d), trap (27b,67b,132b,149b), trip (85c), trop (62d,167a), tryp (114a), tump (60a,76d,103d), turp, tymp (20c), typp (185b)

TR - -   tram (170a), tran (7a), trap (27b,67b,132b149b), tray (128c, 136d,142d,143c), tree (11d,37a,66a,184b), tref (172b), trek (85c, 93c,99d,168b), tres (19a,52b,63a,152d,165a,175c), tret (9a,178b, 179d), trey (26c,165a), trig (106a,148d,154b,169d), trim (40a,106a,154b,160a,165c,169d), trin (169d), trio (104d,165a, 169c), trip (85c), tris (122d), trit (34d,164c), trod, tron (140d, 180a), trop (62d,167a), trot (85b,93d,112d), trow (18a,21a,159d,

164c,170b), **troy** (161c,180a), **Troy, true** (7a,8d,37b,54b,94c,149c), **tryp** (114a)

- TR -   **Atri, atry** (141b), **etre** (61a,c,62d,166c)

- - TR   **natr** (189)

T - - R   **faar** (12b), **tahr** (68a,76d), **tair** (68a,76d), **tear** (67c,87b,130a), **teer** (25b,69d), **tehr** (27c,68a), **thar** (68a,76d), **Thor** (7c,68c,99c, 100c,109c,165b), **tiar** (39a,75a,121a), **tier** (118a,134b), **tour** (31b, 85c), **tsar** (42d,49d,60b,135c), **turr** (24d,105a), **tyer, Tyrr** (68c, 109c,163d,178a), **tzar** (42d,49d,60b,135c)

TS - -   **tsar** (42d,49d,60b,135c), **tshi, Tshi** (69c), **tsia** (162c), **Tsin** (30b), **tsun** (30b)

- - TS   **Acts, arts** (138c), **cits, eats, lots, orts** (60d), **rats**

T - - S   **Taos** (192), **Tass** (107a,135d,151b), **Tees** (108a), **Teos** (82a), **Tess** (73d,164c,183d), **this** (42b,124b), **Thos** (84a,181c), **thus** (149c), **togs** (32c), **tops** (159c), **toss** (24a,132d), **tres** (19a,52b,63a,152d,165a, 175c), **tris** (122d)

- TT -   **atta** (58d,90c,97d,160c,173d), **Atta** (94d,95d,100a,106b,117a), **Attu, Etta** (183c), **ette** (158a,c,d), **otto** (58d,116b,134a), **Otto** (14c,66d,67a,96a)

- - TT   **batt** (37c), **bitt** (54d,175c), **bott** (32a,88d), **butt** (27a,77b,127d, 162a,182b), **Catt** (9d), **gett** (44d), **Lett** (16a,90a,93a), **Matt, mitt** (56c), **mutt** (39c,101d), **Natt** (107b), **nett, Nott** (107b), **Pitt** (50d,155d), **pott** (113d), **putt** (69d), **sett** (115a,156d), **tatt** (87c), **watt** (173b,177c), **Watt** (82a)

T - - T   **tact** (43c,d,116a), **Taft** (29d), **tait** (14d), **takt** (105a,163a), **tart** (114d), **tatt** (87c), **taut** (163b,165c), **tent** (26b,115a), **test** (26a, 51c,144a,169c,170c), **text** (21c,140d), **that** (42b,124b,129c), **tilt** (26b,d,166a), **tint** (33c,d,114d), **todt** (66b), **tolt, toot, tort** (31c,91a,185c), **tout** (61a,127a), **tret** (9a,178b,179d), **trit** (34d,164c), **trot** (85b,93d,112d), **tuft** (24b,32d,38c), **twit** (162b,c)

TU - -   **tuan** (95d,147b,166c), **tuba** (105a,137d), **tube** (118b,158a), **tuck** (156b), **tuel, tufa** (121b,177a), **tuff** (121b,177a), **tuft** (24b,32d, 38c), **tuke** (26b,53b), **tula** (9a), **Tula, tule** (24b,27c), **Tulu** (45d), **tump** (60a,76d,103d), **tuna** (57a,b,123b,170d), **tund** (121d), **tune** (8b,12c,98c), **tung** (110a,168c), **tuno** (28b,168c), **tunu** (28b), **tuny, Tupi** (192), **turf** (115c,149d,160b), **Turi** (191), **Turk** (101d,102d, 106a,111d), **turm** (132d), **turn** (28d,131a,175a), **turp, turr** (24d, 105a), **tush** (167b), **tusk** (167b), **tute** (171b), **tutu** (16a,106d,147d), **tuwi** (117a,168c), **tuza** (119d)

- TU -   **atua** (120d), **Atum** (143a,159b), **etui** (27a,29b,62c,106b,148d, 166d,174b), **Otus** (67a), **stub** (156c), **stud** (22b,25a,42d,54d,111c, 143a,174a), **stum** (70c,105c,131a,173a), **stun** (145a,157d), **Utug** (159b), **utum** (19b,112c)

- - TU   **actu** (7a,89a), **Attu, datu** (95c,102c,117a), **Ketu** (48b), **latu** (190), **mitu** (39d), **patu** (179b), **tatu** (12d), **Tatu, tutu** (16a,106d,147d), **yutu** (19b,166a)

T - - U   **tabu** (59d,111d), **Taku** (80c), **tapu, tatu** (12d), **Tatu, tchu, teju** (151b), **thou** (124b), **Tibu** (191), **Tiou** (192), **tolu** (16a), **Tulu** (45d), **tunu** (28b), **tutu** (16a,106d,147d)

TW - -   **twee, twig, twin** (45c,171d), **twit** (162b,c)

T - - W   **thaw, thew** (104c), **trow** (18a,21a,159d,164c,170b)

TY - -   **Tybi** (102a), **tyee** (29d), **tyer, tyke** (29d), **tymp** (20c), **tyne, Tyne** (108a), **type** (31d,115a,155a), **typo** (35c,51b,123d), **typp** (185b), **typy, tyre** (15a), **Tyre** (31b,90d,117b), **tyro** (9b,17d,108c), **Tyrr** (68c,109c,163d,178a), **Tyto** (16c)

- TY -   **etym** (133d), **Itys** (163b), **Styx** (29b,73a,105c)

- - TY   **arty, city, Coty** (63c), **doty** (43d), **duty** (109b,162b), **Katy** (183d), **maty** (80c), **mity, pity** (35b), **toty** (87b)

T - - Y   **taky, Tavy** (183d), **they** (124b), **tidy** (106a,111b), **tiny** (100c,148c), **toby** (8c,85c,104b), **Toby** (96b,125c), **tody** (19b,d,59a,166a), **tony, Tony** (96b), **tory, Tory** (23c,36b,94c,172a), **toty** (87b), **towy** (58b), **tray** (128c,136d,142d,143c), **trey** (26c,165a), **troy** (161c,180a), **Troy, tuny, typy**

TZ - -   **tzar** (42d,49d,60b,135c)

- TZ -   **Itza** (192)

- - TZ   **batz** (190), **litz** (127b), **untz** (189)

UA - -   **uang** (131a)

- UA -   **bual** (182c), **duab** (157c), **duad** (171d), **dual** (45c,171d), **duan** (64b), **duar, Duat** (172d), **Fuad** (54d), **Guam, guan** (151b), **guao** (168c,169b), **guar** (46c,59d), **juan** (113a), **Juan** (96a), **juar** (100a), **kuan** (30b), **Kuan** (30c), **Kuar** (102a), **Muav** (66a), **quad** (33c,172a), **quae** (176b), **quag** (21c,102c), **quai** (88b,117c,180c), **quan** (190), **quas** (135c), **quay** (88b,117c,180c), **ruay** (189), **tuan** (95d,147b, 166c), **yuan** (190), **Yuan** (30b,101d)

- - UA   **agua** (152d,166c,178c), **akua** (120d), **aqua** (90a,178c), **atua** (120d), **Erua** (103c), **skua** (19b,72c,84a,141a), **ulua** (57a,74c), **Ulua** (141b)

U - - A   **ueba** (188), **ulna** (21d,39b), **ulua** (57a,74c), **Ulua** (141b), **Ulva** (141b), **unca** (49a), **upla, Urfa** (99a), **Uria** (14c,16d), **urna** (133a), **Ursa** (17b,36b,43d), **urva** (38b), **Usha** (16a,150c), **uvea** (53c,82b)

UB - -   **uber** (66b), **Ubii** (191)

- UB -   **buba** (170a), **Bube** (180b), **Bubi** (180b), **Bubo** (112c), **cuba** (189), **Cuba** (180b), **cube** (66b,150a), **cubi** (188), **dubb** (161c), **hubb** (118b), **juba** (106b), **jube** (28d), **kuba** (26d,189), **Luba** (191), **lube** (110a), **Lubs** (94c), **Nuba** (108c), **nubk** (30d,164d), **rube** (37d, 135d,185d), **Rube** (96b), **ruby** (20a,65d,179c), **tuba** (105a,137d), **tube** (118b,158a)

- - UB   **blub, chub** (40c,154c), **club** (39c), **daub** (148d), **doub** (189), **drub** (17b,39c), **flub** (22b), **gaub** (116c), **glub, grub** (43c,88d), **knub** (178b), **slub** (171c), **snub** (128c,148b), **stub** (156c)

- UC -   **Auca** (192), **buck, cuca** (33a,105d), **duce** (29d), **duck** (26b,53b, 179c), **Duco, duct** (170c), **fuci** (132c), **huck** (167d), **juca** (27a), **juck** (114c), **iuce** (58c,117d), **Luce** (7b,35a), **luck** (28d), **lucy, Lucy** (183c), **much, muck, ouch!, puca** (68a), **puce** (33c,d,52a), **puck** (44b,68a,77c,100c), **Puck** (99d,143b), **ruck** (39a,185a), **such** (146d), **suck, tuck** (156b), **yuca** (27a)

- - UC   **douc** (101d), **eruc** (37a,56a)

U - - C   **Udic** (108a), **Utac** (22d)

UD - -   udad (143d,144a,181c), udal (76b,88b,131c), Udic (108a)

- UD -   Aude, buda (83d), Buda, dude (40d), duds (32c,166d), Juda, Jude (11c,96a), judo (84b,85c,142b), Judy (125c,183d), kudu (11a), Ludd (23c), ludi (133b), ludo (65a,112b), mudd (188), nuda (39b), Nudd (23c), nude (16c,172d), pudu (41d), rudd (26d,57a,b), rude (134b,172b), sudd (40b,58c,107b), suds (59a), wudu (102d)

- - UD   baud (162d), Chud (191), feud (55d,126b,175b), foud (54d,144b), gaud (169d), laud (122a), loud (156a), maud (53d,71a,136d,143c), Maud (181a,183c), Phud (110b), puud (189), roud (57a,b), scud (32c,126c,135b,160c), spud (121d,151c), stud (22b,25a,42d,54d, 111c,143a,174a), syud (103b), thud

U - - D   udad (143d,144a,181c), used (6d,73a), uvid (101a)

UE - -   ueba (188)

- UE -   Auer (79a), duel, duet (104d,171d), euer (66d), fuel (65c), hued, juez (152b), kuei (44a), quei (189), ruer, suer (124d), suet (54d), tuel

- - UE   ague (30a,55d,95c), blue (33c,98c,102c,150d,173a), clue, flue (8b,30a), gaue (67a), glue (7b,156a), moue (61d,62b), neue (66c), Niue (137d), roue (41b,44c,127c,134b), slue (97b,148b,160a), true (7a,8d,37b,54b,94c,149c)

U - - E   ulme (49c), unde (179a), unie (173a), unze (189), urde (86b), urge (42d,46b,79d,80a,b,81c,150a), usee

- UF -   buff (134c,161d), Bufo (166c), cuff (148a), duff (125b), Dufy (63a), gufa (21b,99a), guff, huff (58a), kufa (21b,99a), luff (136b), muff, puff, (180d), ruff (19b,33b,63d,137a), sufi (103a, 116c), tufa (121b,177a), tuff (121b,177a), tuft (24b,32d,38c), yuft (135c)

- - UF   pouf, souf (146b)

UG - -   ugly

- UG -   auge (123c,132b), Bugi (191), euge (180a), fuga, fugu (84b), gugu, huge, Hugh (96a), Hugo (63a,96a), juga (27a), kuge (84c), luge (148a), Lugh (28b), muga, ough, pugh, ruga (59b,185a), sugi (84b), vugg (28a,66a,132b), vugh (28a,66a,132b), Yuga (76d)

- - UG   chug (53a), drug (105d), glug, joug (138d), plug (156d,184d), slug (46b,99b,157c), smug, snug (35a,38b,165c), Snug (99d), thug (65a), toug (171a), Utug (159b)

U - - G   uang (131a), Utug (159b)

- UH -   buhl (81a), buhr (180d), Duhr (155b), Guha (191), guhr (47d), kuhl (53c), Ruhr

- - UH   bruh (95a)

U - - H   umph, Urth (68d,107d,163d), Utah (180b)

- UI -   cuif (139a,d,140c), cuir (45c,62a), duim (188), duit (190), Duit (192), guib (11a), huia (19a,106d), luif, Muir (8b,142c), nuit (62b), quid (39b,166d), quip (183a,b), quit (90d,130c), quiz, ruin (42d), suit (38a,58a,91a,112a,119c,137c), Yuit (51c)

- - UI   arui (11b,143d,144a,181c), equi (122d), etui (27a,29b,62c,106b, 148d,166d,174b), Maui (120d)

410

U - - I   Ubii (191), unci (31d)

- UJ -   fuji (84b), Fuji (84d), juju (29b,55d), puja (77a), suji (180c)

- UK -   bukh (122a), bukk (122a), cuke (39b), duke (107c), duku (95d, 168c), juke (114c), Kuki (191), kuku (19a,106d), luke, Luke (52a,96a), puka (107a,168c), puku (11a), rukh (53b,54a), Suku (191), tuke (26b,53b), wukf (103a)

- - UK   cauk (139b), dauk (95c), Sauk (192), souk (22a,97a)

UL - -   Ulam (67b), ulan (27d,88a), Ulex (153c), ullo (6a,144a), Ullr (146b,164d), ulme (49c), ulna (21d,39b), ulua (57a,74c), Ulua (141b), Ulva (141b)

- UL -   aula (66c,73b), aulu (74c,168c), bulb 37a,172c), bulk (97b), bull (113c), bult (76d), cull (117c), culm (11a,32d,70d,145a,156a), cult (141d,161c), dull (21a,32c,173a), Dull (94b), fulk (173a), full (7b, 130b), gula (90a,101a,165b), gulf (6c), gull (32d,41c,42a,72c,99b, 141a), Gulo (183c), gulp (46a,79d,160a), hula (74b) hule, (23a, 134c), hulk (144d,173d), hull (141d,142a,144c,d), hulu (55b), jula, Jule (183d), July, kula (189), Kuli (27b), lull (25c,126d,150c), lulu (19a,57b,112c), Lulu (183d), mule (45b,148b,153c,180b), mulk (60d), mull (53b,135a,164c), null (108c,177a), pule (180d), pulk (37c,88d), puli (45a,78d), pull (45d,167d), pulp, pulu (74c), puly, rule (11b,26b,90b), rull (170b), Sula (65a), suld (188), sulk (159a), Sulu (102c), tula (9a), Tula, tule (24b,27c), Tulu (45d), vuln (184d), Yule (30d), zulu (171d,175d), Zulu (86a)

- - UL   Aoul (191), azul (151d), baul (18b), caul (16d,74d), deul (77b), Elul (102b), foul (173a), Gaul (10a,60d,63c), goul (102a), haul (27b,45d), maul (73c,96b), paul, Paul (96a), poul (190), saul (48a, 168c), Saul (18c,86d,115a), shul (161a), soul (10d,125a,153c, 176d)

U - - L   udal (76b,88b,131c), unal (147a), Ural (135c), uval (70c)

UM - -   umbo (22b), umph

- UM -   bump, Duma (135c), dumb (153b), dump, fume (129a,149a,157a), fumy, Gump (43b), Hume (50c), hump (124d), jump, lump (45a, 160c), mump (29b,153d), Numa (133a), numb, puma (27b,37c,55b, 103d), Pume (137b,175b,185b), pump, rumb (120b), rump, Sumo, sump (28c,45d), tump (60a,76d,103d), Yuma

- - UM   ahum, alum (14a,45c), arum (13a,39b,58d,92b,155c), Arum (66a), Atum (143a,159b), Baum (9c,112c), chum (38d), doum (168c), drum (105a), Geum (76b), glum (102c,159a), grum (102c), jhum, meum (27a,89c), Meum, odum (168c,180a), ogum (82b), ovum (48d), plum, rhum (8c), saum (189), scum (129b), slum, stum (70c,105c,131a,173a), swum, Ulam (67b), utum (19b,112c)

U - - M   urim (18d,23a,110a), utum (19b,112c)

UN - -   unal (147a), unau (148c,171d), unca (49a), unci (31d), unco (140c), unde (179a), undo (11a,93d), undy (179a), unie (173a), Unio (105c), unis (91b), unit (101c,110c,147a), unto (166c), untz (189), unze (189)

- UN -   aune (188), aunt (129c), buna (161c), bund (49c,66c,90c), bung (119d,156d), bunk, bunn (25b), bunt (15d,180c), Cuna (193), dune (137a), dunk (43c,79d), Duns, dunt, fund (6d,101c,130c), Fung

411

(191), **Funj, funk** (63d,113c), **guna** (106a,137b), **gunj** (70c), **hung, hunh?, hunk, hunt** (141c), **June** (183c), **Jung** (125a), **junk** (30a, 134c), **Juno** (69c,85d,100c,126b), **kung** (125b), **kunk** (188), **luna** 103c), **Luna** (102b), **lune** (38c,73b,74d), **lung, luny** (38b), **mund** (124d), **mung** (70d), **munj** (70d), **paun** (18b), **puna** (10b,33b,104a, 119b,182a), **pund** (189), **pung** (22c,148b), **punk** (9b,166a,167c), **puno** (182a), **punt** (21a,58b), **puny** (55b,179a), **Qung** (191), **rune** (9b,67a,94a,105c,107d,120a,141d,163d), **rung** (28c,39a), **runt** (47a172d), **sung, Sung** (30b), **sunk, sunn** (56a), **tuna** (57a,b,123b, 170d), **tund** (121d), **tune** (8b,12c,98c), **tung** (110a,168c), **tuno** (28b,168c), **tunu** (28b), **tuny, Yunx** (184a), **Zuni** (125b)

- - **UN** **Amun** (86d,127d,159b,164a), **Chun** (30c), **drun** (132b), **faun** (56a, 68b,137c,161a,184a), **Idun** (107d), **jaun** (113a), **kaun** (93d), **laun** (146b), **loun** (19a,b), **maun** (139d), **noun** (114b,158a), **paun** (18b), **shun** (15a,51b,52a), **spun, stun** (145a,157d), **taun** (188), **tsun** (30b), **Usun** (191), **whun** (64c,70a)

U - - N **ulan** (27d,88a), **upon** (6b), **uran** (101d), **Usun** (191), **uzan** (189)

- UO - **buoy** (28d,58c), **quod** (123d)

U - - O **ullo** (6a,144a), **umbo** (22b), **unco** (140c), **undo** (11a,93d), **Unio** (105c), **unto** (166c), **upgo** (13c)

UP - - **upas** (84d,120b,168c,d), **upgo** (13c), **Upis** (13b), **upla, upon** (6b)

- UP - **dupe** (27c,41c,72c,160c), **Hupa** (192), **jupe** (62b,84a), **lupe** (19a, 64a), **Nupe** (191), **pupa** (30d,81b,c), **rupa** (60b), **supa** (168c), **supe** (53a,154d), **Tupi** (192)

- - UP **blup, caup, coup** (20d,97c,157b,c,162d), **gaup, loup** (61d,62a,90c, 139d), **Loup** (193), **noup** (124b), **plup, roup** (44a,121d), **scup** (57a, 121b), **snup** (149b), **soup, toup** (95d), **yaup, youp** (185d)

UR - - **Ural** (135c), **uran** (101d), **urde** (86b), **Urdu** (77b), **urdy** (86b), **Urey** (17b,36b,43d), **Urth** (68d,107d,163d), **urus** (14d,53a,112c), **urva** 150a), **Uria** (14c,16d), **urim** (18d,23a,110a), **urna** (133a), **Ursa** (17b,36b,43d), **Urth** (68d,107d,163d), **urus** (14d,53a,112c), **urva** (38b)

- UR - **aura** (44c,49c,66a,96b,158a,170d,177c), **auri** (34a), **bura** (182b), **bure** (61b), **burg** (22b,73c), **buri** (56b), **burl** (87c,169a), **burn, burr** (123b), **bury** (81d), **cura** (152c), **curb** (130c,146b), **curd** (99d), **cure** (123b), **curl** (38d,73b,131d), **curr** (104c), **curt** (145b,c), **dura** (153c), **duro** (190), **durr** (70b), **furl** (132d), **fury** (157a), **guru** (77b), **hura** (20a,137a), **Hura, hurl** (167c), **hurt, jura, Jura, jure** (90b), **jury** (38a), **Kurd** (48b,82a), **Kure** (84c), **Kuri** (191), **kurk** (31a,139b), **lura** (22d,82a), **lure** (41c,51a,54b,163a), **lurg** (96d,141b,184d), **Luri** (191), **lurk** (92a,147d), **mura** (84d), **Mura** (192), **mure** (177d), **murk** (41a,67d), **murr** (72b,128b), **nurl** (33b,87c), **nurr** (67d), **ours** (124c), **pure** (29b,172b,173c), **puri** (80d), **purl** (87c,104c), **purr** (104c), **Puru** (192), **ruru** (19b,102c,106d), **sura** (87c,113b,166d), **surd** (82c,177a), **sure** (173d), **surf** (23a), **turf** (115c,149d,160b), **Turi** (191), **Turk** (101d,102d,106a,111d), **turm** (132d), **turn** (28d, 131a,175a), **turp, turr** (24d,105a), **Wurd, wurm** (67c), **yurt** (101d)

- - UR **Alur** (191), **Asur** (68c), **biur** (35a), **blur, caur** (139a), **Daur** (139b), **dour** (67d,159a), **ebur** (89c), **four** (26c), **gaur** (112c,181c), **gour** (112c,181c), **hour, knur** (67d,87c,107c), **lour** (13d,63d), **peur** (61c),

pour (162d), **scur** (78b), **slur** (44b,124c,148b,168a), **smur** (32c,46b, 100c), **sour, spur** (10d,67d,167d,168a,181b), **tour** (31b,85c), **your** (124c)

U - - R **uber** (66b), **Ullr** (146b,164d), **usar** (8d,16c), **user** (49d), **utor** (90a, 166c)

US - - **usar** (8d,16c), **Usas** (68d), **used** (6d,73a), **usee, user** (49d), **uses** (18a), **Usha** (16a,150c), **Usun** (191)

- US - **Ausa, ausu** (168c,180b), **bush, busk** (17b,37b,55d,161b), **buss** (87a,148c), **bust, busy, cush** (101c), **Cush** (51d,73c), **cusk** (57b), **cusp** (38c,78b,119a,120a,b), **cuss, duse** (83c), **dusk** (171c), **dust, fuse** (98c), **fuss** (22b,35b), **fust** (105c,143b), **gush** (35a,154c), **gust, huse** (180c), **hush** (17b,146c), **husk** (53a,78d,142a), **huso** (180c), **just** (51b,54b), **kusa, Kush, lush** (94d), **lust** (41b), **Musa** (16a), **muse** (65b,93d,120d,164c), **Muse** (68d), **mush** (97d), **musk** (116b), **Muso** (192), **muss** (135b,173d), **must** (70c,101a,106d,157d,182c), **Ouse** (132a,185d), **oust** (44c,49a,52b,125d), **push,** (145c) **puss, rusa, Rusa** (41d,136d), **ruse** (13b,77c,157b,169c), **rush, rusk** (23a), **Russ** (135b), **rust** (37b,112c,119a), **Susa** (49a), **susi** (53b,d), **susu** (20c), **Susu** (191), **Susy** (183d), **tush** (167b), **tusk** (167b),

- - US **acus** (89d,118a), **Apus** (36b,c), **avus** (89b), **cous** (38a), **crus** (91a, 143c), **deus** (68a,89b), **Esus, gaus** (67a), **Grus** (36b,c,38b), **Ilus** (88d,170b), **irus** (109d), **nous** (81d,100a,128b), **onus** (24c,93b,109b), **opus** (35c,105a,184c), **Otus** (67a), **Pius** (121a), **plus** (10b, 102c), **pous** (188), **Rhus** (159a), **sous** (62d,172c), **thus** (149c), **urus** (14d,53a,112c), **Zeus** (135a)

U - - S **unis** (91b), **upas** (84d,120b,168c,d), **Upis** (13b), **urus** (14d,53a, 112c), **uses** (18a), **Usas** (68d), **utas** (49a,109c)

UT - - **utac** (22d), **Utah** (180b), **utas** (49a,109c), **utor** (90a,166c), **Utug** (159b), **utum** (19b,112c)

- UT - **auto** (34d), **Buto** (142d), **butt** (27a,77b,127d,162a,182b), **cute** (39c), **duty** (109b,162b), **fute** (51c), **Guti, jute** (37a,48a,56a,133d, 136a), **Jute, lute** (11c,28b,84d,105a,131d), **muta** (28d,103a), **mute** (146c,153b), **muth** (188), **mutt** (39c,101d), **putt** (69d), **Ruta** (76b, 134d), **rute** (188), **ruth** (35b,118c), **Ruth** (105b,183c), **tute** (171b), **tutu** (16a,106d,147d), **yutu** (19b,166a)

- - UT **abut** (22a,167c), **bhut** (67a), **blut** (66b), **bout** (36c), **brut** (182c), **Brut** (23c), **chut!, Cnut** (40d,50c), **gaut** (88b,103d,132a), **glut** (52c,70a,137c,159d), **gout, knut, Knut** (40d,50c,96a), **lout** (15c, 22a,24b,45b,109a,157d), **naut** (141b), **paut** (140a), **phut** (24b), **Phut** (110b), **pout** (159a), **prut!, Prut** (41a), **rout** (41d,44b,46b), **scut** (145c,161b), **shut, smut** (32d,44a,119a,150c), **sput** (21c), **taut** (163b,165c), **tout** (61a,127a)

U - - T **unit** (101c,110c,147a)

- UU - **puud** (189)

U - - U **unau** (148c,171d), **Urdu** (77b)

UV - - **uval** (70c), **uvea** (53c,82b), **uvic** (70c), **uvid** (101a)

- UV - **cuvy** (141a)

- UW - **tuwi** (117a,168c)

- - UW **bouw** (188), **dauw** (24c)

413

- UX -   buxy (115b), luxe (61c,62d,159c), puxy

- - UX   crux (39a,151b), eaux (178c), flux (28d,58d), jeux (61d), Vaux (63b)

U - - X   Ulex (153c)

- UY -   buyo (18b), cuya (39b), Puya (118b)

U - - Y   ugly, undy (179a), urdy (86b), Urey (14b,107c,138c)

UZ - -   uzan (189)

- UZ -   auzu (168c,180b), buzz, fuze (98c), fuzz (45d), guze (128d), huzz, Juza (155b), Muzo (192), tuza (119d), wuzu (102d), zuza (189)

- - UZ   Ghuz (171a)

U - - Z   untz (189)

VA - -   Vach (153b), vade (42c,67d,89b), vagi (38b), vail (94b,124a,174b), vain (81a), vair (64c,154c), vale (54c,128a,174b), Vale (7c,109c), vali (171a,176a), Vali (7c,109c), vamp (80a,145a), vane (179b, 182a), vang (72d,134a,140b), Vans (107d), vara (151d), vare 179b), vari (34d,91b,134d,174d), vary (28d,43c), vasa (46d,114a, 160b,175d), Vasa, vase, vast (78d,79d), vasu (106c), Vasu (176d), Vaux (63b), Vayu (68c,182a), vaza (114a)

- VA -   aval (70c), Avar (27d,108a), Evan (96a), Ivah (18d), Ivan (40c, 85b,96a), kvas (135c), oval (48d,49c,127a), Svan (27d), uval (70c)

- - VA   Alva (151d), cava (116a,175b), Civa (56d), deva (23d,42a,42b, 56d,77a), diva (100d,123c), Hova (95a), Java (33a), jiva (77a), Jova (193), kava (18c,116a), kiva (28c,125b), lava (101c,151a, 177a), Neva (91b,132a), nova (20c,106d,155c,174d), peva (12d), siva (67a), Siva (56d,77a), Ulva (141b), urva (38b), viva (93d), Xova (193), yava

V - - A   vara (151d), vasa (46d,114a,160b,175d), Vasa, vaza (114a), Veda (77a,b), vega (110d,152c), Vega (155b), vela (98c,136b,149d), Vela (36b,c), vena (90a,175a), vera (140c,151b,175c), Vera (183c), veta (104a), Vida (183c), vila (54b), vina (77a,105a), Vira (191), visa (114d), vita (89c,92a), viva (93d), vola (89d,150a), vota (133b)

V - - B   verb (7a,114b,184b)

- - VD   NKVD (135d)

V - - D   veld (151a), vend (97a,115c,142b), Vend (10b,148a), verd (71d), void (11a,49d,108d,174b)

VE - -   veal, Veda (77a,b), veer (28d,144c,171b), vega (110d,152c), Vega (155b), veil (74d,76c), vein (20d,157b), vela (98c,136b,149d), Vela (36b,c), veld (151a), velo (175b), vena (90a,175a), vend (97a, 115c,142b), Vend (10b,148a), vent (8b,11b,110d,112a), Veps (191), vera (140c,151b,175c), Vera (183c), verb (7a,114b,184b), verd (71d), veri (28b), vert (71d,166a,171b), very (149c), vest (32c, 177b), veta (104a), veto (94a,124a), Veto

- VE -   avec (63a,183a), aver (7c,14a,15c,41c,95c,140d,155c,160b,184c), Aves (19d), evea (82a,95a), even (51a,58b,79d,91d,149a,173a), ever (9b,14b,80b), evet (48d,107a,136c,169d), Ives (9c,90b), oven (15d,78c,86b), over (6b,38c,80a,114d,130a), uvea (53c,82b)

- - VE   bave (61d,146c), cave (27d), cive (110c), cove (17a,73d,107d),

Dave (96b), **dive** (42b,74b,119d), **dove** (19a,117d), **eave** (133c), **five**, **gave**, **give** (79d,123a), **gyve** (55d,143b), **have** (92a), **hive** (17c), **hove** (92a), **Jave** (84d), **jive** (160c), **jove** (85d), **kive** (174d), **lave** (16d,178b), **leve** (62a), **live** (47c), **love** (163a), **move**, **nave** (30d,31a,78d,114b,180c), **neve** (56d,67c,70c,149b), **nove** (83b), **pave** (85a), **rave** (41c,157a,161d), **reve** (61c,104d), **rive** (32a,153d), **rove** (127d,132b,178a), **save** (52b,110c,123a,173c), **seve** (63a, 182c), **sive** (146a), **Tave** (183d), **vive** (93d), **wave** (19a,59a,111c, 131d,160c,172d), **wive** (97a), **wove**

V - - E   **vade** (42c,67d,89b), **vale** (54c,128a,174b), **Vale** (7c,109c), **vane** (179b,182a), **vare** (179b), **vase**, **vice** (31d,158a), **vide** (89d,126a, 142a), **vile** (16c,56c), **vine** (32b), **vire** (11a,13b), **vise** (31d,77d, 114d), **vite** (62b), **vive** (93d), **voce** (83c,177a), **vole** (97d,104a, 148a,149b), **vote** (60b), **Vote** (56d)

V - - G   **vang** (72d,134a,140b), **voog** (28a,66a,132b), **vugg** (28a,66a,132b)

- - VH   **IHVH** (159d), **JHVH** (159d), **YHVH** (159d)

V - - H   **Vach** (153b), **Voth** (191), **vugh** (28a,66a,132b)

VI - -   **vial** (148c), **vice** (31d,158a), **Vida** (183c), **vide** (89d,126a,142a), **vier** (66c), **view** (93d,138b), **vila** (54b), **vile** (16c,56c), **vili** (54b), **Vili** (109c), **vill** (176b), **vily** (54b), **vina** (77a,105a), **vine** (32b), **vino** (92d,182b), **vint** (26c,182c), **viny**, **viol** (105a), **Vira** (191), **vire** (11a,13b), **visa** (114d), **vise** (31d,77d,114d), **viss** (189), **vita** (89c, 92a), **vite** (62b), **viti** (176b), **viva** (93d), **vive** (93d), **vivo** (93a)

- VI -   **avid** (47b,71a,186b), **avis** (89a), **Avis** (183c), **evil** (79c,95d,147a, 181a,185c), **Ovid** (132d,133b), **Ovis** (143d), **uvic** (70c), **uvid** (101a)

- - VI   **Devi** (147b,153b), **divi**, **favi** (138a,165d), **hevi** (111d), **Kavi** (84d), **Levi** (84a,90c), **ravi** (61b), **Ravi** (16b)

V - - I   **vagi** (38b), **vali** (171a,176a), **Vali** (7c,109c), **vari** (34d,91b,134d, 174d), **veri** (28b), **vili** (54b), **Vili** (109c), **viti** (176b), **vlei** (38c,160a)

V - - K   **volk** (66c,105d,116a,184c)

VL - -   **vlei** (38c,160a), **vley** (160a)

V - - L   **vail** (94b,124a,174b), **veal**, **veil**, (74d,76c), **vial** (148c), **vill** (176b), **viol** (105a)

V - - N   **vain** (81a), **vein** (20d,157b), **vuln** (184d)

VO - -   **voce** (83c,177a), **voet** (188), **Vogt**, **void** (11a,49d,108d,174b), **vola** (89d,150a), **vole** (97d,104a,148a,149b), **volk** (66c,105d,116a,184c), **volt** (49b,78c,173b), **voog** (28a,66a,132b), **vota** (133b), **vote** (60b), **Vote** (56d), **Voth** (191), **Voto** (192)

- VO -   **Avon** (143b), **Avow** (6d,36a,41c,112c), **evoe** (15b,130d,181c)

- - VO   **levo** (91a), **pavo** (115b), **Pavo** (36b,c), **vivo** (93a)

V - - O   **velo** (175b), **veto** (94a,124a), **Veto**, **vino** (92d,182b), **vivo** (93a), **Voto** (192)

V - - P   **vamp** (80a,145a)

V - - R   **vair** (64c,154c), **veer** (28d,144c,171b), **vier** (66c)

- - VS   **revs** (131a)

V - - S   **Vans** (107d), **Veps** (191), **viss** (189)

V - - T   **vast** (78d,79d), **vent** (8b,11b,110d,112a), **vert** (71d,166a,171b), vest (32c,177b), **vint** (26c,182c), **voet** (188), **Vogt, volt** (49b,78c, 173b)

VU - - vugg (28a,66a,132b), vugh (28a,66a,132b), vuln (184d)

- VU - avus (89b), ovum (48d)

- - VU kivu (170c)

V - - U vasu (106c), Vasu (176d), Vayu (68c,182a)

V - - W view (93d,138b)

V - - X Vaux (63b)

- - VY bevy (38a,58c), **cavy** (72b,120d,132c,157b), **cuvy** (141a), **Davy** (96b,136b), **envy** (41b), **levy** (14a,162b), **Livy** (132d,133a), **navy** (33c,58b), **pavy** (115b), **pevy** (91d,94c), **Tavy** (183d), **wavy** (147b, 172d)

V - - Y vary (28d,43c), **very** (149c), vily (54b), viny, vley (160a)

WA - - Waac, waag (71d,101d), **Wabi** (192), **Waco, wadd** (109c), **wade, wadi** (46c,106a,109a,128a,132a), **wady** (109a,128a,132a), waeg (19b,72c,87a), **waer** (40b), **Wafd** (49a), **waft** (20d,58c), **wage** (27a, 115b), **waif** (157b), **wail** (39b,88a), **wain** (177b), **Wain, wait** (26d, 42b,92c,155d,162a), **waka** (26a), **wake** (134b,168a), **wakf** (103a), **waky, wale** (70b,131b,157c,163d,179a,180a,c,d), **wali** (171a), **walk, wall, Walt** (96b), **wand** (120b,132c,156a), **wane** (41c,43c), **wang** (189), **want** (41b,42d,87b,106b,122a), **wany, wapp** (54b,133d, 145d), **waqf** (103a), **ward** (31c,55c,86b), **ware** (27d,35a), **warf, warm** (7c,75b,163b), **warn** (7b), **warp** (36c,165a,171c), **wart** (124d), **wary** (27d,176b), **wash, wasp, wast, Wate** (141a), **watt** (173b, 177c), **Watt** (82a), **wave** (19a,59a,111c,131d,160c,172d), **wavy** (147b,172d), **waxy** (119c,149d), **ways**

- WA - Awan (191), **away** (6b,69d,76a,109d,111d), **Ewan, kwan** (30b), **swab** (102b), **swad** (94d), **swag** (22a,156c), **swam, swan** (19b,33a), **swap** (168a), **swat** (15d,20d,32d,157c), **Swat** (103a), **sway** (104a)

- - WA biwa (93d,168c), **dewa, Iowa** (193), **kawa** (18c,116a), **Iowa** (19a), **pawa** (189), **tawa** (160d,168c), **Tewa** (193)

W - - A waka (26a), **Wega** (155b), **weka** (58c,106d,107a,127b), **weta** (93c), **whoa** (156d)

W - - C Waac

- - WD dowd (143b), **gawd** (169c)

W - - D wadd (109c), **Wafd** (49a), **wand** (120b,132c,156a), **ward** (31c,55c, 86b), **week, weld** (47c,85b,173c), **wend** (67d,123d), **Wend** (10b, 148a), **wild** (38b,173d), **wind** (33b,39d,171c,185a), **woad** (20d,47c), **wold** (47c,60a,118d,174a,184a), **wood, word** (124b,165c), **Wurd, Wyrd** (107d)

WE - - weak (55b), **weal** (124d,157c,180c,d), **wean** (8d,42d), **wear** (50b), **weed, week, weel** (16d,57d,140d,180d), **weep** (39b,88a,104a), **weet** (19d), **weft** (39a,165a,184b), **Wega** (155b), **Wegg** (111d), **weir** ('40b,57d), **weka** (58c,106d,107a,127b), **weki** (55c), **weld** (47c,85b, 173c), **Welf** (67a), **welk** (65c,96d,141b), **well welt** (36d,131b,145a, b,177b,d), **wend** (67d,123d), **Wend** (10b,148a), **went** (42c), **wept, were** (139b), **werf** (54d), **weri** (15c,27c), **wert, west, West** (9c,50b, 109b), **weta** (93c)

- WE - ewer (84d,85c,118c,181b), kwei (44a), Owen (96a,183c), sweb (160d), twee

- - WE howe (77d), Howe (17a,82a), powe

W - - E wade, wage (27a,115b), wake (134b,168a), wale (70b,131b,157c, 163d,179a,180a,c,d), wane (41c,43c), ware (27d,35a), Wate (141a), wave (19a,59a,111c,131d,160c,172d), were (139b), whee, wide (133d), wife (154a), wile (13b,41c,157b,169c), wine, wipe, wire, wise (136b), wive (97a), woke, wore, Wote (191), wove

W - - F waif (157b), wakf (103a), waqf (103a), warf, Welf (67a), werf (54d), wolf, woof (39a,163d,165a,179d), Wraf, wukf (103a)

W - - G waag (71d,101d), waeg (19b,72c,87a), wang (189), Wegg (111d), Whig wigg, wing (10d,58c,59a,118b,d), wong (56a)

WH - - wham (157c), what (129c), whau (107a,168c), whee!, when (180d), whet (143c,156b), whew, whey (100a), Whig, whim (26c, 54c,108c), whin (64c,70a,132b,181d), whip (58c,88d), whir (25c, 181a), whit (166c), whiz (25c), whoa (156d), whom (42b), whoo!, whun (64c,70a), whyo (59d,65a)

- - WH JHWH (159d), YHWH (159c)

W - - H wash, wish (42d), with (10b)

WI - - wick, wide (133d), widu (102d), wiel (140d,180d), wies (185a), wife (154a), wigg, wild (38b,173d), wile (13b,41c,157b,169c), wilk (65c,96d,141b), will (18b,43a,163c,177c), wilt (46b), wily (13b,38b,39c), wind (33b,39d,171c,185a), wine, wing (10d,58c, 59a,118b,d), wink (107a), winy (176c), wipe, wire, wiry (147a, 167c), wise (136b), wish (42d), wisp (24b,148c), wist (87c), with (10b), wive (97a)

- WI - swig (46a,72c), swim (58c), swiz (160c), twig, twin (45c,171d), twit (162b,c)

- - WI iiwi (19a,74b), Kawi (84d), kiwi (11d,19a,58c), tuwi (117a,168c)

W - - I Wabi (192), wadi (46c,106a,109a,128a,132a), wali (171a), weki (55c), weri (15c,27c)

- - WK bowk (155d), cawk (133c), dawk (95c), gawk (146d), gowk (146d), hawk (19c,115c), sawk (188)

W - - K walk, weak (55b), week, welk (65c,96d,141b), wick, wilk (65c, 96d,141b), wink (107a), work (64c,76b)

- - WL bawl, bowl, cowl (101d), dowl, fowl, gowl (102a,140d,185b), howl (39b), jowl (29b), mewl (180d), pawl (43a,95a), yawl (136b,171d, 175d), yowl

W - - L wail (39b,88a), wall, weal (124d,157c,180c,d), weel (16d,57d,140d, 180d), well, wiel (140d,180d), will (18b,43a,163c,177c), wool (58b, 179c)

- - WM dawm (190)

W - - M warm (7c,75b,163b), wham (157c), whim (26c,54c,108c), whom (42b), worm, wurm (67c),

- - WN bawn (181a), dawn (14d,41b), down (149d), fawn (33c), gown, hewn, kawn (93d), lawn (20a,37c,53b,92c), lown (157d), mown, pawn (29c,119c), sawn, sewn, town (73c), yawn

W - - N wain (177b), Wain, warn (7b), wean (8d,42d), when (180d), whin

(64c,70a,132b,181d), **whun** (64c,70a), **woon** (24c), **worn** (143b),
wren (19b,c), **Wren** (50b), **wynn** (165d)

WO - - **woad** (20d,47c), **woke**, **wold** (47c,60a,118d,174a,184a), **wolf**,
wong (56a), **wont** (6d,40a,73a,174c), **wood woof** (39a,163d,165a,
179d), **wool** (58b,179c), **woon** (24c), **word** (124b,165c), **wore**,
work (64c,76b), **worm**, **worn** (143b), **wort** (76a,95d,121d), **Wote**
(191), **wove**

- WO - **Lwow**, **swob** (102b), **swop** (168a), **swot**, **swow** (100a)

W - - O **Waco**, **whoo**, **whyo** (59d,65a)

- - WP **gawp**, **lowp** (90c,139d), **yawp**

W - - P **wapp** (54b,133d,145d), **warp** (36c,165a,171c), **wasp**, **weep** (39b,
88a,104a), **whip** (58c,88d), **wisp** (24b,148c), **wrap** (32b,51a)

WR - - **Wraf**, **wrap** (32b,51a), **wren** (19b,c), **Wren** (50b), **writ** (91a)

- WR - **awry** (13d,38d,171c), **ewry** (133c)

W - - R **waer** (40b), **wear** (50b), **weir** (40b,57d), **whir** (25c,181a)

- WS - **owse**

- - WS **mews** (154c), **news** (165c)

W - - S **ways**, **wies** (185a)

- - WT **newt** (48d,136c,169d), **nowt** (106a,139a), **yowt** (139c)

W - - T **waft** (20d,58c), **wait** (26d,42b,92c,155d,162a), **Walt** (96b), **want**
(41b,42d,87b,106b,122a), **wart** (124d), **wast**, **watt** (173b,177c),
Watt (82a), **weet** (19d), **weft** (39a,165a,184b), **welt** (36d,131b,
145a,b,177b,d), **went** (42c), **wept**, **wert**, **west**, **West** (9c,50b,109b),
what (129c), **whet** (143c,156b), **whit** (166c), **wilt** (46b), **wist** (87c),
wont (6d,40a,73a,174c), **wort** (76a,95d,121d), **writ** (91a)

WU - - **wudu** (102d), **wukf** (103a), **Wurd**, **wurm** (67c), **wuzu** (102d)

- WU - **swum**

W - - U **whau** (107a,168c), **widu** (102d), **wudu** (102d), **wuzu** (102d)

W - - W **whew!**

WY - - **wynn** (165d), **Wyrd** (107d)

- WY - **Gwyn** (40c,50b)

- - WY **dewy** (101a), **jawy**, **nowy** (194), **rowy** (157b), **towy** (58b)

W - - Y **wady** (109a,128a,132a), **waky**, **wany**, **wary** (27d,176b), **wavy**
(147b,172d), **waxy** (119c,149d), **whey** (100a), **wily** (13b,38b,39c),
winy (176c), **wiry** (147a,167c)

W - - Z **whiz** (25c)

- XA - **axal** (120b), **exam**, **oxan** (65c)

- - XA **Bixa** (145d), **coxa** (77b), **doxa** (48b), **moxa** (27d,30c), **myxa** (168c,
169a), **noxa**, **toxa** (153d)

X - - A **xema** (72c), **Xema** (12c), **Xina** (183d), **Xosa** (86a), **Xova** (193)

XE - - **xema** (72c), **Xema** (12c), **xeno** (34d)

- XE - **oxea** (153d), **oxen** (10c), **oxer** (55c)

- - XE **luxe** (61c,62d,159c), **Mixe** (192), **saxe** (20d,33c)

X - - E **Xipe** (15c)

XI - - **Xina** (183d), **Xipe** (15c)

- XI - axil (10c), **axis** (28b,41d,77c,153c), **exit** (114d), **ixia** (37a), **Ixil** (192), **oxid** (112c)

- - XI **dixi**, **taxi** (13a,125b)

- XL - **axle** (153c,180c), **ixle** (56a)

XM - - **Xmas**

XO - - **Xosa** (86a), **Xova** (193)

- XO - **axon** (106c,153c)

- - XO **Moxo** (192), **myxo**, **taxo** (13a)

X - - O **xeno** (34d), **xylo** (35a,183d)

X - - S **Xmas**

- - XT **next** (106a), **sext** (26b,111b,147b), **text** (21c,140d)

XY - - **xylo** (35a,183d)

- XY - **oxyl** (112c)

- - XY **boxy**, **buxy** (115b), **doxy** (129d), **foxy** (38b,39c,181d), **mixy**, **pixy** (154b), **puxy**, **Roxy** (183d), **waxy** (119c,149d)

YA - - **yage** (23a), **yaje** (23a), **Yaka** (191), **Yaki** (193), **Yale** (173c), **yali** (171a), **Yama** (57a,68a), **Yana** (192,193), **yang** (30b,70a), **yank**, **Yank**, **Yaou** (30c), **yapa** (113b), **Yapp** (22a), **yard** (152d), **yare** (96b,124b,128b), **yark** (22c), **yarl** (40d,107d), **yarn** (154b,161b, 184b), **yarr** (72a), **Yaru** (48d), **yate** (51d,168c), **yati** (76d), **yaup**, **yava**, **yawl** (136b,171d,175d), **yawn**, **yawp**, **yaya** (113c,168c)

- YA - **ayah** (108d), **cyan**, **dyad** (113a), **Dyak** (22b), **Dyas** (66a), **eyah** (95b, 108d,111c), **eyas** (106c,173a), **Iyar** (102b), **kyah** (19a), **kyak** (51c), **kyar** (33a), **kyat** (189), **Iyam** (139a), **Lyas** (66a), **pyal** (175c), **pyat** (95b), **ryal** (110a,190)

- - YA **Alya** (155b,c), **Arya** (80d), **baya** (179b), **Baya** (191), **cuya** (39b), **Goya** (151d), **Hoya** (14d), **maya** (77a,179b), **Maya** (23d,186c), **Puya** (118b), **raya** (19b,23c,76d,107d), **saya** (117a), **soya** (151b), **yaya** (113c,168c)

Y - - A **Yaka** (191), **Yama** (57a,68a), **Yana** (192,193), **yapa** (113b), **yava**, **yaya** (113c,168c), **yeta** (84c), **Yima** (84a,116b,c), **Ynca** (193), **yoga** (10b,13c,77a), **yuca** (27a), **Yuga** (76d), **Yuma**

- YB - **gybe** (144c), **Tybi** (102a)

- YC - **syce** (71d)

- YD - **hyde** (188), **Hyde** (45a)

- - YD **emyd** (163c,167c)

Y - - D **yard** (152d), **yond** (164d)

YE - - **yeah**, **yean** (88a), **year**, **yeas** (177c), **Yedo** (166d), **yegg** (24c), **yell** (145c), **yelp**, **yelt** (151b), **yeni** (19b,161d), **yeso** (72d), **yeta** (84c)

- YE - **ayes** (177c), **byee** (189), **dyer**, **eyer**, **eyey** (74b), **oyer** (38a,75b, 119c), **oyes** (38a,39b,75b), **oyez** (38a,39b,75b), **pyet** (95b), **ryel** (190), **syed** (103b), **tyee** (29d), **tyer**

- - YE **Daye** (123d), **Skye** (163c)

Y - - E **yage** (23a), **yaje** (23a), **Yale** (173c), **yare** (96b,124b,128b), **yate** (51d,168c), **yoke** (85b,92d,173c), **yore** (10b,69d,93c,110b,165d), **Yule** (30d)

419

- YG -   **bygo** (114c), **zyga** (134b)

Y - - G   **yang** (30b,70a), **yegg** (24c)

YH - -   **YHVH** (159d), **YHWH** (159d)

Y - - H   **yeah**, **YHVH** (159d), **YHWH** (159d), **yodh** (91d), **yogh** (10c,185a)

YI - -   **Yima** (84a,116b,c)

- YI -   **ayin** (91c)

- - YI   **kiyi** (185d)

Y - - I   **Yaki** (193), **yali** (171a), **yati** (76d), **yeni** (19b,161d), **Yobi, yogi** (76d)

- YK -   **cyke** (40c), **dyke** (49c,91d), **fyke** (15d), **hyke!**, **syke** (194), **tyke** (29d)

Y - - K   **yank, Yank, yark** (22c), **yolk, york** (38c), **York** (50b,c)

- YL -   **gyle** (23b,174d), **Hyla** (10a,166d,169b), **hyle** (97c), **kyle** (57a, 139c), **pyla** (22d), **pyle** (34b), **Pyle** (9c,178a), **Xylo** (35a,183d)

- - YL   **acyl** (6d), **amyl** (155c), **idyl** (114d), **noyl** (87c), **odyl** (59d,79c), **oxyl** (112c), **teyl** (92b,c,168c)

Y - - L   **yarl** (40d,107d), **yawl** (136b,171d,175d), **yell** (145c), **yowl, ypil** (117a,168c)

YM - -   **Ymer** (67a,131c), **Ymir** (67a,131c)

- YM -   **cyma** (101a,b), **cyme** (58d,69c), **hymn** (150c), **ryme** (178d), **tymp** (20c), **zyme** (55c)

- - YM   **clym** (12b), **etym** (133d), **onym** (162c)

YN - -   **Ynca** (193)

- YN -   **dyna** (34c), **dyne** (59d,173b), **gyne** (34b,55b,183c), **jynx** (78a), **Jynx** (184a), **lynx** (26c,181d), **Lynx** (36b), **myna** (19a,c,70b), **rynd** (100a), **syne** (140b,147a), **tyne, Tyne** (108a), **wynn** (165d)

- - YN   **coyn** (37a), **Gwyn** (40c,50b), **llyn** (120d,140a)

Y - - N   **yarn** (154b,161b,184b), **yawn, yean** (88a), **yuan** (190), **Yuan** (30b, 101d)

YO - -   **Yobi, yodh** (91d), **yoga** (10b,13c,77a), **yogh** (10c,185a), **yogi** (76d), **yoke** (85b,92d,173c), **yolk, yond** (164d), **yoop, yore** (10b,69d,93c, 110b,165d), **york** (38c), **York** (50b,c), **youp** (185d), **your** (124c), **yowl, yowt** (139c)

- YO -   **eyot** (82d), **ryot** (115c)

- - YO   **buyo** (18b), **cayo, coyo** (15a,30c), **Enyo** (12c,69c,178a), **Idyo** (191), **kayo** (87c), **Mayo** (193), **whyo** (59d,65a)

Y - - O   **Yedo** (166d), **yeso** (72d)

YP - -   **ypil** (117a,168c)

- YP -   **gyps, Gyps** (71d), **hype** (185a), **hypo** (117b), **hyps, rype** (19b,125a), **sype** (110c), **type** (31d,115a,155a), **typo** (35c,51b), **typp** (185b), **typy**

- - YP   **tryp** (114a)

Y - - P   **Yapp** (22a), **yaup, yawp, yelp, yoop, youp** (185d)

- YR -   **Byrd** (9c,120b), **byre** (38a), **eyra** (181d), **eyre** (23c,31b,85c), **Eyre, eyry** (47b,106c), **fyrd** (110a), **gyre** (31b,171b), **gyri** (22d,

131b), **gyro** (34d), **Lyra** (36b,74a), **lyre** (11c,81c,105a,111c), **Myra** (10a,31b,183c), **pyre** (64c), **pyro, Syra, tyre** (15a), **Tyre** (31b,90d, 117b), **tyro** (9b,17d,108c), **Tyrr** (68c,109c,163d,178a), **Wyrd** (107d)

- - YR skyr (21d,151a)

Y - - R yarr (72a), year, **Ymer** (67a,131c), **Ymir** (67a,131c), your (124c), **Yser**

YS - - Yser

- YS - cyst, lyse, myst (71c,123b)

- - YS Alys (183c), **Emys** (167c,171b), days, **Itys** (163b), ways

Y - - S yeas (177c)

- YT - myth (8b,91a), **Tyto** (16c)

- - YT skyt (138c,140b)

Y - - T yelt (151b), yowt (139c), yuft (135c), **Yuit** (51c), yurt (101d)

YU - - yuan (190), **Yuan** (30b,101d), yuca (27a), yuft (135c), **Yuga** (76d), **Yuit** (51c), **Yule** (30d), **Yuma, Yunx** (184a), yurt (101d), yutu (19b,166a)

- YU - syud (103b)

- - YU Vayu (68c,182a)

Y - - U Yaou (30c), **Yaru** (48d), yutu (19b,166a)

- YV - gyve (55d,143b)

- YX - myxa (168c,169a), myxo

- - YX Ceyx (73b), eryx (137a), onyx (25d,28d,65d,142b), oryx (11a), **Pnyx** (71c), **Styx** (29b,73a,105c)

Y - - X Yunx (184a)

- - YZ hayz

ZA - - Zach (96b), zaim (170d), zain (41a), **Zama** (73d,141d), zany (24a, 32d,59c), zarf (39c,155a), zarp (120c), zati (21d)

- ZA - Azam (166c), azan (102d), czar (42d,49d,60b,135c), izar (65b, 103b), **Izar** (155b), tzar (42d,49d,60b,135c), **Uzan** (189)

- - ZA boza (12a), caza, **Daza** (191), **Gaza** (117a), **Itza** (192), **Juza** (155b), onza (189), tiza (172a), tuza (119d), vaza (114a), zuza (189)

Z - - A Zama (73d,141d), zeta (71b,91c), **Zipa** (29d), zira (188), **Zola** (63a), zona (144c,186d), zuza (189), zyga (134b)

- ZB - ezba (188)

Z - - B Zimb (6c)

Z - - C zinc (21a)

Z - - D Zend, zoid

ZE - - zeal (12c,55d), zebu (22d,80d,112c), zein, **Zeke** (96b), zeme (55d,161b,180b), zemi (55d,161b,180b), **Zend, Zeno** (71b), zenu (143d), zero (31a,84c,108c), **Zero** (118d), zest (55d,72d), zeta (71b,91c), **Zeus** (135a)

- ZE - ezel (47a,85d)

- - ZE adze (40c,167a), bize (182a), coze (29b), daze (157d), doze (148a), faze (43d), fuze (98c), gaze, guze (128d), haze (100c,174d), laze (79b), **Laze** (191), maze (87b,157d), naze (26b,124b), noze (75a),

421

ooze (53c,104b,116a), raze (42b,d,91d), size, unze (189)

Z - - E   Zeke (96b), zeme (55d,161b,180b), zone (44c,50a,160a), zyme (55c)

Z - - F   zarf (39c,155a)

Z - - G   zing

- ZH -   Azha (155b)

Z - - H   Zach (96b)

ZI - -   Zimb (6c), zinc (21a), zing, Zion (75b,c,83a,157d), Zipa (29d), zipp, Zips (40c), zira (188), zizz (181a)

- - ZI   cazi (103a), gazi, kazi (103a), Lazi (191), Nazi

Z - - I   zati (21d), zemi (55d,161b,180b), Zuni (125b)

Z - - L   zeal (12c,55d)

Z - - M   zaim (170d), zoom

Z - - N   zain (41a), zein, Zion (75b,c,83a,157d), zoon (43a)

ZO - -   Zoar, Zoas (20b), zobo (186b), zodi, zogo (136a), zoid, Zola (63a), zona (144c,186d), zone (44c,50a,160a), zoom, zoon (43a)

- ZO -   Azof (20b,135d), azon (127b), Azov (20b,135d), mozo (152b), Muzo (192)

- - ZO   bozo (55b), Idzo (191), kozo (113d,168c), lazo (88d,128b,133d)

Z - - O   Zeno (71b), zero (31a,84c,108c), Zero (118d), zobo (186b), zogo (136a)

Z - - P   zarp (120c), zipp

- ZR -   Ezra (96a)

Z - - R   Zoar

Z - - S   Zeus (135a), Zips (40c), Zoas (20b)

Z - - T   zest (55d,72d)

ZU - -   zulu (171d,175d), Zulu (86a), Zuni (125b), zuza (189)

- ZU -   azul (151d)

- - ZU   anzu (11d), auzu (168c,180b), Enzu (102b), wuzu (102d)

Z - - U   zebu (22d,80d,112c), zenu (143d), zulu (171d,175d), Zulu (86a)

ZY - -   zyga (134b), zyme (55c)

- - ZY   cazy (103a), cozy (149c), dazy, dozy, gazy, hazy (174b), Jozy, kazy (103a), lazy, oozy (148b), sizy (176d)

Z - - Y   zany (24a,32d,59c)

- - ZZ   bizz, buzz, fuzz (45d), huzz, jazz, razz (131b), sizz, zizz (181a)

Z - - Z   zizz (181a)